2005 BROOKMAN

UNITED STATES
& CANADA
STAMPS & POSTAL COLLECTIBLES

Including
SPECIALIZED LISTINGS
OF
STATE DUCK & INDIAN RESERVATION STAMPS
PLATE NO. COILS & UNEXPLODED BOOKLETS
U.S. SOUVENIR CARDS • PAGES • PANELS
AND FEATURING
UNITED STATES FIRST DAY COVERS
AND
AUTOGRAPH SECTION

Plus
Confederate States
U.S. Possessions
Marshall Island, Micronesia, Palau
Canadian Provinces

2005 BROOKMAN PRICE GUIDE

TERMS AND INFORMATION

CONDITION - We price United States stamps issued prior to 1890 in two grades - Average and Fine. From 1890 to 1934, we list a price for F-VF and VF quality. From 1935 to date, we price F-VF NH quality. **FOR INFORMATION ON GRADING SEE PAGE iv.**

GUM AND HINGING

Original Gum (O.G.)
Prior to 1870, Unused stamps may have partial or no gum. If you require o.g., add the percentage indicated in ( ). **Example** (OG + 25%). From 1910 to 1934, o.g. can be expected, but stamps may have been hinged or have hinge remnants. From 1935 to date, deduct 20% from NH price for hinged copies.

Never Hinged (N.H.)
Most issues are priced in F-VF, Never Hinged condition. Premiums for Average, NH usually run about half the F-VF premium. Prices for Never Hinged stamps on issues prior to 1882 will be quoted where available.

SPECIAL PRICING INSTRUCTIONS

Average - From 1890-1934 **Average perforated** stamps, when available, will be priced at 60-70% of the F-VF price depending upon the general quality of the issue.

Average imperforate stamps, when available, will be priced at 70-75% of the F-VF price depending upon the general quality of the issue.

From 1935 to present, average quality, when available, will be priced at 20% below the F-VF price.

Very Fine NH, 1935-Date
VF NH singles, plate blocks, line pairs, etc. are available. Unless otherwise noted, these are priced at a 20% premium over the F-VF price, unless specifically priced at the following premiums: Add 10¢ to any item priced under 50¢. Add 20% to any item priced at 50¢ and up. Unless priced as Very Fine, sets are not available Very Fine and stamps should be listed individually with appropriate premium.

Very Fine Unused O.G. Plate Blocks & Line Pairs
Very Fine Unused Plate Blocks and Line Pairs prior to #749 & 723 (and selected Back-of-the-Book Issues) are generally available at the respective F-VF NH price.

Very Fine Used
From 1847-1934, Very Fine Used stamps, when available, are priced by adding the % indicated to the appropriate Fine or F-VF price. **Example** (VF + 50%).
From 1935 to date, the premiums are the same as for VF NH copies.

MINIMUM ORDER OF $20 - Present day costs force us to require that mail orders total a minimum of $20.00. Send payment with order.

PRICES - Every effort will be made to maintain these prices throughout the life of this edition. However, prices are subject to change if market conditions require. We are not responsible for typographical errors.

BROOKMAN/BARRETT & WORTHEN
10 Chestnut Drive
Bedford, NH 03110
Phone (603) 472-5575
Fax (603) 472-8795
PRINTED IN USA

Arlene Dunn, Publisher
Edited By David S. Macdonald

First Day Covers Contributing Editors:
Robert G. Driscoll
Mike Zoeller
Rebecca Zoeller

Autograph Contributing Editors:
Robert G. Driscoll
Phillip Marks
Greg Tucker

TABLE OF CONTENTS
STAMPS

INDEX TO ADVERTISERS

Postal Reply Cards, Covers and Color Inserts

Featured Articles

We wish to thank the advertisers who help keep the Brookman Price Guide available at the lowest possible price. We urge you to support our advertisers and let them know their ads were helpful to you.

BROOKMAN GRADING GUIDE

The following guide is a simplified approach to stamp grading designed to help you better understand the quality you can expect to receive when you order a specific grade. All grades listed below are for undamaged stamps free of faults such as tears, thin spots, creases, straight edges, scrapes, etc. Stamps with those defects are considered "seconds" and sell for prices below those listed. The stamps you receive may not always match the criteria given since each stamp must be judged on its own special merits such as freshness, color, cancellation, etc. For example: a well centered stamp may be graded only as "Average" because of a very heavy cancellation. Grading stamps is an art, not a science, and frequently the cliche "beauty is in the eye of the beholder" applies. Stamps offered throughout this price list fall into the "Group A" category unless the heading contains a (B) or (C).

GROUP A - WELL CENTERED ISSUES

| Average | Average | Average | Average |

| F-VF | F-VF | F-VF | F-VF |

| Very Fine | Very Fine | Very Fine | Very Fine |

GROUP A	AVERAGE	F-VF	VERY FINE
PERFORATED STAMPS	Perforations touch or barely clear of design on one or two sides.	Perforations well clear of design on all sides.	Design very well centered within perforations.
IMPERFORATE STAMPS	One edge may touch design.	All four edges are clear of design.	Four edges are well clear of and well centered around design.
COILS AND BOOKLET PANES	Perforated and imperforate edge may touch design on one or two edges.	Perforated and imperforate edges are clear of the design.	Design very well centered within perforated and imperforate edges.

NOTE: Stamps of poorer centering than "Average" grade are considered seconds.

"**EXTREMELY FINE**" is a grading term used to descibe stamps that are almost "Perfect" in centering, color, freshness, cancellations, etc. This grade, when available, is priced substantially higher than Very Fine quality.

WASHINGTON 2006
World Philatelic Exhibition
May 27-June 3, 2006
See you there!
www.washington-2006.org

GROUP B - MEDIAN CENTERED ISSUES

| Average | Average | Average | Average | Average |

| F-VF | F-VF | Very Fine | Very Fine | Very Fine |

GROUP B	AVERAGE	F-VF	VERY FINE
PERFORATED STAMPS	Perforations touch or barely cut into design on one or two sides.	Perforations clear of design on all four sides.	Design well centered within perforations.
IMPERFORATE STAMPS	One or two edges may touch or barely cut into design.	All four edges are clear of design as in "A".	Four edges are well clear of and well centered around design as in "A".
COILS AND BOOKLET PANES	Perforated and imperforate edge may touch or barely cut into design.	Perforated and imperforate edges are clear of design as in "A".	Design well centered within perforated and imperforated edges.

GROUP C - POORLY CENTERED ISSUES

| Average | Average | Average | Average | Average |

| Fine | Fine | Very Fine | Very Fine | Very Fine |

GROUP C	AVERAGE	FINE	VERY FINE
PERFORATED STAMPS	Perforations may cut into design on one or more sides.	Perforations touch or just clear of design on one or more sides.	Perforations will clear design on all four sides.
IMPERFORATE STAMPS	One or more edges may cut into design.	One or more edges touch the design.	All four edges clear of the design.
COILS AND BOOKLET PANES	Perforated and imp. edge may cut into design on one or more sides.	Perforated and imperforate edges may touch or just clear design.	Perfoforated and imperforated edges well clear of design on all four sides.

Welcome to Stamp Collecting!

Challenge....information....friendship.... and just plain fun are part of "the World's Most Popular Hobby," stamp collecting! For more than 150 years, stamp collecting has been the hobby of choice of royalty, movie stars, sport celebrities, and hundreds of thousands of other people. Why do so many different people like stamps? One reason is, the hobby of stamp collecting suits almost anybody -- it's very personal. You fit the hobby to yourself, instead of forcing yourself to fit rules, as with many hobbies. There is not much free choice about how to play golf or softball or square dance -- there are many rules.

But stamp collecting can be done in a very simple way using your stamps you find on your everyday mail and place on plain paper in a three-ring binder. Or you can give a "want list" to a stamp dealer. He will pull the stamps you want from his stock, and you mount them in the correct spaces in a custom-made album that you bought.

Or you can go to stamp shows or stamp shops and spend hours looking through boxes of stamps and envelopes in search of a particular stamp with a certain postal marking or a special first-day cover that has a meaning to suit your own interests.

Stamp collecting is a special mix of the structured and the unstructured, and you can make it a personal hobby that will not be like anyone else's. It's a world all its own, and anyone can find a comfortable place in it.

"Stamp Collector" or "Philatelist"?

Some people think that a "philatelist" (fi-LAT-uh-list) means someone who is more expert or serious than someone who is a "stamp collector." That is not true! But one advantage of using the word "philately" (fi-LAT-uh-lee) is that it includes all areas of the hobby -- not just stamps -- such as postal markings, postal history, postal stationery, and the postal items from the time before there were stamps, such as folder letters.

Finding Material for Your Collection

You can easily find everything for your stamp hobby by mail. Stamps, other philatelic material, catalogues, albums, and so on are easy to get by mail order. The philatelic press carries advertising for all these hobby needs, and stamp shows in your area also will have dealers there. If you are lucky, you also may have a retail stamp store nearby.

Stamps shows may be small one-or-two day events in your local area, or very large events in big city convention halls lasting several days and featuring hundreds of dealers and thousands of pages of exhibits to see. Stamp shows also provide chances to meet other collectors, some of whom you may have "met" only by mail before.

How to Learn About Your New Hobby

Organizations, publications, and other collectors can help you grow in the hobby. The hobbies/recreation section of your local library may have basic books about stamp collecting, and the free reference department may have a set of catalogs.

If your local library has no books on stamp collecting, you can borrow some from the huge collection of the American Philatelic Research Library through the interlibrary loan or by becoming a member of the American Philatelic Society.

The APS/APRL are the largest stamp club and library in the United States and offer many services to collectors, including a 100-page monthly magazine, insurance for stamp collections, and a Sale Division through which members can buy sell stamps by mail among themselves. The APS/APRL are at P.O. Box 8000, State College, PA 16803, or call (814) 237-3803.

There also are many newspapers and magazines in the stamp hobby, including Linn's Stamp News, Stamp Collector, Scott Monthly Journal, Mekeel's, Global Stamp News, and Stamps. Some can be found on a large newsstands.

Taking Care of Your Collection

Paper is very fragile and must be handled with care. Stamp collectors use special tools and materials to protect their collectibles. Stamp tongs may look like cosmetic tweezers, but they have special tips that will not damage stamps, so be sure to buy your tongs from a stamp dealer and not in the beauty section at the drugstore!

Stamp albums and other storage methods (temporary file folders and boxes, envelopes, etc.) should be archival quality and acid-free paper, and any plastic used on or near stamps and covers (postally-used envelopes of philatelic interest) also should be archival -- as used for safe storage by museums. Plastic that is not archivally safe has oil based softeners that can leach out and do much damage to the stamps. In recent years philatelic manufacturers have become more careful about their products, and it is easy to find safe paper and plastic for hobby use.

Never use cellophane or other tapes around your stamps. Even so-called "magic tape" will cause damage that can not be undone. Stamps should be put on pages either with hinges (small rectangles of special gummed paper) or with mounts (little self adhesive plastic envelopes in many sizes to fit stamps on covers). Mounts keep stamps in the condition in which you bought them. Also available are pages with strips of plastic attached to them; these are "self-mounting" pages, meaning all you have to do is slip your stamp into the plastic strip.

Other hobby tools include gauges, for measuring the perforations on the stamps, and watermark fluid, which makes the special marks in some stamp papers visible momentarily. "Perfs" and watermarks are important if you decide to do some types of specialized collecting.

A Stamp Is a Stamp?

Not really -- a stamp can be many things: a feast for the eye with beautiful design and color printing technique...a mystery story, as you try to find out about the person, place or event behind the stamp... a mystery story, as you try to find out how and why this stamp and envelope traveled and received certain postal markings. Collectors who enjoy postal history always want the stamp with its envelope, which is one reason why you should no be quick to soak stamps off their covers. If you find an old hoard of envelopes, get some advice before you take the stamps off!

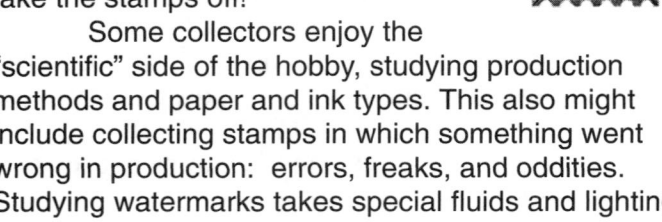

Some collectors enjoy the "scientific" side of the hobby, studying production methods and paper and ink types. This also might include collecting stamps in which something went wrong in production: errors, freaks, and oddities. Studying watermarks takes special fluids and lighting equipment, also needed to study the luminescent inks used on modern stamps to trigger high-tech canceling equipment in the post office.

Other branches of collecting includes first-day covers (FDCs), which carry a stamp on the first day it was sold with the day's postmark. Some FDCs have cachet (ca-SHAY), which is a design on the envelope that relates to the stamp and adds an attractive quality to the cover. Some clubs, catalogues, dealers specialize in FDCs.

Clubs, etc.

It is possible to collect for a lifetime and never leave home -- get everything you need by mail -- but a lot of enjoyment can be added if you join a club or go to stamp shows and exhibitions, and meet other collectors like yourself. Local clubs usually have a general focus, have meetings, and may organize stamp shows as part of their activities. Specialty-collecting groups, which may focus on stamps of one country or one type of stamp, will have a publication as the main service to members, but may have other activities and occasional meetings at large stamp shows. The American Philatelic Society, America's Stamp Club," is the oldest and largest stamp organization in the United States and has served hundreds of thousands of collectors since 1886.

Again, Welcome to Stamp Collecting!

The more you know about it, the more you will like it -- Happy Collecting!

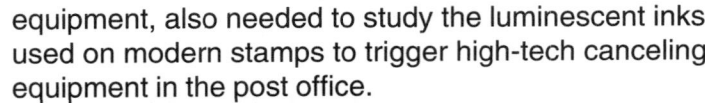 *This production was prepared by the American Philatelic Society, the oldest and largest national stamp organization in the United States. Information on member benefits and services is available from APS, 100 Match Factory Place, Bellefonte, Pa., 16823-1367; phone 814-933-3803; website: www.stamps.org.*

Commemorative, Special Issue & Air Mail Identifier

Commemorative, Special Issue & Air Mail Identifier

Commemorative, Special Issue & Air Mail Identifier

ix

Commemorative, Special Issue & Air Mail Identifier

x

Commemorative, Special Issue & Air Mail Identifier

Commemorative, Special Issue & Air Mail Identifier

DEFINITIVE ISSUE IDENTIFIER

The purpose of these listings is to aid the novice and intermediate collector in identifying U.S. definitive issues.
The first step in identification should be to note the stamp's denomination, color, and subject and then locate it on the list below. If that
step does not provide you with a definitive Scott No., you will have to do some additional work.
If the identification can only be made by determining the stamp's "type", grill size or press from which the stamp was printed, it will
be necessary to check the appropriate pages of the Brookman or Scott catalogs for this information.
If the identification can only be made by determining the stamp's perf measurements or watermark, you will then have to use your perf gauge and/or watermark
detector. If you do not own these "tools," contact your favorite dealer.

    * With few exceptions, this list features major Scott Nos. and omits Reprints, Re-issues and Special Printings.
    * Watermark and Press notations are not listed when they do not contribute to the stamp's identification.
    * Scott nos. followed by "**" were also issued Bullseye Perf. 11.2
    * Scott nos. followed by a "*" were issued both Untagged and Tagged.
    * All bklt. singles are perforated on two or three sides only.

Den.	Color	Subject	Type / Comment	Press	Perf.	Wmk.	Scott #
½¢	olive brn	N. Hale		F	11		551
½¢	olive brn	N. Hale		R	11x10.5		653
½¢	dp orng	B. Franklin	1938 Prexie Issue		11x10.5		803
½¢	rd orng	B. Franklin	1954 Liberty Issue		11x10.5		1030
1¢	**blue**	**B. Franklin**	**Ty I**		**Imperf**		**5**
1¢	blue	B. Franklin	Ty Ib		Imperf		5A
1¢	blue	B. Franklin	Ty II		Imperf		6
1¢	blue	B. Franklin	Ty III		Imperf		7
1¢	blue	B. Franklin	Ty IIIa		Imperf		8
1¢	blue	B. Franklin	Ty IIIa		Imperf		8A
1¢	blue	B. Franklin	Ty IV		Imperf		9
1¢	blue	B. Franklin	Ty I		15		18
1¢	brt. bl	B. Franklin	Ty I, reprint, w/o gum		12		40
1¢	blue	B. Franklin	Ty Ia		15		19
1¢	blue	B. Franklin	Ty II		15		20
1¢	blue	B. Franklin	Ty III		15		21
1¢	blue	B. Franklin	Ty IIIa		15		22
1¢	blue	B. Franklin	Ty IV		15		23
1¢	blue	B. Franklin	Ty V		15		24
1¢	blue	B. Franklin			12		63
1¢	blue	B. Franklin	"Z" Grill		12		85A
1¢	blue	B. Franklin	"E" Grill		12		86
1¢	blue	B. Franklin	"F" Grill		12		92
1¢	buff	B. Franklin	Issue of 1869 "G grill"		12		112
1¢	buff	B. Franklin	w/o grill, original gum		12		112b
1¢	buff	B. Franklin	Re-iss/wht crackly gum		12		123
1¢	buff	B. Franklin	Same, soft porous paper		12		133
1¢	brn. orng.	B. Franklin	Same, w/o gum		12		133a
1¢	ultra	B. Franklin	hard paper, w/grill		12		134
1¢	ultra	B. Franklin	Same, w/o grill		12		145
1¢	ultra	B. Franklin	Same, w/Secret mark		12		156
1¢	dk. ultra	B. Franklin	Soft porous paper		12		182
1¢	gray bl.	B. Franklin	Same, re-engraved		12		206
1¢	ultra	B. Franklin			12		212
1¢	dull bl.	B. Franklin	w/o Triangles		12		219
1¢	ultra	B. Franklin	w/ Tri. in Top corners		12	NW	246
1¢	ultra	B. Franklin	w/ Tri. in Top corners		12	NW	247
1¢	blue	B. Franklin	w/ Tri. in Top corners		12	DL	264
1¢	dp. grn	B. Franklin	w/ Tri. in Top corners		12	DL	279
1¢	blue grn	B. Franklin	"Series 1902"		12	DL	300
1¢	blue grn	B. Franklin	"Series 1902"		Imperf	DL	314
1¢	blue grn	B. Franklin	"Series 1902" B. Pn./6		12	DL	300b
1¢	blue grn	B. Franklin	"Series 1902" Coil		12 Hz	DL	316
1¢	blue grn	B. Franklin	"Series 1902" Coil		12 Vert	DL	318
1¢	green	B. Franklin			12	DL	331
1¢	green	B. Franklin	Blue Paper		12	DL	357
1¢	green	B. Franklin			12	SL	374
1¢	green	B. Franklin			Imperf	DL	343
1¢	green	B. Franklin			Imperf	SL	383
1¢	green	B. Franklin	Bklt. Pn. of 6		12	DL	331a
1¢	green	B. Franklin	Bklt. Pn. of 6		12	SL	374a
1¢	green	B. Franklin	Coil		12 Hz	DL	348
1¢	green	B. Franklin	Coil		12 Hz	SL	385
1¢	green	B. Franklin	Coil		12 Vert	DL	352
1¢	green	B. Franklin	Coil		12 Vert	SL	387
1¢	green	B. Franklin	Coil		8.5 Hz	SL	390
1¢	green	B. Franklin	Coil		8.5 Vert	SL	392
1¢	green	Washington			12	SL	405
1¢	green	Washington			10	SL	424
1¢	green	Washington		F	10	NW	462
1¢	green	Washington		R	10	NW	543
1¢	green	Washington		F	11	NW	498
1¢	gray grn	Washington	Offset	F	11	NW	525
1¢	green	Washington	19mm x 22.5mm	R	11	NW	544
1¢	green	Washington	19.5-20mm x 22mm	R	11	NW	545
1¢	gray grn	Washington	Rossbach Press		12.5	NW	536
1¢	green	Washington		R	11x10	NW	538
1¢	green	Washington		R	10x11	NW	542
1¢	green	Washington			Imperf	SL	408
1¢	green	Washington			Imperf	NW	481
1¢	green	Washington	Offset		Imperf	NW	531
1¢	green	Washington	Bklt. Pn. of 6		12	SL	405b
1¢	green	Washington	Bklt. Pn. of 6		10	SL	424d

Den.	Color	Subject	Type / Comment	Press	Perf.	Wmk.	Scott #
1¢	green	Washington	Bklt. Pn. of 6		10	NW	462a
1¢	green	Washington	Bklt. Pn. of 6		11	NW	498e
1¢	green	Washington	Bklt. Pn. of 30		11	NW	498f
1¢	green	Washington	Coil		8.5 Hz	SL	410
1¢	green	Washington	Coil		8.5 Vert	SL	412
1¢	green	Washington	Coil	F	10 Hz	SL	441
1¢	green	Washington	Coil	R	10 Hz	SL	448
1¢	green	Washington	Coil	R	10 Hz	SL	441
1¢	green	Washington	Coil	R	10 Hz	NW	486
1¢	green	Washington	Coil	F	10 Vert	SL	443
1¢	green	Washington	Coil	R	10 Vert	SL	452
1¢	green	Washington	Coil	R	10 Vert	NW	490
1¢	deep grn	B. Franklin		F	11		552
1¢	green	B. Franklin	19¾ x 22¼mm	R	11		594
1¢	green	B. Franklin	19¼ x 22¾mm	R	11		596
1¢	green	B. Franklin		R	11x10		578
1¢	green	B. Franklin		R	10		581
1¢	green	B. Franklin		R	11x10.5		632
1¢	green	B. Franklin		F	Imperf		575
1¢	deep grn	B. Franklin	Bklt. Pn. of 6	F	11		552a
1¢	green	B. Franklin	Bklt. Pn. of 6	R	11x10.5		632a
1¢	green	B. Franklin	Coil	R	10 Vert		597
1¢	yel. grn.	B. Franklin	Coil	R	10 Hz		604
1¢	green	B. Franklin	Kansas Ovpt.		11x10.5		658
1¢	green	B. Franklin	Nebraska Ovpt.		11x10.5		669
1¢	green	Washington	1938 Prexie Issue		11x10.5		804
1¢	green	Washington	Bklt. Pn. of 6		11x10.5		804b
1¢	green	Washington	Coil		10 Vert		839
1¢	green	Washington	Coil		10 Hz		848
1¢	dk green	Washington	1954 Liberty Issue		11x10.5		1031
1¢	dk green	Washington	Coil		10 Vert		1054
1¢	green	A. Jackson			11x10.5		1209*
1¢	green	A. Jackson	Coil		10 Vert		1225*
1¢	green	T. Jefferson			11x10.5		1278
1¢	green	T. Jefferson	Bklt. Pn. of 8		11x10.5		1278a
1¢	green	T. Jefferson	B.Pn./4 + 2 labels		11x10.5		1278b
1¢	green	T. Jefferson	Coil		10 Vert		1299
1¢	dk blue	Inkwell & Quill			11x10.5		1581
1¢	dk blue	Inkwell & Quill	Coil		10 Vert		1811
1¢	black	Dorothea Dix			11		1844**
1¢	violet	Omnibus	Coil		10 Vert		1897
1¢	violet	Omnibus	Coil, re-engraved		10 Vert	B	2225
1¢	brnish verm	Margaret Mitchell			11		2168
1¢	multi	Kestrel	No "¢" Sign		11		2476
1¢	multi	Kestrel	'¢' sign added		11		2477
1¢	multi	Kestrel	Self-adhesive Coil "1999" Date		Die-cut 10.5 Vert		3031
1¢	multi	Kestrel	Self-adhesive Coil "2000" Date		Die-cut 10.5 Vert		3031A
1¢	multi	Kestrel	Coil		10 Vert		3044
1¢	multi	Tiffany Lamp	Self-adhesive Coil		Die-cut Vert.		3757
1¼¢	**turquoise**	**Palace of Governors**			**10.5x11**		**1031A**
1¼¢	turquoise	Palace of Governors	Coil		10 Hz		1054A
1¼¢	lt. grn	Albert Gallatin			11x10.5		1279
1½¢	**yel brn**	**W.G. Harding**		**F**	**11**		**553**
1½¢	yel brn	W.G. Harding		R	10		582
1½¢	yel brn	W.G. Harding		R	11x10.5		633
1½¢	brown	W.G. Harding	"Full Face"	R	11x10.5		684
1½¢	yel brn	W.G. Harding		F	Imperf		576
1½¢	yel brn	W.G. Harding		R	Imperf		631
1½¢	brown	W.G. Harding	Coil		10 Vert		598
1½¢	yel brn	W.G. Harding	Coil		10 Hz		605
1½¢	brown	W.G. Harding	"Full Face," Coil		10 Vert		686
1½¢	brown	W.G. Harding	Kansas Ovpt.		11x10.5		659
1½¢	brown	W.G. Harding	Nebraska Ovpt.		11x10.5		670
1½¢	bstr brn	M. Washington			11x10.5		805
1½¢	bstr brn	M. Washington	Coil		10 Vert		840
1½¢	bstr brn	M. Washington	Coil		10 Hz		849
1½¢	brn carm	Mount Vernon			10.5x11		1032
2¢	**black**	**A. Jackson**			**12**		**73**
2¢	black	A. Jackson			12		84
2¢	black	A. Jackson	"Z" Grill		12		85B
2¢	black	A. Jackson	"E" Grill		12		87

DEFINITIVE ISSUE IDENTIFIER

Den.	Color	Subject	Type / Comment	Press	Perf.	Wmk.	Scott #
2¢	black	A. Jackson	"F" Grill		12		93
2¢	brown	Horse & Rider	Issue of 1869 "G grill"		12		113
2¢	brown	Horse & Rider	w/o grill, original gum		12		113b
2¢	brown	Horse & Rider	Re-iss/wht crackly gum		12		124
2¢	red brown	A. Jackson	Hard paper, w/grill		12		135
2¢	red brown	A. Jackson	Hard paper,w/o grill		12		146
2¢	brown	A. Jackson	Same, w/secret mark		12		157
2¢	vermillion	A. Jackson	Yellowish wove (hard)		12		178
2¢	vermillion	A. Jackson	Soft porous paper		12		183
2¢	red brown				12		210
2¢	pl rd brn	Washington	Special Printing		12		211B
2¢	green	Washington			12		213
2¢	lake	Washington	w/o Triangles		12		219D
2¢	carmine	Washington	w/o Tri.		12		220
2¢	pink	Washington	Ty I Tri. in Top corners		12	NW	248
2¢	carm. lake	Washington	Ty I Tri. "		12	NW	249
2¢	carmine	Washington	Ty I Tri. "		12	NW	250
2¢	carmine	Washington	Ty I Tri. "		12	DL	265
2¢	carmine	Washington	Ty II Tri. "		12	NW	251
2¢	carmine	Washington	Ty II Tri. "		12	DL	266
2¢	carmine	Washington	Ty III Tri. "		12	NW	252
2¢	carmine	Washington	Ty III Tri. "		12	DL	267
2¢	red	Washington	Ty III Tri. "		12	DL	279B
2¢	carm rose	Washington	Ty III Tri. "		12	DL	279Bc
2¢	red	Washington	Bklt. Pn. of 6		12	DL	279Be
2¢	carmine	Washington	"Series 1902"		12	DL	301
2¢	carmine	Washington	"Series 1902" B.Pn./6		12	DL	301c
2¢	carmine	Washington	"Shield" Design, Die I		12	DL	319
2¢	carmine	Washington	"Shield", Die II		12	DL	319i
2¢	carmine	Washington	"Shield", B.Pn./6, Die I		12	DL	319g
2¢	carmine	Washington	"Shield", B.Pn./6, Die II		12	DL	319h
2¢	lake	Washington	"Shield", B.Pn./6, Die II		12	DL	319q
2¢	carmine	Washington	"Shield" Design	Imperf		DL	320
2¢	lake	Washington	"Shield" Design	Imperf		DL	320a
2¢	carmine	Washington	"Shield" Coil		12 Hz	DL	321
2¢	carmine	Washington	"Shield" Coil		12 Vert	DL	322
2¢	carmine	Washington	"TWO CENTS" Design		12	DL	332
2¢	carmine	Washington	"TWO..." Blue Paper		12	DL	358
2¢	carmine	Washington	"TWO..."		12	SL	375
2¢	lake	Washington	"TWO..."		12	SL	375v
2¢	carmine	Washington	"TWO..."	F	11	DL	519
2¢	carmine	Washington	"TWO..."		Imperf	DL	344
2¢	carmine	Washington	"TWO..."		Imperf	SL	384
2¢	dark carm	Washington	"TWO..."		Imperf	SL	384v
2¢	carmine	Washington	"TWO..." Bklt. Pn. of 6		12	DL	332a
2¢	carmine	Washington	"TWO..." Bklt. Pn. of 6		12	SL	375a
2¢	carmine	Washington	"TWO..." Coil		12 Hz	DL	349
2¢	carmine	Washington	"TWO..." Coil		12 Hz	SL	386
2¢	carmine	Washington	"TWO..." Coil		12 Vert	DL	353
2¢	carmine	Washington	"TWO..." Coil		12 Vert	SL	388
2¢	carmine	Washington	"TWO..." Coil		8.5 Hz	SL	391
2¢	carmine	Washington	"TWO..." Coil		8.5 Vert	SL	393
2¢	carmine	Washington	"2 CENTS" Design		12	SL	406
2¢	lake	Washington	"2..."		12	SL	406v
2¢	carmine	Washington	"2..."		10	SL	425
2¢	carmine	Washington	"2..."		10	NW	463
2¢	carm rd	Washington	"2..."		11	SL	461
2¢	carmine	Washington	"2..." Ty I	F	11	NW	499
2¢	carmine	Washington	"2..." Ty Ia	F	11	NW	500
2¢	carmine	Washington	"2..." Offset Ty. IV		11	NW	526
2¢	carmine	Washington	"2..." Offset Ty. V		11	NW	527
2¢	carmine	Washington	"2..." Offset Ty. Va		11	NW	528
2¢	carmine	Washington	"2..." Offset Ty. VI		11	NW	528A
2¢	carmine	Washington	"2..." Offset Ty. VII		11	NW	528B
2¢	carm rose	Washington	"2..." Coil Waste:				
2¢	carm rose	Washington	Ty III	R	11	NW	546
2¢	carm rose	Washington	Ty II	R	11x10	NW	539
2¢	carm rose	Washington	Ty III	R	11x10	NW	540
2¢	carmine	Washington	"2 CENTS"	F	Imperf	SL	409
2¢	carm rose	Washington	"2..."	F	Imperf	NW	482
2¢	carm rose	Washington	"2..." Offset Ty IV		Imperf	NW	532
2¢	carmine	Washington	"2..." Offset Ty V		Imperf	NW	533
2¢	carmine	Washington	"2..." Offset Ty Va		Imperf	NW	534
2¢	carmine	Washington	"2..." Offset Ty VI		Imperf	NW	534A
2¢	carmine	Washington	"2..." Offset Ty VII		Imperf	NW	534B
2¢	carmine	Washington	"2..." Bklt. Pn. of 6		12	SL	406a
2¢	carmine	Washington	"2..." Bklt. Pn. of 6		10	SL	425e
2¢	carmine	Washington	"2..." Bklt. Pn. of 6		10	NW	463a
2¢	carmine	Washington	"2..." Bklt. Pn. of 6	F	11	NW	499e
2¢	carmine	Washington	"2..." Bklt. Pn. of 30	F	11	NW	499f
2¢	carmine	Washington	"2 CENTS" Coil		8.5 Hz	SL	411
2¢	carmine	Washington	"2..." Coil		8.5 Vert	SL	413
2¢	carmine	Washington	"2..." Coil Ty I	F	10 Hz	SL	442
2¢	red	Washington	"2..." Coil Ty I	R	10 Hz	SL	449
2¢	carmine	Washington	"2..." Coil Ty II	R	10 Hz	NW	487
2¢	carmine	Washington	"2..." Coil Ty III	R	10 Hz	SL	450
2¢	carmine	Washington	"2..." Coil Ty III	R	10 Hz	NW	488
2¢	carmine	Washington	"2..." Coil Ty I	F	10 Vert	SL	444
2¢	carm red	Washington	"2..." Coil Ty I	R	10 Vert	SL	453
2¢	red	Washington	"2..." Coil Ty II	R	10 Vert	SL	454
2¢	carmine	Washington	"2..." Coil Ty II	R	10 Vert	NW	491
2¢	carmine	Washington	"2..." Coil Ty III	R	10 Vert	SL	455
2¢	carmine	Washington	"2..." Coil Ty III	R	10 Vert	NW	492
2¢	carmine	Washington	"2..." Hz Coil Ty I	R	Imperf	SL	459
2¢	deep rose	Washington	"2..." Hz Coil Ty Ia/ Shermack Ty IIPerfsF			*NW	482A
2¢	carmine	Washington		F	11		554
2¢	carmine	Washington	19¾ x 22¼ mm	R	11		595
2¢	carmine	Washington	19¾ x 22¼ mm	R	11x10		579
2¢	carmine	Washington	Die I	R	11x10.5		634
2¢	carmine	Washington	Die II	R	11x10.5		634A
2¢	carmine	Washington		R	10		583
2¢	carmine	Washington		F	Imperf		577
2¢	carmine	Washington	Bklt. Pn. of 6	F	11		554c
2¢	carmine	Washington	Bklt. Pn. of 6	R	10		583a
2¢	carmine	Washington	Bklt. Pn. of 6	R	11x10.5		634d
2¢	carmine	Washington	Coil		10 Vert		599
2¢	carmine	Washington	Coil Die II		10 Vert		599A
2¢	carmine	Washington	Coil		10 Hz		606
2¢	carmine	Washington	Kansas Ovpt.		11x10.5		660
2¢	carmine	Washington	Nebraska Ovpt.		11x10.5		671
2¢	rose carm	J. Adams			11x10.5		806
2¢	rose carm	J. Adams	Bklt. Pn. of 6		11x10.5		806b
2¢	rose carm	J. Adams	Coil		10 Vert		841
2¢	rose carm	J. Adams	Coil		10 Hz		850
2¢	carm rose	T. Jefferson			11x10.5		1033
2¢	carm rose	T. Jefferson	Coil		10 Vert		1055*
2¢	dk bl gray	Frank Lloyd Wright			11x10.5		1280
2¢	dk bl gray	Frank Lloyd Wright	B. Pn. of 5 + Label		11x10.5		1280a
2¢	dk bl gray	Frank Lloyd Wright	Booklet Pn. of 6		11x10.5		1280c
2¢	red brn	Speaker's Stand			11x10.5		1582
2¢	brn black	Igor Stravinsky			10.5x11		1845
2¢	black	Locomotive	Coil		10 Vert		1897A
2¢	black	Locomotive	Coil, "Re-engraved"	B	10 Vert		2226
2¢	brt blue	Mary Lyon			11		2169
2¢	multi	Red-headed Woodpecker			11.1		3032
2¢	multi	Red-headed Woodpecker	Coil		9¾ Vert		3045
2.5¢	gray bl	Bunker Hill			11x10.5		1034
2.5¢	gray bl	Bunker Hill	Coil		10 Vert		1056
3¢	orng brn	Washington	Ty I		Imperf		10
3¢	dull red	Washington	Ty I		Imperf		11
3¢	rose	Washington	Ty I		15		25
3¢	dull red	Washington	Ty II		15		26
3¢	dull red	Washington	Ty IIa		15		26a
3¢	pink	Washington			12		64
3¢	pgn bld pink	Washington			12		64a
3¢	rose pink	Washington			12		64b
3¢	rose	Washington			12		65
3¢	lake	Washington			12		66
3¢	scarlet	Washington			12		74
3¢	rose	Washington	"A" Grill		12		79
3¢	rose	Washington	"B" Grill		12		82
3¢	rose	Washington	"C" Grill		12		83
3¢	rose	Washington	"D" Grill		12		85
3¢	rose	Washington	"Z" Grill		12		85C
3¢	rose	Washington	"E" Grill		12		88
3¢	rose	Washington	"F" Grill		12		94
3¢	ultra	Locomotive	"G grill"		12		114
3¢	ultra	Locomotive	w/o grill, Original gum		12		114a
3¢	green	Washington	Hard paper, w/grill		12		136
3¢	green	Washington	Same, w/o grill		12		147
3¢	green	Washington	Same, w/secret mark		12		158
3¢	green	Washington	Same, Soft porous paper		12		184
3¢	blue grn	Washington	Same, re-engraved		12		207
3¢	vermillion	Washington			12		214
3¢	purple	A. Jackson	w/o Triangles		12		221
3¢	purple	A. Jackson	w/ Tri. in Top corners		12	NW	253
3¢	purple	A Jackson	w/ Tri. in Top corners		12	DL	268
3¢	violet	A. Jackson	"Series 1902"		12	DL	302
3¢	dp violet	Washington		F	12	DL	333
3¢	dp violet	Washington	Blue paper	F	12	DL	359
3¢	dp violet	Washington		F	12	SL	376
3¢	dp violet	Washington		F	10	SL	426
3¢	violet	Washington		F	10	NW	464
3¢	lt violet	Washington	Ty I	F	11	NW	501
3¢	dk violet	Washington	Ty II	F	11	NW	502
3¢	violet	Washington	Ty III Offset		11	NW	529
3¢	purple	Washington	Ty IV Offset		11	NW	530
3¢	violet	Washington	Ty II Coil Waste	R	11x10	NW	541
3¢	dp violet	Washington			Imperf	DL	345
3¢	violet	Washington	Ty I	F	Imperf	NW	483
3¢	violet	Washington	Ty II	F	Imperf	NW	484

DEFINITIVE ISSUE IDENTIFIER

Den.	Color	Subject	Type / Comment	Press	Perf.	Wmk.	Scott #
3¢	violet	Washington	Ty IV Offset		Imperf	NW	535
3¢	lt violet	Washington	B. Pn. of 6, Ty I	F	11	NW	501b
3¢	dk violet	Washington	B. Pn. of 6, Ty II	F	11	NW	502b
3¢	dp violet	Washington	Coil "Orangeburg"	F	12 Vert	SL	389
3¢	dp violet	Washington	Coil	F	8.5 Vert	SL	394
3¢	violet	Washington	Coil, Ty I	F	10 Vert	SL	445
3¢	violet	Washington	Coil, Ty I	R	10 Vert	SL	456
3¢	violet	Washington	Coil, Ty I	R	10 Hz	NW	489
3¢	dp violet	Washington	Coil, Ty I	R	10 Vert	NW	493
3¢	dull violet	Washington	Coil, Ty II	R	10 Vert	NW	494
3¢	violet	A. Lincoln		F	11		555
3¢	violet	A. Lincoln		R	10		584
3¢	violet	A. Lincoln		R	11x10.5		635
3¢	violet	A. Lincoln	Coil		10 Vert		600
3¢	violet	A. Lincoln	Kansas Ovpt.		11x10.5		661
3¢	violet	A. Lincoln	Nebraska Ovpt.		11x10.5		672
3¢	dp violet	Washington	Stuart Portrait		11x10.5		720
3¢	dp violet	Washington	Stuart B. Pn. of 6		11x10.5		720b
3¢	dp violet	Washington	Stuart Coil		10 Vert		721
3¢	dp violet	Washington	Stuart Coil		10 Hz		722
3¢	dp violet	T. Jefferson			11x10.5		807
3¢	dp violet	T. Jefferson	Bklt. Pn. of 6		11x10.5		807a
3¢	dp violet	T. Jefferson	Coil		10 Vert		842
3¢	dp violet	T. Jefferson	Coil		10 Hz		851
3¢	dp violet	Statue of Liberty			11x10.5		1035*
3¢	dp violet	Liberty	Bklt. Pn. of 6		11x10.5		1035a
3¢	dp violet	Liberty	Coil		10 Vert		1057*
3¢	violet	F. Parkman			10.5x11		1281
3¢	violet	F. Parkman	Coil		10 Vert		1297
3¢	olive	Early Ballot Box			11x10.5		1584
3¢	olive grn	Henry Clay			11x10.5		1846
3¢	dark grn	Handcar	Coil		10 Vert		1898
3¢	brt blue	Paul D. White MD			11		2170
3¢	claret	Conestoga Wagon	Coil		10 Vert		2252
3¢	multi	Bluebird			11		2478
3¢	multi	Eastern Bluebird			11.1		3033
3¢	red,blue,black	Star	Self-adhesive		Die-cut 11		3613
3¢	red,blue,black	Star	Self-adhesive		Die-cut 10		3614
3¢	red,blue,black	Star	Coil				3615
3.1¢	**brn (yel)**	**Guitar**	**Coil**		**10 Vert**		**1613**
3.4¢	**dk blsh grn**	**School Bus**	**Coil**		**10 Vert**		**2123**
3.5¢	**prpl (yel)**	**Weaver Violins**	**Coil**		**10 Vert**		**1813**
4¢	**blue grn**	**A. Jackson**			**12**		**211**
4¢	carmine	A. Jackson			12		215
4¢	dk brn	A. Lincoln	w/ Triangles		12		222
4¢	dk brn	A. Lincoln	w/ Tri. in Top corners		12	NW	254
4¢	dk brn	A. Lincoln	w/ Tri. in Top corners		12	DL	269
4¢	rose brn	A. Lincoln	w/ Tri. in Top corners		12	DL	280
4¢	brown	U.S. Grant	"Series 1902"		12	DL	303
4¢	brown	U.S. Grant	Coil, Shermack Ty III		*	DL	314A
4¢	orng brn	Washington		F	12	DL	334
4¢	orng brn	Washington	Blue Paper	F	12	DL	360
4¢	brown	Washington		F	12	SL	377
4¢	brown	Washington		F	10	SL	427
4¢	brown	Washington		F	10	NW	465
4¢	brown	Washington		F	11	NW	503
4¢	orng brn	Washington		F	Imperf	DL	346
4¢	orng brn	Washington	Coil	F	12 Hz	DL	350
4¢	orng brn	Washington	Coil	F	12 Vert	DL	354
4¢	brown	Washington	Coil	F	8.5 Vert	SL	395
4¢	brown	Washington	Coil	F	10 Vert	SL	446
4¢	brown	Washington	Coil	R	10 Vert	SL	457
4¢	orng brn	Washington	Coil	R	10 Vert	NW	495
4¢	yel brn	M. Washington		F	11		556
4¢	yel brn	M. Washington		R	10		585
4¢	yel brn	M. Washington		R	11x10.5		636
4¢	yel brn	M. Washington	Coil		10 Vert		601
4¢	yel brn	M. Washington	Kansas Ovpt.		11x10.5		662
4¢	yel brn	M. Washington	Nebraska Ovpt.		11x10.5		673
4¢	brown	W.H. Taft			11x10.5		685
4¢	brown	W.H. Taft	Coil		10 Vert		687
4¢	red violet	J. Madison			11x10.5		808
4¢	red violet	J. Madison	Coil		10 Vert		843
4¢	red violet	A. Lincoln			11x10.5		1036*
4¢	red violet	A. Lincoln	Bklt. Pn. of 6		11x10.5		1036a
4¢	red violet	A. Lincoln	Coil		10 Vert		1058
4¢	black	A. Lincoln			11x10.5		1282*
4¢	black	A. Lincoln	Coil		10 Vert		1303
4¢	rose mag	"Books, etc."			11x10.5		1585
4¢	violet	Carl Schurz			10.5x11		1847
4¢	rdsh brn	Stagecoach	Coil		10 Vert		1898A
4¢	rdsh brn	Stagecoach	Coil, re-engr.	B	10 Vert		2228
4¢	bl violet	Father Flanagan			11		2171
4¢	claret	Steam Carriage	Coil		10 Vert		2451
4¢	multi	Chippendale Chair, SA			Diecut 10 3/4 x 10¼		3750
4½¢	**dark gray**	**White House**			**11x10.5**		**809**
4½¢	dark gray	White House	Coil		10 Vert		844
4½¢	blue grn	The Hermitage			10.5x11		1037
4½¢	blue grn	The Hermitage	Coil		10 Hz		1059
4.9¢	brn blk	Buckboard	Coil		10 Vert		2124
5¢	**rd brn**	**B. Franklin**			**Imperf**		**1**
5¢	rd brn	B. Franklin	Bluish paper (reprint)		Imperf		3
5¢	rd brn	T. Jefferson	Ty I		Imperf		12
5¢	brick red	T. Jefferson	Ty I		15		27
5¢	rd brn	T. Jefferson	Ty I		15		28
5¢	brt rd brn	T. Jefferson	Ty I		15		28b
5¢	Indian red	T. Jefferson	Ty I		15		28A
5¢	brown	T. Jefferson	Ty I		15		29
5¢	orng brn	T. Jefferson	Ty II		15		30
5¢	brown	T. Jefferson	Ty II		15		30A
5¢	buff	T. Jefferson			12		67
5¢	red brn	T. Jefferson			12		75
5¢	brown	T. Jefferson			12		76
5¢	brown	T. Jefferson	"A" Grill		12		80
5¢	brown	T. Jefferson	"F" Grill		12		95
5¢	blue	Z. Taylor	Yellowish wove (hard)		12		179
5¢	blue	Z. Taylor	Soft Porous Paper		12		185
5¢	yel brn	J. Garfield			12		205
5¢	indigo	J. Garfield			12		216
5¢	choc	U.S. Grant	w/o Triangles		12		223
5¢	choc	U.S. Grant	w/ Tri. in Top corners		12	NW	255
5¢	choc	U.S. Grant	w/ Tri. in Top corners		12	DL	270
5¢	dk blue	U.S. Grant	w/ Tri. in Top corners		12	DL	281
5¢	blue	A. Lincoln	"Series 1902"		12	DL	304
5¢	blue	A. Lincoln	"Series 1902"		Imperf	DL	315
5¢	blue	Washington			12	DL	335
5¢	blue	Washington	Blue Paper		12	DL	361
5¢	blue	Washington			12	SL	378
5¢	blue	Washington			10	SL	428
5¢	blue	Washington			10	NW	466
5¢	blue	Washington			11	NW	504
5¢	blue	Washington			Imperf	DL	347
5¢	blue	Washington	Coil		12 Hz	DL	351
5¢	blue	Washington	Coil		12 Vert	DL	355
5¢	blue	Washington	Coil		8.5 Vert	SL	396
5¢	blue	Washington	Coil	F	10 Vert	SL	447
5¢	blue	Washington	Coil	R	10 Vert	SL	458
5¢	blue	Washington	Coil	R	10 Vert	NW	496
5¢	carmine	Washington	Error of Color		10	NW	467
5¢	rose	Washington	Error of Color		11	NW	505
5¢	carmine	Washington	Error of Color		Imperf	NW	485
5¢	dk blue	T. Roosevelt		F	11		557
5¢	blue	T. Roosevelt		R	10		586
5¢	dk blue	T. Roosevelt	Coil	R	10 Vert		602
5¢	dk blue	T. Roosevelt		R	11x10.5		637
5¢	dp blue	T. Roosevelt	Kansas Ovpt.		11x10.5		663
5¢	dp blue	T. Roosevelt	Nebraska Ovpt.		11x10.5		674
5¢	brt blue	J. Monroe			11x10.5		810
5¢	brt blue	J. Monroe	Coil		10 Vert		845
5¢	blue	J. Monroe			11x10.5		1038
5¢	dk bl gray	Washington			11x10.5		1213*
5¢	dk bl gray	Washington	Bklt. Pn. of 5 + "Mailman" Label		11x10.5		1213a
			"Use Zone Nos." Label		11x10.5		1213a*
			"Use Zip Code" Label		11x10.5		1213a*
5¢	dk bl gray	Washington	Coil		10 Vert		1229*
5¢	blue	Washington			11x10.5		1283*
5¢	blue	Washington	Re-engr. (clean face)		11x10.5		1283B
5¢	blue	Washington	Coil		10 Vert		1304
5¢	henna brn	Pearl Buck			10.5x11		1848
5¢	gray grn	Motorcycle	Coil		10 Vert		1899
5¢	dk olv grn	Hugo Black			11		2172
5¢	carmine	Luis Munoz Marin			11		2173*
5¢	black	Milk Wagon	Coil		10 Vert		2253
5¢	red	Circus Wagon	Coil Engraved		10 Vert		2452
5¢	carmine	Circus Wagon	Coil Gravure		10 Vert		2452B
5¢	brown	Canoe	Coil Engraved		10 Vert		2453
5¢	red	Canoe	Coil Gravure		10 Vert		2454
5¢	multi.	Toleware	Coil Gravure		10 Vert.		3612
5.2¢	**carmine**	**Sleigh**	**Coil**		**10 Vert**		**1900**
5.3¢	**black**	**Elevator**	**Coil**		**10 Vert**		**2254**
5.5¢	**dp mag**	**Star Rt Truck**	**Coil**		**10 Vert**		**2125**
5.9¢	**blue**	**Bicycle**	**Coil**		**10 Vert**		**1901**
6¢	**ultra**	**Washington**	**"G" Grill**		**12**		**115**
6¢	carmine	A. Lincoln	hard wh paper, w/grill		12		137
6¢	carmine	A. Lincoln	Same, w/o grill		12		148
6¢	dull pink	A. Lincoln	Same, secret mark		12		159
6¢	pink	A. Lincoln	Same, sft porous pap		12		186
6¢	rose	A. Lincoln	Same, re-engraved		12		208
6¢	brn red	A. Lincoln	Same, re-engraved		12		208a
6¢	brn red	J. Garfield	w/o Triangles		12		224
6¢	dull brn	J. Garfield	w/ Tri. in Top corners		12	NW	256
6¢	dull brn	J. Garfield	w/ Tri. in Top corners		12	DL	271
6¢	dull brn	J. Garfield	w/ Tri. in Top corners		12	USIR	271a

DEFINITIVE ISSUE IDENTIFIER

Den.	Color	Subject	Type / Comment	Press	Perf.	Wmk.	Scott #
6¢	lake	J. Garfield	w/ Tri. in Top corners		12	DL	282
6¢	claret	J. Garfield	"Series 1902"		12	DL	305
6¢	rd orng	Washington			12	DL	336
6¢	rd orng	Washington	Blue paper		12	DL	362
6¢	rd orng	Washington			12	SL	379
6¢	rd orng	Washington			10	SL	429
6¢	rd orng	Washington			10	NW	468
6¢	rd orng	Washington			11	NW	506
6¢	rd orng	J. Garfield		F	11		558
6¢	rd orng	J. Garfield		R	10		587
6¢	rd orng	J. Garfield		R	11x10.5		638
6¢	rd orng	J. Garfield	Kansas Ovpt.		11x10.5		664
6¢	rd orng	J. Garfield	Nebraska Ovpt.		11x10.5		675
6¢	dp orng	J. Garfield	Coil		10 Vert		723
6¢	red orng	J.Q. Adams			11x10.5		811
6¢	red orng	J.Q. Adams	Coil		10 Vert		846
6¢	carmine	T. Roosevelt			11x10.5		1039
6¢	gray brn	F.D. Roosevelt			10.5x11		1284*
6¢	gray brn	F.D. Roosevelt	Bklt. Pn. of 8		11x10.5		1284b
6¢	gray brn	F.D. Roosevelt	Bklt. Pn. of 5 + Label		11x10.5		1284c
6¢	gray brn	F.D. Roosevelt	Coil		10 Hz		1298
6¢	gray brn	F.D. Roosevelt	Coil		10 Vert		1305
6¢	dk bl,rd & grn	Flag & White House			11		1338
6¢	dk bl,rd & grn	Flag & White House			11x10.5		1338D
6¢	dk bl,rd & grn	Flag & White House	Coil		10 Vert		1338A
6¢	dk bl gray	D.D. Eisenhower			11x10.5		1393
6¢	dk bl gray	Eisenhower	Bklt. Pn of 8		11x10.5		1393a
6¢	dk bl gray	Eisenhower	Bklt. Pn of 5 + Label		11x10.5		1393b
6¢	dk bl gray	Eisenhower	Coil		10 Vert		1401
6¢	orng verm	Walter Lippmann			11		1849
6¢	multi	Circle of Stars	Bklt. Single		11		1892
6¢	red brn	Tricycle	Coil		10 Vert		2126
6.3¢	brick red	Liberty Bell	Coil		10 Vert		1518
7¢	vermilion	E.M. Stanton	Hard wh paper, w/grill		12		138
7¢	vermilion	E.M. Stanton	Same, w/o grill		12		149
7¢	orng verm	E.M. Stanton	Same, w/secret mark		12		160
7¢	black	Washington			12	SL	407
7¢	black	Washington			10	SL	430
7¢	black	Washington			10	NW	469
7¢	black	Washington			11	NW	507
7¢	black	Wm. McKinley		F	11		559
7¢	black	Wm. McKinley		R	10		588
7¢	black	Wm. McKinley		R	11x10.5		639
7¢	black	Wm. McKinley	Kansas Ovpt.		11x10.5		665
7¢	black	Wm. McKinley	Nebraska Ovpt.		11x10.5		676
7¢	sepia	A. Jackson			11x10.5		812
7¢	rose carm	W. Wilson			11x10.5		1040
7¢	brt blue	B. Franklin			10.5x11		1393D
7¢	brt carm	Abraham Baldwin			10.5x11		1850
7.1¢	lake	Tractor	Coil		10 Vert		2127
7.4¢	brown	Baby Buggy	Coil		10 Vert		1902
7.6¢	brown	Carreta	Coil		10 Vert		2255
7.7¢	brn (brt yl)	Saxhorns	Coil		10 Vert		1614
7.9¢	carm (yl)	Drum	Coil		10 Vert		1615
8¢	lilac	W.T. Sherman	w/o Triangles		12		225
8¢	violet brn	W.T. Sherman	w/ Tri. in Top corners		12	NW	257
8¢	violet brn	W.T. Sherman	w/ Tri. in Top corners		12	DL	272
8¢	violet brn	W.T. Sherman	w/ Tri. in Top corners		12	USIR	272a
8¢	violet blk	M. Washington	"Series 1902"		12	DL	306
8¢	olive grn	Washington			12	DL	337
8¢	olive grn	Washington	Blue Paper		12	DL	363
8¢	olive grn	Washington			12	SL	380
8¢	pl olv grn	B. Franklin			12	SL	414
8¢	pl olv grn	B. Franklin			10	SL	431
8¢	olv grn	B. Franklin			10	NW	470
8¢	olv grn	B. Franklin			11	NW	508
8¢	olv grn	U.S. Grant		F	11		560
8¢	olv grn	U.S. Grant		R	10		589
8¢	olv grn	U.S. Grant		R	11x10.5		640
8¢	olv grn	U.S. Grant	Kansas Ovpt.		11x10.5		666
8¢	olv grn	U.S. Grant	Nebraska Ovpt.		11x10.5		677
8¢	olv grn	M. Van Buren			11x10.5		813
8¢	dk viol bl & carm	Statue of Liberty		Flat	11		1041
		Statue of Liberty		Rotary	11		1041B
		Statue of Liberty Redrawn		Giori	11		1042
8¢	brown	Gen. J.J. Pershing		R	11x10.5		1042A
8¢	violet	Albert Einstein			11x10.5		1285*
8¢	multi	Flag & Wh House			11x10.5		1338F
8¢	multi	Flag & Wh House	Coil		10 Vert		1338G
8¢	blk,rd & bl gry	Eisenhower			11		1394
8¢	dp claret	Eisenhower	Bklt. sgl./B.Pn. of 8		11x10.5		1395a
8¢	dp claret	Eisenhower	Bklt. Pn. of 6		11x10.5		1395b
8¢	dp claret	Eisenhower	Bklt. Pn. of 4 + 2 Labels		11x10.5		1395c
8¢	dp claret	Eisenhower	Bklt. Pn. of 7 + Label		11x10.5		1395d
8¢	multi	Postal Service Emblem			11x10.5		1396
8¢	dp claret	Eisenhower	Coil		10 Vert		1402
8¢	olive blk	Henry Knox			10.5x11		1851
8.3¢	green	Ambulance	Coil		10 Vert		2128
8.3¢	green	Ambulance	Coil Precan.	B	10 Vert		2231
8.4¢	dk bl (yel)	Grand Piano	Coil		10 Vert		1615C
8.4¢	dp claret	Wheel Chair	Coil		10 Vert		2256
8.5¢	dk pris grn	Tow Truck	Coil		10 Vert		2129
9¢	salmn rd	B. Franklin			12	SL	415
9¢	salmn rd	B. Franklin			10	SL	432
9¢	salmn rd	B. Franklin			10	NW	471
9¢	salmn rd	B. Franklin			11	NW	509
9¢	rose	T. Jefferson		F	11		561
9¢	rose	T. Jefferson		R	10		590
9¢	orng red	T. Jefferson		R	11x10.5		641
9¢	lt rose	T. Jefferson	Kansas Ovpt.		11x10.5		667
9¢	lt rose	T. Jefferson	Nebraska Ovpt.		11x10.5		678
9¢	rose pink	W.H. Harrison			11x10.5		814
9¢	rose lilac	Alamo			10.5x11		1043
9¢	slate grn	Capitol Dome			11x10.5		1591
9¢	slate grn	Capitol Dome	Bklt. Single		11x10.5		1590
9¢	slate grn	Capitol Dome	Bklt. Single		10		1590a
9¢	slate grn	Capitol Dome	Coil		10 Vert		1616
9¢	dark grn	Sylvanus Thayer			10.5x11		1852
9.3¢	carm rose	Mail Wagon	Coil		10 Vert		1903
10¢	black	Washington			Imperf		2
10¢	black	Washington	Bluish paper (reprint)		Imperf		4
10¢	green	Washington	Ty I		Imperf		13
10¢	green	Washington	Ty II		Imperf		14
10¢	green	Washington	Ty III		Imperf		15
10¢	green	Washington	Ty IV		Imperf		16
10¢	green	Washington	Ty I		15		31
10¢	green	Washington	Ty II		15		32
10¢	green	Washington	Ty III		15		33
10¢	green	Washington	Ty IV		15		34
10¢	green	Washington	Ty V		15		35
10¢	dark grn	Washington	Premier Gravure, Ty I		12		62B
10¢	yel grn	Washington	Ty II		12		68
10¢	green	Washington	"Z" Grill		12		85D
10¢	green	Washington	"E" Grill		12		89
10¢	yel grn	Washington	"F" Grill		12		96
10¢	yellow	Eagle & Shield	"G" Grill		12		116
10¢	brown	T. Jefferson	w/grill, Hard wh paper		12		139
10¢	brown	T. Jefferson	Same, w/o grill		12		150
10¢	brown	T. Jefferson	Same, w/secret mark		12		161
10¢	brown		Soft porous paper:				
			w/o secret mark		12		187
			w/secret mark		12		188
10¢	brown	T. Jefferson	Soft paper, re-engr.		12		209
10¢	green	D. Webster	w/o Triangles		12		226
10¢	dark grn	D. Webster	w/ Tri. in Top corners		12	NW	258
10¢	dark grn	D. Webster	w/ Tri. in Top corners		12	DL	273
10¢	brown	D. Webster	Ty I "		12	DL	282C
10¢	orng brn/brn	D. Webster	Ty II "		12	DL	283
10¢	pl rd brn	D. Webster	"Series 1902"		12	DL	307
10¢	yellow	Washington			12	DL	338
10¢	yellow	Washington	Blue Paper		12	DL	364
10¢	yellow	Washington			12	SL	381
10¢	yellow	Washington	Coil		12 Vert	DL	356
10¢	orng yel	B. Franklin			12	SL	416
10¢	orng yel	B. Franklin			10	SL	433
10¢	orng yel	B. Franklin			10	NW	472
10¢	orng yel	B. Franklin			11	NW	510
10¢	orng yel	B. Franklin	Coil	R	10 Vert	NW	497
10¢	yel orng	J. Monroe		F	11	NW	562
10¢	yel orng	J. Monroe		R	10	NW	591
10¢	orange	J. Monroe		R	11x10.5	NW	642
10¢	orange	J. Monroe	Coil	R	10 Vert	NW	603
10¢	orng yel	J. Monroe	Kansas Ovpt.		11x10.5	NW	668
10¢	orng yel	J. Monroe	Nebraska Ovpt.		11x10.5	NW	679
10¢	brn red	J. Tyler			11x10.5		815
10¢	brn red	J. Tyler	Coil		10 Vert		847
10¢	rose lake	Indep. Hall			10.5x11		1044*
10¢	lilac	A. Jackson			11x10.5		1286*
10¢	red & bl	Crossed Flags			11x10.5		1509
10¢	red & bl	Crossed Flags	Coil		10 Vert		1519
10¢	blue	Jefferson Mem.			11x10.5		1510
10¢	blue	Jefferson Mem.	Bklt. Pn. of 5 + Label		11x10.5		1510b
10¢	blue	Jefferson Mem.	Bklt. Pn. of 8		11x10.5		1510c
10¢	blue	Jefferson Mem.	Bklt. Pn. of 6		11x10.5		1510d
10¢	blue	Jefferson Mem.	Coil		10 Vert		1520
10¢	multi	"Zip Code"			11x10.5		1511
10¢	violet	Justice			11x10.5		1592
10¢	violet	Justice	Coil		10 Vert		1617
10¢	prus bl	Richard Russell			10.5x11		1853
10¢	lake	Red Cloud			11		2175
10¢	sky blue	Canal Boat	Coil		10 Vert		2257
10¢	green	Tractor Trailer	Coil Intaglio		10 Vert		2457

DEFINITIVE ISSUE IDENTIFIER

Den.	Color	Subject	Type / Comment	Press	Perf.	Wmk.	Scott #
10¢	green	Tractor Trailer	Coil Gravure		10 Vert		2458
10¢	red&black	Joseph W. Stilwell			11		3420
10¢	multi	American Clock	Self-adhesive				3751
10.1¢	**slate blue**	**Oil Wagon**	**Coil**		**10 Vert**		**2130**
10.9¢	**purple**	**Hansom Cab**	**Coil**		**10 Vert**		**1904**
11	**dark grn**	**B. Franklin**			**10**	**SL**	**434**
11¢	dark grn	B. Franklin			10	NW	473
11¢	light grn	B. Franklin			11	NW	511
11¢	lt bl/bl grn	R.B. Hayes		F	11		563
11¢	light blue	R.B. Hayes		R	11x10.5		692
11¢	ultra	J.K. Polk			11x10.5		816
11¢	carm & dk viol bl	Statue of Liberty			11		1044A*
11¢	orange	Printing Press			11x10.5		1593
11¢	dk blue	Alden Partridge			11		1854
11¢	red	RR Caboose	Coil		10 Vert		1905
11¢	dk green	Stutz Bearcat	Coil		10 Vert		2131
12¢	**black**	**Washington**			**Imperf**		**17**
12¢	black	Washington	Plate 1		15		36
12¢	black	Washington	Plate 3		15		36b
12¢	black	Washington			12		69
12¢	black	Washington	"Z" Grill		12		85E
12¢	black	Washington	"E" Grill		12		90
12¢	black	Washington	"F" Grill		12		97
12¢	green	S.S. Adriatic	"G grill"		12		117
12¢	dull violet	H. Clay	Hard wh paper, w/grill		12		140
12¢	dull violet	H. Clay	Same, w/o grill		12		151
12¢	blksh viol	H. Clay	Same, w/secret mark		12		162
12¢	claret brn	B. Franklin			12	SL	417
12¢	claret brn	B. Franklin			10	SL	435
12¢	copper rd	B. Franklin			10	SL	435a
12¢	claret brn	B. Franklin			10	NW	474
12¢	claret brn	B. Franklin			11	NW	512
12¢	brn carm	B. Franklin			11	NW	512a
12¢	brn violet	G. Cleveland		F	11		564
12¢	brn violet	G. Cleveland		R	11x10.5		693
12¢	bright viol	Z. Taylor			11x10.5		817
12¢	red	B. Harrison			11x10.5		1045*
12¢	black	Henry Ford			10.5x11		1286A*
12¢	rd brn (bge)	Liberty Torch	Coil		10 Vert		1816
12¢	dk blue	Stanley Stmr	Ty I Coil		10 Vert		2132
12¢	dk blue	Stanley Stmr	Ty II Coil, precanc.		10 Vert		2132b
12.5¢	**olive grn**	**Pushcart**	**Coil**		**10 Vert**		**2133**
13¢	**purp blk**	**B. Harrison**	**"Series 1902"**		**12**	**DL**	**308**
13¢	blue grn	Washington			12	DL	339
13¢	blue grn	Washington	Blue Paper		12	DL	365
13¢	apple grn	B. Franklin			11	NW	513
13¢	green	B. Harrison		F	11		622
13¢	yel grn	B. Harrison		R	11x10.5		694
13¢	bue grn	M. Fillmore			11x10.5		818
13¢	brown	J.F. Kennedy			11x10.5		1287*
13¢	brown	Liberty Bell			11x10.5		1595
13¢	brown	Liberty Bell	Bklt. Pn. of 6		11x10.5		1595a
13¢	brown	Liberty Brll	Bklt. Pn. of 7 + Label		11x10.5		1595b
13¢	brown	Liberty Bell	Bklt. Pn. of 8		11x10.5		1595c
13¢	brown	Liberty Bell	Bklt. Pn of 5 + Label		11x10.5		1595d
13¢	brown	Liberty Bell	Coil		10 Vert		1618
13¢	multi	Eagle & Shield	Bullseye Perfs		11x10.5		1596
13¢	multi	Eagle & Shield	Line Perfs		11		1596d
13¢	dk bl & rd	Flag Over Indep. Hall			11x10.5		1622
13¢	dk. bl & rd	Flag Over Indep. Hall			11		1622c
13¢	dk bl & rd	Flag Over Indep. Hall	Coil		10 Vert		1625
13¢	bl & rd	Flag Over Captl	Bklt. Single		11x10.5		1623
13¢	bl & rd	Flag Over Captl	Bklt. Single		10		1623b
13¢	bl & rd	Flag Over Capt	B. Pn. of 8				
		(7 #1623 (13¢) + 1 # 1590 (9¢))			11X10.5		1623a
13¢	bl & rd	Flag Over Capt	B. Pn. of 8				
		(7 #1623b (13¢) + 1 #1590a (9¢))			10		1623c
13¢	brn & bl (grn bistr)	Indian Head Penny			11		1734
13¢	lt maroon	Crazy Horse			10.5x11		1855
13¢	black	Patrol Wagon	Coil		10 Vert		2258
13.2¢	**slate grn**	**Coal Car**	**Coil**		**10 Vert**		**2259**
14¢	**blue**	**American Indian**		**F**	**11**		**565**
14¢	dk blue	American Indian		R	11x10.5		695
14¢	blue	F. Pierce			11x10.5		819
14¢	gray brn	Fiorello LaGuardia			11x10.5		1397
14¢	slate grn	Sinclair Lewis			11		1856
14¢	sky blue	Iceboat	Coil, overall tag		10 Vert		2134
14¢	sky blue	Iceboat, Ty II	Coil, block tag	B	10 Vert		2134b
14¢	crimson	Julia Ward Howe			11		2176
15¢	**black**	**A. Lincoln**			**12**		**77**
15¢	black	A. Lincoln	"Z" Grill		12		85F
15¢	black	A. Lincoln	"E" Grill		12		91
15¢	black	A. Lincoln	"F" Grill		12		98
15¢	**brn & bl**	**Landing of Columbus:**					
			Ty I Frame, "G grill"		12		118
			Same, w/o grill, o.g.		12		118a
			Ty II Frame, "G grill"		12		119
			Ty III, wh crackly gum		12		129
15¢	orange	D. Webster	Hard wh paper, w/grill		12		141
15¢	brt orng	D. Webster	Same, w/o grill		12		152
15¢	yel orng	D. Webster	Same, w/secret mark		12		163
15¢	red orng	D. Webster	Soft porous paper		12		189
15¢	indigo	H. Clay	w/o Triangles		12		227
15¢	dk blue	H. Clay	w/ Tri. in Top corners		12	NW	259
15¢	dk blue	H. Clay	w/ Tri. in Top corners		12	DL	274
15¢	olive grn	H. Clay	w/ Tri. in Top corners		12	DL	284
15¢	olive grn	H. Clay	"Series 1902"		12	DL	309
15¢	pl ultra	Washington			12	DL	340
15¢	pl ultra	Washington	Blue Paper		12	DL	366
15¢	pl ultra	Washington			12	SL	382
15¢	gray	B. Franklin			12	SL	418
15¢	gray	B. Franklin			10	SL	437
15¢	gray	B. Franklin			10	NW	475
15¢	gray	B. Franklin			11	NW	514
15¢	gray	Statue of Liberty		F	11		566
15¢	gray	Statue of Liberty		R	11x10.5		696
15¢	blue gray	J. Buchanan			11x10.5		820
15¢	rose lake	John Jay			11x10.5		1046*
15¢	maroon	O.W. Holmes			11x10.5		1288
15¢	dk rse clrt	O.W. Holmes	Type II		11x10.5		1288d
15¢	dk rse clrt	O.W. Holmes	Bklt. sgl./B.Pn. of 8		10		1288Bc
15¢	gray, dk bl & red	Ft McHenry Flag			11		1597
15¢		Ft McHenry Flag	Bklt. sgl./B. Pn. of 8		11x10.5		1598a
15¢		Ft McHenry Flag	Coil		10 Vert		1618C
15¢	multi	Roses	Bklt. sgl./B. Pn. of 8		10		1737a
15¢	sepia (yel)		Windmills Bklt. Pn. of 10		11		1742a
15¢	rd brn &						
	sepia	Dolley Madison			11		1822
15¢	claret	Buffalo Bill Cody			11		2177
15¢	violet	Tugboat	Coil		10 Vert		2260
15¢	multi	Beach Umbrella	Bklt. sgl./B. Pn. of 10		11.5x11		2443a
16¢	**black**	**A. Lincoln**			**11x10.5**		**821**
16¢	brown	Ernie Pyle			11x10.5		1398
16¢	blue	Statue of Liberty			11		1599
16¢	blue	Statue of Liberty	Coil		10 Vert		1619
16.7¢	**rose**	**Popcorn Wagon**	**Coil**		**10 Vert**		**2261**
17¢	**black**	**W. Wilson**		**F**	**11**		**623**
17¢	black	W. Wilson		R	10.5x11		697
17¢	rose red	A. Johnson			11x10.5		822
17¢	green	Rachel Carson			10.5x11		1857
17¢	ultra	Electric Auto	Coil		10 Vert		1906
17¢	sky blue	Dog Sled	Coil		10 Vert		2135
17¢	dk bl grn	Belva Ann Lockwood			11		2178
17.5¢	**dk violet**	**Racing Car**	**Coil**		**10 Vert**		**2262**
18¢	**brn carm**	**U.S. Grant**			**11x10.5**		**823**
18¢	violet	Dr. Elizabeth Blackwell			11x10.5		1399
18¢	dark bl	George Mason			10.5x11		1858
18¢	dark brn	Wildlife Animals	Bklt. Pn. of 10		11		1889a
18¢	multi	Flag/Amber Waves...			11		1890
18¢	multi	Flag/Sea to...Sea	Coil		10 Vert		1891
18¢	multi	Flag/Purple Mtns...Bklt. Single			11		1893
18¢	multi	Flag/Purple Mnts...Bklt. Pn. of 8					
		(7 #1893 (18¢) + 1 #1892 (6¢))			11		1893a
18¢	dk brn	Surrey	Coil		10 Vert		1907
18¢	multi	Washington & Monument	Coil		10 Vert		2149
19¢	**brt violet**	**R.B. Hayes**			**11x10.5**		**824**
19¢	brown	Sequoyah			10.5x11		1859
19¢	multi	Fawn			11.5x11		2479
19¢	multi	Fishing Boat	Coil Type I		10 Vert		2529
19¢	multi	Fishing Boat	Coil Type III		9.8 Vert		2529C
19¢	multi	Balloon	Bklt. sgl./B. Pn. of 10		10		2530,a
20¢	**ultra**	**B. Franklin**			**12**	**SL**	**419**
20¢	ultra	B. Franklin			10	SL	438
20¢	lt. ultra	B. Franklin			10	NW	476
20¢	lt. ultra	B. Franklin			11	NW	515
20¢	carm rse	Golden Rose		F	11		567
20¢	carm rse	Golden Gate		R	10.5x11		698
20¢	brt bl grn	J. Garfield			11x10.5		825
20¢	ultra	Monticello			10.5x11		1047
20¢	dp olive	George C. Marshall			11x10.5		1289*
20¢	claret	Ralph Bunche			10.5x11		1860
20¢	green	Thomas H. Gallaudet			10.5x11		1861
20¢	black	Harry S. Truman			11		1862**
20¢	blk, dk bl & red						
		Flag/Supreme Court			11		1894
20¢		Flag/Sup. Ct. Coil			10 Vert		1895
20¢		Flag/Sup. Ct. Bklt. sgl./Pns. of 6 & 10			11x10.5		1896,a,b
20¢	vermilion	Fire Pumper	Coil		10 Vert		1908
20¢	dk blue	Rocky Mtn. Bighorn	Bklt. sgl./Pn. of 10		11		1949a
20¢	sky blue	Consumer Ed.	Coil		10 Vert		2005

DEFINITIVE ISSUE IDENTIFIER

Den.	Color	Subject	Type / Comment	Press	Perf.	Wmk.	Scott #
20¢	bl violet	Cable Car	Coil		10 Vert		2263
20¢	red brown	Virginia Agpar			11.1x11		2179
20¢	green	Cog Railway	Coil		10 Vert		2463
20¢	multi	Blue Jay	Bklt. Sgl./B. Pn. of 10		11x10		2483,a
20¢	multi	Blue Jay	Self-adhesive		Die-Cut		3048
20¢	multi	Blue Jay	Coil		11.6 Vert		3053
20¢	multi	Ring necked Pheasant Blkt. Sgl.	Die-cut		11.2		3050
20¢	multi	Ring necked Pheasant	Bklt.Sgle.Die-cut		10.5x11		3051
20¢	multi	Ring neck Pheasant	Bk.Sgle.Die-cut 10.6x10.4 on 3 sides				3051A
20¢	multi	Ring necked Pheasant	Coil		Die-cut9.8 Vert		3055
20¢	dark carmine	George Washington	S.A. Booklet Stamp		Die-cut 11.25		3482
20¢	dark carmine	George Washington	S.A. Booklet Stamp		Die-cut 10.5x11.25		3483
20.5¢	**rose**	**Fire Engine**	**Coil**		**10 Vert**		**2264**
21¢	**dull blue**	**Chester A. Arthur**			**11x10.5**		**826**
21¢	green	Amadeo Giannini			11x10.5		1400
21¢	bl violet	Chester Carlson			11		2181
21¢	olive grn	RR Mail Car	Coil		10 Vert		2265
21¢	multi	Bison			11.25		3467
21¢	multi	Bison	Self-adhesive		Die-cut 11		3468
21¢	multi	Bison	Self-adhesive		Die-cut 8.5 Vert		3475
21¢	multi	Bison	S.A Booklet Stamp		Die-cut 11.25		3484
21¢	multi	Bison	S.A.Booklet Stamp		Die-cut 10.5x11.25		3484A
21.1¢	**multi**	**Envelopes**	**Coil**		**10 Vert**		**2150**
22¢	**vermilion**	**G. Cleveland**			**11x10.5**		**827**
22¢	dk chlky bl	John J. Audubon			11		1863**
22¢	bl rd blk	Flag/Capitol			11		2114
22¢	bl rd blk	Flag/Capitol	Coil		10 Vert		2115
22¢	bl rd blk	Flag/Capitol/"of the People"	Bklt. Sgl.		10 Hz		2116
22¢	bl rd blk	Flag/Capitol/"of the People"	B. Pn. of 5		10 Hz		2116a
22¢	blk & brn	Seashells	Bklt. Pn. of 10		10		2121a
22¢	multi	Fish	Bklt. Pn. of 5		10 Hz		2209a
22¢	multi	Flag & Fireworks			11		2276
22¢	multi	Flag & Fireworks	Bklt. Pn. of 20		11		2276a
22¢	multi	Uncle Sam	Self-adhesive		Die-cut 10.8		3259
22¢	multi	Uncle Sam	Self-adhesive Coil		Die-cut9.9 Vert		3263
22¢	multi	Uncle Sam	Coil		9¾ Vert		3353
23¢	**purple**	**Mary Cassatt**			**11**		**2181**
23¢	dk blue	Lunch Wagon	Coil		10 Vert		2464
23¢	multi	Flag & Presorted First Class	Coil		10 Vert		2605
23¢	multi	USA & Flag Presort First Cl	Coil		10 Vert	ABNC	2606
23¢	multi	USA & Flag Presort First Cl	Coil		10 Vert	BEP	2607
23¢	multi	USA & Flag Presort First Cl	Coil		10 Vert	SVS	2608
23¢	green	George Washington	Self-adhesive		Die-cut 11.25x11.75		3468A
23¢	green	George Washington	S.A. Coil		Die-cut 8.5 Vert.		3475A
23¢	green	G.Washington	WA		11¼		3616
23¢	green	G.Washington	S.A. Coil		Die-cut 8.5 Vert.		3617
23¢	green	G.Washington	S.A. Booklet stamp		Die-cut 11¼		3618
23¢	green	G.Washington	S.A. Booklet stamp		Die-cut 10½x11¼		3619
23¢	gray green	G. Washington	S.A. Bk.Sgle. "2003"		Die-cut 11		3819
24¢	**gray lilac**	**Washington**	**"Twenty Four Cents"**		**15**		**37**
24¢	red lilac	Washington	"24 Cents"		12		70
24¢	brn lilac	Washington			12		70a
24¢	steel blue	Washington			12		70b
24¢	violet	Washington			12		70c
24¢	grayish lil	Washington			12		70d
24¢	lilac	Washington			12		78
24¢	grayish lil	Washington			12		78a
24¢	gray	Washington			12		78b
24¢	blkish viol	Washington			12		78c
24¢	gray lilac	Washington	"F" Grill		12		99
24¢	grn & viol	Decl. of Indep.	"G grill"		12		120
24¢	grn & viol	Decl. of Indep.	w/o grill, original gum		12		120a
24¢	purple	Gen'l. W. Scott	Hard wh paper, w/grill		12		142
24¢	purple	Gen'l. W. Scott	Same, w/o grill		12		153
24¢	gray blk	B. Harrison			11x10.5		828
24¢	red (blue)	Old North Church			11x10.5		1603
24.1¢	**dp ultra**	**Tandem Bicycle**	**Coil**		**10 Vert**		**2266**
25¢	**yel grn**	**Niagara Falls**		**F**	**568**		
25¢	blue grn	Niagara Falls		R	10.5x11		699
25¢	dp rd lil	Wm. McKinley			11x10.5		829
25¢	green	Paul Revere			11x10.5		1048
25¢	green	Paul Revere	Coil		10 Vert		1059A*
25¢	rose	Frederick Douglass			11x10.5		1290*
25¢	orng brn	Bread Wagon	Coil		10 Vert		2136
25¢	blue	Jack London			11		2182
25¢	blue	Jack London	Bklt. Pn. of 10		11		2182a
25¢	blue	Jack London	Bklt. Sgl./B. Pn. of 6		10		2197,a
25¢	multi	Flag & Clouds			11		2278
25¢	multi	Flag & Clouds	Bklt. Sgl./B. Pn. of 6		10		2285Ac
25¢	multi	Flag/Yosemite	Coil		10 Vert		2280
25¢	multi	Honeybee	Coil		10 Vert		2281
25¢	multi	Pheasant	Bklt. Sgl./B. Pn. of 10		11		2283,a
25¢	multi	Pheasant	Same, w/o red in sky		11		2283b,c
25¢	multi	Grossbeak	Bklt. Single		10		2284
25¢	multi	Owl	Bklt. Single		10		2285
25¢	multi	Grossbk & Owl	Bklt. Pn. of 10 (5 ea.)		10		2285b
25¢	multi	Eagle & Shield	Self-adhesive		Die cut		2431
25¢	dk rd & bl	Flag	Self-adhesive		Die cut		2475
28¢	**brn (bl)**	**Ft. Nisqually**			**11x10.5**		**1604**
28¢	myrtle grn	Sitting Bull			11		2183
29¢	**blue (bl)**	**Sandy Hook Lighthouse**			**11x10.5**		**1605**
29¢	blue	Earl Warren			11		2184
29¢	dk violet	T. Jefferson			11		2185
29¢	multi	Red Squirrel	Self-adhesive		Die cut		2489
29¢	multi	Rose	Self-adhesive		Die cut		2490
29¢	multi	Pine Cone	Self-adhesive		Die cut		2491
29¢	blk & multi	Wood Duck	Bklt. sgl./B. Pn. of 10		10		2484,a
29¢	red & multi	Wood Duck	Bklt. sgl./B. Pn. of 10		11		2485,c
29¢	multi	African Violet	Bklt. sgl./B. Pn. of 10		10x11		2486,a
29¢	bl,rd,clar	Flag/Rushmore	Coil, Engraved		10		2523
29¢	bl,rd,brn	Flag/Rushmore	Coil, Gravure		10		2523A
29¢	multi	Tulip			11		2524
29¢	multi	Tulip			12.5x13		2524a
29¢	multi	Tulip	Coil	Roulette	10 Vert		2525
29¢	multi	Tulip	Coil		10 Vert		2526
29¢	multi	Tulip	Bklt. sgl./B. Pn. of 10		11		2527,a
29¢	multi	Flag/Rings	Bklt. sgl./B. Pn. of 10		11		2528
29¢	multi	Flags on Parade			11		2531
29¢	blk,gld,grn	Liberty/Torch	Self-adhesive		Die cut		2531A
29¢	multi	Flag & Pledge	blk. denom Bklt. sgl., Bklt. Pn. of 10		10		2593,a
29¢	multi	Flag & Pledge	red denom., Bklt. sgl., Bklt. Pn. of 10		10		2594,a
29¢	brn,multi	Eagle & Shield	Self-adhesive		Die cut		2595
29¢	grn,multi	Eagle & Shield	Self-adhesive		Die cut		2596
29¢	red,multi	Eagle & Shield	Self-adhesive		Die cut		2597
29¢	multi	Eagle	Self-adhesive		Die cut		2598
29¢	blue,red	Flag/White House	Coil		10 Vert		2609
29¢	multi	Liberty	Self-adhesive		Die cut		2599
30¢	**orange**	**B. Franklin**	**Numeral at bottom**	**15**			**38**
30¢	orange	B. Franklin	Numerals at Top	12			71
30¢	orange	B. Franklin	"A" Grill	12			81
30¢	orange	B. Franklin	"F" Grill	12			100
30¢	bl & carm	Eagle, Shield & Flags,	"G" Grill	12			121
30¢			w/o grill, original gum	12			121a
30¢	black	A. Hamilton	Hard wh paper, w/grill	12			143
30¢	black	A. Hamilton	Same, w/o grill	12			154
30¢	gray blk	A. Hamilton	Same	12			165
30¢	full blk./grnish blk	A. Hamilton	Soft porous paper	12			190
30¢	orng brn	A. Hamilton		12			217
30¢	black	T. Jefferson		12			228
30¢	orng red	B. Franklin		12		SL	420
30¢	orng red	B. Franklin		10		SL	439
30¢	orng red	B. Franklin		10		NW	476A
30¢	orng red	B. Franklin		11		NW	516
30¢	olive brn	Buffalo		F	11		569
30¢	brown	Buffalo		R	10.5x11		700
30¢	dp ultra	T. Roosevelt			11x10.5		830
30¢	blue	T. Roosevelt			11x10.5		830 var
30¢	dp blue	T. Roosevelt			11x10.5		830 var
30¢	black	R.E. Lee			11x10.5		1049
30¢	red lilac	John Dewey			10.5x11		1291*
30¢	green	Morris School			11x10.5		1606
30¢	olv gray	Frank C. Laubach			11		1864**
30¢	multi	Cardinal			11		2480
32¢	**blue**	**Ferryboat**	**Coil**		**10 Vert**		**2466**
32¢	multi	Peach	Booklet Single		10x11		2487
32¢	multi	Peach	Self-adhesive		Die cut		2493
32¢	multi	Peach	Self-adhesive Coil		Die cut		2495
32¢	multi	Pear	Booklet Single		10x11		2488
32¢	multi	Pear	Self-adhesive		Die cut		2494
32¢	multi	Pear	Self-adhesive Coil		Die cut		2495A
32¢	multi	Peach & Pear	Bklt. Pane of 10		10x11		2488A
32¢	multi	Peach & Pear	Self-adhesive Pane		Die cut		2494A
32¢	multi	Peach & Pear	Self-adhesive Coil		Die-cut		2495-95A
32¢	multi	Pink Rose	Self-adhesive		Die cut		2492
32¢	red-brown	James K. Polk			11.2		2587
32¢	multi	Flag over Porch			10.04		2897
32¢	multi	Flag over Porch	Coil	BEP	9.9 Vert		2913
32¢	multi	Flag over Porch	Coil	SVS	9.9 Vert		2914
32¢	multi	Flag over Porch	Self-adhesive Coil		Die cut 8.7		2915
32¢	multi	Flag over Porch	Self-adhesive Coil		Die cut 9.7		2915A
32¢	multi	Flag over Porch	Self-adhesive Coil		Die cut 11.5		2915B
32¢	multi	Flag over Porch	Self-adhesive Coil		Die cut 10.9		2915C
32¢	multi	Flag over Porch	Self-adhesive Coil		Die cut 9.8		2915D
32¢	multi	Flag over Porch	Bklt.Sgle./P.Pn. of 10		11x10		2916a
32¢	multi	Flag over Porch	Self-adhesive		Die-cut 8.8		2920,20b
32¢	multi	Flag over Porch	Self-adhesive		Die-cut 11.3		2920d
32¢	multi	Flag over Porch	Self-adhesive		Die-cut 9.8		2921a
32¢	multi	Flag over Porch	Linterless SA Coil		Die-cut		3133

DEFINITIVE ISSUE IDENTIFIER

Den.	Color	Subject	Type / Comment	Press	Perf.	Wmk.	Scott #
32¢	multi	Flag over Field	Self-adhesive		Die cut		2919
32¢	lake	Henry R. Luce			11		2935
32¢	blue	Lila & DeWitt Wallace			11		2936
32¢	brown	Milton S. Hershey			11		2933
32¢	green	Cal Farley			11		2934
32¢	multi	Yellow Rose	Self-adhesive		Die-cut 9.9 Vert		3049
32¢	multi	Yellow Rose	Self-adhesive Coil		Die-cut 9.8 Vert.		3054
32¢	multi	Statue of Liberty			Die-cut 11		3122
32¢	multi	Statue of Liberty			Die-cut 11.5x11.8		3122E
32¢	multi	Citron, Moth	Self-adhesive		Die-cut		3126,28a
32¢	multi	Flowering Pineapple, Cockroaches Self-adhesive			Die-cut		3127,29a
33¢	multi	Flag and City			11.2		3277
33¢	multi	Flag and City	Self-adhesive		Die-cut 11.1		3278
33¢	multi	Flag and City	SA Bklt.Single		Die-cut 11½x11¾		3278F
33¢	multi	Flag and City	SA Bklt.Single		Die-cut 9.8		3279
33¢	multi	Flag and City Coil			9.9 Vert.		3280
33¢	multi	Flag and City	SA Coil, square corner		Die-cut 9.8		3281
33¢	multi	Flag and City	SA Coil, rounded corner		Die-cut 9.8		3282
33¢	multi	Flag and Chalkboard	SA Bklt.Single		Die-cut 7.9		3283
33¢	multi	Fruit Berries SA Booklet Singles			Die-cut 11.2x11.7		3294-97
33¢	multi	Fruit Berries SA Booklet Singles			Die-cut 9.5x10		3298-3301
33¢	multi	Fruit Berries, SA Coils			Die-cut 8.5 Vert		3302-5
33¢	multi	Fruit Berries, SA Coils			Die-cut 8.5 Horiz.		3404-7
33¢	multi	Coral Pink Rose SA Bklt. Single			Die-cut 11½x11¼		3052
33¢	multi	Coral Pink Rose SA Bklt. Single			Die-cut 10.75x10.5		3052E
33¢	red & black	Claude Pepper			11		3426
34¢	multi	Statue of Liberty	S.A. Coil (rounded corners)		Die-cut 9.75 Vert.		3466
34¢	multi	Statue of Liberty	Coil		9.75 Vert.		3476
34¢	multi	Statue of Liberty	S.A. Coil (square corners)		Die-cut 9.75 Vert.		3477
34¢	multi	Statue of Liberty S.A. Booklet Single	Die-cut				3484
34¢	multi	Statue of Liberty S.A. Single from Conv. Pane			Die-cut 11		3485
34¢	multi	Flag over Farm			11.25		3469
34¢	multi	Flag over Farm	Self-adhesive		Die-cut 11.25		3470
34¢	multi	Flag over Farm	S.A. Booklet Stamp		Die-cut 8		3495
34¢	multi	Flowers	Self-adhesive Coils		Die-cut 8.5 Vert.		3478-81
34¢	multi	Flowers	S.A. Booklet Stamps		Die-cut 10.25x10.75		3487-90
34¢	multi	Apple & Orange	S.A. Booklet Stamps		Die-cut 11.25		3491-92
34¢	multi	Apple & Orange	S.A. Bklt. Stamps		Die-cut 11.5x10.75		3493-94
34¢	multi	United We Stand	S.A. Booklet Stamp		Die-cut 11.25		3549
34¢	multi	United We Stand	S.A. Booklet Stamp		Die-cut 10.5x10.75		3549B
34¢	multi	United We Stand Self-adhesive Coil Square Corners			Die-cut 9.75 Vert.		3550
34¢	multi	United We Stand Self-adhesive Coil Rounded Corners			Die-cut 9.75 Vert.		3550A
35¢	gray	Charles R. Drew M.D.			10.5x11		1865
35¢	black	Dennis Chavez			11		2186
37¢	blue	Robert Millikan			10.5x11		1866
37¢	multi	Flag	"2003" Date		11¼		3629F
37¢	multi	Flag	Self-adhesive		Die-cut 11¼x11		3630
37¢	multi	Flag	Coil		10 Vert.		3631
37¢	multi	Flag	S.A. Coil "2002"		Die-cut 10 Vert.		3632
37¢	multi	Flag	S.A. Coil "2003"		Die-cut 10 Vert.		3632A
37¢	multi	Flag	S.A. Coil "2004"		Die-cut 11 3/4 Vert.		3632C
37¢	multi	Flag	S.A. Coil "2002"		Die-cut 8.5 Vert.		3633
37¢	multi	Flag	S.A. Coil "2003"		Die-cut 8.5 Vert.		3633A
37¢	multi	Flag	S.A. Booklet Stamp		Die-cut 11		3634
37¢	multi	Flag	S.A. Booklet Stamp		Die-cut 11¼		3635
37¢	multi	Flag	S.A. Booklet Stamp		Die-cut 10½x10 3/4		3636
37¢	multi	Flag	S.A. Booklet Stamp "2003"		Die-cut 11		3634b
37¢	multi	Flag	S.A. Booklet Stamp		Die-cut		3637
37¢	multi	Antique Toys	Self-adhesive Coils		Die-cut 8½		3638-41
37¢	multi	Antique Toys	S.A. Booklet Stamp		Die-cut 11		3642-45
37¢	multi	Snowy Egret	S.A. Coil "2003" date		Die-cut 8½ Vert.		3829
37¢	multi	Snowy Egret	S.A. Coil "2004" date		Die-cut 8½ Vert.		3829A
37¢	multi	Snowy Egret	S.A. Booklet Stamp		Die-cut		3830
39¢	rose lilac	Grenville Clark			11		1867**
40¢	brn red	J. Marshall			11x10.5		1050
40¢	bl black	Thomas Paine			11x10.5		1292*
40¢	dk grn	Lillian M. Gilbreth			11		1868**
40¢	dk blue	Claire Chennault			11		2187
45¢	brt blue	Harvey Cushing, MD			11		2188
45¢	multi	Pumpkinseed Fish			11		2481
46¢	carmine	Ruth Benedict			11		2938
50¢	orange	T. Jefferson	w/ Tri. in Top corners	12		NW	260
50¢	orange	T. Jefferson	w/ Tri. in Top corners	12		DL	275
50¢	orange	T. Jefferson	"Series 1902"	12		DL	310
50¢	violet	Washington		12		DL	341
50¢	violet	B. Franklin		12		SL	421
50¢	violet	B. Franklin		12		DL	422
50¢	violet	B. Franklin		10		SL	440
50¢	lt violet	B. Franklin		10		NW	477
50¢	rd violet	B. Franklin		11		NW	517

Den.	Color	Subject	Type / Comment	Press	Perf.	Wmk.	Scott#
50¢	lilac	Arlington Amph		F	11		570
50¢	lilac	Arlington Amph		R	10.5x11		701
50¢	lt rd viol	W.H. Taft			11x10.5		831
50¢	brt prpl	S.B. Anthony			11x10.5		1051
50¢	rose mag	Lucy Stone			11x10.5		1293*
50¢	blk & orng	Iron "Betty" Lamp			11		1608
50¢	brown	Chester W. Nimitz			11		1869**
52¢	purple	Hubert Humphrey			11		2189
55¢	green	Alice Hamilton			11		2940
55¢	black	Justin Morrill	SA	Die-cut 11½			2941
55¢	multi	Art-Deco Eagle	Self-adhesive		Die-cut 10.75		3471
56¢	scarlet	John Harvard			11		2190
57¢	multi	Art-Deco Eagle Self-adhesive			Die-cut 10.75		3471A
60¢	multi	Coverlet Eagle Self-adhesive			Die-cut 11x11¼		3646
65¢	dk blue	"Hap" Arnold			11		2191
75¢	dp mag	Wendell Wilkie			11		2192
76¢	red & black	Hattie Caraway Self-adhesive			Die-cut 11		3431
76¢	red & black	Hattie Caraway Self-adhesive			Die-cut 11½x11		3432
77¢	blue	Mary Breckenridge			11.8x11.6		2942
78¢	purple	Alice Paul			11.2		2943
83¢	multi	Edna Ferver			11.2		3433
90¢	blue	Washington	"Ninety Cents"		15		39
90¢	blue	Washington	"90 Cents"		12		72
90¢	blue	Washington	Same, "F" Grill		12		101
90¢	carm & blk	A. Lincoln	"G grill"		12		122
90¢	carm & blk	A. Lincoln	w/o grill, o.g.		12		122a
90¢	carmine	Com. Perry	Hard wh paper, w/grill		12		144
90¢	carmine	Com. Perry	Same, w/o grill		12		155
90¢	rose carm	Com. Perry	Same		12		166
90¢	carmine	Com. Perry	Soft porous paper		12		191
90¢	purple	Com. Perry	Soft porous paper		12		218
90¢	orange	Com. Perry			12		229
$1.00	black	Com. Perry	Ty I		12	NW	261
$1.00	black	Com. Perry	Ty I		12	DL	276
$1.00	black	Com. Perry	Ty II		12	NW	261A
$1.00	black	Com. Perry	Ty II		12	DL	276A
$1.00	black	D.G. Farragut			12	DL	311
$1.00	violet brn	Washington			12	DL	342
$1.00	violet brn	B. Franklin			12	DL	423
$1.00	violet blk	B. Franklin			10	DL	460
$1.00	violet blk	B. Franklin			10	NW	478
$1.00	violet brn	B. Franklin			11	NW	518
$1.00	deep brn	B. Franklin			11	NW	518b
$1.00	violet blk	Lincoln Memorial			11		571
$1.00	prpl & blk	W. Wilson			11		832
$1.00	prpl & blk	W. Wilson			11	USIR	832b
$1.00	rd viol & blk	W. Wilson	Dry Print, smooth gum		11		832c
$1.00	purple	P. Henry			11x10.5		1052
$1.00	dl purple	Eugene O'Neill			11x10.5		1294*
$1.00	dl purple	Eugene O'Neill	Coil		10 Vert		1305
$1.00	brn,orng&yel (tan)	Rush Lamp & Candle Holder			11		1610
$1.00	dk prus grn	Bernard Revel			11		2193
$1.00	dk blue	Johns Hopkins			11		2194
$1.00	bl & scar	Seaplane	Coil		10 Vert		2468
$1.00	gold,multi	Eagle & Olympic Rings			11		2539
$1.00	blue	Burgoyne			11.5		2590
$1.00	multi	Red Fox	Self-adhesive		Die-cut 11.5x11.3		3036
$1.00	multi	Red Fox	Self-adhesive		Die-cut 11 3/4x11		3036a
$1.00	multi	Wisdom	Self-adhesive		Diecut 11¼x11		3766
$2.00	brt blue	J. Madison	w/ Tri. in Top corners	12		NW	262
$2.00	brt blue	J. Madison	w/ Tri. in Top corners	12		DL	277
$2.00	dk blue	J. Madison	"Series 1902"	12		DL	312
$2.00	dk blue	J. Madison	"Series 1902"	10		NW	479
$2.00	orng rd & blk	B. Franklin			11		523
$2.00	carm & blk	B. Franklin			11		547
$2.00	dp blue	U.S. Capitol			11		572
$2.00	yel grn&blk	W.G. Harding			11		833
$2.00	dk grn&rd (tan)	Kerosene Table Lamp			11		1611
$2.00	brt viol	William Jennings Bryan			11		2195
$2.00	multi	Bobcat			11		2482
$2.90	multi	Eagle			11		2540
$2.90	multi	Space Shuttle			11x10½		2543
$3.00	multi	Challenger Shuttle			11.2		2544, 2544a
$3.00	multi	Mars Pathfinder			Souv. Sheet		3178
$3.20	multi	Space Shuttle Landing	Self-adhesive		Die-cut 11.5		3261
$3.50	multi	Capitol Dome Self-adhesive			Die-cut 11.25x11.5		3472
$3.85	multi	Jefferson Memorial S.A.			Die-cut 11¼		3647
$3.85	multi	Jefferson Meml.,S.A. "2003" Date			Die-cut 11x10 3/4		3647A
$5.00	dk green	J. Marshall	w/ Tri. in Top corners	12		NW	263
$5.00	dk green	J. Marshall	w/ Tri. in Top corners	12		DL	278
$5.00	dk green	J. Marshall	"Series 1902"	12		DL	313
$5.00	lt green	J. Marshall	"Series 1902"	10		NW	480
$5.00	dp grn & blk	B. Franklin			11		524
$5.00	carm & bl	Freedom Statue/Capitol			11		573
$5.00	carm & blk	C. Coolidge			11		834
$5.00	rd brn & blk	C. Coolidge			11		834a

DEFINITIVE ISSUE IDENTIFIER

Den.	Color	Subject	Type / Comment	Press	Perf.	Wmk.	Scott #
$5.00	black	A. Hamilton			11		1053
$5.00	gray blk	John Bassett Moore			11x10.5		1295*
$5.00	rd brn,yel&orng (tan)	RR Conductors Lantern			11		1612
$5.00	copper rd	Bret Harte			11		2196
$5.00	slate grn	Washington & Jackson			11.5		2592
$8.75	multi	Eagle & Moon			11		2394
$9.35	multi	Eagle & Moon	Bklt. sgl./B. Pn. of 3		10 Vert		1909,a
$9.95	multi	Eagle			11		2541
$9.95	multi	Moon Landing			10.7x11.1		2842
$10.75	multi	Eagle & Moon	Bklt. sgl./B. Pn. of 3		10 Vert		2122,a
$10.75	multi	Endeavor Shuttle			11		2544A
$11.75	multi	Piggyback Space Shuttle					
			Self-adhesive		Die-cut 11.5		3262
$12.25	multi	Washington Monument					
			Self-adhesive		Die-cut 11.25x11.5		3473
$13.65	multi	Capitol Dome	Self-adhesive		Die-cut 11¼		3648
$14.00	multi	Spread winged Eagle			11		2542

NON-DENOMINATED ISSUES (Stamps without numerical values)

Den.	Color	Subject	Type / Comment	Press	Perf.	Wmk.	Scott #
(1¢)	multi	Weather Vane, Blue Date			11.2		3257
(1¢)	multi	Weather Vane, Black Date			11.2		3258
(3¢)	multi	Dove	ABN		11x10.8		2877
(3¢)	multi	Dove	SVS		10.8x10.9		2878
* (4¢)	gold,carm	Text only	Make-up rate		11		2521
(5¢)	multi	Butte	Coil		9.8 Vert		2902
(5¢)	multi	Butte	Self-adhesive Coil		Die-cut 11.5		2902B
(5¢)	multi	Mountain	Coil	BEP	9.8 Vert		2903
(5¢)	multi	Mountain	Coil	SVS	9.8 Vert		2904
(5¢)	multi	Mountain	Self-adhesive Coil		Die-cut 11.5		2904A
(5¢)	multi	Mountain	Self-adhesive Coil		Die-cut 9.8		2904B
(5¢)	multi	Wetlands	Coil		10 Vert		3207
(5¢)	multi	Wetlands	Self-adhesive Coil		Die-cut 9.7 Vert		3207A
(5¢)	multi	Sea Coast	Self-adhesive Coil		Die-cut 8.5 Vert		3693
(5¢)	multi	Sea Coast	Coil		9.8 Vert		3775
(5¢)	multi	Sea Coast	Self-adhesive Coil		Die-cut 9½x10		3875
(10¢)	multi	Automobile	Coil		9.8 Vert		2905
(10¢)	multi	Automobile	Self-adhesive Coil		Die-cut 11.5		2907
(10¢)	multi	Eagle & Shield	Coil "Bulk Rate, USA"		10 Vert		2602
(10¢)	multi	Eagle & Shield	Coil "USA Bulk Rate"		10 Vert	BEP	2603
(10¢)	multi	Eagle & Shield	Coil "USA Bulk Rate"		10 Vert	SVS	2604
(10¢)	multi	Eagle & Shield	Self-adhesive Coil		Die-cut 11.5		2906
(10¢)	multi	Eagle & Shield	Coil "Presorted"		9.9 Vert		3270
(10¢)	multi	Eagle & Shield	Coil "Presorted"		Die-cut 9.9 Vert		3271
(10¢)	multi	Green Bicycle	Self-adhesive Coil		Die-cut 9.8 Vert		3228
(10¢)	multi	Green Bicycle	Coil		9.9 Vert		3229
(10¢)	multi	New York Public Library Lion	Self-adhesive Coil		Die-cut 11.5 Vert.		3447
(10¢)	multi	New York Public Library Lion	Coil		Water-activated		3769
(10¢)	multi	Atlas Statue	Self-adhesive Coil		Die-cut 8.5 Vert.		3520
(10¢)	multi	Atlas Statue	SA Coil "2003" Date		Die-cut 11 Vert.		3770
A (15¢)	orange	Eagle			11		1735
A (15¢)	orange	Eagle	Bklt. Sgl./Pn. of 8		11x10.5		1736,a
A (15¢)	orange	Eagle	Coil		10 Vert		1743
(15¢)	multi	Auto Tail Fin	Coil	BEP	9.8 Vert		2908
(15¢)	multi	Auto Tail Fin	Coil	SVS	9.8 Vert		2909
(15¢)	multi	Auto Tail Fin	Self-adhesive Coil		Die-cut 11.5		2910
(15¢)	multi	Woody Wagon	Self-adhesive Coil		Die-cut 11.5 Vert.		3522
B (18¢)	violet	Eagle			11x10.5		1818
B (18¢)	violet	Eagle	Bklt. sgl./Pn of 8		10		1819,a
B (18¢)	violet	Eagle	Coil		10 Vert		1820
C (20¢)	brown	Eagle			11x10.5		1946
C (20¢)	brown	Eagle	Coil		10 Vert		1947
C (20¢)	brown	Eagle	Bklt. sgl./Pn. of 10		11x10.5		1948,a
G (20¢)	multi	Flag Black "G"		BEP	11.2x11.1		2879
G (20¢)	multi	Flag Red "G"		SVS	11x10.9		2880
D (22¢)	green	Eagle			11		2111
D (22¢)	green	Eagle	Coil		10 Vert		2112
D (22¢)	green	Eagle	Bklt. sgl./Pn. of 10		11		2113,a
E (25¢)	multi	Earth			11		2277
E (25¢)	multi	Earth	Coil		10 Vert		2279
E (25¢)	multi	Earth	Bklt. sgl./Pn. of 10		11		2282a
(25¢)	multi	Juke Box	Coil	BEP	9.8 Vert		2911
(25¢)	multi	Juke Box	Coil	SVS	9.8 Vert		2912
(25¢)	multi	Juke Box	Self-adhesive Coil		Die-cut 11.5		2912A
(25¢)	multi	Juke Box	Self-adhesive Coil		Die-cut 9.8		2912B
(25¢)	multi	Juke Box	Linerless SA Coil		Die-cut		3132
(25¢)	multi	Diner	Coil		10 Vert		3208
(25¢)	multi	Diner	Self-adhesive Coil		Die-cut 9.7 Vert		3208A
G (25¢)	multi	Flag, Black "G"	Coil	SVS	9.8 Vert		2888
(25¢)	multi	American Eagle	Self-adhesive Coil		Die-cut 11 3/4 Vt.		3792-3801
F (29¢)	multi	Tulip			13		2517
F (29¢)	multi	Tulip	Coil		10		2518
F (29¢)	multi	Tulip	Bklt. Stamp	BEP	11 bullseye		2519
F (29¢)	multi	Tulip	Bkt. Stamp	KCS	11		2520
F (29¢)	blk,dk bl,red	Flag	Self-adhesive		Die cut		2522

Den.	Color	Subject	Type / Comment	Press	Perf.	Wmk.	Scott #
G (32¢)	multi	Flag, Black "G"		BEP	11.2x11.1		2881
G (32¢)	multi	Flag, Red "G"		SVS	11x10.9		2882
G (32¢)	multi	Flag, Black "G"	Bklt. Stamp	BEP	10x9.9		2883
G (32¢)	multi	Flag, Blue "G"	Bklt. Stamp	ABN	10.9		2884
G (32¢)	multi	Flag, Red "G"	Bklt. Stamp	SVS	11x10.9		2885
G (32¢)	multi	Flag	Self-adhesive		Die cut		2886,87
G (32¢)	multi	Flag, Black "G"	Coil	BEP	9.8 vert.		2889
G (32¢)	multi	Flag, Blue "G"	Coil	ABN	9.8 vert.		2890
G (32¢)	multi	Flag, Red "G"	Coil	SVS	9.8 vert.		2891
G (32¢)	multi	Flag, Red "G"	Coil	Roulette	9.8 vert.		2892
H (33¢)	multi	Uncle Sam's Hat			11.2		3260
H (33¢)	multi	Uncle Sam's Hat	Coil		9.8 Vert		3264
H (33¢)	multi	Uncle Sam's Hat					
			Self-adhesive Coil		Die-cut 9.9 Vert		3265
H (33¢)	multi	Uncle Sam's Hat					
			Self-adhesive Coil		Die-cut 9.7 Vert		3266
H (33¢)	multi	Uncle Sam's Hat, Small Date					
			S.A.Bklt. Stamp		Die-cut 9.9		3267
H (33¢)	multi	Uncle Sam's Hat, Large Date					
			S.A.Bklt. Stamp		Die-cut 11.2x11.1		3268
H (33¢)	multi	Uncle Sam's Hat					
			S.A. Bklt. Stamp		Die-cut 8		3269
(34¢)	multi	Flag over Farm			11.25		3448
(34¢)	multi	Flag over Farm	Self-adhesive		Die-cut 11.25		3449
(34¢)	multi	Flag over Farm	S.A. Booklet Stamp		Die-cut 8		3450
(34¢)	multi	Statue of Liberty	S.A. Booklet Stamp		Die-cut 11		3451
(34¢)	multi	Statue of Liberty	Coil		9.75 Vert.		3452
(34¢)	multi	Statue of Liberty	Self-adhesive Coil		Die-cut 10 Vert.		3453
(34¢)	multi	Flowers	S.A. Booklet Stamps				
					Die-cut 10.25x10.75		3454-57
(34¢)	multi	Flowers	S.A. Booklet Stamp				
					Die-cut 11.25x11.75		3458-61
(34¢)	multi	Flower	Self-adhesive Coils				
					Die-cut 8.5 Vert.		3462-65
(37¢)	multi	Flag			11¼x11		3620
(37¢)	multi	Flag	Self-adhesive		Die-cut 11¼x11		3621
(37¢)	multi	Flag	Self-adhesive Coil		Die-cut 10 Vert.		3622
(37¢)	multi	Flag	S.A. Booklet Stamp		Die-cut 11¼		3623
(37¢)	multi	Flag	S.A. Booklet Stamp		Die-cut 10½x10¾		3624
(37¢)	multi	Flag	S.A. Booklet Stamp		Die-cut 8		3625
(37¢)	multi	Antique Toys	S.A. Booklet Stamp		Die-cut 11		3626-29

Adventures in Topicals

By George Griffenhagen
Editor of *Topical Time*

There is much more to topical stamp collecting than accumulating postage stamps picturing something or some one associated with a theme. To experience the adventure of topical collecting, you need to expand your horizons by including a variety of philatelic elements in your collection. We will review the variety of philatelic elements that awaits your discovery.

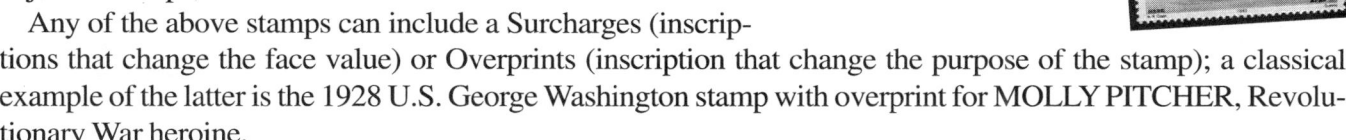

To most people, a postage stamp is something they stick on a envelope to mail a letter. However, stamp collectors know that postage stamps come in a variety of forms. There are Definitives (most 19th century stamps were definitives); Commemoratives (they made there appearance at the close of the 19th century); Semi-Postals (also called charity stamps); Provisionals (to fill an urgent need); and Locals (for use in a limited geographical area). The stamp design is generally limited to a single stamp, but Composites are those in which the design extends over two or more adjacent stamps differing in design or denomination, while Tete-beche is a term describing adjacent stamps, one of which is inverted.

Any of the above stamps can include a Surcharges (inscriptions that change the face value) or Overprints (inscription that change the purpose of the stamp); a classical example of the latter is the 1928 U.S. George Washington stamp with overprint for MOLLY PITCHER, Revolutionary War heroine.

Perfins and Watermarks offer interesting philatelic elements. Among the thousands of Perfins (named for PERForated INSignia), topical collectors can find designs for anchors, bells, coffee grinders, dancers, eagles, fish, flags, spinning wheels, swans, and windmills. Watermarks (patterns impressed into the paper during manufacture) also come in a variety of images including anchors, birds, coats-of-arms, flowers, lions, moons, posthorns, pyramids, stars, swans, and trees.

Marginal inscriptions frequently include more than plate numbers or other post office inscriptions. Design on tabs and margins (selvage) of stamps and souvenir sheets often supplement a theme as much as the design of the stamp itself. Equally interesting are the tabs and marginal advertisements attached to postage stamps.

The introduction of postage stamp booklets in 1895 offered opportunities for governmental promotional messages and commercial advertising on covers, interleaves, and labels required to make total face value of a booklet a convenient multiple of the local currency. Commercial advertising was introduced into the stamp booklets during the first decade of the 19th century. By the 1920s, entire stamp booklets were devoted to advertisements of a single firm.

There are, of course, many stamps that are not postage stamps. Revenues (also called fiscals or tax stamps) are stamps indicating the payment of a fee or collection of a tax. They predate postage stamps by several centuries, having been used in The Netherlands as early as 1627 and in Spain as early as 1637. Even though revenues are not postage stamps, they lay claim to being the "most historic stamp of all time." It was a 1765 revenue stamp imposing a tax on legal documents in the British colonies in America which ignited the American Revolutionary War. Cinderellas are virtually any item that looks like a postage stamp but is not a postage stamp. They include such material as advertising seals, bogus stamps, charity seals, fantasy stamps, food rationing stamps, political seals, poster stamps, and propaganda seals. There are even Test Stamps issued by various postal administrations for use in developing stamp vending machines.

Covers (envelopes that have passed through the mail bearing appropriate postal markings) were used centuries before the introduction of the postage stamp. Today they are classified either as Commercial or Philatelic. Many adventures lies ahead for the collector who searches for a particular stamp that belongs in a topical collection. By the second half of the 19th century, envelopes were imprinted with a wide range of colorful advertisements (called Corner Cards referring to the return address). Patriotic Cover became popular during the American Civil War, and Mourning Covers (with their black boarders) were widely used during the Victorian era. Other interesting covers include Balloon Mail (which preceded First Flight Covers), Paquebots (mail posted on the high seas), Crash/Wreck Covers, Free Frank Covers, and censored Covers. First Day Covers (FDCs) comprise a great portion of philatelic covers.

Postal Stationary includes all forms of stationary bearing a printed stamp (indicium). Pre-stamped letter sheets were used as early as the 17th century, but it was British Mulready which was introduced in 1840 that popularized postal stationery. The first Postal card bearing an indicium was issued in Austria 1869, and the Aerogramme (air letter) led to subsequent use of the British Airgraph and American V-Mail during World War II.

Cancellations (called postmarks when they include date and place of posting) come in variety of forms. The most desirable for the topical collector are Fancy Cancels applied by oblterators made of cork or wood. The rarest were produced in Waterbury, Connecticut, from 1865 to 1869. With the introduction of rapid cancelling machines, Slogan Cancels, Pictorial Cancels, and First Day of Issue Cancels were created. The introduction of the postage meter in the early 20th century also led to a variety of advertising slogans.

Other philatelic elements of interest to the topical collector are Maximum Cards (introduced around 1900); Autographs on stamps and covers; and the Telephone Card (which was used as early as the 1800s to prepay telephone calls). The scope of material for the topical collector is limited only by one's imagination.

SELECTED and ANNOTATED BIBLIOGRAPHY

The volumes listed below are recommended for the library of any collector who wishes to gain more knowledge in the areas covered by the current Brookman. While the main emphasis is on stamps, many of these volumes contain good postal history information. Check with your favorite dealer for availability and price. (To conserve space, some bibliographic notations have been abbreviated).

19th & 20th Century

Cummings, William W., ed., *Scott 1995 Specialized Catalogue of U.S. Stamps*
This annual publication offers a treasure trove of information on virtually every area of the postage and revenue stamps of the US, UN & US Possessions. A "must have."

Sloane, George B., *Sloane's Column*, arr. by George Turner, 1961, (BIA 1980)
A subject by subject arrangement of Sloane's 1350 columns which appeared in "STAMPS" magazine from 1932-1958 covering virtually every facet of U.S. philately.

White, Roy, *Encyclopedia of the Colors of U.S. Postage Stamps*, Vol 1-5, 1981, 86.
The first four volumes cover US stamps from 1847-1918 plus a few selected issues. Volume five covers the US Postage Dues from 1879-1916. They are the finest available works for classifying the colors of U.S. postage stamps.

19th Century
General

Brookman, Lester G., *The United States Postage Stamps of the 19th Century*, 3 vol., 1966. (Reprinted in 1989 by D.G.Phillipps Co.)
This is the finest and most informative work on 19th Century issues. Each stamp, from the 5¢ Franklin of 1847 thru the $2 Trans-Mississippi of 1898, is given separate, and often in-depth treatment. This is a must for any collector.

Luff, John N., *The Postage Stamps of the United States*, 1902.
While much of Luff's information has been superseded by Brookman, his treatment of Postmaster Provisionals and several Back-of-the-book sections make this a worthwhile volume. (The "Gossip Reprint", 1937, is more useful and recommended.)

Perry, Elliot, *Pat Paragraphs*, arr by George Turner & Thomas Stanton, BIA, 1981.
A subject by subject arrangement of Perry's 58 pamphlets which were published from 1931-1958. The emphasis is on the 19th century classics as well as carriers & locals.

Baker, Hugh J. and J. David, *Bakers' U.S. Classics*, 1985
An annotated compilation of the Bakers' columns from "STAMPS" magazine which appeared from 1962-1969. This major work provides extensive coverage of nearly all aspects of U.S. and Confederate philately.

By Issue or Subject

Ashbrook, Stanley B., *The United States One Cent Stamp of 1851-57*, 2 vol, 1938.
Although most of stamp and plating information in Volume 1 has been superseded by Mortimer Neinken's great work, Vol. 2 features an indispensible amount of information on the postal history of the period.

Neinken, Mortimer L., *The United States One Cent Stamp of 1851 to 1861*, 1972. *United States, The 1851-57 Twelve Cent Stamp*, 1964.
The One cent book supplements and updates, but does not replace, Ashbrook's study. The Twelve cent booklet deals almost exclusively with the plating of this issue. Both are fundamental works.

Chase, Dr. Carroll, *The 3¢ Stamp of the U.S. 1851-57 Issue*, Rev. ed., 1942.
This outstanding work provides the most comprehensive information available in one place on this popular issue. (The Quarterman reprint, 1975, contains a new forward, corrections, additions and a selected bibliography of articles.

Hill, Henry W., *The United States Five Cent Stamps of 1856-1861*, 1955.
This extensively illustrated volume is the only work dealing exclusively with this issue. It includes studies on stamps, plating, cancels, and postal history.

Neinken, Mortimer L., *The United States Ten Cent Stamps of 1855-1859*, 1960.
This work not only provides an indispensable amount of stamp and plating information, but it also reprints Chapters 50-53 from Ashbrook Vol. 2 dealing with California, Ocean and Western Mails.

Cole, Maurice F., *The Black Jacks of 1863-1867*, 1950.
A superb study of the issue with major emphasis on postal history.

Lane, Maryette B., *The Harry F. Allen Collection of Black Jacks, A Study of the Stamp and it's Use*, 1969
The title says it all. This book beautifully complements, but does not replace, Cole.

Ashbrook, Stanley B., *The U.S. Issues of 1869, Preceded by Some Additional Notes on "The premieres Gravures of 1861"*, 1943
This work concentrates on the design sources and production of the 1869 issue. Ashbrook concludes with his "Addendum" attacking Scott for listing the Premieres.

Willard, Edward L., *The U.S. Two Cent Red Brown of 1883-1887*, 2 vol., 1970.
Volume I deals with the background, production and varieties of the stamp. Vol. II deals exclusively with the cancellations found on the stamp. A good Banknote intro.

20th Century
General

King, Beverly S. and Johl, Max G. *The United States Postages Stamps of the Twentieth Century*, Vol. 1 revised, Vol. 2-4, 1934-38.
These volumes are still the standard work on 20th Century U.S. postage stamps from 1901 to 1937. (The 1976 Quarterman reprint contains only the regular issue, air mail and Parcel Post sections from the original volumes. It is highly recommended.

By Issue or Subject

Armstrong, Martin A., *Washington-Franklins, 1908-1921*, 2nd Edition, 1979.
Armstrong, Martin A., *US Definitive Series, 1922-1938*, 2nd Edition, 1980.
Armstrong, Martin A., *United States Coil Issues, 1906-38*, 1977
Each of these volumes not only supplements the information found in Johl, but expands each area to include studies of essays, proofs, booklet panes, private perfs, Offices in China and the Canal Zone. One major plus is the wealth of illustrations, many of rare and unusual items, which were not included in Johl's work due to laws restricting the publication of stamp pictures prior to 1938.

20th Century
By Issue or Subject (cont.)

Schoen, DeVoss & Harvey, *Counterfeit Kansas-Nebraska Overprints on 1922-34 Issue plus First Day Covers of the Kansas-Nebraska Overprints*, 1973.
A fine pamphlet covering K-N varieties, errors and First Day covers, plus important information pointing out the differences between genuine and fake overprints.

Datz, Stephen, *U.S. Errors: Inverts, Imperforates, Colors Omitted*, 1992 Ed., 1991.
This volume does a superb job covering the subjects listed in its title, It is extensively illustrated and provides price, quantity and historical information.

Air Mail & Back-of-the-Book

Amercian Air Mail Society, *American Air Mail Catalog*, Fifth Ed., 5 vols + 1990 Pricing Supplement, 1974-1990.
Virtually everything there is to know about air mail stamps and postal history.

Arfken, George B., *Postage Due, The United States Large Numeral Postage Due Stamps, 1879-1894*, 1991.
A Comprehensive study of virtually every aspect of these interesting stamps. Additionally, about half the book is devoted to their extensive usage which helps to clarify some of the more complex markings and routings found on "Due" covers.

Gobie, Henry M. *The Speedy, A History of the U.S. Special Delivery Service*, 1976
Gobie, Henry M., *U.S. Parcel Post, A Postal History*, 1979.
Each of these volumes includes information on the stamps, but their main thrust is on the postal history of the respective services. Official documents and Postal Laws & Regulations have been extensively reproduced and numerous covers illustrating the various aspects of the services are pictured.

Markovits, Robert L., *United States, The 10¢ Registry Stamp of 1911*, 1973.
This pamphlet provides a superb blueprint for the formation of specialized collection around a single stamp. It is extensively illustrated and concludes with an extensive bibliography which touches upon a multitude of additional subjects.

McGovern, Edmund C., ed, *Catalog of the 19th Century Stamped Envelopes and Wrappers of the United States*, USPSS 1984

Haller, Austin P., ed., *Catalog of the 20th Century Stamped Envelopes and Wrappers of the United States*, USPSS 1990

Beachboard, John H., ed., *United States Postal Card Catalog*, USPSS 1990
Each of the three previous volumes contains the finest available information in their respective fields. They are indispensable to the postal stationery collector.

First Day Covers & Related Collectibles

Planty, Dr. Earl & Mellone, Michael, *Planty's Photo Encyclopedia of Cacheted FDCs, 1923-1939*, Vol. 1-10, 1976-1984

Mellone, Mike, *Specialized Catalog of First Day Covers of the 1940's (2nd ed.), 1950's and 1960's*, 2 vol., 2 vol., 3 vol. respectively, 1983-1985.

Pelcyger, Dr. Scott, *Mellone's Specialized Catalog of First Day Ceremony Programs & Events*, 1989
Each of these volumes illustrates virtually every known cachet and ceremony program for the stamps listed within. They each provide an invaluable resource.

Radford, Dr. Curtis D., *The Souvenir Card Collectors Society Numbering System for Forerunner and Modern Day Souvenir Card*, 1989.
The most informative work on this popular collecting area.

Revenues

Toppan, Deats and Holland, *'An Historical Reference List of the Revenue Stamps of the United States...'*, 1899.
The information in this volume, while almost 100 years old, still provides the collector with much of the basic knowledge available today on US Revenues and "Match and Medicines" from 1862-1898. (The "Gossip" reprint is recommended.)

Confederate States

Dietz, August, *The Postal Service of the Confederate States of America*, 1929
This monumental work has been the "Bible" for Confederate collectors. Covering virtually every aspect of Confederate philately, its content remains useful, even after 60+ years. (A 1989 reprint makes this work more affordable for the average collector.)

Skinner, Gunter and Sanders, *The New Dietz Confederate States Catalog and Handbook*, 1986.
This volume makes an effort to cover every phase of Confederate philately and postal history. Despite the presence of some flaws, it is highly recommended.

Possessions

Plass, Brewster and Salz, *Canal Zone Stamps*, 1986.
Published by the Canal Zone Study Group, this outstanding well written and extensively illustrated volume, is now the "bible" for these fascinating issues.

Meyer, Harris, et. at, *Hawaii, Its Stamps and Postal History*, 1948.
After 45 years, this volume, which deals with virtually every facet of Hawaiian stamps and postal history, remains the finest work written on the subject.

Palmer, Maj. F.L., *The Postal Issues of the Philippines*, 1912
An ancient, but still useful study, with interesting information on the U.S. overprints.

British North America

Boggs, Winthrop S., *The Postage Stamps and Postal History of Canada*, 2 vol., 1945. (Quarterman reprint, One vol., 1975)
For almost 50 years the standard work on Canadian stamps and postal history. One of the "must have" books. (The reprint omits most of the Vol. 2 appendices.)

Lowe, Robson, *The Encyclopedia of British Empire Postage Stamps*, Vol. 5, North America, 1973
This work continues the fine tradition of Robson Lowe's earlier volumes dealing with British Empire. Covering all of BNA, it is an essential tool for the collector.

1847 General Issue, Imperforate VF + 50%, OG +150% (C)

1,3,948a   2,4,948b

Scott's No.		Unused Fine	Ave.	Used Fine	Ave.
1	5¢ Franklin, Red Brown	2500.00	1600.00	525.00	350.00
1	5¢ Red Brown, Pen Cancel			250.00	175.00
2	10¢ Washington, Black	13500.00	8750.00	1200.00	750.00
2	10¢ Black, Pen Cancel			700.00	475.00

1875 Special Printing: Reproductions of 1847 Issue (VF+50%)

3	5¢ Red Brown, 1875 Reproduction ...	750.00	550.00	...	...
4	10¢ Black, 1875 Reproduction	900.00	675.00	...	...

5¢ Franklin: #1 Top of white shirt on left is even with "F" of "FIVE".
#3 Top of white shirt on left is even with top of "5".
10¢ Washington: #2 Left line on coat points to "T" of "TEN"
#4 Left line on coat is more rounded and points toward the upper right corner oi the left "X"

NOTE: SEE #948 FOR 5¢ BLUE AND 10¢ BROWN ORANGE.

1851-57 Issue, Imperforate, "U.S. Postage" at Top (VF,OG+200%, VF+75%) (C)

5-9   10-11   12   13-16   17

		Unused Fine	Ave.	Used Fine	Ave.
5	1¢ Franklin, Blue, Type I	...		...	
5A	1¢ Blue, Type Ib	...		6500.00	4000.00
6	1¢ Blue, Type Ia	...		8500.00	5250.00
7	1¢ Blue, Type II.................................	500.00	300.00	150.00	90.00
8	1¢ Blue, Type III	...		2950.00	1750.00
8A	1¢ Blue, Type IIIa	2000.00	1200.00	850.00	500.00
9	1¢ Blue, Type IV	300.00	185.00	110.00	65.00
10	3¢ Wash., Orange Brown, Ty. I......	1350.00	800.00	97.50	60.00
11	3¢ Dull Red, Type I	95.00	60.00	9.75	5.75
12	5¢ Jefferson, Red Brown, Ty. I	...		950.00	550.00
13	10¢ Washington, Green, Type I	...		750.00	450.00
14	10¢ Green, Type II	1600.00	975.00	210.00	145.00
15	10¢ Green, Type III	1600.00	975.00	210.00	145.00
16	10¢ Green, Type IV	...		1350.00	800.00
17	12¢ Washington, Black	2100.00	1300.00	300.00	180.00

1¢ Franklin: #5,18 Type I Complete design at top and bottom.
#6,19 Type Ia Same as I with design partly cut away.
#5A Type Ib Same as I with design at bottom slightly cut away.
#7,20 Type II Lines complete top and bottom, lower parts of bottom scrolls and ornaments are missing.
#8,21 Type III Top and bottom lines are broken in the middle.
#8A,22 Type IIIa Top or bottom lines (not both) are broken in middle.
#9,23 Type IV Like type II with top and/or bottom lines recut.
#24 Type V Like type III with side ornaments partly cut away.
3¢ Washington: #10-11,25 Type I Outer frame line around entire design.
#26 Type II Outer frame line missing at top and bottom of design, side frame lines extend beyond top and bottom of design.
#26a Type IIa Same as Type II except that side frame lines do not extend beyond top and bottom of design.
5¢ Jefferson: #12,27-29 Type I Full design at top and bottom
#30-30A Type II Design partly cut away at top and bottom.
10¢ Washington: #13,31 Type I Shells in lower corners are almost complete, outer line at bottom is nearly complete, outer lines at top are broken.
#14,32 Type II Top of design is complete but outer line at bottom is broken in middle and bottom shells are partly cut away.
#15,33 Type III Top and bottom outer lines are partly cut away.
#16,34 Type IV Outer top and bottom lines are recut (strengthened).
#35 Type V Side ornaments are partly cut away. These are complete on Types I-IV with three circles at outer edge of bottom panel.

1857-61 Designs as above but Perf. 15½ (VF,OG+225%,VF+100%) (C)

18-24 ,40   25-26, 41   27-30A, 42   31-35, 43

36, 44    37, 45   38, 46   39, 47

1857-61 Designs as above but Perf. 15½ (VF,OG+225%,VF+100%) (C)

Scott's No.		Unused Fine	Ave.	Used Fine	Ave.
18	1¢ Franklin, Blue, Type I	750.00	450.00	500.00	300.00
19	1¢ Blue, Type Ia	...	...	5750.00	3500.00
20	1¢ Blue, Type II	475.00	275.00	210.00	125.00
21	1¢ Blue, Type III	5500.00	3500.00	2250.00	1350.00
22	1¢ Blue, Type IIIa	800.00	500.00	400.00	250.00
23	1¢ Blue, Type IV	3500.00	2100.00	625.00	375.00
24	1¢ Blue, Type V	80.00	50.00	35.00	20.00
25	3¢ Washington, Rose, Type I	1100.00	675.00	85.00	52.50
26	3¢ Dull Red, Type II	45.00	27.50	6.75	4.25
26a	3¢ Dull Red, Type IIa	100.00	60.00	57.50	35.00
27	5¢ Jefferson, Brick Red, Type I ...	11000.00	6500.00	1250.00	750.00
28	5¢ Red Brown, Type I	2000.00	1200.00	750.00	450.00
28A	5¢ Indian Red, Type I	...	...	2500.00	1500.00
29	5¢ Brown, Type I	1000.00	575.00	325.00	195.00
30	5¢ Orange Brown, Type II	525.00	325.00	950.00	550.00
30A	5¢ Brown, Type II	750.00	450.00	265.00	160.00
31	10¢ Washington, Green, Type I	7750.00	4500.00	875.00	525.00
32	10¢ Green, Type II	2275.00	1300.00	235.00	150.00
33	10¢ Green, Type III	2275.00	1300.00	235.00	150.00
34	10¢ Green, Type IV	...	...	1750.00	950.00
35	10¢ Green, Type V	120.00	75.00	65.00	40.00
36	12¢ Washington, Black, Plate 1	625.00	375.00	250.00	150.00
36b	12¢ Black, Plate 3	325.00	185.00	160.00	95.00
37	24¢ Washington, Gray Lilac	550.00	325.00	295.00	180.00
38	30¢ Franklin, Orange	750.00	435.00	365.00	215.00
39	90¢ Washington, Blue	1200.00	750.00	...	...

12¢ Washington #17,36 Plate I Outer frame lines are more complete than with Plate III
#36b Plate III Outer frame lines are uneven or broken.
NOTE: #5A THROUGH 38 WITH PEN CANCELS USUALLY SELL FOR 50-60% OF LISTED USED PRICES. USED EXAMPLES OF #39 SHOULD ONLY BE PURCHASED WITH, OR SUBJECT TO, A CERTIFICATE OF AUTHENTICITY.

1875 Reprints of 1857-60 Issue, Perf.12, Bright Colors, White Paper, Without Gum (VF+75%) (C)

		Fine	Ave.		
40	1¢ Franklin, Bright blue	500.00	335.00	..	..
41	3¢ Washington, Scarlet	2800.00	1800.00	..	..
42	5¢ Jefferson, Orange Brown	1150.00	750.00	..	..
43	10¢ Washington, Blue Green	2500.00	1650.00	..	..
44	12¢ Washington, Greenish Black	2750.00	1850.00	..	..
45	24¢ Washington, Blackish Violet ...	3000.00	2000.00	..	..
46	30¢ Franklin, Yellow Orange	2900.00	1950.00	..	..
47	90¢ Washington, Deep Blue	4000.00	2700.00	..	..

1861 New Designs, Perf.12, Thin Paper (VF,OG+225%, VF+100% OG+125%) (C)

		Fine	Ave.	Fine	Ave.
62B	10¢ Washington, Dark Green	2750.00	1650.00	1075.00	650.00

1861-62 Modified Designs, Perf. 12 (VF,OG+225%, VF+100%) (C)

63,86,92,102   73,84,85B,87, 93,103   64-65,79,83,85, 85C,88,94,104   67,75-76, 95, 105   68,89,96,106

69,85E,90,97,107   77,91,98,108   70,78,99,109   71,100,110   72,101,111

		Fine	Ave.	Fine	Ave.
63	1¢ Franklin, Blue	125.00	75.00	30.00	18.00
64	3¢ Washington, Pink	3500.00	2200.00	675.00	385.00
64b	3¢ Rose Pink	235.00	140.00	125.00	75.00
65	3¢ Rose	60.00	35.00	2.40	1.50
67	5¢ Jefferson, Buff	7750.00	5000.00	750.00	500.00
68	10¢ Washington, Yellow Green	325.00	185.00	42.50	25.00
69	12¢ Washington, Black	575.00	350.00	80.00	45.00
70	24¢ Washington, Red Lilac	800.00	475.00	175.00	110.00
70b	24¢ Steel Blue	3500.00	2500.00	700.00	425.00
70c	24¢ Violet, Thin Paper	4750.00	3000.00	1250.00	750.00
71	30¢ Franklin, Orange	675.00	385.00	140.00	85.00
72	90¢ Washington, Blue	1200.00	700.00	350.00	215.00

Former #66 3¢ Lake is considered a Trial Color Proof.

1861-66 New Values or Designs, Perf. 12 (VF,OG+225%,VF+100%) (C)

		Fine	Ave.	Fine	Ave.
73	2¢ Jackson, Black (1863)	145.00	75.00	45.00	25.00
75	5¢ Jefferson, Red Brown	1800.00	1075.00	400.00	240.00
76	5¢ Brown (1863)	500.00	300.00	100.00	60.00
77	15¢ Lincoln, Black (1866)	900.00	525.00	125.00	75.00
78	24¢ Washington, Lilac/Gray Lilac ..	550.00	325.00	125.00	75.00

Former #74 3¢ Scarlet is considered a Trial Color Proof.

UNUSED STAMPS WITH ORIGINAL GUM

Scott No.	Original Gum Fine	Ave.	Scott No.	Original Gum Fine	Ave.	Scott No.	Original Gum Fine	Ave.
7	1100.00	650.00	30	1150.00	700.00	68	700.00	400.00
9	650.00	400.00	35	270.00	165.00	69	1350.00	800.00
11	250.00	150.00	36	1375.00	825.00	70	2000.00	1200.00
18	1750.00	1050.00	36b	700.00	425.00	71	1500.00	850.00
20	1050.00	600.00	37	1400.00	825.00	73	350.00	185.00
22	1850.00	1100.00	38	1700.00	1150.00	76	1200.00	750.00
24	175.00	110.00	63	275.00	165.00	77	2250.00	1350.00
26	100.00	60.00	64b	500.00	300.00	78	1650.00	975.00
29	2500.00	1500.00	65	130.00	75.00			

1867 Designs of 1861-66 with Grills of Various Sizes (VF,OG+225%, VF+100%) (C)

Grills consist of small pyramids impressed on the stamp and are classified by area, shape of points and number of rows of points. On Grilled-All-Over and "C" Grills, points thrust upward on FACE of stamp; on all other grills points thrust upward on BACK of stamp. Points of "Z" grill show horizontal ridges (-); other grills from "D" through "I" show vertical (I) ridges or come to a point. It is important to see a Scott catalog for details of these interesting stamps.

1867 "A" Grill (Grill All Over)

Scott's No.		Unused Fine	Unused Ave.	Used Fine	Used Ave.
79	3¢ Washington, Rose	2300.00	1400.00	1150.00	700.00
	1867 "C" Grill 13 x 16mm Points Up				
83	3¢ Washington, Rose	2250.00	1375.00	875.00	525.00
	1867 "D" Grill 12 x 14mm Points Down				
84	2¢ Jackson, Black	7000.00	4500.00	3000.00	1800.00
85	3¢ Washington, Rose	2500.00	1500.00	875.00	525.00
	1867 "Z" Grill 11 x 14mm				
85B	2¢ Jackson, Black	3350.00	1950.00	1000.00	625.00
85C	3¢ Washington, Rose	5000.00	3000.00	2750.00	1650.00
85E	12¢ Washington, Black	5000.00	3000.00	1300.00	825.00
	1867 "E" Grill 11 x 13mm				
86	1¢ Franklin, Blue	1250.00	750.00	400.00	240.00
87	2¢ Jackson, Black	525.00	325.00	125.00	75.00
88	3¢ Washington, Rose	300.00	165.00	20.00	12.50
89	10¢ Washington, Green	1900.00	1100.00	250.00	150.00
90	12¢ Washington, Black	1800.00	1050.00	300.00	185.00
91	15¢ Lincoln, Black	3750.00	2200.00	525.00	325.00
	1867 "F" Grill 9 x 13mm				
92	1¢ Franklin, Blue	550.00	325.00	300.00	180.00
93	2¢ Jackson, Black	175.00	100.00	40.00	24.00
94	3¢ Washington, Red	140.00	80.00	6.00	3.50
95	5¢ Jefferson, Brown	1200.00	675.00	675.00	425.00
96	10¢ Washington, Yellow Green	1000.00	575.00	200.00	120.00
97	12¢ Washington, Black	1175.00	700.00	210.00	130.00
98	15¢ Lincoln, Black	1350.00	750.00	265.00	160.00
99	24¢ Washington, Gray Lilac	2250.00	1200.00	800.00	500.00
100	30¢ Franklin, Orange	2500.00	1500.00	650.00	400.00
101	90¢ Washington, Blue	4250.00	2500.00	1350.00	800.00

1875 Re-issue of 1861-66 Issues, Hard Very White Paper, White Gum, Deep Colors, Without Grills (VF,OG+150%, VF+75%, OG + 100%) (C)

102	1¢ Franklin, Blue	400.00	240.00	..	..
103	2¢ Jackson, Black	1600.00	1100.00	..	..
104	3¢ Washington, Brown Red	1750.00	1200.00	..	..
105	5¢ Jefferson, Brown	1400.00	950.00	..	..
106	10¢ Washington, Green	1600.00	1100.00	..	..
107	12¢ Washington, Black	2000.00	1350.00	..	..
108	15¢ Lincoln, Black	2100.00	1400.00	..	..
109	24¢ Washington, Deep Violet	2700.00	1800.00	..	..
110	30¢ Franklin, Brownish Orange	2700.00	1800.00	..	..
111	90¢ Washington, Blue	3500.00	2300.00	..	..

1869 Pictorial Issues-"G" Grill 9½ mm., Hard Wove Paper, Perf.12 (VF,OG+225%, VF+100%) (C)

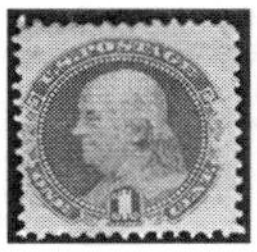
112,123,133

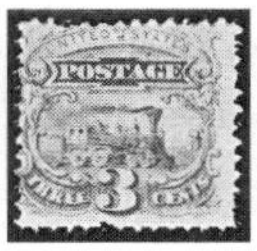
113,124

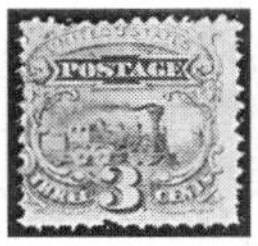
114,125

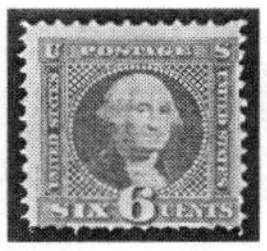
115,126

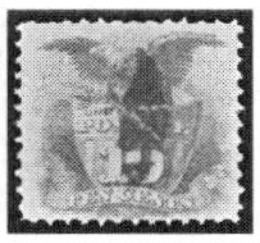
116,127

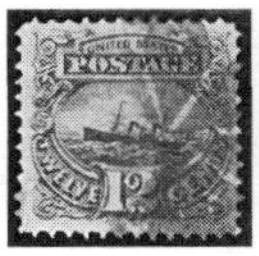
117,128

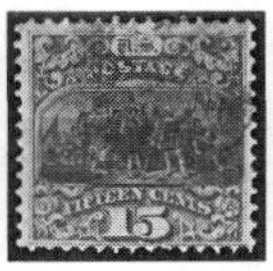
118

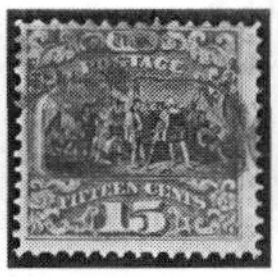
119,129

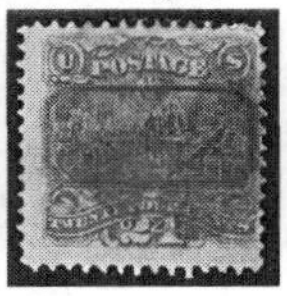
120,130

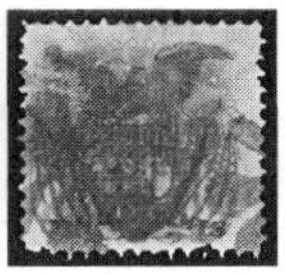
121,131

90¢ Abraham Lincoln #122, 132

112	1¢ Franklin, Buff	300.00	175.00	140.00	85.00
113	2¢ Post Horse & Rider, Brown	265.00	160.00	70.00	42.50
114	3¢ Locomotive, Ultramarine	130.00	80.00	16.50	10.00
115	6¢ Washington, Ultramarine	1150.00	700.00	180.00	110.00
116	10¢ Shield & Eagle, Yellow	800.00	475.00	120.00	70.00
117	12¢ "S.S. Adriatic", Green	900.00	550.00	135.00	80.00
118	15¢ Landing of Columbus, Brown & Blue,Type I	3100.00	1800.00	550.00	325.00
119	15¢ Brown & Blue, Type II	1375.00	825.00	215.00	135.00
120	24¢ Declaration of Independence, Green & Violet	3000.00	1800.00	625.00	375.00
121	30¢ Shield, Eagle & Flags, Ultramarine & Carmine	2800.00	1650.00	450.00	275.00
122	90¢ Lincoln, Carmine & Black	4000.00	2300.00	1875.00	1200.00

15¢ Columbus #118 Type I No frame line around central design.
#119 Type II Diamond shaped ornament in middle above central design, frame line around central design.
#129 Type III Same as Type I except that it is missing ffringe of brown shading lines around sides and bottom of picture.

1875 Re-issues of 1869 Issue, Without Grill, Hard White Paper, White Crackly Gum (VF,OG+150%, VF+75%) (C)

123	1¢ Franklin, Buff	250.00	150.00	275.00	160.00
124	2¢ Post Horse & Rider, Brown	365.00	200.00	425.00	250.00
125	3¢ Locomotive, Blue	2800.00	1850.00	..	..
126	6¢ Washington, Ultramarine	900.00	575.00	..	..
127	10¢ Shield & Eagle, Yellow	1100.00	775.00	..	..
128	12¢ "S.S.Adriatic",Green	1350.00	900.00	..	..
129	15¢ Columbus, Type III	1000.00	700.00	..	..
130	24¢ Decl.of Indep.,Green & Violet	1100.00	775.00	..	..
131	30¢ Shield, Eagle & Flags	1400.00	950.00	..	..
132	90¢ Lincoln,Carmine & Black	2500.00	1700.00	..	..

1880-81 Re-issues of 1869 Issue, Without Grill, Soft Porous Paper, (VF,OG+175%, VF+75%) (C)

Scott's No.		Unused Fine	Unused Ave.	Used Fine	Used Ave.
133	1¢ Franklin, Buff	140.00	85.00	165.00	95.00
133a	1¢ Brown Orange, Issued without Gum (1881)	200.00	130.00	175.00	110.00

UNUSED STAMPS WITH ORIGINAL GUM

Scott No.	Original Gum Fine	Original Gum Ave.	Scott No.	Original Gum Fine	Original Gum Ave.	Scott No.	Original Gum Fine	Original Gum Ave.
87	1300.00	800.00	94	350.00	210.00	116	2000.00	1200.00
88	750.00	450.00	112	650.00	385.00	117	2150.00	1300.00
92	2000.00	1200.00	113	625.00	365.00	123	500.00	300.00
93	425.00	250.00	114	275.00	170.00	124	700.00	385.00
						133	325.00	200.00

IMPORTANT NOTICE

PRIOR TO #134, UNUSED PRICES ARE FOR STAMPS WITH PARTIAL OR NO GUM, FOR ORIGINAL GUM, SEE SPECIAL LISTINGS. MORE EXPENSIVE ISSUES WITH ORIGINAL GUM SELL FOR VARYING PREMIUMS.
FROM #134 TO #293, UNUSED PRICES ARE FOR STAMPS WITH FULL ORIGINAL GUM WHICH ARE OR HAVE BEEN HINGED. STAMPS WITH PARTIAL GUM OR NO GUM ARE LISTED SEPARATELY.

1870-72 National Printing - Without Secret Marks #134-40, 145-52,

1¢ 2¢ 3¢ 6¢ 7¢ 10¢ 12¢

Arrows point to distinguishing characteristics: 1¢ ball is clear; 2¢ no spot of color; 3¢ light shading; 6¢ normal vertical lines; 7¢ no arcs of color cut around lines; 10¢ ball is clear; 12¢ normal 2.

1873-79 Continental and American Printings - Secret Marks #156-62, 167-73, 178, 182-84, 186-88, 192-98

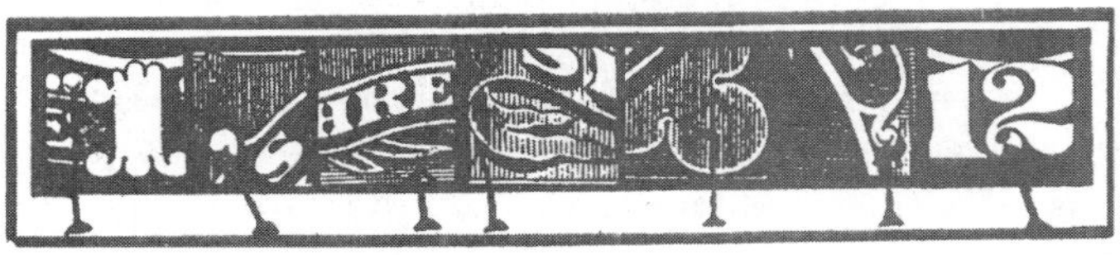

1¢ 2¢ 3¢ 6¢ 7¢ 10¢ 12¢

Arrows point to distinguishing characteristics: 1¢ dash in ball; 2¢ spot of color where lines join in scroll ornaments; 3¢ under part of ribbon heavily shaded; 6¢ first four vertical lines strengthened; 7¢ arcs of color cut around lines; 10¢ a crescent in the ball; 12¢ ball of 2 is crescent shaped.

1870-71 National Bank Note Company Printing -Grilled-Hard Paper (VF+75%) (C)

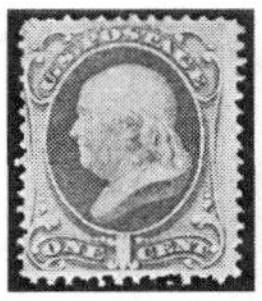
134,145,156,167, 182,192,206

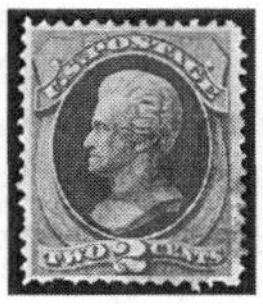
135,146,157,168, 178,180,183,193,203

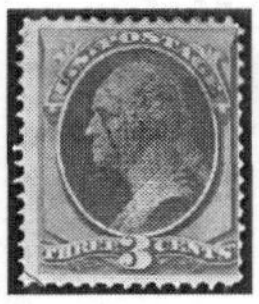
136,147,158,169, 184,194,207,214

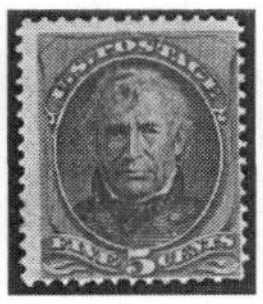
179,181,185,204

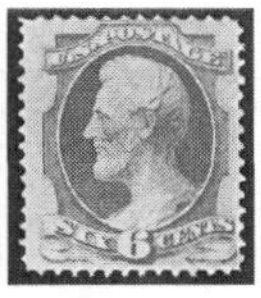
137,148,159,170, 186195,,208

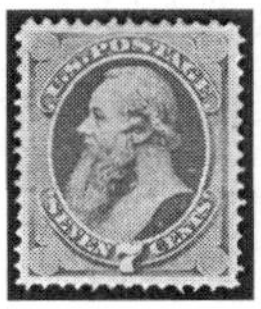
138,149,160,171 196

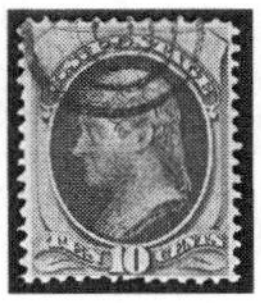
139,150,161,172, 187-88,197,209

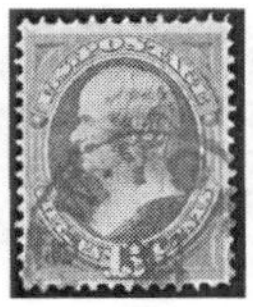
141,152,163,174 189,199

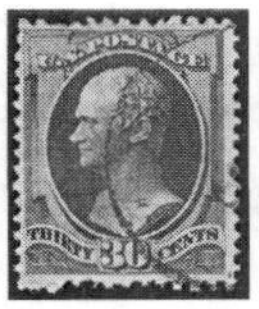
143,154,165,176, 190,201,217

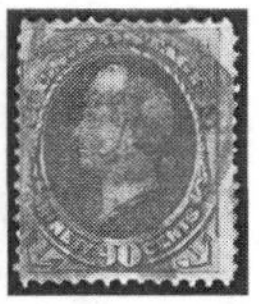
144,155,166,177 191,202,218

24¢ General Winfield Scott #142, 153,175

Scott's No.		Unused,OG Fine	Unused,OG Ave.	Used Fine	Used Ave.
134	1¢ Franklin, Ultramarine	1850.00	1100.00	125.00	75.00
135	2¢ Jackson, Red Brown	1050.00	650.00	57.50	35.00
136	3¢ Washington, Green	600.00	350.00	18.00	11.00
137	6¢ Lincoln, Carmine	4000.00	2400.00	450.00	270.00
138	7¢ Stanton, Vermilion (1871)	3000.00	1800.00	375.00	225.00
139	10¢ Jefferson, Brown	4000.00	2400.00	550.00	325.00
140	12¢ Clay, Dull Violet	...	...	2500.00	1500.00
141	15¢ Webster, Orange	6500.00	4000.00	975.00	575.00
142	24¢ Scott, Purple	..	..	5500.00	3500.00
143	30¢ Hamilton, Black	13500.00	8000.00	2350.00	1400.00
144	90¢ Perry, Carmine	12000.00	7000.00	1500.00	900.00

Note: We do not list prices for Never HInged stamps prior to 1881. Depending on issue, Never HInged stamps can sell for 2 to 5 times the price of unused stamps.

1870-72 National Bank Note Company Printing
Without Grill (VF+75%) (C)

Scott's No.		Unused,OG Fine	Ave.	Used Fine	Ave.
145	1¢ Franklin, Ultramarine	475.00	285.00	12.00	7.00
146	2¢ Jackson, Red Brown	275.00	165.00	9.50	5.50
147	3¢ Washington, Green	250.00	150.00	1.35	.85
148	6¢ Lincoln, Carmine	700.00	425.00	21.00	12.50
149	7¢ Stanton, Vermilion (1871)	825.00	500.00	75.00	45.00
150	10¢ Jefferson, Brown	1000.00	600.00	20.00	12.00
151	12¢ Clay, Dull Violet	1850.00	1100.00	135.00	80.00
152	15¢ Webster, Bright Orange	2000.00	1200.00	135.00	80.00
153	24¢ Scott, Purple	1450.00	850.00	110.00	65.00
154	30¢ Hamilton, Black (1871)	4850.00	3000.00	170.00	100.00
155	90¢ Perry, Carmine (1872)	3750.00	2250.00	250.00	150.00

1873 Continental Printing White Hard Paper (VF+75%)(C)
Same designs as preceding issue but with secret marks as shown below.

156	1¢ Franklin, Ultramarine	225.00	110.00	3.25	1.95
157	2¢ Jackson, Brown	300.00	180.00	15.75	9.50
158	3¢ Washington, Green	110.00	65.00	.60	.35
159	6¢ Lincoln, Dull Pink	365.00	220.00	16.50	10.00
160	7¢ Stanton, Org. Vermilion	1100.00	650.00	75.00	45.00
161	10¢ Jefferson, Brown	750.00	450.00	16.50	10.00
162	12¢ Clay, Blackish Violet	2000.00	1200.00	85.00	52.50
163	15¢ Webster, Yellow Orange	2000.00	1200.00	100.00	60.00
164	24¢ Scott, Purple				
165	30¢ Hamilton, Gray Black	2500.00	1500.00	90.00	50.00
166	90¢ Perry, Rose Carmine	2300.00	1400.00	225.00	135.00

1875 Special Printing of 1873 Issue, Hard White Wove Paper, Without Gum (VF + 75%) (C)

167	1¢ Franklin, Ultramarine	10000.00	6500.00	..	..
168	2¢ Jackson, Dark Brown	5000.00	3300.00	..	..
169	3¢ Washington, Blue Green	12000.00	8000.00	..	..
170	6¢ Lincoln, Dull Rose	12000.00	8000.00	..	..
171	7¢ Stanton, Reddish Vermilion	3000.00	2000.00	..	..
172	10¢ Jefferson, Pale Brown	12000.00	8000.00	..	..
173	12¢ Clay, Dark Violet	4000.00	2700.00	..	..
174	15¢ Webster, Bright Orange	12000.00	8000.00	..	..
175	24¢ Scott, Dull Purple	3000.00	2000.00	..	..
176	30¢ Hamilton, Greenish Black	9500.00	6500.00	..	..
177	90¢ Perry, Violet Carmine	11500.00	7750.00	..	..

1875 Continental Printing-Yellowish Hard Paper (VF+75%) (C)

178	2¢ Jackson, Vermilion	350.00	210.00	8.50	5.25
179	5¢ Taylor, Blue	475.00	300.00	17.00	10.00

1875 Special Printing of 1875 Issue, Hard White Wove Paper, Without Gum

180	2¢ Jackson, Carmine Vermilion	....	..	..	..
181	5¢ Taylor, Bright Blue	..	..	..	..

1879-87 American Printing - Continental Design, Soft Porous Paper (VF+75%) (C)
Soft porous paper is less transparent than hard paper.
When held to the light it usually appears mottled, somewhat like newsprint.

182	1¢ Franklin, Dark Ultramarine	275.00	165.00	3.00	1.80
183	2¢ Jackson, Vermilion	125.00	75.00	2.50	1.50
184	3¢ Washington, Green	95.00	60.00	.50	.30
185	5¢ Taylor, Blue	450.00	275.00	10.75	6.50
186	6¢ Lincoln, Pink	875.00	525.00	19.00	11.50
187	10¢ Brown (no secret mark)	2650.00	1600.00	21.00	13.00
188	10¢ Brown (secret mark)	1800.00	1100.00	21.00	13.00
189	15¢ Webster, Red Orange (1881)	280.00	170.00	18.00	11.00
190	30¢ Hamilton, Full Black (1881)	900.00	550.00	55.00	32.50
191	90¢ Perry, Carmine (1887)	1800.00	1100.00	230.00	140.00

UNUSED STAMPS WITHOUT GUM

Scott No.	Fine	Ave.	Scott No.	Fine	Ave.	Scott No.	Fine	Ave.
134	750.00	450.00	152	900.00	550.00	178	165.00	110.00
135	450.00	275.00	153	625.00	375.00	179	225.00	140.00
136	275.00	170.00	156	95.00	55.00	182	115.00	67.50
137	1750.00	1050.00	157	150.00	90.00	183	50.00	30.00
138	1250.00	750.00	158	50.00	30.00	184	40.00	25.00
145	185.00	110.00	159	165.00	100.00	185	200.00	120.00
146	125.00	75.00	160	475.00	285.00	186	375.00	225.00
147	115.00	67.00	161	350.00	210.00	187	1200.00	725.00
148	275.00	165.00	162	850.00	515.00	188	800.00	500.00
149	350.00	215.00	163	875.00	525.00	189	140.00	85.00
150	425.00	250.00	166	1050.00	625.00	190	450.00	275.00
151	825.00	500.00				191	900.00	550.00

1880 Special Printing of 1879 Issue, Soft Porous Paper, Without Gum (VF+75%) (C)

192	1¢ Franklin, Dark Ultramarine	....	..	..	..
193	2¢ Jackson, Black Brown	....	..	..	..
194	3¢ Washington, Blue Green	....	..	..	..
195	6¢ Lincoln, Dull Rose	....	..	..	..
196	7¢ Stanton, Scarlet Vermilion	4500.00	3000.00	..	..
197	10¢ Jefferson, Deep Brown	....	..	..	..
198	12¢ Clay, Blackish Purple	6500.00	4250.00	..	..
199	15¢ Webster, Orange	....	..	..	..
200	24¢ Scott, Dark Violet	6500.00	4250.00	..	..
201	30¢ Hamilton, Greenish Black	....	..	..	..
202	90¢ Perry, Dull Carmine	....	..	..	..
203	2¢ Jackson, Scarlet Vermilion	....	..	..	..
204	5¢ Taylor, Deep Blue	....	..	..	..

212	210,213	211,215	205,216

1882 New Design (VF NH, VF OG & VF, Used+75%) (C)

Scott's No.		NH Fine	Unused,OG Fine	Ave.	Used Fine	Ave.
205	5¢ Garfield, Yellow Brown	550.00	250.00	150.00	7.25	4.50

1882 Special Printing of 1882 Issue, Soft Porous Paper, Without Gum (C)

205C	5¢ Garfield, Gray Brown	..	..	..	..	..

1881-82 Re-engraved Designs (VF NH, VF OG & VF, Used+75%) (C)

206	1¢ Franklin, Gray Blue	160.00	70.00	42.50	1.10	.65
207	3¢ Washington, Blue Green	160.00	70.00	42.50	.55	.35
208	6¢ Lincoln, Rose (1882)	1150.00	525.00	325.00	75.00	45.00
208a	6¢ Brown Red (1883)	1050.00	475.00	285.00	110.00	65.00
209	10¢ Jefferson, Brown (1882)	350.00	150.00	90.00	5.25	3.15
209b	10¢ Black Brown	2500.00	1100.00	650.00	165.00	100.00

#206 1¢ Re-engraved: Strengthened vertical lines at top of design appear almost solid. Lines of shading added to curved ornaments in upper corners.
#207 3¢ Re-engraved: Short horizontal line added below the "TS" of "CENTS" Shading lines at sides of central oval are about one-half previous width.
#208 6¢ Re-engraved: Three vertical lines from edge of panel to the outside left margin instead of four lines as on the original designs.
#209 10¢ Re-engraved: Four vertical lines between edge of shield and left side of oval instead of five. Horizontal lines of background are strengthened.

1883-87 New Designs (VF NH, VF OG & VF, Used + 75%) (C)

210	2¢ Washington Red Brown	100.00	42.50	25.00	.50	.30
211	4¢ Jackson, Blue Green	600.00	250.00	150.00	16.50	10.00
212	1¢ Franklin, Ultramarine (1887)	235.00	100.00	60.00	1.65	1.00

1883-85 Special Printings, Soft Porous Paper (VF+75%) (C)

211B	2¢ Wash., Pale Red Brown	650.00	400.00	265.00		
211D	4¢ Jackson, Deep Blue Green, Without Gum	..	..	..	..	..

1887-88 Revised Colors (VF NH, VF OG & VF, Used +75%) (C)

213	2¢ Washington, Green (1887)	85.00	42.50	25.00	.45	.30
214	3¢ Wash., Vermilion (1887)	150.00	65.00	40.00	47.50	28.50
215	4¢ Jackson, Carmine (1888)	525.00	200.00	120.00	18.00	11.00
216	5¢ Garfield, Indigo (1888)	575.00	225.00	135.00	11.00	6.50
217	30¢ Hamilton, Orange Brown (1888)	1050.00	400.00	240.00	100.00	60.00
218	90¢ Perry, Purple (1888)	2750.00	1000.00	600.00	200.00	120.00

NOTE: Most Special Printings are very rare and some are not priced as there is no current retail price information available.

UNUSED STAMPS WITHOUT GUM

Scott No.	Fine	Ave.	Scott No.	Fine	Ave.	Scott No.	Fine	Ave.
205	115.00	70.00	209	60.00	37.50	214	32.50	20.00
206	32.50	20.00	210	19.50	11.50	215	90.00	55.00
207	32.50	20.00	211	115.00	70.00	216	95.00	55.00
208	225.00	135.00	212	42.50	25.00	217	175.00	110.00
208a	200.00	120.00	213	18.75	11.50	218	500.00	300.00

1890-1893 No Triangles, Perforated 12 (VF Used + 75%) (C)

	219	219D,220	221	222
	223	224	225	226
	227	228	229	

Scott's No.		Unused, NH VF	F-VF	Unused, OG VF	F-VF	Used F-VF
219	1¢ Franklin, Dull Blue	90.00	52.50	40.00	22.50	.50
219D	2¢ Washington, Lake	750.00	425.00	325.00	185.00	1.30
220	2¢ Carmine	77.50	45.00	31.50	19.00	.45
220a	2¢ Cap on left "2"	475.00	275.00	200.00	115.00	7.50
220c	2¢ Cap on both "2's"	1900.00	1100.00	800.00	475.00	16.50
221	3¢ Jackson, Purple	250.00	150.00	110.00	65.00	5.75
222	4¢ Lincoln, Dark Brown	300.00	180.00	130.00	80.00	2.25
223	5¢ Grant, Chocolate	275.00	160.00	120.00	70.00	2.25
224	6¢ Garfield, Brown Red	250.00	150.00	110.00	65.00	17.50
225	8¢ Sherman, Lilac (1893)	195.00	115.00	80.00	50.00	10.75
226	10¢ Webster, Green	600.00	350.00	250.00	150.00	2.85
227	15¢ Clay, Indigo	875.00	495.00	335.00	200.00	18.75
228	30¢ Jefferson, Black	1275.00	750.00	525.00	325.00	25.00
229	90¢ Perry, Orange	2000.00	1200.00	825.00	500.00	100.00

UNUSED STAMPS WITHOUT GUM

Scott No.	VF	F-VF	Scott No.	VF	F-VF	Scott No.	VF	F-VF
219	22.50	12.50	221	60.00	35.00	226	130.00	80.00
219D	175.00	100.00	222	75.00	45.00	227	180.00	110.00
220	16.50	10.00	223	70.00	40.00	228	285.00	175.00
220a	110.00	60.00	224	60.00	35.00	229	475.00	275.00
220c	425.00	250.00	225	45.00	27.50			

Greetings
FROM EVERYWHERE.

Greg Manning Auctions will travel anywhere. From the highest mountains, most tropical beaches, to the coolest climates and everywhere in between. Our philatelic experts will venture near and far to meet with you — whether your collection is worth $3,000 or $10 Million.

We will guide you on how to achieve the highest prices for your collections or stock, by taking the worry out of selling. The choice is yours to decide to go with consignment to our world-renowned auctions or an immediate cash sale.

Whether we need to come by air, train, boat, car or even by foot, Greg Manning Auctions, with our team of experts are flexible to meet with you at your home, bank, office, or other convenient location in any climate, time zone or altitude.

Call today to learn more. We welcome the opportunity to travel to you!

775 Passaic Avenue West Caldwell, NJ 07006 Phn: 973.882.0887 Phn: 800.782.6771 Fax: 973.882.3499
Email: info@gregmanning.com
Greg Manning Auctions, Inc. is a publicly traded company, NASDAQ Symbol GMAI

GREG MANNING AUCTIONS, INC.

1893 Columbian Exposition Issue (VF Used + 60%) (B)

230   231   232

233   234   235

236   237   238

239   240   241

242   243   244

245

Scott's No.		Unused, NH VF	F-VF	Unused, OG VF	F-VF	Used F-VF
230	1¢ Blue	57.50	35.00	27.50	17.50	.45
230	Plate Block of 6	650.00	400.00	400.00	250.00	...
231	2¢ Violet	47.50	31.50	24.00	15.75	.30
231	Plate Block of 6	550.00	350.00	335.00	215.00	...
231v	2¢ Violet, "Broken Hat" 3rd person to left of Columbus has a triangular "cut" in his hat	165.00	100.00	80.00	50.00	1.00
232	3¢ Green	195.00	120.00	95.00	60.00	13.75
233	4¢ Ultramarine	225.00	135.00	105.00	65.00	6.75
234	5¢ Chocolate	265.00	160.00	125.00	80.00	7.00
235	6¢ Purple	240.00	145.00	110.00	70.00	18.50
236	8¢ Magenta	200.00	120.00	95.00	60.00	9.50
237	10¢ Black Brown	375.00	225.00	175.00	110.00	7.00
238	15¢ Dark Green	650.00	400.00	315.00	200.00	55.00
239	30¢ Orange Brown	925.00	550.00	400.00	250.00	77.50
240	50¢ Slate Blue	1700.00	1000.00	725.00	450.00	145.00
241	$1 Salmon	4250.00	2800.00	1700.00	1100.00	550.00
242	$2 Brown Red	5000.00	3000.00	1900.00	1200.00	525.00
243	$3 Yellow Green	7500.00	4500.00	2875.00	1800.00	1000.00
244	$4 Crimson Lake	11000.00	6500.00	4000.00	2500.00	1150.00
245	$5 Black	12000.00	7000.00	4400.00	2750.00	1400.00

UNUSED STAMPS WITHOUT GUM

Scott No.	Without Gum VF	F-VF	Scott No.	Without Gum VF	F-VF	Scott No.	Without Gum VF	F-VF
230	15.00	9.50	235	60.00	37.50	241	925.00	600.00
231	13.50	8.50	236	52.50	32.50	242	1000.00	650.00
231v	45.00	27.50	237	95.00	60.00	243	1600.00	1000.00
232	52.50	32.50	238	175.00	110.00	244	2200.00	1350.00
233	55.00	35.00	239	225.00	135.00	245	2350.00	1500.00
234	70.00	45.00	240	400.00	250.00			

1894 Issue - Triangles - No Watermark (VF Used + 75%) (C)

246-47,264 279   248-52,265-67, 279B   253,268   254,269,280   255,270,281

1894 Issue - Triangles - No Watermark (VF Used + 75%) (C)

256,271,282   257,272   258,273,282C-83   259,274,284

260,275   261-61A,276-76A   262,277   263,278

Scott's No.		Unused, NH VF	F-VF	Unused, OG VF	F-VF	Used F-VF
246	1¢ Franklin, Ultramarine	95.00	55.00	41.50	25.00	4.75
246	Plate Block of 6	1000.00	600.00	575.00	350.00	...
247	1¢ Blue	210.00	120.00	90.00	55.00	2.25
247	Plate Block of 6	2000.00	1200.00	1100.00	700.00	...
248	2¢ Washington, Pink, Tri. A	82.50	47.50	36.50	21.00	4.75
248	Plate Block of 6	700.00	425.00	375.00	225.00	...
249	2¢ Carmine Lake, Tri. A	475.00	275.00	210.00	125.00	4.25
250	2¢ Carmine, Triangle A	82.50	47.50	38.50	23.00	.60
250	Plate Block of 6	850.00	500.00	500.00	300.00	...
251	2¢ Carmine, Triangle B	875.00	500.00	375.00	225.00	5.75
252	2¢ Carmine, Tri C, Type III	365.00	210.00	165.00	100.00	8.50
253	3¢ Jackson, Purple	325.00	185.00	150.00	90.00	8.25
254	4¢ Lincoln, Dark Brown	465.00	265.00	185.00	110.00	4.75
255	5¢ Grant, Chocolate	315.00	180.00	145.00	85.00	5.50
256	6¢ Garfield, Dull Brown	525.00	300.00	225.00	135.00	21.00
257	8¢ Sherman, Violet Brown	385.00	220.00	185.00	110.00	13.50
258	10¢ Webster, Dark Green	825.00	475.00	375.00	225.00	10.75
259	15¢ Clay, Dark Blue	900.00	525.00	395.00	235.00	50.00
260	50¢ Jefferson, Orange	1750.00	1000.00	750.00	450.00	100.00
261	$1 Perry, Black, Type I	3150.00	1800.00	1250.00	750.00	275.00
261A	$1 Black, Type II	7000.00	4000.00	2800.00	1700.00	575.00
262	$2 Madison, Bright Blue	9750.00	5750.00	4150.00	2500.00	900.00
263	$5 Marshall, Dark Green	16000.00	9000.00	6200.00	3750.00	1575.00

UNUSED STAMPS WITHOUT GUM

Scott No.	Without Gum VF	F-VF	Scott No.	Without Gum VF	F-VF	Scott No.	Without Gum VF	F-VF
246	21.50	12.50	253	75.00	45.00	259	200.00	120.00
247	45.00	27.50	254	95.00	55.00	260	375.00	225.00
248	18.50	11.00	255	75.00	45.00	261	500.00	300.00
249	110.00	65.00	256	115.00	70.00	261A	1100.00	650.00
250	20.00	12.00	257	95.00	55.00	262	1700.00	1000.00
251	185.00	115.00	258	190.00	115.00	263	3350.00	2000.00
252	85.00	50.00						

Triangle Varieties on the 2¢ Stamps

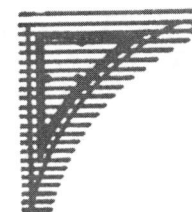 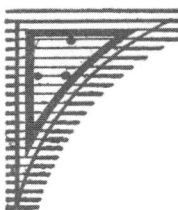 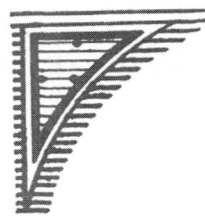

Triangle A   Triangle B   Triangle C

TRIANGLE A - The horizontal background lines run across the triangle and are of the same thickness within the triangle as the background lines.

TRIANGLE B - Horizontal lines cross the triangle but are thinner within the triangle than the background lines.

TRIANGLE C - The horizontal lines do not cross the triangle and the lines within the triangle are as thin as in Triangle B.

Circle Varieties on the $1 Stamps

Type I   Type II

Types of $1.00 stamps. Type I, the circles enclosing "$1" are broken where they meet the curved lines below "One Dollar". Type II, the circles are complete.

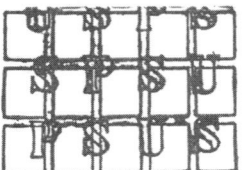

DOUBLE-LINE WATERMARK
This illustration shows a block of 15 with the Double Line watermark. Since only 90 letters were used per 100 stamps, they appear in various positions on the stamps.

IMPORTANT NOTICE
FROM #134 TO #293, UNUSED PRICES ARE FOR STAMPS WITH FULL ORIGINAL GUM WHICH ARE OR HAVE BEEN HINGED. STAMPS WITH PARTIAL GUM OR NO GUM ARE LISTED SEPARATELY.

1895 Triangle Designs - Double Line Watermark (VF Used + 60%) (C)

Scott's No.		Unused, NH VF	F-VF	Unused, OG VF	F-VF	Used F-VF
264	1¢ Franklin, Blue	17.50	10.50	8.50	5.25	.40
264	Plate Block of 6	475.00	300.00	275.00	175.00	...
265	2¢ Washington, Carmine, Triangle A	85.00	50.00	40.00	25.00	2.25
265	Plate Block of 6	975.00	575.00	475.00	300.00	...
266	2¢ Carmine, Triangle B	80.00	47.50	37.50	24.00	3.75
266	Plate Block of 6	1000.00	600.00	500.00	325.00	...
267	2¢ Carmine,Triangle C Type III	15.00	9.00	6.75	4.25	.30
267	Plate Block of 6	375.00	225.00	240.00	150.00	...
268	3¢ Jackson, Purple	100.00	60.00	47.50	30.00	1.50
268	Plate Block of 6	1500.00	900.00	800.00	500.00	...
269	4¢ Lincoln, Dark Brown	115.00	67.50	53.50	33.50	2.30
269	Plate Block of 6	1575.00	950.00	875.00	550.00	...
270	5¢ Grant, Chocolate	100.00	60.00	46.50	29.50	2.25
270	Plate Block of 6	1575.00	950.00	750.00	475.00	...
271	6¢ Garfield, Dull Brown	300.00	180.00	130.00	80.00	5.75
272	8¢ Sherman, Violet Brn	190.00	110.00	80.00	50.00	1.90
273	10¢ Webster, Dark Green	265.00	160.00	120.00	75.00	1.50
274	15¢ Clay, Dark Blue	675.00	400.00	285.00	180.00	11.00
275	50¢ Jefferson, Orange	875.00	525.00	365.00	230.00	23.00
276	$1 Perry, Black, Type I	2350.00	1400.00	800.00	500.00	70.00
276A	$1 Black, Type II	4500.00	2650.00	1750.00	1100.00	150.00
277	$2 Madison, Bright Blue	3350.00	2000.00	1375.00	875.00	275.00
278	$5 Marshall, Dark Green	7500.00	4500.00	2850.00	1800.00	400.00

1897-1903 NEW Colors - Double Line Watermark (VF Used + 60%) (C)

Scott's No.		Unused, NH VF	F-VF	Unused, OG VF	F-VF	Used F-VF
279	1¢ Franklin, Green (1898)	27.50	16.00	12.75	8.00	.40
279	Plate Block of 6	400.00	250.00	225.00	140.00	...
279B	2¢ Washington, Red. Triangle C, Type IV	27.50	16.00	12.75	8.00	.35
279B	Plate Block of 6	435.00	275.00	240.00	150.00	...
279Be	2¢ Booklet Pane of 6, Triangle C, Type IV	1050.00	600.00	550.00	325.00	...
280	4¢ Lincoln,Rose Brown (1898)	90.00	52.50	42.50	26.00	1.50
280	Plate Block of 6	1300.00	775.00	800.00	475.00	...
281	5¢ Grant, Dark Blue (1898)	100.00	60.00	47.50	29.50	1.40
281	Plate Block of 6	1300.00	775.00	800.00	475.00	...
282	6¢ Garfield, Lake (1898)	135.00	80.00	57.50	36.50	3.75
282	Plate Block of 6	1900.00	1150.00	1050.00	675.00	...
282a	6¢ Purplish Lake	190.00	115.00	80.00	50.00	7.50
282C	10¢ Webster, Brown, Type I (1898)	575.00	335.00	240.00	150.00	3.75
283	10¢ Orange Brown., Type II (1898)	375.00	225.00	160.00	100.00	3.50
284	15¢ Clay, Olive Green (1898)	475.00	285.00	190.00	100.00	7.50

2¢ Washington #252,267 Type III Toga button without shading.
#279B Type IV Toga button is shaded. Many other minor differences
10¢ Webster #282C Type I Oval lines intact where they contact "10"s.
#283 Type II Ornaments around "10'"s break the curved line below the
"E" of "TEN" and "T" of "CENT"

UNUSED STAMPS WITHOUT GUM

Scott No.	VF	F-VF	Scott No.	VF	F-VF	Scott No.	VF	F-VF
264	4.25	2.75	273	60.00	37.50	279B	6.50	4.00
265	20.00	12.50	274	150.00	90.00	280	21.50	13.00
266	19.00	12.00	275	185.00	115.00	281	24.00	15.00
267	3.50	2.25	276	325.00	200.00	282	30.00	19.00
268	24.00	15.00	276A	650.00	400.00	282a	40.00	25.00
269	27.00	17.00	277	600.00	375.00	282C	1.20	.75
270	23.50	15.00	278	1275.00	800.00	283	60.00	50.00
271	65.00	40.00	279	6.50	4.00	284	95.00	60.00
272	40.00	25.00						

1898 Trans-Mississippi Exposition Issue (VF Used + 60%) (B)

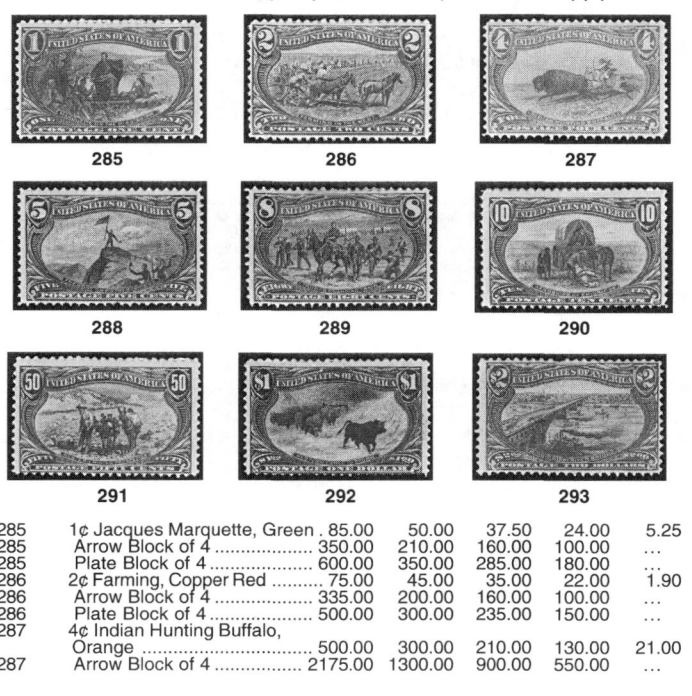

285	286	287
288	289	290
291	292	293

Scott's No.		Unused, NH VF	F-VF	Unused, OG VF	F-VF	Used F-VF
285	1¢ Jacques Marquette, Green	85.00	50.00	37.50	24.00	5.25
285	Arrow Block of 4	350.00	210.00	160.00	100.00	...
285	Plate Block of 4	600.00	350.00	285.00	180.00	...
286	2¢ Farming, Copper Red	75.00	45.00	35.00	22.00	1.90
286	Arrow Block of 4	335.00	200.00	160.00	100.00	...
286	Plate Block of 4	500.00	300.00	235.00	150.00	...
287	4¢ Indian Hunting Buffalo, Orange	500.00	300.00	210.00	130.00	21.00
287	Arrow Block of 4	2175.00	1300.00	900.00	550.00	...

1898 Trans-Mississippi Exposition Issue (VF Used + 60%) (B)

Scott's No.		Unused, NH VF	F-VF	Unused, OG VF	F-VF	Used F-VF
288	5¢ John Fremont on the Rocky Mountains, Dull Blue	450.00	260.00	200.00	125.00	18.00
288	Arrow Block of 4	1975.00	1175.00	875.00	550.00	...
289	8¢ Troops Guarding Wagon Train, Violet Brown.	550.00	315.00	240.00	150.00	35.00
289	Arrow Block of 4	2500.00	1400.00	1075.00	675.00	...
290	10¢ Emigration, Gray Violet	550.00	315.00	240.00	150.00	23.00
290	Arrow Block of 4	2500.00	1400.00	1075.00	675.00	...
291	50¢ Western Mining Prospector, Sage Green	2000.00	1200.00	850.00	525.00	150.00
292	$1 Cattle in Storm, Black	3750.00	2250.00	1500.00	950.00	435.00
293	$2 Mississippi River Bridge, Orange Brown	6350.00	3800.00	2650.00	1650.00	750.00

Note: See # 3209-3210 for multi-color issues

UNUSED STAMPS WITHOUT GUM

Scott No.	VF	F-VF	Scott No.	VF	F-VF	Scott No.	VF	F-VF
285	19.50	12.00	288	110.00	65.00	291	400.00	250.00
286	18.00	11.00	289	120.00	75.00	292	850.00	525.00
287	110.00	65.00	290	120.00	75.00	293	1350.00	850.00

1901 Pan-American Exposition Issue VF Used + 75% (B)

294	295	296
297	298	299

Scott's No.		Unused, NH VF	F-VF	Unused, OG VF	F-VF	Used F-VF
294-99	Set of 6	1275.00	750.00	650.00	385.00	90.00
294	1¢ Lake Navigation Steamship, Green & Black	52.50	30.00	27.50	16.00	2.95
294	Arrow Block of 4	225.00	135.00	120.00	75.00	...
294	Plate Block of 6	550.00	325.00	300.00	180.00	...
295	2¢ Train, Carmine & Black.	47.50	27.50	25.00	15.00	.95
295	Arrow Block of 4	210.00	135.00	110.00	67.50	...
295	Plate Block of 6	575.00	350.00	315.00	190.00	...
296	4¢ Electric Automobile, Chocolate & Black	240.00	140.00	120.00	70.00	14.00
296	Arrow Block of 4	1000.00	600.00	500.00	300.00	...
297	5¢ Bridge at Niagara Falls, Ultramarine & Black	260.00	150.00	135.00	77.50	13.00
297	Arrow Block of 4	1100.00	650.00	575.00	335.00	...
298	8¢ Canal Locks at Sault Ste. Marie, Brown Violet & Black	315.00	185.00	160.00	95.00	42.50
298	Arrow Block of 4	1350.00	800.00	675.00	415.00	...
299	10¢ Ocean Navigation Steamship, Brown & Black	435.00	250.00	220.00	130.00	21.50
299	Arrow Block of 4	1850.00	1075.00	925.00	550.00	...

1902-03 Issue Perf. 12 VF Used + 60% (C)

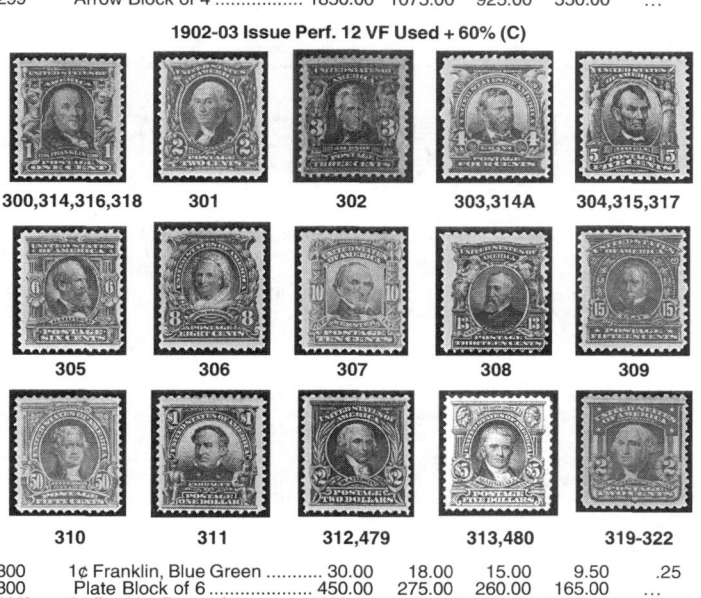

300,314,316,318	301	302	303,314A	304,315,317
305	306	307	308	309
310	311	312,479	313,480	319-322

Scott's No.		Unused, NH VF	F-VF	Unused, OG VF	F-VF	Used F-VF
300	1¢ Franklin, Blue Green	30.00	18.00	15.00	9.50	.25
300	Plate Block of 6	450.00	275.00	260.00	165.00	...
300b	1¢ Booklet Pane of 6	1400.00	850.00	725.00	450.00	...
301	2¢ Washington, Carmine	36.50	21.50	18.50	11.75	.25
301	Plate Block of 6	500.00	300.00	275.00	175.00	...
301c	2¢ Booklet Pane of 6	1275.00	750.00	625.00	375.00	...
302	3¢ Jackson, Bright Violet	150.00	85.00	70.00	45.00	2.75
302	Plate Block of 6	1675.00	1000.00	950.00	600.00	...
303	4¢ Grant, Brown	150.00	85.00	70.00	45.00	1.75
303	Plate Block of 6	1700.00	1025.00	1000.00	625.00	...

1902-03 Issue Perf. 12 VF Used + 60% (C)

Scott's No.		Unused, NH VF	Unused, NH F-VF	Unused, OG VF	Unused, OG F-VF	Used F-VF
304	5¢ Lincoln, Blue	180.00	110.00	87.50	55.00	1.60
304	Plate Block of 6	1800.00	1100.00	1100.00	700.00	...
305	6¢ Garfield, Claret	190.00	115.00	87.50	55.00	2.75
305	Plate Block of 6	1850.00	1100.00	1100.00	675.00	...
306	8¢ Martha Washington, Violet Black	110.00	65.00	56.50	35.00	2.25
306	Plate Block of 6	1600.00	975.00	900.00	575.00	...
307	10¢ Webster, Red Brown	190.00	110.00	87.50	55.00	2.15
307	Plate Block of 6	2400.00	1400.00	1350.00	825.00	...
308	13¢ B. Harrison, Purple Black	125.00	75.00	60.00	37.50	7.00
308	Plate Block of 6	1500.00	900.00	875.00	550.00	...
309	15¢ Clay, Olive Green	465.00	275.00	215.00	130.00	5.75
309	Arrow Block of 4	2100.00	1250.00	950.00	575.00	...
310	50¢ Jefferson, Orange	1350.00	800.00	600.00	375.00	22.00
311	$1 Farragut, Black	2250.00	1350.00	900.00	575.00	57.50
312	$2 Madison, Dark Blue	3600.00	2150.00	1450.00	900.00	150.00
313	$5 Marshall, Dark Green	8500.00	5000.00	3600.00	2250.00	575.00

1906-08 Same Designs, Imperforate VF Used + 30% (B)

314	1¢ Franklin, Blue Green	46.50	35.00	24.50	18.50	17.50
314	Pair	100.00	75.00	51.50	38.50	...
314	Arrow Block of 4	210.00	150.00	110.00	85.00	...
314	Center Line Block of 4	335.00	250.00	185.00	140.00	...
314	Plate Block of 6	385.00	290.00	215.00	165.00	...
314A	4¢ Grant, Brown	..	..	..	..	..
315	5¢ Lincoln, Blue	750.00	550.00	400.00	300.00	650.00
315	Pair	1600.00	1200.00	875.00	650.00	...

1908 Same Designs, Coils, Perforated 12 Horizontally (C)

316	1¢ Franklin, Blue Green	..	..	..	..	..
317	5¢ Lincoln, Blue	..	..	..	4500.00	..

1908 Same Designs, Coil, Perf. 12 Vertically (C)

318	1¢ Franklin, Blue Green	..	..	..	4250.00	..

1903 Washington & Shield Issue, Perforated 12 VF Used + 60% (C)

319	2¢ Carmine, Type I	15.75	9.00	8.00	5.00	.25
319	Plate Block of 6	230.00	135.00	130.00	80.00	...
319g	2¢ Booklet Pane of 6, Ty.I	335.00	195.00	175.00	110.00	...
319f	2¢ Lake, Type II	36.50	21.00	18.50	11.50	.75
319f	Plate Block of 6	975.00	600.00	575.00	350.00	...
319h	2¢ Booklet Pane of 6, Ty.II	1000.00	600.00	600.00	375.00	...

2¢ Shield #319,320,321 Type I Border line normal in lower left corner.
#319f,320a,333 Type II Enlarged border line in lower left corner.

1906 Shield Issue, Imperforate VF Used + 30% (B)

320	2¢ Carmine, Type I	47.50	35.00	26.50	20.00	17.50
320	Pair	100.00	75.00	57.50	43.50	...
320	Arrow Block of 4	215.00	160.00	120.00	90.00	...
320	Center Line Block of 4	325.00	235.00	180.00	135.00	...
320	Plate Block of 6	375.00	280.00	225.00	170.00	...
320a	2¢ Lake, Type II	130.00	95.00	70.00	52.50	40.00
320a	Pair	285.00	210.00	155.00	115.00	...
320a	Arrow Block of 4	600.00	450.00	325.00	240.00	...
320a	Center Line Block of 4	950.00	725.00	525.00	400.00	...
320a	Plate Block of 6	1300.00	1000.00	850.00	650.00	...

1908 Shield Issue, Coil, Perf. 12 Horizontally (C)

321	2¢ Carmine, Type I	..	..	..	..	..

1908 Shield Issue, Coil, Perf. 12 Vertically (C)

322	2¢ Carmine, Type II	..	..	..	4250.00	..

1904 Louisiana Purchase Exposition Issue VF Used + 60% (B)

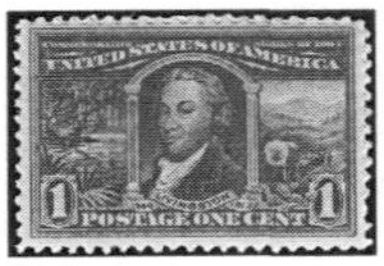
323
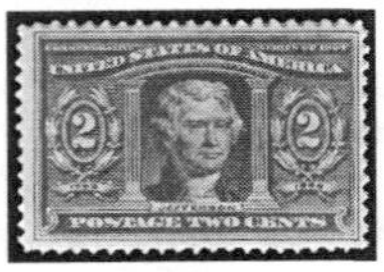
324
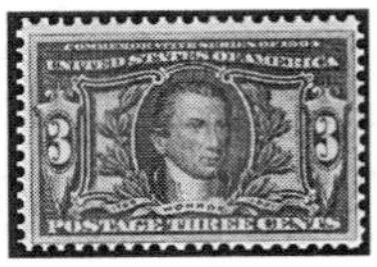
325
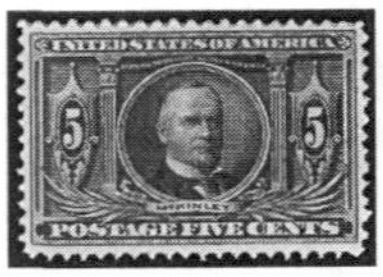
326
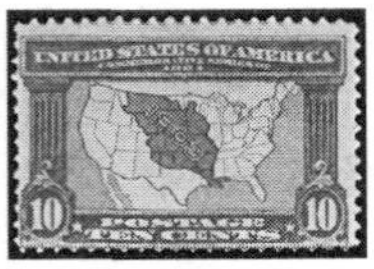
327

323-27	**Set of 5**	**11125.00**	**675.00**	**550.00**	**340.00**	**80.75**
323	1¢ Robert Livingston, Green	75.00	45.00	40.00	25.00	4.25
323	Arrow Block of 4	325.00	200.00	175.00	110.00	...
323	Plate Block of 4	385.00	235.00	215.00	135.00	...
324	2¢ Thomas Jefferson, Carmine	66.50	40.00	31.50	20.00	1.75
324	Arrow Block of 4	285.00	175.00	140.00	90.00	...
324	Plate Block of 4	400.00	240.00	215.00	135.00	...
325	3¢ James Monroe, Violet	250.00	150.00	120.00	75.00	29.50
325	Arrow Block of 4	1100.00	650.00	515.00	325.00	...
325	Plate Block of 4	1850.00	1100.00	1050.00	650.00	...
326	5¢ William McKinley, Blue	270.00	160.00	130.00	880.00	21.00
326	Arrow Block of 4	1150.00	700.00	550.00	350.00	...
326	Plate Block of 4	2100.00	1200.00	1125.00	700.00	...
327	10¢ Map, Brown	550.00	325.00	260.00	160.00	28.50
327	Arrow Block of 4	2350.00	1375.00	1150.00	700.00	...
327	Plate Block of 4	4500.00	2700.00	2650.00	1700.00	...

1907 Jamestown Exposition Issue VF Used + 100% (C)

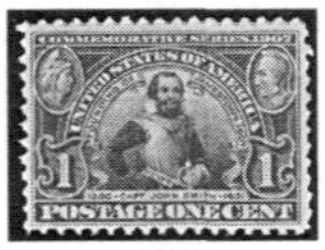
328
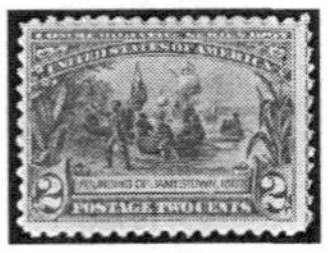
329
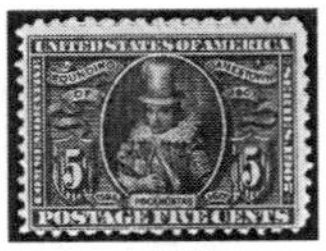
330

1907 Jamestown Exposition Issue VF Used + 100% (C)

Scott's No.		Unused, NH VF	Unused, NH F-VF	Unused, OG VF	Unused, OG F-VF	Used F-VF
328-30	**Set of 3**	**540.00**	**270.00**	**270.00**	**135.00**	**30.00**
328	1¢ John Smith, Green	80.00	40.00	40.00	20.00	3.50
328	Arrow Block of 4	335.00	175.00	175.00	90.00	...
328	Plate Block of 6	650.00	325.00	375.00	190.00	...
329	2¢ Founding of Jamestown, Carmine	100.00	50.00	50.00	25.00	3.25
329	Arrow Block of 4	435.00	220.00	215.00	110.00	...
329	Plate Block of 6	900.00	450.00	500.00	250.00	...
330	5¢ Pocahontas, Blue	395.00	200.00	195.00	100.00	25.00
330	Arrow Block of 4	1700.00	865.00	865.00	435.00	...
330	Plate Block of 6	7000.00	3500.00	3650.00	1850.00	...

1908-09 Washington-Franklins, Double Line Watermark - Perforated 12 VF Used + 60% (B)

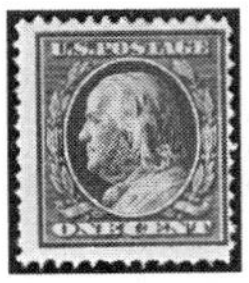
331,343,348,352, 357,374,383,385, 387,390,392,519
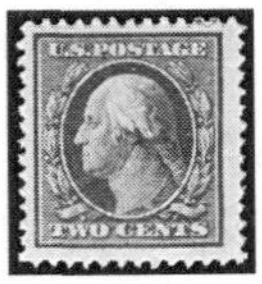
332,344,349,353, 358,375,384,386, 388,391,393
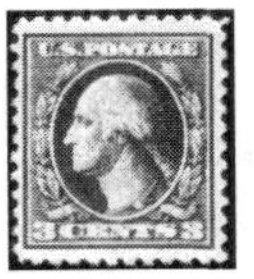
333,345,359,376, 389,394,426,445, 456,464,483,489, 493-94,501-2, 529-30,535,541
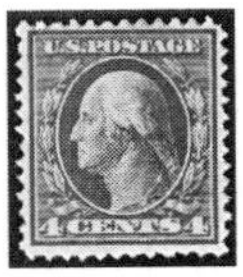
334,346,350,354, 377,395,427,446, 457,465,495,503
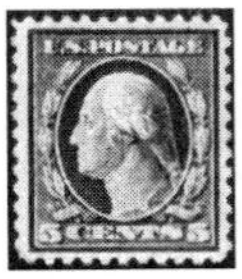
335,347,351.355, 361,378,396,428, 447,458,466,496, 504-5
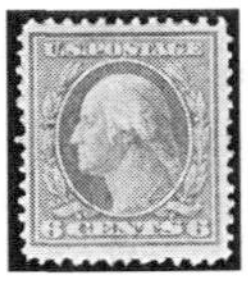
336,362,379,429, 468,506
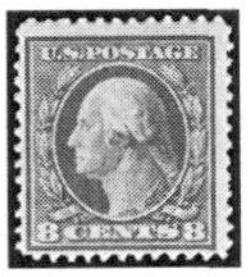
337,380
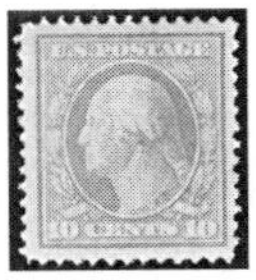
338,356,364,381
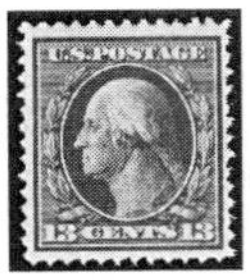
339,365
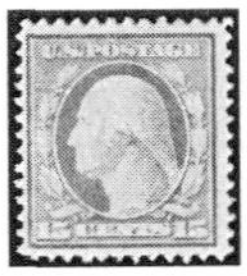
340,366,382
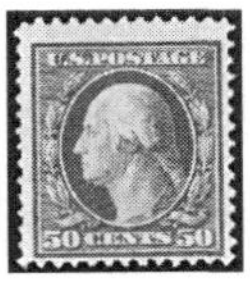
341
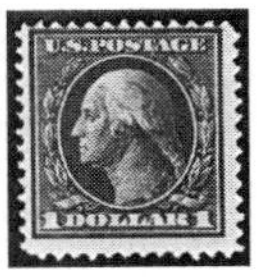
342

331	1¢ Franklin, Green	18.50	11.00	9.50	6.00	.30
331	Plate Block of 6	170.00	100.00	85.00	55.00	...
331a	1¢ Booklet Pane of 6	350.00	215.00	210.00	130.00	...
332	2¢ Washington, Carmine	17.50	10.00	8.75	5.50	.25
332	Plate Block of 6	150.00	82.50	80.00	50.00	...
332a	2¢ Booklet Pane of 6	325.00	190.00	180.00	115.00	...
333	3¢ Deep Violet	92.50	55.00	45.00	27.50	2.85
333	Plate Block of 6	750.00	450.00	425.00	275.00	...
334	4¢ Orange Brown	105.00	60.00	52.50	32.50	1.15
334	Plate Block of 6	950.00	550.00	525.00	325.00	...
335	5¢ Blue	130.00	80.00	65.00	40.00	2.00
335	Plate Block of 6	1175.00	675.00	650.00	400.00	...
336	6¢ Red Orange (1909)	165.00	95.00	82.50	52.50	5.50
336	Plate Block of 6	2350.00	1350.00	1200.00	750.00	...
337	8¢ Olive Green	130.00	75.00	65.00	40.00	3.50
337	Plate Block of 6	1100.00	650.00	550.00	350.00	...
338	10¢ Yellow (1909)	185.00	105.00	90.00	57.50	1.50
338	Plate Block of 6	1750.00	1000.00	875.00	550.00	...
339	13¢ Blue Green (1909)	110.00	65.00	55.00	35.00	15.00
339	Plate Block of 6	1150.00	700.00	600.00	375.00	...
340	15¢ Ultramarine (1909)	175.00	100.00	87.50	55.00	6.25
340	Plate Block of 6	1400.00	800.00	700.00	450.00	...
341	50¢ Violet (1909)	875.00	500.00	435.00	270.00	18.50
342	$1 Violet Brown (1909)	1425.00	825.00	675.00	425.00	75.00

1908-09 Series, Double Line Watermark - Imperforate VF Used + 30% (B)

343	1¢ Franklin, Green	15.00	11.00	7.95	6.00	5.00
343	Pair	31.50	23.00	17.00	12.75	...
343	Arrow Block of 4	70.00	50.00	36.00	27.50	...
343	Center Line Block or 4	85.00	60.00	42.50	32.50	...
343	Plate Block of 6	100.00	75.00	59.50	45.00	...
344	2¢ Washington, Carmine	23.00	16.00	12.00	8.50	3.50
344	Pair	48.50	33.50	25.75	18.00	...
344	Arrow Block of 4	100.00	70.00	55.00	40.00	...
344	Center Line Block of 4	115.00	80.00	60.00	45.00	...
344	Plate Block of 6	200.00	145.00	120.00	90.00	...
345	3¢ Deep Violet (1909)	45.00	33.50	25.00	18.50	19.50
345	Pair	95.00	70.00	52.50	38.50	...
345	Arrow Block of 4	200.00	150.00	110.00	85.00	...
345	Center Line Block of 4	210.00	165.00	130.00	100.00	...
345	Plate Block of 6	385.00	295.00	240.00	180.00	...
346	4¢ Orange Brown (1909)	60.00	45.00	33.50	25.00	22.50
346	Pair	130.00	95.00	70.00	52.50	...
346	Arrow Block of 4	270.00	200.00	160.00	120.00	...
346	Center Line Block of 4	325.00	250.00	195.00	150.00	...
346	Plate Block of 6	485.00	375.00	300.00	225.00	...
347	5¢ Blue	110.00	80.00	60.00	45.00	32.50
347	Pair	230.00	170.00	125.00	95.00	...
347	Arrow Block of 4	500.00	365.00	280.00	215.00	...
347	Center Line Block of 4	535.00	400.00	325.00	250.00	...
347	Plate Block of 6	775.00	575.00	475.00	350.00	...

9

1908-10 Coils, Double Line Watermark. - Perf. 12 Horiz. VF Used + 60% (C)

Scott's No.		Unused, NH VF	F-VF	Unused, OG VF	F-VF	Used F-VF
348	1¢ Franklin, Green	95.00	55.00	47.50	30.00	18.50
348	Pair	235.00	135.00	120.00	75.00	...
348	Line Pair	700.00	400.00	350.00	225.00	...
349	2¢ Wash.,Carmine(1909)	190.00	110.00	95.00	60.00	13.50
349	Pair	475.00	275.00	240.00	150.00	...
349	Line Pair	1275.00	725.00	650.00	400.00	...
350	4¢ Orange Brown (1910)	375.00	220.00	190.00	120.00	115.00
350	Pair	875.00	500.00	425.00	275.00	...
351	5¢ Blue (1909)	425.00	250.00	215.00	135.00	135.00
351	Pair	1125.00	635.00	565.00	350.00	...

1909 Coils, Double Line Watermark - Perf. 12 Vert. VF Used + 60% (C)

Scott's No.		Unused, NH VF	F-VF	Unused, OG VF	F-VF	Used F-VF
352	1¢ Franklin, Green	225.00	130.00	110.00	70.00	45.00
352	Pair, 2mm Spacing	550.00	325.00	275.00	175.00	...
352	Pair, 3mm Spacing	535.00	315.00	265.00	170.00	...
352	Line Pair	1750.00	1000.00	875.00	550.00	...
353	2¢ Washington, Carmine	225.00	135.00	110.00	70.00	11.75
353	Pair, 2mm Spacing	550.00	325.00	275.00	175.00	...
353	Pair, 3mm Spacing	535.00	315.00	265.00	170.00	...
353	Line Pair	1750.00	1000.00	875.00	550.00	...
354	4¢ Orange Brown	535.00	315.00	270.00	170.00	95.00
354	Pair, 2mm Spacng	1250.00	725.00	650.00	400.00	...
354	Pair, 3mm Spacing	1200.00	700.00	625.00	385.00	...
355	5¢ Blue	575.00	325.00	290.00	180.00	100.00
355	Pair	1450.00	825.00	725.00	450.00	...
356	10¢ Yellow	6650.00	3750.00	3350.00	2100.00	2000.00

(#348-56, should be purchased with, or subject to, a certificate of authenticity.)

1909 "Blue Papers", Double Line Watermark, Perf. 12 VF Used + 60% (B)

Scott's No.		Unused, NH VF	F-VF	Unused, OG VF	F-VF	Used F-VF
357	1¢ Franklin, Green	265.00	150.00	130.00	80.00	90.00
358	2¢ Washington, Carmine	265.00	150.00	130.00	80.00	90.00
359	3¢ Deep Violet	5250.00	2950.00	2600.00	1600.00	2000.00
360	4¢ Orange Brown	...	...	...	...	...
361	5¢ Blue	11750.00	6750.00	5650.00	3650.00	...
362	6¢ Red Orange	3750.00	2100.00	1950.00	1175.00	3750.00
363	8¢ Olive Green	...	...	...	...	...
364	10¢ Yellow	4500.00	2500.00	2300.00	1400.00	4250.00
365	13¢ Blue Green	7000.00	4000.00	3600.00	2300.00	2000.00
366	15¢ Pale Ultramarine	3500.00	2000.00	1800.00	1100.00	...

*** Blue Papers, which were printed on experimental paper with approxi-mately 35% rag content, actually have a grayish appearance which can best be observed by looking at the stamps from the gum side. Additionally, the watermark is more clearly visible than on the stamps printed on regular paper (#331-340). The stamps are also noted for having carbon specks imbedded in the texture of the paper.**
Blue papers should be purchased with, or subject to, a certificate of authenticity.

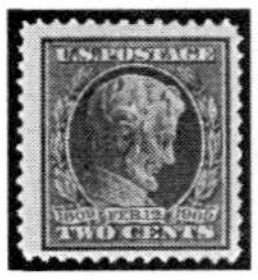
367-69

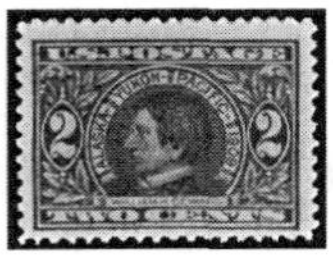
370-71

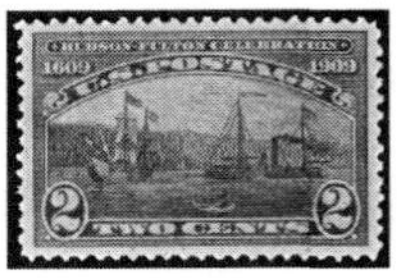
372-73

1909 Lincoln Birth Centenary (Used Perf.VF+50%, Imperf.VF+30%) (B)

Scott's No.		Unused, NH VF	F-VF	Unused, OG VF	F-VF	Used F-VF
367	2¢ Perforated 12	16.50	11.50	8.25	5.75	1.75
367	Plate Block of 6	285.00	190.00	180.00	120.00	...
368	2¢ Imperforate	50.00	37.50	30.00	22.50	19.50
368	Pair	110.00	80.00	65.00	47.50	...
368	Arrow Block of 4	225.00	165.00	135.00	100.00	...
368	Center Line Block of 4	275.00	210.00	175.00	130.00	...
368	Plate Block of 6	365.00	265.00	215.00	160.00	...
369	2¢ Bluish Paper, Perf. 12	500.00	315.00	265.00	175.00	230.00

1909 Alaska-Yukon-Pacific Exposition Issue (Used Perforated VF+50%, Imperforate VF+30%) (B)

Scott's No.		Unused, NH VF	F-VF	Unused, OG VF	F-VF	Used F-VF
370	2¢ Perforated 12	19.50	12.50	11.25	7.50	1.65
370	Plate Block of 6	425.00	275.00	240.00	165.00	...
371	2¢ Imperforate	85.00	57.50	45.00	33.50	24.50
371	Pair	175.00	120.00	95.00	70.00	...
371	Arrow Block of 4	350.00	240.00	200.00	150.00	...
371	Center Line Block of 4	400.00	300.00	240.00	190.00	...
371	Plate Block of 6	585.00	425.00	360.00	275.00	...

1909 Hudson-Fulton Celebration (Used Perf.VF+40%, Imperf.VF+30%) (B)

Scott's No.		Unused, NH VF	F-VF	Unused, OG VF	F-VF	Used F-VF
372	2¢ Perforated 12	30.00	19.50	16.50	11.00	3.75
372	Plate Block of 6	575.00	375.00	335.00	225.00	...
373	2¢ Imperforate	90.00	65.00	45.00	35.00	24.50
373	Pair	195.00	140.00	95.00	75.00	...
373	Arrow Block of 4	400.00	290.00	210.00	160.00	...
373	Center Line Block of 4	550.00	425.00	315.00	240.00	...
373	Plate Block of 6	700.00	500.00	365.00	275.00	...

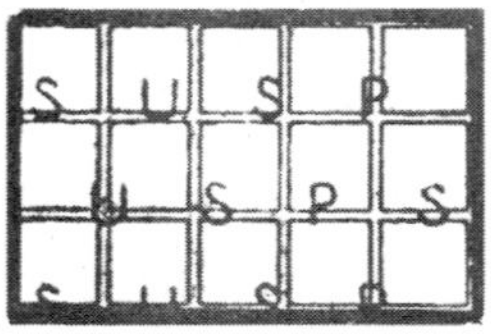

SINGLE-LINE WATERMARK
This illustration shows a block of 15 stamps with the Single Line Watermark. The watermark appears in various positions on the stamps.

1910-11 Single Line Watermark Perf 12, VF Used + 60% (B)

Scott's No.		Unused, NH VF	F-VF	Unused, OG VF	F-VF	Used F-VF
374	1¢ Franklin, Green	17.50	10.00	8.75	5.50	.25
374	Plate Block of 6	170.00	100.00	95.00	60.00	...
374a	1¢ Booklet Pane of 6	400.00	240.00	225.00	140.00	...
375	2¢ Washington, Carmine	17.50	10.00	8.75	5.50	.25
375	Plate Block of 6	185.00	110.00	110.00	65.00	...
375a	2¢ Booklet Pane of 6	275.00	160.00	150.00	95.00	...
376	3¢ Deep Violet (1911)	52.50	30.00	26.50	16.50	2.00
376	Plate Block of 6	425.00	250.00	240.00	150.00	...
377	4¢ Brown (1911)	77.50	45.00	40.00	25.00	1.00
377	Plate Block of 6	485.00	285.00	285.00	175.00	...
378	5¢ Blue (1911)	77.50	45.00	40.00	25.00	.70
378	Plate Block of 6	625.00	375.00	360.00	225.00	...

1910-11 Single Line Watermark Perf 12, VF Used + 60% (B)

Scott's No.		Unused, NH VF	F-VF	Unused,OG VF	F-VF	Used F-VF
379	6¢ Red Orange (1911)	90.00	52.50	45.00	28.50	.90
379	Plate Block of 6	900.00	550.00	535.00	335.00	...
380	8¢ Olive Green (1911)	275.00	160.00	135.00	85.00	12.50
381	10¢ Yellow (1911)	285.00	165.00	145.00	90.00	4.75
382	15¢ Pale Ultramarine (1911)	695.00	395.00	340.00	215.00	16.00

1910 Single Line Watermark, Imperforate VF Used + 30% (B)

Scott's No.		Unused, NH VF	F-VF	Unused,OG VF	F-VF	Used F-VF
383	1¢ Franklin, Green	7.25	5.50	4.00	3.00	2.75
383	Pair	15.75	11.75	8.50	6.50	...
383	Arrow Block of 4	35.00	25.00	19.00	14.00	...
383	Center Line Block of 4	57.50	45.00	32.50	25.00	...
383	Plate Block of 6	87.50	65.00	52.50	40.00	...
384	2¢ Washington, Carmine	15.00	11.00	8.00	6.00	2.75
384	Pair	32.50	23.50	17.00	12.75	...
384	Arrow Block of 4	65.00	50.00	37.50	27.50	...
384	Center Line Block of 4	110.00	80.00	65.00	50.00	...
384	Plate Block of 6	240.00	180.00	145.00	110.00	...

1910 Coils Single Line Watermark - Perf. 12 Horiz. VF Used + 60% (C)

Scott's No.		Unused, NH VF	F-VF	Unused,OG VF	F-VF	Used F-VF
385	1¢ Franklin, Green	95.00	55.00	47.50	30.00	16.00
385	Pair	235.00	135.00	120.00	75.00	...
385	Line Pair	1100.00	650.00	550.00	350.00	...
386	2¢ Washington, Carmine	180.00	110.00	90.00	57.50	21.50
386	Pair	650.00	365.00	325.00	200.00	...
386	Line Pair	2230.00	13500.00	1200.00	750.00	...

1910-11 Coils Single Line Wtmk. - Perf. 12 Vert. VF Used + 60% (C)

Scott's No.		Unused, NH VF	F-VF	Unused,OG VF	F-VF	Used F-VF
387	1¢ Franklin, Green	500.00	290.00	260.00	160.00	57.50
387	Pair, 2mm Spacing	1100.00	650.00	575.00	350.00	...
387	Pair, 3mm Spacing	1200.00	700.00	600.00	375.00	...
387	Line Pair	2100.00	1250.00	1075.00	675.00	...
388	2¢ Washington, Carmine	2600.00	1500.00	1300.00	800.00	400.00
389	3¢ Washington, Deep Violet (1911)	...	**USED FINE**			**9500.00**

(Examples of #388 and 389 should be purchased with, or subject to, a certificate.)

1910 Coils S. Line Wmk. - Perf. 8½ Horizontally VF Used + 60% (B)

Scott's No.		Unused, NH VF	F-VF	Unused,OG VF	F-VF	Used F-VF
390	1¢ Franklin, Green	12.00	7.50	6.25	4.00	6.00
390	Pair	27.50	17.00	14.50	9.25	...
390	Line Pair	90.00	55.00	47.50	30.00	...
391	2¢ Washington, Carmine	95.00	55.00	46.50	29.50	12.75
391	Pair	240.00	150.00	120.00	80.00	...
391	Line Pair	625.00	365.00	325.00	200.00	...

1910-13 Coils S. Line Wmk. - Perf. 8½ Vertically VF Used + 60% (B)

Scott's No.		Unused, NH VF	F-VF	Unused,OG VF	F-VF	Used F-VF
392	1¢ Franklin, Green	60.00	35.00	30.00	19.00	21.00
392	Pair	155.00	90.00	80.00	50.00	...
392	Line Pair	475.00	275.00	240.00	150.00	...
393	2¢ Washington, Carmine	110.00	65.00	55.00	35.00	10.75
393	Pair	270.00	170.00	140.00	90.00	...
393	Line Pair	700.00	400.00	350.00	225.00	...
394	3¢ Deep Violet (1911)	160.00	90.00	80.00	50.00	50.00
394	Pair, 2mm Spacing	400.00	225.00	200.00	125.00	...
394	Pair, 3mm Spacing	390.00	215.00	195.00	120.00	...
394	Line Pair	925.00	550.00	475.00	300.00	...
395	4¢ Brown (1912)	155.00	90.00	75.00	47.50	47.50
395	Pair, 2mm Spacing	375.00	220.00	180.00	115.00	...
395	Pair, 3mm Spacing	360.00	210.00	175.00	110.00	...
395	Line Pair	975.00	600.00	500.00	325.00	...
396	5¢ Blue (1913)	155.00	90.00	75.00	47.50	47.50
396	Pair	375.00	220.00	180.00	115.00	...
396	Line Pair	875.00	550.00	475.00	275.00	...

1913 Panama-Pacific Exposition, Perforated 12 VF Used + 60% (B)

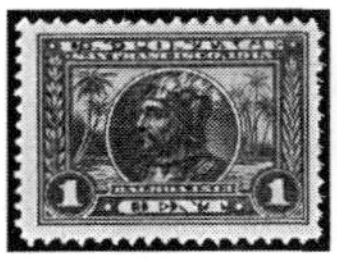
397,401

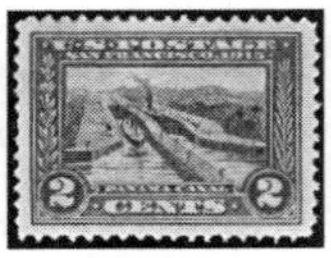
398,402

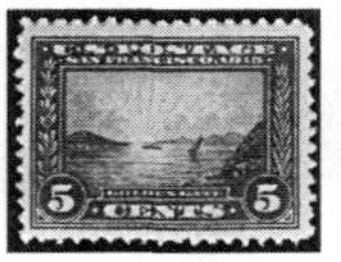
399,403

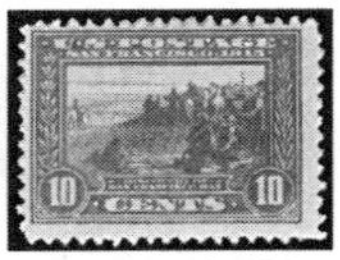
400,400A,404

Scott's No.		Unused, NH VF	F-VF	Unused,OG VF	F-VF	Used F-VF
397-400A	**Set of 5**	**1175.00**	**685.00**	**600.00**	**375.00**	**46.50**
397	1¢ Vasco Nunez de Balboa, Green	46.50	27.50	23.50	15.00	1.50
397	Plate Block of 6	375.00	235.00	225.00	140.00	...
398	2¢ Pedro Miguel Locks at Panama Canal, Carmine	52.50	30.00	26.50	16.50	.60
398	Plate Block of 6	600.00	350.00	325.00	210.00	...
399	5¢ Golden Gate, Blue	185.00	110.00	95.00	60.00	8.50
399	Plate Block of 6	4000.00	2500.00	2400.00	1500.00	...
400	10¢ San Francisco Bay, Orange Yellow	350.00	200.00	175.00	110.00	21.50
400A	10¢ Orange	625.00	360.00	315.00	195.00	16.50

1914-15 Panama-Pacific Exposition, Perf. 10 VF Used + 60% (B)

Scott's No.		Unused, NH VF	F-VF	Unused,OG VF	F-VF	Used F-VF
401-04	**Set of 4**	**3300.00**	**1900.00**	**1625.00**	**1025.00**	**79.50**
401	1¢ Balboa, Green	70.00	40.00	35.00	22.50	6.00
401	Plate Block of 6	775.00	450.00	425.00	260.00	...
402	2¢ Panama, Carmine (1915)	180.00	105.00	90.00	57.50	1.90
402	Plate Block of 6	4000.00	2500.00	2400.00	1500.00	...
403	5¢ Golden Gate, Blue(1915)	495.00	275.00	240.00	150.00	16.00
404	10¢ San Fran.,Orange(1915)	2750.00	1600.00	1350.00	850.00	60.00

NOTE: PRIOR TO 1935, TO DETERMINE VERY FINE USED PRICE, ADD VF% AT BEGINNING OF EACH SET TO THE APPROPRIATE FINE PRICE. MINIMUM 10¢ PER STAMP.
NOTE: STAMP ILLUSTRATIONS INDICATE DESIGNS, PERFORATIONS AND TYPES MAY VARY

NOTE: PRICES THROUGHOUT THIS LIST ARE SUBJECT TO CHANGE WITHOUT NOTICE IF MARKET CONDITIONS REQUIRE. MINIMUM MAIL ORDER MUST TOTAL AT LEAST $20.00.

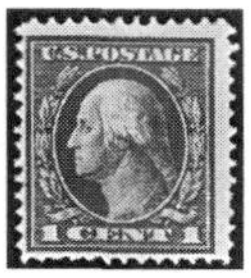

405,408,410,412, 424,441,443,448, 452,462,481,486, 490,498,525,531, 536,538,542-45

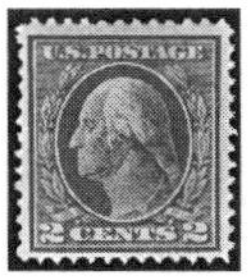

406,409,411,413, 425,442,444, 449-50,453-55, 463,482,487-88, 491-92,499-500, 526-28B,532-34B, 539-40,546

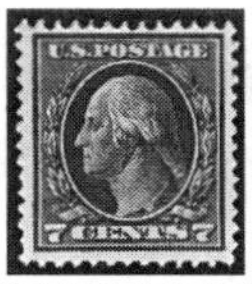

407,430,469,507

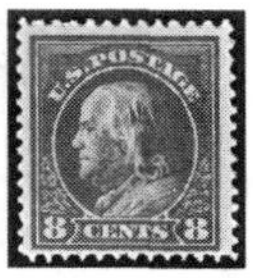

414,431,470,508

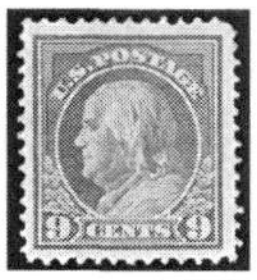

415,432,471,509

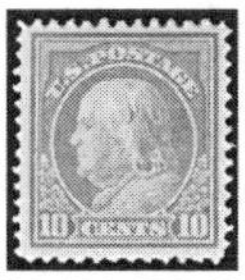

416,433,472,497

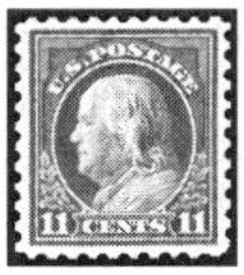

434,473,511

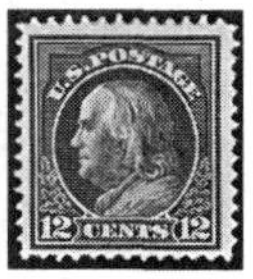

417,435,474,512

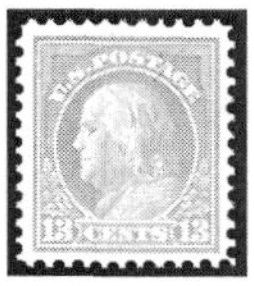

513

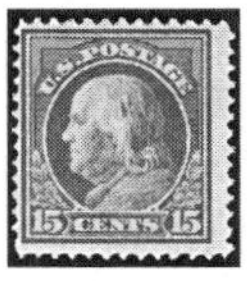

418,437,475,514

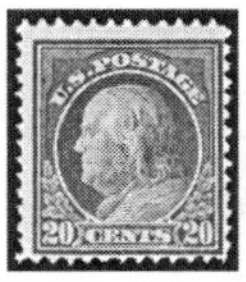

419,438,476,515

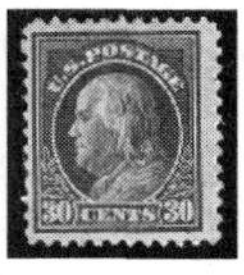

420,439,516

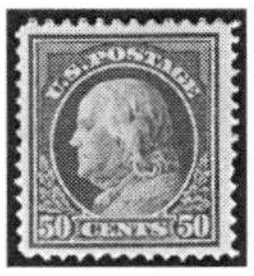

421-22,440,477,517

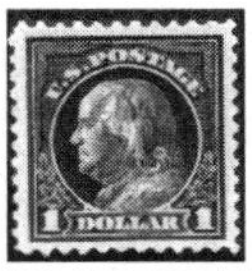

423,460,478,518

NOTE: THE 1¢ TO 7¢ STAMPS FROM 1912-21 PICTURE WASHINGTON. THE 8¢ TO $5 STAMPS PICTURE FRANKLIN.

1912-14 Single Line Watermark, Perforated 12 VF Used + 60% (B)

Scott's No.		Unused, NH VF	Unused, NH F-VF	Unused,OG VF	Unused,OG F-VF	Used F-VF
405	1¢ Washington, Green	17.50	10.00	8.75	5.50	.20
405	Plate Block of 6	200.00	125.00	120.00	75.00	...
405b	1¢ Booklet Pane of 6	160.00	100.00	95.00	60.00	...
406	2¢ Carmine, Type I	17.50	10.00	8.75	5.50	.20
406	Plate Block of 6	225.00	135.00	130.00	80.00	...
406a	2¢ Booklet Pane of 6	160.00	100.00	95.00	60.00	...
407	7¢ Black (1914)	200.00	120.00	100.00	65.00	10.50

1912 Single Line Wmk. - Imperforate VF Used + 30% (B)

408	1¢ Washington, Green	3.00	2.25	1.65	1.25	.65
408	Pair	6.25	4.75	3.50	2.65	...
408	Arrow Block of 4	13.50	10.00	7.25	5.50	...
408	Center Line Block of 4	21.50	16.50	12.50	9.50	...
408	Plate Block of 6	33.00	25.00	21.00	15.75	...
409	2¢ Carmine, Type I	2.85	2.15	1.65	1.25	.75
409	Pair	6.25	4.75	3.50	2.65	...
409	Arrow Block of 4	13.50	9.50	7.25	5.50	...
409	Center Line Block of 4	22.75	16.50	13.00	10.00	...
409	Plate Block of 6	62.50	46.50	39.00	30.00	...

1912 Coils Single Line Wtmk. - Perforated 8½ Horiz. VF Used + 60% (B)

410	1¢ Washington, Green	17.00	10.00	8.75	5.50	4.00
410	Pair	42.50	25.00	22.50	13.75	...
410	Line Pair	95.00	57.50	50.00	32.50	...
411	2¢ Carmine, Type I	23.00	13.50	12.00	7.50	3.75
411	Pair	57.50	35.00	30.00	18.75	...
411	Line Pair	135.00	80.00	67.50	42.50	...

1912 Coils Single Line Wtmk. - Perforated 8½ Vert. VF Used + 60% (B)

412	1¢ Washington, Green	65.00	37.50	31.50	20.00	5.50
412	Pair	170.00	95.00	78.50	50.00	...
412	Line Pair	290.00	170.00	140.00	90.00	...
413	2¢ Carmine, Type I	130.00	75.00	65.00	40.00	1.75
413	Pair	290.00	165.00	145.00	90.00	...
413	Line Pair	700.00	395.00	350.00	215.00	...

1912-14 Franklin Design. Single Line Wmk. - Perf. 12 VF Used + 60% (B)

414	8¢ Franklin, Olive Green	125.00	72.50	60.00	38.50	1.60
414	Plate Block of 6	975.00	575.00	550.00	350.00	...
415	9¢ Salmon Red (1914)	140.00	82.50	72.50	45.00	11.75
415	Plate Block of 6	1350.00	850.00	800.00	500.00	...
416	10¢ Orange Yellow	110.00	65.00	55.00	35.00	.60
416	Plate Block of 6	1000.00	625.00	600.00	375.00	...
417	12¢ Claret Brown (1914)	130.00	77.50	67.50	42.50	4.00
417	Plate Block of 6	1275.00	800.00	750.00	475.00	...
418	15¢ Gray	225.00	130.00	110.00	70.00	3.50
418	Plate Block of 6	1800.00	1000.00	850.00	550.00	...
419	20¢ Ultramarine (1914)	500.00	300.00	260.00	165.00	14.50
420	30¢ Orange Red (1914)	300.00	180.00	160.00	100.00	16.00
421	50¢ Violet (1914)	1075.00	650.00	550.00	350.00	18.00

#421 usually shows an offset on the back; #422 usually does not.

1912 Franklin Design. Double Line Wmk. - Perf. 12 VF Used + 60% (B)

422	50¢ Franklin, Violet	675.00	400.00	335.00	210.00	18.00
423	$1 Violet Brown	1200.00	725.00	650.00	400.00	57.50

AVERAGE QUALITY

From 1890 to date, Average Quality, when available, can usually be supplied at 30% discount from the Fine to Very Fine prices.

1914 Washington, Single Line Wtmk., Perf.12x10 VF Used +60% (C)

Scott's No.		Unused, NH VF	Unused, NH F-VF	Unused,OG VF	Unused,OG F-VF	Used F-VF
423A	1¢ Green	...	...	...	5750.00	3750.00
423B	2¢ Rose red	...	...	...	...	7500.00
423C	5¢ Blue	...	...	...	...	9500.00

1914 Washington, Single Line Wtmk.,Perf.10x12 VF Used + 60% (C)

423D	1¢ Green	...	...	...	...	5750.00

1914-15 Flat Press Single Line Watemark, Perf. 10 VF Used + 60% (B)

424	1¢ Washington, Green	6.75	4.00	3.65	2.25	.20
424	Plate Block of 6	90.00	55.00	52.50	32.50	...
424	Pl.Bk. of 10 "COIL STAMPS"	300.00	190.00	175.00	110.00	...
424d	1¢ Booklet Pane of 6	11.00	6.50	6.50	4.00	...
425	2¢ Rose Red, Type I	5.75	3.50	3.25	2.00	.20
425	Plate Block of 6	56.50	37.50	36.50	22.50	...
425	Pl.Bk.of 10 "COIL STAMPS"	350.00	210.00	200.00	125.00	...
425e	2¢ Booklet Pane of 6	55.00	33.50	31.50	20.00	...
426	3¢ Deep Violet, Type I	35.00	21.00	18.50	11.50	1.35
426	Plate Block of 6	400.00	250.00	240.00	150.00	...
427	4¢ Brown	95.00	55.00	47.50	30.00	.75
427	Plate Block of 6	1075.00	650.00	650.00	400.00	...
428	5¢ Blue	85.00	50.00	46.50	27.50	.75
428	Plate Block of 6	825.00	500.00	475.00	300.00	...
429	6¢ Red Orange	135.00	80.00	67.50	42.50	1.65
429	Plate Block of 6	875.00	525.00	575.00	325.00	...
430	7¢ Black	210.00	125.00	105.00	67.50	4.75
430	Plate Block of 6	2000.00	1250.00	1150.00	725.00	...
431	8¢ Franklin, Olive Green	100.00	60.00	50.00	31.50	2.35
431	Plate Block of 6	1050.00	625.00	600.00	375.00	...
432	9¢ Salmon Red	115.00	70.00	60.00	38.50	10.75
432	Plate Block of 6	1550.00	950.00	875.00	550.00	...
433	10¢ Orange Yellow	125.00	75.00	65.00	40.00	.80
433	Plate Block of 6	1375.00	850.00	800.00	500.00	...
434	11¢ Dark Green (1915)	65.00	39.50	34.00	21.50	7.50
434	Plate Block of 6	500.00	300.00	285.00	180.00	...
435	12¢ Claret Brown	65.00	39.50	34.00	21.50	6.50
435	Plate Block of 6	575.00	375.00	350.00	225.00	...
435a	12¢ Copper Red	75.00	45.00	40.00	25.00	6.75
435a	Plate Block of 6	650.00	415.00	400.00	250.00	...
437	15¢ Gray	350.00	210.00	175.00	110.00	7.75
437	Plate Block of 6	2200.00	1350.00	1300.00	800.00	...
438	20¢ Ultramarine	550.00	325.00	280.00	175.00	5.00
439	30¢ Orange Red	665.00	395.00	335.00	210.00	15.75
440	50¢ Violet (1915)	1600.00	950.00	785.00	495.00	17.50

1914 Coils Flat Press Single Line Watermark - Perforated 10 Horizontally VF Used + 60% (B)

441	1¢ Washington, Green	2.80	1.75	1.50	.95	1.10
441	Pair	7.00	4.50	3.75	2.50	...
441	Line Pair	19.50	12.00	10.50	6.50	...
442	2¢ Carmine, Type I	24.00	15.00	13.00	8.00	6.50
442	Pair	60.00	37.50	32.50	19.75	...
442	Line Pair	145.00	90.00	75.00	47.50	...

1914 Coils Flat Press S.L. Wmk. - Perf. 10 Vert. VF Used + 60% (B)

443	1¢ Washington, Green	60.00	36.50	31.00	19.50	5.75
443	Pair	150.00	95.00	77.50	50.00	...
443	Line Pair	375.00	225.00	190.00	120.00	...
444	2¢ Carmine, Type I	95.00	55.00	47.50	30.00	2.25
444	Pair	275.00	160.00	140.00	90.00	...
444	Line Pair	650.00	400.00	340.00	215.00	...
445	3¢ Violet, Type I	625.00	365.00	325.00	200.00	110.00
445	Pair	1575.00	900.00	800.00	500.00	...
446	4¢ Brown	335.00	200.00	175.00	110.00	43.50
446	Pair	850.00	500.00	450.00	275.00	...
446	Line Pair	1800.00	1100.00	950.00	575.00	...
447	5¢ Blue	135.00	80.00	67.50	42.50	37.50
447	Pair	325.00	200.00	170.00	105.00	...
447	Line Pair	615.00	365.00	315.00	200.00	...

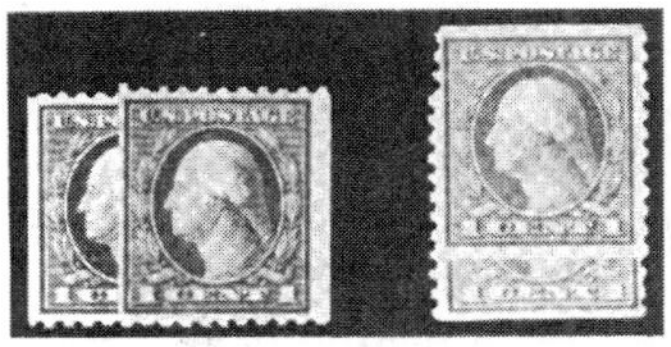

The two top stamps are Rotary Press while the underneath stamps are Flat Press. Note that the designs of the Rotary Press stamps are a little longer or Wider than Flat Press stamps. Flat Press Stamps usually show spots of color on back.

Perf. Horizontally **Perf. Vertically**

1915 Coils Rotary Single Line Wmk. - Perf. 10 Horiz. VF Used + 60% (B)

448	1¢ Washington, Green	18.50	11.00	9.50	6.00	3.75
448	Pair	47.50	27.50	23.50	15.00	...
448	Line Pair	125.00	75.00	65.00	40.00	...
449	2¢ Red, Type I	6500.00	4000.00	3250.00	2000.00	475.00
450	2¢ Carmine, Type III	26.50	16.00	13.50	8.50	4.00
450	Pair	67.50	40.00	34.00	21.50	...
450	Line Pair	225.00	135.00	120.00	75.00	...

1914-16 Coils Rotary Single Line Wmk. - Perf. 10 Vert. VF Used + 60% (B)

452	1¢ Washington, Green	32.50	20.00	17.50	11.00	2.75
452	Pair	82.50	50.00	43.50	27.50	...
452	Line Pair	180.00	110.00	92.50	57.50	...
453	2¢ Carmine Rose, Type I	375.00	220.00	195.00	120.00	4.75
453	Pair	850.00	500.00	435.00	270.00	...
453	Line Pair	1575.00	950.00	875.00	550.00	...
454	2¢ Red, Type II (1915)	285.00	175.00	145.00	90.00	9.75
454	Pair	625.00	385.00	325.00	200.00	...
454	Line Pair	1125.00	675.00	600.00	375.00	...
455	2¢ Carmine, Type III (1915)	27.50	16.50	14.00	8.75	1.70
455	Pair	70.00	42.50	35.00	21.50	...
455	Line Pair	140.00	85.00	70.00	45.00	...
456	3¢ Violet (1916)	750.00	450.00	385.00	240.00	95.00
456	Pair	1850.00	1100.00	950.00	600.00	...
457	4¢ Brown (1915)	75.00	45.00	40.00	25.00	21.50
457	Pair	190.00	115.00	100.00	62.50	...
457	Line Pair	375.00	225.00	190.00	120.00	...

1914-16 Coils Rotary Single Line Wmk. - Perf. 10 Vert. VF Used + 60% (B)

Scott's No.		Unused, NH VF	F-VF	Unused,OG VF	F-VF	Used F-VF
458	5¢ Blue (1916)	85.00	52.50	45.00	28.50	19.50
458	Pair	210.00	125.00	110.00	70.00	...
458	Line Pair	450.00	265.00	225.00	140.00	...

1914 Imperforate Coil, Rotary Press Single Line Wmk. - VF Used + 40% (B)

459	2¢ Washington, Carmine, Type I	725.00	525.00	475.00	350.00	875.00

Genuinely used examples of #459 are rare. Copies should have contemporary cancels and be purchased with, or subject to, a certificate of authenticity.

1915 Flat Press Double Line Wmk. - Perforated 10 VF Used + 75% (B)

460	$1 Franklin, Violet Black	2250.00	1300.00	1150.00	675.00	80.00

1915 Flat Press Single Line Wmk. - Perf. 11 VF Used + 100% (B)

461	2¢ Pale Carmine Red, Ty.I	475.00	230.00	240.00	120.00	250.00

(Counterfeits of #461 are common. Purchase with, or subject to, a certificate.)

1916-17 Flat Press, No Watermark - Perforated 10 (VF Used + 60%) (B)

462	1¢ Washington, Green	21.00	13.00	11.50	7.25	.45
462	Plate Block of 6	325.00	195.00	195.00	120.00	...
462a	1¢ Booklet Pane of 6	25.00	15.00	14.50	9.00	...
463	2¢ Carmine, Type I	12.50	7.50	6.50	4.00	.35
463	Plate Block of 6	265.00	170.00	160.00	100.00	...
463a	2¢ Booklet Pane of 6	210.00	125.00	120.00	75.00	...
464	3¢ Violet, Type I	180.00	110.00	100.00	60.00	13.75
465	4¢ Orange Brown	125.00	75.00	63.50	40.00	2.00
465	Plate Block of 6	1375.00	825.00	800.00	500.00	...
466	5¢ Blue	180.00	110.00	100.00	60.00	2.10
466	Plate Block of 6	1900.00	1150.00	1100.00	700.00	...
467	5¢ Carmine ERROR	1500.00	900.00	800.00	500.00	600.00
467	5¢ Single in Block of 9	2230.00	1400.00	1300.00	800.00	...
467	5¢ Pair in Block of 12	3850.00	2300.00	2100.00	1375.00	...
468	6¢ Red Orange	250.00	150.00	130.00	80.00	7.50
469	7¢ Black	295.00	180.00	160.00	100.00	11.50
470	8¢ Franklin, Olive Green	140.00	85.00	75.00	47.50	6.50
470	Plate Block of 6	1175.00	725.00	675.00	425.00	...
471	9¢ Salmon Red	160.00	95.00	82.50	52.50	15.00
471	Plate Block of 6	1650.00	975.00	925.00	575.00	...
472	10¢ Orange Yellow	250.00	150.00	135.00	82.50	1.90
473	11¢ Dark Green	110.00	65.00	55.00	35.00	16.50
473	Plate Block of 6	825.00	500.00	475.00	300.00	...
474	12¢ Claret Brown	135.00	80.00	70.00	45.00	6.50
474	Plate Block of 6	1350.00	800.00	750.00	475.00	...
475	15¢ Gray	450.00	270.00	240.00	150.00	12.75
476	20¢ Ultramarine	600.00	365.00	325.00	200.00	13.75
476A	30¢ Orange Red	...	5500.00	...	3500.00	...
477	50¢ Light Violet (1917)	2700.00	1650.00	1400.00	875.00	62.50
478	$1 Violet Black	1850.00	1150.00	975.00	600.00	20.00

1917 Flat Press, No Watermark-Perf. 10, Designs of 1902-3 VF used 35% (B)

479	$2 Madison, Dark Blue	925.00	550.00	475.00	300.00	45.00
480	$5 Marshall, Light Green	750.00	450.00	400.00	250.00	45.00

NOTE: #479 & 480 have the same designs as #312 & 313

1916-17 Flat Press, No Watermark - Imperforate VF Used + 30% (B)

481	1¢ Washington, Green	2.25	1.70	1.20	.90	1.00
481	Pair	4.75	3.60	2.50	1.90	...
481	Arrow Block of 4	10.50	7.50	5.75	4.25	...
481	Center Line Block of 4	16.00	12.00	9.00	7.00	...
481	Plate Block of 6	25.00	19.00	15.00	11.50	...
482	2¢ Carmine, Type I	4.00	2.85	2.10	1.60	1.35
482	Pair	8.50	5.95	4.35	3.30	...
482	Arrow Block of 4	17.50	13.00	9.25	7.00	...
482	Center Line Block of 4	21.00	15.75	11.50	8.75	...
482	Plate Block of 6	49.50	37.50	29.50	22.50	...
482A	2¢ Deep Rose, Type Ia	...	...	...	...	...
483	3¢ Violet, Type I (1917)	31.50	23.50	17.50	13.00	8.00
483	Pair	66.50	49.50	36.50	27.00	...
483	Arrow Block of 4	140.00	110.00	77.50	60.00	...
483	Center Line Block of 4	160.00	120.00	91.50	70.00	...
483	Plate Block of 6	240.00	180.00	150.00	115.00	...
484	3¢ Violet, Type II (1917)	23.50	17.50	13.50	10.00	5.00
484	Pair	49.50	37.50	28.50	21.00	...
484	Arrow Block of 4	105.00	75.00	60.00	45.00	...
484	Center Line Block of 4	135.00	100.00	80.00	60.00	...
484	Plate Block of 6	200.00	150.00	120.00	90.00	...
485	5¢ Carmine ERROR (1917)	...	...	...	...	...

1916-19 Coils Rotary, No Watermark - Perf. 10 Horiz. VF Used + 50% (B)

486	1¢ Washington, Green (1918)	2.40	1.50	1.30	.85	.30
486	Pair	5.25	3.30	2.75	1.85	...
486	Line Pair	12.00	7.75	6.50	4.25	...
487	2¢ Carmine, Type II	37.50	25.00	20.75	13.75	5.00
487	Pair	85.00	55.00	43.75	30.75	...
487	Line Pair	285.00	175.00	140.00	95.00	...
488	2¢ Carmine, Type III (1919)	8.00	5.00	4.15	2.75	1.70
488	Pair	18.00	11.75	9.75	6.50	...
488	Line Pair	48.50	31.50	26.50	17.50	...
489	3¢ Violet, Type I (1917)	12.50	8.25	6.75	4.50	1.65
489	Pair	27.50	18.00	15.00	10.00	...
489	Line Pair	77.50	50.00	42.50	27.50	...

1916-22 Coils, Rotary, No Wmk. - Perf. 10 Vert. VF Used + 50% (B)

490	1¢ Washington, Green	1.50	1.00	.85	.55	.25
490	Pair	3.50	2.30	2.00	1.30	...
490	Line Pair	10.50	7.00	5.75	3.75	...
491	2¢ Carmine, Type II	4500.00	3000.00	2500.00	1650.00	575.00
492	2¢ Carmine, Type III	26.00	17.00	13.50	9.00	.30
492	Pair	58.50	37.50	30.00	20.00	...
492	Line Pair	130.00	87.50	70.00	47.50	...
493	3¢ Violet, Type I (1917)	45.00	26.50	23.00	14.50	3.25
493	Pair	100.00	58.50	50.00	32.50	...
493	Line Pair	275.00	175.00	140.00	95.00	...
494	3¢ Violet, Type II (1918)	26.00	16.50	13.50	9.00	1.10
494	Pair	57.50	37.50	32.00	21.00	...
494	Line Pair	165.00	110.00	90.00	60.00	...
495	4¢ Orange Brown (1917)	26.50	17.50	14.00	9.50	3.75
495	Pair	65.00	42.50	32.50	22.75	...
495	Line Pair	190.00	125.00	100.00	70.00	...

1916-22 Coils, Rotary, No Wmk. - Perf. 10 Vert. VF Used + 50% (B)

Scott's No.		Unused, NH VF	F-VF	Unused,OG VF	F-VF	Used F-VF
496	5¢ Blue (1919)	9.25	6.00	4.75	3.25	1.00
496	Pair	21.50	13.50	10.50	7.25	...
496	Line Pair	75.00	47.50	39.50	26.50	...
497	10¢ Franklin, Orange Yellow (1922)	51.50	33.50	27.50	18.50	11.00
497	Pair	125.00	80.00	65.00	42.50	...
497	Line Pair	300.00	200.00	160.00	110.00	...

1917-19 Flat Press, No Watermark - Perf. 11 VF Used + 50% (B)

498	1¢ Washington, Green	1.20	.75	.65	.45	.25
498	Plate Block of 6	35.00	22.50	20.00	13.50	...
498e	1¢ Booklet Pane of 6	6.50	4.00	3.75	2.50	...
498f	1¢ Booklet Pane of 30	2000.00	1300.00	1250.00	800.00	...
499	2¢ Carmine, Type I	1.20	.75	.65	.45	.25
499	Plate Block of 6	35.00	22.50	20.00	13.50	...
499e	2¢ Booklet Pane of 6	11.50	7.50	7.25	4.75	...
500	2¢ Deep Rose,Ty.Ia(VF+75%)	650.00	385.00	360.00	210.00	180.00
501	3¢ Light Violet, Type I	30.00	19.50	16.50	11.00	.25
501	Plate Block of 6	250.00	165.00	150.00	100.00	...
501b	3¢ Booklet Pane of 6	150.00	100.00	90.00	60.00	...
502	3¢ Dark Violet, Type II	37.50	25.00	20.75	14.00	.65
502	Plate Block of 6	300.00	195.00	175.00	120.00	...
502b	3¢ Booklet Pane of 6 (1918)	115.00	75.00	67.50	45.00	...
503	4¢ Brown	27.50	17.50	15.00	10.00	.35
503	Plate Block of 6	315.00	210.00	185.00	125.00	...
504	5¢ Blue	22.00	14.50	12.00	8.00	.35
504	Plate Block of 6	260.00	170.00	150.00	100.00	...
505	5¢ Rose ERROR	975.00	650.00	525.00	350.00	450.00
505	5¢ ERROR in Block of 9	1500.00	1000.00	900.00	600.00	...
505	5¢ Pair in Block of 12	2750.00	1850.00	1650.00	1100.00	...
506	6¢ Red Orange	30.00	19.50	16.50	11.00	.45
506	Plate Block of 6	375.00	250.00	225.00	150.00	...
507	7¢ Black	63.50	41.50	35.00	23.50	1.25
507	Plate Block of 6	575.00	375.00	350.00	225.00	...
508	8¢ Franklin, Olive Bistre	30.00	19.50	16.50	11.00	1.00
508	Plate Block of 6	300.00	200.00	180.00	120.00	...
509	9¢ Salmon Red	34.50	22.50	18.50	12.50	2.00
509	Plate Block of 6	300.00	200.00	180.00	120.00	...
510	10¢ Orange Yellow	45.00	28.50	24.00	15.75	.25
510	Plate Block of 6	350.00	250.00	225.00	150.00	...
511	11¢ Light Green	22.00	14.50	12.50	8.25	3.25
511	Plate Block of 6	260.00	180.00	165.00	110.00	...
512	12¢ Claret Brown	22.00	14.50	12.50	8.25	.60
512	Plate Block of 6	260.00	180.00	165.00	110.00	...
513	13¢ Apple Green (1919)	27.50	18.00	15.00	10.00	6.50
513	Plate Block of 6	250.00	170.00	150.00	100.00	...
514	15¢ Gray	100.00	63.50	52.50	35.00	1.15
514	Plate Block of 6	1200.00	800.00	725.00	475.00	...
515	20¢ Light Ultramarine	115.00	75.00	65.00	42.50	.50
515	Plate Block of 6	1300.00	850.00	775.00	525.00	...
516	30¢ Orange Red	100.00	65.00	52.50	35.00	1.15
516	Plate Block of 6	1175.00	775.00	700.00	475.00	...
517	50¢ Red Violet	185.00	120.00	100.00	65.00	.85
517	Plate Block of 6	3350.00	2200.00	1950.00	1300.00	...
518	$1 Violet Brown	160.00	100.00	85.00	55.00	1.75
518	Arrpw Block of 4	700.00	450.00	365.00	240.00	...
518	Plate Block of 6	2600.00	1800.00	1700.00	1100.00	...
518b	$1 Deep Brown	...	2500.00	2000.00	1350.00	875.00

1917 Same Design as #332, Double Line Wmk. - Perf. 11 VF Used + 100% (C)

519	2¢ Washington, Carmine	1100.00	550.00	600.00	300.00	950.00

(* Mint and used copies of #519 have been extensively counterfeited. Examples of either should be purchased with, or subject to, a certificate of authenticity.)

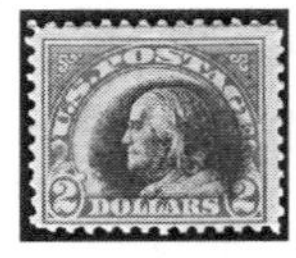

523,547

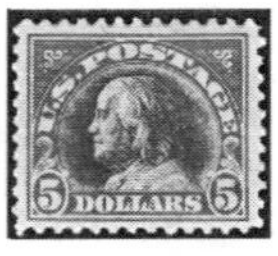

524

1918 Franklin, Flat Press, No Watermark, Perf. 11 VF Used + 50% (B)

523	$2 Orange Red & Black	1650.00	1075.00	900.00	600.00	265.00
524	$5 Deep Green & Black	565.00	370.00	295.00	195.00	32.50

1918-20 Offset Printing, Perforated 11 VF Used + 60% (B)

525	1¢ Washington, Gray Green	6.50	4.00	3.50	2.25	.95
525	Plate Block of 6	55.00	34.00	31.50	20.00	...
526	2¢ Carmine, Type IV (1920)	65.00	40.00	35.00	22.50	5.00
526	Plate Block of 6	475.00	300.00	290.00	185.00	...
527	2¢ Carmine, Type V (1920)	52.50	32.50	28.50	18.00	1.50
527	Plate Block of 6	350.00	215.00	210.00	130.00	...
528	2¢ Carmine, Type Va (1920)	23.50	14.50	12.75	8.00	.70
528	Plate Block of 6	180.00	115.00	110.00	70.00	...
528A	2¢ Carmine, Type VI (1920)	140.00	85.00	75.00	47.50	1.80
528A	Plate Block of 6	850.00	600.00	535.00	350.00	...
528B	2¢ Carmine, Type VII (1920)	57.50	35.00	31.00	19.50	.65
528B	Plate Block of 6	395.00	250.00	225.00	140.00	...
529	3¢ Violet, Type III	8.50	5.25	4.75	3.00	.40
529	Plate Block of 6	125.00	75.00	70.00	45.00	...
530	3¢ Purple, Type IV	5.00	3.00	2.70	1.70	.35
530	Plate Block of 6	43.50	27.50	27.00	17.00	...

1918-20 Offset Printing, Imperforate VF Used + 30% (B)

531	1¢ Washington, Green (1919)	19.50	15.00	12.00	9.00	8.50
531	Pair	41.50	31.50	25.00	19.00	...
531	Arrow Block of 4	85.00	65.00	53.50	39.50	...
531	Center Line Block of 4	110.00	85.00	68.50	52.50	...
531	Plate Block of 6	145.00	110.00	90.00	70.00	...
532	2¢ Carmine Rose, Type IV (20)	97.50	75.00	52.50	40.00	27.50
532	Pair	210.00	160.00	110.00	85.00	...
532	Arrow Block of 4	435.00	330.00	225.00	175.00	...
532	Center Line Block of 4	465.00	360.00	265.00	200.00	...
532	Plate Block of 6	725.00	550.00	395.00	300.00	...

1918-20 Offset Printing, Imperforate VF Used + 30% (B)

Scott's No.		Unused, NH VF	F-VF	Unused,OG VF	F-VF	Used F-VF
533	2¢ Camine, Type V (1920)	425.00	315.00	230.00	175.00	95.00
533	Pair	925.00	675.00	485.00	375.00	...
533	Arrow Block of 4	1900.00	1400.00	1050.00	775.00	...
533	Center Line Block of 4	2375.00	1800.00	1300.00	1000.00	...
533	Plate Block of 6	3000.00	2250.00	1650.00	1250.00	...
534	2¢ Carmine, Type Va (1920) ...	31.00	23.50	17.00	13.00	8.50
534	Pair	65.00	48.50	36.50	27.50	...
534	Arrow Block of 4	125.00	95.00	75.00	60.00	...
534	Center Line Block of 4	145.00	110.00	85.00	65.00	...
534	Plate Block of 6	215.00	165.00	120.00	90.00	...
534A	2¢ Carmine, Type VI (1920)	82.50	62.50	45.00	35.00	30.00
534A	Pair	175.00	130.00	95.00	75.00	...
534A	Arrow Block of 4	350.00	260.00	195.00	150.00	...
534A	Center Line Block of 4	385.00	285.00	225.00	170.00	...
534A	Plate Block of 6	600.00	450.00	360.00	275.00	...
534B	2¢ Carmine, Type VII (1920)	4000.00	3000.00	2300.00	1750.00	975.00
535	3¢ Violet, Type IV	20.00	15.00	11.00	8.50	7.50
535	Pair	42.50	31.50	23.50	18.00	...
535	Arrow Block of 4	87.50	65.00	52.50	39.50	...
535	Center Line Block of 4	100.00	75.00	60.00	45.00	...
535	Plate Block of 6	135.00	100.00	82.50	62.50	...

Types of the 2¢ and 3¢ Washington Issues

2¢ Washington: **Type I**, Flat and Rotary - One shading line in first curve of ribbon above left "2". One shading line in second curve of ribbon above right "2". Toga button and top line of toga rope have faint outline. Shading lines of face end in front of the ear are not joined and form a lock of hair.

Type Ia, Flat - Similar to Type I except that lines are stronger. Toga button and rope shading lines are heavier.

Type II, Rotary - Ribbons similar to Type I. Toga button and rope lines are heavy. Shading lines in front of ear at lock of hair end in strong vertical curved line. Similar to Type Ia but only occurs on rotary printings.

Type III, Rotary - Similar to Type II except that there are two shading lines in ribbons above "2"'s instead of one as described in Type I.

Type IV, Offset - Top line of toga rope is broken. Shading lines inside toga button form "DID" (first D is reversed). Line of color in left "2" is broken.

Type V, Offset - Top line of toga rope is complete. Toga button has five vertical shade lines. Shading dots on nose are complete. Line of color in left "2" is broken as in Type IV.

Type Va, Offset - Similar to Type V except that the third row of dots from the bottom on the nose has only four dots instead of six and appears incomplete. Height of design is 1/3 millimeter shorter than Type V.

Type VI, Offset - Similar to Type V with line of color in left "2" very heavy.

Type VII, Offset - Line of color in left "2" is continuous but heavier than in Type V or Va and lighter than in Type VI. Three vertical rows of dots on upper lip instead of two rows on other types. Dots added to top of head.

3¢ Washington: **Type I**, Flat and Rotary - Top line of toga rope is weak and rope shading lines are thin. 5th shading line from the left in rope is missing. Line between lips is thin.

Type II, Flat and Rotary - Top line of toga rope is strong and shading lines of rope are complete. The line between lips is much heavier than in Type I.

Type III, Offset - Top line of toga rope is strong but 5th shading line is missing as in Type I. Two short vertical lines in toga button with a dot in the middle. "P" & "O" of "POSTAGE" are separated by line of color.

Type IV, Offset - The shading lines of toga rope are complete. The center line of toga button is an unbroken vertical line running through the dot. The "P" & "O" of "POSTAGE" are joined (no color line in between).

See Scott Catalogs for more details and illustrations.

1919 Offset Printing, Perforated 12½ VF Used + 75% (B)

536	1¢ Washington, Gray Green ...	55.00	30.00	31.50	17.50	18.50
536	Plate Block of 6	400.00	240.00	250.00	150.00	...

1919 Victory in World War I Issue VF Used + 50% (B)

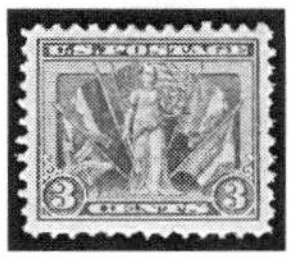
537

537	3¢ Violet	21.00	13.00	11.50	7.50	3.50
537	Plate Block of 6	235.00	150.00	135.00	90.00	...
537a	3¢ Deep Red Violet	2750.00	1800.00	1600.00	1050.00	...
537c	3¢ Red Violet	170.00	105.00	87.50	57.50	12.50

1919 Rotary Press Printing - Perforated 11x10 VF Used + 75% (C)

Stamp designs 19½-20 x 22-22¼ mm

538	1¢ Washington. Green	30.00	17.00	16.50	9.50	9.50
538	Plate Block of 4	210.00	125.00	130.00	75.00	...
539	2¢ Carmine Rose, Type II, ...	3750.00	...	2500.00		...
540	2¢ Carmine Rose,Type III	36.50	20.00	19.00	11.50	9.50
540	Plate Block of 4	240.00	135.00	140.00	80.00	...
541	3¢ Violet, Type II	120.00	65.00	62.50	35.00	30.00
541	Plate Block of 4	795.00	450.00	465.00	265.00	...

1920 Rotary Press - Perforated 10x11 VF Used +75% (C)

Stamp design 19 x 22½-22 3/4 mm

542	1¢ Washington, Green	35.00	20.00	20.75	11.75	1.35
542	Plate Block of 6	350.00	200.00	210.00	120.00	...

1921 Rotary Press - Perforated 10 VF Used +75% (C)

Stamp design 19 x 22½ mm

543	1¢ Washington, Green	2.40	1.35	1.30	.75	.35
543	Plate Block of 4	35.00	20.00	21.00	12.00	...
543	Plate Block of 6	80.00	45.00	47.50	27.50	...

1921-22 Rotary Press - Perforated 11 VF Used + 75% (C)

544	1¢ Green (19x22½ mm) (1922)	...		...		2750.00
545	1¢ Green (19½x22 mm)	525.00	275.00	265.00	150.00	145.00
546	2¢ Carmine Rose, Ty.III	280.00	160.00	160.00	90.00	135.00

1920 Flat Press, No Watermark, Perforated 11 VF Used + 50% (B)

547	$2 Franklin,Carmine & Black .	525.00	350.00	285.00	190.00	40.00
547	Arrow Block of 4	2250.00	1500.00	1250.00	800.00	...
547	Center Line Block of 4	2500.00	1650.00	1350.00	900.00	...

1920 Pilgrim Tercentenary Issue VF Used + 40% (B)

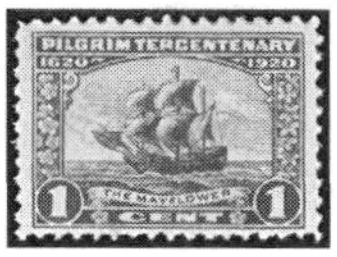
548

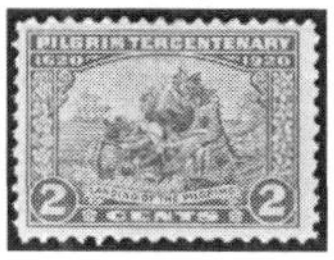
549

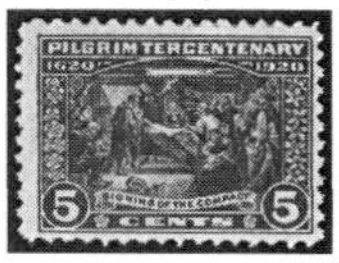
550

Scott's No.		Unused, NH VF	F-VF	Unused,OG VF	F-VF	Used F-VF
548-50	**Set of 3 ....**	**107.50**	**77.50**	**62.50**	**44.75**	**18.50**
548	1¢ Mayflower, Green	9.25	6.50	5.25	3.75	2.65
548	Plate Block of 6	77.50	55.00	48.50	35.00	...
549	2¢ Landing of the Pilgrims, Carmine Rose	14.00	10.00	8.50	6.00	1.75
549	Plate Block of 6	130.00	85.00	77.50	55.00	...
550	5¢ Signing of the Compact, Deep Blue	90.00	65.00	52.50	37.50	15.00
550	Plate Block of 6	850.00	600.00	565.00	400.00	...

1922-25 Regular Issue, Flat Press, Perforated 11 VF Used + 40% (B)

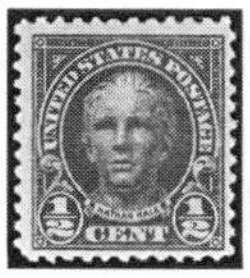
551,653

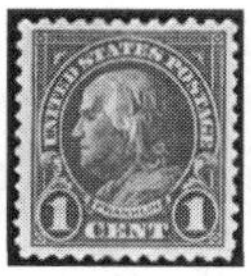
552,575,578, 581,594,596, 597,604,632

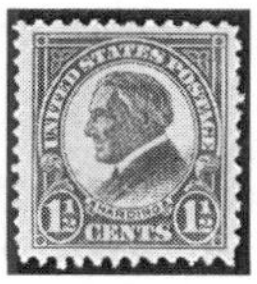
553,576,582, 598,605,631, 633

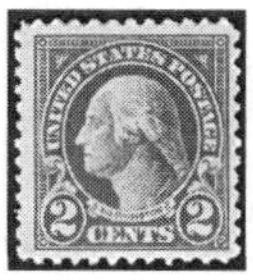
554,577,579, 583,595,599-9A 606,634-34A

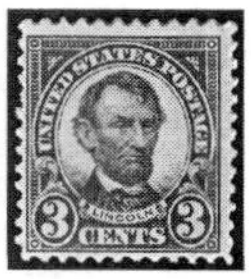
555,584,600, 635

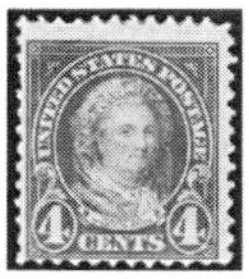
556,585,601, 636

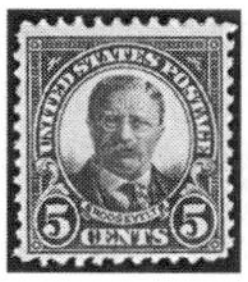
557,586,602, 637

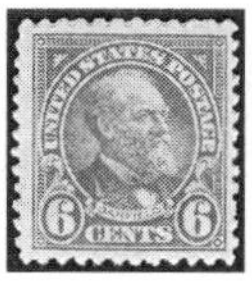
558,587,638, 723

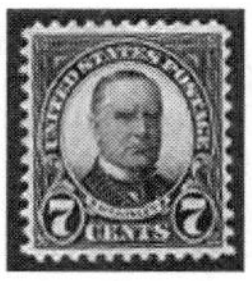
559,588,639

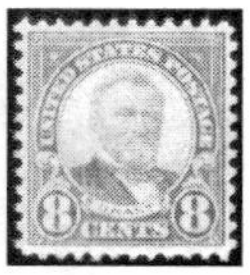
560,589,640

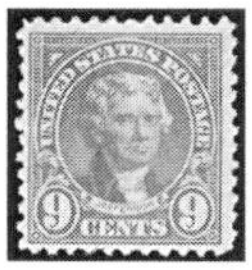
561,590,641

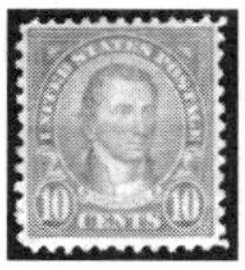
562,591,603, 642

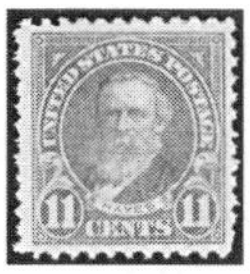
563,692

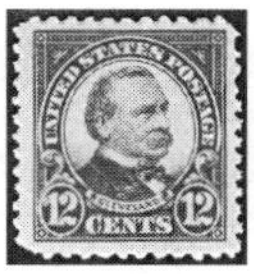
564,693

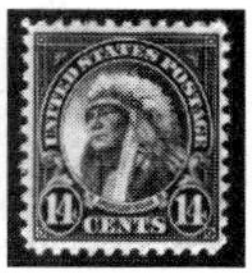
565,695

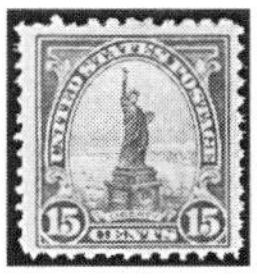
566,696

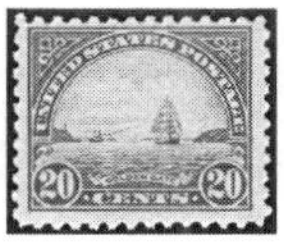
567,698

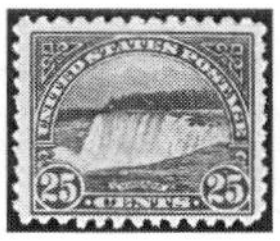
568,699

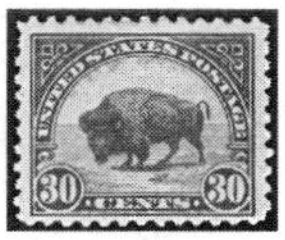
569,700

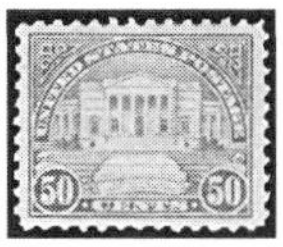
570,701

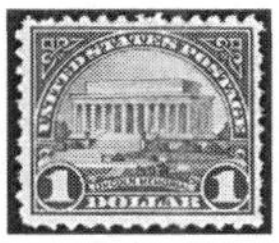
571

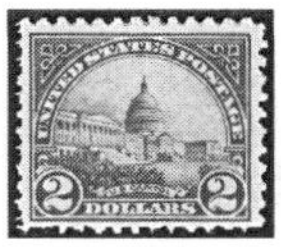
572

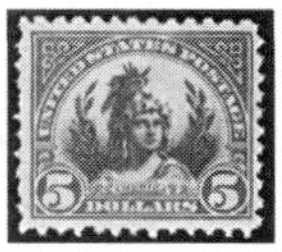
573

551-73	**Set of 23 ....**	**1400.00**	**965.00**	**795.00**	**575.00**	**32.50**
551	½¢ Hale, Olive Brown (1925)	.40	.30	.30	.20	.20
551	Plate Block of 6	10.00	6.75	6.50	4.50	...
552	1¢ Franklin, Green (1923)	3.75	2.50	2.10	1.50	.20
552	Plate Block of 6	39.50	26.50	26.00	18.00	...
552a	1¢ Booklet Pane of 6	17.50	12.00	10.50	7.50	...
553	1½¢ Harding, Yellow Brown ('25)	6.00	4.25	3.50	2.50	.30
553	Plate Block of 6	56.50	40.00	37.50	26.50	...
554	2¢ Washington, Carmine (1923)	4.25	2.85	2.40	1.70	.20
554	Plate Block of 6	39.50	26.50	26.00	18.00	...
554c	2¢ Booklet Pane of 6	21.00	15.00	12.50	8.75	...
555	3¢ Lincoln, Violet (1923)	40.00	27.50	22.75	16.50	1.40
555	Plate Block of 6	280.00	200.00	185.00	135.00	...
556	4¢ Martha Washington, Yellow Brown(1923)	40.00	27.50	22.75	16.50	.40
556	Plate Block of 6	280.00	200.00	185.00	135.00	...
557	5¢ T. Roosevelt, Dark Blue	40.00	27.50	22.75	16.50	.30
557	Plate Block of 6	290.00	200.00	190.00	135.00	...
558	6¢ Garfield, Red Orange	75.00	50.00	41.50	30.00	.85
558	Plate Block of 6	625.00	450.00	420.00	300.00	...
559	7¢ McKinley, Black (1923)	19.50	13.50	11.00	8.00	.80
559	Plate Block of 6	130.00	90.00	85.00	60.00	...
560	8¢ Grant, Olive Green (1923) .	95.00	65.00	56.50	40.00	1.00
560	Plate Block of 6	950.00	675.00	625.00	450.00	...
561	9¢ Jefferson, Rose (1923)	32.50	22.50	18.75	13.50	1.50
561	Plate Block of 6	280.00	200.00	185.00	130.00	...
562	10¢ Monroe, Orange (1923)	45.00	30.75	25.75	18.50	.30
562	Plate Block of 6	375.00	265.00	250.00	180.00	...
563	11¢ Hayes, Greenish Blue	4.00	2.75	2.30	1.65	.50
563	Plate Block of 6	55.00	37.50	35.00	25.00	...

1922-25 Regular Issue, Flat Press, Perforated 11 VF Used + 40% (B)

Scott's No.		Unused, NH VF	F-VF	Unused,OG VF	F-VF	Used F-VF
564	12¢ Cleveland, Brown Violet (9123)	16.50	11.00	9.00	6.50	.25
564	Plate Block of 6	140.00	100.00	90.00	65.00	...
565	14¢ American Indian, Blue (1923)	11.00	7.50	6.35	4.50	1.00
565	Plate Block of 6	95.00	70.00	62.50	45.00	...
566	15¢ Statue of Liberty, Gray	55.00	37.50	29.75	21.75	.25
566	Plate Block of 6	500.00	350.00	315.00	225.00	...
567	20¢ Golden Gate, Carmine Rose (1923)	55.00	37.50	29.75	21.75	.25
567	Plate Block of 6	435.00	300.00	280.00	200.00	...
568	25¢ Niagara Falls, Yellow Green	42.50	29.00	25.00	17.50	.75
568	Plate Block of 6	400.00	275.00	260.00	185.00	...
569	30¢ American Buffalo, Olive Brown (1923)	70.00	50.00	42.50	30.00	.55
569	Plate Block of 6	425.00	300.00	285.00	200.00	...
570	50¢ Arlington Amphitheater, Lilac	110.00	75.00	65.00	45.00	.30
570	Plate Block of 6	1050.00	750.00	700.00	500.00	...
571	$1 Lincoln Memorial, Violet Black (1923)	100.00	67.50	56.50	40.00	.55
571	Arrow Block of 4	450.00	285.00	260.00	175.00	...
571	Plate Block of 6	700.00	485.00	450.00	315.00	...
572	$2 U.S. Capitol, Blue (1923)	210.00	140.00	115.00	80.00	8.75
572	Arrow Block of 4	875.00	600.00	500.00	350.00	...
572	Plate Block of 6	1650.00	1110.00	950.00	650.00	...
573	$5 Head of Freedom Statue, Carmine & Blue (1923)	415.00	285.00	230.00	165.00	13.50
573	Arrow Block of 4	1750.00	1250.00	975.00	700.00	...
573	Center Line Block of 4	1950.00	1375.00	1075.00	775.00	...
573	Plate Block of 8	4150.00	2850.00	2750.00	1800.00	...

1923-25 Flat Press - Imperforate VF Used + 30% (B)

Scott's No.		Unused, NH VF	F-VF	Unused,OG VF	F-VF	Used F-VF
575-77	**Set of 3**	**23.50**	**17.75**	**13.85**	**10.75**	**7.75**
575	1¢ Franklin, Green	16.50	12.50	9.75	7.50	4.75
575	Pair	35.00	26.50	20.75	16.00	...
575	Arrow Block of 4	75.00	57.50	45.00	35.00	...
575	Center Line Block of 4	90.00	67.50	52.50	40.00	...
575	Plate Block of 6	120.00	90.00	77.50	60.00	...
576	1½¢ Harding, Yellow Brown (1925)	3.60	2.70	2.10	1.60	1.60
576	Pair	7.75	5.75	4.50	3.50	...
576	Arrow Block of 4	16.00	12.50	9.75	7.50	...
576	Center Line Block of 4	24.00	18.00	14.50	11.00	...
576	Plate Block of 6	35.00	27.00	23.00	17.50	...
577	2¢ Washington, Carmine	4.75	3.50	2.75	2.10	1.80
577	Pair	10.50	7.50	6.00	4.50	...
577	Arrow Block of 4	22.50	16.50	12.50	9.50	...
577	Center Line Block of 4	33.75	25.00	19.50	15.00	...
577	Plate Block of 6	47.50	35.00	29.50	22.50	...

1923 Rotary Press, Perforated 11 x 10 VF Used + 75% (C)

Scott's No.		Unused, NH VF	F-VF	Unused,OG VF	F-VF	Used F-VF
578	1¢ Franklin, Green	230.00	130.00	130.00	75.00	130.00
578	Plate Block of 4	1750.00	975.00	1050.00	600.00	...
579	2¢ Washington, Carmine	190.00	110.00	115.00	65.00	110.00
579	Plate Block of 4	1175.00	685.00	725.00	425.00	...

1923-26 Rotary Press, Perforated 10 VF Used + 60% (B)

Scott's No.		Unused, NH VF	F-VF	Unused,OG VF	F-VF	Used F-VF
581-91	**Set of 11**	**430.00**	**270.00**	**250.00**	**160.00**	**22.75**
581	1¢ Franklin, Green	22.50	14.00	13.50	8.50	1.10
581	Plate Block of 4	240.00	150.00	150.00	95.00	...
582	1½¢ Harding, Brown (1925)	12.50	7.50	7.25	4.50	.90
582	Plate Block of 4	87.50	55.00	55.00	35.00	...
583	2¢ Washington, Carmine (1924)	6.00	3.75	3.60	2.25	.30
583	Plate Block of 4	77.50	50.00	47.50	30.00	...
583a	2¢ Booklet Pane of 6	175.00	110.00	110.00	70.00	...
584	3¢ Lincoln, Violet (1925)	65.00	40.00	38.50	24.00	2.50
584	Plate Block of 4	535.00	330.00	335.00	210.00	...
585	4¢ M.Wash., Yellow Brown ('25)	40.00	25.00	24.00	15.00	.80
585	Plate Block of 4	500.00	300.00	295.00	180.00	...
586	5¢ T. Roosevelt, Blue (1925)	37.50	23.50	22.00	14.00	.50
586	Plate Block of 4	500.00	300.00	295.00	180.00	...
587	6¢ Garfield, Red Orange(1925)	18.50	11.50	11.00	7.00	.85
587	Plate Block of 4	230.00	145.00	140.00	85.00	...
588	7¢ McKinley, Black (1926)	28.50	17.50	17.00	10.50	6.50
588	Plate Block of 4	250.00	160.00	150.00	95.00	...
589	8¢ Grant, Olive Green (1926)	62.50	38.75	37.50	23.00	4.50
589	Plate Block of 4	450.00	280.00	280.00	180.00	...
590	9¢ Jefferson, Rose (1926)	12.00	7.50	7.00	4.50	2.50
590	Plate Block of 4	120.00	75.00	62.50	45.00	...
591	10¢ Monroe, Orange (1925)	150.00	95.00	87.50	55.00	.80
591	Plate Block of 4	1050.00	650.00	675.00	425.00	...

1923 Rotary Press, Perforated 11 VF Used + 100% (C)

Scott's No.		Unused, NH VF	F-VF	Unused,OG VF	F-VF	Used F-VF
594	1¢ Franklin, Green, Stamp design 19 3/4 x 22¼mm	...	...	FINE	USED	6000.00
595	2¢ Washington, Carmine	675.00	365.00	425.00	215.00	275.00
596	1¢ Green, design 19¼x22½mm	...	...	...	...	...

1923-29 Rotary Press Coils, VF Used + 40% (B), (599A VF Used + 100% (C))

Scott's No.		Unused, NH VF	F-VF	Unused,OG VF	F-VF	Used F-VF
597-99,600-06	**Set of 10**	**37.50**	**26.00**	**22.50**	**16.00**	**2.50**
597-99,600-06	**Set of 10 Pairs**	**80.00**	**56.50**	**47.50**	**34.50**	**...**
597-99,600-06	**Set of 10 Line Pairs**	**260.00**	**175.00**	**150.00**	**105.00**	**...**
	Perforated 10 Vertically					
597	1¢ Franklin, Green	.65	.45	.45	.30	.20
597	Pair	1.40	1.00	1.00	.65	...
597	Line Pair	4.50	3.25	2.90	2.10	...
598	1½¢ Harding, Brown (1925)	1.80	1.25	1.15	.80	.20
598	Pair	4.00	2.75	2.50	1.75	...
598	Line Pair	12.75	8.25	7.50	5.25	...
599	2¢ Washington, Carmine, Type I	.85	.60	.50	.35	.20
599	Pair	1.85	1.30	1.10	.75	...
599	Line Pair	4.25	2.95	2.60	1.80	...
599A	2¢ Carmine, Type II (1929)	335.00	170.00	185.00	95.00	11.75
599A	Pair	700.00	365.00	400.00	200.00	...
599A	Line Pair	1500.00	800.00	950.00	500.00	...
599A	2¢ Average Quality	...	100.00	...	60.00	7.50
599,599A	Combination Line Pair	1800.00	950.00	1100.00	600.00	...

1923-29 Rotary Press Coils, VF Used + 40% (B), (599A VF Used + 100% (C)

Scott's No.		Unused, NH VF	F-VF	Unused,OG VF	F-VF	Used F-VF
600	3¢ Lincoln, Violet (1924)	13.50	9.25	8.00	5.75	.30
600	Pair	28.50	20.00	17.50	12.50	...
600	Line Pair	70.00	47.50	40.00	27.50	...
601	4¢ Martha Washington, Yellow Brown	8.25	5.75	5.00	3.50	.50
601	Pair	18.00	12.50	10.75	7.50	...
601	Line Pair	70.00	50.00	42.50	30.00	...
602	5¢ Theodore Roosevelt, Dark Blue (1924)	3.85	2.75	2.30	1.65	.25
602	Pair	8.50	6.00	5.00	3.50	...
602	Line Pair	30.00	18.00	15.00	10.75	...
603	10¢ Monroe, Orange (1924)	8.00	5.75	4.75	3.50	.30
603	Pair	17.50	12.50	10.50	7.50	...
603	Line Pair	57.50	41.50	35.00	25.00	...
	Perforated 10 Horizontally					
604	1¢ Franklin, Green (1924)	.75	.55	.50	.35	.20
604	Pair	1.60	1.20	1.10	.75	...
604	Line Pair	8.25	5.75	4.95	3.50	...
605	1½¢ Harding, Yellow Brown ('25)	.75	.55	.50	.35	.25
605	Pair	1.60	1.20	1.10	.75	...
605	Line Pair	7.00	5.00	4.25	3.00	...
606	2¢ Washington, Carmine	.75	.55	.50	.35	.20
606	Pair	1.60	1.20	1.10	.75	...
606	Line Pair	5.50	4.00	3.25	2.35	...

NOTE: Type I, #599, 634 - No heavy hair lines at top center of head.
Type II, #599A, 634A - Three heavy hair lines at top center of head.

1923 Harding Memorial Issues

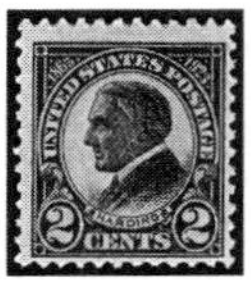
610

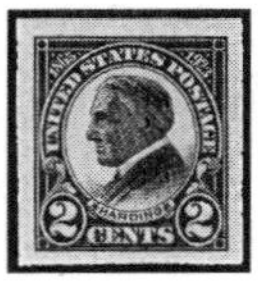
611

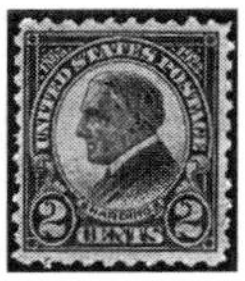
612-613

1923 Harding Memorial (#610 VF Used + 40% (B), #612-13 VF Used + 60% (C)) #611 Imperforate VF Used + 30% (B)

Scott's No.		Unused, NH VF	F-VF	Unused,OG VF	F-VF	Used F-VF
610-12	**Set of 3**	**47.50**	**30.75**	**29.75**	**19.75**	**6.95**
610-12	**Set of 3 Plate Blocks**	**715.00**	**450.00**	**475.00**	**325.00**	**...**
610	2¢ Black, Flat Press, Perf. 11	1.35	.95	.85	.60	.25
610	Plate Block of 6	37.50	27.50	25.00	18.00	...
611	2¢ Black, Flat, Imperforate	12.00	9.00	7.50	5.75	4.75
611	Pair	26.50	20.00	16.50	13.00	...
611	Arrow Block of 4	55.00	41.50	34.00	27.00	...
611	Center Line Block of 4	130.00	95.00	70.00	55.00	...
611	Plate Block of 6	155.00	115.00	100.00	75.00	...
612	2¢ Black, Rotary, Perf. 10	36.50	22.50	23.00	14.50	2.25
612	Plate Block of 4	550.00	350.00	375.00	240.00	...
613	2¢ Black, Rotary, Perf.11	...	...	...	...	...

#610-11 design 19¼x22 mm, #612-13 design 19¼x22½ mm
Mint Sheet of 100 F-VF, NH #610 140.00

1924 Huguenot - Walloon Tercentenary Issue VF Used + 35% (B)

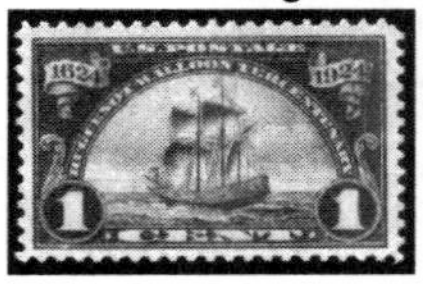
614

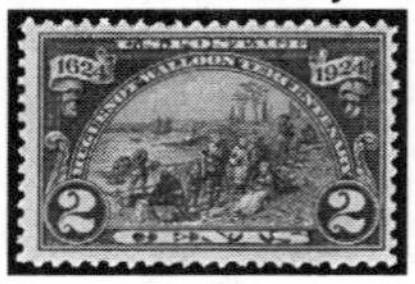
615

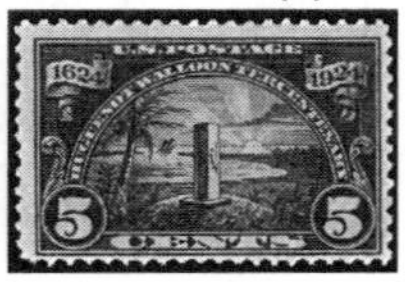
616

Scott's No.		Unused, NH VF	F-VF	Unused,OG VF	F-VF	Used F-VF
614-16	**Set of 3**	**70.00**	**51.50**	**45.00**	**33.50**	**21.00**
614-16	**Set of 3 Plate Blocks**	**650.00**	**475.00**	**450.00**	**325.00**	**...**
614	1¢ Ship "New Netherlands"	6.75	5.00	4.50	3.25	3.50
614	Plate Block of 6	75.00	55.00	48.75	36.50	...
615	2¢ Walloons Landing at Fort Orange	10.50	7.50	6.75	5.00	2.50
615	Plate Block of 6	110.00	80.00	70.00	52.50	...
616	5¢ Jan Ribault Monument	56.50	41.50	36.50	27.00	16.00
616	Plate Block of 6	515.00	365.00	350.00	250.00	...

Mint Sheets of 50 F-VF, NH #614 315.00 #615 475.00 #616 2400.00

1925 Lexington - Concord Battles Issue VF Used + 35% (B)

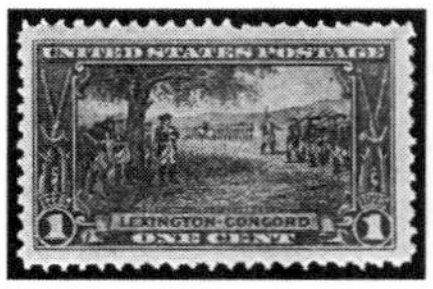
617

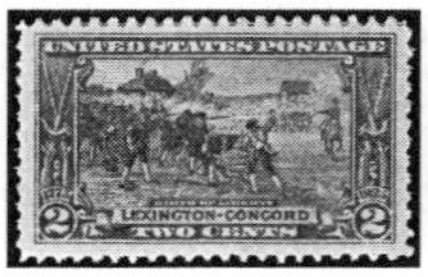
618

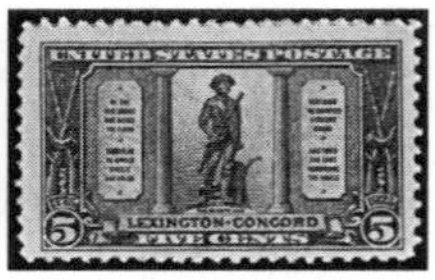
619

Scott's No.		Unused, NH VF	F-VF	Unused,OG VF	F-VF	Used F-VF
617-19	**Set of 3**	**68.50**	**49.50**	**44.50**	**32.75**	**20.75**
617-19	**Set of 3 Plate Blocks**	**665.00**	**495.00**	**440.00**	**325.00**	**...**
617	1¢ Washington at Cambridge	6.75	5.00	4.35	3.25	2.50
617	Plate Block of 6	75.00	55.00	47.50	35.00	...
618	2¢ "Birth of Liberty"	10.50	7.75	6.75	5.00	4.25
618	Plate Block of 6	120.00	90.00	80.00	60.00	...
619	5¢ "The Minute Man"	55.00	39.50	36.00	26.50	15.00
619	Plate Block of 6	500.00	375.00	335.00	250.00	...

Mint Sheets of 50 F-VF, NH #617 325.00 #618 475.00 #619 2300.00

NOTE: PRIOR TO 1935, TO DETERMINE VERY FINE USED PRICE, ADD VF% AT BEGINNING OF EACH SET TO THE APPROPRIATE FINE PRICE. MINIMUM 10¢ PER STAMP.
NOTE: STAMP ILLUSTRATIONS INDICATE DESIGNS, PERFORATIONS AND TYPES MAY VARY

NOTE: PRICES THROUGHOUT THIS LIST ARE SUBJECT TO CHANGE WITHOUT NOTICE IF MARKET CONDITIONS REQUIRE. MINIMUM MAIL ORDER MUST TOTAL AT LEAST $20.00.

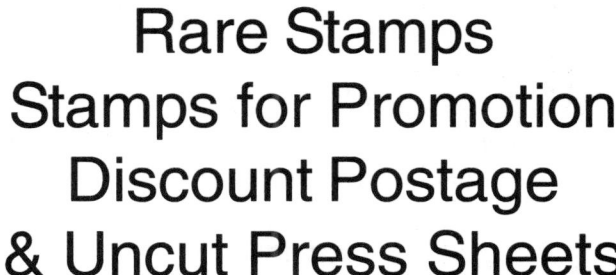

| 620 | 621 | 622,694 | 623,697 |

1925 Norse American Centennial VF Used + 35% (B)

Scott's No.		Unused, NH VF	F-VF	Unused, OG VF	F-VF	Used F-VF
620-21	Set of 2	35.00	25.75	21.75	16.50	15.00
620-21	Set of 2 Plate Blocks	1350.00	1000.00	950.00	700.00	...
620	2¢ Sloop, Carmine & Black	8.50	6.50	5.35	4.00	3.50
620	Arrow Block of 4	37.50	29.00	23.50	18.00	...
620	Center Line Block of 4	48.50	36.50	30.00	22.50	...
620	Plate Block of 8	350.00	250.00	250.00	180.00	...
621	5¢ Viking Ship, Blue & Black	29.00	21.00	18.00	13.50	13.00
621	Arrow Block of 4	135.00	100.00	87.50	65.00	...
621	Center Line Block of 4	145.00	110.00	100.00	75.00	...
621	Plate Block of 8	1075.00	800.00	750.00	550.00	...

Mint Sheet of 100 F-VF, NH #620 950.00 #621 2750.00

1925-26 Designs of 1922-25, Flat Press, Perf. 11 VF Used + 40% (B)

622	13¢ Harrison, Green (1926)	29.50	21.00	18.00	13.00	.70
622	Plate Block of 6	280.00	200.00	180.00	130.00	...
623	17¢ Wilson, Black	35.00	25.00	21.00	15.00	.40
623	Plate Block of 6	335.00	240.00	225.00	160.00	...

1926 Commemoratives

| 627 | 628 | 629 |

1926 Commemoratives VF Used + 30% (B)

627-29,643-44	1926-27 Set of 5	27.50	19.75	19.50	14.50	9.25
627	2¢ Sesquicentennial Exposition & 150th Anniversary of Declaration of Independence	5.25	4.00	3.75	2.75	.60
627	Plate Block of 6	65.00	50.00	45.00	35.00	...
628	5¢ John Ericsson Memorial	11.00	8.50	7.50	5.75	3.35
628	Plate Block of 6	125.00	95.00	95.00	70.00	...
629	2¢ Battle of White Plains 150th Anniversary	3.85	2.95	2.75	2.10	1.95
629	Plate Block of 6	62.50	47.50	43.50	32.50	...

Mint Sheets F-VF, NH #627 (50) 250.00 #628 (50) 550.00 #629 (100) 375.00

1926 International Philatelic Exhibition Souvenir Sheet VF Used + 35%

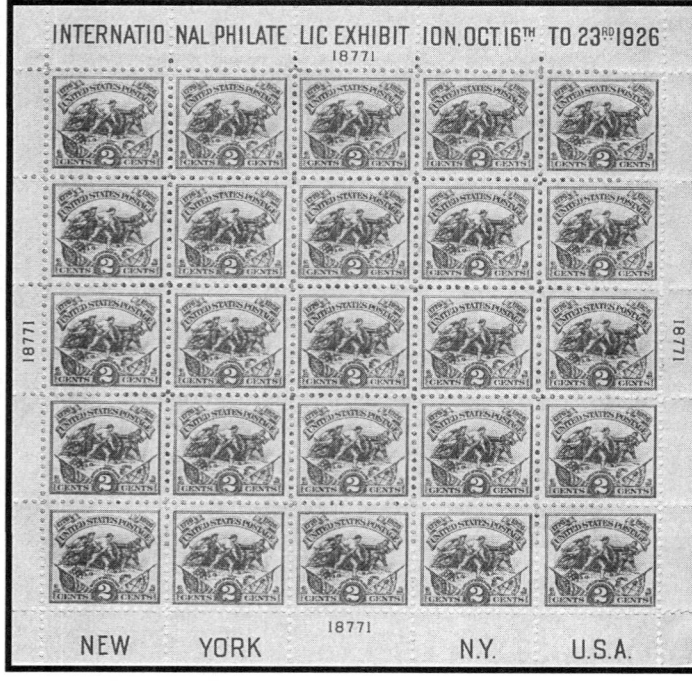

630	2¢ White Plains Sheet of 25	925.00	700.00	600.00	450.00	475.00
630v	2¢ "Dot over S" Var. Sheet	10000.00	775.00	635.00	475.00	500.00

#630v Dot over "S" of "States" on #18774 LL9 and #1873 LL11

1926 Rotary Press, Imperforate VF Used + 30% (B)

Scott's No.		Unused, NH VF	F-VF	Unused, OG VF	F-VF	Used F-VF
631	1½¢ Harding, Brown	3.50	2.65	2.40	1.85	1.85
631	Pair	7.50	5.60	5.00	3.95	...
631	Arrow Block of 4	17.00	13.00	12.00	9.00	...
631	Center Line Block of 4	33.75	27.50	25.00	19.50	...
631	Plate Block of 4	100.00	80.00	70.00	55.00	...
631v	1½¢ Vert. Pair, Horiz. Gutter	9.00	7.00	6.50	5.00	...
631h	1½¢ Horiz. Pair, Vert. Gutter	9.00	7.00	6.50	5.00	...

1926-1928 Rotary. Perforated 11x10½, Same as 1922-25 VF Used +35% (B) (634A VF Used +100% (C))

632-34,635a,36-42	Set of 11	37.50	27.50	26.50	19.75	1.95
632	1¢ Franklin, Green (1927)	.40	.30	.30	.20	.20
632	Plate Block of 4	3.50	2.50	2.30	1.75	...
632a	1¢ Booklet Pane of 6	11.50	8.00	7.50	5.50	...
633	1½¢ Harding, Yellow Brown ('27)	3.75	2.75	2.65	2.00	.20
633	Plate Block of 4	120.00	85.00	82.50	60.00	...
634	2¢ Washington, Carmine, Type I	.40	.30	.30	.20	.20
634	Plate Block of 4	3.75	2.75	2.60	1.95	...
634	Electric Eye Plate Block of 10	9.50	6.75	6.75	5.00	...
634d	2¢ Booklet Pane of 6 (1927)	3.65	2.35	2.50	1.65	...
634A	2¢ Carmine, Type II (1928)	850.00	475.00	525.00	275.00	14.50
635	3¢ Lincoln, Violet (1927)	.90	.65	.60	.45	.20
635	Plate Block of 4	20.00	15.00	14.50	10.75	...
635a	3¢ Bright Violet Reissue (1934)	.70	.50	.50	.35	.20
635a	Plate Block of 4	12.50	9.00	8.25	6.00	...
636	4¢ Martha Washington, Yellow Brown (1927)	4.75	3.50	3.35	2.50	.20
636	Plate Block of 4	130.00	95.00	90.00	67.50	...
637	5¢ T. Roosevelt, Dark Blue ('27)	4.25	3.15	3.00	2.25	.20
637	Plate Block of 4	28.50	21.00	20.00	15.00	...
638	6¢ Garfield, Red Orange(1927)	4.25	3.15	3.00	2.25	.20
638	Plate Block of 4	28.50	21.00	20.00	15.00	...
639	7¢ McKinley, Black (1927)	4.25	3.15	3.00	2.25	.20
639	Plate Block of 4	28.50	21.00	20.00	15.00	...
640	8¢ Grant, Olive Green (1927)	4.25	3.15	3.00	2.25	.20
640	Plate Block of 4	28.50	21.00	20.00	15.00	...
641	9¢ Jefferson, Orange Red ('27)	4.25	3.15	3.00	2.25	.20
641	Plate Block of 4	28.50	21.00	20.00	15.00	...
642	10¢ Monroe, Orange (1927)	8.25	6.00	5.75	4.25	.20
642	Plate Block of 4	47.50	35.00	33.50	25.00	...

Mint Sheets of 100 F-VF, NH #632 35.00 #633 350.00 #634 28.50 #635 77.50 #635a 57.50 #636 435.00 #637 325.00 #638 325.00 #639 325.00 #640 325.00 #641 325.00 #642 635.00

| 643 | 644 | 645 | 646 |

| 647 | 648 | 649 | 650 |

1927 Commemoratives VF Used + 30% (B)

643	2¢ Vermont 150th Anniversary of Independence	2.65	1.95	1.70	1.30	1.10
643	Plate Block of 6	65.00	48.50	50.00	37.50	...
644	2¢ Burgoyne Campaign: Battles of Bennington, Oriskany, Fort Stanwix and Saratoga	6.75	4.75	4.75	3.50	2.65
644	Plate Block of 6	68.50	52.50	51.50	39.50	...

Mint Sheets F-VF, NH #643 100 285.00 #644 50 285.00

1928 Commemoratives VF Used +30%, #646-48 VF Used +50% (B)

645-50	Set of 6	47.50	33.00	34.75	23.85	22.00
645	2¢ Valley Forge 150th Anniv.	1.65	1.30	1.30	1.00	.55
645	Plate Block of 6	46.50	35.00	33.50	25.00	...
646	2¢ Battle of Monmouth "Molly Pitcher" overprint (on #634)	2.25	1.50	1.65	1.10	1.10
646	Plate Block of 4	60.00	40.00	40.00	27.50	...
647	2¢ Hawaii Discovery 150th Anniv. "Hawaii" ovpt. (on #634)	10.50	6.75	6.75	4.50	4.25
647	Plate Block of 4	240.00	160.00	165.00	110.00	...
648	5¢ "Hawaii" ovpt. (on #637)	28.00	18.50	18.50	12.50	12.50
648	Plate Block of 4	485.00	325.00	370.00	240.00	...
649	2¢ Aeronautics Conf., Wright Brothers Flight 25th Anniversary	2.10	1.60	1.60	1.20	1.00
649	Plate Block of 6	21.00	16.00	15.75	12.00	...
650	5¢ Aeronautics	8.50	6.50	6.50	5.00	3.75
650	Plate Block of 6	105.00	77.50	75.00	55.00	...

Mint Sheets F-VF, NH #645 (100) 185.00 #646 (100) 195.00 #647 (100) 875.00 #648 (100) 2150.00 #649 (50) 95.00 #650 (50) 425.00

| 651 | 654-656 | 657 |

Looking For Those Missing Stamps, Covers
And At Bargain Prices Too !!!
Do You Enjoy Great Articles From The Leading Philatelic Writers?
You'll Find The Answer In The

BROOKMAN TIMES

"The Brookman Times" is published 6 times a year and has ads from leading stamp dealers and articles from leading Philatelic writers, such as Les Winick, Marjory Sente, George Griffenhagen, Lloyd de Vries, James Graue, David Straight, and APS Director of Education Kim Kowalczyk. There are bargains galore and of particular note is that only dealers who advertise in the Brookman Price Guide can advertise in "The Brookman Times". We feel these dealers are the "cream of the crop" and can heartily endorse them.

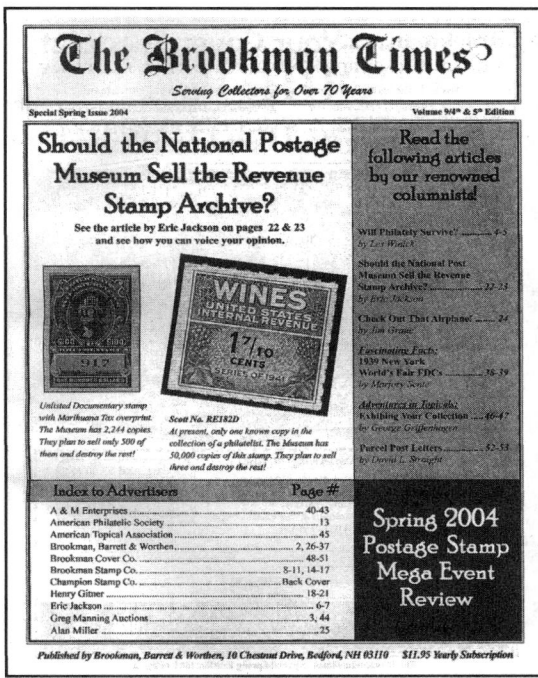

SOME OF THE LEADING DEALERS YOU WILL FIND IN "THE BROOKMAN TIMES"

A & M Enterprises	Eric Jackson
Alexander Autographs	Michael Jaffe Stamps, Inc.
American First Day Cover Society	Kenmore Stamp Co.
American Philatelic Society	Lindner Publications
American Stamp Dealer Assoc.	Linn's Stamp News
American Topical Assoc.	Greg Manning Auctions
Artmaster, Incorporated	Markeast Stamp Co.
BJ's Stamps	Phillip Marks
Brooklyn Gallery	Alan Miller Stamps
Brookman/Barrett & Worthen	Mystic Stamp Co.
Brookman Cover Co.	Nutmeg Stamp Sales
Brookman Stamp Co.	Philatelic Arts
Brookman Times	Plate Block Stamp Co.
Champion Stamp Co., Inc.	Gary Posner, Inc.
Collectibles Insurance Agency	Professional Stamp Experts
Steve Crippe	Scott Publishing
Dale Enterprises, Inc.	Spectrum Numismatic Auctions
Michael Damsky	Greg Tucker
Henry Gitner Philatelists, Inc.	Vidiforms Co., Inc.
Have Tongs, Will Travel	Washington 2006
	Scott Winslow Assoc.

Now You Can Get This $11.95 Value FREE !!!

Everyone who purchases a Brookman Price Guide can receive the **"Brookman Times" FREE**.
All you have to do is fill out the coupon below (or a copy of the coupon).
(If you purchased your price guide directly from Brookman/Barrett & Worthen you will automatically receive the "Brookman Times".)

BROOKMAN
Barrett & Worthen

Dept. - PG
10 Chestnut Drive
Bedford, NH 03110

E-mail: sales@coverspecialist.com
www.coverspecialist.com

Please send me 6 issues of the "Brookman Times".
(I am enclosing $4.00 for Postage & Handling)

Name : _____

Address : _____

_____

NO PHONE ORDERS PLEASE - MAIL ONLY

1929 Commemorative VF Used + 30% (B)

Scott's No.		Unused, NH VF	Unused, NH F-VF	Unused,OG VF	Unused,OG F-VF	Used F-VF
651, 654-57, 680-81	**Set of 7**	**32.00**	**22.75**	**21.50**	**16.00**	**5.50**
651	2¢ George Rogers Clark, Fort Sackville 150th Anniversary	1.15	.85	.80	.60	.55
651	Arrow Block of 4	5.35	3.75	3.60	2.70	...
651	Plate Block of 6	18.50	13.50	14.00	10.00	...
	1929 Rotary, Perf. 11x10½, Design of #551 VF Used + 35% (B)					
653	½¢ Nathan Hale, Olive Brown	.40	.30	.30	.20	.15
653	Plate Block of 4	2.85	2.10	2.00	1.50	...
	1929 Thomas Alva Edison, First Lamp VF Used + 35% (B)					
	Rotary design is taller than Flat Press, Coil design is wider.					
654	2¢ Flat Press, Perforated 11	1.35	1.00	1.00	.75	.75
654	Plate Block of 6	45.00	33.50	34.75	25.75	...
655	2¢ Rotary, Perf. 11x10½	1.45	.95	1.00	.70	.25
655	Plate Block of 4	62.50	45.00	46.50	32.50	...
656	2¢ Coil, Perf. 10 Vertically	28.50	21.00	18.00	13.50	1.95
656	Pair	60.00	45.00	38.50	28.50	...
656	Line Pair	140.00	105.00	85.00	65.00	...
	1929 Commemoratives (continued) VF Used +30% (B)					
657	2¢ Sullivan Expedition	1.20	.95	.90	.70	.70
657	Plate Block of 6	38.75	30.00	30.00	23.50	...

Mint Sheets F-VF,NH #651 (50) 65.00 #653 (100) 22.50 #654 (100) 150.00 #655 (100) 150.00 #657 (100) 140.00

1929 KANSAS - NEBRASKA ISSUES

658

665

668

671

677

1929 "Kans." Overprints on Stamps #632-42 VF Used + 60% (C)

Scott's No.		Unused, NH VF	Unused, NH F-VF	Unused,OG VF	Unused,OG F-VF	Used F-VF
658-68	**Set of 11**	**565.00**	**335.00**	**350.00**	**225.00**	**150.00**
658	1¢ Franklin, Green	6.25	3.75	3.95	2.50	2.25
658	Plate Block of 4	70.00	42.50	50.00	30.00	...
659	1½¢ Harding, Brown	10.00	5.95	6.25	3.95	2.75
659	Plate Block of 4	83.50	52.50	58.50	37.50	...
660	2¢ Washington, Carmine	10.00	6.00	6.35	4.00	1.10
660	Plate Block of 4	85.00	52.50	56.50	35.00	...
661	3¢ Lincoln, Violet	50.00	30.00	31.50	20.00	13.50
661	Plate Block of 4	385.00	230.00	260.00	160.00	...
662	4¢ M. Washington, Yel. Brn	45.00	27.50	29.50	18.50	9.50
662	Plate Block of 4	385.00	230.00	260.00	160.00	...
663	5¢ T. Roosevelt, Deep Blue	28.50	17.00	18.00	11.00	9.75
663	Plate Block of 4	280.00	170.00	190.00	120.00	...
664	6¢ Garfield, Red Orange	67.50	40.00	42.50	26.50	16.50
664	Plate Block of 4	875.00	525.00	550.00	350.00	...
665	7¢ McKinley, Black	62.50	37.50	40.00	25.00	22.50
665	Plate Block of 4	865.00	550.00	600.00	375.00	...
666	8¢ Grant, Olive Green	225.00	135.00	145.00	90.00	60.00
666	Plate Block of 4	1500.00	900.00	1050.00	650.00	...
667	9¢ Jefferson, Light Rose	33.50	20.00	21.75	13.50	10.75
667	Plate Block of 4	425.00	260.00	280.00	175.00	...
668	10¢ Monroe, Orange Yellow	53.50	32.50	34.00	21.50	11.00
668	Plate Block of 4	675.00	400.00	435.00	275.00	...

1929 "Nebr." Overprints on Stamps #632-42 VF Used + 60% (C)

Scott's No.		Unused, NH VF	Unused, NH F-VF	Unused,OG VF	Unused,OG F-VF	Used F-VF
669-79	**Set of 11**	**750.00**	**445.00**	**470.00**	**290.00**	**145.00**
669	1¢ Franklin, Green	9.25	5.50	5.75	3.65	2.00
669	Plate Block of 4	90.00	55.00	60.00	37.50	...
670	1½¢ Harding, Brown	8.75	5.25	5.50	3.50	2.25
670	Plate Block of 4	100.00	60.00	65.00	40.00	...
671	2¢ Washington, Carmine	8.75	5.25	5.50	3.50	1.25
671	Plate Block of 4	80.00	47.50	52.50	32.50	...
672	3¢ Lincoln, Violet	36.50	22.00	23.00	14.50	10.50
672	Plate Block of 4	335.00	195.00	230.00	140.00	...
673	4¢ M. Washington, Yel. Brn	50.00	29.50	31.50	19.50	13.50
673	Plate Block of 4	485.00	290.00	315.00	195.00	...
674	5¢ T. Roosevelt, Deep Blue	45.00	26.50	27.50	17.50	13.50
674	Plate Block of 4	525.00	325.00	360.00	225.00	...
675	6¢ Garfield, Red Orange	95.00	57.50	60.00	38.50	22.50
675	Plate Block of 4	950.00	575.00	635.00	400.00	...
676	7¢ McKinley, Black	56.50	34.00	35.00	22.50	17.50
676	Plate Block of 4	560.00	335.00	350.00	225.00	...
677	8¢ Grant, Olive Green	80.00	47.50	51.50	31.50	22.75
677	Plate Block of 4	775.00	475.00	500.00	325.00	...
678	9¢ Jefferson, Light Rose	95.00	55.00	57.50	36.50	24.00
678	Plate Block of 4	950.00	575.00	625.00	400.00	...
679	10¢ Monroe, Orange Yellow ..	300.00	180.00	190.00	120.00	21.50
679	Plate Block of 4	1950.00	1175.00	1250.00	800.00	...

NOTE: IN 1929, SOME 1¢-10¢ STAMPS WERE OVERPRINTED "Kans." AND "Nebr." AS A MEASURE OF PREVENTION AGAINST POST OFFICE ROBBERIES IN THOSE STATES, THEY WERE USED ABOUT ONE YEAR, THEN DISCONTINUED.
Genuine unused, o.g. K-N's have either a single horiz. gum breaker ridge or two widely spaced horiz. ridges (21 mm apart). Unused, o.g. stamps with two horiz. ridges spaced 10 mm apart have counterfeit ovpts. Unused stamps without ridges are regummed and/or have a fake ovpt.

680

681

682

683

1929 Commemoratives (continued) VF Used + 30% (B)

Scott's No.		Unused, NH VF	Unused, NH F-VF	Unused,OG VF	Unused,OG F-VF	Used F-VF
680	2¢ Battle of Fallen Timbers, General "Mad" Anthony Wayne	1.25	.95	1.00	.75	.80
680	Plate Block of 6	39.50	29.00	28.50	22.00	...
681	2¢ Ohio River Canalization	1.00	.85	.70	.60	.70
681	Plate Block of 6	30.00	22.50	22.00	16.50	...
	1930 Commemoratives VF Used + 30% (B)					
682-83,688-90,702-3	**Set of 7 (1930-31)**	**6.75**	**5.25**	**4.75**	**3.50**	**3.40**
682	2¢ Massachusetts Bay Colony 300th Anniversary	.95	.75	.70	.55	.55
682	Plate Block of 6	45.00	35.00	32.50	25.00	...
683	2¢ Carolina-Charleston 250th ...	2.00	1.50	1.40	1.10	1.10
683	Plate Block of 6	67.50	52.50	52.00	40.00	...

Mint Sheets of 100 F-VF, NH #680 150.00 #681 135.00 #682 115.00 #683 190.00

684,686

685,687

688

689

690

1930 Regular Issues, Rotary Press Perf.11x10½ VF Used + 35% (B)

Scott's No.		Unused, NH VF	Unused, NH F-VF	Unused,OG VF	Unused,OG F-VF	Used F-VF
684	1½¢ Harding,Full Face, Brown, ...	.60	.45	.40	.30	.15
684	Plate Block of 4	3.95	2.95	2.70	2.10	...
685	4¢ Taft, Brown	1.75	1.30	1.20	.90	.20
685	Plate Block of 4	21.75	16.00	13.75	11.00	...
	Mint Sheets of 100 F-VF, NH #684 45.00 #685 140.00					
	1930 Regular Issue Coils, Perf.10 Vertically VF Used + 35% (B)					
686	1½¢ Harding,Full Face,Brown ...	3.35	2.50	2.35	1.75	.25
686	Pair	7.25	5.50	5.00	3.75	...
686	Line Pair	15.50	11.50	11.00	8.25	...
687	4¢ Taft, Brown	5.75	4.25	4.00	3.00	.65
687	Pair	12.50	9.25	8.75	6.50	...
687	Line Pair	30.00	23.50	21.50	16.50	...

1930-31 Commemoratives (cont.) VF Used + 30% (B)

Scott's No.		Unused, NH VF	Unused, NH F-VF	Unused,OG VF	Unused,OG F-VF	Used F-VF
688	2¢ Battle of Braddock's Field 175th Anniversary	1.60	1.20	1.20	.90	.85
688	Plate Block of 6	52.50	40.00	40.00	30.00	...
689	2¢ Baron Von Steuben	.95	.70	.65	.50	.50
689	Plate Block of 6	39.50	29.50	30.00	22.50	...
690	2¢ General Casimir Pulaski Polish Patriot (1931)	.45	.35	.35	.25	.25
690	Plate Block of 6	17.50	13.00	13.50	10.00	...

Mint Sheets of 100 F-VF, NH #688 160.00 #689 95.00 #690 45.00

1931 Rotary Press, Perforated 11x10½ or 10½x11 VF Used + 35% (B)
Designs of #563-70, 622-23

Scott's No.		Unused, NH VF	Unused, NH F-VF	Unused,OG VF	Unused,OG F-VF	Used F-VF
692-701	**Set of 10**	**190.00**	**140.00**	**135.00**	**100.00**	**2.25**
692	11¢ Hayes,Light Blue	4.70	3.50	3.35	2.50	.20
692	Plate Block of 4	22.75	16.75	16.00	12.00	...
693	12¢ Cleveland, Brown Violet ...	10.00	7.75	7.25	5.50	.20
693	Plate Block of 4	50.00	36.50	33.50	25.00	...
694	13¢ Harrison, Yellow Green	4.25	3.25	3.00	2.25	.30
694	Plate Block of 4	23.75	17.50	16.75	12.50	...
695	14¢ Indian, Dark Blue	6.50	4.75	4.50	3.25	.75
695	Plate Block of 4	41.50	30.00	29.50	21.50	...
696	15¢ Liberty, Gray	14.00	10.50	10.00	7.50	.20
696	Plate Block of 4	66.50	48.50	47.50	35.00	...
697	17¢ Wilson, Black	10.50	7.75	7.25	5.25	.35
697	Plate Block of 4	60.00	42.50	41.50	30.00	...
698	20¢ Golden Gate, Carm. Rose	17.00	12.75	12.00	9.00	.20
698	Plate Block of 4	77.50	56.50	55.00	40.00	...
699	25¢ Niagara Falls, Blue Green	19.00	14.00	13.50	10.00	.25
699	Plate Block of 4	87.50	66.50	62.50	47.50	...
700	30¢ Buffalo, Brown	33.50	25.00	24.00	17.50	.25
700	Plate Block of 4	150.00	110.00	110.00	77.50	...
701	50¢ Amphitheater, Lilac	82.50	60.00	57.50	42.50	.20
701	Plate Block of 4	390.00	285.00	275.00	200.00	...

Mint Sheets of 100 F-VF, NH #692 350.00 #693 800.00 #694 325.00 #695 485.00 #696 1075.00 #697 750.00 #698 1300.00 #699 1450.00

702

703

704

705

706

707

708

709

710

711

712

713

714

715

Scott's No.		Unused, NH VF	F-VF	Unused, OG VF	F-VF	Used F-VF
702	2¢ Red Cross 50th Anniversary	.40	.30	.30	.20	.20
702	Arrow Block of 4	1.50	1.10	1.30	.85	…
702	Plate Block of 4	3.95	2.95	2.80	2.25	…
703	2¢ Battle of Yorktown 150th	.55	.45	.45	.35	.30
703	Arrow Block of 4	2.95	2.25	2.20	1.75	…
703	Center Line Block of 4	3.25	2.50	2.50	1.95	…
703	Plate Block of 4	4.25	3.25	3.25	2.50	…
703	Plate Block of 6	5.75	4.50	4.50	3.50	…
703	Plate Block of 8	7.50	5.75	5.75	4.25	…

Mint Sheets F-VF, NH #702 (100) 27.50 #703 (50) 25.00

1932 Washington Birth Bicentennial VF Used + 40% (B)
Various Portraits of George Washington

Scott's No.		Unused, NH VF	F-VF	Unused, OG VF	F-VF	Used F-VF
704-15	Set of 12	48.75	34.50	35.00	24.50	2.60
704-15	Set of 12 Plate Blocks	650.00	450.00	485.00	350.00	…
704	½¢ Peale, Olive Brown	.35	.25	.30	.20	.15
704	Plate Block of 4	11.00	7.50	7.75	5.50	…
705	1¢ Houdon, Green	.35	.25	.30	.20	.15
705	Plate Block of 4	8.25	5.75	6.00	4.25	…
706	1½¢ Peale, Brown	.80	.55	.55	.40	.20
706	Plate Block of 4	32.50	23.00	24.00	17.00	…
707	2¢ Stuart, Carmine Rose	.35	.25	.30	.20	.15
707	Plate Block of 4	2.85	2.00	2.10	1.50	…
708	3¢ Peale, Deep Violet	1.10	.75	.75	.55	.20
708	Plate Block of 4	27.50	19.50	21.00	15.00	…
709	4¢ Polk, Light Brown	.65	.45	.40	.30	.20
709	Plate Block of 4	11.00	8.00	8.50	6.00	…
710	5¢ Peale, Blue	3.35	2.40	2.40	1.75	.20
710	Plate Block of 4	31.75	22.50	24.00	17.00	…
711	6¢ Trumbull, Red Orange	7.25	5.00	5.15	3.65	.20
711	Plate Block of 4	100.00	72.50	77.50	55.00	…
712	7¢ Trumbull, Black	.65	.45	.40	.30	.25
712	Plate Block of 4	15.00	10.75	11.50	8.25	…
713	8¢ Saint Memim, Olive Bistre	6.00	4.15	4.50	3.15	.70
713	Plate Block of 4	100.00	72.50	77.50	55.00	…
714	9¢ Williams, Pale Red	5.50	3.85	3.85	2.75	.25
714	Plate Block of 4	75.00	52.50	56.50	40.00	…
715	10¢ Stuart, Orange Yellow	25.00	17.50	17.50	12.50	.25
715	Plate Block of 4	210.00	145.00	150.00	110.00	…

Mint Sheets of 100 F-VF, NH #704 19.50 #705 22.50 #706 75.00 #707 20.00 #708 90.00 #709 52.50 #710 265.00 #711 575.00 #712 55.00 #713 495.00 #714 435.00 #715 1900.00

1932 Commemoratives VF Used + 30% (B)

| 716 | 717 | 718 | 719 |

Scott's No.		Unused, NH VF	F-VF	Unused, OG VF	F-VF	Used F-VF
716-19, 724-25	Set of 6	8.75	6.50	6.50	4.95	1.30
716	2¢ Winter Olympics, Lake Placid	.75	.55	.60	.45	.25
716	Plate Block of 6	20.00	15.00	15.00	11.50	…
717	2¢ Arbor Day 60th Anniversary	.35	.25	.30	.20	.20
717	Plate Block of 4	12.50	9.50	9.75	7.50	…
718	3¢ Summer Olympics	2.65	2.00	1.95	1.50	.25
718	Plate Block of 4	25.00	18.50	18.50	14.00	…
719	5¢ Summer Olympics	3.95	3.00	3.00	2.25	.30
719	Plate Block of 4	45.00	33.50	33.50	25.00	…

Mint Sheets of 100 F-VF, NH #716 70.00 #717 35.00 #718 220.00 #719 330.00

| 720 | 721 | 722 | 723 |

1932 Regular Issue, Rotary Press VF Used + 35% (B)

720	3¢ Washington, Deep Violet	.35	.25	.30	.20	.15
720	Plate Block of 4	2.60	2.00	2.00	1.50	…
720b	3¢ Booklet Pane of 6	95.00	70.00	66.50	49.50	…

1932 Regular Issue Rotary Press Coils VF Used + 35%)B)

721	3¢ Washington, Perf. 10 Vert.	4.25	3.25	3.35	2.50	.25
721	Pair	9.00	6.85	7.00	5.25	…
721	Line Pair	13.00	9.50	10.00	7.50	…
722	3¢ Washington, Perf. 10 Horiz.	2.40	1.80	1.85	1.35	.70
722	Pair	5.25	3.85	4.00	2.90	…
722	Line Pair	8.75	6.50	6.75	5.00	…
723	6¢ Garfield, Orange, Pf.10 Vert.	20.00	15.00	14.00	10.50	.30
723	Pair	45.00	33.00	30.00	23.00	…
723	Line Pair	100.00	75.00	75.00	55.00	…

| 724 | 725 | 726 | 727,752 |

1932 Commemoratives (cont.) VF Used + 30% (B)

724	3¢ William Penn, Quaker	.65	.50	.45	.35	.25
724	Plate Block of 6	19.50	15.00	15.00	11.50	…
725	3¢ Daniel Webster, Statesman	.95	.70	.65	.50	.35
725	Plate Block of 6	33.75	26.00	26.00	20.00	…

Sheets of 100 F-VF, NH #720 27.50 #724 65.00 #725 95.00

1933 Commemoratives VF Used + 30% (B)

Scott's No.		Unused, NH VF	F-VF	Unused, OG VF	F-VF	Used F-VF
726-29,732-34	Set of 7	4.15	3.15	3.35	2.40	1.80
726	3¢ Georgia Bicentennial, James E. Oglethorpe	.80	.60	.60	.45	.25
726	Plate Block of 6	25.00	19.50	19.50	15.00	…
726	Plate Block of 10 with "CS"	36.50	27.50	27.50	21.50	…
727	3¢ Peace, Newburgh, NY	.35	.25	.30	.20	.20
727	Plate Block of 4	8.25	6.50	6.65	5.00	…

| 728,730a, 766a | 729,731a, 767a | 732 | 733,735a, 753 | 734 |

730, 766

731, 766

728	1¢ Century of Progress, Chicago, Fort Dearborn	.45	.35	.35	.25	.20
728	Plate Block of 4	3.50	2.60	2.65	2.00	…
729	3¢ Chicago, Federal Building	.50	.40	.40	.30	.20
729	Plate Block of 4	5.50	4.00	4.00	3.00	…

Mint Sheets of 100 F-VF, NH #726 82.50 #727 25.00 #728 37.50 #729 38.75

1933 American Philatelic Society Souvenir Sheets, Without Gum

730	1¢ Chicago, Imperforate Souvenir Sheet of 25	…	…	37.50	37.50
730a	1¢ Single Stamp from sheet	…	.90	.75	.65
731	3¢ Chicago, Imperforate Souvenir Sheet of 25	…	…	32.50	32.50
731a	3¢ Single Stamp from Sheet	…	…	.70	.60	.60

1933 Commemoratives (continued) VF Used + 30% (B)

732	3¢ Natl. Recovery Act (NRA)	.35	.25	.30	.20	.15
732	Plate Block of 4	2.65	2.00	2.10	1.60	…
733	3¢ Byrd Antarctic Expedition	.95	.70	.75	.55	.55
733	Plate Block of 6	24.00	18.50	18.00	14.50	…
734	5¢ General Tadeusz Kosciuszko, Polish Soldier	1.10	.80	.80	.60	.35
734	Plate Block of 6	57.50	42.50	42.50	32.50	…

Mint Sheets F-VF, NH #732 (100) 22.50 #733 (50) 55.00 #734 (100) 125.00

1934 National Stamp Exhibition (Byrd Antarctic) Souvenir Sheet

735, 768

Scott's No.		Unused, NH VF	F-VF	Unused, OG VF	F-VF	Used F-VF
735	3¢ Byrd, Imperforate Souvenir Sheet of 6....	...	...	...	16.00	15.00
735a	3¢ Single Stamp from sheet	...	...	2.75	2.50	2.40

NOTE: #730, 731 AND 735 WERE ISSUED WITHOUT GUM.

1934 Commemoratives VF Used + 30% (B)

736   737,738,754   739,755

736-39	Set of 4 .... 1.85	1.30	1.35	.95	.75
736	3¢ Maryland Founding 300th .... .55	.40	.40	.30	.20
736	Plate Block of 6 .... 15.50	11.75	11.75	9.00	...
737	3¢ Mother's Day "Whistler's Mother" Rotary, Perforated 11x10½ 40	.30	.30	.20	.20
737	Plate Block of 4 .... 2.30	1.80	1.85	1.40	...
738	3¢ Mother's Day, Flat Press, Perforated 11 .... .45	.35	.35	.25	.25
738	Plate Block of 6 .... 8.00	6.00	6.25	4.75	...
739	3¢ Wisconsin Discovery by Jean Nicolet 300th Anniversary 60	.45	.45	.35	.20
739	Plate Block of 6 .... 7.75	6.25	6.50	5.00	...

Mint Sheets F-VF, NH #736 (100) 50.00 #737 (50) 15.00 #738 (50) 21.50 #739 (50) 25.00

1934 National Parks Year Issue - Perf. 11 VF Used + 30% (B)

740,751   744   747   749

741   742,750   743

745   746   748

740-49	Set of 10 .... 18.50	14.00	14.75	11.00	7.15
740-49	Set of 10 Plate Blocks 185.00	140.00	145.00	110.00	...
740	1¢ Yosemite, Green .... .35	.25	.30	.20	.20
740	Plate Block of 6 .... 2.20	1.70	1.75	1.35	...
741	2¢ Grand Canyon, Red .... .35	.25	.30	.20	.20
741	Plate Block of 6 .... 2.50	1.95	2.00	1.50	...
742	3¢ Mt. Rainier, Violet .... .40	.30	.35	.25	.20
742	Plate Block of 6 .... 3.25	2.50	2.60	2.00	...
743	4¢ Mesa Verde, Brown .... .65	.50	.55	.40	.45
743	Plate Block of 6 .... 14.00	10.75	11.00	8.50	...
744	5¢ Yellowstone, Blue 1.50	1.10	1.20	.90	.70
744	Plate Block of 6 .... 16.00	12.00	12.50	9.50	...
745	6¢ Crater Lake, Dark Blue 2.10	1.60	1.65	1.25	1.00
745	Plate Block of 6 .... 29.50	22.50	24.00	18.00	...

1934 National Parks Year Issue - Perf. 11 VF Used + 30% (B)

Scott's No.		Unused, NH VF	F-VF	Unused, OG VF	F-VF	Used F-VF
746	7¢ Acadia, Black 1.40	1.10	1.15	.85	.80
746	Plate Block of 6 .... 18.50	14.50	15.00	11.50	...
747	8¢ Zion, Sage Green 3.50	2.65	2.75	2.10	2.10
747	Plate Block of 6 .... 31.00	23.50	24.00	18.50	...
748	9¢ Glacier, Red Orange 3.25	2.50	2.60	1.95	.75
748	Plate Block of 6 .... 31.00	23.50	24.00	18.50	...
749	10¢ Great Smoky Mountains, Gray Black 6.00	4.65	4.85	3.65	1.10
749	Plate Block of 6 .... 45.00	35.00	36.50	27.50	...

Mint Sheets of 50 F-VF, NH **#740-49 Set of 10 735.00** #740 9.75 #741 11.00 #742 13.50 #743 37.50 #744 57.50 #745 100.00 #746 60.00 #747 150.00 #748 140.00 #749 245.00

1934 National Parks Souvenir Sheets

750, 770

751, 769

750	3¢ American Philatelic Society, Mt. Rainier, Imperf. Sheet of 6 ...	52.50	...	42.50	40.00
750a	3¢ Single Stamp from Sheet 5.75	5.25	5.00	4.50	4.00
751	1¢ Trans-Mississippi Philatelic Exposition, Yosemite, Impf.Sheet of 6 19.50	...	16.00	15.00	
751a	1¢ Single Stamp from Sheet 2.70	2.35	2.30	2.00	1.95

NOTE: PRIOR TO 1935, TO DETERMINE VERY FINE USED PRICE, ADD VF% AT BEGINNING OF EACH SET TO THE APPROPRIATE FINE PRICE. MINIMUM 10¢ PER STAMP.
NOTE: STAMP ILLUSTRATIONS INDICATE DESIGNS, PERFORATIONS AND TYPES MAY VARY

NOTE: PRICES THROUGHOUT THIS LIST ARE SUBJECT TO CHANGE WITHOUT NOTICE IF MARKET CONDITIONS REQUIRE. MINIMUM MAIL ORDER MUST TOTAL AT LEAST $20.00.

1935 Farley Special Printing Issue, Without Gum

754

755

757

756

760

763

765

758

759

761

762

764

771

These stamps were issued imperforate (except #752 & 753) and without gum.
Horiz. and Vert. Gutter or Line Blocks are available at double the pair price.
NOTE: #752, 766A-70A HAVE GUTTERS INSTEAD OF LINES.

Scott's No.		Plate Blocks	Hz. Pair Vert.Line	Vert. Pr. Hz.Line	Singles Unused	Used
752-71	**Set of 20 .... (15)**	400.00	135.00	92.50	29.75	29.50
752	3¢ Newburgh, Perf.10½x11					
	(Design of #727)	25.00	8.75	5.25	.20	.25
753	3¢ Byrd, Perf. 11(#733) (6)	17.50	39.50	1.95	.55	.55
754	3¢ Mother's Day, (#738) (6)	17.50	1.85	2.10	.60	.60
755	3¢ Wisconsin, (#739) .... (6)	19.50	2.00	2.40	.70	.70

National Parks, Imperforate

756-65	**Set of 10 .... (6)**	275.00	42.50	41.50	16.00	16.00
756	1¢ Yosemite (#740) (6)	5.00	.65	.55	.25	.25
757	2¢ Grand Canyon(#741) (6)	6.00	.70	.80	.25	.25
758	3¢ Mt. Rainier (#742) .... (6)	15.00	1.50	1.60	.55	.55
759	4¢ Mesa Verde (#743) . (6)	20.00	2.50	2.95	1.10	1.10
760	5¢ Yellowstone (#744) ... (6)	25.00	5.25	4.75	2.10	2.10
761	6¢ Crater Lake (#745) .... (6)	40.00	6.00	7.00	2.50	2.50
762	7¢ Acadia (#746) .... (6)	33.50	4.50	5.00	1.80	1.80
763	8¢ Zion (#747) .... (6)	42.50	7.50	5.75	2.35	2.35
764	9¢ Glacier (#748) .... (6)	45.00	5.50	6.00	2.25	2.25
765	10¢ Great Smoky(#749) (6)	55.00	11.50	10.00	3.95	3.95

Singles And Pairs From Souvenir Sheets, Imperforate

766a-70a	**Set of 5 ....**	...	40.75	35.75	10.75	9.75
766a	1¢ Chicago (#730a)	...	8.75	6.00	1.10	.70
766	1¢ Chicago, Pane of 25 ..	...	(Pair 95.00)		35.00	...
767a	3¢ Chicago.(#731a(.....	...	9.00	6.50	1.10	.70
767	3¢ Chicago, Pane of 25 ..	...	(Pair 95.00)		35.00	...
768a	3¢ Byrd (#735a)	...	8.50	7.50	3.00	3.00
768	3¢ Byrd, Pane of 6	...	(Pair 50.00)		22.50	...
769a	1¢ Yosemite (#751a)	...	5.25	4.75	1.85	1.80
769	1¢ Yosemite, Pane of 6 ...	...	(Pair 32.50)		13.00	...
770a	3¢ Mt. Rainier (#750a)	...	11.00	12.50	4.25	4.00
770	3¢ Mt. Rainier, Pane of 6 ..	...	(Pair 85.00)		37.50	...

NOTE: #766-70 Pairs are two panes with gutter in between).

Airmail Special Delivery, Imperforate (Design of CE1)

771	16¢ Dark Blue (#CE1) . (6)	75.00	6.75	8.50	2.75	2.75

**Horizontal Pairs
Vertical Gutters**

**Vertical Pair
Horizontal Line**

FARLEY SPECIAL PRINTING SHEETS AND POSITION BLOCKS

Scott's No.		Stamps in Sheets	Uncut Sheet	Center Line Block	T or B Arrow Block	L or R Arrow Block
752-71	**Set of 20 (Arrow Bks.15)**	...	8300.00	470.00	215.00	132.50
752	3¢ Newburgh, Pf.10½x11	(400)	450.00	65.00	18.75	11.50
753	3¢ Byrd, Perf.11	(200)	595.00	90.00	85.00	4.25
754	3¢ Mother's Day	(200)	185.00	9.00	4.00	4.50
755	3¢ Wisconsin	(200)	210.00	10.75	4.75	5.25
756-65	**Set of 10 Parks ....**	...	4150.00	155.00	95.00	95.00
756	1¢ Yosemite	(200)	65.00	3.75	1.45	1.20
757	2¢ Grand Canyon	(200)	75.00	5.25	1.50	1.70
758	3¢ Mount Rainier	(200)	160.00	6.50	3.35	3.75
759	4¢ Mesa Verde	(200)	285.00	11.00	5.50	6.75
760	5¢ Yellowstone	(200)	500.00	16.00	11.50	10.50
761	6¢ Crater Lake	(200)	625.00	22.50	13.50	15.75
762	7¢ Acadia	(200)	475.00	17.00	10.00	11.50
763	8¢ Zion	(200)	575.00	21.50	16.00	13.00
764	9¢ Glacier	(200)	595.00	25.00	12.50	13.50
765	10¢ Great Smoky	(200)	975.00	35.00	25.00	22.00
766a-770a	**Set of 5 ....**		2200.00	95.00	...	...
766a	1¢ Chicago	(225)	375.00	21.00	...	...
767a	3¢ Chicago	(225)	375.00	22.50	...	...
768a	3¢ Byrd	(150)	550.00	18.50	...	...
769a	1¢ Yosemite	(120)	275.00	11.75	...	...
770a	3¢ Mount Rainier	(120)	750.00	28.50	...	...
771	16¢ Airmail Special Del. ..	(200)	825.00	75.00	14.50	18.00

**VERY FINE COPIES OF #752 TO THE PRESENT ARE
AVAILABLE FOR THE FOLLOWING PREMIUMS:
ADD 10¢ TO ANY ITEM PRICED UNDER 50¢. ADD 20% TO ANY ITEM PRICED AT 50¢ & UP.
UNLESS PRICED AS VERY FINE, SETS ARE NOT AVAILABLE VERY FINE AND STAMPS
SHOULD BE LISTED INDIVIDUALLY WITH APPROPRIATE PREMIUM.
SOME BOOKLET PANES & COILS MAY REQUIRE HIGHER PREMIUMS.**

Cross Gutter Block

Center Line Block

Arrow Block

772, 778a 773, 778b 775, 778c

774 784 777

778

776, 778d 782 783

1935 Commemoratives

Scott's No.		Mint Sheet	Plate Block	F-VF NH	F-VF Used
772-75	Set of 4	...	...	1.50	.55
772	3¢ Connecticut Settlement Tercen.	19.50	2.75	.40	.15
773	3¢ California-Pacific Exposition ..	17.00	2.00	.35	.15
774	3¢ Boulder Dam	14.75 (6)	2.50	.30	.15
775	3¢ Michigan Statehood Centenary	26.50	3.25	.55	.15

1936 Commemoratives

Scott's No.		Mint Sheet	Plate Block	F-VF NH	F-VF Used
776-78,782-84	Set of 6	...	...	5.25	3.65
776	3¢ Texas Independence Centennial	26.50	3.15	.55	.15
777	3¢ Rhode Island Settlement Terc.	31.50	3.25	.65	.15
778	3¢ (TIPEX) Third International Philatelic Exhibition Souvenir Sheet of 4 ...	...	...	3.25	3.00
778a	3¢ Connecticut, Imperforate	...	...	.85	.80
778b	3¢ California-Pacific, Imperforate ..	...	...	.85	.80
778c	3¢ Michigan, Imperforate	...	...	.85	.80
778d	3¢ Texas, Imperforate	...	...	.85	.80
782	3¢ Arkansas Statehood Centennial	33.50	3.50	.70	.15
783	3¢ Oregon Territory Centennial ...	11.75	1.50	.25	.15
784	3¢ Susan B. Anthony .... (100)	22.50	1.20	.25	.15

1936-1937 Army - Navy Series

785 786 787

788 789

790 791 792

793 794

1936-1937 Army - Navy Series

Scott's No.		Mint Sheet	Plate Block	F-VF NH	F-VF Used
785-94	Set of 10	260.00	52.50	4.95	1.70
785-94	Very Fine Set of 10	...	62.50	5.95	2.50
	#785-89 Army Issues				
785	1¢ Washington & Greene	14.00	1.50	.30	.15
786	2¢ Jackson & Scott (1937)	17.00	1.75	.35	.15
787	3¢ Sherman,Grant,Sheridan (1937)	26.50	2.85	.55	.15
788	4¢ Lee & Jackson (1937)	40.00	11.00	.60	.25
789	5¢ West Point (1937)	47.50	12.00	.80	.30
	#790-94 Navy Issues				
790	1¢ Jones & Barry	5.75	1.10	.20	.15
791	2¢ Decatur & MacDonough (1937)	18.75	2.00	.40	.15
792	3¢ Farragut & Porter (1937)	22.00	2.30	.45	.15
793	4¢ Sampson, Dewey, Schley (1937)	47.50	12.50	.70	.25
794	5¢ U.S. Naval Academy (1937) ..	47.50	12.00	.80	.30

1937 Commemoratives

795 796 798

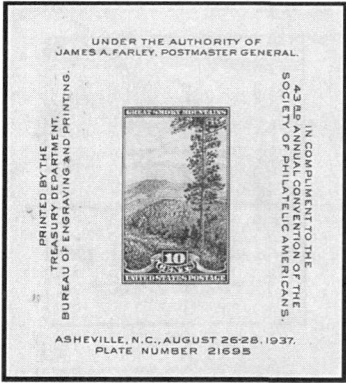 

797 799

800 801 802

Scott's No.		Mint Sheet	Plate Block	F-VF NH	F-VF Used
795-802	Set of 8	...	...	3.65	1.50
795	3¢ Northwest Territory Ordinance of 1787	26.50	2.85	.55	.15
796	5¢ Virginia Dare .... (48)	22.50 (6)	9.50	.35	.25
797	10¢ Society of Philatelic Americans Souvenir Sheet..	...	...	.85	.70
798	3¢ Constitution Signing 150th Ann.	45.00	5.00	.95	.15
799-802	Territorials Set of 4	55.00	7.25	1.20	.55
799	3¢ Hawaii Territory	14.00	1.85	.30	.15
800	3¢ Alaska Territory	14.00	1.85	.30	.15
801	3¢ Puerto Rico Territory	16.50	2.00	.35	.15
802	3¢ Virgin Islands Territory	14.00	1.85	.30	.15

NOTE: FROM 1935 TO DATE, WITH FEW LISTED EXCEPTIONS, UNUSED PRICES ARE FOR NEVER HINGED STAMPS. HINGED STAMPS, WHEN AVAILABLE, ARE PRICED AT APPROXIMATELY 15% BELOW THE NEVER HINGED PRICE.

1938 Presidential Series (B) (VF+25%)

803	804,839,848	805,840,849	806,841,850	807,842,851
808,843	809,844	810,845	811,846	812
813	814	815,847	816	817
818	819	820	821	822
823	824	825	826	827
828	829	830	831	
832	833	834		

Scott's No.		Mint Sheet	Plate Block	F-VF NH	F-VF Used
803-34	Set of 32	...	850.00	185.00	15.95
803-34	Very Fine Set of 32	...	1025.00	22.00	20.75
803-31	Set of 29 (½¢-50¢)	...	187.50	38.00	5.25
803-31	Very Fine Set of 29	...	235.00	47.50	7.75
803	½¢ Benjamin Franklin .... (100)	13.50	.70	.20	.15
804	1¢ George Washington .... (100)	12.00	.70	.20	.15
804b	1¢ Booklet Pane of 6, 2½ mm (1942)	...	...	2.25	1.95
804bv	same, 3 mm Gutter (1939)	...	...	7.50	...
805	1½¢ Martha Washington .... (100)	12.50	.70	.20	.15
806	2¢ John Adams .... (100)	12.75	.70	.20	.15
806	2¢ Electric Eye Plate Block of 10	...	7.50	...	...
806b	2¢ Booklet Pane of 6, 2½ mm (1942)	...	...	7.50	...
806bv	same, 3 mm Gutter (1939)	...	...	10.00	...
807	3¢ Thomas Jefferson .... (100)	27.50	1.25	.30	.15
807	3¢ Electric Eye Plate Block of 10	...	45.00	...	...
807a	3¢ Booklet Pane of 6, 2½ mm (1942)	...	...	8.50	8.25
807av	same, 3 mm Gutter (1939)	...	...	14.95	...
808	4¢ James Madison .... (100)	95.00	4.25	.90	.15
809	4½¢ White House .... (100)	25.00	1.50	.25	.15
810	5¢ James Monroe .... (100)	32.50	1.50	.30	.15
811	6¢ John Quincy Adams .... (100)	39.50	1.90	.40	.15
812	7¢ Andrew Jackson .... (100)	67.50	3.50	.70	.15
813	8¢ Martin Van Buren .... (100)	55.00	2.80	.55	.15
814	9¢ William Henry Harrison ...... (100)	52.50	2.25	.45	.15
815	10¢ John Tyler .... (100)	52.50	2.40	.50	.15
816	11¢ James K. Polk .... (100)	72.50	4.00	.75	.15
817	12¢ Zachary Taylor .... (100)	155.00	7.75	1.60	.20
818	13¢ Millard Fillmore .... (100)	200.00	9.00	2.00	.20
819	14¢ Franklin Pierce .... (100)	145.00	8.00	1.50	.20
820	15¢ James Buchanan .... (100)	62.50	2.50	.55	.15
821	16¢ Abraham Lincoln .... (100)	145.00	8.00	1.50	.55
822	17¢ Andrew Johnson .... (100)	145.00	8.00	1.50	.20
823	18¢ Ulysses S. Grant .... (100)	225.00	11.00	2.25	.20
824	19¢ Rutherford B. Hayes .... (100)	180.00	8.75	1.85	.60
825	20¢ James A. Garfield .... (100)	100.00	4.50	1.00	.15
826	21¢ Chester A. Arthur .... (100)	230.00	11.50	2.30	.20
827	22¢ Grover Cleveland .... (100)	165.00	12.50	1.75	.75
828	24¢ Benjamin Harrison .... (100)	475.00	21.50	4.75	.35

1938 Presidential Series (continued)

Scott's No.		Mint Sheet	Plate Block	F-VF NH	F-VF Used
829	25¢ William McKinley .... (100)	115.00	5.25	1.10	.15
830	30¢ Theodore Roosevelt .... (100)	600.00	27.00	6.00	.20
831	50¢ William Howard Taft .... (100)	800.00	37.50	8.00	.20
832	$1 Wood.Wilson, Purple & Black(100)	1000.00	45.00	10.00	.20
832b	$1 Wilson, Wtmk. "USIR" (1951)	...	1750.00	300.00	65.00
832c	$1 Dry Printing,Red Violet & Black(1954) .... (100)	835.00	37.50	8.50	.20
833	$2 Warren G. Harding	...	125.00	25.00	5.75
833	$2 Harding, Very Fine	...	150.00	30.00	6.75
834	$5 Calvin Coolidge Carmine & Black	...	550.00	125.00	5.50
834	$5 Coolidge, Very Fine	...	650.00	150.00	6.50
834	$5 Coolidge, F-VF, Lightly Hinged	...	475.00	100.00	...
834a	$5 Red Brown & Black	...	...	2750.00	...

$1 Wilson: #832,832b Standard printing with similar paper, etc. as #833, 834.
#832c Dry Printing, thick white paper, smooth, colorless gum

Scott #	ARROW BLOCKS Never Hinged VF	F-VF	CENTER LINE BLOCKS Never Hinged VF	F-VF	TOP PLATE BLOCK OF 20 Never Hinged VF	F-VF
832	52.50	45.00	57.50	50.00	500.00	500.00
833	140.00	115.00	150.00	120.00	900.00	750.00
834	685.00	575.00	775.00	650.00	3250.00	2750.00

1938 Commemoratives

835	836	837	838

Scott's No.		Mint Sheet	Plate Block	F-VF NH	F-VF Used
835-38	Set of 4	...	...	1.60	.50
835	3¢ Constitution Ratification 150th	30.00	5.25	.60	.15
836	3¢ Swedish-Finnish Tercentenary(48)	13.50 (6)	3.25	.30	.15
837	3¢ Northwest Territory Sesqui. (100)	35.00	10.50	.30	.15
838	3¢ Iowa Territory Centennial	30.00	7.50	.45	.15

1939 Presidential Coils (B) (VF+25%)

Scott's No.		Line Pairs NH	F-VF NH	F-VF Used
839-51	Set of 13	140.00	32.50	5.25
839-51	Very Fine Set of 13	170.00	40.00	6.75
Perforated 10 Vertically				
839	1¢ George Washington	1.35	.30	.15
840	1½¢ Martha Washington	1.30	.30	.15
841	2¢ John Adams	1.40	.30	.15
842	3¢ Thomas Jefferson	1.75	.50	.20
843	4¢ James Madison	30.00	7.25	.75
844	4½¢ White House	5.00	.60	.50
845	5¢ James Monroe	27.50	5.00	.45
846	6¢ John Quincy Adams	7.00	1.25	.25
847	10¢ John Tyler	51.50	12.00	.85
Perforated 10 Horizontally				
848	1¢ George Washington	3.00	.85	.25
849	1½¢ Martha Washington	4.00	1.35	.55
850	2¢ John Adams	7.50	3.00	.70
851	3¢ Thomas Jefferson	6.25	2.50	.70

1939 Commemoratives

852	853	854	857

855	856	858

Scott's No.		Mint Sheet	Plate Block	F-VF NH	F-VF Used
852-58	Set of 7	...	...	4.65	1.00
852	3¢ Golden Gate Exposition	15.00	1.85	.30	.15
853	3¢ New York World's Fair	14.50	2.50	.30	.15
854	3¢ Washington Inaugural Sesqui.	47.50 (6)	7.50	.95	.15
855	3¢ Baseball Centennial	120.00	11.00	2.25	.20
856	3¢ Panama Canal 25th Anniv. ..	24.00 (6)	4.00	.50	.20
857	3¢ Printing 300th Anniversary ...	12.00	1.60	.25	.15
858	3¢ North & South Dakota, Montana, Washington Statehood 50th Anniv.	15.00	1.80	.30	.15

1940 Famous Americans Series

(Stamp images 859 through 893 shown in left column)

Scott's No.		Mint Sheet	Plate Block	F-VF NH	F-VF Used
859-93	Set of 35	2950.00	435.00	38.75	18.75
859-93	Very Fine Set of 35	...	515.00	46.50	22.75
859/91	1¢,2¢,3¢ Values (21)	...	42.50	5.95	2.95
Authors					
859	1¢ Washington Irving .... (70)	15.75	1.40	.25	.15
860	2¢ James Fenimore Cooper ... (70)	18.50	1.65	.30	.15
861	3¢ Ralph Waldo Emerson .... (70)	16.50	1.60	.25	.15
862	5¢ Louisa May Alcott .... (70)	40.00	11.75	.45	.35
863	10¢ Samuel L. Clemens .... (70)	190.00	47.50	2.25	1.90

1940 Famous Americans (continued)

Scott's No.		Mint Sheet	Plate Block	F-VF NH	F-VF Used
Poets					
864	1¢ Henry W. Longfellow .... (70)	42.50	4.00	.60	.15
865	2¢ John G. Whittier .... (70)	16.50	2.50	.25	.15
866	3¢ James Russell Lowell .... (70)	17.50	3.00	.25	.15
867	5¢ Walt Whitman .... (70)	55.00	12.00	.60	.35
868	10¢ James Whitcomb Riley .... (70)	235.00	52.50	2.75	2.25
Educators					
869	1¢ Horace Mann .... (70)	13.50	2.75	.20	.15
870	2¢ Mark Hopkins .... (70)	13.00	1.60	.20	.15
871	3¢ Charles W. Eliot .... (70)	18.50	3.15	.25	.15
872	5¢ Frances E. Willard .... (70)	57.50	15.00	.60	.15
873	10¢ Booker T. Washington ...... (70)	215.00	39.50	2.70	1.85
Scientists					
874	1¢ John James Audubon .... (70)	17.50	1.60	.25	.15
875	2¢ Dr. Crawford W. Long .... (70)	14.50	1.40	.25	.15
876	3¢ Luther Burbank .... (70)	19.50	1.65	.30	.15
877	5¢ Dr. Walter Reed .... (70)	31.50	8.75	.35	.35
878	10¢ Jane Addams .... (70)	130.00	27.50	1.65	1.50
Composers					
879	1¢ Stephen C. Foster .... (70)	19.50	1.50	.30	.15
880	2¢ John Philip Sousa .... (70)	14.00	1.50	.20	.15
881	3¢ Victor Herbert .... (70)	17.00	1.75	.25	.15
882	5¢ Edward A. MacDowell .... (70)	48.50	12.50	.60	.35
883	10¢ Ethelbert Nevin .... (70)	335.00	47.50	4.50	2.00
Artists					
884	1¢ Gilbert C. Stuart .... (70)	24.00	1.80	.35	.15
885	2¢ James A. Whistler .... (70)	13.50	1.30	.20	.15
886	3¢ Augustus Saint-Gaudens .... (70)	22.50	1.75	.35	.15
887	5¢ Daniel Chester French .... (70)	52.50	10.75	.70	.35
888	10¢ Frederic Remington .... (70)	190.00	35.00	2.40	1.85
Inventors					
889	1¢ Eli Whitney .... (70)	35.00	3.50	.50	.15
890	2¢ Samuel F.B. Morse .... (70)	34.50	3.00	.50	.15
891	3¢ Cyrus H. McCormick .... (70)	28.50	2.00	.40	.15
892	5¢ Elias Howe .... (70)	105.00	16.50	1.40	.45
893	10¢ Alexander Graham Bell ..... (70)	1050.00	85.00	15.00	3.25

1940 Commemoratives

(Stamps 894, 895, 896, 897)

(Stamps 898, 899, 900, 901, 902)

Scott's No.		Mint Sheet	Plate Block	F-VF NH	F-VF Used
894-902	Set of 9	...	...	2.60	1.40
894	3¢ Pony Express 80th Anniv.	27.50	4.25	.55	.20
895	3¢ Pan American Union 50th Ann.	21.50	3.65	.40	.15
896	3¢ Idaho Statehood 50th Anniv.	16.50	2.50	.30	.15
897	3¢ Wyoming Statehood 50th Anniv.	16.00	1.95	.30	.15
898	3¢ Coronado Expedition 400th Ann.	16.00	1.95	.30	.15
899	1¢ Defense, Statue of Liberty .. (100)	14.75	.65	.20	.15
900	2¢ Defense, Anti-Aircraft Gun . (100)	14.75	.65	.20	.15
901	3¢ Defense, Torch .... (100)	17.00	.85	.20	.15
902	3¢ 13th Amendment 75th Anniv. .	20.75	4.25	.35	.25

1941-1943 Commemoratives

(Stamps 903, 904, 905)

(Stamps 906, 907, 908)

24

Scott's No.	Mint Sheet	Plate Block	F-VF NH	F-VF Used
903-08 Set of 6	...	...	2.50	.95
903 3¢ Vermont Statehood 150th Ann.	31.50	3.50	.60	.15
904 3¢ Kentucky Statehood 150th(1942)	16.00	1.60	.30	.15
905 3¢ Win the War, Eagle (1942) (100)	19.50	.85	.20	.15
906 5¢ Chinese Resistance (1942) ...	65.00	15.00	1.20	.30
907 2¢ Allied Nations (1943) .... (100)	11.75	.85	.20	.15
908 1¢ Four Freedoms (1943) .... (100)	11.75	.85	.20	.15

1943-44 Overrun Nations (Flags)

909

910

911

912

913

914

915

916

917

918

919

920

921

Scott's No.	Mint Sheet	Plate Block	F-VF NH	F-VF Used
909-21 Set of 13	240.00	65.00	4.75	3.15
909-21 Very Fine Set of 13	...	75.00	5.75	3.95
909 5¢ Poland	17.50	8.00	.30	.25
910 5¢ Czechoslovakia	16.50	3.75	.30	.25
911 5¢ Norway	12.00	2.25	.30	.25
912 5¢ Luxembourg	12.00	1.80	.30	.25
913 5¢ Netherlands	12.00	1.80	.30	.25
914 5¢ Belgium	12.00	1.80	.30	.25
915 5¢ France	12.00	1.80	.30	.25
916 5¢ Greece	42.50	16.00	.85	.40
917 5¢ Yugoslavia	26.50	7.50	.45	.25
918 5¢ Albania	26.50	7.50	.45	.25
919 5¢ Austria	22.50	6.00	.35	.25
920 5¢ Denmark	26.00	7.00	.45	.25
921 5¢ Korea (1944)	17.00	6.50	.40	.25
921v 5¢ "KORPA" Variety (1 per sheet)	50.00	...	27.50	...

(On #909-21, the country name rather than a plate number appears in the margin.)

1944 Commemoratives

922

923

924

925

926

Scott's No.	Mint Sheet	Plate Block	F-VF NH	F-VF Used
922-26 Set of 5	...	...	1.60	.65
922 3¢ Transcontinental Railroad 75th	17.50	1.80	.30	.15
923 3¢ Steamship "Savannah" 125th	22.50	2.50	.45	.15
924 3¢ Telegraph Centennial	19.50	2.00	.40	.15
925 3¢ Corregidor, Philippines	12.75	1.35	.25	.15
926 3¢ Motion Pictures 50th Anniv. ...	17.00	1.50	.30	.15

1945 Commemoratives

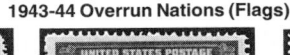

927

928

929

930

931

932

933

934

935

936

937

938

Scott's No.	Mint Sheet	Plate Block	F-VF NH	F-VF Used
927-38 Set of 12	...	...	3.00	1.40
927 3¢ Florida Statehood Centennial	19.50	1.80	.40	.15
928 5¢ United Nations Conference	10.00	.85	.20	.15
929 3¢ Iwo Jima (Marines)	22.50	2.25	.35	.15
930-33 Franklin.D.Roosevelt Set of 4	29.50	3.00	.80	.55
930 1¢ F.D.R., Hyde Park Residence ..	5.00	.60	.20	.15
931 2¢ F.D.R., Warm Springs, GA	7.50	.70	.20	.15
932 3¢ F.D.R., White House	9.00	.85	.20	.15
933 5¢ F.D.R., Map, Four Freedoms (1946)	12.00	1.15	.25	.15
934 3¢ Army in World War II	12.00	1.15	.25	.15
935 3¢ Navy in World War II	14.50	1.40	.30	.15
936 3¢ Coast Guard in World War II ..	11.50	1.00	.25	.15
937 3¢ Alfred E. Smith, Governor .. (100)	21.50	1.00	.25	.15
938 3¢ Texas Statehood 100th Anniv.	19.50	1.80	.40	.15

1946 Commemoratives

939

940

941

942

943

944

Scott's No.	Mint Sheet	Plate Block	F-VF NH	F-VF Used
939-44 Set of 6	...	...	1.50	.75
939 3¢ Merchant Marine in W.War II .	9.00	.85	.20	.15
940 3¢ World War II Veterans .... (100)	23.50	1.00	.25	.15
941 3¢ Tennessee Statehood 150th ..	17.00	1.50	.35	.15
942 3¢ Iowa Statehood Centennial	18.75	1.75	.40	.15
943 3¢ Smithsonian Institution 100th .	13.50	1.25	.30	.15
944 3¢ Santa Fe, Kearny Expedition 100th Anniversary	12.75	1.25	.30	.15

NOTE: FROM 1935 TO DATE, WITH FEW LISTED EXCEPTIONS, UNUSED PRICES ARE FOR NEVER HINGED STAMPS. HINGED STAMPS, WHEN AVAILABLE, ARE PRICED AT APPROXIMATELY 15% BELOW THE NEVER HINGED PRICE.

1947 Commemoratives

945

946

947

1948 Commemoratives (continued)

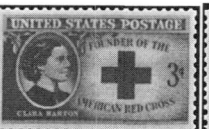
965

966

967

968

970

971

948

952

969

972

973

974

949

950

951

975

976

977

Scott's No.		Mint Sheet	Plate Block	F-VF NH	F-VF Used
945-52	**Set of 8**	...	..	2.50	1.60
945	3¢ Thomas A. Edison,Inventor . (70)	19.50	1.30	.30	.15
946	3¢ Joseph Pulitzer, Publisher	13.50	1.30	.30	.15
947	3¢ Postage Stamp Centenary	9.00	.85	.20	.15
948	5¢ & 10¢ (CIPEX) Centenary International Philatelic Exhibition Souvenir Sheet	...	...	1.20	.90
948a	5¢ Franklin, Blue	...	...	.50	.35
948b	10¢ Wash., Brown Orange	...	...	.60	.40
949	3¢ Doctors "The Doctor"	9.00	.85	.20	.15
950	3¢ Utah Settlement Centennial ...	14.00	1.30	.30	.15
951	3¢ Frigate Constitution 150th Ann.	11.00	1.10	.25	.15
952	3¢ Everglades Park Dedication ..	18.75	1.85	.40	.15

1948 Commemoratives

953

954

955

978

979

980

956

957

958

1949 Commemoratives

Scott's No.		Mint Sheet	Plate Block	F-VF NH	F-VF Used
953-80	**Set of 28**	...	...	7.50	3.25
953	3¢ George W. Carver,Botanist . (70)	22.75	1.50	.35	.15
954	3¢ California Gold Rush Centennial	13.50	1.30	.30	.15
955	3¢ Mississippi Territory 150th Ann.	16.00	1.50	.35	.15
956	3¢ Four Chaplains	13.50	1.30	.30	.15
957	3¢ Wisconsin Statehood Centennial	18.50	1.80	.40	.15
958	5¢ Swedish Pioneers Centennial	13.50	1.30	.30	.15
959	3¢ Progress of Women; E.Stanton, C.Chapman Catt, L.Mott	18.50	1.80	.40	.15
960	3¢ William A. White, Writer ...... (70)	17.50	1.30	.30	.15
961	3¢ U.S. - Canada Friendship	9.00	.85	.20	.15
962	3¢ Francis Scott Key	13.50	1.30	.30	.15
963	3¢ American Youth Month	9.00	.85	.20	.15
964	3¢ Oregon Territory Centennial ...	13.50	1.30	.30	.15
965	3¢ Harlan F. Stone, Justice ...... (70)	15.00	1.10	.25	.15
966	3¢ Palomar Mt. Observatory .... (70)	17.50	1.50	.30	.15
967	3¢ Clara Barton, Red Cross	9.00	.85	.20	.15
968	3¢ Poultry Industry Centennial	13.50	1.30	.30	.15
969	3¢ Gold Star Mothers	9.00	.85	.20	.15
970	3¢ Fort Kearny, Nebraska Cent. .	14.50	1.40	.30	.15
971	3¢ Volunteer Firemen 300th Ann.	15.00	2.00	.30	.15
972	3¢ Indian Centennial, Five Tribes	14.00	1.40	.30	.15
973	3¢ Rough Riders 50th Anniv.	9.00	.85	.20	.15
974	3¢ Juliette Low, Girl Scouts	17.00	1.50	.35	.15
975	3¢ Will Rogers, Humorist .... (70)	19.75	1.40	.30	.15
976	3¢ Fort Bliss, Texas .... (70)	23.50	1.60	.35	.15
977	3¢ Moina Michael, Educator	13.50	1.30	.30	.15
978	3¢ Gettysburg Address 85th Anniv.	18.50	1.75	.40	.15
979	3¢ Turners Society Centennial	11.00	1.10	.25	.15
980	3¢ Joel Chandler Harris,Writer (70)	21.75	1.50	.35	.15

959

960

961

962

963

964

1949 Commemoratives

981

982

983

1949 Commemoratives (continued)

984

985

986

Scott's No.		Mint Sheet	Plate Block	F-VF NH	F-VF Used
981-86	**Set of 6**	...	...	**1.50**	**.70**
981	3¢ Minnesota Territory Centennial	13.50	1.30	.30	.15
982	3¢ Washington & Lee University .	11.50	1.10	.25	.15
983	3¢ Puerto Rico Election	9.00	.85	.20	.15
984	3¢ Annapolis Tercentenary	11.50	1.10	.25	.15
985	3¢ Grand Army of the Republic ...	11.50	1.10	.25	.15
986	3¢ Edgar Allan Poe, Writer ...... (70)	23.50	1.75	.35	.15

1950 Commemoratives

987

988

990

989

991

992

993

994

995

996

997

Scott's No.		Mint Sheet	Plate Block	F-VF NH	F-VF Used
987-97	**Set of 11**	...	...	**2.90**	**1.30**
987	3¢ Bankers Association 75th Ann.	18.75	1.70	.40	.15
988	3¢ Samuel Gompers, Labor .... (70)	12.75	.85	.20	.15
989-92	National Capitol, Set of 4	42.50	3.95	.90	.55
989	3¢ Freedom Statue, Capitol Dome	9.00	.85	.20	.15
990	3¢ Executive Mansion	11.50	1.10	.25	.15
991	3¢ Supreme Court	13.50	1.30	.30	.15
992	3¢ U.S. Capitol	11.50	1.10	.25	.15
993	3¢ Railroad Engineers, Casey Jones	16.50	1.50	.35	.15
994	3¢ Kansas City, MO Centenary ...	18.50	1.75	.40	.15
995	3¢ Boy Scouts of America	13.75	1.30	.30	.15
996	3¢ Indiana Territory 150th Anniv. .	16.50	1.50	.35	.15
997	3¢ California Statehood Centennial	13.75	1.30	.30	.15

1951 Commemoratives

998

999

1000

1001

1002

1003

1951 Commemoratives (continued)

Scott's No.		Mint Sheet	Plate Block	F-VF NH	F-VF Used
998-1003	**Set of 6**	...	...	**1.70**	**.70**
998	3¢ Confederate Veterans	18.50	1.75	.40	.15
999	3¢ Nevada Settlement Centennial	13.50	1.30	.30	.15
1000	3¢ Landing of Cadillac, Detroit	16.50	1.50	.35	.15
1001	3¢ Colorado Statehood 75th Ann.	13.50	1.30	.30	.15
1002	3¢ Chemical Society 75th Anniv.	13.50	1.30	.30	.15
1003	3¢ Battle of Brooklyn 175th Ann.	11.50	1.10	.25	.15

1952 Commemoratives

1004

1005

1006

1007

1008

1009

1011

1010

1012

1013

1014

1015

1016

Scott's No.		Mint Sheet	Plate Block	F-VF NH	F-VF Used
1004-16	**Set of 13**	...	...	**3.35**	**1.50**
1004	3¢ Betsy Ross 200th Birthday	13.50	1.30	.30	.15
1005	3¢ 4-H Clubs	28.50	2.50	.60	.15
1006	3¢ B & O Railroad 125th Anniv. ..	16.50	1.50	.35	.15
1007	3¢ Amer. Automobile Assoc 50th	13.50	1.30	.30	.15
1008	3¢ North Atlantic Treaty Organ. (100)	18.00	.85	.20	.15
1009	3¢ Grand Coulee Dam 50th Ann.	13.50	1.30	.30	.15
1010	3¢ Marquis de Lafayette	17.00	1.50	.35	.15
1011	3¢ Mt. Rushmore Memorial 25th	13.50	1.30	.30	.15
1012	3¢ Civil Engineers Society Cent.	13.50	1.30	.30	.15
1013	3¢ Service Women	9.00	.85	.20	.15
1014	3¢ Gutenberg Bible 500th Anniv.	9.00	.85	.20	.15
1015	3¢ Newspaper Boys	9.00	.85	.20	.15
1016	3¢ International Red Cross	9.00	.85	.20	.15

1953 Commemoratives

1017

1018

1019

1020

1021

1022

Scott's No.		Mint Sheet	Plate Block	F-VF NH	F-VF Used
1017-28	**Set of 12**	...	...	**3.15**	**1.50**
1017	3¢ National Guard	11.50	1.10	.25	.15
1018	3¢ Ohio Statehood 150th Anniv. (70)	19.50	1.30	.30	.15
1019	3¢ Washington Territory Centennial	13.50	1.30	.30	.15
1020	3¢ Louisiana Purchase 150th Ann.	18.50	1.75	.40	.15
1021	5¢ Opening of Japan Cent., Perry	16.50	1.50	.35	.15
1022	3¢ American Bar Association 75th	13.50	1.30	.30	.15

1953 Commemoratives (cont.)

1023

1024

1025

1026

1027

1028

Scott's No.		Mint Sheet	Plate Block	F-VF NH	F-VF Used
1023	3¢ Sagamore Hill, T. Roosevelt ..	11.50	1.10	.25	.15
1024	3¢ Future Farmers Assoc. 25th ..	11.50	1.10	.25	.15
1025	3¢ Trucking Industry 50th Anniv. .	9.00	.85	.20	.15
1026	3¢ General George S. Patton	13.50	1.30	.30	.15
1027	3¢ New York City 300th Anniv.	11.50	1.10	.25	.15
1028	3¢ Gadsden Purchase Centennial	13.50	1.30	.30	.15

1954 Commemoratives

1029

1060

1061

1062

1063

1029,1060-63	**Set of 5 ....**	**...**	**...**	**1.40**	**.60**
1029	3¢ Columbia University 200th Ann.	13.50	1.30	.30	.15

1954-1968 Liberty Series, Perf.11x10½, 10½x11 (B) (VF+25%)
(Sheets of 100)

1030

1031,1054

1031A,1054A

1032

1033,1055

1034,1056

1035,1057

1036,1058

1037,1059

1038

1039

1040

1041,1041B

1042

1042A

1030-53	**Set of 27 (No #1041B) ....**	**...**	**515.00**	**120.00**	**11.50**
1030-53	**Very Fine Set of 27 (No #1041B)**	**...**	**615.00**	**145.00**	**14.00**
1030-51	½¢-50¢ Values only (25) (No#1041B)	...	72.50	15.75	3.00
1030	½¢ Benjamin Franklin, Dry (1958)	9.00	.70	.20	.15
1030a	½¢ Wet Printing (1955)	9.00	.70	.20	.15
1031	1¢ George Washington, Dry (1956)	7.50	.60	.20	.15
1031b	1¢ Wet Printing (1954)	12.00	1.10	.25	.15
1031A	1¼¢ Palace of Governors (1960)	8.00	.60	.20	.15
1032	1½¢ Mount Vernon (1956)	27.50	1.95	.30	.15
1033	2¢ Thomas Jefferson	12.00	.65	.20	.15
1034	2½¢ Bunker Hill (1959)	22.50	1.10	.25	.15
1035	3¢ Statue of Liberty, Dry	14.00	.70	.20	.15
1035f	3¢ Booklet Pane of 6, Dry Printing	...	...	6.50	3.50
1035b	3¢ Tagged, Dry Printing (1966) ...	40.00	9.00	.35	.30
1035e	3¢ Wet Printing	22.50	1.25	.25	.20
1035a	3¢ Booklet Pane of 6, Wet Printing	...	...	6.00	3.50
1036	4¢ Abraham Lincoln, Dry	27.50	1.25	.30	.15
1036a	4¢ Booklet Pane of 6 (1958)	...	...	3.00	2.50
1036b	4¢ Tagged, Dry Printing (1963) ...	80.00	11.95	.70	.55

1954-1968 Liberty Series (continued) (B)
(Sheets of 100)

Scott's No.		Mint Sheet	Plate Block	F-VF NH	F-VF Used
1036c	4¢ Wet Printing	27.50	1.25	.30	.20
1037	4½¢ The Hermitage (1959)	27.50	1.30	.30	.15
1038	5¢ James Monroe	27.50	1.25	.30	.15
1039	6¢ Theodore Roosevelt, Dry	42.50	1.95	.45	.15
1039a	6¢ Wet Printing (1955)	55.00	2.50	.55	.20
1040	7¢ Woodrow Wilson (1956)	32.50	1.50	.35	.15
1041	8¢ Liberty, Original, Flat, Perf.11 .	33.50	2.75	.35	.15
1041B	8¢ Liberty, Original, Rotary,Pf.11 .	52.50	4.25	.55	.25
#1041B is slightly taller than #1041. #1041 22.7mm tall; #1041B 22.9mm tall.					
1042	8¢ Liberty, Redrawn,Perf.11 (1958)	33.50	1.50	.35	.15
#1041,1041B: Torch Flame between "U.S." and "POSTAGE".					
#1042: Torch Flame goes under "P" of "POSTAGE".					
1042A	8¢ John J. Pershing (1961)	38.50	1.70	.40	.15

1043

1044

1044A

1045

1046

1047

1048,1059A

1049

1050

1051

1052

1053

1043	9¢ The Alamo (1956)	57.50	2.75	.60	.15
1044	10¢ Independence Hall (1956) ...	50.00	2.50	.55	.15
1044b	10¢ Tagged (1966)	...	45.00	3.75	2.50
1044A	11¢ Statue of Liberty,Perf.11 (1961)	40.00	1.95	.40	.15
1044Ac	11¢ Tagged (1967)	...	47.50	2.25	1.75
1045	12¢ Benjamin Harrison (1959) ...	60.00	2.85	.60	.15
1045a	12¢ Tagged (1968)	65.00	5.00	.65	.35
1046	15¢ John Jay (1958)	100.00	4.50	1.00	.15
1046a	15¢ Tagged (1966)	...	11.75	1.50	.75
1047	20¢ Monticello (1956)	70.00	3.50	.70	.15
1048	25¢ Paul Revere (1958)	175.00	7.95	1.80	.15
1049	30¢ Robert E. Lee, Dry (1957)	180.00	8.50	1.85	.15
1049a	30¢ Wet Printing (1955)	...	11.50	2.75	1.25
1050	40¢ John Marshall, Dry (1958)	275.00	13.00	2.75	.15
1050a	40¢ Wet Printing (1955)	...	17.50	3.75	1.75
1051	50¢ S.B. Anthony, Dry (1958)	220.00	10.00	2.25	.15
1051a	50¢ Wet Printing (1955)	...	14.75	2.50	1.25
1052	$1 Patrick Henry, Dry (1958)	...	31.50	7.00	.25
1052a	$1 Wet Printing (1955)	...	36.50	8.50	2.95
1053	$5 Alexander Hamilton,Perf.11 (1956)	...	425.00	100.00	8.50
1053	$5 Hamilton, Very Fine	...	500.00	120.00	10.00

NOTE: SETS CONTAIN OUR CHOICE OF WET OR DRY, TAGGED OR UNTAGGED.

1954-80 Liberty Series Coil Stamps, Perforated 10 (B) (VF+25%)

		Line Pairs	F-VF NH	F-VF Used
1054-59A	**Set of 8 ....**	**25.75**	**3.50**	**2.40**
1054-59A	**Very Fine Set of 8 ....**	**30.75**	**4.35**	**3.00**
#1054A and #1059 are Perforated Horizontally.				
1054	1¢ Washington, Dry, Small Holes (1960)	1.10	.25	.15
1054l	1¢ Washington, Dry, Large Holes (1957)	4.50	1.75	.60
1054c	1¢ Wet Printing, Large Holes (1954) .	4.25	.85	.25
1054A	1¼¢ Palace of Governors, Small Holes (1960)	2.50	.20	.15
1054Al	1¼¢ Large Holes	175.00	12.50	.90
1055	2¢ Jefferson, Dry, Large Holes (1957)	3.00	1.00	.25
1055a	2¢ Tagged, Small Holes,Shiny Gum (1968)	.60	.20	.15
1055av	2¢ Tagged, Small Holes, Dull Gum	2.25	.25	...
1055d	2¢ Wet Printing, Large Holes, Yellow Gum (1954)	5.00	.50	.40
1055dw	2¢ Wet,Large Holes, White Gum	32.50	4.25	...
1056	2½¢ Bunker Hill, Large Holes (1959) .	3.50	.25	.20
1056s	2½¢ Small Holes, Precancelled(1961)	...	525.00	150.00
1057	3¢ Liberty, Dry Printing, Large Holes (1956)	7.00	.60	.30
1057s	3¢ Liberty, Dry, Small Holes (1958)	.60	.20	.15
1057b	3¢ Tagged, Small Holes (1967)	37.50	2.00	1.75
1057d	3¢ Tagged, "Look Magazine" (1966) ..	...	10.75	...
1057c	3¢ Wet Printing,Large Holes (1954) ..	4.25	.75	.50
1058	4¢ Lincoln, Dry Printing, Large Holes (1958)	3.50	1.10	.40
1058s	4¢ Lincoln, Dry, Small Holes (1958) ...	1.40	.25	.15
1058b	4¢ Wet, Large Holes, Precancelled ...	475.00	45.00	1.00
1059	4½¢ Hermitage, Large Holes (1959) .	15.00	1.40	1.30
1059s	4½¢ Small Holes	525.00	29.50	...
1059A	25¢ Paul Revere (1965)	2.50	.85	.30
1059Ab	25¢ Tagged, Shiny Gum (1973)	5.00	1.00	.50
1059Ad	25¢ Tagged, Dull Gum (1980)	7.50	2.00	...

NOTE: SETS INCLUDE OUR CHOICE OF LARGE OR SMALL HOLES, TAGGED OR UNTAGGED.)

1954 Commemoratives (continued) (see also No.1029)

Scott's No.		Mint Sheet	Plate Block	F-VF NH	F-VF Used
1060	3¢ Nebraska Territory Centennial	13.50	1.30	.30	.15
1061	3¢ Kansas Territory Centennial ...	13.50	1.30	.30	.15
1062	3¢ George Eastman, Inventor .. (70)	16.00	1.10	.25	.15
1063	3¢ Lewis & Clark Expedition 150th	18.50	1.75	.40	.15

1955 Commemoratives

1064   1065   1068

1066   1067   1069

1070   1071   1072

1064-72 Set of 9	...	...	2.95	1.10

Scott's No.		Mint Sheet	Plate Block	F-VF NH	F-VF Used
1064	3¢ Penn. Academy of Fine Arts, Charles Wilson Peale	16.00	1.50	.35	.15
1065	3¢ Land Grant Colleges Centennial	18.50	1.75	.40	.15
1066	8¢ Rotary International 50th Ann.	28.50	2.65	.60	.15
1067	3¢ Armed Forces Reserves	9.00	.85	.20	.15
1068	3¢ Old Man of the Mtns, NH	16.00	1.50	.35	.15
1069	3¢ Soo Locks Centennial	18.50	1.75	.40	.15
1070	3¢ Atoms for Peace	11.50	1.10	.25	.15
1071	3¢ Fort Ticonderoga, NY Bicent. .	13.50	1.30	.30	.15
1072	3¢ Andrew Mellon, Financier ... (70)	23.75	1.50	.35	.15

1956 Commemoratives

1073   1074   1076

1075

1073-85 Set of 13	...	...	5.25	3.95
1073	3¢ B. Franklin 250th Anniv of Birth	13.50	1.35	.30	.15
1074	3¢ Booker T. Washington, Educator	13.50	1.35	.30	.15
1075	3¢ & 8¢ (FIPEX) Fifth International Philatelic Exhibition Souvenir Sheet	...	...	2.50	2.65
1075a	3¢ Liberty Single	...	...	1.00	1.10
1075b	8¢ Liberty Single	...	...	1.25	1.35
1076	3¢ FIPEX Stamp	9.00	.85	.20	.15

NOTE: WE HAVE ESTABLISHED A MINIMUM PRICE OF .20 FOR UNUSED STAMPS AND .15 PER USED STAMP. THIS INCLUDES THE VALUE OF THE STAMP PLUS THE COST INVOLVED IN PROCESSING. YOU CAN USUALLY SAVE SUBSTANTIALLY WHEN PURCHASING COMPLETE SETS.

1956 Commemoratives (continued)

1077   1078   1079

1080   1081   1082

1083   1084   1085

Scott's No.		Mint Sheet	Plate Block	F-VF NH	F-VF Used
1077	3¢ Wildlife - Wild Turkey	13.50	1.35	.30	.15
1078	3¢ Wildlife - Antelope	13.50	1.35	.30	.15
1079	3¢ Wildlife - King Salmon	16.50	1.50	.35	.15
1080	3¢ Pure Food & Drug Act 50th Ann.	11.50	1.10	.25	.15
1081	3¢ Wheatland, James Buchanan	13.50	1.30	.30	.15
1082	3¢ Labor Day, AFL-CIO	13.50	1.30	.30	.15
1083	3¢ Nassau Hall, Princeton 200th	13.50	1.30	.30	.15
1084	3¢ Devils Tower, Wyoming	13.50	1.30	.30	.15
1085	3¢ Children of the World	9.00	.85	.20	.15

1957 Commemoratives

1086   1087   1088

1089   1090   1091

1092   1093   1094

1095   1096   1097

1957 Commemoratives (cont.)

1098

1099

Scott's No.		Mint Sheet	Plate Block	F-VF NH	F-VF Used
1086-99	Set of 14	...	...	2.80	1.65
1086	3¢ Alexander Hamilton	9.00	.85	.20	.15
1087	3¢ Polio, March of Dimes	9.00	.85	.20	.15
1088	3¢ Coast & Geodetic Society 150th	9.00	.85	.20	.15
1089	3¢ Architects Institute Centennial	9.00	.85	.20	.15
1090	3¢ Steel Industry Centennial	9.00	.85	.20	.15
1091	3¢ Naval Review, Jamestown	9.00	.85	.20	.15
1092	3¢ Oklahoma Statehood 50th Ann.	13.50	1.30	.30	.15
1093	3¢ School Teachers	10.75	1.20	.25	.15
1094	4¢ 48-Star U.S. Flag	9.00	.85	.20	.15
1095	3¢ Shipbuilding 350th Anniv .... (70)	19.50	1.30	.30	.15
1096	8¢ Ramon Magsaysay .... (48)	10.75	1.10	.25	.15
1097	3¢ 200th Birth of Lafayette	13.50	1.30	.30	.15
1098	3¢ Wildlife - Whooping Crane	11.50	1.10	.25	.15
1099	3¢ Religious Freedom, Flushing Remonstrance 300th Anniv.	9.00	.85	.20	.15

Champions of Liberty Series: #1096,1110-11, 1117-18, 1125-26, 1137-38, 1147-48, 1159-60, 1165-66, 1168-69 and 1174-75.

1958 Commemoratives

1100

1104

1105

1106

1107

1108

1109

1110

1112

1113

1114

1115

1116

1118

1119

1958 Commemoratives (cont.)

1120

1121

1122

1123

Scott's No.		Mint Sheet	Plate Block	F-VF NH	F-VF Used
1100,1104-1123	Set of 21	...	...	4.50	2.50
1100	3¢ Gardening & Horticulture	9.00	.85	.20	.15
1104	3¢ Brussels World Fair	9.00	.85	.20	.15
1105	3¢ James Monroe .... (70)	12.75	.85	.20	.15
1106	3¢ Minnesota Statehood Centennial	13.50	1.30	.30	.15
1107	3¢ Geophysical Year 1957-58	9.00	.85	.20	.15
1108	3¢ Gunston Hall, VA, George Mason	9.00	.85	.20	.15
1109	3¢ Mackinac Bridge, MI Dedication	16.50	1.50	.35	.15
1110	4¢ Simon Bolivar, South America(70)	12.75	.85	.20	.15
1111	8¢ Simon Bolivar .... (72)	17.50	1.75	.25	.15
1112	4¢ Atlantic Cable Centennial	9.00	.85	.20	.15

1958-59 Abraham Lincoln Commemoratives

1113-16	Set of 4	47.50	4.65	1.10	.55
1113	1¢ Beardless Lincoln (1959)	4.00	.60	.20	.15
1114	3¢ Bust of Lincoln (1959)	13.50	1.30	.30	.15
1115	4¢ Lincoln-Douglas Debates	18.75	1.70	.40	.15
1116	4¢ Statue of Lincoln (1959)	13.50	1.30	.30	.15

1958 Commemoratives (continued)

1117	4¢ Lajos Kossuth, Hungary ...... (70)	12.75	.85	.20	.15
1118	8¢ Lajos Kossuth .... (72)	17.50	1.45	.25	.15
1119	4¢ Freedom of Press	9.00	.85	.20	.15
1120	4¢ Overland Mail Centennial	11.50	1.10	.25	.15
1121	4¢ Noah Webster, Author .... (70)	16.00	1.10	.25	.15
1122	4¢ Forest Conservation	13.50	1.30	.30	.15
1123	4¢ Fort Duquesne, Pittsburgh	13.50	1.30	.30	.15

1959 Commemoratives

1124

1126

1127

1134

1128

1129

1130

1131

1132

1133

1124-38	Set of 15	...	...	3.35	1.80
1124	4¢ Oregon Statehood 100th Ann.	13.50	1.30	.30	.15
1125	4¢ Jose San Martin, S.America (70)	12.50	.85	.20	.15
1126	8¢ Jose San Martin .... (72)	17.50	1.20	.25	.15
1127	4¢ N.A.T.O. 10th Anniv. .... (70)	12.50	.85	.20	.15
1128	4¢ Arctic Explorations	13.50	1.30	.30	.15
1129	8¢ World Peace through Trade ..	14.50	1.40	.30	.15
1130	4¢ Silver Discovery, NV Cent.	13.50	1.30	.30	.15
1131	4¢ St. Lawrence Seaway Opening	11.50	1.10	.25	.15
1132	4¢ 49-Star Flag	8.75	.85	.20	.15
1133	4¢ Soil Conservation	11.50	1.10	.25	.15
1134	4¢ Petroleum Industry Centennial	13.50	1.30	.30	.15

1959 Commemoratives (continued)

1135   1136   1137   1138

Scott's No.		Mint Sheet	Plate Block	F-VF NH	F-VF Used
1135	4¢ Dental Health, ADA Centennial	11.50	1.10	.25	.15
1136	4¢ Ernst Reuter. Berlin .... (70)	12.50	.85	.20	.15
1137	8¢ Ernst Reuter .... (72)	17.50	1.20	.25	.15
1138	4¢ Dr. Ephraim McDowell, Ovarian Operation 150th Anniv. .... (70)	19.50	1.30	.30	.15

1960 Commemoratives

1139   1140   1141

1142   1143   1144

Scott's No.		Mint Sheet	Plate Block	F-VF NH	F-VF Used
1139-73	Set of 35	...	...	8.25	4.25
1139-44	Credoes Set of 6	63.50	6.25	1.40	.80
1139	4¢ G.Washington Credo	11.50	1.10	.25	.15
1140	4¢ B.Franklin Credo	11.50	1.10	.25	.15
1141	4¢ T.Jefferson Credo	11.50	1.10	.25	.15
1142	4¢ F.S. Key Credo	13.50	1.30	.30	.15
1143	4¢ A.Lincoln Credo	11.50	1.10	.25	.15
1144	4¢ P.Henry Credo (1961)	11.50	1.10	.25	.15

1145   1146   1147   1151

1149   1150   1152

1153   1154   1155

1156   1157   1158   1159

1960 Commemoratives (continued)

Scott's No.		Mint Sheet	Plate Block	F-VF NH	F-VF Used
1145	4¢ Boy Scout Jubilee	21.00	2.00	.45	.15
1146	4¢ Winter Olympics, Squaw Valley	13.50	1.30	.30	.15
1147	4¢ Thomas G. Masaryk, Czech. (70)	12.50	.85	.20	.15
1148	8¢ Thomas G. Masaryk .... (72)	17.50	1.20	.25	.15
1149	4¢ World Refugee Year	8.75	.85	.20	.15
1150	4¢ Water Conservation	11.50	1.10	.25	.15
1151	4¢ (SEATO)Southeast Asia Treaty(70)	12.50	.85	.20	.15
1152	4¢ The American Woman	8.75	.85	.20	.15
1153	4¢ 50-Star Flag	8.75	.85	.20	.15
1154	4¢ Pony Express Centennial	21.00	2.00	.35	.15
1155	4¢ Employ the Handicapped	8.75	.85	.20	.15
1156	4¢ World Forestry Congress	13.50	1.30	.30	.15
1157	4¢ Mexican Independence 150th	8.75	.85	.20	.15
1158	4¢ U.S. - Japan Treaty Cent.	8.75	.85	.20	.15
1159	4¢ Ignacy Paderewski, Poland (70)	12.50	.85	.20	.15
1160	8¢ Ignacy Jan Paderewski .... (72)	19.75	1.40	.30	.15

1161   1162   1163   1167

1164   1165   1169

1170   1171   1172   1173

1161	4¢ Robert A. Taft, Senator .... (70)	19.50	1.30	.30	.15
1162	4¢ Wheels of Freedom	8.75	.85	.20	.15
1163	4¢ Boys' Club of America Cent. ..	13.50	1.30	.30	.15
1164	4¢ First Automated Post Office ...	18.50	1.70	.40	.15
1165	4¢ Gustaf Mannerheim,Finland (70)	12.50	.85	.20	.15
1166	8¢ Gustaf Mannerheim .... (72)	17.50	1.20	.25	.15
1167	4¢ Camp Fire Girls 50th Anniv. ...	22.50	2.25	.50	.15
1168	4¢ Guiseppe Garibaldi, Italy ..... (70)	11.50	.80	.20	.15
1169	8¢ Guiseppe Garibaldi .... (72)	17.50	1.20	.25	.15
1170	4¢ Walter F. George, Senator .. (70)	26.50	1.70	.40	.15
1171	4¢ Andrew Carnegie .... (70)	19.50	1.30	.30	.15
1172	4¢ John Foster Dulles .... (70)	19.50	1.30	.30	.15
1173	4¢ "Echo I" Communications Satellite	16.00	1.50	.35	.15

1961 Commemoratives

1174   1175   1176   1177

1178   1179   1180

1181   1182   1183

Scott's No.		Mint Sheet	Plate Block	F-VF NH	F-VF Used
1174-1190	Set of 17		...	5.35	2.00
1174	4¢ Mahatma Gandhi, India ...... (70)	12.50	.85	.20	.15
1175	8¢ Mahatma Gandhi .... (72)	17.50	1.20	.25	.15
1176	4¢ Range Conservation	11.50	1.10	.25	.15
1177	4¢ Horace Greeley, Publisher .. (70)	19.50	1.30	.30	.15

1961-1965 Civil War Centennial

1178-82	Set of 5	110.00	11.00	2.35	.55
1178	4¢ Fort Sumter (1961)	28.50	2.60	.60	.15
1179	4¢ Battle of Shiloh (1962)	16.00	1.50	.35	.15
1180	5¢ Gettysburg (1963)	21.00	2.10	.45	.15
1181	5¢ The Wilderness (1964)	18.75	1.85	.40	.15
1182	5¢ Appomattox (1965)	31.75	3.35	.65	.15

1184

1185

1186

1187

1188
1189
1190

1183	4¢ Kansas Statehood Centennial	13.50	1.30	.30	.15
1184	4¢ George W. Norris, Senator	16.00	1.50	.35	.15
1185	4¢ Naval Aviation 50th Anniv.	13.50	1.30	.30	.15
1186	4¢ Workmen's Compensation 50th	16.50	1.50	.35	.15
1186v	Plate Number Inverted	18.00	1.65	...	...
1187	4¢ Frederic Remington, Artist	13.50	1.30	.30	.15
1188	4¢ Republic of China, Sun Yat-sen	16.00	1.50	.35	.15
1189	4¢ Basketball - James Naismith .	16.00	1.50	.35	.15
1190	4¢ Nursing Profession	16.00	1.50	.35	.15

1962 Commemoratives (See also 1179)

1191

1192

1193

1195

1194

1196

1197

1198

1199

1200

1201

Scott's No.		Mint Sheet	Plate Block	F-VF NH	F-VF Used
1191-1207	Set of 17	...	...	3.95	2.00
1191	4¢ New Mexico Statehood 50th ..	13.50	1.10	.30	.15
1192	4¢ Arizona Statehood 50th Anniv.	13.50	1.10	.30	.15
1193	4¢ Project Mercury	12.00	1.10	.25	.15
1194	4¢ Malaria Eradication, WHO	8.75	.85	.20	.15
1195	4¢ Charles Evans Hughes	8.75	.85	.20	.15
1196	4¢ Seattle World's Fair	13.50	1.30	.30	.15
1197	4¢ Louisiana Statehood 150th Ann.	16.00	1.50	.35	.15
1198	4¢ Homestead Act Centennial	11.50	1.10	.25	.15
1199	4¢ Girl Scouts 50th Anniversary .	8.75	.85	.20	.15
1200	4¢ Brien McMahon, Senator; Atomic Energy Act	13.50	1.30	.30	.15
1201	4¢ Apprenticeship Act 25th Ann. .	8.75	.85	.20	.15

1202

1203

1205

1206

1207

1202	4¢ Sam Rayburn, Speaker-House	16.50	1.50	.35	.15
1203	4¢ Dag Hammarskjold, U.N.	8.75	.85	.20	.15
1204	4¢ Hammarskjold "Error"	9.00	1.60	.20	.15

Note: The yellow background is inverted on #1204

1205	4¢ Christmas Wreath .... (100)	17.50	.90	.20	.15
1206	4¢ Higher Education	8.75	.85	.20	.15
1207	4¢ Winslow Homer "Breezing Up"	12.00	1.10	.25	.15

1962-1963 Regular Issues, Perf.11x10½, Coils Perf.10 Vert.

1208

1209,1225

1213,1229

1208	5¢ Flag & White House (1963) (100)	18.50	.90	.20	.15
1208a	5¢ Flag Tagged (1966) .... (100)	28.50	2.00	.30	.20
1209	1¢ Andrew Jackson (1963) .... (100)	7.00	.60	.20	.15
1209a	1¢ Tagged (1966) .... (100)	7.50	.65	.20	.20
1213	5¢ George Washington .... (100)	18.50	.90	.20	.15
1213a	5¢ Pane of 5 "Mailman", Slogan 1	...	...	6.25	5.25
1213a	5¢ Pane of 5 "Use Zone", Slogan 2	...	...	19.75	12.50
1213a	5¢ Pane of 5 "Use Zip Code", Slogan 3	...	...	3.25	2.50
1213b	5¢ Tagged (1963) .... (100)	60.00	8.00	.65	.50
1213c	5¢ Pane of 5 "Zone" Tagged, Slogan 2	...	...	100.00	...
1213c	5¢ Pane of 5 "Zip" Tagged, Slogan 3	...	...	1.65	...
1225	1¢ A.Jackson Coil	Line Pr.		.25	.15
1225a	1¢ Coil, Tagged (1966)	Line Pr.		.75	.20	.15
1229	5¢ G.Washington Coil	Line Pr.		3.25	1.10	.15
1229a	5¢ Coil, Tagged (1963)	Line Pr.		9.75	1.65	.25

1963 Commemoratives (See also 1180)

1230

1231

1232

1235

1233
1234

1230-41	Set of 12	...	...	2.95	1.45
1230	5¢ Carolina Charter Tercentenary	18.50	1.70	.40	.15
1231	5¢ Food for Peace, Freedom-Hunger	8.75	.85	.20	.15

1236

1237

1238

1239

1240

1241

Scott's No.		Mint Sheet	Plate Block	F-VF NH	F-VF Used
1232	5¢ West Virginia Statehood Cent.	13.50	1.30	.30	.15
1233	5¢ Emancipation Proclamation Cent.	11.00	1.10	.25	.15
1234	5¢ Alliance for Progress	8.75	.85	.20	.15
1235	5¢ Cordell Hull, Secreatary of State	16.50	1.50	.35	.15
1236	5¢ Eleanor Roosevelt	13.50	1.30	.30	.15
1237	5¢ The Sciences, National Academy of Sciences Centenary	8.75	.85	.20	.15
1238	5¢ City Mail Delivery Centennial	8.75	.85	.20	.15
1239	5¢ Int'l. Red Cross Centenary	8.75	.85	.20	.15
1240	5¢ Christmas Tree .... (100)	27.50	1.30	.30	.15
1240a	5¢ Christmas, Tagged .... (100)	70.00	7.50	.70	.50
1241	5¢ John J. Audubon-Columbia Jays	13.75	1.30	.30	.15

1964 Commemoratives (See also 1181)

1243

1242

1244

1245

1246

1247

1248

1249

1250

1251

1242-60	Set of 19	...	...	5.75	2.25
1242	5¢ Sam Houston, Texas	18.50	1.75	.40	.15
1243	5¢ Charles M. Russell, "Jerked Down"	16.00	1.50	.35	.15
1244	5¢ New York World's Fair	13.50	1.30	.30	.15
1245	5¢ John Muir, Naturalist	13.50	1.30	.30	.15
1246	5¢ John F. Kennedy Memorial	23.50	2.25	.50	.15
1247	5¢ New Jersey Tercentenary	16.00	1.50	.35	.15
1248	5¢ Nevada Statehood Centennial	13.50	1.30	.30	.15
1249	5¢ Register and Vote	8.75	.85	.20	.15
1250	5¢ William Shakespeare	8.75	.85	.20	.15
1251	5¢ Doctors Mayo	14.50	1.40	.30	.15

FOR INFORMATION CONCERNING VERY FINE SEE PAGE II

1252

1254 1255
1256 1257

1253

1258

1259

1260

Scott's No.		Mint Sheet	Plate Block	F-VF NH	F-VF Used
1252	5¢ American Music, ASCAP 50th	8.75	.85	.20	.15
1253	5¢ Homemakers, Sampler	8.75	.85	.20	.15
1254-7	5¢ Christmas Flowers, Block of 4(100)	35.00	1.75	1.50	1.10
1254-7	5¢ Set of 4 Singles	...	...	1.30	.60
1254-7a	5¢ Christmas Tagged, Block of 4(100)	80.00	8.75	3.25	2.95
1254-7a	5¢ Set of 4 Singles	...	...	2.95	2.40
1258	5¢ Verrazano-Narrows Bridge	13.50	1.30	.30	.15
1259	5¢ Fine Arts - Stuart Davis	8.75	.85	.20	.15
1260	5¢ Amateur Radio 50th Anniv.	16.00	1.60	.35	.15

1965 Commemoratives

1262

1261

1263

1265

1264

1266

1267

1268

1269

1270

1261-76	Set of 16	...	...	4.00	2.15
1261	5¢ Battle of New Orleans 150th	21.50	1.95	.45	.15
1262	5¢ Physical Fitness - Sokol Cent.	8.75	.85	.20	.15
1263	5¢ Crusade Against Cancer	8.75	.85	.20	.15
1264	5¢ Wintston Churchill Memorial	13.50	1.30	.30	.15
1265	5¢ Magna Carta 750th Anniv.	8.75	.85	.20	.15
1266	5¢ Int'l. Cooperation Year, United Nations 20th Anniv.	8.75	.85	.20	.15
1267	5¢ Salvation Army Centennial	8.75	.85	.20	.15
1268	5¢ Dante Alighieri	8.75	.85	.20	.15
1269	5¢ Herbert Hoover	18.50	1.75	.40	.15
1270	5¢ Robert Fulton, The "Clermont"	8.75	.85	.20	.15

1965 Commemoratives (cont.)

1271

1272

1273

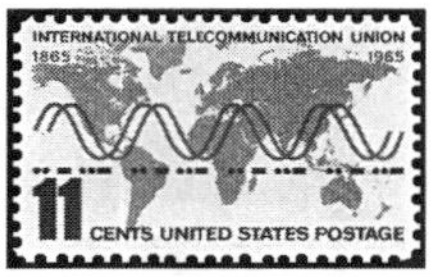

1274

1276

1275

Scott's No.		Mint Sheet	Plate Block	F-VF NH	F-VF Used
1271	5¢ Florida Settlement 400th Ann.	18.50	1.75	.40	.15
1272	5¢ Traffic Safety	8.75	.85	.20	.15
1273	5¢ John S. Copley Painting	13.50	1.30	.30	.15
1274	11¢ Telecommunication Union 100th	27.50	5.50	.50	.30
1275	5¢ Adlai Stevenson	8.75	.85	.20	.15
1276	5¢ Christmas Angel .... (100)	17.50	.90	.20	.15
1276a	5¢ Christmas, Tagged .... (100)	65.00	8.75	.65	.35

1965-79 Prominent Americans Series, Perf.11x10½, 10½x11

(Sheets of 100)

1278,1299

1279

1280

1281,1297

1282,1303

1283,1304

1283B,1304C

1284,1298

1285

1286

1286A

1287

1288/1305E

1289

1290

Scott's No.		Mint Sheet	Plate Block	F-VF NH	F-VF Used
1278-88,1289-95	**Set of 20 ....**	**...**	**112.50**	**24.00**	**5.25**
1278-88, 1289-95	**Very Fine Set of 20 ...**	**...**	**135.00**	**28.75**	**7.25**
	NOTE: SETS WILL CONTAIN OUR CHOICE OF TAGGED OR UNTAGGED.				
1278	1¢ Thomas Jefferson (1968)	7.00	.60	.20	.15
1278a	1¢ Booklet Pane of 8	...	...	1.10	1.10
1278ae	1¢ Pane of 8, Dull Exp. Gum	...	...	1.80	...
1278b	1¢ Booklet Pane of 4 (1971)	...	...	.80	.80
1279	1¼¢ Albert Gallatin (1967)	18.75	10.75	.20	.15
1280	2¢ Frank Lloyd Wright (1968)	8.00	.60	.20	.15
1280a	2¢ Booklet Pane of 5 (S4 or S5) ('68)	...	...	1.20	1.30
	S4 is "Mail Early", S5 is "Use Zip Code"				
1280c	2¢ Booklet Pane of 6 (1971)	...	...	1.10	1.30
1280ce	2¢Pane of 6, Dull Exp. Gum	...	...	1.10	...
1281	3¢ Francis Parkman (1967)	12.00	.75	.20	.15
1282	4¢ Abraham Lincoln	31.50	1.50	.35	.15
1282a	4¢ Lincoln, Tagged	27.50	1.30	.30	.15
1283	5¢ Washington, Dirty Face ('66) .	18.75	.80	.20	.15
1283a	5¢ Washington, Tagged	17.50	.80	.20	.15
1283B	5¢ Washington,Clean Face ('67)	16.00	.90	.20	.15
1283Bv	5¢ Clean Face, Dull Gum	39.50	3.25	.40	...
1284	6¢ Franklin D.Roosevelt (1966) ..	24.00	.95	.25	.15
1284a	6¢ F.D.R., Tagged	24.50	1.10	.25	.15
1284b	6¢ Booklet Pane of 8 (1967)	...	...	1.75	1.50
1284c	6¢ Pane of 5 (S4 or S5) (1968) ...	...	...	1.75	1.50
	S4 = Mail Early in the Day S5 = Use Zip Code				
1285	8¢ Albert Einstein (1966)	36.50	1.70	.40	.15
1285a	8¢ Einstein, Tagged	36.50	1.70	.40	.20
1286	10¢ Andrew Jackson (1967)	47.50	2.10	.50	.15
1286A	12¢ Henry Ford (1968)	67.50	3.00	.70	.15
1287	13¢ John F. Kennedy (1967)	55.00	2.50	.60	.15
1288	15¢ O.W. Holmes, Type I (1968)	42.50	2.10	.45	.15
1288d	15¢ Holmes, Type II (1979)	105.00	13.50	1.00	.20
1288B	15¢ Bklt. Single, Perforated 10 Type III	...	...	.50	.15
1288Bc	15¢ Bk. Pane of 8, Type III (1978)	...	...	3.75	4.00

1965-79 Prominent Americans Series (continued)

Scott's No.		Mint Sheet	Plate Block	F-VF NH	F-VF Used
1289	20¢ George C. Marshall (1967) ..	72.50	3.25	.75	.15
1289a	20¢ Tagged, Shiny Gum (1973) .	70.00	3.00	.70	.30
1289ad	20¢ Tagged, Dull Gum, ...	165.00	8.75	1.75	...
1290	25¢ Frederick Douglass, Rose Lake (1967)	100.00	4.75	1.10	.15
1290a	25¢ Tagged, Shiny Gum (1973) ..	95.00	4.25	1.00	.15
1290ad	25¢ Tagged, Dull Gum	140.00	8.50	1.50	...
1290b	25¢ F. Douglass, Magenta	...	175.00	27.50	...

1291

1292

1293

1294,1305C

1295

Scott's No.		Mint Sheet	Plate Block	F-VF NH	F-VF Used
1291	30¢ John Dewey (1968)	130.00	5.75	1.35	.15
1291a	30¢ Dewey, Tagged(1973)	110.00	5.00	1.20	.15
1292	40¢ Thomas Paine (1968)	125.00	5.95	1.35	.15
1292a	40¢ Tagged, Shiny Gum (1973) ..	110.00	5.00	1.20	.25
1292ad	40¢ Tagged, Dull Gum	140.00	7.50	1.50	...
1293	50¢ Lucy Stone (1968)	165.00	7.50	1.75	.15
1293a	50¢ Stone, Tagged (1973)	150.00	7.00	1.60	.25
1294	$1 Eugene O'Neill (1967)	350.00	15.75	3.75	.20
1294a	$1 O'Neill, Tagged (1973)	275.00	12.50	3.00	.20
1295	$5 John B. Moore (1966)	...	67.50	15.00	2.95
1295a	$5 Moore, Tagged (1973)	...	57.50	13.00	2.75

#1288 and 1305E: Die I top bar of "5" is horiz., tie touches lapel.
#1288d and 1305Ei: Die II top bar of "5" slopes down to right, tie does not touch lapel.
#1288B and 1288Bc: Die III booklets only, design shorter than Die I or II.

1297

1298

1304 Line Pair

1305

1966-81 Prominent Americans, Coils, Perforated 10 (B) (25%)

Scott's No.		Line Pair	F-VF NH	F-VF Used
1297-1305C	**Prominent Am. Coils (9) ....**	**14.50**	**5.25**	**2.10**
1297-1305C	**Very Fine Set of 9 ....**	**17.75**	**6.50**	**3.00**
1297	3¢ Francis Parkman, Shiny Gum (1975)	.60	.20	.15
1297d	3¢ Parkman, Dull Gum	5.00	.50	...
1297b	3¢ Bureau Precancel, Dull Gum	4.35	.50	.25
1297bs	3¢ Bureau Precancel, Shiny Gum	42.50	2.25	...
1298	6¢ F.D. Roosevelt, Perf. Horiz. 1967) .	1.50	.25	.15
1299	1¢ Thomas Jefferson (1968)	.50	.20	.15
1299a	1¢ Bureau Precancel	325.00	11.00	1.65
1303	4¢ Abraham Lincoln	.80	.30	.15
1303a	4¢ Bureau Precancel	300.00	10.00	.95
1304	5¢ Washington,Original, Shiny Gum ...	.50	.20	.15
1304d	5¢ Original, Dull Gum	8.50	1.10	...
1304a	5¢ Bureau Precancel	300.00	9.75	.75
1304C	5¢ Redrawn, Clean Face (1981)	2.00	.25	.15
1305	6¢ F.D.Roosevelt, Pf. Vert. ('68)	.75	.30	.15
1305b	6¢ Bureau Precancel	600.00	25.00	1.25
1305E	15¢ O.W.Holmes, Shiny Gum, Type I (1978)	1.30	.45	.15
1305Ed	15¢ Type I, Dull Gum	8.25	2.25	...
1305Ef	15¢ Bureau Precancel	...	45.00	42.50
1305Ei	15¢ Holmes, Type II, Dull Gum (1979)	3.00	.80	.25
1305C	$1 Eugene O'Neill, Shiny Gum (1973)	8.50	3.50	1.10
1305Cd	$1 O'Neill, Dull Gum	10.50	4.25	...

NOTE: F.VF, NH Bureau Precancels have full original gum and have never been used.

1966 Commemoratives

1306

1307

1308

1309

1310

1312

1966 Commemoratives

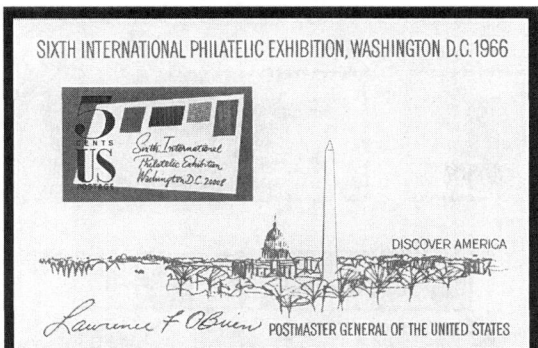

1311

Scott's No.		Mint Sheet	Plate Block	F-VF NH	F-VF Used
1306-22	Set of 17	8.75	...	3.80	2.10
1306	5¢ Migratory Bird Treaty 50th	8.75	.85	.20	.15
1307	5¢ Humane Treatment of Animals	8.75	.85	.20	.15
1308	5¢ Indiana Statehood 150th Ann.	23.00	2.15	.50	.15
1309	5¢ American Circus (Clown)	21.50	2.00	.45	.15
1310	5¢ (SIPEX) Sixth International Philatelic Exhibition Stamp	8.75	.85	.20	.15
1311	5¢ SIPEX Souvenir Sheet	...	...	.20	.20
1312	5¢ Bill of Rights	8.75	.85	.20	.15

1313

1314

1315

1316

1317

1318

1319

1320

1321   **1322**

1313	5¢ Polish Christianity Millenium ..	8.75	.85	.20	.15
1314	5¢ National Park Service 50th Ann.	11.50	1.10	.25	.15
1314a	5¢ Parks, Tagged	16.50	2.00	.35	.30
1315	5¢ Marine Corps Reserve 50th Ann.	8.75	.85	.20	.15
1315a	5¢ Marines, Tagged	16.50	2.00	.35	.30
1316	5¢ Fed. of Women's Clubs 75th .	8.75	.85	.20	.15
1316a	5¢ Women's Clubs, Tagged	16.50	2.00	.35	.30
1317	5¢ Folklore: Johnny Appleseed ...	13.50	1.30	.30	.15
1317a	5¢ Appleseed, Tagged	18.50	2.25	.40	.30
1318	5¢ Beautification of America	8.75	.85	.20	.15
1318a	5¢ Beautification, Tagged	16.50	2.00	.50	.30
1319	5¢ Great River Road	21.50	1.95	.45	.15
1319a	5¢ Great River Road, Tagged	23.50	2.25	.50	.30
1320	5¢ Savings Bond - Servicemen ..	8.75	.85	.20	.15
1320a	5¢ Savings Bonds, Tagged	16.50	2.00	.35	.30
1321	5¢ Christmas, Madonna and Child by Hemming .... (100)	17.50	.90	.20	.15
1321a	5¢ Christmas, Tagged .... (100)	32.50	2.25	.35	.30
1322	5¢ Mary Cassatt "The Boating Party"	8.75	.85	.20	.15
1322a	5¢ Cassatt, Tagged	16.50	2.00	.35	.30

NOTE: FROM #752 TO DATE, AVERAGE QUALITY STAMPS, WHEN AVAILABLE, WILL BE PRICED AT APPROX. 20% BELOW THE APPROPRIATE FINE QUALITY PRICE. VERY FINE COPIES OF #752-DATE ARE AVAILABLE FOR THE FOLLOWING PREMIUMS: ADD 10¢ TO ANY ITEM PRICED UNDER 50¢. ADD 20% TO ANY ITEM PRICED AT 50¢ & UP. UNLESS PRICED AT VERY FINE, SETS ARE NOT AVAILABLE VERY FINE STAMPS SHOULD BE LISTED INDIVIDUALLY WITH APPROPRIATE PREMIUM.

1967 Commemoratives

1323

1324

1325

1326

1327

1328

1329

1330

1333

1334

1331   1332

1335   **1337**   **1336**

Scott's No.		Mint Sheet	Plate Block	F-VF NH	F-VF Used
1323-37	Set of 15	...	...	5.50	1.85
1323	5¢ National Grange Centennial ..	11.50	1.10	.25	.15
1324	5¢ Canada Nationhood Centenary	8.75	.85	.20	.15
1325	5¢ Erie Canal 150th Anniversary	16.00	1.50	.35	.15
1326	5¢ Search for Peace - Lions 50th	13.50	1.30	.30	.15
1327	5¢ Henry David Thoreau, Writer .	16.00	1.50	.35	.15
1328	5¢ Nebraska Statehood Centennial	16.00	1.50	.35	.15
1329	5¢ Voice of America 25th Anniv. .	8.75	.85	.20	.15
1330	5¢ Folklore: Davy Crockett	16.00	1.50	.35	.15
1331-2	5¢ Accomplishments in Space, Pair	50.00	5.25	2.25	1.50
1331-2	5¢ Set of 2 Singles	...	...	1.80	.40
1333	5¢ Urban Planning	8.75	.85	.20	.15
1334	5¢ Finnish Independence 50th Ann.	8.75	.85	.20	.15
1335	5¢ Thomas Eakins "The Biglin Brothers Racing" Painting	13.50	1.30	.30	.15
1336	5¢ Christmas, Madonna	8.75	.85	.20	.15
1337	5¢ Mississippi Statehood 150th Ann.	22.50	2.15	.50	.15

1968-71 Regular Issues

1338

1338A,D

1338F,G

1338	6¢ Flag & White House, Giori . (100)	18.00	.85	.20	.15
1338D	6¢ Flag, Huck Press (1970) .... (100)	18.50 (20)	4.25	.20	.15
1338F	8¢ Flag & White House (1971) (100)	27.50 (20)	6.25	.30	.15
1338A	6¢ Flag & W.House Coil (1969) .. Full Line Pr.	5.50		.25	.15
1338A	6¢ Flag & W.House Coil (1969) .. Partial Line Pr.	1.25		...	...
1338G	8¢ Flag & W.House Coil (1971) .. Partial Line Pr.	2.75		.25	.15

NOTE: #1338 is 19mm x 22mm, Perforated 11, #1338A-G are18¼mm x 21 mm. #1338D,38F Perforated 11x10½. #1338A,G Perforated 10 Vertically.

1339

1341

1340

1968 Commemoratives

Scott's No.		Mint Sheet	Plate Block	F-VF NH	F-VF Used
1339-40,42-64	Set of 25	...	...	8.95	4.75
1339	6¢ Illinois Statehood 150th Anniv.	18.50	1.70	.40	.15
1340	6¢ HemisFair '68, San Antonio ...	9.00	.85	.20	.15

1968 Airlift to Servicemen

1341	$1 Eagle Holding Pennant	150.00	12.75	3.00	2.25

1968 Commemoratives (cont.)

1342

1343

1344

1345

1346

1347

1348

1349

1350

1351

1352

1353

1354

1355

1356

1342	6¢ Support Our Youth - Elks	9.00	.85	.20	.15
1343	6¢ Law and Order, Policeman	16.75	1.70	.35	.15
1344	6¢ Register and Vote	9.00	.85	.20	.15

1968 Historic American Flags

1345-54	6¢ Historic Flags, Strip/10	21.50 (20)	9.75	4.50	4.75
1345-46	6¢ Plate Blk. of 4	...	2.00	...	...
1345-54	6¢ Set of 10 Singles	...	...	4.00	3.25
1345	6¢ Fort Moultrie	...	...	.50	.35
1346	6¢ Fort McHenry	...	...	.50	.35
1347	6¢ Washington's Cruisers	...	...	.45	.35
1348	6¢ Bennington	...	...	.45	.35
1349	6¢ Rhode Island	...	...	.45	.35
1350	6¢ First Stars & Stripes	...	...	.45	.35
1351	6¢ Bunker Hill	...	...	.45	.35
1352	6¢ Grand Union	...	...	.45	.35
1353	6¢ Philadelphia Light Horse	...	...	.45	.35
1354	6¢ First Navy Jack	...	...	.45	.35

1968 Commemoratives (continued)

1355	6¢ Walt Disney, Animator	42.50	4.00	.90	.20
1356	6¢ Father Marquette, Jesuit	18.50	1.70	.40	.15

1968 Commemoratives (continued)

1357

1358

1359

1360

1362

1361

1363

1364

1357	6¢ Folklore: Daniel Boone	16.00	1.50	.35	.15
1358	6¢ Arkansas River Navigation	28.50	2.50	.60	.15
1359	6¢ Leif Erikson, Norse Explorer ..	11.50	1.10	.25	.15
1360	6¢ Cherokee Strip Opening 75th	13.50	1.30	.30	.15
1361	6¢ John Trumbull "The Battle of Bunker Hill"	18.50	1.70	.40	.15
1362	6¢ Waterfowl Conservation	13.50	1.35	.30	.15
1363	6¢ Christmas, Angel Gabriel	9.00 (10)	2.25	.20	.15
1363a	6¢ Christmas, Untagged	21.50 (10)	4.75	.45	.25
1364	6¢ American Indian: Chief Joseph	16.00	1.50	.35	.15

1969 Commemoratives

1365 **1366**

1367 **1368**

1369

1370

1371

1373

1372

1374

1375

1365-86	Set of 22 (no precancels)	...	...	9.25	3.15
1365-8	6¢ Beautification, Block of 4	25.00	2.50	2.10	2.25
1365-8	6¢ Set of 4 Singles	...	...	1.75	.75
1369	6¢ American Legion 50th Anniv. .	9.00	.85	.20	.15
1370	6¢ Grandma Moses "July Fourth"	9.00	.85	.20	.15
1371	6¢ Apollo 8 Mission	16.00	1.50	.35	.15
1372	6¢ W.C. Handy, Jazz	18.50	1.70	.40	.15
1373	6¢ California Settlement 200th Ann.	16.00	1.50	.35	.15
1374	6¢ John Wesley Powell, Geologist	18.50	1.70	.40	.15
1375	6¢ Alabama Statehood 150th Ann.	18.50	1.70	.40	.15

1969 Commemoratives (continued)

1376 1377
1378 1379

1381   1380   1382

1383   1385   1386

1384   1384 Precancel

Scott's No.		Mint Sheet	Plate Block	F-VF NH	F-VF Used
1376-9	6¢ Botanical Congress, Block of 4	30.75	3.00	2.75	2.65
1376-9	6¢ Set of Singles	...	...	2.50	.80
1380	6¢ Dartmouth College, D.Webster	16.50	1.50	.35	.15
1381	6¢ Professional Baseball 100th ..	42.50	4.25	.90	.20
1382	6¢ College Football 100th Anniv.	26.50	2.40	.55	.15
1383	6¢ D.D. Eisenhower Memorial . (32)	9.00	1.30	.30	.15
1384	6¢ Christmas, Winter Sunday	11.50 (10)	2.75	.25	.15
1384a	6¢ Precancelled (Set of 4 Cities)	210.00(10)	120.00	3.00	2.50

NOTE: #1384a EXISTS WITH "ATLANTA, GA"; "BALTIMORE, MD", MEMPHIS, TN"
AND "NEW HAVEN, CT" PRECANCELS.

1385	6¢ Hope for Crippled Children	9.00	.85	.20	.15
1386	6¢ William M. Harnett "Old Models"(32)	6.00	.85	.20	.15

1970 Commemoratives

1387   1388
1389   1390

1391   1392

1970 Commemoratives

Scott's No.		Mint Sheet	Plate Block	F-VF NH	F-VF Used
1387-92,1405-22	Set of 24 (no precan.)	...	...	7.75	3.00
1387-90	6¢ Natural History, Block of 4 (32)	7.75	1.20	1.00	1.10
1387-90	6¢ Set of 4 Singles	...	...	.95	.70
1391	6¢ Maine Statehood 150th Anniv.	23.50	2.15	.50	.15
1392	6¢ Wildlife Conservation - Buffalo	13.50	1.50	.30	.15

1970-74 Regular Issue, Perforated 11x10½, 10½x11

1393,1401   1393D   1394-95,1402   1396

1397   1398   1399   1400

Scott's No.				F-VF NH	F-VF Used
1393-94,1396-1400	Set of 8	...	...	3.35	1.10
1393	6¢ Eisenhower, Shiny Gum .... (100)	22.50	1.10	.25	.15
1393a	6¢ Booklet Pane of 8, Shiny Gum			2.10	2.25
1393v	6¢ Eisenhower, Dull Gum .... (100)	39.50	4.00	.40	.15
1393ae	6¢ Pane of 8, Dull Experimental Gum	...	...	1.75	...
1393b	6¢ Bklt. Pane of 5, (S4 or S5) (1971)			1.50	1.40
1393D	7¢ B. Franklin, Shiny Gum ('72)(100)	27.50	1.30	.30	.15
1393Dv	7¢ Franklin, Dull Gum .... (100)	39.50	2.75	.40	...
1394	8¢ Eisenhower,Multicolored, Perforated 11 (1971) .... (100)	27.50	1.30	.30	.15
1395	8¢ Eisenhower, Deep Claret, Shiny Gum, Booklet Single			.35	.15
1395a	Booklet Pane of 8, Shiny Gum (1971)	...	...	2.40	2.25
1395b	Booklet Pane of 6, Shiny Gum (1971)	...	...	1.95	1.80
1395v	8¢ Booklet Single, Dull Gum	...	...	.35	...
1395c	Booklet Pane of 4 Dull (1972)	...	...	1.95	1.75
1395d	Booklet Pane of 7, Dull (S4) (1972)	...	...	3.25	2.50
1395d	Booklet Pane of 7, Dull (S5) (1972)	...	...	2.10	1.95
	S4 is "Mail Early", S5 is "Use Zip Code"				
1396	8¢ U.S. Postal Service (1971) (100)	22.50 (12)	3.25	.25	.15
1396	8¢ U.S. Postal Service	...	(20) 5.25	...	...
1397	14¢ Fiorello La Guardia (1972) (100)	35.00	1.60	.40	.15
1398	16¢ Ernie Pyle (1971) .... (100)	85.00	3.75	.90	.20
1399	18¢ Elizabeth Blackwell (1974)(100)	52.50	2.25	.55	.15
1400	21¢ Amadeo P. Giannini (1973)(100)	67.50	3.00	.70	.25

NOTE: #1395 ONLY EXISTS WITH ONE OR MORE STRAIGHT EDGES SINCE IT COMES FROM BOOKLET PANES.

1970-71 Dwight D. Eisenhower, Coils, Perf. 10 Vertically

Scott's No.		Line Pair	F-VF NH	F-VF Used
1401	6¢ Gray, Shiny Gum	.60	.25	.15
1401d	6¢ Dull Gum	3.00	.65	...
1401a	6¢ Bureau Precancel	500.00	27.50	2.95
1402	8¢ Deep Claret ('71)	.75	.30	.15
1402b	8¢ Bureau Precancel	210.00	8.50	.95

1970 Commemoratives (continued)

1405   1406   1407

1408   1409   1419

1414   1414a   1420

1970 Commemoratives (continued)

1410 1411
1412 1413

1415 1416
1417 1418

1421 1422

Scott's No.		Mint Sheet	Plate Block	F-VF NH	F-VF Used
1405	6¢ Edgar Lee Masters, Poet	16.00	1.50	.35	.15
1406	6¢ Women Suffrage 50th Anniv. .	11.75	1.10	.25	.15
1407	6¢ South Carolina Founding Tercen.	18.50	1.70	.40	.15
1408	6¢ Stone Mountain Memorial	16.00	1.50	.35	.15
1409	6¢ Fort Snelling, Minnesota 150th	16.00	1.50	.35	.15
1410-13	6¢ Anti-Pollution, Block of 4	18.75 (10)	4.75	1.75	1.70
1410-13	6¢ Set of 4 Singles	...	...	1.60	.65
1414	6¢ Christmas, Nativity, Ty. I	9.00 (8)	1.65	.20	.15
1414a	6¢ Christmas, Nativity, Precancel	11.75 (8)	2.75	.25	.20
1414d	6¢ Type II, Horiz. Gum Breakers .	52.50 (8)	10.75	1.10	.30
1414e	6¢ Type II, Precancelled	60.00 (8)	12.50	1.25	.35
Type I - blurry impression, snowflakes in sky, no gum breakers					
Type II – sharper impression, no snowflakes in sky, with gum breakers					
1415-18	6¢ Christmas Toys, Block of 4 ..	25.00 (8)	5.00	2.35	2.25
1415-18	6¢ Set of 4 Singles	...	...	1.95	.60
1415a-18a	6¢ Toys, Precancelled, Block-4	37.50 (8)	7.50	3.50	3.50
1415a-18a	6¢ Set of 4 Singles	...	...	2.75	1.00
1419	6¢ United Nations 25th Anniv	9.00	.85	.20	.15
1420	6¢ Landing of the Pilgrims 350th	9.00	.85	.20	.15
1421-22	6¢ Disabled American Veterans - Servicemen, Pair	10.75	1.40	.50	.50
1421-22	6¢ Set of 2 Singles	...	...	.45	.30

1971 Commemoratives

1423

1425

1424

1427 1428
1429 1430

1971 Commemoratives (cont.)

1426

1432

1431

1433 1434 1435

1436

1437

1438

1439

1440 1441
1442 1443

1444

1445

1446

1447

Scott's No.		Mint Sheet	Plate Block	F-VF NH	F-VF Used
1423-45	Set of 23	...	...	6.50	3.15
1423	6¢ American Wool Industry	9.00	.85	.20	.15
1424	6¢ Gen. Douglas MacArthur	23.50	2.15	.50	.15
1425	6¢ Blood Donor Program	9.00	.85	.20	.15
1426	8¢ Missouri Statehood 150th Ann .	26.50 (12)	6.75	.55	.15
1427-30	8¢ Wildlife, Block of 4 .... (32)	9.25	1.35	1.20	1.10
1427-30	8¢ Set of 4 Singles	...	...	1.10	.70
1431	8¢ Antarctic Treaty	11.50	1.10	.25	.15
1432	8¢ American Revolution Bicentennnial Emblem	13.50	1.25	.30	.15
1433	8¢ John Sloan "The Wake of the Ferry" Painting	11.50	1.10	.25	.15
1434-5	8¢ Space Achievement, Pair	12.75	1.15	.55	.55
1434-5	8¢ Set of 2 Singles	...	...	.50	.30
1436	8¢ Emily Dickinson, Poet	16.00	1.50	.35	.15
1437	8¢ San Juan, Puerto Rico 450th ...	13.50	1.30	.30	.15
1438	8¢ Prevent Drug Abuse	11.50 (6)	1.60	.25	.15
1439	8¢ CARE 25th Anniversary	11.50 (8)	2.10	.25	.15
1440-3	8¢ Historic Preservation,Block-4(32)	10.75	1.50	1.35	1.10
1440-3	8¢ Set of 4 Singles	...	...	1.30	.70
1444	8¢ Christmas, Adoration	11.50 (12)	3.25	.25	.15
1445	8¢ Christmas, Partridge	11.50 (12)	3.25	.25	.15

1972 Commemoratives

1448 1449
1450 1451

1452

1454

National Parks Centennial

1453

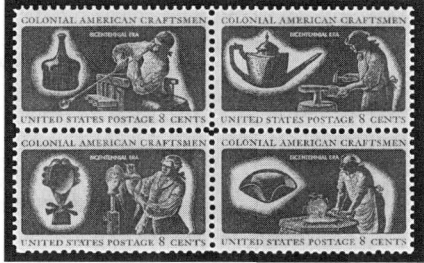

1456 1457
1458 1459

Family Planning

1455

Scott's No.		Mint Sheet	Plate Block	F-VF NH	F-VF Used
1446-74	**Set of 29**	...	...	**8.75**	**3.95**
1446	8¢ Sidney Lanier, Poet	18.00	1.70	.40	.15
1447	8¢ Peace Corps	11.75 (6)	1.60	.25	.15
1448-54,C84	National Parks Set of 8	72.50	7.00	2.00	1.15
1448-51	2¢ Cape Hatteras, Block of 4 (100)	9.75	.75	.60	.55
1448-51	2¢ Set of 4 Singles	...	...	.55	.45
1452	6¢ Wolf Trap Farm, VA	13.50	1.30	.30	.15
1453	8¢ Old Faithful, Yellowstone .... (32)	10.75	1.50	.35	.15
1454	15¢ Mt. McKinley, Alaska	25.00	2.35	.55	.25
	See #C84 for 11¢ City of Refuge National Park Issue				
1455	8¢ Family Planning	11.50	1.10	.25	.15
1456-9	8¢ Colonial Craftsmen, Block of 4	13.50	1.30	1.20	1.10
1456-9	8¢ Set of 4 Singles	...	...	1.10	.60

1460

1461

1462

1463

1464 1465
1466 1467

1469

1468

1470

1460-62,C85	Olympics Set of 4	55.00	12.50	1.20	.75
1460	6¢ Olympics - Bicycling	9.00 (10)	2.10	.20	.15
1461	8¢ Olympics - Bobsledding	11.50 (10)	2.65	.25	.15
1462	15¢ Olympics - Running	21.00 (10)	4.75	.45	.35
	See #C85 for 11¢ Olympics				

1973 Commemoratives (continued)

Scott's No.		Mint Sheet	Plate Block	F-VF NH	F-VF Used
1463	8¢ Parent Teacher Assn 75th Ann.	16.00	1.50	.35	.15
1463r	8¢ P.T.A. Error Plate # Reversed	17.00	1.65	...	...
1464-7	8¢ Wildlife Conservation, Block-4(32)	9.25	1.40	1.20	1.10
1464-7	8¢ Set of 4 Singles	...	...	1.10	.70
1468	8¢ Mail Order Business	16.50 (12)	4.35	.35	.15
1469	8¢ Osteopathic Medicine	28.50 (6)	3.75	.60	.15
1470	8¢ Folklore: Tom Sawyer	18.00	1.75	.40	.15

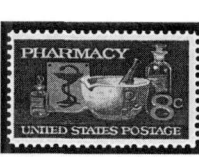

1471 1472 1473 1474

1471	8¢ Christmas Angel	11.50 (12)	3.25	.25	.15
1472	8¢ Christmas, Santa Claus	13.75 (12)	3.75	.30	.15
1473	8¢ Pharmacy	18.75	2.00	.40	.15
1474	8¢ Stamp Collecting .... (40)	9.25	1.10	.25	.15

1973 Commemoratives

1475 1476 1477

1478 1479 1488

1480 1481
1482 1483

1484

1485 1486 1487

1475-1508	**Set of 34**	...	...	**9.85**	**5.00**
1475	8¢ Love	11.50 (6)	1.60	.25	.15
1476-79	Communications in Colonial America(4)	43.75	4.15	.95	.55
1476	8¢ Printers and Patriots	11.50	1.10	.25	.15
1477	8¢ Posting a Broadside	11.50	1.10	.25	.15
1478	8¢ Postrider	11.50	1.10	.25	.15
1479	8¢ Drummer	11.50	1.10	.25	.15
1480-83	8¢ Boston Tea Party, Block of 4	15.00	1.50	1.35	1.10
1480-83	Set of 4 Singles	...	...	1.25	.60
1484-87	Arts Set of 4	42.50	14.50	1.10	.55
1484	8¢ George Gershwin,Composer (40)	9.00 (12)	3.25	.25	.15
1485	8¢ Robinson Jeffers, Poet .... (40)	11.50 (12)	3.75	.25	.15
1486	8¢ Henry Tanner, Painter .... (40)	9.00 (12)	3.25	.25	.15
1487	8¢ Willa Cather, Novelist .... (40)	15.00 (12)	5.00	.40	.15
1488	8¢ Nicolaus Copernicus	11.50	1.10	.25	.15

VERY FINE COPIES OF #752-DATE ARE AVAILABLE FOR THE FOLLOWING PREMIUMS:
ADD 10¢ TO ANY ITEM PRICED UNDER 50¢. ADD 20% TO ANY ITEM PRICED AT 50¢ & UP.

1973 Postal Service Employees

1488	1490	1491	1492	1493

1494	1495	1496	1497	1498

Scott's No.		Mint Sheet	Plate Block	F-VF NH	F-VF Used
1489-98	8¢ Postal Employees, Strip of 10 .	15.75 (20)	7.00	3.25	2.50
1489-98	8¢ Set of 10 Singles	...	...	3.00	2.00

1973 Commemoratives (continued)

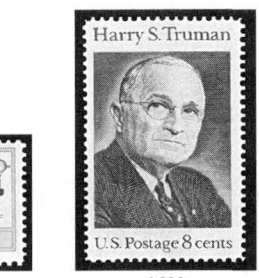

1500	1499	1501

1502	1503	1504

1505	1507	1508
1506		

1499	8¢ Harry S Truman .... (32)	16.75	2.35	.55	.15
1500-2,C86 Electronics Set of 4		59.50	5.15	1.25	.80
1500	6¢ Marconi's Spark Coil	11.50	1.00	.25	.15
1501	8¢ Transistors & Circuit Board	11.75	1.00	.25	.15
1502	15¢ Various Inventions	21.75	1.85	.45	.35
See #C86 for 11¢ Electronics					
1503	8¢ Lyndon B. Johnson .... (32)	15.00 (12)	6.50	.50	.15
1504-6	Rural America				
1504	8¢ Angus & Longhorn Cattle	16.50	1.50	.35	.15
1505	10¢ Chautauqua Tent (1974)	13.50	1.30	.30	.15
1506	10¢ Wheat Fields & Train(1974) ...	18.50	1.75	.40	.15
1507	8¢ Christmas, Madonna	11.50 (12)	3.25	.25	.15
1508	8¢ Christmas, Needlepoint Tree ...	11.50 (12)	3.25	.25	.15

1973-1974 Regular Issues, Perforated 11x10½

1509,1519	1510,1520	1511	1518

Scott's No.		Mint Sheet	Plate Block	F-VF NH	F-VF Used
1509	10¢ Crossed Flags .... (100)	33.50 (20)	7.50	.35	.15
1510	10¢ Jefferson Memorial .... (100)	28.50	1.35	.30	.15
1510b	Booklet Pane of 5	...	...	2.25	2.15
1510c	Booklet Pane of 8	...	...	2.40	2.50
1510d	Booklet Pane of 6 (1974)	...	...	10.00	5.25
1511	10¢ Zip Code (1974) .... (100)	28.00 (8)	2.50	.30	.15

1973-74 Regular Issue Coils, Perf. 10 Vertically

Scott's No.		Line Pair	F-VF NH	F-VF Used
1518	6.3¢ Liberty Bell (1974)	.70	.25	.15
1518a	6.3¢ Bureau Precancel	1.50	.35	.20
1519	10¢ Crossed Flags .... Full 6.75 Part 2.75		.35	.15
1520	10¢ Jefferson Memorial	.75	.30	.15
1520a	10¢ Bureau Precancel	170.00	6.00	1.50

1974 Commemoratives (See also 1505-06)

1525	1526	1527

1528	1529

1530	1531	1532	1533
1534	1535	1536	1537

Scott's No.		Mint Sheet	Plate Block	F-VF NH	F-VF Used
1525-52	**Set of 28**	...	...	**9.25**	**4.35**
1525	10¢ Veterans of Foreign Wars	13.50	1.30	.30	.15
1526	10¢ Robert Frost, Poet	21.00	1.90	.45	.15
1527	10¢ Expo '74, Spokane .... (40)	15.00 (12)	5.00	.40	.15
1528	10¢ Horse Racing: Kentucky Derby and Churchill Downs Centennial ..	21.00 (12)	5.50	.45	.15
1529	10¢ Skylab I	13.50	1.30	.30	.15
1530-37	10¢ Universal Postal Union Centenary Block of 8 .... (32)	11.50 (10)	3.50	2.75	2.50
1530-37	10¢ Strip of 8	...	...	2.75	2.50
1530-37	10¢ Plate Block of 16	... (16)	5.95		
1530-37	10¢ Set of 8 Singles	...	...	2.65	2.00

❑ Membership Application/Information (<u>Dealers Only</u>)

❑ A list of stamp dealers in my geographic area

❑ A list of dealers specializing in my area of collecting

❑ A list of retail stores

Name: _____

Address: _____

City: _____

State: _____ Zip: _____

Speciality Area: _____

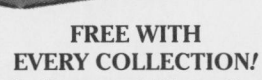

40C

1538
1539

1540
1541

1542

1543
1545

1544
1546

1547

1548

1549

1551

1550

1552

Scott's No.	Mint Sheet	Plate Block	F-VF NH	F-VF Used
1538-41 10¢ Mineral Heritage Block of 4 (48)	15.00	1.50	1.35	1.10
1538-41 10¢ Strip of 4	...	...	1.30	1.00
1538-41 10¢ Set of 4 Singles	...	...	1.20	.60
1542 10¢ Kentucky Settlement 150th	18.00	1.70	.40	.15
1543-46 10¢ First Continental				
Congress, Block of 4	18.50	1.80	1.60	1.20
1543-46 10¢ Set of 4 Singles	...	...	1.50	.60
1547 10¢ Energy Conservation	13.50	1.30	.30	.15
1548 10¢ Folklore: Sleepy Hollow	13.50	1.30	.30	.15
1549 10¢ Retarded Children	13.50	1.30	.30	.15
1550-52 Christmas Issues				
1550 10¢ Angel	13.50 (10)	3.25	.30	.15
1551 10¢ Currier & Ives "The Road Winter"	13.50 (12)	3.75	.30	.15
1552 10¢ Peace on Earth, Self-adhesive	16.00 (20)	7.25	.35	.25
1552 10¢ Same - Plate Block of 12	...	(12) 4.50	...	...

NOTE: MOST UNUSED COPIES OF #1552 ARE DISCOLORED FROM THE ADHESIVE. PRICE IS FOR DISCOLORED COPIES.

1975 Commemoratives

1553

1555

1554

1556

1557

1558

1559

1560

1561

1562

1563

1564

1567
1565

1568
1566

1569
1570

1571

1573
1575

1572
1574

Scott's No.	Mint Sheet	Plate Block	F-VF NH	F-VF Used
1553-80 Set of 28 (No #1580B)	...	...	9.25	3.95
1553-55 American Arts Issue				
1553 10¢ Benjamin West Self Portrait	20.75 (10)	4.75	.45	.15
1554 10¢ Paul Laurence Dunbar, Poet	20.75 (10)	4.75	.45	.15
1555 10¢ D.W. Griffith, Motion Pictures	20.75	1.90	.45	.15
1556 10¢ Space Pioneer - Jupiter	16.00	1.50	.35	.15
1557 10¢ Space Mariner 10	16.00	1.50	.35	.15
1558 10¢ Collective Bargaining	13.50 (8)	2.50	.30	.15
1559-62 Contributors to the Cause (4)	65.00	15.00	1.40	.80
1559 8¢ Sybil Ludington	11.50 (10)	2.65	.25	.20
1560 10¢ Salem Poor	16.00 (10)	3.75	.35	.15
1561 10¢ Haym Salomon	16.00 (10)	3.75	.35	.15
1562 18¢ Peter Francisco	25.00 (10)	6.25	.55	.40
1563 10¢ Lexington-Concord 200th (40)	15.00 (12)	4.95	.40	.15
1564 10¢ Battle of Bunker Hill 200th (40)	13.50 (12)	4.50	.35	.15
1565-68 10¢ Revolutionary War Military				
Uniforms, Block of 4	16.00 (12)	4.75	1.40	1.20
1565-68 10¢ Set of 4 Singles			1.30	.60
1569-70 10¢ Apollo Soyuz, Pair (24)	7.25 (12)	4.00	.65	.50
1569-70 10¢ Set of 2 Singles			.60	.30
1571 10¢ International Women's Year	13.50 (6)	1.90	.30	.15
1572-75 10¢ Postal Service Bicent., Block-4	17.50 (12)	4.75	1.50	1.40
1572-75 10¢ Set of 4 Singles	...	...	1.40	.60

1975 Commemoratives (cont.)

1576   1577   1578

1579   1580

Scott's No.		Mint Sheet	Plate Block	F-VF NH	F-VF Used
1576	10¢ World Peace through Law	16.00	1.60	.35	.15
1577-78	10¢ Banking & Commerce, Pair (40)	15.00	1.95	.85	.55
1577-78	10¢ Set of 2 Singles	...	...	.80	.30
1579	10¢ Christmas, Madonna and Child by Ghirlandaio	16.00 (12)	4.25	.35	.15
1580	10¢ Christmas Card, Perf. 11.2	18.50 (12)	5.00	.40	.20
1580c	10¢ Christmas, Perf. 10.9	16.00 (12)	4.25	.35	.15
1580B	10¢ Christmas, Perf. 10½ x 11	45.00 (12)	14.50	.85	.50

1975-1981 Americana Issue, Perforated 11 x 10½

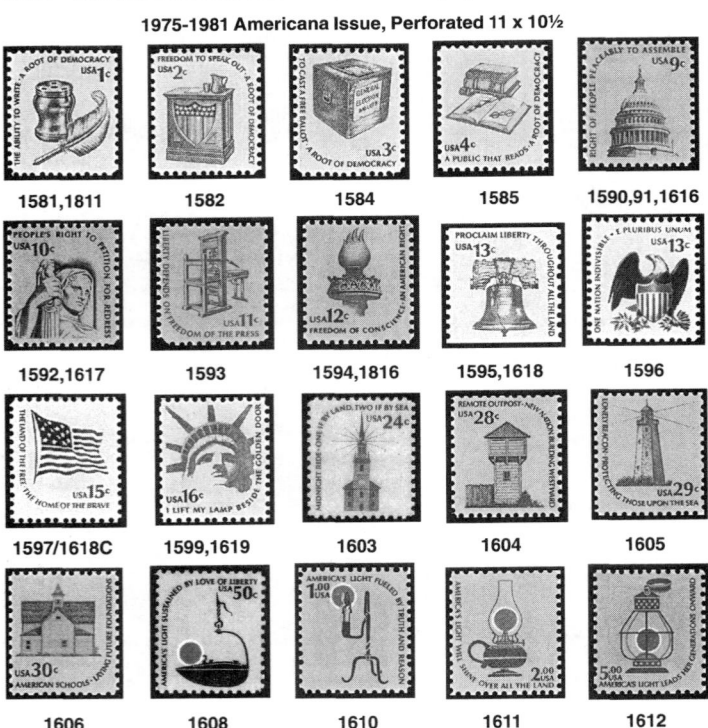

1581,1811   1582   1584   1585   1590,91,1616

1592,1617   1593   1594,1816   1595,1618   1596

1597/1618C   1599,1619   1603   1604   1605

1606   1608   1610   1611   1612

Scott's No.		Mint Sheet	Plate Block	F-VF NH	F-VF Used
1581-85,91-94,96-97,99-1612	Set of 19 ..	...	140.00	29.75	5.85
1581	1¢ Ability to Write, Shiny Gum (1977)	6.50	.60	.20	.15
1581v	1¢ Dull Gum	17.50	1.25	.25	...
1582	2¢ Freedom to Speak Out, Shiny Gum (1977)	8.00	.60	.20	.15
1582v	2¢ Dull Gum, white paper	33.50	2.50	.35	...
1582b	2¢ Dull Gum, cream paper (1981)	22.50	2.75	.25	.20
1584	3¢ Cast a Free Ballot,Shiny Gum ('77)	12.00	.60	.20	.15
1584v	3¢ Dull Gum	22.50	1.50	.25	...
1585	4¢ Public That Reads,Shiny Gum ('77)	15.00	.70	.20	.15
1585v	4¢ Dull Gum	23.75	1.50	.25	...
1590	9¢ Assembly, Booklet Single Perf.11x10½, Size 17½x20½ (1977)	...	...	.85	.85
1590 & 1623 attached Pair (from 1623A) ..		...	...	1.40	1.65
1590A	9¢ Booklet Single, Perf. 10x9 3/4 .	...	...	32.50	22.50
1590A & 1623B attd. Pair (from 1623C)		...	...	35.00	25.00
1591	9¢ Assemble, Large Size, 18½x22½ mm, Shiny Gum	27.50	1.25	.30	.15
1591v	9¢ Dull Gum	120.00	8.95	1.25	...
1592	10¢ Right to Petition,Shiny Gum ('77)	28.50	1.40	.30	.15
1592v	10¢ Dull Gum	67.50	3.75	.70	...
1593	11¢ Freedom of Press	37.50	1.75	.40	.15
1594	12¢ Freedom of Conscience ('81)	37.50	2.00	.40	.15

1975-1981 Americana Issue (continued)
(Sheets of 100)

Scott's No.		Mint Sheet	Plate Block	F-VF NH	F-VF Used
1595	13¢ Liberty Bell, Booklet Single	...	...	.40	.15
1595a	13¢ Booklet Pane of 6	...	...	2.60	2.00
1595b	13¢ Booklet Pane of 7	...	...	2.75	2.75
1595c	13¢ Booklet Pane of 8	...	...	2.75	2.85
1595d	13¢ Booklet Pane of 5 (1976)	...	...	2.25	2.10
1596	13¢ Eagle & Shield, Bullseye Perfs.	38.50 (12)	5.00	.40	.15
1596d	13¢ Line Perfs.	... (12)	595.00	40.00	...

#1596 Bullseye Perforations line up perfectly where horiz. and vertical rows meet. Pf 11.2.
#1596d Line Perfs. do not meet evenly. Perforated 11.

1597	15¢ McHenry Flag, Perf. 11 (1978)	47.50 (20)	10.50	.50	.15
1598	15¢ McHenry Flag, Booklet Single, Pef. 11x10½ (1978)	...	...	.75	.15
1598a	15¢ Booklet Pane of 8	...	...	5.50	2.75
1599	16¢ Statue of Liberty (1978)	57.50	2.75	.60	.20
1603	24¢ Old North Church (1978)	70.00	3.50	.75	.20
1604	28¢ Fort Nisqually, Shiny Gum (1978)	75.00	3.75	.80	.20
1604v	28¢ Dull Gum	180.00	15.00	1.85	...
1605	29¢ Lighthouse, Shiny Gum (1978)	90.00	4.50	.95	.50
1605v	29¢ Dull Gum	215.00	17.50	2.25	...
1606	30¢ Schoolhouse (1979)	105.00	5.00	1.10	.15
1608	50¢ Iron "Betty" (1979)	140.00	6.50	1.50	.30
1610	$1 Rush Lamp (1979)	295.00	13.00	3.00	.30
1611	$2 Kerosene Table Lamp ('78)	535.00	23.00	5.50	.65
1612	$5 Railroad Lantern (1979)	1400.00	62.50	14.50	2.50

Note: #1608-1612 are Lithographed and Engraved, Perforated 11.

1975-79 Americana Coil Issues - Perf. 10 Vertically

1613   1614    1615   1615C

Scott's No.		Line Pair	F-VF NH	F-VF Used
1613-19,1811-16	Americana Coils (12) .... (11)	12.25	3.70	2.15
1613	3.1¢ Guitar (1979)	.85	.20	.15
1613a	3.1¢ Bureau Precancel, Lines Only	6.50	.30	.25
1614	7.7¢ Saxhorns (1976)	1.20	.30	.20
1614a	7.7¢ Bureau Precancel	3.75	.70	.45
1615	7.9¢ Drum Shiny Gum (1976)	.95	.30	.20
1615a	7.9¢ Bureau Precancel Shiny Gum	3.25	.40	.25
1615v	7.9¢ Dull Gum	5.50	.45	...
1615va	7.9¢ Bureau Precancel, Dull Gum	4.75	.50	...
1615C	8.4¢ Steinway Grand Piano Shiny Gum (1978)	2.50	.35	.20
1615Cd	8.4¢ Bureau Precancel, Shiny Gum	6.75	.55	.30
1615Cdv	8.4¢ Precancel, Dull Gum	3.75	.50	...
1616	9¢ Right to Assemble (1976)	.85	.35	.20
1616b	9¢ Bureau Precancel	40.00	1.25	.75
1617	10¢ Right to Petition, Shiny Gum (1977)	.95	.35	.15
1617a	10¢ Bureau Precancel, Dull Gum	45.00	2.25	1.25
1617v	10¢ Dull Gum	1.60	.40	...
1618	13¢ Liberty Bell, Shiny Gum	.95	.35	.15
1618a	13¢ Bureau Precancel	80.00	7.00	1.00
1618v	13¢ Dull Gum	2.75	1.00	...
1618va	13¢ Bureau Precancel, Dull Gum	32.75	1.40	...
1618C	15¢ Fort McHenry Flag (1978) (No Lines) ..	...	.65	.15
1619	16¢ Statue of Liberty Overall Tagging (1978)	1.60	.55	.35
1619a	16¢ Block Tagging (No Lines)	...	.90	.75

Note: Also see #1811-1816 for 1980-81 issues.

1975-77 Regular Issue

1622,1625   1623

Scott's No.		Mint Sheet	Plate Block	F-VF NH	F-VF Used
1622	13¢ Flag over Independence Hall, Perf. 11x10 3/4	(100) 47.50 (20)	10.50	.50	.15
1622C	13¢ Perf. 11¼ (1981)	(100) 175.00 (20)	90.00	1.10	.95

Plate Blocks of #1622 have Pl. #'s at Top or Bottom.
Plate Blocks of #1622C have Pl. #'s at Left or Right.

1623	13¢ Flag over Capitol, Booklet Single Perforated 11 x 10½ (1977)	...	...	.45	.20
1623a	13¢ & 9¢ Bklt. Pane of 8 (7#1623,1#1590)...	...	...	3.75	2.75
1623B	13¢ Booklet Single, Perf. 10x9 3/4 (1977)...	...	...	.70	.70
1623c	13¢ & 9¢ Bklt .Pane of 8 (7#1623B,1#1590A)	...	...	37.50	26.50
1625	13¢ Flag over Independence Hall, Coil Perf.10 Vert. .... (Partial Line)	5.75	.45	.15
1625	Full Line Pair	21.75	...	...

1976 Commemoratives

1629   1630   1631

1632

Scott's No.	Sheet	Mint Block	Plate NH	F-VF Used	F-VF
1629-32,83-85,90-1703 Set of 21		...	...	10.50	3.00
1629-31 13¢ The Spirit of '76, Strip of 3		22.75 (12)	6.00	1.45	1.00
1629-31 Set of 3 Singles		...	...	1.35	.50
1632 13¢ Interphil '76, Philadelphia		18.50	1.70	.40	.15

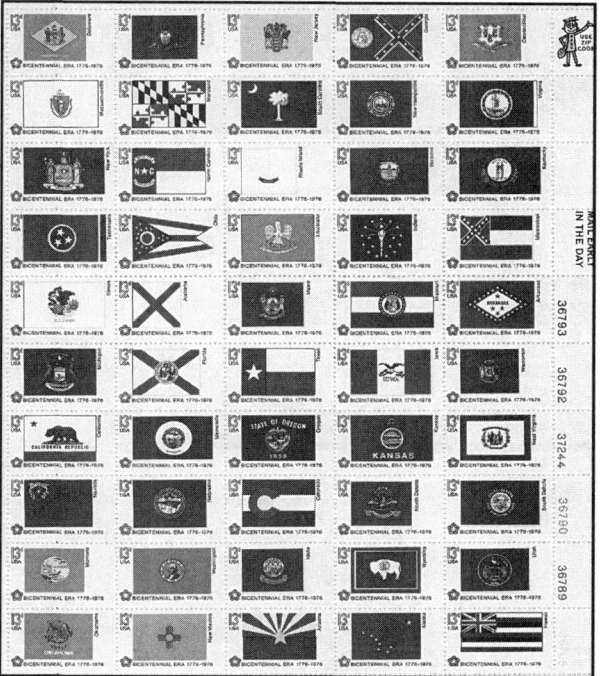

1633-82 Sheet

1976 U.S. Bicentennial: State Flags Issue

		Mint Block	Plate	F-VF	F-VF
1633-82 13¢ State Flags attd		28.75 (12) 8.75		...	...
1633-82 Set of 50 Singles		...	...	27.75	16.50
1633-82 13¢ Individual Singles		...	...	.80	.40

1633	DE	1646	VT	1659	FL	1671	ND
1634	PA	1647	KY	1660	TX	1672	SD
1635	NJ	1648	TN	1661	IA	1673	MT
1636	GA	1649	OH	1662	WI	1674	WA
1637	CT	1650	LA	1663	CA	1675	ID
1638	MA	1651	IN	1664	MN	1676	WY
1639	MD	1652	MS	1665	OR	1677	UT
1640	SC	1653	IL	1666	KS	1678	OK
1641	NH	1654	AL	1667	WV	1679	NM
1642	VA	1655	ME	1668	NV	1680	AZ
1643	NY	1656	MO	1669	NE	1681	AK
1644	NC	1657	AR	1670	CO	1682	HI
1645	RI	1658	MI				

1976 Commemoratives (continued)

1683   1684   1685

1683	13¢ Telephone Centennial, A.Bell .	21.50	1.85	.45	.15
1684	13¢ Commercial Aviation 50th Ann.	18.50 (10)	4.65	.40	.15
1685	13¢ American Chemistry Soc.Cent.	22.50 (12)	6.25	.50	.15

1976 American Bicentennial Souvenir Sheets

1686

The Surrender of Lord Cornwallis at Yorktown
From a Painting by John Trumbull

1687

The Declaration of Independence, 4 July 1776 at Philadelphia
From a Painting by John Trumbull

1688

Washington Crossing the Delaware
From a Painting by Emanuel Leutze / Eastman Johnson

1689

Washington Reviewing His Ragged Army at Valley Forge
From a Painting by William T. Trego

Scott's No.	Mint Sheet	Plate Block	F-VF NH	F-VF Used
1686-89 Set of Four Souvenir Sheets	...	...	28.75	25.00
1686a-89e Set of 20 Singles	...	...	28.00	23.75
1686 13¢ Surrender of Cornwallis at Yorktown	...	...	4.75	4.00
1686a-e 13¢ Any Single	...	...	1.10	.90
1687 18¢ Declaration of Independence .	...	...	6.75	5.75
1687a-e 18¢ Any Single	...	...	1.50	1.30
1688 24¢ Washington Crossing Delaware	...	...	9.25	8.00
1688a-e 24¢ Any Single	...	...	1.95	1.70
1689 31¢ Washington at Valley Forge ...	...	...	12.00	10.50
1689a-e 31¢ Any Single	...	...	2.50	2.15

1976 Commemoratives (continued)

| 1691 | 1692 | 1693 | 1694 |

1699

1690

1700

| 1695 | 1696 |
| 1697 | 1698 |

1701

1702,1703

1690	13¢ Benjamin Franklin and Map ...	23.50	2.10	.50	.15
1691-94	13¢ Declaration of Independence, Strip of 4	36.50 (16)	13.75	3.25	1.75
1691-94	13¢ Set of 4 Singles	...	...	3.15	.70
1695-98	13¢ Winter Olympic Games, Block-4	22.50 (12)	6.50	1.90	1.65
1695-98	13¢ Set of 4 Singles	...	...	1.80	.70
1699	13¢ Clara Mass, Yellow Fever ... (40)	19.50 (12)	6.50	.50	.15
1700	13¢ Adolph S. Ochs, Publisher .. (32)	15.00	2.10	.50	.15
1701	13¢ Christmas, Nativity	21.50 (12)	5.50	.45	.15
1702	13¢ Christmas "Winter Pastime", Andriotti Press	21.50 (10)	4.75	.45	.15
1703	13¢ Same, Gravure-Intaglio	21.50 (20)	9.25	.45	.15

#1702: Andriotti Press, lettering at Base is Black, No Snowflakes in Sky.
#1703: Intaglio-Gravure, lettering at Base is Gray Black, Snowflakes in Sky.

1977 Commemoratives

1704

| 1706 | 1707 |
| 1708 | 1709 |

1977 Commemoratives (continued)

1705

1710

1711

| 1712 | 1713 |
| 1714 | 1715 |

1716

1717
1719

| 1718 |
| 1720 |

1721

1725

1722

1723
1724

1726

Scott's No.		Mint Sheet	Plate Block	F-VF NH	F-VF Used
1704-1730	Set of 27	...	...	11.25	3.85
1704	13¢ Washington at Princeton .... (40)	22.50 (10)	6.25	.60	.15
1705	13¢ Sound Recording Centennial .	22.50	2.10	.50	.15
1706-09	13¢ Pueblo Art, Block of 4 .... (40)	15.75 (10)	4.50	1.65	1.25
1706-09	13¢Strip of 4	...	...	1.65	1.25
1706-09	13¢ Set of 4 Singles	...	...	1.50	.70
1710	13¢ Lindbergh's Flight 50th Anniv.	28.00 (12)	7.50	.60	.15
1711	13¢ Colorado Statehood Centennial, Line Perforated 11	28.00 (12)	7.50	.60	.15
1711c	13¢ Bullseye Perfs 11.2	57.50 (12)	19.50	1.15	.95
1712-15	13¢ American Butterflies, Block of 4	18.50 (12)	5.50	1.65	1.50
1712-15	13¢ Set of 4 Singles	...	...	1.50	.70
1716	13¢ Lafayette's Landing 200th ... (40)	18.00	2.10	.50	.15
1717-20	13¢ Revolutionary War Civilian Skills, Block of 4	18.50 (12)	5.50	1.65	1.50
1717-20	13¢ Set of 4 Singles	...	...	1.50	.70
1721	13¢ Peace Bridge 50th Ann.	21.00	1.85	.45	.15
1722	13¢ Herkimer at Oriskany .... (40)	15.00 (10)	4.25	.40	.15
1723-24	13¢ Energy Conservation and Development, Pair .... (40)	17.00 (12)	5.75	.90	.60
1723-24	13¢ Set of 2 Singles	...	...	.85	.30
1725	13¢ Alta California Settlement 200th	23.50	2.10	.50	.15
1726	13¢ Articles of Confederation 200th	21.50	1.85	.45	.15

NOTE: MODERN BOOKLET PANES ARE GLUED INTO BOOKLETS AND PRICES LISTED ARE FOR PANES WITHOUT SELVEDGE OR WITH DISTURBED SELVEDGE AND, USUALLY, FOLDED. LIMITED QUANTITIES EXIST UNFOLDED WITH FULL SELVEDGE—THESE ARE USUALLY PRICED ANYWHERE FROM 1½ TO 4 TIMES THESE PRICES WHEN AVAILABLE.
NOTE: PRICES THROUGHOUT THIS LIST ARE SUBJECT TO CHANGE WITHOUT NOTICE IF MARKET CONDITIONS REQUIRE.   MIN. MAIL ORDER MUST TOTAL AT LEAST $20.00.

1977 Commemoratives (continued)

| 1727 | 1728 | 1729 | 1730 |

Scott's No.		Mint Sheet	Plate Block	F-VF NH	F-VF Used
1727	13¢ Talking Pictures 50th Anniv. ...	23.50	2.10	.50	.15
1728	13¢ Surrender at Saratoga 200th (40)	15.00 (10)	4.25	.40	.15
1729	13¢ Christmas, Washington at Valley Forge .... (100)	37.50 (20)	8.50	.40	.15
1730	13¢ Christmas - Rural Mailbox . (100)	37.50 (10)	4.25	.40	.15

| 1731 | 1732 | 1733 | 1734 | 1735-36,1743 |

| 1737 | 1738 | 1739 | 1740 | 1741 | 1742 |

1978 Commemoratives

1731-33,44-69	Set of 29	...	...	15.00	6.25
1731	13¢ Carl Sandburg, Poet	28.50	2.50	.60	.15
1732-33	13¢ Captain Cook, Pair	23.50 (20)	10.50	1.00	.75
1732	13¢ Captain Cook Portrait, Alaska	...	2.10	.50	.15
1733	13¢ Hawaii "Resolution" & "Discovery"	...	2.10	.50	.15

1978-80 Regular Issues

1734	13¢ Indian Head Penny .... (150)	55.00	1.70	.40	.15
1735	(15¢) "A" & Eagle, Perf. 11 ... (100)	42.50	1.90	.45	.15
1735c	(15¢) Bullseye Perf. 11.2 .... (100)	52.50	2.75	.55	.35
1736	(15¢) "A" & Eagle, Perf. 11x10½ Booklet Single	...	...	.55	.15
1736a	15¢ Booklet Pane of 8	...	...	3.75	3.00
1737	15¢ Roses, Perf. 10, Booklet Single	...	...	.45	.15
1737a	15¢ Booklet Pane of 8	...	...	3.25	3.00
1738-42	15¢ Windmills, Strip of 5 (1980) ..	...	...	2.50	2.25
1738-42	15¢ Set of 5 Singles	...	...	2.40	.90
1742a	15¢ Booklet Pane of 10 (2 ea. #1738-42) (1980)	...	...	4.95	4.25
1743	(15¢) "A" & Eagle, Coil, Pf. Vert. ... Line Pr.	...	1.15	.45	.15

1978 Commemoratives (continued)

| 1744 | 1745 1746 |
| | 1747 1748 |

1978 Commemoratives (continued)

| 1749 | 1750 | 1753 |
| 1751 | 1752 | |

| 1754 | 1755 | 1756 |

| 1757 |

Scott's No.		Mint Sheet	Plate Block	F-VF NH	F-VF Used
1744	13¢ Harriet Tubman	26.50 (12)	6.75	.55	.15
1745-48	13¢ Folk Art: Quilts, Block of 4 . (48)	19.00 (12)	5.50	1.65	1.25
1745-48	13¢ Set of 4 Singles	...	...	1.50	.70
1749-52	13¢ American Dance, Block of 4(48)	19.00 (12)	5.50	1.65	1.25
1749-52	13¢ Set of 4 Singles	...	...	1.50	.70
1753	13¢ French Alliance .... (40)	15.00	1.70	.40	.15
1754	13¢ Cancer Detection, Pap Test George Papanicolaou	23.50	2.10	.50	.15
#1755-56	Performing Arts				
1755	13¢ Jimmie Rodgers	27.50 (12)	7.50	.60	.15
1756	15¢ George M. Cohan	35.00 (12)	9.50	.75	.15

1978 Canadian International Philatelic Exhibition Souvenir Sheet

1757	13¢x8 ($1.04) CAPEX'78 Souvenir Sheet .... (6)	17.50	...	3.00	2.75
1757	13¢ Souvenir Sheet with Plate Number ...		3.25	...	...
1757a-h	13¢ Set of 8 Singles	...	...	2.95	2.00
1757a-d	13¢ Strip of Four (a-d)	...	...	1.60	1.50
1757e-h	13¢ Strip of Four (e-h)	...	...	1.60	1.50
1757a-h	13¢ Block of 8, attached	...	...	3.50	3.25

1757a Cardinal	1757d Blue Jay	1757g Red Fox
1757b Mallard	1757e Moose	1757h Raccoon
1757c Canada Goose	1757f Chipmunk	

1971-83 American Revolution Bicentennial Issues

1432, 1456-59, 1476-83, 1543-46, 1559-68, 1629-82, 1686-89, 1691-94, 1704, 1716-20, 1722, 1728, 1753, 1789-89B, 1826, 1937-38, 2052.

NOTE: PRICES THROUGHOUT THIS LIST ARE SUBJECT TO CHANGE WITHOUT NOTICE IF MARKET CONDITIONS REQUIRE. MINIMUM ORDER MUST TOTAL AT LEAST $20.00.

1978 Commemoratives (continued)

1758	1759	1760 1762	1761 1763

1764 1766	1765 1767	1768	1769

Scott's No.		Mint Sheet	Plate Block	F-VF NH	F-VF Used
1758	15¢ Photography .... (40)	16.75 (12)	5.75	.45	.15
1759	15¢ Viking Mission to Mars	21.00	2.10	.45	.15
1760-63	15¢ American Owls, Block of 4	21.00	2.00	1.80	1.80
1760-63	15¢ Set of 4 Singles	...	...	1.70	.70
1764-67	15¢ American Trees, Block of 4 (40)	17.50 (12)	6.00	1.80	1.80
1764-67	15¢ Set of 4 Singles	...	...	1.70	.70
1768	15¢ Christmas Madonna	(100) 41.50 (12)	5.50	.45	.15
1769	15¢ Christmas Hobbyhorse	(100) 41.50 (12)	5.50	.45	.15

1979 Commemoratives

1770	1771	1772

1774	1775 1777	1776 1778	1773

1979 Commemoratives (continued)

Scott's No.		Mint Sheet	Plate Block	F-VF NH	F-VF Used
1770-1802	Set of 33 (No#1789A,B,1795A-98A)...	...		16.50	5.35
1770	15¢ Robert F. Kennedy .... (48)	25.00	2.30	.55	.15
1771	15¢ Martin Luther King, Jr.	28.50 (12)	7.50	.60	.15
1772	15¢ Int'l. Year of the Child	23.50	2.10	.50	.15
1773	15¢ John Steinbeck, Novelist	28.50	2.50	.60	.15
1774	15¢ Albert Einstein, Physicist........	27.50	2.50	.60	.15
1775-78	15¢ PA Toleware, Block of 4 .... (40)	18.00 (10)	5.00	1.90	1.50
1775-78	15¢ Set of 4 Singles	...	...	1.80	.80

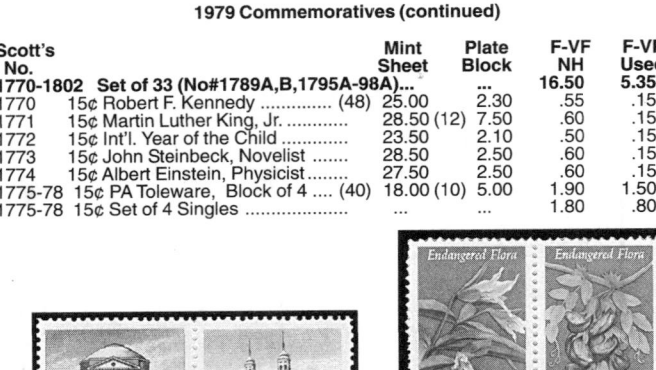

1779 1781	1780 1782	1783 1785	1784 1786

1787	1788	1789

1790	1791 1793	1792 1794

1795 1797	1796 1798	1800

1779-82	15¢ Architecture, Block of 4 ...... (48)	28.50	2.95	2.50	2.25
1779-82	15¢ Set of 4 Singles	...	...	2.40	.80
1783-86	15¢ Endangered Flowers, Block-4	24.75 (12)	6.50	2.10	1.50
1783-86	15¢ Set of 4 Singles	...	...	2.00	.80
1787	15¢ Seeing Eye Dog 50th Ann.	27.50 (20)	12.50	.60	.15
1788	15¢ Special Olympics	23.50 (10)	5.25	.50	.15
1789	15¢ John P. Jones, Perf. 11x12	23.50 (10)	5.25	.50	.15
1789A	15¢ Perforated 11	38.50 (10	8.75	.80	.25
1789B	15¢ Perforated 12	...	...	3250.00	3250.00
1790	10¢ Olympics - Decathalon	14.50 (12)	4.50	.30	.20
1791-94	15¢ Summer Olympics, Block-4	21.00 (12)	6.50	2.10	1.95
1791-94	Set of 4 Singles	...	...	1.95	.80

46

1979 Commemoratives (continued)

1801

1802

Scott's No.		Mint Sheet	Plate Block	F-VF NH	F-VF Used
1795-98	15¢ Winter Olympics, Perf. 11 x 10½, Block of 4 (1980)	24.00 (12)	6.50	2.10	1.50
1795-98	15¢ Set of 4 Singles	...	...	1.95	.80
1795A-98A	15¢ Perforated 11,Block of 4	47.50 (12)	14.00	4.00	3.95
1795A-98A	15¢ Set of 4 Singles	...	...	3.75	3.60
1799	15¢ Christmas Madonna ...... (100)	41.50 (12)	5.50	.45	.15
1800	15¢ Christmas Ornament ..... (100)	41.50 (12)	5.50	.45	.15
1801	15¢ Will Rogers, Humorist	21.00 (12)	6.00	.45	.15
1802	15¢ Vietnam Veterans	26.50 (10)	5.95	.55	.15

1980 Commemoratives (See also 1795-98)

1803

1804

1805
1806

1807
1808

1809
1810

Scott's No.		Mint Sheet	Plate Block	F-VF NH	F-VF Used
1803-10,21-43	Set of 31	...	...	16.50	5.25
1803	15¢ W.C. Fields, Actor-Comedian	26.50 (12)	7.00	.55	.15
1804	15¢ Benjamin Banneker	33.50 (12)	8.50	.70	.15
1805-10	15¢ Letter Writing Week, Strip of 6	(60) 26.50	(36) 23.50	3.75	3.50
1805-10	15¢ Set of 6 Singles	...	...	3.50	1.40

1811

1813

1816

1818-1820

1980-81 Americana Coils, Perf. 10 Vertically

Scott's No.		Line Pair	F-VF NH	F-VF Used
1811	1¢ Inkwell & Quill, Shiny Gum	.50	.20	.15
1811v	1¢ Dull Gum	.70	.25	...
1813	3.5¢ Two Violins, Coil	1.10	.20	.15
1813a	3.5¢ Bureau Precancel	2.50	.30	.25
1816	12¢ Conscience, Coil (1981)	2.25	.40	.30
1816a	12¢ Bureau Precancel	42.50	1.65	1.50

1981 "B" Eagle Regular Issue

Scott's No.		Mint Sheet	Plate Block	F-VF NH	F-VF Used
1818	(18¢) Perf. 11x10½ .... (100)	52.50	2.25	.55	.15
1819	(18¢) Perf. 10, Booklet Single	...	...	.75	.15
1819a	(18¢) Booklet Pane of 8	...	...	5.50	3.75
1820	(18¢) Coil, Perf. 10 Vert.	Line Pr.	1.65	.60	.15

1980 Commemoratives (continued)

1821

1822

Emily Bissell

1823

1824

1825

1826

1827
1829

1828
1830

1834
1836

1835
1837

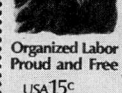

1831

1832

1833

1842

1838
1840

1837
1841

1843

Scott's No.		Mint Sheet	Plate Block	F-VF NH	F-VF Used
1821	15¢ Frances Perkins, Sec. of Labor	21.00	1.95	.45	.15
1822	15¢ Dolley Madison, First Lady . (150)	70.00	2.25	.50	.15
1823	15¢ Emily Bissell, Social Worker ..	27.50	2.50	.60	.15
1824	15¢ Helen Keller/Anne Sullivan	35.00	3.25	.75	.15
1825	15¢ Veterans Administration	21.00	1.80	.45	.15
1826	15¢ Gen. Bernardo de Galvez, Battle of Mobile	42.50	3.75	.90	.15
1827-30	15¢ Coral Reefs, Block of 4	22.75 (12)	6.50	1.95	1.35
1827-30	15¢ Set of 4 Singles	...	...	1.80	.80
1831	15¢ Organized Labor, Bald Eagle .	21.50 (12)	6.25	.50	.15

1980 Commemoratives (continued)

Scott's No.		Mint Sheet	Plate Block	F-VF NH	F-VF Used
1832	15¢ Edith Wharton, Novelist	23.75	2.10	.50	.15
1833	15¢ Education in America	26.00 (6)	3.50	.55	.15
1834-37	15¢ Pacific Northwest Indian Masks, Block of 4	(40) 26.50 (10)	7.50	2.75	1.85
1834-37	15¢ Set of 4 Singles	...	...	2.65	.80
1838-41	15¢ Architecture, Block of 4	(40) 24.00	2.85	2.50	1.95
1838-41	15¢ Set of 4 Singles	...	...	2.25	.80
1842	15¢ Christmas Madonna	21.50 (12)	5.50	.45	.15
1843	15¢ Christmas Toys	21.50 (20)	10.00	.45	.15

1980-85 Great Americans Series

1844	1845	1846	1847	1848

1849	1850	1851	1852	1853

1854	1855	1856	1857	1858

1859	1860	1861	1862	1863

1864	1865	1866	1867

1868	1869

Perf. 11 x 10½ or Perf.11 (Sheets of 100)

Scott's No.		Mint Sheet	Plate Block	F-VF NH	F-VF Used
1844-69	Set of 26	...	...	15.00	3.95
1844	1¢ Dorothea Dix, Bullseye Perfs., Perforated 11.2 (1983)	8.75 (20)	2.75	.20	.15
1844c	1¢ Line Perfs.10.9, Small Block Tagging (1983)	6.75 (20)	2.25	.20	.15
1844d	1¢ Perf.10.9, Large Block Tagging ('85)	10.00 (20)	2.75	.25	.15
1845	2¢ Igor Stravinsky (1982)	8.50	.60	.20	.15
1846	3¢ Henry Clay (1983)	11.75	.75	.20	.15
1847	4¢ Carl Schurz (1983)	15.00	.75	.20	.15
1848	5¢ Pearl Buck (1983)	27.50	1.25	.30	.15
1849	6¢ Walter Lippmann (1985)	18.00 (20)	4.15	.20	.15
1850	7¢ Abraham Baldwin (1985)	27.50 (20)	6.25	.30	.15
1851	8¢ Gen. Henry Knox (1985)	23.00	1.25	.25	.15
1852	9¢ Sylvanus Thayer (1985)	32.50 (20)	7.25	.35	.20
1853	10¢ Richard Russell Perf. 11, Small Block Tagging (1984)	47.50 (20)	10.75	.50	.15
1853a	10¢ Large Block Tagging	62.50 (20)	14.50	.65	.15
1854	11¢ Alden Partridge (1985)	45.00	2.75	.60	.15
1855	13¢ Crazy Horse (1982)	52.50	2.50	.55	.25
1856	14¢ Sinclair Lewis, Small Block Tagging (1985)	52.50 (20)	11.75	.55	.15
1856a	14¢ Large Block Tagging	62.50 (20)	13.75	.65	.15
1857	17¢ Rachel Carson (1981)	47.50	2.15	.50	.15
1858	18¢ George Mason (1981)	47.50	2.50	.50	.20
1859	19¢ Sequoyah	70.00	3.25	.75	.25
1860	20¢ Dr. Ralph Bunche (1982)	75.00	3.50	.80	.15
1861	20¢ Thomas Gallaudet (1983)	70.00	3.75	.75	.15

1980-85 Great Americans Series (continued)

Scott's No.		Mint Sheet	Plate Block	F-VF NH	F-VF Used
1862	20¢ Harry Truman, Line Perf. 10.9, Small Block Tagging,Dull Gum (1984)	62.50 (20)	13.00	.65	.15
1862a	20¢ Bullseye, Perf 11.2, Large Block Tagging,Dull Gum	72.50 (4)	4.50	.75	.30
1862b	20¢ Perf.11.2,Overall Tagging, Dull Gum (1990)	82.50	5.75	.85	.50
1862d	20¢ Perf. 11.2, Mottled Tagging, Shiny Gum (1993)	87.50	5.50	.90	.70
1863	22¢ John J. Audubon, Line Perf 11, Small Block Tagging (1985)	72.50 (20)	16.50	.75	.15
1863a	22¢ Perf.11, Large Block Tagging	97.50 (20)	21.50	1.00	.15
1863b	22¢ Bullseye Perfs., Perf. 11.2, Large Block Tagging (1987)	72.50 (4)	5.75	.75	.20
1864	30¢ Frank .C. Laubach, Line Perf. 11, Small Block Tagging (1984)	85.00 (20)	19.75	.90	.15
1864a	30¢ Bullseye Perf. 11.2, Large Block Tagging	87.50	5.75	.90	.20
1864b	30¢ Perf. 11.2, Overall Tagging	...	45.00	3.00	2.00
1865	35¢ Dr. Charles Drew (1981)	105.00	5.00	1.10	.20
1866	37¢ Robert Millikan (1982)	105.00	4.75	1.10	.20
1867	39¢ Grenville Clark, Line Perf 10.9, Small Block Tagging (1985)	105.00 (20)	24.50	1.10	.20
1867c	39¢ Perf.10.9, Large Block Tagging	130.00 (20)	29.50	1.35	.20
1867d	39¢ Bullseye Perf 11.2, Large Block Tagging	100.00 (4)	6.75	1.10	.20
1868	40¢ Lillian Gilbreth, Line Perf. 10.9, Small Block Tagging (1984)	110.00 (20)	25.00	1.20	.20
1868a	40¢ Bullseye Perf.11.2, Large Block Tagging	120.00	7.25	1.30	.20
1869	50¢ Chester W. Nimitz, Line Perf. 10.9, Overall Tagging, Shiny Gum (1985)	150.00 (4)	10.00	1.50	.20
1869a	50¢ Bullseye Perf. 11.2, Large Block Tagging, Dull Gum	160.00	8.25	1.60	.25
1869d	50¢ Perf.11.2,Overall Tagging, Dull Gum	240.00	14.00	2.50	.40
1869e	50¢ Pf.11.2,Mottled Tagging, Shiny Gum (1992)	190.00	11.50	2.00	.40

TAGGING VARIATIONS

Tagging is a usually invisible coating applied to postage stamps which can be "read" by the automated mail-handling equipment used by the post office. After a period of years of testing, tagging has since been applied to most stamps. This tagging can be detected by use of a short-wave ultra-violet lamp.

Overall Tagging: The tagging has been applied to the entire surface of the stamp.

Block Tagging: The tagging is applied over the center area of the stamp with the outside edges untagged. Comes in small or large sized block tagging.

Solid Tagging: The tagging is applied as part of the process of coating prephosphored paper making it very smooth. Also known as surface tagging.

Mottled Tagging: Also applied to prephosphored paper without a coating. Appears to have a mottled or blotchy appearance. Experts disagree on details of mottled tagging.

1981 Commemoratives

1874	1875	1876 1878	1877 1879

Scott's No.		Mint Sheet	Plate Block	F-VF NH	F-VF Used
1874-79,1910-45	Set of 42	...	...	27.50	7.00
1874	15¢ Everett Dirksen, Senator	23.50	2.15	.50	.15
1875	15¢ Whitney Young, Civil Rights	23.50	2.10	.50	.15
1876-79	18¢ Flowers, Block of 4	(48) 31.75	3.25	2.75	2.25
1876-79	18¢ Set of 4 Singles	...	...	2.30	.80

ZIP, MAIL EARLY & COPYRIGHT BLOCKS

Due to space limitations, we do not list individual prices for Zip Code, Mail Early, Copyright and other inscription blocks. With the exception of those items listed below, these are priced at the total price for the single stamps plus one additional stamp. For example, if the single stamp retailed for 45¢, a zip block of 4 would retail for $2.25 (5x.45). Se-tenants should be based on the attached price plus 25%. (blocks of 6 would be 75% over attached block prices)

Scott's No.		Copyright Block	Mail Early Block	Zip Code Block
1274	1965 11¢ Telecommunication	...	...	3.75
1284	1966 6¢ F. D. Roosevelt	...	4.50	3.75
1284a	Same, tagged	...	2.75	2.25
1347-49	1968, 6¢ Historic Flags	...	3.50	...
1353-54	1968, 6¢ Historic Flags	...	...	2.50
C72	1968, 10¢ 50 State Runway	...	5.50	4.50
C95-96	1979, 25¢ Wiley Post	7.50	...	7.50

1981-82 Regular Issues

1890

1891

1892

1893

1894-96

1880	1881
1882	1883
1884	1885
1886	1887
1888	1889

Scott's No.		Mint Sheet	Plate Block	F-VF NH	F-VF Used
1880-89	18¢ American Wildlife Booklet Singles	...	...	10.00	2.00
1889a	18¢ Wildlife Booklet Pane of 10 .			10.75	8.50
1890	18¢ Flag & "For Amber Waves of Grain" .... (100)	62.50 (20)	14.00	.65	.15
1891	18¢ Flag "From Sea to Shining Sea", Coil Perf.10 Vert. ..... (Pl. # Strip)	7.25 (5)	6.00 (3)	.65	.15
1892	6¢ Circle of Stars, Booklet Single	...	...	1.10	.50
1893	18¢ Flag & "For Purple Mountain Majesties" Booklet Single	...	...	.60	.15
1892-93	6¢ & 18¢, Vertical Pair	...	...	1.75	1.75
1893a	Booklet Pane of 8 (2 #1892, 6 #1893)	...	...	5.00	4.25
1894	20¢ Flag over Supreme Court, Line Pf. 11, Dull Gum .... (100)	95.00 (20)	21.00	1.00	.25
1894e	20¢ Bullseye Perf. Perforated 11.2, Shiny Gum .. (100)	62.50 (20)	13.50	.65	.15
1895	20¢ Flag over Supreme Court, Wide Block Tagging, Coil ... Pl. # Strip	6.00 (5)	4.25 (3)	.60	.15
1895a	20¢ Narrow Block Tagging .. Pl. # Strip	6.00 (5)	4.25 (3)	.65	.15
1895b	20¢ Flag, Precancelled .... Pl. # Strip	95.00 (5)	90.00 (3)	1.50	.75
1896	20¢ Flag over Supreme Court, Booklet Single	...	...	.75	.15
1896a	20¢ Booklet Pane of 6	...	...	3.95	3.50
1896b	20¢ Booklet Pane of 10 (1982) ...	...	...	6.50	5.25

1981-91 Transportation Coil Series

1897

1897A

1898

1898A

1899

1900

1901

1902

1903

1904

1905

1906

1907

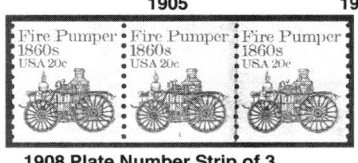
1908 Plate Number Strip of 3

11¢ RR Untagged Issue not included in Set.
Pl. #s must appear on center stamp

1981-91 Transportation Coils (continued)

Scott's No.		Pl# Strip of 5	Pl# Strip of 3	F-VF NH	F-VF Used
1897-1908	Set of 14 (No #1905b)	115.00	52.50	4.25	2.10
1897	1¢ Omnibus (1983)	.70	.50	.20	.15
1897A	2¢ Locomotive (1982)	.75	.55	.20	.15
1898	3¢ Handcar (1983)	.95	.75	.20	.15
1898A	4¢ Stagecoach (1982)	1.60	1.25	.20	.15
1899	5¢ Motorcycle (1983)	1.30	1.00	.20	.15
1900	5.2¢ Sleigh (1983)	12.75	5.25	.25	.15
1901	5.9¢ Bicycle (1982)	16.50	6.50	.25	.20
1902	7.4¢ Baby Buggy (1984)	12.50	7.00	.30	.20
1903	9.3¢ Mail Wagon (1984)	16.50	7.50	.30	.20
1904	10.9¢ Hansom Cab (1982)	42.50	13.50	.50	.20
1905	11¢ RR Caboose (1984)	5.00	3.75	.40	.15
1905b	11¢ Untagged, not precanc. ('91) ..	4.00	3.25	.35	.25
1906	17¢ Electric Car	3.00	2.25	.50	.15
1907	18¢ Surrey	3.75	2.50	.60	.15
1908	20¢ Fire Pumper	3.75	2.75	.60	.15

#1897-97A: See #2225-26 for designs without "¢" signs.
#1898A: See #2228 for "B" Press

1981-91 Transportation Coil Series Precancelled Stamps

1898Ab

1900a

1901a

1902a

1903a

1904a

1905a

1906a

Scott's No.		Pl# Strip of 5	Pl# Strip of 3	F-VF NH	F-VF Used
1898Ab/1906a	Precancelled Set of 8	130.00	125.00	2.95	1.80
1898Ab	4¢ Stagecoach (1982)	8.25	7.50	.30	.20
1900a	5.2¢ Sleigh (1983)	15.00	13.50	.25	.20
1901a	5.9¢ Bicycle (1982)	50.00	47.50	.40	.25
1902a	7.4¢ Baby Buggy (1984)	7.00	6.50	.35	.25
1903a	9.3¢ Mail Wagon	4.00	3.25	.40	.25
1904a	10.9¢ Hansom Cab (1982)	42.50	40.00	.55	.25
1905a	11¢ RR Caboose (1984)	5.25	4.25	.40	.25
1906a	17¢ Electric Car, Type "A"	6.00	5.00	.50	.35
1906ab	17¢ Type "B"	37.50	35.00	1.50	.75
1906ac	17¢ Type "C"	18.00	15.00	1.10	.50

Type "A" - "Presorted" 11.5mm Length
Type "B" - "Presorted" 12.5mm Length
Type "C" - "Presorted" 13.5mm Length

1983 Express Mail Issue

1909

Scott's No.		Mint Sheet	Plate Block	F-VF NH	F-VF Used
1909	$9.35 Eagle & Moon, Booklet Single	...	...	30.00	22.50
1909a	$9.35 Booklet Pane of 3	...	...	88.50	...

1981 Commemoratives (continued)

1912	1913	1914	1915
1916	1917	1918	1919

1981 Commemoratives (continued)

1910

1911

1920

1921  1922

1923  1924

Scott's No.		Mint Sheet	Plate Block	F-VF NH	F-VF Used
1910	18¢ American Red Cross Centennial	26.50	2.80	.55	.15
1911	18¢ Savings & Loan Sesquicent. ..	25.00	2.50	.55	.15
1912-19	18¢ Space Achievement, Blk-8 . (48)	32.50 (8)	6.00	5.50	4.25
1912-19	18¢ Set of 8 Singles	...	...	5.25	2.00
1920	18¢ Professional Management Education Centennial	25.00	2.40	.55	.15
1921-24	18¢ Wildlife Habitats, Block of 4 ..	29.50	2.75	2.50	2.00
1921-24	18¢ Set of 4 Singles	...	...	2.40	.70

1925

1926

1927

1928 1929
1930 1931

1932

1934

1933

1935

1936

1939

1981 Commemoratives (continued)

1937 1938

1940

1941

1942 1943
1944 1945

Scott's No.		Mint Sheet	Plate Block	F-VF NH	F-VF Used
1925	18¢ Year of the Disabled	25.00	2.40	.55	.15
1926	18¢ Edna St. Vincent Millay, Poet	30.00	2.75	.65	.15
1927	18¢ Alchoholism	55.00 (20)	40.00	.60	.15
1928-31	18¢ Architecture, Block of 4 .... (40)	29.50	3.35	3.00	2.25
1928-31	18¢ Set of 4 Singles	...	...	2.75	.70
1932	18¢ Mildred "Babe" Didrikson Zaharias, Athlete	37.50	4.00	.80	.15
1933	18¢ Robert "Bobby" Jones, Golf .	65.00	7.50	1.40	.20
1934	18¢ Frederic Remington "Coming Through the Rye" Sculpture	33.50	3.00	.70	.15
1935	18¢ James Hoban, White House	25.00	2.40	.55	.15
1936	20¢ James Hoban	26.00	2.50	.55	.15
1937-38	18¢ Yorktown & VA Capes, Pair	28.75	3.00	1.40	1.00
1937-38	18¢ Set of Singles	...	...	1.30	.40
1939	(20¢) Botticelli Madonna .... (100)	50.00	2.50	.55	.15
1940	(20¢) Christmas-Teddy Bear	26.00	2.50	.55	.15
1941	20¢ John Hanson, President of Continental Congress	36.00	3.75	.75	.15
1942-45	20¢ Desert Plants, Block of 4 . (40)	28.50	3.25	3.25	2.00
1942-45	20¢ Set of 4 Singles	...	...	3.00	.70

1981-82 Regular Issues

1946-1948

1949

1946	(20¢) "C" & Eagle, Pf. 11x10½ .. (100)	52.50	2.50	.55	.15
1947	(20¢) "C" & Eagle, Coil, Perf.10 Vert.	Line Pr.	2.25	.75	.15
1948	(20¢) "C" & Eagle, Perf.11, Booklet Single...			.70	.15
1948a	(20¢) Booklet Pane of 10, Perf.11 .	...	...	6.75	5.00

#1948 design is substantially smaller than #1946-47 design.

1949	20¢ Type I, Bighorn Sheep, Booklet Single...			.75	.15
1949a	20¢ Type I, Booklet Pane of 10	...	...	7.25	4.50
1949c	20¢ Type II, Booklet Single	...	...	1.75	.50
1949d	20¢ Type II, Booklet Pane of 10	...	...	16.50	...

Ty. I is 18¾ mm wide and has overall tagging.
Ty. II is 18½ mm wide and has block tagging.

1982 Commemoratives

1950

1951

1952

1950-52, 2003-4, 2006-30	Set of 30 (No #1951A) ...		...	22.50	4.65
1950	20¢ Franklin D. Roosevelt, 100th Anniversary of Birth .... (48)	26.50	2.50	.55	.15
1951	20¢ "LOVE", Perf. 11 1/4	29.50	2.50	.60	.15
1951A	20¢ Perf. 11 1/4x 10½	45.00	5.50	.95	.35
1952	20¢ George Washington. 250th Annversary of Birth	28.50	2.75	.60	.15

1982 State Birds & Flowers Issue

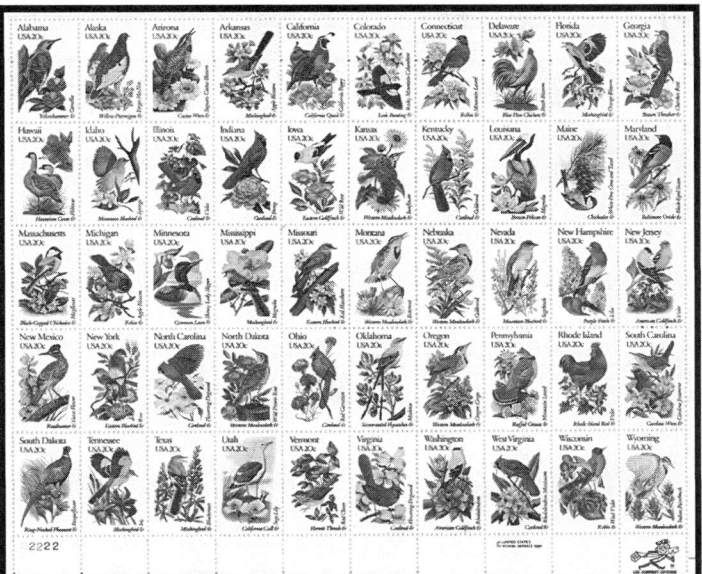

1953-2002 Sheet

1957

1961

1966

1972

Scott's No.		Mint Sheet	Plate Block	F-VF NH	F-VF Used
1953-2002	20¢ 50 States, Sheet of 50, Perf. 10½ x 11 1/4	41.50	...	...	...
1953-2002	20¢ Set of Singles, ...	...	...	39.50	23.50
1953-2002	20¢ Individual Singles ...	...	...	1.10	.60
1953A-2002A	20¢ 50 States, Sheet of 50, Perforated 11 1/4 x 11 ..	47.50	...	...	...

NOTE: Sets of singles may contain mixed perforation sizes.

1953 Alabama	1970 Louisiana	1987 Ohio
1954 Alaska	1971 Maine	1988 Oklahoma
1955 Arizona	1972 Maryland	1989 Oregon
1956 Arkansas	1973 Massachusetts	1990 Pennsylvania
1957 California	1974 Michigan	1991 Rhode Island
1958 Colorado	1975 Minnesota	1992 South Carolina
1959 Connecticut	1976 Mississippi	1993 South Dakota
1960 Delaware	1977 Missouri	1994 Tennessee
1961 Florida	1978 Montana	1995 Texas
1962 Georgia	1979 Nebraska	1996 Utah
1963 Hawaii	1980 Nevada	1997 Vermont
1964 Idaho	1981 New Hampshire	1998 Virginia
1965 Illinois	1982 New Jersey	1999 Washington
1966 Indiana	1983 New Mexico	2000 West Virginia
1967 Iowa	1984 New York	2001 Wisconsin
1968 Kansas	1985 North Carolina	2002 Wyoming
1969 Kentucky	1986 North Dakota	

2003

2004

2005

1982 Commemoratives (continued)

2003	20¢ U.S. & Netherlands	32.50 (20)	13.95	.60	.15
2004	20¢ Library of Congress	27.50	2.50	.55	.15

1982 Consumer Education Coil

2005	20¢ Clothing Label	(Pl# Strip) 150.00(5)	25.00(3)	1.10	.15

1982 Commemoratives (continued)

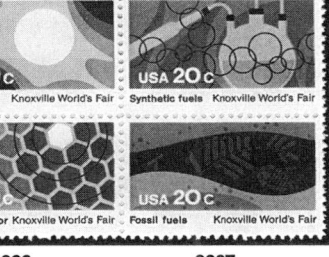
2006 2007
2008 2009

2010

2012

2011

2013

2015

2016

2019 2020
2021 2022

2017

2018

2023 **2024** **2025**

Scott's No.		Mint Sheet	Plate Block	F-VF NH	F-VF Used
2006-09	20¢ Knoxville Fair, Block of 4 ...	41.50	3.95	3.50	1.50
2006-09	20¢ Set of 4 Singles	...	...	3.40	.80
2010	20¢ Horatio Alger, Newspaper .	26.50	2.50	.55	.15
2011	20¢ "Aging Together"	26.50	2.50	.55	.15
2012	20¢ John, Ethel and Lionel Barrymore, Performing Arts	26.50	2.50	.55	.15
2013	20¢ Mary Walker, Surgeon	28.75	2.75	.60	.15
2014	20¢ Peace Garden Manitoba ...	41.50	3.75	.85	.15
2015	20¢ Libraries of America	26.50	2.50	.55	.15
2016	20¢ Jackie Robinson, Baseball, Black Heritage	95.00	8.95	2.00	.20
2017	20¢ Touro Synagogue	50.00 (20)	21.50	1.00	.15
2018	20¢ Wolf Trap Farm Park	26.50	2.50	.55	.15
2019-22	20¢ Architecture, Block of 4 .. (40)	32.50	4.00	3.50	1.75
2019-22	20¢ Set of 4 Singles	...	...	3.25	.80
2023	20¢ St. Francis of Assisi	28.50	2.75	.60	.15
2024	20¢ Ponce de Leon, Explorer ...	47.50 (20)	21.00	1.00	.15
#2025-30	Christmas Issues				
2025	13¢ Christmas, Kitten & Puppy	21.75	2.00	.45	.15

2026

2027
2029

2028
2030

Scott's No.		Mint Sheet	Plate Block	F-VF NH	F-VF Used
2026	20¢ Christmas, Tiepolo Madonna	29.50 (20)	13.75	.60	.15
2027-30	20¢ Christmas Winter Scenes, Block of 4	41.50	4.25	3.75	2.00
2027-30	20¢ Set of 4 Singles	...	...	3.60	.80

1983 Commemoratives

2032

2033
2034

2035

2036

2031

2037

2039

2038

2040

2041

2042

2043

2044

2045

2046

2047

Scott's No.		Mint Sheet	Plate Block	F-VF NH	F-VF Used
2031-65	Set of 35	...	...	25.00	5.50
2031	20¢ Science & Industry	26.50	2.50	.55	.15
2032-35	20¢ Ballooning, Block of 4 (40)	26.00	3.00	2.75	2.00
2032-35	20¢ Set of 4 Singles	...	...	2.50	.80
2036	20¢ Sweden, Benjamin Franklin	26.50	2.50	.55	.15
2037	20¢ Civilian Conservation C.50th	26.50	2.50	.55	.15
2038	20¢ Joseph Priestley, Oxygen	29.00	2.75	.60	.15
2039	20¢ Voluntarism	29.00 (20)	13.95	.60	.15
2040	20¢ German Immigration Tricent. "Concord"	26.50	2.50	.55	.15
2041	20¢ Brooklyn Bridge Centennial	26.50	2.50	.55	.15
2042	20¢ Tennessee Valley Authority	31.75 (20)	14.95	.65	.15
2043	20¢ Physical Fitness, Runner	29.75 (20)	13.95	.60	.15
2044	20¢ Scott Joplin, Black Heritage	32.50	3.00	.70	.15
2045	20¢ Medal of Honor (40)	29.50	3.25	.75	.15
2046	20¢ George Herman "Babe" Ruth	105.00	9.75	2.25	.20
2047	20¢ Nathaniel Hawthorne	31.50	2.95	.65	.15

2048
2050

2049
2051

2052

2053

2054

2055
2057

2056
2058

2059
2061

2060
2062

		Mint Sheet	Plate Block	F-VF NH	F-VF Used
2048-51	13¢ Los Angeles Summer Olympics, Block of 4	29.50	3.25	3.00	1.50
2048-51	13¢ Set of 4 Singles	...	...	2.90	.80
2052	20¢ Signing of Treaty of Paris (40)	23.50	2.75	.60	.15
2053	20¢ Civil Service Centennial	29.75 (20)	13.95	.60	.15
2054	20¢ Metropolitan Opera Cent.	29.50	2.75	.60	.15
2055-58	20¢ Inventors, Block of 4	39.50	4.25	3.75	2.75
2055-58	20¢ Set of 4 Singles	...	...	3.60	.80
2059-62	20¢ Streetcars, Block of 4	39.50	4.25	3.75	2.75
2059-62	20¢ Set of 4 Singles	...	...	3.60	.80

1983 Commemoratives (continued)

2063

2064

2065

Scott's No.		Mint Sheet	Plate Block	F-VF NH	F-VF Used
2063	20¢ Christmas, Raphael Madonna	26.50	2.50	.55	.15
2064	20¢ Christmas, Santa Claus	30.00 (20)	13.95	.60	.15
2065	20¢ Martin Luther, Founder of Lutheran Church	26.50	2.50	.55	.15

1984 Commemoratives

2067
2069

2068
2070

2066

2071

2072

2073

2074

2075

2076
2078

2077
2079

2066-2109	Set of 44	...	...	32.95	6.85
2066	20¢ Alaska Statehood 25th Ann.	26.50	2.50	.55	.15
2067-70	20¢ Winter Olympics, Sarajevo, Block of 4	38.50	3.85	3.50	1.75
2067-70	20¢ Set of 4 Singles	...	...	3.25	.80
2071	20¢ Federal Deposit Insurance Corporation 50th Anniversary ..	26.50	2.50	.55	.15
2072	20¢ Love, Hearts	29.50 (20)	14.50	.60	.15
2073	20¢ Carter G. Woodson, Historian, Black Heritage	29.50	2.75	.60	.15
2074	20¢ Soil & Water Conservation	26.50	2.50	.55	.15
2075	20¢ Credit Union Act 50th Ann.	26.50	2.50	.55	.15
2076-79	20¢ Orchids, Block of 4 .... (48)	30.00	3.50	2.75	2.25
2076-79	20¢ Set of 4 Singles	...	...	2.50	.80

1984 Commemoratives (cont.)

2080

2082   2083
2084   2085

2086

2081

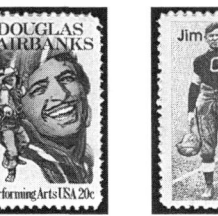

2087

2091

2092

2088

2089

2090

2093

2094

2095

2096

2097

Scott's No.		Mint Sheet	Plate Block	F-VF NH	F-VF Used
2080	20¢ Hawaii Statehood 25th Ann.	29.50	2.75	.65	.15
2081	20¢ National Archives 50th Ann.	29.50	2.75	.65	.15
2082-85	20¢ Los Angeles Summer Olympics, Block of 4	47.50	5.00	4.65	3.75
2082-85	20¢ Set of 4 Singles	...	...	4.50	.90
2086	20¢ Louisiana World's Expo. . (40)	38.50	4.25	1.00	.15
2087	20¢ Health Research	31.50	3.00	.65	.15
2088	20¢ Douglas Fairbanks, Performing Arts	39.50 (20)	17.50	.80	.15
2089	20¢ Jim Thorpe, Athlete	37.50	3.50	.80	.15
2090	20¢ John McCormack, Performing Arts	26.50	2.50	.55	.15
2091	20¢ St. Lawrence Seaway 25th	26.50	2.50	.55	.15
2092	20¢ Waterfowl Preservation Act	42.50	4.25	.90	.15
2093	20¢ Roanoke Voyages 400th ...	42.50	4.25	.90	.15
2094	20¢ Herman Melville, Author	26.50	2.50	.55	.15
2095	20¢ Horace Moses, Founder of Junior Achievement	40.00 (20)	17.75	.85	.15
2096	20¢ Smokey Bear	32.50	3.00	.70	.15
2097	20¢ Roberto Clemente, Baseball	130.00	11.75	2.75	.20

1978 - to Date Black Heritage Series

#1744, 1771, 1804, 1875, 2016, 2044, 2073, 2137, 2203, 2249, 2371, 2402, 2442, 2567, 2617, 2746, 2816, 2956, 3058, 3121, 3181, 3273, 3371, 3557, 3746, 3834

NOTE: PRICES THROUGHOUT THIS LIST ARE SUBJECT TO CHANGE WITHOUT NOTICE IF MARKET CONDITIONS REQUIRE. MINIMUM ORDER MUST TOTAL AT LEAST $20.00.

1984 Commemoratives (continued)

2098
2100

2099
2101

2102

2104

2103

2105

2109

2106

2107

2108

2110

Scott's No.		Mint Sheet	Plate Block	F-VF NH	F-VF Used
2098-2101	20¢ Dogs, Block of 4 .... (40)	29.50	4.25	3.50	2.75
2098-2101	20¢ Set of 4 Singles	...	...	3.00	.80
2102	20¢ Crime Prevention, McGruff, Crime Dog	26.50	2.50	.55	.15
2103	20¢ Hispanic Americans .... (40)	21.50	2.50	.55	.15
2104	20¢ Family Unity	40.00	(20) 17.75	.85	.15
2105	20¢ Eleanor Roosevelt .... (48)	26.50	2.75	.60	.15
2106	20¢ A Nation of Readers	32.50	2.95	.70	.15
#2107-8	Christmas Issues				
2107	20¢ Lippi Madonna & Child	26.50	2.50	.55	.15
2108	20¢ Santa Claus	26.50	2.50	.55	.15
2109	20¢ Vietnam Veterans Memorial(40)	35.00	4.25	.90	.15

1985 Commemoratives

2110,2137-47,52-66	Set of 27	...	...	35.00	5.50
2110	22¢ Jerome Kern, Composer, Performing Arts	31.50	3.00	.65	.15

1985-87 Regular Issues

2111-2113

2114-2115

2115b

2116

2111	(22¢) "D" & Eagle Perf 11 .... (100)	100.00	(20) 32.50	.85	.15

Scott's No.		Pl. # Strip of 5	Pl # Strip of 3	F-VF NH	F-VF Used
2112	(22¢) "D" & Eagle Coil,Pf.10 Vert.	9.50	6.50	.70	.15

Scott's No.		Mint Sheet	Plate Block	F-VF NH	F-VF Used
2113	(22¢) "D" Booklet Single, Perf.11	...	...	1.15	.15
2113a	(22¢) "D" Booklet Pane of 10 ..	...	...	10.75	4.50

#2113 design is substantially smaller than #2111-12 design.

2114	22¢ Flag over Capitol Dome(100)	72.50	3.50	.75	.15

Scott's No.		Pl. # Strip of 5	Pl # Strip of 3	F-VF NH	F-VF Used
2115	22¢ Flag over Capitol Wide Block Tagging Coil,Pf.10 Vert.	4.50	3.50	.65	.15
2115a	22¢ Narrow Block Tagging	4.50	3.50	.65	.15
2115b	22¢ Flag "T" Test Coil (1987) ..	5.75	4.50	.70	.25

#2115b has a tiny "T" below capitol building

2116	22¢ Flag over Capitol Booklet Single	...	...	.90	.15
2116a	22¢ Booklet Pane of 5	...	...	4.25	2.25

1985-89 Regulars

2117

2118

2119

2120

2121

2122

Scott's No.		Mint Sheet	Plate Block	F-VF NH	F-VF Used
2117-21	22¢ Seashells, Strip of 5	...	...	3.70	3.25
2117-21	22¢ Set of 5 Singles	...	...	3.50	1.00
2121a	22¢ Booklet Pane of 10	...	...	6.50	6.50
2122	$10.75 Express Mail, Eagle & Moon, Booklet Single, Type I	...	...	29.50	10.75
2122a	$10.75 Booklet Pane of 3, Type I (Pl. #11111)	...	...	87.50	...
2122b	$10.75 Type II, Booklet Single (1989)	...	...	45.00	17.50
2122c	$10.75 Type II Booklet Pane of 3(Pl.#22222)...	...	...	135.00	...

Ty. I: washed out appearance; "$10.75" is grainy.
Ty. II: brighter colors; "$10.75" is smoother and less grainy.

1985-89 TRANSPORTATION COIL SERIES II

2123

2124

2125

2126

2127

2128

2129

2130

2131

2132

2133

2134

2135

2136

* Plate Numbers must appear on center stamp.

Scott's No.		Pl.# Strip of 5	Pl.# Strip of 3	F-VF NH	F-VF Used
2123-36	Set of 14 (No #2134b)	42.50	33.50	5.25	2.10
2123	3.4¢ School Bus	1.70	1.30	.25	.15
2124	4.9¢ Buckboard	1.50	1.10	.25	.15
2125	5.5¢ Star Route Truck (1986) .	2.65	2.10	.25	.15
2126	6¢ Tricycle	2.25	1.85	.25	.20
2127	7.1¢ Tractor (1987)	2.95	2.50	.35	.20
2128	8.3¢ Ambulance	2.50	1.85	.35	.20
2129	8.5¢ Tow Truck (1987)	4.25	3.50	.35	.20
2130	10.1¢ Oil Wagon	3.25	2.65	.35	.20
2131	11¢ Stutz Bearcat	2.60	2.00	.35	.15
2132	12¢ Stanley Steamer, Type I ...	3.75	2.75	.60	.20
2133	12.5¢ Pushcart	4.00	3.25	.40	.25
2134	14¢ Iceboat, Type I	2.85	2.25	.40	.20
2134b	14¢ "B" Press, Type II (1986) ..	6.00	5.00	.50	.25

#2134 17½mm Wide, Overall Tagging, Line in Plate Strip
#2134b 17¼mm Wide, Block Tagging, No line in Plate Strip

2135	17¢ Dog Sled (1986)	5.50	4.25	.70	.20
2136	25¢ Bread Wagon (1986)	5.75	4.25	.75	.15

1985-89 TRANSPORTATION COIL SERIES II
PRECANCELLED COILS

 2123a    2124a    2125a    2126a    2127a

 2127b    2128a    2129a   2130a   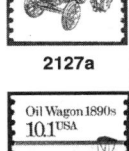 2130b

 2132a    2132b   2133a

Scott's No.		Pl.# Strip of 5	Pl.# Strip of 3	F-VF NH	F-VF Used
2123a/33a	Precan. Set of 12 (No#2132b)	40.75	33.00	3.95	2.60
2123a	3.4¢ School Bus	5.50	4.75	.30	.25
2124a	4.9¢ Buckboard	2.25	1.75	.25	.20
2125a	5.5¢ Star Route Truck (1986) .	2.95	2.50	.25	.20
2126a	6¢ Tricycle	2.65	2.15	.30	.20
2127a	7.1¢ Tractor (1987)	4.50	3.75	.35	.20
2127b	7.1¢ Zip + 4 Precancel (1989)	3.25	2.50	.35	.25
2128a	8.3¢ Ambulance	2.50	1.85	.35	.25
2129a	8.5¢ Tow Truck (1987)	4.25	3.50	.35	.25
2130a	10.1¢ Oil Wagon,Red Prec.(1988)	3.35	2.75	.35	.25
2130av	10.1¢ Oil Wagon, Black Precan.	3.35	2.75	.35	.25
2132a	12¢ Stanley Steamer, Type I ...	4.00	3.00	.60	.25
2132b	12¢ "B" Press,Type II (1987) ...	30.00	26.50	2.00	.75
	#2132, 2132a "Stanley Steamer 1909" 18mm, Line in Plate Strip				
	#2132b "Stanley Steamer 1909" 17½ mm, No line in Plate Strip				
2133a	12.5¢ Pushcart	4.25	3.50	.40	.30

1985 Commemoratives (cont.)

 2137

 2138 2140   2139 2141

 2142    2143   2146

 2144   2145   2147

Scott's No.		Mint Sheet	Plate Block	F-VF NH	F-VF Used
2137	22¢ Mary Mcleod Bethune, Educator, Black Heritage	45.00	4.25	.95	.15
2138-41	22¢ Duck Decoys, Block of 4	95.00	10.00	8.75	6.50
2138-41	22¢ Set of 4 Singles	...	...	8.25	1.00
2142	22¢ Winter Special Olympics .. (40)	25.00	2.95	.65	.15

1985 Commemoratives (continued)

Scott's No.		Mint Sheet	Plate Block	F-VF NH	F-VF Used
2143	22¢ Love	33.50	3.25	.70	.15
2144	22¢ Rural Electrification Admin.50th	52.50 (20)	29.50	.80	.15
2145	22¢ Ameripex '86, Chicago ..... (48)	28.75	2.75	.60	.15
2146	22¢ Abigail Adams	28.50	3.25	.70	.15
2147	22¢ Frederic A. Bartholdi Statue of Liberty	28.50	2.75	.60	.15

1985 Regular Issue Coil Stamps Perf. 10 Vertically

 2149    2149a    2150    2150a

Scott's No.		Pl# Strip of 5	Pl# Strip of 3	F-VF NH	F-VF Used
2149	18¢ Washington, Pre-Sort, Low Gloss Gum	4.65	3.25	.75	.20
2149a	18¢ Precancelled	4.50	3.50	.55	.35
2149d	18¢ Precancelled, Dull Gum ..	7.50	6.00	.80	...
2150	21.1¢ Envelope	4.75	3.50	.70	.25
2150a	21.1¢ Zip + 4 Precancel	5.00	4.00	.75	.50

1985 Commemoratives (continued)

 2152    2153    2154

 2155 2157   2156 2158    2159

 2160 2162   2161 2163    2165

 2164   2166   2167

Scott's No.		Mint Sheet	Plate Block	F-VF NH	F-VF Used
2152	22¢ Korean War Veterans	39.50	3.95	.85	.15
2153	22¢ Social Security Act 50th Ann.	28.50	2.75	.60	.15
2154	22¢ World War I Veterans	39.50	3.95	.85	.15
2155-58	22¢ Horses, Block of 4 .... (40)	110.00	13.75	12.00	7.00
2155-58	22¢ Set of 4 Singles	...	...	11.00	1.60
2159	22¢ Public Education	67.50	5.75	1.35	.15
2160-63	22¢ Int'l. Youth Year, Block of 4 ..	59.50	7.00	5.25	3.00
2160-63	22¢ Set of 4 Singles	...	...	4.00	1.20
2164	22¢ Help End Hunger	31.50	3.00	.65	.15
2165	22¢ Genoa Madonna and Child ..	28.50	2.75	.60	.15
2166	22¢ Christmas Poinsettia Plants	28.50	2.75	.60	.15

1986 Commemoratives

Scott's No.		Mint Sheet	Plate Block	F-VF NH	F-VF Used
2167,2202-04,2210-11, 2220-24,2235-45	**Set of 22 (1986)**	...	...	**20.75**	**3.85**
2167	22¢ Arkansas Statehood	72.50	6.50	1.50	.15

1986-94 Great Americans, Perforated 11, Tagged

(Sheets of 100)

2168 2169 2170 2171

2172 2173 2175 2176

2177 2178 2179 2180 2181

2182,2197 2183 2184 2185 2186

2187 2188 2189 2190 2191

2192 2193 2194 2195 2196

Scott's No.		Mint Sheet	Plate Block	F-VF NH	F-VF Used
2168/96	**Set of 28**	...	**197.50**	**42.00**	**7.25**
2168	1¢ Margaret Mitchell	9.00	.75	.20	.15
2169,	2¢ Mary Lyon, Block Tagging (1987)	8.25	.70	.20	.15
2169a	2¢ Untagged (1996)	12.75	1.10	.25	.20
2170	3¢ Dr.Paul Dudley White,Dull Gum	12.00	.70	.20	.15
2170a	3¢ Untagged, Dull Gum	15.00	1.10	.25	.15
2170s	3¢ Untagged, Shiny Gum (1995)	15.00	1.10	.25	...
2171	4¢ Father Flanagan, Large Block Tagging, Blue Violet...................	14.50	.85	.20	.15
2171a	4¢ Untagged, Grayish Violet	17.50	1.10	.25	.20
2171b	4¢ Untagged,Deep Grayish Blue('93)	17.50	1.10	.25	.20
2172	5¢ Hugo Black	38.50	1.85	.40	.15
2173	5¢ Luis Munoz Marin Overall Tagging (1990)	17.50	.90	.20	.15
2173a	5¢ Marin, Untagged (1991)	22.50	1.10	.25	.20
2175	10¢ Red Cloud, Large Block Tagging, Lake, Dull Gum (1987)	47.50	2.25	.50	.20
2175a	10¢ Overall Tagging, Dull Gum ('90)	100.00	9.50	.90	.35
2175c	10¢ Solid Tagging, Dull Gum(1991)	...	11.50	2.00	.50
2175d	10¢ Mottled Tagging, Shiny Gum(1993)...		11.50	2.00	.50
2175e	10¢ Carmine, Mottled Tagging, Shiny Gum (1994)	47.50	2.35	.50	.20
2176	14¢ Julia Ward Howe (1987)	42.50	2.25	.45	.20
2177	15¢ Buffalo Bill Cody, Large Block Tagging (1988)	75.00	8.25	.75	.25
2177a	15¢ Overall Tagging (1990)	50.00	3.50	.50	...
2177b	15¢ Solid Tagging, Prephosp.	...	6.50	1.00	...
2178	17¢ Belva Ann Lockwood	53.50	2.75	.55	.20
2179	20¢ Virginia Agpar, Red Brown, Perf. 11 x 11.1 (1994)	52.50	3.00	.55	.20
2179a	20¢ Orange Brown	62.50	3.50	.65	.20
2180	21¢ Chester Carlson (1988)	57.50	3.25	.60	.40

1986-94 Great Americans, Perforated 11 (continued)

(Sheets of 100)

Scott's No.		Mint Sheet	Plate Block	F-VF NH	F-VF Used
2181	23¢ Mary Cassatt, Large Block Tagging, Dull Gum (1988)	62.50	3.50	.65	.20
2181a	23¢ Overall Tagging, Dull Gum ..	90.00	5.50	.95	.30
2181b	23¢ Solid Tagging, Dull Gum	75.00	4.25	.80	.20
2181c	23¢ Mottled Tagging, Shiny Gum	90.00	5.50	.95	.50
2182	25¢ Jack London, Perf. 11	75.00	3.75	.80	.20
2182v	25¢ Booklet Single,Perf.11(1988)	...	...	.80	.20
2182a	25¢ Booklet Pane of 10, Perf. 11 (1988)...		...	7.25	4.50
2183	28¢ Sitting Bull (1989)	115.00	5.50	1.20	.40
2184	29¢ Earl Warren (1992)	95.00	4.75	1.00	.20
2185	29¢ Jefferson Pf 11½ x 11 (1993)	85.00	4.50	.90	.20
2185	29¢ Jefferson, Plate Block of 8 ...	...	8.50	...	...
2186	35¢ Dennis Chavez (1991)	95.00	5.00	1.00	.40
2187	40¢ Claire Chennault, Overall Tagging, Dull Gum (1990)	105.00	5.50	1.10	.25
2187a	40¢ Solid Tagging, Dull Gum	135.00	6.75	1.40	.40
2187b	40¢ Grainy Solid Tagging, Low Gloss Gum (1998)	120.00	6.00	1.25	...
2187c	40¢ Mottled Tagging,Shiny Gum('94)	130.00	9.50	1.30	.35
2188	45¢ Dr. Harvey Cushing, Bright Blue, Large Block Tagging (1988)	125.00	5.75	1.30	.25
2188a	45¢ Blue, Overall Tagging (1990)	270.00	15.75	2.75	.75
2189	52¢ Hubert Humphrey, Solid Tagging, Dull Gum (1991)	155.00	9.00	1.60	.25
2189a	52¢ Mottled Tagging, Shiny Gum (1993)	195.00	9.75	2.00	...
2190	56¢ John Harvard	155.00	8.50	1.60	.25
2191	65¢ Gen. H.H."Hap" Arnold (1988)	170.00	8.75	1.75	.25
2192	75¢ Wendell Willkie, Solid Tagging, Dull Gum (1992)	190.00	9.75	1.95	.25
2192a	75¢ Mottled Tagging, Shiny Gum	220.00	11.50	2.25	...
2193	$1 Dr. Bernard Revel	370.00	19.50	3.75	.40
2194	$1 Johns Hopkins, Intense Deep Blue, Large Block Tagging, Dull Gum (1989) .... (20)	57.50	13.75	3.00	.40
2194b	$1 Deep Blue, Overall Tagging, Dull Gum (1990) ...... (20)	62.50	14.75	3.25	.40
2194d	$1 Dark Blue, Solid Tagging, Dull Gum (1992) .... (20)	62.50	14.75	3.25	.40
2194e	$1 Blue, Mottled Tagging, Shiny Gum (1993) .... (20)	67.50	16.00	3.50	.50
2194f	$1 Blue, Grainy Solid Tagging, Low Gloss Gum (1998) .... (20)	67.50	16.00	3.50	...
2195	$2 William Jennings Bryan	515.00	25.00	5.25	.65
2196	$5 Bret Harte, Large Block Tagging (1987) .... (20)	240.00	55.00	12.50	2.65
2196b	$5 Solid Tagging (1992) .... (20)	255.00	57.50	13.00	3.00
2197	25¢ J. London Booklet Single, Perf.10 (1988)	...	...	.75	.15
2197a	25¢ Booklet Pane of 6, Perf.10 (1988) ...		...	4.50	3.00

NOTE: SETS CONTAIN OUR CHOICE OF TAGGED OR UNTAGGED, ETC.

1986 Commemoratives (continued)

2198 2199 2200 2201

2202 2203 2204 2211

2205 2206 2207

2208 2209 2210

1986 Commemoratives (continued)

Scott's No.		Mint Sheet	Plate Block	F-VF NH	F-VF Used
2198-2201	22¢ Stamp Collecting Set of 4 Booklet Singles	...	...	2.60	1.20
2201a	22¢ Stamp Coll. Booklet Pane of 4	...	...	2.75	2.65
2202	22¢ Love, Puppy	32.50	2.95	.70	.15
2203	22¢ Sojourner Truth, Human Rights, Black Heritage	42.50	3.75	.90	.15
2204	22¢ Republic of Texas, 150th Ann.	57.50	5.50	1.20	.15
2205-09	22¢ Fish Set of 5 Booklet Singles	...	...	10.50	1.00
2209a	22¢ Fish Booklet Pane of 5	...	...	10.75	5.75
2210	22¢ Public Hospitals	33.50	3.25	.70	.15
2211	22¢ Duke Ellington, Performing Arts	31.50	3.00	.65	.15

1986 Presidents Miniature Sheets of 9

2216a George Washington
2216b John Adams
2216c Thomas Jefferson
2216d James Madison
2216e James Monroe
2216f John Quincy Adams
2216g Andrew Jackson
2216h Martin Van Buren
2216i William H. Harrison
2217a John Tyler
2217b James Knox Polk
2217c Zachary Taylor
2217d Millard Fillmore
2217e Franklin Pierce
2217f James Buchanan
2217g Abraham Lincoln
2217h Andrew Johnson
2217i Ulysses S. Grant
2218a Rutherfor B. Hayes
2218b James A. Garfield
2218c Chester A. Arthur
2218d Grover Cleveland
2218e Benjamin Harrison
2218f William McKinley
2218g Theodore Roosevelt
2218h William H. Taft
2218i Woodrow Wilson
2219a Warren G. Harding
2219b Calvin Coolidge
2219c Herbert Hoover
2219d Franklin Roosevelt
2219e White House
2219f Harry S Truman
2219g Dwight Eisenhower
2219h John F. Kennedy
2219i Lyndon B. Johnson

2216-2219

2216-19	22¢ Ameripex '86, Set of 4 Sheets of 9...	...	...	28.75	27.50
2216	22¢ Washington-Harrison Sheet of 9	...	...	7.50	7.25
2217	22¢ Tyler - Grant Sheet of 9	...	...	7.50	7.25
2218	22¢ Hayes-Wilson Sheet of 9	...	...	7.50	7.25
2219	22¢ Harding-Johnson Sheet of 9	...	...	7.50	7.25
2216a-19i	22¢ Presidents, Set of 36 Singles	...	...	27.75	17.50

1986 Commemoratives (continued)

2220 **2222**		**2221** **2223**	**2224**

		Mint Sheet	Plate Block	F-VF NH	F-VF Used
2220-23	22¢ Arctic Explorers, Block of 4 ..	65.00	6.75	5.50	4.25
2220-23	22¢ Set of 4 Singles	...	...	5.00	1.20
2224	22¢ Statue of Liberty 100th Anniv.	36.50	3.25	.75	.15

1986-96 Transportation "B" Press Coils

2225	**2226**	**2228**	**2231**

1986-96 Transportation "B" Press Coils (continued)

Scott's No.		Pl.# Strip of 5	Pl.# Strip of 3	F-VF NH	F-VF Used
2225-31	Set of 4	14.50	10.75	2.00	.65
2225	1¢ Omnibus,Large Block Tagging, Dull Gum	1.00	.70	.20	.15
2225a	1¢ Mottled Tagging, Shiny Gum ..	18.50	17.50	.35	.20
2225b	1¢ Untagged, Dull Gum	1.20	.80	.25	.20
2225s	1¢ Untagged, Shiny Gum (1996)	1.40	.90	.25	...
2225l	1¢ Untagged, Low Gloss Gum	2.75	2.00	.40	...
2226	2¢ Locomotive, Tagged, Dull (1987)	1.00	.75	.20	.15
2226a	2¢ Untagged, Dull Gum (1994) ...	1.25	.85	.25	.20
2226s	2¢ Untagged, Shiny Gum	2.50	2.00	.30	...
2228	4¢ Stagecoach, Reduced Size, Large Block Tagging	1.65	1.30	.20	.20
2228a	4¢ Overall Tagging (1990)	14.00	12.75	.65	.30
1898A:	"Stagecoach 1890s" is 19½ mm. long				
2228:	"Stagecoach 1890s" is 17 mm. long				
2231	8.3¢ Ambulance, Precancel	11.50	8.50	1.50	.25
2128:	"Ambulance 1860s" is 18½ mm. long				
2231:	"Ambulance 1860s" is 18 mm. long				

1986 Commemoratives (continued)

2235 **2237**	**2236** **2238**	**2239**	**2240** **2242**	**2241** **2243**

2244	**2245**	**2247**	**2248**

2246	**2249**	**2250**	**2251**

Scott's No.		Mint Sheet	Plate Block	F-VF NH	F-VF Used
2235-38	22¢ Navajo Art, Block of 4	52.50	5.50	4.50	4.25
2235-38	22¢ Set of 4 Singles	...	...	4.25	.80
2239	22¢ T.S. Eliot, Poet	38.50	3.75	.80	.15
2240-43	22¢ Woodcarved Figurines., Blk-4	45.00	4.25	3.75	3.50
2240-43	22¢ Set of 4 Singles	...	...	3.50	.80
2244-45	Christmas Issues				
2244	22¢ Perugino Madonna & Child(100)	57.50	2.95	.60	.15
2245	22¢ Village Scene .... (100)	57.50	2.95	.60	.15

1987 Commemoratives

		Mint Sheet	Plate Block	F-VF NH	F-VF Used
2246-51,75,2336-38,2349-54,2360-61,2367-68 Set of 20		...	...	17.25	3.25
2246	22¢ Michigan Statehood 150th An.	52.50	4.75	1.10	.15
2247	22¢ Pan American Games	28.50	2.75	.60	.15
2248	22¢ Love, Heart .... (100)	57.50	2.95	.60	.15
2249	22¢ Jean Baptiste Pointe du Sable, Pioneer Trader, Black Heritage ...	32.50	3.25	.70	.15
2250	22¢ Enrico Caruso, Opera, Performing Arts	28.50	2.75	.60	.15
2251	22¢ Girl Scouts 75th Anniv.	32.50	3.25	.70	.15

Scott's No.		Pl.# Strip of 5	Pl.# Strip of 3	F-VF NH	F-VF Used
2252-66	Set of 15	66.00	52.50	7.50	3.35
2252	3¢ Conestoga Wagon, Dull Gum (1988)	1.40	1.10	.20	.15
2252a	3¢ Untagged, Dull Gum (1992) ..	1.65	1.35	.20	.20
2252s	3¢ Untagged, Shiny Gum (1995)	1.85	1.50	.25	...
2252l	3¢ Untagged, Low Gloss Gum ...	11.00	10.00	.45	...
2253	5¢ Milk Wagon	2.25	1.85	.25	.15
2254	5.3¢ Elevator, Precancel (1988) .	2.30	1.85	.30	.20
2255	7.6¢ Carretta, Precancel (1988) ..	3.15	2.65	.30	.20
2256	8.4¢ Wheelchair, Precancel (1986)	3.00	2.50	.30	.20
2257	10¢ Canal Boat, Large Block Tagging, Dull Gum	3.85	3.25	.35	.15
2257a	10¢ Overall Tagging, Dull (1993) .	5.75	4.75	.45	.30
2257s	10¢ Overall Tagging, Shiny (1994)	6.00	5.25	.45	...
2257b	10¢ Mottled Tagging, Shiny	5.50	4.75	.40	.30
2257c	10¢ Solid Tagging, Low Gloss Gum	5.50	4.75	.40	.30
2258	13¢ Police Wagon, Prec. (1988) ..	7.25	6.00	.70	.25
2259	13.2¢ Railroad Coal Car, Precancelled (1988)	4.25	3.65	.40	.20
2260	15¢ Tugboat, Large Block Tagging (1988)	3.25	2.50	.45	.20
2260a	15¢ Overall Tagging (1990)	6.50	5.50	.65	.25
2261	16.7¢ Popcorn Wagon, Prec.('88)	4.75	3.75	.50	.25
2262	17.5¢ Marmon Wasp	5.75	4.75	.70	.30
2262a	17.5¢ Precancelled, Untagged ...	6.75	5.25	.80	.35
2263	20¢ Cable Car, Large Block Tagging (1988)	4.75	3.75	.65	.20
2263b	20¢ Overall Tagging (1990)	12.00	9.75	1.30	.35
2264	20.5¢ Fire Engine, Prec. (1988) .	10.00	7.50	1.35	.40
2265	21¢ Railroad Mail Car, Precancelled (1988)	6.50	4.75	.65	.40
2266	24.1¢ Tandem Bicycle, Precancelled (1988)	6.75	5.25	.85	.40

1987 Special Occasions Issue

2267 Congratulations! **2268** Get Well! **2269** Thank You! **2270** Love You, Dad!

2271 Best Wishes! **2272** Happy Birthday! **2273** Love You, Mother! **2274** Keep In Touch!

2275 Uniting Communities USA 22 · **2276** · **2277,79,82** Earth Domestic USA E

2278,2285A · **2280** Yosemite · **2281** · **2283**

2284 · **2285**

Scott's No.		Mint Sheet	Plate Block	F-VF NH	F-VF Used
	1987 Special Occasions Issue				
2267-74	22¢ Special Occasions Booklet Singles (8)...	...	...	14.50	2.95
2274a	22¢ Booklet Pane of 10	...	...	15.75	14.75
	Booklet Pane contains 2 each of # 2267 and # 2272				
	1987 Commemoratives (continued)				
2275	22¢ United Way 100th Anniv.	28.50	2.75	.60	.15
	1987-89 Regular Issues				
2276	22¢ Flag & Fireworks .... (100) 57.50		3.00	.60	.15
2276a	22¢ Fireworks Booklet Pane of 20	...	...	12.50	11.00
2276v	22¢ Flag, Booklet Single (1 or 2 straight edges)	...		.70	.20
2277	(25¢) "E" & Earth Issue (1988) (100) 80.00		4.25	.85	.15
2278	25¢ Flag & Clouds (1988) ...... (100) 70.00		3.75	.75	.15

Scott's No.		Pl.# Strip of 5	Pl.# Strip of 3	F-VF NH	F-VF Used
2279	(25¢) "E" Earth Coil (1988)	5.00	3.75	.70	.15
2280	25¢ Flag & Yosemite Coil. Large Block Tagging (1988)	4.75	3.50	.80	.15
2280a	25¢ Mottled Tagging (1989)	5.75	4.25	.90	.15
2281	25¢ Honeybee Coil	5.25	3.75	.85	.15
2282	(25¢) "E" & Earth Booklet Single (1988)...	...	...	.85	.20
2282a	(25¢) Booklet Pane of 10	...	...	7.75	6.50
2283	25¢ Pheasant Booklet Single, **red & blue sky** (1988)	...	...	.85	.15
2283a	25¢ Booklet Pane of 10	...	...	7.75	6.50
2283b	25¢ Blue Sky, **(red omitted)**, Booklet Single (1989)	...	...	9.00	2.00
2283c	25¢ Booklet Pane 10 **(Pl# A3111,A3222)**...	...	...	85.00	...
2284	25¢ Grosbeak Booklet Single (1988)	...	...	.75	.20
2285	25¢ Owl Booklet Single (1988) ...	...	...	.75	.20
2284-85	25¢ Attached Pair	...	...	1.50	1.25
2285b	25¢ Booklet Pane of 10 (5 ea. #2284,2285)...	...	...	6.75	5.75
2285A	25¢ Flag & Clouds Booklet Single (1988)...	...	...	.85	.15
2285Ac	25¢ Booklet Pane of 6	...	...	4.75	4.00

1987 North American Wildlife Series

2286-2335 Sheet

58

1987 North American Wildlife Series (continued)

2287   **2288**   **2289**

Scott's No.		Mint Sheet	Plate Block	F-VF NH	F-VF Used
2286-2335	22¢ American Wildlife Sheet of 50	69.50	...	...	...
2286-2335	22¢ Set of 50 Singles	....	...	65.00	22.50
2286-2335	22¢ Individual Singles	....	...	1.50	.60

2286 Barn Swallow	2303 Blackbird	2320 Bison
2287 Monarch Butterfly	2304 Lobster	2321 Snowy Egret
2288 Bighorn Sheep	2305 Jack Rabbit	2322 Gray Wolf
2289 Hummingbird	2306 Scarlet Tanager	2323 Mountain Goat
2290 Cottontail	2307 Woodchuck	2324 Deer Mouse
2291 Osprey	2308 Spoonbill	2325 Prairie Dog
2292 Mountain Lion	2309 Bald Eagle	2326 Box Turtle
2293 Luna Moth	2310 Brown Bear	2327 Wolverine
2294 Mule Deer	2311 Iiwi	2328 American Elk
2295 Gray Squirrel	2312 Badger	2329 Sea Lion
2296 Armadillo	2313 Pronghorn	2330 Mockingbird
2297 Eastern Chipmunk	2314 River Otter	2331 Raccoon
2298 Moose	2315 Ladybug	2332 Bobcat
2299 Black Bear	2316 Beaver	2333 Ferret
2300 Tiger Swallowtail	2317 Whitetailed Deer	2334 Canada Goose
2301 Bobwhite	2318 Blue Jay	2335 Red Fox
2302 Ringtail	2319 Pika	

2336   **2337**   **2338**   **2339**

2340   **2341**   **2342**   **2343**

2344   **2345**   **2346**   **2347**

2348   **2349**   **2350**

1987-90 Ratification of the Constitution Bicentennial

Scott's No.			Plate Block	F-VF NH	F-VF Used
2336-48	Set of 13	575.00	56.50	12.00	2.40
2336	22¢ Delaware.	45.00	4.50	.95	.20
2337	22¢ Pennsylvania	45.00	4.50	.95	.20
2338	22¢ New Jersey	45.00	4.50	.95	.20
2339	22¢ Georgia (1988)	45.00	4.50	.95	.20
2340	22¢ Connecticut (1988)	45.00	4.50	.95	.20
2341	22¢ Massachusetts (1988)	45.00	4.50	.95	.20
2342	22¢ Maryland (1988)	47.50	4.75	1.00	.20
2343	25¢ South Carolina (1988)	46.50	4.50	.95	.20
2344	25¢ New Hampshire (1988)	46.50	4.50	.95	.20
2345	25¢ Virginia (1988)	46.50	4.50	.95	.20

1987-90 Ratification of the Constitution Bicentennial (continued)

Scott's No.		Mint Sheet	Plate Block	F-VF NH	F-VF Used
2346	25¢ New York (1988)	46.50	4.50	.95	.20
2347	25¢ North Carolina (1989)	46.50	4.50	.95	.20
2348	25¢ Rhode Island (1990)	52.50	5.25	1.10	.20

1987 Commemoratives (continued)

2351   **2352**
2353   **2354**

2355
2356
2357
2358
2359

2362
2363
2364
2365
2366

2360   **2361**   **2367**   **2368**

		Mint Sheet	Plate Block	F-VF NH	F-VF Used
2349	22¢ U.S.-Morocco Diplomatic Relations 200th Anniversary	28.50	2.75	.60	.15
2350	22¢ William Faulkner, Novelist .	53.50	5.00	1.10	.15
2351-54	22¢ Lacemaking, Block of 4 .. (40)	35.00	5.00	3.50	3.00
2351-54	22¢ Set of 4 Singles	...	...	3.35	1.00
2355-59	22¢ Drafting of Constitution, Booklet Singles (5)	...	...	6.50	1.10
2359a	22¢ Booklet Pane of 5	...	...	6.75	5.75
2360	22¢ Signing the Constitution 200th	53.50	5.00	1.10	.15
2361	22¢ Certified Public Accounting	150.00	13.00	3.00	.20
2362-66	22¢ Locomotives Booklet Singles (5)	...	...	4.25	1.10
2366a	22¢ Booklet Pane of 5	...	...	4.50	4.25
#2367-68	Christmas Issues				
2367	22¢ Moroni Madonna & Child (100)	57.50	2.95	.60	.15
2368	22¢ Ornaments .... (100)	57.50	2.95	.60	.15

1988 Commemoratives

2369　　　　　　2370　　　　　　2371

2372　　　　　2373　　　　　2376
2374　　　　　2375

2377　　　2378　　　2379　　　2380

Scott's No.		Mint Sheet	Plate Block	F-VF NH	F-VF Used
2339-46,69-80,86-93,99-2400 Set of 30		...	...	28.75	5.50
2369	22¢ 1988 Winter Olympics, Calgary, Skiing	35.00	3.50	.75	.15
2370	22¢ Australia Bicentennial ..... (40)	23.00	2.75	.60	.15
2371	22¢ J.W. Johnson, Author, Black Heritage	33.00	3.25	.70	.15
2372-75	22¢ Cats, Block of 4 .... (40)	38.50	5.75	4.00	3.75
2372-75	22¢ Set of 4 Singles	...	...	3.75	1.00
2376	22¢ Knute Rockne, Football	47.50	4.50	1.00	.20
2377	25¢ Francis Ouimet, Golf	52.50	4.95	1.10	.20
2378	25¢ Love, Roses .... (100)	67.50	3.50	.70	.15
2379	45¢ Love, Roses	65.00	6.25	1.35	.20
2380	25¢ Summer Olympics, Seoul ..	37.50	3.75	.80	.15

2381　　　　　　　2382

2383　　　　　　　2384

2385

2381-85	25¢ Classic Cars, Booklet Singles	...	...	11.50	1.25
2385a	25¢ Booklet Pane of 5	...	...	11.75	7.50

1988 Commemoratives (continued)

2386　　　　2387　　　　2390　　　2391
2388　　　　2389　　　　2392　　　2393

Scott's No.		Mint Sheet	Plate Block	F-VF NH	F-VF Used
2386-89	25¢ Antarctic Explorers, Block of 4	59.50	6.75	5.25	4.25
2386-89	25¢ Set of 4 Singles	...	...	4.75	1.00
2390-93	25¢ Carousel Animals, Block of 4	58.50	6.25	5.25	4.25
2390-93	25¢ Set of 4 Singles	...	...	4.75	1.00

2394　　　　　　2399　　　　　　2400

2395　　　　　2396

2397　　　　　2398

1988 Express Mail Issue
2394	$8.75 Eagle & Moon .... (20)	500.00	115.00	26.50	8.75

1988 Special Occasions Issue
2395-98	25¢ Special Occasions, Booklet Singles...	...	...	3.75	1.00
2396a	25¢ Happy Birthday & Best Wishes Booklet Pane of 6 (3&3) with gutter .	...	...	5.00	4.75
2398a	25¢ Thinking of You & Love You Booklet Pane of 6 (3&3) with gutter .	...	...	5.00	4.75

1988 Commemoratives (continued)
2399	25¢ Botticelli Madonna & Child	31.50	3.25	.65	.15
2400	25¢ Horse & Sleigh with Village	31.50	3.25	.65	.15

2401　　　　　2402　　　　　2403

1989 Commemoratives
2347,2401-4,10-18,20-28,34-37 Set of 27		...	...	26.50	4.50
2401	25¢ Montana Statehood Cent ...	47.50	4.65	1.00	.15
2402	25¢ A. Philip Randolph, Labor & Civil Rights, Black Heritage ..	47.50	4.50	1.00	.15
2403	25¢ North Dakota Statehoo. Cent.	47.50	4.50	1.00	.15

1989 Issues (continued)

2404

2410

2405

2406

2407

2408

2409

2411

2416

2412

2413

2414

2415

2417

2418

2421

2426

2419

2422
2424

2423
2425

2420

2427

2428, 2429

2431

1989 Commemoratives (continued)

Scott's No.		Mint Sheet	Plate Block	F-VF NH	F-VF Used
2404	25¢ Washington Statehood Cent.	42.50	4.00	.90	.15
2405-09	25¢ Steamboats, Booklet Singles	...		5.00	1.10
2409a	25¢ Booklet Pane of 5 (Unfolded 8.50)	...		5.25	4.50
2410	25¢ World Stamp Expo '89	35.00	3.50	.75	.15
2411	25¢ Arturo Toscanini, Conductor	35.00	3.50	.75	.15
2412-15	25¢ Constitution Bicent., Set of 4	160.00	17.75	3.75	.55
2412	25¢ House of Representatives	47.50	4.65	1.00	.15
2413	25¢ U.S. Senate	57.50	5.50	1.20	.15
2414	25¢ Executive Branch/ George Washington Inauguration	42.50	4.25	.90	.15
2415	25¢ U.S. Supreme Court (1990)	40.00	3.95	.85	.15
2416	25¢ South Dakota Statehood Centennial	53.50	5.00	1.10	.15
2417	25¢ Henry Louis "Lou" Gehrig	55.00	5.25	1.10	.20
2418	25¢ Ernest Hemingway, Writer	38.50	3.75	.80	.15

1989 Priority Mail Issue

2419	$2.40 Moon Landing 20th Ann.(20)	150.00	35.00	7.75	3.50

1989 Commemoratives (continued)

2420	25¢ Letter Carriers (40)	25.00	3.00	.65	.15
2421	25¢ Drafting Bill of Rights Bicent.	45.00	4.75	.95	.15
2422-25	25¢ Prehistoric Animals, Blk.-4(40)	55.00	6.50	5.75	4.50
2422-25	25¢ Set of 4 Singles	...		5.50	1.00
2426	25¢ Pre-Columbian America, Southwest Carved Figures	31.50	3.00	.65	.15

1989 Christmas Issues

2427	25¢ Caracci Madonna & Child	33.50	3.25	.70	.15
2427v	25¢ Madonna, Booklet Single	...	...	.90	.20
2427a	25¢ Booklet Pane of 10 (Unfolded 15.00)			8.25	7.50
2428	25¢ Sleigh & Presents, Perf.11	33.50	3.25	.70	.15
2429	25¢ Sleigh, Booklet Single, Perf.11½	...		.90	.20
2429a	25¢ Booklet Pane of 10 (Unfolded 19.50)			8.25	7.50

1989 Regular Issue

2431	25¢ Eagle & Shield, self adhesive	...	...	1.10	.30
2431a	25¢ Pane of 18	...	...	17.50	
2431v	25¢ Eagle & Shield, Coil (No #) Plain Strip of 3	2.70		.90	...

1989 World Stamp Expo '89, Washington, DC

2433

2438

2434

2435

2436

2437

Scott's No.		Mint Sheet	Plate Block	F-VF NH	F-VF Used
2433	90¢ World Stamp Expo Souvenir Sheet of 4	...	...	19.50	15.00
2433a-d	90¢ Set of 4 singles	...	...	19.00	13.00
2434-37	25¢ Traditional Mail Delivery,				
	Block of 4	(40) 47.50	6.00	5.00	4.25
2434-37	Set of 4 Singles	...	...	4.75	1.20
2438	25¢ Traditional Mail Souvenir Sheet of 4	...	...	7.25	5.00
2438a-d	25¢ Set of 4 singles	...	...	7.00	4.00

Also see #C122-26

2439

2440,2441

2442

2443

2444

2449

2445
2447

2446
2448

Scott's No.		Mint Sheet	Plate Block	F-VF NH	F-VF Used
1990 Commemoratives					
2348,2439-40,2442,44-49,96-2500,2506-15 Set of 25		...		27.75	4.65
2439	25¢ Idaho Statehood Centennial	47.50	4.50	1.00	.15
2440	25¢ Love, Doves, Perf.12½x13	31.50	3.00	.65	.15
2441	25¢ Love, Booklet Single Perf.11½	...	...	1.15	.20
2441a	25¢ Booklet Pane of 10	(Unfolded 48.50)	...	10.75	9.50
2442	25¢ Ida B. Wells, Black Heritage	72.50	7.00	1.50	.15
1990 Regular Issue					
2443	15¢ Beach Umbrella, Booklet Single	...	...	.45	.15
2443a	15¢ Booklet Pane of 10	(Unfolded 8.75)	...	4.35	3.50
1990 Commemoratives (continued)					
2444	25¢ Wyoming Statehood Centen.	47.50	4.50	1.00	.15
2445-48	25¢ Classic Films, Block of 4	(40) 77.50	9.50	8.00	6.50
2445-48	25¢ Set of 4 Singles	...	...	7.75	1.00
2449	25¢ Marianne Moore, Poet	31.50	3.00	.65	.15

1990-95 Transportation Coils IV

2451

2452,2452B

2452D

2453,2454

2457

2458

2463

2464

2466

2468

Scott's No.		Pl# Strip of 5	Pl# Strip of 3	F-VF NH	F-VF Used
2451/2468	Set of 12 values	56.50	42.75	7.15	2.30
2451	4¢ Steam Carriage (1991)	1.20	.90	.20	.15
2451b	4¢ Untagged	1.65	1.25	.25	.20
2452	5¢ Circus Wagon, Engraved,				
	Dull Gum	2.10	1.75	.20	.15
2452a	5¢ Untagged, Dull Gum	2.50	2.00	.25	.20
2452l	5¢ Untagged, Low Gloss Gum	2.50	2.00	.25	...
2452B	5¢ Circus Wagon, Gravure (1992)	2.50	1.95	.25	.15
2452Bf	5¢ Circus Wagon, Luminescent	4.75	4.00	.35	...
#2452 Short letters and date,#2452B Taller, thinner letters & date					
2452D	5¢ Circus Wagon(¢ sign)				
	Low Gloss Gum (1995)	2.25	1.85	.25	.15
2452Dg	5¢ Circus Wagon, Luminescent,				
	Shiny Gum	2.95	2.25	.40	...
2453	5¢ Canoe, Brown, Precan. (1991)	2.30	1.85	.25	.15
2454	5¢ Canoe, Red, Precancelled,				
	Shiny Gum(1991)	2.35	1.90	.25	.15
2454l	5¢ Low Gloss Gum	13.00	12.00	.65	...
2457	10¢ Tractor Trailer, Intaglio,				
	Precancelled (2991)	3.25	2.75	.30	.20
#2457"Additional Presort Postage Paid" In Gray.					
2458	10¢ Tractor Trailer, Gravure (1994)	4.85	4.00	.45	.25
#2458	"Additional, etc." in black. Whiter paper.				
2463	20¢ Cog Railway (1995)	6.00	5.00	.55	.20
2464	23¢ Lunch Wagon, Solid				
	Tagging, Dull Gum (1991)	5.00	3.95	.65	.15
2464a	23¢ Mottled Tagging, Dull Gum(1993)	16.75	13.00	2.00	.35
2464s	23¢ Mottled Tagging,Shiny Gum('93)	7.50	6.00	.80	...
2466	32¢ Ferryboat,Blue,Mottled				
	Tagging, Shiny Gum (1995)	8.50	6.75	.90	.15
2466l	32¢ Mottled Tagging,Low Gloss Gum	16.00	13.75	1.10	.35
2466b	32¢ Bright "Bronx" blue, Mottled	180.00	165.00	6.75	5.75
2468	$1 Seaplane, Overall				
	Tagging, Dull Gum	19.75	13.00	3.50	.70
2468b	$1 Mottled Tagging,Shiny Gum(1993)	20.75	14.00	3.75	1.00
2468c	$1 Grainy Solid Tagging,				
	Low Gloss Gum (1998)	29.50	21.50	4.00	1.00

2470   2471   2472   2473   2474

2475

1990 Commemorative Booklet Pane

Scott's No.		Mint Sheet	Plate Block	F-VF NH	F-VF Used
2470-74	25¢ Lighthouse Booklet Singles	...	...	8.75	1.00
2474a	25¢ Booklet Pane of 5	(Unfolded 14.75)		9.00	6.50
1990 Flag Regular Issue					
2475	25¢ ATM Self Adhesive, Plastic Stamp	...	...	1.10	.50
2475a	25¢ Pane of 12	...	...	10.75	...

1990-95 Flora and Fauna

2476   2477   2478   2479

2480   2481   2482

2476-82	Set of 7		...	35.00	7.65	2.00
2476	1¢ Kestrel (1991)	(100)	7.50	.75	.20	.15
2477	1¢ Redesign with "¢" sign (1995)(100)		7.50	.75	.20	.15
2478	3¢ Eastern Bluebird (1991)	(100)	12.00	.85	.20	.15
2479	19¢ Fawn (1991)	(100)	47.50	2.50	.50	.15
2480	30¢ Cardinal (1991)	(100)	72.50	3.75	.75	.25
2481	45¢ Pumpkinseed					
	Sunfish(1992)	(100)	115.00	5.95	1.20	.35
2482	$2.00 Bobcat	(20)	95.00	22.50	5.00	1.10

See #3031-3055 for additional designs and denominations.

1991-95 Flora and Fauna Booklet Stamps

| 2483 | 2484,2485 | 2486 | 2487,2493, 2495 | 2488,2494, 2495A |

Scott's No.		F-VF NH	F-VF Used
2483	20¢ Blue Jay, Booklet Single (1995)	.80	.15
2483a	20¢ Booklet Pane of 10 .... (Unfolded 8.95)	7.00	4.95
2484	29¢ Wood Duck, BEP Booklet Single Pf 10.9x9.8.....	.90	.20
2484a	29¢ BEP Booklet Pane of 10(1991)(Unfolded 9.95)...	7.95	6.95
2485	29¢ Wood Duck, KCS Booklet Single Perf.11... ...	1.00	.20
2485a	29¢ KCS Booklet Pane of 10 (1991)(Unfolded 11.95)...	8.75	8.75
2486	29¢ African Violet Booklet Single	1.10	.20
2486a	29¢ Booklet Pane of 10 (1993) ... (Unfolded 11.50)...	9.50	8.25
2487	32¢ Peach, Booklet Single	1.10	.20
2488	32¢ Pear, Booklet Single	1.10	.20
2487-88	32¢ Peach & Pear, Attached Pair	2.20	1.75
2488a	32¢ Booklet Pane of 10 (1995) ... (Unfolded 11.50)...	9.75	8.50

1993-96 Self Adhesive Convertible Panes & Coils

| 2489 | 2490 | 2491 | 2492 |

			F-VF NH	F-VF Used
2489	29¢ Red Squirrel		1.00	.40
2489a	29¢ Convertible Pane of 18		16.50	...
2489v	29¢ Squirrel Coil (No Plate #) ..... Plain Strip of 3	2.70	.90	...
2490	29¢ Rose		1.00	.40
2490a	29¢ Convertible Pane of 18		16.50	...
2490v	29¢ Rose Coil (No Plate #) .... Plain Strip of 3	2.70	.90	...
2491	29¢ Pine Cone		1.00	.40
2491a	29¢ Convertible Pane of 18 (1993)		16.50	...
2491v	Pine Cone Coil .... Pl.#Strip (5) 10.50	(3) 8.75	.90	...
2492	32¢ Pink Rose		1.10	.30
2492a	32¢ Convertible Pane of 20 (1995) ...		17.50	...
2492r	32¢ Pane of 20 with Die-cut "Time to Reorder" (1995)		17.75	...
2492g	32¢ Pink Rose, Coil ..... Pl.#Strip (5) 8.75	(3) 7.00	.90	...
2492b	32¢ Pink Rose, Folded Pane of 15 (1996) ...		15.95	...
2492e	32¢ Pink Rose, Folded Pane of 14 (1996)...		32.75	...
2492f	32¢ Pink Rose, Folded Pane of 16 (1996)...		37.50	...
2493	32¢ Peach, Self-adhesive single		1.00	.30
2494	32¢ Pear, Self-adhesive single ...		1.00	.30
2493-94	32¢ Peach & Pear, Attached Pair...		2.00	...
2494a	32¢ Convertible Pane of 20, Self-adhesive (1995) ...		19.50	...
2495	32¢ Peach, Coil, Self-adhesive		2.15	...
2495A	32¢ Pear, Coil, Self-adhesive		2.15	...
2495-95A	32¢ Peach & Pear, Coil Pair (1995) Pl # Strip (5) 18.75	(3)13.50	4.25	...

1990 Commemoratives (continued)

| 2496 | 2497 | 2498 |

| 2499 | 2500 |

Scott's No.		Mint Sheet	Plate Block	F-VF NH	F-VF Used
2496-2500	25¢ Olympians,Strip of 5 ...... (35)	38.50	(10)13.00	5.75	4.75
2496-2500	25¢ Set of 5 Singles	...	...	5.50	1.25
2496-2500	25¢ Tab Strip of 5, Top or Bottom	...	...	6.75	5.75

1990 Commemoratives (continued)

| 2501 | 2502 | 2503 |

| 2504 | 2505 |

| 2506 | 2507 |

| 2508 | 2509 |
| 2510 | 2511 |

| 2512 | 2513 |

| 2514, 2514v | 2515,2516 |

Scott's No.		Mint Sheet	Plate Block	F-VF NH	F-VF Used
2501-05	25¢ Indian Headdresses Booklet Singles...		...	7.50	1.00
2505a	25¢ Booklet Pane of 10 (2 ea.) ... (Unfolded 19.50)...			15.00	12.75
2506-07	25¢ Micronesia/Marshall Isl., Pair	47.50	4.75	1.95	1.25
2506-07	25¢ Set of 2 Singles	...	...	1.85	.40
2508-11	25¢ Sea Creatures, Block of 4 (40)	38.50	4.75	4.00	3.50
2508-11	25¢ Set of 4 Singles	...	...	3.75	1.00
2512	25¢ Pre-Columbian America, Grand Canyon	38.50	3.75	.80	.15
2513	25¢ Dwight Eisenhower Birth Centenary .... (40)	45.00	5.50	1.20	.15
#2514-16	Christmas Issues				
2514	25¢ Antonello Madonna & Child .	36.00	3.50	.75	.15
2514v	25¢ Madonna, Booklet Single	...	...	.95	.20
2514b	25¢ Booklet Pane of 10 .... (Unfolded 14.75)...			8.75	7.75
2515	25¢ Christmas Tree, Perf. 11	36.00	3.50	.75	.15
2516	25¢ Tree, Booklet Single, Perf. 11½x11	...	...	1.20	.20
2516a	25¢ Booklet Pane of 10 .... (Unfolded 16.95)...			10.95	9.95

1991-94 Regular Issues

2517-2520	2521	2522

2523	2523A	2524-27	2528

2529	2529C	2530	2531	2531A

Scott's No.		Mint Sheet	Plate Block	F-VF NH	F-VF Used
2517	(29¢) "F" Flower, Perf.13 .... (100)	82.50	4.25	.85	.15

Scott's No.		Pl. Strip of 5	Pl. Strip of 3	F-VF NH	F-VF Used
2518	(29¢) "F" Flower Coil, Perf.10 Vert.	5.00	3.75	.80	.15

Scott's No.		Mint Sheet	Plate Block	F-VF NH	F-VF Used
2519	(29¢) "F" Flower, BEP Booklet Single	...	...	1.10	.20
2519a	(29¢) Booklet Pane of 10,BEP,bullseye perfs...			9.50	7.50
2520	(29¢) "F" Flower, KCS Booklet Single	...	...	3.15	.35
2520a	(29¢) Booklet Pane of 10, KCS ..			29.50	24.95

#2519: Bullseye perforations (11.2). Horizontal and vertical perforations meet exactly in stamp corners.
#2520: Normal (line) perforations, Perf. 11

2521	(4¢) Non-Denom. "make-up" .. (100)	13.50	.95	.20	.15
2522	(29¢) "F" Flag Stamp, ATM self adhesive...			1.30	.60
2522a	(29¢) ATM Pane of 12			14.95	...

Scott's No.		Pl. Strip of 5	Pl. Strip of 3	F-VF NH	F-VF Used
2523	29¢ Flag & Mt. Rushmore, Blue, Red, Claret, Intagllo, Mottled Tagging,Pf.10 Vert.	7.25	5.00	1.10	.20
2523c	29¢ Blue, Red, Brown (Toledo Brown) Mottled Tagging	225.00	210.00	4.25	...
2523d	29¢ Solid Tagging (Lenz Paper) .	250.00	225.00	6.00	...
2523A	29¢ Flag, Coil, Gravure, Perf.10 Vert.	6.75	5.25	1.10	.45

On # 2523A, "USA" & "29" are not outlined in white. #2523 outlined in white.

Scott's No.		Mint Sheet	Plate Block	F-VF NH	F-VF Used
2524	29¢ Flower, Perf. 11 .... (100)	75.00	3.95	.80	.20
2524A	29¢ Flower, Perf. 13x12 3/4 .... (100)	100.00	8.75	.95	.25

Scott's No.		Pl. Strip of 5	Pl. Strip of 3	F-VF NH	F-VF Used
2525	29¢ Flower Coil, Rouletted 10 Vert.	7.00	5.25	.90	.20
2526	29¢ Flower Coil, Perf. 10 Vert. (1992)	7.50	5.25	1.00	.20
2527	29¢ Flower Booklet Single			.90	.20
2527a	29¢ Booklet Pane of 10 .... (Unfolded 10.75)			8.25	6.75
2528	29¢ Flag with Olympic Rings, Booklet Single...			.95	.20
2528a	29¢ Booklet Pane of 10 .... (Unfolded 10.75)			8.75	7.25
2529	19¢ Fishing Boat Coil, Pf.10 Vert.,Ty.I	4.75	3.75	.60	.15
2529a	19¢ Boat Coil, Type II (1993)	5.00	3.75	.60	.35
2529b	19¢ Type II, Untagged (1993)	13.50	11.50	1.10	.50
2529C	19¢ Boat Coil, Type III (1994)	10.00	8.25	1.00	.40

#2529 Type I: Darker color & large color cells, coarser dot pattern, Perf. 10
#2529a,b Type II: Lighter color & small color cells, finer dot pattern, Perf. 10
#2529C Type III: Letters taller & thinner, only 1 loop of rope around piling, Perf.9.8

2530	19¢ Hot-Air Balloons, booklet single	...	...	.60	.20
2530a	19¢ Booklet Pane of 10 ..... (Unfolded 7.50)			5.25	4.00

Scott's No.		Mint Sheet	Plate Block	F-VF NH	F-VF Used
2531	29¢ Flags on Parade & Memorial Day Anniv .... (100)	90.00	4.75	.95	.20
2531A	29¢ Liberty & Torch, ATM self adhesive ...			1.00	.30
2531Ab	29¢ ATM Pane of 18, Original back	...		16.75	...
2531Av	29¢ ATM Pane of 18, Revised back	...		16.75	...

1991 Commemoratives

2533	2532	2534

2532-35,37-38,50-51,53-58,60-61, 2567,78-79 Set of 19 (No #2535A)		...	17.75	3.60
2532	50¢ Switzerland 700th Anniv. .. (40)	62.50	7.25	1.60	.35
2533	29¢ Vermont Statehood Bicent. ..	72.50	7.00	1.50	.20
2534	29¢ Savings Bond, 50th Anniv ...	37.50	3.75	.80	.20

1991 Commemoratives (continued)

  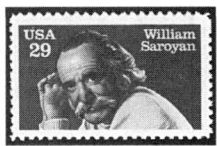

2535,2536	2537	2538

Scott's No.		Mint Sheet	Plate Block	F-VF NH	F-VF Used
2535	29¢ Love Stamp, Perf. 12½x13 ..	37.50	3.75	.80	.15
2535A	29¢ Love, Perf. 11	47.50	5.00	1.00	.25
2536	29¢ Booklet Single, Pf. 11 on 2-3 sides...		...	.95	.20
2536a	29¢ Booklet Pane of 10 .... (Unfolded 9.50)	...		8.50	6.50

NOTE: "29" is further from edge of design on #2535 than on #2536.

2537	52¢ Love Stamp, two ounces	72.50	7.00	1.50	.35
2538	29¢ William Saroyan, Writer	36.50	3.50	.75	.20

1991-96 Regular Issues

2539	2540	2541

2542	2543

2544	2544A

2539	$1.00 USPS Logo&Olympic Rings(20)	55.00	12.50	2.75	.75
2540	$2.90 Priority Mail, Eagle .... (20)	185.00	41.50	9.50	3.00
2541	$9.95 Express Mail, Eagle and Olympic Rings, Domestic Rate .. (20)	525.00	115.00	26.50	9.75
2542	$14.00 Express Mail, Eagle in Flight, International Rate. .... (20)	675.00	150.00	35.00	21.50
2543	$2.90 Priority Mail, Futuristic Space Shuttle (1993) .... (40)	335.00	37.50	8.50	2.75
2544	$3 Priority Mail, Challenger Shuttle (1995) .... (20)	150.00	33.50	7.50	2.75
2544b	$3 with 1996 Date ('96) .... (20)	160.00	36.00	8.00	3.25
2544A	$10.75 Express Mail, Endeavor Shuttle (1995) .... (20)	535.00	120.00	27.50	9.75

1991 Commemoratives (continued)

2545	2546	2547

2548	2549

2545-49	29¢ Fishing Flies, Booklet Singles	...	...	10.50	1.10
2549a	29¢ Booklet Pane of 5 .... (Unfolded 16.50)...			10.75	8.75

1991 Commemoratives (continued)

2550

2551, 2552

2553

2554

2555

2556   **2557**

2558

2561

2560

Scott's No.		Mint Sheet	Plate Block	F-VF NH	F-VF Used
2550	29¢ Cole Porter, Composer	45.00	4.50	.95	.20
2551	29¢ Desert Shield/Desert Storm, Southwest Asia Service Medal ..	45.00	4.50	.95	.20
2552	29¢ Desert Storm, Booklet Single, ABNCo...	...		1.10	.20
2552a	29¢ Booklet Pane of 5 .... (Unfolded 6.50)			5.00	4.25
2553-57	29¢ Summer Olympics, Barcelona, Strip of 5 .... (40)	37.50	(10) 10.75	4.75	4.25
2553-57	29¢ Set of 5 Singles	...	...	4.50	1.00
2558	29¢ Numismatics	47.50	4.50	1.00	.20

1991 World War II Souvenir Sheet of 10

2559

2559	29¢ 1941 World War II Events (20)	23.50	...	11.75	9.75
2559a-j	29¢ Set of 10 Singles	...	...	11.50	5.50
2559s	29¢ Se-Tenant Center Block of 10 ...	...	...	13.50	13.00

2559a Burma Road
2559b Recruits
2559c Lend-Lease Act
2559d Atlantic Charter

2559e Arsenal of Democracy
2559f Reuben James
2559g Gas Mask, Helmet

2559h Liberty Ship
2559i Pearl Harbor
2559j U.S. Declares War

1991 Commemoratives (continued)

2562

2563

2564

2565

2566

2568

2569

2570

2571

2572   **2573**

2574   **2575**

2567

2576   **2577**

2567

2578

2579

2580   **2581**

2582

2583

2584

2585

Scott's No.		Mint Sheet	Plate Block	F-VF NH	F-VF Used
2560	29¢ Basketball Centennial	47.50	4.50	1.00	.20
2561	29¢ District of Columbia Bicent ..	36.50	3.50	.75	.20
2562-66	29¢ Comedians, Booklet Singles ..	...	...	4.75	1.10
2566a	29¢ Booklet Pane of 10 (2 each) (Unfolded 11.75)			9.50	8.50
2567	29¢ Jan Matzeliger, Inventor, Black Heritage	40.00	4.25	.85	.20
2568-77	29¢ Space Exploration Booklet Singles...			14.50	3.25
2577a	29¢ Booklet Pane of 10 .... (Unfolded 18.75)...			14.75	12.75
1991 Christmas Issues					
2578	(29¢) Roman Madonna & Child ..	36.50	3.50	.75	.15
2578v	(29¢) Madonna, Booklet Single ..	...	...	.90	.20
2578a	(29¢) Booklet Pane of 10 .... (Unfolded 10.75)			8.00	6.50
2579	(29¢) Santa & Chimney	36.50	3.50	.75	.15
2580-85	(29¢) Santa & Chimney, Set of 6 Booklet Singles			12.50	1.95
2580-81	(29¢) Booklet Pair, Type I & II, ...	...	...	10.00	...
Type II, the far left brick from the top row of the chimney is missing from #2581					
2582-85	Booklet singles, Set of 4	...	...	3.00	...
2581b-2585a	Booklet Panes of 4, Set of 5 (Unfolded 31.75)			24.95	22.50

1994-95 Definitives Designs of 1869 Essays

2587

2590

2592

Scott's No.		Mint Sheet	Plate Block	F-VF NH	F-VF Used
2587-92	Set of 3	...	68.50	15.75	5.00
2587	32¢ James S. Polk (1995) ...... (100)	82.50	4.25	.85	.20
2590	$1 "Surrender of Burgoyne+" by John Trumbull .... (20)	52.50	11.75	2.65	1.20
2592	$5 Washington & Jackson .... (20)	250.00	55.00	12.75	3.95

2593,2594

2595-97

2598

2599

1992-93 Pledge of Allegiance

2593	29¢ Black denom. Booklet Single,Perf.10	...	.90	.15
2593a	29¢ Booklet Pane of 10, Perf. 10 (Unfolded 9.75)	...	8.25	7.50
2593B	29¢ Black denom.,Booklet Single,Perf.11x10	...	1.75	.85
2593Bc	29¢ Booklet Pane of 10, Perf. 11x10	...	16.50	12.75
2593Bl	29¢ Booklet Single, Perf.11x10, low gloss gum	...	2.75	...
2593Bcl	29¢ Booklet Pane of 10, Pf.11x10, low gloss gum	...	25.00	...
2594	29¢,Red denomination Booklet Single (1993)	...	.95	.20
2594a	29¢ Booklet Pane of 10 .... (Unfolded 11.75)	...	8.75	6.75

1992 Eagle & Shield Self-Adhesive Stamps

2595	29¢ "Brown" denomination		...	1.10	.30
2595a	29¢ Convertible Pane of 17	...	...	16.50	...
2595v	29¢ "Brown" Coil	Plain Strip of 3	3.00	1.00	...
2596	29¢ "Green" denomination		...	1.10	.30
2596a	29¢ Convertible Pane of 17	...	...	16.50	...
2596v	29¢ "Green" Coil	Plain Strip of 3	3.00	1.00	...
2597	29¢ "Red" denomination		...	1.10	.30
2597a	29¢ Convertible Pane of 17	...	...	16.50	...
2597v	29¢ "Red" Coil	PlainStrip of 3	3.00	1.00	...

NOTE: #2595v-2597v do not have plate numbers.

1994 Eagle Self-Adhesive Issue

Scott's No.		Pl# Strip of 5	Pl# Strip of 3	F-VF NH	Used
2598	29¢ Eagle, self-adhesive			1.10	.30
2598a	29¢ Convertible Pane of 18			17.50	...
2598v	29¢ Eagle Coil, self-adhesive	9.75	8.00	1.00	...

1994 Statue of Liberty Self-Adhesive Issue

2599	29¢ Statue of Liberty, self-adhesive	...	...	1.00	.30
2599a	29¢ Convertible Pane of 18	...	...	16.00	...
2599v	29¢ Liberty Coil,Self-adhesive	9.75	8.00	.95	...

2596a Sample of Self-Adhesive Pane

1991-93 Coil Issues, Perforated 10 Vertically

2602

2603,2604,2907

2605

2606, 2607, 2608

2609

Scott's No.		Pl# Strip of 5	Pl# Strip of 3	F-VF NH	Used
2602	(10¢) Eagle, Bulk rate **ABNCo**	2.85	2.25	.30	.20
2603	(10¢) Eagle,Bulk rate,Shiny Gum, **BEP** (1993)	3.65	3.00	.30	.20
2603l	(10¢) Low Gloss Gum	5.00	4.00	.45	...
2603b	(10¢) Tagged, Shiny Gum	20.75	17.50	1.75	1.25
2604	(10¢) Eagle, Bulk rate,Shiny Gum,**SVS**	3.95	3.25	.30	.25
2604l	(10¢) Low Gloss Gum	3.95	3.25	.30	...

#2603 Orange yellow & multicolored, #2604 Gold & multicolored.

2605	23¢ Flag, Pre-sort First Class	5.25	3.95	.65	.35
2606	23¢ USA, Pre-sort 1st Cl., **ABNCo**('92)	5.50	4.25	.65	.35
2607	23¢ USA, Pre-sort 1st Cl.,Shiny Gum **BEP** (1992)	6.75	5.50	.70	.35
2607l	23¢ Low Gloss Gum	7.75	6.25	.85	...
2607a	23¢ Tagged, Shiny Gum	125.00	115.00	3.75	...
2608	23¢ USA, Pre-sort 1st Class,**SVS**(1993)	7.75	6.00	.90	.35

#2606 Light blue at bottom, "23" 6 mm wide, "First Class" 9½ mm wide.
#2607 Dark blue at bottom, "23" 6½ mm wide, "First Class" 9 mm wide.
#2608 Violet blue at bottom, "23" 6½ mm wide, "First Class" 8½ mm wide.

2609	29¢ Flag & White House (1992) ...	6.75	5.00	.90	.15

1992 Commemoratives

2611

2612

2613

2614

2615

2616

2617

2618

2619

Scott's No.		Mint Sheet	Plate Block	F-VF NH	F-VF Used
2611-23,2630-41,2698-2704,2710-14,2720	Set of 38		...	34.50	8.35
2611-15	29¢ Winter Olympics, Strip of 5 (35)	35.00 (10)	10.75	5.00	4.25
2611-15	29¢ Set of 5 Singles	...	...	4.75	1.25
2616	29¢ World Columbian Stamp Expo	36.50	3.50	.75	.20
2617	29¢ W.E.B. DuBois, Civil Rights, Black Heritage	45.00	4.50	.95	.20
2618	29¢ Love, Heart Envelope	36.50	3.50	.75	.20
2619	29¢ Olympic Baseball	57.50	5.50	1.20	.20

2620
2622
2621
2623

2624

2625

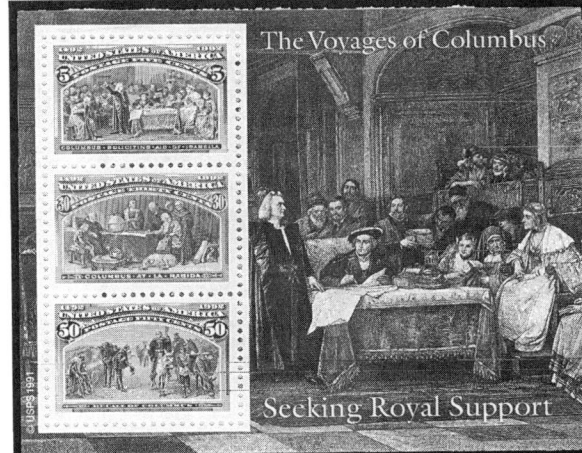

2626

2627

2628

2629

Scott's No.		Mint Sheet	Plate Block	F-VF NH	F-VF Used
2620-23	29¢ Voyage of Columbus, Block-4(40)	37.50	4.75	3.95	3.50
2620-23	29¢ Set of 4 Singles	...		3.75	1.10
2624-29	1¢-$5 Columbian Expo Souv. Sheet Set of 6	...		42.50	39.50
2624	1¢,4¢,$1 Sheet of 3	...	...	2.95	2.95
2625	2¢,3¢,$4 Sheet of 3	...	...	10.75	10.75
2626	5¢,30¢,50¢ Sheet of 3	...	...	2.40	2.40
2627	6¢,8¢,$3 Sheet of 3	...	...	8.95	8.95
2628	10¢,15¢,$2 Sheet of 3	...	...	6.50	6.50
2629	$5 Sheet of 1	...	...	13.50	13.50
2624a-29	1¢-$5 Set of 16 Singles	...	...	41.50	37.50

2624a 1¢ Deep Blue	2626a 5¢ Chocolate	2628a 10¢ Black Brown
2624b 4¢ Ultramarine	2626b 30¢ Orange Brown	2628b 15¢ Dark Green
2624c $1 Salmon	2626c 50¢ Slate Blue	2628c $2 Brown Red
2625a 2¢ Brown Violet	2627a 6¢ Purple	2629 $5 Black
2625b 3¢ Green	2627b 8¢ Magenta	
2625c $4 Crimson Lake	2627c $3 Yellow Green	

1992 Commemoratives (continued)

2630

2631 2632 2635
2633 2634

2636

2637

2638

2639

2640 2641

2642 2643 2644 2645 2646

Scott's No.		Mint Sheet	Plate Block	F-VF NH	F-VF Used
2630	29¢ New York Stock Exchange Bicentennial .... (40)	29.00	3.50	.75	.20
2631-34	29¢ Space Accomplishments, Bk.-4	47.50	4.95	4.25	3.75
2631-34	29¢ Set of 4 Singles	...	...	4.15	1.10
2635	29¢ Alaska Highway 50th Anniv. .	36.50	3.50	.75	.20
2636	29¢ Kentucky Statehood Bicent.	36.50	3.50	.75	.20
2637-41	29¢ Summer Olympics, Strip-5 (35)	32.50	(10) 10.75	4.75	4.50
2637-41	29¢ Set of 5 Singles	...	...	4.50	1.30
2642-46	29¢ Hummingbirds, Set of 5 Booklet Singles	...	...	4.35	1.10
2646a	29¢ Booklet Pane of 5 .... (Unfolded 5.75)			4.50	4.00

1992 Wildflowers of America

2652 2658 2672 2688

1992 Wildflowers of America (continued)

2647-96 Sheet

Scott's No.		Mint Sheet	Plate Block	F-VF NH	F-VF Used
2647-96	29¢ Wildflowers, Sheet of 50	52.50	...	...	...
2647-96	Set of 50 Singles	...	...	50.00	24.75
2647-96	29¢ Individual Singles	...	...	1.35	.60

2647 Indian Paintbrush
2648 Fragrant Water Lily
2649 Meadow Beauty
2650 Jack-in-the-Pulpit
2651 California Poppy
2652 Large-Flowered Trillium
2653 Tickseed
2654 Shooting Star
2655 Stream Violet
2656 Bluets
2657 Herb Robert
2658 Marsh Marigold
2659 Sweet White Violet
2660 Claret Cup Cactus
2661 White Mountain Avens
2662 Sessile Beltwort
2663 Blue Flag
2664 Harlequin Lupine

2665 Twinflower
2666 Common Sunflower
2667 Sego Lily
2668 Virginia Bluebells
2669 Ohi'a Lehua
2670 Rosebud Orchid
2671 Showy Evening Primrose
2672 Fringed Gentian
2673 Yellow Lady's Slipper
2674 Passionflower
2675 Bunchberry
2676 Pasqueflower
2677 Round-lobed Hepatica
2678 Wild Columbine
2679 Fireweed
2680 Indian Pond Lily
2681 Turk's Cap Lily

2682 Dutchmans' Breeches
2683 Trumpet Honeysuckle
2684 Jacob's Ladder
2685 Plains Prickly Pear
2686 Moss Campion
2687 Bearberry
2688 Mexican Hat
2689 Harebell
2690 Desert Five-spot
2691 Smooth Solomon's Seal
2692 Red Maids
2693 Yellow Skunk Cabbage
2694 Rue Anemone
2695 Standing Cypress
2696 Wild Flax

1992 World War II Souvenir Sheet of 10

2697

2697	29¢ 1942 World War II Events (20)	23.50	...	11.75	9.75
2697a-j	29¢ Set of 10 Singles	...	...	11.50	5.50
2697s	29¢ Se-Tenant Center Block of 10	...	...	13.50	13.00

2697a Raid on Tokyo
2697b Ration Coupons
2697c Coral Sea
2697d Corregidor

2697e Aleutian Islands
2697f Enemy Codes
2697g Midway
2697h Women in War

2697i Guadalcanal
2697j North Africa Landings

1992 Commemoratives (continued)

2698

2699

2704

2700   2701

2702   2703

Giraffe

Giant Panda

Flamingo

King Penguins

White Bengal Tiger

2705
2706
2707
2708
2709

2710

2719

2711, 2715
2713, 2717
2712, 2716
2714, 2718

2720

1993 Commemoratives

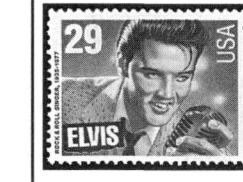
2721

2722

2723

2724, 31   2725, 32   2726, 33

2727, 34

2728, 35

2729, 36

2730, 37

Scott's No.		Mint Sheet	Plate Block	F-VF NH	F-VF Used
2721-30,2746-59,2766,2771-74,2779-89,2791-94,					
2804-06	Set of 47(No #2723A)	...	...	47.50	11.25
2721	29¢ Elvis Presley .... (40)	36.50	4.50	.95	.25
2722	29¢ "Oklahoma!" .... (40)	29.00	3.50	.75	.25
2723	29¢ Hank Williams, Perf. 10 ... (40)	67.50	8.25	1.75	.25
2723A	29¢ Williams, Perf. 11.2 x 11.5 (40)	950.00	150.00	23.95	14.95
2724-30	29¢ Rock 'n Roll, Rythym & Blues, Vertical Strip of 7 .... (35)47.50 (8)12.00			9.75	6.50
2724-30	29¢ Top Horiz. Plate Block of 10 .	...	15.75	...	...
2724-30	29¢ Rock 'n Roll, R & B, set of 7 singles....	...	...	9.50	2.80
2731-37	29¢ Rock 'n Roll, R & B, 7 Booklet Singles...	...	...	6.50	2.40
2737a	29¢ Booklet Pane of 8 (Unfolded 10.75)	...	...	7.50	7.25
2737b	29¢ Booklet Pane of 4 (Unfolded 5.50)	...	...	4.50	4.25

2741

2742

2743

2744

2745

2747

2746

2748

Scott's No.		Mint Sheet	Plate Block	F-VF NH	F-VF Used
2698	29¢ Dorothy Parker, Writer	36.50	3.50	.75	.20
2699	29¢ Dr. Theodore von Karman, Aerospace Scientist	36.50	3.50	.75	.20
2700-03	29¢ Minerals, Block of 4 .... (40)	38.50	4.75	4.00	3.75
2700-03	29¢ Strip of 4	...	...	4.00	3.75
2700-03	29¢ Set of 4 Singles	...	...	3.75	1.10
2704	29¢ Juan Rodriguez Cabrillo, California Explorer	36.50	3.50	.75	.20
2705-09	29¢ Wild Animals, Booklet Singles	...	...	4.50	1.10
2709a	29¢ Booklet Pane of 5 .... (Unfolded 6.00)			4.75	4.25
#2710-19a Christmas Issues					
2710	29¢ Bellini Madonna & Child	36.50	3.50	.75	.15
2710v	29¢ Madonna, booklet single	...	...	.90	.20
2710a	29¢ Booklet Pane of 10 .... (Unfolded 10.75)			7.95	7.50
2711-14	29¢ Toys, Litho, Block of 4	45.00	4.75	4.00	3.75
2711-14	29¢ Set of 4 Singles	...	...	3.75	1.00
2715-18	29¢ Toys, gravure, 4 Booklet Singles ...	...	...	5.50	1.00
2718a	29¢ Booklet Pane of 4 .... (Unfolded 8.00)			6.50	5.25
2719	29¢ Locomotive, ATM, self adhesive single...	...	...	1.10	.45
2719a	29¢ Locomotive, ATM, Convertible Pane of 18...	...	17.50	...	...
#2711-14 Lithographed, "GREETINGS" 27mm wide.					
#2715-18 Photogravure, "GREETINGS" 25mm. #2719 "GREETINGS" 21½ mm wide.					
2720	29¢ Year of the Rooster .... (20)	22.50	5.00	1.15	.25

2741-45	29¢ Space Fantasy, Booklet Singles	...	...	4.35	1.30
2745a	29¢ Booklet Pane of 5 .... (Unfolded 5.50)			4.50	4.25
2746	29¢ Percy Lavon Julian, Chemist, Black Heritage	38.50	3.75	.80	.20
2747	29¢ Oregon Trail 150th Anniv.	55.00	5.00	1.15	.20
2748	29¢ World University Games	38.50	3.75	.80	.20

1993 Commemoratives (continued)

2749   2754   2755

2752   2753

2750   2751

2756   2757

2758   2759

2760   2761   2762   2763   2764

Scott's No.		Mint Sheet	Plate Block	F-VF NH	F-VF Used
2749	29¢ Grace Kelly (1929-1982)	36.50	3.50	.75	.20
2750-53	29¢ Circus, Block of 4 .... (40)	40.00	(6) 8.25	4.25	3.75
2750-53	29¢ Set of 4 Singles	...	...	4.15	1.10
2754	29¢ Cherokee Strip Land Run Centennial .... (20)	15.75	3.50	.80	.20
2755	29¢ Dean Acheson, Diplomat	36.50	3.50	.75	.20
2756-59	29¢ Sporting Horses,Block of 4 (40)	38.50	4.75	4.00	3.50
2756-59	29¢ Set of 4 Singles	...	...	3.80	1.10
2760-64	29¢ Spring Garden Flowers, 5 Booklet Singles...	...	...	4.35	1.30
2764a	29¢ Booklet Pane of 5 .... (Unfolded 5.50)	...	...	4.50	4.00

1993-1999 American Music Series
#2724-37, 2767-78, 2849-61, 2982-92, 3096-99, 3154-65, 3212-19, 3339-50.

1993 World War II Souvenir Sheet of 10

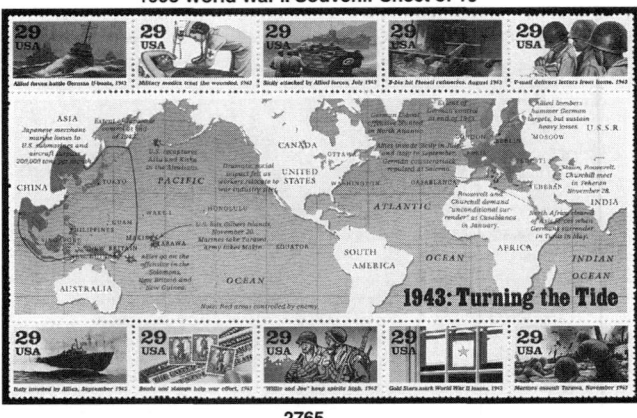

1943: Turning the Tide

2765

Scott's No.		Mint Sheet	Plate Block	F-VF NH	F-VF Used
2765	29¢ 1943 WWII Events .... (20)	23.50	...	11.75	9.75
2765a-j	29¢ Set of 10 Singles	...	...	11.50	6.50
2765s	29¢ Se-Tenant Center Block of 10	...	...	13.50	13.00

2765a Destroyers/U-Boats   2765d B-24's hit Ploesti   2765g Bonds & Stamps
2765b Military Medics   2765e V-Mail Delivers Letters   2765h "Willie & Joe"
2765c Sicily Attacked   2765f Italy Invaded   2765i Gold Stars
   2765j Marines at Tarawa

1993 Commemoratives (cont.)

2766

2771, 2775   2773, 2776
2772, 2777   2774, 2778

2767
2768
2769
2770

2779   2780
2781   2782

2766	29¢ Joe Louis, Boxer	47.50	4.50	1.00	.20
2767-70	29¢ Broadway Musicals, 4 Booklet Singles...	...	...	3.75	1.00
2770a	29¢ Booklet Pane of 4 .... (Unfolded 4.95)...	...	...	3.85	3.35
2771-74	29¢ Country Music, Block of 4 ... (20)	23.75	5.75	5.00	4.25
2771-74	29¢ Horizontal Strip of 4	...	...	5.00	4.25
2771-74	29¢ Horiz. Pl. Block of 8 with Label...	...	11.00	...	...
2771-74	29¢ Set of 4 Singles	...	...	4.75	1.20
2775-78	29¢ Country Music, 4 Booklet Singles	...	...	3.90	1.00
2778a	29¢ Booklet Pane of 4 .... (Unfolded 5.50)...	...	...	4.00	3.75
2779-82	29¢ National Postal Museum, Block of 4 .... (20)	21.75	5.25	4.50	4.00
2779-82	29¢ Horizontal Strip of 4	...	...	4.50	4.00
2779-82	29¢ Set of 4 Singles	...	...	4.35	1.20

1993 Commemoratives (continued)

2783   2784   2789, 2790   2803

2785   2786
2787   2788

2793,96,2799   2794,95,2800
2791,98,2801   2792,97,2802

2804   2805   2806

Scott's No.		Mint Sheet	Plate Block	F-VF NH	F-VF Used
2783-84	29¢ Deaf Communication, Pair . (20)	17.50	3.95	1.80	1.15
2783-84	29¢ Set of 2 Singles	...	...	1.70	.40
2785-88	29¢ Children's Classics, Block-4 (40)	42.50	5.25	4.50	4.00
2785-88	29¢ Horizontal Strip of 4	...	...	4.50	4.00
2785-88	29¢ Set of 4 Singles	...	...	4.35	1.00
#2789-2803 Christmas Issues					
2789	29¢ Cimi Madonna & Child	36.50	3.50	.75	.15
2790	29¢ Madonna, Booklet Single	...	...	1.10	.20
2790a	29¢ Booklet Pane of 4 .... (Unfolded 4.95)	...		3.85	3.25
2791-94	29¢ Christmas Designs, Block of 4 .	45.00	4.50	4.00	3.50
2791-94	29¢ Strip of 4	...	...	4.00	3.50
2791-94	29¢ Set of 4 Singles	...	...	3.85	.80
2795-98	29¢ Christmas Designs, set of 4 Booklet Singles	...		4.50	
2798a	29¢ Booklet Pane of 10 (3 Snowmen)(Unfolded 12.75)			10.50	7.50
2798b	29¢ Booklet Pane of 10 (2 Snowmen)(Unfolded 12.75)			10.50	7.50
2799-2802	29¢ Christmas Designs, self adhesive,4 singles	...		5.50	1.80
2802a	29¢ Convertible Pane of 12, self-adhesive...	...		15.00	...
2799-2802 var. Coils, self-adhesive	Plate Strip of 8 13.95			6.50	...
#2791-94 Perforated 11½. #2795-98 Perforated 11x10 on 2 or 3 sides					
#2795-98 18x21 mm. #2799-2802 19½x26½mm.					
2803	29¢ Snowman, self adhesive	...	...	1.10	.60
2803a	29¢ Convertible Pane of 18, self-adhesive...	...		17.50	...
2804	29¢ Northern Mariana Is. Commonwealth. .... (20)	15.75	3.75	.80	.20
2805	29¢ Columbus at Puerto Rico 500th	36.50	3.50	.75	.20
2806	29¢ AIDS Awareness, Perf.11.2	41.50	3.95	.85	.20
2806a	29¢ AIDS Booklet Single, Perf.11	...	...	1.00	.20
2806b	29¢ Booklet Pane of 5 .... (Unfolded 5.75)			4.50	4.00

1994 Commemoratives

2807   2808   2809   2810   2811

2807-12,2814C-28,2834-36,2839, 2848-68,2871-72,2876 Set of 49 (No #2871A)		...	...	33.75	13.25
2807-11	29¢ Winter Olympics, Strip of 5 .... (20)	17.50	(10)9.50	4.50	4.00
2807-11	29¢ Plate Blocks wiith Inscriptions ..		(10)10.75	...	...
2807-11	29¢ Set of 5 Singles	...	...	4.35	1.40

1994 Commemoratives (continued)

2812   2813   2814,2814C   2815

2816   2817   2818

2819   2820   2821   2822   2823
2824   2825   2826   2827   2828

2829   2830   2831   2832   2833

Scott's No.		Mint Sheet	Plate Block	F-VF NH	F-VF Used
2812	29¢ Edward R. Murrow, Journalist ...	36.50	3.50	.75	.20
2813	29¢ Love & Sunrise, self adhesive ..	...	...	1.00	.30
2813a	29¢ Convertible Pane of 18	...	...	16.50	...
2813v	29¢ Love Coil, self adhesive Plate # Strip .... (5)	10.50 (3)	8.50	1.30	...
2814	29¢ Love & Dove, Booklet Single Perf.10.9x11.1......			.95	.20
2814a	29¢ Booklet Pane of 10 .... (Unfolded 10.75)			8.75	7.50
2814C	29¢ Love & Dove, Perf 11.1	48.50	4.50	1.00	.20
2815	52¢ Love & Doves	72.50	6.75	1.50	.35
2816	29¢ Dr. Allison Davis, Social Anthropologist, Black Heritage . (20)	16.00	3.75	.85	.20
2817	29¢ Year of the Dog .... (20)	33.75	8.00	1.75	.20
2818	29¢ Buffalo Soldiers .... (20)	16.00	3.75	.85	.20
2819-28	29¢ Silent Screen Stars, Blk.-10 (40)	47.50 (10)13.75		12.50	11.50
2819-28	29¢ Half-Pane of 20 with selvedge	...	...	24.50	22.50
2819-28	29¢ Set of 10 singles	...	...	12.00	3.25
2829-33	29¢ Summer Garden Flowers, set of 5 booklet singles...	...	...	4.15	1.35
2833a	29¢ Booklet Pane of 5 .... (Unfolded 5.50)			4.25	4.00

2834   2835   2836

71

1994 World Cup Soccer Championships USA94

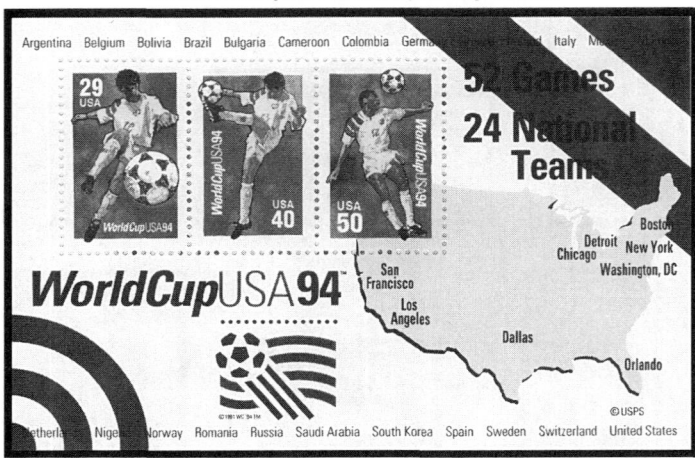

2837

Scott's No.		Mint Sheet	Plate Block	F-VF NH	F-VF Used
2834	29¢ World Cup Soccer .... (20)	17.50	4.00	.90	.20
2835	40¢ World Cup Soccer .... (20)	21.50	4.95	1.10	.35
2836	50¢ World Cup Soccer .... (20)	28.75	6.75	1.50	.50
2837	29¢,40¢,50¢ World Cup Soccer, Souvenir Sheet of 3	...	...	4.75	4.00
2837a-c	29¢-50¢ Set of 3 singles	...	...	4.75	3.00

#2834-36 are overall tagged. #2837a-c are block tagged.

1994 World War II Souvenir Sheet of 10

2838

2838	29¢ 1944 WWII Events .... (20)	27.00	...	13.50	11.50
2838a-j	29¢ Set of 10 Singles	...	...	13.00	7.00
2838v	29¢ Se-Tenant Center Block of 10 ..	...	...	14.75	14.00

2838a Retake New Guinea   2838d Airborne Units   2838g Saipan Bunkers
2838b P51's and B-17's   2838e Submarines in Pacific   2838h Red Ball Express
2838c Normandy   2838f Allies Free Rome   2838i Battle Leyte Gulf
                                                         2838j Battle of the Bulge

2840

2839

2841a

2842

2848

2843

2844

2845

2846   2847

Scott's No.		Mint Sheet	Plate Block	F-VF NH	F-VF Used
1994 Norman Rockwell Issues					
2839	29¢ Norman Rockwell	42.50	4.00	.90	.20
2840	50¢ Norman Rockwell, Souvenir Sheet of 4 ...	...	...	5.95	5.50
2840a-d	50¢ Rockwell, Set of 4 Singles	...	...	5.75	4.00
	2840a Freedom from Want 2840b Freedom from Fear				
	2840c Freedom of Speech 2840d Freedom of Religion				
1994 Moon Landing, 25th Anniversary					
2841	29¢ Moon Landing Miniature Sheet of 12 ...	...	...	12.95	11.50
2841a	29¢ Single Stamp from sheet	...	...	1.15	.30
2842	$9.95 Moon Landing Express Mail .... (20)	635.00	140.00	32.50	12.50
1994 Commemoratives (continued)					
2843-47	29¢ Locomotives, set of 5 Booklet Singles...	...	...	5.85	1.20
2847a	29¢ Booklet Pane of 5	(Unfolded 7.25)		6.00	4.75
2848	29¢ George Meany, Labor Leader	36.50	3.50	.75	.20

2849

2850

2851

2852

2853

2854

2855

2856

2857

2858

2859

2860   2861

Families
have their own
special memories.

So do Stamp Collections.

We value them all.

Brookman.......Your Cover Specialist
LEADER IN 20TH CENTURY POSTAL HISTORY

Large Holding of Pan American Clippers Available from Brookman!

Brookman/Barrett & Worthen has just issued the most comprehensive sales catalog of Pan American Clipper covers. This 68-page full-color, fully-illustrated catalog is divided into 2 volumes. Volume 1 contains 36 pages of Pacific Clipper Flights and Atlantic Clipper Flights, along with Philippine Island Flights, Australia, New Zealand, China, Hawaii and Pacific Rim covers. Volume 2 contains the largest collection ever known of Crosby Pacific and Atlantic Clipper covers in its 32 pages. Because of its comprehensiveness, this will be a valuable reference guide for years to come.

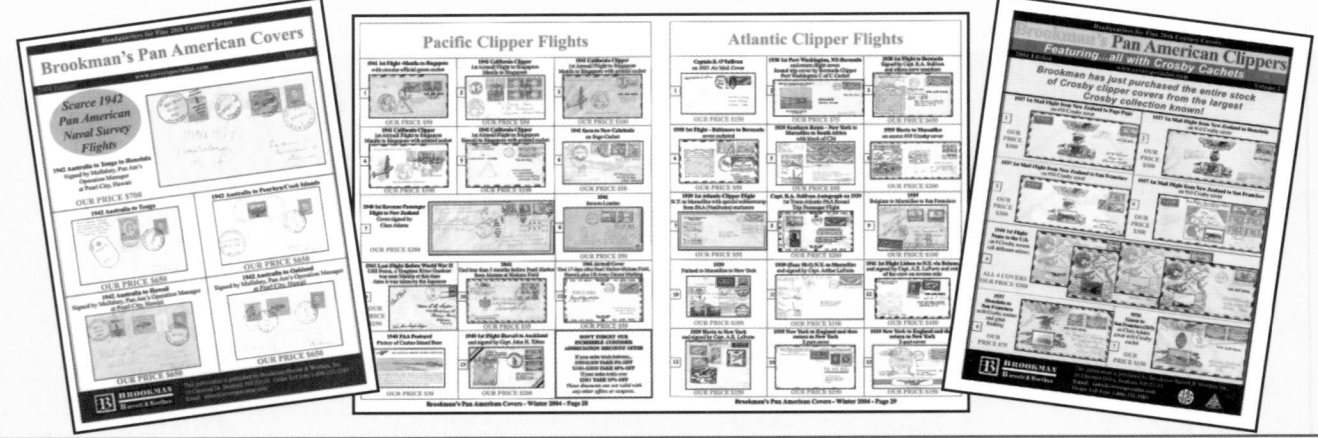

Brookman regularly publishes fully-illustrated, full-color cover catalogs.

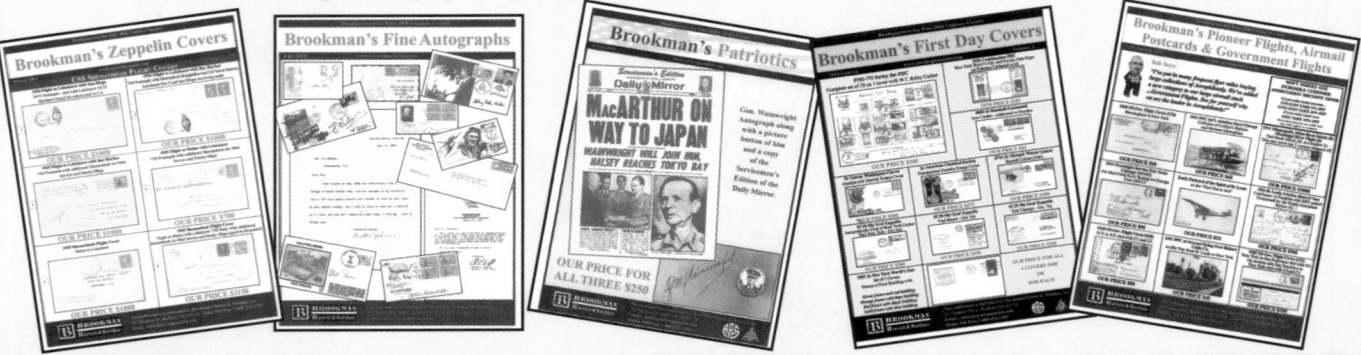

Please check off your collecting interest:

- ☐ Zeppelin Flights
- ☐ Pan American Clippers
- ☐ Pioneer Flights
- ☐ Early Government Flights
- ☐ Philippine Flights

- ☐ Canadian Semi-Officials
- ☐ Autographs
- ☐ Early First Days
- ☐ Australia & New Zealand Flights
- ☐ WWII Patriotics

Please send $3.00 to cover mailing costs, which will be refunded with your first order.

Name_____

Address_____

_____

Phone #_____

Card #_____

(Mastercard or Visa only - **MC Visa** *(circle one)*

Exp. Date_____

BROOKMAN
Barrett & Worthen

10 Chestnut Drive, Bedford, NH 03110
Email: sales@coverspecialist.com
Order Toll Free 1-800-332-3383

Scott's No.		Mint Sheet	Plate Block	F-VF NH	F-VF Used
2849-53	29¢ Popular Singers, Strip of 5 ..... (20)	23.50	(6)9.75	6.00	5.25
2849-53	29¢ Top Plate Block of 12	...	19.50		
2849-53	29¢ Set of 5 Singles	...	...	5.75	2.25
2854-61	29¢ Blues & Jazz Artists, Blk.-8 . (35)	42.50	(10)15.00	(9)13.00	11.95
2854-61	29¢ Top Plate Block of 10 with Label...	...	16.50		
2854-61	29¢ Set of 8 Singles	...	...	11.00	4.00

NOTE: BECAUSE OF SHEET LAYOUT THERE ARE NO BLOCKS OF EIGHT POSSIBLE.

2862

2867

2868

2863

2864

2865

2866

2862	29¢ James Thurber, Cartoonist	36.50	3.50	.75	.20
2863-66	29¢ Wonders of the Sea,Block-4 .. (24)	28.50	4.25	3.75	3.25
2863-66	29¢ Set of 4 Singles	...	...	3.60	1.00
2867-68	29¢ Cranes, Pair .... (20)	18.95	4.50	2.00	1.75
2867-68	29¢ Set of 2 Singles	...	...	1.90	.45

1994 Legends of the West Miniature Sheet

2869

2869	29¢ Revised Sheet of 20	...	...	19.95	18.75
2869a-t	Set of 20 Singles	...	...	19.75	13.75

2869a Home on the Range	2869h Bat Masterson	2869o Wild Bill Hickok
2869b Buffalo Bill Cody	2869i John C. Fremont	2869p Western Wildlife
2869c Jim Bridger	2869j Wyatt Earp	2869q Jim Beckwourth
2869d Annie Oakley	2869k Nellie Cashman	2869r Bill Tilghman
2869e Native American	2869l Charles Goodnight	2869s Sacagawea
2869f Chief Joseph	2869m Geronimo	2869t Overland Mail
2869g Bill Pickett	2869n Kit Carson	

2870

Scott's No.		Mint Sheet	Plate Block	F-VF NH	F-VF Used
2870	29¢ Original (recalled) sheet of 20 with blue envelope..			395.00	...
2870	29¢ Without original blue envelope .	...	...	375.00	...

NOTE; #2870 was the original sheet-it contained an incorrect picture of Bill Pickett (second stamp in second row). It was withdrawn and released only via lottery. #2869 contains the correct picture of Bill Pickett.

1994 Commemoratives (continued)

2871

2872

2873

2874

2875

2876

#2871-74a Christmas Issues

2871	29¢ Sira Madonna & Child, Perf.11¼ ...	36.50	3.50	.75	.15
2871A	29¢ Madonna & Child, Booklet Single, Perf.9 3/4x11 ...			.95	.20
2871Ab	29¢ Booklet Pane of 10 . (Unfolded 10.95)			8.50	5.75
2872	29¢ Christmas Stocking	36.50	3.50	.75	.15
2872v	29¢ Stocking Booklet Single	...	...	.90	.20
2872a	29¢ Booklet Pane of 20 .... (Unfolded 21.50)			16.50	10.75
2873	29¢ Santa Claus, self-adhesive	...	...	1.15	.25
2873a	29¢ Convertible Pane of 12, self-adhesive	...	...	12.75	...
2873v	29¢ Santa Claus Coil, self-adhesive				
	Pl# Strip (5)10.50 (3)8.50			1.00	...
2874	29¢ Cardinal in Snow, self-adhesive	...	...	1.10	.40
2874a	29¢ Convertible Pane of 18, self-adhesive	...	...	17.50	...
2875	$2 Bureau of Engraving & Printing Centennial Souvenir Sheet of 4	...	...	22.75	18.75
2875a	$2 Madison, Single Stamp from Souvenir Sheet...			6.00	3.75
2876	29¢ Year of the Boar, New Year .... (20)	21.75	4.95	1.10	.25

1994 Interim Regular Issues

2877,2878

2879,2880

2881-87,2889-92

2888

2893

Scott's No.		Mint Sheet	Plate Block	F-VF NH	F-VF Used
2877	(3¢) Dove, ABN, Perf. 11x10.8 .... (100)	9.75	.95	.20	.15
2878	(3¢) Dove, SVS, Perf. 10.8x10.9 ...... (100)	15.75	1.25	.25	.15

#2877 Light blue, thin, taller letters. #2878 Darker blue, heavy, shorter letters.

Scott's No.		Mint Sheet	Plate Block	F-VF NH	F-VF Used
2879	(20¢) "G",Postcard, BEP, Black"G" .. (100)	67.50	7.50	.65	.15
2880	(20¢) "G",Postcard, SVS, Red "G" ... (100)	69.50	10.95	.65	.15
2881	(32¢) "G",BEP, Black "G" .... (100)	225.00	89.95	1.50	.25
2881v	(32¢) Black "G" Booklet Single	...	...	1.25	.25
2881a	(32¢) Booklet Pane of 10, Perf. 11.2 x 11.1	...	...	11.50	9.95
2882	(32¢) "G", SVS, Red "G" Pf.11x10.9 . (100)	90.00	7.95	.90	.20
2883	(32¢) "G", BEP, Black "G", Booklet Single	...	...	1.20	.20
2883a	(32¢) Booklet Pane of 10, BEP, Perf. 10 x 9.9...		...	10.95	9.50
2884	(32¢) "G", ABN, Blue "G", Booklet Single	...	...	1.20	.20
2884a	(32¢) Booklet Pane of 10, ABN, Perf.10.9	...	...	10.95	9.50
2885	(32¢) "G", KCS, Red "G", Booklet Single	...	...	1.40	.20
2885a	(32¢) Booklet Pane of 10, KCS Perf.11x10.9...		...	12.95	11.50
2886	(32¢) "G", Surface Tagged, self-adhesive	...	...	1.15	.30
2886a	(32¢) Convertible Pane of 18, self-adhesive, AD...		...	19.00	...
2886b	(32¢) "G", Coil, self-adhesive Pl.# Strip	(5)11.50	(3) 9.50	1.10	...
2887	(32¢) "G", Overall Tagging, self-adhesive, AD...		...	1.35	.35
2887a	(32¢) Convertible Pane of 18, self-adhesive, thin paper...			22.75	...

#2886 Limited amount of blue shading in the whitestripes below field of stars.
#2887 Stronger blue shading in the white stripes. Paper thinner and duller.

1994-95 Interim Coil Stamps, Perforated Or Roulетted 9.8 Vert.

Scott's No.		Pl.Strip of 5	Pl.Strip of 3	F-VF NH	F-VF Used
2888-93	**Set of 6**	**55.00**	**42.50**	**7.25**	...
2888	(25¢) "G" Presort, Coil, SVS	7.50	6.00	1.15	.30
2889	(32¢) "G" Coil, BEP, Black "G" .	16.50	11.75	2.50	.25
2890	(32¢) "G" Coil, ABN, Blue "G"...........	7.75	6.00	.90	.20
2891	(32¢) "G" Coil, SVS, Red "G" ...	11.50	8.75	1.50	.25
2892	(32¢) "G" Coil, SVS, Rouletted, Red "G"	11.00	9.00	1.25	.20
2893	(5¢) "G" Non-Profit, green ABN (1995) .	2.75	2.25	.30	.25

BEP=Bureau of Engraving and Printing ABN=American Bank-Note Co.
SVS=Stamp Venturers KCS=KCS Industries AD = Avery Dennison

1995-97 Regular Issues

2897,2913-16

2902,2902B

2903-4B

2905,6

2908-10

2911-12B

2919

Scott's No.		Mint Sheet	Plate Block	F-VF NH	F-VF Used
2897	32¢ Flag over Porch, Shiny gum.....(100)	92.50	6.75	.95	.15
2897l	32¢ Low Gloss Gum........................(100)	97.50	7.50	1.00	...
2897v	Folded Block of 15 in Booklet (BK243) .	...	...	14.95	...

1995-97 Coil Stamps, Perf. Or Die-cut Vertically

Scott's No.		Pl.Strip of 5	Pl.Strip of 3	F-VF NH	F-VF Used
2902	(5¢) Butte, Perf. 9.8............................	1.80	1.50	.20	.20
2902B	(5¢) Butte, SA, Die-cut 11.5 (1996)	2.65	2.25	.25	.20
2903	(5¢) Mountain, BEP, Perf. 9.8 (1996) ..	2.25	1.95	.20	.15
2903a	(5¢) Mountain, Tagged	110.00	100.00	4.50	...
2904	(5¢) Mountain, SVS, Perf. 9.8 (1996) ..	2.65	2.25	.20	.15
2904A	(5¢) Mountain, SA Die-cut 11.5 (1996) .	3.00	2.50	.25	.20
2904B	(5¢) Mountain, SA Die-cut 9.8 (1997) ...	3.00	2.50	.25	.20

#2903, 2904B Letters outlined in purple. #2904, 2904A No outline on letters.

Scott's No.		Pl.Strip of 5	Pl.Strip of 3	F-VF NH	F-VF Used
2905	(10¢) Automobile, Perf. 9.8	3.25	2.75	.30	.25
2906	(10¢) Automobile, SA, Die-cut 11.5 (1996)	3.25	2.75	.35	.25
2907	(10¢) Eagle & Shield, SA, (Design of 1993) Die-cut 11.5 (1996)	4.50	3.75	.45	.25
2908	(15¢) Auto Tail Fin, BEP, Perf. 9.8	3.75	3.00	.45	.30
2909	(15¢) Auto Tail Fin, SVS, Perf. 9.8	3.75	3.00	.45	.30
2910	(15¢) Auto Tail Fin, SA Die-cut 11.5 (1996)	3.95	3.25	.50	.30

#2908 has darker colors and heavier shading than #2909 or 2910

Scott's No.		Pl.Strip of 5	Pl.Strip of 3	F-VF NH	F-VF Used
2911	(25¢) Juke Box, BEP, Perf. 9.8	6.75	5.25	.75	.40
2912	(25¢) Juke Box, SVS, Perf. 9.8	6.75	5.25	.75	.40
2912A	(25¢) Juke Box, SA, Die-cut 11.5 (1996)	7.75	6.25	.90	.40
2912B	(25¢) Juke Box, SA, Die-cut 9.8 (1997)	7.75	6.25	.90	.40

#2911 & 2912B have darker colors and heavier shading than #2912 or 2912A

Scott's No.		Pl.Strip of 5	Pl.Strip of 3	F-VF NH	F-VF Used
2913	32¢ Flag-Porch, BEP, Perf. 9.8, Shiny gum	7.25	5.50	.95	.15
2913l	32¢ Low Gloss Gum	8.25	6.50	.95	...
2914	32¢ Flag over Porch, SVS, Perf. 9.8	8.25	6.50	.95	.25

#2913 has Red "1995" Date. #2914 has Blue "1995" Date.
Note: S.A. indicates Self-adhesive. Otherwise, stamps are moisture activated.

1995-97 Regular Issue Coils (continued)

Scott's No.		Pl.Strip of 5	Pl.Strip of 3	F-VF NH	F-VF Used
2915	32¢ Flag over Porch, SA, Die-cut 8.7 ...	18.75	15.75	1.60	.30
2915A	32¢ Flag over Porch, SA, Die-cut 9.8 ... Red "1996", multiple stamps touch (1996)	8.75	6.75	1.10	.30
2915B	32¢ Flag-Porch, SA, Die-cut 11.5(1996)	15.75	13.00	1.40	.80
2915C	32¢ Flag-Porch,SA,Die-cut 10.9(1996)	19.50	16.00	1.80	.80
2915D	32¢ Flag over Porch, SA, Die-cut 9.8, Red "1997" Stamps separate on backing (1997)	17.75	15.00	1.50	.75

Note: See #3133 for Blue "1996" Date Die-cut 9.9

1995-97 Booklets and Panes

Scott's No.		Mint Sheet	Plate Block	F-VF NH	F-VF Used
2916	32¢ Flag over Porch, Booklet Single	...	...	1.10	.20
2916a	32¢ Booklet Pane of 10, Pf.10.8x9.8 .... (Unfolded 11.75)			9.50	7.75
2919	32¢ Flag over Field, self-adhesive single	...	...	1.00	.30
2919a	32¢ Convertible Pane of 18, Self-adhesive	...	...	15.75	...
2920	32¢ Flag over Porch, self-adhesive single large Blue "1995" date Die-cut 8.7	...	...	1.25	.30
2920a	32¢ Convertible Pane of 20, Self-adhesive, large "1995"	...	...	21.75	...
2920f	32¢ Flag over Porch, Folded Booklet of 15(1996)		...	17.50	...
2920h	32¢ Flag over Porch, Folded Booklet of 16 with lower right stamp removed (1996)	...	...	75.00	...

Note: #2920f and 2920h have large "1995" dates like #2920

Scott's No.		Mint Sheet	Plate Block	F-VF NH	F-VF Used
2920b	32¢ Flag over Porch, self adhesive single, small Blue "1995" date Die-cut 8.7	...	...	9.50	1.00
2920c	32¢ Convertible Pane of 20, SA, small "1995"...		...	170.00	...
2920D	32¢ Flag over Porch, self-adhesive, Blue "1996" date (1996) Die-cut 11.3	...	...	1.40	.35
2920De	32¢ Convertible Pane of 10, self-adhesive ...		...	12.50	...
2921	32¢ Flag over Porch, self-adhesive Booklet Single, Red "1996" Date (1996)	...	...	1.20	.30
2921a	32¢ Booklet Pane of 10, self-adhesive Die-cut 9.8 Red "1996" Date (1996) ..... (Unfolded 11.75)			10.50	...
2921b	32¢ Flag over Porch, self-adhesive Booklet Single, Red "1997" Date (1997)	...	...	1.40	.30
2921c	32¢ Booklet Pane of 10, self-adhesive Die-cut 9.8 Red "1997" Date (1997)	...	...	12.75	...
2921d	32¢ Booklet Pane of 5, self-adhesive Die-cut 9.8 Red "1997" Date (1997) ..... (Unfolded 8.25)			6.75	...

1995-99 Great American Series

2933

2934

2935

2936

2938

2940

2941

2942

2943

Scott's No.		Mint Sheet	Plate Block	F-VF NH	F-VF Used
2933-43	**Set of 9**	...	**53.50**	**10.00**	**2.50**
2933	32¢ Milton S. Hershey .... (100)	77.50	4.75	.80	.25
2934	32¢ Cal Farley (1996) .... (100)	77.50	4.75	.80	.20
2935	32¢ Henry R.Luce (1998) .... (20)	15.50	3.50	.80	.25
2936	32¢ Lila & DeWitt Wallace (1998) . (20)	15.50	3.50	.80	.25
2938	46¢ Ruth Benedict .... (100)	110.00	6.75	1.15	.25
2940	55¢ Alice Hamilton, MD .... (100)	125.00	7.75	1.30	.30
2941	55¢ Justin S. Morrill (1999) .... (20)	25.00	5.75	1.30	.30
2942	77¢ Mary Breckenridge, SA (1998) (20)	35.00	8.00	1.80	.40
2943	78¢ Alice Paul, Bright Violet, Solid Tagging .... (100)	180.00	11.50	1.85	.50
2943a	78¢ Dull Violet, Grainy Solid Tag. .. (100)	190.00	12.00	1.95	.50
2943b	78¢ Pale Violet,Grainy Solid Tag. .. (100)	220.00	13.50	2.25	.60

1995 Commemoratives

2948

2949

2950

Scott's No.		Mint Sheet	Plate Block	F-VF NH	F-VF Used
2948,2950-58,2961-68,2974,2976-80, 2982-92,2998-99,3001-7,3019-23 Set of 49 No #3003A	....	...	...	**51.00**	**15.50**
2948	(32¢) Love & Cherub	38.50	3.75	.80	.25
2949	(32¢) Love & Cherub, Self-adhesive ...	...	...	1.00	.25
2949a	(32¢) Convertible Pane of 20, Self-adhesive ...		...	18.75	...
2950	32¢ Florida Statehood 150th Anniv. .. (20)	33.50	8.00	1.75	.25

1995 Commemoratives (continued)

2951
2953

2952
2954

2955

2956

2957,2959

2958

2960

2965

2961

2962

2963

2964

2966

2967

2968

2969   2970   2971   2972   2973

Scott's No.		Mint Sheet	Plate Block	F-VF NH	F-VF Used
2951-54	32¢ Earth Day/Kids Care, Block of 4(16)	15.75	4.50	4.00	3.50
2951-54	32¢ Set of 4 Singles	...	...	3.75	1.20
2955	32¢ Richard Nixon	53.50	5.50	1.10	.25
2956	32¢ Bessie Coleman, Aviator, Black Heritage	38.50	3.75	.80	.25
2957	32¢ Love Cherub, Perf. 11.2	38.50	3.75	.80	.25
2957v	Folded Block of 15 in Booklet (BK244)	...	...	14.95	...
2958	55¢ Love Cherub	72.50	6.75	1.50	.60
2959	32¢ Love Cherub, Booklet Single Perf.9.8x10.8	...	...	.95	.25
2959a	32¢ Booklet Pane of 10	(Unfolded 9.95)		8.75	7.95
2960	55¢ Love Cherub, Self-Adhesive single	...	...	1.60	.65
2960a	55¢ Convertible Pane of 20, Self-Adhesive	...	...	28.50	...
2960v	55¢ Convertible Pane of 20 with Die-cut "Time to Reorder" (1996)	...	...	28.50	...
2961-65	32¢ Recreational Sports Strip of 5 .. (20)20.00 (10)11.50			5.25	4.75
2961-65	32¢ Set of 5 Singles	...	...	5.00	1.75

1995 Commemoratives (continued)

Scott's No.		Mint Sheet	Plate Block	F-VF NH	F-VF Used
2966	32¢ Prisoners of War (POW)& Missing in Action (MIA) .... (20)	15.00	3.50	.80	.25
2967	32¢ Marilyn Monroe, Legends of Hollywood .... (20)	29.50	7.00	1.50	.25
2968	32¢ Texas Statehood 150th Anniv. .... (20)	27.50	6.50	1.40	.25
2969-73	32¢ Great Lakes Lighthouses 5 Booklet Singles	...	...	6.75	1.50
2973a	32¢ Booklet Pane of 5 .... (Unfolded 8.25) …			7.00	6.25

2974

2980

2975

2977
2979

2976
2978

2974	32¢ United Nations 50th Anniv. .... (20)	15.00	3.50	.80	.25

1995 Civil War Miniature Sheet

2975	32¢ Civil War, Miniature Sheet of 20		...	35.00	29.75
2975a-t	32¢ Set of 20 Singles		...	34.50	15.95

2975a Monitor & Virginia	2975h Frederick Douglass	2975o Mary Chesnut
2975b Robert E. Lee	2975i Raphael Semmes	2975p Chancellorsville
2975c Clara Barton	2975j Abraham Lincoln	2975q William T. Sherman
2975d Ulysses S. Grant	2975k Harriet Tubman	2975r Phoebe Pember
2975e Battle of Shiloh	2975l Stand Watie	2975s "Stonewall" Jackson
2975f Jefferson Davis	2975m Joseph E. Johnston	2975t Gettysburg
2975g David Farragut	2975n Winfield Hancock	

1995 Commemoratives (cont.)

2976-79	32¢ Carousel Horses, Block of 4 ... (20)	21.75	5.25	4.50	4.00
2976-79	32¢ Set of 4 Singles	...	...	4.35	1.20
2980	32¢ Woman Suffrage, 19th Amendmt.(40)	31.00	3.75	.80	.25

1995 World War II Souvenir Sheet of 10

2981

2981	32¢ 1945 W.War II Events .... (20)	27.00	...	13.50	11.50
2981a-j	32¢ Set of 10 Singles	...	...	13.00	7.00
2981v	32¢ Se-Tenant Center Block of 10...	...	...	14.75	14.00

2981a Iwo Jima	2981d U.S. & Soviets Meet	2981g Refugees
2981b Manila	2981e Holocaust	2981h Japan Surrender
2981c Okinawa	2981f German Surrender	2981i Victory Hits Home
		2981j Returning Veterans

 **2982**
 **2983**
 **2984**

 **2985**
 **2986**
 **2987**

 **2988**
 **2989**
 **2990**

 **2991**
 **2992**
 **2999**

2993 **2994** **2995** **2996** **2997**

3000

2998

Scott's No.		Mint Sheet	Plate Block	F-VF NH	F-VF Used
2982	32¢ Louis Armstrong .... (20)	25.00	5.85	1.30	.25
2983-92	32¢ Jazz Musicians, Block of 10 .... (20)	26.50 (10)	14.75	13.75	12.75
2983-92	32¢ Set of 10 Singles	...	...	13.00	5.00
2993-97	32¢ Fall Garden Flowers, 5 Booklet Singles...	...	...	4.60	1.50
2997a	32¢ Booklet Pane of 5 .... (Unfolded 5.75)	...	...	4.75	4.00
2998	60¢ Eddie Rickenbacker, original	82.50	7.75	1.70	.50
2998a	60¢ Rickenbacker, reprint (1999)	82.50	7.75	1.70	.50

The original has a 1mm wide "1995" date while the reprint "1995" is 1½mm wide.
The 1999 reprint is less sharp than the original and has paler colors.

2999	32¢ Republic of Palau	38.50	3.75	.80	.25

1995 Comic Strips Miniature Sheet

Scott's No.		Mint Sheet	Plate Block	F-VF NH	F-VF Used
3000	32¢ Comic Strips, Miniature Sheet of 20	...	...	18.50	16.50
3000a-t	32¢ Set of 20 Singles	...	...	18.00	11.95

3000a The Yellow Kid
3000b Katzenjammer Kids
3000c Little Nemo
3000d Bringing Up Father
3000e Krazy Kat
3000f Rube Goldberg

3000g Toonerville Folks
3000h Gasoline Alley
3000i Barney Google
3000j Little Orphan Annie
3000k Popeye
3000l Blondie
3000m Dick Tracy

3000n Alley Oop
3000o Nancy
3000p Flash Gordon
3000q Li'l Abner
3000r Terry and the Pirates
3000s Prince Valiant

1995 Commemoratives (continued)

 **3001**
 **3003**
 **3002**

 **3004,3010,3016**
 **3005,3009,3015**
3006,3011,3017
 **3007,3008,3014**

3012,3018
3013

3001	32¢ U.S. Naval Academy 150th An. .. (20)	15.00	3.50	.80	.25
3002	32¢ Tennessee Williams, Writer .... (20)	25.00	5.75	1.30	.25
#3003-18 Christmas Issues					
3003	32¢ Bondone Madonna/Child, Perf.11.2	38.50	3.95	.80	.20
3003A	32¢ Madonna and Child, Booklet Single, Perf.9.8x10.9...			1.10	.20
3003Ab	32¢ Booklet Pane of 10 .... (Unfolded 11.50)			9.95	5.95
3004-7	32¢ Santa & Children, Block of 4	42.50	4.50	3.50	3.00
3004-7	32¢ Strip of 4	...	...	3.50	3.00
3004-7	32¢ Set of 4 Singles	...	...	3.35	1.20
3004v-7v	32¢ Set of 4 Booklet Singles (3007b or c) ...			4.50	1.40
3007b	32¢ Booklet Pane of 10, 3 each #3004-5, 2 each #3006-7 .... (Unfolded 11.75)			10.50	8.95
3007c	32¢ Booklet Pane of 10, 2 each #3004-5, 3 each #3006-7 .... (Unfolded 11.75)			10.50	8.95
Self-Adhesive Stamps					
3008-11	32¢ Santa & Children, Block of 9	...	...	9.75	...
3008-11	32¢ Set of 4 Singles	...	...	4.50	1.40
3011a	32¢ Convertible Pane of 20	...	...	19.50	...
3012	32¢ Midnight Angel	...	...	1.00	.40
3012a	32¢ Convertible Pane of 20	...	...	18.00	...
3012c	Folded Block of 15 in Booklet	...	...	15.75	...
3012d	Folded Pane of 16 with one stamp missing (15)...	...	...	19.75	...
3013	32¢ Children Sledding	...	...	1.10	.45
3013a	32¢ Convertible Pane of 18	...	...	16.50	...
Self-Adhesive Coil Stamps					
3014-17	32¢ Santa & Children Strip of 4 Pl.Strip of 8	28.75		12.75	...
3014-17	32¢ Set of 4 Singles			12.50	3.00
3018	32¢ Midnight Angel .... Pl.# Strip (5)10.50	(3)8.00		1.30	.40

 **3019**
 **3020**
 **3021**

3022
3023

3019-23	32¢ Antique Automobiles, Strip of 5 (25)	20.75 (10)	9.75	4.25	4.00
3019-23	32¢ Set of 5 Singles	...	...	4.15	2.00

 **1996 Commemoratives**

3024

3030

3025  3026  3027 3028  3029

Scott's No.	Mint Sheet	Plate Block	F-VF NH	F-VF Used
3024,3058-67,3069-70,3072-88				
3090-3104,3106-11,3118 Set of 52	...	...	52.75	14.75
3024 32¢ Utah Statehood Centennial	38.50	3.75	.80	.25
3024v Folded Block of 15 in Booklet(BK 245)	...	...	17.95	...
3025-29 32¢ Winter Garden Flowers, 5 Booklet Singles	...	...	4.85	1.75
3029a 32¢ Booklet Pane of 5 .... (Unfolded 6.00)	...	...	5.00	4.50
3030 32¢ Love Cherub, Self-adhesive single	...	...	1.10	.30
3030a 32¢ Convertible Pane of 20, Self-adhesive	...	...	20.00	...
3030b 32¢ Folded Pane of 15 + Label	...	...	16.50	...

1996-2002 Flora and Fauna Series

3031,31A,44 3032,3045 3033 3036

3048,3053  3049,3054  3050-51A,3055  3052

Scott's No.			F-VF NH	F-VF Used
3031 1¢ Kestrel, SA, Black 1999 Date,DC10 3/4	6.00	.80	.20	.15
3031A 1¢ Kestrel,SA, Blue 2000 Date,DC 11 1/4	6.00	.80	.20	.15
3032 2¢ Red-headed Woodpecker .... (100)	9.75	1.25	.20	.15
3033 3¢ Eastern Bluebird .... (100)	10.75	1.30	.20	.15
3036 $1 Red Fox, SA, DC 11½x11¼('98) (20)	46.50	10.25	2.35	.50
3036a $1 Red Fox,SA, DC 11 3/4x11(2002)(20)	49.50	11.00	2.50	.60

Scott's No.	Pl.Strip of 5	Pl.Strip of 3	F-VF NH	F-VF Used
3044 1¢ Kestrel, Coil, "1996" 1mm Wide ...	.80	.60	.20	.15
3044a 1¢ Reprint, Deep Shade,"1996"1½mm (1999)	1.20	.90	.20	.15
3045 2¢ Woodpecker Coil (1999)	1.20	.90	.20	.15
3048 20¢ Blue Jay, Self-adhesive Single	...	...	.70	.25
3048a 20¢ Convertible Pane of 10	...	...	6.50	...
3048b 20¢ Booklet Pane of 4	...	...	4.00	...
3048c 20¢ Booklet Pane of 6	...	...	6.00	...
3049 32¢ Yellow Rose, Self-adhesive Single	...	...	1.00	.25
3049a 32¢ Convertible Pane of 20	...	...	17.50	...
3049b 32¢ Booklet Pane of 4	...	...	4.75	...
3049c 32¢ Booklet Pane of 5 + Label	...	...	5.95	...
3049d 32¢ Booklet Pane of 6	...	...	5.95	...
3050 20¢ Ringnecked Pheasant, SA Single, Die-cut 11¼...	...	...	.75	.20
3050a 20¢ Pane of 10, Diecut 11¼ (1998) ...	...	...	6.95	...
3050b 20¢ Pheasant, SA Single, Die-cut 11 .	...	...	.80	.25
3050c 20¢ Pane of 10, Diecut 11 (1998) ...	...	...	7.50	...
#3050a, c All stamps upright #3051 Upright #3051A Turned sideways				
3051 20¢ Ringnecked Pheasant, Die-cut 10½x11 on 3 sides, booklet single, upright, SA (1999)	...	...	.85	.20
3051A 20¢ Die-cut 10.6x10.4 on 3 sides, bklt single, sideways,SA	4.50	...	1.25	...
3051Ab 20¢ Pheasant, Booklet Pane of 5 with 4 #3051 and 1 #3051A turned sideways at top, SA	...	...	7.50	...
3051Ac 20¢ Booklet Pane of 5 with 4 #3051 and 1 #3051A turned sideways at bottom, SA	...	...	7.50	...
3052 33¢ Coral Pink Rose, Booklet Single (3052a,b,c), Die-cut 11½x11¼, SA (1999)	...	...	1.25	.30
3052a 33¢ Booklet Pane of 4	...	...	4.75	...
3052b 33¢ Booklet Pane of 5	...	...	6.00	...
3052c 33¢ Booklet Pane of 6	...	...	7.25	...
3052v 33¢ SA Single from Pane of 20 (3052d)	...	...	.95	...
3052d 33¢ Convertible Pane of 20, Diecut 11½x11¼, SA...	...	...	16.75	...
3052E 33¢ Rose, Booklet Single, Die-cut 10 3/4x 10½ (3052Ef)...	...	...	1.10	.30
3052E 33¢ Double-sided Pair	...	...	2.20	...
3052Ef 33¢ Conv.Double-sided Pane of 20, . Die-cut 10 3/4 x 10½ (2000)	...	...	17.50	...
3053 20¢ Blue Jay Coil, SA	7.75	6.00	.90	.20
3054 32¢ Yellow Rose Coil, SA (1997)	8.50	6.50	1.00	.20
3055 20¢ Ringnecked Pheasant Coil, SA (1998)	7.50	5.75	.70	.20

1996 Commemoratives (continued)

3059 3058 3060

 3065

3061 3062
3063 3064

3066

3067

Scott's No.	Mint Sheet	Plate Block	F-VF NH	F-VF Used
3058 32¢ Ernest E. Just, Marine Biologist, Black Heritage .... (20)	18.50	4.25	.95	.25
3059 32¢ Smithsonian Institution 150th .... (20)	18.50	4.25	.95	.25
3060 32¢ Year of the Rat .... (20)	23.75	5.75	1.25	.25
3061-64 32¢ Pioneers of Communication, Block of 4 .... (20)	18.50	4.50	3.85	3.35
3061-64 32¢ Strip of 4	...	...	3.85	3.35
3061-64 32¢ Set of 4 singles	...	...	3.75	1.20
3065 32¢ Fulbright Scholarships, 50th Anniv.	85.00	8.50	1.75	.25
3065v Folded Block of 15 in Booklet (BK246)	...	...	26.50	...
3066 50¢ Jacqueline Cochran, Pilot	63.50	6.25	1.30	.45
3067 32¢ Marathon .... (20)	15.00	3.50	.80	.25

1996 Atlanta '96 Summer Olympics Miniature Sheet

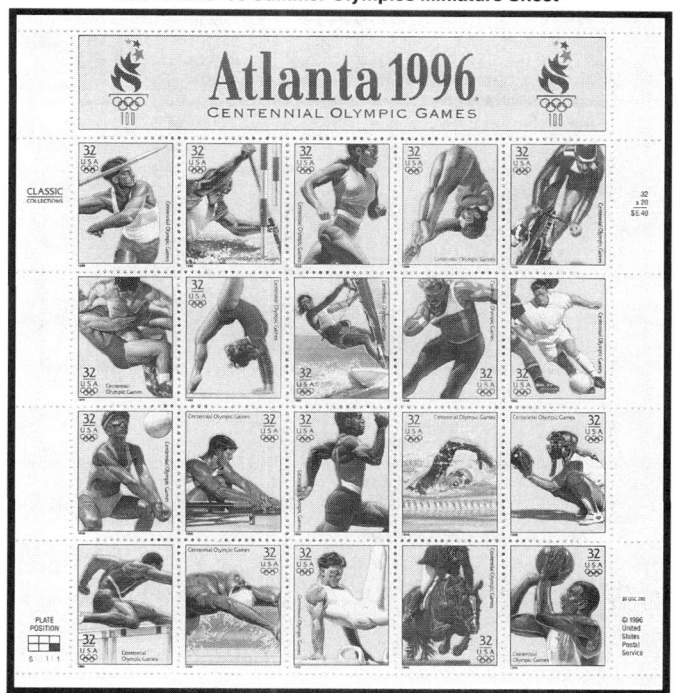

3068

77

Scott's No.	Mint Sheet	Plate Block	F-VF NH	F-VF Used
3068 32¢ Olympic Games, Miniature Sheet of 20 ...	...	...	19.95	18.75
3068a-t 32¢ Olympics Set of 20 Singles	...	...	19.75	13.75

3068a Decathlon	3068h Women's Sailboarding	3068n Women's Swimming
3068b Men's Canoeing	3068i Men's Shot Put	3068o Women's Softball
3068c Women's Running	3068j Women's Soccer	3068p Men's Hurdles
3068d Women's Diving	3068k Beach Volleyball	3068q Men's Swimming
3068e Men's Cycling	3068l Men's Rowing	3068r Men's Gymnastics
3068f Freestyle Wrestling	3068m Men's Sprints	3068s Equestrian
3068g Women's Gymnastic		3068t Men's Basketball

1996 Commemoratives (continued)

3069   3070, 3071

3072   3073   3074   3075   3076

3079   3078   3083   3084
3077   3080   3085   3086

3081   3082   3087

Scott's No.	Mint Sheet	Plate Block	F-VF NH	F-VF Used
3069 32¢ Georgia O'Keeffe .... (15)	20.00	6.50	1.40	.25
3069v Folded Block of 15 in Booklet (BK247)	...	...	19.95	...
3070 32¢ Tennessee Statehood Bicentennial	38.50	3.85	.80	.25
3070v Folded Block of 15 in Booklet (BK248)	...	...	16.50	...
3071 32¢ Tennessee Self-adhesive single	...	...	1.20	.30
3071a Convertible Pane of 20 SA	...	...	21.95	...
3072-76 32¢ American Indian Dances, Strip of 5	(20)19.50	(10)10.75	5.00	4.50
3072-76 32¢ Set of 5 Singles	...	...	4.85	1.75
3072-76v Folded Block of 15 in Booklet (BK249)	...	...	15.75	...
3077-80 32¢ Prehistoric Animals, Block of 4 (20)	18.00	4.15	3.75	3.25
3077-80 32¢ Strip of 4	...	...	3.75	3.25
3077-80 32¢ Set of 4 singles	...	...	3.65	1.20
3081 32¢ Breast Cancer Awareness .... (20)	20.75	4.75	1.10	.25
3082 32¢ James Dean, Legends of Hollywood .... (20)	26.75	6.50	1.40	.25
3082v Folded Block of 15 in Booklet (BK250)	...	...	21.50	...

1996 Commemoratives (continued)

Scott's No.	Mint Sheet	Plate Block	F-VF NH	F-VF Used
3083-86 32¢ Folk Heroes, Block of 4 .... (20)	19.50	4.50	4.00	3.75
3083-86 32¢ Strip of 4	...	...	4.00	3.75
3083-86 32¢ Set of 4 Singles	...	...	3.90	1.20
3083-86v Folded Block of 15 in Booklet (BK251)	...	...	15.95	...
3087 32¢ Olympic Games, Discobolus ...... (20)	19.50	4.50	1.00	.25
3087v Folded Block of 15 in Booklet (BK252)	...	...	20.95	...

3090   3088-89   3104

3096   3097
3098   3099

3095   3091   3092   3093   3094

3102   3103
3100   3101

Scott's No.	Mint Sheet	Plate Block	F-VF NH	F-VF Used
3088 32¢ Iowa Statehood 150th Anniv.	77.50	7.75	1.60	.25
3088v Folded Block of 15 in Booklet (BK253)	...	...	24.95	...
3089 32¢ Iowa Self-Adhesive single	...	...	1.40	.30
3089a Iowa Convertible Pane of 20 SA	...	...	25.75	...
3090 32¢ Rural Free Delivery Centennial .. (20)	15.00	3.50	.80	.25
3090v Folded Block of 30 in Booklet (BK254)	...	...	31.95	...
3091-95 32¢ Riverboats, SA, Strip of 5 .... (20)	21.00	(10)11.50	5.50	4.75
3091-95 32¢ Set of 5 singles	...	...	5.35	1.75
3091-95v Folded Block of 15 in Booklet (BK255)	...	...	17.95	...
3091-95 32¢ Riverboats, self-adhesive attd, with "missing 3 perforations" special die cutting. .... (20)	295.00	(10)160.00	79.50	...
3096-99 32¢ Big Band Leaders, Block of 4 .. (20)	21.50	5.00	4.50	4.00
3096-99 32¢ Strip of 4	...	...	4.50	4.00
3096-99 32¢ Horiz. Pl. Block of 8 with selvedge	...	9.75	...	...
3096-99 32¢ Set of 4 Singles	...	...	4.25	1.40
3100-3 32¢ Songwriters Block of 4 .... (20)	21.50	5.00	4.50	4.00
3100-3 32¢ Strip of 4	...	...	4.50	4.00
3100-3 32¢ Horiz. Pl. Block of 8 with selvedge	...	9.75	...	...
3100-3 32¢ Set of 4 Singles	...	...	4.25	1.40
3104 23¢ F. Scott Fitzgerald, Writer	33.50	3.25	.70	.25

NOTE: S.A.=SELF ADHESIVE STAMPS WHICH DON'T REQUIRE MOISTURE-ACTIVATION

996 Endangered Species Miniature Sheet

3105

Scott's No.		Mint Sheet	Plate Block	F-VF NH	F-VF Used
3105	32¢ Endangered Species,Miniature Sheet of 15	...		13.75	12.75
3105a-o	32¢ Set of 15 Singles			13.50	8.95
3105v	Folded Block of 15 in Booklet (BK256)	...	...	14.95	...

3105a Black-footed Ferret	3105f Schaus	3105j Gila Trout
3105b Thick-Billed Parrot	Swallowtail Butterfly	3105k San Francisco
3105h Brown Pelican	3105g Wyoming Toad	Garter Snake
3105c Hawaiian Monk Seal	3105i California Condor	3105m Florida Panther
3105d American Crocodile	3105l Woodland Caribou	3105n Piping Plover
3105e Ocelot		3105o Florida Manatee

1996 Commemoratives (cont.)

3106

3108,3113
3110,3115

3109,3114
3111,3116

3107,3112

3118

3106	32¢ Computer Technology	(40) 30.95	3.95	.80	.25
#3107-3117a Christmas Issues					
3107	32¢ Matteis Madonna and Child	37.50	3.95	.80	.25
3107v	Folded Block of 15 in Booklet (BK257)	...	...	14.95	...
3108-11	32¢ Family Scenes, Block of 4	55.00	5.75	4.50	4.00
3108-11	32¢ Strip of 4	...	...	4.50	4.00
3108-11	32¢ Set of 4 Singles	...	...	4.35	1.20
Self-Adhesive Booklet Stamps					
3112	32¢ Madonna and Child Single	...	...	1.00	.30
3112a	32¢ Convertible Pane of 20	...	...	17.75	...
3113-16	32¢ Family Scenes Set of 4 Singles ..	...	...	4.75	1.40
3116a	32¢ Convertible Pane of 20	...	...	21.50	...
3117	32¢ Skaters single	...	...	1.00	.35
3117a	32¢ Convertible Pane of 18	...	...	16.95	...
1996 Commemoratives (cont.)					
3118	32¢ Hanukkah, Self-adhesive	(20) 15.00	3.50	.80	.25
3118v	Folded Block of 15 in Booklet (BK258)	...	...	14.95	...
3118r	32¢ Hanukkah, revised backing SA (1997) ..	(20) 15.00	3.50	.80	...

#3118 Die-cut with continuous horizontal wavy line.
#3118r Die-cut with two short lines on each side of semi-circle.

1996 Cycling Souvenir Sheet

3119

Scott's No.		Mint Sheet	Plate Block	F-VF NH	F-VF Used
3119	50¢ Cycling Souvenir Sheet of 2	...	...	3.00	2.75
3119a-b	50¢ Set of 2 Singles	...	...	2.90	1.95

3119a Orange & Multicolored, 3119b Blue Green & Multicolored

3120   **3121**   **3122**

1997 Commemoratives
3120-21, 3125, 3130-31, 3134-35, 3141, 3143-50, 3152-75

Set of 40		...	...	38.75	13.50
3120	32¢ Year of the Ox	(20) 21.50	5.00	1.10	.25
3121	32¢ Benjamin O. Davis Sr., Brigadier General, Black Heritage S.A.	(20) 18.50	4.25	.95	.25

1997 Statue of Liberty Self-Adhesive Regular Issue

3122	32¢ Liberty, Die-cut 11 from #3122b, c or d ...	...	...	1.20	.25
3122b	32¢ Booklet Pane of 4	...	...	4.75	...
3122c	32¢ Booklet Pane of 5 + Label	...	...	5.50	...
3122d	32¢ Booklet Pane of 6, die-cut 11 ...	...	...	6.25	...
3122v	32¢ Die-cut 11 from #3122a	...	...	1.20	...
3122a	32¢ Convertible Pane of 20	...	...	18.50	...
3122E	32¢ Die-cut 11.5x11.8 from #3122Eg ...	...	...	2.50	.40
3122Eg	32¢ Booklet Pane of 6, 11.5x11.8 ..	...	...	13.50	...
3122Ev	32¢ Die-cut 11.5x11.8 from #3122Ef ...	...	...	3.00	...
3122Ef	32¢ Convertible Pane of 20, 11.5x11.8	...	...	45.00	...

#3122Ev is die-cut on all four sides.

1997 Commemoratives (continued)

3123   **3124**   **3125**

3123	32¢ Love, Swans, SA Single	...	...	1.10	.30
3123a	32¢ Convertible Pane of 20, SA	...	...	18.50	...
3124	55¢ Love, Swans, SA Single	...	...	1.90	.45
3124a	55¢ Convertible Pane of 20, SA	...	...	35.75	...
3125	32¢ Helping Children Learn, SA	(20) 18.00	4.25	.95	.25

CONVERTIBLE PANES
Convertible Panes are sheets (usually of 18 or 20 stamps) that can be folded into complete booklets with the peelable backing forming the booklet cover.

UNCUT SHEETS AND POSITION PIECES
Many modern issues are released by the Postal Service in complete uncut sheets as they appear before being cut down to the panes normally available to the public. The gutters between the panes create a variety of position pieces. The uncut sheets and position pieces are offered in special listings after the postage listings.

1997 Merian Botanical Prints Booklets, Self-Adhesive

| 3126 | 3127 | 3128 | 3129 |

Scott's No.		Mint Sheet	Plate Block	F-VF NH	F-VF Used
#3126-27a Serpentine Die Cut 10.9 x 10.2 on 2,3,4 sides. Design 20x27mm.					
3126	32¢ Citron, Moth, Beetlet Booklet Single	...	...	1.00	.30
3127	32¢ Flowering Pineapple, Cockroaches, Booklet Single...	...	...	1.00	.30
3127a	32¢ Convertible Pane of 20	...	...	18.00	
#3128-29b Serpentine Die Cut 11.2 x 10.8 on 2 or 3 sides. Design 18½x24mm.					
3128	32¢ Citron, Moth, Beetle, Booklet Single	...	...	1.50	.40
3128a	32¢ Large perforation on right side .	...	...	3.00	1.75
3128b	32¢ Booklet Pane of 5, 2-#3128-29, 1-#3128a	...	...	10.75	
3129	32¢ Flowering Pineapple, Cockroaches, Booklet Single...	...	...	1.50	.40
3129a	32¢ Large Perforations on right side	...	...	9.75	2.50
3129b	32¢ Booklet Pane of 5, 2-#3128-29, 1-#3129a	...	...	14.75	
3128-29	32¢ Attached Pair	...	...	3.00	

#3128a and #3129a are placed sideways on pane. Die-cut 10.8 on left side/

1997 Pacific '97 Commemoratives

| 3130 | 3131 |

3130-31	32¢ Pacific'97 Pair	(16) 15.75	4.50	2.00	1.80
3130-31	32¢ Set of 2 Singles	...	...	1.95	.60

1997 Linerless Coil Stamps

| 3132 | 3133 |

Scott's No.		Pl.Strip of 5	Pl.Strip of 3	F-VF NH	F-VF Used
3132	(25¢) Juke Box, SA, Imperf.	14.50	10.75	1.75	.50
3133	32¢ Flag over Porch, SA, Die-cut 9.9	10.00	7.75	1.10	.40

NOTE: #3133 has Blue "1996" Date at bottom

1997 Commemoratives (continued)

| 3134 | 3135 |

3136

1997 Commemoratives (continued)

Scott's No.		Mint Sheet	Plate Block	F-VF NH	F-VF Used
3134	32¢ Thornton Wilder. Writer	(20) 15.00	3.50	.80	.25
3135	32¢ Raoul Wallenberg & Jewish Refugees	(20) 15.00	3.50	.80	.25

1997 World of Dinosaurs Miniature Sheet

3136	32¢ World of Dinosaurs, Miniature Pane of 15...	...	...	14.50	13.50
3136a-o	32¢ Dinosaurs Set of 15 Singles .	...	...	14.25	9.50

3136a Ceratosaurus	3136f Stegosaurus	3136k Daspletosaurus
3136b Camptosaurus	3136g Allosaurus	3136l Paleosaniwa
3136c Camarasaurus	3136h Opisthias	3136m Corythosaurus
3136d Brachiosaurus	3136i Edmontonia	3136n Ornithominus
3136e Goniopholis	3136j Einiosaurus	3136o Parasaurolophus

1997 Bugs Bunny Self-Adhesive Souvenir Sheet

3137

3137	32¢ Souvenir Sheet of 10	...	...	8.25	...
3137a	32¢ Single stamp	...	...	.95	.35
3137b	32¢ Booklet Pane of 9 (left side)	...	...	6.75	...
3137c	32¢ Booklet Pane of 1 (right side) ...	...	...	2.25	...
3138	32¢ Souvenir Sheet of 10 with special Die-cut that extends thru paper backing	...	...	250.00	...
3138a	32¢ Single stamp	...	...	7.50	...
3138b	32¢ Booklet Pane of 9 (left side)	...	...	65.00	...
3138c	32¢ Booklet Pane of 1 imperf (right side)	...	...	195.00	...

NOTE: Souvenir sheets from the uncut sheet do not have vertical roulette lines dividing the two halves of the souvenir sheet. They are listed with the Uncut Sheets.

1997 Pacific '97 Souvenir Sheets

3139

3140

1997 Pacific'97 Souvenir Sheets (continued)

Scott's No.		Mint Sheet	Plate Block	F-VF NH	F-VF Used
3139	50¢ Benjamin Franklin Sheet of 12 .	...	...	18.00	16.50
3139a	50¢ single stamp from souvenir sheet			1.65	.80
3140	60¢ George Washington Sheet of 12			21.50	19.50
3140a	60¢ single stamp from souvenir sheet	...	...	2.00	.95

1997 Commemoratives (continued)

3141

3141	32¢ Marshall Plan 50th Anniv.	(20) 15.00	3.50	.80	.25

1997 Classic American Aircraft Miniature Sheet

3142

3142	32¢ Classic American Aircraft, Mini Sheet of 20	...	18.50	17.00
3142a-t	Aircraft Set of 20 Singles	...	...	18.00	12.75

3142a Mustang	3142h Stratojet	3142o Peashooter
3142b Model B	3142i GeeBee	3142p Tri-Motor
3142c Cub	3142j Staggerwing	3142q DC-3
3142d Vega	3142k Flying Fortress	3142r 314 Clipper
3142e Alpha	3142l Stearman	3142s Jenny
3142f B-10	3142m Constellation	3142t Wildcat
3142g Corsair	3142n Lightning	

3143, 3148   **3144, 3149**   **3145, 3147**

3146, 3150   **3152**   **3153**

1997 Legendary Football Coaches

3143-46	32¢ Football Coaches, Block of 4	(20) 19.50	4.50	4.00	3.50
3143-46	32¢ Strip of 4		...	4.00	3.50
3143-46	32¢ Top Plate Block of 8 with Label	...	8.50	...	...
3143-46	32¢ Set of 4 Singles			3.85	1.40
3147-50	32¢ Coaches set of 4	79.50	19.50	4.35	2.30
3147	32¢ Vince Lombardi	(20) 22.50	5.50	1.20	.60
3148	32¢ Bear Bryant	(20) 19.50	5.00	1.10	.60
3149	32¢ Pop Warner	(20) 19.50	5.00	1.10	.60
3150	32¢ George Halas	(20) 19.50	5.00	1.10	.60

#3147-50 HAVE A RED BAR ABOVE THE COACHES NAME.
THIS BAR IS MISSING ON THE SE-TENANT ISSUE #3143-46

1997 American Dolls Miniature Sheet

3151

Scott's No.		Mint Sheet	Plate Block	F-VF NH	F-VF Used
3151	32¢ American Dolls, Miniature Sht of 15	...	...	17.50	15.75
3151a-o	32¢ Set of 15 Singles	...	...	17.00	9.75
3151v	Folded Block of 15 in Booklet (BK266)	...	...	19.75	...

3151a "Alabama Baby"	3151g Plains Indian	3151l "Betsy McCall"
3151b "Columbian Doll"	3151h Izannah Walker Doll	3151m "Skippy"
3151c "Raggedy Ann"	3151i "Babyland Rag"	3151n "Maggie Mix-up"
3151d Martha Chase Doll	3151j "Scootles"	3151o Albert Schoenhut Doll
3151e "American Child"	3151k Ludwig Greiner Doll	
3151f "Baby Coos"		

1997 Commemoratives (continued)

3152	32¢ Humphrey Bogart, Legends of Hollywood	(20) 18.50	4.35	.95	.25
3152v	Folded Block of 15 in Booklet (BK267)	...	...	14.95	...
3153	32¢ The Stars and Stripes Forever	38.75	3.75	.80	.25
3153v	Folded Block of 15 in Booklet (BK268)	...	...	14.95	...

3154   **3155**
3156   **3157**

3158   **3159**   **3160**

3161   **3162**   **3163**

3164

3165

3166

3167

3173

3168

3169

3170

3171

3172

Scott's No.		Mint Sheet	Plate Block	F-VF NH	F-VF Used
3154-57	32¢ Opera Singers, Block of 4 ...	(20) 21.75	5.00	4.50	4.00
3154-57	32¢ Strip of 4	...	...	4.50	4.00
3154-57	32¢ TopPlate Block of 8 with Label	...	9.50	...	...
3154-57	32¢ Set of 4 Singles	...	...	4.35	1.40
3158-65	32¢ Classical Conductors & Composers, Block of 8	(20) 22.75	(8) 11.00	9.50	7.75
3158-65	32¢ Set of 8 Singles	...	...	9.25	3.75
3166	32¢ Padre Felix Varela	(20) 15.00	3.50	.80	.30
3167	32¢ U.S. Air Force 50th Anniv. ...	(20) 15.00	3.50	.80	.25
3168-72	32¢ Movie Monsters, Strip of 5 ...	(20) 21.50	(10) 11.75	5.50	4.75
3168-72	32¢ Set of 5 Singles	...	...	5.35	1.75
3168/72v	Folded Block of 15 in Booklet(BK 269)	...	...	17.50	...
3173	32¢ First Supersonic Flight 1947 self-adhesive 50th Anniv.(20)	15.00	3.50	.80	.25

3174

3175

3176

3177

3178

3174	32¢ Women in the Military	(20) 15.00	3.50	.80	.25
3175	32¢ Kwanzaa, self-adhesive	38.50	3.75	.80	.30
3176	32¢ Pietro Madonna & Child, self-adhesive	...	...	1.00	.25
3176a	32¢ Convertible Pane of 20	...	...	18.00	...

Scott's No.		Mint Sheet	Plate Block	F-VF NH	F-VF Used
3177	32¢ American Holly , SA Single from #3177a	...	...	1.00	.25
3177a	32¢ Convertible Pane of 20	...	...	18.50	...
3177v	32¢ Holly, SA Single from #3177b, c or d	...	...	1.15	...
3177b	32¢ Booklet Pane of 4	...	...	4.95	...
3177c	32¢ Booklet Pane of 5 plus label...	...	...	5.95	...
3177d	32¢ Booklet Pane of 6	...	...	6.50	...

1997 Priority Rate Mars Pathfinder Souvenir Sheet

3178	$3 Mars Rover Sojourner	...	...	7.75	7.50
3178a	$3 Single Stamp	...	...	7.50	3.00

NOTE: #3178 IS IMPERFORATE ON ALL 4 SIDES AND MEASURES 146mm WIDE BY 82mm TALL. #3178v IS AN UNCUT SHEET OF 18 WITH VERTICAL PERFORATIONS BETWEEN THE SOUVENIR SHEETS AND WIDE HORIZONTAL GUTTERS. AN INDIVIDUAL SOUVENIR SHEET MEASURES APPROX. 152mm WIDE BY 87mm TALL. See uncut sheet listings.

1998 Commemoratives

3179

3180

3181

3179-81, 3192-3203, 3206, 3211-27, 3230-35, 3237-43, 49-52 Set of 51		...	...	46.50	12.75
3179	32¢ Year of the Tiger	(20) 20.75	4.95	1.10	.25
3180	32¢ Alpine Skiing	(20) 18.50	4.25	.95	.25
3181	32¢ Madam C.J. Walker, Entrepreneur,Black Heritage SA	(20) 18.50	4.25	.95	.25

1998-2000 Celebrate the Century Souvenir Sheets

3182

3182-91	Set of 10 Souvenir Sheets	...	...	140.00	...
3182	32¢1900's, Sheet of 15	...	...	14.50	12.75
3182a-o	32¢ Set of 15 Singles	...	...	14.50	8.95

3182a Model T Ford	3182e St.Louis World's Fair	3182j John Muir
3182b Theodore Roosevelt	3182f Pure Food & Drug Act	3182k "Teddy" Bear
3182c "Great Train Robbery"	3182g Wright Brothers	3182l W.E.B.DuBois
3182d Crayola Crayons	3182h Boxing Match	3182m Gibson Girl
	3182i Immigrants Arrive	3182n Baseball World

Series

3182o Robie House

3183	32¢1910's, Sheet of 15	...	...	14.50	12.75
3183a-o	32¢ Set of 15 Singles	...	...	14.50	8.95

3183a Charlie Chaplin	3183f Panama Canal	3183l Crossword Puzzle
3183b Federal Reserve	3183g Jim Thorpe	3183m Jack Dempsey
3183c George W. Carver	3183h Grand Canyon	3183n Construction Toys
3183d Avant-Garde Art	3183i World War I	3183o Child Labor Reform
3183e Transcontinental Telephone Line	3183j Boy & Girl Scouts 3183k Woodrow Wilson	

1998-2000 Celebrate the Century Souvenir Sheets (continued)

Scott's No.		Mint Sheet	Plate Block	F-VF NH	F-VF Used
3184	32¢1920's, Sheet of 15	...	...	14.50	12.75
3184a-o	32¢ Set of 15 Singles	...	...	14.50	8.95

3184a Babe Ruth   3184g Margaret Mead   3184l Four Horsemen of
3184b The Gatsby Style   3184h Flappers   Notre Dame
3184c Prohibition   3184i Radio Entertains   3184m Lindbergh Flies the
3184d Electric Toy Trains   3184j Art Deco   Atlantic
3184e 19th Amendment   3184k Jazz Flourishes   3184n American Realism
3184f Emily Post

| 3185 | 32¢1930's, Sheet of 15 .... | ... | ... | 14.50 | 12.75 |
| 3185a-o | 32¢ Set of 15 Singles .... | ... | ... | 14.50 | 8.95 |

3185a F. D.Roosevelt   3185f Superman   3185j Jesse Owens
3185b Empire State Bldg   3185g Household   3185k Streamline Design
3185c Life Magazine   Conveniences   3185l Golden Gate Bridge
3185d Eleanor Roosevelt   3185h "Snow White and   3185m The Depression
3185e New Deal   the Seven Dwarfs"   3185n Bobby Jones
               3185i "Gone with the Wind"

| 3186 | 33¢1940's, Sheet of 15 (1999) ... | ... | ... | 14.75 | 12.75 |
| 3186a-o | 33¢ Set of 15 Singles .... | ... | ... | 14.75 | 8.95 |

3186a World War II   3186f TV Entertains America   3186k UN Headquarters
3186b Antibiotics   3186g Jitterbug   3186l Postwar Baby Boom
3186c Jackie Robinson   3186h Jackson Pollock   3186m Slinky
3186d Harry S Truman   3186i GI Bill   3186n "A Streetcar named
3186e Women War Effort   3186j Big Band Sound   Desire"
                                   3186o "Citizen Kane"

| 3187 | 33¢1950's, Sheet of 15 (1999) ... | ... | ... | 14.75 | 12.75 |
| 3187a-o | 33¢ Set of 15 Singles .... | ... | ... | 14.75 | 8.95 |

3187a Polio Vaccine   3187e Korean War   3187i Drive-In Movies
3187b Teen Fashions   3187f Desegrating Public   3187j World Series
3187c The "Shot Heard   Schools   3187k Rocky Marciano
      Round the World"   3187g Tail Fins   3187l "I Love Lucy"
3187d Satellites Launched   3187h "The Cat in the Hat"   3187m Rock n'Roll
                                 3187n Stock Car Racing

| 3188 | 33¢ 1960's, Sheet of 15 (1999) .. | ... | ... | 14.75 | 12.75 |
| 3188a-o | 33¢ Set of 15 Singles .... | ... | ... | 14.75 | 9.95 |

3188a M. L. King, Jr.   3188f The Peace Corps   3188l Super Bowl
3188b Woodstock   3188g Viet Nam War   3188m Peace Symbol
3188c Man Walks - Moon   3188h Ford Mustang   3188n Roger Maris
3188d Green Bay Packers   3188i Barbie Doll   3188o The Beatles
3188e Star Trek   3188j Integrated Circuit   "Yellow Submarine"
           3188k Lasers

| 3189 | 33¢ 1970's, Sheet of 15 (2000) .. | ... | ... | 14.75 | 12.75 |
| 3189a-o | 33¢ Set of 15 Singles .... | ... | ... | 14.75 | 9.95 |

3189a Earth Day   3189f U.S. 200th Birthday   3189l Monday Night
3189b "All in the Family"   3189g Secretariat   Football
3189c "Seasame Street"   3189h VCR's   3189m Smiley Face
3189d Disco Music   3189i Pioneer 10   3189n Jumbo Jets
3189e Pittsburgh Steelers   3189k 1970's Fashion   3189o Medical Imaging

| 3190 | 33¢ 1980's, Sheet of 15 (2000) .. | ... | ... | 14.75 | 12.75 |
| 3190a-o | 33¢ Set of 15 Singles .... | ... | ... | 14.75 | 9.95 |

3190a Space Shuttle   3190f Cable TV   3190k Fall of Berlin Wall
3190b "Cats" Broadway   3190g Viet Nam Veterans   3190l Video Games
3190c San Francisco 49ers   Memorial   3190m "E.T."
3190d Hostages in Iran   3190h Compact Dics   3190n Personal
      Come Home   3190i Cabbage Patch Kids   Computers
3190e Figure Skating   3190j "The Crosby Show"   3190o Hip-Hop Culture

| 3191 | 33¢ 1990's, Sheet of 15 (2000) .. | ... | ... | 14.75 | 12.75 |
| 3191a-o | 33¢ Set of 15 Singles .... | ... | ... | 14.75 | 9.95 |

3191a Baseball Records   3191f Computer Art and   3191k "Jurassic Park"
3191b Gulf War   Graphics   3191l "Titanic"
3191c "Seinfeld"   3191g Species Recovery   3191m Sports Utility
3191d Extreme Sports   3191h Space Exploration   Vehicle
3191e Education   3191i Special Olympics   3191n World Wide Web
           3191j Virtual Reality   3191o Cellular Phones

1998 Commemoratives (continued)

3192

3193

3194

WA = Water-Activated (Perforated)   SA = Self-Adhesive (Die-cut)

1998 Commemoratives (continued)

3195

3196

3197

3198   **3199**

3200

3201   **3202**   **3203**

Scott's No.		Mint Sheet	Plate Block	F-VF NH	F-VF Used
3192	32¢ "Remember the Maine" Cent.	(20) 18.50	4.25	.95	.25
3193-97	32¢ Flowering Trees, SA, Strip-5	(20) 17.00	(10) 9.75	4.50	4.25
3193-97	32¢ Set of 5 Singles	...	...	4.35	1.75
3198-3202	32¢ Alexander Calder,				
	Sculptor, Strip of 5	(20) 18.50	(10)10.50	4.75	4.25
3198-3202	32¢ Set of 5 Singles	...	...	4.65	1.75
3203	32¢ Cinco de Mayo, SA.	(20) 18.50	4.25	.95	.25

1998 Tweety & Sylvester Self-Adhesive Souvenir Sheets

3204

3204	32¢ Souvenir Sheet of 10	...	...	8.00	7.50
3204a	32¢ Single Stamp			.85	.35
3204b	32¢ Booklet Pane of 9 (left side)	...	...	6.50	...
3204c	32¢ Booklet Pane of 1(right side)	...	...	2.25	...
3205	32¢ Souvenir Sheet of 10 with special				
	Die-cut that extends thru paper backing	...	...	15.75	...
3205a	32¢ Single Stamp	...	...	1.35	...
3205b	32¢ Booklet Pane of 9 (left side)	...	...	10.95	...
3205c	32¢ Imperf Bklt. Pane of 1(right side)	...	...	5.50	...

NOTE: Souvenir sheets from the uncut sheet do not have vertical roulette lines dividing thetwo halves of the souvenir sheet. See uncut sheet listings.

3206   3207   3208

1998 Commemoratives (continued)

Scott's No.		Mint Sheet	Plate Block	F-VF NH	F-VF Used
3206	32¢ Wisconsin Statehood 150th Anniversary SA .... (20)	15.00	3.50	.80	.25

1998 Nondenominated Coil Stamps, Perf. 10 or Die-cut 9.8 Vertical

Scott's No.		Pl.Strip of 5	Pl.Strip of 3	F-VF NH	F-VF Used
3207	(5¢) Wetlands, Non-Profit, WA	2.75	2.30	.25	.20
3207A	(5¢) Wetlands, Self Adhesive	2.75	2.30	.25	.20
3208	(25¢) Diner, Water-Activated	6.75	5.25	.70	.40
3208A	(25¢) Diner, Self-Adhesive	6.75	5.25	.70	.40

1998 Trans-Mississippi Centennial Souvenir Sheets

3209

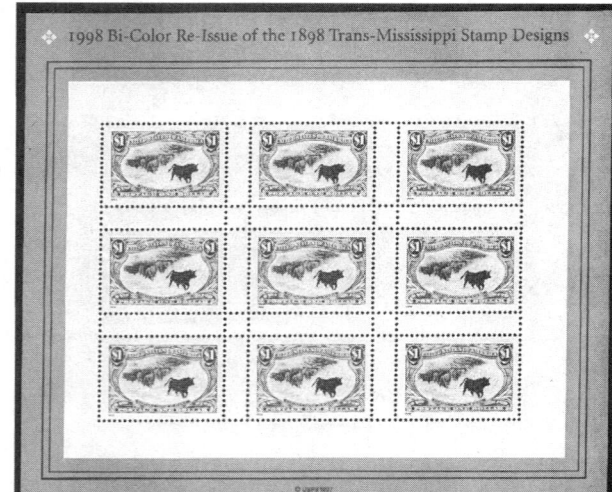

3210

Scott's No.		Mint Sheet	Plate Block	F-VF NH	F-VF Used
3209	1c-$2 Souvenir Sheet of 9	...	...	9.95	8.95
3209a-i	1c-$2 Set of 9 Singles	...	...	9.75	7.25
3210	$1 Cattle in Storm, Souvenir Sheet of 9	...	...	22.75	20.75
3210a	$1 Single from Souvenir Sheet ...	...	...	2.75	1.75

NOTE: #3209-10 contain bicolored versions of the designs of the 1898 Trans-Mississippi issue. (#285-93)

3209a 1¢ Green & Black	3209d 5¢ Blue & Black	3209g 50¢ Green & Black
3209b 2¢ Red Brown & Black	3209e 8¢ Dark Lilac & Black	3209h $1 Red & Black
3209c 4¢ Orange & Black	3209f 10¢ Purple & Black	3209i $2 Red Brown &Black

1998 Commemoratives (continued)

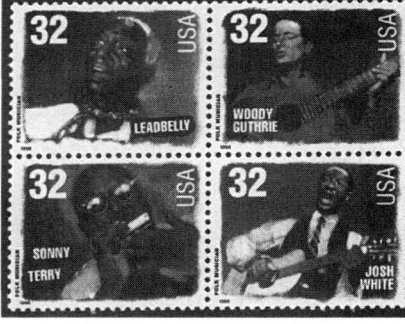

3211   3214   3215
      3212   3213

3219   3218   3220
3216   3217

3221   3224   3225
      3222   3223

Scott's No.		Mint Sheet	Plate Block	F-VF NH	F-VF Used
3211	32¢ Berlin Airlift 50th Anniv. .... (20)	15.00	3.50	.80	.25
3212-15	32¢ Folk Musicians, Block of 4 ... (20)	20.00	4.75	4.25	3.75
3212-15	32¢ Strip of 4	...	...	4.25	3.75
3212-15	32¢ Top Plate Block of 8 with label	...	9.50	...	...
3212-15	32¢ Set of 4 Singles	...	...	4.15	1.40
3216-19	32¢ Gospel Singers, block of 4 ... (20)	20.00	4.75	4.25	3.75
3216-19	32¢ Strip of 4	...	...	4.25	3.75
3216-19	32¢ Top Plate Block of 8 with label	...	9.50	...	...
3216-19	32¢ Set of 4 Singles	...	...	4.15	1.40
3220	32¢ Spanish Settlement of Southwest in 1598 400th Anniv. . (20)	18.50	4.15	.95	.25
3221	32¢ Stephen Vincent Benet .... (20)	18.50	4.15	.95	.25
3222-25	32¢ Tropical Birds, Block of 4. .... (20)	21.50	5.25	4.50	4.00
3222-25	32¢ Set of 4 Singles	...	...	4.35	1.20
3222-25v	Folded Block of 15 in Booklet (BK272)	...	...	18.75	...

3226   3227   3228-29

Scott's No.		Mint Sheet	Plate Block	F-VF NH	F-VF Used
3226	32¢ Alfred Hitchcock, Legends of Hollywood .... (20)	17.00	4.00	.90	.25
3227	32¢ Organ & Tissue Donation, SA .... (20)	15.00	3.50	.80	.25

1998-2000 Nondenominated Coil Stamps, Diecut 9.8 or Perf.9.9 Vertical

Scott's No.		Pl.Strip of 5	Pl.Strip of 3	F-VF NH	F-VF Used
3228	(10¢) Green Bicycle, Small 1mm "1998" Date,Self-adhesive	3.75	3.00	.35	.15
3228a	(10¢) Large 1½mm "1998" Date,SA('00)	8.25	6.75	.70	.20
3229	(10¢) Green Bicycle, Water-Activated	4.50	3.75	.35	.15

3235

3231

3232

3233

3234

3230

3237

3236

| 3238 | 3239 | 3240 | 3241 | 3242 |

1998 Commemoratives (continued)

Scott's No.		Mint Sheet	Plate Block	F-VF NH	F-VF Used
3230-34	32¢ Bright Eyes, SA, Strip of 5 ...	(20) 19.50	(10)11.00	5.25	4.75
3230-34	32¢ Set of 5 Singles	...	...	5.15	1.75
3235	32¢ Klondike Gold Rush Cent. ...	(20) 18.50	4.15	.95	.25

1998 Four Centuries of American Art Miniature Sheets

3236	32¢ American Art, Pane of 20	...	...	25.75	23.75
3236-a-t	32¢ Art, Set of 20 Singles	...	...	25.50	15.75

3236a John Foster Church	3236g Asher B. Durand	3236n Frederic Edwin
3236b The Freake Limner	3236h Joshua Johnson	3236o Mary Cassatt
3236c Ammi Phillips	3236i William Harnett	3236p Edward Hopper
3236d Rembrandt Peale	3236j Winslow Homer	3236q Grant Wood
3236e John James Audubon	3236k George Catlin	3236r Charles Sheelet
3236f George Caleb Bingham	3236l Thomas Moran	3236s Franz Kline
	3236m Alfred Bierstadt	3236t Mark Rothko

3243

3244

3245

3246

3249   3250

3247   3248

3251   3252

Scott's No.		Mint Sheet	Plate Block	F-VF NH	F-VF Used
3237	32¢ Ballet	(20) 16.00	3.75	.85	.25
3237v	Folded Block of 15 in Booklet (BK273)	...	...	17.50	...
3238-42	32¢ Space Discovery, Strip of 5 ..	(20) 18.50	(10)10.50	4.75	4.25
3238-42	32¢ Set of 5 Singles	...	...	4.65	1.75
3238-42v	Folded Block of 15 in Booklet (BK274)	...	...	19.50	...
3243	32¢ Giving and Sharing	(20) 15.00	3.50	.80	.25
#3244-52b Christmas Issues					
3244	32¢ Florence Madonna & Child, SA	...	...	1.00	.20
3244a	32¢ Convertible Pane of 20	...	...	18.00	...
3245-48	32¢ Wreaths, Set of 4 Booklet Singles, DC 11.3x11.6...	...	...	25.00	1.80
3248a	32¢ Booklet Pane of 4	...	...	30.75	...
3248b	32¢ Booklet Pane of 5	...	...	39.50	...
3248c	32¢ Booklet Pane of 6	...	...	47.50	...
3249-52	32¢ Wreaths, SA, Block of 4	(20) 20.00	4.75	4.25	4.00
3249-52	32¢ Set of 4 Singles, DC 11.4x11.6 ...	...	4.00	1.60	...
3249v-52v	32¢ Wreaths, from #3252b booklet of 20...	...	...	4.75	...
3252b	32¢ Convertible Pane of 20, Diecut 11.4x11.6...	...	...	22.50	...
#3245-48 designs 21 x 24 mm. #3249-52 designs 23 x 30 mm.					

1998 Regular Issues

3257-58

3259,3263

3260,3264-69

3270-71

3261

3262

1998 Regular Issue Sheet Stamps

Scott's No.		Mint Sheet	Plate Block	F-VF NH	F-VF Used
3257-62	Set of 6	...	157.50	35.75	13.50
3257	(1¢) Weather Vane, Make-Up Stamp, White "USA," Black "1998" Date, BCA	5.00	.75	.20	.15
3258	(1¢) Weather Vane, Pale blue "USA," Blue "1998" Date, AP	5.00	.75	.20	.15
#3257 design is 18mm high with thin letters					
#3258 design is 17mm high with thick letters					
3259	22¢ Uncle Sam, self-adhesive, Die-cut 10.8	(20) 10.75	2.75	.55	.20
3259a	22¢ Die-cut 10.8x10.5	(20) 26.50	7.50	2.50	1.25
Note: Panes of #3259a mainly consist of 15 #3259 and 5 #3259a.					
Plate blocks contain 2 #3259 and 2 #3259a.					
3260	(33¢) Hat, water-activated,shiny gum	42.50	4.25	.90	.20
3260a	(33¢) Hat, low gloss gum	42.50	4.25	.90	...
3261	$3.20 Priority Mail, Space Shuttle Landing	(20)160.00	35.00	8.00	2.50
3262	$11.75 Express Mail, Piggyback Space Shuttle	(20)535.00	120.00	27.50	10.75

Used Self-adhesive Issues

Prices for used Self-adhesive stamps are for on or off piece. Attached used se-tenant pieces are often on paper to keep the stamps attached.

1998-2000 Regular Issues

Scott's No.		Pl. Strip of 5	Pl. Strip of 3	F-VF NH	F-VF Used
3263	22¢ Uncle Sam Coil, Self-adhesive	6.50	5.25	.70	.20
3264	(33¢) Hat Coil, WA, shiny gum ...	9.25	7.50	.90	.25
3264l	(33¢) Hat, low gloss gum	10.00	8.00	.95	...
3265	(33¢) Hat Coil, SA, Die-cut 9.9 vertical	11.00	8.75	1.10	.25
3266	(33¢) Hat Coil, SA, Die-cut 9.7 vertical	11.00	8.75	1.10	.35

Note: Unused #3266 is on paper larger than stamp, #3265 is same size as stamp
#3265 has sharp corners. #3266 has rounded corners.

3267	(33¢) Hat, Booklet single, SA, BEP, Small "1998" Date, Die-cut 9.9 ..	...	...	1.10	.30
3267a	(33¢) Hat, Booklet Pane of 10	...	...	10.00	...
3268	(33¢) Hat, single from pane of 10 SA, AV, Large "1998" Date, Die-cut 11 1/4	...	...	1.20	.25
3268a	(33¢) Hat, Pane of 10	10.00	...	11.00	...
3268b	(33¢) Hat, single from pane of 20, SA, AV, Large "1998" Date, Die-cut 11 ...	...	...	2.10	.50
3268c	(33¢) Hat, Pane of 20	...	...	18.75	...
3269	(33¢) Hat, single from pane of 18,SA, AV	...	...	1.00	.40
3269a	(33¢) Hat, Pane of 18, Die-cut 8 .	...	...	17.50	...
3270	(10¢) Eagle & Shield Coil, Water-activated, Small 1¼mm "1998" Date	4.35	3.75	.30	.20
3270a	(10¢) Large 1 3/4mm "1998" Date(2000)	12.75	11.00	.60	.40
3271	(10¢) Eagle & Shield Coil, Self-adhesive, Small 1¼mm "1998" Date, Untagged	4.25	3.50	.35	.20
3271b	(10¢) Tagged "Error"	12.50	10.00	1.10	...
3271a	(10¢) Large 1 3/4mm "1998"Date(2000)	11.50	9.50	.95	.25

#3270-71b "Presorted Std.". #2602-4 "Bulk Rate".

3273	3274	3275	3276

3272	3277-82	3283

1999 Commemoratives

Scott's No.		Mint Sheet	Plate Block	F-VF NH	F-VF Used
3272-73,75-76,86-92,3308-9,14-50,52,54,56-59,3368-69 (58)...				53.50	17.50
3272	33¢ Year of the Rabbit	(20) 21.50	5.00	1.10	.25
3273	33¢ Malcolm X, Civil Rights Activist, Black Heritage, SA	(20) 26.50	6.25	1.35	.25
3274	33¢ Victorian-Love SA		...	1.10	.25
3274a	33¢ Convertible Pane of 20		...	19.50	...
3275	55¢ Victorian-Love SA	(20) 27.00	6.25	1.40	.50
3276	33¢ Hospice-Care, SA	(20) 16.00	3.75	.85	.25

1999 Flag over City Regular Issues

3277	33¢ Red date, Water-activated ...	(100) 115.00	35.00	.85	.25
3278	33¢ Black date, SA, Die-cut 11 ...	(20) 17.00	5.50	.85	.20
3278v	33¢ Black date, Booklet Single, SA, Die-cut 11			1.15	...
3278a	33¢ Booklet Pane of 4	...	...	4.50	...
3278b	33¢ Booklet Pane of 5	...	...	5.50	...
3278c	33¢ Booklet Pane of 6	...	...	6.50	...
3278dv	33¢ Single from Convertible Pane of 10, SA...	...	...	1.10	...
3278d	33¢ Convertible Pane of 10, Die-cut 11 ...	...	...	9.75	...
3278ev	33¢ Single from Convertible Pane of 20, SA...	...	...	1.00	...
3278e	33¢ Convertible Pane of 20. Die-cut 11, BEP	...	...	17.50	...
3278i	33¢ Single from Conv. Pane of 10, Diecut 11¼	...	...	2.95	1.00
3278j	33¢ Convertible Pane of 10, Diecut 11¼ ...	...	...	27.50	...
3278F	33¢ Single from Reprint Pane Die-cut 11½x11 3/4	...	...	1.35	.35
3278Fg	33¢ Convertible Pane of 20, Reprint, SA, AVR...	...	...	25.00	...

Note: The reprint is a bluer shade than the original - slight die-cutting differences.

3279	33¢ Red date, Booklet Single, SA, Die-cut 9.8	...	...	1.10	.25
3279a	33¢ Booklet Pane of 10	...	...	9.75	...

1999-2000 Flag over City Regular Issue Coils

Scott's No.		Pl. Strip of 5	Pl. Strip of 3	F-VF NH	F-VF Used
3280	33¢ Red date, Water Activated, Small 1¼mm "1999" Date	8.25	6.50	.90	.25
3280a	33¢ Large 1 3/4mm "1999" Date(2000)	13.75	10.00	1.95	.25
3281	33¢ Red date, SA Square, large 1 3/4mm date	10.50	8.25	1.10	.25
3281c	33¢ Reprint with smaller 1¼m date	17.50	13.50	1.95	.25
3282	33¢ Red date, SA, Rounded	10.75	8.50	1.10	.30

#3281 has square corners with backing same size as stamp.
#3282 has rounded corners with backing larger than the stamp.

1999 Flag Over Chalkboard, Self-adhesive

Scott's No.		Mint Sheet	Plate Block	F-VF NH	F-VF Used
3283	33¢ Flag. Self-adhesive single ...	...	...	1.30	.30
3283a	33¢ Convertible Pane of 18	...	...	19.75	...

1999 Commemoratives (continued)

3286	3287

3288	3289	3290	3291	3292

Scott's No.		Mint Sheet	Plate Block	F-VF NH	F-VF Used
3286	33¢ Irish Immigration	(20) 19.00	4.50	1.00	.25
3287	33¢ Alfred Lunt & Lynn Fontaine, Actors	(20) 16.00	3.75	.85	.25
3288-92	33¢ Arctic Animals, Strip of 5	(15) 15.00	(10) 11.50	5.25	4.25
3288-92	33¢ Set of 5 Singles	...	...	5.15	1.75

1999 Sonoran Desert Miniature Sheet

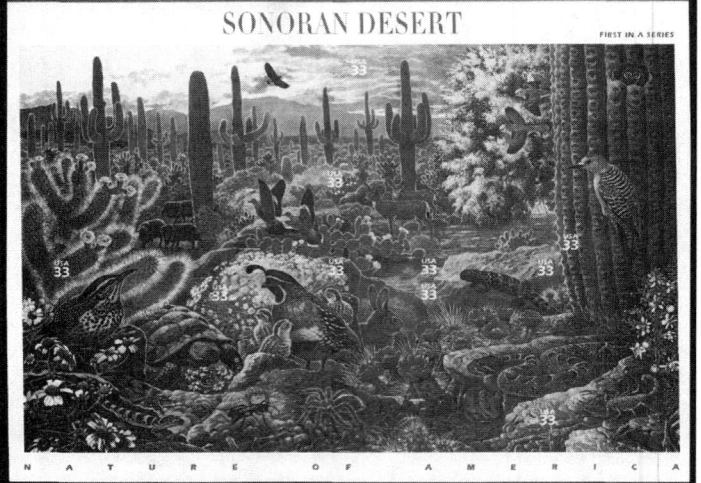

3293

3293	33¢ Sonoran Desert, SA Miniature Sheet of 10...	...	8.50	8.25
3293a-j	33¢ Set of 10 Singles	...	8.50	5.75

3293a Cactus Wren, Brittlebush,Teddy Bear Cholla	3293d Gambel Quail	3293h Gila Monster
	3293e Saquaro Cactus	3293i W. Diamondback Rattlesnake, Cactus Mouse
3293b Desert Tortoise	3293f Desert Mule Deer	
3293c White-winged Dove Prickly Pear	3293g Desert Cottontail Hedgehog Cactus	3293j Gila Woodpecker

1999 Fruit Berries Self-Adhesive Regular Issues

3296,99,3305	3294,98,3302	3295,3300,3303	3297,3301,3304

3294-97	33¢ Block of 4, Die-cut 11¼x11½ from #3297b	...	...	4.00	3.75
3294-97	33¢ Set of 4 Singles, Die-cut 11¼ x 11½	...	...	3.75	1.00
3297b	33¢ Convertible Pane of 20 (1999 Date) ...	...	...	17.50	...
3294a-97a	33¢ Block of 4 from 3297d (2000 Dates)...	...	...	5.25	...
3294a-97a	33¢ Set of 4 Singles (2000 Dates)	...	...	5.00	1.20
3297d	33¢ Double-sided Pane of 20 (2000 Dates)	...	...	22.50	...

#3294-97, 97b have "1999" dates, #3249a-97a, 97d have "2000" dates.

3298-3301	33¢ Booklet Block of 4 Die-cut 9½x10	...	...	6.50	4.25
3298-3301	33¢ Booklet Singles, Die-cut 9½ x 10	...	...	6.25	1.20
3301a	33¢ Booklet Pane of 4	...	...	6.50	...
3301b	33¢ Booklet Pane of 5	...	...	7.75	...
3301c	33¢ Booklet Pane of 6	...	...	9.00	...
3302-5	33¢ Coils, Die-Cut 8.5, Vertical Strip of 4	(PS9)14.50	(PS5) 8.50	6.25	...
3302-5	33¢ Set of 4 Coil Singles	...	...	6.00	1.20

1999 Daffy Duck Self-adhesive Souvenir Sheets

3306

Scott's No.		Mint Sheet	Plate Block	F-VF NH	F-VF Used
3306	33¢ Souvenir Sheet of 10	...	...	8.50	8.00
3306a	33¢ Single Stamp	...	...	.90	.35
3306b	33¢ Booklet Pane of 9 (left side)	...	...	7.25	...
3306c	33¢ Booklet Pane of 1 (right side)	...	...	2.25	...
3307	33¢ Souvenir Sheet of 10 with Special Die-cut that extends through paper backing...	...	...	15.75	...
3307a	33¢ Single stamp with special Die-cut	...	...	1.35	...
3307b	33¢ Booklet Pane of 9, Special Die-cut (left side)	...	...	10.95	...
3307c	33¢ Imperforate Bklt. Pane of 1 (right side)	...	...	5.50	...

1999 Commemoratives (continued)

| 3308 | | 3310 3312 | | 3311 3313 | | 3309 |

| 3314 | 3315 | 3316 |

| 3321 | 3322 | 3328 | 3327 |
| 3323 | 3324 | 3326 | 3325 |

Scott's No.		Mint Sheet	Plate Block	F-VF NH	F-VF Used
3321-24	33¢ Xtreme Sports, Block-4, SA .	(20) 16.75	4.00	3.50	3.25
3321-24	33¢ Strip of 4	...	...	3.50	3.25
3321-24	33¢ Set of 4 singles	...	...	3.40	1.20
3325-28	33¢ American Glass, Block of 4 .	(15) 13.50	...	4.00	3.75
3325-28	33¢ Strip of 4	...	...	4.00	3.75
3325-28	33¢ Set of 4 Singles	...	...	3.85	1.40
3325-28v	Folded Block of 15 in Booklet (BK277)	...	...	15.75	...

| 3329 | 3330 | 3332 | 3338 |

3334

3335

3336

3337

3333

3343	3344
3339	3340
3341	3342

3331

3308	33¢ Ayn Rand, Writer	(20) 16.00	3.75	.85	.25
3309	33¢ Cinco de Mayo	(20) 16.00	3.75	.85	.25
3310-13	33¢ Tropical Flowers, SA, Block of 4	...	...	4.50	4.25
3310-13	33¢ Set of 4 Singles	...	...	4.35	1.20
3313v	33¢ 2 blocks of 4 back–to–back	...	...	8.95	...
3313b	33¢ Convertible Pane of 20, SA	...	...	19.00	...
3314	33¢ John & William Bartram, Botanists, SA	(20) 16.00	3.75	.85	.25
3315	33¢ Prostate Cancer, SA	(20) 16.00	3.75	.85	.25
3316	33¢ California Gold Rush 150th .	(20) 16.00	3.75	.85	.25
3317-20	33¢ Aquarium Fish, Strip of 4 SA	(20) 16.75 (8)	7.50	3.50	3.25
3317-20	33¢ Set of 4 Singles, Block tagging	...	...	3.40	1.20
3317a-20a	33¢ Fish, Strip of 4	(20)	...	...	...
3317a-20a	33¢ Set of 4 singles, Overall tagging	...	...	...	...

3329	33¢ James Cagney, Legends of Hollywood	(20) 16.00	3.75	.85	.25
3330	55¢ William "Billy" Mitchell, Aviation Pioneer, SA	(20) 27.00	6.25	1.40	.45
3331	33¢ Honoring Those Who Served	(20) 16.00	3.75	.85	.25
3332	45¢ Universal Postal Union	(20) 21.50	5.00	1.10	.60
3333-37	33¢ All Aboard, Trains, Strip of 5	(20) 23.75 (10)	12.75	6.00	5.50
3333-37	33¢ Set of 5 Singles…………….	...	...	5.85	1.75
3333-37v	Folded Block of 15 in Booklet (BK278)	...	...	18.50	...
3338	33¢ Frederick Law Olmstead Landscape Architects	(20) 16.00	3.75	.85	.25
3339-44	33¢ Hollywood Composers,Blk.-6	(20) 18.00 (6)	6.50	5.75	5.25
3339-44	33¢Top Plate Block of 8 with label	...	8.50	...	...
3339-44	33¢ Set of 6 Singles	...	...	5.65	2.70

1999 Commemoratives (continued)

3345 · 3346 · 3347 · 3348 · 3349 · 3350

Scott's No.		Mint Sheet	Plate Block	F-VF NH	F-VF Used
3345-50	33¢ Broadway Songwriters, Blk.-6 (20)	18.00	(6) 6.50	5.75	5.25
3345-50	33¢ Top Plate Block of 8 with label	...	8.50		
3345-50	33¢ Set of 6 Singles	...	...	5.65	2.70

1999 Insects and Spiders Miniature Sheet

3351

3351	33¢ Insects and Spiders Miniature Sheet of 20	...	...	17.50	16.50
3351a-t	33¢ Set of 20 Singles	...	...	17.25	9.95

3351a Black widow
3351b Elderberry longhorn
3351c Lady beetle
3351d Yellow garden spider
3351e Dogbane beetle
3351f Flower fly
3351g Assassin bug
3351h Ebony jewelwing
3351i Velvet ant
3351j Monarch caterpillar
3351k Monarch butterfly
3351l Eastern hercules beetle
3351m Bombantler beetle
3351n Dung beetle
3351o Spotted water beetle
3351p True katydid
3351q Spinybacked spider
3351r Periodical cicada
3351s Scorpionfly
3351t Jumping spider

3352 · 3353 · 3354 · 3355

1999 Commemoratives (continued)

3352	33¢ Hanukkah, #3318 design,SA (20)	16.00	3.75	.85	.25

1999 Regular Issue Coil Stamp

3353	22¢ Uncle Sam, Perf 9 3/4	(PS5)6.25 (PS3)5.00	.65	.20

  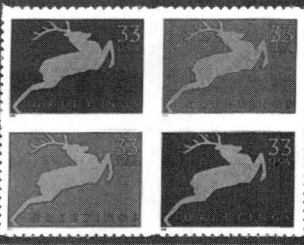

3368

3356, 60 Red · 3357,61 Blue
3358, 62 Purple · 3359, 63 Green

3369 · 3364 Red · 3365 Blue · 3366 Purple · 3367 Green

Scott's No.		Mint Sheet	Plate Block	F-VF NH	F-VF Used
3354	33¢ North Atlantic Treaty Organization 50th Anniversary (20)	16.00	3.75	.85	.25
#3355-3367c	Christmas Issues				
3355	33¢ Vivarini Madonna, Booklet Single, SA...	...	...	1.10	.20
3355v	33¢ Back-to-Back Booklet Singles, SA	...	...	2.20	...
3355a	33¢ Double-sided Convertible Pane of 20...	...	...	18.00	...
3356-59	33¢ Deer, Block of 4,SA,DC 11 1/4 (20)	16.00	3.75	3.50	3.25
3356-59	33¢ Strip of 4	...	...	3.50	3.25
3356-59	33¢ Set of 4 singles	...	...	3.40	1.20
3360-63	33¢ Deer, Block of 4 from Pane of 20	...	...	4.00	3.75
3360-63	33¢ Strip of 4 from Pane of 20	...	...	4.00	3.75
3360-63	33¢ Set of 4 Singles from Pane of 20	...	...	3.95	1.20
3363a	33¢ Convertible Pane of 20, SA, Die-cut 11 1/4			17.50	...

3356-59 have narrow borders. #3360-63 borders are much wider.

3364-67	33¢ Deer, set of 4 Singles from Booklet Panes	...	...	9.75	1.40
3367a	33¢ Booklet Pane of 4, Die-cut 11½x11 1/4	...	...	10.00	...
3367b	33¢ Booklet Pane of 5, Die-cut 11½x11 1/4	...	...	12.50	...
3367c	33¢ Booklet Pane of 6, Die-cut 11½x11 1/4	...	...	15.00	...

Note: Designs of stamps in Deer Booklet of 15 are considerably smaller than those in Sheet of 20 or Convertible Pane of 20

3368	33¢ Kwanzaa, #3175 design, SA (20)	16.00	3.75	.85	.25
3369	33¢ Millennium Baby, SA (20)	16.00	3.75	.85	.25

3370 · 3371 · 3372

3377a2

2000 Commemoratives

3370-72,79-90,93-3402,14-17,38-46 (38)	...	...	32.50	10.95
3370	33¢ Year of the Dragon	21.50	5.00	1.10	.25
3371	33¢ Patricia Roberts Harris, First Black Woman Cabinet Secretary, Black Heritage, SA	16.00	3.75	.85	.25

Note: From #3370 to date, Sheets are Panes of 20 unless otherwise indicated.

USED NOTE: Modern Used U.S. stamps are very difficult to keep in stock and many may not be available when you place your order. Prices are listed on these for when they are in stock and for reference purposes.

2000 U.S. Navy Submarines

Scott's No.		Mint Sheet	Plate Block	F-VF NH	F-VF Used
3372	33¢ U.S. Navy Submarines	16.00	3.75	.85	.25
3377a1	22¢,33¢,55¢,60¢,$3.20 Booklet Pane of 5, Selvedge 1			38.50	...
3377a2	22¢,33¢,55¢,60¢,$3.20 Booklet Pane of 5, Selvedge 2			38.50	...
3377a	Prestige Booklet with 2 Panes (Selvedge 1 & 2)	...		75.00	...

Note: Selvedge 1 "THE DOLPHIN PIN", Selvedge 2 "THE SUBMARINE STAMPS"

3373-77	22¢-$3.20 set of 5 Booklet Singles			37.50	14.95
3373	22¢ S Class Submarines............	...		1.75	1.25
3374	33¢ Los Angeles Class (Design of 3372)...	...		3.00	1.25
3375	55¢ Ohio Class	...		4.50	1.75
3376	60¢ USS Holland	...		5.00	2.25
3377	$3.20 Gato Class	...		29.50	8.95

#3372 with microprinted "USPS" at base of sail. #3374 without microprinting.

2000 Pacific Coast Rain Forest Miniature Sheet of 10

3378

3378	33¢ Rain Forest Miniature Sheet of 10	...	...	8.50	8.25
3378a-j	33¢ Set of 10 Singles	...	...	8.50	5.50

3378a Harlequin Duck
3378b Dwarf Oregongrape
3378c American Dipper
3378d Cutthroat Trout
3378e Roosevelt Elk
3378f Winter Wren

3378g Pacific Giant Salamander, Rough Skinned Newt
3378h Western Tiger Swallowtail

3378i Douglas Squirrel, Foloise Lichen
3378j Foloise Lichen, Banana slug

2000 Commemoratives (continued)

3379   3380   3381   3382   3383

3386   3387   3388   3384   3385

3379-83	33¢ Louise Nevelson, Wood Sculptures, Strip of 5	16.00	(10) 9.25	4.25	3.75
3379-83	33¢ Set of 5 Singles..	...	...	4.20	1.75
3384-88	33¢ Edwin Powell Hubble, Hubble Space Telescope Images, Strip of 5.......	16.00	(10) 9.25	4.25	3.75
3384-88	33¢ Set of 5 Singles......	...	...	4.20	1.75

2000 Commemoratives (continued)

3389   3390   3398

3393   3394   3397
3395   3396

3391

Scott's No.		Mint Sheet	Plate Block	F-VF NH	F-VF Used
3389	33¢ American Samoa................	16.00	3.75	.85	.25
3390	33¢ Library of Congress............	16.00	3.75	.85	.25

2000 Wile E. Coyote and Road Runner Souvenir Sheet of 10

3391	33¢ Souvenir Sheet of 10..........	...	...	8.50	8.00
3391a	33¢ Single stamp......................			.90	.35
3391b	33¢ Booklet Pane of 9 (left side)	...		7.25	...
3391c	33¢ Booklet Pane of 1 (right side)	...		2.25	...
3392	33¢ Souvenir Sheet of 10 with Special Die-cut that extends through paper backing + imperf.single	...		19.75	...
3392a	33¢ Single stamp with special die-cut from left side	...		1.65	...
3392b	33¢ Booklet Pane of 9 with special die-cut (left-side)...			13.75	...
3392c	33¢ Imperforate Booklet Pane of 1 (right side)	...		6.75	...

2000 Commemoratives (continued)

3393-96	33¢ Distinguished Soldiers: John L. Hines, Omar Bradley, Alvin York, Audie Murphy, Block-4	16.00	3.75	3.50	3.25
3393-96	33¢ Strip of 4..........................	...	...	3.50	3.25
3393-96	33¢ Set of 4 Singles.....	...	...	3.40	1.40
3397	33¢ Summer Sports, Runner........	16.00	3.75	.85	.25
3398	33¢ Adoption, SA.......................	16.00	3.75	.85	.25

3399	3400	3401	3402

Scott's No.		Mint Sheet	Plate Block	F-VF NH	F-VF Used
3403	33¢ Historic American Flags, Sheet of 20	…		16.50	15.75
3403a-t	33¢ Set of 20 Singles		…	16.50	9.95

3403a Sons of Liberty	3403h Pierre L'Enfant	3403o Fort Sumter
3403b New England Flag	3403i Indian Peace Flag	3403p Centennial
3403c Forster Flag	3403j Easter Flag	3403q 38-Star FLag
3403d Continental Colors	3403k Star-Spangled Banner	3403r Peace Flag
3403e Francis Hopkinson	3403l Bennington Flag	3403s 48-Star Flag
3403f Brandywine Flag	3403m Great Star Flag	3403t 50-Star Flag
3403g John Paul Jones	3403n 29-Star Flag	

Scott's No.		Mint Sheet	Plate Block	F-VF NH	F-VF Used
3399-3402	33¢ Youth Team Sports, Block of 4	16.00	3.75	3.50	3.25
3399-3402	33¢ Strip of 4	…	…	3.50	3.25
3399-3402	33¢ Set of 4 Singles	…	…	3.40	1.20

3404	3405	3406	3407

2000 Fruit Berries Self-adhesive Linerless Coils with "2000" Date

3404-7	33¢ Blueberry,Raspberry, Strawberry,Blackberry, Strip of 4(PS9)21.75 (PS5) 13.75			8.25	…
3404-7	33¢ Berries, set of 4 singles	…	…	8.00	1.40

2000 Legends of Baseball

3408	33¢ Legends of Baseball Sheet of 20	…	…	18.50	17.50
3408a-t	33¢ Set of 20 Singles	…	…	18.50	10.95

3408a Jackie Robinson	3408h Babe Ruth	3408o Pie Traynor
3408b Eddie Collins	3408i Walter Johnson	3408p Satchel Paige
3408c Christy Mathewson	3408j Roberto Clemente	3408q Honus Wagner
3408d Ty Cobb	3408k Lefty Grove	3408r Josh Gibson
3408e George Sisler	3408l Tris Speaker	3408s Dizzy Dean
3408f Rogers Hornsby	3408m Cy Young	3408t Lou Gehrig
3408g Mickey Cochrane	3408n Jimmie Foxx	

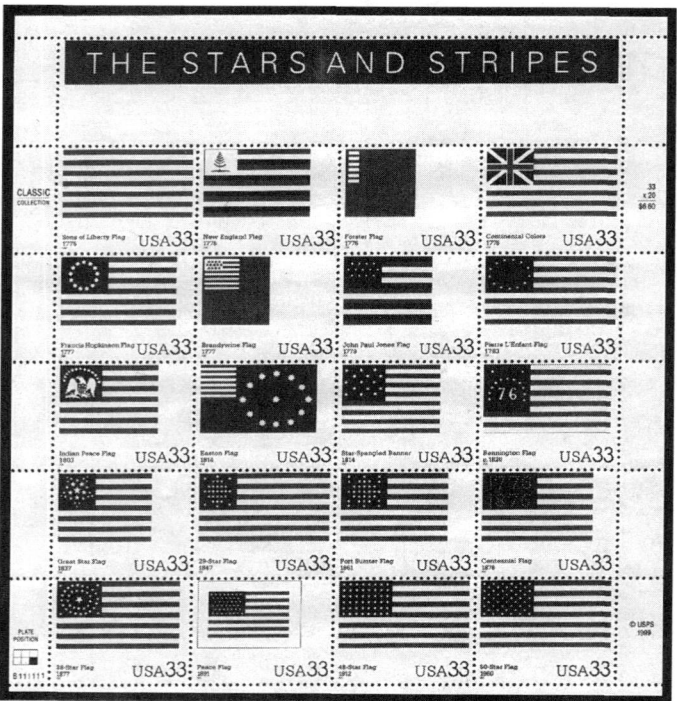

3403

2000 Space Achievement and Exploration Souvenir Sheets

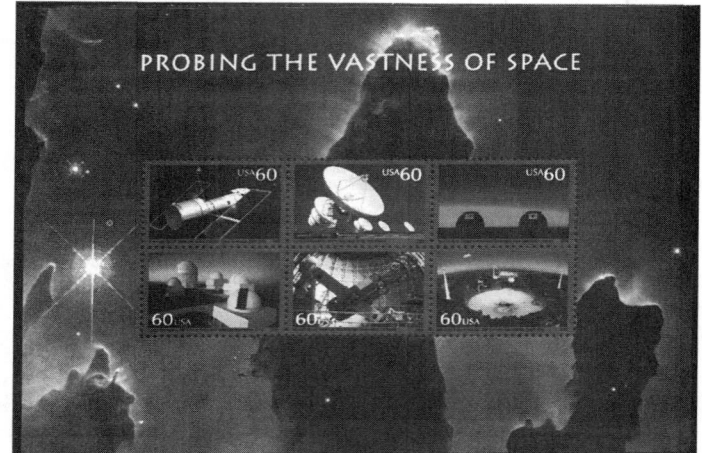

3409

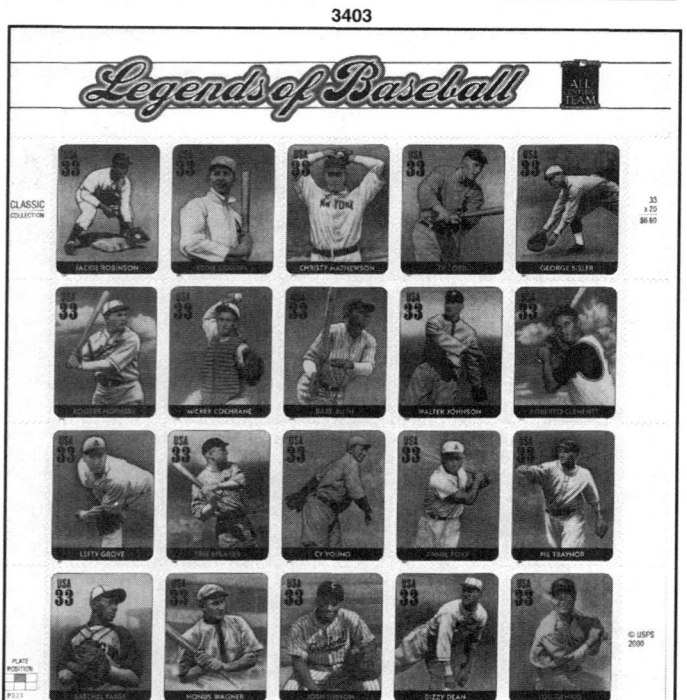

3408

3413

3410

3411

3412

Scott's No.		Mint Sheet	Plate Block	F-VF NH	F-VF Used
3409-13	**60¢-$11.75 set of 5 souvenir sheets**		…	**140.00**	…
3409	60¢ Probing the Vastness of Space, sheet of 6		…	15.00	13.75
3409a-f	60¢ Set of 6 singles.................			15.00	4.50
3410	$1 Exploring the Solar System, sheet of 5		…	22.50	21.50
3410a-e	$1 Set of 5 singles..................			22.50	21.00
3411	$3.20 Escaping the Gravity of Earth, sheet of 2		…	25.00	22.50
3411a-b	$3.20 Set of 2 singles...............		…	25.00	12.00
3412	$11.75 Space Achievement and Exploration, sheet of 1		…	45.00	42.50
3413	$11.75 Landing on the Moon, hologram sheet of 1		…	45.00	42.50

3414	3415	3416	3417

2000 Commemoratives (continued)

3414-17	33¢ "Stampin' the Future, Children's Stamp Designs, Strip of 4, SA	16.00	(8)7.50	3.50	3.25
3414-17	33¢ Set of 4 Singles	…	…	3.40	1.20

2000-2003 Distinguished Americans, Bi-Color

3420	3426	3431-32	3433-34

3420	10¢ General Joseph W. Stilwell	5.50	1.35	.30	.20
3426	33¢ Senator Claude Pepper..........	16.00	3.75	.85	.20
3431	76¢ Hattie W. Caraway, Die-cut 11x11(2001)...	34.75	8.00	1.80	.40
3432	76¢ Caraway, Die-cut 11½x11	70.00	17.50	3.75	3.50
3433	83¢ Edna Ferber,Author, SA (2002)	35.75	8.25	1.85	.75
3434	83¢ Ferber, "2003" Date (2003)	32.50	7.35	1.65	1.00

2000 Commemoratives (continued)

3438	3439	3440

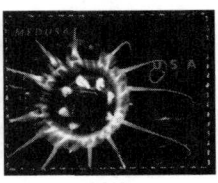

3441	3442	3443

| 3444 | 3445 | 3446 |

Scott's No.		Mint Sheet	Plate Block	F-VF NH	F-VF Used
3438	33¢ California Statehood, SA, 150th	26.50	6.00	1.35	.25
3439-43	33¢ Deep Sea Creatures, Strip-5... (15)	12.00	(10) 9.00	4.25	4.00
3439-43	33¢ Set of 5 Singles	...	...	4.15	1.75
3444	33¢ Thomas Wolfe, Novelist	16.00	3.75	.85	.25
3445	33¢ The White House, 200th SA	26.50	6.25	1.40	.25
3446	33¢ Edward G. Robinson, Legends Of Hollywood	25.00	5.75	1.30	.30

| 3447 | 3448-50 |  3451 | 3452-53 |

2000 Presorted Standard Coil, SA
3447	(10¢) New York Public Library Lion (PS5)4.65 (PS3) 3.75			.45	.20

2000 Non-Denominated Regular Issues
3448	(34¢) Flag over Farm, Perf.11¼...	16.00	3.75	.85	.40
3449	(34¢) Flag over Farm, SA, Die-cut 11¼, Small "2000" Date	20.75	5.00	1.10	.30
3450	(34¢) Flag over Farm, SA Single, Die-cut 8, Large "2000" Date	...	...	1.20	.25
3450a	(34¢) Convertible ATM Pane of 18	...	...	20.75	...
3451	(34¢) Statue of Liberty, Single from Conv. Pane of 20...	...	...	1.00	.35
3451a	(34¢) Convertible Pane of 20, Die-cut 11	...	...	17.50	...
3451v	(34¢) Statue of Liberty, SA, Booklet Single, Die-cut 11	...	...	1.30	.20
3451b	(34¢) Booklet Pane of 4	...	...	4.75	...
3451c	(34¢) Booklet Pane of 6	...	...	7.25	...

Scott's No.		Pl. Strip of 5	Pl. Strip of 3	F-VF NH	F-VF Used
3452	(34¢) Liberty, Perforate Coil	9.75	7.75	.95	.20
3453	(34¢) Liberty, SA Die-cut	12.75	10.75	1.00	.20

| 3454,58,65 |  3455,59,64 | 3456,60,62 | 3457,61,63 |

3454-57	(34¢) Flowers, Block of 4 from #3457e	...	...	4.75	...
3454-57	(34¢) Double-sided Block of 8 from #3457e	...	...	9.50	...
3454-57	(34¢) Set of 4 Singles...	...	...	4.50	1.20
3457e	(34¢) Double-sided Pane of 20,Die-cut 10½ x 10 3/4,...	...	...	19.75	...
3454v-57v	(34¢) Flowers, from Booklet Panes (#3457b-d) Die-cut 10½x10 3/4	...	...	5.25	...
3457b	(34¢) Booklet Pane of 4	...	...	5.25	...
3457c	(34¢) Booklet Pane of 6 #3456v-57v (1), #3454-55v (2)...	...	...	8.00	...
3457d	(34¢) Booklet Pane of 6 #3454-55v (1), #3456v-57v (2)...	...	...	8.00	...
3458-61	(34¢) Flowers, Block of 4 from #3461b or c, Die-cut 11½x11 3/4	...	...	10.95	...
3454-61	(34¢) Back-to-Back Block of 8 with both #3454-57 and #3458-61	...	...	15.75	...
3461b	(34¢) Double-sided Pane of 20 (3-#3454-57, 2-#3458-61)	...	...	29.75	...
3461c	(34¢) Double-sided Pane of 20 (2-#3454-57, 3-#3458-61)	...	...	38.75	...
3462-65	(34¢) Flowers, SA Die-cut Coils (9) 33.50 (5)19.75			14.50	...
3462-65	(34¢) Set of 4 Singles, Die-cut 8½ Vert.	...	...	14.00	2.20

Note: "000" of "2000" are rounder on #3454-61 than on #3462-65.

2001 Regular Issues, With Denominations

| 3466,76-77 | 3467-8,75 / 3484-84A | 3468A,75A |  3469-70, 95 |

| 3471-71A | 3472 | 3473 |

| 3478,89 | 3479,90 |  3480,88 |  3481,87 |

Scott's No.		Mint Sheet	Plate Block	F-VF NH	F-VF Used
3466	34¢ Liberty, SA Die-cut 9 3/4 Coil, Rounded corners, stamps separate on rolls	(PS5)9.50	(PS3) 7.50	1.00	.20
3467	21¢ Bison, WA	(100)59.50	7.75	.55	.20
3468	21¢ Bison, SA, Die-cut 11	10.75	2.50	.55	.20
3468A	23¢ G.Washington, SA,11¼x11 3/4	11.50	2.75	.60	.20
3469	34¢ Flag over Farm, Perf.11¼	(100)90.00	12.50	.85	.20
3470	34¢ Flag over Farm, SA, DC 11¼	16.00	3.50	.85	.20
3471	55¢ Art-Deco Eagle, SA	27.50	6.25	1.40	.35
3471A	57¢ Art-Deco Eagle, SA	28.50	6.50	1.45	.40
3472	$3.50 U.S. Capitol Dome, SA	170.00	37.50	8.75	3.75
3473	$12.25 Washington Monument, SA	585.00	130.00	29.50	10.95

Scott's No.		Pl. Strip of 5	Pl. Strip of 3	F-VF NH	F-VF Used
3475	21¢ Bison, SA Die-cut 8½ Vert.Coil	5.75	4.75	.55	.20
3475A	23¢ Washington,SA Coil,"2001"Date	5.25	4.00	.60	.20
See #3617 for "2002" Date					
3476	34¢ Liberty, Perforated Coil	8.00	6.50	.90	.20
3477	34¢ Liberty, SA Die-cut Coil, Square corners, stamps together on roll	8.50	7.00	1.00	.20
3478-81	34¢ Flowers,SA Die-cut Coil Strip (PS9)15.00	(PS5)9.75		5.75	...
3478-81	34¢ Flowers, Set of 4 singles	...	...	5.50	1.00

Note: #3478,3489 Green Background #3479,3490 Red Background
#3480,3488 Tan Background #3481,3487 Purple Background

| 3482-83 |  3485 |  3491 |  3492 |

#3482-83h George Washington, SA
Scott's No.		Mint Sheet	Plate Block	F-VF NH	F-VF Used
3482	20¢ Die-cut 11 1/4 Single from Conv. Pane (3482a)			.50	.20
3482a	20¢ Die-cut 11 1/4 Convertible Pane of 10	...		4.85	...
3482v	20¢ Die-cut 11 1/4 Single from Booklet Panes 4 and 6 (3482b and c)	...		.65	.20
3482b	20¢ Die-cut 11 1/4 Booklet Pane of 4	...		2.50	...
3482c	20¢ Die-cut 11 1/4 Booklet Pane of 6	...		3.75	...
3483	20¢ Die-cut 10½x11¼ Single from Conv. Pane (3483c)			2.50	...
3483g	20¢ Pair from Convertible Pane, #3483 at right			3.25	...
3483h	20¢ Pair from Convertible Pane, #3483 at left			3.25	..
3483c	20¢ Convertible Pane of 10 (5-#3482 at left, 5-#3483 at right)			14.75	...
3483f	20¢ Convertible Pane of 10 (5-#3483 at left, 5-#3482 at right)			14.75	...
3483v	20¢ Die-cut 10 1/2x11 SA Single from Booklet Panes 4 and 6 (3483a,b,d or e)			4.75	...
3483vr	20¢ #3482v-83v Pair, 3483v at right			5.25	...
3483vl	20¢ #3482v-83v, 3483v at left	...		5.25	...
3483a	20¢ Bk.Pane of 4 (2-#3482v,2-#3483v) #3483v at right			14.00	...
3483b	20¢ Bk.Pane of 6 (3-#3482v,3-#3483v) #3483v at right			21.00	...
3483d	20¢ Bk.Pane of 4 (2-#3482v,2-#3483v) #3483v at left			14.00	...
3483e	20¢ Bk.Pane of 6 (3-#3482v,3-#3483v) #3483v at left			21.00	...

#3484-84A Bison, SA
3484	21¢ Die-cut 11¼ Single from Convertible Pane (3484d)			.85	.20
3484d	21¢ Die-cut 11¼ Convertible Pane of 10	...		8.00	...
3484v	21¢ Die-cut 11¼ Single from Booklet Panes of 4 or 6 (3484a-b)			.60	...
3484b	21¢ Die-cut 11¼ Booklet Pane of 4	...		2.75	...
3484c	21¢ Die-cut 11¼ Booklet Pane of 6	...		4.00	...
3484A	21¢ Die-cut 10½x11¼ Single from Convertible Pane of 10 (3484Ag or Aj)			2.50	...
3484Ak	21¢ Pair from Convertible Pane, #3484A at right	...		3.00	...
3484Al	21¢ Pair from Convertible Pane, #3484A at left	...		3.00	...
3484Ag	21¢ Convertible Pane of 10 (5-#3484 at left, 5-#3484A at right)			13.75	...
3484Aj	21¢ Convertible Pane of 10 (5-#3484A at left, 5-#3484 at right)			13.75	...

2001 Regular Issues, With Denominations (continued)

Scott's No.		Mint Sheet	Plate Block	F-VF NH	F-VF Used
3484Av	21¢ Die-cut 10½x11¼ Single from Booklet Panes of 4 or 6 (3484Ae,f,h,i)....			3.75	...
3484Avr	21¢ 3484v-84Av Pair, 3484Av at right	...	...	4.25	...
3484Avl	21¢ 3484V-84Av Pair, 3484Av at left	...	...	4.25	...
3484Ae	21¢ Bk.Pane of 4 (2-#3484v,2-#3484Av) #3484Av at right			8.25	...
3484Af	21¢ Bk.Pane of 6 (3-#3484v,3-#3484Av) #3484Av at right			12.50	...
3484Ah	21¢ Bk.Pane of 4 (2-#3484v,2-#3484Av) #3484Av at left			8.25	...
3484Ai	21¢ Bk.Pane of 6 (3-#3484v,3-#3484Av) #3484Av at left			12.50	...
3485	34¢ Statue of Liberty, SA Single from Pane (3485a-b)...			1.35	.20
3485a	34¢ Convertible Pane of 10, SA, Die-cut 11			12.50	...
3485b	34¢ Convertible Pane of 20, SA, Die-cut 11			25.00	...
3485v	34¢ Liberty, SA Single from Booklet Pane (3485c-d)			1.10	...
3485c	34¢ Booklet Pane of 4, SA, Die-cut 11	...	...	4.00	...
3485d	34¢ Booklet Pane of 6, SA. Die-cut 11	...	...	6.00	...
3487-90	34¢ Flowers, Block of 4 from Pane of 20 (3490e)...			5.50	...
3487-90	34¢ Set of 4 Singles, Die-cut 10½x10 3/4 ...			5.35	1.20
3487-90	34¢ Double-sided Block of 8			11.00	...
3490e	34¢ Double-sided Pane of 20			25.00	...
3487v-90v	34¢ Flowers, Block of 4 from B.Pane (3490b,c,d)			4.00	...
3490b	34¢ Booklet Pane of 4, Die-cut 10½x10 3/4...			4.00	...
3490c	34¢ Booklet Pane of 6, #3489-90 (1) #3487-88 (2)			6.50	...
3490d	34¢ Booklet Pane of 6, #3487-88 (1), #3489-90 (2)			6.50	...
3491-92	34¢ Apple & Orange Pair from Convertible Pane of 20, Die-cut 11¼.(3492b)			1.90	1.80
3491-92	34¢ Set of 2 Singles	...	...	1.90	.50
3492b	34¢ Convertible Pane of 20,Die-cut 11¼			17.50	...
3493-94	34¢ Apple & Orange Booklet Pair, Die-cut 11½ x10 3/4 (3494b,c or d)	...	...	2.00	...
3493-94	34¢ Set of 2 Singles	...	...	2.00	.50
3494b	34¢ Booklet Pane of 4, Die-cut 11½x10 3/4...			4.00	...
3494c	34¢ Booklet Pane of 6, Apple stamp in top left corner, Die-cut 11½x10 3/4			6.50	...
3494d	34¢ Booklet Pane of 6, Orange stamps in top left corner, Die-cut 11½x10 3/4	...	...	6.50	...
3495	34¢ Flag over Farm, SA Single from Conv. Pane of 18			.85	.20
3495a	34¢ Convertible Pane of 18, Die-cut 8			15.00	...

2001 Rose and Love Letters, Self-Adhesive

3496	3497-98	3499

3496	(34¢) Booklet Single..................	...	...	1.00	.25
3496a	(34¢) Convertible Pane of 20......			18.00	...
3497	34¢ Single from Conv. Pane, Die-cut 11¼ (3497a)	...		1.10	.20
3497a	34¢ Convertible Pane of 20........			20.75	...
3498	34¢ Single from B.Pane, Die-cut 11½x10 3/4 (3498a-b)...			1.10	.25
3498a	34¢ Booklet Pane of 4..............			4.00	...
3498b	34¢ Booklet Pane of 6..............			6.00	...
3499	55¢ Rose & Love Letters...........	27.50	6.25	1.40	.40

2001 Commemoratives

3500	3501

3500-1,3-4,7-19,21,23-33,36-40,45-48 (38)		...	...	32.75	11.50
3500	34¢ Year of the Snake.............	25.00	5.75	1.30	.30
3501	34¢ Roy Wilkins, Civil Rights Leader, Black Heritage SA...............	16.50	3.75	.85	.25

2001 American Illustrators Miniature Sheet of 20

3502	34¢ Illustrators, Sheetlet of 20, SA	...	...	25.00	22.75
3502a-t	34¢ Set of 20 Singles	...	...	25.00	12.95

3502a James Montgomery Flagg	3502k Edwin Austin Abbey
3502b Maxfield Parrish	3502l Jessie Wilcox Smith
3502c J.C.Leyendecker	3502m Neysa McMein
3502d Robert Fawcett```	3502n Jon Whitcomb
3502e Coles Phillips	3502o Harvey Dunn
3502f Al Parker	3502p Frederic Remington
3502g A. B.Frost	3502q Rockwell Kent
3502h Howard Pyle	3502r N.C.Wyeth
3502i Rose O'Neill	3502s Norman Rockwell
3502j Dean Cornwell	3502t John Held Jr.

2001 American Illustrators Miniature Sheet of 20

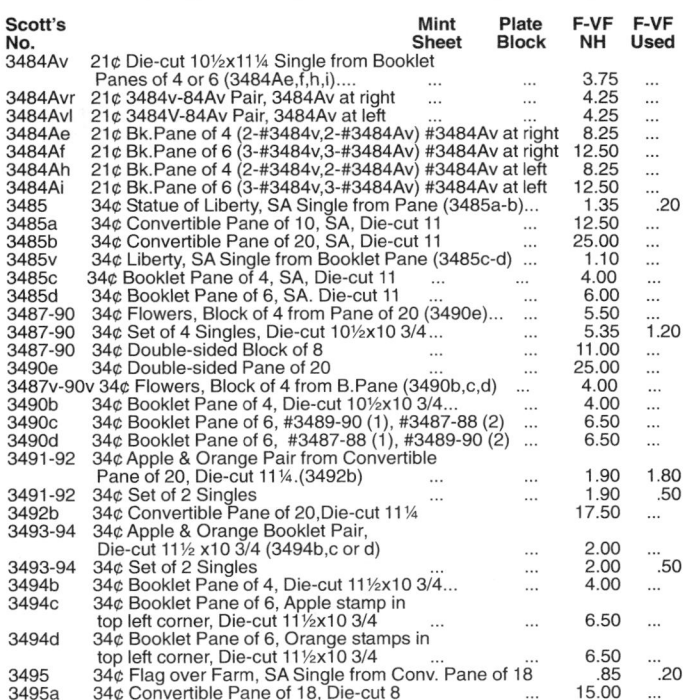

3502

2001 Commemoratives (continued)

3503	3504

Scott's No.		Mint Sheet	Plate Block	F-VF NH	F-VF Used
3503	34¢ Diabetes Awareness, SA	16.50	3.75	.85	.25
3504	34¢ Nobel Prize Centennial	16.50	3.75	.85	.25

2001 Pan-American Inverts Souvenir Sheet

3505

3505	1¢,2¢,4¢,80¢ (4) Souvenir Sheet of 7	...	...	14.75	12.75
3505a	1¢ Pan-American Invert single....	...	...	1.40	.50
3505b	2¢ Pan-American Invert single....	...	...	1.40	.50
3505c	4¢ Pan-American Invert single....	...	...	1.40	.50
3505d	80¢ Pan-American Exposition.....	...	...	2.75	1.10

2001 Great Plains Prairie Miniature Sheet

3506

table

Scott's No.		Mint Sheet	Plate Block	F-VF NH	F-VF Used
3506	34¢ Prairie Miniature Sheet of 10	...	...	8.50	8.00
3506a-j	34¢ Set of 10 Singles	...	...	8.50	6.50

3506a Pronghorns, Canada Geese
3506b Burrowing Owls, American Buffalos
3506c American Buffalo, Black-tailed Prairie Dogs, Wild Alfalfa
3506d Black-tailed Prairie Dog, American Buffalos
3506e Painted Lady Butterfly, American Buffalo, Prairie Coneflowers, Prairie Wild Roses
3506f Western Meadowlark, Camel Cricket, Prairie Cornflowers, Prairie Wild Roses
3506g Badger, Harvester Ants
3506h Eastern Short-horned Lizard,
3506i Plains Spadefoot, Dung Beetle, Prairie Wild Roses
3506j Two-striped Grasshopper, Ord's Kangaroo Rat

2001 Commemoratives (continued)

3507

3508

3509

3510-19

3507	34¢ "Peanuts", Snoopy World War I Flying Ace, SA	18.75	4.50	.95	.25
3508	34¢ Honoring U.S. Veterans, Flag, SA	16.50	3.75	.85	.25
3509	34¢ Frida Kahlo, Painter	16.50	3.75	.85	.25

2001 Legendary Major League Baseball Fields

3510-19	34¢ Legendary Baseball Fields	18.50 (10)	10.75	9.50	8.50
3510-19	34¢ Set of 10 Singles	...	...	9.50	6.50

3510 Ebbets Field
3511 Tiger Stadium
3512 Crosley Field
3513 Yankee Stadium
3514 Polo Grounds
3515 Forbes Field
3516 Fenway Park
3517 Comiskey Park
3518 Shibe Park
3519 Wrigley Field

3520

3521

3522

3523

2001 Non-Denominated Regular Issue Coils, SA

Scott's No.		Pl. Strip of 5	Pl. Strip of 3	F-VF NH	F-VF Used
3520	(10¢) Atlas Statue, New York	4.00	3.50	.30	.25
3522	(15¢) Woody Wagon	3.85	3.00	.50	.20

2001 Commemoratives (continued)

Scott's No.		Mint Sheet	Plate Block	F-VF NH	F-VF Used
3521	34¢ Leonard Bernstein, Conductor	16.50	3.75	.85	.25
3523	34¢ Lucille Ball, Legends of Hollywood	16.50	3.75	.85	.25

3524   **3525**   **3526**   **3527**

3524-27	34¢ Amish Quilts, Block of 4, SA	18.00	4.25	3.75	3.50
3524-27	34¢ Strip of 4	...	...	3.75	3.50
3524-27	34¢ Set of 4 Singles	...	...	3.60	1.40

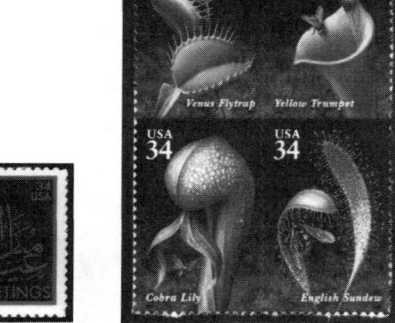

3532   **3528**   **3529**   **3533**
          3530   **3531**

3528-31	34¢ Carnivorous Plants, Block of 4,SA	18.00	4.25	3.75	3.50
3528-31	34¢ Strip of 4	...	...	3.75	3.50
3528-31	34¢ Set of 4 Singles	...	...	3.60	1.40
3532	34¢ Islamic Festival, Eid, SA	16.50	3.75	.85	.25
3533	34¢ Enrico Fermi, Physicist	16.50	3.75	.85	.25

1995 - Legends of Hollywood Series:
#2967, 3082, 3152, 3226, 3329, 3446, 3523

Note: From #3370 to date, Sheets are Panes of 20 unless otherwise indicated.

USED NOTE: Modern Used U.S. stamps are very difficult to keep in stock and many may not be available when you place your order. Prices are listed on these for when they are in stock and for reference purposes.

WASHINGTON 2006
World Philatelic Exhibition
May 27-June 3, 2006
See you there!
www.washington-2006.org

2001 Porky Pig "That's All Folks" Souvenir Sheet

3534

Scott's No.		Mint Sheet	Plate Block	F-VF NH	F-VF Used
3534	34¢ Regular Souvenir Sheet of 10.	...	...	8.50	8.00
3534a	34¢ Porky Pig single from souvenir sheet	...	...	.90	.30
3534b	34¢ Booklet Pane of 9 (left side)	...	...	7.00	...
3534c	34¢ Booklet Pane of 1 (right side)	...	...	2.25	...
3535	34¢ Special Die-cut Souvenir Sheet of 10...	...	...	37.50	...
3535a	34¢ Porky Pig single from souvenir sheet..	...	...	3.50	...
3535b	34¢ Booklet Pane of 9 (left side) ..	...	...	27.50	...
3535c	34¢ Imperforate Booklet Pane of 1 (right side)	...	...	12.50	...

2001 Christmas Issues, Self-Adhesive

3540, 3544 · 3538, 3542
3539, 3543 · 3537, 3541

3536

3536	34¢ Costa Madonna & Child, Booklet Single..	...		.95	.20
3536a	34¢ Convertible Pane of 20	...		17.50	...
3537-40	34¢ Santa Claus, Block of 4,Large date...16.50		3.75	3.50	...
3537-40	34¢ Set of 4 Singles, Die-cut 10 3/4x11..............			3.40	1.00
3537a-40a	34¢ Santa, Small Date, Block of 4 from Pane of 20 (3540d)	4.00			3.75
3537a-40a	34¢ Set of 4 singles	...		3.85	1.20
3537a-40a	34¢ Double-sided Block of 8 (3540d)	...		8.00	...
3540d	34¢ Double-sided Convertible Pane of 20, Small Date..			18.50	...
3537b-40e	34¢ Santa, Large Date, Block of 4 from Pane of 20 (3540g)	4.00			3.75
3537b-40e	34¢ Set of 4 singles	...		3.85	1.40
3537b-40e	34¢ Double-sided Block of 8	...		8.00	...
3540g	34¢ Double-sided, Conv.Pane of 20, Large Date	...		18.50	...
3541-44	34¢ Santa, Block of 4 from Bk.Panes (3544b-d)	...		4.00	3.75
3541-44	34¢ Set of 4 singles	...		3.85	1.20
3544b	34¢ Booklet Pane of 4, Die-cut 11	...		4.00	...
3544c	34¢ Booklet Pane of 6, #3543-44 (1), #3541-42 (2)	...		6.25	...
3544d	34¢ Booklet Pane of 6, #3541-42 (1), #3543-44 (2)	...		6.25	...

Note: #3541-44 designs are smaller than #3537-40 and #3537a-40a.
#3537a-40a designs are slightly taller that #3537-40.

3545 · 3546 · 3547

3548 · 3549-50A · 3551

2001 Commemoratives (continued)

Scott's No.		Mint Sheet	Plate Block	F-VF NH	F-VF Used
3545	34¢ James Madison................	16.50	3.75	.85	.25
3546	34¢ Thanksgiving, SA.........	16.50	3.75	.85	.25
3547	34¢ Hanukkah, Design of #3118,SA.	16.50	3.75	.85	.25
3548	34¢ Kwanzaa, Design of #3175,SA.......	16.50	3.75	.85	.25

2001-2 "United We Stand" Special Issue, SA

3549	34¢ Flag, Single from Convertible Pane, Die-cut 11¼..			1.25	.25
3549a	34¢ Convertible Pane of 20, Die-cut 11¼..		..	23.50	..
3549B	34¢ Single from Bk.Pane of 4 or 6, Die-cut 10½x10 3/4			1.15	.25
3549Bc	34¢ Booklet Pane of 4, Die-cut 10½x 10 3/4 (2002)		..	4.25	..
3549Bd	34¢ Booklet Pane of 6, Die-cut 10½x 10 3/4 (2002)		..	6.25	..
3549Bv	34¢ Single from Double-sided Pane-20,Die-cut 10½ x10 3/4			1.00	..
3549Bv	34¢ Double-sided Pair from Convertible Pane			2.00	..
3549Be	34¢ Double-sided Convertible Pane of 20, Die-cut 10½x10 3/4 (2002)		..	18.00	..

Scott's No.		Pl. Strip of 5	Pl. Strip of 3	F-VF NH	F-VF Used
3550	34¢ Flag, Coil, square corners....	9.00	7.00	1.10	.20
3550A	34¢ Flag, Coil, rounded corners...	9.00	7.00	1.10	.20

Stamps are separated on mint #3550A, adjoining on mint #3550.

2001 Rose and Love Letters Stamps, Self-Adhesive

Scott's No.		Mint Sheet	Plate Block	F-VF NH	F-VF Used
3551	57¢ Rose & Love Letters...........	25.75	5.95	1.35	.45

3556

3555 · 3552 · 3558
3553 · 3554

3557 · 3559 · 3560

2002 Commemoratives

3552-60, 3650-56, 59-74, 76-79, 92, 95 (38)	...	...	33.50	10.95	
3552-55	34¢ Winter Olympic Sports, Block of 4, SA.....	17.00	3.85	3.50	3.35
3552-55	34¢ Strip of 4................	...	...	3.50	3.35
3552-55	34¢ Set of 4 Singles	...	...	3.40	1.20
3556	34¢ Mentoring a Child, SA...................	16.50	3.75	.85	.25
3557	34¢ Langston Hughes, Writer, Black Heritage Series, SA...........	16.50	3.75	.85	.25
3558	34¢ Happy Birthday, SA...........	16.50	3.75	.85	.25
3559	34¢ Year of the Horse, SA...........	16.50	3.75	.85	.25
3560	34¢ U.S. Military Academy, SA....	16.50	3.75	.85	.25

2002 Greetings from America Postcard Designs, Self-adhesive

3561-3610	34¢ 50 States Greeting Card designs in styles of the 1930's. SA.........50	42.50	...	...	...
3561-3610	34¢ Set of 50 Singles.	...	...	42.50	29.50
3561/3610	34¢ Individual singles	...	...	1.00	.75

3561 Alabama	3573 Illinois	3586 Montana	3599 Rhode Island
3562 Alaska	3574 Indiana	3587 Nebraska	3600 South Carolina
3563 Arizona	3575 Iowa	3588 Nevada	3601 South Dakota
3564 Arkansas	3576 Kansas	3589 New Hampshire	3602 Tennessee
3565 California	3577 Kentucky	3590 New Jersey	3603 Texas
3566 Colorado	3578 Louisiana	3591 New Mexico	3604 Utah
3567 Connecticut	3579 Maine	3592 New York	3605 Vermont
3568 Delaware	3580 Maryland	3593 North Carolina	3606 Virginia
3569 Florida	3581 Massachusetts	3594 North Dakota	3607 Washington
3570 Georgia	3582 Michigan	3595 Ohio	3608 West Virginia
3571 Hawaii	3583 Minnesota	3596 Oklahoma	3609 Wisconsin
3572 Idaho	3584 Mississippi	3597 Oregon	3610 Wyoming
	3585 Missouri	3598 Pennsylvania	

2002 Greetings from America (continued)

3561-3610

2002 Longleaf Pine Forest Miniature Sheet of 10

LONGLEAF PINE FOREST

FOURTH IN A SERIES

NATURE OF AMERICA

3611

Scott's No.		Mint Sheet	Plate Block	F-VF NH	F-VF Used
3611	34¢ Pine Forest SA Miniature Sheet of 10...	...	...	8.50	8.00
3611a-j	34¢ Set of 10 Singles	...	...	8.50	6.00

3611a Bachman's Sparrow 3611b Northern bobwhite, yellow pitcher plants
3611c Fox squirrel, red-bellied woodpecker 3611d Brown-heade nuthatch
3611e Broadhead skink, yellow pitcher plants, pipeworts
3611f Eastern towhee, yellow pitcher plants, Savannah meadow beauties
3611g Gray Fox, gopher tortoise, horizontal
3611h Blind click beetle, sweetbay, pine woods treefrog
3611i Rosebud orchid, pipeworts, southern toad, yellow pitcher plants
3611j Grass-pink orchid, yellow-sided skimmer, pipeworts, yellow pitcher plants,hor.

3612	 **3613**	 **3614**	 **3615**

2002 American Designs Coil Stamp

Scott's No.		Pl. Strip of 5	Pl. Strip of 3	F-VF NH	F-VF Used
3612	5¢ American Toleware......................	2.40	2.10	.20	.20

2002 Denominated Make-Up Issue

Scott's No.	#3613 Die-cut 11, #3614 Die-cut 10	Mint Sheet	Plate Block	F-VF NH	F-VF Used
3613	3¢ Star, date in lower left corner, SA	(50) 6.00	.85	.20	.20
3614	3¢ Star, date in lower right corner,SA	(50) 6.00	.85	.20	.20

Scott's No.		Pl. Strip of 5	Pl. Strip of 3	F-VF NH	F-VF Used
3615	3¢ Star Coil, WA, Die-cut 10	2.15	1.75	.20	.20

3616-19	**3620-25**	 **3630-37**

3626	**3627**	**3628**	**3629**

#3616-19 George Washington with 2002 Date, SA

Scott's No.		Mint Sheet	Plate Block	F-VF NH	F-VF Used
3616	23¢ Green, Perf.11¼, WA	(100)65.00	10.75	.60	.15

Scott's No.		Pl. Strip of 5	Pl. Strip of 3	F-VF NH	F-VF Used
3617	23¢ Coil, Die-cut 8½ Vert.,"2002" Date	5.50	4.25	.65	.20

Scott's No.		Mint Sheet	Plate Block	F-VF NH	F-VF Used
3618	23¢ Single from Conv.Pane of 10, Diecut 11¼ (3618c)	...	...	.60	.15
3618c	23¢ Convertible Pane of 10, Diecut 11¼ ...	...	...	5.75	...
3618v	23¢ Booklet Single, SA Die-cut 11¼ (3618a-b)...	...	...	.80	.15
3618a	23¢ Booklet Pane of 4, Diecut 11¼	...	...	2.85	...
3618b	23¢ Booklet Pane of 6, Diecut 11¼	...	...	4.35	...
3619	23¢ Single from Convertible Pane of 10, Diecut 10½x11¼ (3619e or f)	...	...	2.50	...
3619g	23¢ Pair #3619 at left, #3618 at right (3619e)	...	...	3.25	...
3619h	23¢ Pair #3618 at left, #3619 at right (3619f)	...	...	3.25	...
3619e	23¢Conv.-Pane-10 5 #3619 at left, 5 #3618 at right ...	...	...	13.75	...
3619f	23¢ Conv.-Pane-10 5 #3618 at left, 5 #3619 at right ...	...	...	13.75	...
3619v	23¢ Booklet Single, SA, Diecut 10½x11¼ (3619a-d)	...	...	3.50	...
3619vg	23¢ Booklet Pair, #3619v at left, #3618v at right	...	...	4.25	...
3619vh	23¢ Booklet Pair, #3618v at left, #3619v at right	...	...	4.25	...
3619a	23¢ Booklet Pane of 4, 2 #3619 at left, 2 #3618 at right	...	...	7.50	...
3619b	23¢ Booklet Pane of 6, 3 #3619 at left, 3 #3618 at right	...	...	11.25	...
3619c	23¢ Booklet Pane of 4, 2 #3618 at left, 2 #3619 at right	...	...	7.50	...
3619d	23¢ Booklet Pane of 6, 3 #3618 at left, 3 #3619 at right	...	...	11.25	...

Diecut differences are at top & bottom of stamp, Diecut at sides are all 11¼

#3620-25a Flag & USA

3620	(37¢) USA First-Class, WA	(100)97.50	12.50	.95	.20
3621	(37¢) USA First-Class, SA, Die-cut 11¼x11	(20) 18.75	4.25	.95	.20

#3621 Small "2002" and microprinted "USA" at bottom of topmost red stripe.

Scott's No.		Pl. Strip of 5	Pl. Strip of 3	F-VF NH	F-VF Used
3622	(37¢) SA Coil, Diecut 10 Vert.	12.00	8.00	1.10	.20

Scott's No.		Mint Sheet	Plate Block	F-VF NH	F-VF Used
3623	(37¢) SA Single from Convertible Pane of 20 (3623a)..	...	...	1.20	.20
3623a	(37¢) SA Convertible Pane of 20, Die-cut 11¼...	...	...	22.75	...

#3623 small "2002" and microprinted "USPS" at top of topmost red stripe.

3624	(37¢) Single from Double-sided Pane of 20, SA (3624c)..	...	...	1.00	.20
3624	(37¢) Double-sided Pair from Double-sided Pane of 20	...	...	2.00	...
3624c	(37¢) Double-sided Convertible Pane of 20, SA Die-cut 10½x 10 3/4	...	...	18.50	...
3624v	(37¢) Single from Bk.Pane of 4 or 6 (3624a or b)	...	...	1.35	...
3624a	(37¢) Booklet Pane of 4, SA, Die-cut 10½x10 3/4	...	...	5.00	...
3624b	(37¢) Booklet Pane of 6, SA, Die-cut 10½x10 3/4	...	...	7.50	...

#3624-24v Large "2002" Date.

3625	(37¢) Single from ATM Pane of 18, SA, Die-cut 8	...	...	.95	.20
3625a	(37¢) Convertible ATM Pane of 18, SA	...	...	16.75	...

#3626-29d Antique Toys, Die-cut 11

3626-29	(37¢) Block of 4 from Convertible Pane of 20 (3629e)..	...	...	3.95	3.75
3626-29	(37¢) Set of 4 Singles from Conv.Pane of 20	...	...	3.95	1.20
3629e	(37¢) Convertible Pane of 20, SA	...	...	18.75	...
3626-29v	(37¢) Block of 4 from Bk.Panes of 4 or 6 (3629b-d)	...	...	4.95	...
3626-29v	(37¢) Set of 4 singles from Booklet Panes	...	...	4.95	...
3629b	(37¢) Booklet Pane of 4, SA	....	...	5.00	...
3629c	(37¢) Booklet Pane of 6, 2 Taxi Cabs (#3628), SA	...	...	7.50	...
3629d	(37¢) Booklet Pane oi 6, 2 Locomotives (#3627), SA...	...	...	7.50	...

2002-4 Denominated Rate-Change Issues #3629F-37a Flag and "USA"

3629F	37¢ Flag, Sheet, WA "2003" Date (100) 77.50		9.50	.80	.20
3630	37¢ Flag, Sheet, SA, DC 11¼x11	17.50	4.00	.90	.15

#3630 small "2002" and microprinted "USA" at bottom of topmost red stripe.

Scott's No.		Pl. Strip of 5	Pl. Strip of 3	F-VF NH	F-VF Used
3631	37¢ Coil, Perf. 10 Vert, WA	10.00	8.00	1.10	.15
3632	37¢ Coil, Diecut 10,SA, "2002" Date	10.00	8.00	1.10	.15
3632A	37¢ Coil, Die-cut 10,SA, "2003" Date	8.00	6.50	.80	.25
3632C	37¢ Coil, Die-cut 11 3/4,"2004" Date Mottled Tagging, SA	8.00	6.50	.80	.20
3632Cv	37¢ Die-cut 11 3/4,Smooth Tagging,SA	8.00	6.50	.80	.20
3633	37¢ Coil, Diecut 8.5,SA "2002" Date	10.00	8.00	1.10	.15
3633A	37¢ Coil, Diecut 8.5,SA "2003" Date	8.75	7.00	.90	.20

Mint copies of #3633 are separated in strips while #3632,3632A and 3633A are adjoining.

2002-4 Denominated Rate-Change Issues

Scott's No.		Mint Sheet	Plate Block	F-VF NH	F-VF Used
3634	37¢ Single from Convertible Pane of 10 (3634a), SA	..		.90	.15
3634a	37¢ Convertible Pane of 10, SA, Die-cut 11...			8.75	
#3634 Large "2002" Date					
3634b	37¢ Single from Bk.P.-4 or 6 (3634c-d),Die-cut 11,SA...			.80	.20
3634c	37¢ Booklet Pane of 4 with "2003" Date (2003)...			3.00	...
3634d	37¢ Booklet Pane of 6 with "2003" Date (2003)			4.50	...
3635	37¢ Single from Convertible Pane of 20 (3635a), SA..			.90	...
3635a	37¢ Convertible Pane of 20, SA, Die-cut 11¼...			17.00	
#3635 Small "2002" and microprinted "USPS" at top of topmost red stripe.					
3636	37¢ Single from Double-sided Pane of 20 (3636c), SA..			.90	...
3636	37¢ Double-sided Pair from Double-sided Pane of 20			1.80	...
3636c	37¢ Double-sided Convertible Pane of 20, SA Die-cut 10½ x10 3/4			17.00	
3636v	37¢ Single from Bk. Pane of 4 or 6 (3636a-b), SA			1.10	...
3636a	37¢ Booklet Pane of 4, SA, DC 10½x 10 3/4...			4.00	...
3636b	37¢ Booklet Pane of 6, SA, DC 10½x 10 3/4...			6.00	...
#3636-36v Large "2002" Date.					
3637	37¢ Flag, SA Single from ATM Pane of 18...			.90	.20
3637a	37¢ Flag, ATM Pane of 18, SA, Die-cut 8 (2003)			15.00	...

3638, 43   **3639, 42**   **3640, 45**   **3641, 44**

#3638-45h Antique Toys

Scott's No.	Die-cut 8½ Horiz.	Pl. Strip of 5	Pl. Strip of 3	F-VF NH	F-VF Used
3638-41	37¢ Coils, Strip of 4, SA.............	(PS9)15.00	(PS5)9.75	5.50	5.25
3638-41	37¢ Coils, Set of 4 Singles	...	...	5.50	1.20

Scott's No.		Mint Sheet	Plate Block	F-VF NH	F-VF Used
3642-45	37¢ Block of 4 from Conv. Pane of 20, SA (3645e)	...		3.50	3.25
3642-45	37¢ Set of 4 Singles from Conv.Pane of 20			3.50	1.20
3645e	37¢ Convertible Pane of 20, SA ..			17.00	...
3642-45v	37¢ Block of 4 from Bk.Pane of 4 or 6 (3645b-d)			4.95	3.25
3642-45v	37¢ Set of 4 Singles from Bk.Pane of 4 or 6			4.95	1.20
3645b	37¢ Booklet Pane of 4, SA			5.00	...
3645c	37¢ Booklet Pane of 6, 2 Taxi Cabs (3644), SA			7.50	...
3645d	37¢ Booklet Pane of 6, 2 Locomotives (3643), SA			7.50	...
3642a-45f	37¢ Block of 4 from Double-sided Bklt. of 20 "2003" Date			3.00	...
3642a-45f	37¢ Double-sided Blocks of 4 (8 stamps)...			6.00	...
3642a-45f	37¢ Set of 4 singles from Double-sided Booklet of 20			3.00	1.60
3645h	37¢ Double-sided Booklet of 20 "2003" Date			14.75	...
#3642-45d Die-cut 11, #3642a-45h Die-cut 11 x 11 1/4					

3646   **3647-47A**   **3648**

3646	60¢ Coverlet Eagle, SA	23.75	5.50	1.35	.45
3647	$3.85 Jefferson Memorial, SA "2002" Date	165.00	37.00	8.50	3.75
3647A	$3.85 Jefferson Meml."2003" Date	150.00	34.50	7.75	3.75
3648	$13.65 U.S. Capitol, SA	530.00	115.00	27.00	11.75

2002 Masters of American Photography Miniature Sheet of 20

3649
2002 Masters of American Photography Miniature Sheet of 20 (cont.)

Scott's No.		Mint Sheet	Plate Block	F-VF NH	F-VF Used
3649	37¢ Photography, Sheetlet of 20, SA	...	...	17.50	16.75
3649a-t	37¢ Photography, Set of 20 Singles	...	...	17.50	11.75

3649a A.S.Southworth, J.J.Hawes   3649k James VanDer Zee
3649b Timothy H. O'Sullivan   3649l Dorothea Lange
3649c Carleton E. Watkins   3649m Walker Evans
3649d Gertrude Kasebier   3649n W. Eugene Smith
3649e Lewis W. Hine   3649o Paul Strand
3649f Alvin Langdon Coburn   3649p Ansel Adams
3649g Edward Steichen   3649q Imogen Cunningham
3649h Alfred Stieglitz   3649r Andre Kertesz
3649i Man Ray   3649s Garry Winogrand
3649j Edward Weston   3649t Minor White

3650   **3651**   **3652**   **3657**

3654 3653   **3656 3655**   **3660**

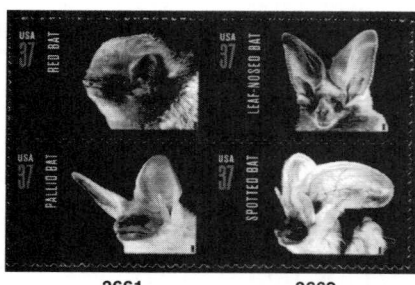  

3661 3662   **3664 3663**   **3658**   **3659**

2002 Commemoratives (continued)

3650	37¢ John James Audunon, Botanist, SA	16.50	3.75	.85	.30
3651	37¢ Harry Houdini, Magician, SA	16.50	3.75	.85	.30
3652	37¢ Andy Warhol, Artist, SA	16.50	3.75	.85	.30
3653-56	37¢ Teddy Bears, Block of 4, SA (4)	25.00	5.85	5.25	4.75
3653-56	37¢ Vertical Strip of 4	...	...	5.25	4.75
3653-56	37¢ Set of 4 Singles	...	...	5.00	1.40

2002 Love Heart, Self-adhesive

3657	37¢ Love, Single from Convertible Pane of 20	..		.85	.25
3657a	37¢ Convertible Pane of 20	...	...	16.50	...
3658	60¢ Love, SA	26.00	6.00	1.35	.40

2002 Commemoratives (continued)

3659	37¢ Ogden Nash, Humorist, SA ..	16.50	3.75	.85	.30
3660	37¢ Duke Kahanamoku, Surfer, SA	16.50	3.75	.85	.30
3661-64	37¢ American Bats, Block of 4	16.50	3.85	3.50	3.25
3661-64	37¢ Horizontal Strip of 4	...	...	3.50	3.25
3661-64	37¢ Bats, Set of 4 singles	...	...	3.40	1.40

Note: From #3370 to date, Sheets are Panes of 20 unless otherwise indicated.

USED NOTE: Modern Used U.S. stamps are very difficult to keep in stock and many may not be available when you place your order. Prices are listed on these for when they are in stock and for reference purposes.
2002 Commemoratives (continued)

2002 Commemoratives (continued)

3665   3666
3667   3668

3669

3670   3671

3673

3672   3674   3675

Scott's No.		Mint Sheet	Plate Block	F-VF NH	F-VF Used
3665-68	37¢ Women in Journalism: Nellie Bly, Ida M. Tarbell, Ethel L. Payne, Marguerite Higgins, Block of 4, SA	16.50	3.85	3.50	3.25
3665-68	37¢ Strip of 4	...	...	3.50	3.25
3665-68	37¢ Women, Set of 4 Singles	...	...	3.40	1.40
3669	37¢ Irving Berlin, Songwriter,SA	16.50	3.75	.85	.30
3670-71	37¢ Neuter and Spay, Pair,SA	16.50	3.75	1.70	1.50
3670-71	37¢ Neuter & Spay, Set of 2 Singles	...	...	1.70	.60
3672	37¢ Hanukkah (Design of #3118), SA	16.50	3.75	.85	.30
3673	37¢ Kwanzaa (Design of #3175), SA	16.50	3.75	.85	.30
3674	37¢ Islamic Festival, Eid, SA	16.50	3.75	.85	.30
3675	37¢ Madonna, Single from Conv. Pane of 20, SA	...	...	.85	.30
3675a	37¢ Convertible Pane of 20, SA	...	...	16.50	...

2002 Holiday Snowmen, Self-adhesive

3676, 84   3677, 85   3678, 86   3679, 87

3683, 88   3680, 89   3681, 90   3682, 91

3676-79	37¢ Snowmen,Die-cut 11,Block of 4(20)	16.50	3.85	3.50	3.25
3676-79	37¢ Vertical Strip of 4 from Sheet	...	...	3.50	3.25
3676-79	37¢ Set of 4 Singles from Sheet	...	...	3.40	1.00

Scott's No.		Pl. Strip of 9	Pl. Strip of 5	F-VF NH	F-VF Used
3680-83	37¢ Linerless Coils, Die-cut 8½ Horizontal Strip of 4, attd.	13.75	8.50	5.50	...
3680-83	37¢ Coils, set of 4 singles	...	...	5.25	1.20
3684-87	37¢ Set of 4 singles from Double-sided Convertible Pane of 20, Die-cut 10½x11(3687b).	...	...	3.50	1.00
3684-87	37¢ Block of 4 from Double-sided Conv. Pane of 20	...	...	3.50	...
3684-87	37¢ Double-sided Blocks of 4 from Conv. Pane of 20	...	...	7.00	...
3687b	37¢ Double-sided Convertible Pane of 20	...	...	16.50	...

2002 Holiday Snowmen (continued)

Scott's No.		Mint Sheet	Plate Block	F-VF NH	F-VF Used
3688-91	37¢ Block of 4 from Bk.Panes of 4 or 6 (3691b-d), DC.11			3.95	...
3688-91	37¢ Set of 4 Singles from Bk.Panes of 4 or 6,Die-cut 11			3.95	1.00
3691b	37¢ Booklet Pane of 4	...	...	4.00	...
3691c	37¢ Booklet Pane of 6 (2 each #3688-89)	...	...	6.00	...
3691d	37¢ Booklet Pane of 6 (2 each #3690-91)	...	...	6.00	...

Note: Designs of #3676-79 and #3684-87 are of deeper color and are larger than the designs for #3680-83 and #3688-91.

3692   3693   3695

3694

2002 Commemoratives (continued)

3692	37¢ Cary Grant, Legends of Hollywood, SA	16.50	3.75	.85	.30

2002 American Scenes Self-Adhesive Coil

Scott's No.		Pl. Strip of 5	Pl. Strip of 3	F-VF NH	F-VF Used
3693	(5¢) Sea Coast, Die-cut 8½ Vert. #See #3775, 3785.	2.40	2.10	.20	.20

2002 Hawaiian Missionaries Stamps of 1851-52 Souvenir Sheet

Scott's No.		Mint Sheet	Plate Block	F-VF NH	F-VF Used
3694	37¢ Missionaries Souvenir Sheet of 4	...	...	3.75	3.50
3694a-d	37¢ Missionaries Set of 4 Singles			3.75	2.00

#3694a 2¢ 1851 #3694b 5¢ 1851 #3694c 13¢ 1851 #3694d 13¢ 1852.

2002 Commemoratives (continued)

3695	37¢ Happy Birthday, SA	16.50	3.75	.85	.30

2002 Greetings from America, Revised Denominations

3696-3745	37¢ 50 States Greeting Cards designs style of the 1930's. SA .. (50)	42.50	...	...	...
3696-3745	37¢ Greetings, Set of 50 Singles, SA	...	...	42.50	29.75

Same designs as the 34¢ sheet of 50 #3561-3610. See next page for photo.

3696 Alabama	3709 Indiana	3722 Nebraska	3735 South Carolina
3697 Alaska	3710 Iowa	3723 Nevada	3736 South Dakota
3698 Arizona	3711 Kansas	3724 New Hampshire	3737 Tennessee
3699 Arkansas	3712 Kentucky	3725 New Jersey	3738 Texas
3700 California	3713 Louisiana	3726 New Mexico	3739 Utah
3701 Colorado	3714 Maine	3727 New York	3740 Vermont
3702 Connecticut	3715 Maryland	3728 North Carolina	3741 Virginia
3703 Delaware	3716 Massachusetts	3729 North Dakota	3742 Washington
3704 Florida	3717 Michigan	3730 Ohio	3743 West Virginia
3705 Georgia	3718 Minnesota	3731 Oklahoma	3744 Wisconsin
3706 Hawaii	3719 Mississippi	3732 Oregon	3745 Wyoming
3707 Idaho	3720 Missouri	3733 Pennsylvania	
3708 Illinois	3721 Montana	3734 Rhode Island	

3696-3745

2003 Commemoratives

| | | 3746 | | 3747 | | 3748 | | 3750 |

Scott's No.		Mint Sheet	Plate Block	F-VF NH	F-VF Used
3746-48, 71, 73-74, 81-82, 86-91, 3803, 3808-18, 21-24 Set of 30		...	...	28.75	9.50
3746	37¢ Thurgood Marshall, SA	15.75	3.65	.80	.30
3747	37¢ Year of the Ram, SA	15.75	3.65	.80	.30
3748	37¢ Zora Neale Hurston, SA	15.75	3.65	.80	.30

| 3751 | 3757 | 3766 | 3769 | 3770 |

2003-4 American Design Regular Issues, SA

Scott's No.		Mint Sheet	Plate Block	F-VF NH	F-VF Used
...	2¢ Navajo Necklace (2004)	1.00	.50	.20	.15
3750	4¢ Chippendale Chair (2004)	2.25	.85	.20	.20
3751	10¢ American Clock	3.95	.95	.20	.15
3766	$1 Wisdom	38.75	8.95	1.95	.95

2003 Regular Issue Coils

Scott's No.		Pl. Strip of 5	Pl. Strip of 3	F-VF NH	F-VF Used
3757	1¢ Tiffany Lamp, SA	.80	.65	.20	.15
3769	(10¢) New York Public Library Lion, WA	2.50	1.95	.25	.20
3769v	(10¢) Lion, Lighter Shade, WA	2.50	1.95	.25	.20

#3769 Darker shade, date almost touches design.
#3769v Lighter shade, date 1/3 mm away from design.

| 3770 | (10¢) Atlas Statue, "2003" Date, SA | 3.50 | 2.75 | .25 | .20 |

#3770 is the same design as #3520 with "2003" date instead of "2001" date.

| | 3771 | | 3773 | | 3774 | | 3775,85 |

Scott's No.		Mint Sheet	Plate Block	F-VF NH	F-VF Used
3771	80¢ Special Olympics, SA	33.75	7.75	1.75	.50

2003 American Filmmaking Souvenir Sheet of 10

3772

3772	37¢ American Filmmaking: Behind the Scenes Souvenir Sheet of 10, SA	...	...	8.00	7.50
3772a-j	37¢ Filmmaking, Set of 10 Singles	...	...	8.00	6.00

3772a Screenwriting	3772e Makeup	3772h Film Editing
3772b Directing	3772f Art Direction	3772i Special Effects
3772c Costume Design	3772g Cinematography	3772j Sound
3772d Musical Composing		

2003 Commemoratives (continued)

3773	37¢ Ohio Statehood, SA	15.75	3.65	.80	.30
3774	37¢ Pelican Island National Wildlife Refuge, SA	15.75	3.65	.80	.30

2003-4 Regular Issue Coil, Water Activated

Scott's No.		Plate Strip-5	Plate Strip-3	F-VF NH	F-VF Used
3775	(5¢) Seacoast "2003" date	1.75	1.40	.20	.15
...	(5¢) Seacoast "2004" date	1.75	1.40	.20	.15

2003 Old Glory Prestige Booklet SA

| 3776 | 3777 | 3778 | 3779 | 3780 |

3776-80	37¢ Old Glory Strip of 5	...	...	4.50	3.85
3776-80	37¢ Old Glory Set of 5 Singles	...	...	4.50	2.00
3780b1	37¢ Old Glory Pane of 10, 1876 Flag	...	...	9.00	...
3780b2	37¢ Old Glory Pane of 10, Old Glory	...	...	9.00	...
3780bv	37¢ Prestige Booklet with 2 Panes of 10 (BK294)	...	...	17.75	...

#3780b1 has 1876 flag on backing paper. #3780b2 has Old Glory Marching.

3781 **3782**

2003 Commemoratives (continued)

Scott's No.		Mint Sheet	Plate Block	F-VF NH	F-VF Used
3781	37¢ Cesar E. Chavez, SA	15.75	3.65	.80	.30
3782	37¢ Louisiana Purchase, SA	15.75	3.65	.80	.30

2003 Powered Flight Souvenir Sheet of 10, SA

3783	37¢ First Powered Flight Souvenir Sheet of 10, SA ...			7.95	...
3783	37¢ Flight Single stamp from Souvenir Sheet		...	.85	.30
3783b	37¢ Flight Top pane of 1		...	2.25	...
3783a	37¢ Flight Bottom Pane of 9		...	6.75	...

3784-84A   **3786**   **3792-3801**   **3803**
3844-53

3787   **3788**   **3789**   **3790**   **3791**

2003 Purple Heart Self-Adhesive

Scott's No.		Mint Sheet	Plate Block	F-VF NH	F-VF Used
3784	37¢ Die-cut 11¼x10 3/4	14.75	3.50	.75	.25
3784A	37¢ Die-cut 10 3/4 x 10¼	14.75	3.50	.75	.50

2003 Sea Coast Coil Stamp Die-cut 9½x10

Scott's No.		Plate Strip-5	Plate Strip-3	F-VF NH	F-VF Used
3785	(5¢) Serpentine die-cuts all around	1.75	1.40	.20	.20

2003 Commemoratives (continued)

Scott's No.		Mint Sheet	Plate Block	F-VF NH	F-VF Used
3786	37¢ Audrey Hepburn, Hollywood, SA	15.75	3.65	.80	.25
3787-91	37¢ Southeastern Lighthouses,Strip-5	37.50 (10)	19.75	9.50	8.50
3787-91	37¢ Lighthouses, set of 5 singles, SA	...	...	9.50	1.75

2003-4 American Eagle Presorted First Class Coil (10 Color combinations)

Scott's No.		Plate Strip-11	F-VF NH	F-VF Used
3792-3801	(25¢) Self-Adhesive Strip of 10 "2003"	7.75	5.50	...
3792-3801	(25¢) Eagle, set of 10 singles "2003" date	...	5.50	3.50

2003 Arctic Tundra Miniature Sheet

3802

Scott's No.		Mint Sheet	Plate Block	F-VF NH	F-VF Used
3802	37¢ Arctic Tundra, Self-adhesive Miniature Sheet of 10			7.95	7.50
3802a-j	37¢ Arctic Tundra, Set of 10 Singles	---	---	7.95	5.00

3802a Gyrfalcon
3802b Gray Wolf
3802c Common Raven
3802d Musk Ox and Caribou
3802e Grizzly Bears, Caribou

3802f Caribou, Willow Ptarmigans
3802g Arctic Ground Squirrel
3802h Willow Ptarmigan, Bearberry
3802i Arctic Grayling
3802j Singing Vole, Thin-legged Wolf Spider, Lingonberry, Labrador Tea

2003 Commemoratives (continued)

3803	37¢ Korean War Veterans Memorial	15.75	3.65	.80	.30

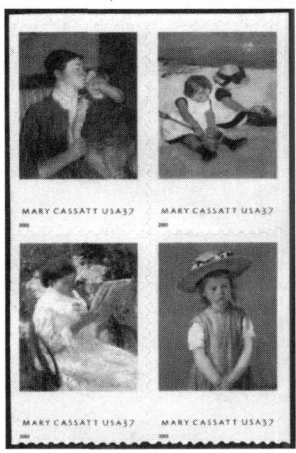 

3804	**3805**	**3808**	**3809**
3806	**3807**	**3810**	**3811**

3804-7	37¢ Mary Cassatt Paintings Block of 4, SA...		3.20	3.00	...
3804-7	37¢ Mary Cassatt Set of 4 singles	...	...	3.20	1.40
3804-7	37¢ Cassatt, Double-sided Blocks of 4 (8 stamps)		...	6.40	...
3807b	37¢ Cassatt, Double-sided Convertible Pane of 20		...	15.75	...
3808-11	37¢ Early Football Heroes: Bronco Nagurski, Ernie Nevers, Walter Camp, Red Grange Block of 4	15.75	3.65	3.20	3.00
3808-11	37¢ Football Heroes Strip of 4	...	...	3.20	3.00
3808-11	37¢ Football Heroes Set of 4 singles	...	...	3.20	1.40

2003 Commemoratives (continued)

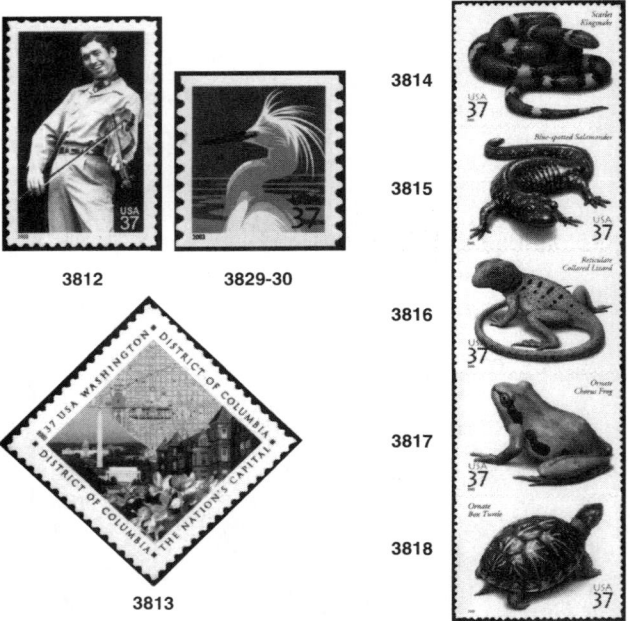

3812   3829-30

3813

3814
3815
3816
3817
3818

Scott's No.		Mint Sheet	Plate Block	F-VF NH	F-VF Used
3812	37¢ Roy Acuff, Country Singer, SA	15.75	3.65	.80	.30
3813	37¢ District of Columbia, SA	(16) 12.75	3.65	.80	.30
3814-18	37¢ Reptiles & Amphibians, Strip-5	15.75	(10) 8.75	4.00	3.75
3814-18	37¢ Reptiles, Set of 5 singles	...	...	4.00	2.00

2003 George Washington Regular Issue

3819	23¢ Washington with "2003" Date	14.75	3.50	.75	.25

#3819 is the same basic design as #3468A which has "2001" date

2003 Commemoratives (continued)

3820	37¢ Madonna & Child Single from Double-sided Pane of 20			.80	.25
3820	37¢ Madonna Double-sided Pair from Pane of 20 (2 stamps)		1.60		...
3820a	37¢ Madonna Double-sided Convertible Pane of 20		...	15.75	...

#3820 is the same design as #3675.

3821	3822		3825	3826
3823	3824		3827	3828

2003 Holiday Music Makers, Self-adhesive

3821-24	37¢ Music Makers, Block of 4	15.75	3.65	3.20	3.00
3821-24	37¢ Music Makers, Vertical Strip of 4	...	...	3.20	3.00
3821-24	37¢ Music Makers, Set of 4 singles			3.20	1.20
3821-24v	37¢ Block of 4 from Double-sided Convertible Pane of 20			3.20	...
3821-24v	37¢ Set of 4 singles from Double-sided Conv.Pane of 20			3.20	...
3821-24v	37¢ Double-sided Blocks of 4 (8 stamps)		...	6.40	...
3824b	37¢ Double-sided Convertible Pane of 20		...	15.75	...
3825-28	37¢ Music Makers, Block of 4 from Vending Booklet	...		3.20	3.00
3825-28	37¢ Set of 4 singles from Vending Booklet (3828b,c,d)			3.20	1.20
3828b	37¢ Music Makers, Booklet Pane of 4		...	3.25	...
3828c	37¢ Booklet Pane of 6, 2 each #3825 & #3826		...	4.95	...
3838d	37¢ Booklet Pane of 6, 2 each #3827 & #3828		...	4.95	...

2003-4 Snowy Egret Regular Issue

Scott's No.		Plate Strip-5	Plate Strip-3	F-VF NH	F-VF Used
3829	37¢ Coil Die-cut 8½ Vert "2003" date	8.00	6.50	.75	.25
3829A	37¢ Coil Die-cut 8½ Vert."2004" date	8.00	6.50	.75	.25
3830	37¢ Single from Convertible Pane of 20	...	...	.75	.25
3830a	37¢ Convertible Pane of 20 (2004)	...	...	14.75	...

2004 Pacific Coral Reefs Miniature Sheet, SA

3831

Scott's No.		Mint Sheet	Plate Block	F-VF NH	F-VF Used
3831	37¢ Pacific Coral Reefs Miniature Sheet of 10	...	7.50	...
3831a-j	37¢ Pacific Coral Reefs Set of 10 singles	...	...	7.50	5.00

3831a Emperor Angelfish, Blue Coral, Mound Coral
3831b Bumphead Wrasse, Moorish Idol   3831c Bumphead Parrotfish
3831d Black-spotted Puffer, Threadfin Butterflyfish, Staghorn Coral
3831e Hawksbill Turtle 3831f Pink Anemonefish, Magnificent Sea Anemone
3831g Snowflake Moray Eel, Spanish Dancer
3831h Lionfish 3831i Triton's Trumpet
3831j Oriental Sweetlips, Bluestreak Cleaner Wrasse, Mushroom Coral

3832   3833   3834

2004 Commemoratives

3832	37¢ Year of the Monkey	14.75	3.50	.75	.30

2004 Love Special Issue

3833	37¢ Candy Hearts, Single from Pane of 20, SA	...		.75	.25
3833a	37¢ Candy Hearts Convertible Pane of 20	14.75	...	...	...

2004 Commemoratives (continued)

3834	37¢ Paul Robeson, SA	14.75	3.50	.75	.30

3835   3836   3837

3835	37¢ Dr. Seuss, SA	14.75	3.50	.75	.30

2004 Garden Blossoms Special Issue

3836	37¢ Garden Bouquet Booklet Single, SA	...	...	.75	.25
3836a	37¢ Convertible Booklet of 20	...	...	14.75	...
3837	60¢ Garden Botanical	23.50	5.25	1.20	.50

3838   3839

3838	37¢ Air Force Academy, SA	14.75	3.50	.75	.30
3839	37¢ Henry Mancini, SA	14.75	3.50	.75	.30

Stop Collecting Stamps!

C ollect plate blocks! Plate blocks are just as much fun to collect as singles, but eminently, more profitable as the examples below indicate.

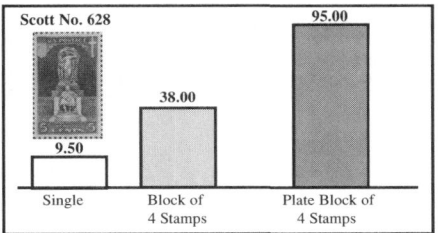
Scott No. 628
- Single: 9.50
- Block of 4 Stamps: 38.00
- Plate Block of 4 Stamps: 95.00

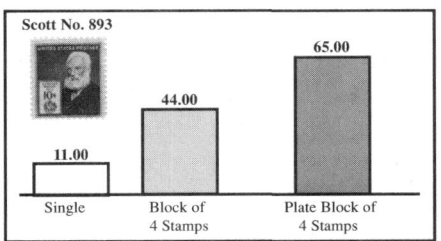
Scott No. 893
- Single: 11.00
- Block of 4 Stamps: 44.00
- Plate Block of 4 Stamps: 65.00

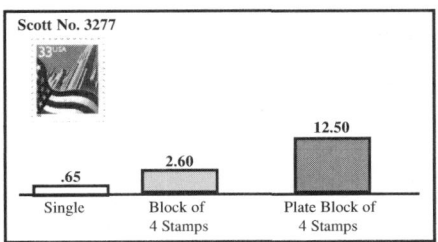
Scott No. 3277
- Single: .65
- Block of 4 Stamps: 2.60
- Plate Block of 4 Stamps: 12.50

These are not isolated examples. There is no instance in which a plate block does not have a higher catalog value than the single stamps that comprise it.

Why now is a great time. . .

The cycles of interest in plate block collecting ebb and flow, as do all collectibles. Right now, demand is powerful, especially for plate blocks of the 1930s and before. One couldn't select a better time to start!

Why buy from us?

The Plate Block Stamp Co. has been in business since 1977 and has grown to be America's premier plate block dealer. Our inventory always exceeds a quarter million plate blocks of consistent Fine-Very Fine Never Hinged condition and always at very competitive prices. Ordering is super-easy with our 20-page catalog, 800 telephone service, and new web site. Orders are routinely processed within hours. And if for any reason you wish to return a stamp, we will happily refund your money in full.

Inside Information

In addition to great prices, our customers receive the information-packed *Plate Block Market Analyst*. Every quarter we tell what's hot and what's not.

Had you been informed by The *Market Analyst* you would have been able to take advantage of some of the following recommendations we made:

In Volume 67, October 1996 the "Black G" stamp, Scott # 2881 was originally recommended. Now it has a catalogue value of $70.00

In Volume 72, January, 1998 Scott # C132 was recommended. Now $25.00 Scott, will be higher in next catalogue

The *Plate Block Market Analyst*...a great opportunity for you to learn more about the hobby you love.

Whatever your goal or interest in collecting stamps might be, plate blocks are the answer. If you collect solely for enjoyment, you certainly can enjoy the beauty of a plate block collection. If you collect for the knowledge to be gained, plate blocks add another dimension. If you are building a legacy for your children or grandchildren, plate blocks add excitement...if you're investing, plate blocks provide a consistent history of appreciation.

So stop collecting stamps! Contact us for a free plate block catalog and newsletter today!

2004 Commemoratives (continued)

3840	3841	
3842	3843	

Scott's No.		Mint Sheet	Plate Block	F-VF NH	F-VF Used
3840-43	37¢ American Choreographers: George Balanchine, Martha Graham, Agnes de Mille, Alvin Ailey, Horizontal Strip of 4, SA	14.75	(8) 6.75	3.00	...
3840-43	37¢ Choreographers, Set of 4 singles	...	...	3.00	1.40
3844-53	(25¢ Water-activated Strip of 10 "2004" date		7.75	5.50	...
3844-53	(25¢) Eagle, set of 10 singles "2004" date	...	...	5.50	3.50

2004 Lewis and Clark Bicentennial

3854		3855	3856

3854	37¢ Lewis & Clark Together, SA ..	14.75	3.50	.75	.30
3855-56	37¢ Lewis & Clark Portraits Booklet Singles (2)	...		1.90	1.00
3856b	37¢ Lewis & Clark Portrait Booklet Pane of 10 (5 ea)...	...	...	9.50	...
...	37¢ Lewis & Clark Portraits Prestige Booklet of 20				
3856v	(2 Booklet Panes of 10) (BK 297)	...	...	17.95	...

2004 Commemoratives (continued)

3857-61

3857-61	37¢ Isamu Noguchi, Sculptor, Horizontal Strip of 5, SA	14.75	(10) 8.00	3.75	...
3857-61	37¢ Isamu Noguchi, Set of 5 singles	...	...	3.75	1.75

3862	3863

3862	37¢ World War II Memorial, SA ...	14.75	3.50	.75	.30
3863	37¢ Athens Summer Olympics, SA	14.75	3.50	.75	.30

2004 Commemoratives (continued)

The Art of Disney

Scott's No.		Mint Sheet	Plate Block	F-VF NH	F-VF Used
...	37¢ The Art of Disney, Friendship, SA Block of 4	14.75	3.50	3.00	2.75
...	37¢ Disney, Vertical Strip of 4	...	...	3.00	2.75
...	37¢ Disney, Set of 4 singles	...	...	3.00	1.40
...	37¢ USS Constellation, 150th, SA	14.75	3.50	.75	.30
...	37¢ R. Buckminster Fuller, SA	14.75	3.50	.75	.30
2004 Distinguished Americans Series, SA					
...	23¢ Wilma Rudolph, Sheet stamp	8.95	2.10	.45	.25
...	23¢ Wilma Rudolph, Single from Convertible Pane of 10			.45	.25
...	23¢ Wilma Rudolph, Convertible Pane of 10			4.50	...
...	23¢ Wilma Rudolph, Booklet Single from Bk.Pane of 10			.45	...
...	23¢ Wilma Rudolph, Booklet Pane of 10 ...		...	4.50	...
2004 Commemoratives (continued)					
...	37¢ James Baldwin, SA	14.75	3.50	.75	.30
...	37¢ Martin Johnson Heade, Single from Double-sided Convertible Pane of 20, SA	...	...	.75	.30
...	37¢ Heade, Double-sided Pair from Pane of 20	...	...	1.50	...
...	37¢ Heade, Double-sided Convertible Pane of 20	...	14.75	...	
...	37¢ American Indian Art Souvenir Sheet of 10, SA	...	7.50	...	
...	37¢ American Indian Art Set of 10 singles...	7.50	5.00		
...	37¢ John Wayne, SA	14.75	3.50	.75	.30

SEMI POSTAL STAMPS

B1

B2

B3

1998 Breast Cancer Research

Scott's No.		Mint Sheet	Plate Block	F-VF NH	F-VF Used
B1	(32¢ + 8¢) Breast Cancer, 1st Class Rate	(20) 20.75	5.00	1.10	.50

2002 Heroes of 2001

Scott's No.		Mint Sheet	Plate Block	F-VF NH	F-VF Used
B2	(34¢+11¢) Non-Denominated	(20) 20.75	5.00	1.10	.50

2003 Stop Family Violence

Scott's No.		Mint Sheet	Plate Block	F-VF NH	F-VF Used
B3	(37¢+8¢) Domestic Violence	(20) 17.75	3.95	.90	.50

MINT COMMEMORATIVE YEAR SETS

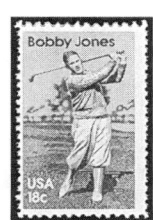

Year	Scott's No.	Qty.	F-VF NH
1926-27	627-29, 43-44	5	20.75
1928	645-50	6	33.00
1929	651, 54-57, 80-81	7	22.75
1930-31	682-3,88-90,702-3	7	5.25
1932	716-19, 24-25	6	6.50
1933	726-29, 32-34	7	3.15
1934	736-39	4	1.30
1935	772-75	4	1.50
1936	776-84	6	5.25
1937	795-802	8	3.65
1938	835-38	4	1.60
1939	852-58	7	4.65
1940	894-902	9	2.60
1941-3	903-08	6	2.50
1944	922-26	5	1.60
1945	927-38	12	3.00
1946	939-44	6	1.50
1947	945-52	8	3.00
1948	953-80	28	7.50
1949	981-86	6	1.50
1950	987-97	11	2.95
1951	998-1003	6	1.70
1952	1004-16	13	3.35
1953	1017-28	12	3.15
1954	1029,60-63	5	1.40
1955	1064-72	9	2.95
1956	1073-85	13	5.25
1957	1086-99	14	2.85
1958	1100,04-23	21	4.50
1959	1124-38	15	3.35

Year	Scott's No.	Qty.	F-VF NH
1960	1139-73	35	8.25
1961	1174-90	17	5.35
1962	1191-1207	17	3.95
1963	1230-41	12	2.95
1964	1242-60	19	5.75
1965	1261-76	16	4.00
1966	1306-22	17	3.85
1967	1323-37	15	5.50
1968	1339-40,42-64	25	8.95
1969	1365-86	22	9.25
1970	1387-92,1405-22	24	7.75
1971	1423-45	23	6.50
1972	1446-74	29	8.75
1973	1475-1508	34	9.85
1974	1525-52	28	9.25
1975	1553-80	28	9.25
1976	1629-32,83-85 1690-1703	21	10.50
1977	1704-30	27	11.25
1978	1731-33,44-69	29	15.00
1979	1770-1802	33	16.50
1980	1803-10,21-43	31	16.50
1981	1874-79,1910-45	42	27.50
1982	1950-52,2003-4,955 2006-30	30	22.50
1983	2031-65	35	25.00
1984	2066-2109	44	32.95
1985	2110,37-47,52-66	27	35.00

Year	Scott's No.	Qty.	F-VF NH
1986	2167,2202-4,10-11, 2220-24,2235-22	45	20.75
1987	2246-51,75, 2336-38,2349-54, 2360-61,2367-68	20	17.25
1988	2339-46,69-80, 86-93,2399-2400	30	28.75
1989	2347,2401-04, 10-18,20-28,34-37..27		26.50
1990	2348,2349-40,2442, 44-49,96-2500, 2506-15	25	27.75
1991	2532-35,37-38,50-51, 2553-58,60-61,67, 2578-79	19	17.75
1992	2611-23,30-41,98-99, 2700-04,10-14,20	38	34.50
1993	2721-30,46-59,66, 2771-74,79-89,91-94, 2804-06	47	47.50
1994	2807-12,14C-28,2834-36, 39,48-68,2871-72, 76	49	33.75

Year	Scott's No.	Qty.	F-VF NH
1995	2948,50-58,61-68,74 76-80,82-92,98-99 3001-7,19-23	49	51.00
1996	3024,30,58-67,69-70 3072-88,90-3104, 3106-11,18	53	52.75
1997	3120-21,3125,30-31, 3134-35, 3141,43-50, 3152-75	40	38.75
1998	3179-81,3192-3203,3206 3211-27,30-35,37-48	51	46.50
1999	3272-73, 75-76, 86-92, 3308-9, 14-50, 54, 3356-59, 68-69	58	53.50
2000	3370-72, 79-90, 93-2402, 3414-17, 38-46	38	32.50
2001	3500-1, 3-4, 7-19, 21, 3523-33. 36-40, 3545-48	38	32.75
2002	3552-60, 3650-56, 59-74, 3676-79, 92,95	38	33.50
2003	3746-48,71,73-74,81-82, 3786-91,3803,8-18, 3821-24	30	28.75

C1-3   C4   C5   C6

1918 First Issue VF Used + 50% (B)

Scott's No.		Unused, NH VF	F-VF	Unused, OG VF	F-VF	Used F-VF
C1-3	Set of 3	625.00	415.00	365.00	240.00	110.00
C1-3	Plate Blocks, set of 3	7250.00	4850.00	4600.00	3150.00	...
C1	6¢ Curtiss Jenny, Orange	150.00	100.00	85.00	60.00	29.50
C1	Arrow Block of 4	650.00	425.00	380.00	260.00	...
C1	Center Line Block of 4	700.00	465.00	415.00	275.00	...
C1	Plate Block of 6	1500.00	1000.00	1000.00	700.00	...
C2	16¢ Green	240.00	160.00	145.00	95.00	40.00
C2	Arrow Block of 4	1050.00	700.00	650.00	425.00	...
C2	Center Line Block of 4	1175.00	775.00	725.00	475.00	...
C2	Plate Block of 6	2450.00	1650.00	1600.00	1150.00	...
C3	24¢ Carmine Rose & Blue	250.00	170.00	150.00	100.00	45.00
C3	Arrow Block of 4	1075.00	725.00	650.00	435.00	...
C3	Center Line Block of 4	1225.00	815.00	750.00	495.00	...
C3	Plate Block of 12	3500.00	2350.00	2100.00	1400.00	...

1923 Second Issue VF Used +40% (B)

		VF	F-VF	VF	F-VF	F-VF
C4-6	Set of 3	435.00	300.00	260.00	185.00	69.50
C4-6	Plate Blocks, set of 3	8000.00	5850.00	5000.00	3650.00	...
C4	8¢ Propeller, Dark Green	52.50	36.50	30.00	21.50	13.00
C4	Plate Block of 6	525.00	365.00	300.00	215.00	...
C5	16¢ Emblem, Dark Blue	195.00	135.00	115.00	80.00	30.00
C5	Plate Block of 6	3600.00	2500.00	2150.00	1500.00	...
C6	24¢ Biplane, Carmine	210.00	150.00	125.00	90.00	30.00
C6	Plate Block of 6	4350.00	3250.00	2850.00	2100.00	...

C7-9   C10

1926-27 Map & Mail Planes VF Used + 40% (B)

		VF	F-VF	VF	F-VF	F-VF
C7-9	Set of 3	32.75	22.50	19.50	13.50	5.25
C7-9	Plate Blocks set of 3	340.00	240.00	230.00	160.00	...
C7	10¢ Map, Dark Blue	5.95	4.25	3.50	2.50	.50
C7	Plate Block of 6	82.50	60.00	55.00	40.00	...
C8	15¢ Map, Olive Brown	6.95	4.95	4.25	2.95	2.75
C8	Plate Block of 6	82.50	60.00	55.00	40.00	...
C9	20¢ Map, Yellow Green (1927)	21.50	14.50	12.75	8.75	2.25
C9	Plate Block of 6	195.00	135.00	130.00	90.00	...

Mint Sheets of 50, F-VF, NH #C7 300.00 #C8 325.00 #C9 850.00

Scott's No.		Unused, NH VF	F-VF	Unused, OG VF	F-VF	Used F-VF

1927 Lindbergh Tribute VF + 40% (B)

C10	10¢ Lindbergh, Dark Blue	16.00	11.50	9.75	7.00	2.25
C10	Plate Block of 6	250.00	175.00	165.00	115.00	...
C10a	10¢ Booklet Pane of 3	175.00	125.00	115.00	80.00	...

C11   C12,C16-17,C19

1928 Beacon VF Used + 50% (B)

C11	5¢ Carmine & Blue	10.50	7.00	6.25	4.25	.70
C11	Arrow Block of 4	45.00	30.00	28.00	19.00	...
C11	Plate Block of 6	85.00	55.00	57.50	40.00	...
C11	Pl.Block of 6 Double "TOP"	185.00	125.00	130.00	90.00	...
C11	Pl.Block of 8 No "TOP"	300.00	215.00	225.00	165.00	...

1930 Winged Globe, Flat Press, Perf. 11 VF Used + 40% (B)

C12	5¢ Violet	19.50	14.00	12.00	8.75	.50
C12	Plate Block of 6	295.00	210.00	200.00	150.00	...

Mint Sheets of 50 F-VF, NH #C10 775.00 #C11 395.00 #C12 750.00

1930 GRAF ZEPPELIN ISSUE VF Used + 30% (B)

C13   C14

C15   C18

C13-15	Set of 3	3250.00	2575.00	2250.00	1700.00	1300.00
C13-15	Plate Blocks set of 3 ..	34,500.00	26000.00	23000.00	17500.00	...
C13	65¢ Zeppelin, Green	550.00	425.00	365.00	285.00	225.00
C13	Plate Block of 6	4950.00	3750.00	3250.00	2500.00	...
C14	$1.30 Zeppelin, Brown	1150.00	875.00	775.00	575.00	450.00
C14	Plate Block of 6	12000.00	9000.00	8000.00	6000.00	...
C15	$2.60 Zeppelin, Blue	1750.00	1350.00	1175.00	900.00	700.00
C15	Plate Block of 6	18500.00	14000.00	12750.00	9500.00	...

OG = With original gum, has been or is hinged. NH = Never has been hinged.

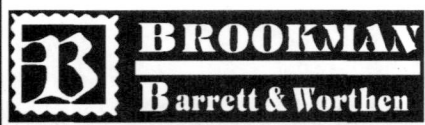

C38

C40

C42

C43

C44

C45

Scott's No.		Unused, NH VF	F-VF	Unused, OG VF	F-VF	Used F-VF
1931-32 Rotary Press, Perf. 10½x11, Designs of #C12 VF Used + 40% (B)						
C16	5¢ Winged Globe, Violet	11.00	8.25	7.00	5.00	.55
C16	Plate Block of 4	150.00	110.00	105.00	75.00	...
C17	8¢ Winged Globe (1932)	4.85	3.35	3.00	2.15	.35
C17	Plate Block of 4	55.00	40.00	38.50	27.50	...
1933 Century of Progress VF Used + 30% (B)						
C18	50¢ Graf Zeppelin, Green	185.00	140.00	125.00	95.00	87.50
C18	Plate Block of 6	1475.00	1125.00	1000.00	775.00	...
1934 Winged Globe, Design of #C12 VF Used +40% (B)						
C19	6¢ Dull Orange	4.25	3.00	3.35	2.40	.20
C19	Plate Block of 4	39.50	28.50	29.50	21.75	...
	Mint Sheets of 50 F-VF, NH #C16 475.00 #C17 225.00 #C19 200.00					

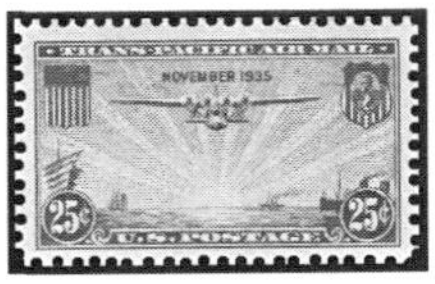

C20

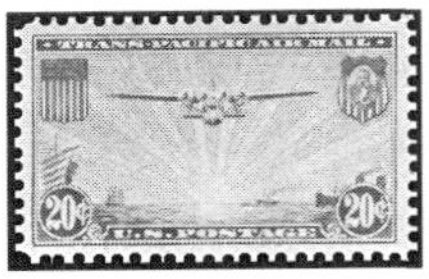

C21-22

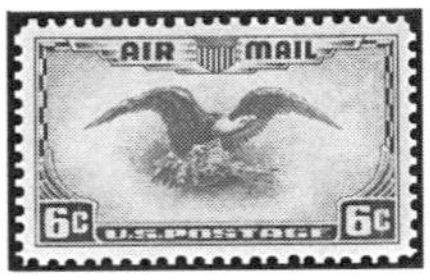

C23

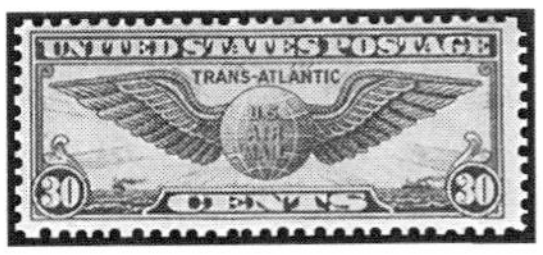

C24

Scott's No.		VF	F-VF	VF	F-VF	Used
1935-37 Trans-Pacific Issue (VF Used + 30%)						
C20-22	**Clipper Set of 3 ....**	**28.75**	**22.00**	**22.50**	**17.50**	**7.25**
C20-22	**Plate Block set of 3 ....**	**360.00**	**265.00**	**275.00**	**215.00**	...
C20	25¢ China Clipper	2.10	1.60	1.60	1.25	1.20
C20	Plate Block of 6	36.50	27.50	29.00	22.50	...
C21	20¢ China Clipper (1937)	14.00	10.75	11.00	8.50	1.50
C21	Plate Block of 6	170.00	125.00	130.00	100.00	...
C22	50¢ China Clipper (1937)	14.00	10.75	11.00	8.50	5.00
C22	Plate Block of 6	170.00	125.00	130.00	100.00	...
	Mint Sheets of 50 F-VF, NH #C20 110.00 #C21 650.00 #C22 675.00					
1938 Eagle (VF Used + 30%)						
C23	6¢ Dark Blue & Carmine	.75	.55	.55	.40	.20
C23	Arrow Block of 4	3.25	2.75	2.60	2.00	...
C23	Center Line Block of 4	3.75	3.00	2.90	2.25	...
C23	Plate Block of 4	13.00	10.00	9.75	7.50	...
C23	Top Plate Block of 10	22.00	16.50	17.00	12.50	...
C23v	6¢ Ultramarine & Carmine	200.00	150.00	160.00	120.00	...
1939 Trans-Atlantic Issue (VF Used + 40%)						
C24	30¢ Winged Globe, Blue .	15.50	11.00	12.00	8.75	1.35
C24	Plate Block of 6	245.00	175.00	195.00	140.00	...
	Mint Sheets of 50 F-VF, NH #C23 40.00 #C24 675.00					

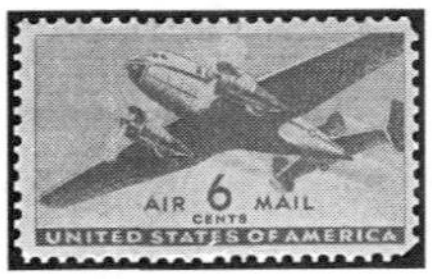

C25-31

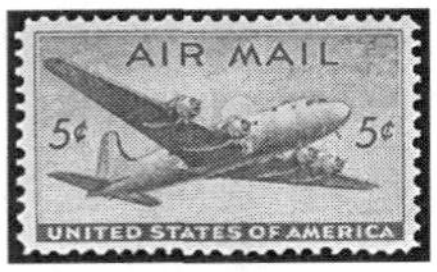

C32

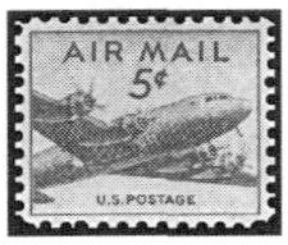

C33,C37,C39,C41

1941-44 Transport Plane

Scott's No.		Mint Sheet	Plate Block	F-VF NH	F-VF Used
C25-31	**Set of 7 ....**	...	125.00	23.50	4.85
C25	6¢ Carmine	9.75	1.00	.20	.20
C25a	6¢ Booklet Pane of 3	...	...	4.25	3.75
C26	8¢ Olive Green (1944)	11.50	1.85	.25	.20
C27	10¢ Violet	75.00	9.00	1.50	.20
C28	15¢ Brown Carmine	150.00	13.50	3.00	.35
C29	20¢ Bright Green	115.00	10.75	2.30	.35
C30	30¢ Blue	135.00	12.75	2.75	.40
C31	50¢ Orange	700.00	80.00	13.00	3.75

1946-1947 Issues

C32	5¢ DC-4 Skymaster	7.50	.80	.20	.20
C33	5¢ DC-4 Small Plane (1947) ... (100) 15.00		.80	.20	.20

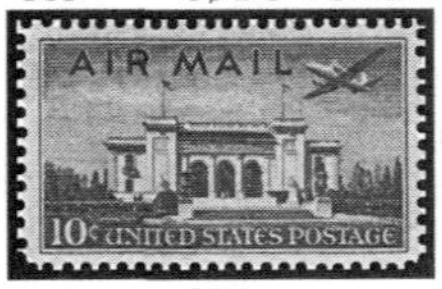

C34

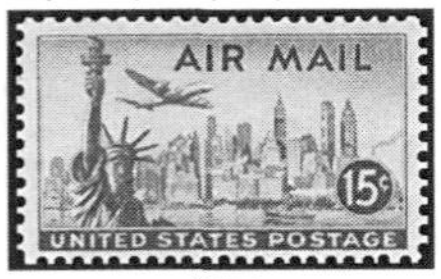

C35

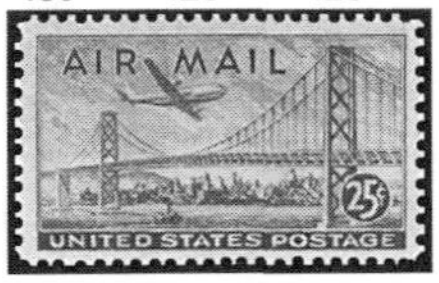

C36

C34-36	**Views Set of 3 (1947) ....**	**82.50**	**7.50**	**1.75**	**.50**
C34	10¢ Pan-Am Building, Wet	13.75	1.50	.30	.20
C34a	10¢ Dry Printing	21.75	2.10	.45	.25
C35	15¢ New York Skyline, Wet	21.50	2.00	.45	.20
C35b	15¢ Dry Printing	32.50	3.00	.66	.25
C36	25¢ Oakland Bay Bridge, Wet	52.50	4.50	1.10	.20
C36a	25¢ Dry Printing	65.00	5.75	1.35	.30

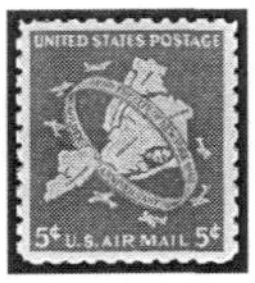

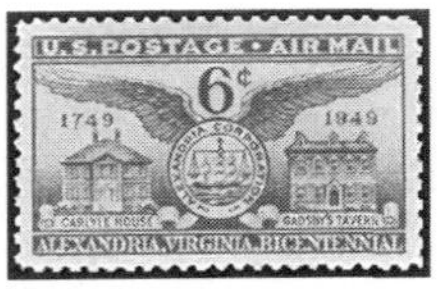

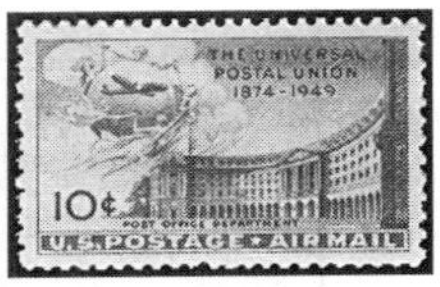

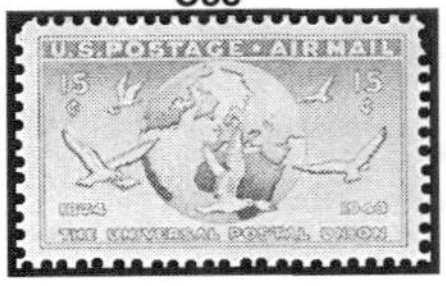

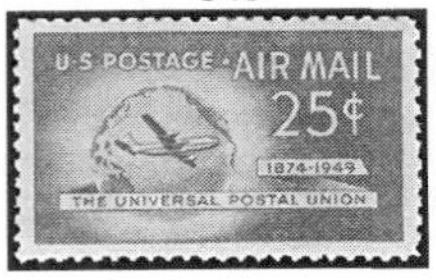

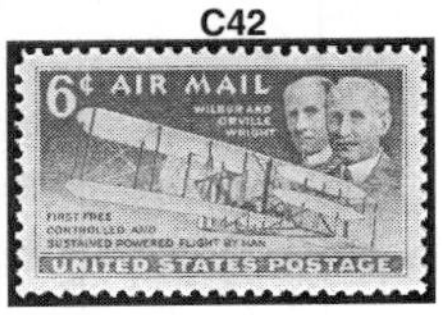

1948-49 Issues

Scott's No.		Mint Sheet	Line Pair	F-VF NH	F-VF Used
C37	5¢ Small Plane, Coil		9.00	1.10	1.10
	Plate Blocks				
C38	5¢ New York City Jubilee .... (100)	21.50	4.25	.25	.20
C39	6¢ DC-4 (Design of C33) ('49) .. (100)	18.50	.80	.20	.20
C39a	6¢ Booklet Pane of 6		...	10.75	9.75
C39b	6¢ Dry Printing .... (100)	90.00	5.50	.95	.40
C39c	6¢ Bk. Pane of 6, Dry Printing ...	...	...	25.00	...
C40	6¢ Alexandria Bicentennial ('49) .	10.75	1.00	.25	.20
	Line Pair				
C41	6¢ Small Plane, Coil (1949)	...	14.50	3.25	.20
	Plate Blocks				
C42-44	**Univ. Postal Union Set of 3 (1949)**	...	9.50	1.40	1.00
C42	10¢ Post Office Building	14.50	1.50	.30	.25
C43	15¢ Globe & Doves	21.75	2.00	.45	.35
C44	25¢ Stratocruiser & Globe	36.50	5.75	.75	.50
C45	6¢ Wright Brothers Flight (1949)	18.75	1.85	.40	.20

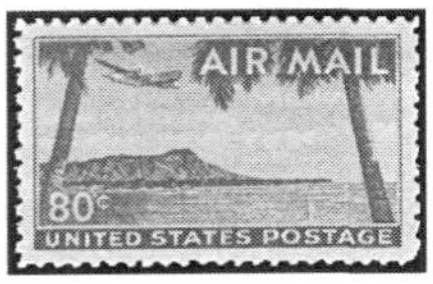

C46

1952 Hawaii Issue

C46	80¢ Diamond Head	335.00	31.75	6.75	1.50

1953-58 Issues

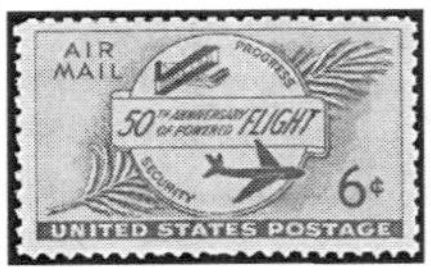

C47

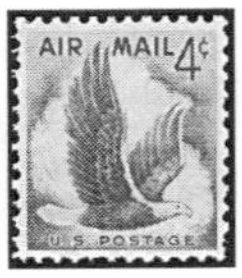

C48, C50

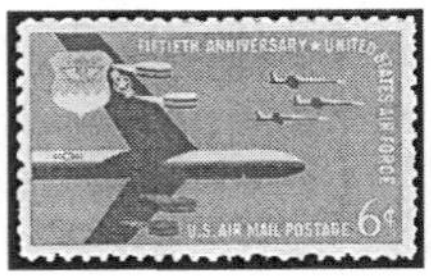

C49

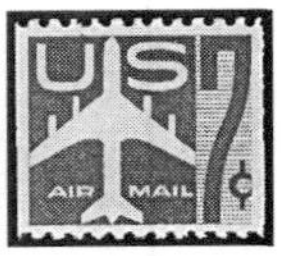

C51,C52,C60,C61

C47	6¢ Powered Flight 50th Anniv.	8.75	.80	.20	.20
C48	4¢ Eagle in Flight (1954) .... (100)	14.75	1.60	.20	.15
C49	6¢ Air Force 50th Anniv.(1957) ...	9.75	.95	.20	.20
C50	5¢ Eagle in Flight (1958) .... (100)	16.50	1.40	.20	.15
C51	7¢ Jet Silhouette, Blue (1958) (100)	17.50	.90	.20	.15
C51a	7¢ Booklet Pane of 6	...	...	11.75	9.50
			Line Pair		
C52	7¢ Jet Blue Coil, LargeHoles (1958)	...	19.75	2.10	.20
C52s	7¢ Small Holes	...	150.00	9.75	...

1959-61 Issues

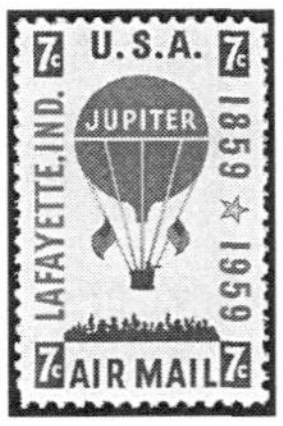

C54

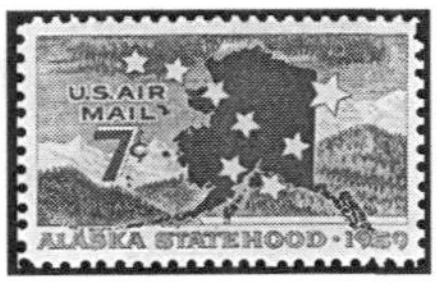

C53

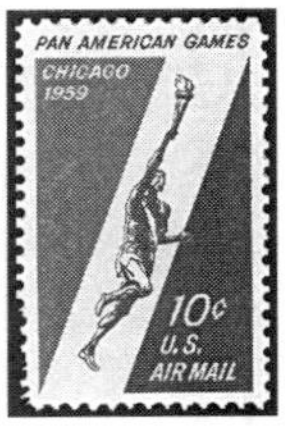

C56

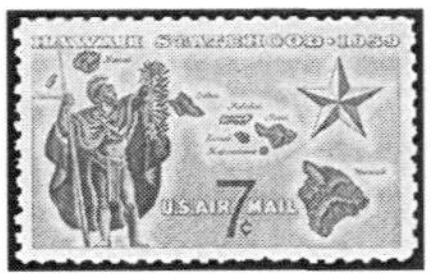

C55

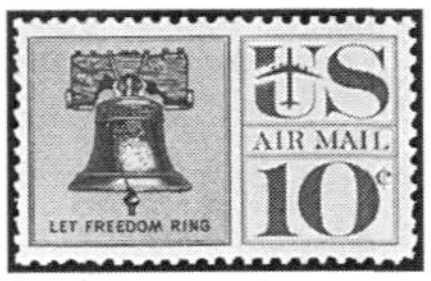

C57

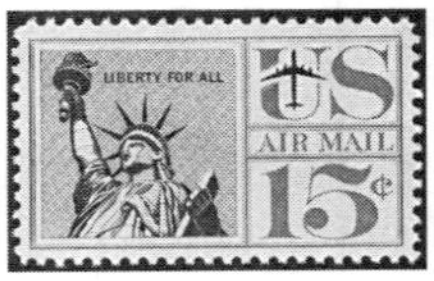

C58

1959-61 Issues (continued)

C59

C62

C63

Scott's No.		Mint Sheet	Plate Block	F-VF NH	F-VF Used
C53-56	1959 Commemoratives Set of 4	75.00	5.85	1.55	.80
C53	7¢ Alaska Statehood	14.50	1.30	.30	.20
C54	7¢ Balloon Jupiter	21.50	2.00	.45	.20
C55	7¢ Hawaii Statehood	14.50	1.30	.30	.20
C56	10¢ Pan-Am Games, Chicago	28.75	2.60	.60	.30
C57-59, C62-63	Regulars Set of 5	165.00	14.75	3.35	1.45
C57	10¢ Liberty Bell (1960)	70.00	6.25	1.50	.90
C58	15¢ Statue of Liberty (1959)	23.75	2.10	.45	.20
C59	25¢ Abraham Lincoln	35.00	3.25	.75	.20
C59a	25¢ Tagged (1966)	40.00	3.75	.85	.35
C60	7¢ Jet Silhouette, Carmine ..... (100)	21.50	1.10	.25	.15
C60a	7¢ Bk. Pane of 6	...	...	15.75	12.75
C61	7¢ Jet, Carmine Coil	Line Pair 45.00	4.00	.30	
C62	13¢ Liberty Bell (1961)	21.00	1.80	.40	.20
C62a	13¢ Tagged (1967)	45.00	9.00	.95	.65
C63	15¢ Liberty, Re-engraved (1961)	22.50	1.95	.45	.20
C63a	15¢ Tagged (1967)	24.00	2.35	.50	.25

#C58 has wide border around statue, #C63 is divided in center.

1962-67 Issues

C64,C65

C66

C67

C68

C69

C70

C71

C64	8¢ Jet over Capitol (1962) ...... (100)	22.75	1.00	.25	.15
C64b	8¢ B. Pane of 5, Slogan 1, "Your Mailman"	...	5.95	4.75	
C64b	8¢ B. Pane of 5, Sl. 2, "Use Zone Numbers"	...	80.00	...	
C64b	8¢ B. Pane of 5, Sl. 3, "Always Use Zip"	...	13.75		
C64a	8¢ Jet, Tagged (1963) .... (100)	27.50	1.20	.30	.20
C64c	8¢ Booklet Pane of 5, Tagged, Slogan 3 (1964)	...	1.65	1.25	
C65	8¢ Capitol & Jet Coil (1962)	Line Pair 7.25	.60	.20	
C65a	8¢ Tagged (1965)	Line Pair 2.75	.35	.15	
C66	15¢ Montgomery Blair (1963)	35.00	3.25	.75	.65
C67	6¢ Bald Eagle (1963) .... (100)	18.50	1.75	.20	.15
C67a	6¢ Eagle, Tagged (1967)	...	75.00	3.75	3.00
C68	8¢ Amelia Earhart (1963)	19.00	1.75	.40	.20
C69	8¢ Robert H. Goddard (1964)	26.50	2.50	.55	.20
C70	8¢ Alaska Purchase (1967)	18.75	1.85	.40	.20
C71	20¢ Columbia Jays (1967)	45.00	3.75	.90	.20

1968-73 Issues

C72,C73

C74

C75

C76

C77

C78,C82

C79,C83

C80

C81

1968-73 Issues (continued)

Scott's No.		Mint Sheet	Plate Block	F-VF NH	F-VF Used
C72	10¢ 50-Star Runway (1968) .... (100)	28.75	1.30	.30	.15
C72b	10¢ Booklet Pane of 8	...	...	2.35	2.25
C72c	10¢ B. Pane of 5 with Slogan 4 or Slogan 5	...	...	4.25	4.00
	Slogan 4 = Mail Early in the Day Slogan 5 = Use Zip Code				
C72v	10¢ Congressional Precancel	...	110.00	2.00	...
C73	10¢ 50-Star Runway Coil (1968) .	Line Pair 2.25	.40	.20	
C74	10¢ Air Mail Service 50th Anniv ('68)	15.00	2.20	.30	.20
C75	20¢ "USA" and Jet (1968)	27.00	2.65	.55	.20
C76	10¢ Moon Landing (1969) .... (32)	12.50	1.75	.40	.20
C77-81	Regulars Set of 5	140.00	9.25	1.95	1.10
C77	9¢ Delta Wing Plane Silh. (1971)(100)	28.50	1.50	.30	.25
C78	11¢ Jet Airliner Silhouette ('71) . (100)	33.50	1.75	.35	.15
C78a	11¢ Booklet Pane of 4	...	...	1.50	1.30
C78b	11¢ Congressional Precancel	...	25.75	.65	.40
C79	13¢ Winged Envelope (1973) .... (100)	33.50	1.75	.35	.15
C79a	13¢ Booklet Pane of 5	...	...	1.60	1.50
C79b	13¢ Congressional Precancel	...	9.50	.60	.35
C80	17¢ Statue of Liberty Head (1971)	22.50	2.10	.45	.25
C81	21¢ "USA" and Jet (1971)	28.75	2.65	.60	.20
C82	11¢ Jet Silhouette Coil (1971)	Line Pair .90	.40	.15	
C83	13¢ Winged Envelope Coil (1973).	Line Pair 1.25	.45	.15	

1972-1979 Issues

C85

C84

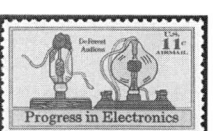
C86

C87

C88

C89

C90

C91

C93

C95

C92

C94

C96

C97

C84	11¢ City of Refuge National Park, Hawaii (1972)	21.50	2.00	.45	.20
C85	11¢ Olympic Games - Skiing ('72)	16.50	(10) 3.65	.35	.20
C86	11¢ Electronics (1973)	23.75	2.25	.50	.20
C87	18¢ Statue of Liberty (1974)	24.50	2.30	.50	.40
C88	26¢ Mt. Rushmore Memorial (1974)	48.50	4.50	1.00	.20
C89	25¢ Plane & Globes (1976)	34.50	3.00	.70	.20
C90	31¢ Plane, Globe and Flag (1976)	41.50	3.65	.85	.20
C91-96	Aviators Set of 6, attd. .... (3)	315.00	(3)17.50	6.50	5.25
C91-96	Set of 6 Singles	...	...	6.25	3.00
C91-92	31¢ Wright Brothers, attd (1978)(100)	95.00	4.50	1.95	1.75
C91-92	Set of 2 Singles	...	...	1.90	.80
C93-94	21¢ Octave Chanute, attd. ('79) (100)	90.00	4.50	1.90	1.80
C93-94	Set of 2 Singles	...	...	1.85	1.00
C95-96	25¢ Wiley Post, attd. (1979) ..... (100)	145.00	9.25	2.95	2.75
C95-96	Set of 2 Singles	...	...	2.85	1.40
C97	31¢ Olympics - High Jump (1979)	45.00	(12)11.50	.90	.40

From 1935 to date, add 20% for Very Fine quality unless otherwise noted.
Minimum premium of 10¢ per stamp.

1980 Issues

C99

C98

C100

Scott's No.		Mint Sheet		Plate Block	F-VF NH	F-VF Used
C98	40¢ Philip Mazzei, Perf. 11	58.50	(12)	15.75	1.20	.25
C98A	40¢ Mazzei, Perf. 10½x11¼ (1982)	...	(12)	110.00	6.00	2.00
C99	28¢ Blanche Stuart Scott (1980)	46.50	(12)	12.75	.95	.25
C100	35¢ Glenn Curtiss	47.50	(12)	13.50	1.00	.25

1983 Los Angeles Summer Olympic Issues

C101   C102
C103   C104

C105   C106
C107   C108

C109   C110
C111   C112

C101-12	Olympics Set of 12, attd.	(3)180.00	(3)	19.75	15.50	13.50
C101-12	Set of 12 Singles	...	...		13.75	7.15
C101-4	28¢ Summer Olympics, attd	62.50		6.25	5.50	4.75
C101-4	Set of 4 Singles	...		...	5.25	2.00
C105-8	40¢ Summer Olympics,					
	Bullseye Perfs Pf. 11.2, attd	60.00		6.00	5.25	4.50
C105-8	Set of 4 Singles	...		...	5.00	1.80
C105a-8a	40¢ Line Perfs Pf. 11, attd	110.00		12.75	8.75	8.00
C105a-8a	Set of 4 Singles	...		...	8.00	4.00
C109-12	35¢ Summer Olympics, attd	67.50		8.00	5.25	5.00
C109-12	Set of 4 Singles	...		...	4.75	2.60

1985-1989 Issues

C113

C114

C115

C116

C117

C118

C119

C120

C121

Scott's No.		Mint Sheet	Plate Block	F-VF NH	F-VF Used
C113-16	**1985 Commems., Set of 4 ......**	215.00	22.75	4.35	1.35
C113	33¢ Alfred Verville	45.00	4.35	.95	.25
C114	39¢ Lawrence & Elmer Sperry ..	52.50	5.00	1.10	.35
C115	44¢ Transpacific Airmail	57.50	5.50	1.20	.35
C116	44¢ Father Junipero Serra	67.50	9.00	1.35	.50
C117	44¢ New Sweden (1988)	73.50	9.00	1.50	.75
C118	45¢ Samuel Langley, Large				
	Block Tagging (1988)	65.00	6.00	1.35	.30
C118a	45¢ Overall Tagging	165.00	33.50	3.00	2.00
C119	36¢ Igor Sikorsky (1988)	52.50	4.95	1.10	.35
C120	45¢ French Revolution (1989) (30)	37.50	5.75	1.30	.55
C121	45¢ Pre-Columbian Customs ('89)	85.00	8.00	1.75	.50

1989 Universal Postal Congress Issues

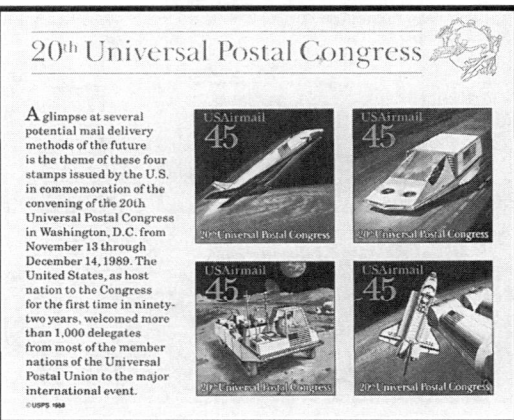

C122   C123
C124   C125

C126

C122-25	45¢ Futuristic Mail				
	Delivery, Attached .... (40)	63.50	7.50	6.50	5.75
C122-25	Set of 4 Singles	...	...	6.25	3.00
C126	45¢ Future Mail Delivery Souvenir				
	Sheet of 4, Imperforate	...	...	6.50	5.75
C126a-d	45¢ Set of 4 singles	...	...	6.35	5.00

1990-1993 Airmail Issues

C127

C128

C129

C130

C131

C132

Scott's No.		Mint Sheet	Plate Block	F-VF NH	F-VF Used
C127	45¢ America, Caribbean Coast ...	80.00	9.00	1.60	.50
C128	50¢ Harriet Quimby, Pf. 11 (1991)	70.00	7.00	1.50	.45
C128b	H.Quimby, Perf. 11.2 (1993)	75.00	7.50	1.60	.50
C129	40¢ William T. Piper (1991)	60.00	5.75	1.25	.45
C130	50¢ Antarctic Treaty (1991)	67.50	6.75	1.40	.65
C131	50¢ Pre-Columbian America (1991)	67.50	6.75	1.40	.55
C132	40¢ W.T. Piper, new design ('93)	260.00	65.00	4.75	.85

#C129: Blue sky clear along top of design, Perf. 11
#C132: Piper's hair is touching top of design, Bullseye Perf. 11.2

1999-2003 American Landmarks International Rate Regular Issues

C133

C134

C135

C137

C138

C136

Scott's No.			Plate Block	F-VF NH	F-VF Used
C133-38	Landmarks, Set of 6	160.00	38.50	8.50	2.50
C133	48¢ Niagara Falls, SA	(20) 22.75	5.50	1.20	.35
C134	40¢ Rio Grande, SA	(20) 18.50	4.25	1.00	.50
C135	60¢ Grand Canyon, SA (2000) ...	(20) 28.50	7.00	1.50	.35
C136	70¢ Nine Mile Prairie, SA (2001)	(20) 33.75	7.75	1.75	.50
C137	80¢ Mount McKinley, SA (2001)	(20) 38.50	8.75	2.00	.50
C138	60¢ Acadia, SA, Die-cut 11¼x11½ (2001)	(20) 28.50	6.75	1.50	.40
C138a	60¢ Die-cut 11½x 11 3/4 (2003) ..	(20) 26.50	6.25	1.40	.50

1934-36 AIR MAIL SPECIAL DELIVERY VF Used +30%

CE1,CE2

Scott's No.		Unused, NH VF	F-VF	Unused, OG VF	F-VF	F-VF Used
CE1	16¢ Great Seal, Dark Blue	1.15	.90	.95	.70	.75
CE1	Plate Block of 6	27.00	22.50	22.00	18.00	...
CE2	16¢ Seal, Red & Blue	.75	.55	.55	.45	.30
CE2	Arrow Block of 4	3.15	2.50	2.50	2.00	...
CE2	Center Line Block of 4	3.50	2.75	2.80	2.35	...
CE2	Plate Block of 4	10.50	8.50	8.65	6.75	...
CE2	Top Plate Block of 10	18.50	15.00	14.50	12.50	...

Mint Sheets of 50 F-VF, NH #CE1 60.00; #CE2 40.00

SPECIAL DELIVERY STAMPS

E1

E2,E3

E4,E5

1885 "At A Special Delivery Office", Unwatermarked, Perf. 12 (VF+70%)(C)

Scott's No.		NH Fine	Unused, OG Fine	Ave.	Used Fine	Ave.
E1	10¢ Messenger, Blue	725.00	325.00	195.00	40.00	24.50
E1	10¢ Unused, without gum	...	175.00	100.00	...	...

1888-93 "At Any Post Office", No Line Under "TEN CENTS" Unwatermarked, Perf. 12 VF + 70% (C)

E2	10¢ Blue	650.00	300.00	180.00	16.00	9.75
E2	10¢ Unused, without gum	...	160.00	95.00	...	...
E3	10¢ Orange (1893)	375.00	180.00	110.00	22.50	13.75
E3	10¢ Unused, without gum	...	95.00	55.00	...	...

1894 Line Under "TEN CENTS", Unwatermarked, Perf. 12 VF + 70% (C)

E4	10¢ Blue	1350.00	625.00	375.00	27.50	17.00
E4	10¢ Unused, without gum	...	325.00	190.00	...	...

1895 Line Under "TEN CENTS, Double Line Watermark, Perf. 12 VF+70% (C)

E5	10¢ Blue	270.00	135.00	85.00	3.75	2.25
E5	10¢ Unused, without gum	...	70.00	45.00	...	...

E6,E8-11

E7

Scott No.		Unused, NH VF	F-VF	Unused,OG VF	F-VF	Used F-VF
	1902-08 Double Line Watermark, VF Used + 60% (B)					
E6	10¢ Ultramarine, Perf. 12	395.00	250.00	175.00	110.00	3.50
E7	10¢ Mercury, Green (1908) ...	155.00	95.00	77.50	48.50	32.50
	1911-14 Single Line Watermark VF Used + 50% (B)					
E8	10¢ Ultramarine, Perf. 12	240.00	150.00	120.00	80.00	5.75
E9	10¢ Ultra., Perf. 10 (1914)	450.00	300.00	220.00	150.00	6.00
	1916 Unwatermarked, Perf.10 VF Used + 50% (B)					
E10	10¢ Pale Ultramarine	700.00	450.00	350.00	240.00	24.00
	1917 Unwatermarked, Perf. 11 VF Used +40% (B)					
E11	10¢ Ultramarine	42.50	29.50	23.50	16.75	.50
E11	Plate Block of 6	385.00	275.00	240.00	175.00	...

E12-13,E15-18

E14,E19

	1922-1925 Flat Press Printings, Perf. 11 VF Used + 30% (B)					
E12	10¢ Motorcycle, Gray Violet ...	62.50	46.50	35.00	26.50	.50
E12	Plate Block of 6	575.00	425.00	390.00	300.00	...
E13	15¢ Deep Orange (1925)	50.00	35.00	28.00	21.50	1.20
E13	Plate Block of 6	475.00	350.00	325.00	250.00	...
E14	20¢ P.O. Truck, Black (1925) ...	4.75	3.65	2.80	2.15	1.50
E14	Plate Block of 6	60.00	47.50	45.00	32.50	...
	1927-1951 Rotary Press Printings, Perf. 11x10½ VF Used + 25%					
E15-19	Set of 5	10.65	8.35	8.25	6.50	3.15
E15	10¢ Motorcycle, Gray Violet	1.50	1.20	1.10	.85	.20
E15	Plate Block of 4	7.50	5.75	5.75	4.25	...
E16	15¢ Orange (1931)	1.70	1.35	1.25	1.00	.20
E16	Plate Block of 4	8.00	6.25	5.75	4.75	...
E17	13¢ Blue (1944)	1.10	.90	.90	.70	.20
E17	Plate Block of 4	5.25	4.00	4.25	3.25	...
E18	17¢ Orange Yellow (1944)	4.50	3.50	3.65	2.75	2.50
E18	Plate Block of 4	35.00	26.50	27.00	19.50	...
E19	20¢ P.O. Truck, Black (1951) ..	2.40	1.85	1.85	1.50	.20
E19	Plate Block of 4	11.50	8.75	8.75	7.00	...

MINT SHEETS OF 50, F-VF, NH
#E14 165.00, E15 55.00, E16 65.00, E17 42.50, E18 175.00, E19 95.00

E20,E21

E22,E23

1954-1971

Scott's No.		Mint Sheet	Pl. Block NH	F-VF NH	F-VF Used
E20-23	Set of 4	...	19.50	4.25	.85
E20	20¢ Letter & Hands	32.50	3.15	.65	.20
E21	30¢ Letter & Hands (1957)	40.00	3.75	.85	.20
E22	45¢ Arrows (1969)	67.50	6.25	1.40	.40
E23	60¢ Arrows (1971)	72.50	6.50	1.50	.20

F1

FA1

J1-28

J29-68

1911 REGISTRATION VF Used + 50% (B)

Scott's No.		Unused, NH VF	F-VF	Unused,OG VF	F-VF	Used F-VF
F1	10¢ Eagle, Ultramarine	165.00	110.00	90.00	60.00	6.50

1955 CERTIFIED MAIL

Scott's No.		Mint Sheet	Pl.Block NH	F-VF NH	F-VF Used
FA1	15¢ Postman, Red	25.00	4.75	.50	.40

POSTAGE DUE STAMPS

1879 Perforated 12 (NH + 150%, VF OG & Used + 70%, VF NH + 250%) (C)

Scott's No.		Unused,OG Fine	Ave.	Used Fine	Ave.
J1	1¢ Brown	55.00	32.50	8.00	4.75
J2	2¢ Brown	300.00	180.00	7.50	4.50
J3	3¢ Brown	47.50	30.00	4.00	2.40
J4	5¢ Brown	525.00	315.00	37.50	23.00
J5	10¢ Brown	600.00	365.00	40.00	24.00
J6	30¢ Brown	285.00	170.00	39.50	25.00
J7	50¢ Brown	450.00	270.00	57.50	35.00

1879 Special Printing of 1879 Issue, Soft Porous Paper VF+50% (C)

Scott's No.					
J8	1¢ Deep Brown	..	..	..	..
J9	2¢ Deep Brown	..	..	..	..
J10	3¢ Deep Brown	..	..	..	..
J11	5¢ Deep Brown	..	..	..	..
J12	10¢ Deep Brown	3750.00	2350.00	..	..
J13	30¢ Deep Brown	3750.00	2350.00	..	..
J14	50¢ Deep Brown	3750.00	2350.00	..	..

1884 Same Design Perf. 12 (NH + 125%, VF OG & Used + 70%, VF NH + 210%)

Scott's No.		Fine	Ave.	Fine	Ave.
J15	1¢ Red Brown	50.00	30.00	4.50	2.75
J16	2¢ Red Brown	57.50	35.00	4.25	2.65
J17	3¢ Red Brown	850.00	525.00	170.00	110.00
J18	5¢ Red Brown	450.00	275.00	27.50	16.50
J19	10¢ Red Brown	450.00	275.00	22.50	13.50
J20	30¢ Red Brown	140.00	85.00	42.50	25.00
J21	50¢ Red Brown	1350.00	800.00	150.00	90.00

1891 Same Design Pf.12 (NH+125%,VF OG & Used+70%,VF NH+210%)

Scott's No.		Fine	Ave.	Fine	Ave.
J22	1¢ Bright Claret	27.50	16.50	1.15	.70
J23	2¢ Bright Claret	29.50	17.50	1.20	.75
J24	3¢ Bright Claret	55.00	32.50	11.50	7.00
J25	5¢ Bright Claret	70.00	42.50	11.50	7.00
J26	10¢ Bright Claret	115.00	70.00	18.75	11.00
J27	30¢ Bright Claret	450.00	270.00	140.00	85.00
J28	50¢ Bright Claret	450.00	270.00	135.00	80.00

UNUSED STAMPS WITHOUT GUM

Scott No.	Without Gum Fine	Ave.	Scott No.	Without Gum Fine	Ave.	Scott No.	Without Gum Fine	Ave.
J1	38.50	23.00	J15	35.00	21.00	J22	18.75	11.50
J2	210.00	125.00	J16	40.00	25.00	J23	20.00	12.50
J3	32.50	21.50	J17	600.00	385.00	J24	39.50	22.75
J4	365.00	225.00	J18	315.00	190.00	J25	50.00	30.00
J5	415.00	250.00	J19	315.00	190.00	J26	80.00	50.00
J6	200.00	120.00	J20	100.00	60.00	J27	315.00	190.00
J7	315.00	190.00	J21	950.00	575.00	J28	315.00	190.00

1894-95 Unwatermarked, Perforated 12 VF Used + 60% (C)

Scott's No.		Unused, NH VF	F-VF	Unused,OG VF	F-VF	Used F-VF
J29	1¢ Vermilion	5000.00	3250.00	2400.00	1500.00	400.00
J30	2¢ Vermilion	1750.00	1000.00	875.00	550.00	120.00
J31	1¢ Claret	150.00	95.00	72.50	45.00	6.25
J32	2¢ Claret	125.00	75.00	60.00	37.50	4.50
J33	3¢ Claret (1895)	500.00	300.00	240.00	150.00	30.00
J34	5¢ Claret (1895)	825.00	500.00	400.00	250.00	35.00
J35	10¢ Claret (1895)	825.00	500.00	400.00	250.00	22.50
J36	30¢ Claret (1895)	1300.00	800.00	625.00	395.00	135.00
J36b	Pale Rose	1100.00	650.00	525.00	325.00	110.00
J37	50¢ Claret (1895)	4350.00	2650.00	2100.00	1300.00	450.00
J37a	Pale Rose	3950.00	2400.00	1900.00	1200.00	375.00

1895-97, Double Line Watermark, Perf. 12 VF Used + 60% (C)

Scott's No.		VF	F-VF	VF	F-VF	F-VF
J38	1¢ Claret	25.75	15.00	12.75	8.00	.60
J39	2¢ Claret	25.75	15.00	12.75	8.00	.55
J40	3¢ Claret	170.00	100.00	85.00	52.50	2.25
J41	5¢ Claret	185.00	110.00	92.50	57.50	2.25
J42	10¢ Claret	185.00	110.00	92.50	57.50	3.75
J43	30¢ Claret (1897)	1475.00	900.00	700.00	450.00	45.00
J44	50¢ Claret (1896)	1100.00	650.00	525.00	325.00	30.00

1910-12, Single Line Watermark, Perf. 12 VF Used + 60% (C)

Scott's No.		VF	F-VF	VF	F-VF	F-VF
J45	1¢ Claret	90.00	52.50	45.00	27.50	2.85
J46	2¢ Claret	90.00	52.50	45.00	27.50	1.15
J47	3¢ Claret	1450.00	850.00	725.00	450.00	30.00
J48	5¢ Claret	265.00	150.00	130.00	80.00	6.75
J49	10¢ Claret	325.00	190.00	160.00	100.00	11.50
J50	50¢ Claret (1912)	2750.00	1650.00	1350.00	850.00	110.00

OG = With original gum, has been or is hinged. NH = Never has been hinged.

1914 Single Line Watermark, Perf. 10 VF Used + 60% (C)

Scott's No.		Unused, NH VF	F-VF	Unused,OG VF	F-VF	Used F-VF
J52	1¢ Carmine Lake	160.00	90.00	80.00	50.00	9.75
J53	2¢ Carmine Lake	110.00	62.50	55.00	35.00	.55
J54	3¢ Carmine Lake	2400.00	1350.00	1200.00	750.00	45.00
J55	5¢ Carmine Lake	95.00	52.50	47.50	28.75	2.75
J56	10¢ Carmine Lake	145.00	82.50	72.50	45.00	1.90
J57	30¢ Carmine Lake	550.00	315.00	275.00	175.00	15.00
J58	50¢ Carmine Lake				9500.00	900.00

1916 Unwatermarked, Perf. 10 VF Used + 60% (B)

Scott's No.		VF	F-VF	VF	F-VF	F-VF
J59	1¢ Rose		5750.00	4750.00	3000.00	425.00
J60	2¢ Rose	575.00	325.00	285.00	175.00	45.00

1917-25 Unwatermarked, Perf. 11 VF Used + 50% (B)

Scott's No.		VF	F-VF	VF	F-VF	F-VF
J61	1¢ Carmine Rose	6.50	4.00	3.50	2.25	.25
J61	Plate Block of 6	95.00	60.00	52.50	35.00	...
J62	2¢ Carmine Rose	6.50	4.00	3.50	2.25	.35
J62	Plate Block of 6	95.00	60.00	52.50	35.00	...
J63	3¢ Carmine Rose	27.50	17.50	14.00	9.50	.35
J63	Plate Block of 6	195.00	130.00	120.00	80.00	...
J64	5¢ Carmine Rose	27.50	17.50	14.00	9.50	.35
J64	Plate Block of 6	195.00	130.00	120.00	80.00	...
J65	10¢ Carmine Rose	37.50	25.00	20.00	13.50	.50
J66	30¢ Carmine Rose	185.00	125.00	100.00	67.50	.80
J67	50¢ Carmine Rose	275.00	175.00	140.00	95.00	.45
J68	½¢ Dull Red (1925)	1.95	1.30	1.15	.75	.35

J69-76,J79-86

J77-78,J87

J88-99J102-4

J100-1

1930-31 Flat Press, Perf. 11 VF Used + 40% (B)

Scott's No.		VF	F-VF	VF	F-VF	F-VF
J69	½¢ Carmine	8.75	6.00	5.25	3.75	1.10
J69	Plate Block of 6	75.00	52.50	50.00	35.00	...
J70	1¢ Carmine	5.75	4.00	3.50	2.50	.35
J70	Plate Block of 6	55.00	37.50	35.00	25.00	...
J71	2¢ Carmine	7.25	4.75	4.25	3.00	.35
J71	Plate Block of 6	75.00	52.50	50.00	35.00	...
J72	3¢ Carmine	46.50	32.50	27.50	19.50	1.65
J73	5¢ Carmine	42.50	28.00	25.00	17.50	2.30
J74	10¢ Carmine	110.00	75.00	65.00	47.50	1.20
J75	30¢ Carmine	280.00	195.00	170.00	120.00	2.25
J76	50¢ Carmine	400.00	275.00	250.00	175.00	1.10
J77	$1 Carmine	52.50	36.50	31.50	22.50	.40
J77a	$1 Scarlet	45.00	31.50	27.00	19.00	.40
J78	$5 Carmine	75.00	50.00	45.00	31.50	.45
J78a	$5 Scarlet, Dry Printing	66.50	43.50	38.50	27.50	.45
J78b	$5 Scarlet, Wet Printing	70.00	47.50	42.50	30.00	.50

1931-56 Rotary Press, Perf. 11x10½ or 10½x11 (VF+30%)

Scott's No.		Mint Sheet	Pl.Blk NH	F-VF NH	F-VF Used
J79-87	Set of 9	...	...	65.00	1.90
J79	½¢ Carmine .... (100)	125.00	27.50	1.10	.20
J80	1¢ Carmine, dry printing .... (100)	27.50	2.00	.25	.20
J80b	1¢ Carmine, wet printing .... (100)	28.50	2.25	.25	.20
J81	2¢ Carmine, dry printing .... (100)	27.50	2.00	.25	.20
J81b	2¢ Carmine, wet printing .... (100)	28.50	2.25	.25	.20
J82	3¢ Carmine, dry printing .... (100)	32.50	3.00	.30	.25
J82b	3¢ Carmine, wet printing .... (100)	37.50	3.25	.35	.25
J83	5¢ Carmine, dry printing .... (100)	55.00	4.50	.50	.25
J83b	5¢ Carmine, wet printing .... (100)	60.00	5.50	.60	.25
J84	10¢ Carmine, dry printing .... (100)	170.00	9.50	1.60	.25
J84b	10¢ Carmine, wet printing .... (100)	195.00	10.75	1.80	.25
J85	30¢ Carmine	...	57.50	8.50	.30
J86	50¢ Carmine	...	77.50	14.00	.25
J87	$1 Scarlet (1956)	...	225.00	42.50	.35

1959-85 Rotary Press, Perf. 11x10½ (VF+25%)

Scott's No.		Mint Sheet	Pl.Blk NH	F-VF NH	F-VF Used
J88-104	Set of 17			21.00	5.50
J88	½¢ Carmine Rose & Black ...... (100)	375.00	195.00	1.65	1.65
J89	1¢ Carmine Rose & Black .... (100)	7.00	.75	.20	.15
J89v	1¢ Dull Gum .... (100)	27.50	4.00	.25	...
J90	2¢ Carmine Rose & Black .... (100)	8.50	.75	.20	.20
J90v	2¢ Dull Gum .... (100)	27.50	4.25	.25	...
J91	3¢ Carmine Rose & Black .... (100)	11.75	.85	.20	.15
J91v	3¢ Dull Gum .... (100)	26.50	3.00	.25	...
J92	4¢ Carmine Rose & Black .... (100)	16.50	1.10	.20	.15
J93	5¢ Carmine Rose & Black .... (100)	18.75	.85	.20	.15
J93v	5¢ Dull Gum .... (100)	27.50	4.75	.25	...
J94	6¢ Carmine Rose & Black .... (100)	20.00	1.30	.20	.20
J94v	6¢ Dull Gum .... (100)	...	...	165.00	...
J95	7¢ Carmine Rose & Black .... (100)	30.00	2.00	.30	.15
J95v	7¢ Dull Gum .... (100)	...	...	650.00	...
J96	8¢ Carmine Rose & Black .... (100)	30.00	2.00	.30	.15
J97	10¢ Carmine Rose & Black ..... (100)	25.00	1.50	.25	.25
J97v	10¢ Dull Gum .... (100)	39.50	4.75	.35	...
J98	30¢ Carmine Rose & Black ..... (100)	85.00	4.75	.85	.20
J98v	30¢ Dull Gum .... (100)	100.00	10.75	1.00	...
J99	50¢ Carmine Rose & Black ..... (100)	130.00	6.75	1.25	.20
J99v	50¢ Dull Gum .... (100)	160.00	17.00	1.50	...
J100	$1 Carmine Rose & Black .... (100)	275.00	12.00	2.50	.20
J100v	$1 Dull Gum .... (100)	325.00	22.50	3.00	...
J101	$5 Carmine Rose & Black	...	55.00	12.50	.35
J101v	$5 Dull Gum	...	90.00	15.00	...
J102	11¢ Carmine Rose & Blk. ('78) (100)	36.50	3.50	.35	.50
J103	13¢ Carmine Rose & Blk. ('78) (100)	37.50	2.75	.35	.50
J104	17¢ Carmine Rose & Blk. ('85) (100)	110.00	39.50	.60	.60

U.S. OFFICES IN CHINA

K1-16

K17-18

1919 U.S. Postal Agency in China
VF Used + 50% (B)

Scott's No.		Unused, NH VF	F-VF	Unused, OG VF	F-VF	Used F-VF
K1	2¢ on 1¢ Green (on #498)	53.50	33.50	27.00	18.00	25.00
K2	4¢ on 2¢ Rose (on #499)	53.50	33.50	27.00	18.00	25.00
K3	6¢ on 3¢ Violet (#502)	120.00	75.00	60.00	40.00	55.00
K4	8¢ on 4¢ Brown (#503)	130.00	80.00	65.00	42.50	55.00
K5	10¢ on 5¢ Blue (#504)	140.00	87.50	72.50	47.50	55.00
K6	12¢ on 6¢ Red Orange(#506)	200.00	120.00	100.00	65.00	85.00
K7	14¢ on 7¢ Black (#507)	200.00	120.00	100.00	65.00	95.00
K8	16¢ on 8¢ Olive Bister (#508)	150.00	95.00	75.00	50.00	60.00
K8a	16¢ on 8¢ Olive Green	145.00	90.00	72.50	47.50	55.00
K9	18¢ on 9¢ Salmon Red (#509)	150.00	95.00	75.00	50.00	65.00
K10	20¢ on 10¢ Or. Yellow (#510)	135.00	85.00	67.50	45.00	55.00
K11	24¢ on 12¢ Brn. Carm. (#512)	175.00	110.00	90.00	60.00	60.00
K11a	24¢ on 12¢ Claret Brown	240.00	150.00	120.00	80.00	95.00
K12	30¢ on 15¢ Gray (#514)	200.00	120.00	100.00	65.00	110.00
K13	40¢ on 20¢ Deep Ultra (#515)	300.00	190.00	150.00	100.00	175.00
K14	60¢ on 30¢ Or. Red (#516)	270.00	170.00	135.00	90.00	135.00
K15	$1 on 50¢ Lt. Violet (#517)	1300.00	775.00	650.00	425.00	475.00
K16	$2 on $1 Vlt. Brown (#518)	1000.00	600.00	500.00	325.00	400.00
	1922 Surcharged in Shanghai, China					
K17	2¢ on 1¢ Green (#498)	290.00	175.00	145.00	95.00	100.00
K18	4¢ on 2¢ Carmine (#528B)	240.00	150.00	120.00	80.00	85.00

OFFICIAL DEPARTMENTAL STAMPS

O1-9,O94-5

O15-24,O96-103

O25-34,O106-7

O35-45

1873 Continental Bank Note Co. - Thin Hard Paper
(NH + 150%, VF OG & Used + 70%, VF NH + 250%) (C)

DESIGNS: Busts are same as 1873 Regulars with exception of Post Office Dept.

Scott's No.		Unused,OG Fine	Ave.	Used Fine	Ave.
	AGRICULTURE DEPARTMENT				
O1	1¢ Franklin, Yellow	135.00	85.00	120.00	72.50
O2	2¢ Jackson	110.00	65.00	52.50	32.50
O3	3¢ Washington	95.00	55.00	10.00	6.00
O4	6¢ Lincoln	110.00	65.00	40.00	24.00
O5	10¢ Jefferson	225.00	135.00	135.00	80.00
O6	12¢ Clay	300.00	180.00	180.00	110.00
O7	15¢ Webster	250.00	150.00	165.00	100.00
O8	24¢ Scott	250.00	150.00	150.00	90.00
O9	30¢ Hamilton	300.00	180.00	190.00	115.00
	EXECUTIVE DEPARTMENT				
O10	1¢ Franklin, Carmine	500.00	300.00	325.00	195.00
O11	2¢ Jackson	350.00	210.00	160.00	100.00
O12	3¢ Washington	375.00	225.00	135.00	80.00
O13	6¢ Lincoln	575.00	350.00	375.00	225.00
O14	10¢ Jefferson	550.00	325.00	425.00	260.00
	INTERIOR DEPARTMENT				
O15	1¢ Franklin, Vermilion	32.50	19.50	6.50	4.00
O16	2¢ Jackson	27.50	16.50	7.75	4.75
O17	3¢ Washington	40.00	24.00	4.25	2.50
O18	6¢ Lincoln	32.50	19.50	5.75	3.50
O19	10¢ Jefferson	32.50	19.50	12.50	7.50
O20	12¢ Clay	42.50	26.50	6.75	4.00
O21	15¢ Webster	75.00	45.00	13.75	8.25
O22	24¢ Scott	57.50	35.00	11.75	7.00
O23	30¢ Hamilton	75.00	45.00	11.75	7.00
O24	90¢ Perry	160.00	95.00	30.00	18.00

UNUSED STAMPS WITHOUT GUM

Scott No.	Without Gum Fine	Ave.	Scott No.	Without Gum Fine	Ave.	Scott No.	Without Gum Fine	Ave.
O1	95.00	60.00	O9	210.00	125.00	O17	28.00	17.00
O2	75.00	45.00	O10	350.00	210.00	O18	22.50	13.75
O3	65.00	38.50	O11	250.00	150.00	O19	22.50	13.75
O4	75.00	45.00	O12	270.00	160.00	O20	29.50	18.75
O5	160.00	100.00	O13	415.00	250.00	O21	52.50	32.50
O6	210.00	125.00	O14	385.00	225.00	O22	40.00	24.00
O7	175.00	110.00	O15	22.50	13.75	O23	52.50	32.50
O8	175.00	110.00	O16	19.50	11.50	O24	110.00	65.00

	JUSTICE DEPARTMENT				
O25	1¢ Franklin, Purple	100.00	60.00	70.00	42.50
O26	2¢ Jackson	165.00	100.00	70.00	42.50
O27	3¢ Washington	165.00	100.00	18.75	11.00
O28	6¢ Lincoln	150.00	90.00	28.50	17.00
O29	10¢ Jefferson	175.00	105.00	57.50	35.00

OFFICIAL DEPARTMENTAL STAMPS (continued)

1873 Continental Bank Note Co. - Thin Hard Paper
(NH + 150%, VF OG & Used + 70%, VF NH + 250%) (C)

Scott's No.		Unused,OG Fine	Ave.	Used Fine	Ave.
	JUSTICE DEPARTMENT				
O30	12¢ Clay	140.00	85.00	45.00	27.50
O31	15¢ Webster	275.00	165.00	125.00	75.00
O32	24¢ Scott	675.00	400.00	275.00	165.00
O33	30¢Hamilton	675.00	400.00	210.00	125.00
O34	90¢ Perry	1000.00	600.00	400.00	240.00
	NAVY DEPARTMENT				
O35	1¢ Franklin, Ultramarine	65.00	40.00	32.50	19.50
O36	2¢ Jackson	55.00	32.50	15.00	9.00
O37	3¢ Washington	90.00	55.00	8.75	5.25
O38	6¢ Lincoln	50.00	30.00	13.75	8.75
O39	7¢ Stanton	350.00	210.00	150.00	90.00
O40	10¢ Jefferson	70.00	42.50	27.50	16.50
O41	12¢ Clay	85.00	50.00	27.50	16.50
O42	15¢ Webster	150.00	90.00	45.00	27.50
O43	24¢ Scott	165.00	100.00	55.00	33.50
O44	30¢ Hamilton	120.00	75.00	30.00	18.00
O45	90¢ Perry	575.00	350.00	190.00	115.00

UNUSED STAMPS WITHOUT GUM

Scott No.	Without Gum Fine	Ave.	Scott No.	Without Gum Fine	Ave.	Scott No.	Without Gum Fine	Ave.
O25	70.00	42.50	O32	475.00	285.00	O39	250.00	150.00
O26	115.00	70.00	O33	475.00	285.00	O40	50.00	30.00
O27	115.00	70.00	O34	700.00	425.00	O41	60.00	36.50
O28	105.00	65.00	O35	45.00	28.00	O42	110.00	65.00
O29	125.00	75.00	O36	40.00	23.50	O43	115.00	70.00
O30	100.00	60.00	O37	63.50	38.50	O44	85.00	52.50
O31	195.00	115.00	O38	35.00	21.50	O45	415.00	250.00

O47-56,O108

O57-67

O68-71

O72-82, O109-13

O83-93, O114-20

	POST OFFICE DEPARTMENT				
O47	1¢ Numeral, Black	11.50	7.00	7.50	4.50
O48	2¢	15.00	9.00	5.75	3.50
O49	3¢	5.00	3.00	1.00	.60
O50	6¢	15.00	9.00	5.00	3.00
O51	10¢	62.50	37.50	35.00	21.50
O52	12¢	30.00	18.00	7.00	4.25
O53	15¢	42.50	26.00	11.50	7.00
O54	24¢	52.50	32.50	14.50	8.75
O55	30¢	57.50	35.00	14.50	8.75
O56	90¢	75.00	45.00	13.50	8.00
	STATE DEPARTMENT				
O57	1¢ Franklin, Green	110.00	65.00	45.00	27.50
O58	2¢ Jackson	175.00	110.00	67.50	40.00
O59	3¢ Washington	85.00	50.00	15.00	9.00
O60	6¢ Lincoln	75.00	45.00	18.75	11.00
O61	7¢ Stanton	140.00	85.00	40.00	24.00
O62	10¢ Jefferson	110.00	65.00	35.00	21.00
O63	12¢ Clay	170.00	100.00	85.00	50.00
O64	15¢ Webster	180.00	110.00	57.50	35.00
O65	24¢ Scott	350.00	210.00	150.00	90.00
O66	30¢ Hamilton	325.00	195.00	115.00	70.00
O67	90¢ Perry	650.00	400.00	230.00	140.00
O68	$2 Seward Green & Black	950.00	550.00	625.00	375.00
O69	$5 Green & Black	4750.00	2850.00	3250.00	1950.00
O70	$10 Green & Black	3500.00	2100.00	2750.00	1650.00
O71	$20 Green & Black	2750.00	1650.00	1950.00	1150.00
	TREASURY DEPARTMENT				
O72	1¢ Franklin, Brown	31.50	19.00	4.50	2.75
O73	2¢ Jackson	40.00	24.00	4.50	2.75
O74	3¢ Washington	37.50	22.50	1.25	.75
O75	6¢ Lincoln	37.50	22.50	2.50	1.50
O76	7¢ Stanton	75.00	45.00	22.50	13.50
O77	10¢ Jefferson	75.00	45.00	7.00	4.25
O78	12¢ Clay	67.50	40.00	5.00	3.00
O79	15¢ Webster	70.00	42.50	7.00	4.25
O80	24¢ Scott	375.00	225.00	57.50	35.00
O81	30¢ Hamilton	150.00	90.00	7.75	4.65
O82	90¢ Perry	150.00	90.00	8.50	5.00

UNUSED STAMPS WITHOUT GUM

Scott No.	Without Gum Fine	Ave.	Scott No.	Without Gum Fine	Ave.	Scott No.	Without Gum Fine	Ave.
O47	8.00	5.00	O58	125.00	75.00	O72	22.50	13.50
O48	10.75	6.50	O59	60.00	37.50	O73	27.50	16.50
O49	3.50	2.10	O60	55.00	33.50	O74	26.50	16.00
O50	10.75	6.50	O61	100.00	60.00	O75	26.50	16.00
O51	43.50	26.50	O62	75.00	45.00	O76	52.50	32.00
O52	21.50	13.00	O63	120.00	70.00	O77	52.50	32.00
O53	30.00	18.00	O64	125.00	75.00	O78	46.50	28.00
O54	37.50	22.50	O65	250.00	150.00	O79	50.00	30.00
O55	42.50	26.00	O66	225.00	135.00	O80	275.00	165.00
O56	52.50	32.50	O67	450.00	275.00	O81	110.00	65.00
O57	75.00	45.00	O68	650.00	400.00	O82	110.00	65.00

OFFICIAL DEPARTMENTAL STAMPS (continued)

1873 Continental Bank Note Co. - Thin Hard Paper
(NH + 150%, VF OG & Used + 70%, VF NH + 250%) (C)
WAR DEPARTMENT

Scott's No.		Unused,OG Fine	Ave.	Used Fine	Ave.
O83	1¢ Franklin, Rose	115.00	70.00	9.00	5.50
O84	2¢ Jackson	100.00	60.00	9.00	5.50
O85	3¢ Washington	110.00	65.00	3.00	1.80
O86	6¢ Lincoln	375.00	225.00	5.75	3.50
O87	7¢ Stanton	100.00	60.00	60.00	35.00
O88	10¢ Jefferson	37.50	22.50	13.50	8.25
O89	12¢ Clay	140.00	85.00	7.50	4.50
O90	15¢ Webster	35.00	21.00	9.50	5.50
O91	24¢ Scott	35.00	21.00	7.50	4.50
O92	30¢ Hamilton	37.50	22.50	7.00	4.25
O93	90¢ Perry	75.00	45.00	32.50	19.50

UNUSED STAMPS WITHOUT GUM

Scott No.	Without Gum Fine	Ave.	Scott No.	Without Gum Fine	Ave.	Scott No.	Without Gum Fine	Ave.
O83	80.00	50.00	O87	70.00	42.50	O91	25.00	15.00
O84	70.00	42.50	O88	27.50	16.50	O92	26.50	16.00
O85	75.00	45.00	O89	100.00	60.00	O93	52.50	32.50
O86	260.00	1605.00	O90	25.00	15.00			

1879 American Bank Note Co. - Soft Porous Paper
(NH + 150%, VF OG & Used + 70%, VF NH + 250%) (C)
AGRICULTURE DEPARTMENT

Scott's No.		Unused,OG Fine	Ave.	Used Fine	Ave.
O94	1¢ Franklin (Issued w/o gum)	3250.00	2000.00	...	...
O95	3¢ Washington, Yellow	300.00	180.00	57.50	35.00
	INTERIOR DEPARTMENT				
O96	1¢ Franklin, Vermilion	190.00	115.00	180.00	110.00
O97	2¢ Jackson	4.75	2.85	1.85	1.10
O98	3¢ Washington	4.50	2.70	1.15	.70
O99	6¢ Lincoln	7.50	4.50	5.00	3.00
O100	10¢ Jefferson	70.00	42.50	50.00	30.00
O101	12¢ Clay	140.00	85.00	80.00	47.50
O102	15¢ Webster	270.00	165.00	180.00	110.00
O103	24¢ Scott	3150.00	1850.00	...	...
	JUSTICE DEPARTMENT				
O106	3¢ Washington, Purple	85.00	50.00	57.50	35.00
O107	6¢ Lincoln	210.00	125.00	150.00	90.00
	POST OFFICE DEPARTMENT				
O108	3¢ Numeral, Black	15.00	9.00	5.00	3.00
	TREASURY DEPARTMENT				
O109	3¢ Washington, Brown	50.00	30.00	5.75	3.50
O110	6¢ Lincoln	75.00	45.00	30.00	18.00
O111	10¢ Jefferson	135.00	80.00	50.00	30.00
O112	30¢ Hamilton	1250.00	750.00	250.00	150.00
O113	90¢ Perry	1850.00	1150.00	250.00	150.00
	WAR DEPARTMENT				
O114	1¢ Franklin, Rose	3.50	2.10	3.00	1.80
O115	2¢ Jackson	5.50	3.25	2.75	1.65
O116	3¢ Washington	5.50	3.25	1.15	.70
O117	6¢ Lincoln	5.50	3.25	1.85	1.15
O118	10¢ Jefferson	35.00	21.50	30.00	18.00
O119	12¢ Clay	27.50	16.50	9.00	5.50
O120	30¢ Hamilton	90.00	55.00	60.00	37.50

OG = With original gum, has been or is hinged. NH = Never Hinged

UNUSED STAMPS WITHOUT GUM

Scott No.	Without Gum Fine	Ave.	Scott No.	Without Gum Fine	Ave.	Scott No.	Without Gum Fine	Ave.
O95	210.00	125.00	O106	60.00	36.50	O115	4.00	2.40
O96	135.00	80.00	O107	150.00	87.50	O116	4.00	2.40
O97	3.50	2.10	O108	10.75	6.50	O117	4.00	2.40
O98	3.50	2.10	O109	35.00	21.50	O118	25.00	15.00
O99	5.25	3.25	O110	52.50	32.50	O119	20.00	12.00
O100	50.00	30.00	O111	95.00	55.00	O120	65.00	40.00
O101	100.00	60.00	O112	875.00	525.00			
O102	190.00	115.00	O114	2.50	1.50			

OFFICIAL POSTAL SAVINGS

O121, 25   O124   O126

1910-11 Double-line Watermark VF Used + 50% (B)

Scott's No.		Unused, NH VF	F-VF	Unused,OG VF	F-VF	Used F-VF
O121	2¢ Black	35.00	21.50	17.50	11.75	1.35
O121	Plate Block of 6	700.00	450.00	375.00	250.00	...
O122	50¢ Dark Green (1911)	325.00	200.00	165.00	110.00	37.50
O123	$1 Ultramarine (1911)	300.00	180.00	150.00	100.00	9.75

1911 Single-line Watermark VF Used + 50% (B)

Scott's No.		Unused, NH VF	F-VF	Unused,OG VF	F-VF	Used F-VF
O124	1¢ Dark Violet	17.50	11.00	9.00	6.00	1.15
O124	Plate Block of 6	400.00	250.00	210.00	140.00	...
O125	2¢ Black	110.00	70.00	56.50	37.50	4.50
O126	10¢ Carmine	37.50	25.00	20.00	13.75	2.00
O126	Plate Block of 6	800.00	525.00	435.00	285.00	...

MODERN OFFICIAL ISSUES

O127-32   O133   O135-36   O138   O139

| O138A | 0138B,41,45 | 0140 | 0143 | 0144 |

| 0146-51 | 0152 | 0153,57-59 | 0154-55 | 0156 |

1983-85 Official Stamps

Scott's No.		Mint Sheet	Pl# Blk. F-VF NH	F-VF NH	F-VF Used
O127-33	Set of 7	...	...	17.75	...
O127	1¢ Eagle (100)	10.00	.80	.20	.20
O128	4¢ Eagle (100)	15.00	.80	.20	.25
O129	13¢ Eagle (100)	45.00	2.25	.45	.70
O129A	14¢ Eagle (No Pl.#) (1985) (100)	45.00	...	.45	.50
O130	17¢ Eagle (100)	55.00	2.95	.55	.45
O132	$1 Eagle($1.00) (100)	295.00	13.50	3.00	1.00
O133	$5 Eagle	...	60.00	13.75	8.75
O135	20¢ Eagle Coil (with ¢ sign) (Pl.# Strip)	90.00(5)	15.00(3)	1.40	1.80
O136	22¢ Eagle Coil (No Plate #) (1985)			1.30	1.75
O138	(14¢) "D" Postcard rate (1985) (100)	450.00	38.50	4.50	4.25

1985-88 Official Coil Stamps

Scott's No.		Mint Sheet	Pl# Blk. F-VF NH	F-VF NH	F-VF Used
O138A-B,O139-41	Set of 5	...	...	7.50	...
O138A	15¢ Eagle (1988)	...	...	.55	.55
O138B	20¢ Eagle (No ¢ sign) (1988)	...	...	.65	.60
O139	(22¢) "D" Eagle (1985) (Pl.# Strip)	90.00(5)	47.50(3)	4.50	2.75
O140	(25¢) "E" Eagle (1988)	...	...	1.25	1.85
O141	25¢ Eagle (1988)	...	...	.90	.50

1989-1993 Official Stamps

Scott's No.		Mint Sheet	Pl# Blk. F-VF NH	F-VF NH	F-VF Used
O143	1¢ Offset (No ¢ sign) (100)	9.50	...	.20	.20
O144	(29¢) "F" Eagle Coil (1991)	...	...	1.60	.75
O145	29¢ Eagle Coil(1991)	...	...	1.15	.45
O146-51	Set of 5	...	...	5.25	...
O146	4¢ Make-up rate (1991) (100)	14.75	...	.20	.30
O146A	10¢ Eagle (1993) (100)	28.75	...	.30	.50
O147	19¢ Postcard rate (1991) (100)	52.50	...	.55	.55
O148	23¢ 2nd Ounce rate (1991) (100)	67.50	...	.70	.50
O151	$1 Eagle ($1)(1993) (100)	370.00	...	3.75	1.75

1994-2002 Official Stamps

Scott's No.		Mint Sheet	Pl# Blk. F-VF NH	F-VF NH	F-VF Used
O152	(32¢) "G" Eagle Coil	...	...	1.10	1.25
O153	32¢ Eagle Coil (1995)	...	...	2.50	.95
O154	1¢ "¢" Sign added,No "USA"('95)(100)	8.75	...	.20	.20
O155	20¢ Sheet Stamp (1995) (100)	52.50	...	.55	.50
O156	23¢ Reprint,Line above "23"('95)(100)	62.50	...	.65	.60
O157	33¢ Eagle Coil (1999)	...	...	1.10	.95
O158	34¢ Great Seal Coil (2001)	...	...	1.10	.75
O159	37¢ Great Seal Coil(2002) (Pl.# Strip)	6.50(5)	4.75(3)	1.00	.90

1945 POSTAL NOTE STAMPS

PN1-18 Examples

Scott's No.			F-VF NH	F-VF Used
PN1-18	set of 18	...	32.75	3.35
PN1	1¢ Black	2.50	.20	.20
PN2	2¢ Black	2.50	.20	.20
PN3	3¢ Black	2.75	.20	.20
PN4	4¢ Black	3.75	.25	.20
PN5	5¢ Black	4.25	.30	.20
PN6	6¢ Black	5.00	.35	.20
PN7	7¢ Black	7.00	.50	.20
PN8	8¢ Black	8.50	.60	.20
PN9	9¢ Black	9.00	.65	.20
PN10	10¢ Black	11.00	.75	.20
PN11	20¢ Black	21.50	1.50	.20
PN12	30¢ Black	28.50	2.00	.20
PN13	40¢ Black	35.00	2.50	.20
PN14	50¢ Black	47.50	3.25	.20
PN15	60¢ Black	60.00	4.25	.20
PN16	70¢ Black	72.50	5.00	.20
PN17	80¢ Black	75.00	5.50	.20
PN18	90¢ Black	90.00	6.25	.20

NEWSPAPER AND PERIODICAL STAMPS

1865 National Bank Note, Thin Hard Paper , Without Gum, Perf.12 Various Shades (VF+ 75%) (C)

Scott's No.		Unused Fine	Unused Ave.	Used Fine	Used Ave.
PR1	5¢ Blue, colored border	400.00	240.00	...	...
PR2	10¢ Green, colored border	170.00	110.00	...	...
PR3	25¢ Red, colored border	215.00	130.00	...	...
PR4	5¢ Blue, white border	115.00	70.00	...	...
	1875 Reprints, Hard White Paper, Without Gum, Perf.12 (VF+75%) (C)				
PR5	5¢ Blue, white border	100.00	60.00	...	...
PR6	10¢ Green, colored border	115.00	70.00	...	...
PR7	25¢ Carmine, colored border	150.00	90.00	...	...
	1881 American Bank Note,Soft Porous Paper,Without Gum, Pf.12 (VF+75%)(C)				
PR8	5¢ Dark blue, white border	300.00	180.00	...	...

PR9/91

PR11/92

PR102/114

PR108/120

1875 Continental, Thin Hard Paper, Perf. 12 (VF+75%) (C)

Scott's No.		Unused,OG Fine	Unused,OG Ave.	Used Fine	Used Ave.
PR9	2¢ Freedom, Black	57.50	35.00	20.00	12.00
PR10	3¢ Black	60.00	37.50	22.50	13.50
PR11	4¢ Black	60.00	37.50	20.00	12.00
PR12	6¢ Black	75.00	45.00	22.50	13.50
PR13	8¢ Black	95.00	55.00	32.50	19.50
PR14	9¢ Black	180.00	110.00	70.00	42.50
PR15	10¢ Black	110.00	65.00	25.00	15.00
PR16	12¢ Justice, Rose	250.00	150.00	65.00	40.00
PR17	24¢ Rose	285.00	175.00	80.00	50.00
PR18	36¢ Rose	350.00	210.00	85.00	52.50
PR19	48¢ Rose	575.00	350.00	140.00	85.00
PR20	60¢ Rose	425.00	250.00	80.00	50.00
PR21	72¢ Rose	700.00	425.00	180.00	110.00
PR22	84¢ Rose	900.00	550.00	275.00	165.00
PR23	96¢ Rose	750.00	450.00	175.00	105.00
PR24	$1.92 Ceres, Dark brown	850.00	500.00	235.00	140.00
PR25	$3 Victory, Vermilion	1100.00	675.00	250.00	150.00
PR26	$6 Clio, Ultramarine	1600.00	1000.00	375.00	225.00
PR27	$9 Minerva, Yellow orange	2100.00	1275.00	400.00	240.00
PR28	$12 Vesta, Blue green	2750.00	1650.00	525.00	315.00
PR29	$24 Peace, Dark gray violet	2875.00	1750.00	550.00	335.00
PR30	$36 Commerce, Brown rose	3000.00	1800.00	700.00	425.00
PR31	$48 Hebe, Red brown	3500.00	2100.00	775.00	475.00
PR32	$60 Indian Maiden, Violet	4000.00	2400.00	875.00	525.00

UNUSED STAMPS WITHOUT GUM

Scott No.	Without Gum Fine	Without Gum Ave.	Scott No.	Without Gum Fine	Without Gum Ave.	Scott No.	Without Gum Fine	Without Gum Ave.
PR9	40.00	24.00	PR13	65.00	40.00	PR17	200.00	120.00
PR10	42.50	26.50	PR14	130.00	80.00	PR18	250.00	150.00
PR11	42.50	26.50	PR15	75.00	45.00	PR19	400.00	240.00
PR12	52.50	31.50	PR16	175.00	110.00	PR20	260.00	160.00

1875 Special Printing , Hard White Paper, Without Gum (VF+75%) (C)

Scott's No.		Unused Fine	Unused Ave.	Used Fine	Used Ave.
PR33	2¢ Freedom, Gray black	375.00	225.00	...	...
PR34	3¢ Gray black	400.00	240.00	...	...
PR35	4¢ Gray black	450.00	275.00	...	...
PR36	6¢ Gray black	500.00	300.00	...	...
PR37	8¢ Gray black	575.00	350.00	...	...
PR38	9¢ Gray black	650.00	395.00	...	...
PR39	10¢ Gray black	800.00	650.00	...	...
PR40	12¢ Justice, Pale rose	950.00	575.00	...	...
PR41	24¢ Pale rose	1350.00	800.00	...	...
PR42	36¢ Pale rose	1650.00	1000.00	...	...
PR43	48¢ Pale rose	2150.00	1275.00	...	...
PR44	60¢ Pale rose	2500.00	1500.00	...	...
PR45	72¢ Pale rose	2900.00	1750.00	...	...
PR46	84¢ Pale rose	3000.00	1800.00	...	...
PR47	96¢ Pale rose	5000.00	3000.00	...	...
PR48	$1.92 Ceres, Dark brown	...	...	...	...
PR49	$3 Victory, Vermilion	...	...	...	...
PR50	$6 Clio, Ultramarine	...	...	...	...
PR51	$9 Minerva, Yellow orange	...	...	...	...
PR52	$12 Vesta, Blue green	...	...	...	...
PR53	$24 Peace, Dark gray violet	...	...	...	...
PR54	$36 Commerce, Brown rose	...	...	...	...
PR55	$48 Hebe, Red brown	...	...	...	...
PR56	$60 Indian Maiden, Violet	...	...	...	...

1879 American Bank Note, Soft Porous Paper, Perf.12 (VF+75%) (C)

Scott's No.		Unused,OG Fine	Unused,OG Ave.	Used Fine	Used Ave.
PR57	2¢ Freedom, Black	27.50	16.50	5.00	3.00
PR58	3¢ Black	30.00	18.00	6.00	3.75
PR59	4¢ Black	30.00	18.00	6.00	3.75
PR60	6¢ Black	57.50	35.00	12.50	7.50
PR61	8¢ Black	57.50	35.00	12.50	7.50
PR62	10¢ Black	57.50	35.00	12.50	7.50
PR63	12¢ Justice, Red	290.00	175.00	50.00	30.00
PR64	24¢ Red	290.00	175.00	50.00	30.00

1879 American Bank Note, Soft Porous Paper, Perf.12 (VF+75%) (C)

Scott's No.		Unused,OG Fine	Unused,OG Ave.	Used Fine	Used Ave.
PR65	36¢ Red	575.00	350.00	140.00	85.00
PR66	48¢ Red	525.00	315.00	110.00	65.00
PR67	60¢ Red	450.00	270.00	90.00	55.00
PR68	72¢ Red	800.00	475.00	180.00	110.00
PR69	84¢ Red	800.00	475.00	135.00	80.00
PR70	96¢ Red	650.00	395.00	95.00	57.50
PR71	$1.92 Ceres, Pale brown	350.00	210.00	80.00	47.50
PR72	$3 Victory, Red vermilion	375.00	225.00	90.00	55.00
PR73	$6 Clio, Blue	750.00	450.00	140.00	85.00
PR74	$9 Minerva, Orange	500.00	300.00	95.00	57.50
PR75	$12 Vesta, Yellow green	575.00	350.00	120.00	75.00
PR76	$24 Peace, Dark violet	600.00	365.00	150.00	90.00
PR77	$36 Commerce, Indian red	650.00	390.00	165.00	100.00
PR78	$48 Hebe, Yellow brown	675.00	400.00	225.00	135.00
PR79	$60 Indian Maiden, Purple	650.0	390.00	210.00	125.00

UNUSED STAMPS WITHOUT GUM

Scott No.	Without Gum Fine	Without Gum Ave.	Scott No.	Without Gum Fine	Without Gum Ave.	Scott No.	Without Gum Fine	Without Gum Ave.
PR57	20.00	12.00	PR65	400.00	240.00	PR73	550.00	325.00
PR58	21.50	13.00	PR66	365.00	215.00	PR74	350.00	210.00
PR59	21.50	13.00	PR67	325.00	195.00	PR75	400.00	240.00
PR60	40.00	24.00	PR68	565.00	350.00	PR76	425.00	260.00
PR61	40.00	24.00	PR69	565.00	350.00	PR77	450.00	270.00
PR62	40.00	24.00	PR70	450.00	270.00	PR78	475.00	285.00
PR63	210.00	125.00	PR71	250.00	150.00	PR79	450.00	270.00
PR64	210.00	125.00	PR72	275.00	165.00			

1883 American Bank Note Special Printing of 1879 Issue (VF+75%) (C)

Scott's No.		Unused,OG Fine	Unused,OG Ave.	Used Fine	Used Ave.
PR80	2¢ Freedom, Intense black	800.00	475.00	...	...
	1885 American Bank Note, Soft Porous Paper, Perf. 12 (VF + 75%) (C)				
PR81	1¢ Freedom, Black	35.00	21.00	6.00	3.75
PR82	12¢ Justice, Carmine	100.00	60.00	14.00	8.50
PR83	24¢ Carmine	100.00	60.00	15.00	9.00
PR84	36¢ Carmine	135.00	80.00	25.00	15.00
PR85	48¢ Carmine	190.00	110.00	37.50	22.50
PR86	60¢ Carmine	250.00	150.00	55.00	32.50
PR87	72¢ Carmine	250.00	150.00	57.50	35.00
PR88	84¢ Carmine	500.00	300.00	140.00	85.00
PR89	96¢ Carmine	425.00	260.00	110.00	65.00
	1894 Bureau Issue, Soft Wover Paper, Perforated 12 (VF+75%) (C)				
PR90	1¢ Freedom, Intense black	210.00	125.00	500.00	300.00
PR91	2¢ Intense black	225.00	135.00	...	...
PR92	4¢ Intense black	275.00	165.00	...	...
PR93	6¢ Intense black	3250.00	1950.00	...	...
PR94	10¢ Intense black	600.00	365.00	...	...
PR95	12¢ Justice, Pink	1500.00	900.00	1250.00	750.00
PR96	24¢ Pink	1950.00	1150.00	1400.00	850.00
PR97	36¢ Pink	...	...	...	...
PR98	60¢ Pink	...	...	...	...
PR99	96¢ Pink	...	...	...	...
PR100	$3 Victory, Scarlet	...	...	...	...
PR101	$6 Clio, Pale blue	...	...	...	...

UNUSED STAMPS WITHOUT GUM

Scott No.	Without Gum Fine	Without Gum Ave.	Scott No.	Without Gum Fine	Without Gum Ave.	Scott No.	Without Gum Fine	Without Gum Ave.
PR81	25.00	15.00	PR86	175.00	110.00	PR91	160.00	95.00
PR82	70.00	42.50	PR87	175.00	110.00	PR92	200.00	120.00
PR83	70.00	42.50	PR88	350.00	210.00	PR94	425.00	260.00
PR84	95.00	55.00	PR89	300.00	180.00			
PR85	130.00	80.00	PR90	150.00	90.00			

1895 New Designs, Unwatermarked, Perf.12 (VF + 75%, NH +100%)

Scott's No.		Unused,OG Fine	Unused,OG Ave.	Used Fine	Used Ave.
PR102	1¢ Freedom, Black	100.00	60.00	16.00	10.00
PR103	2¢ Black	100.00	60.00	16.00	10.00
PR104	5¢ Black	150.00	90.00	27.50	16.50
PR105	10¢ Black	300.00	180.00	60.00	36.50
PR106	25¢ Justice, Carmine	425.00	260.00	70.00	42.50
PR107	50¢ Carmine	950.00	575.00	160.00	95.00
PR108	$2 Victory, Scarlet	1150.00	700.00	160.00	95.00
PR109	$5 Clio, Ultramarine	1350.00	800.00	240.00	140.00
PR110	$10 Vesta, Green	1700.00	1000.00	265.00	160.00
PR111	$20 Peace, Slate	1850.00	1100.00	475.00	285.00
PR112	$50 Commerce, Dull rose	1850.00	1100.00	400.00	240.00
PR113	$100 Indian Maiden, Purple	2250.00	1350.00	575.00	350.00
	1895-97 Double-line Watermark, Perf.12 (VF + 75%, NH + 100%)				
PR114	1¢ Freedom, Black	5.00	3.00	5.75	3.50
PR115	2¢ Black	5.00	3.00	5.75	3.50
PR116	5¢ Black	7.50	4.50	7.50	4.50
PR117	10¢ Black	5.75	3.50	5.75	3.50
PR118	25¢ Justice, Carmine	9.50	5.75	13.50	8.00
PR119	50¢ Carmine	11.75	7.00	15.00	9.00
PR120	$2 Victory, Scarlet	15.00	9.00	25.00	15.00
PR121	$5 Clio, Dark blue	27.50	16.50	35.00	21.00
PR122	$10 Vesta, Green	27.50	16.50	35.00	21.00
PR123	$20 Peace, Slate	29.50	17.75	40.00	24.00
PR124	$50 Commerce, Dull rose	37.50	22.50	47.50	28.50
PR125	$100 Indian Maiden, Purple	42.50	25.00	60.00	36.50

UNUSED STAMPS WITHOUT GUM

Scott No.	Without Gum Fine	Without Gum Ave.	Scott No.	Without Gum Fine	Without Gum Ave.	Scott No.	Without Gum Fine	Without Gum Ave.
PR102	70.00	42.50	PR114	3.50	2.10	PR120	11.00	6.50
PR103	70.00	42.50	PR115	3.50	2.10	PR121	20.00	12.00
PR104	110.00	65.00	PR116	5.25	3.25	PR122	20.00	12.00
PR105	210.00	125.00	PR117	4.00	2.40	PR123	22.00	13.50
PR106	275.00	165.00	PR118	6.75	4.25	PR124	27.50	16.50
PR107	650.00	400.00	PR119	8.25	5.00	PR125	30.00	18.00

1913 PARCEL POST STAMPS, Carmine Rose VF Used + 50% (B)

Q1 Q2 Q3
Q4 Q5 Q6
Q7 Q8 Q9
Q10 Q11 Q12

Scott's No.		Unused, NH VF	F-VF	Unused,OG VF	F-VF	Used F-VF
Q1-12	Parcel Post Set of 12	2800.00	1800.00	1325.00	865.00	145.00
Q1	1¢ Post Office Clerk	13.50	8.50	6.75	4.50	1.35
Q1	Plate Block of 6	200.00	135.00	120.00	80.00	...
Q2	2¢ City Carrier	17.00	10.50	8.25	5.50	1.00
Q2	Plate Block of 6	250.00	165.00	150.00	100.00	...
Q3	3¢ Railway Postal Clerk	30.00	19.00	15.00	10.00	5.00
Q3	Plate Block of 6	450.00	300.00	275.00	185.00	...
Q4	4¢ Rural Carrier	87.50	55.00	42.50	28.50	2.75
Q4	Plate Block of 6	1950.00	1250.00	1150.00	750.00	...
Q5	5¢ Mail Train	77.50	50.00	37.50	25.00	2.00
Q5	Plate Block of 6	1850.00	1200.00	1100.00	725.00	...
Q6	10¢ Steamship & Tender	125.00	80.00	60.00	40.00	2.50
Q6	Plate Block of 6	1950.00	1250.00	1150.00	750.00	...
Q7	15¢ Automobile Service	170.00	110.00	82.50	55.00	10.75
Q8	20¢ Airplane Carrying Mail ...	335.00	220.00	165.00	110.00	22.50
Q9	25¢ Manufacturing	160.00	100.00	75.00	50.00	6.00
Q10	50¢ Dairying	800.00	525.00	375.00	250.00	35.00
Q11	75¢ Harvesting	240.00	150.00	115.00	75.00	28.75
Q12	$1 Fruit Growing	850.00	550.00	415.00	275.00	31.75

JQ1-5 QE1-4

1912 PARCEL POST DUE VF + 50% (B)

JQ1-5	Parcel Post Due Set of 5	915.00	585.00	435.00	290.00	72.50
JQ1	1¢ Dark Green	27.50	17.50	13.50	8.75	4.00
JQ1	Plate Block of 6	1100.00	700.00	650.00	425.00	...
JQ2	2¢ Dark Green	210.00	130.00	100.00	65.00	15.00
JQ3	5¢ Dark Green	37.50	24.00	18.00	12.00	4.50
JQ3	Plate Block of 6	1150.00	750.00	675.00	450.00	...
JQ4	10¢ Dark Green	425.00	275.00	210.00	140.00	47.50
JQ5	25¢ Dark Green	250.00	165.00	120.00	80.00	8.00

1925-1955 SPECIAL HANDLING STAMPS VF + 30% (B)

QE1-4	Special Handling Set of 4	46.75	34.50	28.50	21.50	8.50
QE1	10¢ Yellow Green, Dry (1955) ...	2.65	2.00	1.65	1.25	1.00
QE1	Plate Block of 6	49.50	37.50	32.50	25.00	...
QE1a	10¢ Wet Printing (1928)	5.35	4.00	3.25	2.50	1.10
QE1a	Plate Block of 6	37.50	29.50	25.00	19.50	...
QE2	15¢ Yellow Green, Dry (1955) ...	3.25	2.40	1.95	1.50	1.00
QE2	Plate Block of 6	65.00	55.00	43.50	32.50	...
QE2a	15¢ Wet Printing (1928)	6.00	4.35	3.65	2.75	1.10
QE2a	Plate Block of 6	55.00	40.00	32.50	25.00	...
QE3	20¢ Yellow Green, Dry (1955) ...	5.00	3.60	2.95	2.25	1.50
QE3	Plate Block of 6	75.00	55.00	45.00	35.00	...
QE3a	20¢ Wet Printing (1928)	7.50	5.50	4.50	3.50	1.75
QE3a	Plate Block of 6	70.00	52.50	42.50	32.50	...
QE4	25¢ Yellow Green (1929)	37.50	27.50	23.00	17.50	7.50
QE4	Plate Block of 6	435.00	325.00	275.00	210.00	...
QE4a	25¢ Deep Green (1925)	52.50	40.00	32.50	25.00	5.50
QE4a	Plate Block of 6	525.00	390.00	325.00	250.00	...

Used sets of #QE1-4 usually contain #QE4a.

U.S. AUTOPOST ISSUES
Computer Vended Postage

Washington, DC **Kensington, MD**

Washington, D.C., Machine 82
CVP1a	25¢ First Class, Ty. 1	
	$1.00 3rd Class, Ty. 1	
	$1.69 Parcel Post, Ty. 1	
	$2.40 Priority Mail, Ty. 1	
CVP5a	$8.75 Express Mail, Ty. 1	
	Set of 5	**95.00**

Kensington, MD, Machine 82
CVP11a	25¢ First Class, Ty. 1 CVP2a	
CVP12a	$1.00 3rd Class, Ty. 1CVP3a	
CVP13a	$1.69 Parcel Post, Ty. 2CVP4a	
CVP14a	$2.40 Priority Mail, Ty. 1	
CVP15a	$8.75 Express Mail, Ty. 1	
	Set of 5	**77.50**

Washington, D.C., Machine 83
CVP6a	25¢ First Class, Ty. 1	
CVP7a	$1.00 3rd Class, Ty. 1	
CVP8a	$1.69 Parcel Post, Ty. 2	
CVP9a	$2.40 Priority Mail, Ty. 1	
CVP10a	$8.75 Express Mail, Ty. 1	
	Set of 5	**77.50**

Kensington, MD, Machine 83
CVP16a	25¢ First Class, Ty. 1	
CVP17a	$1.00 3rd Class, Ty. 1	
CVP18a	$1.69 Parcel Post, Ty. 2	
CVP19a	$2.40 Priority Mail, Ty. 1	
CVP20a	$8.75 Express Mail, Ty. 1	
	Set of 5	**77.50**

CVP31,31a,31b,31c CVP32, CV33

1992-2002 Variable Rate Coils (Computer Vending)

Scott's No.		Pl# Strip of 5	Pl# Strip of 3	F-VF NH	F-VF Used
CVP31	29¢ Shield, Pf.10 Horiz., Dull Gum	15.75	12.50	1.65	.50
CVP31a	29¢ Shield, Shiny Gum	15.75	12.50	1.65	...
CVP31b	32¢ Shield, Dull Gum (1994)	16.50	13.00	1.50	.65
CVP31c	32¢ Shield, Shiny Gum (1995)	16.50	13.00	1.65	...
CVP32	29¢ Shield, Perf. 9.9 Vert. (1994)	15.00	12.50	1.50	.60
CVP33	32¢ Shield, Perf. 9.9 Vert. (1996)	15.00	12.50	1.50	.60
CVP33v	37¢ Shield, Perf.9.9 Vert.(2002)	12.50	10.00	1.25	...

NOTE: VARIABLE RATE COILS COME IN A NUMBER DIFFERENT DENOMINATIONS BUT THE FIRST CLASS RATE OF 29¢ AND 32¢ ARE THE ONLY RATES REGULARLY AVAILABLE.

U.S. TEST COILS

T11 etc. T31etc. T41 etc. SV1

Scott's No.		Line Pair	Pair	F-VF NH

BUREAU OF ENGRAVING & PRINTING TEST COILS

Blank Coils
T11	Imperforate	...	57.50	27.50
T15	Perforated 10, shiny Gum	...	1.30	.65
T17	Perforated 11	...	9.00	4.50
T18	Perf. 10, Tagged, dull Gum (1980)	65.00	11.50	5.75
T21	Perf. 10, Two Horiz. Red Lines	...	14.00	7.00

1938-60 Solid Design Coil
T31	Purple	30.00	11.00	5.50
T32	Carmine (1954)	...	...	...
T33	Red Violet, Small Holes (1960)	30.00	6.00	3.00
T33l	Red Violet, Large Holes	...	25.00	12.50

1962-98 "FOR TESTING PURPOSES ONLY"
T41	Black, untagged, shiny gum	11.75	2.70	1.35
T41a	Black, tagged, shiny gum	6.00	2.00	1.00
T41b	Black, tagged, pebble-surfaced gum	25.00	3.50	1.75
T41d	Black, tagged, dull gum	45.00	11.50	5.75
T41e	Black, untagged, dull gum	8.75	2.20	1.10
T42	Carmine, tagged (1970)	...	...	...
T43	Green, tagged, pebble-surfaced gum	600.00	250.00	125.00
T43c	Green, untagged, dull gum	600.00	250.00	125.00
T44	Brown, untagged	37.50	5.50	2.75
T45	Orange, tagged	...	...	...
T46	Black, "B" Press, 19mm wide (1988)	...	1.70	.85
T47	Blue, untagged,shiny gum (1995) ...	...	500.00	250.00
T48	Gray black, untagged, dull gum	...	400.00	200.00
T48a	Black, on white paper,self-adhesive(1998) ...		1.40	.70
T48a	Same, Plate #V1, Strip of 5		12.95	...
T49	Black,on blue paper, self-adhesive (1996) ...		1.40	.70
T49	Same, Plate #1111, Strip of 5		12.95	...
T50	Same, Serpentine Die-cut 9.8 Vert.		1.90	.95
T50	Same, Plate #1111, Strip of 5		14.95	...

STAMP VENTURERS TEST COILS
SV1	Eagle, Perforated	...	2.20	1.10
SV2	Eagle, Rouletted	...	6.50	3.25

POSTAL SAVINGS, SAVINGS & WAR SAVINGS STAMPS

| PS1, 4, 6 | PS7-10 | PS11-14 | S1-5 | S7 |

1911-36 Postal Savings Stamps VF Used + 30% (B)

Scott's No.		Unused, NH VF	F-VF	Unused, OG VF	F-VF	Used F-VF
PS1	10¢ Orange	19.50	14.50	10.00	7.75	1.25
PS2	10¢ Orange Imprint on Deposit Card	...	200.00	160.00	37.50	
PS4	10¢ Blue,Single-line Wk.,Pf.12	9.50	6.50	5.50	4.00	1.10
PS4	Plate Block of 6	275.00	215.00	195.00	150.00	...
PS5	10¢ Blue Imprint on Deposit Card...	...	175.00	140.00		25.00
PS6	10¢ Blue, Unwmk., Perf.11(1936)	7.75	6.00	6.00	4.75	1.15
PS6	Plate Block of 6	160.00	125.00	110.00	85.00	...

1940 Postal Savings - Numerals VF Used +30% (B)

Scott's No.		Unused, NH VF	F-VF	Unused, OG VF	F-VF	Used F-VF
PS7	10¢ Deep Ultramarine	20.75	15.75	16.50	12.50	5.00
PS7	Plate Block of 6	300.00	225.00	230.00	175.00	...
PS8	25¢ Dark Carmine Rose	25.00	18.50	18.50	14.00	8.00
PS8	Plate Block of 6	325.00	250.00	240.00	180.00	...
PS9	50¢ Dark Blue Green	65.00	50.00	52.50	40.00	15.00
PS10	$1 Gray Black	195.00	150.00	145.00	110.00	15.00

1941 Postal Savings - Minute Man VF Used + 30% (B)

Scott's No.		Unused, NH VF	F-VF	Unused, OG VF	F-VF	Used F-VF
PS11	10¢ Rose Red	.80	.60	.60	.45	...
PS11	Plate Block of 4	9.75	7.50	7.25	5.50	...
PS11b	10¢ Booklet Pane of 10	57.50	45.00	43.50	35.00	...
PS12	25¢ Blue Green	2.25	1.75	1.70	1.40	...
PS12	Plate Block of 4	25.00	18.75	18.50	15.00	...
PS12b	25¢ Booklet Pane of 10	70.00	55.00	57.50	45.00	...
PS13	50¢ Ultramarine	8.50	6.50	6.50	5.00	...
PS13	Plate Block of 4	65.00	50.00	52.50	40.00	...
PS14	$1 Gray Black	14.50	11.00	10.75	8.25	...
PS14	Plate Block of 4	97.50	75.00	75.00	57.50	...
PS15	$5 Sepia, Size 36mm x 46mm	49.50	37.50	38.50	30.00	...
PS15	Plate Block of 5	550.00	425.00	415.00	325.00	...

1954-61 Savings Stamps - Minute Man VF + 25% (B)

Scott's No.		Plate Block	F-VF NH	F-VF Used
S1	10¢ Rose Red	3.00	.45	...
S1a	10¢ Booklet Pane of 10 (1955) ...	...	140.00	...
S2	25¢ Blue Green	32.50	6.75	...
S2a	25¢ Booklet Pane of 10 (1955) ...	...	775.00	...
S3	50¢ Ultramarine (1956)	47.50	8.00	...

1954-61 Savings Stamps - Minute Man VF + 25% (B)

Scott's No.		Plate Block	F-VF NH	F-VF Used
S4	$1 Gray Black (1957)	110.00	21.50	...
S5	$5 Sepia (1956)	650.00	85.00	...
S6	25¢ 48 Star Flag, Blue & Carmine (1958)	8.75	1.75	...
S6a	25¢ Booklet Pane of 10	...	67.50	...
S7	25¢ 50 Star Flag, Blue & Carmine (1961)	10.00	1.35	...
S7a	25¢ Booklet Pane of 10	...	275.00	...

| WS7-13 |

1917 War Savings Thrift Stamps VF Used + 40% (B)

Scott's No.		NH VF	F-VF	Unused, OG VF	F-VF	Used F-VF
WS1	25¢ Deep Green	33.50	22.50	20.75	14.50	2.00

1917-19 War Savings Certificate Stamps VF Used + 40% (B)

Scott's No.		NH VF	F-VF	Unused, OG VF	F-VF	Used F-VF
WS2	$5 Washington, Green,Pf.11	165.00	115.00	105.00	75.00	22.50
WS3	$5 Green, Rouletted 7	...	...	1400.00	1000.00	600.00
WS4	$5 Franklin, Deep Blue (1919)	600.00	425.00	375.00	270.00	140.00
WS5	$5 Washington,Carmine('19)	1500.00	1000.00	950.00	650.00	225.00
WS6	$5 Lincoln, Orange (1920)	..	..	..	..	1100.00

1942-45 War Savings Stamps VF Used + 25% (B)

Scott's No.		NH VF	F-VF	Unused, OG VF	F-VF	Used F-VF
WS7	10¢ Rose Red	.55	.45	.45	.35	.20
WS7	Plate Block of 4	5.75	4.75	4.50	3.75	...
WS7b	10¢ Booklet Pane of 10	60.00	47.50	45.00	35.00	...
WS8	25¢ Blue Green	1.25	1.00	1.00	.80	.30
WS8	Plate Block of 4	10.00	8.00	7.75	6.50	...
WS8b	25¢ Booklet Pane of 10	57.50	45.00	42.50	33.50	...
WS9	50¢ Deep Ultramarine	4.65	3.75	3.75	3.00	1.15
WS9	Plate Block of 4	26.50	21.50	19.75	16.50	...
WS10	$1 Gray Black	13.75	11.00	10.75	8.50	3.25
WS10	Plate Block of 4	80.00	65.00	65.00	52.50	...
WS11	$5 Violet Brown (1945)	62.50	50.00	50.00	40.00	16.50
WS11	Plate Block of 4	575.00	450.00	450.00	350.00	...

1943 War Savings Coil Stamps Perf.10 Vert. VF Used + 25% (B)

Scott's No.		NH VF	F-VF	Unused, OG VF	F-VF	Used F-VF
WS12	10¢ Rose Red	3.15	2.50	2.50	2.00	.80
WS12	Line Pair	13.00	9.50	9.25	7.50	...
WS13	25¢ Dark Blue Green	5.75	4.50	4.35	3.50	1.50
WS13	Line Pair	24.00	19.50	19.50	16.00	...

UNITED STATES POSTAL SERVICE MINT SETS
Commemoratives and Definitives

These are complete with folder or hard cover albums as produced by the U.S. Postal Service

Year	Scott's Nos.	# Stamps	Price
	Commemoratives		
1968 (1)	"Cover #334-890", #1339-40, 1342-64,C74	26	225.00
1968 (2)	"Cover #369-245", Contents same as (1)		165.00
1969	#1365-86,C76	23	150.00
1970	#1387-92,1405-22	24	225.00
1971 (1)	"Mini Album" #1396,1423-45	24	40.00
1971 (2)	Black strips, Contents same as (1)		150.00
1972	#1446-74,C84-85	31	25.00
1973	#1475-1504,1507-08,C86	33	20.00
1974	#1505-06,1525-51	29	15.00
1975	#1553-80	28	17.50
1976	#1629-32,1633/82 (1 single), 1683-85,1690-1702	21	32.50
1977	#1704-30	28	15.00
1978	#1731-33,44-56,58-69	28	17.50
1979	#1770-94,1799-1802,C97	30	18.50
1980	#1795-98,1803-04,21,23-43	28	23.50
1981	#1874-79,1910-26,28-45	41	30.00
1982	#1950,52,1953/2002 (1 single), 2003-04,06-24,26-30	29	26.50
1983	#2031-65,C101-12	47	50.00
1984	#2066-71,73-2109	43	45.00
1985	#2110,37-47,52-66	27	35.00
1986	#2167,2201a,2202-04,2209a, 2210-11,2216a-9i (1 single), 2220-24,35-45	25	27.50
1987	Soft Cover, #2246-51,2274a,75, 2286/2335 (1 single), 2336-38, 2349-54,59a,60-61,66a,67-6824		60.00
1987	Hard Cover, Same contents		120.00
1988	Soft Cover, #2339-46,69-80, 85a,86-93,95-99,2400,C117	37	60.00
1988	Hard Cover, Same contents		120.00
1989	#2347,2401-04,09a,10-14, 2416-18,20-28	22	75.00

Year	Scott's Nos.	# Stamps	Price
1990	#2348,2415,39-40,42,44-49,74a, 2496-2515	32	95.00
1991	#2532-35,37-38,49a,50-51,53-67, 2577a,78,80 or 81,82-85, C130-31	33	95.00
1992	Hard Cover, #2611-23,30-41,46a, 2647/96 (1 single), 2697-99, 2700-04,2709a,10-14	41	80.00
1993	Hard Cover, #2721-23,31-37,45a, 2746-59,64a,65-66,70a,78a,79-89, 2791-94,2804-05	47	95.00
1994	Hard Cover, #2807-12,2814-28, 2833a,34-36,38-40,2841a,2847a, 2848-69,71-72	52	95.00
1995	Hard Cover, #2587,2876,2948, 2950-58,61-68,73a,74-92,97a, 2999-3007,3019-23	55	90.00
1996	Hard Cover #3024-29,58-65,67-70 3072-88,90-3111,3118-19	59	110.00
1996	Soft Cover,#3024,3025-29(1),3058-60 ,61-64(1),65,67,68a-t(1),3069-70,72-76(1), 77-80(1),81-82, 3083-86(1),87-88,90, 91-95(1),3096-99(1),3100-3(1),3104, 3105a-o(1)3106-7, 3108-11(1),18, 19a-b(1)	29	70.00
1997	Hard Cover #3120-21, 23-27, 3130-31, 34-37, 39a, 40a 3141-46, 51-52, 54-77	47	90.00
1998	Hard Cover #3179-81, 92-3204, 3206 10a, 11-19, 21-27, 30-44, 3249-52	52	90.00
1999	Hard Cover #3272-76, 86-93 3306, 3308, 10-29, 37-51, 54, 3355(4), 3356-59	59	90.00

Year	Scott's Nos.	# Stamps	Price
2000	Hard Cover #3369-72,78-91, 3393-3402,3408,14-17,38-46	78	110.00
2001	Hard Cover #3500-19, 21-33, 3535a, 36-40,45-46	72	85.00
2002	Hard Cover #3552-60, 61/3610 (1) 3611, 49-56, 59-71, 75-79, 3692, 94	70	95.00
2003	Hard Cover #3657-58,3746,48,72-74, 3780b,81-83,86-91,3802-18, 3821-24	65	95.00
	Definitives & Stationery		
1980	#1738-42,1805-11,13,22,59,C98-100, U590,U597-99,UC53,UX82-86	27	60.00
1981	#1582b,1818,1819-20 PRS,57-58, 65,89a,90,91 PR,93a,94,95 PR, 96a,1903 PR,1906-08 PRS,1927, 46,47-48 PRS	22	47.50
1982	#1615v PR,1845,55,60,66,97A PR, 1698A PR,1901 PR,1904 PR,49a, 1951,2005 PR,2025,U591,U602-03, UC55,UX94-97,UXC20	22	22.50
1983	#1844,46-48,61,97 PR,98 PR,99 PR, 1900 PR,O127-29,O130,32,35 PR, U604-05,UC56-57,UO73,UX98-100, UXC21,UZ2	25	22.50
1984	#1853,62,64,68,1902 PR,1905 PR, 2072,U606,UX101-04	12	17.50
1987-88	#2115b,2127,29,30av,69,76-78,80, 2182,83,88,92,2226,52-66,C118-19, O138A-B,40-41	35	70.00
1989-90	#2127av,73,84,86,94A,2280v,2419, 2431 (6),43a,52,75a,76,O143,U611, U614-18,UC62,UO79-80,UX127-38, UX143-48, UX150-52	44	85.00

PLATE NUMBER COIL STRIPS

1897

2127

Scott No.	F-VF,NH	Pl.Strip of 5	Pl.Strip of 3
	1981		
1891	**18¢ Flag**		
	Pl# 1	350.00	85.00
	Pl# 2	65.00	21.50
	Pl# 3	875.00	225.00
	Pl# 4	10.75	6.50
	Pl# 5	7.25	6.00
	Pl# 6	...	...
	Pl# 7	42.50	32.50
1895	**20¢ Flag, Wide Block Tagging**		
	Pl# 1	100.00	6.50
	Pl# 2,11	10.75	6.00
	Pl# 3,5,13-14	6.00	4.25
1895a	20¢ Flag, Narrow Block Tagging		
	Pl# 4	750.00	32.50
	Pl# 6	225.00	80.00
	Pl# 8	16.00	5.00
	Pl# 9-10	6.00	4.25
	Pl# 12	10.75	6.00
1895b	20¢ Flag, Untagged		
	Pl# 14	95.00	90.00
	1981-91 Transportation Coils		
1897	**1¢ Omnibus**		
	Pl# 1,2,5,6	.70	.50
	Pl# 3,4	.95	.75
1897A	**2¢ Locomotive**		
	Pl# 2,3,4,6,8,10	.75	.55
1898	**3¢ Handcar**		
	Pl# 1-4	.95	.75
1898A	**4¢ Stagecoach**		
	Pl# 1,2,3,4	1.60	1.25
	Pl# 5,6	2.75	2.25
1898Ab	Pl# 3,4,5,6	8.25	7.50
1899	**5¢ Motorcycle**		
	Pl# 1-4	1.30	1.00
1900	**5.2¢ Sleigh**		
	Pl# 1,2	12.75	5.25
	Pl# 3	395.00	195.00
	P1#5	240.00	165.00
1900a	Pl# 1-3, 5	15.00	13.50
	P1#4,6	18.50	17.00
1901	**5.9¢ Bicycle**		
	Pl# 3,4	16.50	6.50
1901a	Pl# 3,4	50.00	47.50
	Pl# 5,6	125.00	100.00
1902	**7.4¢ Baby Buggy**		
	Pl# 2	14.50	7.00
1902a	Pl# 2	6.50	5.95
1903	**9.3¢ Mail Wagon**		
	Pl# 1,2	16.50	7.50
	Pl# 3,4	45.00	19.50
	Pl# 5,6	500.00	375.00
1903a	Pl# 1,2	13.00	12.00
	Pl# 3	45.00	40.00
	Pl# 4	22.50	17.50
	Pl# 5,6	4.00	3.25
	Pl# 8	350.00	325.00
1904	**10.9¢ Hansom Cab**		
	Pl# 1,2	42.50	13.50
1904a	Pl# 1,2	42.50	40.00
	Pl# 3,4	600.00	575.00
1905	**11¢ Caboose**		
	Pl# 1	5.00	3.75
1905b	Pl# 2, untagged	4.00	3.25
1905a	Pl# 1	5.25	4.25
1906	**17¢ Electric Car**		
	Pl# 1-5	3.00	2.25
	Pl# 6	18.75	17.50
	Pl# 7	7.75	7.00
1906a	Pl# 3A-5A	6.00	5.00
	Pl# 6A,7A	16.50	15.00
1906ab	Pl# 3B,5B,6B	42.50	39.50
	Pl# 4B	37.50	35.00
1906ac	Pl# 1C,2C,3C,4C	18.00	14.00
	Pl# 7C	43.50	40.00
1907	**18¢ Surrey**		
	Pl# 1	120.00	65.00
	Pl# 2,5,6,8	3.75	2.50
	Pl# 3,4	110.00	65.00
	Pl# 7	40.00	35.00
	Pl# 9-12	17.00	15.00
	Pl# 13-14,17-18	3.75	2.50
	Pl# 15-16	32.50	30.00

Scott No.	F-VF,NH	Pl.Strip of 5	Pl.Strip of 3
1908	**20¢ Fire Pumper**		
	Pl# 1	185.00	22.50
	Pl# 2	1175.00	180.00
	Pl# 3,4,13,15,16	5.25	4.25
	Pl# 5,9,10	3.75	2.75
	Pl# 6	50.00	30.00
	Pl# 7,8	195.00	60.00
	Pl# 11	115.00	22.50
	Pl# 12,14	8.50	7.50
	1982-1987		
2005	**20¢ Consumer**		
	Pl# 1,2	200.00	25.00
	Pl# 3,4	150.00	25.00
2112	**(22¢) "D" Eagle Coil**		
	Pl# 1,2	9.50	6.50
2115	**22¢ Flag/Capitol, Wide Block Tagging**		
	Pl# 2, 10, 15	4.50	3.50
	Pl# 4, 6, 16	8.50	7.50
	Pl# 13	15.00	9.00
	Pl# 14	42.50	40.00
2115a	22¢ Flag, Narrow Block Tagging		
	Pl# 1,7	15.00	9.00
	Pl# 3	75.00	13.00
	Pl# 5,11,17,18,20,21	8.50	7.50
	Pl# 8, 12, 19, 22	4.50	3.50
2115b	22¢ Flag Test Coil		
	Pl# T1	5.75	4.50
	1985-89 Transportation Coils		
2123	**3.4¢ School Bus**		
	Pl# 1,2	1.70	1.30
2123a	Pl# 1,2	5.50	4.75
2124	**4.9¢ Buckboard**		
	Pl# 3,4	1.50	1.10
2124a	Pl# 1-6	2.25	1.75
2125	**5.5¢ Star Route Truck**		
	Pl# 1	2.65	2.10
2125a	Pl# 1,2	2.95	2.50
2126	**6¢ Tricycle**		
	Pl# 1	2.25	1.85
2126a	Pl# 1	2.65	2.15
	Pl# 2	9.75	9.00
2127	**7.1¢ Tractor**		
	Pl# 1	2.95	2.50
2127a	Pl# 1	4.50	3.75
2127b	Zip + 4		
	Pl# 1	3.25	2.50
2128	**8.3¢ Ambulance**		
	Pl# 1,2	2.50	1.85
2128a	Pl# 1,2	2.50	1.85
	Pl# 3,4	6.50	5.50
2129	**8.5¢ Tow Truck**		
	Pl# 1	4.25	3.50
2129a	Pl# 1	4.25	3.50
	Pl# 2	13.50	12.50
2130	**10.1¢ Oil Wagon**		
	Pl# 1	3.25	2.65
2130a	Pl# 2,3 **Red Prec.**	3.35	2.50
2130av	Pl# 1,2 **Black Prec.**	3.35	2.75
2131	**11¢ Stutz Bearcat**		
	Pl# 1-4	2.60	2.00
2132	**12¢ Stanley Steamer**		
	Pl# 1,2	3.75	2.75
2132a	Pl# 1,2	4.00	3.00
2132b	12¢ "B" Press, Prec.		
	Pl# 1	30.00	26.50
2133	**12.5¢ Pushcart**		
	Pl# 1	4.00	3.25
	P1#2	6.25	5.75
2133a	Pl# 1, 2	4.25	3.50
2134	**14¢ Iceboat**		
	Pl# 1-4	2.85	2.25
2134b	"B" Press		
	Pl# 2	6.00	5.00
2135	**17¢ Dog Sled**		
	Pl# 2	5.50	4.25
2136	**25¢ Bread Wagon**		
	Pl# 1-5	5.75	4.25
	1985		
2149	**18¢ GW Monument**		
	Pl# 1112,3333	4.65	3.25
2149a	Pl# 11121	8.25	7.50
	Pl# 33333	4.50	3.50
2149d	Pl# 33333 Dry Gum	7.50	6.00
	Pl# 43444 Dry Gum	8.25	7.50

Scott No.	F-VF,NH	Pl.Strip of 5	Pl.Strip of 3
2150	**21.1¢ Pre-Sort**		
	Pl# 111111	4.75	3.50
	Pl# 111121	6.50	5.25
2150a	Pl# 111111	5.00	4.00
	Pl# 111121	6.25	5.00
	1986-96 Transportation Coils		
2225	**1¢ Omnibus "B" Press**		
	Pl# 1,2	1.00	.70
2225a	Pl# 3 mottled tagging	18.50	17.50
2225b	Pl# 2,3 untagged, Dull	1.20	.80
2225s	Pl# 3 Shiny, untagged	1.40	1.00
2225l	Pl# 3 Low gloss,untag.	2.75	2.00
2226	**2¢ Locomotive "B" Press**		
	Pl# 1 Tagged, Dull	1.00	.75
2226a	Pl# 2 untagged, Dull	1.25	.85
2226s	P1# 2, untagged,Shiny	2.50	2.00
2228	**4¢ Stagecoach "B"**		
	Pl# 1, block tagging	1.65	1.30
2228a	Pl# 1, overall tagging	14.00	12.75
2231	**8.3¢ Ambul."B" Press,Precancel**		
	Pl# 1	11.50	8.50
	Pl# 2	13.50	9.75
	1987-94 Transportation Coils		
2252	**3¢ Conestoga Wagon**		
	Pl# 1	1.40	1.10
2252a	Pl# 2,3 untagged, Dull	1.65	1.35
2252s	Pl# 3 untagged, Shiny	1.85	1.50
	Pl# 5,6 untagged,Shiny	3.00	2.50
2252l	Pl# 3 untag.,Low gloss	11.00	10.00
2253	**5¢ Milk Wagon**		
	Pl# 1	2.25	1.85
2254	**5.3¢ Elevator, Precancel**		
	Pl# 1	2.30	1.85
2255	**7.6¢ Carreta, Precancel**		
	Pl# 1,2	3.15	2.65
	Pl# 3	6.50	6.00
2256	**8.4¢ Wheel Chair, Precancel**		
	Pl# 1,2	3.00	2.50
	Pl# 3	15.75	14.50
2257	**10¢ Canal Boat**		
	Pl# 1 block tagging,Dull	3.85	3.25
2257a	Pl# 1 overall tag.,Dull	5.75	4.75
2257s	Pl# 5 Overall tag,Shiny	6.00	5.25
2257b	Pl# 1-4 mottled tagging, Shiny gum	5.50	4.75
2257c	Pl# 5 solid tag,low gloss	5.50	4.75
2258	**13¢ Patrol Wagon, Precancel**		
	Pl# 1	7.25	6.00
2259	**13.2¢ Coal Car, Precancel**		
	Pl# 1,2	4.25	3.65
2260	**15¢ Tugboat**		
	Pl# 1,2 large block tag.	3.25	2.50
2260a	Pl# 2, overall tagging	5.50	4.50
2261	**16.7¢ Popcorn Wagon, Precancel**		
	Pl# 1	4.75	3.75
	P1# 2	5.50	4.50
2262	**17.5¢ Marmon Wasp**		
	Pl# 1	5.75	4.75
2262a	Pl# 1	6.75	5.25
2263	**20¢ Cable Car**		
	Pl# 1,2 block tag	4.75	3.75
2263b	Pl# 2, overall tag	12.00	9.75
2264	**20.5¢ Fire Engine, Prec.**		
	Pl# 1	10.00	7.50
2265	**20.5¢ RR Mail Car, Prec.**		
	Pl# 1,2	6.50	4.75
2266	**24.1¢ Tandem Bike, Prec.**		
	Pl# 1	6.75	5.25
	1988		
2279	**(25¢) "E" Series**		
	Pl# 1111,1222	5.00	3.75
	Pl# 1211, 2222	6.50	5.25
2280	**25¢ Yosemite Block tagged**		
	Pl# 1,7	8.50	7.50
	Pl# 2-5,8	4.75	3.50
	Pl# 9	16.50	14.50
2280a	25¢ Yosemite mottled tagging		
	Pl# 1	50.00	42.50
	Pl# 2-3,7-11,13-14	5.75	4.25
	Pl# 5,15	8.50	7.50
	Pl# 6	16.75	15.00
2281	**25¢ Honeybee**		
	Pl# 1,2	5.25	3.75

PLATE NUMBER COIL STRIPS

Scott No.	F-VF,NH	Pl.Strip of 5	Pl.Strip of 3
	1990-95 Transportation Coils		
2451	**4¢ Steam Carriage**		
	Pl# 1	1.20	.90
2451b	Pl# 1, untagged	1.65	1.25
2452	**5¢ Circus Wagon, Engraved, Dull gum**		
	Pl# 1	2.10	1.75
2452a	Pl# 1, untagged, Dull	2.50	2.00
2452l	Pl# 2 untagg.,Low gloss	2.50	2.00
2452B	**5¢ Circus Wagon, Gravure**		
	Pl# A1,A2	2.50	1.95
2452Bf	Pl# A3 Hi-brite	4.75	4.00
2452D	**5¢ Circus Wagon (¢ sign)**		
	Pl# S1,S2, Low gloss	2.25	1.85
2452Dg	Pl# S2 Hi-brite, Shiny	2.95	2.25
2453	**5¢ Canoe, Brown, Engraved**		
	Pl# 1,2,3	2.30	1.85
2454	**5¢ Canoe, Red, Gravure**		
	Pl# S11	2.35	1.90
2454l	Pl# S11 Low gloss .	13.00	12.00
2457	**10¢ Tractor Trailer,intaglio**		
	Pl# 1	3.25	2.75
2458	**10¢ Tractor Trailer, Gravure**		
	Pl#11, 22	4.85	4.00
2463	**20¢ Cog Railway**		
	Pl# 1,2	6.00	5.00
2464	**23¢ Lunch Wagon**		
	Pl# 2,3 overall tagging	5.00	3.95
2464a	23¢ Dull Gum		
	Pl# 3 mottled tagging	16.75	13.00
2464s	23¢ Shiny Gum		
	Pl# 3, 4, 5 mottled tag	7.50	6.00
2466	**32¢ Ferry Boat,Shiny gum**		
	Pl# 2,3,4	8.50	6.75
	Pl# 5	14.75	13.50
2466l	32¢ Mottled tagging, Low gloss Gum		
	Pl# 3,5	16.00	13.75
	Pl# 4	23.75	21.75
2466b	32¢ Bronx Blue		
	P1# 5	180.00	165.00
2468	**$1 Seaplane, Overall tag, Dull Gum**		
	Pl# 1	19.75	13.00
2468b	$1 mottled tagging, Shiny Gum		
	Pl# 3	20.75	14.00
2468c	$1 solid tagging, Low gloss Gum		
	P1# 3	29.50	21.50
	1993-95 Flora & Fauna		
2491c	**29¢ Pine Cone, SA**		
	Pl# B1	10.50	8.75
2492g	**32¢ Pink Rose, SA**		
	Pl# S11	8.75	7.00
2495-95Av	**32¢ Peach & Pear, SA**		
	Pl# V11111	18.75	13.50
	1991-1994		
2518	**(29¢) "F" Flower**		
	Pl# 1111,1222,,2222	5.00	3.75
	Pl# 1211	17.00	15.00
	Pl# 2211	6.25	5.00
2523	**29¢ Flag/Mt. Rushmore**		
	Pl# 1-8 mottled tagging	7.25	5.00
	Pl# 9	11.50	9.50
2523c	29¢ Toledo Brown		
	P1#7	225.00	210.00
2523d	29¢ Solid tag (Lenz) ...		
	Pl# 6	250.00	225.00
2523A	**29¢ Rushmore/Gravure**		
	Pl# A11111,A22211	6.75	5.25
2525	**29¢ Flower, rouletted**		
	Pl# S1111,S2222	7.00	5.25
2526	**29¢ Flower, perforated**		
	Pl# S2222	7.50	5.25
2529	**19¢ Fishing Boat, Type I**		
	Pl# A1111,A1212,A2424	4.75	3.75
	Pl# A1112	10.00	8.75
2529a	19¢ Type II, Andreotti Gravure		
	Pl# A5555, A5556, A6667	5.00	3.75
	P1# A7667, A7679 A7766, A7779	6.50	5.50
2529b	19¢ Type II,untagged		
	A5555	13.50	11.50
2529C	**19¢ Type III, S111 ......**	10.00	8.25
2598v	**29¢ Eagle, SA**		
	Pl# 111	9.75	8.00
2599v	**Statue of Liberty, SA**		
	Pl# D1111	9.75	8.00
2602	**(10¢) Eagle &Shield**		
	A11111,A11112,A21112, A22112,A22113,A33333, A43334,A43335,A53335	2.85	2.25
	A12213	16.50	15.00
	A21113,A33335, A43324,A43325,A43326, A43426,A54444,A54445	2.85	2.25
	A34424,A34426,.............	10.50	9.50
	A32333	450.00	425.00
	A33334	120.00	110.00

Scott No.	F-VF,NH	Pl.Strip of 5	Pl.Strip of 3
2602	(10¢) Eagle & Shield		
	A77777,A88888,A88889, A89999,A99998,A99999	2.85	2.25
	A1010101010,A1110101010, A1011101011,etc.	5.00	4.00
	A111101011011	15.00	14.00
2603	**(10¢) Eagle & Shield (BEP)**		
	Pl# 11111,22221, 22222	3.65	3.00
2603l	(10¢) Low Gloss Gum, Pl# 22222, 44444, 33333	5.00	4.00
2603b	(10¢) Tagged, Shiny Pl# 11111, 22221	20.75	17.50
2604	**(10¢) Eagle & Shield (SV)**		
	Pl# S22222	3.95	3.25
2604l	(10¢) Low Gloss Gum, Pl# S11111, S22222	3.95	3.25
2605	**23¢ Flag, Bulk Rate**		
	Pl# A111,A112,A122, A212,A222,A333	5.25	3.95
2606	**23¢ USA Pre-sort, ABNCo.**		
	Pl# A1111,A2222,A2232, A2233,A3333,A4443, A4444,A4453,A4364	5.50	4.25
2607	**23¢ USA Pre-sort, BEP, Shiny**		
	Pl# 1111	6.75	5.50
2607l	23¢ Low gloss Gum #1111	7.75	6.25
2607a	23¢ Tagged,Shiny #1111 ..	125.00	115.00
2608	**23¢ USA Pre-sort, S.V.**		
	Pl# S1111	7.75	6.00
2609	**29¢ Flag/White House**		
	Pl# 1-11	6.75	5.00
	Pl# 13-15,17-18	8.00	6.25
	1993 Self-Adhesive		
2799-2802v	**29¢ Christmas**		
	Pl#V1111111 .... (8)	13.95	...
2813v	**29¢ Love**		
	Pl# B1	10.50	8.50
2873v	**29¢ Santa Claus**		
	Pl# V1111	10.50	8.50
2886b	**(32¢) "G"**		
	Pl# V1111	11.50	9.50
	1994-95 "G" Coils		
2888	**(25¢) "G"**		
	Pl# S11111	7.50	6.00
2889	**(32¢) Black "G"**		
	Pl# 1111, 2222	16.50	11.75
2890	**(32¢) Blue "G"**		
	Pl# A1111,A1112,A1211, A1212,A1311,A1313,A1324, A2211,A2212,A2213,A2214, A2313,A3113,A3314,A3323, A3324,A3433,A3435,A3436, A4427,A5327,A5417, A5427	7.75	6.00
	P1# A1113,A1222,A1313, A1314,A1417,A1433,A2223, A3314,A3315,A3423,A3426, A4426, A5437	8.50	6.00
	Pl# A4435	395.00	375.00
2891	**(32¢) Red "G"**		
	Pl# S1111	11.50	8.75
2892	**(32¢) "G" Rouletted**		
	Pl# S1111,S2222	11.00	9.00
2893	**(5¢) "G" Non-Profit**		
	Pl# A11111,A21111	2.75	2.25
	1995-97 Non Denominated Coils		
2902	**(5¢) Butte,**		
	Pl# S111,S222, S333 ..	1.80	1.50
2902B	**(5¢) Butte, SA**		
	Pl# S111	2.65	2.25
2903	**(5¢) Mountain, BEP**		
	Pl# 11111	2.25	1.95
2903a	(5¢) Mountain, Tagged Pl# 11111	110.00	100.00
2904	**(5¢) Mountain, SVS**		
	Pl# S111	2.65	2.25
2904A	**(5¢) Mountain, 11.5**		
	Pl# V222222, V333333, V333333	3.00	2.50
	Pl# V333323, V333342, V333343	5.75	4.75
2904B	**(5¢) Mountain, 9.8**		
	Pl# 11111	3.00	2.50
2905	**(10¢) Automobile**		
	Pl# S111,S222,S333	3.25	2.75
2906	**(10¢) Automobile**		
	Pl# S111	3.25	2.75
2907	**(10¢) Eagle & Shield**		
	Pl# S11111	4.50	3.75
2908	**(15¢) Auto Tail Fin, BEP**		
	Pl# 11111	3.75	3.00
2909	**(15¢) Auto Tail Fin, SVS**		
	Pl# S11111	3.75	3.00

Scott No.	F-VF,NH	Pl.Strip of 5	Pl.Strip of 3
2910	**(15¢) Auto Tail Fin, SA**		
	Pl# S11111	3.95	3.25
2911	**(25¢) Juke Box, BEP**		
	Pl# 111111,212222, 222222,332222	6.75	5.25
2912	**(25¢) Juke Box, SVS**		
	Pl# S11111, S22222	6.75	5.25
2912A	**(25¢) Juke Box, 11.5, SA**		
	Pl# S11111, S22222	7.75	6.25
2912B	**(25¢) Juke box, 9.8, SA**		
	Pl# 111111,222222	7.75	6.25
	1995-97 Flag over Porch		
2913	**32¢ Flag over Porch, BEP, Shiny**		
	Pl# 11111,22221,22222	7.25	5.50
2913l	32¢ Low Gloss Gum		
	Pl# 11111, 22222, 33333, 34313, 44444, 45444, 66646, 77767, . 78767, 91161, 99969	8.25	6.50
	Pl# 22322, 66666	15.00	12.50
2914	**32¢ Flag over Porch, SVS**		
	Pl# S11111	8.25	6.50
2915	**32¢ Flag over Porch, 8.7, SA**		
	Pl# V11111	18.75	15.75
2915A	**32¢ Flag over Porch, 9.7,SA**		
	Pl#11111,22222,23222, 33333,44444,45444, 55555,66666,78777, 88888,89878,97898 99999,11111A,13231A, 22222A,33333A,444 44A, 55555A,66666A,77777A, 88888A	8.75	6.75
	Pl# 78777A	23.50	21.50
	P1#87898, 89898	35.00	32.50
	P1#87888	70.00	67.50
	P1#88898	435.00	425.00
	Pl# 89888	62.50	60.00
	Pl# 89899	725.00	700.00
	Pl# 99899	45.00	42.50
	P1#13231A	95.00	90.00
2915B	**32¢ Flag over Porch, 11.5, SA**		
	Pl# S11111	15.75	13.00
2915C	**32¢ Flag over Porch, 10.9, SA**		
	Pl# 66666	19.50	16.00
	Pl# 55555	33.50	30.00
2915D	**32¢ Flag over Porch, 9.8,SA**		
	Stamps Separate		
	Pl# 11111	17.75	15.00
	1995-99		
3014-17	**32¢ Santa & Children, SA**		
	Pl# V1111 .... (8)	28.75	...
3018	**32¢ Midnight Angel, SA**		
	Pl# B1111	10.50	8.00
3044	**1¢ Kestrel**		
	Pl # 1111	.80	.60
3044a	1¢ Kestrel, Reprint		
	Pl# 1111,2222,3333,4444	1.20	.90
3045	**2¢ Woodpecker**		
	Pl# 11111	1.20	.90
	Pl# 22222	2.85	2.50
3053	**20¢ Blue Jay, SA**		
	Pl# 11111	7.75	6.00
3054	**32¢ Yellow Rose, SA**		
	Pl # 1111, 1112, 1122 2222, 2223,2333, 3444, 4455, 5455, 5555, 5556, 5566, 5666,6666,7777	8.50	6.50
	Pl# 2233, 3444,6677, 6777,8888	15.00	13.00
3055	**20¢ Ringnecked Pheasant, SA**		
	Pl#1111,2222	7.50	5.75
3132	**(25¢) Juke Box, SA**		
	Linerless Pl #M11111 ...	14.50	10.75
3133	**32¢ Flags over Porch, SA**		
	Linerless Pl #M11111 ...	10.00	7.75
3207	**(5¢) Wetlands**		
	Pl#S1111	2.75	2.30
3207A	(5¢) Wetlands, SA		
	Pl#1111,2222,3333, 4444, 5555	2.40	2.10
3208	**(25¢) Diner, SA**		
	Pl#S11111	6.75	5.25
3208A	(25¢) Diner, SA		
	Pl#11111,22211,22222, 33333,44444,55555	6.75	5.25
3228	**(10¢) Green Bicycle,Small Date, SA**		
	Pl# 111,221,222,333,344, 444,555,	3.75	3.00
3228a	(10¢) Bicycle, Large Date, SA Pl# 666,777,888,999 .	8.25	6.75
3229	(10¢) Green Bicycle Pl#S111	4.50	3.75
	1998 Regular Issues		
3263	**22¢ Uncle Sam**, SA		
	Pl#1111	6.50	5.25

PLATE NUMBER COIL STRIPS

3132

0135

Scott No.	F-VF, NH	Pl. Strip of 5	Pl. Strip of 3
3264	**(33¢) Hat, Shiny Gum**		
	Pl#1111,3333,3343,		
	3344,3444	9.25	7.50
3264l	(33¢) Low gloss Gum		
	Pl# 1111	10.00	8.00
3265	(33¢) Hat, SA, Die-cut 9.9		
	Pl#1111,1131,2222,3333	11.00	8.75
3266	(33¢) Hat, SA Die-cut 9.7		
	Pl# 1111	11.00	8.75
3270	**(10¢) Eagle, Pre-sorted, Small Date**		
	Pl#11111	4.35	3.75
3270a	(10¢) Eagle, Pre-sorted, Large Date		
	Pl#22222	12.75	11.00
3271	**(10¢) Eagle, Pre-sorted, Small Date,SA**		
	Pl#11111, 22222	4.25	3.50
3271a	(10¢) Eagle, Pre-sorted, Large Date		
	Pl# 33333	11.50	9.50
3271b	(10¢) Eagle, Tagged		
	Pl# 11111	12.50	10.00
	1999-2000		
3280	**33¢ Flag over City, WA, Small Date**		
	Pl# 1111,2222	8.25	6.50
3280a	33¢ Flag over City,WA, Large Date		
	Pl# 3333	13.75	10.00
3281	33¢ Flag over City, SA, Square		
	Corners, Large Date		
	Pl# 1111A,2222A,3333A,		
	3433A,4444A,5555A,6666,		
	6666A,7777,7777A,8888,		
	8888A,9999,9999A,		
	1111B,2222B	10.50	8.25
3281c	33¢ Smaller 1¼mm date		
	Pl# 1111,2222,3333,3433,		
	4443,4444,5555,9999A	17.50	13.50
3282	33¢ Flag over City, SA, Rounded		
	Corners		
	Pl# 1111,2222	10.75	8.50
3302-5	**33¢ Fruit Berries**		
	Pl# B1111,B1112,B2211,		
	B2221,B2222 (9)	14.50	(5)8.50
3353	**22¢ Uncle Sam**		
	Pl# 1111	6.25	5.00
3404-7	**33¢ Fruit Berries**		
	Pl# G1111 (9)	21.75	(5)13.75
3447	**(10¢) N.Y.Public Library Lion**		
	Pl# S11111,S22222	4.65	3.75
3452	**(34¢) Statue of Liberty**, Perforated		
	Pl# 1111	9.75	7.75
3453	(34¢) Statue of Liberty, SA,Die-cut		
	Pl# 1111	13.50	11.50

Scott No.	F-VF, NH	Pl. Strip of 5	Pl. Strip of 3
	2000-2004 Coils		
3462-65	**(34¢) Flowers, SA Die-cut**		
	Pl# B1111 (9)	33.50	(5)19.75
3466	**34¢ Liberty, SA , Rounded Corners**		
	Pl# 1111,2222	9.50	7.50
3475	**21¢ Bison, SA**		
	Pl# V1111, V2222	5.75	4.75
3475A	**23¢ Washington, SA "2001" date**		
	Pl# B11	5.25	4.00
3476	**34¢ Liberty, Perforated**		
	Pl# 1111	8.00	6.50
3477	34¢ Liberty, Die-cut, Square Corners		
	Pl# 1111,2222,3333,		
	4444,5555,6666.7777 .	8.50	7.00
3478-81	**34¢ Flowers, SA Die-cut**		
	Pl# B1111,B2111,B2122,		
	B2211,B2222 (9)	15.00	(5)9.75
3520	**(10¢) Atlas Statue, SA**		
	Pl# B1111	4.00	3.50
3522	**(15¢) Woody Wagon, SA**		
	Pl# S11111	3.85	3.00
3550	**34¢ United We Stand, Square Corners**		
	Pl# 1111,2222,3333	9.00	7.00
3550A	**34¢ United We Stand, Rounded Corners**		
	Pl# 1111	9.00	7.00
3612	**5¢ American Toleware, WA**		
	Pl# S1111111	2.40	2.10
3615	**3¢ Star, WA**		
	Pl# S111	2.15	1.75
3617	**23¢ Washington, "2002" Date, SA**		
	Pl# V11,V13,V21,V22,		
	V24, V35, V46	5.50	4.25
3622	**(37¢) Flag, SA**		
	Pl# 1111,2222	12.00	8.00
3631	**37¢ Flag, WA**		
	Pl# S1111	10.00	8.00
3632	**37¢ Flag, SA, Diecut 10**		
	Pl# 1111,2222,3333,4444,		
	5555,6666,7777	10.00	8.00
3632A	37¢ SA, Die-cut 10 "2003" Date		
	Pl# S1111	8.00	6.50
3632C	37¢ SA, Die-cut 11 3/4		
	Mottled Tagging "2004" Date		
	Pl#S1111	8.00	6.50
3632Cv	37¢ SA, Die-cut 11 3/4		
	Smooth Tagging "2004" Dat		
	Pl#S1111	8.00	6.50
3633	37¢ Flag, SA, Diecut 8.5 2002 Date		
	Pl# B1111	10.00	8.00
3633A	37¢ Flag, SA, Diecut 8.5 2003 Date		
	Pl#B1111	8.75	7.00

Scott No.	F-VF, NH	Pl. Strip of 5	Pl. Strip of 3
3638-41	**37¢ Antique Toys**		
	Pl# B11111,B12222, .. (9)	15.00	(5) 9.75
3680-83	**37¢ Holiday Snowmen, SA**		
	Pl# G1111 (9)	13.75	(5) 8.50
3693	**(5¢) Sea Coast**		
	Pl# B111	2.40	2.10
3757	**1¢ Tiffany Lamp, WA**		
	Pl# B111	.80	.65
3769	**(10¢)Library Lion, WA**		
	Pl# S11111	2.50	1.95
3769v	(10¢) Library Lion, Lighter shade		
	Pl# S11111	2.50	1.95
3770	**(10¢) Atlas Statue "2003" Date**		
	Pl# V11111	3.50	2.75
3775	**(5¢) Sea Coast, WA, Perf. 9¾ vert.**		
	Pl# B111	1.75	1.40
3785	(5¢) Sea Coast, Die-cut all around		
	Pl# S1111	1.75	1.40
3792-3801	**(25¢) American Eagle, SA**		
	Pl# S1111111 (11)	7.75	...
3829	**37¢ Snowy Egret, "2003" Date, SA**		
	Pl# V1111	8.00	6.50
3829A	37¢ Snowy Egret, "2004" Date, SA		
	Pl#P11111	8.00	6.50
	1983-85 Official Stamps		
O135	**20¢ Official**		
	Pl# 1	90.00	15.00
O139	**(22¢) "D" Official**		
	Pl# 1	90.00	47.50
O159	**37¢ Official**		
	Pl# S1111	6.50	4.75
	VARIABLE RATE COILS		
CVP31	**29¢ Shield, Dull Gum**		
	Pl# 1	15.75	12.50
CVP31a	**29¢ Shiny Gum**		
	Pl# 1	15.75	12.50
CVP31b	**32¢ Dull Gum**		
	Pl# 1	16.50	13.00
CVP31c	**32¢ Shiny Gum**		
	Pl# 1	16.50	13.00
CVP32	**29¢ Vertical Design**		
	Pl# A11	15.00	12.50
CVP33	**32¢ Vertical Design**		
	Pl# 11	15.00	12.50
CVP33v	37¢ Vertical Design		
	Pl#	12.50	10.00

CONVERTIBLE SELF-ADHESIVE PANES (Complete Unfolded Booklets)

3116a

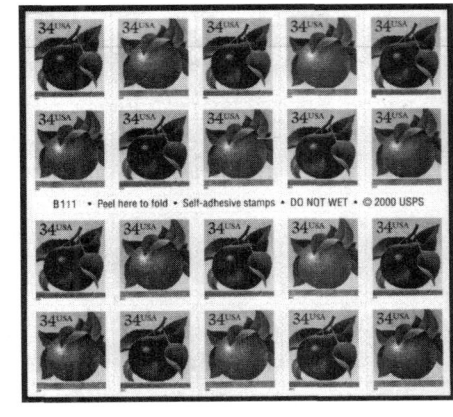

3492b

Scott No.	Description	F-VF,NH
2431a	25¢ Eagle & Shield (18)	
	Pl# A1111	17.50
2475a	25¢ Flag, Plastic (12) No #	10.75
2489a	29¢ Red Squirrel (18)	
	Pl# D11111,D22211	16.50
	Pl#D22221,D22222,D23133	19.75
2490a	29¢ Rose (18)	
	Pl# S111	16.50
2491a	29¢ Pine Cone (18)	
	Pl# B3-11,B13-14, B16	16.50
	Pl# B1-2, B12, B15	18.75
2492a	32¢ Pink Rose (20)	
	Pl# S111,S112,S333	17.50
2492r	32¢ Die-Cut "Time to Reorder"	
	S444, S555	17.75
2494a	32¢ Peach & Pear (20)	
	Pl# V11111,V11122, V11132,	
	V12132, V12211, V22212,	
	V22221, V22222, V33333, V33353,	
	V33363, V44424, V44454	19.50
	Pl# V11131, V12131, V12221,	
	V33142, V33143, V33243,	
	V33343, V33453, V44434, V45434,	
	V45464, V54565, V55365	21.75
	Pl# V33323	27.50
2522a	(29¢) "F" Flag (12) No Pl#	14.95
2531Ab	29¢ Liberty & Torch (18) No Pl#	16.75
2531Av	29¢ Revised back No Pl#	16.75
2595a	29¢ Eagle, Brown (17)	
	Pl# B1111-1,B1111-2,B3434-1	16.50
	Pl# B2222-1,B2222-2,B3333-1,	
	B3333-3,B3434-3, B4344-1,	
	B4444-1,B4444-3	27.50
2596a	29¢ Eagle, Green (17)	
	Pl# D11111,D21221,D22322,	
	D23322,D32322,D43352,	
	D43452,D43453,D54563,	
	D54571,D54573,D65784	16.50
	Pl# D54561,D54673,D61384	25.00
	Pl# D32342,D42342	35.00
2597a	29¢ Eagle, Red (17)	
	Pl# S1111	16.50
2598a	29¢ Eagle (18)	
	Pl# M111,M112	17.50
2599a	29¢ Statue of Liberty (18)	
	Pl# D1111,D1212	16.00
2719a	29¢ Locomotive (18)	
	Pl# V11111	17.50
2802a	29¢ Christmas (12)	
	Pl# V111-1111,V222-1222,	
	V222-2112,V222-2122,V222-2221,	
	V222-2222	15.00
	Pl# V333-3333	18.75
2803a	29¢ Snowman (18)	
	Pl# V1111,V2222	17.50
2813a	29¢ Love & Sunrise (18)	
	Pl# B111-1,B111-2,B111-3,B111-4,	
	B222-4,B222-5,B222-6, B333-9,	
	B333-10,B333-11,B333-12, B333-17,	
	B344-12,B344-13,B444-10, B444-13,	
	B444-15,B444-17,B444-18,	
	B444-19,B555-20, B555-21	16.50
	Pl# B121-5,B221-5,B444-7,B444-8,	
	B444-9,B444-14,B444-16	19.75
	Pl# B333-5,B333-7,B333-8	25.00
	Pl# B344-11	50.00
	Pl# B111-5,B333-14,B434-10	110.00
2873a	29¢ Santa Claus (12)	
	Pl# V1111	12.75
2874a	29¢ Cardinal in Snow (18)	
	Pl# V1111,V2222	17.50
2886a	(32¢) "G" Surface (18)	
	Pl# V11111,V22222	19.00
2887a	(32¢) "G" Overall (18)	
	No Plate Number	22.75
2919a	32¢ Flag over Field (18)	
	Pl# V1111,V1311,V1433,V2111,	
	V2222,V2322	15.75

Scott No.	Description	F-VF,NH
2920a	32¢ Flag over Porch, Large "1995"(20)	
	Pl# V12211,V12212,V12312,V12321,	
	V12322,V12331,V13322,V13831,	
	V13834,V13836,V22211,V23322,	
	V34743,V34745,V36743,V42556,	
	V45554,V56663,V56665,V56763,	
	V57663,V65976,V78989	21.75
	Pl# V23422	32.50
	Pl# V23522	50.00
2920c	32¢ Flag over Porch, Small "1995"(20)	
	Pl# V11111	170.00
2920De	32¢ Flag over Porch, 11.3 (10)	
	Pl# V11111,V12111,V23222,	
	V31111,V32111,V32121,V44322,	
	V44333,V44444,V55555,V66666,	
	V66886,V67886,V68886,V68896,	
	V76989,V77666,V77668,V77766,	
	V78698,V78886,V78896,V78898,	
	V78986,V78989,V89999	12.50
2949a	(32¢) Love & Cherub (20)	
	Pl# B1111-1,B2222-1	
	B2222-2,B3333-2	18.75
2960a	55¢ Love Cherub (20)	
	Pl# B1111-1,B2222-1	28.50
3011a	32¢ Santa & Children (20)	
	Pl# V1111,V1211,	
	V3233,V3333,V4444	19.50
	Pl# V1212	29.50
3012a	32¢ Midnight Angel (20)	
	Pl# B1111,B2222,B3333	18.00
3013a	32¢ Children Sledding (20)	
	Pl# V1111	16.50
3030a	32¢ Love Cherub (20)	
	Pl#B1111-1,B1111-2	
	B2222-1,B2222-2	20.00
3048a	20¢ Blue Jay (10) SA	
	Pl# S1111, S2222	6.50
3049a	32¢ Yellow Rose)20)	
	Pl# S1111, S2222, S3333	17.50
3050a	20¢ Pheasant, Diecut 11 1/4 (10) SA	
	Pl# V2232,V2333,V2342,V2343,	
	V3232,V3243,V3333	6.95
3050c	2017 Pheasant, Diecut 11	
	Pl# V1111,V2222,V3233	7.50
3052d	33¢ Rose, Die-cut 11½x11¾ (20)	
	Pl# S222	16.75
3052Ef	33¢ Rose, Die-cut 11½x11¼ (20)	
	Pl# S111	17.50
3071a	32¢ Tennessee (20)	
	Pl# S11111	21.95
3089a	32¢ Iowa (20), Pl# B11111	25.75
3112a	32¢ Madonna (20)	
	Pl# 11111,12111,22121,22221,	
	23231,33231,33331,33341,	
	44441,55441,55562,56562,66661,	
	66662,67661,78871,78872,	
	78882,79882	17.75
	Pl# 6656-2	25.00
	Pl# 5556-1	30.00
	Pl# 5555-1	70.00
3116a	32¢ Family Scenes (20)	
	Pl# B1111,B2222,B3333,	21.50
3117a	32¢ Skaters (18)	
	Pl# V1111,V2111	16.95
3122a	32¢ Liberty & Torch, Die-cut 11 (20)	
	Pl# V1111,V1211,V1311,V2122,	
	V2222,V2311,V2331,V3233,V3333,	
	V3513,V4532	18.50
3122Ef	32¢ Liberty & Torch,Die-cut 11.5x11.8(20)	
	Pl# V1111,V1211,V2122,V2222	45.00
3123a	32¢ Love & Swans (20)	
	Pl# B1111,B2222,B3333,B4444,	
	B5555,B6666,B7777	18.50
3124a	55¢ Love & Swans (20)	
	Pl#B1111,B2222,B3333,B4444	35.75
3127a	32¢ Merian Botanical,SA	
	Prints (20) Pl#S11111,S22222,	
	S33333	18.00

Scott No.	Description	F-VF,NH
3176a	32¢ Madonna (20)	
	Pl# 1111, 2222, 3333	18.00
3177a	32¢ American Holly (20)	
	Pl# B1111, B2222, B3333	18.50
3244a	32¢ Madonna (20)	
	Pl# 11111, 22222, 33333	18.00
3252b	32¢ Wreaths (20)	
	Pl#B111111, B222222,	
	B333333, B444444,	
	B555555	22.50
3268a	(33¢) Hat, Die-cut 11¼ (10)	
	Pl# V1111, V1211, V2211, V2222	11.00
3268c	(33¢) Hat. Die-cut 11 (20)	
	Pl# V1111, V1112, V1113, V1122,	
	V1213, V1222, V2113, V2122,	
	V2213, V2222, V2223	18.75
3269a	(33¢) Hat, Die-cut 8 (18)	
	Pl# V1111	17.50
3274a	33¢ Victorian-Love (20)	
	Pl #V1111,V1112,V1117,V1118,V1211,	
	V1212,V1213,V1233,V1313,V1314,	
	V1333,V1334,V1335,V1323,V2221,	
	V2222,V2223,V2424,V2425,V2426,	
	V2324,V3123,V3124,V3133,V3133,	
	V3134,V3323,V3327,V3333,V3334,	
	V3336,V4529,V5650	19.50
3278d	33¢ Flag over City, Die-cut 11 (10)	
	Pl# V1111, V1112,V1113,V2222,	
	V2322,V3434,V3433, V4444	9.75
3278e	33¢ Flag over City, Die-cut 11 (20)	
	Pl#V1111, V1211, V2122,V2222,	
	V2223,V3333,V4444	17.50
3278j	33¢ Flag over City Diecut 11¼ (10)	
	Pl#V1111,V1112,V2222	27.50
3278Fg	33¢ Flag over City, Reprint (20)	
	Pl# V1111,V1131,V2222,V2223,	
	V2323,V2423,V2443,V3333,V4444,	
	V5428,V5445,V5576,V5578,V6423,	
	V6456,V6546,V6556,V6575,V6576,	
	V7567,V7667	25.00
3283a	33¢ Flag over Chalkboard (20)	
	Pl# V1111	19.75
3297b	33¢ Fruit Berries, "1999" Date (20)	
	Pl# B1111, B1112, B2211, B2222,	
	B3331, B3332, B3333,B4444	
	B5555	17.50
3297d	33¢ Fruit Berries, "2000" Date (20)	
	Pl# B1111	22.50
3313b	33¢ Tropical Flowers (20)	
	Pl# S11111, S22222, S22244, S22344,	
	S22444,S22452,S22462,S23222,	
	S24222,S24224,S24242,S24244,	
	S24422,S24442,S24444, S26462,	
	S32323,S32333,S32444,S33333,	
	S44444,S45552,S46654,S55452,	
	S55552,S56462,S62544,S62562,	
	S64452,S64544,S65552,S66462,	
	S66544,S66552,S66562,S66652	19.00
3355a	33¢ Madonna (20)	
	Pl# B1111,B2222,B3333	18.00
3363a	33¢ Deer (20) Pl#B111111,B222222,	
	B33333, B444444,B555555,	
	B666666, B777777, B888888,	
	B999999, B000000, BAAAAAA,	
	BBBBBBB	17.50
3450a	(34¢) Flag over Farm (18)	
	Pl# V1111	15.75
3451a	(34¢) Statue of Liberty (20)	
	Pl# V1111, V2222	17.50
3457e	(34¢) Flowers, Die-cut 10¼x10 3/4 (20)	
	Pl# S1111	19.75
3482a	20¢ G. Washington, Die-cut 11¼x11 (10)	
	Pl# P1, P2, P3	4.85
3483c	20¢ G. Washington, Mixed Die-cuts(10)	
	Pl# P1, P2, P3	14.75
3483f	20¢ G. Washington, Mixed Die-cuts (10)	
	Pl# P1, P2, P3	14.75

CONVERTIBLE SELF-ADHESIVE PANES (Complete Unfolded Booklets)

Scott No.	Description	F-VF,NH
3484d	21¢ Bison, Die-cut 11¼x11 (10) PI# P111111, P222222, P333333, P444444, P555555	8.00
3484Ag	21¢ Bison, Mixed Die-cuts (10) PI# P111111, P222222, P333333, P444444, P555555	13.75
3484Aj	21¢ Bison, Mixed Die-cuts (10) PI# P111111, P222222, P333333, P444444, P555555	13.75
3485a	34¢ Statue of Liberty (10) PI# V1111, V1221	12.50
3485b	34¢ Statue of Liberty (20) PI# V1111, V1211, V1221, V2111, V2112, V2121, V2122, V2212, V2222	25.00
3490e	34¢ Flowers (20) PI# S1111, S2222	25.00
3492b	34¢ Apples & Oranges (20) PI# B1111, B2222, B3333, B4444, B5555, B6666, B7777	17.50
3495a	34¢ Flag over Farm (18) PI# V1111	15.00
3496a	(34¢) Rose & Love Letters (20) PI# B1111, B2222	18.00
3497a	34¢ Rose & Love Letters (20) PI# B1111, B2222, B3333, B4444, B5555	15.75
3536a	34¢ Madonna (20) PI# B1111	17.50

Scott No.	Description	F-VF,NH
3549a	34¢ United We Stand (20) PI# B1111, B222, B3333, B4444	23.50
3549Be	34¢ United -Stand,Double-sided(20) PI# S1111	18.00
3618c	23¢ Washington (10) PI# P1, P2, P3	5.75
3619e	23¢ Washington, Mixed Diecuts(10) PI# P1, P2, P3	13.75
3619f	23¢ Washington, Mixed Diecuts(10) PI# P1, P2, P3	13.75
3623a	(37¢) Flag (20) PI# B1111, B2222, B3333	22.75
3624c	(37¢) Flag, Double-sided (20) PI# S1111	18.50
3625a	(37¢) Flag, ATM (18) PI# V1111	16.75
3629e	(37¢) Antique Toys (20) PI# V1111, V1112, V2222	18.75
3634a	37¢ Flag (10) PI# V1111	8.75
3635a	37¢ Flag (20) PI# B1111, B2222, B3333, B4444, B5555, B6666, B7777	17.00
3636c	37¢ Flag, Double-sided (20) PI# S1111, S2222, S3333, S4444	17.00
3637a	37¢ Flag, ATM (18) PI# V1111	15.00

Scott No.	Description	F-VF,NH
3645e	37¢ Antique Toys (20) PI# V1111, V1112, V2221, V2222	17.00
3645h	37¢ Toys,Double-sided (20) PI# V1111	14.75
3657a	37¢ Love (20) PI# B11111, B22222, B33333, B44444, B55555, B66666, B77777	16.50
3675a	37¢ Madonna & Child (20) PI# B1111, B2222	16.50
3687b	37¢ Holiday Snowmen (20) PI# S1111, S1113, S2222, S4444	16.50
3807b	37¢ Mary Cassatt, Double-sided (20) PI# S11111	15.75
3820a	37¢ Madonna, Double-sided (20) PI# S1111	15.75
3824a	37¢ Music Makers, Double-sided (20) PI# S1111	15.75
3830a	37¢ Snowy Egret (20) PI# P11111	14.75
3833a	37¢ Candy Hearts (20) PI# V1111	14.75
3836a	37¢ Garden Bouquet (20) PI# P22222	14.75

UNFOLDED BOOKLET PANES WITH PLATE NUMBERS

2474a

3029a

Scott No.	Description	FVF,NH
2409a	25¢ Steamboats, PI#1	8.50
	PI# 2	22.50
2427a	25¢ Madonna (10) PI# 1	15.00
2429a	25¢ Sleigh (10) PI# 1111	19.50
2441a	25¢ Love (10), PI# 1211	48.50
2443a	15¢ Beach Umbrella (10) PI#111111	8.75
2474a	25¢ Lighthouse (5) PI# 1,3,5	14.75
	PI# 2	16.75
2483a	20¢ Blue Jay (10) PI# S1111	8.95
2484a	29¢ Wood Duck, BEP(10) PI#1111	9.95
2485a	29¢ Wood Duck, KCS (10) PI#K1111	11.95
2486a	29¢ African Violet (10) PI# K1111	11.50
2488a	32¢ Peach & Pear (10) PI# S1111	11.50
2505a	25¢ Indian Headresses (10) PI# 1,2	19.50
2514b	25¢ Madonna (10) PI# 1	14.75
2516a	25¢ Christmas Tree (10) PI#1211	16.95
2527a	29¢ Flower (10) PI# K1111	10.75
2528a	29¢ Flag & Rings (10) PI# K11111	10.75
2530a	19¢ Hot-Air Balloons (10) PI# 1111	7.50
2536a	29¢ Love (10) PI# 1111,1112	9.50
2549a	29¢ Fishing Flies (5) PI# A23213	16.50
	PI# A23133	22.50
	PI# A23124	57.50
	PI# A33225,A33233	30.00
2552a	29¢ Desert Storm (5) PI# A11121111	6.50
2566a	29¢ Comedians (10) PI#1	11.75
2577a	29¢ Space (10) PI# 111111	18.75
2578a	(29¢) Madonna (10) PI# 1	10.75
2581b-85a	(29¢) Santa, never bound set of 5 Panes of 4, PI# A11111	31.75
2593a	29¢ Pledge, black (10) PI# 1111	9.75
2594a	29¢ Pledge, red (10) PI# K1111	11.75
2646a	29¢ Hummingbirds (5) PI# A2212112,A2212122,A2222222	5.75
	PI# A1111111, A2212222	10.95
2709a	29¢ Wild Animals (5) PI# K1111	6.00
2710a	29¢ Madonna (10) PI# 1	10.75
2718a	29¢ Toys, never bound (4) PI# A111111,A222222	8.00

Scott No.	Description	FVF,NH
2737a	29¢ Rock'n Roll (8) PI#A22222	10.75
2737b	29¢ Rock'n Roll (4) PI#A22222	5.50
2745a	29¢ Space Fantasy (5) PI# 1111,1211	5.50
	PI# 2222	7.75
2764a	29¢ Spring Flowers (5) PI# 1	5.50
2770a	29¢ Broadway Musicals (4) PI# A11111,A11121,A22222	4.95
2778a	29¢ Country Music (4) PI# A222222	5.50
2790a	29¢ Madonna, never bound (4) PI# K1-11111, K1-44444	4.95
	PI# K1-33333	7.50
2798a	29¢ 3 Snowmen (10) PI#111111	12.75
2798b	29¢ 2 Snowmen (10) PI#111111	12.75
2806b	29¢ Aids (5) PI# K111	5.75
2814a	29¢ Love & Dove (10) PI# A11111	10.75
2833a	29¢ Summer Flowers (5) PI# 2	5.50
2847a	29¢ Locomotives (5) PI# S11111	7.25
2871Ab	29¢ Madonna (10) PI# 1,2	10.95
2872a	29¢ Stocking (20) PI# P11111,P44444	21.50
	PI# P22222	27.50
2916a	32¢ Flag over Porch (10) PI# 11111	11.75
2921a	32¢ Flag over Porch SA, (10) PI# 21221, 22221, 22222	11.75
2921d	32¢ Flag over porch SA, (10) P1# 11111	8.25
2959a	32¢ Love & Cherub (10) PI# 1	9.95
2973a	32¢ Great Lakes Lighthouses (5) PI# S11111	5.75
2997a	32¢ Fall Flowers (5) PI# 2	5.75
3003Ab	32¢ Madonna (10) PI# 1	11.50
3007a	32¢ Santa (10) PI# P1111	11.75
3007c	32¢ Santa (10) PI# P1111	11.75
3029a	32¢ Winter Flowers, SA (5) PI #1	6.00
3049c	32¢ Yellow Rose (5), SA PI#S1111	5.95

Scott No.	Description	FVF,NH
3049d	32¢ Yellow Rose (6) SA PI# S1111	7.50
3122c	32¢ Liberty (5), SA PI# V1111	5.50
3122d	32¢ Liberty (6), #V1111, SA	7.50
3128b	32¢ Merian Botanical (5) PI# S11111	6.75
3129b	32¢ Merian Botanical (5) PI# S11111	8.75
3177d	32¢ Holly (6) PI# B11111, SA	8.25
3248c	32¢ Wreaths (6) #B111111	39.00
3278b	33¢ Flag over City (5) #V1111,V1112, V1121,V1122,V1212,V2212, SA	5.50
3301c	33¢ Fruit Berries(6)#B1111,B1112, B2212, B2221, B2222,SA	6.50
3367c	33¢ Deer (6) #B111111, B222222 SA	12.50
3451b	(34¢) Liberty (4) PI# V1111	4.75
3482b	20¢ G.Washington (4) PI# P1,P2,P3	2.10
3483a	20¢ G.Washington (4) PI# P1,P2,P3	10.00
3483d	20¢ G.Washington (4) PI# P1,P2,P3	10.00
3484b	21¢ Bison (4) PI# P111111, P333333, P444444	2.40
3484Ae	21¢ Bison (4) PI# P111111, P333333, P444444	8.25
3484Ah	21¢ Bison (4) PI# P111111, P333333, P444444	8.25
3485c	34¢ Liberty (4) PI# V111, V1122, V2212, V2222	4.75
3494b	34¢ Apple & Orange (4) PI# B1111	4.75
3498b	34¢ Love (6) PI# B1111	6.75
3618a	23¢ G.Washington (4) PI# P1,P2,P4	2.40
3619a	23¢ G.Washington (4) PI# P1,P2,P4	7.50
3619c	23¢ G.Washington (4) PI# P1,P2,P4	7.50

COMPLETE BOOKLETS

BK81

BK115

Scott No.	Cover Value, Pane No. and Description(Number of Panes)	F-VF NH
1914 Flat Press, Perf. 10, Single-Line Wtmk.		
BK41	25¢ #424d,1¢ Washington (4)	325.00
BK42	97¢ #424d,1¢ Washington (16)	150.00
BK43	73¢ #424d,1¢(4) + #425e,2¢ (4)	350.00
BK44	25¢ #425e,2¢ Washington (2)	500.00
1916 Flat Press, Perf. 10, Unwatermarked		
BK47	25¢ #462a,1¢ Washington(4)	700.00
BK48	97¢ #462a 1¢ Washington(16)	450.00
BK49	73¢ #462a,1¢(4)& #463a,2¢ (4)	950.00
BK50	25¢ #463a,2¢ Washington(2)	600.00
1917-23 Flat Press, Perforated 11		
BK53	25¢ #498e,1¢ Wash.,"POD"(4)	450.00
BK54	97¢ #498e,1¢ Washington(16)	85.00
BK55	25¢ #498e,1¢ "City Carrier"(4)	90.00
BK56	73¢ #498e,1¢(4) + #499e,2¢(4)	77.50
BK57	73¢ #498e,1¢(4) + #554c,2¢(4)	125.00
BK58	25¢ #499e,2¢ Washington(2)	300.00
BK59	49¢ #499e,2¢ Washington(4)	525.00
BK60	97¢ #499e,2¢ Washington(8)	750.00
BK61	97¢ #498e,2¢ Wash.,"97¢"Cover(8)	1375.00
BK62	37¢ #501b,3¢ Wash.,Type I(2)	625.00
BK63	37¢ #502b,3¢ Wash., Type II(2)	250.00
1923 Flat Press, Perforated 11		
BK66	25¢ #552a,1¢ Franklin(4)	80.00
BK67	97¢ #552a,1¢ Franklin(16)	625.00
BK68	73¢ #552a,1¢(4) + #554c,2¢(4)	125.00
BK69	25¢ #554c,2¢ Washington (2)	400.00
BK70	49¢ #554c,2¢ Washington (4)	975.00
BK71	97¢ #554c,2¢ Washington (8)	1650.00
1926 Rotary Press, Perforated 10		
BK72	25¢ #583a,2¢ Washington(2)	600.00
BK73	49¢ #583a,2¢ Washington(4)	850.00
BK74	97¢ #583a,2¢ Washington(8)	1250.00
1927-32 Rotary Press, Perf. 11 x 10½		
BK75	25¢ #632a,1¢ Franklin(4)	92.50
BK76	97¢ #632a,1¢ "P.O.D."cvr.(16)	565.00
BK77	97¢ #632a,1¢ "Postrider"cvr.(16)	775.00
BK79	73¢ #632a,1¢(4) + #634a,2¢(4) "Postrider" Cover	85.00
BK80	25¢ #634d,2¢ Washington(2)	10.00
BK81	49¢ #634d,2¢ Washington(4)	16.50
BK82	97¢ #634d,2¢ "Postrider"cvr.(8)	57.50
BK83	97¢ #634d,2¢ Wash.,"97¢"Cover	950.00
BK84	37¢ #720b,3¢ Washington(2)	165.00
BK85	73¢ #720b,3¢ Washington(4)	395.00
1939-42 Presidential Series		
BK86	25¢ #804bv,1¢ Washington(4)	50.00
BK87	97¢ #804bv,1¢ Washington(16)	600.00
BK89	73¢ #804bv,1¢(4) + #806bv,2¢(4)	180.00
BK90	25¢ #804b,1¢ Washington(4)	7.75
BK91	97¢ #804b,1¢ "P.O.D."cover(16)	550.00
BK92	73¢ #804b,1¢(4) + #806b,2¢(4) "Postrider" cover	35.00
BK93	73¢ #804b,1¢(4) + #806b,2¢(4)] "P.O. Seal" cover	42.50
BK94	97¢ #806bv,2¢ John Adams(8)	550.00
BK95	97¢ #806b,2¢ Adams (8)	1400.00
BK96	25¢ #806b,2¢ Adams "Postrider"(2)	20.00
BK97	25¢ #806b,2¢ Adams "P.O.Seal"(2)	110.00
BK98	49¢ #806b,2¢ Adams "Postrider"(4)	60.00
BK99	49¢ #806b,2¢ Adams "P.O. Seal"(4)	85.00
BK100	37¢ #807av,3¢ Jefferson(2)	95.00
BK101	73¢ #807av,3¢ Jefferson (4)	**975.00**
BK102	37¢ #807a,3¢ Jefferson(2)	22.50
BK103	73¢ #807a,3¢ Jefferson(4)	45.00

Scott No.	Cover Value, Pane No. and Description(Number of Panes)	F-VF NH
1954-58 Liberty Series		
BK104	37¢ #1035a,3¢ Liberty, Wet(2)	17.50
BK104a	37¢ #1035f,3¢ Dry Printing(2)	19.50
BK105	73¢ #1035a,3¢ Liberty, Wet(4)	29.50
BK105a	73¢ #1035f,3¢ Dry Printing(4)	35.00
BK106	97¢ on 37¢ #1036a,4¢ Lincoln(4)	75.00
BK107	97¢ on 73¢ #1036a,4¢ Lincoln(4)	42.50
BK108	97¢ "Yellow" paper #1036a(4)	125.00
BK109	97¢ "Pink" paper #1036a(4)	13.50
BK109a	same, with Experimental Silicone Interleaving	150.00
1962-64 George Washington Issue		
BK110	$1 #1213a,5¢ Slog.1 "Mailman"(4)	32.50
BK111	$1 #1213a,5¢ Slogan 2 "Zone"(4) "Postrider" Cover	150.00
BK112	$1 #1213a,5¢ Slogan 2 "Zone"(4) "Mr. Zip" Cover	125.00
BK113	$1 #1213a,5¢ Slogan 3 "Zip"(4)	16.50
BK114	$1 #1213c,5¢ Tagged, Slogan 2(4)	425.00
BK115	$1 #1213c,5¢ Tagged, Slogan 3(4)	7.50
1967-78 Regular Issues		
BK116	$2 #1278a,1¢ (1) + 1284b,6¢(4)	8.50
BK117	$1 #1280c,2¢ (1) + #1284c,6¢(3)	6.50
BK117A	$3.60 #1288Bc,15¢ Holmes(3)	11.75
BK117B	$2 #1278a,1¢(1) + #1393d,6¢(4) "P.O. Seal" Cover	13.50
BK118	$2 #1278a,1¢(1) + #1393d,6¢(4) "Eisenhower" Cover	9.50
BK119	$2 #1278ae,1¢(1) + #1393d,6¢(4) Dull Gum,"Eisenhower"Cover	9.00
BK120	$1 #1280c,2¢(1) + #1393b,6¢(3)	5.95
BK121	$1.92 #1395a,8¢ Eisenhower-8(3)	7.75
BK122	$1 #1278b,1¢(1) + #1395b,8¢(3)	5.75
BK123	$2 #1395c,8¢(1) + #1395d,8¢(3)	9.50
BK124	$1 #1510b,10¢ Jeff. Meml. - 5(2)	4.75
BK125	$4 #1510c,10¢ Jeff. Meml. - 8(5)	12.00
BK126	$1.25 #1510d,10¢(1)+#C79a,13¢(1)	14.75
1975-80 Regular Issues		
BK127	90¢ #1280c,2¢(1) +1595a,13¢(1)	3.75
BK128	$2.99 #1595b,13¢(1)+#1595c,13¢(2)	8.50
BK129	$1.30 #1595d,13¢ Liberty Bell-5(2)	6.00
BK130	$1.20 #1598a,15¢ McHenry Flag-8(1)	5.75
BK131	$1 #1623a,9¢ + 13¢, Pf. 11x10½(1)	4.00
BK132	$1 #1623c,9¢ + 13¢, Perf. 10(1)	39.50
BK133	$3.60 #1736a,(15¢) "A"(3)	12.00
BK134	$2.40#1737a,15¢ Roses(2)	6.50
BK135	$3 #1742a,15¢ Windmills(2)	10.50
BK136	$4.32 #1819a,(18¢) "B"(3)	16.50
1981-83 Regular Issues		
BK137	$3.60 #1889a,18¢Wildlife(2)Pl#1-10	22.50
BK137	Pl# 11-13	50.00
BK137	Pl# 14-16	45.00
BK138	$1.20 #1893a,6¢ + 18¢ Flag(1)Pl# 1	5.75
BK139	$1.20 #1896a,20¢ Flag - S.C. -6(1)	
BK139	Pl# 1	4.25
BK140	$2 #1896b,20¢ Flag-S. Court-10(1)	
BK140	Pl# 1	7.00
BK140	Pl#4	52.50
BK140A	$4 #1896b,20¢ Flag-S. Court-10(2)	
BK140A	Pl# 2	13.50
BK140A	Pl#3	20.00
BK140B	$28.05#1909a,$9.35 Exp.Mail(1) #1111	89.50
BK141	$4#1948a,(20¢) "C"(2)No Pl#	13.75
BK142	$4 #1949a,20¢ Bighorn Sheep(2)	
BK142	Pl#1-6, 9-10	14.50
BK142	Pl# 11,12,15	37.50
BK142	Pl# 14	30.00
BK142	Pl# 16	85.00
BK142	Pl# 17-19	70.00
BK142	Pl# 20, 22-24	110.00

Scott No.	Cover Value, Pane No. and Description(Number of Panes)	F-VF NH
BK142	Pl# 21,28,29	375.00
BK142	Pl# 25-26	175.00
BK142a	$4 #1949d,20¢ Sheep, Type II(2)	
BK142a	Pl# 34	33.50
1985-89 Regular Issues		
BK143	$4.40 #2113a,(22¢) "D"(2)Pl#1,3,4	23.50
BK144	$1.10 #2116a,22¢ Flag - Capitol(1)	
BK144	Pl# 1,3	4.50
BK145	$2.20 #2116a,22¢ Flag - Capitol(2)	
BK145	Pl# 1,3	9.00
BK146	$4.40 #2121a,22¢ Seashells(2) Multi-Seashells Cover (7 covers needed for all 25 shells)Pl#1,3	13.95
BK146	Pl# 2	15.75
BK147	$4.40 #2121a,22¢(2)"Beach"Cover Pl#1,3,5,7,10	12.95
BK147	Pl# 8	15.00
BK148	$32.25 #2122a,$10.75 Express Mail Type I(1) Pl#11111	89.50
BK149	$32.25 #2122c,Type II(1)Pl# 22222	140.00
BK150	$5 #2182a, 25¢ Jack London-10(2)	
BK150	Pl# 1,2	14.50
BK151	$1.50 #2197a,25¢ Jack London-6(1)	
BK151	Pl# 1	4.75
BK152	$3 #2197a,25¢ Jack London-6(2)	
BK152	Pl#1	9.25
1986 Commemoratives		
BK153	$1.76 #2201a,22¢ Stamp Coll(2)	
BK153	Pl# 1	5.50
BK153a	same, #2201b Black Omitted (2)	175.00
BK154	$2.20 #2209a,22¢ Fish(2)	
BK154	Pl# 11111,22222	21.75
1987-88 Regular Issues		
BK155	$2.20 #2274a,22¢ Sp. Occasions(1)	
BK155	Pl# 111111,222222	16.50
BK156	$4.40 #2276a,22¢ Flag-Fireworks(1)	
BK156	No Pl#	13.00
BK156	Pl# 1111,2222	15.75
BK156	Pl# 2122	22.50
BK157	$5 #2282a,(25¢) "E"(2)	
BK157	Pl#1111,2222	16.00
BK157	Pl# 2122	20.75
BK158	$5 #2283a,25¢ Pheasant(2)	
BK158	Pl# A1111	16.00
BK159	$5 #2283c Bluer sky(2)	
BK159	Pl# A3111,A3222	175.00
BK160	$5 #2285b,25¢ Owl-Grosbeak(2)	
BK160	Pl#1111,1112,1211,1433,1434 1734,2121,2321,3333,5955	13.50
BK160	Pl# 1133,2111,2122,2221,2222, 3133,3233,3412,3413,3422,3521 4642,4644,4911,4941	22.75
BK160	Pl# 1414	100.00
BK160	Pl# 1634,3512,3822	47.50
BK160	Pl# 5453	170.00
BK161	$3 #2285Ac,25¢ Flag-Clouds(2)	
BK161	Pl# 1111	9.50
1987-90 Commemoratives		
BK162	$4.40 #2359a,22¢ Constitution (4)	
BK162	Pl# 1111,1112	26.95
BK163	$4.40 #2366a,22¢ Locomotives (4)	
BK163	Pl# 1,2	17.95
BK164	$5 #2385a,25¢ Classic Cars(4)	
BK164	Pl#1	47.50
BK165	$3 #2396a(1),2398a(1), 25¢ Special OccasionsPl# A1111	10.00
BK166	$5 #2409a,25¢ Steamboats(4)	
BK166	Pl#1,2	20.75
BK167	$5 #2427a,25¢ 1989 Madonna(2)	
BK167	Pl#1	16.50
BK168	$5 #2429a,25¢ Sleigh(2)	
BK168	Pl# 1111,2111	16.50

COMPLETE BOOKLETS

BK215

BK176

BK191

Scott No.	Cover Value, Pane No. and Description(Number of Panes)	F-VF NH
BK169	$5 #2441a,25¢ Love,Doves(2)	
	Pl# 1211	21.50
BK169	Pl# 2111,2222	29.50
BK169	Pl# 2211	35.00

1990 Regular Issue

BK170	$3 #2443a,15¢ Beach Umbrella(2)	
	Pl#111111	8.75
BK170	Pl# 221111	11.75

1990 Commemorative

BK171	$5 #2474a,25¢ Lighthouses(4)	
	Pl#1-5	35.95

1991-96 Flora and Fauna Regular Issues

BK172	$2 #2483a,20¢ Blue Jay(1)Pl# S1111 . 7.25	
BK173	$2.90 #2484a,29¢ Duck,BEP(1)	
	Pl# 4444	8.50
BK174	$5.80 #2484a,29¢ Duck,BEP(2)	
	Pl# 1111,2222,4444	15.95
BK174	Pl# 1211,3221	130.00
BK174	Pl# 2122,3222,3333	22.50
BK175	$5.80 #2485a,29¢ Duck,KCS(2)	
	Pl# K11111	17.50
BK176	$2.90 #2486a,29¢ African Violet(1)	
	Pl# K11111	9.75
BK177	$5.80 #2486a,29¢ African Violet(2	
	Pl# K11111)	19.00
BK178	$6.40 #2488a,32¢ Peach-Pear(2)	
	Pl# 11111	19.50
BK178A	$4.80 #2492b,32¢ Pink Rose(1)	15.95
BK178B	$4.80 #2492f (1) 32¢ Pink Rose	65.00
BK178C	$9.60 #2492b,32¢ Pink Rose (2)	
	No Pl#	31.75
BK178D	$9.60 #2492f,32¢ Pink Rose (2)	
	2 Panes of #2492f with missing	
	stamp (15 stamps) No Pl#	77.50
BK178E	$9.60 #2492e (1), 2492f (1)	
	32¢ Pink Rose No Pl#	75.00
BK178F	$9.60 #2492b (1), 2492f (1)	
	32¢ Pink Rose No Pl#	425.00

1990 Commemoratives

BK179	$5 #2505a,25¢ Indian Headdress(2)	
	Pl# 1,2	29.75
BK180	$5 #2514b,25¢ Madonna(2) Pl# 1	17.50
BK181	$5 #2516a,25¢ Christmas Tree(2)	
	Pl# 1211	21.75

1991 Regular Issues

BK182	$2.90 #2519a,(29¢) "F",BEP(1)	
	Pl # 2222	9.50
BK183	$5.80 #2519a,(29¢) "F",BEP(2)	
	Pl# 1111,2121,2222	19.00
BK183	Pl# 1222,2111,2212	35.00
BK184	$2.90 #2520a,(29¢) "F",KCS(1)	
	Pl# K1111	30.00
BK185	$5.80 #2527a,29¢ Flower(2)	
	Pl# K1111,K2222,K3333	16.50
BK186	$2.90 #2528a,29¢ Olympic(1)	
	Pl# K11111 (Blue Cover)	8.75
BK186A	$2.90 #2528a, 29¢ Olympic (1)	
	Pl# K11111 (Red Cover)	10.75
BK186Ab	$2.90 #2528a, WCSE Ticket Cover	20.75
BK187	$3.80 #2530a,19¢ Balloons(2)	
	Pl# 1111,2222	10.50
BK187	Pl# 1222	35.00

1991 Commemoratives

Scott No.	Cover Value, Pane No. and Description(Number of Panes)	F-VF NH
BK188	$5.80 #2536a,29¢ Love(2)	
	Pl# 1111,1112	16.95
BK188	Pl# 1113,1123,2223	18.95
BK188	Pl# 1212	45.00
BK189	$5.80 #2549a,29¢ Fishing Flies(4)	
	Pl# A22122,A23123,A23124,A33235	
	A44446,A45546,A45547	42.75
BK189	Pl# A11111,A22113,A23133,	
	A23313	57.50
BK189	Pl#A22132,A32224,A32225,	
	A33233	49.50
BK190	$5.80 #2552a,29¢ Desert Storm(4)	
	Pl# A11111111,A11121111	19.95
BK191	$5.80 #2566a,29¢ Comedians(2)	
	Pl# 1,2	18.95
BK192	$5.80 #2577a,29¢ Space(2)	
	Pl#111111,111112	29.50
BK193	$5.80 #2578a,(29¢) Madonna(2)	
	Pl# 1	15.95
BK194	$5.80 #2581b-85a,(29¢)	
	Santa & Chimney(5 Panes, 1 each)	
	Pl# A11111,A12111	25.00

1992-93 Regular Issues

BK195	$2.90 #2593a,29¢ Pledge,Pf.10(1)	
	Pl# 1111,2222	10.95
BK196	$5.80 #2593a,29¢ Pledge,Pf.10(2)	
	Pl# 1111,2222	16.50
BK197	$5.80 #2593Bc,29¢ Perf. 11x10(2)	
	Pl# 1111,1211, 2122, 2222,	
	2232, 3333,	32.95
BK197I	$5.80 #2593Bcl,29¢ Low gloss gum (2)	
	Pl# 2232, 4444	52.50
BK197I	Pl# 3333 (2)	135.00
BK198	$2.90 #2594a,29¢ Pledge, Red(1)	
	Pl# K1111	11.95
BK199	$5.80 #2594a,29¢ Pledge, Red(2)	
	Pl# K1111	18.00

1992 Commemoratives

BK201	$5.80 #2646a 29¢ Hummingbirds(4)	
	Pl# A1111111,A2212112,A2212222	
	A2222222	17.95
BK201	Pl# A2212122	21.95
BK202	$5.80 #2709a,29¢ Wild Animals(4)	
	Pl# K1111	18.95
BK202A	$5.80 #2710a,29¢ Madonna(2)Pl# 1	15.95
BK203	$5.80 #2718a,29¢ Toys(5)	
	Pl# A111111,A112211,A222222	32.50

1993 Commemoratives

BK204	$5.80 #2737a(2),2737b(1)	
	29¢ Rock'n Roll, Rythym & Blues	
	Pl# A11111,A22222	19.50
BK204	Pl# A13113,A44444	22.75
BK207	$5.80 #2745a,29¢ Space Fantasy(4)	
	Pl# 1111,1211,2222	17.95
BK208	$5.80 #2764a,29¢ Garden Flowers(4)	
	Pl# 1,2	17.95
BK209	$5.80 #2770a,29¢ Broadway(5)	
	Pl# A11111, A11121,A22222,	
	A23232,A23233	19.50
BK210	$5.80 #2778a,29¢ Country Music(5)	
	Pl# A111111,A222222,A333333	
	A422222	19.75
BK211	$5.80 #2790a,29¢ Madonna(5)	
	Pl# A111111,K133333,K144444	
	K255555,K266666	19.50
BK211	Pl# K222222	42.50
BK212	$5.80 #2798a(1),2798b(1)	
	29¢ Christmas Designs	
	Pl# 111111,222222	20.95
BK213	$2.90 #2806b,29¢ AIDS(2) Pl# K111	8.95

1994 Commemoratives

BK214	$5.80 #2814a,29¢ Love & Dove(2)	
	Pl# A11111,A11311,A12112	
	A21222,A22122,A22222,A22322	17.50
BK214	Pl# A12111,A12211,A12212,	
	A21311	27.50
BK215	$5.80 #2833a,29¢ Garden Flowers(4)	
	Pl# 1,2	16.95

Scott No.	Cover Value, Pane No. and Description(Number of Panes)	F-VF NH
BK216	$5.80 #2847a,29¢ Locomotives(4)	
	Pl# S11111	23.95
BK217	$5.80 #2871Ab,29¢ Madonna(2)Pl#1,2	16.95
BK218	$5.80 #2872a,29¢ Stocking(1)	
	Pl# P11111,P22222,P33333,P44444	16.50

1994 "G" Regular Issues

BK219	$3.20 #2881a,(32¢) BEP,Pf.11(1)	
	Pl# 1111	11.75
BK220	$3.20 #2883a,(32¢) BEP,Pf.10(1)	
	Pl# 1111,2222	11.75
BK221	$6.40 #2883a,(32¢)BEP,Pf.10(2)	
	Pl# 1111,2222	21.75
BK222	$6.40 #2884a,(32¢)ABN,Blue(2)	
	Pl# A1111,A1211,A2222	
	A3333,A4444	21.75
BK223	$6.40 #2885a,(32¢)KCS,Red(2)	
	Pl# K1111	25.75

1995-97 Regular Issues

BK225	$3.20 #2916a,32¢ Flag-Porch(1)	
	Pl# 11111,22222,33332	11.75
BK226	$6.40 #2916a,32¢ Flag-Porch(2)	
	Pl# 11111,22222,23222,33332,	
	44444	18.95
BK226A	$4.80#2920f 32¢ Flag-Porch (1)No Pl#	17.50
BK226B	$4.80 #2920h 32¢ Flag-Porch(1)No Pl#	75.00
BK227	$9.60#2920f 32¢ Flag-Porch(2)No Pl#	34.50
BK227A	$4.80#2921c(1), 2921d(1)	
	32¢ Flag-Porch Pl# 11111	19.50
BK228	$6.40 2921a 32¢ Flag-Porch (2)	
	Pl# 11111,13111,21221,22221,22222,	
	44434,44444,55555,55556,66666,	
	77777,88788,88888,99999	20.95
BK228A	$9.60 2921c 32¢ Flag-Porch (3)	
	Pl# 11111	38.50

1995 Commemoratives

BK229	$6.40 #2959a,32¢ Love (2) Pl#1	17.50
BK230	$6.40 #2973a,32¢ Great Lakes	
	Lighthouses(4) Pl# S11111	27.95
BK231	$6.40 #2997a,32¢ Garden Flowers(4)	
	Pl #2	18.95
BK232	$6.40 #3003Ab,32¢ Madonna(2) Pl# 1	19.75
BK233	$6.40 #3007b(1),3007c(1),	
	32¢ Santa & Children	
	Pl# P1111,P2222	20.95
BK233A	$4.80 #3012c,32¢ Midnight Angel(1)	
	Pl# B1111,B2222,B3333	15.75
BK233B	$4.80 #3012d 32¢ Midnight Angel (1)	
BK233C	$9.60 #3012c,32¢ Midnight Angel(2)	
	Pl# B1111,B2222,B3333	31.50
BK233D	$9.60 #3012d,32¢ Midnight Angel(2)	
	No Pl#	39.50
BK233E	$9.60 #3012c,3012d	77.50

1996 Commemoratives

BK234	$6.40 #3029a,32¢ Winter	
	Garden Flowers(4) Pl# 1	19.95
BK235	$4.80 3030b 32¢ Love (1)	17.50
BK236	$9.60 3030b 32¢ Love (2)	32.75

1996-97 Issues

BK237	$2 3048b (1), 3048c (1) 20¢	
	Blue Jay Pl# S1111, S2222	10.00
BK241	$4.80 3049b (1), 3049c (1), 3049d (1)	
	32¢ Yellow Rose Pl# S1111	16.75
BK242	$9.60 3049d 32¢ Yellow Rose (5)	
	Pl# S1111	29.75

1999 Flora & Fauna Issues

BK242A	$4 3051Ab (1), 3051Ac(1) 20¢ Pheasant	
	Pl# V1111	15.00
BK242B	$4.95 3052a (1), 3052b (12), 3052c (1)	
	33¢ Coral Pink Rose Pl# S111	17.50

1996 Makeshift Vending Machine Booklets

BK243	$4.80 2897 32¢ Flag Over Porch (15)	14.95
BK244	$4.80 2957 32¢ Love Cherub (15)	14.95
BK245	$4.80 3024 32¢ Utah Statehood (15)	17.95
BK246	$4.80 3065 32¢ Fulbright (15)	26.50
BK247	$4.80 3069 32¢ Geo. O'Keefe (15)	19.95
BK248	$4.80 3070 32¢ Tennessee (15)	16.50
BK249	$4.80 3072-76 32¢Indian Dances(15)	15.75
BK250	$4.80 3082 32¢ James Dean (15)	21.50

COMPLETE BOOKLETS

BK246

BKC19

QI2

BK264

Scott No.	Cover Value, Pane No. and Description(Number of Panes)	F-VF NH
BK251	$4.80 3083-86 32¢ Folk Heroes (15)	15.95
BK252	$4.80 3087 32¢ Discobolus (15)	20.95
BK253	$4.80 3088 32¢ Iowa (15)	24.95
BK254	$4.80 3090 32¢ Rural Free (30)	31.95
BK255	$4.80 3091-95 32¢ Riverboats (15)	17.95
BK256	$4.80 3105a/o 32¢ End Species (15)	14.95
BK257	$4.80 3107 32¢ Madonna (15)	14.95
BK258	$4.80 3118 32¢ Hanukkah (15)	14.95

1997 Issues

BK259	$4.80 3122b (1), 3122c (1), 3122d (1) 32¢ Statue of Liberty Pl# V1111	16.00
BK260	$9.60 3122d 32¢ Statue of Liberty(5) Pl# V1111	29.75
BK260A	$9.60 3122Eg 32¢ Statue of Liberty(5) Pl# V1111	67.50
BK261	$4.80 3128b (2), 3129b (1), 32¢ Merian Botanical Prints Pl#S11111	35.00
BK264	$4.80 3177b (1) 3177c (1) 3177d (1) 32¢ Holly, Pl# B1111	17.00
BK265	$9.60 3177d (5) 32¢ Holly,Pl# B1111	31.75

1997 Makeshift Vending Machine Booklets

BK266	$4.80 3151a-o 32¢ Dolls	19.75
BK267	$4.80 3152 32¢ Bogart	14.95
BK268	$4.80 3153 32¢ Stars & Stripes	14.95
BK269	$4.80 3168-72 32¢ Monsters	17.50

1998 Issues

BK270	$4.80 3248a(1), 3248b(1) 3248c(1) 32¢ Wreaths Pl# B111111	110.00
BK271	$6.60 3267a (33¢) Hat (2) Pl.#1111, 2222,3333	19.95

1998 Makeshift Vending Booklets

BK272	$4.80 3222-25 32¢ Tropical Birds	18.75
BK273	$4.80 3237 32¢ Ballet	17.50
BK274	$4.80 3238-42 32¢ Space Discovery	19.50

1999 Flag and City

BK275	$4.95 3278a (1), 3278b (1), 3278c (1) 33¢ Flag, Pl# V1111,V1112,V1121, V1212,V2212	15.95
BK276	$6.60 3279a (2) Pl.# 1111,1121	19.50

1999 Fruits and Berries

BK276A	$4.95 3301a (1), 3301b (1), 3301c(1)33¢ Pl.# B1111, B1112, B2212, B2222	22.50

1999 Christmas Deer

BK276B	$4.95 3367a (1), 3367b (1), 3367c (1) 33¢ Deer Pl.# B111111, B222222	35.75

1999 Makeshift Vending Booklets

BK277	$4.95 3325,27-28 (4 each), 3326 (3) 33¢ Glass	15.75
BK278	$4.95 3333-37 (3 each) 33¢ Trains	18.50

2000 U.S. Navy Submarines Prestige Booklet

BK279	$9.80 3377a (2) 22¢-$3.20	75.00

Scott No.	Cover Value, Pane No. and Description(Number of Panes)	F-VF NH
	2000-2001 Regular Issues	
BK280	$6.80 3451b (2), 3451c (2) (34¢) Statue of Liberty Pl# V1111, V2222	22.75
BK281	$6.80 3457b (2), 3457c(1),3457d(1) 34¢ Flowers Pl# S1111	25.75
BK281A	$2 3482b (1), 3482c (1) 20¢ G. Washington Pl# P1,P2,P3	6.00
BK282	$2 3483a (1), 3483b (1) 20¢ G. Washington Pl# P1,P2,P3	32.75
BK282A	$2 3482d(1), 3482e(1) 20¢ G. Washington Pl# P1,P2,P3	32.75
BK282B	$2.10 3484b (1), 3484c (1) 21¢ Bison Pl# P111111, P333333, P444444	6.25
BK282C	$2.10 3484Ae (1), 3484Af (1) 21¢ Bison Pl# P111111, P333333, P444444	19.75
BK282D	$2.10 3484Ah (1), 3484Ai (1) 21¢ Bison Pl# P111111, P333333, P444444	19.75
BK283	$6.80 3485c (2), 3485d (2) 34¢ Liberty Pl# V1111, V1122, V2212, V2222	19.75
BK284	$6.80 3490b (2),3490c (1),3490d(1), 34¢ Flowers Pl# S1111	19.75
BK284A	$6.80 3494b (2), 3494c (1), 3494d (1) 34¢ Apples & Oranges Pl# B1111	19.75
BK285	$6.80 3498a (2), 3498b (2), 34¢ Rose & Love Letter Pl# B1111	19.75
	2001 Christmas Issue	
BK286	$6.80 3544b (2), 3544c (1),3544d(1) 34¢ Santa Claus Pl# V1111	19.75
	2002 United We Stand	
BK287	$6.80 #3549Bc (2), 3549Bd (2) 34¢ Flag Pl# S1111	19.75
	2002-3 Issues	
BK288	$2.30 #3618a (1), 3618b (1) 23¢ Washington,Diecut 11¼ Pl# P1, P2, P4	6.95
BK289	$2.30 #3619a (1), 3619b (1) 23¢ Wash., Mixed Diecuts Pl# P1, P2, P4	17.50
BK289A	$2.30 #3619c (1), 3619d (1) 23¢ Wash., Mixed Diecuts Pl# P1, P2, P4	17.50
BK290	($7.40) #3624a(2), 3624b(2) (37¢) Flag, First Class Pl# S11111	23.75
BK291	($7.40) #3629b(2),3629c(1), 3629d(1) (37¢) Toys, First Class	23.75
BK291A	$7.40 #3634c(2), 3634d(2) 37¢ Flag "2003" Date Pl#V1111	14.75
BK291B	$7.40 #3636a(2), 3636b(2) 37¢ Flag Pl# S11111	18.75
BK292	$7.40 #3645b(2),3645c(1),3645d(1) 37¢ Antique Toys Pl# V1111	23.75
BK293	$7.40 #3691b (2), 3691c (1), 3691d (1) 37¢ Snowmen (20) Pl# V1111	18.75

Scott No.	Cover Value, Pane No. and Description(Number of Panes)	F-VF NH
	2003-2004 Issues	
BK294	$7.40 #3780b (2) 37¢ Old Glory Booklet No Pl#	17.75
BK295	$3.70 #3783a(1), 3783b (1), 37¢ Powered Flight No Pl#	7.95
BK296	$7.40 #3828b(2),3828c(1)3828d(1) 37¢ Music Makers Pl# S11111	15.75
BK297	$7.40 #3856b(2) 37¢ Lewis & Clark Booklet	17.95
	1927-60 Airmail Issues	
BKC1	61¢ #C10a.10¢ Lindbergh(2)	295.00
BKC2	37¢ #C25a,6¢ Transport(2)	9.00
BKC3	73¢ #C25a,6¢ Transport(4)	17.50
BKC4	73¢ #C39a,6¢ Small Plane, Wet(2)	25.00
BKC4a	73¢ #C39c,6¢ Small Plane, Dry(2)	50.00
BKC5	85¢ on 73¢ #C51a,7¢ Blue Jet(2)	45.00
BKC6	85¢ #C51a,7¢ Blue Jet(2)	25.00
BKC7	85¢ #C60a,7¢ Red Jet(2),Blue Cvr.	32.50
BKC8	85¢ #C60a,7¢ Red Jet (2),Red Cvr.	40.00
	1962-64 Jet over Capitol	
BKC9	80¢ #C64b,8¢ Slog.1,"Mailman"(2)	15.75
BKC10	$2 #C64b,8¢ Slog.1,"Mailman"(5)	30.00
BKC11	80¢ #C64b,8¢ Slogan 3, "Zip"(2)	28.50
BKC12	$2 #C64b,8¢ Slogan 3, "Zone"(5) "Wings" Cover	425.00
BKC13	$2 #C64b,8¢ Slog.2,8¢ Mr. Zip Cover	435.00
BKC15	$2 #C64b,8¢ Slogan 3, "Zip"(5)	100.00
BKC16	80¢ #C64c,8¢ Tagged Slogan 3(2)	47.75
BKC17	80¢ #C64c, 8¢ Pink Cover (2)	1650.00
BKC18	$2 #C64c, 8¢ Tagged, Sl.3,Pink(5)	395.00
BKC19	$2 #C64c, 8¢ Tagged, Sl.3,Red(5)	8.50
	1968-73 Airmail Issues	
BKC20	$4 #C72b,10¢ 50-Star Runway-8(5)	12.00
BKC21	$1 #C72c,10¢ 50-Star Runway-5(2)	8.95
BKC22	$1 #1280c,2¢(1) + #C78a,11¢(2)	4.50
BKC23	$1.30 #C79a,13¢ Envelope (2)	3.50
	1965-81 Postal Insurance Booklets	
QI1	(10¢) "Insured P.O.D. V"	165.00
QI2w	(20¢) "Insured U.S.Mail" White on Black Back Cover	6.00
QI2b	(20¢) "Insured U.S.Mail" Black on White Back Cover	3.50
QI3	(40¢) "Insured U.S.Mail" Black (1977)	7.00
QI4	(50¢) "Insured U.S.Mail" Green (1978)	6.00
QI5	(45¢) "Insured U.S.Mail" Red (1981)	6.00

UNCUT PRESS SHEETS AND POSITION PIECES

Scott No.	Description	F-VF,NH
2869	**1994 29¢ Legends of the West**	
	Uncut Sheet of 120 (6 Panes of 20)	120.00
	Block of 10 with Horizontal Gutter .	16.50
	Block of 8 with Vertical Gutter	11.95
	Horizontal Pair with Vertical Gutter	2.25
	Vertical Pair with Horizontal Gutter	2.65
	Center Gutter Block of 4	16.00
	Cross Gutter Block of 20	27.75
2967	**1995 32¢ Marilyn Monroe**	
	Uncut Sheet of 120 (6 Panes of 20)	195.00
	Block of 8 with Vertical Gutter	57.50
	Cross Gutter Block of 8	70.00
	Vertical Pair with Horizontal Gutter	5.50
	Horizontal Pair with Vertical Gutter	9.75
2975	**1995 32¢ Civil War**	
	Uncut Sheet of 120 (6 Panes of 20)	225.00
	Block of 10 with Horizontal Gutter	35.00
	Block of 8 with Vertical Gutter	32.50
	Horizontal Pair with Vertical Gutter	5.75
	Vertical Pair with Horizontal Gutter	5.75
	Center Gutter Block of 4	25.00
	Cross Gutter Block of 20	50.00
3000	**1995 32¢ Comic Strips**	
	Uncut Sheet of 120 (6 Panes of 20)	120.00
	Block of 8 with Horizontal Gutter ...	21.75
	Block of 10 with Vertical Gutter	26.75
	Horizontal Pair with Vertical Gutter	4.50
	Vertical Pair with Horizontal Gutter	4.50
	Center Gutter Block of 4	17.50
	Cross Gutter Block of 20	37.50
3068	**1996 32¢ Atlanta Olympic Games**	
	Uncut Sheet of 120 (6 Panes of 20)	130.00
	Block of 8 with Vertical Gutter	21.75
	Block of 10 with Horizontal Gutter .	25.75
	Horizontal Pair with Vertical Gutter	4.50
	Vertical Pair with Horizontal Gutter	4.50
	Center Gutter Block of 4	18.75
	Cross Gutter Block of 20	33.50
3082	**1996 32¢ James Dean**	
	Uncut Sheet of 120 (6 Panes of 20)	170.00
	Block of 8 with Vertical Gutter	26.75
	Cross Gutter Block of 8	35.00
	Vertical Pair with Horizontal Gutter	4.25
	Horizontal Pair with Vertical Gutter	6.50
3130-31	**1997 Pacific'97 Triangles**	
	Uncut Sheet of 96 (6 Panes of 16)	100.00
	Block of 32 (2Panes)	36.50
	Vertical Pair with Horizontal Gutter	9.75
	Horizontal Pair with Vertical Gutter	6.75
	Cross Gutter Block of 16	29.50
3137v	**1997 32¢ Bugs Bunny**	
	Top Uncut Sheet of 60 (6 Panes of 10)	500.00
	Bottom Uncut Sheet of 60 with Plate Number (6 Panes of 10)	750.00
	Souvenir Sheet from uncut sheet ..	90.00
	Souvenir Sheet with plate number	450.00
	Vertical Pair with Horizontal Gutter	30.00
	Horizontal Pair with Vertical Gutter	60.00
3142	**1997 32¢ Classic American Aircraft**	
	Uncut Sheet of 120 (6 Panes of 20)	120.00
	Block of 10 with Vertical Gutter	14.50
	Block of 8 with Horizontal Gutter ...	12.50
	Horizontal Pair with Vertical Gutter	3.25
	Vertical Pair with Horizontal Gutter	3.25
	Center Gutter Block of 4	17.75
	Center Gutter Block of 20	26.50
3152	**1997 32¢ Humphrey Bogart**	
	Uncut Sheet of 120 (6 Panes of 20)	120.00
	Block of 8 with Vertical Gutter	17.50
	Cross Gutter Block of 8	20.00
	Vertical Pair with Horizontal Gutter	3.50
	Horizontal Pair with Vertical Gutter	5.00
3168-72	**1997 32¢ Classic Movie Monsters**	
	Uncut Sheet of 180 (9 Panes of 20)	210.00
	Block of 8 with Vertical Gutter	13.00
	Block of 10 with Horizontal Gutter	16.50
	Horizontal Pair with Vertical Gutter	3.75
	Vertical Pair with Horizontal Gutter	3.75
	Center Gutter Block of 8.............	21.75
3175	**1997 32¢ Kwanzaa**	
	Uncut Sheet of 250 (5 Panes of 50)	700.00
	Horizontal Pair with Vertical Gutter	13.50
3178	**1997 $3 Mars Pathfinder, Rover Sojourner.** Uncut Sht of 18 Souvenir Sheets	175.00
	Vertical Pair with Horizontal Gutter	20.00
	Horizontal Pair with Vertical Gutter	20.00
	Block of 6 (3 wide by 2 tall)	75.00
3178c	Souvenir Sheet perforated 2 sides	12.50
3178c	Vertical Pair with Horiz. Gutter	25.00
3178l	Souv.Sheet perforated on left side	12.50
3178l	Vertical Pair with Horiz. Gutter	25.00
3178r	Souv.Sheet perforated on right side	12.50
3178r	Vertical Pair with Horiz. Gutter	25.00
3182	**1998 32¢ Celebrate the Century 1900's**	
	Uncut Sheet of 60 (4 Panes of 15)	67.50
3183	**1998 32¢ Celebrate the Century 1910's**	
	Uncut Sheet of 60 (4 Panes of 15)	67.50
3184	**1998 32¢ Celebrate the Century 1920's**	
	Uncut Sheet of 60 (4 Panes of 15)	67.50
3185	**1998 32¢ Celebrate the Century 1930's**	
	Uncut Sheet of 60 (4 Panes of 15)	67.50
3186	**1999 33¢ Celebrate the Century 1940's**	
	Uncut Sheet of 60 (4 Panes of 15)	68.50
3187	**1999 33¢ Celebrate the Century 1950's**	
	Uncut Sheet of 60 (4 Panes of 15)	68.50
3188	**1999 33¢ Celebrate the Century 1960's**	
	Uncut Sheet of 60 (4 Panes of 15)	68.50
3189	**1999 33¢ Celebrate the Century 1970's**	
	Uncut Sheet of 60 (4 Panes of 15)	68.50
3190	**2000 33¢ Celebrate the Century 1980's**	
	Uncut Sheet of 60 (4 Panes of 15)	68.50
3191	**2000 33¢ Celebrate the Century 1990's**	
	Uncut Sheet of 60 (4 Panes of 15)	68.50
3198-3202	**1998 32¢ Alexander Calder**	
	Uncut Sheet of 120 (6 Panes of 20)	130.00
	Vertical Pair with Horizontal Gutter	4.50
	Block of 10 with Horizontal Gutter .	26.50
	Block of 8 with Vertical Gutter	29.50
	Cross Gutter Block of 20	45.00
3203	**1998 32¢ Cinco de Mayo**	
	Uncut Sheet of 180 (9 Panes of 20)	175.00
	Cross Gutter Block of 4	15.00
	Vertical Pair with Horizontal Gutter	2.75
	Horizontal Pair with Vertical Gutter	2.75
3204v	**1998 32¢ Tweety & Sylvester**	
	Top Uncut Sheet of 60 (6 Panes of 10)	95.00
	Bottom Uncut Sheet of 60 with Plate Number (6 Panes of 10)	160.00
	Souvenir Sheet from uncut sheet ..	17.50
	Souvenir Sheet with plate number	75.00
	Vertical Pair with Horizontal Gutter	8.75
	Horizontal Pair with Vertical Gutter	17.50
3209-10	**1998 1¢-$2 Trans-Mississippi**	
	Uncut Sheet of 54 (3 each #3209 & 3210)	160.00
	Block of 18 with Vertical Gutter between & selvage on 4 sides	67.50
	Block of 9 with Horizontal Gutter ...	55.00
	Block of 12 with Vertical Gutter	45.00
	Cross Gutter Block of 12	77.50
	Vertical Pair with Horizontal Gutter	12.50
	Horizontal Pair with Vertical Gutter	12.00
3226	**1998 32¢ Alfred Hitchcock**	
	Uncut Sheet of 120 (6 Panes of 20)	115.00
	Block of 8 with Vertical Gutter	17.75
	Cross Gutter Block of 8	24.50
	Horizontal Pair with Vertical Gutter	5.50
	Vertical Pair with Horizontal Gutter	4.25
3236	**1998 32¢ American Art**	
	Uncut Sheet of 120 (6 Panes of 20)	165.00
	Block of 8 with Vertical Gutter	25.00
	Block of 10 with Horizontal Gutter	30.00
	Cross Gutter Block of 20	38.50
	Vertical Pair with Horizontal Gutter	6.75
	Horizontal Pair with Vertical Gutter	8.25
3237	**1998 32¢ Ballet**	
	Uncut Sheet of 120 (6 Panes of 20)	110.00
	Cross Gutter Block of 4	12.50
	Vertical Pair with Horizontal Gutter	2.75
	Horizontal Pair with Vertical Gutter	2.75
3238-42	**1998 32¢ Space Discovery**	
	Uncut Sheet of 180 (9 Panes of 20)	175.00
	Cross Gutter Block of 10	25.00
	Block of 10 with Horizontal Gutter .	20.00
	Horizontal Pair with Vertical Gutter	3.25
	Vertical Pair with Horizontal Gutter	3.25
3293	**1999 33¢ Sonoran Desert**	
	Uncut Sheet of 60 (6 Panes of 10)	57.50
3306v	**1999 33¢ Daffy Duck**	
	Top Uncut Sheet of 60 (6 Panes-10)	75.00
	Bottom Uncut Sheet of 60 with Plate Number (6 Panes of 10)	110.00
	Souvenir Sheet from uncut sheet ..	15.00
	Souvenir Sheet with plate number	75.00
	Vertical Pair with Horizontal Gutter	5.50
	Horizontal Pair with Vertical Gutter	10.00
3317-20	**1999 33¢ Aquarium Fish**	
	Uncut Sheet of 120 (6 Panes of 20)	110.00
	Block of 8 with Horizontal Gutter ...	11.00
	Cross Gutter Block of 8	17.50
	Horizontal Pair with Vertical Gutter	2.50
	Vertical Pair with Horizontal Gutter	2.00
3321-24	**1999 33¢ Xtreme Sports**	
	Top Uncut Sheet of 80 (4 Panes-20)	75.00
	Bottom Uncut Sheet of 80 with Plate Number (4 Panes of 20)	95.00
	Cross Gutter Block of 8	17.50
	Vertical Pair with Horizontal Gutter	2.75
	Horizontal Pair with Vertical Gutter	2.75
	Block of 4 with Horizontal Gutter ...	6.00
	Block of 8 with Vertical Gutter	11.00
3329	**1999 33¢ James Cagney**	
	Uncut Sheet of 120 (6 Panes of 20)	110.00
	Block of 8 with Vertical Gutter	13.50
	Cross Gutter Block of 8	20.00
	Horizontal Pair with Vertical Gutter	3.50
	Vertical Pair with Horizontal Gutter	2.50
3333-37	**1999 33¢ All Aboard, Trains**	
	Uncut Sheet of 120 (6 Panes of 20)	160.00
	Block of 10 with Vertical Gutter	21.75
	Block of 8 with Horizontal Gutter ..	20.75
	Cross Gutter Block of 8	23.50
	Vertical Pair with Horizontal Gutter	3.50
	Horizontal Pair with Vertical Gutter	3.50
3351	**1999 33¢ Insects and Spiders**	
	Uncut Sheet of 80 (4 Panes of 20)	75.00
	Block of 10 with Vertical Gutter	18.00
	Block of 8 with Horizontal Gutter ...	17.00
	Cross Gutter Block of 20	35.00
	Vertical Pair with Horizontal Gutter	3.00
	Horizontal Pair with Vertical Gutter	3.00
3378	**2000 33¢ Pacific Coast Rain Forest**	
	Uncut Sheet of 60 (6 Panes of 10)	57.50
3391v	**2000 33¢ Wile E. Coyote and Road Runner**	
	Top Uncut Sheet of 60 with plate number on reverse(6 Panes - 10)	75.00
	Bottom Uncut Sheet of 60 with Plate Number (6 Panes of 10)	90.00
	Souvenir Sheet from uncut sheet ..	13.50
	Souvenir Sheet with plate number	60.00
	Vertical Pair with Horizontal Gutter	3.50
	Horizontal Pair with Vertical Gutter	6.50
3403	**2000 33¢ Stars and Stripes**	
	Uncut Sheet of 120 (6 Panes of 20)	110.00
	Blockof 10 with Vertical Gutter	18.75
	Block of 8 with Horizontal Gutter ...	15.00
	Center Gutter Block of 20	35.00
	Horizontal Pair with Vertical Gutter	4.00
	Vertical Pair with Horizontal Gutter	4.00
3408	**2000 33¢ Legends of Baseball**	
	Uncut Sheet of 120 (6 Panes of 20)	125.00
	Block of 10 with Horizontal Gutter	21.75
	Block of 8 with Vertical Gutter	20.00
	Center Gutter Blockof 20	40.00
	Vertical Pair with Horizontal Gutter	3.50
	Horizontal Pair with Vertical Gutter	4.25
3409-13	**2000 60¢-$11.75 Space Achievement and Exploration**	
	Uncut Sheet of 15 designs (5 Souvenir Sheets)	160.00
3439-43	**2000 33¢ Deep Sea Creatures**	
	Uncut Sheet of 135 (9 Panes of 15)	120.00
	Cross Gutter Block of 10	20.00
	Block of 10 with Vertical Gutter	13.00
	Horizontal Pair with Vertical Gutter	2.65
	Vertical Pair with Horizontal Gutter	2.35
3446	**2000 33¢ Edward G. Robinson**	
	Uncut Sheet of 120 (6 Panes of 20)	165.00
	Cross Gutter Block of 8	30.00
	Block of 8 with Vertical Gutter	22.50
	Horizontal Pair with Vertical Gutter	5.25
	Vertical Pair with Horizontal Gutter	3.75

UNCUT PRESS SHEETS AND POSITION PIECES

Scott No.	Description	FVF,NH
3502	**2001 34¢ American Illiustrators**	
	Uncut Sheet of 80 (4 Panes of 20)	110.00
	Cross Gutter Block of 20	57.50
	Block of 8 with Horizontal Gutter ..	35.00
	Block of 10 with Vertical Gutter	35.00
	Vertical Pair with Horizontal Gutter	6.00
	Horizontal Pair with Vertical Gutter	6.00
3505	**2001 1¢,2¢,4¢,80¢ Pan-Am Inverts**	
	Uncut Sheet of 28 (4 Panes of 7) .	70.00
3506	**2001 34¢ Great Plains Prairie**	
	Uncut Sheet of 60 (6 Panes of 10)	60.00
3510-19	**2001 34¢ Legendary Baseball Fields**	
	Uncut Sheet of 160 (8 Panes of 20)	160.00
	Cross Gutter Block of 12	21.00
	Block of 10 with Vertical Gutter	14.00
	Block of 4 with Horizontal Gutter ..	6.50
	Vertical Pair with Horizontal Gutter	3.25
	Horizontal Pair with Vertical Gutter	3.25
3523	**2001 34¢ Lucille Ball**	
	Uncut Sheet of 180 (9 Panes of 20)	165.00
	Cross Gutter Block of 8	25.00
	Block of 8 with Vertical Gutter	14.00
	Horizontal Pair with Vertical Gutter	4.00
	Vertical Pair with Horizontal Gutter	2.75
3534v	**2001 34¢ Porky Pig**	
	Top Uncut Sheet of 60 with plate number on reverse (6 Panes of 10)	75.00
	Bottom Uncut Sheet of 60 with Plate Number (6 Panes of 10)	90.00
	Souvenir Sheet from Uncut Sheet	13.50
	Souvenir Sheet with Plate Number	60.00
	Vertical Pair with Horizontal Gutter	3.50
	Horizontal Pair with Vertical Gutter	6.50
3545	**2001 34¢ James Madison**	
	Uncut Sheet of 120 (6 Panes of 20)	110.00
	Cross Gutter Block of 4	11.00
	Horizontal Pair with Vertical Gutter	3.75
	Vertical Pair with Horizontal Gutter	2.75
3552-55	**2002 34¢ Winter Sports**	
	Uncut Sheet of 180 (9 Panes of 20)	175.00
	Cross Gutter Block of 8	20.00
	Block of 4 with Vertical Gutter	5.75
	Block of 8 with Horizontal Gutter ..	9.75
	Vertical Pair with Horizontal Gutter	2.75
	Horizontal Pair with Vertical Gutter	2.75
3561-3610	**2002 34¢ Greetings from America**	
	Uncut Sheet of 100 (2 Panes of 50)	95.00
3611	**2002 34¢ Longleaf Pine Forest**	
	Uncut Sheet of 90 (9 Panes of 10)	90.00
3649	**2002 37¢ American Photographers**	
	Uncut Sheet of 120 (6 Panes of 20)	120.00
	Cross Gutter Block of 20	38.50
	Block of 8 with Vertical Gutter.	14.50
	Block of 10 with Horizontal Gutter	17.00
	Vertical Pair with Horizontal Gutter	3.25
	Horizontal Pair with Vertical Gutter	3.25
3653-56	**2002 37¢ Teddy Bears**	
	Uncut Sheet of 120 (6 Panes of 20)	165.00
	Cross Gutter Block of 8	27.50
	Block of 8 with Vertical Gutter	18.75
	Block of 4 with Horizontal Gutter ..	10.00
	Vertical Pair with Horizontal Gutter	3.75
	Horizontal Pair with Vertical Gutter	3.75
3692	**2002 37¢ Cary Grant**	
	Uncut Sheet of 120 (6 Panes of 20)	110.00
	Cross Gutter Block of 8	21.75
	Block of 8 with Vertical Gutter	13.00
	Horizontal Pair with Vertical Gutter	3.75
	Vertical Pair with Horizontal Gutter	2.75
3694	**2002 37¢ Hawaiian Missionaries**	
	Uncut Sheet of 24 (6 Panes of 4) ..	85.00
3772	**2003 37¢ Filmmaking**	
	Uncut Sheet of 60 (6 Panes of 10)	55.00
	Block of 10 with Vertical Gutter	12.50
3786	**2003 37¢ Audrey Hepburn**	
	Uncut Sheet of 120 (6 Panes of 20)	100.00
	Cross Gutter Block of 8	19.75
	Block of 8 with Vertical Gutter	12.00
	Horizontal Pair with Vertical Gutter	3.50
	Vertical Pair with Horizontal Gutter	2.50
3802	**2003 37¢ Arctic Tundra**	
	Uncut Sheet of 80 (8 Panes of 10)	70.00
3831	**2004 37¢ Pacific Coral Reef**	
	Uncut Sheet of 80 (8 Panes of 10)	70.00

LEGENDS OF THE WEST POSITION PIECE EXAMPLES

#2869 Block of 10 with Horizontal Gutter

#2869 Block of 8 with Vertical Gutter

#2869 Center Gutter Block of 4

#2869 Horizontal Pair w/Vertical Gutter

#2869 Vertical Pair w/Horizontal Gutter

MODERN ERRORS

The following listings include the most popular and affordable errors and are not intended to be complete. New listings are added each year to bring this section up-to-date. We do not include "Printer's Waste" Errors.

1519a   **1895a**

IMPERFORATE MAJOR ERRORS

Scott's No.		F-VF NH
498a	1¢ Washington, Vertical Pair, Imperforate Horizontally	500.00
498b	1¢ Washington, Horizontal Pair, Imperforate Between	300.00
498c	1¢ Washington, Vertical Pair, Imperforate Between	425.00
499a	2¢ Washington, Vertical Pair, Imperforate Horizontally	165.00
499b	2¢ Washington, Horizontal Pair, Imperforate Vertically	325.00
499c	2¢ Washington, Vertical Pair, Imperforate Between	750.00
501c	3¢ Washington, Vertical Pair, Imperforate Horizontally	1150.00
502c	3¢ Washington, Vertical Pair, Imperforate Horizontally	500.00
525c	1¢ Washington, Horiz. Pair, Imperf. Between	95.00
527c	2¢ Washington, Vertical Pair, Imperforate Horizontally	925.00
536a	1¢ Washington, Horizontal Pair, Imperforate Vertically	950.00
538a	1¢ Washington, Vert. Pair, Imperf. Horiz.	55.00
540a	2¢ Washington, Vert. Pair, Imperf. Horiz.	55.00
554a	2¢ Washington, Horiz. Pair, Imperf. Vert.	265.00
639a	7¢ McKinley, Vert. Pair, Imperf. Between	300.00
720a	3¢ Washington, Vertical Pair, Imperforate Horizontally	1100.00
739a	3¢ Wisconsin, Vert. Pair, Imperf. Horiz.	350.00
739b	3¢ Wisconsin, Horiz. Pair, Imperf. Vert.	475.00
741a	2¢ Grand Canyon, Vertical Pair, Imperf. Horizontally	550.00
741b	2¢ Grand Canyon, Horizontal Pair, Imperforate Vertically	650.00
742a	3¢ Mount Rainier, Vertical Pair, Imperf. Horizontally	650.00
743a	4¢ Mesa Verde, Vertical Pair, Imperforate Horizontally	950.00
744a	5¢ Yellowstone, Horizontal Pair, Imperforate Vertically	650.00
746a	7¢ Acadia, Horizontal Pair, Imperforate Vertically	675.00
805b	1.5¢ M. Washington, Horiz. Pair, Imperf. Between	160.00
805b	1.5¢ M. Washington, Horiz. Pair, Imperf. Between, precancelled	25.00
899a	1¢ Defense, Vert. Pair, Imperf. Between	600.00
899b	1¢ Defense, Horizontal Pair, Imperf. Between	35.00
900a	2¢ Defense, Horizontal Pair, Imperf. Between	40.00
901a	3¢ Defense, Horizontal Pair, Imperf. Between	27.50
966a	3¢ Palomar, Vert. Pair, Imperf. Between	525.00
1055b	2¢ Jefferson, Coil Pair, Imperf., precancelled	525.00
1055c	2¢ Jefferson, Coil Pair, Imperf.	575.00
1058a	4¢ Lincoln, Coil Pair, Imperf	110.00
1058a	4¢ Same, Line Pair	195.00
1059Ac	25¢ Revere, Coil Pair, Imperf.	50.00
1059Ac	Same, Line Pair	85.00
1125a	4¢ San Martin, Horizontal Pair, Imperf. Between	1450.00
1138a	4¢ McDowell, Vert. Pair, Imperf. Between	475.00
1138b	4¢ McDowell, Vert. Pair, Imperf. Horizontal	325.00
1151a	4¢ SEATO, Vertical Pair, Imperf. Between	150.00
1229b	5¢ Washington, Coil Pair, Imperf	450.00
1297a	3¢ Parkman, Coil Pair, Imperf	27.50
1297a	Same, Line Pair	50.00
1297c	Same, Precancelled	7.50
1297c	Same, Precancelled, Line Pair	22.50
1299b	1¢ Jefferson, Coil Pair, Imperf	27.50
1299b	Same, Line Pair	60.00
1303b	4¢ Lincoln, Coil Pair, Imperf	875.00
1304b	5¢ Washington, Coil Pair Imperf	175.00
1304e	Same, Precancelled	375.00
1304Cd	5¢ Washington, Redrawn, Coil Pair, Imperf.	725.00
1305a	6¢ FDR, Coil Pair, Imperf	70.00
1305a	Same, Line Pair	125.00
1305Eg	15¢ Holmes, Shiny Gum, Coil Pair, Imperf	29.50
1305Eg	Same, Line Pair	65.00
1305Ej	Holmes, Type II, Dry Gum, Coil Pair, Imperf	80.00
1305Ej	Same, Line Pair	275.00
1305Eh	Same, Horizontal Pair, Imperf. Between	195.00
1338k	6¢ Flag, Vert. Pair, Imperf. Between	550.00
1338Ab	6¢ Flag, Coil Pair, Imperf	500.00
1338De	6¢ Flag, Horiz. Pair, Imperf. Between	165.00
1338Fi	8¢ Flag, Vert. Pair, Imperf	45.00
1338Fj	8¢ Flag, Horiz. Pair, Imperf. Between	55.00
1338Gh	8¢ Flag, Coil Pair	55.00
1355b	6¢ Disney, Vert. Pair, Imperf. Horiz	675.00
1355c	6¢ Disney, Imperf. Pair	650.00
1362a	6¢ Waterfowl, Vertical Pair, Imperf. Between	525.00
1363b	6¢ Christmas, Imperf. Pair, tagged	225.00
1363d	6¢ Christmas, Imperf. Pair, untagged	295.00
1370a	6¢ Grandma Moses, Horiz. Pair, Imperf. Between	225.00
1384b	6¢ Winter Sunday, Imperforate Pair	975.00
1402a	8¢ Eisenhower, Coil Pair, Imperf	45.00
1402a	Same, Line Pair	70.00
1484a	8¢ Gershwin, Vert. Pair, Imperf. Horiz	235.00
1485a	8¢ Jeffers, Vert. Pair, Imperf. Horiz	250.00
1487a	8¢ Cathers, Vert. Pair, Imperf. Horiz	275.00
1503a	8¢ Johnson, Horiz. Pair, Imperf. Vert	350.00
1508a	8¢ Christmas, Vert. Pair, Imperf. Between	300.00

IMPERFORATE MAJOR ERRORS (cont.)

Scott's No.		F-VF NH
1509a	10¢ Flags, Horiz. Pair, Imperf. Between	50.00
1509c	10¢ Flags, Vertical Pair, Imperforate	950.00
1510e	10¢ Jefferson Memorial, Vert. Pair, Imperf. Horiz	525.00
1510f	10¢ Jefferson Memorial, Vertical Pair, Imperf. Between	800.00
1518b	6.3¢ Bell Coil Pair, Imperf	200.00
1518c	Same, Precancelled Pair	95.00
1518c	Same, Line Pair	225.00
1519a	10¢ Flag Coil Pair, Imperf	37.50
1520b	10¢ Jefferson Memorial, Coil Pair, Imperf	40.00
1520b	Same, Line Pair	70.00
1563a	10¢ Lexington-Concord, Vert. Pair, Imperf. Horiz	400.00
1579a	10¢ Madonna, Imperf. Pair	100.00
1580a	10¢ Christmas Card, Imperf. Pair	100.00
1596a	13¢ Eagle & Shield, Imperf. Pair	50.00
1597a	15¢ Flag (from Sheet), Imperf. Pair	20.00
1615b	7.9¢ Drum, Coil, Pair, Imperf.	575.00
1615Ce	8.4¢ Piano, Coil, Precancelled Pr., Imperf. Between	55.00
1615Ce	Same, Line Pair	120.00
1615Cf	8.4¢ Piano, Coil, Precancelled Pair, Imperf	17.50
1615Cf	Same, Line Pair	30.00
1616a	9¢ Capitol, Coil Pair, Imperf.	160.00
1616a	Same, Line Pair	375.00
1616c	9¢ Capitol, Coil, Precancelled Pair, Imperf.	750.00
1617b	10¢ Petition, Coil Pair, Imperf	60.00
1617b	Same, Line Pair	125.00
1617bd	Same, Pair, dull finish gum	75.00
1618b	13¢ Liberty Bell, Coil Pair, Imperf	25.00
1618b	Same, Line Pair	65.00
1618Cd	15¢ Flag, Coil Pair, Imperf	25.00
1618Ce	Same, Coil Pair, Imperf. Between	150.00
1622a	13¢ Flag, Horiz. Pair, Imperf. Between	55.00
1622Cd	Same, Imperf. Pair	175.00
1625a	13¢ Flag, Coil Pair, Imperf	25.00
1695-98b	13¢ Winter Olympics, Imperf. Block of 4	675.00
1699a	13¢ Maass, Horiz. Pair, Imperf. Vert	450.00
1701a	13¢ Nativity, Imperf. Pair	100.00
1702a	13¢ Currier & Ives, Overall Tagging, Imperf. Pair	100.00
1703a	13¢ Currier & Ives, Block Tagging, Imperf. Pair	110.00
1704a	13¢ Princeton, Horiz. Pair, Imperf. Vert.	550.00
1711a	13¢ Colorado, Horiz. Pair, Imperf. Between	675.00
1711b	13¢ Colorado, Horizontal Pair, Imperf. Vertically	875.00
1729a	13¢ G.W. at Valley Forge, Imperf. Pair	70.00
1730a	13¢ Christmas Mailbox, Imperf. Pair	295.00
1734a	13¢ Indian Head Penny, Horiz. Pair, Imperf. Vert	300.00
1735a	(15¢) "A" Eagle, Vert. Pair, Imperf	90.00
1735b	(15¢) "A" Eagle, Vert. Pair, Imperf. Horiz.	700.00
1743a	(15¢) "A" Eagle, Coil Pair, Imperf	90.00
1743a	Same, Line Pair	195.00
1768a	15¢ Christmas Madonna, Imperf. Pair	90.00
1769a	15¢ Hobby Horse, Imperf. Pair	95.00
1783-86b	15¢ Flora, Block of 4, Imperf	575.00
1787a	15¢ Seeing Eye Dog, Imperf. Pair	425.00
1789c	15¢ J.P.Jones, Perf. 12, Vert. Pair, Imperf. Horiz	175.00
1789Ad	Same, Perf. 11, Vert. Pair, Imperf. Horiz	150.00
1799a	15¢ 1979 Madonna, Imperf. Pair	90.00
1799b	15¢ Madonna, Vertical Pair, Imperforate Horizontally	675.00
1801a	15¢ Will Rogers, Imperf. Pair	225.00
1804a	15¢ B. Banneker, Horiz. Pair, Imperf. Vert.	800.00
1811a	1¢ Quill Pen, Coil Pair, Imperf	175.00
1811a	Same, Line Pair	250.00
1813b	3.5¢ Violin, Coil Pair, Imperf.	225.00
1813b	Same, Line Pair	400.00
1816b	12¢ Torch, Coil Pair, Imperf	185.00
1816b	Same, Line Pair	375.00
1820a	(18¢) "B" Eagle, Coil Pair, Imperf	100.00
1820a	Same, Line Pair	210.00
1823a	15¢ Bissell, Vert. Pair, Imperf. Horiz	400.00
1825a	15¢ Veterans, Horiz. Pair, Imperf. Vert	425.00
1831a	15¢ Organized Labor, Imperf. Pair	375.00
1833a	15¢ Learning, Horiz. Pair, Imperf. Vert	235.00
1842a	15¢ 1980 Madonna, Imperf. Pair	70.00
1843a	15¢ Toy Drum, Imperf. Pair	70.00
1844a	1¢ Dorothea Dix, Imperf. Pair	375.00
1853b	10¢ R. Russell, Vertical Pair, Imperforate Between	875.00
1856b	14¢ S. Lewis, Vert. Pair, Imperf. Horiz	120.00
1856c	14¢ S. Lewis, Horizontal Pair, Imperf. Between	9.00
1867a	39¢ Clark, Vert. Pair, Imperf. Horiz	600.00
1890a	18¢ "Amber" Flag, Imperf. Pair	110.00
1890b	18¢ "Amber" Flag, Vertical Pair, Imperf. Horiz.	825.00
1891a	18¢ "Shining Sea", Coil Pair, Imperf	30.00
1893b	6¢/18¢ Booklet, Imperf. Vertical Between, Perfs at Left	75.00
1894a	20¢ Flag, Vert. Pair, Imperf	35.00
1894b	20¢ Flag, Vert.Pair, Imperf. Horiz.	525.00
1895d	20¢ Flag, Coil Pair, Imperf	11.50
1897b	1¢ Omnibus, Imperf. Pair	650.00
1897Ae	2¢ Locomotive, Coil Pair, Imperf	52.50
1898Ac	4¢ Stagecoach, Imperf. Pair, Precancelled	800.00
1898Ad	4¢ Stagecoach, Imperf. Pair	900.00
1901b	5.9¢ Bicycle, Precancelled Coil Pair, Imperf	180.00
1903b	9.3¢ Mail Wagon, Precancelled Coil Pair, Imperf	130.00
1904b	10.9¢ Hansom Cab, Prec. Coil Pair, Imperf	165.00

2115e   2603a   2913a

IMPERFORATE MAJOR ERRORS (cont.)

Scott's No.		F-VF NH
1906b	17¢ Electric Car, Coil Pair, Imperf	170.00
1906c	Same, Precancelled Pair, Imperf	625.00
1907a	18¢ Surrey, Coil Pair, Imperf	150.00
1908a	20¢ Fire Pumper, Coil Pair, Imperf	120.00
1927a	18¢ Alcoholism, Imperf. Pair	425.00
1934a	18¢ Remington, Vert. Pair, Imperf. Between	265.00
1939a	20¢ 1981 Madonna, Imperf. Pair	115.00
1940a	20¢ Teddy Bear, Imperf. Pair	250.00
1949b	20¢ Ram Bklt. Booklet Pane Vert. Imperf. Btwn., Perfs. at Left	110.00
1951b	20¢ Love, Imperf. Pair	270.00
2003a	20¢ Netherlands, Imperf. Pair	325.00
2005a	20¢ Consumer, Coil Pair, Imperf	120.00
2015a	20¢ Libraries, Vert. Pair, Imperf. Horiz	300.00
2024a	20¢ Ponce de Leon, Imperf. Pair	500.00
2025a	13¢ Puppy & Kitten, Imperf. Pair	650.00
2026a	20¢ Madonna & Child, Imperf. Pair	150.00
2039a	20¢ Voluntarism, Imperf. Pair	700.00
2044a	20¢ Joplin, Imperf. Pair	450.00
2064a	20¢ 1983 Santa Claus, Imperf. Pair	165.00
2072a	20¢ Love, Horiz. Pair, Imperf. Vert	175.00
2092a	20¢ Waterfowl, Horiz. Pair, Imperf. Vert	385.00
2096a	20¢ Smokey Bear, Horiz. Pair, Imperf. Between	300.00
2096b	Same, Vert. Pair, Imperf. Between	225.00
2104a	20¢ Family Unity, Horiz. Pair, Imperf. Vert	550.00
2106a	20¢ Christmas, Horizontal Pair, Imperf. Vertically	950.00
2111a	(22¢) "D" Eagle, Vert. Pair, Imperf	40.00
2112a	(22¢) "D" Eagle, Coil Pair, Imperf	45.00
2112b	(22¢) "D" Eagle, Coil Pair, Tagging Omitted, Imperf.	135.00
2115e	22¢ Flag, Coil Pair, Imperf	15.00
2115e	same, Plate Number Strip of 5	165.00
2121c	22¢ Seashells Booklet Pane, Imperf. Vert.	625.00
2126b	6¢ Tricycle, Precancelled Coil Pair, Imperf	225.00
2130bv	10.1¢ Oil Wagon, Black Precancel, Coil Pair, Imperf	90.00
2130bv	same, Plate Number 1 Strip of 5	425.00
2130b	10.1¢ Oil Wagon, Red Precancel, Coil Pair, Imperf	20.00
3130b	same, Plate Number 3 Strip of 5	175.00
2133b	12.5¢ Pushcart, Precancelled Coil Pair, Imperf	50.00
2133b	same, Plate Number 1 Strip of 5	250.00
2134a	14¢ Iceboat, Coil Pair, Imperf	125.00
2134a	same, Plate Number Strip of 5	525.00
2135a	17¢ Dogsled, Coil Pair, Imperf. Miscut	475.00
2136a	25¢ Bread Wagon, Coil Pair, Imperf	10.00
2136a	same, Plate Number Strip of 5	250.00
2136b	25¢ Bread Wagon, Imperf. Between	700.00
2142a	22¢ Winter Special Olympics, Vert. pair, Imperf. Horiz	525.00
2146a	22¢ A. Adams, Imperf. Pair	270.00
2149b	18¢ G. Washington Coil, Imperforate Pair	950.00
2149c	18¢ G. Washington Coil, Precancel, Imperf. Pair	800.00
2165a	22¢ 1985 Madonna, Imperf. Pair	90.00
2166a	22¢ Poinsettia, Imperf. Pair	125.00
2210a	22¢ Public Hospitals, Vertical Pair, Imperf. Horiz	335.00
2211a	22¢ Duke Ellington, Vertical Pair, Imperf. Horizontally	950.00
2228b	4¢ Stagecoach "B" Press, Coil Pair, Imperf	375.00
2244a	22¢ Madonna, Imperforate Pair	775.00
2256a	8.4¢ Wheel Chair, Coil Pair, Imperf.	875.00
2259a	13.2¢ Coal Car, Coil Pair, Imperf	95.00
2259a	same, Plate Number 1 Strip of 5	275.00
2260c	15¢ Tugboat, Coil Pair, Imperf	800.00
2261a	16.7¢ Popcorn Wagon Pair, Imperf	230.00
2263a	20¢ Cable Car, Coil Pair, Imperf	70.00
2263a	same, Plate Number 2 Strip of 5	300.00
2265a	21¢ Railway Car, Coil Pair, Imperf	60.00
2265a	same, Plate Number 1 Strip of 5	325.00
2279a	(25¢) "E" Earth, Coil Pair, Imperf	80.00
2279a	same, Plate Number Strip of 5	475.00
2280b	25¢ Flag Over Yosemite, Coil Pair, Block Tagged, Imperf	30.00
2280b	same, Plate Number Strip of 5	450.00
2280c	25¢ Flag Over Yosemite, Coil Pair, Prephosphor paper, Impf	15.00
2280c	same, Plate Number Strip of 5	195.00
2280f	25¢ Flag over Yosemite, Pair, Imperforate Between	700.00
2281a	25¢ Honeybee Coil, Imperf. Pair	50.00
2281a	same, Plate Number Strip of 5	250.00
2418a	25¢ Ernest Hemingway, Vert Pair, Imperf. Horizontally	900.00
2419b	$2.40 Moon Landing, Imperf. Pair	750.00
2431b	25¢ Eagle & Shield Pair, Die-cut Omittted	475.00
2440a	25¢ Love, Imperf. Pair	800.00
2451a	4¢ Steam Carriage, Imperf. Pair	875.00
2452c	5¢ Circus Wagon, Coil Pair, Imperf	875.00

IMPERFORATE MAJOR ERRORS (cont.)

Scott's No.		F-VF NH
2452De	5¢ Circus Wagon, Coil Pair, Imperforate	250.00
2453a	5¢ Canoe, Coil Pair, Imperforate	300.00
2457a	10¢ Tractor Trailer, Coil Pair, Imperforate	250.00
2457a	same, Plate Number 1 Strip of 5	750.00
2463a	20¢ Cog Railway, Coil Pair, Imperforate	115.00
2463a	same, Plate Number 1 Strip of 5	300.00
2464b	23¢ Lunch Wagon, Coil Pair, Imperforate	140.00
2466a	32¢ Ferryboat, Coil Pair, Imperforate	575.00
2517a	(29¢) Flower, Imperforate Pair	675.00
2518a	(29¢) "F" Coil, Imperforate Pair	37.50
2518a	same, Plate Number Strip of 5	225.00
2521a	4¢ Non-denominated, Vert. Pair, Imperf. Horiz	110.00
2521b	4¢ Non-denominated Imperf. Pair	80.00
2523b	29¢ Mt. Rushmore, Coil Pair, Imperf	25.00
2523b	same, Plate Number Strip of 5	275.00
2527c	29¢ Flower, Horiz. Pair, Imperf. Vert.	240.00
2550a	29¢ Cole Porter, Vert. Pair, Imperf. Horiz	600.00
2567c	29¢ Jan Matzeliger, Imperforate Pair	700.00
2579a	(29¢) Santa in Chimney, Horiz. Pair, Imperf. Vertically	300.00
2579b	(29¢) Santa in Chimney, Vert. Pair, Imperf. Horiz	500.00
2594b	29¢ Flag, Imperf. Pair	950.00
2595b	29¢ Eagle & Shield Pair, Die-cut Omittted	195.00
2603a	(10¢) Eagle & Shield, Coil Pair, Imperf	27.50
2603a	same, Plate Number Strip of 5	135.00
2607c	23¢ USA Pre-sort, Coil Pair, Imperf	85.00
2609a	29¢ Flag over White House, Coil Pair, Imperf	20.00
2609a	same, Plate Number Strip of 5	175.00
2609b	same, Pair, Imperf. Between	95.00
2618a	29¢ Love, Horizontal Pair, Imperf. Vertically	750.00
2877a	(3¢) Dove, Imperf. Pair	190.00
2889a	(32¢) & Black "G", Imperf. Pair	300.00
2897a	32¢ Flag over Porch, Imperf. Vertical Pair	75.00
2902a	(5¢) Butte Coil Pair. Imperf	700.00
2904c	(5¢) Mountain Imperf. Pair	475.00
2913a	32¢ Flag over Porch Coil, Imperf. Pair	40.00
2913a	same, Plate Number Strip of 5	400.00
2915Ah	32¢ Flag over Porch, Imperf. Pair	40.00
2915Ah	same, Plate Number Strip of 5	200.00
2921e	32¢ Flag over Porch, Bk.Pane of 10, Imperforate	275.00
2967a	32¢ Marilyn Monroe, Imperf. Pair	600.00
3004-7d	32¢ Santa & Children, Imperf. Block	675.00
3054a	32¢ Yellow Rose Pair, Die-cut Omitted	90.00
3055a	20¢ Ring-necked Pheasant Pair, Die-cut Omitted	200.00
3069a	32¢ Georgia O'Keeffe, Imperf. Pair	170.00
3082a	32¢ James Dean, Imperf. Pair	325.00
3112b	32¢ Madonna, Die-cut Omitted	75.00
3123b	32¢ Love Pair, Die-cut Omitted	225.00
3127c	32¢ Merian, Vertical Pair, Imperf. Between	500.00
3281a	33¢ Flag over City, Imperforate Pair	30.00

AIRMAILS & SPECIAL DELIVERY

C23a	6¢ EagleVertical Pair, Imperf. Horizontal	335.00
C73a	10¢ Stars, Coil Pair, Imperf	575.00
C82a	11¢ Jet, Coil Pair, Imperf	275.00
C82a	Same, Line Pair	425.00
C83a	13¢ Winged Env., Coil Pair, Imperf	75.00
C83a	Same, Line Pair	150.00
C113	33¢ Verville, Imperf. Pair	850.00
C115	44¢ Transpacific, Imperf. Pair	825.00
E15c	10¢ Motorcycle, horiz. pair, imperf. between	295.00
O148a	23¢ Official Mail, Imperf. Pair	100.00

COLOR OMISSION & VARIETY ERRORS

Scott's No.		F-VF NH
499h	2¢ Washington, "Boston Lake", with PFC	375.00
1252a	5¢ Music, blue omitted	975.00
1271a	5¢ Florida, ochre omitted	325.00
1331-32 var.	5¢ Space Twins, red stripes of capsule flag omitted, single in block of 9	225.00
1338Fp	8¢ Flag and White House, Slate green omitted	400.00
1355a	6¢ Disney, ochre omitted	600.00
1362b	6¢ Waterfowl, red & dark blue omitted	900.00
1363c	6¢ Christmas, 1968, light yellow omitted	60.00
1370b	6¢ Grandma Moses, black and prussian blue omitted	775.00
1381a	6¢ Baseball, black omitted	1000.00
1384c	6¢ Christmas, 1969, light green omitted	25.00
1384d	6¢ Christmas, yellow, red & light green omitted	875.00
1414b	6¢ Christmas, 1970, black omitted	550.00
1420a	6¢ Pilgrims, orange & yellow omitted	875.00
1432a	8¢ Revolution, gray & black omitted	600.00
1436a	8¢ Emily Dickinson, black & olive omitted	750.00
1444a	8¢ Christmas, gold omitted	500.00
1471a	8¢ Christmas, 1972, pink omitted	150.00
1473a	8¢ Pharmacy, blue & orange omitted	800.00
1474a	8¢ Stamp Collecting, black omitted	650.00
1488a	8¢ Copernicus, yellow omitted	975.00
1488a	8¢ Copernicus, black omitted	875.00
1501a	8¢ Electronics, black omitted	450.00
1504a	8¢ Cattle, green & red brown omitted	950.00
1506a	10¢ Wheat Field, black & blue omitted	750.00
1509b	10¢ Crossed Flags, blue omitted	175.00
1511a	10¢ Zip, yellow omitted	60.00
1528a	10¢ Horse Racing, blue omitted	875.00
1542a	10¢ Kentucky, dull black omitted	750.00
1547a	10¢ Energy Conservation, blue & orange omitted	850.00
1547b	10¢ Energy Conservation, orange & green omitted	675.00
1547c	10¢ Energy Conservation, green omitted	875.00
1551a	10¢ Christmas, buff omitted	32.50
1555a	10¢ D.W. Griffith, brown omitted	625.00
1556b	10¢ Pioneer 10, dark blues omitted	900.00
1557a	10¢ Mariner, red omitted	450.00
1559a	8¢ Ludington, green inscription on gum omitted	225.00
1560a	10¢ Salem Poor, green inscription on gum omitted	225.00
1561a	10¢ Salomon, green inscription on gum omitted	225.00
1561b	10¢ Salomon, red color omitted	250.00
1596b	13¢ Eagle & Shield, yellow omitted	150.00
1597b	15¢ McHenry Flag, gray omitted	575.00
1608a	50¢ Lamp, black color omitted	300.00
1610a	$1.00 Lamp, dark brown color omitted	250.00
1610b	$1.00 Lamp, tan, yellow & orange omitted	325.00
1618Cf	15¢ Flag Coil, grey omitted	40.00
1686g	13¢ Bicentennial SS, "USA 13¢" omitted on 1st & 5th stamp	450.00
1686i	13¢ Bicent. SS, "USA 13¢" omitted on 2nd, 3rd, 4th stamp	500.00
1686k	13¢ Bicent. SS, "USA 13¢" omitted on 3rd & 4th stamp	750.00
1686l	13¢ Bicent. SS, "USA 13¢" omitted on 5th stamp	525.00
1687g	18¢ Bicent. SS, "USA 18¢" omitted on 1st & 3rd stamp	675.00
1687h	18¢ Bicent. SS, "USA 18¢" omitted on 2nd, 4th, 5th stamp	450.00
1687i	18¢ Bicent. SS, "USA 18¢" omitted on 4th stamp	500.00
1687m	18¢ Bicent. SS, "USA 18¢" omitted on 2nd & 5th stamp	500.00
1688g	24¢ Bicent. SS, "USA 24¢" omitted on 4th & 5th stamp	450.00
1688i	24¢ Bicent. SS, "USA 24¢" omitted on 1st, 2nd, 3rd stamp	500.00
1689g	31¢ Bicent. SS, "USA 31¢" omitted on 1st & 3rd stamp	400.00
1689h	31¢ Bicent. SS, "USA 31¢" omitted on 2nd, 4th, 5th stamp	475.00
1689i	31¢ Bicent. SS, "USA 31¢" omitted on 5th stamp	450.00
1690a	13¢ Franklin, light blue omitted	240.00
1800a	15¢ Christmas, green & yellow omitted	600.00
1800b	15¢ Christmas, yellow, green & tan omitted	675.00
1826a	15¢ de Galvez, red, brown & blue omitted	775.00
1843b	15¢ Wreath, buff omitted	25.00
1894c	20¢ Flag, dark blue omitted	85.00
1894d	20¢ Flag, black omitted	325.00
1895f	20¢ Flag Coil, black omitted	50.00
1895 var.	20¢ Flag, Blue "Supreme Court" color var	175.00
1926a	18¢ Millay, black omitted	325.00
1934b	18¢ Remington, brown omitted	450.00
1937-38b	18¢ Yorktown, se-tenant pair, black omitted	395.00
1951c	20¢ Love, blue omitted	225.00
1951d	20¢ Love, yellow omitted	950.00
2014a	20¢ Peace Garden, black, green & brown omitted	250.00
2045a	20¢ Medal of Honor, red omitted	265.00
2055-58b	20¢ Inventors, Block of 4, black omitted	375.00
2059-62b	20¢ Streetcars, Block of 4, black omitted	400.00
2115 var.	22¢ Flag, "Capitol Bldg." "Erie Blue" color var	12.00
2121b	22¢ Seashells, Bk. Pane of 10, violet omitted	750.00
2145a	22¢ Ameripex, black, blue & red omitted	200.00
2201b	22¢ Stamp Collecting Pane of 4, black omitted	50.00
2201b	22¢ Stamp Collecting, cplt. bklt. of 2 panes, black omitted	100.00
2235-38b	22¢ Navajo Art, black omitted	375.00
2281b	25¢ Honeybee, black (engraved) omitted	60.00
2281c	25¢ Honeybee, Black (litho) omitted	450.00
2349a	22¢ U.S./Morocco, black omitted	275.00
2351-54b	22¢ Lacemaking, white omitted	900.00
2361a	22¢ CPA, black omitted	725.00

COLOR OMITTED (continued)

Scott's No.		F-VF NH
2399a	25¢ Christmas, 1988, gold omitted	30.00
2421a	25¢ Bill of Rights, black (engraved) omitted	325.00
2422-25b	25¢ Prehistoric Animals, black omitted	975.00
2427b	25¢ Christmas, red omitted	800.00
2434-37b	25¢ Traditional Mail Delivery, dark blue omitted	700.00
2441c	25¢ Love, Booklet Single, bright pink omitted	195.00
2443c	15¢ Beach Umbrella, Booklet Single, blue omitted	165.00
2474b	25¢ Lighthouse bklt., white omitted, cplt. bklt. of 4 panes	320.00
2474b	Same, Individual Pane	80.00
2479b	19¢ Fawn, red omitted	825.00
2481a	45¢ Sunfish, black omitted	500.00
2482a	$2 Bobcat, black omitted	300.00
2508-11b	25¢ Sea Creatures, black omitted	750.00
2561a	29¢ Washington, DC Bicentennial, black "USA 29¢" omitted	120.00
2562-66b	29¢ Comedians, Booklet Pane, red & violet omitted	750.00
2595c	29¢ Eagle & Shield, brown omitted	425.00
2635a	29¢ Alaska Highway, black omitted	650.00
2764b	29¢ Garden Flowers, booklet pane, black omitted	250.00
2833c	29¢ Garden Flowers, booklet pane, black omitted	250.00
2949b	(32¢) Love, red omitted	475.00
2980a	32¢ Women's Suffrage, black omitted	425.00
3003c	32¢ Madonna, black omitted	250.00
3030c	32¢ Love, red omitted	400.00
3066a	50¢ Jacqueline Cochran, black omitted	65.00
3257a	(1¢) Weather Vane, black omitted	175.00
3281b	33¢ Flag & City, light blue & yellow omitted	600.00
C23v	6¢ Ultramarine & Carmine	140.00
C76a	10¢ Man on the Moon, red omitted	550.00
C76 var.	10¢ Man on the Moon, patch only omitted	300.00
C84a	11¢ City of Refuge, blue & green omitted	900.00
C91-92b	31¢ Wright Bros., ultramarine & black omitted	725.00
C122-25b	45¢ Future Mail Delivery, light blue omitted	875.00
J89a	Postage Due, Black Numeral omitted	285.00

MINT POSTAL STATIONERY

U119

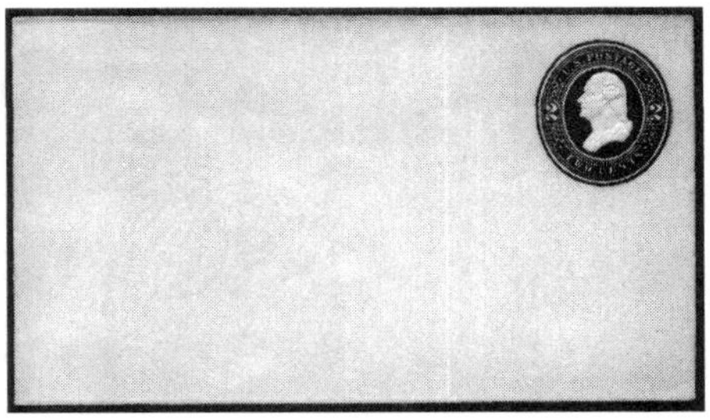

U278

U333

ENTIRE ENVELOPES AND CUT SQUARES

Scott's No.		Entire	Cut Sq.
	1853-61 Issues		
U2	1853 3¢ Red, buff, Die 1	...	275.00
U9	1854 3¢ Red, die 5	125.00	35.00
U10	1854 3¢ Red, buff	65.00	19.50
U12	1853 3¢ Red, buff, Die 6	250.00	140.00
U16	1855 10¢ Green shades, buff	375.00	125.00
U19	1860 1¢ Blue,buff,die 1	80.00	35.00
W20	1861 1¢ Blue,buff,wrapper	110.00	65.00
W21	1861 1¢ Blue,manila, wrapper	110.00	52.50
U26	1860 3¢ Red	55.00	32.50
U27	1860 3¢ Red, buff	40.00	24.00
U34	1861 3¢ Pink	55.00	26.50
U35	1861 3¢ Pink, buff	55.00	25.00
U36	1861 3¢ Pink, blue	250.00	80.00
U38	1861 6¢ Pink	195.00	120.00
U39	1861 6¢ Pink, buff	180.00	70.00
U40	1861 10¢ Yellow green	75.00	40.00
U41	1861 10¢ Yellow green,buff	70.00	37.50
	1863-65 Issues		
U46	1863 2¢ Black,buff,die 1	72.50	43.50
W47	1863 2¢ Black,dark manila	85.00	60.00
U50	1864 2¢ Black,buff,die 3	35.00	14.50
U52	1864 2¢ Black, orange	28.50	15.00
U54	1864 2¢ Black,buff,die 4	30.00	15.75
W55	1864 2¢ Black,wrapper	130.00	80.00
U56	1864 2¢ Black,orange	25.00	16.50
W57	1864 2¢ Black,wrapper	30.00	17.00
U58	1864 3¢ Pink	14.50	8.75
U59	1864 3¢ Pink, buff	13.50	7.50
U60	1865 3¢ Brown	95.00	50.00
U61	1865 3¢ Brown, buff	95.00	50.00
U62	1864 6¢ Pink	150.00	75.00
U63	1864 6¢ Pink, buff	95.00	40.00
U64	1865 6¢ Purple	70.00	50.00
U65	1865 6¢ Purple, buff	75.00	47.50
U67	1865 9¢ Orange, buff	185.00	130.00
U69	1865 12¢ Red brown, buff	185.00	120.00
U70	1865 18¢ Red, buff	200.00	95.00
U71	1865 24¢ Blue, buff	200.00	95.00
U72	1865 30¢ Green, buff	165.00	110.00
U73	1865 40¢ Rose, buff	335.00	110.00
	1870-71 Reay Issue		
U74	1870 1¢ Blue	70.00	40.00
U75	1870 1¢ Blue, amber	57.50	37.50
U76	1870 1¢ Blue, orange	32.50	18.00
W77	1870 1¢ Blue, wrapper	75.00	42.50
U78	1870 2¢ Brown	55.00	39.50
U79	1870 2¢ Brown, amber	37.50	19.00
U80	1870 2¢ Brown, orange	16.50	11.00
W81	1870 2¢ Brown, wrapper	57.50	27.50
U82	1870 3¢ Green	15.00	7.50
U83	1870 3¢ Green, amber	17.00	6.25
U84	1870 3¢ Green, cream	17.00	9.50
U85	1870 6¢ Dark red	38.50	25.00
U86	1870 6¢ Dark red, amber	50.00	28.50
U87	1870 6¢ Dark red, cream	52.50	32.50
U88	1871 7¢ Vermilion, amber	75.00	50.00
U91	1870 10¢ Brown	100.00	77.50
U92	1870 10¢ Brown, amber	110.00	85.00
U93	1870 12¢ Plum	240.00	110.00
U94	1870 12¢ Plum, amber	225.00	115.00
U96	1870 15¢ Red orange	165.00	75.00
U99	1870 24¢ Purple	180.00	125.00
U102	1870 30¢ Black	295.00	80.00
U105	1870 90¢ Carmine	225.00	165.00
	1874-86 Plimpton Issue		
U108	1874 1¢ Dark blue	225.00	170.00
U109	1874 1¢ Dark blue, amber	185.00	150.00
U111	1874 1¢ Dark blue, orange	35.00	22.50
W112	1874 1¢ Dark blue, wrapper	90.00	60.00
U113	1874 1¢ Light blue, die 2	2.50	1.65
U114	1874 1¢ Light blue, amber	7.75	4.25
U115	1874 1¢ Blue, cream	9.00	4.25
U116	1874 1¢ Light blue, orange	.90	.70
U117	1880 1¢ Light blue, blue	11.50	7.00
U118	1879 1¢ Light blue, fawn	12.50	7.00
U119	1886 1¢ Light blue,manila	14.00	7.50
W120	1874 1¢ Light blue,.wrapper	2.65	1.50
U121	1886 1¢ Lt.blue,amber manila	22.50	15.00
U122	1874 2¢ Brown, die 1	140.00	110.00
U123	1874 2¢ Brown, amber	100.00	65.00
W126	1874 2¢ Brown, wrapper	225.00	140.00
U128	1874 2¢ Brown, die 2	90.00	50.00
U129	1874 2¢ Brown, amber	100.00	80.00

Scott's No.		Entire	Cut Sq.
W131	1874 2¢ Brown,wrapper	25.00	18.00
U132	1874 2¢ Brown, die 3	100.00	75.00
U136	1874 2¢ Brown, orange,d.4	75.00	50.00
W137	1874 2¢ Brown,wrap,die 4	95.00	70.00
U139	1875 2¢ Brown, die 5	67.50	50.00
U140	1875 2¢ Brown, amber	110.00	85.00
W141	1875 2¢ Brown, wrapper	42.50	35.00
U142	1875 2¢ Vermilion, die 5	8.50	7.25
U143	1875 2¢ Vermilion,amber	8.50	7.25
U144	1875 2¢ Vermilion,cream	19.50	15.75
U146	1880 2¢ Vermilion, blue	200.00	135.00
U147	1875 2¢ Vermilion,fawn	13.50	8.25
W148	1875 2¢ Vermilion,wrapper	7.50	3.75
U149	1878 2¢ Vermilion, die 6	75.00	52.50
U150	1878 2¢ Vermilion, amber	50.00	35.00
U151	1880 2¢ Vermilion, blue	19.00	13.00
U152	1878 2¢ Vermilion, fawn	15.00	11.50
U153	1876 2¢ Vermilion, die 7	90.00	65.00
W155	1876 2¢ Vermilion,wrapper	45.00	21.50
W158	1881 2¢ Vermilion,wrapper	150.00	90.00
U159	1874 3¢ Green, die 1	50.00	30.00
U160	1874 3¢ Green, amber	57.50	32.50
U161	1874 3¢ Green, cream	60.00	40.00
U163	1874 3¢ Green, die 2	3.25	1.30
U164	1874 3¢ Green, amber	3.50	1.50
U165	1874 3¢ Green, cream	15.00	8.00
U166	1874 3¢ Green, blue	15.00	7.75
U167	1875 3¢ Green, fawn	8.75	5.00
U172	1875 5¢ Blue, die 1	17.00	12.00
U173	1875 5¢ Blue, amber	17.00	12.00
U174	1875 5¢ Blue, cream	150.00	100.00
U175	1875 5¢ Blue, blue	47.50	32.50
U176	1875 5¢ Blue, fawn	250.00	140.00
U177	1875 5¢ Blue, die 2	14.00	8.75
U178	1875 5¢ Blue, amber	16.50	8.50
U179	1875 5¢ Blue, blue	37.50	25.00
U180	1875 5¢ Blue, fawn	180.00	110.00
U181	1874 6¢ Red	12.50	7.50
U182	1874 6¢ Red, amber	20.00	11.00
U183	1874 6¢ Red, cream	70.00	40.00
U184	1875 6¢ Red, fawn	30.00	21.50
U186	1874 7¢ Vermilion, amber	160.00	125.00
U187	1874 10¢ Brown, die 1	57.50	40.00
U188	1874 10¢ Brown, amber	125.00	70.00
U189	1875 10¢ Chocolate, die 2	11.00	6.75
U190	1875 10¢ Chocolate,amber	12.00	7.50
U191	1886 10¢ Brown, buff	15.00	12.00
U192	1886 10¢ Brown, blue	17.50	15.00
U193	1886 10¢ Brown, manila	20.00	16.50
U194	1886 10¢ Brown,amber man.	23.50	17.50
U198	1874 15¢ Orange	85.00	47.50
U199	1874 15¢ Orange, amber	250.00	150.00
U201	1874 24¢ Purple	225.00	175.00
U202	1874 24¢ Purple, amber	240.00	180.00
U203	1874 24¢ Purple, cream	...	165.00
U204	1874 30¢ Black	75.00	62.50
U205	1874 30¢ Black, amber	140.00	75.00
U207	1881 30¢ Black, oriental buff	150.00	100.00
U208	1881 30¢ Black, blue	135.00	110.00
U209	1881 30¢ Black, manila	150.00	95.00
U210	1886 30¢ Black, amber man.	180.00	155.00
U211	1875 90¢ Carmine	160.00	120.00
U212	1875 90¢ Carmine, amber	275.00	200.00
U214	1886 90¢ Carmine,orien.buff	260.00	200.00
U215	1886 90¢ Carmine, blue	240.00	190.00
U216	1886 90¢ Carmine, manila	240.00	160.00
U217	1886 90¢ Carmine,amber man.	225.00	140.00
	1876 Centennial Issue		
U218	1876 3¢ Red	70.00	52.50
U219	1876 3¢ Green, die 1	60.00	47.50
U221	1876 3¢ Green, die 2	80.00	52.50
	1882-86 Issues		
U222	1882 5¢ Brown	8.75	4.50
U223	1882 5¢ Brown, amber	9.50	4.75
U224	1886 5¢ Brown,oriental buff	165.00	120.00
U225	1882 5¢ Brown, blue	100.00	70.00
U227	1883 2¢ Red	8.50	4.00
U228	1883 2¢ Red, amber	9.25	5.00
U229	1883 2¢ Red, blue	11.00	7.50
U230	1883 2¢ Red, fawn	14.00	8.50
U231	1883 2¢ Red, fine lines	8.00	3.75
U232	1883 2¢ Red, amber	9.00	5.00
U233	1883 2¢ Red, blue	13.50	8.00
U234	1883 2¢ Red, fawn	9.00	6.25
W235	1883 2¢ Red,wrapper	26.50	17.50
U236	1884 2¢ Red, coarse lines	16.00	11.00
U237	1884 2¢ Red, amber	22.50	13.00

Scott's No.		Entire	Cut Sq.
U238	1884 2¢ Red, blue	30.00	23.50
U239	1884 2¢ Red, fawn	20.00	14.50
U240	1884 2¢ Red, 3½ links	130.00	85.00
U243	1884 2¢ Red, 2 links	130.00	100.00
U250	1883 4¢ Green, die 1	6.00	3.50
U251	1883 4¢ Green, amber	6.50	4.50
U252	1883 4¢ Green, buff	15.00	11.00
U253	1886 4¢ Green, blue	15.00	10.00
U254	1886 4¢ Green, manila	16.00	12.00
U255	1886 4¢ Green,amber manila	28.50	21.50
U256	1883 4¢ Green, die 2	17.00	8.25
U257	1883 4¢ Green, amber	22.50	12.50
U258	1886 4¢ Green, manila	22.50	12.50
U259	1886 4¢ Green,amber manila	22.50	12.50
U260	1884 2¢ Brown,four wavy lines	18.50	14.50
U261	1884 2¢ Brown, amber	17.00	14.00
U262	1884 2¢ Brown, blue	23.50	17.00
U263	1884 2¢ Brown, fawn	17.50	13.50
W264	1884 2¢ Brown,wrapper	22.50	15.75
U265	1884 2¢ Brown,retouched	22.50	15.75
U266	1884 2¢ Brown, amber	75.00	62.50
U267	1884 2¢ Brown, blue	25.00	19.50
U268	1884 2¢ Brown, fawn	19.50	16.00
W269	1884 2¢ Brown, wrapper	30.00	24.00
U270	1884 2¢ Brown, 2 links	130.00	100.00
U277	1884 2¢ Brown, die 1	.85	.50
U278	1884 2¢ Brown,amber	1.40	.70
U279	1886 2¢ Brown,oriental buff	6.25	4.00
U280	1884 2¢ Brown,blue	4.00	2.75
U281	1884 2¢ Brown,fawn	5.00	3.25
U282	1886 2¢ Brown,manila	16.00	11.75
W283	1884 2¢ Brown,wrapper	10.00	6.75
U284	1886 2¢ Brown,amber manila	13.00	7.50
W287	1884 2¢ Red, wrapper	185.00	130.00
U289	1884 2¢ Brown,amber,die 2	19.50	15.75
U291	1884 2¢ Brown,fawn	35.00	25.00
W292	1884 2¢ Brown,wrapper	30.00	22.50
	1886 Grant Letter Sheet		
U293	1886 2¢ Green, folded	27.50	...
	1887-94 Issues		
U294	1887 1¢ Blue	.95	.55
U295	1894 1¢ Dark blue	11.00	7.75
U296	1887 1¢ Blue, amber	5.50	3.25
U297	1894 1¢ Dk. blue, amber	57.50	47.50
U300	1887 1¢ Blue, manila	1.20	.70
W301	1887 1¢ Blue, wrapper	1.20	.50
U302	1894 1¢ Dark blue, manila	35.00	25.00
W303	1894 1¢ Dark blue, wrapper	25.00	14.00
U304	1887 1¢ Blue, amber manila	13.50	8.00
U305	1887 2¢ Green, die 1	28.50	15.00
U306	1887 2¢ Green, amber	40.00	37.50
U307	1887 2¢ Green, oriental buff	110.00	85.00
U311	1887 2¢ Green, die 2	.75	.35
U312	1887 2¢ Green, amber	.80	.45
U313	1887 2¢ Green, oriental buff	1.10	.60
U314	1887 2¢ Green, blue	1.15	.60
U315	1887 2¢ Green, manila	2.75	1.75
W316	1887 2¢ Green, wrapper	10.75	3.75
U317	1887 2¢ Green,amber manila	5.75	2.50
U318	1887 2¢ Green	185.00	135.00
U319	1887 2¢ Green, manila	225.00	180.00
U320	1887 2¢ Green,oriental buff	210.00	170.00
U321	1887 2¢ Green, blue	270.00	195.00
U322	1887 2¢ Green, manila	265.00	225.00
U324	1887 4¢ Carmine	5.25	2.50
U325	1887 4¢ Carmine, amber	6.75	2.75
U326	1887 4¢ Carmine,oriental buff	11.00	6.50
U327	1887 4¢ Carmine, blue	10.00	5.50
U328	1887 4¢ Carmine, manila	11.00	7.50
U329	1887 4¢ Carmine,amber manila	10.00	5.50
U330	1887 5¢ Blue, die 1	6.75	3.75
U331	1887 5¢ Blue, amber	10.00	5.00
U332	1887 5¢ Blue, oriental buff	13.50	5.00
U333	1887 5¢ Blue, blue	15.00	9.50
U334	1894 5¢ Blue, die 2	35.00	21.50
U335	1894 5¢ Blue, amber	21.50	12.50
U336	1887 30¢ Red brown	57.50	50.00
U337	1887 30¢ Red brown,amber	62.50	55.00
U338	1887 30¢ Red brown, oriental buff	62.50	50.00
U339	1887 30¢ Red brown,blue	60.00	50.00
U340	1887 30¢ Red brown,manila	60.00	52.50
U341	1887 30¢ Red brown, amber manila	65.00	57.50
U342	1887 90¢ Purple	90.00	72.50
U343	1887 90¢ Purple, amber	110.00	90.00
U344	1887 90¢ Purple,oriental buff	120.00	90.00

MINT POSTAL STATIONERY

U350

U510

U546

ENTIRE ENVELOPES AND CUT SQUARES

Scott's No.		Entire	Cut Sq.
U345	1887 90¢ Purple, blue	130.00	90.00
U346	1887 90¢ Purple, manila	135.00	90.00
U347	1887 90¢ Purple, amber man.	140.00	95.00
	1893 Columbian Issue		
U348	1893 1¢ Deep Blue	3.00	2.25
U349	1893 2¢ Violet	3.50	1.75
U350	1893 5¢ Chocolate	14.00	8.00
U351	1893 10¢ Slate Brown	65.00	32.50
	1899 Issues		
U352	1899 1¢ Green	2.10	.80
U353	1899 1¢ Green, amber	8.50	5.25
U354	1899 1¢ Green, oriental buff	16.00	12.50
U355	1899 1¢ Green, blue	16.00	13.00
U356	1899 1¢ Green, manila	6.00	2.15
W357	1899 1¢ Wrapper	9.00	2.35
U358	1899 2¢ Carmine	7.75	2.75
U359	1899 2¢ Carmine, amber	26.75	20.00
U360	1899 2¢ Carmine, orien. buff	29.75	19.50
U361	1899 2¢ Carmine, blue	75.00	62.50
U362	1899 2¢ Carmine	.60	.30
U363	1899 2¢ Carmine, amber	3.00	1.25
U364	1899 2¢ Carmine, orien. buff	3.00	1.15
U365	1899 2¢ Carmine, blue	3.50	1.40
W366	1899 2¢ Wrapper	12.50	7.00
U367	1899 2¢ Carmine	10.00	5.50
U368	1899 2¢ Carmine, amber	16.50	9.00
U369	1899 2¢ Carmine, orien. buff	30.00	25.00
U370	1899 2¢ Carmine, blue	25.00	12.00
U371	1899 4¢ Brown	26.75	17.00
U372	1899 4¢ Brown, amber	32.50	18.50
U374	1899 4¢ Brown	25.00	12.50
U375	1899 4¢ Brown, amber	60.00	52.50
W376	1899 4¢ Wrapper	24.75	17.00
U377	1899 5¢ Blue	15.75	11.50
U378	1899 5¢ Blue, amber	23.75	15.00
	1903-04 Issues		
U379	1903 1¢ Green	1.10	.65
U380	1903 1¢ Green, amber	18.75	13.50
U381	1903 1¢ Green,oriental buff	20.00	15.00
U382	1903 1¢ Green, blue	27.50	19.50
U383	1903 1¢ Green, manila	4.85	3.75
W384	1903 1¢ Green, wrapper	3.75	2.25
U385	1903 2¢ Carmine	.75	.40
U386	1903 2¢ Carmine, amber	3.50	1.85
U387	1903 2¢ Carmine, orien. buff	2.50	1.75
U388	1903 2¢ Carmine, blue	2.75	1.40
W389	1903 2¢ Carmine, wrapper	21.50	16.50
U390	1903 4¢ Chocolate	25.00	21.50
U391	1903 4¢ Chocolate, amber	23.50	19.50
W392	1903 4¢ Chocolate, wrapper	25.00	19.50
U393	1903 5¢ Blue	24.50	19.00
U394	1903 5¢ Blue, amber	27.50	18.00
U395	1904 2¢ Carmine, recut	1.00	.50
U396	1904 2¢ Carmine, amber	11.75	8.00
U397	1904 2¢ Carmine,orien. buff	7.50	5.75
U398	1904 2¢ Carmine, blue	5.25	4.25
W399	1904 2¢ Carmine, wrapper	20.00	11.75
	1907-16 Issues		
U400	1907 1¢ Green	.45	.30
U401	1907 1¢ Green, amber	1.85	1.65
U402	1907 1¢ Green,oriental buff	9.00	6.50
U403	1907 1¢ Green, blue	9.00	7.00
U404	1907 1¢ Green, manila	4.50	3.25
W405	1907 1¢ Green, wrapper	.95	.65
U406	1907 2¢ Brown red	1.65	.80
U407	1907 2¢ Brown red, amber	7.50	5.50
U408	1907 2¢ Brown red, or. buff	9.75	7.50
U409	1907 2¢ Brown red, blue	6.50	4.50
W410	1907 2¢ Brown, wrapper	57.50	45.00
U411	1907 2¢ Carmine	.60	.25
U412	1907 2¢ Carmine, amber	.85	.25
U413	1907 2¢ Carmine, orien. buff	.65	.45
U414	1907 2¢ Carmine, blue	1.10	.50
W415	1907 2¢ Carmine, wrapper	7.50	4.50
U416	1907 4¢ Black	8.75	4.25
U417	1907 4¢ Black, amber	10.50	6.25
U418	1907 5¢ Blue	11.50	7.00
U419	1907 5¢ Blue, amber	19.50	15.00
	1915-32 Issues		
U420	1916 1¢ Green	.35	.20
U421	1916 1¢ Green, amber	.65	.45
U422	1916 1¢ Green, or. buff	2.60	1.90
U423	1916 1¢ Green, blue	.70	.50
U424	1916 1¢ Green, manila	9.50	7.00
W425	1916 1¢ Green, wrapper	.35	.25

Scott's No.		Entire	Cut Sq.
U426	1920 1¢ Green (Glazed)	50.00	37.50
W427	1920 1¢ Green (Glazed)	85.00	65.00
U428	1920 1¢ Green, brown	18.50	13.50
U429	1915 2¢ Carmine	.35	.25
U430	1916 2¢ Carmine, amber	.45	.30
U431	1916 2¢ Carmine, orien. buff	4.50	2.10
U432	1916 2¢ Carmine, blue	.50	.30
W433	1916 2¢ Carmine, wrapper	.50	.30
W434	1920 2¢ Carmine (Glazed)	115.00	85.00
W435	1920 2¢ Carmine, brown	120.00	90.00
U436	1932 3¢ Purple	.60	.35
U436a	1915 3¢ Dark violet	.70	.50
U437	1932 3¢ Purple, amber	.65	.35
U437a	1915 3¢ Dark violet, amber	7.50	4.25
U438	1915 3¢ Dark violet, buff	30.00	23.50
U439	1932 3¢ Purple, blue	.80	.35
U439a	1915 3¢ Dark violet, blue	12.50	7.50
U440	1916 4¢ Black	3.25	1.50
U441	1916 4¢ Black, amber	5.00	3.00
U442	1921 4¢ Black, blue	5.50	3.25
U443	1916 5¢ Blue	6.00	3.25
U444	1916 5¢ Blue, amber	6.00	3.75
U445	1921 5¢ Blue, blue	8.50	4.00
	1920-21 Surcharge Issues		
U446	1920 2¢ on 3¢ (U436)	20.00	13.75
U447	1920 2¢ on 3¢ (U436)	9.50	8.25
U448	1920 2¢ on 3¢ (U436)	3.50	2.40
U449	1920 2¢ on 3¢ (U437)	8.75	6.25
U450	1920 2¢ on 3¢ (U438)	21.50	16.50
U451	1920 2¢ on 3¢ (U439)	19.75	12.00
U458	1920 2¢ on 3¢ (U436)	.70	.50
U459	1920 2¢ on 3¢ (U437)	4.25	3.00
U460	1920 2¢ on 3¢ (U438)	4.25	3.25
U461	1920 2¢ on 3¢ (U439)	7.50	5.50
U468	1920 2¢ on 3¢ (U436)	1.00	.70
U469	1920 2¢ on 3¢ (U437)	5.25	3.50
U470	1920 2¢ on 3¢ (U438)	7.75	5.25
U471	1920 2¢ on 3¢ (U439)	10.50	6.00
U472	1920 2¢ on 4¢ (U390)	25.00	11.50
U473	1920 2¢ on 4¢ (U391)	23.50	16.00
U476	1920 2¢ on 3¢ (U437)	350.00	225.00
U477	1920 2¢ on 3¢ (U436)	165.00	120.00
	1925 Issues		
U481	1925 1½¢ Brown	.55	.20
U482	1925 1½¢ Brown, amber	1.60	1.00
U483	1925 1½¢ Brown, blue	2.25	1.65
U484	1925 1½¢ Brown, manila	13.75	6.75
W485	1925 1½¢ Brown, wrapper	1.35	.85
U489	1925 1½¢ on 1¢ (U353)	170.00	110.00
U490	1925 1½¢ on 1¢ (U400)	7.75	5.25
U491	1925 1½¢ on 1¢ (U401)	11.50	8.00
U493	1925 1½¢ on 1¢ (U403)	135.00	90.00
U495	1925 1½¢ on 1¢ (U420)	.95	.65
U496	1925 1½¢ on 1¢ (U421)	25.00	18.75
U497	1925 1½¢ on 1¢ (U422)	6.00	3.50
U498	1925 1½¢ on 1¢ (U423)	2.25	1.25
U499	1925 1½¢ on 1¢ (U424)	18.50	12.00
U500	1925 1½¢ on 1¢ (U428)	85.00	75.00
U501	1925 1½¢ on 1¢ (U426)	85.00	75.00
U508	1925 1½¢ on 1¢ (U353)	70.00	60.00
U509	1925 1½¢ on 1¢ (U380)	27.50	13.75
U509B	1925 1½¢ on 1¢ (U381)	65.00	55.00
U510	1925 1½¢ on 1¢ (U400)	4.00	2.50
U512	1925 1½¢ on 1¢ (U402)	12.00	8.00
U513	1925 1½¢ on 1¢ (U403)	8.50	5.75
U514	1925 1½¢ on 1¢ (U404)	40.00	27.50
U515	1925 1½¢ on 1¢ (U420)	.60	.35
U516	1925 1½¢ on 1¢ (U421)	57.50	47.50
U517	1925 1½¢ on 1¢ (U422)	7.00	5.50
U518	1925 1½¢ on 1¢ (U423)	6.50	5.25
U519	1925 1½¢ on 1¢ (U424)	32.50	25.00
U521	1925 1½¢ on 1¢ (U420)	5.25	4.00
	1926-1932 Issues		
U522	1926 2¢ Sesquicentennial	1.85	1.30
U522a	1926 2¢ Sesquic. Die 2	11.75	7.50
U523	1932 1¢ Washington Bicent.	1.90	1.10
U524	1932 1½¢ Wash. Bicent	3.50	2.10
U525	1932 2¢ Washington Bicent.	.60	.45
U525a	1932 2¢ Wash.Bic., Die 2	90.00	75.00
U526	1932 3¢ Washington Bicent.	3.00	2.25
U527	1932 4¢ Washington Bicent.	25.00	20.00
U528	1932 5¢ Washington Bicent.	6.50	5.00
U529	1932 6¢ Circle, Orange	9.00	5.75
U530	1932 6¢ Orange, amber	16.50	12.00
U531	1932 6¢ Orange, blue	16.50	12.00

MINT ENTIRE ENVELOPES

Scott's No.		Entire
	1950-1958 Issues	
U532	1950 1¢ Franklin	8.50
U533	1950 2¢ Washington	1.35
U534	1950 3¢ Washington	.55
U535	1952 1½¢ Washington	6.25
U536	1958 2¢ Franklin	.95
U537	1958 2¢ + 2¢ Surch., Circle	3.95
U538	1958 2¢ + 2¢ Surch., Oval	1.00
U539	1958 3¢ + 1¢ Surch., Circle	19.50
U539a	1958 3¢ + 1¢ Surch., Die 7	16.50
U540	1958 3¢ + 1¢ Surch., Oval	.65
	1960-1974 Issues	
U541	1960 1¼¢ Franklin	.90
U542	1960 2½¢ Washington	.95
U543	1960 4¢ Pony Express	.80
U544	1962 5¢ Lincoln	1.10
U545	1962 4¢ + 1¢ Surcharge (U536)	1.65
U546	1964 5¢ New York World's Fair	.70
U547	1965 1¼¢ Liberty Bell	1.00
U548	1968 1-4/10¢ Liberty Bell	1.00
U548A	1969 1 6/10¢ Liberty Bell	.90
U549	1965 4¢ Old Ironsides	1.15
U550	1965 5¢ Eagle	.90
U551	1968 6¢ Liberty Head	.90
U552	1968 4¢ + 2¢ Surcharge (U549)	4.50
U553	1968 5¢ + 1¢ Surcharge (U550)	4.25
U554	1970 6¢ Moby Dick, Herman Melville	.65
U555	1971 6¢ Youth Conference, Brotherhood	.90
U556	1971 1 7/10¢ Liberty Bell	.40
U557	1971 8¢ Eagle	.50
U561	1971 6¢ + 2¢ Liberty (U561)	1.15
U562	1971 6¢ + 2¢ Brotherhood (U555)	2.75
U563	1971 8¢ Bowling	.85
U564	1971 8¢ AgingConference	.65
U565	1972 8¢ Transpo. '72	.75
U566	1973 8¢ + 2¢ Surcharge (U557)	.50
U567	1973 10¢ Liberty Bell	.50
U568	1974 1 8/10¢ Volunteer	.35
U569	1974 10¢ Tennis Centenary	.75
	1975-1982 Issues	
U571	1975 10¢ Seafaring, Bicentennial	.50
U572	1976 13¢ Homemaker, Bicentennial	.55
U573	1976 13¢ Farmer, Bicentennial	.55
U574	1976 13¢ Doctor, Bicentennial	.55
U575	1976 13¢ Craftsman, Bicentennial	.55
U576	1975 13¢ Liberty Tree, Boston	.50
U577	1976 2¢ Star & Pinwheel	.40
U578	1977 2.1¢ Hexagon	.35
U579	1978 2.7¢ U.S.A	.40
U580	1978 (15¢) "A" & Eagle	.60
U581	1978 15¢ Uncle Sam	.60
U582	1976 13¢ Bicentennial 1876 Envelope	.50
U583	1977 13¢ Golf	.95
U584	1977 13¢ Conservation	.55
U585	1977 13¢ Development	.55
U586	1978 15¢ on 16¢ Surcharge	.55
U587	1978 15¢ Auto Racing	.75
U588	1978 15¢ on 13¢ Tree (U576)	.55
U589	1979 3.1¢ Non Profit	.30
U590	1980 3.5¢ Violins	.30
U591	1982 5.9¢ Circle	.35
U592	1981 (18¢) "B" & Eagle	.60
U593	1981 18¢ Star	.60
U594	1981 (20¢) "C" & Eagle	.60
U595	1979 15¢ Veterinary Medicine	.60
U596	1979 15¢ Moscow Olympics,Soccer	.80
U597	1980 15¢ Highwheeler Bicycle	.65
U598	1980 15¢ America's Cup, Yacht	.65
U599	1980 15¢ Honeybee	.55
U600	1981 18¢ Blinded Veteran	.60
U601	1981 20¢ Capitol Dome	.60
U602	1982 20¢ Great Seal	.60
U603	1982 20¢ Purple Heart 1782-1982	.80
	1983-1989 Issues	
U604	1983 5.2¢ Non Profit	.45
U605	1983 20¢ Paralyzed Veterans	.60
U606	1984 20¢ Small Business	.70
U607	1985 (22¢) "D" & Eagle	.75
U608	1985 22¢ American Buffalo	.70
U609	1985 6¢ U.S.S. Constitution	.35
U610	1986 8.5¢ The Mayflower	.35
U611	1988 25¢ Stars in Circle	.80
U612	1988 8.4¢ U.S.S. Constellation	.35
U613	1988 25¢ Snowflake	1.10
U614	1989 25¢ Philatelic Mail, Stars	.65

MINT POSTAL STATIONERY

UC17

UC16

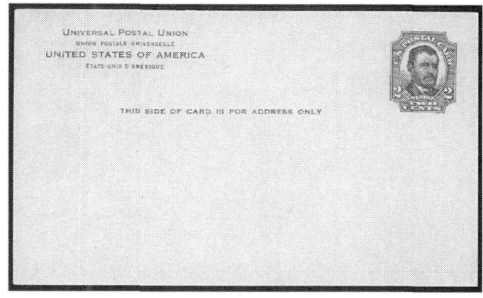

UX25

MINT ENTIRE ENVELOPES

Scott's No.		Entire
U615	1989 25¢ Stars Security Envelope	.70
U616	1989 25¢ Love	.70
U617	1989 25¢ WSE Space Station Hologram	.90
1990-1994 Issues		
U618	1990 25¢ Football, Lombardi Trophy ..	.80
U619	1991 29¢ Star	.85
U620	1991 11.1¢ Non Profit, Birds	.40
U621	1991 29¢ Love	.80
U622	1991 29¢ Magazine Industry	.80
U623	1991 29¢ Stars & Bars	.80
U624	1991 29¢ Country Geese	.80
U625	1992 29¢ Space Station	.80
U626	1992 29¢ Western Americana	.80
U627	1992 29¢ Environment, Hillebrandia ..	.80
U628	1992 19.8¢ Bulk Rate, Star	.55
U629	1992 32¢ Disabled Americans	.80
U630	1993 29¢ Kitten	.85
U631	1994 29¢ Football	.80
1995-1996 Issues		
U632	1995 32¢ Liberty Bell	.85
U633	1995 (32¢) "G" & Flag #6 ¾	1.20
U634	1995 (32¢) "G",Security Envelope #10	1.20
U635	1995 (5¢) Sheep	.30
U636	1995 (10¢) Graphic Eagle	.40
U637	1995 (32¢) Spiral Heart	.90
U638	1995 32¢ Liberty Bell, Security Env. .	.90
U639	1995 32¢ Space Shuttle	.95
U640	1996 32¢ Save our Environment	.90
U641	1996 32¢ Paralympics	.90
1999-2003 Issues		
U642	1999 33¢ Flag	.95
U643	1999 33¢ Flag, Security Envelope	.95
U644	1999 33¢ Love	.95
U645	1999 33¢ Lincoln	.95
U646	2001 34¢ Federal Eagle	.95
U647	2001 34¢ Lovebirds	.95
U648	2001 34¢ Community Colleges	.95
U649	2002 37¢ Ribbon Star	1.00
U649s	2002 37¢ Ribbon Star,Security	1.00
U650	2002 (10¢) Graphic Eagle	.50
U651	2003 37¢ Nurturing Love	.90
U652	2003 $3.85 Jefferson Memorial	7.75
---	2004 37¢ Art of Disney Stamped Stationery Letter Sheets (4)	9.95
---	Same, pad of 12 sheets	28.75

AIR MAIL ENTIRES & CUT SQUARES

1929-44 Issues

Scott's No.		Entire	Cut Sq.
UC1	1929 5¢ Blue, Die 1	5.25	3.25
UC2	1929 5¢ Blue, Die 2	15.00	12.00
UC3	1934 6¢ Orange, Die 2a	1.80	1.30
UC3v	1934 6¢ No Border	2.75	1.30
UC4	1942 6¢ Orange, Die 2b	57.50	...
UC4v	1942 6¢ No Border	4.50	3.00
UC5	1944 6¢ No Border, Die 2c ..	1.25	.90
UC6	1942 6¢ Orange, Die 3	1.75	1.10
UC6v	1942 6¢ Die 3, No Border	2.75	1.40
UC7	1932 8¢ Olive Green	17.00	13.00
1945-47 Issues			
UC8	1945 6¢ on 2¢ Wash. (U429)	1.75	1.35
UC9	1945 6¢on2¢ Wash.Bic.(U525)	110.00	80.00
UC10	1946 5¢ on 6¢ Org.Die 2a(UC3v)	3.75	3.00
UC11	1946 5¢ on 6¢ Org.Die 2b(UC4v)	11.00	10.00
UC12	1946 5¢ on 6¢ Org.Die 2c(UC5)	1.40	.85
UC13	1946 5¢ on 6¢ Org.Die 3 (UC6v)	1.15	.90
UC14	1946 5¢ Plane, Die 1	1.10	.75
UC15	1946 5¢ Plane, Die 2	1.15	.75
UC17	1947 5¢ CIPEX, Stamp Cent.	.60	.50

MINT AIRMAIL ENTIRE ENVELOPES

1950-58 Issues

Scott's No.		Entire
UC18	1950 6¢ DC-4 Skymaster	.65
UC19	1951 6¢ on 5¢, Die 1 (UC14)	1.40
UC20	1951 6¢ on 5¢, Die 2 (UC15)	1.30
UC21	1952 6¢ on 5¢, Die 1 (UC14)	35.00
UC22	1952 6¢ on 5¢, Die 2 (UC15)	6.00
UC25	1956 6¢ FIPEX Philatelic Exhibition ..	1.00
UC26	1958 7¢ DC-4 Skymaster	1.00
UC27	1958 6¢ + 1¢ Orange, Die 2a (UC3v)	325.00
UC28	1958 6¢ + 1¢ Orange, Die 2b (UC4v)	110.00

Scott's No.		Entire
UC29	1958 6¢ + 1¢ Orange, Die 2c (UC5) .	45.00
UC30	1958 6¢ + 1¢ Skymaster (UC18)	1.25
UC31	1958 6¢ + 1¢ FIPEX (UC25)	1.50
UC33	1958 7¢ Jet Silhouette, Blue	.80
1960-73 Issues		
UC34	1960 7¢ Jet Silhouette, Carmine	.75
UC36	1962 8¢ Jet Airliner	.80
UC37	1965 8¢ Jet, Triangle	.55
UC37a	1967 8¢ Jet, Triangle, Tagged	5.25
UC40	1968 10¢ Jet, Triangle	.80
UC41	1968 8¢ + 2¢ Surcharge (UC37)	.90
UC43	1971 10¢ Three Circles	.65
UC45	1971 10¢ + 1¢ Triangle (UC40)	2.00
UC47	1973 13¢ Bird in Flight	.50

MINT AIRLETTER SHEETS

1947-71 Issues

Scott's No.		Unfolded	Folded
UC16	1947 10¢ DC3, 2 Lines, "Air Letter"	...	8.50
UC16a	1951 10¢ 4 Lines,"Air Letter"	...	17.00
UC16c	1953 10¢ "Aerogramme, 4 Lines	...	52.50
UC16d	1955 10¢ Aerogramme, 3 Lines	10.00	8.50
UC32	1959 10¢ Jet Airliner, 2 Lines	8.00	6.50
UC32a	1958 10¢ Jet Airliner, 3 Lines	12.50	10.75
UC35	1961 11¢ Jet Airliner & Globe	3.50	3.00
UC38	1965 11¢ J.F. Kennedy & Jet	4.00	3.50
UC39	1967 13¢ J.F. Kennedy & Jet	3.75	3.25
UC42	1968 13¢ Human Rights Year	10.00	8.00
UC44	1971 15¢ Birds in Flight,Letter	2.00	1.50
UC44a	1971 15¢ "Aerogramme"added	2.00	1.50
1973-81 Issues			
UC46	1973 15¢ Hot Air Ballooning	1.35	.85
UC48	1974 18¢ "USA"	1.60	.95
UC49	1974 18¢ NATO 25th Anniv.	1.60	.95
UC50	1976 22¢ "USA" "usa/22¢" ..	1.60	.95
UC51	1978 22¢ "USA" "22¢USA" ..	1.35	.85
UC52	1979 22¢ Moscow Olympics	2.10	1.65
UC53	1980 30¢ "USA", Blue,Red,Brown	1.35	.85
UC54	1981 30¢ "USA",Yellow,Blue,Black.	1.35	.85
1982-99 Issues			
UC55	1982 30¢ World Trade, Globe	1.35	.85
UC56	1983 30¢ Communication Year	1.35	.85
UC57	1983 30¢ Los Angeles Olympics	1.35	.85
UC58	1985 36¢ Landsat Satellite ..	1.35	.85
UC59	1985 36¢ National Tourism Week	1.35	.85
UC60	1985 36¢ M.Twain/ Halley's Comet	1.50	1.00
UC61	1988 39¢ Stylized Aero	1.50	1.00
UC62	1989 39¢ Montgomery Blair .	1.50	1.00
UC63	1991 45¢ Eagle, blue paper .	1.60	1.10
UC63a	1991 45¢ Eagle, white paper	1.60	1.10
UC64	1995 50¢Thad. Lowe,Balloonist	1.75	1.20
UC65	1999 60¢ Voyaguers Natl. Park	2.00	1.50

OFFICIAL ENVELOPES & CUT SQUARES

Scott's No.		Entire	Cut Sq.
1873-79 Post Office Department			
UO1	1873 2¢ Black, lemon,small #	27.50	19.50
UO2	1873 3¢ Black, lemon	23.00	15.00
UO4	1873 6¢ Black, lemon	28.50	24.00
UO5	1874 2¢ Black, lemon,large#	12.00	8.50
UO6	1874 2¢ Black	135.00	110.00
UO7	1874 3¢ Black, lemon	4.50	3.25
UO9	1874 3¢ Black, amber	125.00	90.00
UO12	1874 6¢ Black, lemon	20.00	12.50
1877 Postal Service			
UO14	1877 Black	10.00	7.50
UO17	1877 Black, blue	11.50	8.50
1873 War Dept., Reay Issue			
UO20	1873 3¢ Dark red	90.00	65.00
UO26	1873 12¢ Dark red	210.00	150.00
UO27	1873 15¢ Dark red	190.00	140.00
UO28	1873 24¢ Dark red	195.00	150.00
WO31	1873 1¢ Vermilion, wrapper .	26.50	16.50
UO34	1873 3¢ Vermilion	160.00	90.00
UO35	1873 3¢ Vermilion, amber ...	315.00	110.00
UO36	1873 3¢ Vermilion, cream ...	37.50	16.00
UO37	1873 6¢ Vermilion	150.00	85.00
UO40	1873 12¢ Vermilion	180.00	160.00
1875 War Dept., Plimpton Issue			
UO44	1875 1¢ Red	185.00	150.00
WO46	1875 1¢ Red, wrapper	8.75	4.00
UO47	1875 2¢ Red	150.00	110.00
UO48	1875 2¢ Red, amber	40.00	32.50
UO49	1875 2¢ Red, orange	60.00	52.50
WO50	1875 2¢ Red, wrapper	170.00	85.00

Scott's No.		Entire	Cut Sq.
UO51	1875 3¢ Red	17.00	15.00
UO52	1875 3¢ Red, amber	21.50	17.50
UO53	1875 3¢ Red, cream	9.00	7.00
UO54	1875 3¢ Red, blue	5.00	4.00
UO55	1875 3¢ Red, fawn	9.00	5.50
UO56	1875 6¢ Red	85.00	52.50
UO57	1875 6¢ Red, amber	100.00	85.00
UO61	1875 12¢ Red	150.00	52.50
UO67	1875 30¢ Red	210.00	180.00
1911 Postal Savings			
U070	1911 1¢ Green	85.00	67.50
U071	1911 1¢ Green, Oriental buff	250.00	200.00
U072	1911 2¢ Carmine	20.00	12.50

OFFICIAL MAIL MINT ENTIRES

Scott's No.		Entire
UO73	1983 20¢ Great Seal	1.35
UO74	1985 22¢ Great Seal	.90
UO75	1987 22¢ Savings Bond Envelope	1.00
UO76	1988 (25¢) "E" Bond Envelope	1.10
UO77	1988 25¢ Great Seal	.90
UO78	1988 25¢ Savings Bond Envelope	1.00
UO79	1990 45¢ Passport Envelope 2 oz	1.50
UO80	1990 65¢ Passport Envelope 3 oz	1.80
UO81	1990 45¢ Self-sealing Passport 2 oz	1.30
UO82	1990 65¢ Self-sealing Passport 3 oz	1.80
UO83	1991 (29¢) "F" Savings Bond	1.25
UO84	1991 29¢ Great Seal	.85
UO85	1991 29¢ Savings Bond Envelope	.85
UO86	1992 52¢ Consular Service	5.00
UO86a	1992 52¢ Recycled heavier paper	2.25
UO87	1992 75¢ Consular Service	12.00
UO87a	1992 75¢ Recycled heavier paper	3.75

#UO86,87 "USPS Copyright" on left under flap.
#UO86a, 87a "USPS Copyright" on right under flap.

UO88	1995 32¢ Great Seal	.95
UO89	1999 33¢ Great Seal	1.00
UO90	2001 34¢ Great Seal	.90
UO91	2002 37¢ Great Seal	.90

MINT & PREPRINTED POSTAL CARDS
Preprinted cards are unused with printed or written address or messages.

1873-1898 Issues

Scott's No.		Preprinted	Mint
UX1	1873 1¢ Liberty, brown, large watermark	60.00	375.00
UX3	1873 1¢ small watermark	25.00	90.00
UX5	1875 1¢ Liberty, black, "Write"	8.00	75.00
UX6	1879 2¢ Liberty, buff	11.00	30.00
UX7	1881 1¢ Liberty, black,"Nothing"	7.50	67.50
UX8	1885 1¢ Jefferson, brown	11.00	57.50
UX9	1886 1¢ Jefferson, black	1.95	22.50
UX10	1891 1¢ Grant, black	8.00	40.00
UX11	1891 1¢ Grant, blue	4.25	17.50
UX12	1894 1¢ Jefferson, black, small wreath	2.50	40.00
UX13	1897 2¢ Liberty,blue on cream	80.00	180.00
UX14	1897 1¢ Jefferson, black, large wreath	3.00	32.50
UX15	1898 1¢ Adams, black	12.75	47.50
UX16	1898 2¢ Liberty, black, "No Frame"	6.00	12.50
1902-1918 Issues			
UX18	1902 1¢ McKinley, oval	2.00	13.00
UX19	1907 1¢ McKinley, circle	2.50	40.00
UX20	1908 1¢ Correspondence Space at Left	9.50	50.00
UX21	1910 1¢ McKinley, shaded	19.50	100.00
UX22	1910 1¢ McKinley, white background	1.80	15.00
UX23	1911 1¢ Lincoln, red	3.75	8.75
UX24	1911 1¢ McKinley, red	1.50	11.50
UX25	1911 2¢ Grant, red	.85	1.50
UX26	1913 1¢ Lincoln, green	3.00	11.50
UX27	1914 1¢ Jefferson, Die 1	.20	.35
UX28	1917 1¢ Lincoln, green	.35	.75
UX29	1917 2¢ Jefferson, Die 1	7.00	45.00
UX30	1918 2¢ Jefferson, Die 2	5.50	32.50
1920-64 Issues			
UX32	1920 1¢ on 2¢ red,die 1(UX29)	16.00	60.00
UX33	1920 1¢ on 2¢ red,die 2(UX30)	3.00	15.00
UX37	1926 3¢ McKinley	2.00	4.50
UX38	1951 2¢ Franklin	.30	.40
UX39	1952 2¢ on 1¢ Jefferson, green	.40	.65
UX40	1952 2¢ on 1¢ Lincoln, green	.50	.75

133

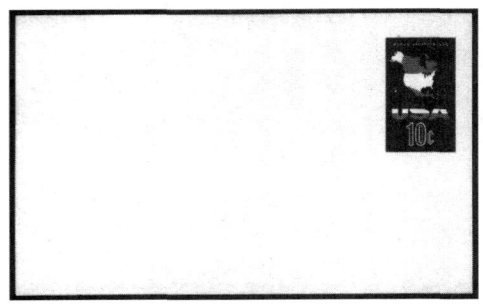

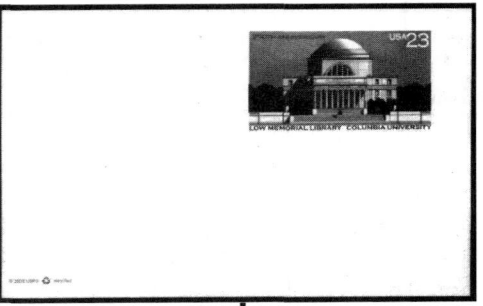

UX59   UX174   UX405

MINT POSTAL CARDS

Scott's No.		Mint Card
UX41	1952 2¢ on 1¢ Jeff, dark green	5.50
UX42	1952 2¢ on 1¢ Lincoln, dk grn	5.75
UX43	1952 2¢ Lincoln, carmine	.30
UX44	1956 2¢ FIPEX, Liberty Torch	.30
UX45	1956 4¢ Statue of Liberty	1.60
UX46	1958 3¢ Statue of Liberty	.50
UX46d	1961 3¢ Precancelled	4.00
UX48	1962 4¢ Lincoln, precancelled	.35
UX48a	1966 4¢ Lincoln, Tagged	.55
UX49	1963 7¢ "USA" & Map	4.50
UX50	1964 4¢ Customs- Flags & Map	.50
UX51	1964`4¢ Social Security	.50

1965-1973 Issues

UX52	1965 4¢ U.S. Coast Guard	.35
UX53	1965 4¢ Bureau of the Census	.35
UX54	1967 8¢ "USA" & Map	4.50
UX55	1968 5¢ Lincoln	.30
UX56	1968 5¢ Women Marines	.40
UX57	1970 5¢ Weather Services	.35
UX58	1971 6¢ Paul Revere	.35
UX59	1971 10¢ "USA" & Map	4.75
UX60	1971 6¢ Hospitals, NY Hospital	.35
UX61	1972 6¢ U.S.F. Constellation	.90
UX62	1972 6¢ Monument Valley	.45
UX63	1972 6¢ Gloucester, Mass.	.45
UX64	1972 6¢ John Hanson	.35
UX64a	1972 6¢ Hanson, coarse paper	1.25
UX65	1973 6¢ Liberty (design of UX1)	.30
UX66	1973 8¢ Samuel Adams	.40

1974-1979 Issues

UX67	1974 12¢ Ship's Figurehead, 1883	.40
UX68	1975 7¢ Charles Thomson	.35
UX69	1975 9¢ John Witherspoon	.35
UX70	1976 9¢ Caesar Rodney	.35
UX71	1977 9¢ Galveston	.35
UX72	1977 9¢ Nathan Hale	.35
UX73	1978 10¢ Cincinnati Music Hall	.35
UX74	1978 (10¢) John Hancock	.35
UX75	1978 10¢ John Hancock	.35
UX76	1978 14¢ Coast Guard Cutter "Eagle"	.45
UX77	1978 10¢ Molly Pitcher, Monmouth	.35
UX78	1979 10¢ George.R. Clark,Vincennes	.35
UX79	1979 10¢ Casimir Pulaski,Savannah	.35
UX80	1979 10¢ Moscow Olympics	.65
UX81	1979 10¢ Iolani Palace, Honolulu	.35

1980-1983 Issues

UX82	1980 14¢ Lake Placid Olympics	.60
UX83	1980 10¢ Salt Lake Temple	.35
UX84	1980 10¢ Landing of Rochambeau	.35
UX85	1980 10¢ Battle of Kings Mountain	.35
UX86	1980 19¢ Drake's "Golden Hinde"	.70
UX87	1981 10¢ Battle of Cowpens	.35
UX88	1981 (12¢) Eagle	.35
UX89	1981 12¢ Isaiah Thomas	.35
UX90	1981 12¢ N. Greene, Eutaw Springs	.35
UX91	1981 12¢ Lewis & Clark Expedition	.35
UX92	1981 (13¢) Robert Morris	.35
UX93	1981 13¢ Robert Morris	.35
UX94	1982 13¢ "Swamp Fox" F. Marion	.35
UX95	1982 13¢ LaSalle Claims Lousiana	.35
UX96	1982 13¢ Music Academy, Philadelphia	.35
UX97	1982 13¢ Old Post Office, St. Louis	.35
UX98	1983 13¢ Oglethorpe, Georgia	.35
UX99	1983 13¢ Old Post Office,Wash.,DC	.35
UX100	1983 13¢ Olympics '84, Yachting	.35

1984-1988 Issues

UX101	1984 13¢ Ark & Dove,Maryland	.35
UX102	1984 13¢ Olympic Torch & Runner	.35
UX103	1984 13¢ Frederic Baraga,Michigan	.35
UX104	1984 13¢ Rancho San Pedro	.35
UX105	1985 (14¢) Charles Carroll	.35
UX106	1985 14¢ Charles Carroll	.55
UX107	1985 25¢ Clipper Flying Cloud	.75
UX108	1985 14¢ George Wythe	.35
UX109	1985 14¢ Connecticut Settlement	.35
UX110	1986 14¢ Stamp Collecting	.35
UX111	1986 14¢ Francis Vigo, Vincennes	.35
UX112	1986 14¢ Settling of Rhode Island	.35
UX113	1986 14¢ Wisconsin Territory, 1836.	.35
UX114	1986 14¢ National Guard Heritage	.35
UX115	1987 14¢ Self-scouring Steel Plow	.35
UX116	1987 14¢ Constitution Convention	.35
UX117	1987 14¢ Stars and Stripes	.35
UX118	1987 14¢ Take Pride in America	.35
UX119	1987 14¢ Timberline Lodge, Oregon	.35

Scott's No.		Mint Card
UX120	1988 15¢ America the Beautiful, Bison and Prairie	.35
UX121	1988 15¢ Blair House	.35
UX122	1988 28¢ "Yorkshire" Packet Ship	.70
UX123	1988 15¢ Iowa Territory	.35
UX124	1988 15¢ Northwest/Ohio Territory	.35
UX125	1988 15¢ Hearst Castle, San Simeon	.35
UX126	1988 15¢ Federalist Papers	.35

1989-1992 Issues

UX127	198915¢ America the Beautiful, Hawk and Sonora Desert	.35
UX128	1989 15¢ Healy Hall, Georgetown Un.	.35
UX129	1989 15¢ America the Beautiful, Great Blue Heron, Marsh	.35
UX130	1989 15¢ Settling of Oklahoma	.35
UX131	1989 21¢ America the Beautiful, Canada Geese and Mountains	.60
UX132	1989 15¢ America the Beautiful, Seashore, Lighthouse, Gull	.35
UX133	1989 15¢ America the Beautiful, Woodlands, Deer, Waterfall	.35
UX134	1989 15¢ Hull House, Chicago	.35
UX135	1989 15¢ America the Beautiful, Independence Hall,Philadelphia	.35
UX136	1989 15¢ America the Beutiful, Baltimore Inner Harbor	.35
UX137	1989 15¢ America the Beautiful, 59th St.Bridge, New York	.35
UX138	1989 15¢ America the Beautiful, Capitol Bldg, Washington, DC	.35
UX139-42	198915¢ Cityscape sheet of 4 postcards, designs of #UX135, UX136, UX137, UX138	15.00
UX143	1989 15¢ The White House	1.25
UX144	1989 15¢ Jefferson Memorial	1.25
UX145	1990 15¢ Rittenhouse Paper Mill,PA	.35
UX146	1990 15¢ World Literacy Year.	.35
UX147	1990 15¢ Fur Traders on Missouri	1.25
UX148	1990 15¢ Isaac Royall House	.40
UX150	1990 15¢ Quadrangle, Stanford Univ	.40
UX151	1990 15¢ DAR/Constitution Hall, DC	1.25
UX152	1990 15¢ Chicago Orchestra Hall	.40
UX153	1991 19¢ Flag	.50
UX154	1991 19¢ Carnegie Hall Centennial	.50
UX155	1991 19¢ "Old Red", Univ. of Texas	.50
UX156	1991 19¢ Bill of Rights Ratification	.50
UX157	1991 19¢ Main Building, Notre Dame	.50
UX158	1991 30¢ America the Beautiful, Niagara Falls	.90
UX159	1991 19¢ Old Mill, Univ. of Vermont	.50
UX160	1992 19¢ Wadsworth Atheneum, CT	.50
UX161	1992 19¢ Cobb Hall, Univ. of Chicago	.50
UX162	1992 19¢ Waller Hall, Willamette Univ.	.50
UX163	1992 19¢ America's Cup	1.10
UX164	1992 19¢ Columbia River Gorge	.50
UX165	1992 19¢ Great Hall, Ellis Island	.50

1993-1994 Issues

UX166	1993 19¢ Washington National Cathedral	.50
UX167	1993 19¢ Wren Building,William & Mary	.50
UX168	1993 19¢ Holocaust Memorial Museum	1.20
UX169.	1993 19¢ Fort Recovery, Ohio	.50
UX170	1993 19¢ Playmaker's Theater, University of North Carolina	.50
UX171	1993 19¢ O'Kane Hall, Holy Cross	.50
UX172	1993 19¢ Beecher Hall, Illinois College	.50
UX173	1993 19¢ Massachusetts Hall, Bowdoin	.50
UX174	1994 19¢ Abraham Lincoln Home, IL	.50
UX175	1994 19¢ Myers Hall, Wittenberg Univ.	.50
UX176	1994 19¢ Canyon de Chelly, AZ	.50
UX177	1994 19¢ St. Louis Union Station	.50
UX178-97	1994 19¢ Legends of the West (20)	25.00

1995-1996 Issues

UX198	1995 20¢ Red Barn, Williamsburg,PA	.50
UX199	1995 (20¢) "G" Old Glory	2.50
UX200-19	1995 20¢ Civil War (20)	36.50
UX220	1995 20¢ Clipper Ship	.50
UX221-40	1995 20¢ Comic Strips (20)	47.50
UX241	1996 20¢ Winter Farm Scene	.50
UX242-61	1996 20¢ Atlanta Olympics (20)	50.00
UX262	1996 20¢ McDowell Hall, St.John's Coll.	.50
UX263	1996 20¢ Alexander Hall, Princeton	.50
UX264-78	1996 20¢ Endangered Species (15)	50.00

1997-1998 Issues

UX279	1997 20¢ Love-Swans	4.25
UX279a	same, Package of 12	45.00

Note: UX279 is sold in packages of 12 with 8 different stamp designs without values.

Scott's No.		Mint Card
UX280	1997 20¢ City College of New York	.50
UX281	1997 20¢ Bugs Bunny	1.60
UX281a	same, Booklet of 10	14.95
UX282	1997 20¢ Golden Gate Bridge	.50
UX283	1997 50¢ Golden Gate Bridge	1.25
UX284	1997 20¢ Fort McHenry, Maryland	.50
UX285-89	1997 20¢ Movie Monsters (5)	7.50
UX289a	same, Booklet of 20	27.50
UX290	1998 20¢ The Lyceum, University of Mississippi	.50
UX291	1998 20¢ Tweety & Sylvester	1.50
UX291a	same, Booklet of 10	13.95
UX292	1998 20¢ Girard College,Philadelphia	.50
UX293-96	1998 20¢ Tropical Birds (4)	4.25
UX296a	same, Booklet of 20	19.75
UX297	1998 20¢ American Ballet	1.50
UX297a	same, Booklet of 10	14.50
UX298	1998 20¢ Kerr Hall, Northeastern Univ.	.50
UX299	1998 20¢ Usen Castle, Brandeis Univ	.50

1999-2000 Issues

UX300	1999 20¢ Love & Heart	.95
UX300a	same, Booklet of 20	17.50
UX301	1999 20¢ Bascom Hill, Wisconsin Un.	.50
UX302	1999 20¢ Washington & Lee Univ.	.50
UX303	1999 20¢ Redwood Library & Athenaeum, Newport, R.Island	.50
UX304	1999 20¢ Daffy Duck	1.50
UX304a	same, Booklet of 10	13.95
UX305	1999 20¢ Mount Vernon	.50
UX306	1999 20¢ Block Island Lighthouse	.50
UX307-11	1999 20¢ Famous Trains (5)	5.75
UX311a	same, Booklet of 20 (4 each)	19.75
UX312	2000 20¢ University of Utah	.50
UX313	2000 20¢ Ryman Auditorium,Nashville	.50
UX314	2000 20¢ Wile E.Coyote & Road Runner	1.50
UX314a	same, Booklet of 10	13.95
UX315	2000 20¢ Adoption	1.50
UX315	same, Booklet of 10	13.95
UX316	2000 20¢ Old Stone Row, Middlebury College, Vermont	.50
UX317-36	2000 20¢ Stars & Stripes in 5 Sheets of 4 (20)	27.50
UX337-56	2000 20¢ Legends of Baseball 5 sheets of 4 (20)	23.95
UX357-60	2000 20¢ Christmas Deer (4)	5.25
UX360a	same, Booklet of 20 (5 each)	19.95

2001-2002 Issues

UX361	2001 20¢ Connecticut Hall, Yale Univ.	.50
UX362	2001 20¢ UnIV. of South Carolina	.50
UX363	2001 20¢ Northwestern Univ.Sesqui.	.50
UX364	2001 20¢ Waldschmidt Hall, University of Portland	.50
UX365-74	2001 21¢ Legendary Baseball Fields (10)	17.50
UX375	2001 21¢ White Barn	.55
UX376	2001 21¢ Porky Pig, That's All Folks	1.50
UX376a	same, Booklet of 10	13.95
UX377-80	2001 21¢ Santa Claus (4)	5.25
UX380a	same, Booklet of 20 (5 each)	19.75
UX381	2002 23¢ Carlsbad Caverns Park	.60
UX382-85	2002 23¢ Teddy Bears (4)	4.50
UX385a	same, Booklet of 20 (4 each)	21.75
UX386-89	2002 23¢ Christmas Snowmen (4)	4.50
UX389a	same, Booklet of 20	21.75

2003-2004 Postal Cards

UX390-94	2003 23¢ Old Glory (5)	5.50
UX394a	same, Booklet of 20 (4 each)	21.50
UX395-99	2003 23¢ SoutheasternLighthouses (5)	5.50
UX399a	same, Booklet of 20 (4 each)	21.50
UX400	2003 23¢ Ohio University	.50
UX401-4	2003 23¢ Holiday Music Makers (4)	4.00
UX404a	same, Booklet of 20	19.50
UX405	2004 23¢ Columbia University	.50
...	2004 23¢ Harriton House	.50
...	2004 23¢ Art of Disney (4)	4.00
...	same, Booklet of 20 (5 each)	19.50

MINT POSTAL STATIONERY

UXC24

MINT AIRMAIL POSTAL CARDS

Scott's No.		Mint Card
UXC1	1949 4¢ Eagle in Flight	.50
UXC2	1958 5¢ Eagle in Flight	2.00
UXC3	1960 5¢ Eagle in Flight, redrawn	6.50
UXC4	1963 6¢ Bald Eagle, precancelled	.70
UXC5	1966 11¢ SIPEX, Visit the USA	.65
UXC6	1967 6¢ Virgin Islands Purchase	.50
UXC7	1967 6¢ Boy Scouts Jamboree	.50
UXC8	1967 13¢ Visit the USA	1.40
UXC9	1968 8¢ Stylized Eagle, precan	.70
UXC9a	1969 8¢ Eagle, Tagged	2.50
UXC10	1971 9¢ Stylized Eagle, precan	.55
UXC11	1971 15¢ Visit the USA	2.00
UXC12	1972 9¢ Grand Canyon	.55
UXC13	1972 15¢ Niagara Falls	.70
UXC14	1974 11¢ Mail Early in the Day	.75
UXC15	1974 18¢ Weather Vane, Visit USA	.90
UXC16	1975 21¢ Weather Vane, Visit USA	.85
UXC17	1978 21¢ Curtiss Jenny	.80
UXC18	1979 21¢ Moscow Olympics	1.10
UXC19	1981 28¢ 1st Trans-Pacific Flight	1.00
UXC20	1982 28¢ Soaring, Gliders	1.00
UXC21	1983 28¢ Speedskater, Olympics	1.00
UXC22	1985 33¢ China Clipper Seaplane	1.00
UXC23	1986 33¢ Ameripex;86, Chicago	.95
UXC24	1988 36¢ DC-3	.95
UXC25	1991 40¢ Yankee Clipper	1.00
UXC26	1995 50¢ Eagle	1.25
UXC27	1999 55¢ Mt. Rainier, Washington	1.30
UXC28	2001 70¢ Badlands, South Dakota	1.65

OFFICIAL POSTAL CARDS

UZ2	1983 13¢ Great Seal	.80
UZ3	1985 14¢ Great Seal	.80
UZ4	1988 15¢ Great Seal	.80
UZ5	1991 19¢ Great Seal	.80
UZ6	1995 20¢ Great Seal	.85

"POSTAL BUDDY" COMPUTER VENDED CARDS

CVUX1	1990 15¢ Eagle	8.00
CVUX1	same, Sheet of 4	32.50
CVUX2	1991 19¢ Eagle	4.25
CVUX2	same, Sheet of 4	17.00
CVUX3	1992 19¢ Plain, Star & U.S.A.	10.00
CVUX3	same, Sheet of 4	42.50

UY2

POSTAL REPLY CARDS

Unsevered Cards-Unfolded   Folded - deduct 30%

1892-1920 Issues

Scott's No.		Preprinted	Mint
UY1	1892 1¢ + 1¢ Grant, black .	17.50	60.00
UY1m	1¢ Message Card detached	3.25	6.25
UY1r	1¢ Reply Card detached	3.25	6.25
UY2	1893 2¢ + 2¢ Liberty, blue	15.00	29.50
UY2m	2¢ Message Card detached	2.25	5.50
UY2r	2¢ Reply Card detached	2.25	5.50
UY3	1898 1¢ Grant, no frame	15.00	100.00
UY3m	1¢ Message Card detached	5.50	14.00
UY3r	1¢ Reply Card detached	5.50	14.00
UY4	1904 1¢ + 1¢ Sherman and Sheridan	13.50	75.00
UY4m	1¢ Sherman Message Card	5.50	12.50
UY4r	1¢ Sheridan Reply Card	5.50	12.50
UY5	1910 1¢ + 1¢ Martha & George Washington, Blue	55.00	250.00
UY5m	1¢ George Message Card	9.00	13.50
UY5r	1¢ Martha Reply Card det.	9.00	13.50
UY6	1911 1¢ + 1¢ M. & G. Wash., Green, double frame line	80.00	225.00
UY6m	1¢ George Message Card	12.50	25.00
UY6r	1¢ Martha Reply Card det. .	12.50	25.00
UY7	1915 1¢ + 1¢ M & G. Wash., Green, single frame line	.90	1.80
UY7m	1¢ George Message Card	.25	.35
UY7r	1¢ Martha Reply Card det. .	.25	.35
UY8	1918 2¢ + 2¢ Martha &George Washington, red	45.00	130.00
UY8m	2¢ George Message Card	10.00	22.50
UY8r	2¢ Martha Reply Card det. .	10.00	22.50
UY9	1920 1¢ on 2¢ + 1¢ on 2¢ Martha & George Washington, red	15.00	27.50
UY9m	1¢ on 2¢ George Message Cd.	2.75	5.50
UY9r	1¢ on 2¢ Martha Reply Card	2.75	5.50
UY10	1920 1¢ on 2¢ + 1¢ on 2¢ M&G Wash., One Press	200.00	450.00
UY10m	1¢ on 2¢ George Message Cd.	50.00	90.00
UY10r	1¢ on 2¢ Martha Reply Card	50.00	90.00

1924-1952 Issues

UY11	1924 2¢ + 2¢ Liberty, red	2.25	3.50
UY11m	2¢ Message Card detached	.50	.75
UY11r	2¢ Reply Card detached	.50	.75
UY12	1926 3¢ + 3¢ McKinley	8.75	15.00
UY12m	3¢ Message Card detached	1.60	3.25
UY12r	3¢ Reply Card detached	1.60	3.25
UY13	1951 2¢ + 2¢ Martha &George Washington, carmine	.95	2.00
UY13m	2¢ George Message Card	.30	.45
UY13r	2¢ Martha Reply Card det.	.30	.45

UY29

Scott's No.		Preprinted	Mint
UY14	1952 2¢ on 1¢ + 2¢ on 1¢ M.&G. Washington, green surcharge below	.90	1.75
UY14m	2¢ on 1¢ George Message .	.30	.50
UY14r	2¢ on 1¢ Martha Reply Cd.	.30	.50
UY15	1952 2¢ on 1¢ + 2¢ on 1¢, M&G Washington, green surcharge at left	50.00	165.00
UY15m	2¢ on 1¢ George Message .	10.00	17.00
UY15r	2¢ on 1¢ Martha Reply Cd. .	10.00	17.00

1956-1969 Issues

Scott's No.		Mint Card
UY16	1956 4¢ + 4¢ Statue of Liberty	1.50
UY16m	4¢ Liberty Message Card detached	.50
UY16r	4¢ Liberty Reply Card detached	.50
UY17	1958 3¢ + 3¢ Statue of Liberty	5.25
UY18	1962 4¢ + 4¢ Abraham Lincoln	6.00
UY18a	1967 4¢ + 4¢ Lincoln, Tagged	9.00
UY19	1963 7¢ + 7¢ "USA" & Map	3.75
UY19m	7¢ Message Card detached	1.10
UY19r	7¢ Reply Card detached	1.10
UY20	1967 8¢ + 8¢ "USA" & Map	3.75
UY20m	8¢ Message Card detached	1.10
UY20r	8¢ Reply Card detached	1.10
UY21	1968 5¢+5¢ Abraham Lincoln	2.00

1971-1988 Issues

UY22	1971 6¢ + 6¢ Paul Revere	1.25
UY23	1972 6¢ + 6¢ John Hanson	1.35
UY24	1973 8¢ + 8¢ Samuel Adams	1.25
UY25	1975 7¢ + 7¢ Charles Thomson	1.25
UY26	1975 9¢ + 9¢ John Witherspoon	1.25
UY27	1976 9¢ + 9¢ Caesar Rodney	1.25
UY28	1977 9¢ + 9¢ Nathan Hale	1.30
UY29	1978 (10¢+10¢) John Hancock	10.75
UY30	1978 10¢ + 10¢ John Hancock	1.25
UY31	1981 (12¢ + 12¢) Eagle	1.25
UY32	1981 12¢ + 12¢ Isaiah Thomas	2.50
UY33	1981 (13¢ + 13¢) Robert Morris	2.40
UY34	1981 13¢ + 13¢ Robert Morris	1.50
UY35	1985 (14¢ + 14¢) Charles Carroll	3.00
UY36	1985 14¢ + 14¢ Charles Carroll	1.50
UY37	1985 14¢ + 14¢ George Wythe	1.50
UY38	1987 14¢ + 14¢ U.S. Flag	1.50
UY39	1988 15¢ + 15¢ America the Beautiful, Bison and Prairie	1.50

1991-2002 Issues

UY40	1991 19¢ + 19¢ Flag	1.50
UY41	1995 20¢ + 20¢ Red Barn	1.50
UY42	1999 20¢ + 20¢ Block Island Lighthouse	1.50
UY43	2001 21¢ + 21¢ White Barn	1.50
UY44	2002 23¢ + 23¢ Carlsbad Caverns	1.50

UNITED STATES REVENUES

R5a	R25a	R37b	R46a	R60c

1862-71 First Issue (continued) (All Used) (C)

R78a	R85c	R91a

1862-71 First Issue (All Used) (C) (VF Perf. & Part Perf.+80%, Imperf.+ 60%)

Scott's No.		Imperforate(a) Fine	Ave.	Part Perforate(b) Fine	Ave.	Perforated(c) Fine	Ave.
R1	1¢ Express	52.50	27.50	37.50	21.00	1.25	.75
R2	1¢ Playing Cards	1075.00	650.00	1000.00	600.00	150.00	90.00
R3	1¢ Proprietary	700.00	400.00	150.00	90.00	.50	.30
R4	1¢ Telegraph	425.00	250.00	...	...	11.75	7.25
R5	2¢ Bank Check,Blue	1.10	.70	...	...	.30	.20
R6	2¢ Bank Check,Orange	...	...	50.00	27.50	.30	.20
R7	2¢ Certificate,Blue	12.00	7.00	...	...	27.50	16.00
R8	2¢ Certificate,Orange	...	...	...	...	25.00	14.00
R9	2¢ Express,Blue	12.00	7.00	19.50	11.00	.50	.35
R10	2¢ Express,Orange	...	...	...	...	8.75	5.25
R11	2¢ Playing Cards,Blue	...	...	210.00	135.00	3.75	2.25
R12	2¢ Playing Cards,Orange	...	...	...	...	40.00	24.00
R13	2¢ Proprietary, Blue	425.00	245.00	150.00	90.00	.40	.25
R14	2¢ Proprietary,Orange	...	...	...	...	35.00	20.00
R15	2¢ U.S.Internal Revenue	...	...	...	...	.30	.20
R16	3¢ Foreign Exchange	...	...	265.00	160.00	3.95	2.35
R17	3¢ Playing Cards	...	...	...	...	130.00	80.00
R18	3¢ Proprietary	...	...	325.00	200.00	4.75	2.75
R19	3¢ Telegraph	70.00	40.00	25.00	15.00	2.65	1.50
R20	4¢ Inland Exchange	...	...	...	...	2.00	1.20
R21	4¢ Playing Cards	...	...	...	...	525.00	300.00
R22	4¢ Proprietary	...	...	210.00	125.00	5.75	3.50
R23	5¢ Agreement	...	...	...	...	.35	.25
R24	5¢ Certificate	2.50	1.40	12.00	7.00	.30	.20
R25	5¢ Express	5.00	3.00	6.50	4.00	.30	.20
R26	5¢ Foreign Exchange	...	...	...	...	.30	.20
R27	5¢ Inland Exchange	6.50	4.00	4.50	2.75	.30	.20
R28	5¢ Playing Cards	...	...	...	...	22.50	13.00
R29	5¢ Proprietary	...	...	...	...	22.50	13.00
R30	6¢ Inland Exchange	...	...	...	...	1.60	.95
R31	6¢ Proprietary	...	...	...	...	1600.00	1000.00
R32	10¢ Bill of Lading	42.50	25.00	300.00	185.00	.95	.55
R33	10¢ Certificate	140.00	80.00	325.00	200.00	.30	.20
R34	10¢ Contract,Blue	...	...	200.00	120.00	.55	.35
R35	10¢ Foreign Exchange,Blue	...	...	...	...	9.50	6.00
R36	10¢ Inland Exchange	250.00	150.00	3.75	2.15	.30	.20
R37	10¢ Power of Attorney	525.00	300.00	25.00	15.00	.90	.55
R38	10¢ Proprietary	...	...	...	...	19.50	12.00
R39	15¢ Foreign Exchange	...	...	...	...	13.50	8.00
R40	15¢ Inland Exchange	35.00	21.50	13.00	7.50	1.40	.85
R41	20¢ Foreign Exchange	52.50	32.50	...	...	37.50	21.50
R42	20¢ Inland Exchange	16.50	10.00	16.50	9.50	.35	.25
R43	25¢ Bond	185.00	115.00	5.75	3.50	2.25	1.30
R44	25¢ Certificate	11.00	7.00	5.50	3.25	.30	.20
R45	25¢ Entry of Goods	19.50	11.50	75.00	45.00	.70	.45
R46	25¢ Insurance	9.00	5.50	9.75	6.00	.30	.20
R47	25¢ Life Insurance	32.50	18.50	350.00	210.00	6.00	4.00
R48	25¢ Power of Attorney	6.50	4.00	25.00	15.00	.35	.25
R49	25¢ Protest	27.50	16.50	425.00	250.00	7.50	4.50
R50	25¢ Warehouse Receipt	45.00	26.50	350.00	195.00	28.50	17.50
R51	30¢ Foreign Exchange	75.00	45.00	1075.00	650.00	47.50	26.50
R52	30¢ Inland Exchange	55.00	32.50	65.00	40.00	3.75	2.15
R53	40¢ Inland Exchange	700.00	425.00	6.50	3.75	4.25	2.50
R54	50¢ Conveyance,Blue	16.00	9.50	1.50	.95	.30	.20
R55	50¢ Entry of Goods	...	...	11.00	6.50	.40	.25
R56	50¢ Foreign Exchange	52.50	30.00	70.00	40.00	7.00	4.25
R57	50¢ Lease	22.50	13.00	85.00	52.50	8.75	5.25
R58	50¢ Life Insurance	37.50	22.50	55.00	32.50	1.10	.65
R59	50¢ Mortgage	15.75	9.50	2.25	1.35	.55	.35
R60	50¢ Original Process	3.50	2.10	525.00	375.00	.65	.40
R61	50¢ Passage Ticket	67.50	37.50	180.00	110.00	1.15	.70
R62	50¢ Probate of Will	42.50	25.00	85.00	50.00	17.00	10.00
R63	50¢ Surety Bond,Blue	185.00	115.00	2.35	1.30	.35	.25
R64	60¢ Inland Exchange	80.00	45.00	45.00	25.00	6.00	3.65
R65	70¢ Foreign Exchange	400.00	235.00	110.00	65.00	9.75	5.75
R66	$1 Conveyance	15.00	9.00	450.00	275.00	25.00	15.00
R67	$1 Entry of Goods	35.00	21.50	...	...	2.10	1.25
R68	$1 Foreign Exchange	75.00	45.00	...	...	.65	.40
R69	$1 Inland Exchange	13.75	8.50	350.00	210.00	.50	.30
R70	$1 Lease	32.50	18.00	...	...	2.75	1.75
R71	$1 Life Insurance	160.00	100.00	...	...	5.75	3.50
R72	$1 Manifest	40.00	23.50	...	...	32.50	19.00
R73	$1 Mortgage	22.50	13.50	...	...	160.00	95.00
R74	$1 Passage Ticket	260.00	170.00	...	...	225.00	135.00
R75	$1 Power of Attorney	80.00	50.00	...	...	2.00	1.20
R76	$1 Probate of Will	75.00	45.00	...	...	40.00	23.50
R77	$1.30 Foreign Exchange	...	...	...	...	55.00	33.50
R78	$1.50 Inland Exchange	25.00	15.00	...	...	4.25	2.50
R79	$1.60 Foreign Exchange	900.00	550.00	...	...	100.00	60.00
R80	$1.90 Foreign Exchange	...	3500.00	...	...	90.00	52.50

Scott's No.		Imperforate(a) Fine	Ave.	Part Perforate(b) Fine	Ave.	Perforated(c) Fine	Ave.
R81	$2 Conveyance	135.00	80.00	1300.00	750.00	2.50	1.40
R82	$2 Mortgage	110.00	65.00	...	...	4.00	2.35
R83	$2 Probate of Will	...	2500.00	...	...	55.00	32.50
R84	$2.50 Inland Exchange	...	2750.00	...	...	9.75	5.75
R85	$3 Charter Party	150.00	95.00	...	...	5.75	3.50
R86	$3 Manifest	130.00	85.00	...	...	35.00	21.50
R87	$3.50 Inland Exchange	...	2800.00	...	...	55.00	32.50
R88	$5 Charter Party	250.00	150.00	...	...	5.75	3.50
R89	$5 Conveyance	35.00	21.50	...	...	9.00	5.25
R90	$5 Manifest	130.00	85.00	...	...	85.00	50.00
R91	$5 Mortgage	115.00	70.00	...	...	17.00	9.50
R92	$5 Probate of Will	500.00	300.00	...	...	17.00	9.50
R93	$10 Charter Party	575.00	350.00	...	...	28.50	18.00
R94	$10 Conveyance	100.00	60.00	...	...	65.00	37.50
R95	$10 Mortgage	400.00	240.00	...	...	27.50	16.00
R96	$10 Probate of Will	1250.00	775.00	...	...	27.50	16.00
R97	$15 Mortgage,Blue	1600.00	975.00	...	...	160.00	95.00
R98	$20 Conveyance	130.00	80.00	...	...	95.00	60.00
R99	$20 Probate of Will	1400.00	850.00	...	...	1350.00	800.00
R100	$25 Mortgage	950.00	550.00	...	...	135.00	80.00
R101	$50 U.S.Int.Revenue	180.00	110.00	...	...	110.00	65.00
R102	$200 U.S.Int.Rev.	1800.00	1100.00	...	...	675.00	400.00

HANDSTAMPED CANCELLATIONS GENERALLY SELL FOR A 20% PREMIUM.

1871 Second Issue (C) (VF + 80%)

R103	R107, R137	R112	R118, R144

Scott's No.		Used Fine	Used Ave.	Scott's No.		Used Fine	Used Ave.
R103	1¢	45.00	25.00	R119	$1.30	325.00	195.00
R104	2¢	1.75	1.10	R120	$1.50	14.50	9.00
R105	3¢	22.50	13.50	R121	$1.60	400.00	235.00
R106	4¢	65.00	35.00	R122	$1.90	250.00	150.00
R107	5¢	1.30	.70	R123	$2	14.50	8.00
R108	6¢	110.00	60.00	R124	$2.50	30.00	18.00
R109	10¢	.95	.55	R125	$3	30.00	18.00
R110	15¢	30.00	18.50	R126	$3.50	210.00	125.00
R111	20¢	5.50	3.00	R127	$5	20.00	12.00
R112	25¢	.60	.35	R128	$10	140.00	85.00
R113	30¢	75.00	45.00	R129	$20	375.00	225.00
R114	40¢	57.50	35.00	R130	$25	450.00	275.00
R115	50¢	.55	.35	R131	$50	450.00	275.00
R116	60¢	110.00	65.00	R132	$200 Red,blue,bk.	2600.00	
R117	70¢	42.50	25.00	R133	$500 Red orange,		
R118	$1	3.75	2.25		green & black...	...	

R103 through R131 have blue frames and a black center.

1871-72 Third Issue - Same Designs as Second Issue (C) (VF + 80%)

Scott's No.		Fine	Ave.	Scott's No.		Fine	Ave.
R134	1¢ Claret	32.50	19.50	R143	70¢ Green	52.50	31.50
R135	2¢ Orange	.30	.20	R144	$1 Green	1.50	.90
R136	4¢ Brown	42.50	25.00	R145	$2 Vermilion	20.00	11.00
R137	5¢ Orange	.30	.20	R146	$2.50 Claret	37.50	22.50
R138	6¢ Orange	47.50	27.50	R147	$3 Green	40.00	23.50
R139	15¢ Brown	10.50	6.50	R148	$5 Vermilion	35.00	15.00
R140	30¢ Orange	15.00	9.50	R149	$10 Green	110.00	65.00
R141	40¢ Brown	40.00	24.00	R150	$20 Orange	475.00	275.00
R142	60¢ Orange	75.00	45.00				

R134 through R150 have black centers.
Note : Cut cancels are usually priced at 40% to 60% of the above prices.

1874 Fourth Issue (C) (VF+80%)

Scott's No.		Unused Fine	Ave.	Used Fine	Ave.
R151	2¢ Orange and Black, Green Paper	...	...	.30	.20

1875-78 Fifth Issue (C) (VF + 80%)

R152a	2¢ Liberty, Blue, Silk Paper	1.50	.90	.30	.20
R152b	2¢ Blue, Watermarked	1.50	.90	.30	.20
R152c	2¢ Blue, Rouletted, Watermarked	...	...	28.50	16.50

* 1898 Postage Stamps Overprinted "I.R." (C) (VF + 80%)

Scott's No.		Unused Fine	Unused Ave.	Used Fine	Used Ave.
R153	1¢ Green, Small I.R. (#279)	3.50	2.10	2.75	1.65
R154	1¢ Green, Large I.R. (#279)	.30	.20	.30	.20
R155	2¢ Carmine,Ty,III,Large I.R. (#267)	.30	.20	.30	.20
R155A	2¢ Carmine, Type IV (#279B)	.40	.25	.40	.25

*** 1898 Newspaper Stamps Surcharged "INT. REV./$5/DOCUMENTARY" (C)**

R159	$5 Blue, Surcharge down (#PR121)	400.00	240.00	160.00	100.00
R160	$5 Blue, Surcharge up (#PR121)	100.00	60.00	87.50	52.50

*** Used prices are for stamps with contemporary cancels.**

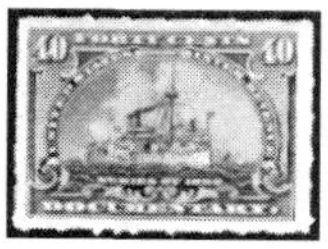
R161-72

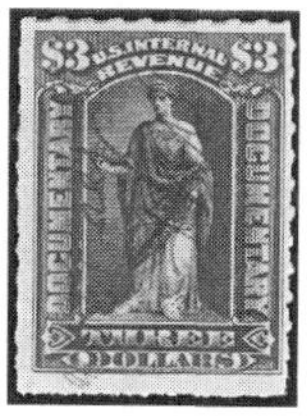
R173-78

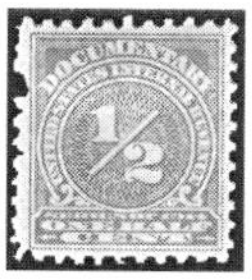
R195-216

1898 Documentary "Battleship" Designs (Rouletted 5½) (C) (VF +40%)

R161	½¢ Orange	2.35	1.50	8.75	5.25
R162	½¢ Dark Gray	.30	.20	.30	.20
R163	1¢ Pale Blue	.30	.20	.25	.15
R163p	1¢ Hyphen Hole Perf. 7	.35	.25	.30	.20
R164	2¢ Carmine	.30	.20	.30	.20
R164p	2¢ Hyphen Hole Perf. 7	.35	.25	.30	.20
R165	3¢ Dark Blue	2.00	1.20	.30	.20
R165p	3¢ Hyphen Hole Perf. 7	17.00	10.00	.90	.55
R166	4¢ Pale Rose	1.30	.80	.30	.20
R166p	4¢ Hyphen Hole Perf. 7	7.00	4.25	1.40	.85
R167	5¢ Lilac	.45	.30	.30	.20
R167p	5¢ Hyphen Hole Perf. 7	7.00	4.25	.30	.20
R168	10¢ Dark Brown	1.50	.90	.25	.15
R168p	10¢ Hyphen Hole Perf. 7	4.75	3.00	.30	.20
R169	25¢ Purple Brown	2.40	1.40	.30	.20
R169p	25¢ Hyphen Hole Perf. 7	8.00	5.00	.35	.25
R170	40¢ Blue Lilac (cut .25)	130.00	85.00	1.50	.85
R170p	40¢ Hyphen Hole Perf. 7	160.00	100.00	32.50	20.00
R171	50¢ Slate Violet	16.00	10.00	.30	.20
R171p	50¢ Hyphen Hole Perf. 7	35.00	21.50	.75	.45
R172	80¢ Bistre (cut .20)	90.00	55.00	.35	.25
R172p	80¢ Hyphen Hole Perf. 7	190.00	115.00	47.50	28.50

Commerce Design (C) (Rouletted 5½) (VF + 40%)

R173	$1 Commerce, Dark Green	10.75	6.50	.25	.15
R173p	1¢ Hyphen Hole Perf. 7	18.50	11.75	.70	.45
R174	$3 Dark Brown (cut .25)	26.50	16.00	.90	.55
R174p	3¢ Hyphen Hole Perf. 7(cut .40) .	37.50	22.50	2.50	1.50
R175	$5 Orange Red (cut .20)	37.50	23.00	1.60	.95
R176	$10 Black (cut .60)	85.00	50.00	2.80	1.70
R177	$30 Red (cut 40.00)	275.00	160.00	110.00	75.00
R178	$50 Gray Brown (cut 1.80)	130.00	80.00	5.50	3.50

1899 Documentary Stamps Imperforate (C) (VF + 40%)

R179	$100 Marshall,Brown.& Bk.(cut 17.50)	170.00	100.00	30.00	19.00
R180	$500 Hamilton,Carmine Lake & Black (cut 275.00)	1000.00	600.00	700.00	425.00
R181	$1000 Madison,Green&Bk.(cut 125.00)	825.00	500.00	300.00	240.00

1900 Documentary Stamps (C) (Hyphen Hole Perf 7) (VF + 40%)

R182	$1 Commerce, Carmine (cut .25)	22.50	13.00	.50	.30
R183	$3 Lake (cut 7.50)	150.00	90.00	45.00	27.50

1900 Surcharged Large Black Open Numerals (C) (VF + 40%)

R184	$1 Gray (cut .25)	15.75	9.50	.35	.25
R185	$2 Gray (cut .20)	15.75	9.50	.30	.20
R186	$3 Gray (cut 3.75)	70.00	42.50	10.00	5.50
R187	$5 Gray (cut 1.30)	47.50	28.50	7.50	4.50
R188	$10 Gray (cut 3.35)	97.50	60.00	18.50	11.00
R189	$50 Gray (cut 80.00)	825.00	500.00	425.00	250.00

1902 Surcharged Large Ornamental Numerals (C) (VF + 40%)

R190	$1 Green (cut .25)	22.50	13.50	3.50	2.15
R191	$2 Green (cut .30)	22.50	13.50	1.50	.90
R192	$5 Green (cut 6.00)	150.00	90.00	26.50	16.50
R193	$10 Green (cut 45.00)	300.00	175.00	130.00	70.00
R194	$50 Green (cut 240.00)	975.00	565.00	725.00	400.00

1914 Documentary Single Line Watermark "USPS" (VF + 60%) (B)
Inscribed "Series of 1914"

R195	½¢ Rose	8.50	5.25	3.50	2.15
R196	1¢ Rose	1.65	.95	.30	.20
R197	2¢ Rose	2.10	1.25	.30	.20
R198	3¢ Rose	50.00	27.50	27.50	16.00
R199	4¢ Rose	15.00	9.00	1.75	1.00
R200	5¢ Rose	4.50	2.65	.30	.20
R201	10¢ Rose	3.75	2.25	.30	.20
R202	25¢ Rose	32.50	19.50	.60	.35
R203	40¢ Rose	18.50	11.00	1.30	.80
R204	50¢ Rose	6.50	3.95	.30	.20
R205	80¢ Rose	110.00	65.00	9.00	5.50

1914 Documentary Double Line Watermark "USIR" (VF + 60%) (B)
Inscribed "Series of 1914" or "Series 1914"

Scott's No.		Unused Fine	Unused Ave.	Used Fine	Used Ave.
R206	½¢ Rose	1.60	.95	.50	.30
R207	1¢ Rose	.30	.20	.25	.15
R208	2¢ Rose	.35	.25	.30	.20
R209	3¢ Rose	1.35	.70	.30	.20
R210	4¢ Rose	3.75	2.25	.50	.30
R211	5¢ Rose	1.60	.90	.35	.25
R212	10¢ Rose	.70	.45	.25	.15
R213	25¢ Rose	4.50	2.70	1.40	.85
R214	40¢ Rose (cut .50)	85.00	52.50	11.00	6.50
R215	50¢ Rose (cut .20)	16.00	10.00	.30	.20
R216	80¢ Rose (cut .90)	130.00	85.00	18.75	11.50

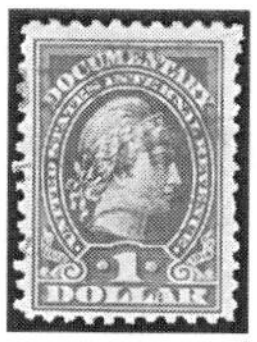
R217-23

R228-39,51-56,60-63

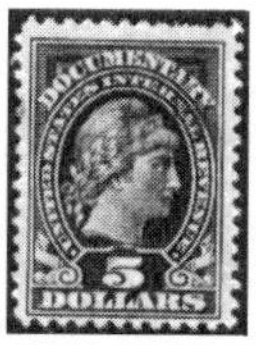
R240-45,57-59

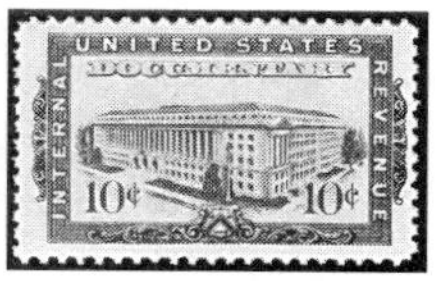
R733-34

R217	$1 Liberty, Green (cut .25)	36.50	21.50	.40	.30
R218	$2 Carmine (cut .25)	50.00	30.00	.70	.45
R219	$3 Purple (cut .45)	65.00	40.00	3.75	2.30
R220	$5 Blue (cut .60)	55.00	33.50	2.50	1.50
R221	$10 Orange (cut .90)	130.00	80.00	4.50	2.65
R222	$30 Vermillion (cut 2.00)	275.00	160.00	15.00	9.00
R223	$50 Violet (cut 300.00)	1200.00	700.00	700.00	385.00

1914-15 Documentary stamps - Perforated 12, Without Gum (VF+60%) (B)
Inscribed "Series of 1915" or "Series of 1914"

R224	$60 Lincoln, Brown (cut 57.50) ...	170.00	110.00	120.00	70.00
R225	$100 Wash., Green (cut 19.50) ..	50.00	32.50	37.50	22.50
R226	$500 Hamilton, Blue (cut 240.00)	...	...	550.00	325.00
R227	$1000 Madison, Orange (cut 250.00)	...	...	500.00	300.00

1917-33 Documentary Stamps - Perforated 11 (VF + 50%) (B)

R228	1¢ Rose	.30	.20	.25	.15
R229	2¢ Rose	.30	.20	.25	.15
R230	3¢ Rose	1.20	.70	.35	.25
R231	4¢ Rose	.60	.35	.30	.20
R232	5¢ Rose	.30	.20	.25	.15
R233	8¢ Rose	1.85	1.10	.35	.25
R234	10¢ Rose	.35	.25	.25	.15
R235	20¢ Rose	.70	.45	.30	.20
R236	25¢ Rose	1.00	.60	.30	.20
R237	40¢ Rose	1.85	1.10	.45	.30
R238	50¢ Rose	2.00	1.20	.25	.15
R239	80¢ Rose	4.75	2.60	.30	.20
	#R240-45 Without "Series 1914"				
R240	$1 Green	5.75	3.50	.30	.20
R241	$2 Rose	10.50	6.50	.25	.15
R242	$3 Violet (cut .25)	33.50	20.00	.95	.60
R243	$4 Brown (cut .25)	23.00	14.00	1.70	1.00
R244	$5 Blue (cut .25)	16.50	9.50	.35	.25
R245	$10 Orange (cut .25)	27.50	16.50	1.15	.70

1917 Documentary Stamps - Perforated 12, Without Gum (VF+50%) (B)
Without "Series of" and Date

R246	$30 Grant, Orange (cut 1.85)	40.00	25.00	11.00	7.00
R247	$60 Lincoln, Brown (cut 1.00)	52.50	32.50	6.50	4.00
R248	$100 Wash., Green (cut .40)	30.00	18.00	1.10	.65
R249	$500 Hamilton, Blue (cut 10.00) .	285.00	175.00	33.50	20.00
R250	$1000 Madison, Orange (cut 4.25)	130.00	80.00	13.00	7.50

1928-29 Documentary Stamps - Perforated 10 (VF + 40%) (B)

R251	1¢ Carmine Rose	1.90	1.15	1.30	.80
R252	2¢ Carmine Rose	.55	.35	.30	.20
R253	4¢ Carmine Rose	6.50	4.00	3.75	2.25
R254	5¢ Carmine Rose	1.40	.85	.55	.35
R255	10¢ Carmine Rose	2.10	1.25	1.10	.70
R256	20¢ Carmine Rose	5.75	3.25	5.00	3.00
	#R257-59 Without "Series 1914"				
R257	$1 Green (cut 4.50)	110.00	62.50	27.50	16.50
R258	$2 Rose	47.50	28.50	2.75	1.65
R259	$10 Orange (cut 22.50)	160.00	95.00	37.50	22.50

1929 Documentary Stamps - Perf. 11x10 (VF + 40%) (B)

R260	2¢ Carmine Rose	2.75	1.50	2.50	1.40
R261	5¢ Carmine Rose	2.00	1.25	1.75	1.10
R262	10¢ Carmine Rose	8.50	5.00	6.50	4.00
R263	20¢ Carmine Rose	16.50	10.00	8.50	5.00

#R264-R732 1940-1958 Dated Documentary Stamps (See Next Two Pages)

1962-1963 Documentary Stamps

Scott's No.		Plate Block	F.VF NH	F.VF Used
R733	10¢ Internal Revenue Building with "Established 1962", IRS Centennail	14.75	1.25	.45
R734	10¢ Bldg."Established 1962" removed (1963)	30.00	4.75	.60

DATED DOCUMENTARY REVENUE STAMPS (VF+30%)

Note: Dated Documentary stamps with cut cancels or perforated initials sell for substantially less than used price.

1940 'SERIES 1940" Overprint on 1917-33 Issues. NH +20%

Scott's No.		F-VF Unused	F-VF Used
R264	1¢ Rose pink	3.00	2.25
R265	2¢ Rose pink	2.75	1.75
R266	3¢ Rose pink	8.50	4.00
R267	4¢ Rose pink	3.75	.55
R268	5¢ Rose pink	4.00	.90
R269	8¢ Rose pink	15.00	12.50
R270	10¢ Rose pink ...	1.80	.55
R271	20¢ Rose pink ...	2.25	.65
R272	25¢ Rose pink ...	5.50	1.25
R273	40¢ Rose pink ...	5.75	.75
R274	50¢ Rose pink ...	6.50	.65
R275	80¢ Rose pink ...	11.50	.90
R276	$1 Green	45.00	.85
R277	$2 Rose	47.50	1.00
R278	$3 Violet	65.00	22.50
R279	$4 Yellow brown .	110.00	27.50
R280	$5 Dark blue	57.50	10.75
R281	$10 Orange	140.00	32.50
R282	$30 Grant	...	650.00
R286	$1000 Madison ..	...	600.00

#R288-653, R679-723 Stamps are Overprinted with Series Date Ex.: "SERIES 1940" or "Series 1949" $30 & up values issued without gum & have straight edges on one/two sides. All are carmine with black overprints.

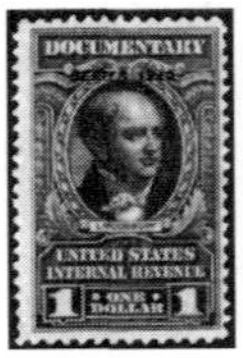

R300

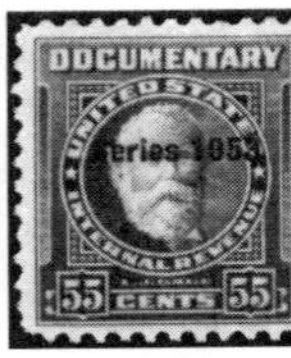

R631

1940

Scott's No.		F-VF NH	F-VF Used
R288	1¢ A.Hamilton	4.50	3.00
R289	2¢ O.Wolcott,Jr.	5.00	3.00
R290	3¢ S.Dexter	23.50	10.00
R291	4¢ A.Gallatin	47.50	22.50
R292	5¢ G.W.Campbell	3.50	.65
R293	8¢ A.Dallas	70.00	47.50
R294	10¢ W.H.Crawford	3.25	.50
R295	20¢ R.Rush	4.50	2.75
R296	25¢ S.D.Ingham	3.00	.55
R297	40¢ L.McLane	50.00	22.50
R298	50¢ W.J.Duane ..	5.25	.45
R299	80¢ R.B.Taney ...	110.00	60.00
R300	$1 L.Woodbury ..	35.00	.50
R301	$2 T.Ewing	50.00	.70
R302	$3 W.Forward	140.00	80.00
R303	$4 J.C.Spencer .	85.00	30.00
R304	$5 G.M.Bibb	55.00	1.85
R305	$10 R.J.Walker ..	100.00	6.00
R305A	$20 W.M.Meredith	...	775.00
R306	$30 T.Corwin	130.00	40.00
R307	$60 H.Cobb	250.00	57.50
R308	$100 P.F.Thomas	180.00	60.00
R310	$1000 S.P.Chase	...	425.00

1941

Scott's No.		F-VF NH	F-VF Used
R311	1¢ A.Hamilton	3.50	2.25
R312	2¢ O.Wolcott,Jr.	3.25	.90
R313	3¢ S.Dexter	8.00	3.50
R314	4¢ A.Gallatin	6.00	1.25
R315	5¢ G.W.Campbell	1.00	.25
R316	8¢ A.Dallas	14.00	7.50
R317	10¢ W.H.Crawford	1.30	.20
R318	20¢ R.Rush	3.00	.45
R319	25¢ S.D.Ingham	1.80	.50
R320	40¢ L.McLane	13.50	2.50
R321	50¢ W.J.Duane ..	2.75	.25
R322	80¢ R.B.Taney ...	55.00	10.00
R323	$1 L.Woodbury ..	10.00	.25
R324	$2 T.Ewing	13.50	.45
R325	$3 W.Forward	20.00	3.00
R326	$4 J.C.Spencer .	35.00	22.50
R327	$5 G.M.Bibb	50.00	.95
R328	$10 R.J.Walker ..	75.00	3.75
R329	$20 W.M.Meredith	...	250.00
R330	$30 T.Corwin	130.00	37.50
R331	$50 J.Guthrie....	375.00	275.00
R332	$60 H.Cobb	175.00	55.00
R333	$100 P.F.Thomas	75.00	27.50
R334	$500 J.A.Dix	...	210.00
R335	$1000 S.P.Chase	...	110.00

1942

Scott's No.		F-VF NH	F-VF Used
R336	1¢ A.Hamilton	.60	.45
R337	2¢ O.Wolcott,Jr.	.50	.45
R338	3¢ S.Dexter	.70	.55
R339	4¢ A.Gallatin	1.25	.90
R340	5¢ G.W.Campbell	.45	.25
R341	8¢ A.Dallas	5.75	4.00

DATED DOCUMENTARY STAMPS (cont.)

Scott's No.		F-VF NH	F-VF Used
R342	10¢ W.H.Crawford	1.35	.25
R343	20¢ R.Rush	1.35	.45
R344	25¢ S.D.Ingham	2.00	.50
R345	40¢ L.McLane	4.75	1.35
R346	50¢ W.J.Duane ..	3.50	.25
R347	80¢ R.B.Taney ...	17.50	9.00
R348	$1 L.Woodbury ..	10.00	.25
R349	$2 T.Ewing	10.50	.25
R350	$3 W.Forward	17.50	2.50
R351	$4 J.C.Spencer .	25.00	4.75
R352	$5 G.M.Bibb	26.50	1.00
R353	$10 R.J.Walker ..	62.50	2.40
R354	$20 W.M.Meredith	125.00	35.00
R355	$30 T.Corwin	70.00	27.50
R356	$50 J.Guthrie	...	575.00
R357	$60 H.Cobb	...	750.00
R358	$100 P.F.Thomas	160.00	100.00
R359	$500 J.A.Dix	...	195.00
R360	$1000 S.P.Chase	...	95.00

1943

Scott's No.		F-VF NH	F-VF Used
R361	1¢ A.Hamilton	.60	.50
R362	2¢ O.Wolcott,Jr.	.45	.40
R363	3¢ S.Dexter	2.75	2.50
R364	4¢ A.Gallatin	1.30	1.10
R365	5¢ G.W.Campbell	.50	.35
R366	8¢ A.Dallas	4.50	3.00
R367	10¢ W.H.Crawford	.70	.25
R368	20¢ R.Rush	1.95	.60
R369	25¢ S.D.Ingham	2.10	.35
R370	40¢ L.McLane	4.75	2.40
R371	50¢ W.J.Duane ..	1.50	.25
R372	80¢ R.B.Taney ...	17.50	5.25
R373	$1 L.Woodbury ..	5.50	.30
R374	$2 T.Ewing	11.50	.25
R375	$3 W.Forward	20.00	2.10
R376	$4 J.C.Spencer .	26.50	4.25
R377	$5 G.M.Bibb	32.50	.60
R378	$10 R.J.Walker ..	55.00	3.75
R379	$20 W.M.Meredith	110.00	27.50
R380	$30 T.Corwin	55.00	17.50
R381	$50 J.Guthrie	110.00	27.50
R382	$60 H.Cobb	240.00	77.50
R383	$100 P.F.Thomas	25.00	11.50
R384	$500 J.A.Dix	...	185.00
R385	$1000 S.P.Chase	...	150.00

1944

Scott's No.		F-VF NH	F-VF Used
R386	1¢ A.Hamilton	.40	.35
R387	2¢ O.Wolcott,Jr.	.45	.45
R388	3¢ S.Dexter	.50	.30
R389	4¢ A.Gallatin	.60	.60
R390	5¢ G.W.Campbell	.30	.25
R391	8¢ A.Dallas	1.75	1.40
R392	10¢ W.H.Crawford	.45	.25
R393	20¢ R.Rush	.70	.25
R394	25¢ S.D.Ingham	1.50	.25
R395	40¢ L.McLane	2.75	.60
R396	50¢ W.J.Duane ..	2.85	.25
R397	80¢ R.B.Taney ...	15.00	3.75
R398	$1 L.Woodbury ..	7.50	.25
R399	$2 T.Ewing	10.50	.40
R400	$3 W.Forward	16.00	2.00
R401	$4 J.C.Spencer .	22.50	8.75
R402	$5 G.M.Bibb	25.00	.40
R403	$10 R.J.Walker ..	47.50	1.30
R404	$20 W.M.Meredith	95.00	14.00
R405	$30 T.Corwin	75.00	27.50
R406	$50 J.Guthrie	35.00	16.50
R407	$60 H.Cobb	200.00	55.00
R408	$100 P.F.Thomas	40.00	9.50
R410	$1000 S.P.Chase	...	210.00

1945

Scott's No.		F-VF NH	F-VF Used
R411	1¢ A.Hamilton	.30	.25
R412	2¢ O.Wolcott,Jr.	.30	.25
R413	3¢ S.Dexter	.50	.40
R414	4¢ A.Gallatin	.35	.30
R415	5¢ G.W.Campbell	.35	.25
R416	8¢ A.Dallas	4.50	1.85
R417	10¢ W.H.Crawford	.85	.25
R418	20¢ R.Rush	5.25	.95
R419	25¢ S.D.Ingham	1.25	.30
R420	40¢ L.McLane	5.50	.95
R421	50¢ W.J.Duane ..	2.75	.25
R422	80¢ R.B.Taney ...	21.00	7.00
R423	$1 L.Woodbury ..	8.00	.25
R424	$2 T.Ewing	9.50	.30
R425	$3 W.Forward	17.00	2.10
R426	$4 J.C.Spencer .	25.00	3.00
R427	$5 G.M.Bibb	25.00	.40
R428	$10 R.J.Walker ..	50.00	1.75
R429	$20 W.M.Meredith	100.00	12.00
R430	$30 T.Corwin	125.00	32.50
R431	$50 J.Guthrie	140.00	35.00
R432	$60 H.Cobb	250.00	52.50
R433	$100 P.F.Thomas	50.00	14.00
R434	$500 J.A.Dix.....	285.00	170.00
R435	$1000 S.P.Chase	200.00	85.00

1946

Scott's No.		F-VF NH	F-VF Used
R436	1¢ A.Hamilton	.25	.25
R437	2¢ O.Wolcott,Jr.	.40	.35
R438	3¢ S.Dexter	.40	.35
R439	4¢ A.Gallatin	.60	.50
R440	5¢ G.W.Campbell	.35	.25
R441	8¢ A.Dallas	1.30	1.00
R442	10¢ W.H.Crawford	.85	.25
R443	20¢ R.Rush	1.25	.40
R444	25¢ S.D.Ingham	4.25	.70

DATED DOCUMENTARY STAMPS (cont.)

Scott's No.		F-VF NH	F-VF Used
R445	40¢ L.McLane	2.50	.65
R446	50¢ W.J.Duane ..	3.75	.25
R447	80¢ R.B.Taney ...	13.00	4.00
R448	$1 L.Woodbury .	10.50	.25
R449	$2 T.Ewing	12.75	.25
R450	$3 W.Forward	18.75	4.50
R451	$4 J.C.Spencer .	25.00	9.50
R452	$5 G.M.Bibb	25.00	.40
R453	$10 R.J.Walker ..	50.00	1.40
R454	$20 W.Meredith .	100.00	12.00
R455	$30 T.Corwin	45.00	12.00
R456	$50 J.Guthrie	32.50	9.50
R457	$60 H.Cobb	72.50	16.50
R458	$100 P.F.Thomas	50.00	8.75
R459	$500 J.A.Dix	...	97.50
R460	$1000 S.P.Chase...	...	110.00

1947

Scott's No.		F-VF NH	F-VF Used
R461	1¢ A.Hamilton	.65	.45
R462	2¢ O.Wolcott,Jr.	.55	.50
R463	3¢ S.Dexter	.65	.45
R464	4¢ A.Gallatin	.70	.60
R465	5¢ G.W.Campbell	.35	.30
R466	8¢ A.Dallas	1.30	.70
R467	10¢ W.H.Crawford	1.10	.25
R468	20¢ R.Rush	1.80	.45
R469	25¢ S.D.Ingham	2.35	.60
R470	40¢ L.McLane	3.50	.80
R471	50¢ W.J.Duane ..	3.00	.30
R472	80¢ R.B.Taney ...	8.50	3.50
R473	$1 L.Woodbury ..	6.25	.30
R474	$2 T.Ewing	9.50	.50
R475	$3 W.Forward	12.50	4.50
R476	$4 J.C.Spencer .	13.50	4.00
R477	$5 G.M.Bibb	20.00	.50
R478	$10 R.J.Walker ..	45.00	2.00
R479	$20 W.M.Meredith	75.00	9.75
R480	$30 T.Corwin	100.00	18.50
R481	$50 J.Guthrie	50.00	13.00
R482	$60 H.Cobb	125.00	37.50
R483	$100 P.F.Thomas	50.00	10.75
R484	$500 J.A.Dix	...	150.00
R485	$1000 S.P.Chase	...	80.00

1948

Scott's No.		F-VF NH	F-VF Used
R486	1¢ A.Hamilton	.30	.30
R487	2¢ O.Wolcott,Jr.	.40	.40
R488	3¢ S.Dexter	.45	.35
R489	4¢ A.Gallatin	.45	.30
R490	5¢ G.W.Campbell	.40	.25
R491	8¢ A.Dallas	.75	.35
R492	10¢ W.H.Crawford	.70	.25
R493	20¢ R.Rush	1.70	.30
R494	25¢ S.D.Ingham	1.40	.25
R495	40¢ L.McLane	4.25	1.75
R496	50¢ W.J.Duane ..	2.25	.25
R497	80¢ R.B.Taney ...	7.50	4.25
R498	$1 L.Woodbury ..	7.00	.25
R499	$2 T.Ewing	12.00	.25
R500	$3 W.Forward	16.50	2.25
R501	$4 J.C.Spencer .	28.50	3.00
R502	$5 G.M.Bibb	21.00	.50
R503	$10 R.J.Walker ..	47.50	.95
R504	$20 W.M.Meredith	90.00	11.50
R505	$30 T.Corwin	65.00	22.50
R506	$50 J.Guthrie	65.00	20.00
R507	$60 H.Cobb	125.00	35.00
R508	$100 P.F.Thomas	65.00	8.75
R509	$500 J.A.Dix......	350.00	110.00
R510	$1000 S.P.Chase	170.00	70.00

1949

Scott's No.		F-VF NH	F-VF Used
R511	1¢ A.Hamilton	.30	.30
R512	2¢ O.Wolcott,Jr.	.55	.40
R513	3¢ S.Dexter	.45	.40
R514	4¢ A.Gallatin	.60	.50
R515	5¢ G.W.Campbell	.40	.25
R516	8¢ A.Dallas	.70	.60
R517	10¢ W.H.Crawford	.45	.30
R518	20¢ R.Rush	1.30	.60
R519	25¢ S.D.Ingham	1.80	.65
R520	40¢ L.McLane	4.25	2.00
R521	50¢ W.J.Duane ..	3.50	.35
R522	80¢ R.B.Taney ...	10.50	4.50
R523	$1 L.Woodbury ..	8.50	.55
R524	$2 T.Ewing	11.00	1.85
R525	$3 W.Forward	17.50	6.00
R526	$4 J.C.Spencer .	20.00	5.50
R527	$5 G.M.Bibb	21.00	2.50
R528	$10 R.J.Walker ..	50.00	3.50
R529	$20 W.M.Meredith	100.00	10.00
R530	$30 T.Corwin	85.00	25.00
R531	$50 J.Guthrie	100.00	37.50
R532	$60 H.Cobb	170.00	42.50
R533	$100 P.F.Thomas	50.00	15.00
R534	$500 J.A.Dix	...	140.00
R535	$1000 S.P.Chase	...	125.00

1950

Scott's No.		F-VF NH	F-VF Used
R536	1¢ A.Hamilton	.30	.25
R537	2¢ O.Wolcott,Jr.	.35	.30
R538	3¢ S.Dexter	.40	.35
R539	4¢ A.Gallatin	.50	.40
R540	5¢ G.W.Campbell	.35	.25
R541	8¢ A.Dallas	1.30	.65
R542	10¢ W.H.Crawford	.70	.25
R543	20¢ R.Rush	1.00	.40
R544	25¢ S.D.Ingham	1.50	.40
R545	40¢ L.McLane	3.25	1.75
R546	50¢ W.J.Duane .	4.25	.25
R547	80¢ R.B.Taney ..	**9.25**	**4.75**

DATED DOCUMENTARY STAMPS (cont.)

Scott's No.		F-VF NH	F-VF Used
R548	$1 L.Woodbury .	9.50	.35
R549	$2 T.Ewing	11.00	1.80
R550	$3 W.Forward	13.00	4.75
R551	$4 J.C.Spencer .	17.50	5.50
R552	$5 G.M.Bibb	21.50	.80
R553	$10 R.J.Walker ..	52.50	7.50
R554	$20 W.M.Meredith	100.00	10.00
R555	$30 T.Corwin	75.00	45.00
R556	$50 J.Guthrie	70.00	16.50
R557	$60 H.Cobb	150.00	52.50
R558	$100 P.F.Thomas	55.00	16.50
R559	$500 J.A.Dix	...	87.50
R560	$1000 S.P.Chase	...	67.50

1951

Scott's No.		F-VF NH	F-VF Used
R561	1¢ A.Hamilton	.30	.25
R562	2¢ O.Wolcott,Jr.	.35	.30
R563	3¢ S.Dexter	.30	.30
R564	4¢ A.Gallatin	.35	.30
R565	5¢ G.W.Campbell	.35	.30
R566	8¢ A.Dallas	1.10	.40
R567	10¢ W.H.Crawford	.55	.25
R568	20¢ R.Rush	1.30	.45
R569	25¢ S.D.Ingham	1.50	.40
R570	40¢ L.McLane	3.50	1.25
R571	50¢ W.J.Duane ..	3.00	.35
R572	80¢ R.B.Taney ...	5.50	2.50
R573	$1 L.Woodbury ..	10.00	.25
R574	$2 T.Ewing	14.50	.45
R575	$3 W.Forward	20.00	3.00
R576	$4 J.C.Spencer .	25.00	5.75
R577	$5 G.M.Bibb	17.50	.60
R578	$10 R.J.Walker ..	42.50	2.25
R579	$20 W.M.Meredith	90.00	9.00
R580	$30 T.Corwin	75.00	12.00
R581	$50 J.Guthrie	85.00	20.00
R582	$60 H.Cobb	135.00	40.00
R583	$100 P.F.Thomas	45.00	10.75
R584	$500 J.A.Dix......	250.00	100.00
R585	$1000 S.P.Chase	...	90.00

1952

Scott's No.		F-VF NH	F-VF Used
R586	1¢ A.Hamilton	.30	.25
R587	2¢ O.Wolcott,Jr.	.40	.30
R588	3¢ S.Dexter	.35	.30
R589	4¢ A.Gallatin	.40	.30
R590	5¢ G.W.Campbell	.30	.25
R591	8¢ A.Dallas	.75	.45
R592	10¢ W.H.Crawford	.45	.25
R593	20¢ R.Rush	1.00	.35
R594	25¢ S.D.Ingham	1.50	.40
R595	40¢ L.McLane ...	3.00	1.30
R596	50¢ W.J.Duane ..	2.75	.30
R597	55¢ L.J.Gage	20.00	9.75
R598	80¢ R.B.Taney ...	13.00	3.00
R599	$1 L.Woodbury ..	5.00	1.40
R600	$1.10 L.J.Gage .	45.00	21.50
R601	$1.65 L.J.Gage .	140.00	45.00
R602	$2 T.Ewing	11.50	.65
R603	$2.20 L.J.Gage .	125.00	60.00
R604	$2.75 L.J.Gage .	140.00	3.50
R605	$3 W.Forward	25.00	3.75
R606	$3.30 L.J.Gage .	130.00	52.50
R607	$4 J.C.Spencer .	22.50	3.75
R608	$5 G.M.Bibb	22.50	1.10
R609	$10 R.J.Walker ..	45.00	1.10
R610	$20 W.M.Meredith	70.00	10.00
R611	$30 T.Corwin	50.00	17.50
R612	$50 J.Guthrie	45.00	14.50
R613	$60 H.Cobb	300.00	52.50
R614	$100 P.F.Thomas	40.00	8.00
R615	$500 J.A.Dix.......	550.00	110.00
R616	$1000 S.P.Chase.	...	28.50
R617	$2500 W.Windom	...	160.00

1953

Scott's No.		F-VF NH	F-VF Used
R620	1¢ A.Hamilton	.30	.30
R621	2¢ O.Wolcott,Jr.	.30	.30
R622	3¢ S.Dexter	.35	.30
R623	4¢ A.Gallatin	.50	.40
R624	5¢ G.W.Campbell	.35	.25
R625	8¢ A.Dallas	.90	.70
R626	10¢ W.H.Crawford	.50	.30
R627	20¢ R.Rush	1.00	.40
R628	25¢ S.D.Ingham	1.10	.50
R629	40¢ L.McLane	2.00	.70
R630	50¢ W.J.Duane ..	2.50	.30
R631	55¢ L.J.Gage	4.25	2.00
R632	80¢ R.B.Taney ...	7.00	1.85
R633	$1 L.Woodbury ..	4.25	.30
R634	$1.10 L.J.Gage .	7.50	2.25
R635	$1.65 L.J.Gage .	7.50	3.75
R636	$2 T.Ewing	6.00	.65
R637	$2.20 L.J.Gage .	14.00	5.25
R638	$2.75 L.J.Gage .	20.00	6.25
R639	$3 W.Forward	12.50	3.25
R640	$3.30 L.J.Gage .	27.50	7.00
R641	$4 J.C.Spencer .	25.00	8.50
R642	$5 G.M.Bibb	20.00	10.00
R643	$10 R.J.Walker ..	45.00	1.75
R644	$20 W.M.Meredith	90.00	16.00
R645	$30 T.Corwin	65.00	14.50
R646	$50 J.Guthrie	130.00	30.00
R647	$60 H.Cobb......	450.00	185.00
R648	$100 P.F.Thomas	40.00	12.50
R649	$500 J.A.Dix......	500.00	130.00
R650	$1000 S.Chase .	250.00	62.50
R651	$2500 W.Windom	...	1000.00

DATED DOCUMENTARY STAMPS (cont.)

Scott's No.		F-VF NH	F-VF Used
	1954 Without Overprint		
R654	1¢ A.Hamilton	.30	.25
R655	2¢ O.Wolcott,Jr.	.30	.25
R656	3¢ S.Dexter	.30	.25
R657	4¢ A.Gallatin	.30	.25
R658	5¢ G.W.Campbell	.30	.25
R659	8¢ A.Dallas	.30	.25
R660	10¢ W.H.Crawford	.30	.25
R661	20¢ R.Rush	.50	.35
R662	25¢ S.D.Ingham	.65	.40
R663	40¢ L.McLane	1.20	.50
R664	50¢ W.J.Duane	1.70	.25
R665	55¢ L.J.Gage	1.50	1.10
R666	80¢ R.B.Taney	2.50	1.65
R667	$1 L.Woodbury	1.40	.30
R668	$1.10 L.J.Gage	3.25	2.25
R669	$1.65 L.J.Gage	95.00	65.00
R670	$2 T.Ewing	1.75	.40
R671	$2.20 L.J.Gage	4.75	3.35
R672	$2.75 L.J.Gage	100.00	57.50
R673	$3 W.Forward	3.00	1.75
R674	$3.30 L.J.Gage	6.75	4.50
R675	$4 J.C.Spencer	4.25	3.25
R676	$5 G.M.Bibb	5.50	.45
R677	$10 R.J.Walker	10.00	1.35
R678	$20 W.M.Meredith	35.00	5.25
	1954 With Date		
R679	$30 T.Corwin	50.00	14.00
R680	$50 J.Guthrie	70.00	19.00
R681	$60 H.Cobb	100.00	21.50
R682	$100 P.F.Thomas	50.00	6.25
R683	$500 J.A.Dix	...	67.50
R684	$1000 S.Chase	285.00	57.50
R685	$2500 W.Windom	...	200.00
R686	$5000 C.J.Folger	...	800.00
	1955		
R688	$30 T.Corwin	67.50	12.00
R689	$50 J.Guthrie	67.50	15.00
R690	$60 H.Cobb	110.00	27.50
R691	$100 P.F.Thomas	55.00	6.75
R692	$500 J.A.Dix	650.00	110.00
R693	$1000 S.P.Chase	...	32.50
R694	$2500 W.Windom	...	120.00
	1956		
R697	$30 T.Corwin	85.00	14.00
R698	$50 J.Guthrie	90.00	19.50
R699	$60 H.Cobb	110.00	37.50
R700	$100 P.F.Thomas	85.00	12.00
R701	$500 J.A.Dix	...	80.00
R702	$1000 S.P.Chase	550.00	59.50
R703	$2500 W.Windom	...	400.00
R705	$10,000 W.Q.Gresham		625.00
	1957		
R706	$30 T.Corwin	115.00	27.50
R707	$50 J.Guthrie	85.00	30.00
R708	$60 H.Cobb	...	165.00
R709	$100 P.F.Thomas	75.00	12.50
R710	$500 J.A.Dix	335.00	95.00
R711	$1000 S.P.Chase	...	72.50
R712	$2500 W.Windom	...	650.00
R714	$10,000 W.Q.Gresham		425.00
	1958		
R715	$30 T.Corwin	80.00	20.00
R716	$50 J.Guthrie	70.00	20.00
R717	$60 H.Cobb	110.00	27.50
R718	$100 P.F.Thomas	55.00	10.00
R719	$500 J.A.Dix	250.00	70.00
R720	$1000 S.P.Chase	...	65.00
R721	$2500 W.Windom	...	800.00
	1958 Without Overprint		
R724	$30 T.Corwin	35.00	6.00
R725	$50 J.Guthrie	37.50	6.50
R726	$60 H.Cobb	75.00	19.50
R727	$100 P.F.Thomas	18.50	4.25
R728	$500 J.A.Dix	80.00	25.00
R729	$1000 S.P.Chase	50.00	19.00
R730	$2500 W.Windom	...	150.00
R731	$5000 C.J.Folger	...	140.00
R732	$10,000 W.Q.Gresham		130.00

DATED STOCK TRANSFER REVENUE STAMPS (VF+30%)

Note: Dated Stock Transfer stamps with cut cancels or perforated initials sell for much less than used price.

1940 'SERIES 1940" and "STOCK TRANSFER" Overprint on 1917-33 Documentary Issues. NH +20%

Scott's No.		F-VF Unused	F-VF Used
RD42	1¢ Rose pink	3.00	.45
RD43	2¢ Rose pink	3.00	.50
RD45	4¢ Rose pink	3.00	.35
RD46	5¢ Rose pink	3.50	.25
RD48	10¢ Rose pink	4.25	.25
RD49	20¢ Rose pink	7.50	.25
RD50	25¢ Rose pink	7.25	.60
RD51	40¢ Rose pink	4.75	.70
RD52	50¢ Rose pink	5.75	.30
RD53	80¢ Rose pink	85.00	52.50
RD54	$1 Green	30.00	.40
RD55	$2 Rose	27.50	.60
RD56	$3 Violet	150.00	11.00
RD57	$4 Yellow brown	57.50	1.10
RD58	$5 Dark blue	55.00	1.25
RD59	$10 Orange	120.00	7.50

DATED STOCK TRANSFERS (cont.)

Scott's No.		F-VF Unused	F-VF Used
RD60	$20 Olive bister	250.00	85.00
RD61	$30 Grant	...	600.00
RD64	$100 Marshall	...	525.00

#RD67-RD372 Stamps are Overprinted with Series Date Ex.: "SERIES 1940" or "Series 1949" $30 & up values issued without gum & have straight edges on one/two sides. All are green with black overprints.

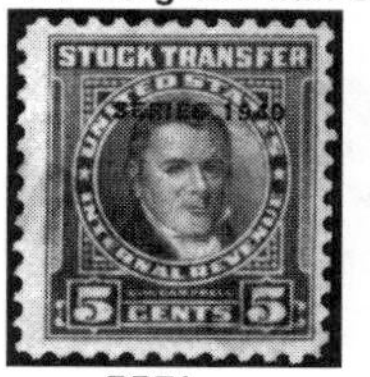

RD71

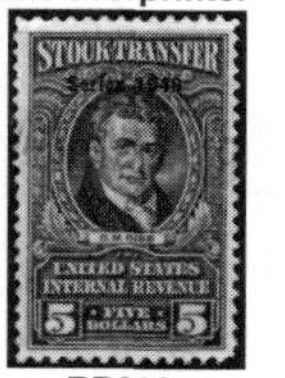

RD223

Scott's No.		F-VF NH	F-VF Used
	1940		
RD67	1¢ A.Hamilton	11.00	3.00
RD68	2¢ O.Wolcott,Jr.	7.25	1.50
RD70	4¢ A.Gallatin	12.50	3.95
RD71	5¢ G.W.Campbell	8.00	1.50
RD73	10¢ W.H.Crawford	11.00	1.95
RD74	20¢ R.Rush	12.75	2.25
RD75	25¢ S.D.Ingham	35.00	8.25
RD76	40¢ L.McLane	65.00	30.00
RD77	50¢ W.J.Duane	11.00	1.90
RD78	80¢ R.B.Taney	85.00	55.00
RD79	$1 L.Woodbury	37.50	3.75
RD80	$2 T.Ewing	42.50	9.00
RD81	$3 W.Forward	65.00	11.00
RD82	$4 J.C.Spencer	265.00	185.00
RD83	$5 G.M.Bibb	57.50	12.50
RD84	$10 R.J.Walker	140.00	35.00
RD85	$20 W.Meredith	800.00	75.00
RD86	$30 T.Corwin	600.00	140.00
RD87	$50 J.Guthrie	650.00	425.00
RD89	$100 P.F.Thomas	...	275.00
	1941		
RD92	1¢ A.Hamilton	.65	.50
RD93	2¢ O.Wolcott,Jr.	.45	.30
RD95	4¢ A.Gallatin	.50	.25
RD96	5¢ G.W.Campbell	.45	.25
RD98	10¢ W.H.Crawford	.75	.25
RD99	20¢ R.Rush	1.75	.30
RD100	25¢ S.D.Ingham	1.75	.40
RD101	40¢ L.McLane	2.50	.75
RD102	50¢ W.J.Duane	4.25	.35
RD103	80¢ R.B.Taney	22.50	7.50
RD104	$1 L.Woodbury	16.50	.25
RD105	$2 T.Ewing	16.00	.30
RD106	$3 W.Forward	23.50	1.50
RD107	$4 J.C.Spencer	42.50	7.25
RD108	$5 G.M.Bibb	45.00	.60
RD109	$10 R.J.Walker	90.00	4.00
RD110	$20 W.Meredith	250.00	60.00
RD111	$30 T.Corwin	225.00	215.00
RD112	$50 J.Guthrie	750.00	375.00
RD113	$60 H.Cobb	...	275.00
RD114	$100 P.F.Thomas	...	160.00
	1942		
RD117	1¢ A.Hamilton	.50	.30
RD118	2¢ O.Wolcott,Jr.	.45	.35
RD119	4¢ A.Gallatin	2.95	1.00
RD120	5¢ G.W.Campbell	.40	.25
RD121	10¢ W.H.Crawford	1.75	.25
RD122	20¢ R.Rush	2.00	.25
RD123	25¢ S.D.Ingham	1.85	.25
RD124	40¢ L.McLane	4.25	.40
RD125	50¢ W.J.Duane	5.25	.25
RD126	80¢ R.B.Taney	21.75	5.75
RD127	$1 L.Woodbury	15.00	.35
RD128	$2 T.Ewing	24.50	.40
RD129	$3 W.Forward	31.50	1.00
RD130	$4 J.C.Spencer	42.50	20.00
RD131	$5 G.M.Bibb	45.00	.40
RD132	$10 R.J.Walker	70.00	8.00
RD133	$20 W.Meredith	160.00	35.00
RD134	$30 T.Corwin	200.00	55.00
RD135	$50 J.Guthrie	325.00	125.00
RD136	$60 H.Cobb	400.00	175.00
RD137	$100 P.F.Thomas	...	70.00
RD139	$1000 S.P.Chase	...	500.00
	1943		
RD140	1¢ A.Hamilton	.40	.30
RD141	2¢ O.Wolcott,Jr.	.45	.35
RD142	4¢ A.Gallatin	1.70	.25
RD143	5¢ G.W.Campbell	.50	.25
RD144	10¢ W.H.Crawford	.95	.25
RD145	20¢ R.Rush	1.65	.25
RD146	25¢ S.D.Ingham	4.50	.30
RD147	40¢ L.McLane	3.75	.25
RD148	50¢ W.J.Duane	3.75	.25
RD149	80¢ R.B.Taney	17.50	4.25
RD150	$1 L.Woodbury	15.00	.25
RD151	$2 T.Ewing	17.00	.35
RD152	$3 W.Forward	20.75	1.25
RD153	$4 J.C.Spencer	42.50	14.00
RD154	$5 G.M.Bibb	62.50	.35
RD155	$10 R.J.Walker	85.00	4.25

DATED STOCK TRANSFERS (cont.)

Scott's No.		F-VF NH	F-VF Used
RD156	$20 W.M.Meredith	...	35.00
RD157	$30 T.Corwin	300.00	130.00
RD158	$50 J.Guthrie	650.00	125.00
RD160	$100 P.Thomas	115.00	55.00
RD162	$1000 S.P.Chase	...	225.00
	1944		
RD163	1¢ A.Hamilton	.60	.55
RD164	2¢ O.Wolcott,Jr.	.50	.25
RD165	4¢ A.Gallatin	.55	.25
RD166	5¢ G.W.Campbell	.50	.25
RD167	10¢ W.H.Crawford	.70	.25
RD168	20¢ R.Rush	1.25	.25
RD169	25¢ S.D.Ingham	2.00	.30
RD170	40¢ L.McLane	8.00	4.50
RD171	50¢ W.J.Duane	4.50	.25
RD172	80¢ R.B.Taney	9.50	4.25
RD173	$1 L.Woodbury	10.50	.40
RD174	$2 T.Ewing	40.00	.55
RD175	$3 W.Forward	37.50	1.25
RD176	$4 J.C.Spencer	40.00	4.75
RD177	$5 G.M.Bibb	37.50	1.00
RD178	$10 R.J.Walker	77.50	4.50
RD179	$20 W.Meredith	125.00	8.25
RD180	$30 T.Corwin	200.00	70.00
RD181	$50 J.Guthrie	135.00	55.00
RD182	$60 H.Cobb	225.00	135.00
RD183	$100 P.F.Thomas	200.00	55.00
RD184	$500 J.A.Dix	...	450.00
RD185	$1000 S.P.Chase	...	725.00
	1945		
RD186	1¢ A.Hamilton	.25	.25
RD187	2¢ O.Wolcott,Jr.	.30	.25
RD188	4¢ A.Gallatin	.25	.25
RD189	5¢ G.W.Campbell	.25	.25
RD190	10¢ W.H.Crawford	.70	.30
RD191	20¢ R.Rush	1.30	.30
RD192	25¢ S.D.Ingham	2.00	.30
RD193	40¢ L.McLane	2.75	.30
RD194	50¢ W.J.Duane	4.25	.30
RD195	80¢ R.B.Taney	8.75	3.00
RD196	$1 L.Woodbury	14.00	.25
RD197	$2 T.Ewing	22.50	.60
RD198	$3 W.Forward	35.00	.90
RD199	$4 J.C.Spencer	37.50	2.50
RD200	$5 G.M.Bibb	25.00	.45
RD201	$10 R.J.Walker	55.00	6.50
RD202	$20 W.Meredith	125.00	11.75
RD203	$30 T.Corwin	135.00	65.00
RD204	$50 J.Guthrie	65.00	22.50
RD205	$60 H.Cobb	230.00	135.00
RD206	$100 P.F.Thomas	85.00	37.50
RD207	$500 J.A.Dix	...	825.00
	1946		
RD209	1¢ A.Hamilton	.25	.25
RD210	2¢ O.Wolcott,Jr.	.35	.25
RD211	4¢ A.Gallatin	.35	.25
RD212	5¢ G.W.Campbell	.35	.25
RD213	10¢ W.H.Crawford	.70	.25
RD214	20¢ R.Rush	1.60	.35
RD215	25¢ S.D.Ingham	1.80	.30
RD216	40¢ L.McLane	3.75	.60
RD217	50¢ W.J.Duane	4.75	.25
RD218	80¢ R.B.Taney	13.00	5.75
RD219	$1 L.Woodbury	10.00	.50
RD220	$2 T.Ewing	11.00	.50
RD221	$3 W.Forward	20.00	1.25
RD222	$4 J.C.Spencer	20.00	5.75
RD223	$5 G.M.Bibb	32.50	1.25
RD224	$10 R.J.Walker	65.00	2.25
RD225	$20 W.Meredith	150.00	42.50
RD226	$30 T.Corwin	130.00	40.00
RD227	$50 J.Guthrie	90.00	45.00
RD228	$60 H.Cobb	200.00	90.00
RD229	$100 P.F.Thomas	125.00	52.50
RD230	$500 J.A.Dix	...	170.00
RD231	$1000 S.P.Chase	...	180.00
	1947		
RD235	1¢ A.Hamilton	1.20	.55
RD236	2¢ O.Wolcott,Jr.	1.30	.50
RD237	4¢ A.Gallatin	.95	.40
RD238	5¢ G.W.Campbell	1.10	.35
RD239	10¢ W.H.Crawford	1.20	.55
RD240	20¢ R.Rush	2.00	.50
RD241	25¢ S.D.Ingham	2.75	.60
RD242	40¢ L.McLane	3.50	.70
RD243	50¢ W.J.Duane	4.00	.30
RD244	80¢ R.B.Taney	20.00	9.50
RD245	$1 L.Woodbury	11.00	.50
RD246	$2 T.Ewing	18.50	.70
RD247	$3 W.Forward	32.50	1.50
RD248	$4 J.C.Spencer	40.00	5.50
RD249	$5 G.M.Bibb	35.00	1.50
RD250	$10 R.J.Walker	55.00	4.75
RD251	$20 W.Meredith	100.00	30.00
RD252	$30 T.Corwin	100.00	50.00
RD253	$50 J.Guthrie	210.00	115.00
RD254	$60 H.Cobb	300.00	135.00
RD255	$100 P.F.Thomas	120.00	40.00
RD256	$500 J.A.Dix	...	375.00
RD257	$1000 S.P.Chase	...	100.00
	1948		
RD261	1¢ A.Hamilton	.30	.25
RD262	2¢ O.Wolcott,Jr.	.25	.25
RD263	4¢ A.Gallatin	.45	.30
RD264	5¢ G.W.Campbell	.35	.25
RD265	10¢ W.H.Crawford	.35	.25
RD266	20¢ R.Rush	1.35	.35

DATED STOCK TRANSFERS (cont.)

Scott's No.		F-VF NH	F-VF Used
RD267	25¢ S.D.Ingham	1.40	.40
RD268	40¢ L.McLane	2.25	.75
RD269	50¢ W.J.Duane	4.25	.30
RD270	80¢ R.B.Taney	17.50	5.75
RD271	$1 L.Woodbury	11.00	.35
RD272	$2 T.Ewing	20.00	.65
RD273	$3 W.Forward	25.00	3.75
RD274	$4 J.C.Spencer	27.50	10.75
RD275	$5 G.M.Bibb	32.50	2.50
RD276	$10 R.J.Walker	55.00	4.50
RD277	$20 W.Meredith	100.00	17.50
RD278	$30 T.Corwin	150.00	57.50
RD279	$50 J.Guthrie	100.00	57.50
RD280	$60 H.Cobb	250.00	130.00
RD281	$100 P.F.Thomas	87.50	22.50
RD282	$500 J.A.Dix	...	225.00
RD283	$1000 S.P.Chase	...	125.00
RD284	$2500 Windom	675.00	350.00
RD285	$5000 C.J.Folger	...	275.00
	1949		
RD287	1¢ A.Hamilton	1.60	.45
RD288	2¢ O.Wolcott,Jr.	1.40	.45
RD289	4¢ A.Gallatin	1.75	.50
RD290	5¢ G.W.Campbell	1.75	.50
RD291	10¢ W.H.Crawford	3.00	./0
RD292	20¢ R.Rush	5.00	.60
RD293	25¢ S.D.Ingham	6.25	.80
RD294	40¢ L.McLane	12.75	1.50
RD295	50¢ W.J.Duane	15.00	.30
RD296	80¢ R.B.Taney	21.00	6.25
RD297	$1 L.Woodbury	17.00	.70
RD298	$2 T.Ewing	25.00	.85
RD299	$3 W.Forward	45.00	4.25
RD300	$4 J.C.Spencer	40.00	7.00
RD301	$5 G.M.Bibb	50.00	2.00
RD302	$10 R.J.Walker	67.50	3.75
RD303	$20 W.Meredith	140.00	14.50
RD304	$30 T.Corwin	175.00	77.50
RD305	$50 J.Guthrie	225.00	125.00
RD306	$60 H.Cobb	375.00	225.00
RD307	$100 P.F.Thomas	150.00	65.00
RD308	$500 J.A.Dix	...	220.00
RD309	$1000 S.P.Chase	...	90.00
RD310	$2500 W.Windom	...	450.00
RD312	$10,000 W.Q.Gresham		375.00
	1950		
RD313	1¢ A.Hamilton	.60	.35
RD314	2¢ O.Wolcott,Jr.	.50	.30
RD315	4¢ A.Gallatin	.40	.35
RD316	5¢ G.W.Campbell	.50	.25
RD317	10¢ W.H.Crawford	2.65	.30
RD318	20¢ R.Rush	4.00	.50
RD319	25¢ S.D.Ingham	4.75	.70
RD320	40¢ L.McLane	7.00	.95
RD321	50¢ W.J.Duane	8.25	.35
RD322	80¢ R.B.Taney	15.75	4.75
RD323	$1 L.Woodbury	15.75	.45
RD324	$2 T.Ewing	28.50	.70
RD325	$3 W.Forward	35.00	3.75
RD326	$4 J.C.Spencer	42.50	8.50
RD327	$5 G.M.Bibb	42.50	1.70
RD328	$10 R.J.Walker	150.00	4.75
RD329	$20 W.Meredith	140.00	23.50
RD330	$30 T.Corwin	140.00	65.00
RD331	$50 J.Guthrie	175.00	85.00
RD332	$60 H.Cobb	250.00	135.00
RD333	$100 P.F.Thomas	100.00	45.00
RD334	$500 J.A.Dix	...	250.00
RD335	$1000 S.P.Chase	...	70.00
RD337	$5000 C.J.Folger	...	675.00
RD338	$10,000 W.Q.Gresham		750.00
	1951		
RD339	1¢ A.Hamilton	2.00	.35
RD340	2¢ O.Wolcott,Jr.	1.65	.30
RD341	4¢ A.Gallatin	2.00	.50
RD342	5¢ G.W.Campbell	1.40	.35
RD343	10¢ W.H.Crawford	2.10	.30
RD344	20¢ R.Rush	5.00	.85
RD345	25¢ S.D.Ingham	7.25	.85
RD346	40¢ L.McLane	30.00	8.50
RD347	50¢ W.J.Duane	12.50	.85
RD348	80¢ R.B.Taney	25.00	9.00
RD349	$1 L.Woodbury	26.50	.80
RD350	$2 T.Ewing	32.50	1.30
RD351	$3 W.Forward	42.50	9.00
RD352	$4 J.C.Spencer	50.00	11.00
RD353	$5 G.M.Bibb	65.00	2.50
RD354	$10 R.J.Walker	120.00	7.75
RD355	$20 W.Meredith	160.00	16.50
RD356	$30 T.Corwin	160.00	70.00
RD357	$50 J.Guthrie	150.00	60.00
RD359	$100 P.F.Thomas	150.00	65.00
RD360	$500 J.A.Dix	...	350.00
RD361	$1000 S.P.Chase	...	100.00
RD364	$10,000 W.Q.Gresham		150.00
	1952		
RD365	1¢ A.Hamilton	32.50	16.00
RD366	10¢ W.H.Crawford	35.00	16.00
RD367	20¢ R.Rush	425.00	...
RD368	25¢ S.D.Ingham	550.00	...
RD369	40¢ L.McLane	110.00	40.00
RD370	$4 J.C.Spencer	...	500.00

NOTE: Unused stamps which have been or are hinged sell for about 20% less than never hinged stamps on Dated Revenues.

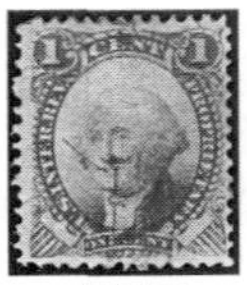
RB1-2

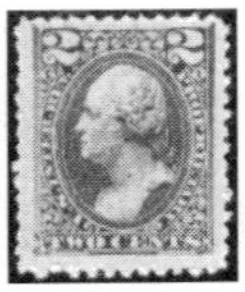
RB11-12

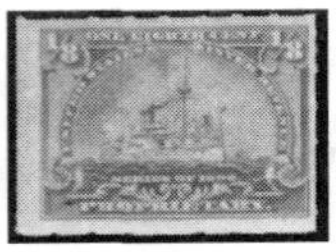
RB20-31

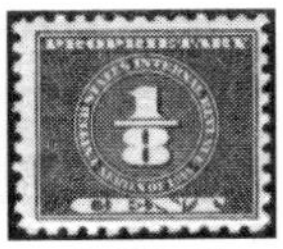
RB32-64

RB65-73

1871-74 Proprietary, G.Washington (All Used) (VF+60%) (C)

Scott's No.		Violet Paper(a) Fine	Ave.	Green Paper(b) Fine	Ave.
RB1	1¢ Green and Black	4.25	2.65	8.50	5.00
RB2	2¢ Green and Black	5.25	3.00	21.00	12.75
RB3	3¢ Green and Black	21.00	12.50	50.00	30.00
RB4	4¢ Green and Black	11.50	7.00	18.00	11.00
RB5	5¢ Green and Black	135.00	80.00	150.00	90.00
RB6	6¢ Green and Black	40.00	24.00	100.00	60.00
RB7	10¢ Green and Black	170.00	105.00	50.00	30.00
RB8	50¢ Green and Black	525.00	300.00	925.00	550.00
RB9	$1 Green and Black	1275.00	750.00	...	...
RB10	$5 Green and Black	...	...	...	...

1875-81 Proprietary (All Used) (VF+60%) (C)

Scott's No.		Silk Paper(s) Fine	Ave.	Perforated(b) Fine	Ave.	Rouletted(c) Fine	Ave.
RB11	1¢ Green	1.85	1.10	.40	.25	85.00	50.00
RB12	2¢ Brown	2.25	1.30	1.35	.75	100.00	60.00
RB13	3¢ Orange	10.75	5.75	3.50	2.10	100.00	60.00
RB14	4¢ Red Brown	6.50	4.00	5.25	2.95	...	...
RB15	4¢ Red	...	...	4.00	2.25	160.00	95.00
RB16	5¢ Black	115.00	70.00	90.00	55.00	...	...
RB17	6¢ Violet Blue	21.50	13.00	18.00	11.00	275.00	165.00
RB18	6¢ Violet	...	...	27.50	17.00	...	...
RB19	10¢ Blue	...	...	265.00	160.00	...	...

1898 Proprietary, Battleship Designs of #R161-72 (C) (VF+40%) (Roulette 5½)

Scott's No.		Unused Fine	Ave.	Used Fine	Ave.
RB20	1/8¢ Yellow Green	.30	.20	.25	.15
RB20p	1/8¢ Hyphen Hole Perf 7	.30	.20	.25	.15
RB21	1/4¢ Pale Brown	.30	.20	.25	.15
RB21p	1/4¢ Hyphen Hole Perf 7	.30	.20	.25	.15
RB22	3/8¢ Deep Orange	.30	.20	.30	.20
RB22p	3/8¢ Hyphen Hole Perf 7	.30	.20	.30	.20
RB23	5/8¢ Deep Ultramarine	.30	.20	.30	.20
RB23p	5/8¢ Hyphen Hole Perf 7	.30	.20	.30	.20
RB24	1¢ Dark Green	1.85	1.15	.30	.20
RB24p	1¢ Hyphen Hole Perf 7	23.50	14.75	14.50	9.00
RB25	1¼¢ Violet	.30	.20	.30	.20
RB25p	1¼¢ Hyphen Hole Perf 7	.30	.20	.30	.20
RB26	1 7/8¢ Dull Blue	10.00	6.25	1.35	.90
RB26p	1 7/8¢ Hyphen Hoe Perf 7	28.50	17.50	7.00	4.50
RB27	2¢ Violet Brown	.95	.60	.30	.20
RB27p	2¢ Hyphen Hole Perf 7	6.00	3.75	.65	.40
RB28	2½¢ Lake	3.75	2.25	.30	.20
RB28p	2½¢ Hyphen Hole Perf 7	4.50	2.85	.30	.20
RB29	3¾¢ Olive Gray	40.00	25.00	8.75	5.75
RB29p	3¾¢ Hyphen Hole Perf 7	65.00	37.50	17.50	10.75
RB30	4¢ Purple	11.00	6.50	.95	.60
RB30p	4¢ Hyphen Hole Perf 7	55.00	32.50	18.00	11.00
RB31	5¢ Brown Orange	11.00	6.50	.95	.60
RB31p	5¢ Hyphen Hole Perf 7	60.00	36.50	18.00	11.00

1914 Black Proprietary Stamps - Single Line Wtmk. "USPS" (VF + 50%) (B)

RB32	1/8¢ Black	.30	.20	.30	.20
RB33	¼¢ Black	1.75	1.10	1.10	.65
RB34	3/8¢ Black	.30	.20	.30	.20
RB35	5/8¢ Black	4.25	2.50	1.75	1.10
RB36	1¼¢ Black	2.65	1.75	1.10	.70
RB37	1 7/8¢ Black	35.00	21.00	15.00	9.50
RB38	2½¢ Black	9.25	5.50	2.35	1.50
RB39	3 1/8¢ Black	80.00	50.00	47.50	27.50
RB40	3 3/4¢ Black	35.00	21.50	20.00	12.50
RB41	4¢ Black	52.50	31.50	26.50	16.00
RB42	4 3/8¢ Black	1250.00	775.00	...	...
RB43	5¢ Black	110.00	67.50	60.00	35.00

1914 Black Proprietary Stamps - Double Line Wtmk. "USIR" (50%) (B)

RB44	1/8¢ Black	.30	.20	.30	.20
RB45	¼¢ Black	.30	.20	.30	.20
RB46	3/8¢ Black	.60	.35	.35	.25
RB47	½¢ Black	3.25	1.95	2.65	1.65
RB48	5/8¢ Black	.30	.20	.30	.20
RB49	1¢ Black	4.50	2.50	4.00	2.25
RB50	1¼¢ Black	.40	.25	.35	.25
RB51	1½¢ Black	3.25	1.90	2.00	1.10
RB52	1 7/8¢ Black	1.10	.65	.60	.35
RB53	2¢ Black	5.50	3.50	3.75	2.35
RB54	2½¢ Black	1.30	.80	1.10	.65
RB55	3¢ Black	3.75	2.10	2.50	1.50
RB56	3 1/8¢ Black	5.00	3.00	2.75	1.65
RB57	3¾¢ Black	10.00	6.00	7.00	4.25
RB58	4¢ Black	.35	.25	.30	.20
RB59	4 3/8¢ Black	14.00	8.50	8.00	4.75
RB60	5¢ Black	3.00	1.80	2.50	1.40
RB61	6¢ Black	47.50	29.50	36.50	21.75
RB62	8¢ Black	18.00	11.00	11.00	6.75
RB63	10¢ Black	10.00	6.00	6.50	4.00
RB64	20¢ Black	20.00	12.50	16.00	9.75

1919 Proprietary Stamps (VF + 50%) (B)

Scott's No.		Unused Fine	Ave.	Used Fine	Ave.
RB65	1¢ Dark Blue	.30	.20	.30	.20
RB66	2¢ Dark Blue	.30	.20	.30	.20
RB67	3¢ Dark Blue	1.10	.65	.65	.40
RB68	4¢ Dark Blue	1.40	.85	.55	.30
RB69	5¢ Dark Blue	1.35	.80	.65	.40
RB70	8¢ Dark Blue	13.00	8.00	9.00	5.50
RB71	10¢ Dark Blue	4.75	3.00	2.10	1.30
RB72	20¢ Dark Blue	7.50	4.50	3.25	1.95
RB73	40¢ Dark Blue	45.00	28.50	10.50	6.50

1918-34 Future Delivery Stamps (VF + 50%) (B)

1917 Documentary Stamps overprinted "FUTURE DELIVERY" in black or red

	Horizontal Overprints (Lines 8mm Apart), Perforated 11				
RC1	2¢ Carmine Rose	5.25	3.25	.30	.20
RC2	3¢ Carmine Rose (cut 10.75)	28.00	17.00	20.00	12.50
RC3	4¢ Carmine Rose (cut .20)	9.00	5.75	.30	.20
RC3A	5¢ Carmine Rose	67.50	40.00	5.50	3.25
RC4	10¢ Carmine Rose	15.00	9.00	.30	.20
RC5	20¢ Carmine Rose (cut .20)	21.75	13.00	.30	.20
RC6	25¢ Carmine Rose (cut .25)	42.50	25.00	.45	.30
RC7	40¢ Carmine Rose (cut .25)	47.50	27.50	.75	.45
RC8	50¢ Carmine Rose (cut .20)	10.75	6.50	.30	.20
RC9	80¢ Carmine Rose (cut 1.00)	87.50	55.00	10.00	6.00
	Vertical Overprints Reading Up (Lines 2mm Apart)				
RC10	$1 Green (cut.20)	37.50	22.50	.35	.25
RC11	$2 Rose (cut .20)	40.00	24.00	.35	.25
RC12	$3 Violet (cut .25)	95.00	57.50	2.50	1.50
RC13	$5 Dark Blue (cut .20)	75.00	45.00	.40	.25
RC14	$10 Orange (cut .25)	95.00	57.50	.75	.45
RC15	$20 Olive Bister (cut .50)	175.00	110.00	6.00	3.50
	Horizontal Overprints, Without Gum (Lines 11 2/3m Apart), Perforated 12				
RC16	$30 Vermilion (cut 1.25)	75.00	45.00	3.25	1.95
RC17	$50 Olive Green (cut .55)	50.00	28.50	1.25	.75
RC18	$60 Brown (cut .80)	75.00	45.00	2.10	1.30
RC19	$100 Yellow Green (cut 7.50)	125.00	75.00	30.00	18.00
RC20	$500 Blue (cut 4.50)	85.00	52.50	10.50	6.25
RC21	$1000 Orange (cut 1.50)	100.00	60.00	5.25	3.25
	1923-24 Horizontal Overprints (Lines 2mm Apart), Perforated 11				
RC22	1¢ Carmine Rose	1.10	.70	.30	.20
RC23	80¢ Carmine Rose (cut .35)	85.00	52.50	1.85	1.15
	1925-34 Horizontal Overprints, Serif Lettering, Perforated 11				
RC25	$1 Green (cut .20)	37.50	22.50	.75	.45
RC26	$10 Orange (cut 8.75)	100.00	60.00	15.00	10.00
	1928-29 Overprints, Perforated 10				
RC27	10¢ Carmine Rose	...	...	1850.00	1150.00
RC28	20¢ Carmine Rose	...	...	1850.00	1150.00

1918-22 Stock Transfer Stamps (VF +50%) (B)

1917 Documentary Stamps overprinted "STOCK TRANSFER" in black or red

	Horizontal Overprints (Lines 8mm Apart) Perforated 11				
RD1	1¢ Carmine Rose	.80	.45	.30	.20
RD2	2¢ Carmine Rose	.30	.20	.25	.15
RD3	4¢ Carmine Rose	.30	.20	.30	.20
RD4	5¢ Carmine Rose	.35	.25	.30	.30
RD5	10¢ Carmine Rose	.35	.25	.30	.30
RD6	20¢ Carmine Rose (cut .20)	.55	.35	.30	.20
RD7	25¢ Carmine Rose (cut .20)	1.40	.80	.30	.20
RD8	40¢ Carmine Rose	1.25	.70	.30	.20
RD9	50¢ Carmine Rose	.65	.40	.30	.20
RD10	80¢ Carmine Rose (cut .20)	3.00	1.80	.35	.25
	Vertical Overprints Reading Up (Lines 2mm Apart)				
RD11	$1 Green, Red Overprint (cut 2.75)	75.00	45.00	18.00	11.00
RD12	$1 Green, Black Overprint	2.50	1.50	.30	.20
RD13	$2 Rose (cut .20)	2.50	1.50	.30	.20
RD14	$3 Violet (cut .25)	16.50	9.50	4.25	2.60
RD15	$4 Yellow Brown (cut .20)	8.50	5.00	.30	.20
RD16	$5 Dark Blue (cut .20)	6.50	4.00	.30	.20
RD17	$10 Orange (cut .20)	14.50	9.00	.35	.25
RD18	$20 Olive Bister (cut 3.00)	80.00	50.00	18.00	11.00
	Horizontal Overprints, Without Gum (Lines 11½mm Apart) Perf.12				
RD19	$30 Vermilion (cut 1.10)	16.00	9.75	4.25	2.50
RD20	$50 Olive Green (cut 17.50)	95.00	52.50	52.50	28.75
RD21	$60 Brown (cut 8.75)	110.00	60.00	20.00	13.00
RD22	$100 Green (cut 2.25)	21.50	13.00	5.25	3.00
RD23	$500 Blue (cut 60.00)	285.00	190.00	100.00	65.00
RD24	$1000 Orange (cut 18.75)	150.00	95.00	65.00	40.00
	1928 Stock Transfer (Lines 8mm Apart), Perf.10 (VF + 50%) (B)				
RD25	1¢ Carmine rose	2.40	1.50	.35	.25
RD26	4¢ Carmine rose	2.40	1.50	.35	.25
RD27	10¢ Carmine rose	1.80	1.20	.35	.25
RD28	20¢ Carmine rose (cut .20)	2.85	1.75	.35	.25
RD29	50¢ Carmine rose	3.35	2.10	.35	.25
	Vertical Overprint Reading Up (Lines 2mm Apart) Perforated 10				
RD30	$1 Green (cut .20)	30.00	21.00	.30	.20
RD31	$2 Carmine rose (cut .20)	30.00	21.00	.30	.20
RD32	$10 Orange (cut .20)	32.50	22.50	.40	.25
	1920 Stock Transfers, Serif Overprints, Perf.11 (VF+50%) (B)				
RD33	2¢ Carmine rose	7.50	4.75	.70	.45
RD34	10¢ Carmine rose	2.50	1.60	.35	.25
RD35	20¢ Carmine rose	4.50	2.65	.30	.20
RD36	50¢ Carmine rose	3.00	2.00	.30	.20
RD37	$1 Green (cut .25)	47.50	30.00	8.50	5.50
RD38	$2 Rose (cut .25)	42.50	26.50	7.50	4.75
	1920 Stock Transfers, Serif Overprints, Perf .10 (VF+ 50%) (B)				
RD39	2¢ Carmine rose	6.00	4.00	.80	.50
RD40	10¢ Carmine rose	1.50	1.00	.55	.35
RD41	20¢ Carmine rose (cut .20)	2.50	1.65	.30	.20

"cut" = Cut cancellation or perforated intial cancellation.

CORDIAL AND WINE STAMPS (VF + 50%)

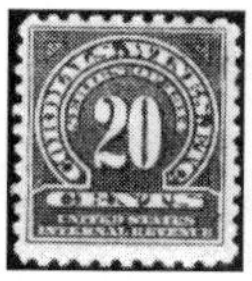

RE1-14, RE16-29,31

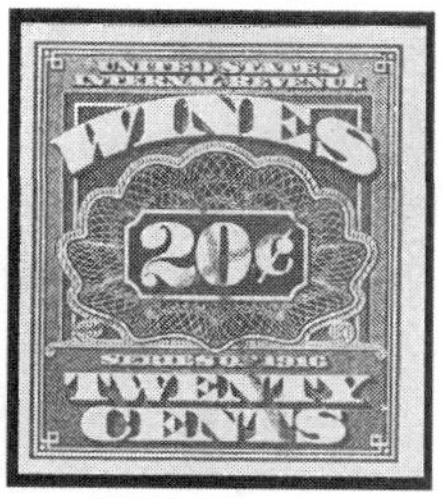

RE32-52,60-80, RE102-5

Scott's No.		Fine Unused	Fine Used
1914 Single-line Wtmk."USPS",Perf.10			
RE1	¼¢ Green	.85	.50
RE2	½¢ Green	.45	.45
RE3	1¢ Green	.45	.35
RE4	1½¢ Green	2.00	1.35
RE5	2¢ Green	3.50	3.50
RE6	3¢ Green	3.00	1.35
RE7	4¢ Green	2.50	1.50
RE8	5¢ Green	1.00	.75
RE9	6¢ Green	7.00	3.75
RE10	8¢ Green	5.25	1.40
RE11	10¢ Green	3.00	2.65
RE12	20¢ Green	4.00	1.65
RE13	24¢ Green	13.00	7.50
RE14	40¢ Green	3.25	.80
RE15	$2 Imperforate	6.50	.25
1914 Double-Line Wtmk."USIR",Perf.10			
RE16	¼¢ Green	5.50	4.50
RE17	½¢ Green	4.00	2.75
RE18	1¢ Green	.30	.20
RE19	1½¢ Green	52.50	33.50
RE20	2¢ Green	.25	.25
RE21	3¢ Green	2.50	2.00
RE22	4¢ Green	.85	.95
RE23	5¢ Green	13.75	10.00
RE24	6¢ Green	.55	.30
RE25	8¢ Green	1.80	.45
RE26	10¢ Green	.60	.25
RE27	20¢ Green	.70	.35
RE28	24¢ Green	12.50	.75
RE29	40¢ Green	27.50	9.50
RE30	$2 Imperforate	35.00	2.95
RE31	$2 Perforated11	72.50	80.00
1916 Rouletted 3½			
Inscribed "Series of 1916"			
RE32	1¢ Green	.35	.35
RE33	3¢ Green	5.00	4.00
RE34	4¢ Green	.30	.30
RE35	6¢ Green	1.75	1.00
RE36	7½¢ Green	7.50	3.75
RE37	10¢ Green	1.25	.40
RE38	12¢ Green	4.00	3.75
RE39	15¢ Green	1.60	1.75
RE40	18¢ Green	23.00	21.00
RE41	20¢ Green	.30	.30
RE42	24¢ Green	4.50	3.25
RE43	30¢ Green	3.00	2.75
RE44	36¢ Green	18.50	14.00
RE45	50¢ Green	.70	.40
RE46	60¢ Green	4.00	2.00
RE47	72¢ Green	32.50	27.50
RE48	80¢ Green	1.20	.75
RE49	$1.20 Green	6.50	6.00
RE50	$1.44 Green	8.00	2.75
RE51	$1.60 Green	23.50	19.50
RE52	$2 Green	1.65	1.60
RE53	$4 Green	.90	.25
RE54	$4.80 Green	3.50	3.25
RE55	$9.60 Green	1.25	.35
RE56	$20 Green,Pf.12	80.00	37.50
RE57	$40 Green,Pf.12	160.00	45.00
RE58	$50 Green,Pf.12	55.00	42.50
RE59	$100 Green,P.12	225.00	130.00
1933 Rouletted 7			
RE60	1¢ Light Green	2.85	.40
RE61	3¢ Light Green	7.50	2.25
RE62	4¢ Light Green	1.75	.40
RE63	6¢ Light Green	10.00	5.25
RE64	7½¢ Lt. Green	4.75	.90
RE65	10¢ Lt. Green	1.75	.20
RE66	12¢ Lt. Green	8.50	5.25
RE67	15¢ Lt. Green	3.50	.30
RE69	20¢ Lt. Green	5.00	.25
RE70	24¢ Lt. Green	4.50	.20
RE71	30¢ Lt. Green	5.50	.20
RE72	36¢ Lt. Green	10.00	.65
RE73	50¢ Lt. Green	4.25	.25
RE74	60¢ Lt. Green	8.00	.20
RE75	72¢ Lt. Green	11.50	.35
RE76	80¢ Lt. Green	11.50	.30
RE77	$1.20 Lt. Green	9.00	1.50
RE78	$1.44 Lt. Green	11.50	4.00
RE79	$1.60 Lt. Green	325.00	185.00
RE80	$2 Light Green	35.00	4.00
RE81	$4 Light Green	31.50	7.00
RE82	$4.80 Lt. Green	30.00	16.00
RE83	$9.60 Lt. Green	150.00	85.00

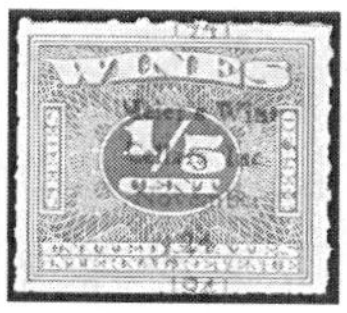

RE83A-101

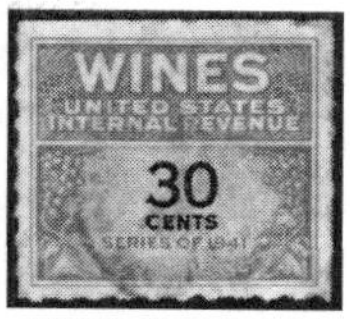

RE108-45,182D-94

1934-40 "Series of 1934" Rouletted 7

Scott No.		Fine Unused	Fine Used
RE83A	1/5¢ Green	.65	.20
RE84	½¢ Green	.50	.45
RE85	1¢ Green	.60	.20
RE86	1¼¢ Green	1.00	.85
RE87	1½¢ Green	6.00	6.00
RE88	2¢ Green	1.75	.70
RE89	2½¢ Green	1.75	.50
RE90	3¢ Green	5.00	3.75
RE91	4¢ Green	2.50	.25
RE92	5¢ Green	.55	.20
RE93	6¢ Green	1.65	.50
RE94	7½¢ Green	2.25	.20
RE95	10¢ Green	.50	.20
RE96	12¢ Green	1.50	.25
RE96A	14 2/5¢ Green	140.00	3.00
RE97	15¢ Green	.75	.20
RE98	18¢ Green	1.40	.20
RE99	20¢ Green	1.25	.20
RE100	24¢ Green	2.00	.20
RE101	30¢ Green	1.50	.20
RE102	40¢ Green	3.00	.25
RE102A	43 1/5¢ Green	12.50	2.50
RE103	48¢ Green	12.75	1.75
RE104	$1 Green	18.50	10.00
RE105	$1.50 Green	28.50	15.00
RE105	Perforated Initials	..	7.50
RE106	$2.50 Green	35.00	17.50
RE106	Perforated Initials	..	9.00
RE107	$5 Green	28.75	6.75
RE107	Perforated Initials	..	2.25
1942 "Series of 1941" Rouletted 7			
RE108	1/5¢ Grn. & Bk.	.75	.55
RE109	¼¢ Green & Bk.	2.40	1.95
RE110	½¢ Green & Bk.	3•2005	1.80
RE111	1¢ Green & Bk.	1.15	1.10
RE112	2¢ Green & Bk.	5.50	5.00
RE113	3¢ Green & Bk.	5.75	4.50
RE115	3¾¢ Green & Bk.	10.75	6.75
RE116	4¢ Green & Bk.	4.25	3.00
RE117	5¢ Green & Bk.	2.75	2.25
RE118	6¢ Green & Bk.	3.50	2.50
RE119	7¢ Green & Bk.	6.75	4.75
RE120	7½¢ Green & Bk.	10.75	6.00
RE121	8¢ Green & Bk.	5.00	4.00
RE122	9¢ Green & Bk.	14.00	9.00
RE123	10¢ Green & Bk.	5.00	1.00
RE124	11¼¢ Green & Bk.	5.50	5.25
RE125	12¢ Green & Bk.	8.25	6.00
RE126	14¢ Green & Bk.	33.50	24.50
RE127	15¢ Green & Bk.	5.75	2.75
RE128	16¢ Green & Bk.	13.50	8.00
RE129	19 1/5¢ Grn & Bk.	160.00	7.50
RE130	20¢ Green & Bk.	6.50	1.75
RE131	24¢ Green & Bk.	5.25	.25
RE132	28¢ Green & Bk.	...	...
RE133	30¢ Green & Bk.	1.40	.20
RE134	32¢ Green & Bk.	160.00	7.00
RE135	36¢ Green & Bk.	3.50	.25
RE136	40¢ Green & Bk.	2.75	.20
RE137	45¢ Green & Bk.	8.00	.25
RE138	48¢ Green & Bk.	20.00	9.00
RE139	50¢ Green & Bk.	12.00	7.50
RE140	60¢ Green & Bk.	3.75	.20
RE141	72¢ Green & Bk.	12.00	1.50
RE142	80¢ Green & Bk.	...	10.00
RE143	84¢ Green & Bk.	...	70.00
RE144	90¢ Green & Bk.	22.50	.20
RE145	96¢ Green & Bk.	15.00	.30

1942 Yellow Green & Black

RE146-72 Denomination in Two Lines

RE146-82, RE195-204

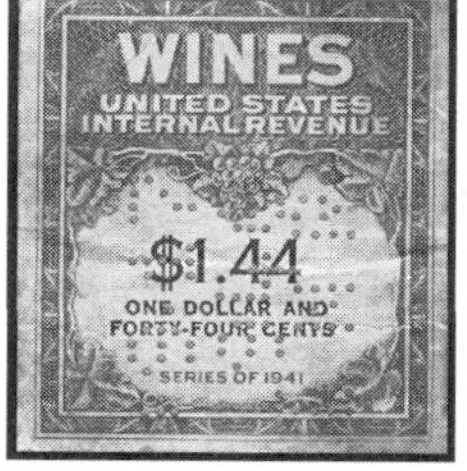

RE146	$1.20	6.75	.25
RE147	$1.44	1.75	.30
RE148	$1.50	115.00	60.00
RE149	$1.60	9.00	1.15
RE150	$1.68	110.00	45.00
RE150	Perforated Initials	...	32.50
RE151	$1.80	3.50	.20
RE152	$1.92	65.00	35.00
RE153	$2.40	11.00	1.15
RE154	$3	75.00	45.00

1942 Yellow Green & Black (continued)

Scott No.		Fine Unused	Fine Used
RE155	$3.36	90.00	27.50
RE156	$3.60	150.00	6.00
RE157	$4	30.00	5.00
RE158	$4.80	150.00	3.50
RE159	$5	16.50	9.00
RE160	$7.20	17.50	.50
RE161	$10	230.00	185.00
RE162	$20	115.00	70.00
RE163	$50	115.00	70.00
RE163	Perforated Initials	...	20.00
RE164	$100	300.00	27.50
RE164	Perforated Initials	...	17.50
RE165	$200	170.00	22.50
RE165	Perforated Initials	...	8.50
RE166	$500	...	140.00
RE166	Perforated Initials	...	35.00
RE167	$600	...	150.00
RE168	$900	...	...
RE169	$1000	...	225.00
RE170	$2000	...	...
RE171	$3000	...	225.00
RE172	$4000	...	750.00

1949 Yellow Green & Black

#RE173-182 Denominations in one line.

RE173	$1	4.00	1.50
RE174	$2	6.50	1.85
RE175	$4	850.00	350.00
RE175	Perforated Initials	...	160.00
RE176	$5	...	90.00
RE177	$6	...	450.00
RE178	$7	...	45.00
RE179	$8	...	425.00
RE179	Perforated Initials	...	75.00
RE180	$10	10.00	5.00
RE180	Perforated Initials	...	2.50
RE181	$20	22.50	4.75
RE181	Perforated Initials	...	2.00
RE182	$30	1400.	700.00

1951-54 Green & Black, Rouletted 7

RE183	3 2/5¢	50.00	45.00
RE184	8½¢	27.50	18.50
RE185	13 2/5¢	90.00	80.00
RE186	17¢	14.00	13.50
RE187	20 2/5¢	100.00	55.00
RE188	33½¢	80.00	80.00
RE189	38¼¢	110.00	80.00
RE190	40 4/5¢	3.50	.70
RE191	51¢	3.75	1.30
RE192	67¢	12.75	4.00
RE193	68¢	3.50	.70
RE194	80 2/5¢	130.00	100.00
RE195-RE197 Denominations in two lines in smaller letters. Yellow Green & Black			
RE195	$1.50¾	45.00	40.00
RE196	$1.60 4/5	4.00	.90
RE197	$1.88 3/10	275.00	80.00
RE197	Perforated Initials	...	32.50
RE198	$1.60 4/5	30.00	6.50
#RE198-204 Denominations in two lines in large letters. Yellow Green & Black			
RE199	$2.01	3.50	.90
RE200	$2.68	3.50	1.40
RE201	$4.08	85.00	30.00
RE202	$5.76	250.00	110.00
RE203	$8.16	16.00	7.00

PLAYING CARD STAMPS (VF+ 50%)

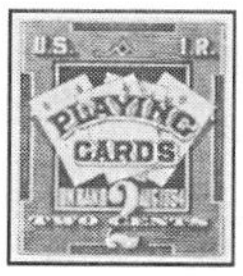

RF1

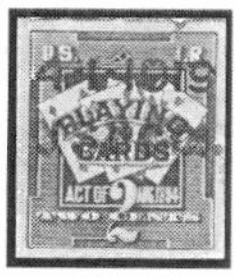

RF16

1894-1902 Rouletted

RF1	2¢ Lake "On Hand.."	.70	.40
RF2	2¢ Ultramarine, "Act of..",Unwmk.	18.75	2.50
RF3	2¢ Blue, Wmtk.	7.00	.60
RF4	2¢ Blue, Perf. 12	...	46.50
1917 Various Surcharges			
RF5	7¢on2¢ Act/1917	700.00	550.00
RF6	7¢ on 2¢ Blue "17 "	...	45.00
RF7	7¢ on 2¢ Blue "7"	...	850.00
RF8	7¢ on 2¢ "7 CTS."	...	1150.00
RF9	7¢ on 2¢ "7 CENTS"	...	8.75
RF10	7¢ on 2¢ Blue "7¢"	...	70.00

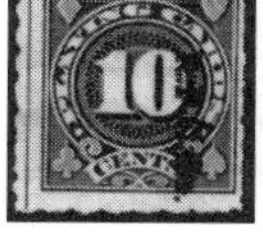

RF19

RF26

1918-1929

Scott No.		Fine Unused	Fine Used
RF11	Blue, Imperf.	40.00	27.50
RF12	Blue, Roulette 14	...	275.00
RF13	7¢ Blue, Roul. 9½	...	47.50
RF14	8¢ on 2¢ Roul. 7	...	100.00
RF15	8¢ on 2¢ Act 1918	...	550.00
RF16	8¢ on 2¢ Blue	130.00	.85
RF17	(8¢) Blue, Roul. 7	18.50	1.40
RF18	8¢ Blue, Roul. 7	...	55.00
RF19	10¢ Blue, Roul. 7	11.50	.40
RF20	10¢ Perf. 10 Coil	...	.30
RF21	10¢ Flat, Perf. 11	24.00	5.00
RF22	10¢ Blue, Perf. 10	15.00	4.00

1929-1940

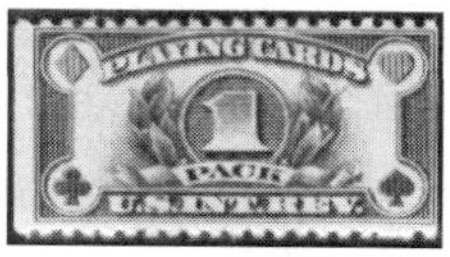

RF27

RF23	10¢ Perf. 10 Coil	...	.25
RF24	10¢ Flat, Perf. 10	15.00	1.25
RF25	10¢ Flat, Perf. 11	11.50	1.25
RF26	Blue, Perf. 10 Coil	...	.40
RF27	Blue, Perf. 10 Coil	2.75	.25
RF28	Blue, Flat. Pf. 11	5.00	.75
RF29	Blue, Perf. 10x11	160.00	85.00

SILVER TAX STAMPS (VF + 50%)

1934 Documentary Stamps of 1917 Overprinted "SILVER TAX" D.L. Wmk., Black Overprint, Perf. 11

RG1	1¢ Carmine Rose	1.30	.85
RG2	2¢ Carmine Rose	1.40	.55
RG3	3¢ Carmine Rose	1.50	.75
RG4	4¢ Carmine Rose	1.85	1.50
RG5	5¢ Carmine Rose	3.00	1.35
RG6	8¢ Carmine Rose	3.75	2.75
RG7	10¢ Carm. Rose	4.00	2.75
RG8	20¢ Carm. Rose	5.50	3.25
RG9	25¢ Carm. Rose	6.00	4.00
RG10	40¢ Carm. Rose	6.75	5.75
RG11	50¢ Carm. Rose	8.50	7.00
RG12	80¢ Carm. Rose	15.00	9.75
RG13	$1 Green	26.50	14.00
RG14	$2 Rose	35.00	22.50
RG15	$3 Violet	62.50	32.50
RG16	$4 Yellow Brown	50.00	22.50
RG17	$5 Dark Blue	70.00	25.00
RG18	$10 Orange	85.00	21.00
Without Gum, Perf. 12			
RG19	$30 Vermillion	160.00	47.50
RG19	Cut cancel	...	17.50
RG20	$60 Brown	175.00	70.00
RG20	Cut cancel	...	25.00
RG21	$100 Green	235.00	31.50
RG22	$500 Blue	500.00	225.00
RG22	Cut cancel	...	95.00
RG23	$1000 Orange	...	100.00
RG23	Cut cancel	...	60.00
1936 Same Overprint, 11 mm between words "SILVER TAX"			
RG26	$100 Green	450.00	75.00
RG27	$1000 Orange	...	775.00
1939 "SILVER TAX" in Violet Large Block Letters			
RG30	5¢ Rose Pink	...	700.00
RG31	10¢ Rose Pink	...	950.00
RG32	80¢ Rose Pink	...	...

DATED SILVER TAX REVENUE STAMPS (VF+30%)

Note: Dated Silver Tax stamps with cut cancels or perforated initials sell for substantially less than used price.

1940 'SERIES 1940" Overprint on 1917-33 Issues. NH +20%

Scott's No.		F-VF Unused	F-VF Used
RG37	1¢ Rose pink	22.50	...
RG38	2¢ Rose pink	22.50	...
RG39	3¢ Rose pink	22.50	...
RG40	4¢ Rose pink	25.00	...
RG41	5¢ Rose pink	17.00	...
RG42	8¢ Rose pink	24.00	...
RG43	10¢ Rose pink	21.50	...
RG44	20¢ Rose pink	25.00	...
RG45	25¢ Rose pink	22.50	...
RG46	40¢ Rose pink	37.50	...
RG47	50¢ Rose pink	37.50	...
RG48	80¢ Rose pink	37.50	...
RG49	$1 Green	150.00	...
RG50	$2 Rose	225.00	...
RG51	$3 Violet	300.00	...
RG52	$4 Yellow brown	575.00	...
RG53	$5 Dark blue	700.00	...
RG54	$10 Orange	800.00	...

#RG58-107 Silver Tax Stamps are Overprinted with Series Date Ex.: "SERIES 1940". $30 & up values were issued without gum & have straight edges on one/two sides. Similar designs as #R288-732

1941

Scott's No.		F-VF NH	F-VF Used
RG58	1¢ A.Hamilton	5.50	2.25
RG59	2¢ O.Wolcott,Jr.	5.50	2.75
RG60	3¢ S.Dexter	5.50	2.75
RG61	4¢ A.Gallatin	7.50	4.75
RG62	5¢ G.W.Campbell	10.00	8.50
RG63	8¢ A.Dallas	12.50	...
RG64	10¢ W.H.Crawford	14.00	8.00
RG65	20¢ R.Rush	22.50	7.50
RG66	25¢ S.D.Ingham	27.50	...
RG67	40¢ L.McLane	45.00	35.00
RG68	50¢ W.J.Duane ..	52.50	30.00
RG69	80¢ R.B.Taney ...	85.00	30.00
RG70	$1 L.Woodbury ..	110.00	40.00
RG71	$2 T.Ewing	275.00	67.50
RG72	$3 W.Forward	225.00	90.00
RG73	$4 J.C.Spencer .	350.00	75.00
RG74	$5 G.M.Bibb	300.00	90.00
RG75	$10 R.J.Walker ..	525.00	90.00
RG76	$20 W.Meredith	775.00	275.00
RG77	$30 T.Corwin.......	375.00	225.00
RG79	$60 H.Cobb	...	250.00
RG80	$100 P.F.Thomas	...	400.00
1942			
RG83	1¢ A.Hamilton	2.50	...
RG84	2¢ O.Wolcott,Jr.	2.50	...
RG85	3¢ S.Dexter	2.50	...
RG86	4¢ A.Gallatin	2.50	...
RG87	5¢ G.W.Campbell	2.00	...
RG88	8¢ A.Dallas	4.75	...
RG89	10¢ W.H.Crawford	5.50	...
RG90	20¢ R.Rush	11.00	...
RG91	25¢ S.D.Ingham	18.75	...
RG92	40¢ L.McLane	28.50	...
RG93	50¢ W.J.Duane ..	32.50	...
RG94	80¢ R.B.Taney ...	87.50	...
RG95	$1 L.Woodbury ..	110.00	65.00
RG96	$2 T.Ewing	110.00	65.00
RG97	$3 W.Forward......	225.00	130.00
RG98	$4 J.C.Spencer....	225.00	130.00
RG99	$5 G.M.Bibb.......	225.00	160.00
RG100	$10 R.J.Walker...	600.00	400.00
RG101	$20 W.Meredith ...	775.00	...
RG105	$100 P.F.Thomas	...	475.00
1944 Without Overprint, Gray			
RG108	1¢ A.Hamilton	.80	.30
RG109	2¢ O.Wolcott,Jr.	.80	.60
RG110	3¢ S.Dexter	1.00	.90
RG111	4¢ A.Gallatin	1.30	1.20
RG112	5¢ G.W.Campbell	2.50	2.50
RG113	8¢ A.Dallas	5.00	2.50
RG114	10¢ W.H.Crawford	5.00	3.00
RG115	20¢ R.Rush	7.75	5.25
RG116	25¢ S.D.Ingham	13.00	5.75
RG117	40¢ L.McLane	20.00	11.00
RG118	50¢ W.J.Duane ..	21.50	12.50
RG119	80¢ R.B.Taney ...	27.50	18.50
RG120	$1 L.Woodbury ..	57.50	20.00
RG121	$2 T.Ewing	80.00	45.00
RG122	$3 W.Forward	90.00	35.00
RG123	$4 J.C.Spencer .	130.00	80.00
RG124	$5 G.M.Bibb	140.00	40.00
RG125	$10 R.J.Walker ..	200.00	30.00
RG126	$20 W.Meredith..	650.00	475.00
RG127	$30 T.Corwin.......	325.00	150.00
RG128	$50 J. Guthrie....	700.00	575.00
RG129	$60 H.Cobb	...	475.00
RG130	$100 P.F.Thomas	...	30.00
RG131	$500 J.A.Dix	...	450.00
RG132	$1000 S.PChase	...	150.00

CIGARETTE TUBE STAMPS
(Very Fine + 50%)

1919-29 Documentary Stamp of 1917 Overprinted "CIGTTE. TUBES".

		Fine Unused	Fine Used
RH1	1¢ Perf.11 (1919) .	.60	.30
RH2	1¢ Perf.10 (1929)	27.50	9.50

1933 Perforated 11

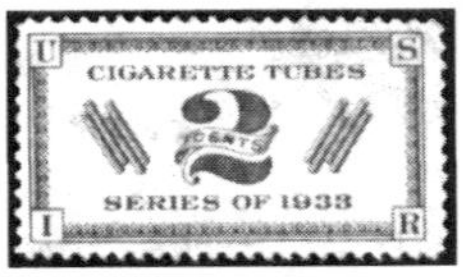

RH3-4

RH3	1¢ Rose	2.50	1.90
RH4	2¢ Rose	7.75	2.85

POTATO TAX STAMPS (VF + 40%)

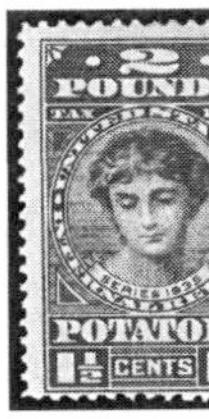

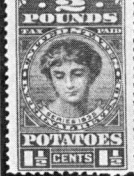

RI1-13

RJA33

1935 Tax Paid Potato Stamps

Scott's No.		F-VF Unused
RI1	¾¢ Carmine Rose	.30
RI2	1¼¢ Black Brown	.50
RI3	2¼¢ Yellow Green	.50
RI4	3¢ Light Violet	.55
RI5	3¾¢ Olive Bister	.60
RI6	7½¢ Orange Brown	1.50
RI7	11¼¢ Deep Orange	1.95
RI8	18¾¢ Violet Brown	4.75
RI9	37½¢ Red Orange	4.50
RI10	75¢ Blue	4.75
RI11	93¾¢ Rose Lake	7.75
RI12	$1.12½¢ Green	14.50
RI13	$1.50 Yellow Brown.......	14.00
1935 Tax Exempt Potato Stamps		
RI14	2 lb Black Brown	1.10
RI15	5 lb Black Brown	20.00
RI16	10 lb Black Brown	20.00
RI17	25 lb Black Brown	...
RI18	50 lb Black Brown	1.25

TOBACCO SALE TAX STAMPS

1934 Documentary Issue of 1917 Overprinted "TOBACCO SALE TAX" D.Line Wtmk., Perf.11 (VF + 50%)

Scott's No.		Fine Unused	Fine Used
RJ1	1¢ Carmine Rose	.35	.20
RJ2	2¢ Carmine Rose	.40	.20
RJ3	5¢ Carmine Rose	1.25	.40
RJ4	10¢ Carm. Rose	1.50	.40
RJ5	25¢ Carm. Rose	4.00	1.50
RJ6	50¢ Carm. Rose	4.00	1.50
RJ7	$1 Green	9.50	1.75
RJ8	$2 Rose	20.00	1.75
RJ9	$5 Dark blue	25.00	4.00
RJ10	$10 Orange	37.50	10.00
RJ11	$20 Olive bister .	90.00	12.50

NARCOTIC TAX STAMPS (VF + 50%)

1919 Documentary Issue of 1914, D.L. Wtmk., Perf. 10, Handstamped "NARCOTIC" in Magenta, Blue or Black

RJA1	1¢ Rose	75.00	70.00

1919 Documentary Issue of 1917, D.L. Wtmk.,Perf. 11, Handstamped "NARCOTIC", "Narcotic", "NARCOTICS", or "ACT/NARCOTIC/1918" in Magenta, Blue, Black, Violet or Red

RJA9	1¢ Carmine Rose	2.25	2.00
RJA10	2¢ Carmine Rose	5.00	3.75
RJA11	3¢ Carmine Rose	28.50	30.00
RJA12	4¢ Carmine Rose	10.00	9.00
RJA13	5¢ Carmine Rose	14.50	14.00
RJA14	8¢ Carmine Rose	12.50	11.75
RJA15	10¢ Carm. Rose	45.00	18.50
RJA16	20¢ Carm. Rose	60.00	55.00
RJA17	25¢ Carm. Rose	37.50	30.00
RJA18	40¢ Carm. Rose	110.00	95.00
RJA19	50¢ Carm. Rose	16.50	17.50
RJA20	80¢ Carm. Rose	95.00	85.00
RJA21	$1 Green	95.00	50.00
RJA22	$2 Rose	...	...
RJA23	$3 Violet	...	...
RJA24	$5 Dark Blue	...	...
RJA25	$10 Orange	...	...

1919 Documentary Issue of 1917, D.L. Wtmk., Perf. 11, Overprinted "NARCOTIC" 17½ mm wide

RJA33	1¢ Carmine Rose	1.00	.70
RJA34	2¢ Carmine Rose	1.85	1.00
RJA35	3¢ Carmine Rose	32.50	22.50
RJA36	4¢ Carmine Rose	5.00	4.00
RJA37	5¢ Carmine Rose	12.00	9.00
RJA38	8¢ Carmine Rose	21.50	16.50
RJA39	10¢ Carm. Rose	3.00	3.00
RJA40	25¢ Carm. Rose	20.00	15.00
Overprint Reading Up			
RJA41	$1 Green	45.00	17.50

Narcotic Issues of 1919-64,D.L.Wmk.

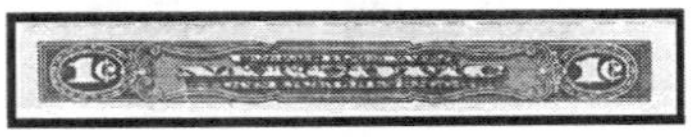

RJA42-45

NARCOTICS TAX (continued)

Scott's No. b.roult.		Fine a.Impf.	Used
RJA42	1¢ Violet	4.50	.25
RJA43	1¢ Violet	.50	.30
RJA44	2¢ Violet	1.20	.50
RJA45	3¢ Violet	...	115.00
RJA46	1¢ Violet	2.50	.75
#RJA47-58 "CENTS" below value			
RJA47	2¢ Violet	1.50	.60
RJA48	3¢ Violet	700.00	...
RJA49	4¢ Violet	...	9.50
RJA50	5¢ Violet	38.50	4.00
RJA51	6¢ Violet	...	.75
RJA52	8¢ Violet	50.00	3.25
RJA53	9¢ Violet	65.00	18.50
RJA54	10¢ Violet	30.00	.50
RJA55	16¢ Violet	52.50	3.50
RJA56	18¢ Violet	100.00	9.50
RJA57	19¢ Violet	120.00	22.50
RJA58	20¢ Violet	350.00	175.00
RJA59	1¢ Violet	45.00	10.00
#RJA60-74 Value Tablet is Solid			
RJA60	2¢ Violet	47.50	18.50
RJA61	4¢ Violet	47.50	55.00
RJA62	5¢ Violet	...	25.00
RJA63	6¢ Violet	60.00	20.00
RJA64	8¢ Violet	...	45.00
RJA65	9¢ Violet	25.00	19.50
RJA66	10¢ Violet	14.00	14.00
RJA67	16¢ Violet	15.00	9.00
RJA68	18¢ Violet	350.00	400.00
RJA69	19¢ Violet	14.00	...
RJA70	20¢ Violet..........	300.00	215.00
RJA71	25¢ Violet	...	19.50
RJA71c	25¢ Rouletted 3½	...	4.00
RJA72	40¢ Violet	375.00	...
RJA72c	40¢ Rouletted 3½	...	75.00
RJA73	$1 Green	...	1.50
RJA74	$1.28 Green	30.00	10.50
Narcotic Issues of 1963-70, Unwmkd.			
RJA75	1¢ Violet	6.75	...
RJA76	1¢ Violet	.95	.95
RJA77	2¢ Violet	4.50	...
RJA78	3¢ Violet	...	115.00
RJA79	1¢ Violet	5.00	1.85
#RJA80-89 "CENTS" Below the Value.			
RJA80	1¢ Violet	...	1.80
RJA81	4¢ Violet	...	9.00
RJA82	5¢ Violet	65.00	...
RJA83	6¢ Violet	...	11.00
RJA84	8¢ Violet	...	4.50
RJA85	9¢ Violet	...	45.00
RJA86	10¢ Violet	...	9.50
RJA87	16¢ Violet	140.00	3.75
RJA88	18¢ Violet	...	45.00
RJA89	20¢ Violet	...	275.00
RJA91	1¢ Violet	60.00	14.00
#RJA92-104 Value Tablet is Solid			
RJA92	2¢ Violet	...	45.00
RJA93	3¢ Violet	77.50	...
RJA94	6¢ Violet	90.00	45.00
RJA95	9¢ Violet	...	120.00
RJA96	10¢ Violet	...	55.00
RJA97	16¢ Violet	37.50	18.00
RJA98	19¢ Violet...........	22.50	375.00
RJA99	20¢ Violet	...	450.00
RJA100	25¢ Violet	...	225.00
RJA101	40¢ Violet	...	...
RJA102	$1 Green	...	30.00
RJA103	$1.28 Green	...	55.00
RJA104	$4 Green	...	...

1963 Denomination added in black by rubber plate (similar to 1959 Postage Dues), Imperforate

		Fine Unused	Fine Used
RJA105	1¢ Violet	95.00	75.00
1964 Denomination on Stamp Plate			
RJA106	1¢ Violet	80.00	5.50

CONSULAR SERVICE FEE STAMPS
(Very Fine + 50%)

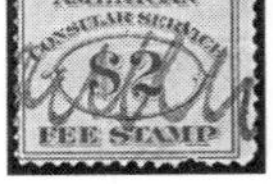

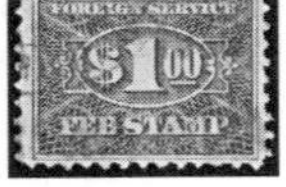

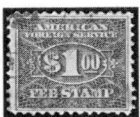

RK1-21 RK27-40

1906 "Consular Service" Perf. 12

Scott No.		Fine Used
RK1	25¢ Dark Green	60.00
RK2	50¢ Carmine	80.00
RK3	$1 Dark Violet	6.75
RK4	$2 Brown	5.25
RK5	$2.50 Dark Blue	1.75
RK6	$5 Brown Red	22.50
RK7	$10 Orange	77.50
Perf. 10		
RK8	25¢ Dark Green	65.00
RK9	50¢ Carmine	75.00
RK10	$1 Dark Violet	375.00
RK11	$2 Brown	90.00
RK12	$2.50 Dark Blue	20.00
RK13	$5 Brown Red	150.00

CONSULAR SERVICE FEE (continued)

Consular Service, Perf. 11

Scott No.		Fine Used
RK14	25¢ Dark Green	72.50
RK15	50¢ Carmine	125.00
RK16	$1 Dark Violet	1.70
RK17	$2 Brown	2.25
RK18	$2.50 Dark Blue	.85
RK19	$5 Brown Red	4.25
RK20	$9 Gray	16.00
RK21	$10 Orange	32.50
1924 "Foreign Service" Pf. 11		
RK22	$1 Dark Violet	80.00
RK23	$2 Brown	87.50
RK24	$2.50 Dark Blue	12.75
RK25	$5 Brown Red	70.00
RK26	$9 Gray	275.00
1925-52 Perf. 10		
RK27	$1 Violet	25.00
RK28	$2 Brown	60.00
RK29	$2.50 Ultramarine	2.25
RK30	$5 Carmine	13.00
RK31	$9 Gray	43.50
Perf. 11		
RK32	25¢ Green	75.00
RK33	50¢ Orange	75.00
RK34	$1 Violet	3.25
RK35	$2 Brown	3.50
RK36	$2.50 Blue	.50
RK36a	$2.50 Ultramarine	.40
RK37	$5 Carmine	3.25
RK38	$9 Gray	16.50
RK39	$10 Blue Gray	85.00
RK40	$20 Violet	90.00

1887 CUSTOMS FEES (VF + 40%)

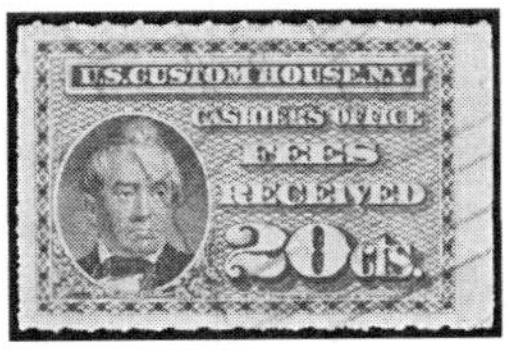

RL 1-8

Scott's No.		Fine Unused	Fine Used
RL1	20¢ Dull Rose	100.00	1.00
RL2	30¢ Orange	130.00	1.75
RL3	40¢ Green	160.00	3.25
RL4	50¢ Dark blue	160.00	5.00
RL5	60¢ Red violet ...	130.00	1.75
RL6	70¢ Brown violet	130.00	30.00
RL7	80¢ Brown	185.00	75.00
RL8	90¢ Black	225.00	90.00

MOTOR VEHICLE USE STAMPS
(Very Fine + 40%)

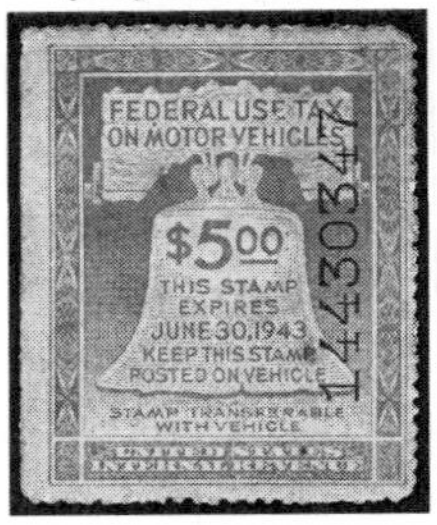

RV1-41

Scott No.		F-VF Unused	F-VF Used
1942 Light Green, Gum on Back			
RV1	$2.09	1.40	.50
Gum on Face, Inscription on Back			
RV2	$1.67	18.50	7.50
RV3	$1.25	13.50	6.50
RV4	84¢	16.00	6.50
RV5	42¢	16.00	6.50
#RV6-29 Gum and Control # on Face, Inscription on Back.			
1942-43 Rose Red			
RV6	$5.00	2.75	1.25
RV7	$4.59	32.50	11.00
RV8	$4.17	38.50	13.50
RV9	$3.75	33.50	11.00
RV10	$3.34	33.50	11.00
RV11	$2.92	33.50	11.00
RV12	$2.50	42.50	13.50
RV13	$2.09	27.50	9.50
RV14	$1.67	25.00	11.00
RV15	$1.25	25.00	8.00
RV16	84¢	25.00	8.00
RV17	42¢	20.00	8.75
1943-44 Yellow			
RV18	$5.00	3.25	1.00
RV19	$4.59	42.50	13.50
RV20	$4.17	55.00	18.00
RV21	$3.75	55.00	18.00

MOTOR VEHICLE USE (continued)

Scott No.	VF Used	F-VF Unused	F-
RV22	$3.34	62.50	19.50
RV23	$2.92	75.00	22.50
RV24	$2.50	75.00	22.50
RV25	$2.09	50.00	16.00
RV26	$1.67	40.00	14.00
RV27	$1.25	40.00	14.00
RV28	84¢	35.00	14.00
RV29	42¢	35.00	14.00

#RV30-53 Gum on Face
Control # and Inscriptions on Back
1944-45 Violet

RV30	$5.00	2.50	1.50
RV31	$4.59	65.00	18.00
RV32	$4.17	45.00	16.00
RV33	$3.75	45.00	16.00
RV34	$3.34	41.50	11.00
RV35	$2.92	41.50	11.00
RV36	$2.50	35.00	11.00
RV37	$2.09	30.00	11.00
RV38	$1.67	30.00	9.50
RV39	$1.25	30.00	9.00
RV40	84¢	22.50	8.00
RV41	42¢	20.00	6.50

RV42-53

1945-46
Bright blue green & Yellow green

RV42	$5.00	2.85	1.25
RV43	$4.59	45.00	16.00
RV44	$4.17	45.00	16.00
RV45	$3.75	42.50	11.00
RV46	$3.34	32.50	11.00
RV47	$2.92	27.50	8.00
RV48	$2.50	30.00	11.00
RV49	$2.09	30.00	11.00
RV50	$1.67	25.00	8.00
RV51	$1.25	20.00	8.00
RV52	84¢	20.00	8.00
RV53	42¢	15.00	1.25

BOATING STAMPS (VF+20%)

RVB1-2

	1960 Rouletted	NH F-VF
RVB1	$1.00 Rose red,blk.# ..	35.00
	Plate Block of 4	160.00
RVB2	$3.00 Blue, red #	50.00
	Plate Block of 4	225.00

CAMP STAMPS (VF + 20%)
National Forest Recreation Fees
1985 "A-D" Serial Numbers.

RVC1	50¢ Black on Pink "A"	45.00
RVC2	$1 Black on Red "B" ...	45.00
RVC3	$2 Black on Yellow"C" .	45.00
RVC4	$3 Black on Green"D" .	45.00

1986 "E-J" Serial Numbers

RVC5	50¢ Black on Pink "E"	70.00
RVC6	$1 Black on Red "F"	70.00
RVC7	$2 Black on Yellow"G"	70.00
RVC8	$3 Black on Green"H" .	70.00
RVC9	$5 Black on Silver"I" ...	275.00
RVC10	$10 Black on Bronze"J"	...

1939 TRAILER PERMIT STAMPS
(VF + 30%)

Scott No.	F-VF Unused	F-VF Used
RVT1	50¢ Bright Blue	550.00
RVT2	$1 Carmine 450.00	175.00

DISTILLED SPIRITS (VF + 30%)

RX1-46

1950
Inscribed "STAMP FOR SERIES 1950"
Yellow, Green & Black

Scott's No.		Fine Used	Punch Cancel
RX1	1¢	27.50	22.50
RX2	3¢	90.00	85.00
RX3	5¢	18.50	17.00
RX4	10¢	16.50	15.00
RX5	25¢	9.50	7.50
RX6	50¢	9.50	7.50
RX7	$1	2.00	1.50
RX8	$3	20.00	16.50
RX9	$5	5.50	4.00
RX10	$10	3.00	1.50
RX11	$25	13.50	10.00
RX12	$50	6.00	5.00
RX13	$100	4.00	2.75
RX14	$300	25.00	20.00
RX15	$500	15.00	10.00
RX16	$1000	9.50	7.50
RX17	$1500	52.50	42.50
RX18	$2000	4.50	3.50
RX19	$3000	20.00	15.00
RX20	$5000	20.00	15.00
RX21	$10,000	27.50	22.50
RX22	$20,000	35.00	31.50
RX23	$30,000	75.00	50.00
RX24	$40,000	900.00	650.00
RX25	$50,000	85.00	75.00

1952 DISTILLED SPIRITS
Inscription
"STAMP FOR SERIES 1950"
omitted
Yellow, Green & Black

RX28	5¢	...	40.00
RX29	10¢	27.50	4.00
RX30	25¢	22.50	15.00
RX31	50¢	27.50	11.50
RX32	$1	18.00	2.25
RX33	$3	32.50	21.50
RX34	$5	35.00	23.50
RX35	$10	18.50	2.25
RX36	$25	22.50	9.50
RX37	$50	60.00	23.50
RX38	$100	18.00	2.25
RX39	$300	22.50	7.50
RX40	$500	...	32.50
RX41	$1000	70.00	6.50
RX43	$2000	...	70.00
RX44	$3000	...	1050.00
RX45	$5000	...	50.00
RX46	$10,000	...	85.00

FIREARMS TRANSFER TAX STAMPS
(VF + 40%)
Documentary Stamp of 1917
Overprinted Vertically in Black
"NATIONAL FIREARMS ACT"

	Without Gum	Fine Unused	Fine Used
RY1	$1 Green (1934)	325.00	...

RY 2,4,6-8

1934-1990 $200 Face Value

RY2	Dark blue & red Serial #1-1500('34)	1250.	750.00
RY4	Dull blue & red Serial #1501-3000 (1950)	500.00	400.00
RY6	Dull blue & red Serial #3001 & up (1974)	225.00	95.00
RY7	Dull Blue, Imperf.(1990)..	475.00	
RY8	Dull Blue, Perf.`1½		70.00

1938-60 With Gum, Perf.11

RY3	$1 Green (1938) ...85.00		
RY5	$5 Red (1960) 22.50	37.50	

1994 Without Gum Perf.12½

RY9	$5 Red	110.00

1946 RECTIFICATION TAX STAMPS
(VF+30%)

Rectification Tax Stamps were for the use of rectifiers for tax on liquor in bottling tanks. **Used stamps have staple holes.**

RZ1-18

Scott's No.		Fine Unused	Fine Used
RZ1	1¢	7.50	3.75
RZ1	Punched Cancel ...		1.85
RZ2	3¢	25.00	8.50
RZ2	Punched Cancel ...		7.50
RZ3	5¢	16.50	2.50
RZ3	Punched Cancel ...		1.20
RZ4	10¢	16.50	2.75
RZ4	Punched Cancel ...		1.20
RZ5	25¢	16.50	3.00
RZ5	Punched Cancel ...		1.85
RZ6	50¢	20.00	5.00
RZ6	Punched Cancel ...		3.50
RZ7	$1	20.00	4.00
RZ7	Punched Cancel ...		2.50
RZ8	$3	90.00	17.50
RZ8	Punched Cancel ...		8.50
RZ9	$5	30.00	10.00
RZ9	Punched Cancel ...		5.75
RZ10	$10	25.00	3.25
RZ10	Punched Cancel ...		1.25
RZ11	$25	90.00	10.50
RZ11	Punched Cancel ...		2.85
RZ12	$50	90.00	8.00
RZ12	Punched Cancel ...		2.85
RZ13	$100	...	9.50
RZ13	Punched Cancel ...		3.25
RZ14	$300	...	9.50
RZ14	Punched Cancel ...		7.00
RZ15	$500	...	9.50
RZ15	Punched Cancel ...		6.50
RZ16	$1000	...	17.50
RZ16	Punched Cancel ...		14.50
RZ17	$1500	...	47.50
RZ17	Punched Cancel ...		35.00
RZ18	$2000	...	75.00
RZ18	Punched Cancel ...		55.00

U.S. HUNTING PERMIT STAMPS

RW1

RW2

On each stamp the words "Void After ..." show a date 1 year later than the actual date of issue. Even though RW1 has on it "Void After June 30, 1935," the stamp was issued in 1934.
RW1-RW25, RW31 Plate Blocks of 6 Must Have Margins on Two Sides

RW1-RW12 VF Used + 50% RW13-RW15 VF Used + 40%

Scott's No.			Never Hinged VF	F-VF	Unused VF	F-VF	Used F-VF
RW1	1934,	$1 Mallards	975.00	690.00	600.00	450.00	135.00
RW2	1935,	$1 Canvasbacks	900.00	625.00	500.00	400.00	160.00
RW3	1936,	$1 Canada Geese	500.00	375.00	325.00	210.00	75.00
RW4	1937,	$1 Scaup Ducks	400.00	300.00	210.00	170.00	50.00
RW5	1938,	$1 Pintails	650.00	375.00	290.00	190.00	50.00
RW6	1939,	$1 Teal	290.00	190.00	145.00	105.00	45.00
RW6		Plate Block of 6	3600.00	2800.00	2700.00	2400.00	...
RW7	1940,	$1 Mallards	290.00	190.00	145.00	100.00	45.00
RW7		Plate Block of 6	3300.00	2800.00	2700.00	2400.00	...
RW8	1941,	$1 Ruddy Ducks	290.00	190.00	145.00	100.00	45.00
RW8		Plate Block of 6	3300.00	2800.00	2700.00	2400.00	...

RW9

RW13

RW9	1942,	$1 Baldplates	300.00	200.00	145.00	115.00	45.00
RW9		Plate Block of 6	3300.00	2800.00	2400.00	2100.00	...
RW10	1943,	$1 Ducks	110.00	80.00	70.00	50.00	45.00
RW10		Plate Block of 6	895.00	725.00	750.00	600.00	...
RW11	1944,	$1 Geese	130.00	80.00	80.00	65.00	30.00
RW11		Plate Block of 6	950.00	775.00	750.00	600.00	...
RW12	1945,	$1 Shovellers	85.00	65.00	50.00	32.50	27.00
RW12		Plate Block of 6	575.00	475.00	490.00	425.00	...
RW13	1946,	$1 Redheads	60.00	43.00	40.00	32.50	15.00
RW13		Plate Block of 6	395.00	340.00	340.00	310.00	...
RW14	1947,	$1 Snow Geese	60.00	43.00	39.00	35.00	15.00
RW14		Plate Block of 6	395.00	340.00	340.00	310.00	...
RW15	1948,	$1 Buffleheads	75.00	55.00	45.00	35.00	15.00
RW15		Plate Block of 6	475.00	400.00	400.00	345.00	...

RW12

RW16

1949-55 Issues VF Used + 40%

RW16	1949,	$2 Goldeneyes	80.00	58.00	55.00	40.00	15.00
RW16		Plate Block of 6	495.00	425.00	425.00	380.00	...
RW17	1950,	$2 Swans	110.00	72.50	65.00	50.00	11.50
RW17		Plate Block of 6	725.00	625.00	625.00	525.00	...
RW18	1951,	$2 Gadwalls	110.00	72.50	60.00	50.00	11.50
RW18		Plate Block of 6	725.00	625.00	625.00	525.00	...
RW19	1952,	$2 Harlequins	110.00	72.50	60.00	50.00	9.00
RW19		Plate Block of 6	725.00	625.00	625.00	525.00	...
RW20	1953,	$2 Teal	125.00	75.00	65.00	50.00	9.00
RW20		Plate Block of 6	750.00	625.00	625.00	550.00	...

RW21

RW25

RW21	1954,	$2 Ring-neckeds	115.00	75.00	65.00	50.00	9.00
RW21		Plate Block of 6	750.00	625.00	625.00	550.00	...
RW22	1955,	$2 Blue Geese	115.00	75.00	65.00	50.00	9.00
RW22		Plate Block of 6	750.00	625.00	625.00	550.00	...

1956-58 Issues VF Used + 40%

RW23	1956,	$2 Merganser	115.00	75.00	65.00	50.00	9.00
RW23		Plate Block of 6	775.00	650.00	650.00	575.00	...

Scott's No.			Never Hinged VF	F-VF	Unused VF	F-VF	Used F-VF
RW24	1957,	$2 Eider	115.00	75.00	65.00	50.00	9.00
RW24		Plate Block of 6	750.00	625.00	625.00	550.00	...
RW25	1958,	$2 Canada Geese	110.00	75.00	65.00	50.00	9.00
RW25		Plate Block of 6	750.00	625.00	625.00	550.00	...

RW27

RW32

1959-71 Issues VF Used + 30%

Scott's No.			Pl# Blocks VF NH	VF NH	F-VF NH	F-VF Unused	F-VF Used
RW26	1959,	$3 Retriever	725.00	160.00	115.00	85.00	9.00
RW27	1960,	$3 Redhead Ducks	635.00	115.00	90.00	65.00	9.00
RW28	1961,	$3 Mallard	650.00	115.00	95.00	65.00	9.00
RW29	1962,	$3 Pintail Ducks	700.00	125.00	100.00	80.00	9.00
RW30	1963,	$3 Brant Landing	700.00	125.00	100.00	80.00	9.00
RW31	1964,	$3 Hawaiian Nene .. (6)	2700.00	125.00	100.00	70.00	9.00
RW32	1965,	$3 Canvasback Ducks	700.00	125.00	100.00	70.00	9.00

RW33

RW35

RW33	1966,	$3 Whistling Swans	700.00	125.00	100.00	75.00	9.00
RW34	1967,	$3 Old Squaw Ducks	725.00	140.00	100.00	75.00	9.00
RW35	1968,	$3 Hooded Mergansers	360.00	85.00	65.00	40.00	9.00
RW36	1969,	$3 White-wing Scooters	360.00	85.00	65.00	40.00	9.00
RW37	1970,	$3 Ross's Geese	360.00	85.00	65.00	40.00	7.00
RW38	1971,	$3 Cinnamon Teals	260.00	50.00	40.00	25.00	7.00

RW39

RW42

1972-83 Issues VF Used + 25%

Scott's No.			VF, NH Pl# Blk	Never Hinged VF	F-VF	Used F-VF
RW39	1972,	$5 Emperor Geese	145.00	35.00	25.00	7.00
RW40	1973,	$5 Steller's Eiders	125.00	28.00	20.00	7.00
RW41	1974,	$5 Wood Ducks	105.00	25.00	17.00	7.00
RW42	1975,	$5 Decoy & Canvasbacks	80.00	20.00	14.00	7.00

RW43

RW46

RW43	1976,	$5 Canada Geese	80.00	20.00	14.00	7.00
RW44	1977,	$5 Pair of Ross's Geese	80.00	20.00	14.00	7.00
RW45	1978,	$5 Hooded Merganser Drake	65.00	16.00	11.00	7.00
RW46	1979,	$7.50 Green-winged Teal	80.00	19.00	14.00	8.00

RW47

RW50

RW47	1980,	$7.50 Mallards	80.00	20.00	16.00	8.00
RW48	1981,	$7.50 Ruddy Ducks	80.00	20.00	16.00	8.00
RW49	1982,	$7.50 Canvasbacks	80.00	20.00	15.00	8.00
RW50	1983,	$7.50 Pintails	80.00	20.00	15.00	8.00

Michael Jaffe Stamps is Your Full Service Duck Dealer

MICHAEL JAFFE STAMPS IS YOUR FULL-SERVICE HEADQUARTERS FOR:
* *Federal Hunting Permit Stamps*
* *State & Foreign Duck Stamps*
* *Duck Stamp Prints*
* *Indian Reservation Stamps*

ALL AT BUDGET-FRIENDLY PRICES!!

Why shop around when you can find 99% of all pictorial Duck stamps ever issued (including foreign) in stock at Michael Jaffe for very competitive prices? Michael Jaffe is also your best source for Duck prints...albums...first day covers... and just about everything else related to Ducks. *And Michael Jaffe guarantees 100% satisfaction on every purchase.*

ASK ABOUT OUR NEW ISSUE SERVICE PROGRAMS FOR ANYTHING "DUCKS"

TOLL FREE 1-800-782-6770 (U.S. & CANADA)
P.O. Box 61484, Vancouver, WA 98666
Phone 360-695-6161 / Fax 360-695-1616
email: mjaffe@brookmanstamps.com
Website: http://www.duckstamps.com

FREE CATALOG ON REQUEST!!
Write, call, fax or e-mail today for your FREE copy of our latest illustrated catalog (a $2 value). It includes all Federal and State Ducks plus the exciting new specialty - Indian Reservation Fish and Game stamps. It also contains special offers on attractive Duck Stamp Prints plus information on how you can subscribe to the Michael Jaffe New Issue Service. If you collect Ducks, or are thinking about expanding into this popular specialty, this catalog will be invaluable.

145

U.S. HUNTING PERMIT STAMPS

RW51

RW54

Scott's No.	VF, NH Pl# Blk	Never Hinged VF	F-VF	Used F-VF

1984-89 Issues VF Used + 25%

Scott's No.		VF, NH Pl# Blk	VF	F-VF	Used F-VF
RW51	1984, $7.50 Wigeon	100.00	25.00	16.00	9.00
RW52	1985, $7.50 Cinnamon Teal	80.00	20.00	14.00	9.00
RW53	1986, $7.50 Fulvous Whistling Duck	80.00	20.00	14.00	9.00
RW54	1987, $10 Red Head Ducks	95.00	23.00	18.00	12.00

RW55

RW57

RW55	1988, $10 Snow Goose	100.00	24.00	18.00	12.00
RW56	1989, $12.50 Lesser Scaups	100.00	25.00	20.00	12.00

1990-2003 Issues VF Used + 25%

RW57	1990, $12.50 Bk-Bellied Whist. Duck	100.00	25.00	20.00	12.00
RW58	1991, $15.00 King Eiders	145.00	36.00	30.00	14.00

RW59

RW60

RW59	1992, $15.00 Spectacled Eider	145.00	35.00	26.00	14.00
RW60	1993, $15.00 Canvasbacks	145.00	35.00	26.00	14.00

RW61

RW62

RW61	1994, $15.00 Redbreast. Merganser	145.00	35.00	26.00	14.00
RW62	1995, $15.00 Mallards	145.00	35.00	26.00	14.00

RW63

RW64

RW63	1996, $15.00 Surf Scoter	145.00	35.00	27.00	14.00
RW64	1997, $15.00 Canada Goose	145.00	35.00	27.00	14.00

RW65

RW66

Scott's No.		VF, NH Pl# Blk	Never Hinged VF	F-VF	Used F-VF
RW65	1998, $15.00 Barrow's Goldeneye	180.00	42.00	32.00	...
RW65A	1998, same, Self-Adhesive	...	42.00	32.00	14.00
RW66	1999, $15.00 Greater Scaup	135.00	32.00	26.00	...
RW66A	1999, same, Self-Adhesive	...	30.00	26.00	14.00

RW67

RW68

RW67	2000, $15.00 Mottled Duck	135.00	33.00	25.00	...
RW67A	2000, same, Self-Adhesive	...	30.00	25.00	14.00
RW68	2001, $15.00 Northern Pintail	130.00	32.00	25.00	...
RW68A	2001 same, Self-Adhesive	...	30.00	25.00	14.00

RW69

RW70

RW69A

RW69	2002, $15.00 Black Scoters	120.00	28.00	24.00	...
RW69A	2002, same, Self-Adhesive	...	28.00	24.00	14.00

RW70A

RW70	2003, $15.00 Snow Geese	120.00	26.00	23.00	...
RW70A	2003. same, Self-Adhesive	...	26.00	23.00	14.00
RW71	2004 $15.00 Redhead	120.00	26.00	23.00	...
RW71A	2004 same, Self-Adhesive	...	26.00	23.00	...

The Beginning of State Duck Stamps

One of the main purposes of the state waterfowl stamp programs have been to generate revenue for waterfowl conservation and restoration project. In addition, waterfowl stamps validate hunting licenses and often serve as a control to limit the harvest within a specific geographical area.

The federal government recognized the need to protect waterfowl in the U.S. with Migratory Bird Treaty Act of 1918. On March 16, 1934 President Franklin Roosevelt signed the Migratory Bird Hunting Stamp Act into law. Sale of federal waterfowl stamps provided funding for the purchase and development of federal waterfowl areas.

Soon, state and local governments began requiring hunters to purchase waterfowl hunting stamps. Since these agencies did not have collectors in mind, most of the early stamps are printed text only. These include Pymatuning, Marion County, Honey Lake and the states of California, Illinois, North and South Dakota as well as several Indian Reservations.

Pictorial state waterfowl stamps saw their beginning in 1971, when California commissioned Paul Johnson to design the state's first duck stamp, a relatively simple rendition of a pair of pintails in flight. California's decision to issue pictorial stamps were prompted by the growing number of collectors interested in fish and game stamps. State officials estimated that any added production costs could be more than made up through the increased sale of stamps to collectors. In 1971, Iowa became the second state to initiate a pictorial waterfowl stamp program.

The appearance of new pictorial issues, combined with the publication of E.L. Vanderford's *Handbook of Fish and Game Stamps* in 1973, led to a surge in waterfowl stamp collecting.

Maryland and Massachusetts began to issue their stamps in 1974. All of Massachusetts stamps depict waterfowl decoys by famous carvers. Illinois started a pictorial stamp program in 1975. The face value of this stamp was $5, and half of the revenue obtained through its sale went to Ducks Unlimited, a private conservation organization which has done much to aid in waterfowl restoration throughout North America.

These pictorial stamp programs were so successful in raising funds for waterfowl conservation projects that many additional states adopted similar stamp programs. Between 1976 and 1980, 13 additional states began issuing pictorial waterfowl stamps. Tennessee became the first state to issue separate pictorial waterfowl stamps for nonresidents. These non-resident stamps were discontinued after only two years.

In response to an increasing demand for waterfowl stamps on the part of stamp collectors, many states started to print there stamps in two different formats in the 1980's. There was one type, usually printed in booklet panes, for license agents to issue to hunters, and a second type, usually printed in sheets, that was sold to collectors.

The 1981 Arkansas stamp was printed in booklet panes of thirty and issued with protective booklet covers to license agents. Sheets of thirty, without protective covers, were kept in Little Rock for sale to collectors. South Carolina issued their first stamp in 1981. They were printed in sheets of thirty. Starting with their second issues in 1982, a portion of the stamps were serially numbered on the reverse and distributed to license agents. Collectors who bought stamps directly from the state were sold stamps from sheets lacking the serial numbers. The agent, or "hunter type" stamps as they are often called, were only sold to those collectors who specially requested them.

When North Dakota introduced their first pictorial stamps in 1982, the first 20,000 stamps were set aside to be sold with prints or to be signed by the artist. These were printed in sheets of ten. Stamps numbered 20,001-150,000 were printed in booklet panes of five and distributed to license agents. Stamps with serial numbers higher than 150,000 were printed in sheets of thirty and reserved for sale to collectors. The stamps that were distributed to license agents were available to collectors for a brief period of time following the end of the hunting season and then destroyed. The collector type stamps, on the other hand, were kept on sale for three years. This accounts for the relative difficulty in obtaining unused examples of early North Dakota Booklet-type (hunter stamps).

New Hampshire's first stamp was printed in two different formats. When collectors placed their orders, they were asked whether they wanted stamps with straight edges on three sides (booklet type) or fully perforated (from sheets printed for collectors). Not understanding the difference between the two types, the majority of collectors requested fully perforated stamps.

Collector interest in state duck stamps exploded in the mid 1980's. This can be attributed to the large number of states issuing stamps by this time and the fact that an album containing spaces for federal and state waterfowl stamps was published in 1987. In the years since, every state has initiated a waterfowl program.

Nearly half of the states print their stamps in two formats today. Hunter stamps from Montana are printed in booklet panes of ten (2x5) with selvage on both sides. These are most often collected in horizontal pairs. (Connecticut 1993-1996 and Virginia 1988-1995 issued stamps in the same format). The selvage on each side of the pair makes it easy to differentiate them from collectors-type stamps, which are printed in sheets of thirty. When the 1986 Montana stamps were issued, some representatives at the state agency did not recognize a difference between the booklet and sheet type stamps. Therefore, only a small number of booklet-type stamps were obtained by collectors.

There have been some occasions when the waterfowl season was ready to begin and the state license sections had not yet received their stamps from the printer. This occurred in 1989 for Oregon and in 1991 for Idaho. In these instances "temporary" non-pictorial stamps were printed and distributed to license agents for issue to hunters until the regular pictorial stamps were received.

In the late 1980's the U.S. Fish and Wildlife Service encouraged many tribal governments to formally organize their fish and wildlife programs. Many of these programs were made to include stamp and license requirements in their general provisions. In 1989 the Crow Creek Sioux of South Dakota became the first tribal government to issue pictorial waterfowl stamps. These stamps were not printed with collectors in mind. Rather, tribal Department of Natural Resources officials were simply attempting to conform to standards set by South Dakota Game, Fish and Parks Commission for their pictorial stamps. Separate stamps were printed for reservations residents, South Dakota residents who did not live on the reservation and nonresidents of the state. For each classification only 200 stamps were printed.

In the last few years, several tribal governments have issued waterfowl stamps that are more readily available to collectors.

-Michael Jaffe

STATE DUCK STAMPS

State Duck Stamps provide a natural area for the person who wishes to expand his or her field of interest beyond the collecting of Federal Ducks. In 1971, California became the first state to issue a pictorial duck stamp. Other states followed with the sales providing a much needed source of revenue for wetlands. By 1994, all 50 states will have issued duck stamps.

Similar to Federal policy, many states hold an art competition to determine the winning design. Other states commission an artist. Beginning in 1987, some states started to issue a "Governor's" stamp. These stamps with high face values were designed to garner additional wetland funds. In 1989, the Crow Creek Sioux Tribe of South Dakota became the first Indian Reservation to issue a pictorial duck stamp.

Hunter or Agent stamps generally come in booklets with a tab attached to the stamp, or specific serial numbers on the stamp issued in sheet format that allows collectors' orders to be filled more easily. Many of these stamps exist with plate numbers in the margin. The items illustrated below represent just a sampling of the interesting varieties which have been produced by the various states.

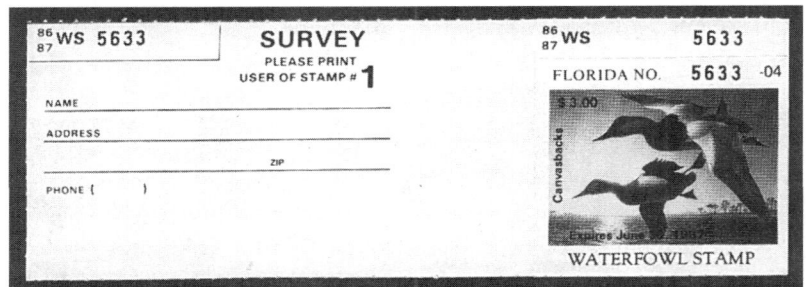

FL 15T SURVEY TAB

OR 3A HUNTER TYPE WITH TAB

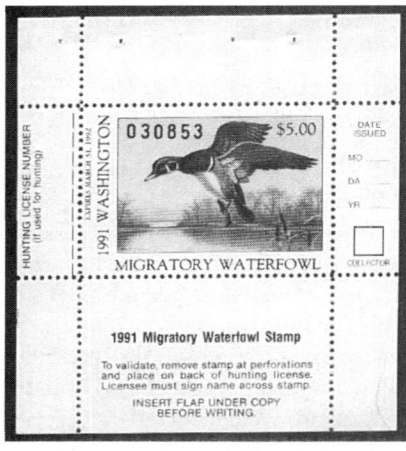

MT 4A HZ. PAIR WITH SIDE MARGINS

WA 6A MINI SHEET   **AR 16 PROOF PAIR, IMPERF.**   **TN 1A NON-RES. LICENSE**

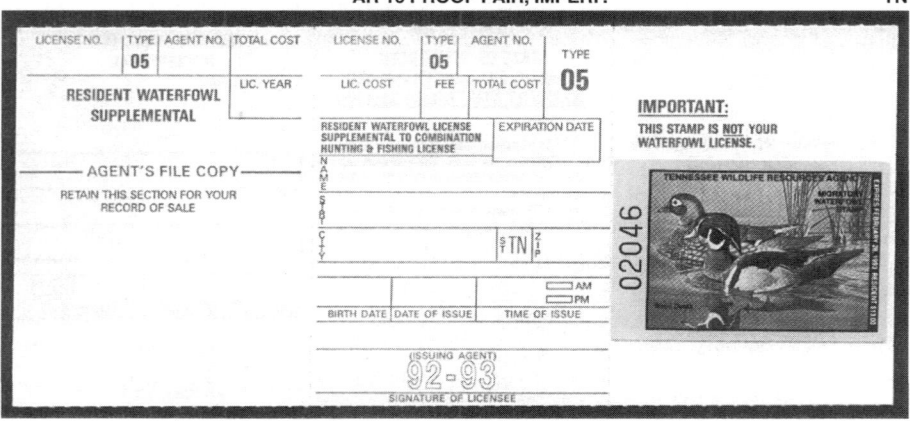

TN 14B 3 PART CARD

STATE HUNTING PERMIT STAMPS

ALABAMA

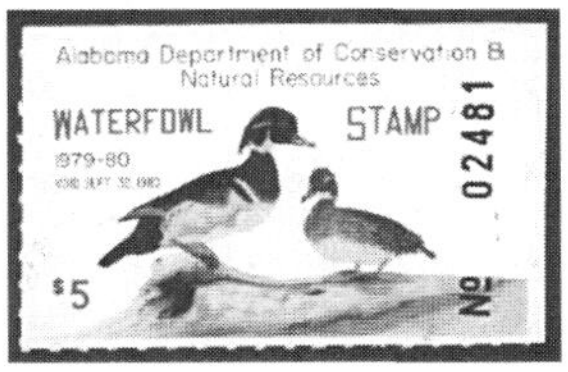

AL 1

No.	Description	F-VF NH
AL 1	1979 $5 Wood Ducks	11.00
AL 2	1980 $5 Mallards	11.00
AL 3	1981 $5 Canada Geese	11.00
AL 4	1982 $5 Green Winged Teal	11.00
AL 5	1983 $5 Widgeon	11.00
AL 6	1984 $5 Buffleheads	11.00
AL 7	1985 $5 Wood Ducks	16.00
AL 8	1986 $5 Canada Geese	16.00
AL 9	1987 $5 Pintails	17.00
AL 10	1988 $5 Canvasbacks	11.00
AL 11	1989 $5 Hooded Merganser	11.00
AL 12	1990 $5 Wood Ducks	11.00
AL 13	1991 $5 Redheads	11.00
AL 14	1992 $5 Cinnamon Teal	11.00
AL 15	1993 $5 Green Winged Teal	11.00
AL 16	1994 $5 Canvasbacks	11.00
AL 17	1995 $5 Canda Geese	11.00
AL 18	1996 $5 Wood Ducks	11.00
AL 19	1997 $5 Snow Goose	11.00
AL 20	1998 $5 Barrow's goldeneye	11.00
AL 21	1999 $5 Redheads	11.00
AL 22	2000 $5 Buffleheads	11.00
AL 23	2001 $5 Ruddy Duck	11.00
AL 24	2002 $5 Pintail	11.00
AL 25	2003 $5 Wood Duck	11.00
AL 26	2004 $5	11.00
Alabama Set 1979-2002 (24)		**260.00**

ALASKA

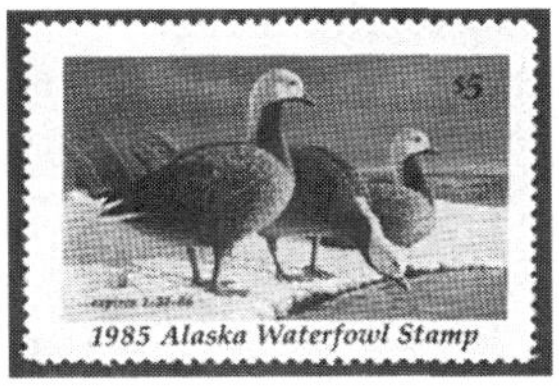

AK1

No.	Description	(A)Hunter Full Tab	F-VF NH
AK 1	1985 $5 Emperor Geese	...	11.00
AK 2	1986 $5 Steller's Elders	...	11.00
AK 3	1987 $5 Spectacled Elders	11.00	11.00
AK 4	1988 $5 Trumpeter Swan	11.00	11.00
AK 5	1989 $5 Goldeneyes	11.00	11.00
AK 6	1990 $5 Oldsquaw	11.00	11.00
AK 7	1991 $5 Snowgeese	11.00	11.00
AK 8	1992 $5 Canvasbacks	11.00	11.00
AK 9	1993 $5 White Fronted Geese	11.00	11.00
AK 10	1994 $5 Harlequin	12.00	14.00
AK 11	1995 $5 Pacific Brant	12.00	14.00
AK 12	1996 $5 Aleutian Canada Geese	12.00	15.00
AK 13	1997 $5 King Eiders	12.00	13.00
AK 14	1998 $5 Barrow's Goldeneye	12.00	13.00
AK 15	1999 $5 Northern Pintails	11.00	12.00
AK 16	2000 $5 Common Eiders	11.00	12.00
AK 17	2001 $5 Buffleheads	11.00	11.00
AK 18	2002 $5 Black Scoter	11.00	11.00
AK 19	2003 $5 Lesser Canada Geese	11.00	11.00
AK 20	2004 $5	11.00	11.00
Alaska Set 1985-2002 (18)		**145.00**	**195.00**

NOTE: Governor's stamps available upon request.

ARIZONA

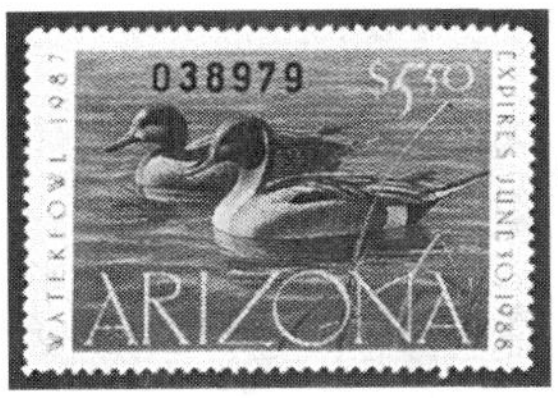

AZ1

No.	Description	(A)Hunter Full Tab	F-VF NH
AZ 1	1987 $5.50 Pintails	12.50	12.50
AZ 2	1988 $5.50 Green Winged Teal	12.50	12.50
AZ 3	1989 $5.50 Cinnamon Teal	12.50	12.50
AZ 4	1990 $5.50 Canada Geese	12.50	12.50
AZ 5	1991 $5.50 Blue Winged Teal	12.50	11.00
AZ 6	1992 $5.50 Buffleheads	12.50	11.00
AZ 7	1993 $5.50 Mexican Duck	11.00	11.00
AZ 8	1994 $5.50 Mallards	11.00	11.00
AZ 9	1995 $5.50 Wigeon	11.00	11.00
AZ 10	1996 $5.50 Canvasback	11.00	11.00
AZ 11	1997 $5.50 Gadwall	11.00	11.00
AZ 12	1998 $5.50 Wood Duck	11.00	11.00
AZ 13	1999 $5.50 Snow Goose	11.00	11.00

ARIZONA (continued)

No.	Description	(A)Hunter Full Tab	F-VF NH
AZ 14	2000 $7.50 Ruddy Ducks	15.00	15.00
AZ 15	2001 $7.50 Redheads	14.00	14.00
AZ 16	2002 $7.50 Ringnecked Duck	13.50	13.50
AZ 17	2003 $7.50 Northern Shoveler	13.50	13.50
AZ 18	2004 $7.50 Lesser Scaup	13.50	13.50
Arizona Set 1987-2002 (16)		**184.00**	**184.00**

NOTE: Governor stamps available upon request

ARKANSAS

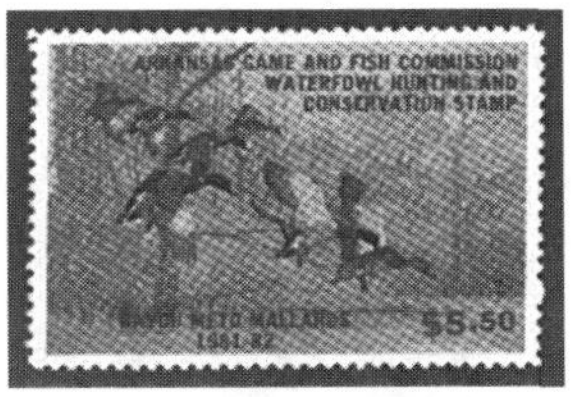

AR1

Arkansas Hunter Serial Numbers
1981-82 110,001-200,000 1983 70,001-160,000
1984-88 25,001-100,000 1989-93 30,001-100,000
1994-95 25,001-100,000 1996-2003 13,001-100,000

No.	Description	(B)Hunter with Serial #	F-VF NH
AR 1	1981 $5.50 Mallards	60.00	55.00
AR 1P	1981 Imperforate Proof Pair		22.00
AR 2	1982 $5.50 Wood Ducks	60.00	45.00
AR 2P	1982 Imperforate Proof Pair		27.50
AR 3	1983 $5.50 Green Wnged Teal	1100.00	70.00
AR 3P	1983 Imperforate Proof Single		80.00
AR 4	1984 $5.50 Pintails	40.00	27.50
AR 4P	1984 Imperforate Proof Pair		22.50
AR 5	1985 $5.50 Mallards	31.00	16.00
AR 5P	1985 Imperforate Proof Pair		22.00
AR 6	1986 $5.50 Black Swamp Mallards	19.00	14.00
AR 6P	1986 Imperforate Proof Pair		22.00
AR 7	1987 $7 Wood Ducks		14.00
AR 7A	1987 $5.50 Wood Ducks	16.00	15.00
AR 7P	1987 Imperforate Proof Pair		22.00
AR 8	1988 $7 Pintails		13.00
AR 8A	1988 $5.50 Pintails	16.00	15.00
AR 8P	1988 Imperforate Proof Pair		25.00
AR 9	1989 $7 Mallards	14.00	13.00
AR 9P	1989 Imperforate Proof Pair		25.00
AR 10	1990 $7 Black Duck/Mallards	14.00	13.00
AR 10P	1990 Imperforate Proof Pair		25.00
AR 11	1991 $7 Widgeons	13.00	13.00
AR 11P	1991 Imperforate Proof Pair		19.00
AR 12	1992 $7 Shovelers	13.00	13.00
AR 12P	1992 Imperforate Proof Pair		19.00
AR 13	1993 $7 Mallards	13.00	13.00
AR 13P	1993 Imperforate Proof Pair		19.00
AR 14	1994 $7 Canada Geese	13.00	13.00
AR 14P	1994 Imperforate Proof Pair		19.00
AR 15	1995 $7 Mallard	13.00	13.00
AR 15P	1995 Imperforate Proof Pair		19.00
AR 16	1996 $7 Black Lab	13.00	13.00
AR 16P	1996 Imperforate Proof Pair		19.00
AR 17	1997 $7 Chocolate Lab	13.00	13.00
AR 17P	1997 Imperforate Proof Pair		19.00
AR 18	1998 Mallards / Yellow Lab	13.00	13.00
AR 18P	1998 Imperforate Proof Pair		19.00
AR 19	1999 $7 Wood Ducks	13.00	13.00
AR 19P	1999 Imperforate Proof Pair		19.00
AR 20	2000 $7 Mallards/Dog	13.00	13.00
AR 20P	2000 Imperforate Proof Pair		19.00
AR 21	2001 $7 Canvasback	13.00	13.00
AR 21P	2001 Imperforate Proof Pair		19.00
AR 22	2002 $7 Mallard	13.00	13.00
AR 22P	2002 Imperforate Proof Pair		19.00
AR 23	2003 $7 Mallard/Chesepeake Bay Retriever	13.00	13.00
AR 23P	2003 Imperforate Proof Pair		19.00
AR 24	2004 $7 Mallards	13.00	13.00
Arkansas Set 1981-2002 (24)			**415.00**
Arkansas Hunter, cplt (22)		**1450.00**	
Arkansas Imperfs, cplt (22)			**495.00**

CALIFORNIA

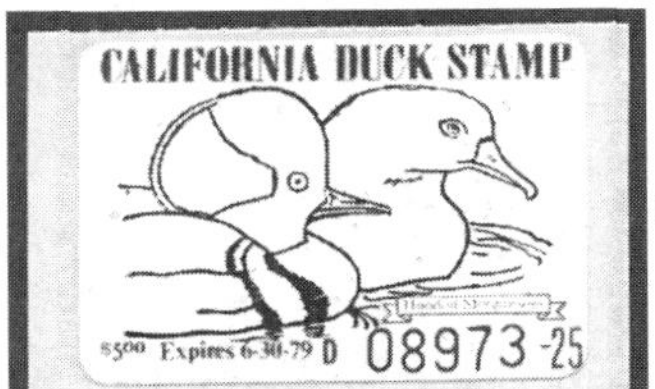

CA8

No.	Description	F-VF NH
CA 1	1971 $1 Pintails Original Backing	795.00
CA 1	1971 $1 Unsigned w/o Orig. Backing	195.00
CA 2	1972 $1 Canvasback Orig.Backing	3200.00
CA 2	1972 $1 Unsigned w/o Orig. Backing	340.00
CA 3	1973 $1 Mallards	14.00
CA 4	1974 $1 White Fronted Geese	3.50
CA 5	1975 $1 Green Winged Teal Clear Wax Back	185.00

CALIFORNIA (continued)

No.	Description	F-VF NH
CA 5R	1975 $1 Same, Ribbed Back	50.00
CA 6	1976 $1 Widgeon	25.00
CA 7	1977 $1 Cinnamon Teal	50.00
CA 7A	1978 $5 Cinnamon Teal	11.00
CA 8	1978 $5 Hooded Merganser	165.00
CA 9	1979 $5 Wood Ducks	11.00
CA 9P	1979 Imperforate Proof Pair	65.00
CA 10	1980 $5 Pintails	11.00
CA 10P	1980 Imperforate Proof Pair	65.00
CA 11	1981 $5 Canvasbacks	11.00
CA 12	1982 $5 Widgeon	11.00
CA 13	1983 $5 Green Winged Teal	11.00
CA 14	1984 $7.50 Mallard Decoy	15.00
CA 15	1985 $7.50 Ring Necked Duck	15.00
CA 16	1986 $7.50 Canada Goose	15.00
CA 17	1987 $7.50 Redheads	15.00
CA 18	1988 $7.50 Mallards	15.00
CA 19	1989 $7.50 Cinnamon Teal	15.00
CA 20	1990 $7.50 Canada Goose	15.00
CA 21	1991 $7.90 Gadwalls	15.00
CA 22	1992 $7.90 White Fronted Goose	15.00
CA 23	1993 $10.50 Pintails	17.50
CA 24	1994 $10.50 Wood Ducks	17.50
CA 25	1995 $10.50 Snow Geese	17.50
CA 25a	Strip of 4 designs	72.00
CA 25m	Mini sheet of 4	210.00
CA 26	1996 $10.50 Mallard	17.50
CA 27	1997 $10.50 Pintails	17.50
CA 28	1998 $10.50 Green Winged Teal (Pair)	35.00
CA 29	1999 $10.50 Wood Duck Pair.	35.00
CA 30	2000 $10.50 Canada Goose & Mallard	18.00
CA 31	2001 $10.50 Redheads	18.00
CA 32	2002 $10.50 Pintails	18.00
CA 33	2003 $10.50 Mallards	18.00
CA34	2004 $10.50	18.00
California Set 1973-2002 (35)		**865.00**

COLORADO

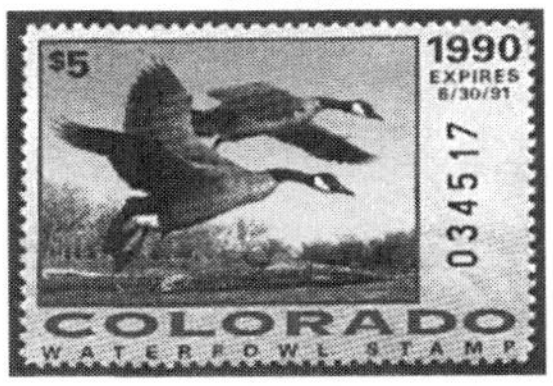

CO1

No.	Description	(A)Hunter Full Tab	F-VF NH
CO 1	1990 $5 Canada Geese	16.00	16.00
CO 2	1991 $5 Mallards	16.00	22.00
CO 3	1992 $5 Pintails	13.00	10.00
CO 4	1993 $5 Green Winged Teal	11.00	10.00
CO 5	1994 $5 Wood Ducks	11.00	10.00
CO 6	1995 $5 Buffleheads	11.00	10.00
CO 7	1996 $5 Cinnamon Teal	11.00	10.00
CO 8	1997 $5 Widgeon	13.00	12.00
CO 9	1998 $5 Cinnamon Teal	11.00	10.00
CO 10	1999 $5 Blue Winged Teal	11.00	10.00
CO 11	2000 $5 Gadwell	11.00	10.00
CO 12	2001 $5 Ruddy Duck	...	10.00
CO 13	2002 $5 Common Goldeneye	...	10.00
CO 14	2003 $5 Canvasbacks	...	10.00
CO 15	2004 $5 Snow Goose	...	10.00
Colorado Set 1990-2002 (13)		...	**142.00**
Colorado Hunter Set (11)		**128.00**	

NOTE: Governor's stamps available upon request.

CONNECTICUT

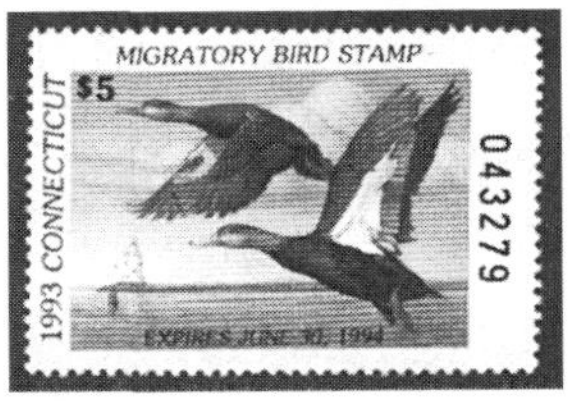

CT1

No.	Description	(A)Hunter Hz. Pair	F-VF NH
CT 1	1993 $5 Black Ducks	24.00	12.00
CT 1M	1993 Commemorative Sheet of 4		85.00
CT 2	1994 $5 Canvasbacks	24.00	12.00
CT 2M	1994 Commemorative Sheet of 4		60.00
CT 3	1995 $5 Mallards	24.00	12.00
CT 4	1996 $5 Old Squaw	24.00	12.00

No.	Description	(A)Hunter "H" Prefix	F-VF NH
CT 5	1997 $5 Green Winged Teal	12.00	12.00
CT 6	1998 $ 5 Mallards	12.00	12.00
CT 7	1999 $5 Canada Goose	12.00	12.00
CT 8	2000 $5 Wood Ducks	12.00	12.00
CT 9	2001 $5 Bufflehead	12.00	12.00
CT 10	2002 $5 Lesser Scaup	12.00	12.00
CT 11	2003 $5 Black Ducks	...	12.00
CT 12	2004 $5	...	12.00
Connecticut Set 1993-2002 (10)		**159.00**	**114.00**

NOTE: Governor's stamps available upon request.

STATE HUNTING PERMIT STAMPS

DELAWARE

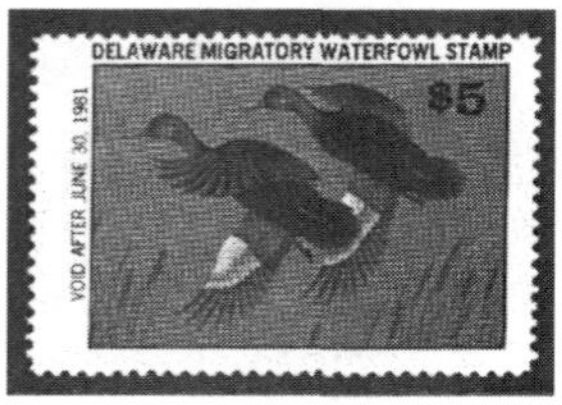

DE1

No.	Description	(A)Hunter S# on back	F-VF NH
DE 1	1980 $5 Black Ducks	...	110.00
DE 2	1981 $5 Snow Geese	...	80.00
DE 3	1982 $5 Canada Geese	...	80.00
DE 4	1983 $5 Canvasbacks	...	50.00
DE 5	1984 $5 Mallards	...	17.00
DE 6	1985 $5 Pintail	...	14.00
DE 7	1986 $5 Widgeon	...	14.00
DE 8	1987 $5 Redheads	...	14.00
DE 9	1988 $5 Wood Ducks	...	11.00
DE 10	1989 $5 Buffleheads	...	11.00
DE 11	1990 $5 Green Winged Teal .	...	11.00
DE 12	1991 $5 Hooded Merganser ..	12.00	11.00
DE 13	1992 $5 Northern Shoveler ..	11.00	11.00
DE 14	1993 $5 Goldeneyes	11.00	11.00
DE 15	1994 $5 Blue Geese	11.00	11.00
DE 16	1995 $5 Scaup	11.00	11.00
DE 17	1996 $6 Gadwall	11.00	11.00
DE 18	1997 $6 White Winged Scoter	11.00	11.00
DE 19	1998 $6 Blue Winged Teal	11.00	11.00
DE 20	1999 $6 Tundra Swan	11.00	11.00
DE 21	2000 $6 American Brandt	11.00	11.00
DE 22	2001 $6 Old Squaw	11.00	11.00
DE 23	2002 $6 Ruddy Duck	11.00	11.00
DE 24	2003 $9 Ring Necked Duck	15.00	15.00
DE 25	2004 $9 Black Scoter	15.00	15.00
Delaware Set 1980-2002 (23)		**...**	**500.00**
Delaware Hunters 1991-2002(12) ...		**126.00**	**...**

NOTE: Governor's stamps available upon request.

FLORIDA

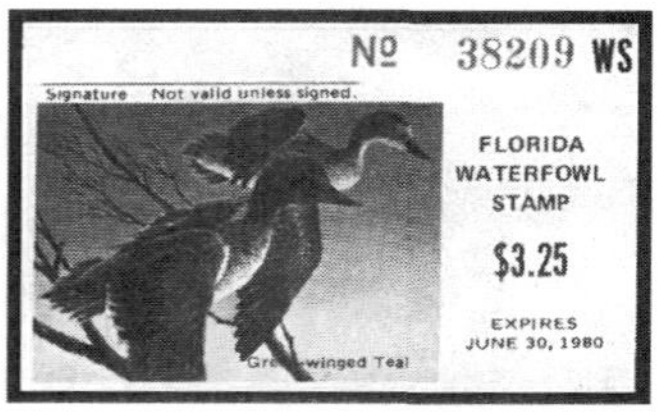

FL1

No.	Description	(T)Full Tab Attached	F-VF NH
FL 1	1979 $3.25 Green Winged Teal	260.00	220.00
FL 2	1980 $3.25 Pintails	24.00	20.00
FL 3	1981 $3.25 Widgeon	24.00	17.00
FL 4	1982 $3.25 Ring-Necked Duck	35.00	24.00
FL 5	1983 $3.25 Buffleheads	70.00	60.00
FL 6	1984 $3.25 Hooded Merganser	20.00	15.00
FL 7	1985 $3.25 Wood Ducks	20.00	15.00

No.	Description	(T)Survey Tab Attached	F-VF NH
FL 8	1986 $3.00 Canvasbacks	20.00	12.00
FL 9	1987 $3.50 Mallards	30.00	11.00
FL 10	1988 $3.50 Redheads	27.00	11.00
FL 11	1989 $3.50 Blue Winged Teal	27.00	8.50
FL 12	1990 $3.50 Wood Ducks	27.00	8.50
FL 13	1991 $3.50 Northern Pintail ..	20.00	8.50
FL 14	1992 $3.50 Ruddy Duck	16.00	8.50
FL 15	1993 $3.50 American Widgeon	16.00	8.00
FL 16	1994 $3.50 Mottled Duck	16.00	7.50
FL 17	1995 $3.50 Fulvous Whistling Duck	16.00	7.50
FL 18	1996 $3.50 Goldeneyes	17.00	7.50
FL 19	1997 $3.50 Hooded Mergansers	17.00	7.50

No.	Description	(T)Top Pair Attached	F-VF NH
FL 20	1998 $3.50 Shoveler	40.00	18.00
FL 21	1999 $3.50 Northern Pintail ..	18.00	7.50
FL 22	2000 $3.50 Ring necked Duck	18.00	7.50
FL 23	2001 $3.50 Canvasback	18.00	7.50
FL 24	2002 $3.50 Mottled Duck	18.00	6.50
FL 24A	2002 $3.50 Reversed Duck ..	...	50.00
FL 25	2003 $3.50 Green Winged Teal.	...	20.00
Florida Set 1979-2002 (24)		**...**	**498.00**

GEORGIA

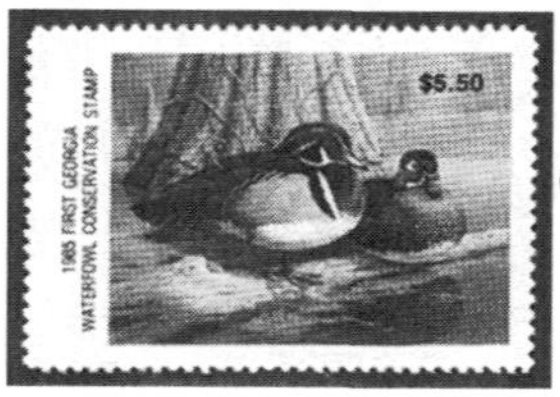

GA 1

GEORGIA (continued)

No.	Description	F-VF NH
GA 1	1985 $5.50 Wood Ducks	17.50
GA 2	1986 $5.50 Mallards	10.00
GA 3	1987 $5.50 Canada Geese	10.00
GA 4	1988 $5.50 Ring Necked Ducks	10.00
GA 5	1989 $5.50 Duckling/Puppy..	16.00
GA 6	1990 $5.50 Wood Ducks	10.00
GA 7	1991 $5.50 Green Winged Teal	10.00
GA 8	1992 $5.50 Buffleheads	14.00
GA 9	1993 $5.50 Mallards	14.00
GA 10	1994 $5.50 Ringnecks	15.00
GA 11	1995 $5.50 Widgeons/Black Lab	24.00
GA 12	1996 $5.50 Black Ducks	19.00
GA 13	1997 $5.50 Lesser Scaup	29.00
GA 14	1998 $5.50 Black Labrador with Ringnecks	20.00
GA 15	1999 $5.50 Pintails	15.00
Georgia Set 1985-99 (15)		**215.00**

HAWAII

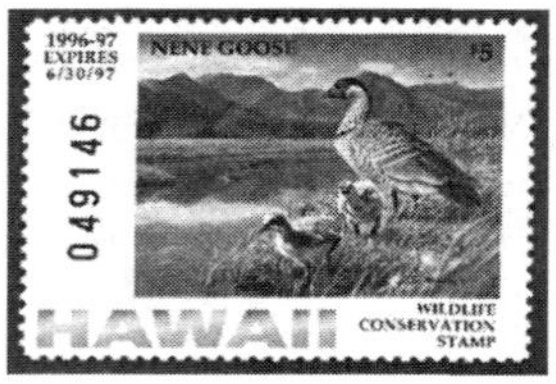

HI 1

No.	Description	(A)Hunter Type	F-VF NH
HI 1	1996 $5 Nene Geese	12.50	12.00
HI 1B	1996 $5 Booklet	...	15.00
HI 1M	1996 $5 Mini Sheet of 4	...	60.00
HI 1P	1996 Imperforate	...	30.00
HI 2	1997 $5 Hawaiian Duck	12.50	12.00
HI 2B	1997 $5 Booklet	...	15.00
HI 2M	1997 $5 Mini Sheet of 4	...	55.00
HI 3	1998 $5 Wild Turkey	12.50	12.00
HI 4	1999 $5 Pheasant	12.50	12.00
HI 5	2000 $5 Erckels Francolin	12.00	12.00
HI 6	2001 $5 Japanese Green Pheasant	12.00	12.00
HI 7	2002 $10 Chucker	...	16.00
HI 8	2003 $10 Nene Goose	...	16.00
HI 8A	2003 $10 Nene Goose Game Bird	...	16.00
HI 9	2004 $10 California Quail	...	16.00
HI 9A	2004 $10 CA Quail Game Bird	...	16.00
Hawaii set 1996-2002 (7)		**79.00**	**79.00**

NOTE: Governor's stamps available upon request.

IDAHO

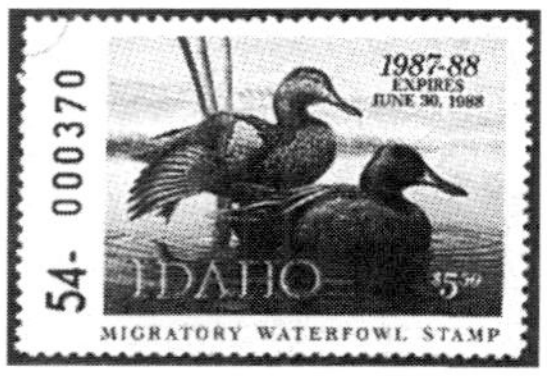

ID 1

No.	Description	(A)Bklt.Sgl. with Tab	F-VF NH
ID 1	1987 $5.50 Cinnamon Teals ..	13.00	17.00
ID 2	1988 $5.50 Green Winged Teal	15.00	15.00
ID 3	1989 $6 Blue Winged Teal	13.00	13.00
ID 4	1990 $6 Trumpeter Swan	13.00	24.00
ID 5	1991 $6 American Widgeons	13.00	11.00
ID 5V	1991 $6 Provisional.	...	150.00
ID 6	1992 $6 Canada Geese	11.00	11.00
ID 7	1993 $6 Common Goldeneye	11.00	12.00
ID 8	1994 $6 Harlequin	11.00	12.00
ID 9	1995 $6 Wood Ducks	11.00	12.00
ID 10	1996 $6 Mallard	...	12.00
ID 11	1997 $6.50 Shovelers	...	12.00
ID 12	1998 $6.50 Canada Geese	...	12.00
Idaho Set 1987-98 (12)		**...**	**130.00**
Idaho Bklt. Set 1987-95 (9)		**90.00**	**...**

ILLINOIS

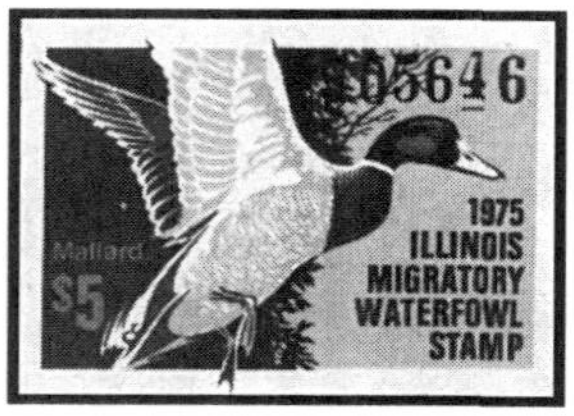

IL 1

No.	Description	(T)Full Tab Attached	F-VF NH
IL 1	1975 $5 Mallard	...	650.00
IL 2	1976 $5 Wood Ducks	...	295.00
IL 3	1977 $5 Canada Goose	...	195.00
IL 4	1978 $5 Canvasbacks	...	140.00
IL 5	1979 $5 Pintail	...	125.00
IL 6	1980 $5 Green Winged Teal .	...	125.00

ILLINOIS (continued)

No.	Description	(T)Full Tab Attached	F-VF NH
IL 7	1981 $5 Widgeon	...	125.00
IL 7A	1981 $5 G.W. Teal Error	...	595.00
IL 8	1982 $5 Black Ducks	...	75.00
IL 9	1983 $5 Lesser Scaup	...	75.00
IL 10	1984 $5 Blue Winged Teal	...	75.00
IL 11	1985 $5 Red Head	22.00	17.00
IL 12	1986 $5 Gadwalls	19.00	17.00
IL 13	1987 $5 Buffleheads	16.00	14.00
IL 14	1988 $5 Common Goldeneye	16.00	14.00
IL 15	1989 $5 Ring Necked Duck ..	13.00	11.00
IL 16	1990 $10 Lesser Snow Goose	19.00	18.00
IL 17	1991 $10 Black Lab/Can.Goose	19.00	18.00
IL 18	1992 $10 Retriever/Mallards	28.00	26.00
IL 19	1993 $10 Puppy/Decoy	28.00	26.00
IL 20	1994 $10 Chessies & Canvasbacks	28.00	26.00
IL 21	1995 $10 Green Winged Teal/Chestnut Lab	28.00	26.00
IL 22	1996 $10 Wood Ducks	...	17.00
IL 23	1997 $10 Canvasbacks	...	17.00
IL 24	1998 $10 Canada Geese	...	17.00
IL 25	1999 $10 Canada Geese/Black Lab		18.00
IL 26	2000 $10 Mallard/Gold Retriever		18.00
IL 27	2001 $10 Canvasback/ Yellow Labrador Retriever	...	18.00
IL 28	2002 $10 Canvasback/ Chestnut Retriever..............	...	18.00
IL 29	2003 $10 Green Winged Teal/ Chocolate Labrador	...	18.00
IL 30	2004 $10	...	18.00

Illinois Set 1975-2002 Without Error (28) 2095.00
NOTE: Governor's stamps available upon request.

INDIANA

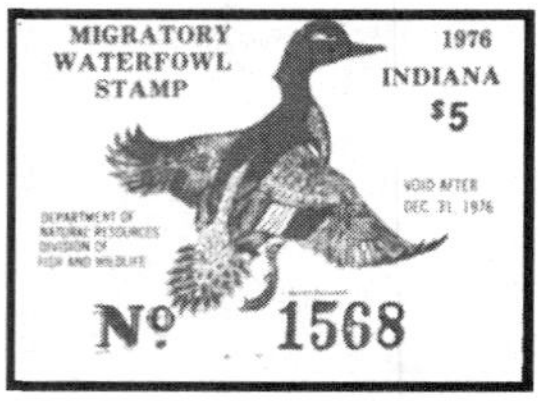

IN 1

No.	Description	(T)Full Tab Attached	F-VF NH
IN 1	1976 $5 Green Winged Teal .	...	10.00
IN 2	1977 $5 Pintail	...	10.00
IN 3	1978 $5 Canada Geese	...	10.00
IN 4	1979 $5 Canvasbacks	...	10.00
IN 5	1980 $5 Mallard Ducklings ...	...	10.00
IN 6	1981 $5 Hooded Merganers .	...	10.00
IN 7	1982 $5 Blue Winged Teal	...	10.00
IN 8	1983 $5 Snow Geese	...	10.00
IN 9	1984 $5 Redheads	...	10.00
IN 10	1985 $5 Pintail	12.00	10.00
IN 11	1986 $5 Wood Duck	12.00	10.00
IN 12	1987 $5 Canvasbacks	12.00	10.00
IN 13	1988 $6.75 Redheads	13.00	12.00
IN 14	1989 $6.75 Canada Goose ...	13.00	12.00
IN 15	1990 $6.75 Blue Winged Teal	13.00	12.00
IN 16	1991 $6.75 Mallards	13.00	12.00
IN 17	1992 $6.75 Green Winged Teal	13.00	12.00
IN 18	1993 $6.75 Wood Ducks	13.00	12.00
IN 19	1994 $6.75 Pintail	13.00	12.00
IN 20	1995 $6.75 Goldeneyes	13.00	12.00
IN 21	1996 $6.75 Black Ducks	13.00	12.00
IN 22	1997 $6.75 Canada Geese ...	13.00	12.00
IN 23	1998 $6.75 Widgeon	13.00	12.00
IN 24	1999 $6.75 Bluebills	13.00	12.00
IN 25	2000 $6.75 Ring Necked Goose	13.00	12.00
IN 26	2001 $6.75 Hooded Merganser	13.00	12.00
IN 27	2002 $6.75 Green Winged Teal	13.00	12.00
IN 28	2003 $6.75 Shoveler	13.00	12.00
IN 29	2004 $6.75 Wood Duck	13.00	12.00
Indiana Set 1976-2002 (27)		**...**	**285.00**

IOWA

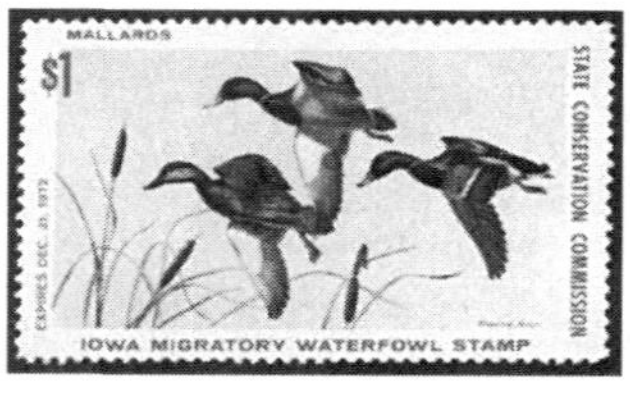

IA 9

No.	Description	F-VF NH
IA 1	1972 $1 Mallards	195.00
IA 2	1973 $1 Pintails	45.00
IA 3	1974 $1 Gadwalls	100.00
IA 4	1975 $1 Canada Geese	110.00
IA 5	1976 $1 Canvasbacks	27.50
IA 6	1977 $1 Lesser Scaup	25.00
IA 7	1978 $1 Wood Ducks	55.00
IA 8	1979 $5 Buffleheads	425.00
IA 9	1980 $5 Redheads	35.00
IA 10	1981 $5 Green Winged Teal	35.00

STATE HUNTING PERMIT STAMPS

IOWA (continued)

No.	Description	F-VF NH
IA 11	1982 $5 Snow Geese	20.00
IA 12	1983 $5 Widgeon	20.00
IA 13	1984 $5 Wood Ducks	40.00
IA 14	1985 $5 Mallard & Decoy	25.00
IA 15	1986 $5 Blue Winged Teal	18.00
IA 16	1987 $5 Canada Goose	16.00
IA 17	1988 $5 Pintails	13.00
IA 18	1989 $5 Blue Winged Teal	13.00
IA 19	1990 $5 Canvasback	10.00
IA 19A	1990 Serial #26001-80000	14.00
IA 20	1991 $5 Mallards	10.00
IA 21	1992 $5 Black Lab/Ducks	14.00
IA 22	1993 $5 Mallards	11.00
IA 23	1994 $5 Green Winged Teal	10.00
IA 24	1995 $5 Canada Geese	10.00
IA 25	1996 $5 Canvasbacks	14.00
IA 26	1997 $5 Canada Geese	10.00
IA 27	1998 $5 Pintails	10.00
IA 28	1999 $5.50 Trumpeter Swans	10.00
IA 29	2000 $5.50 Hooded Merganser	10.00
IA 30	2001 $6 Snow Goose	11.00
IA 31	2002 $8.50 Northern Shoveler	14.00
IA 32	2003 $8.50 Ruddy Duck	14.00
IA 33	2004 $8.50 Wood Ducks	14.00
Iowa Set 1972-2002 (31)		**1300.00**

KANSAS

KS1

No.	Description	(A)Hunter Single	F-VF NH
KS 1	1987 $3 Green Winged Teal	...	9.50
KS 1	1987 $3 Horizontal Pair	...	20.00
KS 1AD	1987 Hunter DD in Serial Number	9.50	...
KS 1AD	1987 Horiz. Pair DD in Serial No.	20.00	...
KS 1AS	1987 Hunter SS in Serial Number	9.50	...
KS 1AS	1987 Horiz. Pair SS in Serial No.	20.00	...
KS 2	1988 $3 Canada Geese	9.50	7.50
KS 2A	1988 $3 Horizontal Pair	20.00	...
KS 3	1989 $3 Mallards	8.00	7.50
KS 3A	1989 $3 Horizontal Pair	16.00	...
KS 4	1990 $3 Wood Ducks	8.00	7.50
KS 4A	1990 $3 Horizontal Pair	16.00	...
KS 5	1991 $3 Pintail	8.00	7.00
KS 5A	1991 $3 Horizontal Pair	16.00	...
KS 6	1992 $3 Canvasbacks	...	7.00
KS 7	1993 $3 Mallards	...	7.00
KS 8	1994 $3 Blue Winged Teal	...	7.00
KS 9	1995 $3 Barrow's Goldeneyes	...	7.00
KS 10	1996 $3 Wigeon	...	7.00
KS 11	1997 $3 Mallard (Blue)	...	7.00
KS 12	1998 $3 Mallard (Green)	...	9.00
KS 13	1999 $3 Mallard (Red)	...	7.00
KS 14	2000 $3 Mallard (Purple)	...	7.00
KS 15	2001 $3 Mallard (Orange)	...	7.00
KS 16	2002 $5 Mallard (Blue)	...	10.00
KS 17	2003 $5 Mallard (Green)	...	10.00
KS 18	2004 $5 Mallard (Red)	...	10.00
Kansas Set 1987-2002 (16)		...	**112.00**
Kansas Hunters Pairs Set 1987-91 (5)	87.00	...	

KENTUCKY

KY1

No.	Description	(T)Full Tab Attached	F-VF NH
KY 1	1985 $5.25 Mallards	17.00	16.00
KY 2	1986 $5.25 Wood Ducks	14.00	11.00
KY 3	1987 $5.25 Black Ducks	14.00	11.00
KY 4	1988 $5.25 Canada Goose	14.00	11.00
KY 5	1989 $5.25 Canvasbacks/ Retriever	17.00	14.00
KY 6	1990 $5.25 Widgeons	14.00	11.00
KY 7	1991 $5.25 Pintails	14.00	11.00
KY 8	1992 $5.25 Green Winged Teal	15.00	14.00
KY 9	1993 $5.25 Canvasback/Decoy	17.00	17.00
KY 10	1994 $5.25 Canada Goose	15.00	14.00
KY 11	1995 $7.50 Ringnecks/Black Lab	18.00	16.00
KY 12	1996 $7.50 Blue Winged Teal	...	14.00
KY 13	1997 $7.50 Shovelers	...	14.00
KY 14	1998 $7.50 Gadwalls	...	14.00
KY 15	1999 $7.50 Goldeneyes	...	14.00
KY 16	2000 $7.50 Redheads	...	14.00
KY 17	2001 $7.50 Mallard	...	14.00
KY 18	2002 $7.50 Pintails	...	14.00
KY 19	2003 $7.50 Snow Goose	...	14.00
KY 20	2004		
Kentucky Set 1985-2002 (18)		...	**229.00**

LOUISIANA

LA 1

No.	Description	(A)$7.50 Non- Resident	F-VF NH
LA 1	1989 $5 Blue Winged Teal	20.00	14.00
LA 2	1990 $5 Green Winged Teal	13.00	9.00
LA 3	1991 $5 Wood Ducks	15.00	11.00
LA 4	1992 $5 Pintails	14.00	11.00
LA 5	1993 $5 American Widgeons	14.00	11.00
LA 6	1994 $5 Mottled Duck	14.00	11.00
LA 7	1995 $5 Speckled Belly Goose	14.00	11.00
LA 8	1996 $5 Gadwall	14.00	11.00

No.	Description	(A)$13.50 Non- Resident	F-VF NH
LA 9	1997 $5 Ring Necked Duck	21.00	11.00
LA 10	1998 $5 Mallard	21.00	11.00
LA 11	1999 $5.50 Snow Goose	21.00	11.00
LA 12	2000 $5.50 Lesser Scaup	40.00	11.00

No.	Description	(A)$25 Non- Resident	F-VF NH
LA 13	2001 $5.50 Northern Shoveler	40.00	11.00
LA 14	2002 $5.50 Canvasbacks	40.00	11.00
LA 15	2003 $5.50 Redhead	40.00	11.00
LA 16	2004 $5.50 Hooded Mergansers	40.00	11.00
Louisiana Set Resident & Non-Resident 1989-2000 (28)			**435.00**

NOTE: Governor's stamps available.

MAINE

ME 1

No.	Description	F-VF NH
ME 1	1984 $2.50 Black Ducks	30.00
ME 2	1985 $2.50 Common Eiders/ Lighthouse	60.00
ME 3	1986 $2.50 Wood Ducks	11.00
ME 4	1987 $2.50 Buffleheads	10.00
ME 5	1988 $2.50 Green Winged Teal	10.00
ME 6	1989 $2.50 Goldeneyes	8.00
ME 7	1990 $2.50 Canada Geese	8.00
ME 8	1991 $2.50 Ring Necked Duck	8.00
ME 9	1992 $2.50 Old Squaw	8.00
ME 10	1993 $2.50 Hooded Merganser	8.00
ME 11	1994 $2.50 Mallards	8.00
ME 12	1995 $2.50 White Winged Scoter	10.00
ME 13	1996 $2.50 Blue Winged Teal	10.00
ME 14	1997 $2.50 Greater Scaup	10.00
ME 15	1998 $2.50 Surf Scoter	7.00
ME 16	1999 $2.50 Black Duck	6.00
ME 17	2000 $2.50 Common Eider	6.00
ME 18	2001 $2.50 Wood Duck	6.00
ME 19	2002 $2.50 Bufflehead	6.00
ME 20	2003 $5.50 Green Winged Teal	10.00
ME 21	2004 $5.50	10.00
Maine Set 1984-2002 (19)		**220.00**

MARYLAND

MD1

No.	Description	F-VF NH
MD 1	1974 $1.10 Mallards	14.00
MD 2	1975 $1.10 Canada Geese	14.00
MD 3	1976 $1.10 Canvasbacks	14.00
MD 4	1977 $1.10 Greater Scaup	14.00
MD 5	1978 $1.10 Redheads	14.00
MD 6	1979 $1.10 Wood Ducks	14.00
MD 7	1980 $1.10 Pintail Decoy	14.00
MD 8	1981 $3 Widgeon	8.00
MD 9	1982 $3 Canvasbacks	11.00
MD 10	1983 $3 Wood Duck	16.00
MD 11	1984 $6 Black Duck	14.00
MD 12	1985 $6 Canada Geese	12.50
MD 13	1986 $6 Hooded Merganser	12.50
MD 14	1987 $6 Redheads	12.50
MD 15	1988 $6 Ruddy Duck	12.50
MD 16	1989 $6 Blue Winged Teal	14.00
MD 17	1990 $6 Lesser Scaup	11.50

MARYLAND (continued)

No.	Description	F-VF NH
MD 18	1991 $6 Shovelers	11.50
MD 19	1992 $6 Bufflehead	11.50
MD 20	1993 $6 Canvasbacks	11.50
MD 21	1994 $6 Redheads	11.50
MD 22	1995 $6 Mallards	12.50
MD 23	1996 $6 Canada Geese	12.50
MD 24	1997 $6 Canvasbacks	12.50
MD 25	1998 $6 Pintail	11.50
MD 26	1999 $6 Wood Ducks	11.50
MD 27	2000 $6 Old Squaws	11.50
MD 28	2001 $6 American Widgeon	11.50
MD 29	2002 $9 Black Scoters	15.00
MD 30	2003 $9 Lesser Scaup	15.00
MD 31	2004 $9	15.00
Maryland Set 1974-2002 (29)		**345.00**

MASSACHUSETTS

MA 1

No.	Description	F-VF NH
MA 1	1974 $1.25 Wood Duck	18.00
MA 2	1975 $1.25 Pintail	18.00
MA 3	1976 $1.25 Canada Goose	18.00
MA 4	1977 $1.25 Goldeneye	18.00
MA 5	1978 $1.25 Black Duck	18.00
MA 6	1979 $1.25 Ruddy Turnstone	18.00
MA 7	1980 $1.25 Old Squaw	18.00
MA 8	1981 $1.25 Red Breasted Merganser	18.00
MA 9	1982 $1.25 Greater Yellowlegs	18.00
MA 10	1983 $1.25 Redhead	18.00
MA 11	1984 $1.25 White Ringed Scooter	18.00
MA 12	1985 $1.25 Ruddy Duck	17.00
MA 13	1986 $1.25 Preening Bluebill	17.00
MA 14	1987 $1.25 American Widgeon	17.00
MA 15	1988 $1.25 Mallard Drake	17.00
MA 16	1989 $1.25 Brant	11.00
MA 17	1990 $1.25 Whistler Hen	11.00
MA 18	1991 $5 Canvasback	12.00
MA 19	1992 $5 Black-Bellied Plover	12.00
MA 20	1993 $5 Red Breasted Merganser	12.00
MA 21	1994 $5 White Winged Scoter	12.00
MA 22	1995 $5 Hooded Merganser	12.00
MA 23	1996 $5 Eider Decoy	12.00
MA 24	1997 $5 Curlew Shorebird	12.00
MA 25	1998 $5 Canada Goose	11.00
MA 26	1999 $5 Old Squaw	11.00
MA 27	2000 $5 Merganser	11.00
MA 28	2001 $5 Black Duck	11.00
MA 29	2002 $5 Bufflehead	11.00
MA 30	2003 $5 Green Winged Teal	10.00
MA 31	2004 $5 Drake Wood Duck	10.00
Mass. Set 1974-2002 (29)		**405.00**

MICHIGAN

MI 1

No.	Description	(T)Full Tab Attached	F-VF NH
MI 1	1976 $2.10 Wood Duck	...	6.00
MI 2	1977 $2.10 Canvasbacks	...	350.00
MI 3	1978 $2.10 Mallards	55.00	30.00
MI 4	1979 $2.10 Canada Geese	75.00	50.00
MI 5	1980 $3.75 Lesser Scaup	37.00	23.00
MI 6	1981 $3.75 Buffleheads	...	30.00
MI 7	1982 $3.75 Redheads	...	30.00
MI 8	1983 $3.75 Wood Ducks	...	30.00
MI 9	1984 $3.75 Pintails	...	30.00
MI 10	1985 $3.75 Ring Necked Duck	...	30.00
MI 11	1986 $3.75 Common Goldeneyes	...	23.00
MI 12	1987 $3.85 Green. Winged Teal	...	14.00
MI 13	1988 $3.85 Canada Goose	...	11.00
MI 14	1989 $3.85 Widgeon	...	11.00
MI 15	1990 $3.85 Wood Ducks	...	11.00
MI 16	1991 $3.85 Blue Winged Teal	...	10.00
MI 17	1992 $3.85 Red Breasted Merganser	...	10.00
MI 18	1993 $3.85 Hooded Merganser	...	10.00
MI 19	1994 $3.85 Black Duck	...	10.00
MI 20	1995 $4.35 Blue Winged Teal	...	10.00
MI 21	1996 $4.35 Canada Geese	...	10.00
MI 22	1997 $5 Canvasbacks	...	10.00
MI 23	1998 $5 Pintail	...	10.00
MI 24	1999 $5 Northern Shoveler	...	10.00
MI 25	2000 $5 Mallard	...	9.00
MI 26	2001 $5 Ruddy Duck	...	9.00

MICHIGAN (continued)

No.	Description	(T)Full Tab Attached	F-VF NH
MI 27	2002 $5 American Wigeon	...	9.00
MI 28	2003 $5 Redhead	...	9.00
MI 29	2004 $5 Wood Duck	...	9.00
Michigan Set 1976-2002 (27)		...	**745.00**

MINNESOTA

MN 1

No.	Description	(T)Full Tab Attached	F-VF NH
MN 1	1977 $3 Mallards	...	20.00
MN 2	1978 $3 Lesser Scaup	...	14.00
MN 3	1979 $3 Pintails	...	14.00
MN 4	1980 $3 Canvasbacks	...	14.00
MN 5	1981 $3 Canada Geese	...	13.00
MN 6	1982 $3 Redheads	...	14.00
MN 7	1983 $3 Bl & Snow Geese	...	14.00
MN 8	1984 $3 Wood Ducks	...	14.00
MN 9	1985 $3 White Fronted Geese	...	10.00
MN 10	1986 $5 Lesser Scaup	...	11.00
MN 11	1987 $5 Goldeneyes	16.00	14.00
MN 12	1988 $5 Buffleheads	16.00	13.00
MN 13	1989 $5 American Widgeons	16.00	13.00
MN 14	1990 $5 Hooded Merganser	50.00	40.00
MN 15	1991 $5 Ross' Goose	10.50	10.00
MN 16	1992 $5 Barrow's Goldeneye	10.50	10.00
MN 17	1993 $5 Blue Winged Teal	10.50	10.00
MN 18	1994 $5 Ring Necked Duck	10.50	10.00
MN 19	1995 $5 Gadwalls	10.50	10.00
MN 20	1996 $5 Scaup	10.50	10.00
MN 21	1997 $5 Shoveler with Decoy	10.50	10.00
MN 22	1998 $5 Harlequin Ducks	10.50	10.00
MN 23	1999 $5 Green Winged Teal	10.50	10.00
MN 24	2000 $5 Red Breasted Morganson	...	10.00
MN 25	2001 $5 Black Duck	...	10.00
MN 26	2002 $5 Ruddy Duck	...	10.00
MN 27	2003 $5 Long Tailed Duck	...	10.00
MN 28	2004 $7.50 Common Merganser	...	14.00
Minnesota Set 1977-2002 (26)		...	**321.00**

MISSISSIPPI

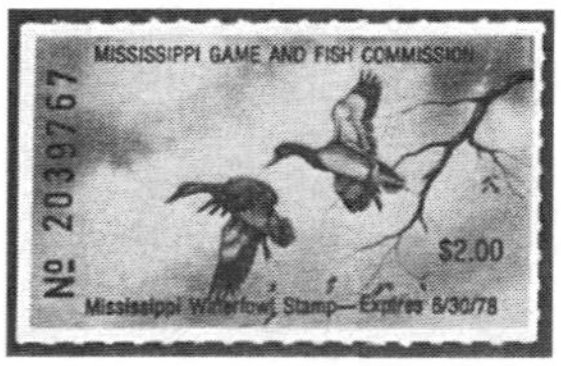

MS 2

No.	Description	F-VF NH
MS 1	1976 $2 Wood Duck	26.00
MS 1B	1976 $2 Full Computer Card	30.00
MS 2	1977 $2 Mallards	12.00
MS 3	1978 $2 Green Winged Teal	12.00
MS 4	1979 $2 Canvasbacks	11.00
MS 5	1980 $2 Pintails	11.00
MS 6	1981 $2 Redheads	11.00
MS 7	1982 $2 Canada Geese	11.00
MS 8	1983 $2 Lesser Scaup	11.00
MS 9	1984 $2 Black Ducks	11.00
MS 10	1985 $2 Mallards	13.00
MS 10A	1985 Serial # Error-No Horizontal #	200.00
MS 10B	1985 Serial # Var.- No Silver Bar	850.00
MS 11	1986 $2 Widgeon	11.00
MS 12	1987 $2 Ring Necked Ducks	11.00
MS 13	1988 $2 Snow Geese	11.00
MS 14	1989 $2 Wood Ducks	8.00
MS 15	1990 $2 Snow Geese	16.00
MS 16	1991 $2 Black Lab/Canvasback Decoy	8.00
MS 17	1992 $2 Green Winged Teal	8.00
MS 18	1993 $5 Mallards	10.00
MS 19	1994 $5 Canvasbacks	10.00
MS 20	1995 $5 Blue Winged Teal	13.00
MS 21	1996 $5 Hooded Merganser	13.00
MS 22	1997 $5 Wood Duck	13.00
MS 23	1998 $5 Pintails	9.00
MS 24	1999 $5 Ring necked Duck	9.00
MS 25	2000 $5 Mallards	9.00
MS 26	2001 $10 Gadwall	16.00
MS 27	2002 $10 Wood Duck Photo	16.00
MS 28	2003 $10 Pintail	16.00
MS 29	2004 $10 Wood Ducks	16.00
Mississippi Set 1976-2002 (27)		**298.00**

NOTE: Governor's stamps available upon request.

MISSOURI

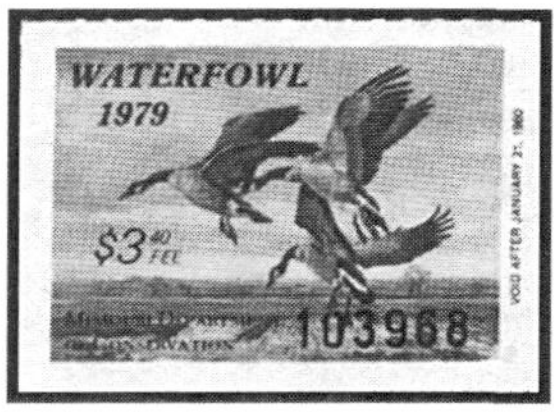

MO 1

No.	Description	(T)Full Tab Attached	F-VF NH
MO 1	1979 $3.40 Canada Geese	975.00	695.00
MO 2	1980 $3.40 Wood Ducks	160.00	140.00
MO 3	1981 $3 Lesser Scaup	90.00	75.00
MO 4	1982 $3 Buffleheads	85.00	70.00
MO 5	1983 $3 Blue Winged Teal	65.00	55.00
MO 6	1984 $3 Mallards	65.00	45.00
MO 7	1985 $3 Widgeon	30.00	27.50
MO 8	1986 $3 Hooded Merganser	20.00	17.00
MO 9	1987 $3 Pintails	17.00	14.00
MO 10	1988 $3 Canvasbacks	13.00	12.00
MO 11	1989 $3 Ring Necked Ducks	10.50	9.50
MO 12	1990 $3 Redheads	11.00	9.00
MO 13	1991 $5 Snow Geese	12.00	9.00
MO 14	1992 $5 Gadwalls	12.00	9.00
MO 15	1993 $5 Green Winged Teal	12.00	9.00
MO 16	1994 $5 White Fronted Geese	12.00	10.00
MO 17	1995 $5 Goldeneyes	15.00	13.00
MO 18	1996 $5 Black Duck	...	14.00
Missouri Set 1979-96 (18)		...	**1175.00**
Missouri Tab Set 1979-95 (17)		**1545.00**	...

NOTE: Governor's stamps available upon request.

MONTANA

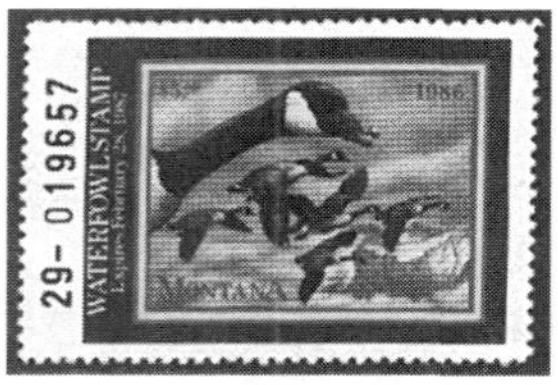

MT 1

No.	Description	(A)Horiz.Pr. side margins	F-VF NH
MT 1	1986 $5 Canada Geese	2800.00	14.00
MT 2	1987 $5 Redheads	38.00	19.00
MT 3	1988 $5 Mallards	28.00	16.00
MT 4	1989 $5 Black Lab & Pintail	38.00	15.00
MT 5	1990 $5 Cinnamon Teal & Blue Winged Teal	25.00	10.00
MT 6	1991 $5 Snow Geese	25.00	10.00
MT 7	1992 $5 Wood Ducks	25.00	10.00
MT 8	1993 $5 Harlequin	25.00	11.00
MT 9	1994 $5 Widgeon	25.00	10.00
MT 10	1995 $5 Tundra Swans	25.00	10.00
MT 11	1996 $5 Canvasbacks	25.00	10.00
MT 12	1997 $5 Golden Retriever	26.00	13.00
MT 13	1998 $5 Gadwalls	20.00	10.00
MT 14	1999 $5 Goldeneyes	20.00	10.00
MT 15	2000 $5 Mallard Decoy	22.00	11.00
MT 16	2001 $5 Canada Geese/ Steamboat	20.00	10.00
MT 17	2002 $5 Sandhill Crane	...	10.00
MT 18	2003 $5 Mallards	...	10.00
Montana Set 1986-2002 (17)		...	**189.00**

NOTE: Governor's stamps available upon request.

NEBRASKA

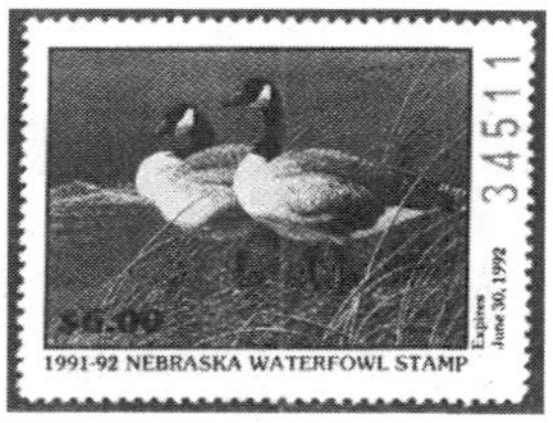

NE 1

No.	Description	F-VF NH
NE 1	1991 $6 Canada Goose	13.00
NE 2	1992 $6 Pintails	12.00
NE 3	1993 $6 Canvasbacks	12.00
NE 4	1994 $6 Mallard	12.00
NE 5	1995 $6 Wood Ducks	12.00
Nebraska Set 1991-95 (5)		**58.00**

NOTE: Governor's stamps available upon request.

Note: Hunting Permit color Illustrations can be found at the following website:
www.duckstamps.com

NEVADA

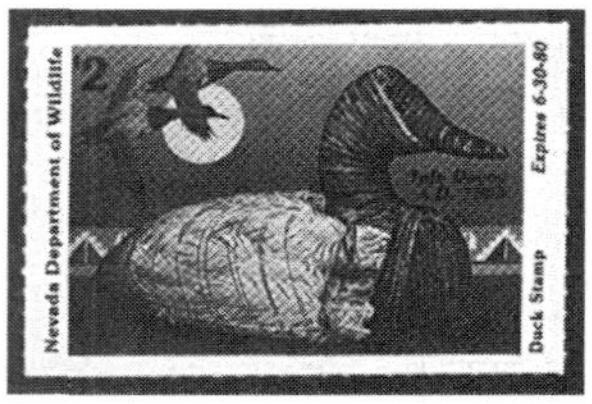

NV1

No.	Description	(T) Serial # Tab Attached	F-VF NH
NV1	1979 $2 Canvasbacks/Decoy	70.00	60.00
NV 2	1980 $2 Cinnamon Teal	10.00	9.00
NV 3	1981 $2 Whistling Swans	13.00	11.00
NV 4	1982 $2 Shovelers	13.00	11.00
NV 5	1983 $2 Gadwalls	14.00	12.00
NV 6	1984 $2 Pintails	14.00	12.00
NV 7	1985 $2 Canada Geese	22.00	20.00
NV 8	1986 $2 Redheads	17.00	16.00
NV 9	1987 $2 Buffleheads	16.00	14.00
NV 10	1988 $2 Canvasback	16.00	14.00
NV 11	1989 $2 Ross' Geese	12.00	11.00
NV 11A	1989 Hunter Tab#50,001-75,000	25.00	...
NV 12	1990 $5 Green Winged Teal	13.00	11.00
NV 12A	1990 Hunter Tab #50,001-75,000	20.00	...
NV 13	1991 $5 White Faced Ibis	13.00	12.00
NV 13A	1991 Hunter Tab #50,001-75,000	15.00	...
NV 14	1992 $5 American Widgeon	11.00	10.00
NV 14A	1992 Hunter Tab#50,001-75,000	14.00	...
NV 15	1993 $5 Common Goldeneye	11.00	10.00
NV 15A	1993 Hunter Tab#50,001-75,000	11.00	...
NV 16	1994 $5 Mallard	14.00	12.00
NV 16A	1994 Hunter Tab#50,001-75,000	11.00	...
NV 17	1995 $5 Wood Ducks	14.00	12.00
NV17A	1995 Hunter Tab#40,001-75,000	11.00	...
NV 18	1996 $5 Ring Necked Duck	14.00	12.00
NV 18A	1996 Hunter Tab#40,001-75,000	11.00	...
NV 19	1997 $5 Ruddy Duck	11.00	10.00
NV 19A	1997 Hunter Tab#40,001-75,000	11.00	...
NV 20	1998 $5 Hooded Merganser	11.00	10.00
NV 20A	1998 Hunter Tab#40,001-75,000	11.00	...
NV 21	1999 $5 Tule Decoy	11.00	10.00
NV 21A	1999 Hunter Tab#40,001-75,000	11.00	...
NV 22	2000 $5 Canvasback	11.00	10.00
NV 22A	2000 Hunter Tab#40,001-75,000	11.00	...
NV 23	2001 $5 Lesser Scaup	11.00	10.00
NV23A	2001 Hunter Tab #40,001-75,000	11.00	...
NV 24	2002 $5 Cinnamon Teal	11.00	10.00
NV 24A	2002 Hunter Tab #40,001-75,000	11.00	...
NV 25	2003 $5 Green Winged Teal	11.00	10.00
NV 25A	2003 Hunter Tab #40,001-75,000	11.00	...
NV 26	2004 $5 Redhead	11.00	10.00
NV 26A	2004 Hunter Tab #40,001-75,000	11.00	...
Nevada Set 1979-2002 (24)		**355.00**	**320.00**

NEW HAMPSHIRE

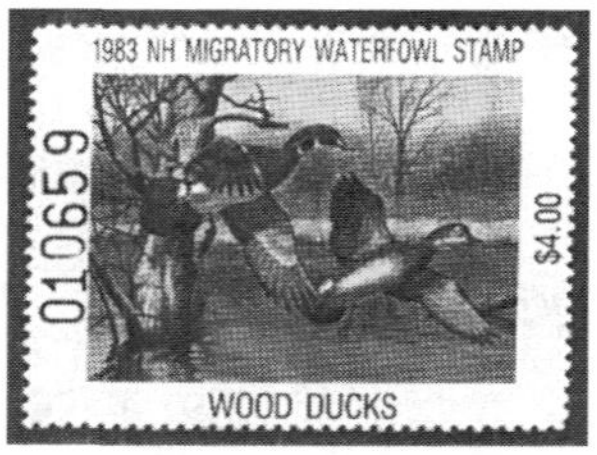

NH 1

No.	Description	(A) 3 Part Booklet Type	F-VF NH
NH 1	1983 $4 Wood Ducks	170.00	160.00
NH 2	1984 $4 Mallards	220.00	140.00
NH 3	1985 $4 Blue Winged Teal	125.00	115.00
NH 4	1986 $4 Mergansers	34.00	28.00
NH 5	1987 $4 Canada Geese	17.00	18.00
NH 6	1988 $4 Buffleheads	14.00	10.00
NH 7	1989 $4 Black Ducks	14.00	10.00
NH 8	1990 $4 Green Winged Teal	10.00	9.00
NH 9	1991 $4 Golden Retriever/Mallard	18.00	18.00
NH 10	1992 $4 Ring Necked Ducks	10.00	9.00
NH 11	1993 $4 Hooded Merganser	9.00	9.00
NH 12	1994 $4 Common Goldeneyes	9.00	9.00
NH 13	1995 $4 Pintails	9.00	9.00
NH 14	1996 $4 Surf Scoters	9.00	9.00
NH 15	1997 $4 Old Squaws	9.00	9.00
NH 16	1998 $4 Canada Goose	9.00	9.00
NH 17	1999 $4 Mallards	9.00	9.00
NH 18	2000 $4 Black Ducks	9.00	9.00
NH 19	2001 $4 Blue Winged Teal	9.00	9.00
NH 20	2002 $4 Pintails	9.00	9.00
NH 21	2003 $4 Wood Ducks	8.00	8.00
NH 22	2004 $4	8.00	8.00
New Hampshire Set 1983-2002 (20)		**6799.00**	**570.00**

NOTE: Governor's stamps available upon request.

STATE HUNTING PERMIT STAMPS

NEW JERSEY

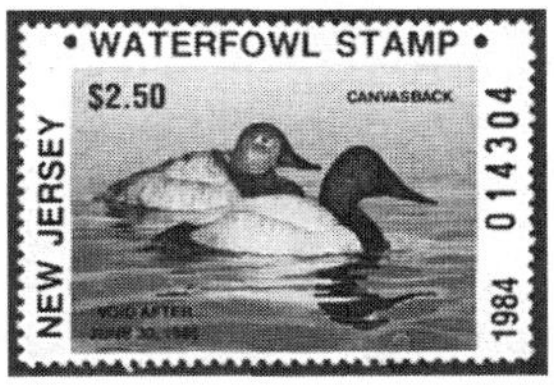

NJ 1

No.	Description	(B) Hunter Booklet Single	F-VF NH
NJ 1	1984 $2.50 Canvasbacks	75.00	55.00
NJ 1A	1984 $5.00 Non-Resident	...	67.00
NJ 2	1985 $2.50 Mallards	35.00	18.00
NJ 2A	1985 $5.00 Non-Resident	...	22.00
NJ 3	1986 $2.50 Pintails	15.00	15.00
NJ 3A	1986 $5.00 Non-Resident	...	17.00
NJ 4	1987 $2.50 Canada Geese	16.00	20.00
NJ 4A	1987 $5.00 Non-Resident	16.00	20.00
NJ 5	1988 $2.50 Green Winged Teal	12.00	10.00
NJ 5A	1988 $5.00 Non-Resident	14.00	12.00
NJ 6	1989 $2.50 Snow Geese	10.00	12.00
NJ 6A	1989 $5.00 Non-Resident	12.00	12.00
NJ 7	1990 $2.50 Wood Ducks	9.00	9.00
NJ 7A	1990 $5.00 Non-Resident	11.00	11.00
NJ 8	1991 $2.50 Atlantic "Brandt"	9.00	9.00
NJ 8A	1991 $5.00 Non-Resident	11.00	11.00
NJ 8V	1991 $2.50 Atlantic"Brandt"	...	26.00
NJ 8AV	1991 $5.00 Atlantic"Brandt"	...	40.00
NJ 9	1992 $2.50 Bluebills	10.00	10.00
NJ 9A	1992 $5.00 Non-Resident	11.00	10.00
NJ 10	1993 $2.50 Buffleheads	10.00	10.00
NJ 10A	1993 $5.00 Non-Resident	11.00	10.00
NJ 10M	1993 $2.50 Mini Sheet	...	35.00
NJ 10AM	1993 $5 Mini Sheet	...	45.00
NJ 11	1994 $2.50 Black Ducks	10.00	10.00
NJ 11A	1994 $5.00 Black Ducks	11.00	10.00
NJ 12	1995 $2.50 Widgeon	10.00	10.00
NJ 12A	1995 $5 Widgeon	10.00	10.00
NJ 13V	1996 $2.50 Goldeneyes NR	8.00	...
NJ 13	1996 $5.00 Goldeneyes	10.00	10.00
NJ 13A	1996 $10 Non Resident	15.00	18.00
NJ 14	1997 $5 Old Squaws	10.00	10.00
NJ 14A	1997 $10 Non Resident	18.00	18.00
NJ 15	1998 $5 Mallards	10.00	10.00
NJ 15A	1998 $10 Non Resident	18.00	18.00
NJ 16	1999 $5 Redheads	10.00	10.00
NJ 16A	1999 $10 Non Resident	18.00	18.00
NJ 17	2000 $5 Canvasbacks	10.00	10.00
NJ 17A	2000 $10 Non Resident	18.00	18.00
NJ 17D	2000 Overprinted "Disabled"	...	12.00
NJ 18	2001 $5 Tundra Swans	10.00	10.00
NJ 18A	2001 $10 Non Resident	18.00	18.00
NJ 19	2002 $5 Wood Duck	10.00	10.00
NJ 19A	2002 $10 Non Resident	18.00	18.00
NJ 19D	2002 Overprinted "Disabled"	...	12.00
NJ 19E	2002 Handstamped "955V"	...	12.00
NJ 20	2003 $5 Pintails/Black Lab	10.00	10.00
NJ 20A	2003 $10 Non Resident	18.00	18.00
NJ 21	2004 $5	10.00	10.00
NJ 21	2004 $10 Non Resident	18.00	18.00
New Jersey Set 1984-2002 (41)		**...**	**639.00**
NJ Bklt. Type Set 1984-2002 (35)		**470.00**	**...**

NOTE: Governor's stamps available upon request.

NEW MEXICO

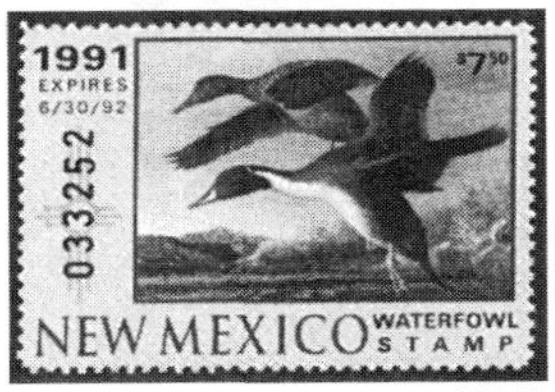

NM 1

No.	Description	(A) Hunter Booklet Single	F-VF NH
NM 1	1991 $7.50 Pintails	15.00	15.00
NM 2	1992 $7.50 American Widgeon	15.00	14.00
NM 3	1993 $7.50 Mallards	15.00	14.00
NM 3M	1993 Commemorative Sheet of 4	...	70.00
NM 3MI	1993 Imperf. Commem.Sht of 4	...	100.00
NM 4	1994 $7.50 Green Winged Teal	20.00	20.00
NM 4	1994 Block of 4 Different	...	80.00
NM 4A	1994 Strip of 4 Different attd	80.00	...
NM 4M	1994 Commemorative Sheet of 4	...	160.00
NM 4MI	1994 Imperf. Commem.Sht of 4	...	275.00
New Mexico Set 1991-94 (7)		**119.00**	**117.00**

NOTE: Governor's stamps available upon request.

NEW YORK

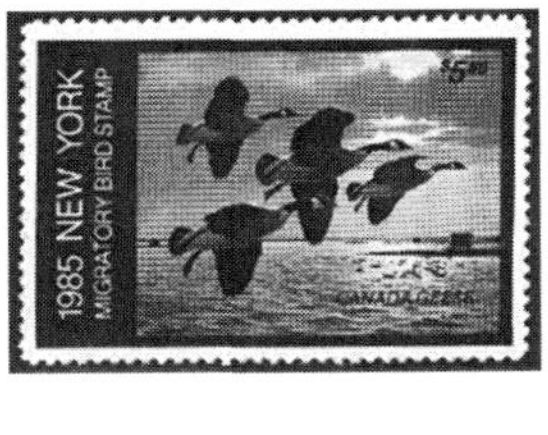

NY 1

NEW YORK (continued)

No.	Description	F-VF NH
NY 1	1985 $5.50 Canada Geese	17.00
NY 2	1986 $5.50 Mallards	10.00
NY 3	1987 $5.50 Wood Ducks	10.00
NY 4	1988 $5.50 Pintails	10.00
NY 5	1989 $5.50 Greater Scaup	10.00
NY 6	1990 $5.50 Canvasbacks	10.00
NY 7	1991 $5.50 Redheads	10.00
NY 8	1992 $5.50 Wood Duck	10.00
NY 9	1993 $5.50 Blue Winged Teal	10.00
NY 10	1994 $5.50 Canada Geese	11.00
NY 11	1995 $5.50 Canada Geese	11.00
NY 12	1996 $5.50 Common Loon	10.00
NY 13	1997 $5.50 Hooded Merganser	10.00
NY 14	1998 $5.50 Osprey	10.00
NY 15	1999 $5.50 Buffleheads	10.00
NY 16	2000 $5.50 Wood Duck	10.00
NY 17	2001 $5.50 Pintails	10.00
NY 18	2002 $5.50 Canvasbacks	10.00
New York Set 1985-2002(18)		**178.00**

NORTH CAROLINA

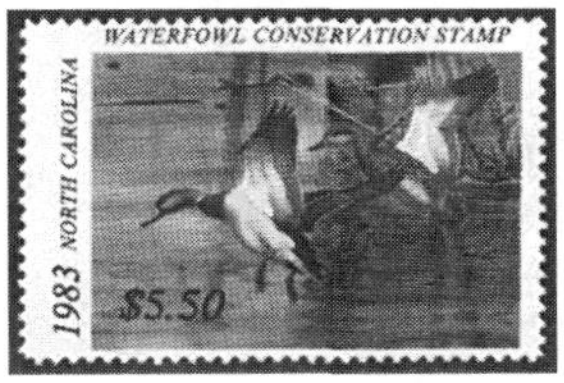

NC 1

No.	Description	(B) Self Adhesive	F-VF NH
NC 1	1983 $5.50 Mallards	...	80.00
NC 2	1984 $5.50 Wood Ducks	...	55.00
NC 3	1985 $5.50 Canvasbacks	...	30.00
NC 4	1986 $5.50 Canada Geese	...	23.00
NC 5	1987 $5.50 Pintails	...	18.00
NC 6	1988 $5 Green Winged Teal	...	12.00
NC 7	1989 $5 Snow Geese/Lighthouse	...	15.00
NC 8	1990 $5 Redheads/Lighthouse	...	15.00
NC 9	1991 $5 Blue Winged Teal/ Lighthouse		15.00
NC 10	1992 $5 American Widgeon/ Lighthouse		15.00
NC 11	1993 $5 Tundra Swan/Lighthouse	...	15.00
NC 12	1994 $5 Buffleheads/Lighthouse	...	15.00
NC 13	1995 $5 Brant/Lighthouse	...	15.00
NC 14	1996 $5 Pintails	...	10.00
NC 15	1997 $5 Wood Ducks	32.00	10.00
NC 16	1998 $5 Canada Geese	20.00	10.00
NC 17	1999 $5 Green Winged Teal	15.00	10.00
NC 18	2000 $10 Canvasbacks	18.00	18.00
NC 19	2001 $10 Black Duck/Lighthouse	18.00	18.00
NC 20	2002 $10 Pintails	18.00	18.00
NC 21	2003 $10 Ring Necked Duck	18.00	18.00
NC 22	2004 $10	18.00	18.00
North Carolina Set 1983-2002 (20)		**...**	**396.00**

NORTH DAKOTA

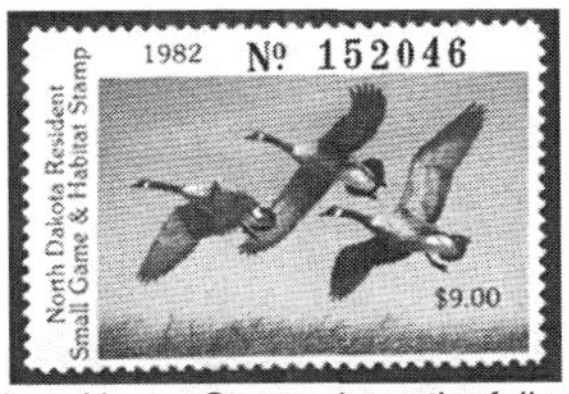

ND 1

North Dakota Hunter Stamps have the following serial #'s:1982-86 #20,001-150,000 1987-95 #20,001-140,000 1982-83 Hunter with Selvedge

No.	Description	(A) Hunter Type	F-VF NH
ND 1	1982 $9 Canada Geese	1750.00	160.00
ND 2	1983 $9 Mallards	3500.00	90.00
ND 3	1984 $9 Canvasbacks	3500.00	45.00
ND 4	1985 $9 Blue Bills	5000.00	25.00
ND 5	1986 $9 Pintails	900.00	22.00
ND 6	1987 $9 Snow Geese	66.00	22.00
ND 7	1988 $9 White Winged Scoter	40.00	15.00
ND 8	1989 $6 Redheads	19.00	14.00
ND 9	1990 $6 Black Labs/Mallards	20.00	18.00
ND 10	1991 $6 Green Winged Teal	16.00	12.50
ND 11	1992 $6 Blue Winged Teal	15.00	10.00
ND 12	1993 $6 Wood Ducks	12.00	10.00
ND 13	1994 $6 Canada Geese	13.00	10.00
ND 14	1995 $6 Widgeon	13.00	10.00
ND 15	1996 $6 Mallards	13.00	10.00
ND 16	1997 $6 White Fronted Geese	13.00	10.00
ND 17	1998 $6 Blue Winged Teal	13.00	10.00
ND 18	1999 $6 Gadwall	13.00	10.00
ND 19	2000 $6 Pintails	13.00	10.00
ND 20	2001 $6 Canada Geese	13.00	10.00
ND 21	2002 $6 Small Game (Text)	...	11.00
ND 22	2003 $6 Small Game (Text)	...	10.00
ND 23	2004 $6 Small Game (Text)	...	10.00
North Dakota Set 1982-2002 (21)		**...**	**507.00**

OHIO

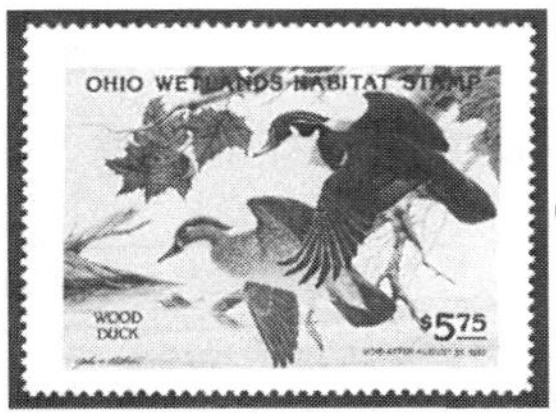

OH 1

No.	Description	F-VF NH
OH 1	1982 $5.75 Wood Ducks	85.00
OH 2	1983 $5.75 Mallards	85.00
OH 3	1984 $5.75 Green Winged Teal	85.00
OH 4	1985 $5.75 Redheads	39.00
OH 5	1986 $5.75 Canvasbacks	33.00
OH 6	1987 $5.75 Blue Winged Teal	14.00
OH 7	1988 $5.75 Goldeneyes	14.00
OH 8	1989 $5.75 Canada Geese	14.00
OH 9	1990 $9 Black Ducks	17.00
OH 10	1991 $9 Lesser Scaup	17.00
OH 11	1992 $9 Wood Ducks	17.00
OH 12	1993 $9 Buffleheads	17.00
OH 13	1994 $11 Mallard	20.00
OH 14	1995 $11 Pintails	20.00
OH 15	1996 $11 Hooded Merganser	20.00
OH 16	1997 $11 Widgeons	20.00
OH 17	1998 $11 Gadwall	20.00
OH 18	1999 $11 Mallard Hen	20.00
OH 19	2000 $11 Buffleheads	20.00
OH 20	2001 $11 Canvasback	20.00
OH 21	2002 $11 Ringnecked Ducks	20.00
OH 22	2003 $11 Hooded Merganser	20.00
OH 23	2004	
Ohio Set 1982-2002 (21)		**575.00**

OKLAHOMA

OK 1

No.	Description	(T) Full Tab Attached	F-VF NH
OK 1	1980 $4 Pintails	...	72.50
OK 2	1981 $4 Canada Goose	...	28.00
OK 3	1982 $4 Green Winged Teal	...	12.00
OK 4	1983 $4 Wood Ducks	...	12.00
OK 5	1984 $4 Ring Necked Ducks	12.00	10.00
OK 6	1985 $4 Mallards	10.00	8.50
OK 7	1986 $4 Snow Geese	10.00	8.50
OK 8	1987 $4 Canvasbacks	10.00	8.50
OK 9	1988 $4 Widgeons	10.00	8.50
OK 9TV	1988 $4 Full Tab Serial #>30,000	24.00	...

No.	Description	(A) Hunter Type With Tab	F-VF NH
OK 10	1989 $4 Redheads	10.00	8.50
OK 11	1990 $4 Hooded Merganser	10.00	8.50
OK 12	1991 $4 Gadwalls	10.00	8.50
OK 13	1992 $4 Lesser Scaup	10.00	8.50
OK 14	1993 $4 White Fronted Geese	9.00	8.00
OK 15	1994 $4 Widgeon	8.00	8.00
OK 16	1995 $4 Ruddy Ducks	8.00	8.00
OK 17	1996 $4 Buffleheads	8.00	8.00
OK 18	1997 $4 Goldeneyes	8.00	8.00
OK 19	1998 $4 Shoveler	...	8.00
OK 20	1999 $4 Canvasbacks	...	8.00
OK 21	2000 $4 Pintail	...	8.00
OK 22	2001 $4 Canada Goose	...	8.00
OK 23	2002 $4 Green Winged Teal	...	8.00
OK 24	2003 $10 Wood Duck	...	15.00
OK 25	2004 $10	...	15.00
Oklahoma Set 1980-2002 (23)		**...**	**270.00**

NOTE: Governor's stamps available upon request.

OREGON

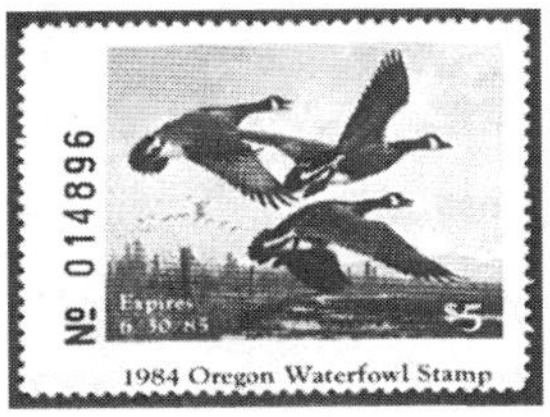

OR1

No.	Description	(A) Hunter Type With Tab	F-VF NH
OR 1	1984 $5 Canada Geese	...	30.00
OR 2	1985 $5 Snow Geese	725.00	42.00
OR 2A	1985 $5 Hunter without Tab	105.00	...
OR 3	1986 $5 Pacific Brant	20.00	17.00
OR 3A	1986 $5 Hunter without Tab	12.00	...

STATE HUNTING PERMIT STAMPS

OREGON (continued)

No.	Description	(A) Hunter Type With Tab	F-VF NH
OR 4	1987 $5 White Fronted Geese	16.00	13.00
OR 4A	1987 $5 Hunter without Tab ..	11.00	...
	1988-90 Hunter 89x197 mm 1992-94 216x152 mm		
OR 5	1988 $5 Great Basin Geese .	19.00	13.00
OR 6	1989 $5 Black Lab/Pintail	18.00	15.00
OR 6VB	1989 $5 Provisional Issue, Black Serial #	36.00	
OR 6VR	1989 $5 Provisional Issue, Red Serial #	14.00	
OR 7	1990 $5 Golden Retriever/Mallard	17.00	17.00
OR 8	1991 $5 Chesepeake Bay Retriever	17.00	17.00
OR 9	1992 $5 Green Winged Teal .	13.00	13.00
OR 10	1993 $5 Mallards	14.00	13.00
OR 10M	1993 Mini. Sheet of 2	...	30.00
OR 10MI	1993 Imperforate Mini Sheet of 2...		200.00
OR 11	1994 $5 Pintails	14.00	13.00
OR 11AN	1994 $25 Hunter Type	60.00	...
OR 12	1995 $5 Wood Ducks	16.00	16.00
OR 12AN	1995 $25 Hunter Booklet ..	80.00	...

No.	Description	(A) Hunter Type Booklet	F-VF NH
OR 13	1996 $5 Mallard/Widgeon/Pintail	18.00	18.00
OR 13AN	1996 $25 NR Hunter Booklet	80.00	...
OR 14	1997 $5 Canvasbacks	18.00	18.00
OR 14AN	1997 $25 NR Hunter Booklet	70.00	...
OR 15	1998 $5 Pintail	16.00	16.00
OR 15AN	1998 $25 NR Hunter Booklet	55.00	...
OR 16	1999 $5 Canada Geese	16.00	16.00
OR 16AN	1999 $25 NR Hunter Booklet	55.00	...

No.	Description	(A) Hunter Mini Sheet	F-VF NH
OR 17	2000 $7.50 Mallard	50.00	16.00
OR 18	2001 $7.50 Canvasbacks	20.00	16.00
OR 19	2002 $7.50 American Widgeon	16.00	16.00
OR 20	2003 $7.50 Wood Duck	16.00	16.00
OR 21	2004 $7.50 Ross' Geese	16.00	16.00
Oregon Set 1984-2002 (19)	....	**...**	**325.00**

NOTE: Governor's stamps available upon request.

PENNSYLVANIA

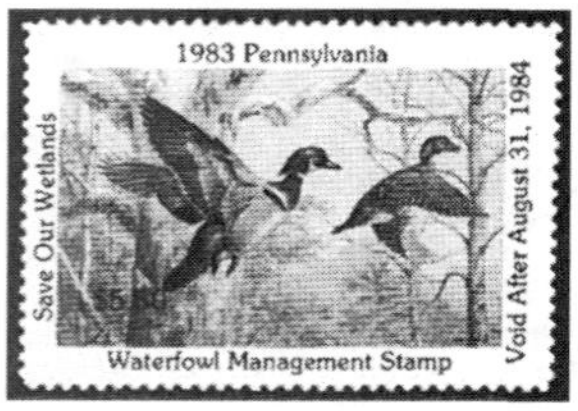

PA 1

No.	Description	F-VF NH
PA 1	1983 $5.50 Wood Ducks	18.00
PA 2	1984 $5.50 Canada Geese	18.00
PA 3	1985 $5.50 Mallards	12.00
PA 4	1986 $5.50 Blue Winged Teal	12.00
PA 5	1987 $5.50 Pintails	12.00
PA 6	1988 $5.50 Wood Ducks	12.00
PA 7	1989 $5.50 Hooded Merganser	12.00
PA 8	1990 $5.50 Canvasbacks	10.00
PA 9	1991 $5.50 Widgeon	10.00
PA 10	1992 $5.50 Canada Geese	10.00
PA 11	1993 $5.50 Northern Shovelers	10.00
PA 12	1994 $5.50 Pintails	10.00
PA 13	1995 $5.50 Buffleheads	10.00
PA 14	1996 $5.50 Black Ducks	10.00
PA 15	1997 $5.50 Hooded Merganser	10.00
PA 16	1998 $5.50 Wood Ducks	10.00
PA 17	1999 $5.50 Ring Necked Duck	10.00
PA 18	2000 $5.50 Green Winged Teal	10.00
PA 19	2001 $5.50 Pintails	10.00
PA 20	2002 $5.50 Snow Goose	10.00
PA 21	2003 $5.50 Canvasbacks	10.00
PA 22	2004 $5.50 Hooded Merganser	10.00
Pennsylvania Set '83-2002 (20)	....	**205.00**

RHODE ISLAND

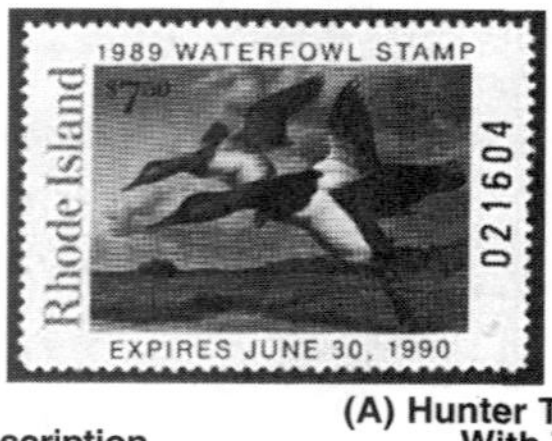

RI 1

No.	Description	(A) Hunter Type With Tab	F-VF NH
RI 1	1989 $7.50 Canvasbacks	20.00	14.00
RI 2	1990 $7.50 Canada Geese ...	17.00	14.00
RI 3	1991 $7.50 Black Lab/ Wood Ducks	19.00	17.00
RI 4	1992 $7.50 Blue Winged Teal	14.00	14.00
RI 5	1993 $7.50 Pintails	14.00	14.00
RI 5M	1993 Commemorative Sheet of 4	...	70.00
RI 5MI	1993 Imperf. Commem. Sht of 4	...	100.00
RI 6	1994 $7.50 Wood Duck	14.00	14.00
RI 7	1995 $7.50 Hooded Merganser	14.00	14.00
RI 8	1996 $7.50 Harlequin	14.00	14.00
RI 9	1997 $7.50 Greater Scaup ...	14.00	14.00
RI 10	1998 $7.50 Black Ducks	14.00	14.00

RHODE ISLAND (continued)

No.	Description	(A) Hunter Type	F-VF NH
RI 11	1999 $7.50 Common Eider & Lighthouse	20.00	15.00
RI 11A	1999 $7.50 Hunter Pair	50.00	...
RI 12	2000 $7.50 Canvasback & Lighthouse	18.00	14.00
RI 12A	2000 $7.50 Hunter Pair	40.00	...
RI 13	2001 $7.50 Mallard	15.00	14.00
RI 13A	2001 $7.50 Hunter Pair	30.00	...
RI 14	2002 $7.50 Winged Scoter	15.00	14.00
RI 14A	2002 $7.50 Hunter Pair	30.00	...
RI 15	2003 $7.50 Old Squaw/ Peregrine Falcon	15.00	14.00
RI 15A	2003 $7.50 Hunter Pair	30.00	...
RI 16	2004		14.00
RI 16A	2004 $7.50 Hunter Pair	30.00	...
Rhode Island Set 1989-2002(14) ..		**195.00**	**190.00**

NOTE: Governor's stamps available upon request.

SOUTH CAROLINA

SC 1

No.	Description	(A) Hunter Serial Number On Reverse	F-VF NH
SC 1	1981 $5.50 Wood Ducks	...	70.00
SC 2	1982 $5.50 Mallards	625.00	115.00
SC 3	1983 $5.50 Pintails	575.00	115.00
SC 4	1984 $5.50 Canada Geese ...	260.00	75.00
SC 5	1985 $5.50 Green Winged Teal	150.00	75.00
SC 6	1986 $5.50 Canvasbacks	50.00	28.00
SC 7	1987 $5.50 Black Ducks	28.00	22.00
SC 8	1988 $5.50 Spaniel/Widgeon	45.00	25.00
SC 9	1989 $5.50 Blue Winged Teal	17.00	11.00
SC 10	1990 $5.50 Wood Ducks	11.00	11.00
SC 11	1991 $5.50 Black Lab/Pintails	12.00	12.00

No.	Description	(A) Hunter Serial Number On Front	F-VF NH
SC 12	1992 $5.50 Buffleheads	17.00	17.00
SC 13	1993 $5.50 Lesser Scaup	17.00	17.00
SC 14	1994 $5.50 Canvasbacks	17.00	17.00
SC 15	1995 $5.50 Shovelers	17.00	17.00
SC 16	1996 $5.50 Redheads/Lightouse	17.00	17.00
SC 17	1997 $5.50 Old Squaws	17.00	17.00
SC 18	1998 $5.50 Ruddy Ducks	17.00	17.00
SC 19	1999 $5.50 Goldeneyes/Light house...		17.00
SC 20	2000 $5.50 Wood Duck/Dog	...	13.00
SC 21	2001 $5.50 Mallard/Decoy/ Dog	...	13.00
SC 22	2002 $5.50 Widgeon/ Chocolate Lab...		12.00
SC23	2003 $5.50 Green Winged Teal .	...	12.00
So. Carolina Set 1981-2002(22) ...		**...**	**695.00**
SC Hunter Type Set 1982-98 (17) ..		**1795.00**	**...**

NOTE: Governor's stamps available upon request.

SOUTH DAKOTA

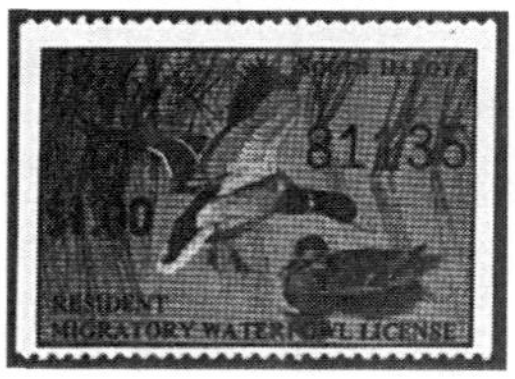

SD 1

No.	Description	(A) Complete Sheet	F-VF NH
SD 1	1976 $1 Mallards	...	40.00
SD 1V	1976 Small Serial # Variety ..	...	90.00
SD 2	1977 $1 Pintails	...	30.00
SD 3	1978 $1 Canvasbacks	...	18.00
SD 4	1986 $2 Canada Geese	...	11.00
SD 5	1987 $2 Blue Geese	...	9.00
SD 6	1988 $2 White Fronted Geese	...	7.00
SD 7	1989 $2 Mallards	...	7.00
SD 8	1990 $2 Blue Winged Teal	...	6.00
SD 9	1991 $2 Pintails	...	6.00
SD 10	1992 $2 Canvasbacks	...	6.00
SD 11	1993 $2 Lesser Scaup	...	6.00
SD 12	1994 $2 Redhead	...	6.00
SD 13	1995 $2 Wood Ducks	...	6.00
SD 14	1996 $2 Canada Goose	...	6.00
SD 15	1997 $2 Widgeons	...	6.00
SD 16	1998 $2 Green Winged Teal .	...	6.00
SD 17	1999 $3 Tundra Swan	...	7.00
SD 18	2000 $3 Buffleheads	12.00	7.00
SD 19	2001 $3 Mallards	12.00	7.00
SD 20	2002 $3 Canvasbacks	12.00	7.00
SD 21	2003 $3 Pintail	11.00	7.00
SD 22	2004 $3 Migratory Bird	10.00	7.00
South Dakota Set 1976-2002 (20) .		**...**	**193.00**

TENNESSEE

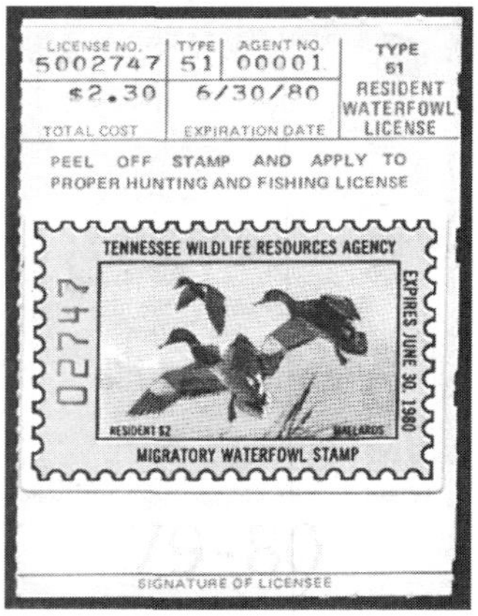

TN 1

No.	Description	(B) 3-Part Card	F-VF NH
TN 1	1979 $2.30 Mallards	...	160.00
TN 1A	1979 $5.30 Non-Resident	...	1100.00
TN 2	1980 $2.30 Canvasbacks	925.00	65.00
TN 2A	1980 $5.30 Non-Resident	...	450.00
TN 3	1981 $2.30 Wood Ducks	..	50.00
TN 4	1982 $6.50 Canada Geese ...	...	65.00
TN 5	1983 $6.50 Pintails	85.00	65.00
TN 6	1984 $6.50 Black Ducks	85.00	65.00
TN 7	1985 $6.50 Bl. Winged Teal ..	60.00	30.00
TN 8	1986 $6.50 Mallards	55.00	17.00
TN 9	1987 $6.50 Canada Geese ...	20.00	14.00
TN 10	1988 $6.50 Canvasbacks	25.00	16.00
TN 11	1989 $6.50 Green Winged Teal	16.00	14.00
TN 12	1990 $13 Redheads	25.00	22.00
TN 13	1991 $13 Mergansers	25.00	22.00
TN 14	1992 $14 Wood Ducks	26.00	23.00
TN 15	1993 $14 Pintail/Decoy	26.00	23.00
TN 16	1994 $16 Mallard	28.00	26.00
TN 17	1995 $16 Ring Necked Ducks	28.00	26.00
TN 18	1996 $18 Black Ducks	31.00	30.00
TN 19	1999 $10 Mallard	...	18.00
TN 20	2000 $10 Bufflehead	...	18.00
TN 21	2001 $10 Wood Ducks	...	18.00
TN 22	2002 $10 Green WingedTeal .	...	18.00
TN 23	2003 $10 Canada Geese	...	18.00
TN 24	2004 $10 Wood Ducks	...	18.00
Tennessee Set 1979-2002 (24)		**...**	**2235.00**
Tennessee Set 1979-2002 (22) without Non-Resident		**...**	**765.00**

TEXAS

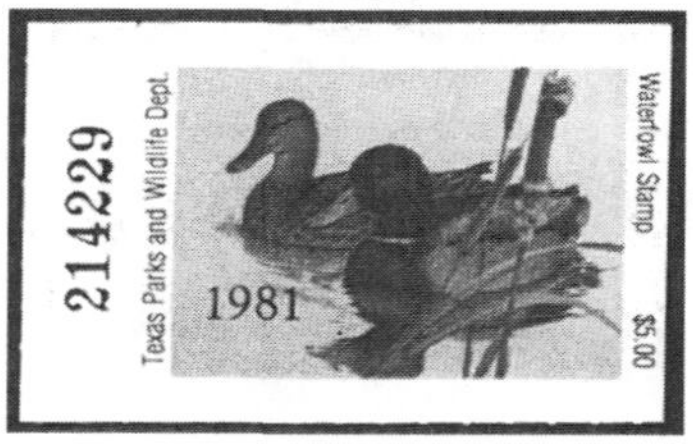

TX 1

No.	Description	(A) Book of 8 Different	F-VF NH
TX 1	1981 $5 Mallards	...	50.00
TX 2	1982 $5 Pintails	...	30.00
TX 3	1983 $5 Widgeon	...	175.00
TX 4	1984 $5 Wood Ducks	...	35.00
TX 5	1985 $5 Snow Geese	...	11.00
TX 6	1986 $5 Green Winged Teal .	...	11.00
TX 7	1987 $5 White Fronted Geese	...	11.00
TX 8	1988 $5 Pintails	...	11.00
TX 9	1989 $5 Mallards	...	11.00
TX 10	1990 $5 Widgeons	...	11.00
TX 11	1991 $7 Wood Duck	...	13.00
TX 12	1992 $7 Canada Geese	...	13.00
TX 13	1993 $7 Blue Winged Teal	...	13.00
TX 14	1994 $7 Shovelers	...	13.00
TX 15	1995 $7 Buffleheads	...	13.00
TX 16	1996 $3 Gadwall	80.00	65.00
TX 17	1997 $3 Cinnamon Teal	60.00	55.00
TX 18	1998 $3 Pintail/Black Lab	55.00	50.00
TX 19	1999 $3 Canvasback	45.00	35.00
TX 20	2000 $3 Hooded Merganser .	35.00	30.00
TX 21	2001 $3Snow Goose	25.00	20.00
TX 22	2002 $3Redhead	25.00	25.00
TX 23	2003 $3Mottled Duck	25.00	25.00
TX 24	2004 $3	25.00	20.00
Texas Set 1981-1995 (15)		**...**	**400.00**

STATE HUNTING PERMIT STAMPS

UTAH

UT 1

No.		Description	(A) Booklet Sgl. with Tab	F-VF NH
UT 1	1986	$3.30 Whistling Swans	...	12.00
UT 2	1987	$3.30 Pintails	...	10.00
UT 3	1988	$3.30 Mallards	...	9.00
UT 4	1989	$3.30 Canada Geese	...	8.00
UT 5	1990	$3.30 Canvasbacks	9.00	8.00
UT 6	1991	$3.30 Tundra Swans	9.00	8.00
UT 7	1992	$3.30 Pintails	9.00	8.00
UT 8	1993	$3.30 Canvasbacks	9.00	8.00
UT 9	1994	$3.30 Chesepeake	95.00	95.00
UT 10	1995	$3.30 Green Winged Teal	9.00	8.00
UT 11	1996	$7.50 White Fronted Goose	...	15.00
UT 12	1997	$7.50 Redheads Pair (2)	...	40.00

Utah Set 1986-97 (13) 217.00
Utah Set Booklet Single 1990-95 (6) 133.00 ...
NOTE: Governor's stamps available upon request.

VERMONT

VT 1

No.		Description	F-VF NH
VT 1	1986	$5 Autumn Wood Ducks	13.00
VT 2	1987	$5 Winter Goldeneyes	10.00
VT 3	1988	$5 Spring Black Ducks	10.00
VT 4	1989	$5 Summer Canada Geese	10.00
VT 5	1990	$5 Green Winged Teal	10.00
VT 6	1991	$5 Hooded Merganser	10.00
VT 7	1992	$5 Snow Geese	10.00
VT 8	1993	$5 Mallards	10.00
VT 9	1994	$5 Ring Necked Duck	10.00
VT 10	1995	$5 Bufflehead	10.00
VT 11	1996	$5 Bluebills	10.00
VT 12	1997	$5 Pintail	10.00
VT 13	1998	$5 Blue Winged Teal	10.00
VT 14	1999	$5 Canvasbacks	10.00
VT 15	2000	$5 Widgeon	9.00
VT 16	2001	$5 Old Squaw	9.00
VT 17	2002	$5 Greater Scaup	9.00
VT 18	2003	$5 Mallard	9.00
VT 19	2004	$5	9.00

Vermont Set 1986-2002 (17) 162.00

VIRGINIA

VA 1

No.		Description	(A) Hunter Bklt.Single	F-VF NH
VA 1	1988	$5 Mallards	16.00	14.00
VA 1A	1988	$5 Horiz. pr./side margins	30.00	...
VA 2	1989	$5 Canada Geese	16.00	14.00
VA 2A	1989	$5 Horiz.pr./side margins	32.00	...
VA 3	1990	$5 Wood Ducks	14.00	14.00
VA 3A	1990	$5 Horiz.pr./side margins	28.00	...
VA 4	1991	$5 Canvasbacks	14.00	10.00
VA 4A	1991	$5 Horiz.pr./side margins	28.00	...
VA 5	1992	$5 Bufflehead	14.00	10.00
VA 5A	1992	$5 Horiz.pr./side margins	26.00	...
VA 6	1993	$5 Black Ducks	10.00	10.00
VA 6A	1993	$5 Horiz.pr./side margins	20.00	...
VA 7	1994	$5 Lesser Scaup	10.00	10.00
VA 7A	1994	$5 Horiz.pr./side margins	20.00	...
VA 8	1995	$5 Snow Geese	10.00	10.00
VA 8A	1995	$5 Horiz.pr./side margins	20.00	...
VA 9	1996	$5 Hooded Merganser	...	10.00
VA 10	1997	$5 Chocolate Lab/Pintail	...	14.00
VA 11	1998	$5 Mallards	...	10.00
VA 12	1999	$5 Green Winged Teal	...	10.00
VA 13	2000	$5 Mallards	...	10.00
VA 14	2001	$5 Blue Winged Teal	...	10.00
VA 15	2002	$5 Canvasbacks	...	10.00
VA 16	2003	$5 Whistling Swan	...	10.00
VA 17	2004	$5	...	10.00

Virginia Set 1988-2002 (15) 154.00
VA Hunter Pairs Set 1988-95 (8) .... 194.00 ...

WASHINGTON

WA 1

Hunter type 1986-97 77x82mm 1998-99 61x137 mm
2000 140x278 mm 2001-3 147x61 mm

No.		Description	(A) Hunter Type	F-VF NH
WA 1	1986	$5 Mallards	17.00	10.00
WA 2	1987	$5 Canvasbacks	12.00	17.00
WA 3	1988	$5 Harlequin	11.00	10.00
WA 4	1989	$5 American Widgeon	11.00	10.00
WA 5	1990	$5 Pintails/Sour Duck	11.00	10.00
WA 6	1991	$5 Wood Duck	11.00	10.00
WA 6V	1991	$6 Wood Duck	11.00	13.00
WA 6VN	1991	$6 Mini Sheet/No Staple Holes		49.00
WA 7	1992	$6 Puppy/Canada Geese	12.00	12.00
WA 7N	1992	$6 Mini Sheet/No Staple Holes		44.00
WA 8	1993	$6 Snow Geese		11.00
WA 8N	1993	$6 Mini Sheet/No Staple Holes		22.00
WA 9	1994	$6 Black Brant		11.00
WA 9N	1994	$6 Mini Sheet/No staple holes		22.00
WA 10	1995	$6 Mallards		12.00
WA 10N	1995	$6 Mini Sheet/No staple holes		19.00
WA 11	1996	$6 Redheads	16.00	17.00
WA 11N	1996	$6 Mini Sheet/No staple holes		20.00
WA 12	1997	$6 Canada Geese	12.00	12.00
WA 12N	1997	$6 Mini Sheet/No staple holes		20.00
WA 13	1998	$6 Goldeneye	12.00	12.00
WA 13N	1998	$6 Mini Sheet/No staple holes		17.00
WA 14	1999	$6 Buffleheads/Pintails	14.00	14.00
WA 14N	1999	$6 Mini Sheet/No staple holes		14.00
WA 15	2000	$6 Widgeon/Canada Goose	12.00	12.00
WA 15N	2000	$6 Mini Sheet/No staple holes		14.00
WA 16	2001	$6 Mallards	12.00	12.00
WA 17	2002	$10 Green Winged Teal	20.00	18.50
WA 18	2003	$10 Pintails	20.00	18.50
WA 19	2004	$10	20.00	18.50

Washington Set 1986-2002 (18) 192.00 193.00

WEST VIRGINIA

WV 1

No.		Description	(A) Non-Resident	F-VF NH
WV 1	1987	$5 Canada Geese	22.00	22.00
WV 1B	1987	$5 HunterBooklet Single	48.00	48.00
WV 2	1988	$5 Wood Ducks	14.00	14.00
WV 2B	1988	$5 Hunter Booklet Single	30.00	30.00
WV 3	1989	$5 Decoys	16.00	16.00
WV 3B	1989	$5 Hunter Booklet Single	16.00	16.00
WV 4	1990	$5 Lab/Decoys	18.00	18.00
WV 4B	1990	$5 Hunter Booklet Single	18.00	18.00
WV 5	1991	$5 Mallards	11.00	11.00
WV 5B	1991	$5 Hunter Booklet Single	13.00	13.00
WV 5S	1991	WV Ohio River Sheet of 6	...	60.00
WV 6	1992	$5 Canada Geese	11.00	11.00
WV 6B	1992	$5 Hunter Booklet Single	11.00	11.00
WV 7	1993	$5 Pintails	11.00	11.00
WV 7B	1993	$5 Hunter Booklet Single	11.00	11.00
WV 8	1994	$5 Green Winged Teal	11.00	11.00
WV 8B	1994	$5 Pintails-Hunter	11.00	11.00
WV 9	1995	$5 Wood Duck	11.00	11.00
WV 9B	1995	$5 Hunter Type	11.00	11.00
WV 10	1996	$5 American Widgeons	11.00	11.00
WV 10B	1996	$5 Hunter Type	11.00	11.00

West Virginia Set 1987-96 (20) 253.00
WV Hunter Type Set 1987-96 (20) 336.00
NOTE: Governor's stamps available upon request.

WISCONSIN

WI 1

No.		Description	(T) Full-Tab Attached	F-VF NH
WI 1	1978	$3.25 Wood Ducks	...	115.00
WI 2	1979	$3.25 Buffleheads	...	30.00
WI 3	1980	$3.25 Widgeon	...	15.00

WISCONSIN (continued)

No.		Description	(T) Full-Tab Attached	F-VF NH
WI 4	1981	$3.25 Lesser Scaup	...	11.00
WI 5	1982	$3.25 Pintails	11.00	9.00
WI 6	1983	$3.25 Blue Winged Teal	13.00	10.00
WI 7	1984	$3.25 Hooded Merganser	13.00	10.00
WI 8	1985	$3.25 Lesser Scaup	14.00	12.00
WI 9	1986	$3.25 Canvasbacks	13.00	11.00
WI 10	1987	$3.25 Canada Geese	9.00	8.00
WI 11	1988	$3.25 Hooded Merganser	9.00	8.00
WI 12	1989	$3.25 Common Goldeneye	9.00	8.00
WI 13	1990	$3.25 Redheads	9.00	8.00
WI 14	1991	$5.25 Green Winged Teal	11.00	10.00
WI 15	1992	$5.25 Tundra Swans	11.00	10.00
WI 16	1993	$5.25 Wood Ducks	11.00	10.00
WI 17	1994	$5.25 Pintails	11.00	10.00
WI 18	1995	$5.25 Mallards	11.00	10.00
WI 19	1996	$5.25 Green Winged Teal	11.00	10.00
WI 20	1997	$7 Canada Goose	13.00	12.00
WI 21	1998	$7 Snow Goose	13.00	12.00
WI 22	1999	$7 Greater Scaup	13.00	12.00
WI 23	2000	$7 Canvasbacks	13.00	12.00
WI 24	2001	$7 Common Goldeneye	13.00	12.00
WI 25	2002	$7 Northern Shoveler	...	12.00
WI 26	2003	$7 Ring Necked Duck	...	12.00
WI 27	2004	$7 Pintail	...	12.00

Wisconsin Set 1978-2002 (25) 380.00

WYOMING

WY1

No.		Description	F-VF NH
WY 1	1984	$5 Meadowlark	75.00
WY 2	1985	$5 Canada Geese	57.00
WY 3	1986	$5 Pronghorn Antelope	68.00
WY 4	1987	$5 Sage Grouse	72.50
WY 5	1988	$5 Cut-Throat Trout	110.00
WY 6	1989	$5 Mule Deer	170.00
WY 7	1990	$5 Grizzly Bear	55.00
WY 8	1991	$5 Big Horn Sheep	50.00
WY 9	1992	$5 Bald Eagle	27.50
WY 10	1993	$5 Elk	20.00
WY 11	1994	$5 Bobcat	18.00
WY 12	1995	$5 Moose	18.00
WY 13	1996	$5 Turkey	18.00
WY 14	1997	$5 Rocky Mountain Goats	18.00
WY 15	1998	$5 Trumpeter Swans	15.00
WY 16	1999	$5 Brown Trout	15.00
WY 17	2000	$5 Buffalo	15.00
WY 18	2001	$10 Whitetailed Deer	19.00
WY 19	2002	$10 River Otter	17.00
WY 20	2003	$10 Bluebirds	17.00
WY 21	2004	$10 Mountain Lion	17.00

NF 1

JR 2

NATIONAL FISH AND WILDLIFE

No.		Description	F-VF NH
NFW 1	1987	$5 Canada Goose	12.00
NFW 2	1988	$5 Mallards	12.00
NFW 3	1989	$5 Wood Ducks	15.00
NFW 4	1990	$7.50 Tundra Swans	17.00
NFW 5	1991	$7.50 Pintails	17.00
NFW 6	1992	$7.50 Snow Geese	17.00
NFW 7	1993-4	$7.50 Canvasbacks	17.00
NFW 8	1995	$7.50 Grn. Winged Teal	17.00
NFW 9	1996	$7.50 Pintails	17.00
NFW 10	1997	$7.50 Common Loon	17.00
NFW 11	1998	$7.50 Barrow's Goldeneyes	17.00

JUNIOR DUCKS

No.		Description	F-VF NH
JR 1	1992	$10 Sheet of 9	70.00
JR 2	1993	$5 Redhead	55.00
JR 3	1994	$5 Hooded Merganser	55.00
JR 4	1995	$5 Pintail	50.00
JR 5	1996	$5 Canvasback	50.00
JR 6	1997	$5 Canada Goose	60.00
JR 7	1998	$5 Black Ducks	110.00
JR 8	1999	$5 Wood Ducks	110.00
JR 9	2000	$5 Northern Pintails	100.00
JR 10	2001	$5 Trumpeter Swan	30.00
JR 11	2002	$5 Mallard	20.00
JR 12	2003	$5 Green Winged Teal	12.00
JR 13	2004	$5 Fulvous Whistling Duck	10.00

INDIAN RESERVATION STAMPS

ARIZONA

NAVAJO

No.	Description	F-VF NH
NA 1	1991 Habitat	75.00
NA 2	1992 Habitat	14.00
NA 3	1993 Habitat	14.00
NA 4	1994 Habitat	11.00
NA 5	1995 Habitat	11.00
NA 6	1996 Habitat	14.00
NA 6A	1996 2nd Printing	18.00
NA 7	1997 Habitat	11.00

MONTANA

CROW

CW 2	1992 Upland Game	65.00
CW 2v	1993 Upland, undated	14.00
CW 3	1992 Waterfowl	120.00
CW 3v	1993 Waterfowl, undated	17.00

FLATHEAD

FH 1	1987 Bird	1700.00
FH 3	1988 Bird/Fish	2200.00
FH 4	1989 Bird/Fish Pr w/Duplicate	20.00
FH 5	1989 Shiny Paper	60.00
FH 7	1990 Shiny Paper	600.00
FH 8	1990 Bird/Fish "Fasson" Backing	45.00
FH 9	1990 Bird/Fish Pr w/Duplicate	20.00
FH 10	1991 Joint Bird	12.00
FH 12	1992 Bird Annual	11.00
FH 13	1992 Bird 3-Day	10.00
FH 16	1993 Bird Annual	10.00
FH 17	1993 Bird 3-Day	10.00
FH 20	1994 Bird Annual	10.00
FH 21	1994 Bird 3-Day	9.00
FH 24	1995 Bird Resident	11.00
FH 25	1995 Bird Non-Resident	17.00
FH 28	1996 Bird Resident	13.00
FH 29	1996 Bird Non-Resident	18.00
FH 33	1997 Bird Resident	13.00
FH 34	1997 Bird Non-Resident	18.00
FH 38	1998 Bird Resident	13.00
FH 39	1998 Bird Non-Resident	16.00
FH 43	1999 Bird Resident	13.00
FH 44	1999 Bird Non-Resident	13.00
FH 48	2000 Bird Resident	13.00
FH 49	2000 Bird Non-Resident	13.00

FORT BELKNAP

No.	Description	F-VF NH
FB 4	1996 Waterfowl	55.00
FB 8	1997 Waterfowl	55.00
FB 11	1998 Waterfowl	45.00
FB 15	1999 Waterfowl	100.00
FB 18	2000 Waterfowl	170.00
FB 21	2001 Waterfowl	...

FORT PECK

FP 3	1975 Bird	1750.00
FP 5	1976 Bird	110.00
FP 9	1978 Bird	375.00
FP 14	1988 $25 Upland Game (yellow)	45.00
FP 15	1988 $50 Upland Game (yellow)	85.00
FP 16	1988 $10 Upland Game (yellow)	27.50
FP 16a	1988 $10 Plate Flaw	140.00
FP 17	1994 $40 Upland Game (yellow)	85.00
FP 18	1994 $15 Upland Game (drawing)	25.00
FP 19	1994 $45 Upland Game (drawing)	65.00
FP 20	1995 $45 Upland Game (white brown)	65.00
FP 25	1996 $25 Upland Game (blue)	27.50
FP 26	1996 $65 Upland Game (brown)	60.00
FP 27	1997 $10 Waterfowl (orange)	22.00
FP 28	1997 $40 Waterfowl (green)	35.00
FP 31	1997 $25 Upland (blue)	25.00
FP 32	1997 $40 Upland (plum)	45.00

NEW MEXICO

JICARILLA

JI 1	1988 Wildlife Stamp (White)	165.00
JI 2	1988 Wildlife Stamp	20.00
JI 14	1996 Wildlife over #9000	90.00
JI 15	1999 $10 Wildlife Blue Seal	100.00
JI 16	2000 $5 Tribal Wildlife (Black Seal)	70.00

ZUNI

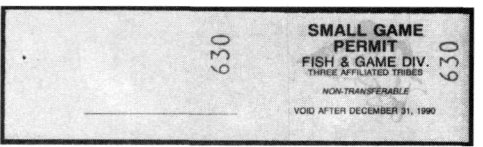

No.	Description	F-VF NH
ZU 1	1995 Habitat	25.00
ZU 2	1996 Habitat	20.00
ZU 3	1997 Habitat	17.00
ZU 4	1998 Habitat	17.00
ZU 5	1999 Habitat	17.00
ZU 6	2000 Habitat	17.00
ZU 7	2001 Habitat	24.00
ZU 8	2002 Habitat	30.00

NORTH DAKOTA

FORT BERTHOLD

TT 12	1990 Small Game	95.00
TT 14	1990 Upland Game	155.00
TT 15	1990 Waterfowl	3000.00
TT 19	1991 Small Game	90.00
TT 21	1991 Upland Game	115.00
TT 22	1991 Waterfowl	1200.00
TT 26	1992 Small Game	90.00
TT 28	1992 Upland Game	95.00
TT 33	1993 Small Game	185.00
TT 35	1993 Upland Game	95.00
TT 36	1993 Waterfowl	675.00
TT 39	1994 Small Game	75.00
TT 41	1994 Upland Game	95.00
TT 42	1994 Waterfowl(#1-60)	775.00
TT 45	1995 Small Game	100.00
TT 47	1995 Upland Bird (Pink)	95.00
TT 47A	1995 Upland Bird (Blue)	95.00
TT 48	1995 Waterfowl (#61-120)	325.00
TT 51	1996 Small Game	55.00
TT 53	1996 Upland Game	65.00
TT 54	1996 Waterfowl (#121-198)	275.00
TT 58	1997 Sand Hill Crane #1-30	1200.00
TT 59	1997 Small Game	55.00
TT 61	1997 Upland Game	55.00
TT 62	1997 Waterfowl (#199-276)	295.00
TT 68	1998 Sand Hil Crane #31-60	1200.00
TT 69	1998 Small Game	45.00
TT 71	1998 Upland Game	55.00
TT 72	1998 Waterfowl (#277-354)	360.00
TT 75	1999 Sand HIll Crane #61-90	1200.00
TT 76	1999 Small Game	40.00
TT 79	1999 Upland Game	50.00
TT 80	1999 Waterfowl (#355-432)	395.00
TT 84	2000 Small Game	40.00
TT 86	2000 Upland Game	150.00
TT 87	2000 Waterfowl (#433-588)	295.00
TT 87A	Printed on Gum	350.00
TT 91	2001 Small Game	40.00
TT 94	2001 Upland Game	175.00
TT 95	2001 Waterfowl (#589-744)	275.00
TT 98	2002 Small Game	35.00
TT 101	2002 Upland Game	225.00
TT 102	2002 Waterfowl (#745-900)	400.00
TT 105	2003 Small Game	...
TT 108	2003 Upland Game	50.00
TT 109	2003 Waterfowl (#901-1056)	400.00

INDIAN RESERVATION STAMPS

SPIRIT LAKE

No.	Description	F-VF NH
SL1-6	1996 set of 6	225.00
SL 7-12	1997 set of 6	175.00
SL13-18	1998 set of 6	175.00
SL19-25	1999 set of 7	160.00
SL 26-32	2000 set of 7	140.00
SL 33-39	2001 set of 7	115.00
SL 40-49	2001-2 set of 10 (color)	90.00
SL 50-59	2002 set of 10 (color)	85.00
SL 60-70	2003 set of 11 (color)	95.00

STANDING ROCK SIOUX TRIBE

SR 10	1992 Waterfowl	19.00
SR 20	1993 Waterfowl	13.00
SR 30	1994 Waterfowl	13.00
SR 39	1995 Waterfowl	17.00
SR 48	1996 Waterfowl	17.00
SR 57	1997 Waterfowl	17.00
SR 73	1998 Waterfowl	17.00
SR73a	1998 Waterfowl (Green backing)	55.00
SR 74	1998 Waterfowl (orange)	120.00
SR 94	1999 Waterfowl	13.00
SR 103	2000 Waterfowl	13.00
SR 116	2001 Waterfowl	13.00
SR 121	2002 Waterfowl	18.00

SOUTH DAKOTA

CHEYENNE RIVER SIOUX TRIBE

CR 2	1984-91 Birds&Small Game, Member	...
CR 7	1984-91 Same,Non-Member	...
CR 12	1989-94 Birds & Small Game Member, Shiny Paper	35.00
CR 18	Non-Member,Shiny Paper	55.00
CR 24	1989-94 Birds & Small Game Member	17.00
CR 34	Same, Non-Member	30.00
CR 32	1994 Waterfowl, Member	20.00
CR 42	1994 Same, Non-Member	30.00
CR 47	1997 Bird, Non-Member, Rouletted	...

CROW CREEK SIOUX TRIBE

No.	Description	F-VF NH
CC 27	1989 $10 Canada Geese Reservat.	650.00
CC 28	1989 $30 SD Resident	...
CC 29	1989 $65 Non-Resident	1750.00
CC 30	1990 $10 Canada Geese Reservat.	450.00
CC 31	1990 $30 SD Resident	400.00
CC 32	1990 $65 Non-Resident	1600.00
1989-1990 Sportsman Set (8 stamps)		
CC 33-40	**($770 Face Value)**	**4500.00**
1989-1990 Upland Game Set		
CC 15-20	**(6 stamps)**	**1150.00**
CC 61	1994 $5 Tribal Member	60.00
CC 62	1994 $15 Resident	90.00
CC 63	1994 $30 Non-Res. Daily	125.00
CC 64	1994 $75 Non-Resident	220.00
CC 91-94	1995 Set of 4	385.00
CC 121-124	1996 Set of 4	335.00
CC 152-155	1997 Set of 4	335.00
CC 170-72	1998 Spring Goose (3)	175.00
CC 187-90	1998 Set of 4	295.00

LAKE TRAVERSE INDIAN RESERVATION
(SISSETON-WAHPETON)

LT 5	1986 Game Bird	225.00
LT 9	1986 Upland Game	525.00
LT 24	1991 Small Game	55.00
LT 26	1991 Upland Bird	75.00
LT 27	1991 Waterfowl-Bright Green	140.00
LT 31	1992 Small Game-Orange	12.50
LT 32	1992 Small Game-Green	30.00
LT 34	1992 Upland Game	4.50
LT 35	1992 Wood Duck	17.00
LT 40	1993 Small Game	13.00
LT 42	1993 Upland Bird	13.00
LT 43	1993 Waterfowl-Bright Red	30.00
LT 52	1994 Small Game	7.00
LT 55	1994 Upland Bird	7.00
LT 56	1994 Waterfowl-Yellow Orange	11.00
LT 59	1995 Small Game	9.00
LT 62	1995 Waterfowl	13.00
LT 65	1996 Small Game	9.00
LT 67	1996 Upland Bird	8.00
LT 68	1996 Waterfowl	12.00
LT 71	1997 Small Game	9.00
LT 72	1997 Sportsman	50.00
LT 73	1997 Upland Bird	8.00
LT 74	1997 Waterfowl	11.00
LT 77	1998 Small Game	8.00
LT 78	1998 Sportsman	45.00
LT 79	1998 Upland Bird	6.00
LT 80	1998 Waterfowl	48.00
LT 85	1999 Sportsman	11.00
LT 86	1999 Upland Bird	7.00
LT 87	1999 Waterfowl	11.00
LT 91	2000 Sportsman	11.00
LT 92	2000 Upland Game	11.00
LT 93	2000 Waterfowl	45.00
LT 96	2001 Small Game	75.00
LT 97	2001 Sportsman	125.00
LT 98	2001 Upland Game	11.00
LT 99	2001 Waterfowl	11.00
LT 102	2002 Small Game	11.00
LT 103	2002 Sportsman	11.00
LT 104	2002 Upland Game	11.00
LT 105	2002 Waterfowl	11.00

LOWER BRULE

No.	Description	F-VF NH
LB 26-30	1995 Set of 5 Waterfowl	55.00
LB 31-33	1996 Set of 3 Waterfowl	40.00
LB 34-36	1997 Set of 3 Waterfowl	40.00
LB 37-39	1998 Set of 3 Waterfowl	40.00
LB 40-42	1999 Set of 3 Waterfowl	40.00

PINE RIDGE (OGLALA SIOUX)

PR 11	1988-92 $4 Waterfowl, Rouletted	400.00
PR 30	1988-92 $4 Waterfowl, Perforated	30.00
PR 47	1992 $4 Canada Geese	14.00
PR 48	1993 $6 Canada Geese	14.00
PR 49	1994 $6 '94 overprint on '93	15.00

ROSEBUD

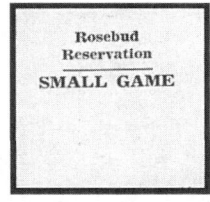

RB 10	1970's Small Game Serial #	2200.00
RB 11	1980's Small Game Serial #	325.00
RB 52	1988 $10 Small Game	50.00
RB 53	1989 $45 Small Game	220.00
RB 90	1996-99 Small Game, Tribal	35.00
RB 91	1996-99 Small Game, Resident	95.00
RB 92	1999-96 Small Game, Non Resident	...
RB 93	2000 $10 Small Game,Tribal (red)	...
RB 94	2000 $30 Small Game,Resident (Red)	450.00
RB 95	2000 $85.00 Small Game, Non-Resident (Red)	130.00

The American First Day Cover Society

. . . is the best source of information, fellowship, education and authority on First Day Cover Collecting. Most importantly, the AFDCS is a nonprofit, non-commercial, international society and the world's largest society devoted to First Day Cover collecting!

A First Day Cover (FDC) is an envelope or card with a new stamp issue that is postmarked on the first day the stamp is sold.

A cachet (pronounced ka-shay) is the design on the envelope. It usually shows something more about the new stamp and is usually on the left side of the envelope. Some cachets cover the entire face of the envelope with the design.

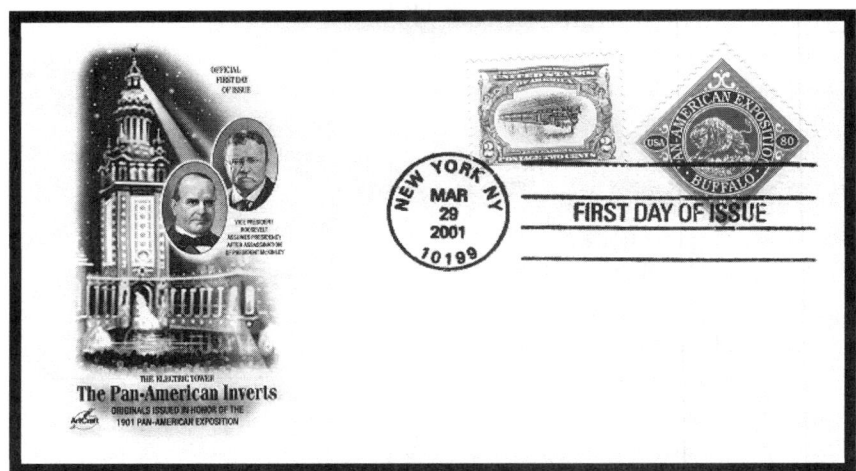

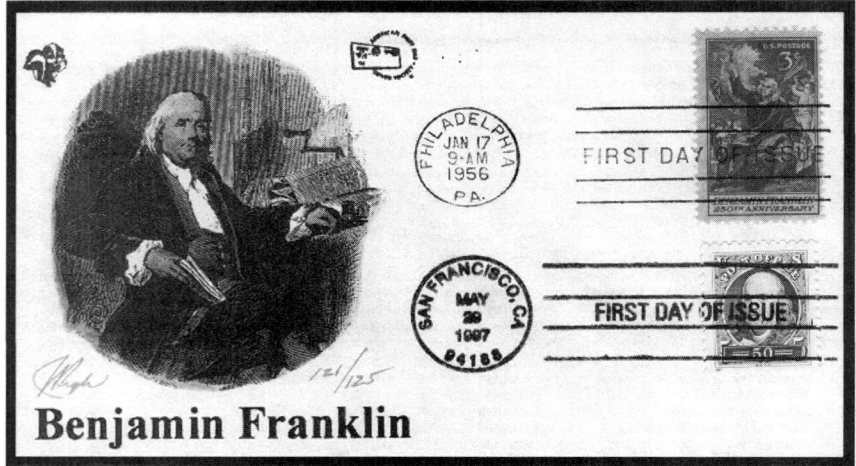

FDC Collecting is a hobby of personal involvement limited only by your own creativity. This FDC has a 50¢ Ben Franklin stamp added to another Franklin FDC made over 40 years earlier. These are called "dual" FDCs. The "AFDCS Glossary of Terms" comes in your FDC collecting package when you join the AFDCS! See the membership information on the opposite page.

A Joint Issue First Day Cover has two or more stamps issued by different countries to commemorate the same person, place or event. You will learn more about Joint Issues when you read *FIRST DAYS,* the award winning journal of the AFDCS. This popular area of collecting has expanded to include dozens of new issues and countries all around the world each year.

Welcome to First Day Cover Collecting!

by Barry Newton, Editor *FIRST DAYS*, the official journal of the American First Day Cover Society

First Day Cover (FDC) Collecting is a hands-on hobby much more than simple collecting. It encourages the individual collector to fully develop a range of interests through cachetmaking, autographs and combo FDCs so that the final collection is a reflection of personal taste. In FDCs, uniqueness is the rule, not the exception. This Chinese New Year FDC was autographed by the stamp designer, Clarence Lee.

FIRST CACHETS

by Marjory J. Sente

Stamp collectors are always interested in the oldest, first, best, rare, most expensive items. So it is not unusual for First Day Cover enthusiasts to search for earliest known cachets by a particular manufacturer or designer. First cachets are fascinating and challenging speciality. They have been researched and documented for thousands of artists and cachet makers. Yet, the search for other first cachets continue.

A first cachet is the initial design commercially produced by a cachet maker. To qualify as commercially produced, the cacheted First Day Cover is made and sold in a quantity greater than maker's personal needs. As an example is the design prepared by Colorano "Silk" cachets for the 1971 American Wool Industry commemorative, issued Janruary 19 at Las Vegas, NV. Ray

Novak had seen silk cachets produced by french firm, Ceres, and decided to market the same type of cachet for United States postal issues. For the first Colorano "Silk" cachet, Ray produced 1200 covers. The press run increased to 2400 in 1972 and by the cachet line's tenth anniversary, production had increased to 10,000 per issue.

Sometimes it is difficult to identify a cachetmaker's initial production, because it is not signed. So researchers need to rely on philatelic publications released about the time the cachet was produced and advertised for distribution. Stuffers in the FDCs also provide good clues as to the cachet's producer. The first Fleetwood cachet, prepared for the Vermont Statehood commemorative, released on March 4, 1941, was not signed, but a stuffer identifies Staehle as the

designer and Fleetwood as the producer. The line has undergone many changes over the years, and today, the colorful Fleetwood designs produced by Unicover are likely the most mass-marketed First Day Covers.

Other cachets are relatively easy to identify, because most designs including the first one are signed. Fluegel cachets, produced from the mid-1940's until 1960's, are nearly always signed "Fluegel." Herman "Cap" Fleugel prepared his first commercial venture for the 3-cent Roosevelt commemorative issued on June 27, 1945. Known for their brilliant colors, his early cachets were printed in letterpress in five or six colors.

Addresses on FDCs are sometimes a tip to their origin. Cachet makers frequently send covers to themselves or relatives. Ernest J.

Weschcke produced his first and only cachet for the Norse-American Centennial commemorative pair, released May 18, 1925. The distinctive red cachet printed on Norwegian Blue envelopes is unsigned but most of the FDCs are addressed to him. It is estimated that Weschcke made about 200 of these FDCs, but few were sold. The others were treasured by the family and kept in pristine condition.

Sometimes a first cachet gives birth to a line with a formal trademark. Of the four major cachet lines that are marked today-- Artcraft, Artmaster, House of Farnam and Fleetwood--only the first Artmaster cachet appeared with its well known script trademark. The other three cachet lines adopted trademarks later.

Robert Schmidt of Louisville, Kentucky, prepared the first Artmaster cachet for the Honor Discharge issue released on May 9, 1946. For this initial cachet 15,000 covers were sold and 10,000 distributed free for advertising and publicity purposes.

Dabbling or creating multiple cachet lines are other confusing issues for the positive identification cachets. Cachetmakers frequently will dabble at making cachets before launching into commercial production. They will design a cachet as an experiment for their own amusement, or as a favor for an organization. Do these forrunners qualify as first cachets? Part of the answer is whether you collect first cachets by artist or designer or cachetmaker or the cachet line.

Sometimes the artist will prepare cachets for earlier FDCs than the one that is considered to be first because it is defined by cachetmaker or the name of the cachet line. For example, Ludwig Staehle prepared his first cachet for the Swedish-Finnish Tercentenary commemorative issued in 1938, several years earlier than the first Fleetwood cachet that he had designed for the 1941 Vermont Statehood issue.

Doris Gold's cachet making career provides another example. She began making one-of-a-kind handrawn/handpainted covers. Her first endeavor for a U.S. issue was for 1975 Benjamin West issue. Her first commercial special events cover was prepared for the 1976 Writer's day INTERPHIL show cancellation. Her first commercial handrawn/handpainted FDC was made for the 1976 Olympics block of four commemorative. The release of the 1977 Lindbergh Transatlantic commemorative was the birth of the DG series. And in 1987 she started the DGHC series beginning with Enrico Caruso commemorative. With this series an outline is printed in black outline, and then the cover is painted by hand. The first cachet for the DGX series, which employs laser color printing was prepared for the 1990 Movie Classics issue.

Sometimes a cachetmaker is involved in commercially producing event covers before making FDCs. This is true for John Adlen, producer of Pilgrim cachets. He started making event covers in the early 1930s. His first cachet on an FDC was for 1937 Constitution commemorative. Most of his covers are signed and include a return address at the bottom of the cachet.

Along with the first cachets come one-time cachets. These designs are the works of cachetmakers who produce only one cachet in their lifetime. Some collectors call them one-timers, first cachets. Others say to have a cachet, you must have second. An excellent discussion on "Collecting First Day Cachets" appeared in September/October 1980 *First Days*.

The systematic compilation of data on first cachets resulted in the publication of *Mellone's First Cachets A FDC Reference Catalog* by Hal Ansink, Lois Hamilton and Dr. Richard A. Monty in 1980. Three years later an updated version was published, followed by a third in 1989. A fourth edition, *First Cachets Revisited*, is the latest comprehensive update of the list. In the interim, *First Days*, the official journal of the American First Day Cover Society, publishes an ongoing column updating research.

Marjory Sente has written about First Day Covers for more than two decades. Her monthly columns have appeared in Linn's Stamp News, Mekeel's Weekly and Stamps, and Stamp Collector. She also teaches an independent learning course on FDCs offered through the American Philatelic Society's StampCampus.

Building Your Collection

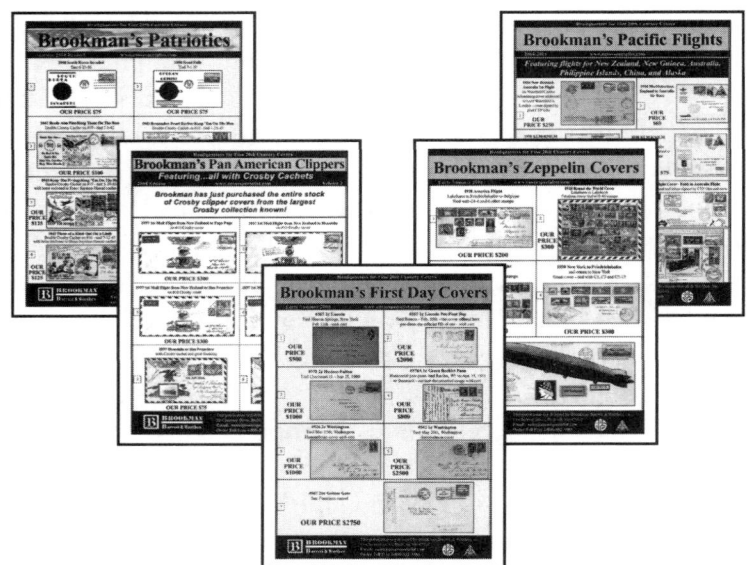

Just a sample of the fine cover catalogs we publish during the year...**now in full color!** Featured areas of collecting are: Zeppelin Flights, PAA Clippers, Pioneer Flights, and Autographs. New covers of interest are: Early Government Flights, Philippine Flights and Canadian Semi-Officials. Please let us know your specific collecting interest so we can send you the appropriate brochure.

Or Disposing Of Your Collection

For Help, Call "Our Man Bob" 1-800-332-3383

"Our Man Bob" has spent over 45 years specializing in covers. From a million covers to individual covers that sell for many thousands of dollars, Brookman/Barrett & Worthen leads the field. Traveling all over the country, we carry want lists for those collectors who want items so scarce that even we don't have them in stock. With a broad base of buyers we are able to pay the fairest prices in the market. To prove this point, over the last several years we have purchased well over 1,000,000 covers from dealers only. They know the best source when they have covers to sell.

BROOKMAN
IS YOUR BEST SOURCE
45 Years And Still No Difference
Being Fair With Both Buyers And Sellers

U.S. First Day Covers

370

569

FDC's will be addressed from #5A-952 and unaddressed from 953 to date. Cacheted prices are for FDC's with common printed cachets. From #704 all FDC's will be cacheted. Multiples are generally priced @ 1.25x for blocks & 2x for plate blks. or line pairs

Scott #	Description	Uncacheted
	1851-1890	
5A	1¢ Franklin, Blue, Type 1b, 7/1/1851 Any City	135,000.00
7	1¢ Franklin, Blue, Type II 7/1/1851 Any City	6,500.00
10	3¢ Washington, Orange Brown 7/1/1851 Any City	17,500.00
64B	3¢ Washington, Rose Pink 8/17/1861 Any City	30,000.00
79	3¢ Washington "A" Grill 8/13/1867 Any City	15,000.00
210	2¢ Washington, Red Brown 10/1/1883 Any City	2,400.00
210-211	2¢ Wash., 4¢ Jackson on one cvr, 10/1/1883	40,000.00
219D	2¢ Washington, Lake 2/22/1890 Any City	20,000.00
	1893 COLUMBIAN ISSUE	
230	1¢ Columbian 1/2/1893 Any City	10,000.00
	Salem, MA 12/31/1892	17,500.00
231	2¢ Columbian 1/2/1893 Any City	6,000.00
	New York, NY or Boston, MA 1/1/1893	7,500.00
	Salem, MA 12/31/1892	17,500.00
232	3¢ Columbian 1/2/1893 Any City	15,000.00
233	4¢ Columbian 1/2/1893 Any City	15,000.00
234	5¢ Columbian 1/2/1893 Any City	20,000.00
235	6¢ Columbian 1/2/1893 Any City	22,500.00
237	10¢ Columbian 1/2/1893 Any City	25,000.00
	East Lexington, MA 12/31/92 bkstp	25,000.00
242	$2.00 Columbian 1/2/1893 New York, NY	65,000.00
265	2¢ Washington 5/2/1895 Any City	9,500.00

*Since Jan. 1, 1893 was a Sunday and few post offices were open, both Jan. 1 and Jan. 2 covers are considered FDC's by collectors.

Scott #	Description	Uncacheted
	1898 TRANS-MISSISSIPPI ISSUE	
285	1¢ Trans-Mississippi 6/17/1898 Any City	14,500.00
286	2¢ Trans-Mississippi 6/17/1898 DC	10,000.00
	6/17/1898 Pittsburgh, PA	13,000.00
287	4¢ Trans-Mississippi 6/17/1898 Any City	22,500.00
288	5¢ Trans-Mississippi 6/17/1898 DC	22,500.00
289	8¢ Trans-Mississippi 6/17/1898 DC	27,500.00
290	10¢ Trans-Mississippi 6/17/1898 Any City	32,500.00
291	50¢ Trans-Mississippi 6/17/1898 DC	35,000.00
292	$1 Trans-Mississippi 6/17/1898 DC	60,000.00
	1901 PAN AMERICAN ISSUE	
294	1¢ Pan-American 5/1/01 Any City	7,500.00
	294,296, 297 on one cover, Boston, MA	30,000.00
295	2¢ Pan-American 5/1/01 Any City	3,500.00
296	4¢ Pan-American 5/1/01 Any City	17,500.00
297	5¢ Pan-American 5/1/01 Any City	25,000.00
298	8¢ Pan-American 5/1/01 Any City	25,000.00
298,296	4¢ & 8¢ on one FDC Boston, MA	27,500.00
294-299	1¢-10¢ Pan-American, cplt. set on one FDC, Any City	40,000.00
	1904 LOUISIANA PURCHASE 1907 JAMESTOWN ISSUES	
323	1¢ Louisiana Purchase 4/30/04 Any City	7,500.00
324	2¢ Louisiana Purchase 4/30/04 Any City	6,000.00
325	3¢ Louisiana Purchase 4/30/04 Any City	18,000.00
326	5¢ Louisiana Purchase 4/30/04 Any City	26,000.00
327	10¢ Louisiana Purchase 4/30/04 Any City	27,500.00
323-327	1¢-10¢ Louisiana Purchase, complete set on 1 FDC	100,000.00
328	1¢ Jamestown Expedition 4/26/07 Any City	12,500.00
329	2¢ Jamestown Expedition 4/26/07 Any City	15,000.00
330	5¢ Jamestown Expedition 5/10/07 Norfolk, VA **(eku)**	20,000.00
328-30	On one cover, 5/10/07 Norwalk, VA **(eku)**	22,000.00
331a	1¢ Franklin, bklt. sgl. 12/2/08 DC	25,000.00
332a	2¢ Washington, bklt. sgl. 11/16/08 DC	35,000.00
	1909 COMMEMORATIVES	
367	2¢ Lincoln 2/12/09 Any City	500.00
367	2¢ Lincoln 2/12/09 Any City on Lincoln-related post-card	600.00
368	2¢ Lincoln Imperf. 2/12/09 Canton, OH	25,000.00
370	2¢ Alaska-Yukon 6/1/09 Any City	5,000.00
370	On related card	6,000.00
370	On card, Any City	5,500.00
372	2¢ Hudson-Fulton, Pre-date 9/23/09, (2 Known)	5,000.00
372	2¢ Hudson-Fulton, Pre-date 9/24/09, (33 Known)	1,500.00
372	Same on related post card/cover	2,500.00

Scott #	Description	Uncacheted
	1909 COMMEMORATIVES (cont.)	
372	2¢ Hudson-Fulton, 9/25/09, Any City, (100-200 Known)	1,000.00
372	2¢ Hudson-Fulton, 9/25/09, Any City on related post-card	1,500.00
373	2¢ Hudson-Fulton Imperf. 9/25/09 Any City	12,500.00
	1913 PAN-PACIFIC ISSUE	
397	1¢ Pan-Pacific Expo 1/1/13 Any City	6,500.00
398	2¢ Pan-Pacific Expo 1/18/13 Washington, D.C.	2,000.00
399	5¢ Pan-Pacific Expo 1/1/13 Any City	22,000.00
400	10¢ Pan-Pacific Expo 1/1/13 Any City	17,500.00
403	5¢ Pan-Pacific Expo, Perf. 10, 2/6/15 Chicago, Ill	7,500.00
397,399,400	1¢,5¢ & 10¢ Pan-Pacific on one FDC, SF, CA	30,000.00
497	10¢ Franklin Coil 1/31/22 DC (all are Hammelman cvrs)	6,500.00
526	2¢ Offset Ty. IV 3/15/20 Any City	1,000.00
537	3¢ Victory 3/3/19 Any City	800.00
542	1¢ Rotary Perf. 10 x 11 5/26/20 Any City	2,500.00
	1920 PILGRIM TERCENTENARY	
548	1¢ "Mayflower" Pair 12/21/20 DC	1,500.00
549	2¢ "Landing of the Pilgrims" 12/21/20 DC	1,200.00
	12/21/20 Philadelphia, PA	4,000.00
	12/21/20 Plymouth, MA	5,000.00
548-50	1¢-5¢ Complete set on one cover, Phila., PA	3,000.00
	Complete set on one cover, DC	3,000.00
	1922-25 FLAT PLATE PERF. 11	
551	½¢ Hale (Block of 4) 4/4/25 DC	18.00
551 cont.	New Haven, CT	23.00
	Unofficial City	175.00
	551 & 576 on one FDC 4/4/25 DC	125.00
552	1¢ Franklin 1/17/23 DC	22.50
	Philadelphia, PA	45.00
	Unofficial City	200.00
553	1½¢ Harding 3/19/25 DC	25.00
554	2¢ Washington 1/15/23 DC	35.00
555	3¢ Lincoln 2/12/23 DC	35.00
	Hodgenville, KY	200.00
	Unofficial City	300.00
556	4¢ Martha Washington 1/15/23 DC	70.00
557	5¢ Teddy Roosevelt 10/27/22 DC	100.00
	New York, NY	150.00
	Oyster Bay, NY	2,000.00
558	6¢ Garfield 11/20/22 DC	175.00
559	7¢ McKinley 5/1/23 DC	125.00
	Niles, OH	175.00
560	8¢ Grant 5/1/23 DC	140.00
	559-560 on one FDC, DC	750.00
	565 & 560 on one FDC, DC	2,500.00
561	9¢ Jefferson 1/15/23 DC	140.00
	556-561 on one FDC, DC	900.00
562	10¢ Monroe 1/15/23 DC	160.00
	562,554,556 & 561 on one FDC	3,200.00
562 & 554	On one FDC	800.00
563	11¢ Hayes 10/4/22 DC	450.00
	Fremont, OH	4,000.00
564	12¢ Cleveland 3/20/23 DC	175.00
	Boston, MA	200.00
	Caldwell, NJ	175.00
	Lynn, MA	4,500.00
565	14¢ Indian 5/1/23 DC	275.00
	Muskogee, OK	2,000.00
566	15¢ Statue of Liberty 11/11/22 DC	400.00
567	20¢ Golden Gate 5/1/23 DC	400.00
	Oakland, CA	8,000.00
	San Francisco, CA	2,200.00
568	25¢ Niagara Falls 11/11/22 DC	450.00
569	30¢ Bison 3/20/23 DC	700.00
	569 & 564 on one FDC, DC	7,250.00
570	50¢ Arlington 11/11/22 DC	1,000.00
	570,566 & 568 on one FDC	6,000.00
571	$1 Lincoln Memorial 2/12/23 DC	6,500.00
	Springfield, IL	6,500.00
	571 & 555 on one FDC, DC	9,500.00
572	$2 U.S. Capitol 3/20/23 DC	22,000.00
573	$5 Freedom Statue 3/20/23 DC	36,000.00

*EKU: Earliest Known Use

164

U.S. First Day Covers

610

Scott #	Description	Uncacheted
	1925-26 ROTARY PRESS PERF. 10	
576	1½¢ Harding Imperf. 4/4/25 DC	40.00
581	1¢ Franklin, unprecancelled 10/17/23 DC	7,500.00
582	1½¢ Harding 3/19/25 DC	40.00
583a	2¢ Washington bklt pane of 6, 8/27/26 DC	1,200.00
584	3¢ Lincoln 8/1/25 DC	50.00
585	4¢ Martha Washington 4/4/25 DC	50.00
585-587	On one FDC	850.00
586	5¢ T. Roosevelt 4/4/25 DC	60.00
587	6¢ Garfield 4/4/25 DC	60.00
588	7¢ McKinley 5/29/26 DC	60.00
589	8¢ Grant 5/29/26 DC	65.00
590	9¢ Jefferson 5/29/26 DC	70.00
	590, 588 & 589 on one FDC	300.00
591	10¢ Monroe 6/8/25 DC	90.00

Scott #	Description	Uncacheted	Line Pairs
	1923-25 Coil Issues		
597	1¢ Franklin 7/18/23 DC	600.00	1,750.00
598	1½¢ Harding 3/19/25 DC	55.00	175.00
*599	2¢ Washington 1/15/23 DC (37 known)	2,000.00	3,500.00
	1/10/23 Lancaster, PA (1 known)	5,000.00	...

*** These are the eku from DC and prepared by Phil Ward.
Other covers are known date 1/10, 1/11 & 1/13.**

600	3¢ Lincoln 5/10/24 DC	100.00	275.00
602	5¢ T. Roosevelt 3/5/24 DC	90.00	275.00
603	10¢ Monroe 12/1/24 DC	110.00	350.00
604	1¢ Franklin 7/19/24 DC	85.00	225.00
605	1½¢ Harding 5/9/25 DC	70.00	175.00
606	2¢ Washington 12/31/23 DC	150.00	450.00

	1923 Issues		
610	2¢ Harding 9/1/23 DC	30.00	...
	Marion, OH	20.00	...
	George W. Linn cachet (1st modern cachet)	...	600.00
611	2¢ Harding Imperf. 11/15/23 DC	75.00	...
612	2¢ Harding Perf. 10 9/12/23 DC	90.00	...

	1924 HUGUENOT-WALLOON ISSUE		
614	1¢ Huguenot-Walloon 5/1/24 DC	30.00	...
	Albany, NY	30.00	...
	Allentown, PA	30.00	...
	Charleston, SC	30.00	...
	Jacksonville, FL	30.00	...
	Lancaster, PA	30.00	...
	Mayport, FL	30.00	...
	New Rochelle, NY	30.00	...
	New York, NY	30.00	...
	Philadelphia, PA	30.00	...
	Reading, PA	30.00	...
	Unofficial City	100.00	...
615	2¢ Huguenot-Walloon 5/1/24 DC	50.00	...
	Albany, NY	50.00	...
	Allentown, PA	50.00	...
	Charleston, SC	50.00	...
	Jacksonville, FL	50.00	...
	Lancaster, PA	50.00	...
	Mayport, FL	50.00	...
	New Rochelle, NY	50.00	...
	New York, NY	50.00	...
	Philadelphia, PA	50.00	...
	Reading, PA	50.00	...
	Unofficial City	125.00	...
616	5¢ Huguenot-Walloon 5/1/24 DC	70.00	...
	Albany, NY	70.00	...
	Allentown, PA	70.00	...
	Charleston, SC	70.00	...
	Jacksonville, FL	70.00	...
	Lancaster, PA	70.00	...
	Mayport, FL	70.00	...
	New Rochelle, NY	70.00	...
	New York, NY	70.00	...
	Philadelphia, PA	70.00	...
	Reading, PA	70.00	...
	Unofficial City	150.00	...
614-16	1¢-5¢ Comp. set on 1 cover, any official city	150.00	...
614-16	Same, Any Unofficial City	400.00	...

Scott #	Description	Uncacheted	Line Pairs
	1925 LEXINGTON-CONCORD ISSUE		
617	1¢ Lexington-Concord 4/4/25 DC	25.00	125.00
	Boston, MA	25.00	125.00
	Cambridge, MA	25.00	125.00
	Concord, MA	25.00	125.00
	Concord Junction, MA	35.00	...
	Lexington, MA	35.00	125.00
	Unofficial City	75.00	...
618	2¢ Lexington-Concord 4/4/25 DC	30.00	125.00
	Boston, MA	30.00	125.00
	Cambridge, MA	30.00	125.00
	Concord, MA	30.00	125.00
	Concord Junction, MA	40.00	...
	Lexington, MA	40.00	125.00
	Unofficial City	100.00	...
619	5¢ Lexington-Concord 4/4/25 DC	70.00	175.00
	Boston, MA	70.00	175.00
	Cambridge, MA	70.00	175.00
	Concord, MA	70.00	175.00
	Concord Junction, MA	90.00	...
	Lexington, MA	90.00	175.00
	Unofficial City	125.00	...
617-19	1¢-5¢ **1st Jackson cachet**		
	(see above listings for prices except #619 which is $750.)		
617-19	1¢-5¢ Lexington-Concord, cplt. set on one cover	125.00	...
	Same, Concord-Junction or Lexington	160.00	...
	Same, Any Unofficial City	250.00	...

	1925 NORSE-AMERICAN ISSUE		
620	2¢ Norse-American 5/18/25 DC	15.00	...
	Algona, IA	15.00	...
	Benson, MN	15.00	...
	Decorah, IA	15.00	...
	Minneapolis, MN	15.00	...
	Northfield, MN	15.00	...
	St. Paul, MN	15.00	...
	Unofficial City	60.00	...
621	5¢ Norse-American 5/18/25 DC	25.00	...
	Algona, IA	25.00	...
	Benson, MN	25.00	...
	Decorah, IA	25.00	...
	Minneapolis, MN	25.00	...
	Northfield, MN	25.00	...
	St. Paul, MN	25.00	...
	Unofficial City	90.00	...
620-21	2¢-5¢ Norse-Amer., one cover 5/18/25 DC	40.00	275.00
	2¢-5¢ Algona, IA	40.00	275.00
	2¢-5¢ Benson, MN	40.00	275.00
	2¢-5¢ Decorah, IA	40.00	275.00
620-1 cont	2¢-5¢ Minneapolis, MN	40.00	275.00
	2¢-5¢ Northfield, MN	40.00	275.00
	2¢-5¢ St. Paul, MN	40.00	275.00
	Unofficial City	150.00	...
	1st Ernest J. Weschcke cachet	...	275.00
	1st A.C. Roessler cachet	...	300.00
622	13¢ Harrison 1/11/26 DC	15.00	...
	Indianapolis, IN	25.00	...
	North Bend, OH	150.00	...
	Unofficial City	200.00	...
623	17¢ Wilson 12/28/25	20.00	275.00
	New York, NY	20.00	275.00
	Princeton, NJ	30.00	275.00
	Staunton, VA	25.00	275.00
	Unofficial City	175.00	...
	1st Nickles cachet	...	275.00
627	2¢ Sesquicentennial 5/10/26 DC	10.00	65.00
	Boston, MA	10.00	65.00
	Philadelphia, PA	10.00	65.00
	1st Griffin cachet	...	150.00
	1st Baxter cachet	...	75.00
628	5¢ Ericsson Memorial 5/29/26 DC	25.00	450.00
	Chicago, IL	25.00	450.00
	Minneapolis, MN	25.00	450.00
	New York, NY	25.00	450.00
629	2¢ White Plains 10/18/26 New York, NY	8.00	70.00
	New York, NY Int. Phil. Ex. Agency	8.00	70.00
	White Plains, NY	8.00	70.00
630a	2¢ White Plains S/S, sgl. 10/18/26 NY, NY	12.00	75.00
	New York, NY Int. Phil. Ex. Agency	12.00	75.00
	White Plains, NY	12.00	75.00
	Block of 10 with selvage	250.00	...
630	Complete Sheet 10/18/26	1,700.00	...
630	10/28/26	1,300.00	...
631	1½¢ Harding Rotary Imperf. 8/27/26 DC	50.00	...

	1926-27 ROTARY PRESS PERF. 11 X 10½		
632	1¢ Franklin 6/10/27 DC	42.50	...
632a	Bklt. Pane of 6 11/27	9,000.00	...
633	1½¢ Harding 5/17/27 DC	42.50	...
634	2¢ Washington 12/10/26 DC	45.00	...
634EE	Experimental Electric Eye 3/28/35	1,000.00	...
635	3¢ Lincoln 2/3/27 DC	45.00	...
635a	3¢ Lincoln Re-issue 2/7/34 DC	25.00	45.00
636	4¢ Martha Washington 5/17/27 DC	55.00	...
637	5¢ T. Roosevelt 3/24/27 DC	55.00	...
638	6¢ Garfield 7/27/27 DC	65.00	...
639	7¢ McKinley 3/24/27 DC	60.00	...

U.S. First Day Covers

658

690

Scott #	Description	Uncacheted	Cacheted
	1926-27 ROTARY PRESS PERF. 11 X 10½ (Cont.)		
639, 637	on one FDC	300.00	...
640	8¢ Grant 6/10/27 DC	65.00	...
	640, 632 on one FDC	300.00	...
641	9¢ Jefferson 5/17/27 DC	70.00	...
	641, 633, & 636 on one FDC	450.00	...
642	10¢ Monroe 2/3/27 DC	85.00	...
	632-42, set of 12	700.00	...
643	2¢ Vermont 8/3/27 DC	8.00	60.00
	Bennington, VT	8.00	60.00
	1st Joshua Gerow cachet	...	200.00
	1st Harris Hunt cachet	...	150.00
	1st Kirkjian cachet	...	275.00
644	2¢ Burgoyne 8/3/27 DC	12.00	75.00
	Albany, NY	12.00	75.00
	Rome, NY	12.00	75.00
	Syracuse, NY	12.00	75.00
	Utica, NY	12.00	75.00
	1st Ralph Dyer cachet	...	300.00
	Unofficial City	40.00	125.00
	1928		
645	2¢ Valley Forge 5/26/28 DC	5.00	60.00
	Cleveland, OH	60.00	140.00
	Lancaster, PA	5.00	60.00
	Norristown, PA	5.00	60.00
	Philadelphia, PA	5.00	60.00
	Valley Forge, PA	5.00	60.00
	West Chester, PA	5.00	60.00
	Cleveland Midwestern Phil. Sta.	5.00	60.00
	1st J.W. Stoutzenberg cachet	...	275.00
	1st Adam K. Bert cachet	...	75.00
	1st Egolf cachet	...	90.00
646	2¢ Molly Pitcher 10/20/28 DC	12.50	85.00
	Freehold, NJ	12.50	85.00
	Red Bank, NJ	12.50	85.00
647	2¢ Hawaii 8/13/28 DC	25.00	125.00
	Honolulu, HI	25.00	125.00
648	5¢ Hawaii 8/13/28 DC	25.00	150.00
	Honolulu, HI	30.00	150.00
647-48	Hawaii on one cover	50.00	250.00
	1st F.W. Reid Cachet	...	325.00
	1st Best Cachet	...	325.00
649	2¢ Aeronautics Conf., green pmk. 12/12/28 DC	6.00	40.00
	Black pmk.	10.00	40.00
650	5¢ Aeronautics Conf., green pmk. 12/12/28 DC	10.00	50.00
	Black pmk	12.50	50.00
649-50	Aero. Conf., one cover, green pmk	15.00	70.00
	One cover, black pmk	17.50	75.00
	1929		
651	2¢ Clark 2/25/29 Vinncennes, in	5.00	30.00
	1st Harry loor cachet	...	150.00
653	½¢ Hale (block of 4) 5/25/29 DC	40.00	...
	Unofficial City	175.00	...
654	2¢ Electric Lt., flat press 6/5/29 Menlo Park, NJ	10.00	45.00
	1st Klotzbach cachet	...	225.00
655	2¢ Electric Light, rotary press 6/11/29 DC	100.00	250.00
656	2¢ Electric Light, coil 6/11/29 DC	100.00	250.00
656	Coil Line Pair	150.00	275.00
655-56	Rotary & Coil sgls. on one FDC	175.00	375.00
657	2¢ Sullivan 6/17/29 Auburn, NY	4.00	30.00
	Binghamton, NY	4.00	30.00
	Canajoharie, NY	4.00	30.00
	Canandaigua, NY	4.00	30.00
	Elmira, NY	4.00	30.00
	Geneva, NY	4.00	30.00
	Geneseo, NY	4.00	30.00
	Horseheads, NY	4.00	30.00
	Owego, NY	4.00	30.00
	Penn Yan, NY	4.00	30.00
	Perry, NY	4.00	30.00
	Seneca Falls, NY	4.00	30.00
	Waterloo, NY	4.00	30.00
	Watkins Glen, NY	4.00	30.00
	Waverly, NY	4.00	30.00
	1st Robert Beazell cachet	...	400.00
	1st A.C. Elliot cachet	...	75.00

Scott #	Description	Uncacheted	Cacheted
	KANSAS OVERPRINTS		
658-68	1¢-10¢ Kansas cplt. set on one FDC 5/1/29 DC	1,500.00	2,000.00
658-68	Kansas Set of 11 covers	1,250.00	2,000.00
658	1¢ Franklin 5/1/29 DC	50.00	...
	4/15/29 Newton, KS	500.00	...
659	1½¢ Harding 5/1/29 DC	60.00	...
660	2¢ Washington 5/1/29 DC	60.00	75.00
661	3¢ Lincoln 5/1/29 DC	75.00	...
662	4¢ Martha Washington 5/1/29 DC	100.00	...
663	5¢ T. Roosevelt 5/1/29 DC	100.00	200.00
664	6¢ Garfield 5/1/29 DC	125.00	...
	4/15/29 Newton, KS	800.00	...
665	7¢ McKinley 5/1/29 DC	150.00	...
666	8¢ Grant 5/1/29 DC	150.00	...
	4/15/29 Newton, KS	800.00	...
667	9¢ Jefferson 5/1/29 DC	150.00	...
668	10¢ Monroe 5/1/29 DC	200.00	...
658,664,666	4/15/29 Newton, KS	1,900.00	...
	NEBRASKA OVERPRINTS		
669-79	1¢-10¢ Nebraska cplt. set on one FDC 5/1/29 DC	1,500.00	1700.00
669-79	Nebraska Set of 11 Covers	1,250.00	2000.00
669	1¢ Franklin 5/1/29 DC	50.00	...
	4/15/29 Beatrice, NE	400.00	...
670	1½¢ Harding 5/1/29 DC	60.00	...
	4/15/29 Hartington, NE	300.00	...
671	2¢ Washington 5/1/29 DC	60.00	...
	4/15/29 Auburn, NE	350.00	...
	4/15/29 Beatrice, NE	350.00	...
	4/15/29 Hartington, NE	350.00	...
672	3¢ Lincoln 5/1/29 DC	75.00	...
	4/15/29 Beatrice, NE	450.00	...
673	4¢ Martha Washington 5/1/29 DC	100.00	...
	4/15/29 Beatrice, NE	500.00	...
	4/15/29 Hartington, NE	500.00	...
674	5¢ T. Roosevelt 5/1/29 DC	100.00	200.00
	4/15/29 Beatrice, NE	500.00	...
	4/15/29 Hartington, NE	500.00	...
675	6¢ Garfield 5/1/29 DC	125.00	...
676	7¢ McKinley 5/1/29 DC	150.00	...
677	8¢ Grant 5/1/29 DC	150.00	...
678	9¢ Jefferson 5/1/29 DC	150.00	...
679	10¢ Monroe 5/1/29 DC	200.00	...
658-79	all 22 values on 1 cover (2 known)	4500.00	...
680	2¢ Fallen Timbers 9/14/29 Erie, PA	3.00	35.00
	Maumee, OH	3.00	35.00
	Perrysburgh, OH	3.00	35.00
	Toledo, OH	3.00	35.00
	Waterville, OH	3.00	35.00
681	2¢ Ohio River 10/19/29 Cairo, IL	3.00	35.00
	Cincinnati, OH	3.00	35.00
	Evansville, IN	3.00	35.00
	Homestead, PA	3.00	35.00
	Louisville, KY	3.00	35.00
	Pittsburgh, PA	3.00	35.00
	Wheeling, WV	3.00	35.00
	1930-31		
682	2¢ Mass. Bay Colony 4/8/30 Boston, MA	3.00	35.00
	Salem, MA	3.00	35.00
683	2¢ Carolina-Charleston 4/10/30 Charleston, SC	3.00	35.00
684	1½¢ Harding 12/1/30 Marion, OH	4.00	45.00
685	4¢ Taft 6/4/30 Cincinnati, OH	6.00	60.00
686	1½¢ Harding, coil 12/1/30 Marion, OH	5.00	60.00
686	Coil Line Pair	15.00	90.00
687	4¢ Taft, coil 9/18/30 DC	40.00	150.00
687	Coil Line Pair	75.00	250.00
688	2¢ Braddock 7/9/30 Braddock, PA	4.00	35.00
689	2¢ Von Steuben 9/17/30 New York, NY	4.00	35.00
690	2¢ Pulaski 1/16/31 Brooklyn, NY	4.00	35.00
	Buffalo, NY	4.00	35.00
	Chicago, IL	4.00	35.00
	Cleveland, OH	4.00	35.00
	Detroit, MI	4.00	35.00

U.S. First Day Covers

737

Scott #	Description	Uncacheted	Cacheted
690	Gary, IN	4.00	35.00
	Milwaukee, WI	4.00	35.00
	New York, NY	4.00	35.00
	Pittsburgh, PA	4.00	35.00
	Savannah, GA	4.00	35.00
	South Bend, IN	4.00	35.00
	Toledo, OH	4.00	35.00
	1st Truby cachet	...	**125.00**

1931 ROTARY PRESS HI-VALUES

692	11¢ Hayes 9/4/31 DC	100.00	...
693	12¢ Cleveland 8/25/31 DC	100.00	...
694	13¢ Harrison 9/4/31 DC	100.00	...
695	14¢ Indian 9/8/31 DC	100.00	...
696	15¢ Statue of Liberty 8/27/31 DC	100.00	...
697	17¢ Wilson 7/27/31 DC	300.00	...
	7/25/31 Brooklyn, NY	3,000.00	...
698	20¢ Golden Gate 9/8/31 DC	250.00	...
699	25¢ Niagara Falls 7/27/31 DC	300.00	...
	7/25/31 Brooklyn, NY	2,500.00	...
	697, 699 on one FDC, Brooklyn, NY	4,000.00	...
700	30¢ Bison 9/8/31 DC	300.00	...
701	50¢ Arlington 9/4/31 DC	400.00	...
701	50¢ Arlington, Woodrich PA	4,500.00	...

1931

702	2¢ Red Cross 5/21/31 DC	3.00	35.00
	Dansville, NY	3.00	35.00
	1st Edward Hacker cachet	...	**150.00**
703	2¢ Yorktown 10/19/31 Wethersfield, CT	3.00	45.00
	Yorktown, VA	3.00	45.00
	Any Predate	200.00	...
	Unofficial City	45.00	...
	1st Crosby cachet	...	**400.00**
	1st Aeroprint cachet	...	**150.00**

1932 WASHINGTON BICENTENNIAL ISSUE

704-15	Bicentennial Set of 12 Covers		220.00
704	½¢ olive brown 1/1/32 DC		20.00
705	1¢ green 1/1/32 DC		20.00
706	1½¢ brown 1/1/32 DC		20.00
707	2¢ carmine rose 1/1/32 DC		20.00
708	3¢ deep violet 1/1/32 DC		20.00
709	4¢ light brown 1/1/32 DC		20.00
710	5¢ blue 1/1/32 DC		20.00
711	6¢ red orange 1/1/32 DC		20.00
712	7¢ black 1/1/32 DC		20.00
713	8¢ olive bistre 1/1/32 DC		20.00
714	9¢ pale red 1/1/32 DC		20.00
715	10¢ orange yellow 1/1/32 DC		20.00
	1st Rice cachet (on any single)		**25.00**
	1st Raley cachet (on any single)		**40.00**
704-15	Wash. Bicent. on one cover		250.00

1932

716	2¢ Winter Olympic Games 1/25/32 Lake Placid, NY		35.00
	1st Beverly Hills cachet		**250.00**
717	2¢ Arbor Day 4/22/32 Nebraska City, NE		25.00
	1st Linnprint cachet		**40.00**
718	3¢ Summer Olympics 6/15/32 Los Angeles, CA		40.00
719	5¢ Summer Olympics 6/15/32 Los Angeles, CA		40.00
718-19	Summer Olympics cplt. set on one FDC		60.00
720	3¢ Washington 6/16/32 DC		40.00
720b	3¢ Booklet Pane 7/25/32 DC		175.00
721	3¢ Washington, coil, vert. 6/24/32 DC		50.00
	Coil Line Pair		90.00
722	3¢ Washington, coil, horiz. 10/12/32 DC		50.00
722	Coil Line Pair		90.00
723	6¢ Garfield, coil 8/18/32 Los Angeles, CA		60.00
723	Coil Line Pair		95.00
724	3¢ William Penn 10/24/32 New Castle, DE		25.00
	Chester, PA		25.00
	Philadelphia, PA		25.00
725	3¢ Daniel Webster 10/24/32 Franklin, NH		25.00
	Exeter, NH		25.00
	Hanover, NH		25.00
726	3¢ Gen'l Oglethorpe 2/12/33 Savannah, GA		25.00
	1st Anderson cachet		**150.00**

Scott #	Description	Cacheted
727	3¢ Peace Proclamation 4/19/33 Newburgh, NY	25.00
	1st Grimsland cachet	**350.00**
728	1¢ Century of Progress 5/25/33 Chicago, IL	20.00
729	3¢ Century of Progress 5/25/33 Chicago, IL	20.00
728-29	Progress on one cover	25.00
730	1¢ Amer. Phil. Soc., sht. of 25 8/25/33 Chicago, IL	200.00
730a	1¢ Amer. Phil. Soc., single 8/25/33 Chicago, IL	20.00
731	3¢ Amer. Phil. Soc., sht. of 25 8/25/33 Chicago, IL	200.00
731a	3¢ Amer. Phil. Soc., single 8/25/33 Chicago, IL	20.00
730-731	On one Uncacheted Cover	850.00
730a-31a	Amer. Phil. Soc. on one cover	25.00
732	3¢ National Recovery Act 8/15/33 DC	20.00
	Nira, IA 8/17/33, unofficial	25.00
733	3¢ Byrd Antarctic 10/9/33 DC	30.00
734	5¢ Kosciuszko 10/13/33 Boston, MA	20.00
	Buffalo, NY	20.00
	Chicago, NY	20.00
	Detroit, MI	20.00
	Pittsburgh, PA	50.00
	Kosciuszko, MS	20.00
	St. Louis, MO	20.00
735	3¢ Nat'l Exhibition, sht. of 6 2/10/34 New York, NY	75.00
735a	3¢ National Exhibition, single 2/10/34 New York NY	20.00
736	3¢ Maryland 3/23/34 St. Mary's City, MD	20.00
	1st Torkel Gundel cachet	**300.00**
	1st Don Kapner cachet	**25.00**
	1st Louis Nix cachet	**250.00**
	1st Top Notch cachet	**25.00**
737	3¢ Mothers of Am., rotary 5/2/34 any city	15.00
738	3¢ Mothers of Am., flat 5/2/34 any city	15.00
737-38	Mothers of Am. on one cover	35.00
739	3¢ Wisconsin 7/7/34 Green Bay, WI	20.00

1934 NATIONAL PARKS ISSUE

740-49	National Parks set of 10 covers	125.00
740-49	On 1 Cover 10/8/34	150.00
740	1¢ Yosemite 7/16/34 Yosemite, CA	12.50
	DC	12.50
741	2¢ Grand Canyon 7/24 34 Grand Canyon, AZ	12.50
	DC	12.50
742	3¢ Mt. Rainier 8/3/34 Longmire, WA	12.50
	DC	12.50
743	4¢ Mesa Verde 9/25/34 Mesa Verde, CO	12.50
	DC	12.50
744	5¢ Yellowstone 7/30/34 Yellowstone, WY	12.50
	DC	12.50
745	6¢ Crater Lake 9/5/34 Crater Lake, OR	12.50
	DC	12.50
746	7¢ Acadia 10/2/34 Bar Harbor, ME	12.50
	DC	12.50
747	8¢ Zion 9/18/34 Zion, UT	12.50
	DC	12.50
748	9¢ Glacier Park 8/27/34 Glacier Park, MT	12.50
	DC	12.50
749	10¢ Smoky Mts. 10/8/34 Sevierville, TN	12.50
	DC	12.50
750	3¢ Amer. Phil. Soc., sheet of 6 8/28/34 Atlantic City, NJ	75.00
750a	3¢ Amer. Phil. Soc., single 8/28/34 Atlantic City, NJ	20.00
751	1¢ Trans-Miss. Phil. Expo., sht. of 6 10/10/34 Omaha, NE	75.00
751a	1¢ Trans-Miss. Phil. Expo., single 10/10/34 Omaha, NE	20.00

Scott #	Description	Center Gutter or Line Blk	Gutter or Line Pair	Singles
1935 FARLEY SPECIAL PRINTING				
752-71	Set of 20 covers	...	...	500.00
752-71	Set on 1 cover 3/15/35	...	...	450.00
752-55,766a-71	10 varieties on 1 cover 3/15/35	...	...	250.00
752	3¢ Peace Proclamation 3/15/35 DC	150.00	50.00	35.00
753	3¢ Byrd 3/15/35 DC	175.00	50.00	35.00
754	3¢ Mothers of America 3/15/35 DC	150.00	45.00	35.00
755	3¢ Wisconsin 3/15/35 DC	150.00	45.00	35.00
756-65	Parks set of 10 covers	1,750.00	400.00	300.00
756-65	Set on 1 cover 3/15/35	...	...	175.00
756	1¢ Yosemite 3/15/35 DC	150.00	40.00	30.00
757	2¢ Grand Canyon 3/15/35 DC	150.00	40.00	30.00
758	3¢ Mount Rainier 3/15/35	150.00	40.00	30.00
759	4¢ Mesa Verde 3/15/35 DC	150.00	40.00	30.00
760	5¢ Yellowstone 3/15/35 DC	150.00	40.00	30.00
761	6¢ Crater Lake 3/15/35 DC	150.00	40.00	30.00
762	7¢ Acadia 3/15/35 DC	150.00	40.00	30.00
763	8¢ Zion 3/15/35 DC	150.00	40.00	30.00
764	9¢ Glacier Park 3/15/35 DC	150.00	40.00	30.00
765	10¢ Smoky Mountains 3/15/35 DC	150.00	40.00	30.00
766	1¢ Century of Progress 3/15/35, DC Imperf, pane of 25,		600.00	...
766a	Strip of 3,	150.00	50.00	40.00
767	3¢ Century of Progress 3/15/35, DC Imperf, pane of 25		600.00	...
767a	Single	150.00	50.00	40.00
768	3¢ Byrd 3/15/35 DC Imperf, pane of 25		600.00	...
768a	Single	175.00	70.00	40.00
769	1¢ Yosemite 3/15/35 DC Imperf, pane of 6		600.00	...
769a	Strip of 3	150.00	55.00	40.00
770	3¢ Mount Rainier 3/15/35 Imperf, pane of 6		600.00	...
770a	Single	150.00	55.00	40.00
771	16¢ Air Mail-Spec. Del. 3/15/35 DC	175.00	60.000	40.00

794

834

Scott #	Description	Price
	1935-36	
772	3¢ Connecticut 4/26/35 Hartford, CT	17.50
	1st Winfred Grandy cachet	**30.00**
773	3¢ Calif. Exposition 5/29/35 San Diego, CA	17.50
	1st W. Espenshade cachet	**30.00**
774	3¢ Boulder Dam 9/30/35 Boulder City, NV	20.00
775	3¢ Michigan 11/1/35 Lansing, MI	17.50
	1st Risko Art Studio cachet	**200.00**
776	3¢ Texas 3/2/36 Gonzales, TX	20.00
	1st John Sidenius cachet	**60.00**
	1st Walter Czubay cachet	**75.00**
777	3¢ Rhode Island 5/4/36 Providence, RI	17.50
	1st J.W. Clifford cachet	**30.00**
778	3¢ TIPEX sheet 5/9/36 New York, NY	17.50
	1st House of Farnam cachet	**500.00**
778a-78d	Single from sheet	10.00
782	3¢ Arkansas 6/15/36 Little Rock, AK	15.00
783	3¢ Oregon 7/14/36 Astoria, OR	12.50
	Daniel, WY	12.50
	Lewiston, ID	12.50
	Missoula, MT	12.50
	Walla Walla, WA	12.50
784	3¢ Susan B. Anthony 8/26/36 DC	17.50
	1st Historic Arts cachet	**25.00**

Scott #	Description	Price
	1936-37 ARMY - NAVY	
785-94	Army-Navy set of 10 covers	75.00
785	1¢ Army 12/15/36 DC	7.50
786	2¢ Army 1/15/37 DC	7.50
787	3¢ Army 2/18/37 DC	7.50
	1st William Von Ohlen cachet	**75.00**
788	4¢ Army 3/23/37 DC	7.50
789	5¢ Army 5/26/37 West Point, NY	7.50
	#785-89, Army set on one cover, 5/26/37	35.00
790	1¢ Navy 12/15/36 DC	7.50
791	2¢ Navy 1/15/37 DC	7.50
792	3¢ Navy 2/18/37 DC	7.50
793	4¢ Navy 3/23/37 DC	7.50
794	5¢ Navy 5/26/37 Annapolis, MD	7.50
	#790-94, Navy set on one cover, 5/26/37	35.00
	#785-94, Army-Navy set on one cover, 5/26/37	75.00

	1937	
795	3¢ Ordinance of 1787 7/13/37 Marietta, OH	12.00
	New York, NY	12.00
	1st Cachet Craft cachet	**60.00**
	1st Linto cachet	**150.00**
796	5¢ Virginia Dare 8/18/37 Manteo, NC	15.00
797	10¢ S.P.A. sheet 8/26/37 Asheville, NC	12.00
798	3¢ Constitution 9/17/37 Philadelphia, PA	12.00
	1st Pilgrim cachet	**90.00**
	1st Fidelity Stamp Co. cachet	**15.00**
799-802	Territory set of 4 covers	60.00
799-802	On 1 Cover 12/15/37	40.00
799	3¢ Hawaii 10/18/37 Honolulu, HI	20.00
800	3¢ Alaska 11/12/37 Juneau, AK	15.00
801	3¢ Puerto Rico 11/25/37 San Juan, PR	15.00
802	3¢ Virgin Islands 12/15/37 Charlotte Amalie, VI	15.00

	1938-1954 PRESIDENTIAL SERIES	
803-34	Presidents set of 32 covers	450.00
803-31	Presidents set of 29 covers	110.00
803	½¢ Franklin 5/19/38 Philadelphia, PA	3.00
804	1¢ Washington 4/25/38 DC	3.00
804b	booklet pane 1/27/39 DC	15.00
805	1½¢ Martha Washington 5/5/38 DC	3.00
806	2¢ J. Adams 6/3/38 DC	3.00
806b	booklet pane 1/27/39 DC	15.00
807	3¢ Jefferson 6/16/38 DC	3.00
807a	booklet pane 1/27/39 DC	15.00
	#804b, 806b, 807a Bklt. set on one cover, 1/27/38 DC	60.00
808	4¢ Madison 7/1/38 DC	3.00
809	4½¢ White House 7/11/38 DC	3.00
810	5¢ Monroe 7/21/38 DC	3.00
811	6¢ J.Q. Adams 7/28/38 DC	3.00
812	7¢ Jackson 8/4/38 DC	3.00

Scott #	Description	Cacheted
	1938-1954 PRESIDENTIAL SERIES (cont.)	
813	8¢ Van Buren 8/11/38 DC	3.00
814	9¢ Harrison 8/18/38 DC	3.00
815	10¢ Tyler 9/2/38 DC	3.00
816	11¢ Polk 9/8/38 DC	5.00
817	12¢ Taylor 9/14/38 DC	5.00
818	13¢ Fillmore 9/22/38 DC	5.00
819	14¢ Pierce 10/6/38 DC	5.00
820	15¢ Buchanan 10/13/38 DC	5.00
821	16¢ Lincoln 10/20/38 DC	6.00
822	17¢ Johnson 10/27/38 DC	6.00
823	18¢ Grant 11/3/38 DC	6.00
824	19¢ Hayes 11/10/38 DC	6.00
825	20¢ Garfield 11/10/38 DC	6.00
	#824-825 on one FDC	40.00
826	21¢ Arthur 11/22/38 DC	7.00
827	22¢ Cleveland 11/22/38 DC	7.00
	#826-827 on one FDC	40.00
828	24¢ Harrison 12/2/38 DC	8.00
829	25¢ McKinley 12/2/38 DC	8.00
	#828-829 on one FDC	40.00
830	30¢ Roosevelt 12/8/38 DC	10.00
831	50¢ Taft 12/8/38 DC	15.00
	#830-831 on one FDC	40.00
832	$1 Wilson 8/29/38 DC	65.00
832c	$1 Wilson, dry print 8/31/54 DC	30.00
833	$2 Harding 9/29/38 DC	125.00
834	$5 Coolidge 11/17/38 DC	210.00

	PRESIDENTIAL ELECTRIC EYE FDC's	
803-31EE	Presidents set of 29 Covers	550.00
803EE	½¢ Electric Eye 9/8/41 DC	10.00
804EE	1¢ Electric Eye 9/8/41 DC	10.00
	#803, 804, E15 on one FDC	30.00
805EE	1½¢ Electric Eye 1/16/41 DC	10.00
806EE	2¢ Electric Eye (Type I) 6/3/38 DC	15.00
806EE	2¢ Electric Eye (Type II) 4/5/39 DC	8.00
807EE	3¢ Electric Eye 4/5/39 DC	8.00
	#806-807 on one FDC 4/5/39	15.00
807EE	3¢ Electric Eye convertible 1/18/40	12.50
808EE	4¢ Electric Eye 10/28/41 DC	17.50
809EE	4½¢ Electric Eye 10/28/41 DC	17.50
810EE	5¢ Electric Eye 10/28/41 DC	17.50
811EE	6¢ Electric Eye 9/25/41 DC	15.00
812EE	7¢ Electric Eye 10/28/41 DC	17.50
813EE	8¢ Electric Eye 10/28/41 DC	17.50
814EE	9¢ Electric Eye 10/28/41 DC	17.50
815EE	10¢ Electric Eye 9/25/41 DC	15.00
	#811, 815 on one FDC	25.00
816EE	11¢ Electric Eye 10/8/41 DC	20.00
817EE	12¢ Electric Eye 10/8/41 DC	20.00
818EE	13¢ Electric Eye 10/8/41 DC	20.00
819EE	14¢ Electric Eye 10/8/41 DC	20.00
820EE	15¢ Electric Eye 10/8/41 DC	20.00
	#816-820 on one FDC	30.00
821EE	16¢ Electric Eye 1/7/42 DC	25.00
822EE	17¢ Electric Eye 10/28/41 DC	25.00
	#808-10, 812-14, 822 on one FDC	60.00
823EE	18¢ Electric Eye 1/7/42 DC	25.00
824EE	19¢ Electric Eye 1/7/42 DC	25.00
825EE	20¢ Electric Eye 1/7/42 DC	25.00
	#824-825 on one FDC	30.00
826EE	21¢ Electric Eye 1/7/42 DC	25.00
	#821, 823-26 on one FDC	60.00
827EE	22¢ Electric Eye 1/28/42 DC	35.00
828EE	24¢ Electric Eye 1/28/42 DC	35.00
829EE	25¢ Electric Eye 1/28/42 DC	40.00
830EE	30¢ Electric Eye 1/28/42 DC	40.00
831EE	50¢ Electric Eye 1/28/42 DC	50.00
	#827-831 on one FDC	75.00

	1938	
835	3¢ Ratification 6/21/38 Philadelphia, PA	15.00
836	3¢ Swedes and Finns 6/27/38 Wilmington, DE	15.00
	1st Staehle cachet	**50.00**
837	3¢ NW Territory 7/15/38 Marietta, OH	15.00
838	3¢ Iowa Territory 8/24/38 Des Moines, IA	15.00

169

U.S. First Day Covers

924

1939 PRESIDENTIAL COILS

Scott #	Description	Line Pr	Price
839-51	Presidents set of 13 covers	...	65.00
839	1¢ Washington, pair 1/20/39 DC	12.00	5.00
840	1½¢ M. Wash., pair 1/20/39 DC	12.00	5.00
841	2¢ J. Adams, pair 1/20/39 DC	12.00	5.00
842	3¢ Jefferson 1/20/39 DC	12.00	5.00
842	Same, pair	...	7.00
843	4¢ Madison 1/20/39 DC	12.00	6.00
844	4½¢ White House 1/20/39 DC	12.00	6.00
845	5¢ Monroe 1/20/39 DC	15.00	6.00
846	6¢ J.Q. Adams, 1/20/39 DC	17.50	7.00
847	10¢ Tyler 1/20/39 DC	20.00	10.00
839-847	On 1 Cover	125.00	60.00
848	1¢ Washington, pair, vert. coil 1/27/39 DC	12.00	6.00
849	1½¢ M. Wash., pair, vert. coil 1/27/39 DC	12.00ea	6.00
850	2¢ J. Adams, pair, vert. coil 1/27/39 DC	12.00	6.00
851	3¢ Jefferson 1/27/39 DC, Vert coil	12.00	6.00
848-51	On 1 Cover	75.00	40.00
839-51	On 1 cover	200.00	110.00

1939

Scott #	Description	Cacheted
852	3¢ Golden Gate 2/18/39 San Francisco, CA	17.50
853	3¢ World's Fair 4/1/39 New York, NY	17.50
	1st Artcraft cachet unaddressed	**300.00**
854	3¢ Wash. Inauguration 4/30/39 NY, NY	17.50
855	3¢ Baseball 6/12/39 Cooperstown, NY	40.00
856	3¢ Panama Canal 8/15/39 USS Charleston	25.00
857	3¢ Printing Tercent. 9/25/39 NY, NY	17.50
858	3¢ 50th Anniv. 4 States 11/2/39 Bismarck, ND	15.00
	11/2/39 Pierre, SD	15.00
	11/8/39 Helena, MT	15.00
	11/11/39 Olympia, WA	15.00

1940 FAMOUS AMERICANS

Scott #	Description	Cacheted
859-93	**Famous Americans set of 35 covers**	**175.00**
859	1¢ Washington Irving 1/29/40 Terrytown, NY	4.00
860	2¢ James Fenimore Cooper 1/29/40 Cooperstown, NY	4.00
861	3¢ Ralph Waldo Emerson 2/5/40 Boston, MA	4.00
862	5¢ Louisa May Alcott 2/5/40 Concord, MA	5.00
863	10¢ Samuel Clemens 2/13/40 Hannibal, MO	10.00
859-63	Authors on one cover 2/13/40	40.00
864	1¢ Henry W. Longfellow 2/16/40 Portland, ME	4.00
865	2¢ John Greenleaf Whittier 2/16/40 Haverhill, MA	4.00
866	3¢ James Russell Lowell 2/20/40 Cambridge, MA	4.00
867	5¢ Walt Whitman 2/20/40 Camden, NJ	5.00
868	10¢ James Whitcomb Riley 2/24/40 Greenfield, IN	6.00
864-68	Poets on one cover 2/24/40	40.00
869	1¢ Horace Mann 3/14/40 Boston, MA	4.00
870	2¢ Mark Hopkins 3/14/40 Williamstown, MA	4.00
871	3¢ Charles W. Eliot 3/28/40 Cambridge, MA	4.00
872	5¢ Frances E. Willard 3/28/40 Evanston, IL	5.00
873	10¢ Booker T. Washington 4/7/40 Tuskegee Inst., AL	13.00
869-73	Educators on one cover 4/7/40	45.00
874	1¢ John James Audubon 4/8/40 St. Francesville, LA	5.00
875	2¢ Dr. Crawford W. Long 4/8/40 Jefferson, GA	5.00
876	3¢ Luther Burbank 4/17/40 Santa Rosa, CA	4.00
877	5¢ Dr. Walter Reed 4/17/40 DC	5.00
878	10¢ Jane Addams 4/26/40 Chicago, IL	6.00
874-78	Scientists on one cover 4/26/40	40.00
879	1¢ Stephen Collins Foster 5/3/40 Bardstown, KY	4.00
880	2¢ John Philip Sousa 5/3/40 DC	4.00
881	3¢ Victor Herbert 5/13/40 New York, NY	4.00
882	5¢ Edward A. MacDowell 5/13/40 Peterborough, NH	5.00
883	10¢ Ethelbert Nevin 6/10/40 Pittsburgh, PA	6.00
879-83	Composers on one cover 6/10/40	40.00
884	1¢ Gilbert Charles Stuart 9/5/40 Narragansett, RI	4.00
885	2¢ James A. McNeill Whistler 9/5/40 Lowell, MA	4.00
886	3¢ Augustus Saint-Gaudens 9/16/40 New York, NY	4.00
887	5¢ Daniel Chester French 9/16/40 Stockbridge, MA	5.00
888	10¢ Frederic Remington 9/30/40 Canton, NY	6.00
884-88	Artists on one cover 9/30/40	40.00
889	1¢ Eli Whitney 10/7/40 Savannah, GA	4.00
890	2¢ Samuel F.B. Morse 10/7/40 NY, NY	4.00
891	3¢ Cyrus Hall McCormick 10/14/40 Lexington, VA	4.00
892	5¢ Elias Howe 10/14/40 Spencer, MA	5.00
893	10¢ Alexander Graham Bell 10/28/40 Boston, MA	7.00
889-93	Inventors on one cover 10/28/40	40.00
859-93	Famous American set on one cover 10/28/40	200.00

1940-43

Scott #	Description	Cacheted
894	3¢ Pony Exxpress 4/3/40 St. Joseph, MO	9.00
	Sacramento, CA	9.00
	1st Aristocrats cachet	**15.00**
895	3¢ Pan American Union 4/14/40 DC	7.00
896	3¢ Idaho Statehood 7/3/40 Boise, ID	7.00
897	3¢ Wyoming Statehood 7/10/40 Cheyenne, WY	7.00
	1st Spartan cachet	**40.00**
898	3¢ Coronado Expedition 9/7/40 Albuquerque, NM	7.00
899	1¢ National Defense 10/16/40 DC	6.00
900	2¢ National Defense 10/16/40 DC	6.00
901	3¢ National Defense 10/16/40 DC	6.00
899-901	National Defense on one cover	10.00
902	3¢ 13th Amend. 10/20/40 World's Fair, NY	12.00
903	3¢ Vermont Statehood 3/4/41 Montpelier, VT	10.00
	1st Fleetwood cachet	**90.00**
	1st Dorothy Knapp hand painted cachet	**1,750.00**
904	3¢ Kentucky Statehood 6/1/42 Frankfort, KY	7.00
	1st Signed Fleetwood cachet	**75.00**
905	3¢ Win the War 7/4/42 DC	7.00
906	5¢ China Resistance 7/7/42 Denver, CO	15.00
907	2¢ United Nations 1/14/43 DC	7.00
908	1¢ Four Freedoms 2/12/43 DC	7.00

1943-44 OVERRUN NATIONS (FLAGS)

Scott #	Description	Name Blks.	Singles
909-21	**Flags set of 13 covers**	**130.00**	**40.00**
909	5¢ Poland 3/22/43 Chicago, IL	10.00	6.00
	DC	10.00	6.00
	1st Penn Arts cachet	...	**20.00**
	1st Smartcraft cachet	...	**15.00**
910	5¢ Czechoslovakia 7/12/43 DC	10.00	5.00
911	5¢ Norway 7/27/43 DC	10.00	5.00
912	5¢ Luxembourg 8/10/43 DC	10.00	5.00
913	5¢ Netherlands 8/24/43 DC	10.00	5.00
914	5¢ Belgium 9/14/43 DC	10.00	5.00
915	5¢ France 9/28/43 DC	10.00	5.00
916	5¢ Greece 10/12/43 DC	10.00	5.00
917	5¢ Yugoslavia 10/26/43 DC	10.00	5.00
918	5¢ Albania 11/9/43 DC	10.00	5.00
919	5¢ Austria 11/23/43 DC	10.00	5.00
920	5¢ Denmark 12/7/43 DC	10.00	5.00
	#909-920 on one cover, 12/7/43	...	70.00
921	5¢ Korea 11/2/44 DC	10.00	6.00
	#909-921 on one cover, 11/2/44	...	85.00

1944

Scott #	Description	Cacheted
922	3¢ Railroad 5/10/44 Ogden, UT	9.00
	Omaha, NE	9.00
	San Francisco, CA	9.00
923	3¢ Steamship 5/22/44 Kings Point, NY	8.00
	Savannah, GA	8.00
924	3¢ Telegraph 5/24/44 DC	8.00
	Baltimore, MD	8.00
925	3¢ Corregidor 9/27/44 DC	9.00
926	3¢ Motion Picture 10/31/44 Hollywood, CA	8.00
	10/31/44 New York, NY	8.00

1945

Scott #	Description	Cacheted
927	3¢ Florida 3/3/45 Tallahassee, FL	7.00
928	5¢ UN Conference 4/25/45 San Francisco, CA	10.00
929	3¢ Iwo Jima 7/11/45 DC	17.50
930	1¢ Roosevelt 7/26/45 Hyde Park, NY	5.00
931	2¢ Roosevelt 8/24/45 Warm Springs, GA	5.00
932	3¢ Roosevelt 6/27/45 DC	5.00
	1st Fluegel cachet	**75.00**
933	5¢ Roosevelt 1/30/46 DC	5.00
	#930-933 on one cover 1/30/46 DC	12.00
934	3¢ Army 9/28/45 DC	10.00
935	3¢ Navy 10/27/45 Annapolis, MD	10.00
936	3¢ Coast Guard 11/10/45 New York, NY	10.00
937	3¢ Alfred E. Smith 11/26/45 New York, NY	6.00
938	3¢ Texas Centennial 12/29/45 Austin, TX	9.00

1946

Scott #	Description	Cacheted
939	3¢ Merchant Marine 2/26/46 DC	10.00
	#929, 934-36, 939 on one cover 2/26/46	30.00
940	3¢ Honorable Discharge 5/9/46 DC	10.00
	1st Artmaster cachet	**20.00**
	#929, 934-36, 939-940 on one cover 5/9/46	35.00
941	3¢ Tennessee Sthd. 6/1/46 Nashville, TN	4.00
942	3¢ Iowa Statehood 8/3/46 Iowa City, IA	4.00
943	3¢ Smithsonian 8/10/46 DC	4.00
944	3¢ New Mexico 10/16/46 Santa Fe, NM	4.00

1947

Scott #	Description	Cacheted
945	3¢ Thomas A. Edison 2/11/47 Milan, OH	4.50
946	3¢ Joseph Pulitzer 4/10/47 New York, NY	4.00
947	3¢ Stamp Centenary Sheet 5/17/47 New York, NY	4.00
	1st Fulton cachet (10 different)	**30.00**
948	5¢-10¢ Stamp Centenary Sheet 5/19/47 New York, NY	4.50
949	3¢ Doctors 6/9/47 Atlantic City, NJ	8.00
950	3¢ Utah Cent. 7/24/47 Salt Lake City, UT	4.00
951	3¢ Constitution 10/21/47 Boston, MA	7.50
	1st C.W. George cachet	**75.00**
	1st Suncraft cachet	**25.00**

U.S. First Day Covers

963

Scott #	Description	Cacheted
	1948	
952	3¢ Everglades 12/5/47 Florida City, FL	4.00
953	3¢ G. Washington Carver 1/5/48 Tuskegee Inst., AL	6.00
	1st Jackson cachet	**35.00**
954	3¢ Discovery of Gold 1/24/48 Coloma, CA	3.00
955	3¢ Mississippi 4/7/48 Natchez, MS	3.00
956	3¢ Four Chaplains 5/28/48 DC	5.00
957	3¢ Wisconsin Cent. 5/29/48 Madison, WI	2.00
958	5¢ Swedish Pioneers 6/4/48 Chicago, IL	2.00
959	3¢ Women's Prog. 7/19/48 Seneca Falls, NY	2.00
960	3¢ William A. White 7/31/48 Emporia, KS	2.00
961	3¢ US-Canada 8/2/48 Niagara Falls, NY	2.00
962	3¢ Francis Scott Key 8/9/48 Frederick, MD	2.25
963	3¢ Youth of America 8/11/48 DC	2.00
964	3¢ Oregon Terr. 8/14/48 Oregon City, OR	2.00
965	3¢ Harlan Fisk Stone 8/25/48 Chesterfield, NH	2.00
966	3¢ Palomar Observatory 8/30/48 Palomar Mt., CA	3.50
967	3¢ Clara Barton 9/7/48 Oxford, MA	3.50
968	3¢ Poultry Industry 9/9/48 New Haven, CT	2.00
969	3¢ Gold Star Mothers 9/21/48 DC	2.00
970	3¢ Fort Kearny 9/22/48 Minden, NE	2.00
971	3¢ Fireman 10/4/48 Dover, DE	5.00
972	3¢ Indian Centennial 10/15/48 Muskogee, OK	2.00
973	3¢ Rough Riders 10/27/48 Prescott, AZ	2.00
974	3¢ Juliette Low 10/29/48 Savannah, GA	7.50
975	3¢ Will Rogers 11/4/48 Claremore, OK	2.00
	1st Kolor Kover cachet	**125.00**
976	3¢ Fort Bliss 11/5/48 El Paso, TX	3.50
977	3¢ Moina Michael 11/9/48 Athens, GA	2.00
978	3¢ Gettysburgh Address 11/19/48 Gettysburg, PA	4.00
979	3¢ Amer. Turners 11/20/48 Cincinnati, OH	2.00
980	3¢ Joel Chandler Harris 12/9/48 Eatonton, GA	2.00
	1949	
981	3¢ Minnesota Terr. 3/3/49 St. Paul, MN	3.00
982	3¢ Washington & Lee Univ. 4/12/49 Lexington, VA	3.00
983	3¢ Puerto Rico 4/27/49 San Juan, PR	4.00
984	3¢ Annapolis 5/23/49 Annapolis, MD	4.00
985	3¢ G.A.R. 8/29/49 Indianapolis, IN	4.00
986	3¢ Edgar Allan Poe 10/7/49 Richmond, VA	4.00
	1950	
987	3¢ Bankers 1/3/50 Saratoga Springs, NY	3.00
988	3¢ Samuel Gompers 1/27/50 DC	2.00
989	3¢ Statue of Freedom 4/20/50 DC	2.00
990	3¢ White House 6/12/50 DC	2.00
991	3¢ Supreme Court 8/2/50 DC	2.00
992	3¢ Capitol 11/22/50 DC	2.00
	#989-992 on one cover 11/22/50	7.50
993	3¢ Railroad Engineers 4/29/50 Jackson, TN	5.00
994	3¢ Kansas City 6/3/50 Kansas City, MO	2.00
995	3¢ Boy Scouts 6/30/50 Valley Forge, PA	7.50
996	3¢ Indiana Terr. 7/4/50 Vincennes, IN	2.00
997	3¢ California Sthd. 9/9/50 Sacramento, CA	3.00
	1951	
998	3¢ Confederate Vets. 5/30/51 Norfolk, VA	4.00
999	3¢ Nevada Territory 7/14/51 Genoa, NY	2.00
1000	3¢ Landing of Cadillac 7/24/51 Detroit, MI	2.00
1001	3¢ Colorado Statehood 8/1/51 Minturn, CO	2.50
1002	3¢ Amer. Chem. Soc. 9/4/51 New York, NY	2.00
1003	3¢ Battle of Brooklyn 12/10/51 Brooklyn, NY	2.00
	1st Velvatone cachet	**75.00**
	1952	
1004	3¢ Betsy Ross 1/2/52 Philadelphia, PA	2.50
	1st Steelcraft cachet	**30.00**
1005	3¢ 4-H Clubs 1/15/52 Springfield, OH	7.50
1006	3¢ B. & O. Railroad 2/28/52 Baltimore, MD	5.00
1007	3¢ Am. Automobile Assoc. 3/4/52 Chicago, IL	2.00
1008	3¢ NATO 4/4/52 DC	2.00
1009	3¢ Grand Coulee Dam 5/15/52 Grand Coulee, WA	2.00
1010	3¢ Lafayette 6/13/52 Georgetown, SC	2.00
1011	3¢ Mount Rushmore 8/11/52 Keystone, SD	2.00
1012	3¢ Civil Engineers 9/6/52 Chicago, IL	2.00
1013	3¢ Service Women 9/11/52 DC	2.50
1014	3¢ Gutenberg Bible 9/30/52 DC	2.00
1015	3¢ Newspaper Boys 10/4/52 Phila., PA	2.00

Scott #	Description	Cacheted
	1953	
1016	3¢ Red Cross 11/21/52 New York, NY	3.00
1017	3¢ National Guard 2/23/53 DC	2.00
1018	3¢ Ohio Statehood 3/2/53 Chillicothe, OH	2.00
	1st Boerger cachet	**25.00**
1019	3¢ Washington Terr. 3/2/53 Olympia, WA	2.00
1020	3¢ Louisiana Pur. 4/30/53 St. Louis, MO	4.00
1021	3¢ Opening of Japan 7/14/53 DC	3.00
	1st Overseas Mailers cachet	**75.00**
1022	3¢ Amer. Bar Assoc. 8/24/53 Boston, MA	6.00
1023	3¢ Sagamore Hill 9/14/53 Oyster Bay. NY	2.00
1024	3¢ Future Farmers 10/13/53 KS City, MO	2.00
1025	3¢ Trucking Ind. 10/27/53 Los Angeles, CA	3.00
1026	3¢ General Patton 11/11/53 Fort Knox, NY	3.00
1027	3¢ Founding of NYC 11/20/53 New York, NY	2.00
1028	3¢ Gadsden Purchase 12/30/53 Tucson, AZ	2.00
	1954	
1029	3¢ Columbia Univ. 1/4/54 New York, NY	2.00
	1954-61 LIBERTY SERIES	
1030-53	Liberty set of 27	100.00
1030	½¢ Franklin 10/20/55 DC	2.00
1031	1¢ Washington 8/26/54 Chicago, IL	2.00
1031A	1¼¢ Palace 6/17/60 Santa Fe, NM	2.00
1032	1½¢ Mt. Vernon 2/22/56 Mt. Vernon, VA	2.00
1033	2¢ Jefferson 9/15/54 San Francisco, CA	2.00
1034	2½¢ Bunker Hill 6/17/59 Boston, MA	2.00
1035	3¢ Statue of Liberty 6/24/54 Albany, NY	2.00
1035a	booklet pane 6/30/54	4.00
1035b	Luminescent 7/6/66 DC	50.00
1035b & 1225a	Luminescent, combo	60.00
1036	4¢ Lincoln 11/19/54 New York, NY	2.00
1036a	booklet pane 7/31/58 Wheeling, WV	3.00
1036b	Luminescent 11/2/63 DC	100.00
1037	4½¢ Hermitage 3/16/59 Hermitage, TN	2.00
1038	5¢ Monroe 12/2/54 Fredericksburg, VA	2.00
1039	6¢ Roosevelt 11/18/55 New York, NY	2.00
1040	7¢ Wilson 1/110/56 Staunton, VA	2.00
1041	8¢ Statue of Liberty 4/9/54 DC	2.00
1042	8¢ Stat. of Lib. (Giori Press) 3/22/58 Cleveland, OH	2.00
1042A	8¢ Pershing 11/17/61 New York, NY	2.25
1043	9¢ The Alamo 6/14/56 San Antonio, TX	2.00
1044	10¢ Independence Hall 7/4/56 Phila., PA	2.00
1044b	Luminescent 7/6/66	50.00
1044A	11¢ Statue of Liberty 6/15/61 DC	2.50
1044Ac	Luminescent 1/11/67	50.00
1045	12¢ Harrison 6/6/59 Oxford, OH	2.00
1045a	Luminescent 5/6/68	40.00
1045a & 1055a	Luminescent, combo	40.00
1046	15¢ John Jay 12/12/58 DC	2.50
1046a	Luminescent 5/6/68	50.00
1047	20¢ Monticello 4/13/56 Charlottesville, VA	2.50
1048	25¢ Paul Revere 4/118/58 Boston, MA	2.50
1049	30¢ Robert E. Lee 9/21/55 Norfolk, VA	4.00
1050	40¢ John Marshall 9/24/55 Richmond, VA	4.00
1051	50¢ Susan Anthony 8/25/55 Louisville, KY	6.00
1052	$1 Patrick Henry 10/7/55 Joplin, MO	10.00
1053	$5 Alex Hamilton 3/19/56 Patterson, NJ	50.00
	1954-65 LIBERTY SERIES COILS	
1054	1¢ Washington 10/8/54 Baltimore, MD	2.00
1054A	1¼¢ Palace 6/17/60 Santa Fe, NM	2.00
1055	2¢ Jefferson 10/22/54 St. Louis, MO	2.00
1055a	Luminescent 5/6/68 DC	40.00
1055a & 1045a	Luminescent, combo	50.00
1056	2½¢ Bunker Hill 9/9/59 Los Angeles, CA	2.00
1057	3¢ Statue of Liberty 7/20/54 DC	2.00
1057b	Luminescent 5/12/67 DC	60.00
1058	4¢ Lincoln 7/31/58 Mandan, ND	2.00
1059	4½¢ Hermitage 5/1/59 Denver, CO	2.00
1059A, & 1289-95	1973 Regular Tagged Issues, set of 8, 4/3/73, NY	450.00
1059A, & 1289-95	1973 Regular Tagged Issues, all 8 on 1 cover, 4/3/73, NY	250.00
1059A	25¢ Paul Revere 2/25/65 Wheaton, MD	2.50
1059b	Luminescent 4/3/73 NY, NY	40.00
1060	3¢ Nebraska Ter. 5/7/54 Nebraska City, NE	2.00
1061	3¢ Kansas Terr. 5/31/54 Fort Leavenworth, KS	2.00
1062	3¢ George Eastman 7/12/54 Rochester, NY	2.00
1063	3¢ Lewis & Clark 7/28/54 Sioux City, IA	4.00
	1955	
1064	3¢ Fine Arts 1/15/55 Philadelphia, PA	2.00
1065	3¢ Land Grant Colleges 2/12/55 East Lansing, MI	3.00
1066	3¢ Rotary Int. 2/23/55 Chicago, IL	4.00
1067	3¢ Armed Forces Reserve 5/21/55 DC	2.00
1068	3¢ New Hampshire 6/21/55 Franconia, NH	2.00
1069	3¢ Soo Locks 6/28/55 Sault St. Marie, MI	2.00
1070	3¢ Atoms for Peace 7/28/55 DC	2.00
1071	3¢ Fort Ticonderoga 9/18/55 Ticonderoga, NY	2.00
1072	3¢ Andrew W. Mellon 12/20/55 DC	2.00
	1956	
1073	3¢ Benjamin Franklin 1/17/56 Phila., PA	2.00
	Poor Richard Station	2.00
1074	3¢ Booker T. Washington 4/5/56	
	Booker T. Washington Birthplace, VA	4.00

U.S. First Day Covers

1129

Scott #	Description	Cacheted
	1956 (cont.)	
1075	11¢ FIPEX Sheet 4/28/56 New York, NY	4.50
1076	3¢ FIPEX 4/30/56 New York, NY	2.00
1077	3¢ Wild Turkey 5/5/56 Fond du Lac, WI	3.00
1078	3¢ Antelope 6/22/56 Gunnison, CO	3.00
1079	3¢ King Salmon 11/9/56 Seattle, WA	3.00
1080	3¢ Pure Food and Drug Laws 6/27/56 DC	2.00
1081	3¢ Wheatland 8/5/56 Lancaster, PA	2.00
1082	3¢ Labor Day 9/3/56 Camden, NJ	2.00
1083	3¢ Nassau Hall 9/22/56 Princeton, NJ	2.00
1084	3¢ Devils Tower 9/24/56 Devils Tower, NY	2.00
1085	3¢ Children 12/15/56 DC	2.00
	1957	
1086	3¢ Alex Hamilton 1/11/57 New York, NY	2.00
1087	3¢ Polio 1/15/57 DC	2.50
1088	3¢ Coast & Geodetic Survey 2/11/57 Seattle, WA	2.00
1089	3¢ Architects 2/23/57 New York, NY	2.25
1090	3¢ Steel Industry 5/22/57 New York, NY	2.00
1091	3¢ Naval Review 6/10/57 USS Saratoga, Norfolk, VA	2.00
1092	3¢ Oklahoma Statehood 6/14/57 Oklahoma City, OK	2.00
1093	3¢ School Teachers 7/1/57 Phila., PA	2.50
	"Philadelpia" error cancel	7.50
1094	4¢ American Flag 7/4/57 DC	2.00
1095	3¢ Shipbuilding 8/15/57 Bath, ME	2.00
1096	8¢ Ramon Magsaysay 8/31/57 DC	2.00
1097	3¢ Lafayette 9/6/57 Easton, PA	2.00
	Fayetteville, NC	2.00
	Louisville, KY	2.00
1098	3¢ Whooping Crane 11/22/57 New York, NY	2.50
	New Orleans, LA	2.50
	Corpus Christi, TX	2.50
1099	3¢ Religious Freedom 12/27/57 Flushing, NY	2.00
	1958-59	
1100	3¢ Horticulture 3/15/58 Ithaca, NY	2.00
1104	3¢ Brussels Exhibit. 4/17/58 Detroit, MI	2.00
1105	3¢ James Monroe 4/28/58 Montross, VA	2.00
1106	3¢ Minnesota Sthd. 5/11/58 St. Paul, MN	2.00
1107	3¢ Int'l. Geo. Year 5/31/58 Chicago, IL	2.00
1108	3¢ Gunston Hall 6/12/58 Lorton, VA	2.00
1109	3¢ Mackinaw Bridge 6/25/58 Mackinaw Bridge, MI	2.00
1110	4¢ Simon Bolivar 7/24/58 DC	2.00
1111	8¢ Simon Bolivar 7/24/58 DC	2.00
1110-11	Bolivar on one cover	2.50
1112	4¢ Atlantic Cable 8/15/58 New York, NY	2.00
1113	1¢ Lincoln 2/12/59 Hodgenville, KY	2.00
1114	3¢ Lincoln 2/27/59 New York, NY	2.00
1115	4¢ Lincoln & Douglas 8/27/58 Freeport, IL	2.00
1116	4¢ Lincoln Statue 5/30/59 DC	2.00
1113-16	On 1 Cover	8.00
1117	4¢ Lajos Kossuth 9/19/58 DC	2.00
1118	8¢ Lajos Kossuth 9/19/58 DC	2.00
1117-18	Kossuth on one cover	2.50
1119	4¢ Freedom of Press 9/22/58 Columbia, MO	2.00
1120	4¢ Overland Mail 10/10/58 San Fran., CA	2.00
	1958-59	
1121	4¢ Noah Webster 10/16/58 W. Hartford, CT	2.00
1122	4¢ Forest Conserv. 10/27/58 Tucson, AZ	2.00
1123	4¢ Fort Duquesne 11/25/58 Pittsburgh, PA	2.00
1124	4¢ Oregon Sthd. 2/14/59 Astoria, OR	2.00
1125	4¢ Jose de San Martin 2/25/59 DC	2.00
1126	8¢ Jose de San Martin 2/25/59 DC	2.00
1125-26	San Martin on one cover	2.50
1127	4¢ NATO 4/1/59 DC	2.00
1128	4¢ Arctic Explorers 4/6/59 Cresson, PA	2.00
1129	8¢ World Trade 4/20/59 DC	2.00
1130	4¢ Silver Cent. 6/8/59 Virginia City, NV	2.00
1131	4¢ St. Lawrence Seaway 6/26/59 Massena, NY	2.00
1131	Joint issue w/Canada	10.00
1131	Joint issue w/Canada, dual cancel	250.00
1132	4¢ 49-Star Flag 7/4/59 Auburn, NY	2.00
1133	4¢ Soil Conserv. 8/26/59 Rapid City, SD	2.00
1134	4¢ Petroleum Ind. 8/27/59 Titusville, PA	3.00
1135	4¢ Dental Health 9/14/59 New York, NY	5.00

Scott #	Description	Cacheted
	1958-59 (cont.)	
1136	4¢ Ernst Reuter 9/29/59 DC	2.00
1137	8¢ Ernst Reuter 9/29/59 DC	2.00
1136-37	Reuter on one cover	2.50
1138	4¢ Dr. McDowell 12/3/59 Danville, KY	2.00
	1960-61	
1139	4¢ Washington Credo 1/20/60 Mt. Vernon, VA	2.00
1140	4¢ Franklin Credo 3/31/60 Phila., PA	2.00
1141	4¢ Jefferson Credo 5/18/60 Charlottesville, VA	2.00
1142	4¢ Francis Scott Key Credo 9/14/60 Baltimore, MD	2.00
1143	4¢ Lincoln Credo 11/19/60 New York, NY	2.00
1144	4¢ Patrick Henry Credo 1/11/61 Richmond, VA	2.00
	#1139-1144 on one cover, 1/11/61	6.00
1145	4¢ Boy Scouts 2/8/60 DC	7.50
1146	4¢ Winter Olympics 2/18/60 Olympic Valley, CA	2.00
1147	4¢ Thomas G. Masaryk 3/7/60 DC	2.00
1148	8¢ Thomas G. Masaryk 3/7/60 DC	2.00
1147-48	Masaryk on one cover	2.50
1149	4¢ World Refugee Year 4/7/60 DC	2.00
1150	4¢ Water Conservation 4/18/60 DC	2.00
1151	4¢ SEATO 5/31/60 DC	2.00
1152	4¢ American Women 6/2/60 DC	2.00
1153	4¢ 50-Star Flag 7/4/60 Honolulu, HI	2.00
1154	4¢ Pony Express Centennial 7/19/60 Sacramento, CA ...	3.00
1155	4¢ Employ the Handicapped 8/28/60 New York, NY	3.00
1156	4¢ World Forestry Co. 8/29/60 Seattle, WA	2.00
1157	4¢ Mexican Indep. 9/16/60 Los Angeles, CA	2.00
1157	Joint issue w/Mexico	20.00
1157	Joint issue w/Mexico, dual cancel	375.00
1158	4¢ US-Japan Treaty 9/28/60 DC	2.00
1159	4¢ Paderewski 10/8/60 DC	2.00
1160	8¢ Paderewski 10/8/60 DC	2.00
1159-60	Paderewski on one cover	2.50
1161	4¢ Robert A. Taft 10/10/60 Cincinnati, OH	2.00
1162	4¢ Wheels of Freedom 10/15/60 Detroit, MI	2.00
1163	4¢ Boys Clubs 10/18/60 New York, NY	2.00
1164	4¢ Automated P.O. 10/20/60 Providence, RI	2.00
1165	4¢ Gustav Mannerheim 10/26/60 DC	2.00
1166	8¢ Gustav Mannerheim 10/26/60 DC	2.00
1165-66	Mannerheim on one cover	2.50
1167	4¢ Camp Fire Girls 11/1/60 New York, NY	4.00
1168	4¢ Giuseppe Garibaldi 11/2/60 DC	2.00
1169	8¢ Giuseppe Garibaldi 11/2/60 DC	2.00
1168-69	Garibaldi on one cover	2.50
1170	4¢ Walter F. George 11/5/60 Vienna, GA	2.00
1171	4¢ Andrew Carnegie 11/25/60 New York, NY	2.00
1172	4¢ John Foster Dulles 12/6/60 DC	2.00
1173	4¢ Echo 1 12/15/60 DC	3.00
	1961-65	
1174	4¢ Mahatma Gandhi 1/26/61 DC	2.00
1175	8¢ Mahatma Gandhi 1/26/61 DC	2.00
1174-75	Gandhi on one cover	2.50
1176	4¢ Range Cons. 2/2/61 Salt Lake City, UT	2.00
1177	4¢ Horace Greeley 2/3/61 Chappaqua, NY	2.00
1178	4¢ Fort Sumter 4/12/61 Charleston, SC	6.00
1179	4¢ Battle of Shiloh 4/7/62 Shiloh, TN	6.00
1180	5¢ Battle of Gettysburg 7/1/63 Gettysburg, PA	6.00
1181	5¢ Battle of Wilderness 5/5/64 Fredericksburg, VA	6.00
1182	5¢ Appomattox 4/9/65 Appomattox, VA	6.00
1178-82	Civil War on 1 cover 4/9/65	12.00
1183	4¢ Kansas Statehood 5/10/61 Council Grove, KS	2.00
1184	4¢ George Norris 7/11/611 DC	2.00
1185	4¢ Naval Aviation 8/20/61 San Diego, CA	2.00
1186	4¢ Workmen's Comp. 9/4/61 Milwaukee, WI	2.00
1187	4¢ Frederic Remington 10/4/61 DC	2.00
1188	4¢ Sun Yat-Sen 10/10/61 DC	6.00
1189	4¢ Basketball 11/6/61 Springfield, MA	8.00
1190	4¢ Nursing 12/28/61 DC	12.00
	1962	
1191	4¢ New Mexico Sthd. 1/6/62 Santa Fe, NM	2.25
1192	4¢ Arizona Sthd. 2/14/62 Phoenix, AZ	2.25
	1st Glory cachet	**35.00**
1193	4¢ Project Mercury 2/20/62 Cape Canaveral, FL	4.00
	1st Marg cachet	**25.00**
1194	4¢ Malaria Eradication 3/30/62 DC	2.00
1195	4¢ Charles Evans Hughes 4/11/62 DC	2.00
1196	4¢ Seattle Fair 4/25/62 Seattle, WA	2.00
1197	4¢ Louisiana 4/30/62 New Orleans, LA	2.00
1198	4¢ Homestead Act 5/20/62 Beatrice, NE	2.00
1199	4¢ Girl Scouts 7/24/62 Burlington, VT	6.00
1200	4¢ Brien McMahon 7/28/62 Norwalk, CT	2.00
1201	4¢ Apprenticeship 8/31/62 DC	2.00
1202	4¢ Sam Rayburn 9/16/62 Bonham, TX	3.00
1203	4¢ Dag Hammarskjold 10/23/62 NY, NY	2.00
1204	4¢ Hammarskjold Invert. 11/16/62 DC	5.00
1205	4¢ Christmas 11/1/62 Pittsburgh, PA	2.00
1206	4¢ Higher Education 11/14/62 DC	2.25
1207	4¢ Winslow Homer 12/15/62 Gloucester, MA	2.25
	1962-63 REGULAR ISSUES	
1208	5¢ 50-Star Flag 1/9/63 DC	2.00
1208a	5¢ Luminescent 8/25/66 DC	35.00
1209	1¢ Andrew Jackson 3/22/63 New York, NY	2.00
1209a	Luminescent 7/6/66 DC	35.00

U.S. First Day Covers

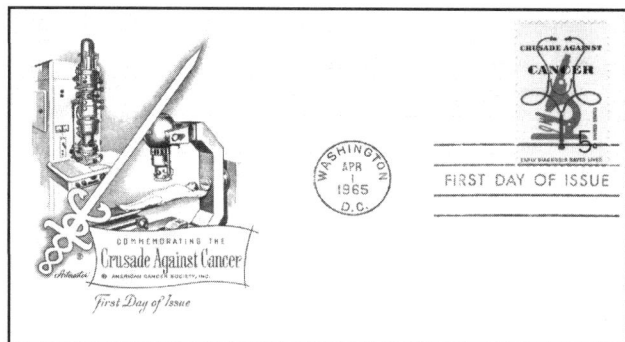

1263

1298

Scott #	Description	Cacheted
	1962-63 REGULAR ISSUES (cont.)	
1213	5¢ Washington 11/23/62 New York, NY	2.00
1213a	Booklet Pane 11/23/62 New York, NY	3.00
1213b	Luminescent 10/28/63 Dayton, OH	35.00
1213c	Luminescent bklt. pair 10/28/63 Dayton, OH	40.00
1213c	Luminescent bklt. pane 10/28/63 Dayton, OH	100.00
	DC	125.00
1225	1¢ Jackson, coil 5/31/63 Chicago, IL	2.00
1225a	Luminescent 7/6/66 DC	35.00
1225a & 1035b Luminescent combo		40.00
1229	5¢ Washington, coil 11/23/62 New York, NY	2.00
1229a	Luminescent 10/28/63 Dayton, OH	35.00
	DC	35.00
1229a,1213b, & 1213c On one FDC 10/28/63 Dayton, OH		60.00
	1963	
1230	5¢ Carolina Charter 4/6/63 Edenton, NC	2.00
1231	5¢ Food for Peace 6/4/63 DC	2.00
1232	5¢ W. Virginia Sthd. 6/20/63 Wheeling, WV	2.00
1233	5¢ Emancipation Proc. 8/16/63 Chicago, IL	4.00
1234	5¢ Alliance for Progress 8/17/63 DC	2.00
1235	5¢ Cordell Hull 10/5/63 Carthage, TN	2.00
1236	5¢ Eleanor Roosevelt 10/11/63 DC	2.00
1237	5¢ Science 10/14/63 DC	2.00
1238	5¢ City Mail Delivery 10/26/63 DC	2.00
1239	5¢ Red Cross 10/29/63 DC	2.50
1240	5¢ Christmas 11/1/63 Santa Claus, IN	2.00
1240a	5¢ Luminescent 11/2/63 DC	60.00
1241	5¢ Audubon 12/7/63 Henderson, KY	2.00
	1964	
1242	5¢ Sam Houston 1/10/64 Houston, TX	4.00
1243	5¢ Charles Russell 3/19/64 Great Falls, MT	2.50
1244	5¢ NY World's Fair 4/22/64 World's Fair, NY	2.00
	1st Sarzin Metallic cachet	**20.00**
1245	5¢ John Muir 4/29/64 Martinez, CA	3.00
1246	5¢ John F. Kennedy 5/29/64 Boston, MA	2.50
	1st Cover Craft cachet	**40.00**
1247	5¢ New Jersey Terc. 6/15/64 Elizabeth, NJ	2.00
1248	5¢ Nevada Sthd. 7/22/64 Carson City, NV	2.00
1249	5¢ Register & Vote 8/1/64 DC	2.00
1250	5¢ Shakespeare 8/14/64 Stratford, CT	2.00
1251	5¢ Doctors Mayo 9/11/64 Rochester, MN	5.00
1252	5¢ American Music 10/15/64 New York, NY	2.50
1253	5¢ Homemakers 10/26/64 Honolulu, HI	2.00
1254-57	5¢ Christmas attd. 11/9/64 Bethlehem, PA	4.00
1254-57	Christmas set of 4 singles	10.00
1254-57a	Luminescent Christmas attd 11/10/64 Dayton, OH	60.00
1254-57a	Luminescent Christmas set of 4 singles	80.00
1258	5¢ Verrazano-Narrows Bridge 11/21/64 Stat. Is., NY	2.00
1259	5¢ Fine Arts 12/2/64 DC	2.00
1260	5¢ Amateur Radio 12/15/64 Anchorage, AK	7.50
	1965	
1261	5¢ Battle of New Orleans 1/8/65 New Orleans, LA	2.00
1262	5¢ Physical Fitness 2/15/65 DC	2.00
1263	5¢ Cancer Crusade 4/1/65 DC	3.50
1264	5¢ Winston Churchill 5/13/65 Fulton, MO	2.25
1265	5¢ Magna Carta 6/15/65 Jamestown, VA	2.00
1266	5¢ Int'l. Cooperation Year 6/26/65 San Francisco, CA	2.00
1267	5¢ Salvation Army 7/2/65 New York, NY	3.00
1268	5¢ Dante 7/17/65 San Francisco, CA	2.00
1269	5¢ Herbert Hoover 8/10/65 West Branch, IA	2.00
1270	5¢ Robert Fulton 8/19/65 Clermont, NY	2.00
1271	5¢ 400th Anniv. of FL 8/28/65 St. Augustine, FL	2.00
1271	Combo w/Spain	90.00
1271	Combo w/Spain, dual cancel	450.00
1272	5¢ Traffic Safety 9/3/65 Baltimore, MD	2.00
1273	5¢ John Copley 9/17/65 DC	2.00
1274	11¢ Int'l. Telecomm. Union 10/6/65 DC	2.00
1275	5¢ A. Stevenson 10/23/65 Bloominton, IL	2.00
1276	5¢ Christmas 11/2/65 Silver Bell, AZ	2.00
1276a	Luminescent 11/16/65 DC	50.00
	1965-68 PROMINENT AMERICANS SERIES	
1278	1¢ Jefferson 1/12/68 Jeffersonville, IN	2.00

Scott #	Description	Cacheted
	1965-68 PROMINENT AMERICANS SERIES (cont.)	
1278a	bklt. pane of 8 1/12/68 Jeffersonville, IN	2.00
1278a	bklt. pane of 8, dull gum 3/1/71 DC	90.00
1278a & 1393a Combo, 3/1/71		150.00
1278b	booklet pane of 4 5/10/71 DC	15.00
1279	1¼¢ Gallatin 1/30/67 Gallatin, MO	2.00
1280	2¢ Wright 6/8/66 Spring Green, WI	2.00
1280a	booklet pane of 5 1/8/68 Buffalo, NY	3.00
1280c	booklet pane of 6 5/7/71 Spokane, WA	15.00
1280c var.	bklt. pane of 6, dull gum 10/31/75 Cleveland, OH	100.00
1281	3¢ Parkman 9/16/67 Boston, MA	2.00
1282	4¢ Lincoln 11/19/65 New York, NY	2.00
1282a	Luminescent 12/1/65 Dayton, OH	40.00
	DC	45.00
1283	5¢ Washington 2/22/66 DC	2.00
1283a	Luminescent 2/23/66 Dayton, OH	100.00
	DC	27.50
1283B	5¢ Washington, redrawn 11/17/67 New York, NY	2.00
1284	6¢ Roosevelt 1/29/66 Hyde Park, NY	2.00
1284a	Luminescent 12/29/66	40.00
1284b	booklet pane of 8 12/28/67 DC	2.50
1284bs	booklet single	2.00
1284c	booklet pane of 5 1/9/68 DC	125.00
1285	8¢ Einstein 3/14/66 Princeton, NJ	4.50
1285a	Luminescent 7/6/66 DC	40.00
1286	10¢ Jackson 3/15/67 Hermitage, TN	2.00
1286A	12¢ Ford 7/30/68 Greenfield Village, MI	3.00
1287	13¢ Kennedy 5/29/67 Brookline, MA	2.50
1288	15¢ Holmes 3/8/68 DC	2.00
1288B	booklet single 6/14/78 Boston, MA	2.00
1288Bc	15¢ bklt. pane of 8 6/14/78 Boston, MA	3.50
1289	20¢ Marshall 10/24/67 Lexington, VA	2.00
1289a	Luminescent 4/3/73 New York, NY	40.00
1290	25¢ Douglass 2/14/67 DC	4.50
1290a	Luminescent 4/3/73 DC	45.00
1291	30¢ Dewey 10/21/68 Burlington, VT	2.50
1291a	Luminescent 4/3/73 New York, NY	45.00
1292	40¢ Paine 1/29/68 Philadelphia, PA	3.00
1292a	Luminescent 4/3/73 New York, NY	45.00
1293	50¢ Stone 8/13/68 Dorchester, MA	4.00
1293a	Luminescent 4/3/73 New York, NY	50.00
1294	$1 O'Neill 10/16/67 New London, CT	7.00
1294a	Luminescent 4/3/73 New York, NY	65.00
1295	$5 Moore 12/3/66 Smyrna, DE	40.00
1295a	Luminescent 4/3/73 New York NY	125.00
#1295 & 1295a on one cover 4/3/73		250.00
	1966-81 PROMINENT AMERICAN COILS	
1297	3¢ Parkman 11/4/75 Pendleton, OR, Vertical coil	2.00
1298	6¢ Roosevelt, vert. coil 12/28/67 DC	2.00
1299	1¢ Jefferson 1/12/68 Jeffersonville, IN	2.00
1303	4¢ Lincoln 5/28/66 Springfield, IL	2.00
1304	5¢ Washington 9/8/66 Cinncinnati, OH	2.00
1304C	5¢ Washington re-engraved 3/31/81 DC	25.00
1305	6¢ Roosevelt, horiz. coil 2/28/68 DC	2.00
1305E	15¢ Holmes 6/14/78 Boston, MA	2.00
1305C	$1 O'Neill 1/12/73 Hampstead, NY	4.00
	1966	
1306	5¢ Migratory Bird 3/16/66 Pittsburgh, PA	2.50
1307	5¢ Humane Treatment 4/9/66 New York, NY	2.00
1308	5¢ Indiana Sthd. 4/16/66 Corydon, IN	2.00
1309	5¢ Circus 5/2/66 Delevan, WI	4.00
1310	5¢ SIPEX 5/21/66 DC	2.00
1311	5¢ SIPEX sheet 5/23/66 DC	2.25
1312	5¢ Bill of Rights 7/1/66 Miami Beach, FL	3.00
1313	5¢ Polish Millenium 7/30/66 DC	2.00
1314	5¢ Nat'l. Park Service 8/25/66 Yellowstone Nat'l. Park	2.00
1314a	Luminescent 8/26/66	50.00
1315	5¢ Marine Corps Reserve 8/29/66 DC	2.50
1315a	Luminescent 8/29/66 DC	50.00
1316	5¢ Women's Clubs 9/12/66 New York, NY	2.00
1316a	Luminescent 9/13/66 DC	50.00
1317	5¢ Johnny Appleseed 9/24/66 Leominster, MA	2.00
1317a	Luminescent 9/26/66 DC	50.00
1318	5¢ Beautification 10/5/66 DC	2.00

U.S. First Day Covers

	1365-68	
Scott #	**Description**	**Cacheted**

1966 (cont.)

Scott #	Description	Cacheted
1318a	Luminescent 10/5/66 DC	50.00
1319	5¢ Great River Road 10/21/66 Baton Rouge, LA	2.00
1319a	Luminescent 10/22/66 DC	50.00
1320	5¢ Savings Bonds 10/26/66 Sioux City, IA	2.00
1320a	Luminescent 10/27/66 DC	50.00
1321	5¢ Christmas 11/1/66 Christmas, MI	2.00
1321a	Luminescent 11/2/66	50.00
1322	5¢ Mary Cassatt 11/17/66 DC	2.00
1322a	Luminescent 11/17/66 DC	50.00

1967

Scott #	Description	Cacheted
1323	5¢ National Grange 4/17/67 DC	2.00
1324	5¢ Canada Centenary 5/25/67 Montreal, CAN	2.00
1325	5¢ Erie Canal 7/4/67 Rome, NY	2.00
1326	5¢ Search for Peace 7/5/67 Chicago, IL	2.00
1327	5¢ Henry Thoreau 7/12/67 Concord, MA	2.00
1328	5¢ Nebraska Statehood. 7/29/67 Lincoln, NE	2.00
1329	5¢ Voice of America 8/1/67 DC	4.00
1330	5¢ Davy Crockett 8/17/67 San Antonio, TX	3.00
1331-32	5¢ Space Twins attd. 9/29/67 Kennedy Space Ctr., FL	8.00
1331-32	Space Twins set of 2 singles	8.00
1333	5¢ Urban Planning 10/2/67 DC	2.00
1334	5¢ Finland Indep. 10/6/67 Finland, MI	2.00
1335	5¢ Thomas Eakins 11/2/67 DC	2.00
1336	5¢ Christmas 11/6/67 Bethlehem, GA	2.00
1337	5¢ Mississippi Statehood 12/11/67 Natchez, MS	2.00

1968-71 REGULAR ISSUES

Scott #	Description	Cacheted
1338	6¢ Flag & White House 1/24/68 DC	2.00
1338A	6¢ Flag & W.H., coil 5/30/69 Chicago, IL	2.00
1338D	6¢ Flag & W.H. (Huck Press) 8/7/70 DC	2.00
1338F	8¢ Flag & White House 5/10/71 DC	2.00
1338G	8¢ Flag & White House, coil 5/10/71 DC	2.00

1968

Scott #	Description	Cacheted
1339	6¢ Illinois Statehood 2/12/68 Shawneetown, IL	2.00
1340	6¢ Hemis Fair '68 3/30/68 San Antonio, TX	2.00
1341	$1 Airlift 4/4/68 Seattle, WA	7.50
1342	6¢ Support Our Youth 5/1/68 Chicago, IL	2.00
1343	6¢ Law and Order 5/17/68 DC	4.00
1344	6¢ Register and Vote 6/27/68 DC	2.50
1345-54	6¢ Historic Flags attd. 7/4/68 Pittsburgh, PA	8.50
1345-54	Historic Flags set of 10 singles	30.00
1355	6¢ Walt Disney 9/11/68 Marceline, MO	40.00
1356	6¢ Marquette 9/20/68 Sault Ste. Marie, MI	2.00
1357	6¢ Daniel Boone 9/26/68 Frankfort, KY	2.00
1358	6¢ Arkansas River 10/1/68 Little Rock, AR	2.00
1359	6¢ Leif Ericson 10/9/68 Seattle, WA	2.00
1360	6¢ Cherokee Strip 10/15/68 Ponca, OK	2.00
1361	6¢ John Trumbull 10/18/66 New Haven, CT	4.00
1362	6¢ Waterfowl Cons. 10/24/68 Cleveland, OH	2.00
1363	6¢ Christmas, tagged 11/1/68 DC	2.00
1363a	6¢ Not tagged 11/2/68 DC	15.00
1364	6¢ American Indian 11/4/68 DC	2.00

1969

Scott #	Description	Cacheted
1365-68	6¢ Beautification attd. 1/16/69 DC	5.00
1365-68	Beautification set of 4 singles	10.00
1369	6¢ American Legion 3/15/69 DC	2.00
1370	6¢ Grandma Moses 5/1/69 DC	2.00
1371	6¢ Apollo 8 5/5/69 Houston, TX	3.00
1372	6¢ W.C. Handy 5/17/69 Memphis, TN	4.00
1373	6¢ California 7/16/69 San Diego, CA	2.00
1374	6¢ John W. Powell 8/1/69 Page, AZ	2.00
1375	6¢ Alabama Sthd. 8/2/69 Huntsville, AL	2.00
1376-79	6¢ Botanical Congress attd. 8/23/69 Seattle, WA	6.00
1376-79	Botanical Congress set of 4 singles	10.00
1380	6¢ Dartmouth Case 9/22/69 Hanover, NH	2.00
1381	6¢ Baseball 9/24/69 Cincinnati, OH	12.00
1382	6¢ Football 9/26/69 New Brunswick, NJ	6.00
1383	6¢ Eisenhower 10/14/69 Abilene, KS	2.00
1384	6¢ Christmas 11/3/69 Christmas, FL	2.00
1384a	6¢ Christmas - Precancel 11/4/69 Atlanta, GA	200.00
	Baltimore, MD	200.00
	Memphis, TN	225.00
	New Haven, CT	200.00
1385	6¢ Hope for Crippled 11/20/69 Columbus, OH	2.00

	1425	
Scott #	**Description**	**Cacheted**

1970

Scott #	Description	Cacheted
1386	6¢ William Harnett 12/3/69 Boston, MA	2.00
1387-90	6¢ Natural History attd. 5/6/70 NY, NY	4.00
1387-90	Natural History set of 4 singles	8.00
1391	6¢ Maine Statehood 7/9/70 Portland, ME	2.00
1392	6¢ Wildlife - Buffalo 7/20/70 Custer, SD	2.00

1970-74 REGULAR ISSUES

Scott #	Description	Cacheted
1393	6¢ Eisenhower 8/6/70 DC	2.00
1393a	booklet pane of 8 8/6/70 DC	2.50
1393a	booklet pane of 8, dull gum 3/1/71 DC	75.00
1393a & 1278a	Combo, 3/1/71	150.00
1393b	booklet pane of 5 8/6/70 DC	3.00
1393bs	booklet single, 8/6/70	2.00
1393D	7¢ Franklin 10/20/72 Philadelphia, PA	2.00
1394	8¢ Eisenhower 5/10/71 DC	2.00
1395	8¢ Eisenhower, claret 5/10/71 DC	2.00
1395a	booklet pane of 8 5/10/71 DC	2.50
1395b	booklet pane of 6 5/10/71 DC	2.50
1395c	bklt. pane of 4 1/28/72 Casa Grande, AZ	2.00
1395cs	Booklet Single 1/28/72 Casa Grande, AZ	2.00
1395d	bklt. pane of 7 1/28/72 Casa Grande, AZ	2.00
1395ds	Booklet Single 1/28/72 Casa Grande, AZ	2.00
1396	8¢ Postal Service Emblem 7/1/71 any city	2.00
1397	14¢ LaGuardia 4/24/72 New York, NY	2.00
1398	16¢ Ernie Pyle 5/7/71 DC	2.50
1399	18¢ Eliz. Blackwell 1/23/74 Geneva, NY	2.00
1400	21¢ Giannini 6/27/73 San Mateo, CA	2.25
1401	6¢ Eisenhower, coil 8/6/70 DC	2.00
1402	8¢ Eisenhower, coil 5/10/71 DC	2.00

1970 COMMEMS

Scott #	Description	Cacheted
1405	6¢ Edgar Lee Masters 8/22/70 Petersburg, IL	2.00
1406	6¢ Woman Suffrage 8/26/70 Adams, MA	2.00
1407	6¢ South Carolina 9/12/70 Charleston, SC	2.00
1408	6¢ Stone Mountain 9/19/70 Stone Mt., GA	2.00
1409	6¢ Ft. Snelling 10/17/70 Ft. Snelling, MT	2.00
1410-13	6¢ Anti-Pollution attd. 10/28/70 San Clemente, CA	5.00
1410-13	Anti-Pollution set of 4 singles	8.00
1414	6¢ Christmas - Religious 11/5/70 DC	2.00
1414a	6¢ Christmas Precancel 11/5/70 DC	3.00
1415-18	6¢ Christmas Toys attd. 11/5/70 DC	6.00
1415-18	Christmas Toys set of 4 singles	10.00
1415a-18a	Christmas Toys-Precancel attd. 11/5/70 DC	15.00
1415a-18a	Christmas Toys-Precancel set of 4 singles	50.00
1414a-18a	Religious & Toys (5) on one FDC 11/5/70 DC	30.00
1419	6¢ UN 25th Anniv. 11/20/70 New York, NY	2.00
1420	6¢ Pilgrims' Landing 11/21/70 Plymouth, MA	2.00
1421-22	6¢ Disabled Vets - US Servicemen attd. 11/24/70 Cincinnati or Montgomery	2.25
1421-22	D.A.V. - Serv. set of 2 singles	4.00

1971

Scott #	Description	Cacheted
1423	6¢ Wool Industry 1/19/71 Las Vegas, NV	2.00
	1st Bazaar cachet	**30.00**
	1st Colorano Silk cachet	**300.00**
1424	6¢ MacArthur 1/26/71 Norfolk, VA	2.00
1425	6¢ Blood Donor 3/12/71 New York, NY	2.00
1426	6¢ Missouri 5/8/71 Independence, MO	2.00
1427-30	8¢ Wildlife Conservation attd. 6/12/71 Avery Island, LA	4.00
1427-30	Wildlife set of 4 singles	8.00
1431	8¢ Antarctic Treaty 6/23/71 DC	2.00
1432	8¢ American Revolution Bic. 7/4/71 DC	2.00
	1st Medallion cachet	**30.00**
1433	8¢ John Sloan 8/2/71 Lock Haven, PA	2.00
1434-35	8¢ Space Achievement Decade attd. 8/2/71	
	Kennedy Space Center, FL	2.50
	Houston, TX	2.50
	Huntsville, AL	2.50
1434-35	Space Achievement set of 2 singles	
	Kennedy Space Center, FL	3.50
	Houston, TX	3.50
	Huntsville, AL	3.50
1436	8¢ Emily Dickinson 8/28/71 Amherst, MA	2.00
1437	8¢ San Juan 9/12/71 San Juan, PR	2.00
1438	8¢ Drug Abuse 10/4/71 Dallas, TX	2.00
1439	8¢ CARE 10/27/71 New York, NY	2.00
1440-43	8¢ Historic Preservation attd. 10/29/71 San Diego, CA	4.00

U.S. First Day Covers

Scott #	Description	Cacheted
	1972	
1440-43	Historic Preservation set of 4 singles	8.00
1444	8¢ Christmas - Religious 11/10/71 DC	2.00
1445	8¢ Christmas - Partridge 11/10/71 DC	2.00
1444-45	Christmas on one cover	2.50
1446	8¢ Sidney Lanier 2/3/72 Macon, GA	2.00
1447	8¢ Peace Corps 2/11/72 DC	2.00
1448-51	2¢ Cape Hatteras 4/5/72 Hatteras, NC	2.00
1452	6¢ Wolf Trap Farm 6/26/72 Vienna, VA	2.00
1453	8¢ Yellowstone 3/1/72 DC	2.00
	Yellowstone Nat'l. Park, WY	2.00
1454	15¢ Mt. McKinley 7/28/72 Mt. McKinley Nat'l. Park, AK	2.00
1448-54,C84	Parks on one cover 7/28/72	6.00
1455	8¢ Family Planning 3/18/72 New York, NY	2.00
1456-59	8¢ Colonial Craftsmen attd. 7/4/72 Williamsburg, VA	4.00
1456-59	Colonial Craftsmen set of 4 singles	8.00
1460	6¢ Olympic - Bicycling 8/17/72 DC	2.00
1461	8¢ Olympic - Bobsledding 8/17/72 DC	2.00
1462	15¢ Olympic - Runners 8/17/72 DC	2.00
1460-62,C85	Olympics on one cover	4.00
1463	8¢ P.T.A. 9/15/72 San Francisco, CA	2.00
1464-67	8¢ Wildlife attd. 9/20/72 Warm Springs, OR	4.00
1464-67	Wildlife set of 4 singles	8.00
1468	8¢ Mail Order 9/27/72 Chicago, IL	2.00
1469	8¢ Osteopathic Medicine 10/9/72 Miami, FL	2.50
1470	8¢ Tom Sawyer 10/13/72 Hannibal, MO	2.50
1471	8¢ Christmas - Religious 11/9/72 DC	2.00
1472	8¢ Christmas - Santa Claus 11/9/72 DC	2.00
1471-72	Christmas on one cover	2.50
1473	8¢ Pharmacy 11/10/72 Cincinnati, OH	10.00
1474	8¢ Stamp Collecting 11/17/72 NY, NY	2.00
	1973	
1475	8¢ Love 1/26/73 Philadelphia, PA	2.25
1476	8¢ Pamphleteer 2/16/73 Portland, OR	2.00
1477	8¢ Broadside 4/13/73 Atlantic City, NJ	2.00
1478	8¢ Post Rider 6/22/73 Rochester, NY	2.00
1479	8¢ Drummer 9/28/73 New Orleans, LA	2.00
1480-83	8¢ Boston Tea Party attd. 7/4/73 Boston, MA	4.00
1480-83	Boston Tea Party set of 4 singles	8.00
1484	8¢ Geo. Gershwin 2/28/73 Beverly Hills, CA	2.00
1485	8¢ Robinson Jeffers 8/13/73 Carmel, CA	2.00
1486	8¢ Henry O. Tanner 9/10/73 Pittsburgh, PA	4.00
1487	8¢ Willa Cather 9/20/73 Red Cloud, NE	2.00
1488	8¢ Nicolaus Copernicus 4/23/73 DC	2.00
1489-98	8¢ Postal People attd. 4/30/73 any city	7.00
1489-98	Postal People set of 10 singles	20.00
1499	8¢ Harry Truman 5/8/73 Independence, MO	2.00
1500	6¢ Electronics 7/10/73 New York, NY	2.00
1501	8¢ Electronics 7/10/73 New York, NY	2.00
1502	15¢ Electronics 7/10/73 New York, NY	2.00
1500-2,C86	Electronics on one cover	7.00
1500-2,C86	Electronics set of 4	8.00
1503	8¢ Lyndon B. Johnson 8/27/73 Austin, TX	2.00
1504	8¢ Angus Cattle 10/5/73 St. Joseph, MO	2.00
1505	10¢ Chautauqua 8/6/74 Chautauqua, NY	2.00
1506	10¢ Wheat 8/16/74 Hillsboro, KS	2.00
1507	8¢ Christmas - Madonna 11/7/73 DC	2.00
1508	8¢ Christmas - Tree 11/7/73 DC	2.00
1507-08	Christmas on one cover	2.75
	1973-74 REGULAR ISSUES	
1509	10¢ Crossed Flags 12/8/73 San Fran., CA	2.00
1510	10¢ Jefferson Memorial 12/14/73 DC	2.00
1510b	booklet pane of 5 12/14/73 DC	2.25
1510bs	booklet pane single, 12/14/73	2.00
1510c	booklet pane of 8 12/14/73 DC	2.50
1510d	booklet pane of 6 8/5/74 Oakland, CA	5.25
1510ds	booklet pane single, 8/5/74	2.00
1511	10¢ Zip Code 1/4/74 DC	2.00
1518	6.3¢ Liberty Bell, coil 10/1/74 DC	2.00
1518	Untagged, 10/2/74 DC	5.00
1519	10¢ Crossed Flags, coil 12/8/73 San Francisco, CA	2.00
1520	10¢ Jefferson Memorial, coil 12/14/73 DC	2.00
	1974	
1525	10¢ Veterans of Foreign Wars 3/11/74 DC	2.00
1526	10¢ Robert Frost 3/26/74 Derry, NH	2.00
1527	10¢ EXPO '74 4/18/74 Spokane, WA	2.00
1528	10¢ Horse Racing 5/4/74 Louisville, KY	5.00
1529	10¢ Skylab 5/14/74 Houston, TX	2.00
1530-37	10¢ UPU Centenary attd. 6/6/74 DC	5.00
1530-37	UPU Centenary set of 8 singles	20.00
1538-41	10¢ Mineral Heritage attd. 6/13/74 Lincoln, NE	4.00
1538-41	Mineral Heritage set of 4 singles	8.00
1542	10¢ Fort Harrod 6/15/74 Harrodsburg, KY	2.00
1543-46	10¢ Continental Congr. attd. 7/4/74 Philadelphia, PA	4.00
1543-46	Continental Congress set of 4 singles	8.00
1547	10¢ Energy Conserv. 9/23/74 Detroit, MI	2.00
1548	10¢ Sleepy Hollow 10/10/74 North Tarrytown, NY	2.00
1549	10¢ Retarded Children 10/12/74 Arlington, TX	2.00
1550	10¢ Christmas - Angel 10/23/74 NY, NY	2.00
1551	10¢ Christmas - Currier & Ives 10/23/74 NY, NY	2.00
1550-51	Christmas on one cover	2.25
1552	10¢ Christmas - Dove 11/15/74 New York, NY	3.00
1550-52	Christmas, dual cancel	5.00

1577-78

Scott #	Description	Cacheted
	1975	
1553	10¢ Benjamin West 2/10/75 Swarthmore, PA	2.00
1554	10¢ Paul Dunbar 5/1/75 Dayton, OH	3.00
1555	10¢ D.W. Griffith 5/27/75 Beverly, Hills, CA	2.00
1556	10¢ Pioneer - Jupiter 2/28/75 Mountain View, CA	2.00
1557	10¢ Mariner 10 4/4/75 Pasadena, CA	2.00
1558	10¢ Collective Bargaining 3/13/75 DC	2.00
1559	8¢ Sybil Ludington 3/25/75 Carmel, NY	2.00
1560	10¢ Salem Poor 3/25/75 Cambridge, MA	3.00
1561	10¢ Haym Salomon 3/25/75 Chicago, IL	2.00
1562	18¢ Peter Francisco 3/25/75 Greensboro, NC	2.00
1559-62	Contributions on one cover, any city	8.00
1563	10¢ Lexington-Concord 4/19/75 Lexington, MA	2.00
	Concord, MA	2.00
1564	10¢ Bunker Hill 6/17/75 Charlestown, MA	2.00
1565-68	10¢ Military Uniforms attd. 7/4/75 DC	4.00
1565-68	Military Uniforms set of 4 singles	8.00
1569-70	10¢ Apollo-Soyuz attd. 7/15/75 Kennedy Sp. Ctr., FL	3.00
1569-70	Apollo-Soyuz set of 2 singles	4.00
1569-70	Apollo-Soyuz, combo, dual cancel	450.00
1571	10¢ Women's Year 8/26/75 Seneca Falls, NY	2.00
1572-75	10¢ Postal Serv. Bicent. attd. 9/3/75 Philadelphia, PA	4.00
1572-75	Postal Service set of 4 singles	8.00
1576	10¢ World Peace through Law 9/29/75 DC	2.00
1577-78	10¢ Banking - Commerce attd. 10/6/75 New York, NY	2.00
1577-78	Banking-Commerce set of 2 singles	3.00
1579	(10¢) Christmas - Madonna 10/14/75 DC	2.00
1580	(10¢) Christmas - Card 10/14/75 DC	2.00
1579-80	Christmas on one cover	2.50
	1975-81 AMERICANA SERIES REGULAR ISSUES	
1581	1¢ Inkwell & Quill 12/8/77 St. Louis, MO	2.00
1582	2¢ Speaker's Stand 12/8/77 St. Louis, MO	2.00
1584	3¢ Ballot Box 12/8/77 St. Louis, MO	2.00
1585	4¢ Books & Eyeglasses 12/8/77 St. Louis, MO	2.00
1581-85	4 values on one cover	3.00
1590	9¢ Capitol Dome, bklt. single	
	perf. 11 x 10½ 3/11/77 New York, NY	10.00
1590a	9¢ Capitol Dome, bklt. single	
	perf. 10 3/11/77 New York, NY	15.00
1591	9¢ Capitol Dome 11/24/75 DC	2.00
1592	10¢ Justice 11/17/77 New York, NY	2.00
1593	11¢ Printing Press 11/13/75 Phila., PA	2.00
1594	12¢ Liberty's Torch 4/8/81 Dallas, TX	2.00
1595	13¢ Liberty Bell, bklt. sgl. 10/31/75 Cleveland, OH	2.00
1595a	bklt. pane of 6 10/31/75 Cleveland, OH	2.25
1595b	bklt. pane of 7 10/31/75 Cleveland, OH	2.50
1595c	bklt. pane of 8 10/31/75 Cleveland, OH	2.75
1595d	bklt. pane of 5 4/2/76 Liberty, MO	2.00
1595ds	bklt. pane single, 4/2/76	2.00
1596	13¢ Eagle & Shield 12/1/75 Juneau, AK	2.00
1597	15¢ Ft. McHenry Flag 6/30/78 Baltimore, MD	2.00
1598	15¢ Ft. McHenry Flag, bklt. sgl. 6/30/78 Baltimore, MD	2.00
1598a	booklet pane of 8 6/30/78 Baltimore, MD	2.75
1599	16¢ Statue of Liberty 3/31/78 NY, NY	2.00
1603	24¢ Old North Church 11/14/75 Boston, MA	2.00
1604	28¢ Ft. Nisqually 8/11/78 Tacoma, WA	2.00
1605	29¢ Lighthouse 4/14/78 Atlantic City, NJ	2.00
1606	30¢ School House 8/27/79 Devils Lake, ND	2.00
1608	50¢ Betty Lamp 9/11/79 San Jaun, PR	2.00
1610	$1 Rush Lamp 7/2/79 San Francisco, CA	3.50
1611	$2 Kerosene Lamp 11/16/78 New York, NY	7.00
1612	$5 Railroad Lantern 8/23/79 Boston, MA	15.00
	1975-79 AMERICANA SERIES COILS	
1613	3.1¢ Guitar 10/25/79 Shreveport, LA	2.00
1614	7.7¢ Saxhorns 11/20/76 New York, NY	2.00
1615	7.9¢ Drum 4/23/76 Miami, FL	2.00
1615C	8.4¢ Grand Piano 7/13/78 Interlochen, MI	2.00
1616	9¢ Capitol Dome 3/5/76 Milwaukee, WI	2.00
1617	10¢ Justice 11/4/77 Tampa, FL	2.00
1618	13¢ Liberty Bell 11/25/75 Allentown, PA	2.00
1618C	15¢ Ft. McHenry Flag 6/30/78 Baltimore, MD	2.00
1619	16¢ Statue of Liberty 3/31/78 NY, NY	2.00

U.S. First Day Covers

1685

Scott #	Description	Cacheted
	1975-77 Regular Series (cont.)	
	1975-77 REGULAR SERIES	
1622	13¢ Flag over Ind. Hall 11/15/75 Philadelphia, PA	2.00
1623	13¢ Flag over Capitol, bklt. single	
	perf. 11 x 10½ 3/11/77 NY, NY	2.50
1623a	13¢ & 9¢ booklet pane of 8 (7 #1623 & 1 #1590)	
	perf. 11 x 10½ 3/11/77 NY, NY	25.00
1623b	13¢ Flag over Capitol, bklt. single	
	perf. 10 3/11/77 New York, NY	2.00
1623c	13¢ & 9¢ booklet pane of 8 (7 #1623b & 1 #1590a)	
	perf. 10 3/11/77 New York, NY	15.00
1625	13¢ Flag over Ind. Hall, coil 11/15/75 Phila., PA	2.00
	1976	
1629-31	13¢ Spirit of '76 attd. 1/1/76 Pasadena, CA	3.00
1629-31	Spirit of '76 set of 3 singles	5.75
1632	13¢ Interphil '76 1/17/76 Phila., PA	2.00
	1976 STATE FLAGS	
1633-82	13¢ State Flags 2/23/76 set of 50 DC	75.00
	State Capitals	80.00
	State Capital & DC cancels, set of 50 combo FDC's	150.00
1682a	Full sheet on one FDC (In Folder)	40.00
1683	13¢ Telephone 3/10/76 Boston, MA	2.00
1684	13¢ Aviation 3/19/76 Chicago, IL	2.00
1685	13¢ Chemistry 4/6/76 New York, NY	2.50
1686-89	13¢-31¢ Bicent. Souv. Shts. 5/29/76 Philadelphia, PA	30.00
1686a-89e	Set of 20 singles from sheets	90.00
1686a-89e	Set of 20 singles on 4 covers	40.00
1690	13¢ Franklin 6/1/76 Philadelphia, PA	2.00
1690	Joint issue w/ Canada	5.00
1690	Joint issue w/ Canada, dual cancel	15.00
1691-94	13¢ Decl. of Indep. attd. 7/4/76 Philadelphia, PA	4.00
1691-94	Decl. of Indep. set of 4 singles	8.00
1695-98	13¢ Olympics attd. 7/16/76 Lake Placid, NY	4.00
1695-98	Olympics set of 4 singles	8.00
1699	13¢ Clara Maass 8/18/76 Belleville, NJ	2.00
1700	13¢ Adolph S. Ochs 9/18/76 New York, NY	2.00
1701	13¢ Nativity 10/27/76 Boston, MA	2.00
1702	13¢ "Winter Pastime" 10/27/76 Boston, MA	2.00
1701-02	Christmas on one cover	2.00
1703	13¢ "Winter Pastime", Grav.-Int. 10/27/76 Boston, MA	2.00
1701,03	Christmas on one cover	2.25
1702-03	Christmas on one cover	2.50
1701-03	Christmas on one cover	3.00
	1977	
1704	13¢ Washington 1/3/77 Princeton, NJ	2.00
	1st Carrollton cachet	**20.00**
1705	13¢ Sound Recording 3/23/77 DC	2.00
1706-09	13¢ Pueblo Pottery attd. 4/13/77 Santa Fe, NM	4.00
1706-09	Pueblo Pottery set of 4 singles	8.00
1710	13¢ Lindbergh 5/20/77 Roosevelt Field Sta., NY	3.00
	1st Doris Gold cachet	**65.00**
	1st GAMM cachet	**50.00**
	1st Spectrum cachet	**25.00**
	1st Tudor House cachet	**20.00**
	1st Z-Silk cachet	**20.00**
1711	13¢ Colorado Sthd. 5/21/77 Denver, CO	2.00
1712-15	13¢ Butterflies attd. 6/6/77 Indianapolis, IN	4.00
1712-15	Butterflies set of 4 singles	8.00
	1st Ham cachet	**450.00**
1716	13¢ Lafayette 6/13/77 Charleston, SC	2.00
1717-20	13¢ Skilled Hands attd. 7/4/77 Cincinnati, OH	4.00
1717-20	Skilled Hands set of 4 singles	8.00
1721	13¢ Peace Bridge 8/4/77 Buffalo, NY	2.00
	US and Canadian stamps on one cover	2.50
	Dual US & Canadian FD cancels	7.50
1722	13¢ Herkimer 8/6/77 Herkimer, NY	2.00
1723-24	13¢ Energy Conservation attd. 10/20/77 DC	2.50
1723-24	Energy Conservation set of 2 singles	3.00
1725	13¢ Alta California 9/9/77 San Jose, CA	2.00
1726	13¢ Articles of Confed. 9/30/77 York, PA	2.00
1727	13¢ Talking Pictures 10/6/77 Hollywood, CA	2.25
1728	13¢ Surrender at Saratoga 10/7/77 Schuylerville, NY	2.00
1729	13¢ Christmas - Valley Forge 10/21/77 Valley Forge, PA	2.00
1730	13¢ Christmas - Mailbox 10/21/77 Omaha, NE	2.00

1760-63

Scott #	Description	Cacheted
	1978	
1729-30	Christmas on one cover, either city	2.50
1729-30	Christmas on one cover, dual FD cancels	4.00
1731	13¢ Carl Sandburg 1/6/78 Galesburg, IL	2.00
	1st Western Silk cachet	**35.00**
1732-33	13¢ Captain Cook attd. 1/20/78 Honolulu, HI	2.00
	Anchorage, AK	2.00
1732-33	Captain Cook set of 2 singles Honolulu, HI	3.50
	Anchorage, AK	3.50
1732-33	Set of 2 on one cover with dual FD cancels	15.00
	1st K.M.C. Venture cachet (set of 3)	**70.00**
1734	13¢ Indian Head Penny 1/11/78 Kansas City, MO	2.00
	1978-80 REGULAR ISSUES	
1735	(15¢) "A" & Eagle 5/22/78 Memphis, TN	2.00
1736	(15¢) "A", booklet single 5/22/78 Memphis, TN	2.00
1736a	(15¢) Booklet Pane of 8 5/22/78 Memphis, TN	3.00
1737	15¢ Roses, booklet single 7/11/78 Shreveport, LA	2.00
1737a	Booklet Pane of 8 7/11/78 Shreveport, LA	3.50
1738-42	15¢ Windmills set of 5 singles 2/7/80 Lubbock, TX	10.00
1742av	15¢ Windmills, strip of 5	5.00
1742a	Windmills booklet pane of 10	5.00
1743	(15¢) "A" & Eagle, coil 5/22/78 Memphis, TN	2.00
	1st Kribbs Kover cachet	**40.00**
1744	13¢ Harriet Tubman 2/1/78 DC	3.00
1745-48	13¢ American Quilts attd. 3/8/78 Charleston, WV	4.00
1745-48	American Quilts set of 4 singles	8.00
	1st Collins cachet	**450.00**
1749-52	13¢ American Dance attd. 4/26/78 New York, NY	4.00
1749-52	American Dance set of 4 singles	8.00
	1st Andrews cachet	**40.00**
1753	13¢ French Alliance 5/4/78 York, PA	2.00
1754	13¢ Dr. Papanicolaou 5/18/78 DC	2.00
1755	13¢ Jimmie Rodgers 5/24/78 Meridian, MS	2.00
1756	15¢ George M. Cohan 7/3/78 Providence, RI	2.00
1757	13¢ CAPEX Sheet 6/10/78 Toronto, Canada	3.50
1757a-h	CAPEX set of 8 singles	16.00
1758	15¢ Photography 6/26/78 Las Vegas, NV	2.00
1759	15¢ Viking Mission 7/20/78 Hampton, VA	2.00
1760-63	15¢ American Owls attd. 8/26/78 Fairbanks, AK	4.00
1760-63	American Owls set of 4 singles	8.00
1764-67	15¢ Amer. Trees attd. 10/9/78 Hot Springs Nat'l. Park, AR	4.00
1764-67	American Trees set of 4 singles	8.00
1768	15¢ Christmas - Madonna 10/18/78 DC	2.00
1769	15¢ Christmas - Hobby Horse 10/18/78 Holly, MI	2.00
1768-69	Christmas on one cover, either City	2.50
1768-69	Dual Cancel	3.00
	1979	
1770	15¢ Robert F. Kennedy 1/12/79 DC	2.25
	1st DRC cachet	**75.00**
1771	15¢ Martin Luther King 1/13/79 Atlanta, GA	3.00
1772	15¢ Int'l. Yr. of the Child 2/15/79 Philadelphia, PA	2.00
1773	15¢ John Steinbeck 2/27/79 Salinas, CA	2.00
1774	15¢ Albert Einstein 3/4/79 Princeton, NJ	3.00
1775-78	15¢ Toleware attd. 4/19/79 Lancaster, PA	4.00
1775-78	Toleware set of 4 singles	8.00
1779-82	15¢ Architecture attd. 6/4/79 Kansas City, MO	4.00
1779-82	Architecture set of 4 singles	8.00
1783-86	15¢ Endangered Flora 6/7/79 Milwaukee, WI	4.00
1783-86	Endangered Flora set of 4 singles	8.00
1787	15¢ Seeing Eye Dogs 6/15/79 Morristown, NJ	2.00
1788	15¢ Special Olympics 8/9/79 Brockport, NY	2.00
1789	15¢ John Paul Jones, perf. 11x12 9/23/79 Annapolis, MD	2.00
1789a	15¢ John Paul Jones, perf. 11 9/23/79 Annapolis, MD	2.00
1789,89a	Both Perfs. on 1 Cover	12.00
1790	10¢ Olympic Javelin 9/5/79 Olympia, WA	2.00
1791-94	15¢ Summer Olympics attd. 9/28/79 Los Angeles, CA	4.00
1791-94	Summer Olympics set of 4 singles	8.00
1795-98	15¢ Winter Olympics attd. 2/1/80 Lake Placid, NY	4.00
1795-98	Winter Olympics set of 4 singles	8.00
1799	15¢ Christmas - Madonna 10/18/79 DC	2.00
1800	15¢ Christmas - Santa Claus 10/18/79 North Pole, AK	2.00
1799-1800	Christmas on one cover, either city	2.50
1799-1800	Christmas on one cover, dual cancel	2.50
1801	15¢ Will Rogers 11/4/79 Claremore, OK	2.00
1802	15¢ Vietnam Vets 11/11/79 Arlington, VA	3.50

U.S. First Day Covers

1833

1906

Scott #	Description	Cacheted
	1980	
1803	15¢ W.C. Fields 1/29/80 Beverly Hills, CA	2.50
	1st Gill Craft cachet	**30.00**
	1st Kover Kids cachet	**20.00**
1804	15¢ Benj. Banneker 2/15/80 Annapolis, MD	3.00
1805-06	15¢ Letters - Memories attd. 2/25/80 DC	2.00
1805-06	Letters - Memories set of 2 singles	3.00
1807-08	15¢ Letters - Lift Spirit attd. 2/25/80 DC	2.00
1807-08	Letters - Lift Spirit set of 2 singles	3.00
1809-10	15¢ Letters - Opinions attd. 2/25/80 DC	2.00
1809-10	Letters - Opinions set of 2 singles	3.00
1805-10	15¢ Letter Writing attd. 2/25/80 DC	4.00
1805-10	Letter Writing set of 6 singles	7.50
1805-10	Letters, Memories, 6 on 3	5.00
	1980-81 REGULAR ISSUES	
1811	1¢ Inkwell, coil 3/6/80 New York, NY	2.00
1813	3½¢ Violins, coil 6/23/80 Williamsburg, PA	2.00
1816	12¢ Liberty's Torch, coil 4/8/81 Dallas, TX	2.00
1818	(18¢) "B" & Eagle 3/15/81 San Fran., CA	2.00
1819	(18¢) "B" & Eagle, bklt. sngl. 3/15/81 San Francisco, CA .	2.00
1819a	(18¢) Bklt. Pane of 8 3/15/81 San Francisco, CA	4.00
1820	(18¢) "B" & Eagle, coil 3/15/81 San Francisco, CA	2.00
1818-20	On One Cover	2.50
	1980	
1821	15¢ Frances Perkins 4/10/80 DC	2.00
1822	15¢ Dolly Madison 5/20/80 DC	2.00
	1st American Postal Arts Society cachet (Post/Art) ...	**35.00**
1823	15¢ Emily Bissell 5/31/80 Wilmington, DE	2.00
1824	15¢ Helen Keller 6/27/80 Tuscumbia, AL	2.00
1825	15¢ Veterans Administration 7/21/80 DC	2.50
1826	15¢ Bernardo de Galvez 7/23/80 New Orleans, LA	2.00
1827-30	15¢ Coral Reefs attd. 8/26/80 Charlotte Amalie, VI	4.00
1827-30	Coral Reefs set of 4 singles	8.00
1831	15¢ Organized Labor 9/1/80 DC	2.00
1832	15¢ Edith Wharton 9/5/80 New Haven, CT	2.00
1833	15¢ Education 9/12/80 Franklin, MA	2.00
1834-37	15¢ Indian Masks attd. 9/25/80 Spokane, WA	4.00
1834-37	Indian Masks set of 4 singles	8.00
1838-41	15¢ Architecture attd. 10/9/80 New York, NY	4.00
1838-41	Architecture set of 4 singles	8.00
1842	15¢ Christmas - Madonna 10/31/80 DC	2.00
1843	15¢ Christmas - Wreath & Toys 10/31/80 Christmas, MI .	2.00
1842-43	Christmas on one cover	2.50
1842-43	Christmas, dual cancel	3.00
	1980-85 GREAT AMERICANS SERIES	
1844	1¢ Dorothea Dix 9/23/83 Hampden, ME	2.00
1845	2¢ Igor Stravinsky 11/18/82 New York, NY	2.00
1846	3¢ Henry Clay 7/13/83 DC	2.00
1847	4¢ Carl Shurz 6/3/83 Watertown, WI	2.00
1848	5¢ Pearl Buck 6/25/83 Hillsboro, WV	2.00
1849	6¢ Walter Lippman 9/19/85 Minneapolis, MN	2.00
1850	7¢ Abraham Baldwin 1/25/85 Athens, GA	2.00
1851	8¢ Henry Knox 7/25/85 Thomaston, ME	2.00
1852	9¢ Sylvanus Thayer 6/7/85 Braintree, MA	2.00
1853	10¢ Richard Russell 5/31/84 Winder, GA	2.00
1854	11¢ Alden Partridge 2/12/85 Norwich Un., VT	2.00
1855	13¢ Crazy Horse 1/15/82 Crazy Horse, SD	2.00
1856	14¢ Sinclair Lewis 3/21/85 Sauk Centre, MN	2.00
1857	17¢ Rachel Carson 5/28/81 Springdale, PA	2.00
1858	18¢ George Mason 5/7/81 Gunston Hall, VA	2.00
1859	19¢ Sequoyah 12/27/80 Tahlequah, OK	2.00
1860	20¢ Ralph Bunche 1/12/82 New York, NY	3.00
1861	20¢ Thomas Gallaudet 6/10/83 West Hartford, CT	2.00
1862	20¢ Harry S. Truman 1/26/84 DC	2.00
1863	22¢ John J. Audubon 4/23/85 New York, NY	2.00
1864	30¢ Frank Laubach 9/2/84 Benton, PA	2.00
1865	35¢ Charles Drew 6/3/81 DC	3.00
1866	37¢ Robert Millikan 1/26/82 Pasadena, CA	2.00
1867	39¢ Grenville Clark 3/20/85 Hanover, NH	2.00
1868	40¢ Lillian Gilbreth 2/24/84 Montclair, NJ	2.00
1869	50¢ Chester W. Nimitz 2/22/85 Fredericksburg, TX	3.00
	1981	
1874	15¢ Everett Dirksen 1/4/81 Pekin, IL	2.00
1875	15¢ Whitney Moore Young 1/30/81 NY, NY	3.00
1876-79	15¢ Flowers attd. 4/23/81 Ft. Valley, GA	4.00

Scott #	Description	Cacheted
	1981 (cont.)	
1876-79	Flowers set of 4 singles	8.00
1880-89	18¢ Wildlife set of 10 sgls. 5/14/81 Boise, ID	17.50
1889a	Wildlife booklet pane of 10	6.00
	1981-82 REGULAR ISSUES	
1890	18¢ Flag & "Waves of Grain" 4/24/81 Portland, ME	2.00
1891	18¢ Flag & "Sea" coil 4/24/81 Portland, ME	2.00
1892	6¢ Circle of Stars, bklt. sngl. 4/24/81 Portland, ME	2.00
1893	18¢ Flag & "Mountain", bklt. sgl. 4/24/81 Portland, ME ...	2.00
1892-93	6¢ & 18¢ Booklet Pair 4/24/81 Portland, ME	3.75
1893a	18¢ & 6¢ B. Pane of 8 (2 #1892 & 6 #1893) 4/24/81 Portland, ME	5.00
1894	20¢ Flag over Supreme Court 12/17/81 DC	2.00
1895	20¢ Flag, coil 12/17/81 DC	2.00
1896	20¢ Flag, bklt. single 12/17/81 DC	2.00
1896a	Flag, bklt. pane of 6 12/17/81 DC	4.00
	#1894, 1895 & 1896a on one FDC	7.00
1896b	Flag, bklt. pane of 10 6/1/82 DC	6.00
1896bv	Reissue-Flag bklt single, 11/17/83, NY	2.50
1896bv	Reissue-Flag, pane of 10, 11/17/83, NY	20.00
	1981-84 TRANSPORTATION COIL SERIES	
1897	1¢ Omnibus 8/19/83 Arlington, VA	2.00
1897A	2¢ Locomotive 5/20/82 Chicago, IL	2.50
1898	3¢ Handcar 3/25/83 Rochester, NY	2.00
1898A	4¢ Stagecoach 8/19/82 Milwaukee, WI	2.00
1899	5¢ Motorcycle 10/10/83 San Francisco, CA	2.50
1900	5.2¢ Sleigh 3/21/83 Memphis, TN	2.00
1900a	Precancelled	150.00
1901	5.9¢ Bicycle 2/17/82 Wheeling, WV	2.00
1901a	Precancelled	200.00
1902	7.4¢ Baby Buggy 4/7/84 San Diego, CA	2.00
1902a	Precancelled	300.00
1903	9.3¢ Mail Wagon 12/15/81 Shreveport, LA	2.00
1903a	Precancelled	300.00
1904	10.9¢ Hansom Cab 3/26/82 Chattanooga, TN	2.00
1904a	Precancelled	300.00
1905	11¢ Caboose 2/3/84 Rosemont, IL	2.50
1906	17¢ Electric Car 6/25/81 Greenfield Village, MI	2.00
1907	18¢ Surrey 5/18/81 Notch, MO	2.00
1908	20¢ Fire Pumper 12/10/81 Alexandria, VA	2.00
1909	$9.35 Express Mail, single 8/12/83 Kennedy Sp. Ctr., FL	60.00
1909a	Express Mail, booklet pane of 3	175.00
	1981 Commemoratives (continued)	
1910	18¢ American Red Cross 5/1/81 DC	2.00
1911	18¢ Savings and Loans 5/8/81 Chicago, IL	2.00
1912-19	18¢ Space Ach. attd. 5/21/81 Kennedy Sp. Ctr., FL	6.00
1912-19	Space Achievement set of 8 singles	16.00
1920	18¢ Professional Management 6/18/81 Philadelphia, PA	2.00
1921-24	18¢ Wildlife Habitats attd. 6/26/81 Reno, NV	4.00
1921-24	Wildlife Habitats set of 4 singles	8.00
1925	18¢ Disabled Persons 6/29/81 Milford, MI	2.00
1926	18¢ Edna St. Vincent Millay 7/10/81 Austeritz, NY	2.00
1927	18¢ Alcoholism 8/19/81 DC	4.00
1928-31	18¢ Architecture attd. 8/28/81 DC	4.00
1928-31	Architecture set of 4 singles	8.00
1932	18¢ Babe Zaharias 9/22/81 Pinehurst, NC	8.00
1933	18¢ Bobby Jones 9/22/81 Pinehurst, NC	12.00
1932-33	Zaharias & Jones on one cover	15.00
1934	18¢ Frederic Remington 10/9/81 Oklahoma City, OK	2.00
1935	18¢ James Hoban 10/13/81 DC	2.00
1936	20¢ James Hoban 10/13/81 DC	2.00
1935-36	Hoban on one cover	3.50
1935-36	Joint issue w/ Ireland	5.00
1935-36	Joint issue w/ Ireland dual cancel	15.00
1937-38	18¢ Battle of Yorktown attd. 10/16/81 Yorktown, VA	2.00
1937-38	Battle of Yorktown set of 2 singles	3.00
1939	(20¢) Christmas - Madonna 10/28/81 Chicago, IL	2.00
1940	(20¢) Christmas - Teddy Bear 10/28/81 Christmas Valley, OR	2.00
1939-40	Christmas on one cover	2.50
1939-40	Christmas, dual cancel	3.00
1941	20¢ John Hanson 11/5/81 Frederick, MD	2.00
1942-45	20¢ Desert Plants attd. 12/11/81 Tucson, AZ	4.00
1942-45	Desert Plants set of 4 singles	8.00
	1st Pugh cachet	**100.00**

U.S. First Day Covers

2036

Scott #	Description	Cacheted
	1981-82 REGULAR ISSUES	
1946	(20¢) "C" & Eagle 10/11/81 Memphis, TN	2.00
1947	(20¢) "C" Eagle, coil 10/11/81 Memphis, TN	2.00
1948	(20¢) "C" Eagle, bklt. single 10/11/81 Memphis, TN	2.00
1948a	(20¢) "C" Booklet Pane of 10	5.50
1949	20¢ Bighorn Sheep, bklt. single 1/8/82 Bighorn, MT	2.00
	1st New Direxions cachet	**25.00**
1949a	20¢ Booklet Pane of 10	6.00
	1982 Commemoratives	
1950	20¢ Franklin D. Roosevelt 1/30/82 Hyde Park, NY	2.00
1951	20¢ Love 2/1/82 Boston, MA	2.00
1952	20¢ George Washington 2/22/82 Mt. Vernon, VA	2.00
	1982 STATE BIRDS AND FLOWERS	
1953-2002	20¢ Birds & Flowers 4/14/82 Set of 50 DC	70.00
	Set of 50 State Capitals	75.00
2002a	Complete pane of 50 (Uncacheted)	45.00
	1982 Commemoratives (continued)	
2003	20¢ US & Netherlands 4/20/82 DC	2.00
2003	Joint issue w/ Netherlands	7.50
...	Joint issue w/ Netherlands, dual cancel	15.00
2004	20¢ Library of Congress 4/21/82 DC	2.00
2005	20¢ Consumer Education, coil 4/27/82 DC	2.00
2006-09	20¢ Knoxville World's Fair, attd. 4/29/82 Knoxville, TN	4.00
2006-09	20¢ Knoxville World's Fair, Knoxville, TN, set of 4 sngls	8.00
2010	20¢ Horatio Alger 4/30/82 Willow Grove, PA	2.00
2011	20¢ "Aging Together" 5/21/82 Sun City, AZ	2.00
2012	20¢ The Barrymores 6/8/82 New York, NY	2.00
2013	20¢ Dr. Mary Walker 6/10/82 Oswego, NY	2.00
2014	20¢ Peace Garden 6/30/82 Dunseith, ND	2.00
2015	20¢ Libraries 7/13/82 Philadelphia, PA	2.00
2016	20¢ Jackie Robinson 8/2/82 Cooperstown, NY	7.00
2017	20¢ Touro Synagogue 8/22/82 Newport, RI	3.00
2018	20¢ Wolf Trap 9/1/82 Vienna, VA	2.00
2019-22	20¢ Architecture attd. 9/30/82 DC	4.00
2019-22	Architecture set of 4 singles	8.00
2023	20¢ St. Francis of Assisi 10/7/82 San Francisco, CA	2.00
2024	20¢ Ponce de Leon 10/12/82 San Juan, PR	2.00
2025	13¢ Christmas - Kitten & Puppy 11/3/82 Danvers, MA	2.00
2026	20¢ Christmas - Madonna & Child 10/28/82 DC	2.00
2027-30	20¢ Christmas - Winter Scene, attd. 10/28/82 Snow, OK	4.00
2027-30	Christmas set of 4 singles	8.00
2026-30	Christmas on one cover either city	3.00
2026-30	Christmas, dual cancel	3.50
	1983 Commemoratives	
2031	20¢ Science & Industry 1/19/83 Chi., IL	2.00
2032-35	20¢ Ballooning 3/31/83 DC	4.00
	Albuquerque, NM	4.00
2032-35	Ballooning set of 4 singles DC	8.00
	Albuquerque, NM	8.00
2036	20¢ Sweden, 3/24/83 Philadelphia, PA	2.00
2036	20¢ US & Sweden, joint Issue, dual cancel	15.00
2036	20¢ US & Sweden, joint issue	5.00
2036	**1st Panda Cachet**	**25.00**
2037	20¢ Civilian Conservation Corps 4/5/83 Luray, VA	2.00
2038	20¢ Joseph Priestley 4/13/83 Northumberland, PA	2.00
2039	20¢ Voluntarism 4/20/83 DC	2.00
2040	20¢ German Immigration 4/29/83 Germantown, PA	2.00
2040	Joint issue w/Germany, dual cancel	15.00
2041	20¢ Brooklyn Bridge 5/17/83 Brooklyn, NY	3.00
2042	20¢ Tennessee Valley Authority 5/18/83 Knoxville, TN	2.00
2043	20¢ Physical Fitness 5/14/83 Houston, TX	2.00
2044	20¢ Scott Joplin 6/9/83 Sedalia, MO	3.00
2045	20¢ Medal of Honor 6/7/83 DC	6.00
2046	20¢ Babe Ruth 7/6/83 Chicago, IL	6.00
2047	20¢ Nathaniel Hawthorne 7/8/83 Salem, MA	2.00
2048-51	13¢ Summer Olympics attd. 7/28/83 South Bend, IN	4.00
2048-51	Summer Olympics set of 4 singles	8.00
2052	20¢ Treaty of Paris 9/2/83 DC	2.00
2052	Joint issue w/France, dual cancel	8.00
2052	French issue only	3.50
2053	20¢ Civil Service 9/9/83 DC	2.00

Scott #	Description	Cacheted
	1983 Commemoratives (cont.)	
2054	20¢ Metropolitan Opera 9/14/83 NY, NY	2.00
2055-58	20¢ Inventors attd. 9/21/83 DC	4.00
2055-58	Inventors set of 4 singles	8.00
2059-62	20¢ Streetcars attd. 10/8/83 Kennebunkport, ME	4.00
2059-62	Streetcars set of 4 singles	8.00
2063	20¢ Christmas - Madonna & Child 10/28/83 DC	2.00
2064	20¢ Christmas - Santa Claus 10/28/83 Santa Claus, IN	2.00
2063-64	Christmas on one cover either city	2.50
2063-64	Christmas, dual cancel	3.00
2065	20¢ Martin Luther 11/11/83 DC	2.00
2065	Joint issue w/Germany, dual cancel	15.00
	1984 Commemoratives	
2066	20¢ Alaska Sthd. 1/3/84 Fairbanks, AK	2.00
2067-70	20¢ Winter Olympics attd. 1/6/84 Lake Placid, NY	4.00
2067-70	Winter Olympics set of 4 singles	8.00
2071	20¢ Fed. Deposit Ins. Corp. 1/12/84 DC	2.00
2072	20¢ Love 1/31/84 DC	2.00
2073	20¢ Carter Woodson 2/1/84 DC	3.00
2074	20¢ Soil & Water Cons. 2/6/84 Denver, CO	2.00
2075	20¢ Credit Union Act 2/10/84 Salem, MA	2.00
2076-79	20¢ Orchids attd. 3/5/84 Miami, FL	4.00
2076-79	Orchids set of 4 singles	8.00
2080	20¢ Hawaii Sthd. 3/12/84 Honolulu, HI	2.00
2081	20¢ National Archives 4/16/84 DC	2.00
2082-85	20¢ Summer Olympics attd. 5/4/84 Los Angeles, CA	4.00
2082-85	Summer Olympics set of 4 singles	8.00
2086	20¢ Louisiana World's Fair 5/11/84 New Orleans, LA	2.00
2087	20¢ Health Research 5/17/84 New York, NY	2.00
2088	20¢ Douglas Fairbanks 5/23/84 Denver, CO	2.00
2089	20¢ Jim Thorpe 5/24/84 Shawnee, OK	5.00
2090	20¢ John McCormack 6/6/84 Boston, MA	2.00
2090	Joint issue w/Ireland, dual cancel	15.00
2091	20¢ St. Lawrence Swy. 6/26/84 Massena, NY	2.00
	Joint issue w/Canada, dual cancel	15.00
2092	20¢ Waterfowl Preservation 7/2/84 Des Moines, IA	2.00
	1st George Van Natta cachet	**40.00**
2093	20¢ Roanoke Voyages 7/13/84 Manteo, NC	2.00
2094	20¢ Herman Melville 8/1/84 New Bedford, MA	2.00
2095	20¢ Horace Moses 8/6/84 Bloomington, IN	2.00
2096	20¢ Smokey the Bear 8/13/84 Capitan, NM	2.00
2097	20¢ Roberto Clemente 8/17/84 Carolina, PR	10.00
2098-2101	20¢ Dogs attd. 9/7/84 New York, NY	4.00
2098-2101	Dogs set of 4 singles	8.00
2102	20¢ Crime Prevention 9/26/84 DC	2.00
2103	20¢ Hispanic Americans 10/31/84 DC	3.00
2104	20¢ Family Unity 10/1/84 Shaker Heights, OH	2.00
2105	20¢ Eleanor Roosevelt 10/11/84 Hyde Park, NY	2.00
2106	20¢ Nation of Readers 10/16/84 DC	2.00
2107	20¢ Christmas - Madonna & Child 10/30/84 DC	2.00
2108	20¢ Christmas - Santa 10/30/84 Jamaica, NY	2.00
2107-08	Christmas on one cover, either city	2.50
2107-08	Christmas, dual cancel	3.00
2109	20¢ Vietnam Memorial 11/10/84 DC	4.50
	1985 REGULARS & COMMEMS.	
2110	22¢ Jerome Kern 1/23/85 New York, NY	2.00
2111	(22¢) "D" & Eagle 2/1/85 Los Angeles, CA	2.00
2112	(22¢) "D" coil 2/1/85 Los Angeles, CA	2.00
2113	(22¢) "D" bklt. single 2/1/85 L.A., CA	2.00
2111-13	(22¢) "D" Stamps on 1	5.00
2113a	(22¢) Booklet Pane of 10	7.00
2114	22¢ Flag over Capitol 3/29/85 DC	2.00
2115	22¢ Flag over Capitol, coil 3/29/85 DC	2.00
2115b	Same, Phosphor Test Coil 5/23/87 Secaucus, NJ	2.50
2116	22¢ Flag over Capitol, bklt. single 3/29/85 Waubeka, WI	2.00
2116a	Booklet Pane of 5	3.00
2117-21	22¢ Seashells set of 5 singles 4/4/85 Boston, MA	10.00
2121a	Seashells, booklet pane of 10	7.00
2122	$10.75 Express Mail, bklt. sgl. 4/29/85 San Francisco, CA	50.00
2122a	Express Mail, booklet pane of 3	135.00
2122b	$10.75 Re-issue, bklt. sgl. 6/19/89 DC	250.00
2122c	Re-issue, booklet pane of 3	700.00
	1985-89 TRANSPORTATION COILS	
2123	3.4¢ School Bus 6/8/85 Arlington, VA	2.00
2123a	Precancelled 6/8/85 (earliest known use)	250.00
2124	4.9¢ Buckboard 6/21/85 Reno, NV	2.00
2124a	Precancelled 6/21/85 DC (earliest known use)	250.00
2125	5.5¢ Star Route Truck 11/1/86 Fort Worth, TX	2.00
2125a	Precancelled 11/1/86 DC	5.00
2126	6¢ Tricycle 5/6/85 Childs, MD	2.00
2127	7.1¢ Tractor 2/6/87 Sarasota, FL	2.00
2127a	Precancelled 2/6/87 Sarasota, FL	5.00
2127av	Zip + 4 Prec., 5/26/89 Rosemont, IL	2.00
2128	8.3¢ Ambulance 6/21/85 Reno, NV	2.00
2128a	Precancelled 6/21/85 DC (earliest known use)	250.00
2129	8.5¢ Tow Truck 1/24/87 Tucson, AZ	2.00
2129a	Precancelled 1/24/87 DC	5.00
2130	10.1¢ Oil Wagon 4/18/85 Oil Center, NM	2.00
2130a	Black Precancel 4/18/85 DC (earliest known use)	250.00
2130av	Red. Prec. 6/27/88 DC	2.00
2131	11¢ Stutz Bearcat 6/11/85 Baton Rouge, LA	2.00
2132	12¢ Stanley Steamer 4/2/85 Kingfield, ME	2.00
2132b	"B" Press cancel 9/3/87 DC	60.00

FIRST DAY COVER COLLECTING MADE EASY!

For over fifty years, Artmaster Incorporated has provided the philatelic community the most courteous and complete First Day Cover services. Our convenient First Day Cover and Self-service Envelope Clubs are automatic shipment plans insuring you never miss another issue, and we offer three distinctive cachet brands from which to choose. **Artmaster** cachets have been produced since 1946 and feature two-color offset printing and include an historical synopsis of the stamp subject on the reverse. **House of Farnam** is the oldest continuously produced cachet in existence and features the timeless beauty of multi-colored registered engraved cachets. And **Cover Craft Cachets** are limited edition versions of the House of Farnam engravings printed on tinted envelopes, and include an informative insert card describing the stamp subject and detailing the exact quantities of covers produced for each issue. Our services are guaranteed - you will be completely satisfied with your covers in every respect, or they will be replaced. Send for a free stamp schedule and sample of our cachets, and see for yourself!

Name _____

Address _____

City _____ **State** _____ **Zip Code** _____

Artmaster
INCORPORATED

P.O. Box 7156 ∗ Louisville, Ky 40257-0156 ∗ Toll Free 1-888-200-6466
email artmaster@firstdaycover.com ∗ visit our website www.firstdaycover.com

U.S. First Day Covers

2155-58

Scott #	Description	Cacheted
	1985-89 TRANSPORTATION COILS (cont.)	
2133	12.5¢ Pushcart 4/18/85 Oil Center, NM	2.00
2134	14¢ Iceboat 3/23/85 Rochester, NY	2.00
2135	17¢ Dog Sled 8/20/86 Anchorage, AK	2.00
2136	25¢ Bread Wagon 11/22/86 Virginia Bch., VA	2.00
	1985 COMMEMS (cont.)	
2137	22¢ Mary McLeod Bethune 3/5/85 DC	3.00
2138-41	22¢ Duck Decoys attd. 3/22/85 Shelburne, VT	4.00
2138-41	Duck Decoys set of 4 singles	8.00
2142	22¢ Winter Special Olympics 3/25/85 Park City, UT	2.00
2143	22¢ Love 4/17/85 Hollywood, CA	2.00
2144	22¢ Rural Electrification Admin. 5/11/85 Madison, SD	2.00
2145	22¢ Ameripex '86 5/25/85 Rosemont, IL	2.00
2146	22¢ Abigail Adams 6/14/85 Quincy, MA	2.00
2147	22¢ Frederic A. Bartholdi 7/18/85 NY, NY	2.00
2149	18¢ Washington Pre-Sort, coil 11/6/85 DC	2.00
2149a	18¢ Washington, Precanceled, pair w/2149	5.00
2150	21.1¢ Zip + 4, coil 10/22/85 DC	2.00
2150a	21.1¢ Zip + 4, Precanceled, pair w/2150	5.00
2152	22¢ Korean War Veterans 7/26/85	3.00
2153	22¢ Social Security Act 8/14/85 Baltimore, MD	2.00
2154	22¢ World War I Vets 8/26/85 Milwaukee, WI	2.25
2155-58	22¢ Horses attd. 9/25/85 Lexington, KY	4.00
2155-58	Horses set of 4 singles	8.00
2159	22¢ Public Education 10/1/85 Boston, MA	2.00
2160-63	22¢ Int'l. Youth Year attd. 10/7/85 Chicago, IL	4.00
2160-63	Set of 4 singles	8.00
2164	22¢ Help End Hunger 10/15/85 DC	2.00
2165	22¢ Christmas - Madonna 10/30/85 Detroit, MI	2.00
2166	22¢ Christmas - Poinsettia 10/30/85 Nazareth, MI	2.00
2165-66	Christmas on one cover, either city	2.50
2165-66	On One Cover, dual cancel	3.00
	1986	
2167	22¢ Arkansas Sthd. 1/3/86 Little Rock, AR	2.00
	1986-94 GREAT AMERICANS SERIES	
2168	1¢ Margaret Mitchell 6/30/86 Atlanta, GA	4.00
2169	2¢ Mary Lyon 2/28/87 South Hadley, MA	2.00
2170	3¢ Dr. Paul Dudley White 9/15/86 DC	2.00
2171	4¢ Father Flanagan 7/14/86 Boys Town, NE	2.00
2172	5¢ Hugo L. Black 2/27/86 DC	2.00
2173	5¢ Luis Munoz Marin 2/18/90 San Juan, PR	2.00
2175	10¢ Red Cloud 8/15/87 Red Cloud, NE	2.00
2176	14¢ Julia Ward Howe 2/12/87 Boston, MA	2.00
2177	15¢ Buffalo Bill Cody 6/6/88 Cody, WY	2.00
2178	17¢ Belva Ann Lockwood 6/18/86 Middleport, NY	2.00
2179	20¢ Virginia Agpar 10/24/94 Dallas, TX	2.00
2180	21¢ Chester Carlson 10/21/88 Rochester, NY	2.00
2181	23¢ Mary Cassatt 11/4/88 Phila., PA	2.00
2182	25¢ Jack London 1/11/86 Glen Ellen, CA	2.00
2182a	Bklt. Pane of 10 Perf, 11 5/3/88 San Francisco, CA	8.00
2182as	Perf. 11 bklt. single 5/3/88 San Francisco, CA	2.00
2183	28¢ Sitting Bull 9/14/89 Rapid City, SD	2.25
2184	29¢ Earl Warren 3/9/92 DC	2.00
2185	29¢ Thomas Jefferson 4/13/93 Charlottesville, VA	2.00
2186	35¢ Dennis Chavez 4/3/91 Albuquerque, NM	2.00
2187	40¢ General Claire Chennault 9/6/90 Monroe, LA	3.00
2188	45¢ Dr. Harvey Cushing 6/17/88 Cleveland, OH	2.00
2189	52¢ Hubert H. Humphrey 6/3/91 Minneapolis, MN	2.00
2190	56¢ John Harvard 9/3/86 Cambridge, MA	3.00
2191	65¢ General "Hap" Arnold 11/5/88 Gladwyne, PA	3.00
2192	75¢ Wendell Wilkie 2/16/92 Bloomington, IN	3.00
2193	$1 Dr. Bernard Revel 9/23/86 NY, NY	6.00
2194	$1 Johns Hopkins 6/7/89 Baltimore, MD	5.00
2195	$2 William Jennings Bryan 3/19/86 Salem, IL	8.00
2196	$5 Bret Harte 8/25/87 Twain Harte, CA	17.50
2197	25¢ Jack London, perf. 10 bklt. sgl. 5/3/88 San Fran., CA	2.00
2197a	Bklt. Pane of 6	4.00
	1986 COMMEMS (cont.)	
2198-2201	22¢ Stamp Coll. set of 4 1/23/86 State College, PA	8.00
	Joint issue, US + Swedish Panes on one Cover	15.00
2201a	Stamp Collecting, bklt. pane of 4	5.00
2201b	Color error, Black omitted on #2198 & 2201	300.00
2201b	Same, set of 4 singles	300.00
2202	22¢ Love 1/30/86 New York, NY	2.00

Scott #	Description	Cacheted
	1986 COMMEMS (cont.)	
2203	22¢ Sojourner Truth 1/4/86 New Paltz, NY	3.00
2204	22¢ Texas 3/2/86 San Antonio, TX	3.00
	Washington-on-the-Brazos, TX	3.00
2205-09	22¢ Fish set of 5 singles 3/21/86 Seattle, WA	10.00
2209a	Fish, booklet pane of 5	6.00
2210	22¢ Public Hospitals 4/11/86 NY, NY	2.00
2211	22¢ Duke Ellington 4/29/86 New York, NY	4.00
2216-19	22¢ U.S. Presidents 4 sheets of 9 5/22/86 Chicago, IL	24.00
2216a-19a	US President set of 36 singles	60.00
2220-23	22¢ Explorers attd. 5/28/86 North Pole, AK	6.00
2220-23	22¢ Explorers set of 4 singles	12.00
2224	22¢ Statue of Liberty 7/4/86 NY, NY	2.00
2224	Joint issue w/France	5.00
2224	Joint issue w/France, dual cancel	15.00
2225	1¢ Omnibus Coil Re-engraved 11/26/86 DC	2.00
2226	2¢ Locomotive Coil Re-engraved 3/6/87 Milwaukee, WI	2.00
2228	4¢ Stagecoach Coil "B" Press 8/15/86 DC (eku)	150.00
2231	8.3¢ Ambulance Coil "B" Press 8/29/86 DC (eku)	150.00
2235-38	22¢ Navajo Art attd. 9/4/86 Window Rock, AZ	4.00
2235-38	Set of 4 singles	8.00
2239	22¢ T.S. Eliot 9/26/86 St. Louis, MO	2.00
2240-43	22¢ Woodcarved Figurines attd. 10/1/86 DC	4.00
2240-43	Set of 4 singles	8.00
2244	22¢ Christmas - Madonna & Child 10/24/86 DC	2.00
2245	22¢ Christmas Village Scene 10/24/86 Snow Hill, MD	2.00
2244-45	Christmas on one Cover, either City	2.50
2244-45	Christmas on one Cover, either City	3.00
	1987 Commeratives	
2246	22¢ Michigan Statehood 1/26/87 Lansing, MI	2.00
2247	22¢ Pan American Games 1/29/87 Indianapolis, IN	2.00
2248	22¢ Love 1/30/87 San Francisco, CA	2.00
2249	22¢ Jean Baptiste Point du Sable 2/20/87 Chicago, IL	3.00
2250	22¢ Enrico Caruso 2/27/87 NY, NY	2.00
2251	22¢ Girl Scouts 3/12/87 DC	4.00
	1987-88 TRANSPORTATION COILS	
2252	3¢ Conestoga Wagon 2/29/88 Conestoga, PA	2.00
2253	5¢ Milk Wagon 9/25/87 Indianapolis, IN	2.00
2254	5.3¢ Elevator, Prec. 9/16/88 New York, NY	2.00
2255	7.6¢ Carretta, Prec. 8/30/88 San Jose, CA	2.00
2256	8.4¢ Wheelchair, Prec. 8/12/88 Tucson, AZ	2.00
2257	10¢ Canal Boat 4/11/87 Buffalo, NY	2.00
2258	13¢ Police Patrol Wagon, Prec. 10/29/88 Anaheim, CA	2.50
2259	13.2¢ RR Car, Prec. 7/19/88 Pittsburgh, PA	2.00
2260	15¢ Tugboat 7/12/88 Long Beach, CA	2.00
2261	16.7¢ Popcorn Wagon, Prec. 7/7/88 Chicago, IL	2.00
2262	17.5¢ Marmon Wasp 9/25/87 Indianapolis, IN	2.00
2262a	Precancelled	5.00
2263	20¢ Cable Car 10/28/88 San Francisco, CA	2.00
2264	20.5¢ Fire Engine, Prec. 9/28/88 San Angelo, TX	2.00
2265	21¢ R.R. Mail Car, Prec. 8/16/88 Santa Fe, NM	2.00
2266	24.1¢ Tandem Bicycle, Prec. 10/26/88 Redmond, WA	2.00
	1987-88 REGULAR & SPECIAL ISSUES	
2267-74	22¢ Special Occasions, bklt. sgls. 4/20/87 Atlanta, GA	16.00
2274a	Booklet Pane of 10	7.00
2275	22¢ United Way 4/28/87 DC	2.00
2276	22¢ Flag and Fireworks 5/9/87 Denver, CO	2.00
2276a	Booklet Pane of 20 11/30/87 DC	12.00
2277	(25¢) "E" Earth Issue 3/22/88 DC	2.00
2278	25¢ Flag & Clouds 6/28/88 Boxborough, MA	2.00
2279	(25¢) "E" Earth Coil 3/22/88 DC	2.00
2280	25¢ Flag over Yosemite Coil 5/20/88 Yosemite, CA	2.00
2280 var.	Phosphor paper 2/14/89 Yosemite, CA	2.00
2281	25¢ Honeybee Coil 9/2/88 Omaha, NE	2.00
2282	(25¢) "E" Earth Bklt. Sgl. 3/22/88 DC	2.00
2282a	Bklt. Pane of 10	7.50
2283	25¢ Pheasant Bklt. Sgl. 4/29/88 Rapid City, SD	2.00
2283a	Bklt. Pane of 10	8.00
2284	25¢ Grosbeak Bklt. Sgl. 5/28/88 Arlington, VA	2.00
2285	25¢ Owl Bklt. Sgl. 5/28/88 Arlington, VA	2.00
2284-85	attached pair	3.50
2285b	Bklt. Pane of 10 (5 of ea.)	8.00

U.S. First Day Covers

2372-75

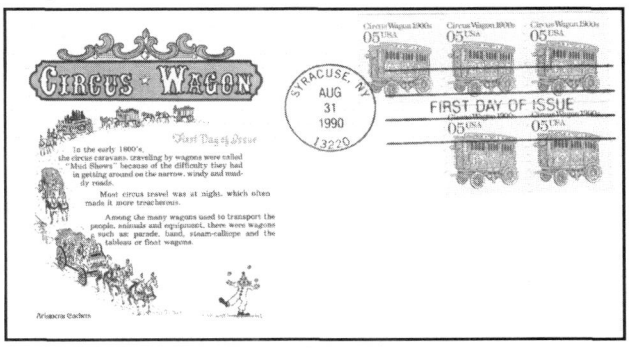

2452

Scott #	Description	Cacheted
	1987-88 REGULAR & SPECIAL ISSUES	
2285A	25¢ Flag & Clouds bklt. sgl. 7/5/88 DC	2.00
2285Ac	Bklt. Pane of 6	4.50
2286-2335	22¢ American Wildlife 6/13/87 Toronto, Canada	
	Set of 50 singles	75.00
2335a	Complete Pane of 50	40.00
	RATIFICATION OF CONSTITUTION STATE BICENTENNIAL ISSUES 1987-90	
2336-48	Set of 13 State Bicent. Issues on one cover each w/ a different First Day cancel	100.00
2336	22¢ Delaware Statehood Bicent. 7/4/87 Dover, DE	2.00
2337	22¢ Pennsylvania Bicent. 8/26/87 Harrisburg, PA	2.00
2338	22¢ New Jersey Bicent. 9/11/87 Trenton, NJ	2.00
2339	22¢ Georgia Bicent. 1/6/88 Atlanta, GA	2.00
2340	22¢ Connecticut Bicent. 1/9/88 Hartford, CT	2.00
2341	22¢ Massachusetts Bicent. 2/6/88 Boston, MA	2.00
2342	22¢ Maryland Bicent. 2/15/88 Annapolis, MD	2.00
2343	25¢ South Carolina Bicent. 5/23/88 Columbia, SC	2.00
2344	25¢ New Hampshire Bicent. 6/21/88 Concord, NH	2.00
2345	25¢ Virginia Bicent. 6/25/88 Williamsburg, VA	2.00
2346	25¢ New York Bicent. 7/26/88 Albany, NY	2.00
2347	25¢ North Carolina Bicent. 8/22/89 Fayetteville, NC	2.00
2348	25¢ Rhode Island Bicent. 5/29/90 Pawtucket, RI	2.00
	1987 COMMEMS (cont.)	
2349	22¢ U.S.-Morocco Relations 7/17/87 DC	2.00
2349	Morocco issue only	5.00
2349	Joint issue w/Morocco, dual cancel	15.00
2349	**1st Anagram cachet**	**25.00**
2350	22¢ William Faulkner 8/3/87 Oxford, MS	2.00
2351-54	22¢ Lacemaking attd. 8/14/87 Ypsilanti, MI	4.00
2351-54	Set of 4 singles	8.00
2355-59	22¢ Drafting of Constitution bklt. sgls. (5) 8/28/87 DC	10.00
2359a	Booklet Pane of 5	5.00
2360	22¢ Signing the Constitution 9/17/87 Philadelphia, PA	2.00
2361	22¢ Certified Public Accounting 9/21/87 NY, NY	12.00
2362-66	22¢ Locomotives, bklt. sgls. (5) 10/1/87 Baltimore, MD	10.00
2366a	Booklet Pane of 5	4.00
2367	22¢ Christmas - Madonna & Child 10/23/87 DC	2.00
2368	22¢ Christmas Ornaments 10/23/87 Holiday, CA	2.00
2367-68	Christmas on one cover, either city	3.00
2367-68	Christmas on one cover, dual cancel	4.00
	1988	
2369	22¢ 1988 Winter Olympics 1/10/88 Anchorage, AK	2.00
2370	22¢ Australia Bicentennial 1/26/88 DC	3.00
2370	Joint issue w/Australia, dual cancel	15.00
2370	Australia issue only	5.00
2371	22¢ James Weldon Johnson 2/2/88 Nashville, TN	3.00
2372-75	22¢ Cats attd. 2/5/88 New York, NY	8.00
2372-75	Set of 4 singles	15.00
2376	22¢ Knute Rockne 3/9/88 Notre Dame, IN	4.00
2377	25¢ Francis Ouimet 6/13/88 Brookline, MA	7.50
2378	25¢ Love, 7/4/88 Pasadena, CA	2.00
2379	45¢ Love, 8/8/88 Shreveport, LA	2.00
2380	25¢ Summer Olympics 8/19/88 Colo. Springs, CO	2.00
2381-85	25¢ Classic Cars, Bklt. Sgls. 8/25/88 Detroit, MI	10.00
2385a	Bklt. Pane of 5	4.00
2386-89	25¢ Antarctic Explorers attd. 9/14/88 DC	4.00
2386-89	Set of 4 singles	8.00
2390-93	25¢ Carousel Animals attd. 10/1/88 Sandusky, OH	4.00
2390-93	Set of 4 singles	8.00
2394	$8.75 Eagle 10/4/88 Terra Haute, IN	30.00
2395-98	25¢ Sp. Occasions Bklt. Sgls. 10/22/88 King of Prussia, PA	7.00
2396a	Happy Birthday & Best Wishes, Bklt. Pane of 6	5.00
2398a	Thinking of You & Love You, Bklt. Pane of 6	5.00
2399	25¢ Christmas Madonna & Child 10/20/88 DC	2.00
2400	25¢ Christmas Sleigh & Village 10/20/88 Berlin, NH	2.00
2399-00	Christmas on one Cover	2.50
2399-00	Christmas on one Cover, dual cancel	3.00
	1989	
2401	25¢ Montana Statehood 1/15/89 Helena, MT	2.00
2402	25¢ A. Philip Randolph 2/3/89 New York, NY	3.00
2403	25¢ North Dakota Statehood 2/21/89 Bismarck, ND	2.00
2404	25¢ Washington Statehood 2/22/89 Olympia, WA	2.00
2405-09	25¢ Steamboats, Bklt. Sgls. 3/3/89 New Orleans, LA	10.00

Scott #	Description	Cacheted
	1989 (cont.)	
2409a	Bklt. Pane of 5	4.00
2410	25¢ World Stamp Expo 3/16/89 New York, NY	2.00
2411	25¢ Arturo Toscanini 3/25/89 New York, NY	2.00
2412	25¢ U.S. House of Representatives 4/4/89 DC	2.00
2413	25¢ U.S. Senate 4/6/89 DC	2.00
2414	25¢ Exec. Branch & George Washington Inaugural 4/16/89 Mt. Vernon, VA	2.00
2412-15	Government combo 2/2/90 Washington, DC	3.50
2415	25¢ U.S. Supreme Court 2/2/90 DC	2.00
2416	25¢ South Dakota Statehood 5/3/89 Pierre, SD	2.00
2417	25¢ Lou Gehrig 6/10/89 Cooperstown, NY	5.50
2418	25¢ Ernest Hemingway 7/17/89 Key West, FL	2.00
2419	$2.40 Moon Landing, Priority Mail, 7/20/89 DC	7.00
2420	25¢ Letter Carriers 8/30/89 Milwaukee, WI	2.00
2421	25¢ Drafting the Bill of Rights 9/25/89 Philadelphia, PA	2.00
2422-25	25¢ Prehistoric Animals attd. 10/1/89 Orlando, FL	5.00
2422-25	Set of 4 singles	10.00
2426, C21	(1) 25¢ Pre-Columbian w/45¢ Air Combo	7.50
2426	25¢ Pre-Columbian Customs 10/12/89 San Juan, PR	2.00
2427	25¢ Christmas Madonna & Child 10/19/89 DC	2.00
2427	Madonna booklet single	2.00
2427a	Booklet Pane of 10	8.00
2428	25¢ Christmas Sleigh & Presents 10/19/89 Westport, CT	2.00
2427-28	Christmas on one Cover, either City	2.50
2427-28	Christmas on one Cover, dual cancel	3.00
2429	25¢ Christmas Sleigh, bklt. sgl. Westport, CT	2.00
2429a	Booklet Pane of 10	8.00
2431	25¢ Eagle & Sheild, pair on backing paper	4.00
2431	25¢ Eagle & Sheild, pane of 6	8.00
2431	25¢ Eagle & Shield, self-adhes. 11/10/89 Virginia Bch., VA	2.00
2431a	Booklet Pane of 18	30.00
2433	90¢ World Stamp Expo S/S of 4 11/17/89 DC	14.50
2434-37	25¢ Traditional Mail Transportation attd. 11/19/89 DC	4.00
2434-37	Set of 4 singles	8.00
2438	25¢ Traditional Mail Transportation, S/S of 4 11/28/89 DC	4.50
	1990	
2439	25¢ Idaho Statehood 1/6/90 Boise, ID	2.00
2440	25¢ Love 1/18/90 Romance, AR	2.00
2441	25¢ Love, bklt. sgl. 1/18/90 Romance, AR	2.00
2441a	Booklet Pane of 10	8.00
2442	25¢ Ida B. Wells 2/1/90 Chicago, IL	3.00
2443	15¢ Beach Umbrella, bklt. sgl. 2/3/90 Sarasota, FL	2.00
2443a	Booklet Pane of 10	6.00
2444	25¢ Wyoming Statehood 2/23/90 Cheyenne, WY	2.00
2445-48	25¢ Classic Films attd. 3/23/90 Hollywood, CA	7.50
2445-48	Set of 4 singles	12.00
2449	25¢ Marianne Moore 4/18/90 Brooklyn, NY	2.00
	1990-95 TRANSPORTATION COILS	
2451	4¢ Steam Carriage 1/25/91 Tucson, AZ	2.00
2452	5¢ Circus Wagon 8/31/90 Syracuse, NY	2.50
2452B	5¢ Circus Wagon, Gravure 12/8/92 Cincinnati, OH	2.50
2452D	5¢ Circus Wagon, Reissue (5¢) 3/20/95, Kansas City, MO	3.00
2453	5¢ Canoe, brown 5/25/91 Secaucus, NJ	2.00
2454	5¢ Canoe, red, Gravure print 10/22/91 Secaucus, NJ	2.00
2457	10¢ Tractor Trailer, Intaglio 5/25/91 Secaucus, NJ	2.00
2458	10¢ Tractor Trailer, Gravure 5/25/94 Secaucus, NJ	2.00
2463	20¢ Cog Railway Car 6/9/95 Dallas, TX	2.00
2464	23¢ Lunch Wagon 4/12/91 Columbus, OH	2.00
2466	32¢ Ferry Boat 6/2/95 McLean, VA	2.00
2468	$1.00 Seaplane 4/20/90 Phoenix, AZ	3.00
	1990-93	
2470-74	25¢ Lighthouse bklt. sgls. 4/26/90 DC	10.00
2474a	Booklet Pane of 5	4.00
2475	25¢ Flag Stamp, ATM self-adhes. 5/18/90 Seattle, WA	2.00
2475a	Pane of 12	10.00
2476	1¢ Kestrel 6/22/91 Aurora, CO	2.00
2477	1¢ Reprint 5/10/95 Aurora, CO w "¢" sign	2.00
2478	3¢ Bluebird 6/22/91 Aurora, CO	2.00
2479	19¢ Fawn 3/11/91 DC	2.00
2480	30¢ Cardinal 6/22/91 Aurora, CO	2.00
2481	45¢ Pumpkinseed Sunfish 12/2/92 DC	2.50

U.S. First Day Covers

2592

1990-93 (cont.)

Scott #	Description	Cacheted
2482	$2 Bobcat 6/1/90 Arlington, VA	7.00
2483	20¢ Blue Jay, Bklt.sgl. 6/15/95 Kansas City, MO	2.00
2483a	Booklet Pane of 10	8.50
2484	29¢ Wood Duck, BEP bklt. single 4/12/91 Columbus, OH	2.00
2484a	BEP Booklet Pane of 10	9.00
2485	29¢ Wood Duck, KCS bklt. single 4/12/91 Columbus, OH	2.00
2485a	KCS Booklet Pane of 10	9.00
2486	29¢ African Violet, Bklt. Sgl. 10/8/93 Beaumont, TX	2.00
2486a	Booklet Pane of 10	8.00
2487	32¢ Peach, Bklt. sgl. 7/8/95 Reno, NV	2.00
2488	32¢ Pear, Bklt. sgl. 7/8/95 Reno, NV	2.00
2487-88	32¢ Peach & Pear, Attached Pair	2.50
2488A	Booklet Pane of 10	8.50

1993-95 SELF ADHESIVE BOOKLETS & COILS

Scott #	Description	Cacheted
2489	29¢ Red Squirrel, Self adhesive,sgl. 6/25/93 Milwaukee, WI	2.00
2489	29¢ Red Squirrel, pair on backing paper	3.00
2489a	Pane of 18	14.00
2490	29¢ Rose, pair on backing paper	3.00
2490	29¢ Rose, Self adhesive sgl. 8/19/93 Houston, TX	2.00
2490a	Pane of 18	14.00
2491	29¢ Pine Cone, pair on backing paper	3.00
2491	29¢ Pine Cone, Self adhesive sgl. 11/5/93 Kansas City, MO	2.00
2491a	Pane of 18	14.00
2492	29¢ Pink Rose, pair on backing paper	3.00
2492	32¢ Pink Rose, Self-adhesive 6/2/95 McLean, VA	2.00
2492a	Pane of 20, Self-adhesive	15.50
2493	32¢ Peach, self-adhesive 7/8/95 Reno, NV	2.00
2494	32¢ Pear, self-adhesive 7/8/95 Reno, NV	2.00
2493-94	32¢ Peach & Pear, attd	2.50
2494a	Pane of 20, self-adhesive	15.50
2495	32¢ Peach, Coil, Self adhesive 7/8/95 Reno, NV	2.00
2495A	32¢ Pear, Coil, Self-adhesive 7/8/95 Reno, NV	2.00
2495-95A	Peach & Pear, Coil Pair	2.50

1990 COMMEMORATIVES (cont.)

Scott #	Description	Cacheted
2496-2500	25¢ Olympians attd. 7/6/90 Minneapolis, MN	7.50
2496-2500	Set of 5 singles	15.00
2496-2500	Olympians with Tab singles attd.	8.00
2496-2500	Set of 5 singles with Tabs	12.00
2501-05	25¢ Indian Headdresses bklt. singles 8/17/90 Cody, WY	10.00
2505a	Booklet Pane of 5	8.00
2506-07	25¢ Micronesia & Marshall Isles 9/28/90 DC	3.00
2506-07	Set of 2 singles	4.00
2506-07	Joint issue w/Micronesia & Marshal Isles.	5.00
2506-07	Joint issue w/Micronesia & Marshal Isles, Triple Cancel	15.00
2506	Micronesia issue only	3.00
2507	Marshal Island issue only, strip of 3	4.00
2508-11	25¢ Sea Creatures attd. 10/3/90 Baltimore, MD	5.00
2508-11	Set of 4 singles	10.00
2508-11	Joint issue w/USSR, attd	5.00
2508-11	Joint issue w/USSR attd, dual cancel	15.00
2508-11	Joint issue w/USSR, set of 4 singles	20.00
2512&C127	Combination on one Cover	4.00
2512	25¢ Pre-Columbian Customs 10/12/90 Grand Canyon, AZ	2.00
2513	25¢ Dwight D. Eisenhower 10/13/90 Abilene, KS	2.00
2514	25¢ Christmas Madonna & Child 10/18/90 DC	2.00
2514	Madonna booklet single	2.00
2514a	Booklet Pane of 10 10/18/90 DC	6.50
2515	25¢ Christmas Tree 10/18/90 Evergreen, CO	2.00
2514-15	Christmas on one Cover, dual cancel	3.00
2516	25¢ Christmas Tree bklt. sgl. 10/18/90 Evergreen, CO	2.00
2516a	Booklet Pane of 10 10/18/90	6.50

1991-94 REGULAR ISSUES

Scott #	Description	Cacheted
2517	(29¢) "F" Flower stamp 1/22/91 DC	2.00
2518	(29¢) "F" Flower coil 1/22/91 DC	2.00
2519	(29¢) "F" Flower, BEP bklt. single 1/22/91 DC	2.00
2519a	Bklt. Pane of 10, BEP	7.50
2517-19	Combination on one Cover	3.00
2520	(29¢) "F" Flower, KCS bklt. single 1/22/91 DC	3.50
2520a	Bklt. Pane of 10, KCS	9.50
2521	(4¢) Make-up rate stamp 1/22/91 DC, non-denom	2.00
2522	(29¢) "F" Flag stamp, ATM self-adhes. 1/22/91 DC	2.00
2522a	Pane of 12	10.00
2523	29¢ Flag over Mt. Rushmore Coil 3/29/91 Mt. Rushmore, SD	2.00

1991-94 REGULAR ISSUES (cont.)

Scott #	Description	Cacheted
2523A	29¢ Same, Gravure print 7/4/91 Mt. Rushmore, SD	2.00

* On #2523A "USA" and "29" are **not** outlined in white

Scott #	Description	Cacheted
2524	29¢ Flower 4/5/91 Rochester, NY	2.00
2525	29¢ Flower coil, rouletted 8/16/91 Rochester, NY	2.00
2526	29¢ Flower coil, perforated 3/3/92 Rochester, NY	2.00
2527	29¢ Flower, bklt. single 4/5/91 Rochester, NY	2.00
2527a	Booklet Pane of 10	7.50
2528	29¢ Flag with Olympic Rings, bklt. sgl. 4/21/91 Atlanta, GA	2.00
2528a	Booklet Pane of 10	7.50
2529	19¢ Fishing Boat, coil 8/8/91 DC	2.50
2529C	19¢ Fishing Boat, coil, Type III 6/25/94 Arlington, VA	2.50
2530	19¢ Ballooning, bklt. sgl. 5/17/91 Denver, CO	2.00
2530a	Booklet Pane of 10	9.00
2531	29¢ Flags/Memorial Day, 125th Anniv. 5/30/91 Waterloo,NY	2.00
2531A	29¢ Liberty Torch, ATM self-adhes. 6/25/91 New York, NY	2.00
2531Ab	Pane of 18	14.00

1991 COMMEMORATIVES

Scott #	Description	Cacheted
2532	50¢ Switzerland, joint issue 2/22/91 DC	2.00
2532	Joint issue w/Switzerland, dual cancel	15.00
2532	Swiss issue only	3.00
2533	29¢ Vermont Statehood 3/1/91 Bennington, VT	2.25
2534	29¢ Savings Bonds 4/30/91 DC	2.00
2535	29¢ Love 5/9/91 Honolulu, HI	2.00
2536	29¢ Love, Booklet Sgl. 5/9/91 Honolulu, HI	2.00
2536a	Booklet Pane of 10	7.50
2537	52¢ Love, 2 ounce rate 5/9/91 Honolulu, HI	2.00
2538	29¢ William Saroyan 5/22/91 Fresno, CA	2.25
2538	Joint issue w/USSR, dual cancel	15.00

1991-95 REGULAR ISSUES

Scott #	Description	Cacheted
2539	$1.00 USPS & Olympic Rings 9/29/91 Orlando, FL	3.00
2540	$2.90 Priority Mail 7/7/91 San Diego, CA	9.00
2541	$9.95 Express Mail,Domestic rate 6/16/91 Sacramento,CA	25.00
2542	$14.00 Express Mail,Internat'l rate 8/31/91 Hunt Valley MD	32.50
2543	$2.90 Priority Mail, Space 6/3/93 Kennedy Space Center FL	7.50
2544	$3 Challenger Shuttle, Priority Mail 6/22/95 Anaheim, CA	7.75
2544A	$10.75 Endeavor Shuttle Express Mail 8/4/95 Irvine, CA	25.00

1991 COMMEMORATIVES (cont.)

Scott #	Description	Cacheted
2545-49	29¢ Fishing Flies, bklt. sgls. 5/31/91 Cudlebackville, NY	10.00
2549a	Booklet Pane of 5	5.00
2550	29¢ Cole Porter 6/8/91 Peru, IN	2.50
2551	29¢ Desert Shield / Desert Storm 7/2/91 DC	2.00
2552	29¢ Desert Shield / Desert Storm bklt. sgl. 7/2/91 DC	2.00
2552a	29¢ Booklet Pane of 5	4.50
2553-57	29¢ Summer Olympics,strip of 5 7/12/91 Los Angeles, CA	4.50
2553-57	Set of 5 singles	10.00
2558	29¢ Numismatics 8/13/91 Chicago, IL	2.00
2559	29¢ World War II S/S of 10 9/3/91 Phoenix, AZ	12.00
2559a-j	Set of 10 singles	30.00
2560	29¢ Basketball 8/28/91 Springfield, MA	3.00
2561	29¢ District of Columbia Bicent. 9/7/91 DC	2.00
2562-66	29¢ Comedians .,set of 5 8/29/91 Hollywood, CA	10.00
2562-66	Set of 5 on 1	4.50
2566a	Booklet Pane of 10	7.50
2567	29¢ Jan Matzeliger 9/15/91 Lynn, MA	3.00
2568-77	29¢ Space Exploration bklt. sgls. 10/1/91 Pasadena, CA	20.00
2577a	Booklet Pane of 10	8.00
2578	(29¢) Christmas, Madonna & Child 10/17/91 Houston,TX	2.00
2578a	Booklet Pane of 10	8.00
2579	(29¢) Christmas, Santa & Chimney 10/19/91 Santa, ID	2.00
2580-85	(29¢) Christmas, bklt. pane sgls. 10/17/91 Santa, ID	12.00
2581b-85a	Booklet Panes of 4, set of 5	20.00

1994-95 DEFINITIVES DESIGNS OF 1869 ESSAYS

Scott #	Description	Cacheted
2587	32¢ James S. Polk 11/2/95 Columbia, TN	1.90
2590	$1 Surrender of Burgoyne 5/5/94 New York, NY	4.00
2592	$5 Washington & Jackson 8/19/94 Pittsburgh, PA	20.00

1992-93 REGULAR ISSUES

Scott #	Description	Cacheted
2593	29¢ "Pledge" Black denom., bklt. sgl. 9/8/92 Rome, NY	2.00
2593a	Booklet Pane of 10	7.00

1992 Eagle & Shield Self-Adhesives Stamps
(9/25/92 Dayton, OH)

Scott #	Description	Cacheted
2595	29¢ "Brown" denomination, sgl	2.00
2595a	Pane of 17 + label	12.00
2596	29¢ "Green" denomination, sgl	2.00
2596a	Pane of 17 + label	12.00
2597	29¢ "Red" denomination, sgl	2.00
2597a	Pane of 17 + label	12.00

1992 Eagle & Shield Self-Adhesive Coils

Scott #	Description	Cacheted
2595v	29¢ "Brown" denomination, pair with paper backing	2.25
2596v	29¢ "Green" denomination, pair with paper backing	2.25
2597v	29¢ "Red" denomination, pair with paper backing	2.25

1994 Eagle Self-Adhesive Issues

Scott #	Description	Cacheted
2598	29¢ Eagle, single 2/4/94 Sarasota, FL	2.00
2598a	Pane of 18	12.50
2598v	29¢ Coil Pair with paper backing	2.25

1994 Statue of Liberty Self-Adhesive Issue

Scott #	Description	Cacheted
2599	29¢ Statue of Liberty, single 6/24/94 Haines, FL	2.00
2599a	Pane of 18	12.50
2599v	29¢ Coil pair with paper backing	2.25

U.S. First Day Covers

2721

Scott #	Description	Cacheted
	1991-93 Coil Issues	
2602	(10¢) Eagle & Shield, bulk-rate 12/13/91 Kansas City, MO	2.00
2603	(10¢) Eagle & Shield, **BEP** 5/29/93 Secaucus, NJ	2.00
2604	(10¢) Eagle & Shld., **Stamp Venturers** 5/29/93 Secaucus, NJ	2.00
2605	23¢ Flag, First Class pre-sort 9/27/91 DC	2.00
2606	23¢ USA, 1st Cl, pre-sort, **ABNCo.** 7/21/92 Kansas City, MO	2.00
2607	23¢ USA, 1st Cl, pre-sort, **BEP** 10/9/92 Kansas City, MO	2.00
2608	23¢ USA, 1st Cl, p.s., **Stamp Venturers** 5/14/93 Denver, CO	2.00
2609	29¢ Flag over White House 4/23/92 DC	2.00
	1992 Commemoratives	
2611-15	29¢ Winter Olympics, strip of 5 1/11/92 Orlando, FL	5.00
2611-15	Set of 5 singles	10.00
2616	29¢ World Columbian Expo 1/24/92 Rosemont, IL	2.00
2617	29¢ W.E.B. DuBois 1/31/92 Atlanta, GA	3.00
2618	29¢ Love 2/6/92 Loveland. CO	2.00
2619	29¢ Olympic Baseball 4/3/92 Atlanta, GA	3.50
	1992 Columbus Commemoratives	
2620-23	29¢ First Voyage of Columbus 4/24/92 Christiansted, VI	4.00
2620-23	Set of 4 singles	8.00
2620-23	Joint issue w/Italy, dual cancel	15.00
2620-23	Joint Issue w/Italy, Dual with blue cancel	450.00
2620-23	Joint Issue w/Italy, set of 4	30.00
2620-23	Italian issue only block of 4	4.00
2624-29	1¢-$5.00 Voyages of Columbus 6 S/S's 5/22/92 Chicago, IL	50.00
2624a-29	Set of 16 singles	90.00
2624-29	Italian issue only, set of 6	35.00
2624-29	Spanish issue only, set of 6	15.00
2624-29	Portugal issue only, set of 6	35.00
	1992 Commemoratives (cont.)	
2630	29¢ New York Stock Exchange 5/17/92 New York, NY	4.00
2631-34	29¢ Space: Accomplishments 5/29/92 Chicago, IL	4.00
2631-34	Set of 4 singles	10.00
2631-34	Joint issue w/Russia,dual cancel, blocks of 4	15.00
2631-34	Joint issue w/Russia, dual cancel, set of 4	20.00
2631-34	Russian issue only, block of 4	3.25
2631-34	Russian issue only, set of 4	12.00
2635	29¢ Alaska Highway 5/30/92 Fairbanks, AK	2.00
2636	29¢ Kentucky Statehood Bicent. 6/1/92 Danville, KY	2.00
2637-41	29¢ Summer Olympics, strip of 5 6/11/92 Baltimore, MD	5.00
2637-41	Set of 5 singles	10.00
2642-46	29¢ Hummingbirds, bklt. sgls. 6/15/92 DC	10.00
2646a	Booklet Pane of 5	5.00
2647-96	29¢ Wildflowers, set of 50 singles 7/24/92 Columbus, OH	87.50
2697	29¢ World War II S/S of 10 8/17/92 Indianapolis, IN	10.00
2697a-j	Set of 10 singles	25.00
2698	29¢ Dorothy Parker 8/22/92 West End, NJ	2.50
2699	29¢ Dr. Theodore von Karman 8/31/92 DC	2.50
2700-03	29¢ Minerals 9/17/92 DC	4.00
2700-03	Set of 4 singles	8.00
2704	29¢ Juan Rodriguez Cabrillo 9/28/92 San Diego, CA	2.00
2705-09	29¢ Wild Animals, bklt. sgls. 10/1/92 New Orleans, LA	10.00
2709a	Booklet Pane of 5	5.00
2710	29¢ Christmas, Madonna & Child 10/22/92 DC	2.00
2710a	Booklet Pane of 10 10/22/92 DC	8.00
2710-14	Christmas on one Cover, dual cancel	4.50
2710-14	Christmason 4 Covers, dual cancel	9.00
2711-14	29¢ Christmas Toys,offset, 10/22/92 Kansas City, MO	4.00
2711-14	Set of 4 singles	10.00
2715-18	29¢ Christmas Toys,gravure,bklt.sgls.10/22/92 Kansas City,MO	10.00
2715-18	Block of 4	4.00
2718a	Booklet Pane of 10	9.00
2719	29¢ Christmas Train self-adhes. ATM 10/28/92 NY, NY	2.00
2719a	Pane of 18	14.00
2720	29¢ Happy New Year 12/30/92 San Francisco, CA	3.00
	1993 Commemoratives	
2721	29¢ Elvis Presley 1/8/93 Memphis, TN	2.00
2722	29¢ Oklahoma! 3/30/93 Oklahoma City, OK	2.00
2723	29¢ Hank Williams 6/9/93 Nashville, TN	2.00
2724-30	29¢ R 'n' R/R & B 6/16/93 on one cover Cleveland, OH & Santa Monica, CA (same cancel ea. city)	10.50

2779-82

Scott #	Description	Cacheted
	1993 Commemoratives (cont.)	
2724-30	Set of 7 singles on 2 covers	12.00
2724-30	Set of 7 singles	21.00
2731-37	29¢ R 'n' R/R & B, Set/7 bklt. sgls. 6/16/93 Cleveland, OH & Santa Monica, CA (same cancel ea. city)	21.00
2731-37	Set of 7 singles on 2 covers	12.00
2737a	Booklet Pane of 8	9.00
2737b	Booklet Pane of 4	5.50
2737a,b	Booklet Panes on 1 cover	14.00
2741-45	29¢ Space Fantasy, bklt. sgls. 1/25/93 Huntsville, AL	10.00
2745a	Booklet Pane of 5	5.00
2746	29¢ Percy Lavon Julian 1/29/93 Chicago, IL	3.00
2747	29¢ Oregon Trail 2/12/93 Salem, OR	2.00
2748	29¢ World University Games 2/25/93 Buffalo, NY	2.00
2749	29¢ Grace Kelly 3/24/93 Hollywood, CA	3.50
2749	Joint issue w/Monaco, dual cancel	15.00
2749	Monaco issue only	2.50
2750-53	29¢ Circus 4/6/93 DC	5.00
2750-53	Set of 4 singles	12.00
2754	29¢ Cherokee Strip 4/17/93 Enid, OK	2.00
2755	29¢ Dean Acheson 4/21/93 DC	2.00
2756-59	29¢ Sport Horses 5/1/93 Louisville, KY	6.00
2756-59	Set of 4 singles	15.00
2760-64	29¢ Garden Flowers, bklt. sgls. 5/15/93 Spokane, WA	10.00
2764a	Booklet Pane of 5	5.00
2765	29¢ World War II S/S of 10 5/31/93 DC	10.00
2765a-j	Set of 10 singles	25.00
2766	29¢ Joe Louis 6/22/93 Detroit, MI	4.00
2767-70	29¢ Broadway Musicals, bkt. sgls. 7/14/93 New York, NY	12.00
2770a	Booklet Pane of 4	6.00
2771-74	29¢ Country Music attd. 9/25/93 Nashville, TN	5.00
2771-74	Set of 4 singles	10.00
2775-78	29¢ Country Music, bklt. sgls. 9/25/93 Nashville, TN	10.00
2778a	Booklet Pane of 4	5.00
2779-82	29¢ National Postal Museum 7/30/93 DC	4.00
2779-82	Set of 4 singles	10.00
2783-84	29¢ Deaf Communication, pair 9/20/93 Burbank, CA	3.00
2783-84	Set of 2 singles	5.00
2785-88	29¢ Children's Classics, block of 4 10/23/93 Louisville, KY	4.00
2785-88	Set of 4 singles	10.00
2789	29¢ Madonna & Child 10/21/93 Raleigh, NC	2.00
2790	Booklet Single	2.00
2790a	Booklet Pane of 4	4.00
2789+91-94	Christmas on one Cover, dual cancel	4.50
2789+91-94	Christmas on 4 Covers, dual cancel	9.00
2791-94	29¢ Christmas Designs attd. 10/21/93 New York, NY	4.00
2791-94	Set of 4 singles	10.00
2795-98	29¢ Contemp. Christmas, 4 bklt.singles 10/21/93 NY, NY	10.00
2798a	Booklet Pane of 10 (3 snowmen)	8.00
2798b	Booklet Pane of 10 (2 snowmen)	8.00
2799-2802	29¢ Contemp. Christmas, self-adhes. Set of 4 10/28/93 NY, NY	9.00
2802a	Pane of 12	10.00
2803	29¢ Snowman, self-adhesive 10/28/93 New York, NY	2.00
2803a	Booklet Pane of 18	14.00
2804	29¢ Northern Mariana Isles 11/4/93 DC	2.00
2805	29¢ Columbus-Puerto Rico 11/19/93 San Juan, PR	2.00
2806	29¢ AIDS Awareness 12/1/93 New York, NY	3.00
2806a	29¢ AIDS, booklet single 12/1/93 New York, NY	3.00
2806b	Booklet Pane of 5	8.00
	1994 Commemoratives	
2807-11	29¢ Winter Olympics, Strip of 5, 1/6/94 Salt Lake City, UT	5.00
2807-11	Set of 5 Singles	10.00
2812	29¢ Edward R. Murrow 1/21/94 Pullman, WA	2.00
2813	29¢ Love & Sunrise, self-adhesive sgl. 1/27/94 Loveland, OH	2.00
2813a	Pane of 18	14.00
2813v	Coil Pair with paper backing	2.25
2814	29¢ Love & Dove, booklet single 2/14/94 Niagara Falls, NY	2.00
2814a	Booklet Pane of 10	7.00
2814C	29¢ Love & Dove, Sheet Stamp 6/11/94 Niagara Falls, NY	2.00
2815	52¢ Love & Doves 2/14/94 Niagara Falls, NY	2.00
2816	29¢ Dr. Allison Davis 2/1/94 Williamstown, MA	3.00
2817	29¢ Chinese New Year, Dog 2/5/94 Pomona, CA	2.50
2818	29¢ Buffalo Soldiers 4/22/94 Dallas, TX	4.00
2819-28	29¢ Silent Screen Stars, attd. 4/27/94 San Francisco, CA	8.00
2819-28	Set of 10 Singles	20.00

U.S. First Day Covers

Scott #	Description	Cacheted
	1994 Commemoratives	
2819-28	Set of 10 on 2 covers	9.50
2829-33	29¢ Summer Garden Flowers 4/28/94 Cincinnati, OH	5.00
2833a	Set of 5 Singles	10.00
2834	29¢ World Cup Soccer 5/26/94 New York, NY	2.00
2834-36	29¢, 40¢, 50¢ Soccer on 1 cover	3.00
2834-36	29¢, 40¢, 50¢ Soccer on 3 covers	5.75
2835	40¢ World Cup Soccer 5/26/94 E. Rutherford, NJ	2.00
2836	50¢ World Cup Soccer 5/26/94 E. Rutherford, NJ	2.00
2837	29¢,40¢,50¢ Soccer Souvenir Sheet of 3 5/26/94 NY,NY	3.50
2838	29¢ World War II Souvenir Sht of 10 6/6/94 U.S.S. Normandy	10.00
2838a-j	Set of 10 Singles	25.00
2839	29¢ Norman Rockwell 7/1/94 Stockbridge, MA	2.00
2840	50¢ Norman Rockwell, S/S of 4 7/1/94 Stockbridge, MA	5.75
2840A-D	Singles from Souvenir Sheet	8.00
	1994 Moon Landing, 25th Anniversary	
2841	29¢ Moon Landing Souvenir Sheet of 12 7/20/94 DC	10.75
2841a	Single from Souvenir Sheet	2.00
2842	$9.95 Moon Landing, Express Mail 7/20/94 DC	25.00
	1994 Commemoratives (cont.)	
2843-47	29¢ Locomotives, booklet singles 7/28/94 Chama, NM	10.00
2847a	Booklet Pane of 5	5.00
2848	29¢ George Meany 8/16/94 DC	2.00
2849-53	29¢ Popular Singers 9/1/94 New York, NY	7.50
2849-53	Set of 5 Singles	15.00
2854-61	29¢ Blues & Jazz Artists 9/17/94 Greenville, MI	12.00
2854-61	Set of 8 on 2 covers	12.00
2854-61	Set of 8 Singles	24.00
2862	29¢ James Thurber 9/10/94 Columbus, OH	2.00
2863-66	29¢ Wonders of the Sea 10/1/94 Honolulu, HI	4.00
2863-66	Set of 4 Singles	8.00
2867-68	29¢ Cranes, attd. 10/9/94 DC	4.00
2867-68	Set of 2 Singles	6.00
2867-68	Joint Issue w/China, dual cancel	20.00
2867-68	Chinese issue only, attd.	2.75
2867-68	Chinese issue only, set of 2	4.50
	1994 Legends of the West Miniature Sheet	
2869	29¢ Legends of the West, Pane of 20 10/18/94 Tucson, AZ, Laramie, WY and Lawton, OK	30.00
2869a-t	Set of 20 Singles	60.00
2869a-t	Set of four covers, 2 blocks of 4 and 2 blocks of 6	25.00
	1994 Commemoratives (cont.)	
2871	29¢ Madonna & Child 10/20/94 DC	2.00
2871a	Booklet single	2.00
2871b	Booklet Pane of 10	8.50
2872	29¢ Christmas Stocking 10/20/94 Harmony, MN	2.00
2872a	Booklet Pane of 20	15.50
2872v	Booklet single	2.00
2873	29¢ Santa Claus, self-adhesive 10/20/94 Harmony, MN	2.00
2873a	Pane of 12	10.00
2873v	Coil pair on paper backing	2.25
2874	29¢ Cardinal in Snow, self-adhesive 10/20/94 Harmony, MN .	2.00
2874a	Pane of 18	14.00
2875	$2 Bureau of Engraving Centennial Souvenir sheet of 4 11/3/94 New York, NY	24.00
2875a	$2 Madison single from souvenir sheet	7.00
2876	29¢ Year of the Boar 12/30/94 Sacramento, CA	2.50
	1994-97 Interim Regular Issues	
2877	(3¢) Dove, ABN, Light blue 12/13/94 DC	2.00
2878	(3¢) Dove, SVS, Darker blue 12/13/94 DC	2.00
2879	(20¢) "G" Postcard Rate, BEP, Black "G" 12/13/94 DC	2.00
2880	(20¢) "G" Postcard Rate, SVS, Red "G" 12/13/94 DC	2.00
2881	(32¢) "G" BEP, Black "G" 12/13/94 DC	2.00
2881a	Booklet Pane of 10	8.50
2882	(32¢) "G" SVS, Red "G" 12/13/94 DC	2.00
2881-82	(32¢) "G" Combo 12/13/94 DC	2.75
2883	(32¢) "G" BEP, Black "G", Booklet Single 12/13/94 DC	2.00
2883a	Booklet Pane of 10, BEP	8.50
2884	(32¢) "G" ABN, Blue "G", Booklet Single 12/13/94 DC	2.00
2884a	Booklet Pane of 10, ABN	8.50
2885	(32¢) "G" KCS, Red "G", Booklet Single 12/13/94 DC	2.00
2885a	Booklet Pane of 10, KCS	8.50
2886	(32¢) "G"Surface Tagged,self-adh.,strip format 12/13/94 DC .	2.00
2886a	Pane of 18, Self-Adhesive	15.00
2887	(32¢) "G" Overall Tagging, self-adhesive 12/13/94 DC	2.00
2887a	Pane of 18, self-adhesive	15.00
2888	(25¢) "G" Presort, Coil 12/13/94 DC	2.00
2888,2393	(25¢) "G" Presort and (5¢) "G" Non-profit Combo 12/13/94 DC	2.40
2889	(32¢) "G" Coil, BEP, Black "G" 12/13/94 DC	2.00
2890	(32¢) "G" Coil, ABN, Blue "G" 12/13/94 DC	2.00
2891	(32¢) "G" Coil, SVS, Red "G" 12/13/94 DC	2.00
2892	(32¢) "G" Coil, Rouletted, Red "G" 12/13/94 DC	2.00
2893	(5¢) "G" Non-Profit, Green, 12/13/94 date, available for mail order sale 1/12/95 DC	2.00
2897	32¢ Flag over Porch, sheet stamp 5/19/95 Denver, CO	2.00
2902	(5¢) Butte 3/10/95 State College, PA	2.00
2902B	(5¢) Butte - S/A Coil 6/15/96 State College, PA	2.00
2903	(5¢) Mountain, Coil, BEP (Letters outlined in purple) 3/16/96, San Jose, Ca	2.00
2904	(5¢) Mountain, Coil, SV, (outlined letters) 3/16/96 San Jose, Ca.	2.00
2904A	(5¢) Mountain, S/A, Coil, 6/15/96	2.00

The Shining Star
Striving to be a serious actress, playing more demanding roles.
FIRST DAY OF ISSUE
UNIVERSAL STUDIOS
UNIVERSAL CITY, CA
JUNE 1 1995
91608

2967

Scott #	Description	Cacheted
	1994-97 Interim Regular Issues (cont.)	
2904B	(5¢) Mountain, S/A, BEP, 1/24/97	2.00
2905	(10¢) Automobile 3/10/95 State College, PA	2.00
2906	(10¢) Auto, S/A. Coil, 6/15/96	2.00
2907	(10¢) Eagle & Shield, S/A, Coil, 5/21/96	2.00
2908	(15¢) Auto Tail Fin, BEP 3/17/95 New York, NY	2.00
2909	(15¢) Auto Tail Fin, SVS 3/17/95 New York, NY	2.00
2908-9	(15¢) Auto Tail Fin, Combo with BEP and SVS Singles	2.25
2910	(15¢) Auto Tail Fin, S/A, Coil, 6/15/96, New York, NY	2.00
2911	(25¢) Juke Box, BEP 3/17/95 New York, NY	2.00
2912	(25¢) Juke Box, SVS 3/17/95 New York, NY	2.00
2912A	(25¢) Juke Box, S/A, Coil, 6/15/96, New York, NY	2.00
2912B	(25¢) Juke Box, S/A, BEP, 1/24/97	2.00
2911-12	(25¢) Juke Box, Combo with BEP and SVS singles	2.50
2913	32¢ Flag over Porch, BEP, coil 5/19/95 Denver, CO	2.00
2914	32¢ Flag over Porch, SVS, coil 5/19/95 Denver, CO	2.00
2913-14	32¢ Flag over Porch, Combo with BEP and SVS singles	2.50
2902B, 2904A, 2906, 2910, 2912A, 2915B	Combo 6/15/96 San Antonio .	5.00
2915	32¢ Flag over Porch, self-adhesive strip format 4/18/95 DC ..	2.00
2915A	32¢ Flag over Porch, S/A, Coil, 5/21/96	2.00
2915B	32¢ Flag over Porch, S/A, Coil, (serpentine diecut 11.5 vert.) SV, 6/15/96, San Antonio, TX	2.00
2915C	32¢ Flag over Porch, Perf II	10.00
2915D	32¢ Flag over Porch, S/A, Coil, BEP, 1/24/97	2.00
2916	32¢ Flag over Porch, booklet single 5/19/95 Denver, CO	2.00
2916a	Booklet Pane of 10	8.50
2919	32¢ Flag over Field, self-adhesive 3/17/95 New York, NY	2.00
2919a	Pane of 18, Self-adhesive	14.50
2920	32¢ Flag over Porch, self-adhesive 4/19/95 DC	2.00
2920a	Pane of 20, self-adhesive w/large "1995"	15.50
2920b	Small Date	10.00
2920c	32¢ Pane of 20 S/A w/small "1995" 4/18/95 (fairly scarce)	45.00
2920d	Serpentine die cut 11.3, S/A, Single, 1/20/96	2.00
2920e	Booklet Pane of 10, S/A, 1/20/96	8.50
2904B, 2912B, 2915D, 2921ds	Combo 1/24/97 Tucson, AZ	4.00
2921	32¢ Flag over Porch, S/A, Booklet Single, (Serpentine die cut 9.8), 5/21/96	2.00
2921a	Booklet Pane of 10, 5/21/96	8.50
2921d-32	32¢ Flag over Porch, booklet pane of 5 1/24/97 Tucson, AZ ..	5.00
2921ds-32	32¢ Flag over Porch, booklet single 1/24/97 Tucson, AZ	5.00
	1995-99 Great American Series	
2933	32¢ Milton S. Hershey 9/13/95 Hershey, PA	2.00
2934	32¢ Cal Farley 4/26/96 Amarillo, TX	2.00
2935	32¢ Henry R. Luce (1998)	2.00
2936	32¢ Lila & DeWitt Wallace (1998)	2.00
2938	46¢ Ruth Benedict 10/20/95 Virginia Beach, VA	2.25
2940	55¢ Alice Hamilton, M.D. 7/11/95 Boston, MA	2.25
2941	55¢ Justin Morrill, 7/17/99 Strafford Vt	2.00
2942	77¢ Mary Breckinridge, 11/9/98, Troy, NY	2.75
2943	78¢ Alice Paul 8/18/95 Mount Laurel, NJ	2.75
	1995 Commemoratives	
2948	(32¢) Love & Cherub 2/1/95 Valentines, VA	2.00
2949	(32¢) Love & Cherub, self-adhesive 2/1/95 Valentines, VA	2.00
2948-49	Love combination on one Cover	3.00
2949a	Pane of 20, self-adhesive	15.50
2950	32¢ Florida Statehood 3/3/95 Tallahassee, FL	2.00
2951-54	32¢ Earth Day/Kids Care attd. 4/20/95 DC	4.35
2951-54	Set of 4 singles	8.00
2955	32¢ Richard Nixon 4/26/95 Yorba Linda, CA	2.00
2956	32¢ Bessie Coleman 4/27/95 Chicago, IL	3.00
2957	32¢ Love-Cherub 5/12/95 Lakeville, PA	2.00
2958	55¢ Love-Cherub 5/12/95 Lakeville, PA	2.25
2959	32¢ Love-Cherub, booklet single	2.00
2959a	Booklet Pane of 10	8.50
2960	55¢ Love-Cherub, self-adhesive single 5/12/95 Lakevilla, PA	2.25
2960a	55¢ Pane of 20, self-adhesive	21.50
2961-65	32¢ Recreational Sports, Strip of 5 5/20/95 Jupiter, FL	6.00
2961-65	Set of 5 singles	15.00
2966	32¢ POW/MIA 5/29/95 DC	3.00
2967	32¢ Monroe 6/1/95 Hollywood, CA	4.00
2967a	Pane of 20 on one cover	16.50
2968	32¢ Texas Statehood 6/16/95 Austin, TX	3.00
2969-73	32¢ Great Lakes Lighthouses,bklt.sgls. 6/17/95 Cheboygan,MI	10.00
2973a	Booklet Pane of 5	5.50

U.S. First Day Covers

Scott #	Description	Cacheted
	1995 Commemoratives (cont.)	
2974	32¢ United Nations 6/26/95 San Francisco, CA	3.00
2975	32¢ Civil War, Miniature Sht. of 20, 6/29/95 Gettysburg, PA	30.00
2975a-t	Set of 20 singles	60.00
2975a-t	Set of 20 singles, Beauvoir, MS	85.00
2975a-t	Set of 20 on 4 covers	20.00
2976-79	32¢ Carousel Horses attd. 7/21/95 Lahaska, PA	4.35
2976-79	Set of 4 singles	8.00
2980	32¢ Women's Suffrage 8/26/95 DC	2.00
2981	32¢ World War II S/S of 10 9/2/95 Honolulu, HI	10.00
2981a-j	Set of 10 singles	25.00
2982	32¢ Louis Armstrong 9/1/95 New Orleans, LA	3.00
2983-92	32¢ Jazz Musicians 9/16/95 Monterey, CA	12.00
2983-92	Set of 10 singles	30.00
2993-97	32¢ Fall Garden Flowers, bklt. sgles. 9/19/95 Encinitas, CA	10.00
2997a	Booklet Pane of 5	5.50
2998	60¢ Eddie Rickenbacker 9/25/95 Columbus, OH	3.00
2999	32¢ Republic of Palau 9/29/95 Agana, Guam	2.00
3000	32¢ Comic Strips, Min. Sheet of 20 10/2/95 Boca Raton, FL	25.00
3000a-t	Set of 20 Singles	50.00
3000a-t	Set of 5 combos (incl. Plate Block)	15.00
3001	32¢ U.S. Naval Academy, 150 Anniv. 10/10/95 Annapolis, MD	3.00
3002	32¢ Tennessee Williams 10/13/95 Clarksdale, MS	2.00
3003	32¢ Madonna and Child 10/19/95 Washington, DC	2.00
3003a	Booklet Single	2.00
3003b	Booklet Pane of 10	8.50
3004-7	32¢ Santa + Children 9/30/95 North Pole, NY, set of 4	8.00
3007a	32¢ Christmas (secular) sheet, 9/30/95, North Pole, NY	3.50
3007b	32¢ Santa & Children, Pane of 10 w/3 of #3004	8.50
3007c	32¢ Santa & Children, Pane of 10 w/2 of #3004	8.50
	1995 Self-Adhesive Stamps	
3008-11	32¢ Santa + Children 9/30/95 North Pole, NY	3.50
3008-11	Set of 4 Singles	7.00
3011a	Pane of 20	15.50
3012	32¢ Midnight Angel 10/19/95 Christmas, FL	2.00
3012a	Pane of 20	15.50
3013	32¢ Children Sledding 10/19/95 Christmas, FL	2.00
3013a	Pane of 18	14.00
	1995 Self-Adhesive Coil Stamps	
3014-17	32¢ Santa + Children 9/30/95 North Pole, NY	3.50
3014-17	Set of 4 Singles	7.00
3018	32¢ Midnight Angel 10/19/95 Christmas, FL	2.00
3018	32¢ Midnight Angle, Pair on backing paper	3.00
	1995 Commemoratives (cont.)	
3019-23	32¢ Antique Automobiles 11/3/95 New York, NY	3.75
3019-23	Set of 5 Singles	8.50
	1996-99 Commemoratives	
3024	32¢ Utah Statehood 1/4/96 Salt Lake City, UT	2.00
3025-29	32¢ Winter Garden Flowers Bklt.Singles 1/19/96 Kennett Sq,PA	10.00
3029a	Booklet Pane of 5	5.50
3030	32¢ Love Cherub, Self-adhesive 1/20/96 New York, NY	2.00
3030a	Booklet Pane of 20	15.50
	1996-99 Flora and Fauna Series	
3031	1¢ Kestrel S/A, 11/19/99, NY,NY	2.00
3032	2¢ Red-headed Woodpecker 2/2/96 Sarasota, FL	2.00
3033	3¢ Eastern Bluebird 4/3/96 DC	2.00
3036	$1.00 Red Fox, 8/14/98	5.00
3044	1¢ Kestrel, Coil 1/20/96 New York, NY	2.00
3045	2¢ Woodpecker coil, 6/22/99, Wash., DC	2.00
3048	20¢ Blue Jay, S/A, 8/2/96 St. Louis, MO	2.00
3048a	Booklet Pane of 10	8.50
3048 + 53	Combo - Blue Jays, 8/2/96, St. Louis, MO	5.00
3049	32¢ Yellow Rose, single, 10/24/96, Pasadena, Ca.	2.00
3049a	Booklet Pane of 20, S/A	15.50
3050	20¢ Ring-Neck Pheasant S/A, 7/31/98, Somerset, NJ	2.00
3050a	20¢ Ring-Neck Pheasant, S/A BP10, 7/31/98	8.50
3050+3055	Combo	3.00
3052	33¢ Pink Coral Rose S/A 8/13/99, Indy, IN	2.00
3052	Convert. BP 20	15.00
3052	Booklet Pane of 4	4.00
3052	Booklet Pane of 5 & Label	4.50
3052	Booklet Pane of 6	5.00
3052E	33c Pink Coral Rose, 4/7/00 New York, NY	2.00
	Pane of 8	8.00
3053	20¢ Blue Jay, Coil, S/A, 8/2/96, St. Louis, MO	2.00
3054	32¢ Yellow Rose, S/A Coil 8/1/97	2.00
3055	20¢ Ring-Neck Pheasant, S/A Coil, 7/31/98, Somerset, NJ	2.00
	1996 Commemoratives (cont.)	
3058	32¢ Ernest E. Just 2/1/96 DC	3.00
3059	32¢ Smithsonian Institution 2/5/96 DC	2.00
3060	32¢ Year of the Rat 2/8/96 San Francisco, CA	2.50
3061-64	32¢ Pioneers of Communication Set of 4 2/22/96 NY, NY	7.00
3061-64a	Block of 4 on one cover	3.50
3065	32¢ Fulbright Scholarship 2/28/96 Fayetteville, AR	2.00
3066	50¢ Jacqueline Cochran 3/9/96 Indio, CA	2.25
3067	32¢ Marathon 4/11/96 Boston, MA	3.00
3068	32¢ Centennial Olympic Games, Min. Sheet of 20 5/2/96 DC	20.00
3068a-t	Set of 20 Singles	40.00
3068a-t	Set of 20 on 4 covers	13.00
3069	32¢ Georgia O'Keeffe 5/23/96 Santa Fe, NM	2.00

2975a-t

Scott #	Description	Cacheted
	1996 Commemoratives (cont.)	
3069	Souvenir Sheet of 15	11.50
3070	32¢ Tennessee Statehood 5/31/96 Nashville, Knoxville or Memphis, TN	2.00
3071	32¢ Tennessee Statehood, Self-adhesive single	2.00
3071a	Booklet Pane of 20	13.00
3076a	32¢ American Indian Dances, 5 designs attached 6/7/96 Oklahoma City, OK	4.00
3072-76	Set of 5 Singles	8.50
3077-80	32¢ Prehistoric Animals, 4 designs attached 6/8/96 Toronto, Canada	4.00
3077-80	Set of 4 Singles	8.00
3081	32¢ Breast Cancer Awareness 6/15/96 DC	2.00
3082	32¢ James Dean 6/24/96 Hollywood, CA	3.00
3082	Pane of 20	17.50
3083-86	32¢ Folk Heroes, 4 designs attached 7/11/96 Anaheim, CA	4.00
3083-86	Set of 4 Singles	8.00
3087	32¢ Olympic Games, Discobolus 7/19 /96	2.00
3088	32¢ Iowa Statehood 8/1/96 Dubuque, IA	2.00
3089	Self-adhesive Single	2.00
3089a	Self-adhesive Pane of 20	15.50
3090	32¢ Rural Free Delivery 8/6/96 Charleston, WV	2.00
3091-95	32¢ River Boats, S/A, 8/22/96, set of 5, Orlando, Fl.	10.00
3095a	Strip of 5	5.50
3096-99	32¢ Big Band Leaders, set of 4, 9/11/96, New York, NY	12.00
3099a	32¢ Big Band Leaders, attd., 9/11/96, New York, NY	6.00
3100-03	32¢ Songwriters, set of 4, 9/11/96, New York, NY	10.00
3103a	32¢ Songwriters, att'd., 9/11/96, New York	5.00
3104	23¢ F. Scott Fitzgerald, 9/27/96, St. Paul, MN	2.00
3105	32¢ Endangered Species, pane of 15,10/2/96, San Diego, Ca.	14.50
3105a-o	Set of 15 covers	30.00
3106	32¢ Computer Tech., 10/8/96, Aberdeen Proving Ground, MD	3.00
3107	32¢ Madonna & Child, 11/1/96, Richmond, Va.	2.00
3107-11	Christmas on one Cover, dual cancel	4.50
3108-11	32¢ Christmas Family Scenes,set of 4,10/8/96,North Pole,AK	8.00
3111a	Block or strip of 4	4.25
3112	32¢ Madonna & Child, single, 11/1/96, Richmond, Va.	2.00
3112a	Pane of 20, S/A	15.50
3116a	Booklet Pane of 20, S/A	15.50
3113-16	32¢ Christmas Family Scene, set of 4, Bklt Pane Singles	8.00
3108-11 + 3117	Combination on one Cover	4.50
3117	32¢ Skaters - for ATM, 10/8/96, North Pole, AK	2.00
3117a	Booklet Pane of 18, S/A	14.75
3118	32¢ Hanukkah, S/A, 10/22/96, Washington, DC	3.00
3118	Joint issue w/Israel, dual cancel	15.00
3118	Israel issue only	4.00
3119	50¢ Cycling, sheet of 2, 11/1/96, New York, NY	3.75
3119	50¢ Cycling, sheet of 2, 11/1/96, Hong Kong	3.75
3119	50¢ Cycling, set of 2, 11/1/96, New York, NY	4.50
3119	50¢ Cycling, set of 2, 11/1/96, Hong Kong	4.50
3119	Joint issue w/Hong Kong, dual cancel, S/S	15.00
	1997 Commemoratives	
3120	32¢ Lunar New Year (Year of the Ox), 1/5/97	2.50
3121	32¢ Benjamin O' Davis Sr., S/A, 1/28/97, Wash. DC	3.00
3122	32¢ Statue of Liberty, S/A, Bklt Single, 2/1/97	2.00
3122a	Pane of 20 w/Label	15.50
3122c	Pane of 5 w/Label	5.50
3122d	Pane of 6	6.00
3123	32¢ Love Swan, S/A, Single, 2/4/97	2.00
3123a	Booklet Pane of 20 w/Label	15.50
3124	55¢ Love Swan, S/A, Single, 2/4/97	2.00
3124a	Booklet Pane of 20 w/Label	15.50
3125	32¢ Helping Children Learn, S/A, 2/18/97	2.00
3123+3124	Combo	3.00
3126-27	Citron Moth & Flowering Pineapple, attd, 3/3/97, Wash. DC	2.50
3126-27	Pane of 20	15.50
3126-27	Set of 2	5.00
3128-29	Slightly smaller than 3126-27, set of 2	5.00
3128-29b	Booklet pane of 5, Vendor Bklt, From booklet of 15	5.50
3128a-29a	(2) Mixed die-cut	6.00
3130-31	32¢ Pacific '97 Stagecoach & Ship, 3/13/97, New York, NY	2.50
3130-31	Set of Singles	4.00
3132	25¢ Jukebox (Linerless Coil) 3/14/97 NY,NY	2.00
3133	32¢ Flag over Porch (LInerless Coil) 3/14/97 NY,NY	2.00

U.S. First Day Covers

3152

3204a

Scott #	Description	Cacheted
	1997 Commemoratives (cont.)	
3132+3132	Combo	3.00
3134	32¢ Thornton Wilder, 4/17/97, Hamden, Ct.	2.00
3135	32¢ Raoul Wallenberg, 4/24/97, Wash. DC	3.50
3136	32¢ The World of Dinosaurs, set of 15, 5/1/97	30.00
3136a-o	15 on 1 miniature pane	12.00
3137	32¢ Bugs Bunny, S/A, pane of 10, 5/22/97	11.00
3137a	32¢ Bugs Bunny, S/A, Single, 5/22/97, Burbank CA	2.50
3137c	32¢ Bugs, single pane (right side) 5/22/97, Burbank,CA	5.00
3138	32¢ Bugs, Pane of 10 (9/1) imperf, 5/22/97, Burbank,CA	275.00
3138c	32¢ Bugs, Pane of 1, imperf, 5/22/97, Burbank,CA	250.00
3139	50¢ Pacific '97 - 1847 Franklin, S/S, 5/29/97, S.F., Ca.	24.00
3139a	50¢ single from S/S	4.00
3140	60¢ Pacific '97 - 1847 Washington, 5/30/97, S.F., Ca.	24.00
3140a	60¢ single from S/S	4.00
3141	32¢ Marshall Plan 6/4/97 Cambridge, MA	2.00
3142a-t	32¢ Classic American Aircraft,set of 20,7/19/97,Dayton, OH .	40.00
3142	Sheet of 20	15.50
3143-46	32¢ Legendary Football Coaches, att'd., 7/25/97	4.00
3146a	Set of 4 singles	8.00
3147-50	32¢ Legendary Football Coaches,set of 4 w/red bar	8.00
3147	32¢ Vince Lombardi,single, Green Bay WI,8/5/97	2.00
3148	32¢ Paul (Bear) Bryant, single, 8/7/97, Tuscaloosa, AL	2.00
3149	32¢ Glenn (Pop) Warner,single, 8/8/97, Phil. PA	2.00
3150	32¢ George Halas, single, 8/16/97, Chicago, IL	2.00
3151a-o	32¢ Classic American Dolls, set of 15, 7/28/97, Anaheim, Ca.	30.00
3151	Sheet of 15	12.00
3152	Pane of 20	17.50
3152	32¢ Humphrey Bogart, Legends of Hollywood series, 7/31/97	2.50
3153	32¢ Stars & Stripes Forever, 8/21/97, Milwaukee, WI	2.00
3154-57	Set of 4	8.00
3157a	32¢ Opera Singers, att'd., 9/10/97 New York, NY	4.25
3158-65	Set of 8	16.00
3165a	32¢ Conductors & Composers, Set of 2, 9/12 /97 Cincinnati, OH	11.00
3166	32¢ Padre Felix Varela 9/15/97 Miami, FL	2.00
3167	32¢ U.S. Air Force, 9/18/97 Washington, DC	4.00
3172a	32¢ Classic Movie Monsters, att'd., 9/30/97 Universal City, CA	5.50
3168-72	Set of 5	10.00
3173	32¢ 1st Supersonic Flight, S/A, 10/14/97,Edwards AF Base,CA	2.50
3174	32¢ Women in the Military, 10/18/97 Wash. DC	2.50
3175	32¢ Kwanzaa 10/22/97, LA,CA	3.00
3176	32¢ Madonna & Child, 10/27/97, Wash. DC	2.00
3176a	32¢ Madonna & Child, Pane of 20, Wash. DC	15.00
3177	32¢ American Holly, S/A, 10/30/97,NY,NY	2.00
3177a	32¢ American Holly, S/A, Pane of 20, 10/30/97,NY,NY	15.50
3177b	32¢ American Holly, S/A, Pane of 6, 10/30/97,NY,NY	6.00
3177b	Pane of 4	4.00
3177c	32¢ American Holly, S/A, Pane of 5&Label,10/30/97,NY,NY	5.50
3177c	Pane of 5	5.00
3177d	Pane of 6	6.00
3176-77	Madonna & Holly on one Cover, dual cancel	3.00
3178	$3 Mars Rover Sojourner, S/S, 12/10/97,Pasadena,CA	12.00
	1998 Commemoratives	
3179	32¢ Year of the Tiger, 1/5/98, Seattle WA	2.50
3180	32¢ Alpine Skiing, 1/22/98, Salt Lake City UT	2.00
3181	32¢ Madam C.J. Walker, 1/28/98, Ind., IN	3.00
	2000 Celebrate The Century Series	
3182	1900's 32¢ Celebrate the Century, Pane of 15,2/3/98, Wash.DC	15.00
3182a-o	1900's 32¢ Celebrate the Century, Set of 15,2/3/98, Wash.DC	35.00
3183	1910's 32¢ Celebrate the Century, Pane of 15,2/3/98, Wash.DC	15.00
3183a-o	1910's 32¢ Celebrate the Century, Set of 15, 2/3/98, Wash.DC	35.00
3184	1920's 32¢ Celebrate the Century, Pane of 15, 5/28/98, Chicago, IL	15.00
3184a-o	1920's 32¢ Celebrate the Century, Set of 15, 5/28/98, Chicago, IL	35.00
3185	1930's 32¢ Celebrate the Century, Pane of 15, 9/10/98, Cleveland, OH	15.00

Scott #	Description	Cacheted
	1998-2000 Celebrate The Century Series (cont.)	
3185a-o	1930's 32¢ Celebrate the Century, Set of 15, 9/10/98, Cleveland, OH	35.00
3186	1940's 33¢ Celebrate the Century, Pane of 15, 2/18/99, Dobins AFB, GA	15.00
3186a-o	1940's 33¢ Celebrate the Century Set of 15, 2/18/99, Dobins AFB, GA	35.00
3187	1950's 33¢ Celebrate the Century, Pane of 15, 5/26/99, Springfield, MA	15.00
3187a-o	1950's 33¢ Celebrate the Century, Set of 15, 5/26/99, Springfield, MA	35.00
3188	1960's 33¢ Celebrate the Century, Pane of 15, 9/17/99, Green Bay, WI	15.00
3188a-o	1960's 33¢ Celebrate the Century Set of 15, 9/17/99, Green Bay, WI	35.00
3189	1970's 33¢ Celebrate the Century, Pane of 15, 11/18/99, NY, NY	15.00
3189a-o	1970's 33¢ Celebrate the Century, Set of 15, 11/18/99, NY, NY	35.00
3190	1980's 33¢ Celebrate the Century, Pane of 15, 1/12/00, Titusville, FL	15.00
3190a-o	1980's 33¢ Celebrate the Century Set of 15, 1/12/00, Titusville, FL	35.00
3191	1990's 33¢ Celebrate the Century, Pane of 15, 5/2/00, Escondido, CA	15.00
3191a-o	1990's 33¢ Celebrate the Century Set of 15, 5/2/00, Escondido, CA	35.00
	1998 Commemoratives (cont.)	
3192	32¢ Remember the Maine, 2/15/98, Key West FL	3.00
3193-97	32¢ Flowering Trees, S/A, Set of 5, 3/19/98, NY,NY	10.00
3197a	32¢ Flowering Trees, S/A, Strip of 5, 3/19/98, NY,NY	5.50
3198-3202	32¢ Alexander Calder, S/A, Set of 5, 3/25/98, Wash, DC	10.00
3202a	32¢ Alexander Calder, S/A, Strip of 5, 3/25/98, Wash, DC	5.50
3203	32¢ Cinco de Mayo, S/A, 4/16/98, San Antonio, TX	2.00
3203	Joint issue w/Mexico, dual cancel	15.00
3203	Mexican issue only	3.00
3204	32¢ Tweety&Sylvester, S/S of 10, perf. 4/27/98, NY, NY	10.00
3204a	32¢ Tweety&Sylvester, single, perf. 4/27/98, NY, NY	2.00
3204c	32¢ Tweety&Sylvester, pane of 1, perf. 4/27/98, NY, NY	5.00
3205	32¢ Tweety&Sylvester, S/S of 10, imperf. 4/27/98, NY, NY	15.00
3205c	Tweety&Sylvester, imperf single	10.00
3205c	32¢ Tweety&Sylvester, pane of 1, imperf. 4/27/98, NY, NY	12.00
3205c	Tweety&Sylvester, perf and imperf Pane on 1 Cover	20.00
3206	32¢ Wisconsin Statehood, 5/29/98, Madison WI	2.25
3207	5¢ Wetlands, Coil, 6/5/98, McLean, VA	2.00
3208	25¢ Diner, coil, 6/5/98, McLean, VA	2.20
3207+3208	Combo	3.00
3209	1¢-$2 Trans Mississippi Cent. 9 diff., 6/18/98, Anaheim,CA	25.00
3209a	1¢-$2 Trans Mississippi Cent. 9 diff., plus pair of $1 issue	30.00
3209	1¢-$2 Trans Mississippi Cent. Full sheet, 6/18/98, Anaheim,CA	10.75
3209	1¢-$2 Trans Mississippi Cent. Full sheet, plus Pair of $1 issue	15.00
3210	$1 Cattle in Storm, pane of 9, 6/18/98, Anaheim,CA	16.50
3211	32¢ Berlin Airlift, 6/26/98, Berlin Station, APOAE	2.00
3215a	32¢ Folk Musicians, 7 designs attd., 6/26/98, (1) Wash. DC ..	6.00
3212-15	32¢ Set of 4 Wash. DC	12.00
3219a	32¢ Gospel Singers, att'd., 7/15/98, New Orleans, LA	6.00
3216-19	32¢ Gospel Singers, Set of 4 7/15/98,	16.00
3220	32¢ Spanish Settlement of SW 1598, 7/11/98 Espanola, NM	2.00
3221	32¢ Stephen Vincent Benet, 7/22/98, Harper's Ferry, WV	2.00
3225a	32¢ Tropical Birds, 7/29/98, Puerto Rico. Block 4	5.50
3222-25	32¢ Tropical Birds, 7/29/98, Set of 4	10.00
3226	32¢ Alfred Hitchcock, 8/3/98, LA, CA	2.00
3226	Pane of 20	17.50
3227	32¢ Organ & Tissue Donation, 8/5/98 coumbus, oh	2.00
3228	(10¢) Bicycle, S/A coil, 8/14/98, Wash. DC (American Transportation)	2.00
3229	(10¢) Bicycle, W/A coil,8/14/98, Wash., DC (American Transporatation)	2.00
3228-29	On one FDC	3.00
3234a	32¢ Bright Eyes, strip of 5, 8/20/98, Boston, MA	5.50
3230-34	32¢ Bright Eyes, Set of 5, 8/20/98,	10.00
3235	32¢ Klondike Gold Rush, 8/21/98, Nome, AK	2.50

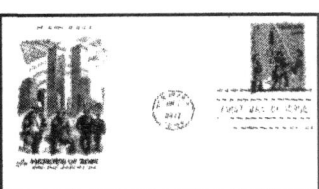

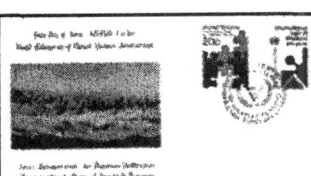

U.S. First Day Covers

$11.75 EXPRESS MAIL

3262

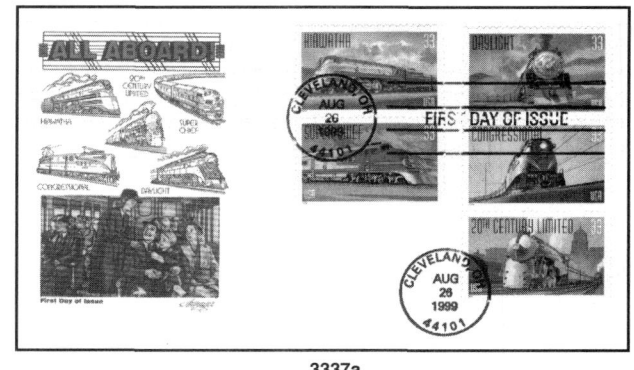

3337a

Scott #	Description	Cacheted
	1998 Commemoratives (cont.)	
3236	32¢ Four Centuries of American Art, pane of 20 8/27/98, Santa Clara, CA	15.50
3236a-t	32¢ Four Centuries of American Art on 4 Covers	20.00
3236a-t	32¢ Four Centuries of American Art, (20), 8/27/98, Santa Clara, CA	40.00
3237	32¢ Ballet, 9/16/98, NY, NY	2.00
3242a	32¢ Space Discovery, Strip of 5, 10/1/98	6.00
3238-42	32¢ Space Discovery, S/A set of 5, 10/1/98	12.00
3243	32¢ Giving & Sharing, 10/7/98, Atlanta GA	2.00
3244	32¢ Madonna and Child, 10/15/98, Wash. DC	2.00
3244a	Pane of 20	15.50
3245-48	32¢ Wreath Set of 4 Vending Bklt sgls, S/A, 10/15/98, Christmas, MI	8.00
3248a	Pane of 4	4.00
3248b	Pane of 5	4.50
3248c	Pane of 6	5.25
3249-52	32¢ Wreaths, set of 4 sheet singles, S/A, (larger than vending) S/A, 10/15/98, Christmas, MI	8.00
3249-52	32¢ Wreaths, attd.	4.00
3252b	32¢ Wreaths, Bklt of 20	15.50
	1998 Regular Issues	
3257	(1¢) Make up Rate – Weathervane, A.P., 11/9/98, Troy, NY	2.00
3258	(1¢) Make up Rate – Weathervane, BCA, 11/9/98, Troy, NY	2.00
3257 &58	On one FDC	2.00
3259	22¢ Uncle Sam, S/A from sheet, 11/9/98, Troy, NY	2.00
3260	(33¢) "H" Hat, W/A from sheet, 11/9/98, Troy, NY	2.00
3261	$3.20 Space Shuttle, Priority Mail, 11/9/98, Troy, NY	8.00
3262	$11.75 Piggyback Space Shuttle, Exp. Mail 11/19/98 NY NY	30.00
3263	22¢ Uncle Sam, coil, pair, S/A, 11/9/98, Troy, NY	2.00
3264	(33¢) "H" Hat, Coil, 11/9/98, Troy, NY	2.00
3265	(33¢) "H" Hat, S/A, single, 11/9/98, Troy, NY	2.00
3266	(33¢) "H" Hat, S/A (w/gaps between stamps) 11-9-98, Troy,NY	2.00
3267	(33¢) "H" Hat, Folded Bklt, Pane of 10, 10/9/98, Troy, NY	8.50
3268	(33¢) "H" Hat, Convertible Bklt Single (A)	2.00
3268a	(33¢) "H" Hat, Convertible Bklt Pane of 10 FDC (B)	8.50
3268b	(33¢) "H" Hat, Convertible Bklt Pane of 20 FDC (C)	15.50
3269	(33¢) "H" Hat, ATM Bklt Single (D)	2.00
3269a	(33¢) "H" Hat, ATM Bklt Pane FDC (E)	14.00
3270	(10¢) Eagle & Shield, W/A, 12/14/98, Wash. DC	2.00
3271	(10¢) Eagle & Shield, S/A Coil, Presort; 12/14/98, Wash. DC	2.00
3270-71	(10¢) Eagle & Shield, Both W/A & S/A on 1	2.20
	1999 Commemoratives	
3272	33¢ Year of the Rabbit, 1/5/99, LA, CA	2.50
3273	33¢ Malcolm X, BH Series, 1/20/99NY, NY	3.00
3274	33¢ Love, S/A, 1/28/99, Loveland, CO	2.00
3274a	33¢ Love, Bklt of 20, 1/28/99	15.50
3274+3275	Combo	3.00
3275	55¢ Love, S/A, 1/28/99, Loveland, CO	2.25
3276	33¢ Hospice Care, 2/9/99, Largo, FL	2.25
	1999 Regular Issues	
3277	33¢ Flag & City, Single W/A sheet, 2/25/99, Orlando, FL	2.00
3278	33¢ Flag & City, S/A Sheet, 2/25/99, Orlando, FL	2.00
3278 a-c	33¢ Flag & City, (3) Convertible Bklts, 2/25/99, Orlando, FL	10.50
3278d	33¢ Flag & City, Convertible Bklt of 10	8.50
3278e	33¢ Flag & City, Convertible Bklt of 20	15.50
3279	33¢ Flag & City, S/A Bklt Stamp, 2/25/99, Orlando, FL	2.00
3279a	33¢ Flag & City, S/A Bklt Pane of 10, 2/25/99, Orlando, FL	8.50
3280	33¢ Flag & City, W/A coil, 2/25/99, Orlando, FL	2.00
3281	33¢ Flag & City, S/A Coil Square die-cut corners, 2/25/99, Orlando, FL	2.00
3282	33¢ Flag & City, S/A Coil Rounded die-cut corners, 2/25/99, Orlando, FL	2.00
3283s	33¢ Flag & Chalkboard, S/A, Cleveland, OH, 3/13/99	2.00
3283	33¢ Flag & Chalkboard, S/A, Pane of 18 OH, 3/13/99	14.50
	1999 Commemoratives (cont.)	
3286	33¢ Irish Immigration, 2/26/99, Boston, MA	2.50
3286	Joint issue w/Ireland, dual cancel	15.00
3286	Irish issue only	4.25
3287	33¢ Alfred Hunt & Lynn Fontanne, 3/2/99	2.00
3292	33¢ Arctic Animals, strip of 5, 3/12/99, Barrow, AK	5.50

Scott #	Description	Cacheted
	1999 Commemoratives (cont.)	
3288-92	33¢ Arctic Animals, set of 5, 3/12/99, Barrow, AK	10.00
3293	33¢ Sonora Desert, pane of 10, 4/6/99	10.00
3294a-3297c	33c Fruit Berries S/A booklet, 3/15/00 Ponchatoula, LA Pane of 8	8.00
	Set of 4 singles	8.00
3293a-j	33¢ Sonora Desert, set of 10, 4/6/99	25.00
3297a	33¢ Fruits & Berries, S/A Pane of 20, 4/10/99	15.50
3294-97	33¢ Fruits & Berries, S/A set of 4, 4/10/99	8.00
3294-97	33¢ Fruits & Berries on one cover	5.50
3301a	33¢ Fruits & Berries, S/A vend. Bklt of 15, 4/10/99	12.50
3302-5	33¢ Fruits & Berries, strip of 4, 4/10/99	4.00
	set of 4 singles from coil, 4/10/99	8.00
3306	Is perf variety	
3306	33¢ Daffy Duck, S/A Imperf Pane of 10, 4/16/99, LA, CA	15.00
3306a	33¢ Daffy Duck, S/A Imperf single, 4/16/99, LA, CA	6.00
3306c	33¢ Daffy Duck, S/A Imperf Pane(right side), 4/16/99, LA, CA	10.00
3307	Is imperf variety	
3307	33¢ Daffy Duck, S/A Perf Pane of 10, 4/16/99, LA, CA	15.00
3307a	33¢ Daffy Duck, S/A Perf Single, 4/16/99, LA, CA	2.50
3307c	33¢ Daffy Duck, S/A Perf Pane (right side), 4/16/99	6.00
3306c&07c	33¢ Daffy Duck combo	15.00
3308	33¢ Ayn Rand, 4/22/99	2.00
3309	33¢ Cinco de Mayo, 4/27/99	2.00
3313a	33¢ Tropical Flowers (1), 5/1/99	5.50
3313b	33¢ Tropical Flowers Bklt Pane of 8 plus label	7.50
3310-13	Set of 4	10.00
3314	33¢ John & William Bartram, 5/18/99	2.00
3315	33¢ Prostrate Cancer Awareness, 5/28/99, Austin, TX	2.00
3316	33¢ Cal. Gold Rush, 6/18/99, Sacramento, CA	2.00
3320a	33¢ Aquarium Fish, 6/24/99, Anaheim, CA	4.50
3317-20	Set of 4	8.00
3324a	33¢ Extreme Sports, 6/25/99, SF., CA	4.25
3321-24	Set of 4	8.00
3328a	33¢ American Glass, 6/29/99, Corning, NY	5.50
3325-28	Set of 4	10.00
3329	33¢ James Cagney, 7/17/99, Burbank, CA	2.00
3329	Sheet of 20	16.00
3330	55¢ Billy Mitchell, 7/30/99, Milwaukee, WI	2.25
3331	33¢ Honoring Those Who Served, 8/16/99, Kansas City, MO	2.00
3332'	45¢ Universal Postal Union, 8/25/99, Beijing, China	2.00
3337a	33¢ Trains (1), 8/26/99, Cleveland, OH	5.50
3333-7	Set of 5	10.00
3338	33¢ F.L. Olmstead, 9/12/99, Boston, MA	2.00
3344a	33¢ Hollywood Composers, 9/16/99, LA, CA	5.50
3339-44	Set of 6	12.00
3350a	33¢ Broadway Songwriters, 9/21/99, NY, NY	5.50
3345-50	Set of 6	12.00
3351	33¢ Insects & Spiders, sheet of 20, 10/1/99, Ind. IN	16.00
3351a-t	Set of 20	40.00
3352	33¢ Hanukkah, 10/8/99, Wash., DC	2.50
3353	22¢ Uncle Sam, W/A Coil, 10/10/99, Wash., DC	2.00
3354	33¢ NATO, 10/13/99, Kansas City, MO	2.00
3355	33¢ Madonna & Child, 10/20/99, Wash., DC	2.00
3355a	33¢ Madonna & Child, Split Pane of 20	15.00
3355b	33¢ Madonna & Child, Pane of 8 (includes tab & plate #)	11.00
3355c	33¢ Madonna & Child, Pane of 12	12.50
3356-9	33¢ Holiday Deer, S/A Sheet Block, 10/20/99,Rudolph, WI	4.25
3356-9	Set of 4	8.00
3360-3	33¢ Holiday Deer, CB Pane 20, 10/20/99, Rudolph, WI	16.00
3360-3	Set of 4	8.00
3368	33¢ Kwanzaa, 10/29/99, LA, CA	3.00
3369	33¢ Year 2000, 12/27/99, Wash., DC and Nation Wide	2.00
	2000 Commemoratives	
3370	33¢ Year of the Dragon, 1/6/00, SF, CA	2.50
3371	33¢ Patricia R. Harris, 1/27/00, Wash., DC	3.00
	33¢ Fruits & Berries S/A Pane of 8,3/15/00, Ponchatoula, LA	8.00
	Set of 4	8.00
3372	33¢ LA Class Submarines,3/27/00, Groton, CT	2.00
3377a	$4.90 US Navy Submarines, BP of 5, Groton, CT	12.00
3373-77	Set of 5	15.00
3378	33¢ Pacific Coast Rain Forest, full sheet, 3/29/00, Seattle, WA	10.00

U.S. First Day Covers

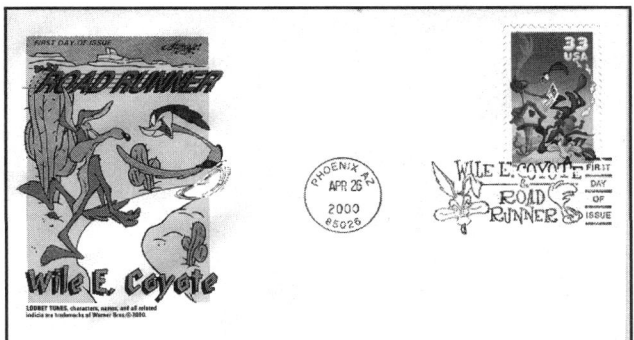

3391

3501

Scott #	Description	Cacheted
	1999 Commemoratives (cont.)	
3378a-j	Set of 10	25.00
3379-83	Set of 5	10.00
3383a	33¢ Louise Nevelson, strip of 5, 4/6/00, NY, NY	5.50
	33¢ Pink Coral Rose, S/A, 4/7/00, NY, NY	2.00
	Pane of 8	8.00
3388a	33¢ Edwin Hubble, strip of 5, 4/10/00, NY, NY	5.50
3384-88	Set of 5	10.00
3389	33¢ American Samoa, 4/17/00, Pago, Pago, AS	2.00
3390	33¢ Library of Congress, 4/24/00, Wash., DC	2.00
3391	33¢ Wile E. Coyote & Roadrunner, Perf. Pane 10, 4/26/00 Phoenix, AZ	10.00
3391a	Perf. Single	2.50
3391c	Perf. Pane (right side)	5.00
3392	33¢ Wile E. Coyote & Roadrunner Imperf. Pane 10, 4/26/00 Phoenix, AZ	12.00
3392a	Imperf. Single	5.00
3392c	Imperf. Pane (right side)	6.00
3391&92	Perf & Imperf Pane Combo	10.00
3396a	33¢ Distinguished Soldiers, block of 4, 5/3/00, Wash., DC	4.25
3393-96	Set of 4	8.00
3397	33¢ Summer Sports, 5/5/00, Spokane, WA	2.00
3398	33¢ Adoption, 5/10/00, LA, CA	2.00
3402a	33¢ Youth Team Sports, block of 4, 5/ /00	4.25
3999-02	Set of 4	8.00
3403	33¢ Stars & Stripes, sheet of 20, 6/14/00, Baltimore, MD	16.00
3403a-t	Set of 20	40.00
3404-07	33¢ Fruits & Berries, Coil Strip of 4, 6/16/00, Buffalo,NY	4.00
3404-07	Set of 4	8.00
3408	33¢ Legends of Baseball, Sheet of 20, 7/6/00, Atlanta, Ga	16.00
3408a-t	Set of 20	45.00
3409	60¢ x 6 Probing the Vastness of Space, 7/10/00, Anaheim, CA	9.00
3409a-f	Set of 6	15.00
3409	Full Souvenir Sheet	12.50
3410	$1.00 x 5 Exploring the Solar System, 7/11/00, Anaheim, CA	12.50
3410	Full Souvenir Sheet	13.50
3410a-e	Set of 5	17.50
3411	$3.20 x 2 Escaping the Gravity of Earth, 7/9/00, Anaheim,CA	13.50
3411a-b	Set of 2	15.00
3411	Full Souvenir Sheet	18.00
3412	$11.75 Achievements in Exploration, 7/6/00, Anaheim, CA	25.00
3412	Full Souvenir Sheet	30.00
3413	$11.75 Landing on the Moon, 7/8/00, Anaheim, CA	25.00
3413	Full Souvenir Sheet	30.00
3417a	33¢ x4 Stampin' the Future, 7/13/00, Anaheim, CA	4.25
3414-17	Set of 4	8.00
3420	10¢ Gen. Joseph Stilwell, Great Amer. Series, 8/24/00, Prov. RI	2.00
3426	33¢ Claude Pepper, 9/ 7/00, Tallahassee, FL	2.00
3431	76c Hattie Caraway S/A, 2/21/01, Little Rock,AR	2.50
3432	83¢ Edna Ferber 07/29/02, Appleton, WI	2.75
3438	33¢ California Statehood, 9/8 /00, Sacramento, CA	2.00
3439-43	33¢ Deep Sea Creatures set 5, 10/2/00, Monterey, CA	10.00
3443a	Strip of 5	5.50
3444	33¢ Thomas Wolfe, 10/3/00, Asheville, NC	2.00
3445	33¢ White House, 10/18/00, Washington, DC	2.00
3446	33¢ Edward G. Robinson, 10/24/00 Los Angeles, CA	2.00
3446	Full Sheet of 20	14.00
	2000-2001 Regular Issues	
3447	(10¢) Lion Statue S/A coil, 11/9/00, New York, NY	2.00
3448	(34¢) Farm Flag W/A, 12/15/00, Washington, DC	2.00
3449	(34¢) Farm Flag S/A, 12/15/00, Washington, DC	2.00
3450	(34¢) Farm Flag ATM, 12/15/00, Washington, DC	2.00
3450a	Pane of 18	13.50
3451	(34¢) Statue of Liberty S/A booklet single	2.00
3451a	Convertible booklet pane of 20	14.50
3451b	Vending booklet pane of 4 w/plate #	5.50
3452	(34¢) Statue of Liberty W/A coil, 12/15/00, New York, NY	2.00
3453	(34¢) Statue ofLiberty S/A coil, 12/15/00, New York, NY	2.00
3454-57	(34¢) Flowers S/A set of 4, 12/15/00, Washington, DC	8.00
	On one Cover	4.50
	Convertible booklet pane of 8	8.00
	Perf. variety set of 4	16.00
	Perf. variety block of 4	9.00

Scott #	Description	Cacheted
	2000-2001 Regular Issues (cont.)	
3458-61	34¢ Flowers S/A coil strip of 4, 12/15/00, Washington, DC	4.50
	Set of 4 coil singles	8.00
3466	34¢ Statueof Liberty S/A coil, 1/1/01, Washington, DC	2.00
3467	21¢ Bison W.A. sheet 9/20/01 DC	2.00
3468A	23¢ George Washington S/A sheet 9/20/01 DC	2.00
3468	21¢ Bison S/A, 2/23/01, Wall, SD	2.25
3469	34¢ Farm Flag W/A, 2/7/01, New York, NY	2.00
3470	34¢ Farm Flag S/A, 3/6/01, Lincoln, NE	2.00
3471	55¢ Art Deco Eagle S/A, 2/22/01, Wall, SC	2.25
3471A	57¢ Art Deco Eagle 9/20/01 DC	2.25
3472	$3.50 Capitol Dome S/A, 1/29/01, Washington, DC	8.00
3473	$12.25 Washington Monument S/A, 1/29/01, Washington, DC	30.00
3475	21¢ Bison S/A coil, 2/22/01, Wall, SD	2.25
3475A	23¢ George Washington S/A coil 9/20/01	2.00
3476	34¢ Statue of Liberty W/A coil, 2/7/01, New York, NY	2.00
3477	34¢ Statue of Liberty S/A coil, 2/7/01, New York, NY	2.00
3478-81	34¢ Flowers S/A coil strip, 2/7/01, New York, NY	4.50
	Set of 4 singles	8.00
3482	20¢ G. Washington S/A, 2/22/01, Little Rock, AR	2.25
3482a	Convertible booklet pane of 10	6.00
3483	20¢ G. Washington S/A, 2/22/01 LR, AR (perf 10.5x11)	2.25
	Vending booklet pane of 10	6.00
3484	21¢ Bison die cut 11.25 9/20/01 DC	2.00
	S/A booklet pane of 10	6.00
	S/A vending booklet pane of 10	6.00
3484A	21¢ Bison die cut 10.5x11.25 9/20/01	5.00
	S/A booklet pane of 10	15.00
	S/A booklet pane of 10	15.00
3485	34¢ Statue of Liberty S/A booklet, 2/7/01, New York, NY	2.00
	Convertible booklet pane of 20	14.50
	Pane of 10	8.50
3487-90	34¢ Flowers set 4 booklet singles, 2/7/01, New York, NY	8.00
	Convertible booklet pane of 12	10.50
	Vending booklet pane of 20 (split on #10 envelope)	17.50
3491-92	34¢ Apple& Orange S/A pair, 3/6/01, Lincoln, NE	2.50
	Set of 2 singles	4.00
	Block of 10 w/pl# from Convertible booklet	8.50
3495	34¢ Farm Flag ATM 12/17/01 DC	2.00
3495a	Pane of 18	12.50
	2001 Commemoratives	
3496	34¢ Love Letter S/A, 1/19/01, Tucson, AZ	2.00
3496a	Convertible booklet pane of 20	14.50
3497	34¢ Love Letter S/A, 2/14/01, Lovejoy, GA	2.00
3497a	Convertible booklet pane of 20	14.50
3498	34¢ Love VB single, 2/14/01, Lovejoy, GA	2.00
	Pane of 4 w/pl# from Vending booklet	5.00
3499	55¢ Love LetterS/A, 2/14/01, Lovejoy, GA	2.25
	Convertible booklet pane of 20	20.00
3497-99	Love combination on one Cover	3.00
3500	34¢ Year of the Snake, 1/20/01, Oakland, CA	2.50
3501	34¢ Roy Wilkins, 1/24/01, Minneapolis, MN	3.00
3502	34¢ American Illustrators Pane 20, 2/1/01, New York, NY	15.00
3502a-t	Set of 20 singles	45.00
	Set on 4 Covers	13.50
3503	34¢ Diabetes Awareness, 3/16/01, Boston, MA	2.00
3504	34¢ Noble Prize, 3/22/01, Washington, DC	2.00
	Joint issue w/Sweden, dual cancel	12.00
	Swedish stamp & cancel only	4.00
3505a-d	1¢, 2¢ & 4¢ Pan American inverts & 80c Buffalo, 3/29/01 Set of 4 singles, New York, NY	12.00
3505	Full Souvenir Sheet	10.00
3506	34¢ Great Plains Prairie Full Sheet, 4/19/01, Lincoln, NE	10.00
3506q-j	Set of 10 singles	20.00
3507	34¢ Peanuts, 5/17/01, Santa Rosa, CA	2.50
3508	34¢ U.S. Veterans, 5/23/01, Washington, DC	2.50
3509	34¢ Frida Kahlo, 6/21/01, Phoenix, AZ	2.00
3510-19	34¢ Baseball's Legendary Playing Fields pane 20, 6/27/01 ...	17.50
	Set of 10 singles	25.00
3520	10¢ Atlas Statue S/A coil, 6/29/01, New York, NY	2.00
3521	34¢ Leonard Bernstein, 7/10/01, New York, NY	2.00
3522	15¢ Woody Wagon coil 8/0/01 Denver, CO	2.00
3523	34¢ Lucille Ball 8/6/01 Los Angeles, CA	2.50
	Full Sheet of 20	14.00

U.S. First Day Covers

3550

3653-56

Scott #	Description	Cacheted
	2001 Commemoratives (cont.)	
3524-27	34¢ Amish Quilts block 8/9/01 Nappanee, IN	3.50
	Set of 4 singles	8.00
3528-31	34¢ Carnivorous Plants block 8/23/01 Des Plaines, IL	3.50
	Set of 4 singles	8.00
3532	34¢ Eid 9/1/01 Des Plaines, IL	2.00
3533	34¢ Enrico Femi 9/29/01 Chicago, IL	2.00
3534	34¢ Porky Pig 10/1/01 Beverly Hills, CA	2.50
	Full sheet of 10	11.00
	Single stamp panel (right side)	7.00
3536	34¢ Madonna & child 10/10/01 Philadelphei, PA	2.00
	Block of 10 w/pl# from booklet pane	7.50
3537-40	34¢ Santas S/A sheet block 10/10/01 Santa Claus, IN	4.00
	Set of 4 singles	9.00
3537a-40a	34¢ Santas set 4 singles	9.00
	Convertible booklet pane of 8	8.00
	Convertible booklet pane of 12	10.00
3541-44	34¢ Santas VB block	4.00
	Set 4 vending booklet singles	9.00
3545	34¢ James madison 10/18/01 New York, NY	2.00
3546	34¢ We Give Thanks 10/21/01 Dallas. TX	2.00
3547	34¢ Hanukkah 10/21/01 New York, NY	2.00
3548	34¢ Kwanzaa 10/21/01 New York, NY	2.00
3549	34¢ United We Stand 10/24/01 New York, NY	2.00
	Block of 10 w/pl# from booklet pane	7.50
3550	34¢ United We Stand S/A coil 10/24/01	2.00
3550A	34¢ United We Stand coil w/gaps 10/24/01	2.00
3551	57¢ Rose & Love Letter 11/19/01 Washington, DC	2.25
3552-55	34¢ Winter Sports 1/8/02 Park City UT, set of 4 singles	9.00
3555a	34¢ Winter Sports, strip of 4	4.00
	2002 Commemoratives/Regular Issues	
3556	34¢ Mentoring 1/10/02 Annapolis, MD	2.00
3557	34¢ Langston Hughes 2/1/02 New York, NY	2.10
3558	34¢ Happy Birthday 2/8/02 Riverside, CA	2.00
3559	34¢ Year of the Horse 2/11/02 New York, NY	2.10
3560	34¢ USMA 3/16/02 West Point, NY	2.00
3561-3610	34¢ Greetings from America 4/4/02 New York, NY	
	Set 50 singles	110.00
	Set of 50 state cancels	120.00
3610a	34¢ Greetings from America, full sheet	26.00
3611a-j	34¢ Longleaf Pine Forest 4/26/02 Tallahassee, FL	
	Set 10 singles	22.00
	Full sheet	9.00
3612	5¢ Toleware Coil 5/31/02 McLean, VA, strip 4 + 4	2.20
3613	3¢ Star BCA 6/7/02 Washington DC, single +34¢	2.10
3614	3¢ Star GL 6/7/02, single+34¢	2.10
	combo 3613-14 + 34¢	2.15
3615	3¢ Star S/A coil 6/7/02, single + 34¢	2.10
	Pair + 34¢	2.15
3616	23¢ Washington W/A sheet 6/7/02 Washington, DC, pair	2.25
3617	23¢ Washington S/A coil 6/7/02, pair	2.25
3618	23¢ Washington 6/7/02 perf 11.75x11, pair	2.25
	convertible bklt pane 10	6.25
3619	23¢ Washington 6/7/02 perf 10.5x11, pair	2.25
	Vending bklt pane 10	6.25
3620	37¢ US Flag 6/7/02 W/A sheet, Washington DC	2.10
3621	37¢ US Flag 6/7/02 S/A pane	2.10
3622	37¢ US Flag 6/7/02 S/A coil	2.10
3623	37¢ US Flag 6/7/02 convertible bklt 20	2.10
	Pl# pane 10	6.25
3624	37¢ US Flag 6/7/02, double-sided & vending bklts	2.10
	Pl# pane 4	3.70
	VB pane 6	4.50
3625	37¢ US Flag 6/7/02 ATM	2.10
	Pl# pane 9	6.00
3626-29	37¢ Antique Toys 6/7/02 Washington DC, set 4 singles	8.50
3629f	37¢ US Flag 11/24/03 Washington DC	2.25
3630	37¢ US Flag 6/7/02 Washington DC, S/A pane	2.10
3631	37¢ US Flag 6/7/02 W/A coil	2.10
3632	37¢ US Flag 6/7/02 S/A coil	2.10
3633	37¢ US Flag 6/7/02 coil separated	2.10
3634	37¢ US Flag 6/7/02 convertible bklt 10	2.10
	Pl# pane 4	3.70
3635	37¢ US Flag 6/7/02 convertible bklt 20	2.10
	Pl# pane 10	6.25

Scott #	Description	Cacheted
3636	37¢ US Flag 6/7/02 double-sided &vending bklts	2.10
	Pl# pane 4	3.70
	VB pane 6	4.50
3638-41	37¢ Antique Toys S/A coil Rochester, NY, strip 4, 7/26/02	4.25
	set 4 singles	8.50
3642-45	37¢ Antique Toys convertible & vending bklts, pane 4, 7/26/02	3.35
	Set 4 singles	8.50
	Pl# pane 10	6.25
3646	60¢ coverlet Eagle 6/12/02 Oak Brook, IL	2.35
3647	$3.85 Jefferson Memorial 7/30/02 Washington DC	9.00
3648	$13.65 US Capitol at Dusk 7/30/02 Washington DC	27.00
3649a-t	37¢ Masters of Photography 6/13/02 San Diego, CA	
	Set 20 singles	50.00
	Full sheet	13.00
3650	37¢ J J Audubon 6/27/02 Santa Clara, CA	2.10
3651	37¢ Harry Houdini 7/3/02 New York, NY	2.10
3652	37¢ Andy Warhol 8/9/02 Pittsburgh, PA	2.10
3653-56	37¢ Teddy Bears 8/15/02 Atlantic City, NJ, Block of 4	5.00
	Set 4 singles	9.00
3657	37¢ LOVE convertible bklt 8/16/02 Atlantic City, NJ	2.10
3657a	37¢ LOVE, Pl#pane 10	6.25
3658	60¢ LOVE 8/16/02, Atlantic City, NJ	2.35
3659	37¢ Ogden Nash 8/19/02 Baltimore, MD	2.10
3660	37¢ Duke Kahanamoku 8/24/02	2.10
3661-64	37¢ American Bats 9/13/02 Austin, TX, set 4 singles	8.50
3664a	37¢ American Bats, block 4	3.50
3665-68	37¢ Women Journalism 9/14/02, Fort Worth, TX, set 4 sngls	8.50
3668a	37¢ Women Journalism, block 4	3.50
3669	37¢ Irving Berlin 9/15/02 New York, NY	2.10
3670-71	37¢ Neuter/Spay 9/20/02 Denver, CO, set 2 singles	4.20
3671a	37¢ Neuter/Spay, pair	2.50
3672	37¢ Hanukkah 10/10/02 Washington DC	2.10
3673	37¢ Kwanzaa 10/10/02 Washington DC	2.10
3674	37¢ Eid 10/10/02 Washington DC	2.10
3675	37¢ Madonna & Child convertible bklt 10/10/02 Chicago, IL	2.10
3675a	37¢ Madonna & Child, Pl#pane 10	6.25
3676-79	37¢ Snowmen convertible bklt 10/28/02 Houghton, MI	
	Set 4 singles	8.50
3679a	Pl# pane 10	6.25
3680-83	37¢ Snowmen S/A coil, set 4 singles	8.50
3683a	Strip 4	3.50
3684-87	37¢ Snowmen double-sided bklt, set 4 singles	8.50
3687a	Pl# pane 6	4.50
3688-91	37¢ Snowmen vending bklt, set 4 singles	8.50
3691a	Pl# pane 6	4.50
3692	37¢ Cary Grant 10/15/02 Hollywood CA	2.10
3693	5¢ Sea Coast 10/21/02, Washington DC, strip 4 + 4	2.20
3694	37¢ Hawaiian Missionaries S/S 10/24/02 New York, NY	5.00
3694 a-d	37¢ Hawaiian Missionaries 10/24/02, set 4 singles	10.00
3695	37¢ Happy Birthday 10/25/02 New York, NY	2.10
3696-3745	37¢ Greetings from America 10/25/02 New York, NY	
	Set 50 singles	120.00
3745a	Full sheet	27.50
	2003-04 Commemoratives/Regular Issues	
3637	37¢ US Flag ATM 2/4/03 Washington, DC	2.10
3642a-45a	37¢ Antique Toys DS bklt 09/03/03 Washington, DC, pane 4	3.50
	Set 4 singles	8.40
3746	37¢ Thurgood Marshall 1/7/03 Washington, DC	2.10
3747	37¢ Year of the Ram 1/15/03 Chicago, IL	2.10
3748	37¢ Zora Neale Hurston 1/24/03 Eatonville, FL	2.10
3750	4¢ Chippendale Chair 3/05/04 New York, NY, block+21¢	2.35
3751	10¢ American Clock 1/24/03, Tucson, AZ, block 4	2.15
3757	1¢ Tiffany Lamp coil 3/1/03, Biloxi, MS, single+37¢	2.10
3766	$1.00 Wisdom 2/28/03 Biloxi, MS	2.75
3769	10¢ Lion Statue coil 2/4/03 Washington, DC, strip 4	2.15
3771	80¢ Special Olympics 2/13/03 Chicago, IL	2.50
3772	37¢ American Filmmaking 2/25/03 Beverly Hills, CA, full sheet	9.25
3772a-j	Set 10 singles	22.00
3773	37¢ Ohio Statehood 3/1/03 Chillicothe, OH	2.10
3774	37¢ Pelican Island Refuge 03/14/03 Sebastian, FL	2.10
3775	5¢ Sea Coast WA coil 03/19/03 Washington DC, strip 4+4	2.15
3776-80	37¢ Old Glory 04/03/03 New York, NY, set 5 singles	10.50
	Strip of 5	4.25
3781	37¢ Cesar Chavez 04/23/03 Los Angeles, CA	2.10

U.S. First Day Covers

Scott #	Description	Cacheted

2003 Commemoratives (cont.)

3782	37¢ Louisiana Purchase 04/30/03 New Orleans, LA	2.10
3783	37¢ First Powered Flight 05/22/03 Dayton, OH, Kill Devil Hills, NC	2.10
3784	37¢ Purple Heart BCA 05/30/03 Mt. Vernon, VA	2.10
3784a	37¢ Purple Heart AP 08/01/03 Somerset, NJ	2.10
3786	37¢ Audrey Hepburn 06/11/03 Los Angeles, CA	2.10
3787-91	37¢ Southeastern Lighthouses 06/13/03 Tybee Island, GA	
	Set 5 singles	10.50
	Strip 3+2	4.00
3792-3801	25¢ American Eagle coil 06/26/03 Santa Clara, CA, strip 5+5 .	4.70
3802a-j	37¢ Arctic Tundra 07/02/03 Barrow, AK, full sheet	9.25
	Set 10 singles	22.00
3803	37¢ Korean War Memorial 04/27/03 Washington, DC	2.10
3804-07	37¢ Mary Cassatt 08/07/03 Columbus, OH, pane 4	3.50
	Set 4 singles	8.40
3808-11	37¢ Early Football Heroes 08/09/03 South Bend, IN, block 4 ..	3.50
	Set 4 singles	8.40
3812	37¢ Roy Acuff 09/13/03 Nashville, TN	2.10
3813	37¢ District of Columbia 09/23/03 Washington DC	2.10
3814-18	37¢ Reptiles & Amphibians 10/07/03 San Diego, CA	
	Set 5 singles	10.50
	Strip 3+2	4.00
3820	37¢ Madonna & Child 10/23/03 New York, NY	2.10
3821-24	37¢ Holiday Music Makers 10/23/03 New York, NY, block 4	3.50
	Set 4 singles	8.40
3821-24b	37¢ Holiday Music Makers DS bklt 10/23/03, set 4 singles .	8.40
	Pane 4	3.50
3825-28	37¢ Holiday Music Makers VB 10/23/03, set 4 singles	8.40
	Pane 4	3.50
3829	37¢ Snowy Egret coil 10/24/03 New York, NY	2.10

2004 Commemoratives/Regular Issues

3830	37¢ Snowy Egret CB 20 01/30/04 Norfolk, VA	2.25
3831a-j	37¢ Pacific Coral Reefs 01/02/04 Honolulu, HI, set 10 singles	22.50
	Full sheet	9.25
3832	37¢ Year of the Monkey 01/13/04 San Francisco, CA	2.25
3833	37¢ LOVE Candy Hearts 01/14/04 Revere, MA	2.25
3834	37¢ Paul Robeson 01/20/04 Princeton, NJ	2.25
3835	37¢ Theodor Geisel 03/02/04 LaJolla, CA	2.25
3836	37¢ Garden Bouquet CB 20 03/04/04 New York, NY	2.25
3837	60¢ Garden Botanical 03/04/04 New York, NY	2.40
3838	37¢ U.S. Air Force Academy 04/01/04 Colorado Springs, CO .	2.25
3839	37¢ Henry Mancini 04/13/04 Los Angeles, CA	2.25
3840-43	37¢ American Choreographers 05/01/04 New York, NY	
	Set 4 singles	9.00
	Block 4	3.50
-----	37¢ Lewis & Clark Bicentennial 05/14/04	2.25
-----	37¢ Lewis & Clark Prestige Booklet 05/14/04, set 2 singles	5.00
	Combo 2	2.50
	Set 2 full panes	12.50
-----	37¢ Isamu Noguchi 05/18/04 Long Island City, NY	
	Set 5 singles	11.25
	Strip 3+2	4.25
-----	37¢ National World War II Memorial 05/29/04 Washington, DC	2.25
-----	37¢ Athens Summer Olympics 06/09/04	2.25
-----	37¢ Art of Disney: Friendship 06/23/04 Anaheim, CA, block 4 .	3.50
	Set 4 singles	9.00
-----	23¢ Wilma Rudolph 07/14/04, New York, NY, pair	2.35
-----	5¢ Toleware 06/25/04, Santa Clara, CA, block+20¢	2.25
-----	37¢ USS Constellation 06/30/04 Baltimore, MD	2.25
-----	37¢ R. Buckminster Fuller 07/12/04 Stanford, CA	2.25
-----	37¢ James Baldwin 07/23/04 New York, NY	2.25
-----	37¢ Heade "Magnolia" DS bklt 08/12/04 Sacramento, CA ...	2.25
-----	2¢ Navajo Jewelry 08/20/04 Indianapolis, IN, block+30¢	2.25
-----	37¢ John Wayne 09/01/04	2.25
	Souvenir sheet	14.00
-----	Sickle Cell Disease Awareness 09/29/04 Atlanta, GA	2.25
-----	37¢ Art of the American Indian 8/21/04 Washington, DC	
	Set 10 singles	22.50
	Full sheet (large envelope)	9.25
-----	37¢ Cloudscapes 10/04/04, set 15 singles	33.75
	Full panes	12.00
-----	37¢ Holiday Ornaments 10/14/04 New York, NY, set 4 singles	9.00
	Block 4	3.50
-----	37¢ Madonna & Child 10/14/04 Washington, DC	2.25
-----	37¢ Hanukkah 10/14/04 New York, NY	2.25
-----	37¢ Kwanzaa 10/16/04 New York, NY	2.25
-----	37¢ Moss Hart 10/24/04 New York, NY	2.25

Semi Postal Stamps

B1	1st Class Rate +8¢ Breast Cancer	2.25
	Research, 8/13/98, Wash. DC	
B2	34¢ &11¢ Heroes of 2001	2.50
B3	45¢ Stop Family Violence 10/08/04 Washington, DC	2.50

WASHINGTON 2006
World Philatelic Exhibition
May 27-June 3, 2006
See you there!
www.washington-2006.org

U.S. First Day Covers

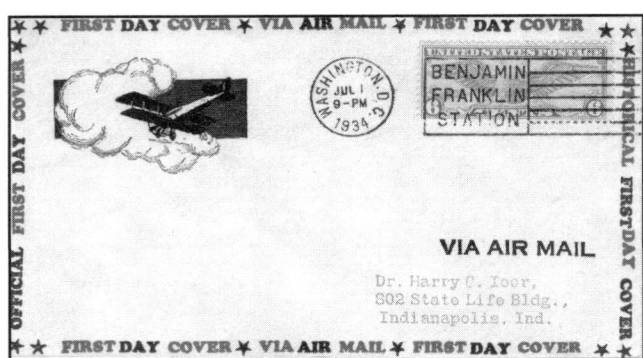

C19

C59

AIR MAIL FIRST DAY COVERS

Cacheted prices are for FDC's with common printed cachets.
From #C4 - C31, FDC's will usually be addressed.
Prices and Dates for #C1-3 are for First Flight Covers, AND FDC's.

Scott #	Description	Uncacheted	Cacheted
C1	6¢ Jenny 12/10/18 Washington, DC FDC	25,000.00	...
C1	6¢ Jenny 12/16/18 NYC; Phila.,PA; DC FFC .	2,000.00	...
C2	16¢ Jenny 7/11/18 Washington, DC FDC	25,000.00	...
C2	16¢ Jenny 7/15/18 NYC; Phila.,PA; DC FFC .	600.00	...
C3	24¢ Jenny 5/15/18 NYC; Phila.,PA; DC FFC .	600.00	...
C4	8¢ Propeller 8/15/23 DC	350.00	...
C5	16¢ Air Service Emblem 8/17/23 DC	600.00	...
C6	24¢ DeHavilland Biplane 8/21/23 DC	650.00	...
C7	10¢ Map 2/13/26 DC	80.00	...
	Chicago, IL	90.00	...
	Detroit, MI	90.00	...
	Cleveland, OH	120.00	...
	Dearborn, MI	120.00	...
	Unofficial city	200.00	...
C8	15¢ Map 9/18/26 DC	90.00	...
C9	20¢ Map 1/25/27 DC	100.00	...
	New York, NY	110.00	...
	1st Albert E. Gorham cachet	...	250.00
C10	10¢ Lindbergh 6/18/27 DC	30.00	175.00
	St. Louis, MO	30.00	175.00
	Detroit, MI	40.00	175.00
	Little Falls, MN	40.00	175.00
	Air Mail Field, Chicago, unofficial	150.00	...
	Unofficial city (other than AMF Chicago)	175.00	...
	1st Milton Mauck cachet	...	250.00
C10a	10¢ **Booklet Single** 5/26/28 DC	100.00	175.00
	Booklet Sgl., Cleveland Midwest Phil. Sta. ...	100.00	175.00
	#C10a sgl. & 645 Cleveland Midwest Sta	150.00	200.00
C10a	10¢ **Booklet Pane of 3** 5/26/28 DC	875.00	1000.00
	B. Pane of 3, Cleveland Midwest Sta.	825.00	1000.00
	#C10a & 645 on one FDC, Clev. Midwst.	900.00	1100.00
	Booklet Pane w/o tab, DC or Cleveland	425.00	750.00
C11	5¢ Beacon, pair 7/25/28 DC	60.00	250.00
	Single on FDC	200.00	...
	Single on FDC with postage due	250.00	...
	Unofficial city (pair)	250.00	...
	Predate 7/24/28	1,500.00	...
C12	5¢ Winged Globe 2/10/30 DC	15.00	90.00
C13	65¢ Graf Zeppelin 4/19/30 DC	1,200.00	2,500.00
	On flight cover, any date	250.00	...
C14	$1.30 Graf Zeppelin 4/19/30 DC	900.00	2,500.00
	On flight cover, any date	400.00	...
C15	$2.60 Graf Zeppelin 4/19/30 DC	1,050.00	2,500.00
	On flight cover, any date	600.00	...
C13-15	Graf Zeppelin, cplt. set on one cover	16,000.00	...
	Complete set on one Flight Cover, any date .	2,400.00	...
C16	5¢ Winged Globe, Rotary 8/19/31 DC	175.00	...
C17	8¢ Winged Globe 9/26/32 DC	16.50	50.00
	Combo with UC7	60.00	...
C18	50¢ Zeppelin 10/2/33 New York, NY	175.00	250.00
	Akron, OH 10/4/33	250.00	400.00
	DC 10/5/33	225.00	425.00
	Miami, FL 10/6/33	250.00	325.00
	Chicago, IL 10/7/33	250.00	400.00
	On flight cover, any date	110.00	150.00
C19	6¢ Winged Globe 6/30/34 Baltimore, MD	300.00	600.00
	New York, NY	**1,250.00**	**1,750.00**
	First Day of Rate 7/1/34 DC	**20.00**	**40.00**
	Combo with UC3	60.00	...

1935-39

Scott #	Description		Cacheted
C20	25¢ China Clipper 11/22/35 DC		45.00
	San Francisco, CA		45.00
C21	20¢ China Clipper 2/15/37 DC		55.00
C22	50¢ China Clipper 2/15/37 DC		60.00
C21-22	China Clipper on one cover		125.00
C23	6¢ Eagle Holding Shield 5/14/38 Dayton, OH		17.50
	St. Petersburg, FL		17.50

AIR MAIL FIRST DAY COVERS

Scott #	Description	Cacheted
C24	30¢ Winged Globe 5/16/39 New York, NY	60.00
C25	6¢ Plane 6/25/41 DC	7.50
C25a	Booklet Pane of 3 (3/18/43) DC	30.00
	Booklet single	10.00
C26	8¢ Plane 3/21/44 DC	6.00
C27	10¢ Plane 8/15/41 Atlantic City, NJ	9.00
C28	15¢ Plane 8/19/41 Baltimore, MD	9.00
C29	20¢ Plane 8/27/41 Philadelphia, PA	12.00
C30	30¢ Plane 9/25/41 Kansas City, MO	20.00
C31	50¢ Plane 10/29/41 St. Louis, MO	30.00
C25-31,C25a	Transport Plane set of 8 covers	95.00

From #C32 - Date, prices are for unaddressed FDC's & common cachets

1946-59

Scott #	Description	Cacheted
C32	5¢ DC-4 Skymaster 9/25/46 DC	2.00
C33	5¢ Small Plane (DC-4) 3/26/47 DC	2.00
C34	10¢ Pan Am. Building 8/30/47 DC	2.00
C35	15¢ New York Skyline 8/20/47 NY, NY	2.00
C36	25¢ Bay Bridge 7/30/47 San Francisco, CA	2.50
C37	5¢ Small Plane, coil 1/15/48 DC	2.00
C38	5¢ NY City Jubilee 7/31/48 New York, NY	2.00
C39	6¢ DC-4 Skymaster 1/18/49 DC	2.00
C39a	Booklet Pane of 6 11/18/49 NY, NY	12.00
C39as	Booklet Pane, single, ...	4.00
C40	6¢ Alexandria 5/11/49 Alexandria, VA	2.00

1946-59

Scott #	Description	Cacheted
C41	6¢ DC-4 Skymaster, coil 8/25/49 DC	2.00
C42	10¢ Post Office Bldg. 11/18/49 New Orleans, LA	2.00
C43	15¢ Globe & Doves 10/7/49 Chicago, IL	3.00
C44	25¢ Boeing 11/30/49 Seattle, WA	4.00
C45	6¢ Wright Brothers 12/17/49 Kitty Hawk, NC	3.00
C46	80¢ Diamond Head 3/26/52 Honolulu, HI	15.00
C47	6¢ Powered Flight 5/29/53 Dayton, OH	2.50
C48	4¢ Eagle in Flight 9/3/54 Phila., PA	2.00
C49	6¢ Air Force 8/1/57 DC	2.00
C50	5¢ Eagle 7/31/58 Colorado Springs, CO	2.00
C51	7¢ Blue Jet 7/31/58 Philadelphia, PA	2.00
C51a	Booklet Pane of 6 7/31/58 San Antonio, TX	7.00
C51as	Booklet Pane, single, ...	4.00
C52	7¢ Blue Jet, coil 7/31/58 Miami, FL	2.00
C53	7¢ Alaska 1/3/59 Juneau, AK	2.00
C54	7¢ Balloon 8/17/59 Lafayette, IN	3.00
C55	7¢ Hawaii Sthd. 8/21/59 Honolulu, HI	2.00
C56	10¢ Pan Am Games 8/27/59 Chicago, IL	2.00

1959-68

Scott #	Description	Cacheted
C57	10¢ Liberty Bell 6/10/60 Miami, FL	2.00
C58	15¢ Statue of Liberty 11/20/59 NY, NY	2.00
C59	25¢ Lincoln 4/22/60 San Francisco, CA	2.00
C59a	Luminescent 12/29/66 DC	60.00
C60	7¢ Red Jet 8/12/60 Arlington, VA	2.00
C60a	Booklet Pane of 6 8/19/60 St. Louis, MO	8.00
C60as	Booklet Pane, single, ...	4.00
C61	7¢ Red Jet, coil 10/22/60 Atlantic City, NJ	2.00
C62	13¢ Liberty Bell 6/28/61 New York, NY	2.00
C62a	Luminescent 2/15/67 DC	60.00
C63	15¢ Statue of Liberty 1/31/61 Buffalo, NY	2.00
C63a	Luminescent 1/11/67 DC	60.00
C64	8¢ Jet over Capitol, single 12/5/62 DC	2.00
C64a	Luminescent 8/1/63 Dayton, OH	2.00
C64b	Booklet Pane of 5 12/5/62 DC	2.00
C64bs	Booklet Pane, single, ...	4.00
C65	8¢ Jet over Capitol, 12/5/62 DC, single	2.00
C65a	Luminescent 1/14/65 New Orleans, LA	60.00
C66	15¢ Montgomery Blair 5/3/63 Silver Springs, MD	2.50
C67	6¢ Bald Eagle 7/12/63 Boston, MA	2.00
C67a	Luminescent 2/15/67 DC	60.00
C68	8¢ Amelia Earhart 7/24/63 Atchinson, KS	4.00
C69	8¢ Robert Goddard 10/5/64 Roswell, NM	3.00
C70	8¢ Alaska Purchase 3/30/67 Sitka, AK	2.00
C71	20¢ Columbia Jays 4/26/67 New York, NY	2.50
C72	10¢ 50-Star Runway 1/5/68 San Fran., CA	2.00
C72	Precancelled, 5/19/71, Wash, DC	75.00

U.S. First Day Covers

C99-100

O133

Scott #	Description	Cacheted
	1969-91	
C72b	Bklt. Pane of 8 1/5/68 San Fran., CA	3.00
C72bs	Booklet Pane, single	4.00
C72c	Bklt. Pane of 5 1/6/68 DC	125.00
C73	10¢ 50-Star Runway, coil 1/5/68 San Francisco, CA	2.00
C74	10¢ Jenny 5/15/68 DC	2.00
C75	20¢ "USA" & Jet 11/22/68 New York, NY	2.00
C76	10¢ First Man on Moon 9/9/69 DC	5.00
C77	9¢ Delta Plane 5/15/71 Kitty Hawk, NC	2.00
C78	11¢ Jet Silhouette 5/7/71 Spokane, WA	2.00
C78	Precancel, 5/19/71, Wash, DC	75.00
C78a	Booklet Pane of 4 5/7/71 Spokane, WA	3.00
C78as	Booklet Pane Single	4.00
C79	13¢ Winged Envelope 11/16/73 NY, NY	2.00
C79	Precancel, 3/4/74, Wash, DC	75.00
C79a	Bklt. Pane of 5 12/27/73 Chicago, IL	3.00
C79as	Blklt.Pane, single	4.00
C80	17¢ Statue of Liberty 7/13/71 Lakehurst, NJ	2.00
C81	21¢ "USA" & Jet 5/21/71 DC	2.00
C82	11¢ Jet Silhouette, coil 5/7/71 Spokane, WA	2.00
C83	13¢ Winged Envelope, coil 12/27/73 Chicago, IL	2.00
C84	11¢ City of Refuge 5/3/72 Honaunau, HI	2.00
C85	11¢ Olympics 8/17/72 DC	2.00
C86	11¢ Electronics 7/10/73 New York, NY	2.00
C87	18¢ Statue of Liberty 1/11/74 Hampstead, NY	2.00
C88	26¢ Mt. Rushmore 1/2/74 Rapid City, SD	2.00
C89	25¢ Plane and Globe 1/2/76 Honolulu, HI	2.00
C90	31¢ Plane, Globe & Flag 1/2/76 Honolulu, HI	2.00
C89-90	On one FDC	3.00
C91-92	31¢ Wright Bros. attd. 9/23/78 Dayton, OH	2.50
C91-92	Wright Bros. set of 2 singles	3.50
C93-94	21¢ Octave Chanute attd. 3/29/79 Chanute, KS	2.50
C93-94	Octave Chanute set of 2 singles	3.50
C95-96	25¢ Wiley Post attd. 11/20/79 Oklahoma City, OK	2.50
C95-96	Wiley Post set of 2 singles	3.50
C97	31¢ Olympic - High Jump 11/1/79 Col. Springs, CO	2.50
C98	40¢ Philip Mazzei 10/13/80 DC	2.50
C99	28¢ Blanche Scott 12/30/80 Hammondsport, NY	2.50
C100	35¢ Glenn Curtiss 12/30/80 Hammondsport, NY	2.50
C99-100	Scott & Curtiss on one cover	3.50
C101-04	28¢ Olympics attd. 6/17/83 San Antonio, TX	4.00
C101-04	Olympics set of 4 singles	10.00
C105-08	40¢ Olympics attd. 4/8/83 Los Angeles, CA	4.50
C105-08	Olympics set of 4 singles	10.00
C109-12	35¢ Olympics attd. 11/4/83 Colorado Springs, CO	4.50
C109-12	Olympics set of 4 singles	10.00
C113	33¢ Alfred Verville 2/13/85 Garden City, NY	2.50
C114	39¢ Sperry Bros. 2/13/85 Garden City, NY	2.50
C115	44¢ Transpacific Airmail 2/15/85 San Francisco, CA	3.00
C116	44¢ Junipero Serra 8/22/85 San Diego, CA	2.50
C117	44¢ New Sweden, 350th Anniv. 3/29/88 Wilmington, DE	2.50
C117	Joint issue w/Sweden, dual cancel	15.00
C117	Swedish issue only, pane of 6	8.00
C118	45¢ Samuel P. Langley 5/14/88 San Diego, CA	2.50
C119	36¢ Igor Sikorsky 6/23/88 Stratford, CT	2.50
C120	45¢ French Revolution 7/14/89 DC	2.50
C121	45¢ Pre-Columbian Customs 10/12/89 San Juan, PR	2.50
C122-25	45¢ Future Mail Transportation attd. 11/27/89 DC	8.00
C122-25	Set of 4 singles	12.00
C126	$1.80 Future Mail Trans. S/S of 4, imperf. 11/24/89 DC	8.00
C127	45¢ America, Caribbean Coast 10/12/90 Grand Canyon, AZ	2.50
C128	50¢ Harriet Quimby 4/27/91 Plymouth, MI	2.50
C129	40¢ William T. Piper 5/17/91 Denver, CO	2.50
C130	50¢ Antarctic Treaty 6/21/91 DC	2.50
C131	50¢ America 10/12/91 Anchorage, AK	2.50
C133	48¢ Niagara Falls, 5/12/99, Niagara Falls, NY	2.00
C134	40¢ Rio Grande, 7/30/99, Milwaukee, WI	2.00
C135	60¢ Grand Canyon, 1/20/00, Grand Canyon, AZ	2.25
C136	70¢ Nine Mile Prairie, 3/6/01, Lincoln, NE	2.50
C137	80c Mt. McKinley, 4/17/01, Fairbanks, AK	2.50
C138	60c Acadia National Park, 5/30/01, Bar Harbor, ME	2.50

1934-36 AIRMAIL SPECIAL DELIVERY ISSUES

CE1	16¢ Great Seal, blue 8/30/34 Chic., IL (AAMS Conv. Sta.)	30.00
CE2	16¢ Great Seal, red & blue 2/10/36 DC	25.00

Scott #	Description	Uncacheted	Cacheted
	1885-1931 SPECIAL DELIVERY		
E1	10¢ Messenger 10/1/85 Any City	12,500.00	...
E12	10¢ Motorcycle,Flat plate,perf. 11 7/12/22 DC	375.00	...
E13	15¢ Motorcycle,Flat plate,perf.11 4/11/25 DC	225.00	...
E14	20¢ Truck, Flat plate, perf. 11 4/25/25 DC	110.00	...
E15	10¢ Motorcycle, Rotary 11/29/27 DC	95.00	...
E15EE	Electric Eye 9/8/41 DC	...	25.00
E16	15¢ Motorcycle, Rotary 8/6/31 Easton, PA	2300.00	...
	Motorcycle, Rotary 8/13/31 DC	125.00	...
	1944-1971 SPECIAL DELIVERY		
E17	13¢ Motorcycle 10/30/44	...	10.00
E18	17¢ Motorcycle 10/30/44	...	10.00
E17-18	Motorcycles on one cover	...	15.00
E19	20¢ Post Office Truck, Rotary 11/30/51 DC	...	4.50
E20	20¢ Letter & Hands 10/13/54 Boston, MA	...	2.00
E21	30¢ Letter & Hands 9/3/57 Indpls., IN	...	2.00
E22	45¢ Arrows 11/21/69 New York, NY	...	2.25
E23	60¢ Arrows 5/10/71 Phoenix, AZ	...	2.50
	1911 REGISTERED MAIL		
F1	10¢ Eagle, blue 12/1/11 Any city	19,500.00	...
	10¢ Eagle, blue 11/28/11 Pre Date	22,000.00	...
	1955 CERTIFIED MAIL		
FA1	15¢ Postman, red 6/6/55 DC	...	2.00

Scott #	Description	4th Class	1st Class
	POSTAGE DUE		
	1925		
J68	½¢ P. Due (4/15/25 EKU) Phil., PA	900.00	...
	Rahway, NJ	2200.00	...
	1959		
J88	½¢ Red & Black 6/19/59 Any city	75.00	...
J89	1¢ Red & Black 6/19/59 Any city	75.00	...
J90	2¢ Red & Black 6/19/59 Any city	75.00	...
J91	3¢ Red & Black 6/19/59 Any city	75.00	...
J92	4¢ Red & Black 6/19/59 Any city	75.00	...
J93	5¢ Red & Black 6/19/59 Any city	115.00	...
J94	6¢ Red & Black 6/19/59 Any city	115.00	...
J95	7¢ Red & Black 6/19/59 Any city	115.00	...
J96	8¢ Red & Black 6/19/59 Any city	115.00	...
J97	10¢ Red & Black 6/19/59 Any city	115.00	...
J98	30¢ Red & Black 6/19/59 Any city	115.00	...

Scott #	Description	Uncacheted	Cacheted
	1959		
J99	50¢ Red & Black 6/19/59 Any city	115.00	...
J100	$1 Red & Black 6/19/59 Any city	125.00	...
J101	$5 Red & Black 6/19/59 Any city	125.00	...
	1978-85		
J102	11¢ Red & Black 1/2/78 Any city	...	5.00
J103	13¢ Red & Black 1/2/78 Any city	...	5.00
	#J102-103 on one FDC	...	7.50
	1978-85		
J104	17¢ Red & Black 6/10/85 Any city	...	5.00
	OFFICIAL MAIL		
O74	3¢ Treasury 7/1/1873 Washington, DC	5,000.00	...
O127	1¢ Eagle 1/12/83 DC	...	2.00
O128	4¢ Eagle 1/12/83 DC	...	2.00
O129	13¢ Eagle 1/12/83 DC	...	2.00
O129A	14¢ Eagle 5/15/85 DC	...	2.00
O130	17¢ Eagle 1/12/83 DC	...	2.00
O132	$1 Eagle 1/12/83 DC	...	5.00
O133	$5 Eagle 1/12/83 DC	...	15.00
O135	20¢ Eagle, with ¢ sign 1/12/83 DC	...	2.00
	#O127-129,O130-135 on one FDC	...	15.00
O136	22¢ Eagle 5/15/85 DC	...	2.00
O138	(14¢) "D" Eagle 2/4/85 DC	...	2.00
O138A	15¢ Official Mail 6/11/88 Corpus Christi, TX	...	2.00

U.S. First Day Covers

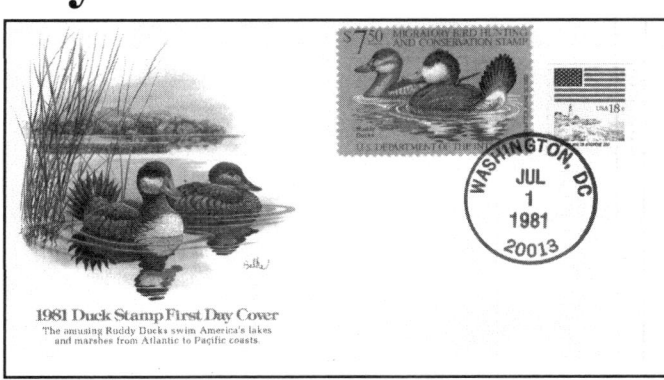

RW48

Scott #	Description	Uncacheted	Cacheted
	OFFICIAL MAIL (cont.)		
O138B	20¢ Official Mail, No ¢ sign 5/19/88 DC	...	2.00
O139	22¢ "D" Eagle 2/4/85 DC	...	2.00
O140	25¢ "E" Official 3/22/88 DC	...	2.00
O141	25¢ Official Mail 6/11/88 Corpus Christi, TX	...	2.00
O143	1¢ Eagle, Offset Printing, No ¢ sign 7/5/89 DC	...	2.00
O144	29¢ "F" Official 1/22/91 DC	...	2.00
O145	29¢ Official Mail 5/24/91 Seattle, WA	...	2.00
O146	4¢ Official Mail 4/6/91 Oklahoma City, OK	...	2.00
O146A	10¢ Official Mail 10/19/93	...	2.00
O147	19¢ Official Postcard rate 5/24/91 Seattle, WA	...	2.00
O148	23¢ Official 2nd oz. rate 5/24/91 Seattle, WA ..	...	2.00
O151	$1 Eagle Sept 1993	...	7.00
O152	32¢ "G" Official 12/13/94	...	2.00
O153	32¢ Official Mail 5/9/95 DC	...	2.00
O154	1¢ Eagle, with ¢ sign 5/9/95 DC	...	2.00
O155	20¢ Eagle, postcard rate 5/9/95 DC	...	2.00
O156	23¢ Eagle, 2nd oz. rate 5/9/95 DC	...	2.00
O154-56	1¢, 20¢, 23¢, 32¢ Coil Combo cover, 5/9/95 DC (1)	...	2.50
O157	33¢ Eagle coil 10/08/99	...	2.00
O158	34¢ Eagle coil, 2/27/01, Washington, DC	...	2.00
O159	37¢ Official mail coil, 8/2/02, Washington, DC .	...	2.10
	POSTAL NOTES		
PN1-18	1¢-90¢ Black, cplt. set on 18 forms	750.00	...
PN1	1¢ Black 2/1/45 on cplt 3 part M.O. form, any city	45.00	...
PN2	2¢ 2/1/45 on cplt 3 part M.O. form, any city	45.00	...
PN3	3¢ 2/1/45 on cplt 3 part M.O. form, any city	45.00	...
PN4	4¢ 2/1/45 on cplt 3 part M.O. form, any city	45.00	...
PN5	5¢ 2/1/45 on cplt 3 part M.O. form, any city	45.00	...
PN6	6¢ 2/1/45 on cplt 3 part M.O. form, any city	45.00	...
PN7	7¢ 2/1/45 on cplt 3 part M.O. form, any city	45.00	...
PN8	8¢ 2/1/45 on cplt 3 part M.O. form, any city	45.00	...
PN9	9¢ 2/1/45 on cplt 3 part M.O. form, any city	45.00	...
PN10	10¢ 2/1/45 on cplt 3 part M.O. form, any city ...	45.00	...
PN11	20¢ 2/1/45 on cplt 3 part M.O. form, any city ...	45.00	...
PN12	30¢ 2/1/45 on cplt 3 part M.O. form, any city ...	45.00	...
PN13	40¢ 2/1/45 on cplt 3 part M.O. form, any city ...	45.00	...
PN14	50¢ 2/1/45 on cplt 3 part M.O. form, any city ...	45.00	...
PN15	60¢ 2/1/45 on cplt 3 part M.O. form, any city ...	45.00	...
PN16	70¢ 2/1/45 on cplt 3 part M.O. form, any city ...	45.00	...
PN17	80¢ 2/1/45 on cplt 3 part M.O. form, any city ...	45.00	...
PN18	90¢ 2/1/45 on cplt 3 part M.O. form, any city ...	45.00	...
	POSTAL SAVINGS		
PS11	10¢ Minuteman, red 5/1/41 Any city	175.00	...

PARCEL POST

Scott #	Description	(1/1/13)	(7/1/13)
Q1	1¢ Post Office Clerk, any city	3500.00	2000.00
Q2	2¢ City Carrier, any city	*4500.00*	2000.00
Q3	3¢ Railway Postal Clerk, any city	...	*4500.00*
Q4	4¢ Rural Carrier, any city	...	*5500.00*
Q5	5¢ Mail Train, any city	40*00.00*	7000.00

1925-28 SPECIAL HANDLING

Scott #	Description	Uncacheted	Cacheted
QE1-3	Set of 3 on one FDC	300.00	
QE1	10¢ Yellow Green 6/25/28 DC	50.00	...
QE2	15¢ Yellow Green 6/25/28 DC	50.00	...
QE3	20¢ Yellow Green 6/25/28 DC	50.00	...
QE4a	25¢ Deep Green 4/11/25 DC	225.00	...

REVENUE STAMPS

Scott #	Description	Uncacheted	Cacheted
R155	2¢ Carmine, 7/1/98	1000.00	...
R733	10¢ Documentary	200.00	...

FEDERAL DUCK STAMP FIRST DAY COVERS

Scott #	Description	Cacheted
RW47	$7.50 Mallards 7/1/80 DC	150.00
RW48	$7.50 Ruddy Ducks 7/1/81 DC	75.00
RW49	$7.50 Canvasbacks 7/1/82 DC	55.00
RW50	$7.50 Pintails 7/1/83 DC	55.00
RW51	$7.50 Widgeons 7/2/84 DC	60.00
RW52	$7.50 Cinnamon Teal 7/1/85	45.00
RW53	$7.50 Fulvous Whistling Duck 7/1/86	45.00
RW54	$10.00 Red Head Ducks 7/1/87	45.00
RW55	$10.00 Snow Goose 7/1/88 Any city	45.00
RW56	$12.50 Lesser Scaups 6/30/89 DC	45.00
RW57	$12.50 Black-Bellied Whistling Duck 6/30/90 DC	45.00
RW58	$15.00 King Eiders 6/30/91 DC	45.00
RW59	$15.00 Spectacled Eiders 6/30/92 DC	45.00
RW60	$15.00 Canvasbacks 6/30/93 DC	40.00
RW60	Same, Mound, MN	40.00
RW61	$15.00 Redbreasted Merganser 6/30/94 DC ...	40.00
RW62	$15.00 Mallard 6/30/95 DC	40.00
RW63	$15.00 Surf Scoter 6/27/96 DC	40.00
RW64	$15.00 Canada Goose 6/21/97 DC	40.00
RW65	$15.00 Barrow's Goldeneye W/A 7/1/98 DC ...	40.00
RW65A	$15.00 Barrow's Goldeneye S/A 7/1/98	40.00
RW66	$15.00 Greater Scaup W/A 7/1/99 DC	40.00
RW66A	$15.00 Greater Scaup S/A 7/1/99 DC	40.00
RW67	$15.00 Mottled Duck W/A 7/1/00 DC	40.00
RW67A	$15.00 Mottled Duck S/A 7/1/00 DC	40.00
RW68	$15.00 Northern Pintail W/A 6/29/2001	40.00
RW68A	$15.00 Northern Pintail S/A 6/29/2001	40.00
RW69	$15.00 Black Scoters W/A 7/1/02	40.00
RW69A	$15.00 Black Scoters S/A 7/1/02	40.00
RW70	$15.00 Snow Geese W/A 7/1/03	40.00
RW70A	$15.00 Snow Geese S/A 7/1/03	40.00

POSTAL STATIONERY FIRST DAY COVERS
Prices are for standard 6¾ size envelopes, unless noted otherwise.

Scott #	Description	Uncacheted	Cacheted
	1925-32		
U436a	3¢ G. Washington, white paper, extra quality 6/16/32 DC, size 5, die 1, wmk. 29	75.00	...
	Size 8, die 1, wmk. 29	18.00	...
U436e	3¢ G. Washington, white paper, extra quality 6/16/32 DC, size 5, die 7, wmk. 29	12.00	30.00
U436f	3¢ G. Washington, white paper, extra quality 6/16/32 DC, size 5, die 9, wmk. 29	12.00	50.00
	Size 12, die 9, wmk. 29	18.00	...
U437a	3¢ G. Washington, amber paper, standard qual. 7/13/32 DC, size 5, wmk. 28	50.00	...
	7/19/32 DC, size 5, wmk. 29, extra qual.	35.00	...
U439	3¢ G. Washington, blue paper, standard qual. 7/13/32, size 5, wmk. 28	40.00	...
	Size 13, die 9, wmk. 28	65.00	...
	9/9/32 DC, size 5, wmk. 28	85.00	...
U439a	3¢ G. Washington, blue paper, extra quality 7/19/32 DC, size 5, die 29	40.00	...
U481	1½¢ G. Wash. 3/19/25 DC, size 5, wmk. 27 ..	35.00	...
	Size 8, wmk. 27	70.00	...
	Size 13, wmk. 26	50.00	...
	Size 5, wmk. 27 with Sc#553, 582 & 598	150.00	...
	Size 8, wmk. 27 with Sc#553, 582 & 598	125.00	...
	Size 13, wmk. 26 with Sc#553	60.00	...
U495	1½¢ on 1¢ B. Franklin 6/1/25 DC, size 5	50.00	...
	6/3/25 DC, size 8	65.00	...
	6/2/25 DC, size 13	60.00	...
U515	1½¢ on 1¢ B. Franklin 8/1/25 Des Moines, IA size 5, die 1	50.00	...
U521	1½¢ on 1¢ B. Franklin 10/22/25 DC size 5, die 1, watermark 25	100.00	...
U522a	2¢ Liberty Bell 7/27/26 Philadelphia, PA Size 5, wmk. 27	20.00	30.00
	Size 5, wmk. 27 DC	22.50	32.50
	Unofficial city, Size 5, wmk. 27	35.00	45.00

U.S. First Day Covers

U532

U564

Scott #	Description	Uncacheted	Cacheted
WASHINGTON BICENTENNIAL ISSUE			
U523	1¢ Mount Vernon 1/1/32 DC, size 5, wmk. 29	10.00	32.50
	Size 8, wmk. 29	12.50	37.50
	Size 13, wmk. 29	10.00	32.50
U524	1½¢ Mount Vernon 1/1/32 DC, size 5, wmk.29	10.00	32.50
	Size 8, wmk. 29	12.50	37.50
	Size 13, wmk. 29	10.00	32.50
U525	2¢ Mount Vernon 1/1/32 DC, size 5, wmk. 29	8.00	30.00
	Size 8, wmk. 29	10.00	30.00
	Size 13, wmk. 29	8.00	30.00
U526	3¢ Mount Vernon 6/16/32 DC, size 5, wmk.29	18.00	40.00
	Size 8, wmk. 29	25.00	80.00
	Size 13, wmk. 29	20.00	60.00
U527	4¢ Mount Vernon 1/1/32 DC, size 8, wmk. 29	30.00	80.00
U528	5¢ Mount Vernon 1/1/32 DC, size 5, wmk. 29	18.00	40.00
	Size 8, wmk. 29	20.00	45.00
1932-71			
U529	6¢ G. Washington, white paper, 8/18/32		
	Los Angeles, CA, size 8,	15.00	...
	8/19/32 DC, size 7	20.00	...
	8/19/32 DC, size 9	20.00	...
U530	6¢ G. Washington, amber paper, 8/18/32		
	Los Angeles, CA, size 8	15.00	...
U530	8/19/32 DC, size 7	20.00	...
	8/19/32 DC, size 9	20.00	...
	size 8, wmk 29 with Sc#723 pair	40.00	...
U531	6¢ G. Washington, blue paper, 8/18/32		
	Los Angeles, CA, size 8	15.00	...
	8/19/32 DC, size 7	20.00	...
	8/19/32 DC, size 9	20.00	...
U532	1¢ Franklin 11/16/50 NY, NY, size 13	2.00	
U533a	2¢ Wash. 11/17/50 NY, NY, size 13	...	2.00
U534a	3¢ Wash.,die 1 11/18/50 NY,NY, size 13	2.00	...
U534b	3¢ Wash.,die 2 11/19/50 NY,NY, size 8	4.00	8.00
POSTAL STATIONERY FIRST DAY COVERS			
U536	4¢ Franklin 7/31/58 Montpelier, VT, size 6 3/4 .	...	2.00
	Size 8	60.00	...
	Size 13, window	25.00	...
	Wheeling, WV, size 6¾, wmk 46, w/#1036a	35.00	...
U540	3¢+1¢ G.Washington (U534c) 7/22/58 Kenvil, NJ		
	Size 8, die 3 (earliest known use)	50.00	...
U541	1¼¢ Franklin 6/25/60 Birmingham, AL		2.00
U542	2½¢ Washington 5/28/60 Chicago, IL		2.00
U543	4¢ Pony Express 7/19/60 St. Joseph, MO		2.00
	Sacramento, CA		3.50
U544	5¢ Lincoln 11/19/62 Springfield, IL		2.00
U546	5¢ World's Fair 4/22/64 World's Fair, NY		2.00
U547	1¼¢ Liberty Bell 1/6/65 DC		2.00
	1/8/65 DC, size 10, wmk 48		15.00
U548	1.4¢ Liberty Bell 3/26/68 Springfield, MA		2.00
	3/27/68 DC, size 10, wmk 48		8.00
U548A	1.6¢ Liberty Bell 6/16/69 DC		2.00

Scott #	Description	Uncacheted	Cacheted
POSTAL STATIONERY FIRST DAY COVERS			
	Size 10, wmk 49		2.00
U549	4¢ Old Ironsides 1/6/65 DC		2.00
	1/8/65, window		15.00
	Size 10		15.00
	Size10, window		15.00
U550	5¢ Eagle 1/5/65 Williamsburg, PA		2.00
	1/8/65, window		15.00
	Size 10		15.00
	Size 10, window		15.00
U550a	5¢ Eagle, tagged 8/15/67 DC, wmk 50		3.50
	Dayton, OH		15.00
	Wmk 48		5.00
	Size 10, wmk 48		5.00
	Size 10, wmk 49, Dayton, OH only		7.50
	Size 10, wmk 49, window		5.00
U551	6¢ Liberty 1/4/68 New York, NY		2.00
	1/5/68 DC, window		3.00
	Size 10, wmk 47		3.00
	Size 10, window, wmk 49		3.00
	11/15/68 DC, shiny plastic window, wmk 48		5.00

Scott #	Description	Uncacheted	Cacheted
POSTAL STATIONERY FIRST DAY COVERS (cont.)			
U552	4 + 2¢ Old Ironsides, revalued 2/5/68 DC, wmk 50		7.50
	Window, wmk 48		7.50
	Size 10, wmk 47		7.50
	Size 10, window, wmk 49		7.50
U553	5 + 1¢ Eagle, revalued 2/5/68 DC		7.50
	Size 10, window		7.50
U553a	5 + 1¢ Eagle, revalued, tagged 2/5/68 DC, wmk 48		10.00
	Size 10, wmk 47 or 49		7.50
	Size 10, window, wmk 49		7.50
U554	6¢ Moby Dick 6/7/70 New Bedford, MA		2.00
U554	**1st Colonial Cachet**		**30.00**
U554	1st Lorstan Cachet		20.00
U555	6¢ Youth Conf. 2/24/71 DC		2.00
U556	1.7¢ Liberty Bell 5/10/71 Balt., MD, wmk 48A		2.00
	5/10/71 DC, wmk 49 with #1394		15.00
	5/10/71 Phoenix, AZ, wmk 48A with #E23		30.00
	5/10/71 DC, with #1283		3.00
	5/11/71 DC, size 10, wmk 47 or 49		12.00
	5/11/71 DC, size 10, wmk 48A		6.00
1971-78			
U557	8¢ Eagle 5/6/71 Williamsburg, PA, wmk 48A		2.00
	Wmk 49		2.50
	DC, window, wmk 48A	15.00	3.50
	Size 10, wmk 48A	15.00	3.50
	Size 10, window, wmk 47	15.00	3.50
U561	6 + 2¢ Liberty Bell, revalued 5/16/71 DC, wmk 47		3.00
	Wmk 48A		25.00
	Wmk 49		4.00
	Window, wmk 47		3.00
	Size 10, wmk 48A		3.00
	Size 10, wmk 49		6.00
	Size 10, window, wmk 47		3.00
	Size 10, window, wmk 49		5.00
U562	6 + 2¢ Youth Conf., revalued 5/16/71 DC, wmk 49		3.00
	Wmk 47		30.00
U563	8¢ Bowling 8/21/71 Milwaukee, WI		1.75
	Size 10		2.00
U564	8¢ Aging Conference 11/15/71 DC		2.00
U565	8¢ Transpo '72 5/2/72 DC, wmk 49		2.00
	Wmk 47		3.00
U566	8 + 2¢ Eagle, revalued 12/1/73 DC		2.50
	Window, wmk 48A	7.50	
	Window, wmk 49		4.50
	Size 10, wmk 47		4.50
	Size 10, window, wmk 47		4.50
U567	10¢ Liberty Bell 12/5/73 Phila., PA, top flap depth 58 mm		2.00
	top flap depth 51 mm		1.75
U567	Window	15.00	...
	Size 10	15.00	...
	Size 10, window	15.00	...
U568	1.8¢ Volunteer 8/23/74 Cincinnati, OH		2.00
	Size 10		2.00
U569	10¢ Tennis 8/31/74 Forest Hills, NY		3.00
	Size 10		3.00
	9/3/74 DC, window		4.00
	Size 10, window		4.00
U571	10¢ Seafaring 10/13/75 Minneapolis, MN		2.00
	Size 10		2.00
U572	13¢ Homemaker 2/2/76 Biloxi, MS		2.00
	Size 10		2.00
U573	13¢ Farmer 3/15/76 New Orleans, LA		2.00
	Size 10		2.00
1971-78			
U574	13¢ Doctor 6/30/76 Dallas, TX		2.50
	Size 10		3.00
U575	13¢ Craftsman 8/6/76 Hancock, MA		2.00
	Size 10		2.00
U576	13¢ Liberty Tree 11/8/75 Memphis, TN		2.00
	Size 10		2.00
U577	2¢ Star & Pinwheel 9/10/76 Hempstead, NY		2.00
	Size 10		2.00
U578	2.1¢ Non-Profit 6/3/77 Houston, TX		2.00
	Size 10		2.00

U.S. First Day Covers

U603

UC25

Scott #	Description	Uncacheted	Cacheted
	1971-78 (cont.)		
U579	2.7¢ Non-Profit 7/5/78 Raleigh, NC		2.00
	Size 10		2.00
U580	(15¢) "A" Eagle 5/22/78 Memphis, TN, wmk 47 ...		2.00
	Wmk 48A		2.00
	Window, wmk 47 or 48A		2.50
	Size 10		2.00
	Size 10, window		2.50
	Size 6¾, wmk 48A with sheet, coil & bklt. pane		10.00
U581	15¢ Uncle Sam 6/3/78 Williamsburg, PA		2.00
	Window		2.50
	Size 10		2.00
	Size 10, window		2.50
U582	13¢ Bicentennial 10/15/76 Los Angeles, CA, wmk 49 ...		2.00
	Wmk 49, dark green		7.50
	Wmk 48A		3.00
	Size 10		2.00
U583	13¢ Golf 4/7/77 Augusta, GA		7.00
	Size 10		7.50
	4/8/77 DC, Size 6¾, window		9.50
	Size 10, window		9.50
	1977-85		
U584	13¢ Conservation 10/20/77 Ridley Park, PA		2.00
	Window		2.50
	Size 10		2.00
	Size 10, window		2.50
U585	13¢ Development 10/20/77 Ridley Park, PA		2.00
	Window		2.50
	Size 10		2.00
	Size 10, window		2.50
U586	15¢ on 16¢ Surcharged USA 7/28/78 Williamsburg, PA .		2.00
	Window	15.00	...
	Size 10, window	15.00	...
	1977-85		
U587	15¢ Auto Racing 9/2/78 Ontario, CA		2.00
	Size 10		2.00
U588	13 + 2¢ Lib. Tree, revalued 11/28/78 Williamsburg, PA ...		2.00
	Window	15.00	...
	Size 10		2.00
	11/29/78 DC, size 6¾, window		2.00
	Size 10, window	15.00	...
U589	3.1¢ Non-Profit 5/18/79 Denver, CO		2.00
	Window		4.00
	Size 10		2.00
	Size 10, window		4.00
U590	3.5¢ Violins 6/23/80 Williamsburg, PA		2.00
	Window		4.00
	Size 10		2.00
	Size 10, window		4.00
U591	5.9¢ Non-Profit 2/17/82 Wheeling, WV		2.00
	Window		4.00
	Size 10		2.00
	Size 10, window		4.00
U592	(18¢) "B" Eagle 3/15/81 Memphis, TN		2.00
	Window		4.00
	Size 10		2.00
	Size 10, window		4.00
U593	18¢ Star 4/2/81 Star City, IN		2.00
	Window		4.00
	Size 10		2.00
	Size 10, window		4.00
U594	(20¢) "C" Eagle 10/11/81 Memphis, TN		2.00
	Window	10.00	...
	Size 10		2.00
	Size 10, window		7.50
U595	15¢ Veterinary Med. 7/24/79 Seattle, WA		2.00
	Window	15.00	...
	Size 10		1.75
	Size 10, window	15.00	...
U596	15¢ Olympics 12/10/79 E. Rutherford, NJ		2.00
	Size 10		2.00
U597	15¢ Bicycle 5/16/80 Baltimore, MD		2.00
	Size 10		2.00
U598	15¢ America's Cup 9/15/80 Newport, RI		2.00
	Size 10		2.00

Scott #	Description	Uncacheted	Cacheted
U599	15¢ Honey Bee 10/10/80 Paris, IL		2.00
	Size 10		2.00
U600	18¢ Blinded Veteran 8/13/81 Arlington, VA		2.00
	Size 10		2.00
U601	20¢ Capitol Dome 11/13/81 Los Angeles, CA		2.00
	Window		4.00
	Size 10		2.00
	Size 10, window		4.00
U602	20¢ Great Seal 6/15/82 DC		2.00
	Size 10		2.00
U603	20¢ Purple Heart 8/6/82 DC		2.00
	Size 10		2.00
U604	5.2¢ Olive Wreaths 3/21/83 Memphis, TN		2.00
	Window		4.00
	Size 10		2.00
	Size 10, window		4.00
U605	20¢ Paralyzed Vets 8/3/83 Portland, OR		2.00
	Size 10		2.00
U606	20¢ Small Business 5/7/84 DC		2.00
	Size 10		2.00
U607	(22¢) "D" Eagle 2/1/85 Los Angeles, CA		2.00
	Window		4.00
	Size 10		2.00
	Size 10, window		4.00
U608	22¢ Bison 2/25/85 Bison, SD		2.00
	Wndow		4.00
	Size 10		2.00
	Size 10, window		4.00
U608A	22¢ Bison precancelled, 11/4/86, DC 10 window	35.00	...
	1985-96		
U609	6¢ Old Ironsides, Non-Profit 5/3/85 Boston, MA		2.00
	Window		4.00
	Size 10		2.00
	Size 10, window		4.00
U610	8.5¢ Mayflower 12/4/86 Plymouth, MA		2.00
	Window		4.00
	Size 10		2.00
	Size 10, window		4.00
U611	25¢ Stars 3/26/88 Star, MS		2.00
	Window		4.00
	Size 10		2.00
	Size 10, window		4.00
U611x	25¢ Stars 8/18/88, Star, ID, 10 double window		5.00
U612	8.4¢ USS Constellation 4/12/88 Baltimore, MD		2.00
	Window		4.00
	Size 10		2.00
	Size 10, window		4.00
U613	25¢ Snowflake 9/8/88 Snowflake, AZ, greeting card size		2.00
U614	25¢ Philatelic Mail Return Env. 3/10/89 Cleveland, OH size 9		2.00
U615	25¢ Security Envelope 7/10/89 DC size 9		3.00
U615x	25¢ Security Envelope 12/29/89, DC, size 9 left window .		4.00
	Size 9, right window		4.00
U616	25¢ Love 9/22/89 McLean, VA size 9		3.50
U617	25¢ Space Station (hologram) 12/3/89, DC, size 9		2.00
U618	25¢ Lombardi Trophy (hologram) 9/9/90 Green Bay, WI size 10		4.00
U619	29¢ Star 1/24/91 DC		2.00
	Size 10		2.00
U619r	29¢ Star, recycled paper 5/1/92, Kansas City, MO		3.00
	Window, recycled paper		3.50
	Size 10, recycled paper		3.50
	Size 10, window, recycled paper		3.50
U620	11.1¢ Swallows 5/3/91 Boxborough, MA		2.00
	Window		4.00
	Size 10, window		4.00
	Size 10		2.00
U620r	11.1¢ Swallows, recycled paper 5/1/92, Kansas City, MO .		3.00
	Window, recycled paper		3.50
	Size 10, recycled paper		3.50
	Size 10, window, recycled paper		3.50
U621	29¢ Love 5/9/91 Honolulu, HI		2.00
	Window		4.00
	Size 10		2.00
	Size 10, window		4.00
U621r	29¢ Love, recycled paper 5/1/92, Kansas City, MO		3.00
	Size 10, recycled paper		3.50

U.S. First Day Covers

Scott #	Description	Cacheted
U622	29¢ Magazine Industry 10/7/91 Naples, FL size 10	2.00
U623	29¢ Star Security 7/20/91, DC, size 9	2.50
	Size 9, left window	4.00
	Size 9, right window	10.00
U623r	29¢ Star Security,s ize 9, recycled paper 5/1/92, Kansas City, MO	3.00
	Size 9, left window, recycled paper	3.50
U624	29¢ Country Geese 11/8/91 Virginia Beach, VA	1.75
	Size 10, 1/21/92 Virginia Beach, VA	2.00
U624r	29¢ Country Geese, recycled paper 5/1/92, Kansas City, MO	2.50
U625	29¢ Space Station (hologram) 1/21/92 Virginia Beach, VA size 10	2.00
U625r	29¢ Space Station (hologram), recycled paper, 5/1/92 Kansas City, MO	2.50
U626	29¢ Western Americana 4/10/92 Dodge City, KS size 10	2.00
U627	29¢ Protect the Environment 4/22/92 Chicago, IL size 10	2.00
U628	19.8¢ Bulk-rate, third class 5/18/92 Las Vegas, NV size 10	2.50
U629	29¢ Disabled Americans 7/22/92 DC	2.00
	Size10	2.00
U630	29¢ Kitten 10/2/93, King of Prussia, PA, size 10	1.75
	Size 10	2.00
U631	29¢ Football size 10 9/17/94 Canton, OH, size 10	3.00
U632	32¢ Liberty Bell 1/3/95 Williamsburg, VA	2.00
	Window	4.00
	Size 10	2.00
	Size 10, window	4.00
U633	32¢ "G" Old Glory 12/13/94, DC	2.00
	Window	4.00
U634	32¢ "G" Old Glory, size 10, 12/13/94, DC	2.00
U635	5¢ Sheep 3/10/95, State College, PA	2.00
	Window	4.00
	Size 10	2.00
	Size 10, window	4.00
U636	10¢ Stylized Eagle, bulk rate 3/10/95, State College,PA size 10	2.00
U637	32¢ Spiral Heart 5/12/95 Lakeville, PA	2.00
	Size 10	2.00
U638	32¢ Liberty Bell Security 5/16/95, DC, size 9	2.00
	Size 9, window	4.00
U639	32¢ Space Station (hologram) 9/22/95, Milwaukee, WI, size 10	2.00
U640	32¢ Environment 4/20/96 Chicago, IL size 10	2.00
U641	32¢ Paralympics 5/2/96 DC size 10	2.00

1999-01

Scott #	Description	Cacheted
U642	33¢ Flag, 3 colors, 1/11/99, Washington DC	2.00
	Window	3.00
	Size 10	2.25
	Size 10, window	3.00
U643	33¢ Flag, 2 colors, 1/11/99, Washington DC size 9	2.00
	Size 9, window	3.00
U644	33¢ Love, 1/28/99, Loveland, CO	2.00
	Size 10	2.25
U645	33¢ Lincoln, 6/5/99	2.00
	Window	3.00
	Size10	2.25
	Size 10, window	3.00
U646	34¢ Federal Eagle 1/7/01, DC	2.00
	Window	3.00
	Size 9, security paper	2.00
	Size 9, window, security paper	3.00
	Size 10	2.00
	Size 10, window	3.00

1999-03

Scott #	Description	Cacheted
U647	34¢ Lovebirds, 2/14/01, Lovejoy, GA	2.00
	Size 10	2.25
U648	34¢ Community Colleges, 2/20/01, Joilet, IL	2.00
	Size 10	2.25
U649	37¢ Ribbon Star 6/7/02, DC	2.00
	Window	3.00
	Size 9, security paper	2.00
	Size 9, window, security	3.00
	Size 10	2.00
	Size 10, window	3.00
U650	10¢ Graphic Eagle, presorted standard 8/8/02, DC, size 10	2.00
U651	37¢ Nurturing Love 1/25/03, Tucson, AZ	2.00
	Size 10	2.00
U652	$3.85 Jefferson Memorial Priority 12/29/03, DC	9.50

AIRMAIL POSTAL STATIONARY

1929-71

Scott #	Description	Uncacheted
UC1	5¢ Monoplane, blue 1/12/29 DC, size 13	30.00
	2/1/29, DC, size 5	60.00
	2/1/29, DC, size 8	85.00
UC3	6¢ Monoplane, orange 7/1/34, DC, size 13	10.00
	6¢ Monoplane, orange 7/1/34, DC, size 13 **(cacheted)**	100.00
	Size 8	20.00
	Size 13 with C19	40.00
UC7	8¢ Monoplane, olive 9/26/32, DC, size 13	10.00
	Size 8	20.00
	Size 13 with C17	50.00
UC10	5¢ on 6¢ Orange 10/1/46 Aiea Hts, HI, die 2a	150.00
UC11	5¢ on 6¢ Orange 10/1/46 Aiea Hts, HI die 2b	200.00
UC12	5¢ on 6¢ Orng. 10/1/46 Aiea Hts, HI, APO & NY, NY die 2c	100.00
UC13	5¢ on 6¢ Orng. 10/1/46 Aiea Hts, HI, die 3	100.00

Scott #	Description	Cacheted
UC14	5¢ Skymaster 9/25/46 DC, size 13	2.50
UC16	10¢ Skymaster Air Letter, 4/27/47	5.00
UC17	5¢ CIPEX, type 1, 5/21/47, New York, NY, size 13	2.25
UC17a	5¢ CIPEX, type 2, 5/21/47, New York, NY, size 13	2.25
UC18	6¢ Skymaster 9/22/50 Philadelphia, PA, size 13	2.25
UC20	6¢ on 5¢ 9/17/51 U.S. Navy Cancel **(uncacheted)**	250.00
UC22	6¢ on 5¢ die 2 (UC15) 8/29/52 Norfolk, VA **(uncacheted)**	35.00
	Cacheted	30.00
UC25a	6¢ FIPEX ,"short clouds" 5/2/56, New York, NY, size 13	2.00
	6¢ FIPEX ,"long clouds" 5/2/56, New York, NY, size 13	2.00

1929-71

Scott #	Description	Cacheted
UC26	7¢ Skymaster 7/31/58 Dayton, OH, "straight left wing"	2.00
	Size 8 **(uncacheted)**	35.00
UC32a	10¢ Jet Air Letter 9/12/58 St. Louis, MO	2.00
UC33	7¢ Jet, blue 11/21/58 New York, NY	2.00
UC34	7¢ Jet, red 8/18/60 Portland, OR	2.00
UC35	11¢ Jet Air Letter 6/16/61 Johnstown, PA	2.00
UC36	8¢ Jet 11/17/62 Chantilly, VA	2.00
UC37	8¢ Jet Triangle 1/7/65 Chicago, IL	2.00
	1/8/65, DC, size 10	15.00
UC37a	8¢ Jet Triangle, tagged 8/15/67 DC	15.00
	Dayton, OH	15.00
	Size 10	7.50
UC38	11¢ Kennedy Air Letter 5/29/65 Boston, MA	2.00
UC39	13¢ Kennedy Air Letter 5/29/67 Chic., IL	2.00
UC40	10¢ Jet Triangle 1/8/68 Chicago, IL	2.00
	1/9/68 DC, size 10	7.50
UC41	8 + 2¢ revalued UC37 2/5/68 DC	10.00
	Size 10	10.00
UC42	13¢ Human Rights Air Letter 12/3/68 DC	2.00
UC43	11¢ Jet & Circles 5/6/71 Williamsburg, PA	2.00
	Size 10	6.00
UC44	15¢ Birds Air Letter 5/28/71 Chicago, IL	2.00
UC44a	15¢ Birds AEROGRAMME 12/13/71 Phila., PA	2.00
UC45	10¢+1¢ revalued UC40 6/28/71 DC	5.00
	Size 10	10.00

1973-99

Scott #	Description	Cacheted
UC46	15¢ Balloon Aerogramme 2/10/73 Albuquerque, NM	2.00
UC47	13¢ Dove 12/1/73 Memphis, TN	2.00
UC48	18¢ USA Aerogramme 1/4/74 Atlanta, GA	2.00
UC49	17¢ NATO Aerogramme 4/4/74 DC	2.00
UC50	22¢ USA Aerogramme 1/16/76 Tempe, AZ	2.00
UC51	22¢ USA Aerogramme 11/3/78 St. Petersburg, FL	2.00
UC52	22¢ Olympics Aerogramme 12/5/79 Bay Shore, NY	2.00
UC53	30¢ Tourism (black& white) Aerogramme 12/29/80 San Francisco, CA	2.00
UC54	30¢ Tourism (color) Aerogramme 9/21/81 Honolulu, HI	2.00
UC55	30¢ World Trade Aerogramme 9/16/82 Seattle, WA	2.00
UC56	30¢ Communications Aerogramme 1/7/83 Anaheim, CA	2.00
UC57	30¢ Olympics Aerogramme 10/14/83 Los Angeles, CA	2.00
UC58	30¢ Landsat Satellite Aerogramme 2/14/85 Goddard Flight Ctr., MD	2.00
UC59	36¢ Travel Aerogramme 5/21/85 DC	2.00
UC60	36¢ Halley's Comet Aerogramme 12/4/85 DC	2.00
UC61	39¢ Letters Aerogramme 5/9/88 Miami, FL	2.00
UC62	39¢ Montgomery Blair Aerogramme 11/20/89 DC	2.00
UC63	45¢ Eagle Aerogramme 5/17/91, Denver, CO, blue paper	2.00
UC63a	45¢ Eagle Aerogramme 5/17/91 Denver, CO, white paper	2.00
UC64	50¢ Thaddeus Lowe Aerogramme 9/23/95 Tampa, FL	2.25
UC65	60¢ Voyager National Park Aerogramme 5/15/99	2.50

OFFICIAL POSTAL STATIONARY

Scott #	Description	Cacheted
UO73	20¢ Eagle 1/12/83 DC, size 10	1.75
	Size 10, window	3.50
UO74	22¢ Eagle 2/26/85 DC, size 10	1.75
	Size 10, window	3.50
UO75	22¢ Eagle, Savings Bond size, window 3/2/87 DC	3.75
UO76	25¢ "E" Eagle Savings Bond size, window 3/22/88 DC	2.00
UO77	25¢ Eagle 4/11/88 DC, size 10	2.00
	Size 10, window	3.50
UO78	25¢ Eagle, Savings Bond size, window, no printing on back flap, 4/11/88, DC	1.75
U078x	25¢ Eagle, Savings Bond size, window, with printing on back flap, 11/28/88, DC	2.00
UO79	45¢ Eagle 3/17/90, Springfield, VA, passport size, gummed flap	2.25
UO80	65¢ Eagle 3/17/90, Springfield, VA, passport size, gummed flap	2.50
UO81	45¢ Eagle 8/10/90, DC, passport size, self-seal flap	2.25
UO82	65¢ Eagle 8/10/90, DC, passport size, self-seal flap	2.50
UO83	29¢ "F" Eagle, Savings Bond size, window, 1/22/91, DC	2.00
UO84	29¢ Eagle 4/6/91 Oklahoma City, OK, size 10	2.00
	Size 10, window	3.50
U084r	29¢ Eagle, size 10, recycled paper 5/1/92, Kansas City, MO	2.50
	Size 10, window, recycled paper	2.50
U085	29¢ Eagle, Savings Bond size, window 4/17/91, DC	1.75
U085r	29¢ Eagle, size 10, recycled paper 5/1/92, Kansas City, MO	2.50
UO86	52¢ Consular Service 7/10/92, DC, passport size, lightweight paper	2.50
U086x	52¢ Consular Service 3/2/94, DC, passport size, heavyweight paper	10.00
UO87	75¢ Consular Service 7/10/92, DC, passport size, lightweight paper	2.75
UO87x	52¢ Consular Service 3/2/94, DC, passport size, heavyweight paper	10.00

U.S. First Day Covers

U089

UX220

Scott #	Description	Uncacheted	Cacheted
	POSTAL CARD FIRST DAY COVERS		
	1973-99 (cont.)		
UO88	32¢ Eagle 5/9/95, DC, size 10		2.00
	Size 10, window		3.50
UO89	33¢ Eagle 2/22/99, DC, size 10		2.00
UO90	34¢ Eagle 2/27/01, DC, size 10		2.00
UO91	37¢ Eagle 7/2/02, DC, size 10		2.00
	1873-1966		
UX1	1¢ Liberty 5/13/1873 Boston, NY, or DC	3000.00	...
UX37	3¢ McKinley 2/1/26 DC	250.00	...
UX38	2¢ Franklin 11/16/51 New York, NY	...	2.00
UX39	2¢ on 1¢ Jefferson (UX27) 1/1/52 DC	12.50	25.00
UX40	2¢ on 1¢ Lincoln (UX28) 3/22/52 DC	40.00	100.00
UX43	2¢ Lincoln 7/31/52 DC	...	2.00
UX44	2¢ FIPEX 5/4/56 New York, NY	...	2.00
UX45	4¢ Liberty 11/16/56 New York, NY	...	2.00
UX46	3¢ Liberty 8/1/58 Philadelphia, PA	...	2.00
UX46a	Missing "I"/"N God We Trust"	125.00	200.00
UX46c	Precancelled 9/15/61	50.00	...
UX48	4¢ Lincoln 11/19/62 Springfield, IL	...	2.00
UX48a	4¢ Lincoln, tagged 6/25/66 Bellevue, OH	35.00	50.00
	7/6/66 DC	4.50	10.00
	Bellevue, OH	20.00	35.00
	Cincinnati, OH	15.00	20.00
	Cleveland, OH	18.00	30.00
	Columbus, OH	20.00	35.00
	Dayton, OH	10.00	18.00
	Indianapolis, IN	20.00	35.00
	Louisville, KY	20.00	35.00
	Overlook, OH	15.00	20.00
	Toledo, OH	20.00	35.00
	1963-87		
UX49	7¢ USA 8/30/63 New York, NY		2.00
UX50	4¢ Customs 2/22/64 DC		2.00
UX51	4¢ Social Security 9/26/64 DC		2.00
UX52	4¢ Coast Guard 8/4/65 Newburyport, MA		2.00
UX53	4¢ Census Bureau 10/21/65 Phila, PA		2.00
UX54	8¢ USA 12/4/67 DC		2.00
UX55	5¢ Lincoln 1/4/68 Hodgenville, KY		2.00
UX56	5¢ Women Marines 7/26/68 San Fran., CA		2.00
UX57	5¢ Weathervane 9/1/70 Fort Myer, VA		2.00
UX58	6¢ Paul Revere 5/15/71 Boston, MA		2.00
UX59	10¢ USA 6/10/71 New York, NY		2.00
UX60	6¢ America's Hospitals 9/16/71 NY, NY		2.00
UX61	6¢ US Frigate Constellation 6/29/72 Any City		2.00
UX62	6¢ Monument Valley 6/29/72 Any City		2.00
UX63	6¢ Gloucester, MA 6/29/72 Any City		2.00
UX64	6¢ John Hanson 9/1/72 Baltimore, MD		2.00
UX65	6¢ Liberty Centenary 9/14/73 DC		2.00
UX66	8¢ Samuel Adams 12/16/73 Boston, MA		2.00
UX67	12¢ Ship's Figurehead 1/4/74 Miami, FL		2.00
UX68	7¢ Charles Thomson 9/14/75 Bryn Mawr, PA		2.00
UX69	9¢ J. Witherspoon 11/10/75 Princeton, NJ		2.00
UX70	9¢ Caeser Rodney 7/1/76 Dover, DE		2.00
UX71	9¢ Galveston Court House 7/20/77 Galveston, TX		2.00
UX72	9¢ Nathan Hale 10/14/77 Coventry, CT		2.00
UX73	10¢ Music Hall 5/12/78 Cincinnati, OH		2.00
UX74	(10¢) John Hancock 5/19/78 Quincy, MA		2.00
UX75	10¢ John Hancock 6/20/78 Quincy, MA		2.00
UX76	14¢ Coast Guard Eagle 8/4/78 Seattle, WA		2.00
UX77	10¢ Molly Pitcher 9/8/78 Freehold, NJ		2.00
UX78	10¢ George R. Clark 2/23/79 Vincennes, IN		2.00
UX79	10¢ Casimir Pulaski 10/11/79 Savannah, GA		2.00
UX80	10¢ Olympics 9/17/79 Eugene, OR		2.00
UX81	10¢ Iolani Palace 10/1/79 Honolulu, HI		1.75
UX82	14¢ Olympic Skater 1/15/80 Atlanta, GA		2.00
UX83	10¢ Mormon Temple 4/5/80 Salt Lake City, UT		2.00
UX84	10¢ Count Rochambeau 7/11/80 Newport, RI		2.00
UX85	10¢ King's Mountain 10/7/80 King's Mountain, NC		2.00
UX86	19¢ Golden Hinde 11/21/80 San Rafael, CA		2.00
UX87	10¢ Battle of Cowpens 1/17/81 Cowpens, SC		2.00
UX88	(12¢) "B" Eagle 3/15/81 Memphis, TN		2.00
UX89	12¢ Isaiah Thomas 5/5/81 Worcester, MA		2.00
UX90	12¢ Nathaniel Greene 9/8/81 Eutaw Springs, SC		2.00
UX91	12¢ Lewis & Clark 9/23/81 St. Louis, MO		2.00
UX92	(13¢) Robert Morris 10/11/81 Memphis, TN		2.00
UX93	13¢ Robert Morris 11/10/81 Phila., PA		2.00

Scott #	Description	Cacheted
	1963-87 (cont.)	
UX94	13¢ Frances Marion 4/3/82 Marion, SC	2.00
UX95	13¢ LaSalle 4/7/82 New Orleans	2.00
UX96	13¢ Philadelphia Academy 6/18/82 Philadelphia, PA	2.00
UX97	13¢ St. Louis P.O. 10/14/82 St. Louis, MO	2.00
UX98	13¢ Oglethorpe 2/12/83 Savannah, GA	2.00
UX99	13¢ Old Washington P.O. 4/19/83 DC	2.00
UX100	13¢ Olympics - Yachting 8/5/83 Long Beach, CA	2.00
UX101	13¢ Maryland 3/25/84 St. Clemente Island, MD	2.00
UX102	13¢ Olympic Torch 4/30/84 Los Angeles, CA	2.00
UX103	13¢ Frederic Baraga 6/29/84 Marquette, MI	2.00
UX104	13¢ Rancho San Pedro 9/16/84 Compton, CA	2.00
UX105	(14¢) Charles Carroll 2/1/85 New Carrollton, MD	2.00
UX106	14¢ Charles Carroll 3/6/85 Annapolis, MD	2.00
UX107	25¢ Flying Cloud 2/27/85 Salem, MA	2.00
UX108	14¢ George Wythe 6/20/85 Williamsburg, VA	2.00
UX109	14¢ Settling of CT 4/18/86 Hartford, CT	2.00
UX110	14¢ Stamp Collecting 5/23/86 Chicago, IL	2.00
UX111	14¢ Frances Vigo 5/24/86 Vincennes, IN	2.00
UX112	14¢ Rhode Island 6/26/86 Providence, RI	2.00
UX113	14¢ Wisconsin Terr. 7/3/86 Mineral Point, WI	2.00
UX114	14¢ National Guard 12/12/86 Boston, MA	2.00
UX115	14¢ Steel Plow 5/22/87 Moines, IL	2.00
UX116	14¢ Constitution Convention 5/25/87 Philadelphia, PA	2.00
UX117	14¢ Flag 6/14/87 Baltimore, MD	2.00
UX118	14¢ Pride in America 9/22/87 Jackson, WY	2.00
UX119	14¢ Historic Preservation 9/28/87 Timberline, OR	2.00
	1988-91	
UX120	15¢ Bison 3/28/88 Buffalo, NY	2.00
UX121	15¢ Blair House 5/4/88 DC	2.00
UX122	28¢ Yorkshire 6/29/88 Mystic, CT	2.00
UX123	15¢ Iowa Territory 7/2/88 Burlington, IA	2.00
UX124	15¢ Northwest/Ohio Territory 7/15/88 Marietta, OH	2.00
UX125	15¢ Hearst Castle 9/20/88 San Simeon, CA	2.00
UX126	15¢ Federalist Papers 10/27/88 New York, NY	2.00
UX127	15¢ The Desert 1/13/89 Tucson, AZ	2.00
UX128	15¢ Healy Hall 1/23/89 DC	2.00
UX129	15¢ The Wetlands 3/17/89 Waycross, GA	2.00
UX130	15¢ Oklahoma Land Run 4/22/89 Guthrie, OK	2.00
UX131	21¢ The Mountains 5/5/89 Denver, CO	2.00
UX132	15¢ The Seashore 4/18/89 Cape Hatteras, NC	2.00
UX133	15¢ The Woodlands 8/26/89 Cherokee, NC	2.00
UX134	15¢ Hull House 9/16/89 Chicago, IL	2.00
UX135	15¢ Independence Hall 9/25/89 Philadelphia, PA	2.00
UX136	15¢ Baltimore Inner Harbor 10/7/89 Baltimore, MD	2.00
UX137	15¢ Manhattan Skyline 11/8/89 New York, NY	2.00
UX138	15¢ Capitol Dome 11/26/89 DC	2.00
UX139-42	15¢ Cityscape, sheet of 4 diff.views,rouletted 12/1/89 DC	10.00
	Separated set of 4 different views	8.00
UX143	15¢ White House, Picture PC, 11/30/89 DC	2.00
UX144	15¢ Jefferson Mem. Pict. PC, 12/2/89 DC	2.00
UX145	15¢ American Papermaking 3/13/90 New York, NY	2.00
UX146	15¢ Literacy 3/22/90 DC	2.00
UX147	15¢ Geo. Bingham Pict.PC, 5/4/90 St. Louis, MO	2.00
UX148	15¢ Isaac Royall House 6/16/90 Medford, MA	2.00
UX150	15¢ Stanford University 9/30/90 Stanford, CA	2.00
UX151	15¢ DAR Mem., Continental/Constitution Hall 10/11/91 DC	2.00
UX152	15¢ Chicago Orchestra Hall 10/19/91 Chicago, IL	2.00
UX153	19¢ Flag 1/24/91 DC	2.00
UX154	19¢ Carnegie Hall 4/1/91 New York, NY	2.00
UX155	19¢ "Old Red" Bldg., U.of Texas 6/14/91 Galveston, TX	2.00
UX156	19¢ Bill of Rights Bicent. 9/25/91 Notre Dame, IN	2.00
UX157	19¢ Notre Dame Admin. Bldg. 10/15/91 Notre Dame, IN	2.00
UX158	30¢ Niagara Falls 8/21/91 Niagara Falls, NY	2.00
UX159	19¢ Old Mill, Univ. of Vermont 10/29/91 Burlington, VT	2.00
	1992-03	
UX160	19¢ Wadsworth Atheneum 1/16/92 Hartford, CT	2.00
UX161	19¢ Cobb Hall, Univ. of Chicago 1/23/92 Chicago, IL	2.00
UX162	19¢ Waller Hall 2/1/92 Salem, OR	2.00
UX163	19¢ America's Cup 5/6/92 San Diego, CA	2.00
UX164	19¢ Columbia River Gorge 5/9/92 Stevenson, WA	2.00
UX165	19¢ Great Hall, Ellis Island 5/11/92 Ellis Island, NY	2.00
UX166	19¢ National Cathedral 1/6/93 DC	2.00

U.S. First Day Covers

Scott #	Description 1992-03 (cont.)	Cacheted
UX167	19¢ Wren Building 2/8/93 Williamsville, VA	2.00
UX168	19¢ Holocaust Memorial 3/23/93 DC	2.00
UX169	19¢ Ft. Recovery 6/13/93 Fort Recovery, OH	2.00
UX170	19¢ Playmaker's Theater 9/14/93 Chapel Hill, NC	2.00
UX171	19¢ O'Kane Hall 9/17/93 Worcester, MA	2.00
UX172	19¢ Beecher Hall 10/9/93 Jacksonville, IL	2.00
UX173	19¢ Massachusetts Hall 10/14/93 Brunswick, ME	2.00
UX174	19¢ Lincoln Home 2/12/94 Springfield, IL	2.00
UX175	19¢ Myers Hall 3/11/94 Springfield, OH	2.00
UX176	19¢ Canyon de Chelly 8/11/94 Canyon de Chelly, AZ	2.00
UX177	19¢ St. Louis Union Station 9/1/94 St. Louis, MO	2.00
UX178-97	19¢ Legends of the West, set of 20 10/18/94, Laramie, WY	40.00
	19¢ Legends of the West, set of 20 10/18/94 Tucson, AZ and Lawton, OK	50.00
	19¢ Legends of the West, Combo w/2689a-t	60.00
UX198	20¢ Red Barn 1/3/95 Williamsburg, PA	2.00
UX199	(20¢) "G" Old Glory, 12/13/94 cancel, released 1/12/95	2.00
UX200-19	20¢ Civil War Set of 20 6/29/95 Gettysburg, PA	40.00
	20¢ Civil War, combo w/2975a-t	60.00
UX220	20¢ Clipper Ship 9/23/95 Hunt Valley, MD	2.00
UX221-40	20¢ Comic Strips Set of 20 10/1/95 Boca Raton, FL	40.00
	20¢ Comic Strips, combo set	60.00
UX241	20¢ Winter Farm Scene 2/23/96 Watertown, NY	2.00
UX242-61	20¢ Olympics, Set of 20 5/2/96 DC	40.00
	20¢ Olympics, combo set	60.00
UX262	20¢ McDowell Hall, Hist.Pres.Series 6/1/96, Anapolis, MD	2.00
UX263	20¢ Alexander Hall, Hist.Pres.Series 9/20/96,Princeton, NJ	2.00
UX264-78	20¢ Endangered Species, Set of 15 10/2/96, San Diego, CA	40.00
	20¢ Endangered Species, combo set	60.00
UX279	20¢ Swans, set of 8 different cards	18.00
	New single card from set of 8	2.25
UX280	20¢ City College of NY, Hist.Pres.Series, NY,NY 5/7/97	2.00
UX281	32¢ Bugs Bunny, 5/22/97, Burbank, CA	2.00
UX282	20¢ Pacific '97, Golden Gate in Daylight 6/2/97 S.F.,Ca.	2.00
UX283	40¢ Pacific '97, Golden Gate at Sunset 6/2/97 S. F., Ca.	2.00
UX284	20¢ Fort McHenry, Hist. Pres. Series 9/97	2.00
UX285-89	20¢ Classic Movie Monsters, 9/30/97, Set of 5, Universal City, CA	11.00
	20¢ Classic Movie Monsters, combo set	16.00
UX290	20¢ University of Mississippi, 4/20/98, Univ. of Ms	2.00
UX291	20¢ Tweety & Sylvester, 4/27/98 NY, NY	2.00
UX292	20¢ Girard College, 5/1/98. Phil.,PA	2.00
UX293–96	20¢ Tropical Birds, Set of 4, 7/29/98, Ponce, PR	9.00
	20¢ Tropical Birds, combo set	13.50
UX297	20¢ Ballet 9/16/98, NY, NY	2.00
UX298	20¢ Northeastern Univ., 10/3/98, Boston, MA	2.00
UX299	20¢ Brandies Univ. 10/17/98, Waltham, MA	2.00
UX300	20¢ Love, 1/28/99, Loveland, CO	2.25
UX301	20¢ Univ. of Wisconsin, 2/5/99, Madison, WI	2.00
UX302	20¢ Washington & Lee Univ., 2/11/99, Lexington, VA	2.00
UX303	20¢ Redwood Library & Anthenaeum, 3/11/99	2.00
UX304	20¢ Daffy Duck, 4/16/99	2.25
UX305	20¢ Mount Vernon, 5/14/99, Mount Vernon, VA	2.00
UX306	20¢ Block Island Lighthouse, 7/24/99, Block Is., RI	2.00
UX307-11	20¢ All Aboard!, set of 5, 8/26/99, Cleveland, OH	10.00
UX307-11	Combo w/#3333-7	15.00
UX312	20¢ Univ. of Utah, 2/28/00, Salt Lake City, UT	2.00
UX313	20¢ Ryman Auditorium, 3/18/00, Nashville, TN	2.00
UX314	20¢ Wile E. Coyote & Roadrunner	2.25
UX314	20¢ Coyote & Roadrunner combo w/stamp	3.00
UX315	20¢ Adoption picture card, 5/10/00	2.25
	20¢ Adoption combo w/stamp	3.00
UX316	20¢ Middlebury College 5/19/00	2.00
UX317-36	20c Stars & Stripes, 6/14/00, Baltimore, MD set of 20	50.00
	Combo w/3403a-t, set of 20	70.00
UX337-56	20¢ Legends of Baseball, 7/6/00, Atlanta, GA set of 20	50.00
	Combo w/3408a-t, set of 20	70.00
UX357-60	20¢ Holiday Deer, 10/12/00, Rudolph, WI set of 4	11.00
	Combo w/3356-59 set of 4	16.00
UX361	20¢ Yale University,, 3/30/01, New Haaven, CT	2.00
UX362	20¢ University of South Carolina, 4/26/01, Columbia, SC	2.00
UX363	20¢ Northwestern University, 4/28/01, Evanston, IL	2.00
UX364	20¢ University of Portland, 5/1/01, Portland, OR	2.00
UX365-74	21¢ Baseball Fields 6/27/01 set of 10	30.00
	FD Cancels from Boston, MA; Chicago, IL; Detroit, MI, and New York, NY	
UX375	21¢ White Barn 9/20/01 DC	2.00
UX376	21¢ Porky Pig 10/1/01 Beverly Hills, CA	2.50
	21¢ Porky Pig combo with stamp	3.00
UX377-80	21¢ Santas 10/1/01 Sata Clause, IN set 4	11.00
	21¢ Santas combo with stamps set 4	16.00
UX381	21¢ Carlsbad Caverns 6/7/02, Carlsbad, NM	2.00
UX382-5	23¢ Teddy Bears 8/15/02, Atlantic City, NJ set of 4	11.00
	Combination with #3653-56	16.00
UX386-89	23¢ Snowmen 10/28/02 Houghton, MI, set of 4	11.00
	Combination with #3676-79	16.00
UX390-94	23¢ Old Glory 4/3/03, New York, NY,set of 5	13.50
	Combination with #3776-80	18.50
UX395-99	23¢ Lighthouses 6/13/03, Tybee Island, GA, set of 5	13.50
	Combination with #3787-91	18.50
UX400	23¢ Ohio University 10/10/03, Athens, OH	2.00
UX401-04	23¢ Music Makers 10/23/03, New York, NY, set of 4	11.00
	Combination with stamps	16.00
UX405	23¢ Columbia U Harriton House 3/25/04, New York, NY	2.00
UX390-94	23¢ Old Glory 1/25/03 New York, NY, set 5 picture cards	14.00
	Combination with stamps	16.00

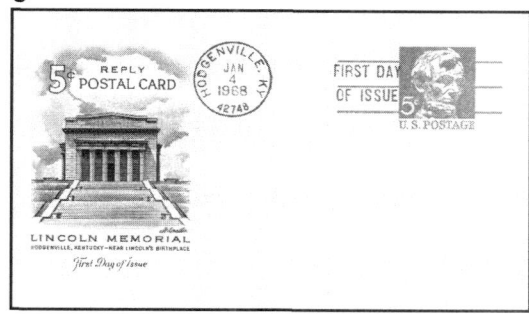

UY21

Scott #	Description 1992-03 (cont.)	Cacheted
UX395-99	23¢ Southeastern Lighthouses 6/13/03 Tybee Island, GA	
	Set 5 picture cards	14.00
	Combination w/stamps	16.00
UX401-04	23¢ Holiday Music Makers 10/23/03 New York, NY	
	Set 4 picture cards	11.00
	Combination w/stamps	13.00
UX---	23¢ Harriton House 6/1/04, Bryn Mawr, PA	2.05

AIRMAIL POST CARDS
1949-01

Scott #	Description	Cacheted
UXC1	4¢ Eagle 1/10/49, DC, in January 10	2.00
	Oval "O" in January 10	5.00
UXC2	5¢ Eagle 7/31/58 Wichita, KS	2.00
UXC3	5¢ Eagle w/border 6/18/60 Minneapolis, MN	2.00
	"Thin dividing line" at top	5.00
UXC4	6¢ Bald Eagle 2/15/63 Maitland, FL	2.00
UXC5	11¢ Visit the USA 5/27/66 DC	2.00
UXC6	6¢ Virgin Islands.3/31/67 Charlotte Amalie, VI	2.00
UXC7	6¢ Boy Scouts 8/4/67 Farragut State Park, ID	2.00
UXC8	13¢ Visit the USA 9/8/67 Detroit, MI	2.00
UXC9	8¢ Eagle 3/1/68 New York, NY	2.00
UXC9a	8¢ Eagle, tagged 5/19/69 Phil.	15.00
UXC10	9¢ Eagle 5/15/71 Kitty Hawk, NC	2.00
UXC11	15¢ Visit the USA 6/10/71 New York, NY	2.00
UXC12	9¢ Grand Canyon 6/29/72 any city	2.00
UXC13	15¢ Niagara Falls 6/29/72 any city	2.00
UXC14	11¢ Modern Eagle 1/4/74 State College, PA	2.00
UXC15	18¢ Eagle Weathervane 1/4/74 Miami, FL	2.00
UXC16	21¢ Angel Weathervane 12/17/75 Kitty Hawk, NC	2.00
UXC17	21¢ Jenny 9/16/78 San Diego, CA	2.00
UXC18	21¢ Olympic-Gymnast 12/1/79 Fort Worth, TX	2.00
UXC19	28¢ First Transpacific Flight 1/2/81 Wenatchee, WA	2.00
UXC20	28¢ Soaring 3/5/82 Houston, TX	2.00
UXC21	28¢ Olympic-Speedskating 12/29/83 Milwaukee, WI	2.00
UXC22	33¢ China Clipper 2/15/85 San Fran., CA	2.00
UXC23	33¢ AMERIPEX '86 2/1/86 Chicago, IL	2.00
UXC24	36¢ DC-3 5/14/88 San Diego, CA	2.00
UXC25	40¢ Yankee Clipper 6/28/91	2.00
UXC26	50¢ Eagle 8/24/95 St. Louis, MO	2.25
UXC27	55¢ Mt. Rainier, 5/15/99	2.25
UXC28	70c Badlands National Park, 2/22/01, Wall, SD	2.50

POSTAL REPLY CARDS

Scott #	Description	Uncacheted	Cacheted
UY1	1¢ + 1¢ U.S. Grant 10/25/1892 any city	350.00	...
UY12	3¢ + 3¢ McKinley 2/1/26 any city	250.00	...
UY13	2¢ + 2¢ Washington 12/29/51 DC	...	2.25
UY14	2¢ on 1¢ + 2¢ on 1¢ G. Wash. 1/1/52 any city	50.00	75.00
UY16	4¢ + 4¢ Liberty 11/16/56 New York, NY	...	2.00
UY16a	Message card printed on both halves	75.00	100.00
UY16b	Reply card printed on both halves	50.00	75.00
UY17	3¢ + 3¢ Liberty 7/31/58 Boise, ID		2.00
UY18	4¢ + 4¢ Lincoln 11/19/62 Springfield, IL		2.00
UY18a	4¢ + 4¢ Lincoln, Tagged 3/7/67 Dayton, OH		500.00
UY19	7¢ + 7¢ USA 8/30/63 New York, NY		2.00
UY20	8¢ + 8¢ USA 12/4/67 DC		2.00
UY21	5¢ + 5¢ Lincoln 1/4/68 Hodgenville, KY		2.00
UY22	6¢ + 6¢ Paul Revere 5/15/71 Boston, MA		2.00
UY23	6¢ + 6¢ John Hanson 9/1/72 Baltimore, MD		2.00
UY24	8¢ + 8¢ Samuel Adams 12/16/73 Boston, MA		2.00
UY25	7¢ + 7¢ Charles Thomson 9/14/75 Bryn Mawr, PA		2.00
UY26	9¢ + 9¢ John Witherspoon 11/10/75 Princeton, NJ		2.00
UY27	9¢ + 9¢ Caeser Rodney 7/1/76 Dover, DE		2.00
UY28	9¢ + 9¢ Nathan Hale 10/14/77 Coventry, CT		2.00
UY29	(10¢ + 10¢) John Hancock 5/19/78 Quincy, MA		2.50
UY30	10¢ + 10¢ John Hancock 6/20/78 Quincy, MA		2.00
UY31	(12¢ + 12¢) "B" Eagle 3/15/81 Memphis, TN		2.00
UY32	12¢ + 12¢ Isaiah Thomas 5/5/81 Worcester, MA		2.00
UY32a	"Small die"		5.00
UY33	(13¢ + 13¢) Robert Morris 10/11/81 Memphis, TN		2.00
UY34	13¢ + 13¢ Robert Morris 11/10/81 Philadelphia, PA		2.00
UY35	(14¢ + 14¢) Charles Carroll 2/1/85 New Carrollton, MD		2.00
UY36	14¢ + 14¢ Charles Carroll 3/6/85 Annapolis, MD		2.00
UY37	14¢ + 14¢ George Wythe 6/20/85 Williamsburg, PA		2.00
UY38	14¢ + 14¢ American Flag 9/1/87 Baltimore, MD		2.00
UY39	15¢ + 15¢ Bison 7/11/88 Buffalo, NY		2.00
UY40	19¢ + 19¢ American Flag 3/27/91 DC		2.00

POSTAL REPLY CARDS

Scott #	Description	Cacheted
UY41	20¢+20¢ Red Barn1/3/95 Williamsburg, PA	2.25
UY42	20¢+20¢ Block Island, 11/10/99, Block Island, RI	2.25
UY43	21¢+21¢ White Barn 9/20/01 DC	2.25
UY44	23¢ Carlsbad Caverns 6/7/02 Carlsbad, NM	2.25

OFFICIAL POSTAL CARDS
1983-95

UZ2	13¢ Eagle 1/12/83 DC	2.00
UZ3	14¢ Eagle 2/26/85 DC	2.00
UZ4	15¢ Eagle 6/10/88 New York, NY	2.00
UZ5	19¢ Eagle 5/24/91 Seattle, WA	2.00
UZ6	20¢ Eagle 5/9/95 DC	2.00

"POSTAL BUDDY" CARDS

PB1	15¢ 7/5/90 Merriifield, VA	5.00
PB2	19¢ 2/3/91 Any city	...
PB3	19¢ Stylized Flag 11/13/92 Any city	30.00

CHRISTMAS SEAL FIRST DAY COVERS

Beginning in 1936, Santa Claus, Indiana has been used as the First Day City of U.S. National Christmas Seals. In 1936 the Postmaster would not allow the seal to be tied to the front of the cover and seals for that year are usually found on the back. Since 1937, all seals were allowed to be tied on the front of the FDC's. **All prices are for cacheted FDC's.**

YEAR	PRICE
1936 (500 processed)	55.00
1937	35.00
1938	35.00
1939	35.00
1940	35.00
1941	30.00
1942	40.00
1943	25.00
1944	30.00
1945	12.00
1946	12.00
1947	12.00
1948	20.00
1949	12.00
1950	12.00
1951	15.00
1952	12.00
1953	10.00
1954	10.00
1955	10.00
1956	10.00
1957	10.00
1958	10.00
1959	10.00
1960	20.00
1961	10.00
1962	10.00
1963	10.00
1964	40.00
1965	10.00
1966	10.00
1967	20.00
1968	10.00

YEAR	PRICE
1968	10.00
1969	10.00
1970	6.00
1971	6.00
1972	6.00
1973	6.00
1974	6.00
1975	7.00
1976	10.00
1977	6.00
1978	10.00
1979	6.00
1980	5.00
1981	5.00
1982	5.00
1983	10.00
1984	5.00
1985	5.00
1986	5.00
1987	5.00

YEAR	PERF	IMPERF
1988	7.50	30.00
1989	7.50	30.00
1990	5.00	20.00
1991	5.00	20.00
1991-Foil	10.00	...
1992	7.50	35.00
1993	5.00	20.00
1994	5.00	20.00
1995	5.00	20.00
1996	5.00	20.00
1997	5.00	20.00
1998	5.00	20.00
1999	5.00	20.00

U.S. Plate No. Coil First Day Covers

1906

2280

The listing below omits prices on FDC's which are extremely rare or where sufficient pricing information is not available. *Due to market volatility, prices are subject to change without notice.* **Prices are for unaddressed FDC's with common cachets and cancels which do not obscure the Pl. #. Strips of 3 must have a plate # on the center stamp.**

Scott #	Description	Pl# Pr.	Pl# Str of 3
1891	18¢ Flag 4/24/81		
	Pl# 1	75.00	120.00
	Pl# 2	180.00	340.00
	Pl# 3	260.00	420.00
	Pl# 4	160.00	280.00
	Pl# 5	125.00	...
1895	20¢ Flag 12/17/81		
	Pl# 1	17.50	36.00
	Pl# 2	100.00	160.00
	Pl# 3	160.00	320.00
1897	1¢ Omnibus 8/19/83		
	Pl# 1,2	7.00	10.50
1897A	2¢ Locomotive 5/20/82		
	Pl# 3,4	10.50	17.00
1898	3¢ Handcar 3/25/83		
	Pl# 1,2,3,4	8.00	17.00
1898A	4¢ Stagecoach 8/19/82		
	Pl# 1,2,3,4	8.00	16.00
1899	5¢ Motorcycle 10/10/83		
	Pl# 1,2	9.00	13.50
	Pl# 3,4	...	...
1900	5.2¢ Sleigh 3/21/83		
	Pl# 1,2	13.50	27.00
1900a	Pl# 1,2	...	...
1901	5.9¢ Bicycle 2/17/82		
	Pl# 3,4	13.50	22.50
1901a	Pl# 3,4	...	...
1902	7.4¢ Baby Buggy 4/7/84		
	Pl# 2	8.50	18.00
1903	9.3¢ Mail Wagon 12/15/81		
	Pl# 1,2	18.00	34.00
	Pl# 3,4	...	...
1904	10.9¢ Hansom Cab 3/26/82		
	Pl# 1,2	14.50	32.50
1904a	Pl# 1,2	...	...
1905	11¢ Caboose 2/3/84, Pl# 1	13.50	32.50
1905a	11¢ Caboose, "B" Press 9/25/91		
	Pl#2	...	...
1906	17¢ Electric Car 6/25/82		
	Pl# 1,2	14.50	27.00
1907	18¢ Surrey 5/18/81		
	Pl# 1	27.00	...
	Pl# 2	17.50	40.00
	Pl# 3,4,7,9,10	...	...
	Pl# 5	100.00	...
	Pl# 6,8	100.00	...
1908	20¢ Fire Pumper 12/10/81		
	Pl# 1,7,8	...	...
	Pl# 2	150.00	240.00
	Pl# 3,4	13.50	36.00
	Pl# 5,6	100.00	175.00
2005	20¢ Consumer 4/27/82		
	Pl# 1,2,3,4	22.50	...
2112	(22¢) "D" Coil 2/1/85		
	Pl# 1,2	8.50	16.00
2115	22¢ Flag over Capitol 3/29/85		
	Pl# 1	32.50	57.50
	Pl# 2	13.50	20.00
2115b	22¢ Test Coil 5/23/87		
	Pl# T1	...	11.00
2123	3.4¢ School Bus 6/8/85		
	Pl# 1,2	5.50	8.50
2124	4.9¢ Buckboard 6/21/85		
	Pl# 3,4	6.00	11.50
2125	5.5¢ Star Route Truck 11/1/86		
	Pl# 1	6.00	11.50
2125a	Pl# 1	...	36.00
2126	6¢ Tricycle 5/6/85		
	Pl# 1	5.50	8.50
2126a	Pl# 1	...	...
2127	7.1¢ Tractor Coil 2/6/87, Pl# 1	6.50	11.50
2127a	Pl# 1	...	32.50
2127a	7.1¢ Zip + 4 Pl# 1 5/26/89	...	6.50
2128	8.3¢ Ambulance 6/21/86		
	Pl# 1,2	6.50	11.00
2128a	Pl# 1,2	...	...
2129	8.5¢ Tow Truck 1/24/87		
	Pl# 1	5.50	8.50

Scott #	Description	Pl# Pr.	Pl# Str of 3
2129a	Pl# 1	...	15.50
2130	10.1¢ Oil Wagon 4/18/85		
	Pl# 1	6.50	10.50
2130a	10.1¢ Red Prec. Pl# 2 6/27/88	...	7.50
2131	11¢ Stutz Bearcat 6/11/85		
	Pl# 3,4	...	11.00
2132	12¢ Stanley Steamer 4/2/85		
	Pl# 1,2	6.50	11.00
2132a	Pl# 1,2	...	...
2133	12.5¢ Pushcart 4/18/85		
	Pl# 1	6.50	11.00
2134	14¢ Iceboat 3/23/85		
	Pl# 1,2	8.50	13.50
2135	17¢ Dog Sled 8/20/86		
	Pl# 2	6.50	10.50
2136	25¢ Bread Wagon 11/22/86		
	Pl# 1	6.50	11.00
2149	18¢ GW Monument 11/6/85		
	Pl# 1112,3333	17.50	32.50
2149a	Pl# 11121	40.00	...
	Pl# 33333	40.00	...
2150	21.1¢ Pre-Sort 10/22/85		
	Pl# 111111	13.50	22.50
2150a	Pl# 111111	35.00	...
2225	1¢ Omnibus Re-engraved 11/26/86		
	Pl# 1	5.50	11.00
2226	2¢ Locomotive Re-engraved 3/6/87		
	Pl# 1	...	7.00
2228	4¢ Stagecoach, "B" Press 8/15/86 (eku)		
	Pl# 1	...	260.00
2231	8.3¢ Ambulance, "B" Press 8/29/86 (eku)		
	Pl# 1	...	...
2252	3¢ Conestoga Wagon 2/29/88		
	Pl# 1	...	6.00
2253	5¢ Milk Wagon 9/25/87		
	Pl# 1	...	6.00
2254	5.3¢ Elevator 9/16/88		
	Pl# 1	...	6.00
2255	7.6¢ Carreta 8/30/88		
	Pl# 1	...	6.50
2256	8.4¢ Wheelchair 8/12/88		
	Pl# 1	...	6.50
2257	10¢ Canal Boat 4/11/87		
	Pl# 1	...	7.50
2258	13¢ Patrol Wagon 10/29/88		
	Pl# 1	...	6.50
2259	13.2¢ Coal Car 7/19/88		
	Pl# 1	...	6.50
2260	15¢ Tugboat 7/12/88		
	Pl# 1	...	6.50
2261	16.7¢ Popcorn Wagon 7/7/88		
	Pl# 1	...	6.50
2262	17.5¢ Racing Car 9/25/87		
	Pl# 1	...	7.50
2263	20¢ Cable Car 10/28/88		
	Pl# 1	...	6.50
	Pl# 2	...	60.00
2264	20.5¢ Fire Engine 9/28/88		
	Pl# 1	...	6.50
2265	21¢ Railroad Mail Car 8/16/88		
	Pl# 1	...	6.50
	Pl# 2	...	...
2266	24.1¢ Tandem Bicycle 10/26/88		
	Pl# 1	...	6.50
2279	(25¢) "E" & Earth 3/22/88		
	Pl# 1111,1222	...	6.50
	Pl# 1211	...	8.50
	Pl# 2222	...	22.50
2280	25¢ Flag over Yosemite 5/20/88		
	Pl# 1,2	...	8.50
	Pl# 3,4	...	125.00
2280v	Pre-Phosphor Paper 2/14/89		
	Pl# 5	...	16.00
	Pl# 6,9	...	32.50
	Pl# 7,8	...	7.50
	Pl# 10	...	...
2281	25¢ Honeybee 9/2/88		
	Pl# 1	...	8.50
	Pl# 2	...	27.00
2451	4¢ Steam Carriage 1/25/91, Pl# 1	...	5.50

U.S. Plate No. Coil First Day Covers

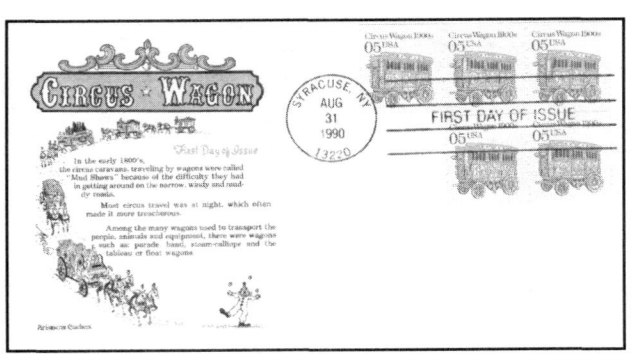

2452

Scott #	Description	Pl# Pr.	Pl# Str of 3
2452	5¢ Circus Wagon 8/31/90, Pl# 1	...	5.50
2452B	5¢ Circus Wagon, Gravure 12/8/92, Pl# A1,A2	...	5.50
2452D	5¢ Circus Wagon, SV 3/20/95, Pl# S1	...	5.50
2453	5¢ Canoe 5/25/91, Pl# 1	...	5.50
2454	5¢ Canoe, Gravure Print 10/22/91, Pl# S11	...	5.50
2457	10¢ Tractor Trailer 5/25/91, Pl# 1	...	5.50
2458	Tractor Trailer 5/25/91, a1 Pl# 1 & 2	...	...
2463	20¢ Cog Railroad 6/9/95, Pl#1	...	6.50
2464	23¢ Lunch Wagon 4/12/91		
	Pl# 2	...	7.50
	Pl# 3	...	6.50
2466	32¢ Ferryboat 6/2/95		
	Pl# 2-3	...	6.50
	Pl# 4	...	13.50
	Pl# 5	...	32.50
2468	$1.00 Seaplane 4/20/90, Pl# 1	...	8.50
2491	29¢ Pine Cone (self-adhesive)11/5/93, Pl# B1	...	8.50
2492	32¢ Rose (self-adhesive) 6/2/95, Pl# S111	...	8.50
2495A	32¢ Peaches and Pears (self-adhesive) 7/8/95		
	Pl# A11111	...	8.50
2518	(29¢) "F" & Flower 1/22/91		
	Pl# 1111,1222,2222,1211	...	8.50
	Pl# 2211	...	22.50
2523	29¢ Flag over Mt. Rushmore 3/29/91, Pl# 1-7	6.50	...
2523A	29¢ Mt. Rushmore, Gravure Print 7/4/91		
	Pl# 11111	...	6.50
2525	29¢ Flower, rouletted 8/16/91, Pl# S1111, S2222	...	6.50
2526	29¢ Flower, perforated 3/3/92, Pl# 2222	6.50	...
2529	(19¢) Fishing Boat 8/8/91		
	Pl# 1111,1212	...	6.50
2529c	(19¢) Fishing Boat 6/25/94, Pl# S111	...	6.50
2599	29¢ Statue of Liberty (self-adhesive) 6/24/94		
	Pl# D1111	...	8.50
2602	10¢ Eagle & Shield, **ABNCo** 12/13/91	...	5.50
	Any Pl# **(except A12213 & A32333)**	...	5.50
	Pl# A12213	...	24.00
	Pl# A32333	...	125.00
2603	10¢ Eagle & Shield, **BEP** 5/29/93, Pl# 11111	...	5.50
2604	10¢ Eagle & Shield, **SV**, Pl# S1111	...	5.50
2607	23¢ Flag, First Class pre-sort 9/27/91	...	6.50
2608	23¢ "USA" First Class pre-sort **ABNCo**, 7/21/92		
	Pl# A1111, A2222	...	6.50
2608A	23¢ "USA" First Class pre-sort **BEP**, 10/9/92		
	Pl# 1111	...	6.50
2608B	23¢ "USA" First Class pre-sort **SV**, 5/14/93		
	Pl# S111	...	6.50
2609	29¢ Flag over White House 4/23/92		
	Pl# 1-7	...	5.25
	Pl# 8	...	...
2799-2809	29¢ Christmas (self-adhesive) 10/28/93		
	Pl# V1111111	...	8.50
2813	29¢ Love (self-adhesive) 1/27/94		
	Pl# B1	...	8.50
2873	29¢ Santa (self-adhesive) 10/20/94		
	Pl# V1111	...	8.50
2886	(32¢) "G" Flag (self-adhesive) 12/13/94		
	Pl# V11111	...	6.50
2888	(32¢) "G" Flag 12/13/94, Pl# S11111	...	6.50
2889	(32¢) "G" Flag 12/13/94		
	Pl# 1111, 2222	...	6.50
2890	(32¢) "G" Flag 12/13/94		
	Pl# A1111, A1112, A1113, A1211, A1212,		
	A1222, A1311, A1313, A1314, A1324, A1417,		
	A1433, A2211, A2212, A2214, A2223,		
	A2313, A3113, A3114, A3315, A3323, A3423,		
	A3324, A3426, A3433, A3435, A3536, A4426,		
	A4427, A5327, A5417, A5427, A5437	...	8.50
2890	(32¢) "G" Flag 12/13/94 ,Pl# A4435	...	200.00
2891	(32¢) "G" Flag 12/13/94, Pl# S111	...	6.50
2892	(32¢) "G" Flag 12/13/94, Pl# S1111,S2222	...	6.50
2893	(32¢) "G" Flag 12/13/94, Pl# A11111, A21111	...	6.50
2902	5¢ Butte 3/10/95	...	5.50
2902b	5¢ ButteSV, self-adhesive 6/15/96		
	Pl# S111	...	5.50
2903	5¢ Mountains, BEP, 3/16/96, Pl# 11111	...	5.50
2904	5¢ Mountains, SV, 3/16/96, Pl# S11	...	5.50
2904a	5¢ Mountains,SA, 6/15/96		
	Pl# V222222, V333333, V333323		
	V333342, V333343	...	5.50
	Pl# S11111	...	6.50

Scott #	Description	Pl# Pr.	Pl# Str of 3
2911	25¢ Juke Box, BEP 3/17/95		
	Pl# S111111	...	6.50
2905	10¢ Auto, 3/10/95, Pl # S111	...	6.50
2906	10¢ Auto,SA 6/15/96, Pl # S111	...	5.50
2907	10¢ Eagle & Shield, SA 5/21/96, Pl # S1111	...	5.50
2908	15¢ Auto Tail Fin, BEP, 3/17/95, Pl# 11111	...	6.50
2909	15¢ Auto Tail Fin, SV, 3/17/95, Pl# S1111	...	6.50
2912	25¢ Juke Box, 3/17/95, Pl# 111	...	6.50
2912a	25¢ Juke Box,SV,SA 6/15/96, Pl# S11111	...	6.50
2912b	25¢ Juke Box,BEP,SA 6/15/96, Pl# 11111	...	6.50
2913	32¢ Flag over Porch 4/18/95		
	Pl# 11111,22222,33333,44444,S11111	...	8.50
	Pl# 22221	...	13.50
	Pl# 45444,66646	...	30.00
2914	32¢ Flag over Porch SV 5/19/95, Pl# S11111	...	8.50
2915A	32¢ Flag over Porch BEP (self-adhesive) 5/21/96		
	Pl# 55555,66666,78777	...	8.50
	Pl# 87888	...	50.00
	Pl# 87898,88888	...	8.50
	Pl# 88898	...	500.00
	Pl# 89878	...	8.50
	Pl# 89888	...	50.00
	Pl# 89898	...	17.50
	Pl# 97898,99999	...	8.50
2915B	32¢ Flag over Porch SV (self-adhesive) 6/15/96		
	Pl# S11111	...	8.50
2915C	32¢ Flag over Porch BEP (self-adhesive) 5/21/96		
	serpentine die-cut Pl# 66666	...	22.50
3017	32¢ Christmas (self-adhesive) 9/30/95		
	Pl# V1111	...	8.50
3018	32¢ Christmas Angel (self-adhesive) 10/31/95		
	Pl# B1111	...	8.50
3044	1¢ Kestrel 1/20/96, Pl# 1111	...	5.50
3045	2¢ Woodpecker, 6/22/99, Pl#11111	...	5.50
3053	20¢ Blue Jay (self-adhesive)8/2/96, Pl# S111	...	6.50
3054	32¢ Yellow Rose, S/A, 8/1/97		
	Pl# 1111,1112,1122,2222,2223,2333,3344,		
	3444,4455,5455,5555,5556,5566,5666	...	8.00
3055	20¢ Ring-Necked Pheasant, 7/31/98, Pl#1111	...	7.00
3207	(5¢) Wetlands, 6/5/98, Pl#S111	...	6.50
3207A	(5¢) Welands S/A, 121/14/98, Pl#1111	...	6.50
3208	(25¢) Diner, 6/5/98, Pl# S111	...	7.00
3208A	(25¢) Diner, 9/30/98, Pl#1111	...	7.00
3228	(10¢) Bicycle S/A, 8/14/98, Pl#111,221,222,333	...	7.00
3229	(10¢) Bicycle, 8/14/98, Pl#S111	...	7.00
3263	22¢ Uncle Sam, 11/9/98, Pl# 111	...	7.50
3264	(33¢) "H" Hat, 11/9/98, Pl#1111,3333,3343,3344,3444	...	8.00
3265	(33¢) "H" Hat S/A, 11/9/98, Pl#1111,1131,2222,3333	...	8.00
3266	(33¢) "H" Hat S/A w/gaps, 11/9/98, Pl#1111	...	8.00
3270	(10¢) Eagle & Shield, 12/14/98, Pl#1111	...	6.50
3271	(10¢) Eagle & Shield S/A, 12/14/98, Pl#11111	...	6.50
3280	33¢ Flag & City, 2/25/99, Pl#1111,2222	...	8.00
3281	33¢ Flag & City S/A, 2/25/99, Pl#1111,2222,3333,3433,		
	4443,4444,5555	...	8.00
3281	33¢ Flag & City S/A w/gaps, 2/25/99, Pl#1111,1222	...	8.00
3404-07	34c Fruit Berries, 6/16/00, Pl#G1111	...	8.00
3447	(10c) Lion Statue, 11/9/00, Pl#S11111	...	6.50
3452	(34c) Statue of Liberty W/A, 12/15/00, Pl#1111	...	7.00
3453	(34c) Statue of Liberty S/A, 21/15/00, Pl#1111	...	7.00
3458-61	(34c) Flowers S/A, 12/15/00, Pl#B1111	...	8.00
3466	34c Statue of Liberty S/A, 1/7/01, Pl#1111	...	7.00
3467	34c Statue of Liberty W/A, 2/7/01, Pl#1111	...	7.00
3468	34c Statue of Liberty S/A, 27/01, Pl#3333	...	7.00
3475	21c Bison S/A, 2/22/01, Pl#V1111	...	6.50
3475A	23c George Washington 9/22/01 Pl#B11	...	6.50
3520	(10c) Atlas Statue 6/29/01 Pl#B111	...	6.00
3522	(15c) Woody Wagon 8/31/01 Pl#S1111	...	6.50
3612	5c Toleware coil 5/31/02, Pl#S1111111	...	6.50
3615	3c Star S/A coil 6/7/02 (+34c), S111	...	6.50
3617	23c Washington S/A coil 6/7/02, V11, V22	...	6.50
3622	37¢ US Flag 6/7/02 S/A coil, 1111, 2222	...	6.50
3631	37¢ US Flag 6/7/02 W/A coil, S1111	...	6.50
3632	37¢ US Flag 6/7/02 S/A coil, 1111, 2222, 3333, 4444	...	6.50
3633	37¢ US Flag 6/7/02 coil separated, B1111	...	6.50
3638-41	37c Antique Toys 7/26/02 S/A coil, B11111, B12222	Strip of 5...	7.25
3680-83	37c Snowmen S/A coil 10/28/02, G1111, G1112	Strip of 3...	7.25
3693	5c Sea Coast coil 10/21/02, B111	...	6.50
3757	1c Tiffany Lamp 3/1/03 (37¢)	...	6.50
3769	10c Lion Statue 2/4/03	...	6.50
3775	5c Sea Coast 3/19/03	...	6.50
3792-3801	25c American Eagle 6/26/03, S1111111, S2222222		
	S3333333, PNC 5+5	...	8.00
3829	37¢ Snowy Egret 10/24/03, V1111, V2111, V3222	...	6.50

Scott #	Description	Pl# Pr.	Pl# Str of 3
	OFFICIAL STAMPS		
O135	20¢ Official, Pl# 1	25.00	75.00
O139	(22¢) "D" Official, Pl# 1	30.00	75.00
O159	37¢ Official Mail coil 8/2/02, S111	6.50	

COMPUTER VENDED POSTAGE

CV31	29¢ Variable Rate Coil 8/20/92		
	Pl# 1	...	7.00
CV31	29¢ Variable Rate 8/20/92, 1st Print		
	Pl# 1	...	7.00
CV31b	29¢ Variable Rate 8/20/92, 2nd Print		
	Pl# 1	...	22.50
CV32	29¢ Variable Rate 8/20/92		
	Pl# A11	...	7.00

U.S. Inauguration Covers

Values listed below from 1901 thru 1925 are for Picture Postcards with Washington DC Cancels
with or without content relating to the Inauguration or Washington DC related items.

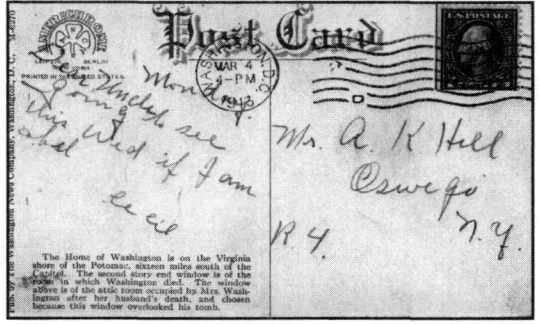

1913 WILSON WITHOUT CONTENT

		Without Content	With Content
1901	McKinley, 3/4/01	1000.00	1500.00
1901	McKinley, 9/7/01, Assassination Day on cover with add-on cachet	...	1650.00
1901	McKinley, 9/14/01, Day of Death with add-on cachet	...	1500.00
1905	Teddy Roosevelt, 3/4/05	350.00	500.00
1909	Taft, 3/4/09	200.00	250.00
1913	Wilson, 3/4/13	300.00	400.00
1917	Wilson, 3/5/17	350.00	450.00
1921	Harding, 3/4/21	400.00	500.00
1925	Coolidge, 3/4/25	400.00	500.00

1937 FRANKLIN D. ROOSEVELT

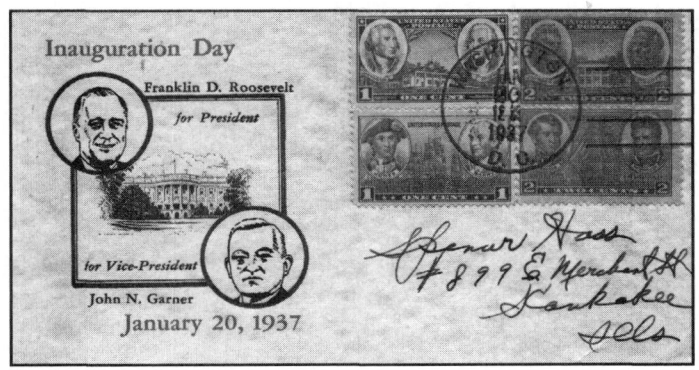

1969 RICHARD NIXON

Prices are for covers with PRINTED CACHETS and Wash, D.C. cancels.
Covers with cancels from other cities, except as noted, sell for somewhat less.

1929	Hoover 3/4/29	250.00
1929	Hoover 3/4/29 **(Rubber Stamp Cachet)**	150.00
1933	Roosevelt 3/4/33	60.00
1937	Roosevelt 1/20/37	225.00
1941	Roosevelt 1/20/41	225.00
1945	Roosevelt 1/20/45	225.00
1945	Truman 4/12/45	250.00
1949	Truman 1/20/49	70.00
1953	Eisenhower 1/20/53	16.00
1957	Eisenhower 1/21/57	12.00

1961	Kennedy 1/20/61	20.00
1963	Johnson 11/22/63 Any City	100.00
1965	Johnson 1/20/65	8.00
1969	Nixon 1/20/69	10.00
1973	Nixon 1/20/73	8.00
1974	Ford 8/9/74	6.00
1977	Carter 1/20/77	4.00
1981	Reagan 1/20/81	4.00
1985	Reagan 1/20/85	3.50
1989	Bush 1/20/89	3.50
1993	Clinton 1/20/93	3.00
1997	Clinton 1/20/97	3.00

Brookman Is Your #1 Source For World War II Patriotic Covers

Brookman carries the broadest stock of World War II Patriotic Covers available. These handsomely cacheted covers depict people, places and events that made history during those momentous days. Order from Pages 205-206 or write/call for our latest list.

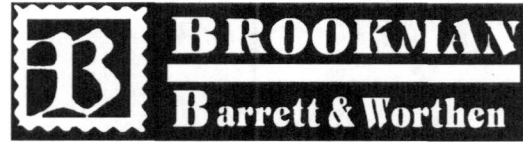

World War II & Korean War Patriotic Covers

3/8/45

The listing below features the dates of significant patriotic events of World War II. The values listed are for standard size covers bearing related, printed cachets, and cancelled on the appropriate date.

Cachets produced by Minkus and others, which feature general patriotic themes such as "Win the War" are valued at 75¢ unused and $2.00 used.

Covers with Naval cancels, when available, usually sell for twice the listed prices.

WORLD WAR II EVENT	CACHETED COVER
Pearl Harbor 12/7/41	100.00
U.S. Declares War on Japan 12/8/41	75.00
Germany and Italy Declare War on U.S. 12/11/41	75.00
U.S. Declares War on Germany and Italy 12/11/41	75.00
Churchill Arrives at the White House 12/22/41	60.00
Manila and Cavite Fall 1/2/42	60.00
Roosevelt's Diamond Jubilee Birthday 1/30/42	60.00
Singapore Surrenders 2/15/42	60.00
Japan Takes Java 3/10/42	60.00
Marshall Arrives in London 4/8/42	60.00
Dedication of MacArthur Post Office 4/15/42	60.00
Doolittle Air Raid on Tokyo 4/18/42	60.00
Fort Mills Corregidor Island Surrenders 5/6/42	60.00
Madagascar Occupied by U.S. 5/9/42	60.00
Mexico at War with Axis 5/23/42	60.00
Bremen Bombed 6/30/42	60.00
Bombing of Cologne 6/6/42	60.00
Japan Bombs Dutch Harbor, AK 6/3/42	60.00
Six German Spies Sentenced to Death 8/7/42	60.00
Brazil at War 8/22/42	60.00
Battle of El Alamein 10/23/42	70.00
Operation Torch (Invasion of North Africa) 11/8/42	50.00
Gas Rationing in U.S. 12/1/42	50.00
The Casablanca Conference 1/14/43	50.00
The Casablanca Conference (You must remember this!) 1/22/43	40.00
Russia takes Rostov 2/14/43	35.00
Point Rationing 3/1/43	50.00
Restoration Day, Honolulu 3/10/43	50.00
Battle of the Bismarck Sea 3/13/43	40.00
U.S. Planes Bomb Naples 4/5/43	50.00
Bizerte & Tunis Occupied 5/8/43	40.00
Invasion of Attu 5/11/43	40.00
U.S. Invades Rendova Island 6/30/43	35.00
Allies Occupy Tobriand + Woodlark 7/1/43	35.00
Siciliy Invaded 7/14/43	35.00
Yanks Bomb Rome 7/19/43	35.00
Mussolini Kicked Out 7/25/43	35.00
Fascist Regime is Dissolved 7/28/43	35.00
The Quebec Conference 8/14/43	40.00
Sicily Encircled 8/17/43	35.00
Japenese Flee From Kiska 8/21/43	35.00
Italy Invaded 9/3/43	40.00
Italy Surrenders 9/8/43	40.00
3rd War Loan Drive 9/9/43	40.00
Mussolini Escapes 9/18/43	35.00
Naples Captured 10/1/43	50.00
U.S. Drives Germans out of Naples 10/2/43	35.00
Italy Declares War on Germany 10/13/43	35.00
Hull, Eden, Stalin Conference 10/25/43	35.00
U.S. Government takes over Coal Mines 11/3/43	35.00
The Cairo Meeting 11/25/43	40.00
The Teheran Meeting 11/28/43	40.00
Roosevelt, Churchill, Kai-Shek at Cairo 12/2/43	40.00
FDR, Stalin, Churchill Agree on 3 fronts 12/4/43	40.00
2nd Anniversary of Pearl Harbor 12/7/43	40.00
US Runs the Railroads 12/28/43	40.00
UN Declaration Signed in Washington 1/1/44	40.00
Soviets Reach Polish Border 1/4/44	35.00
Marshalls Invaded 2/4/44	35.00
Yanks Take Over Kwajalein 2/5/44	35.00
Truk Attacked 2/18/44	35.00
U.S. Captures Cassino 3/16/44	35.00
Last Day of 2 Cent Rate 3/25/44	
Last Day of 2 Cent Rate and First Day of 3 cent Rate-Honolulu 3/26/44	35.00
Title of Military Governor	35.00

WORLD WAR II EVENT	CACHETED COVER
Invasion of Dutch New Guinea 4/24/44	35.00
Sevastopol Seige 5/11/44	35.00
Yanks Finally Capture Cassino 5/18/44	40.00
Rome Falls 6/4/44	35.00
D-Day Single Face Eisenhower 6/6/44	100.00
D-Day Double Face Eisenhower 6/6/44	35.00
D-Day: Invasion of Normandy 6/6/44	35.00
5th War Loan Drive 6/12/44	40.00
B29's Bomb Japan 6/15/44	35.00
Yanks Land on Siepan 6/17/44	35.00
Cherbourg Surrenders 6/27/44	40.00
Paris Revolts 6/23/44	35.00
Caen Falls to Allies 7/10/44	35.00
Relinquished Territory of Hawaii 7/21/44	50.00
Marines Invade Guam 7/21/44	35.00
Waikiki Conference-Honolulu 7/28/44	40.00
Yanks Enter Brest, etc. 8/7/44	35.00
Yanks Capture Guam 8/10/44	40.00
Roosevelt and Mac Aruther in Hawaii 8/10/44	40.00
U.S. Bombs Phillipines 8/10/44	35.00
Alies Invade Southern France 8/15/44	40.00
Invasion of Southern France 8/16/44	25.00
Liberation of Paris 8/23/44	30.00
Romania Joins Allies 8/23/44	35.00
Florence Falls to Allies 8/23/44	30.00
Liberation of Brussels 9/4/44	25.00
Antwerp Liberated 9/4/44	40.00
We Invade Holland, Finland Quits 9/5/44	30.00
Soviets Invade Yugoslavia 9/6/44	30.00
Russians Enter Bulgaria 9/9/44	30.00
We Invade Luxembourg 9/9/44	30.00
Liberation of Luxembourg 9/10	25.00
U.S. First Army Invades Germany 9/11/44	30.00
Lights Go On Again in England 9/17/44	30.00
Albania Invaded 9/27/44	35.00
Phillines, We Will Be Back 9/27/44	25.00
Greece Invaded 10/5/44	35.00
Liberation of Athens 10/14/44	25.00
Liberation of Belgrade 10/16/44	25.00
Flying Tigers Raid Hong Kong 10/16/44	35.00
Russia Invades Czechoslovakia 10/19/44	30.00
Invasion of the Philippines 10/20/44	25.00
The Pied Piper of Leyte-Philippine Invasion 10/21/44	35.00
Martial Law Abolished-Honolulu 10/24/44	40.00
Invasion of Norway 10/25/44	25.00
Cairo Meeting 11/2/44	50.00
Liberation of Tirana 11/18/44	25.00
France Joins UN 1/10/45	50.00
100,000 Yanks Land on Luzon 1/10/45	25.00
Liberation of Warsaw 1/17/45	30.00
Warsaw Recaptured 1/17/45	30.00
Russians Drive to Oder River 2/2/45	25.00
Liberation of Manila 2/4/45	30.00
Yalta Conference 2/12/45	25.00
Liberation of Budapest 2/13/45	25.00
Corregidor Invaded 2/16/45	25.00
Bataan Falls 2/16/45	25.00
Corregidor is Ours 2/17/45	25.00
Turkey Wars Germany and Japan 2/23/45	25.00
US Flag Flies Over Iwo Jima 2/23/45	35.00
Egypt at War 2/25/45	25.00
Palawan Captured 2/28/45	40.00
Yanks Enter Cologne 3/5/45	25.00
Cologne is Taken 3/6/45	25.00
Historical Rhine Crossing 3/8/45	25.00
Mindanao Invaded 3/8/45	40.00
Bombing of Tokyo 3/10/45	25.00
Russia Crosses Oder River 3/13/45	25.00
Capture of Iwo Jima 3/14/45	25.00
Panay Invaded 3/18/45	20.00
Honshu Invaded 3/19/45	20.00
Battle of the Inland Sea 3/20/45	25.00
Crossing of the Rhine 3/24/45	25.00
Kerama Falls 3/26/45	30.00
Danzig Invaded 3/27/45	25.00
Okinawa Invaded 4/1/45	25.00
Vienna Invaded 4/5/45	25.00
Masbate Invaded 4/5/45	30.00
Russia Denounces Jap Treaty 4/5/45	25.00
Japanese Cabinet Resigns 4/7/45	25.00
6 japenese Warships Sunk 4/7/45	25.00
Liberation of Vienna 4/10/45	25.00
We Invade Bremen, etc. 4/10/45	25.00
FDR Dies - Truman becomes President 4/12/45	50.00
Liberation of Vienna 4/13/45	25.00
Patton Invades Czechoslovakia 4/18/45	25.00
Ernie Pyle Dies 4/18/45	25.00
Berlin Invaded 4/21/45	25.00
UN Conference 4/25/45	25.00
Berlin Encircled 4/25/45	25.00
"GI Joe" and "Ivan" Meet at Torgau-Germany 4/26/45	25.00
Patton Enters Austria 4/27/45	20.00
Yanks Meet Reds 4/27/45	25.00
Mussolini Executed 4/28/45	35.00
Hitler Dead 5/1/45	35.00
Liberation of Italy 5/2/45	25.00
Berlin Falls 5/2/45	25.00
Liberation of Rangoon 5/3/45	25.00

World War II & Korean War Patriotic Covers

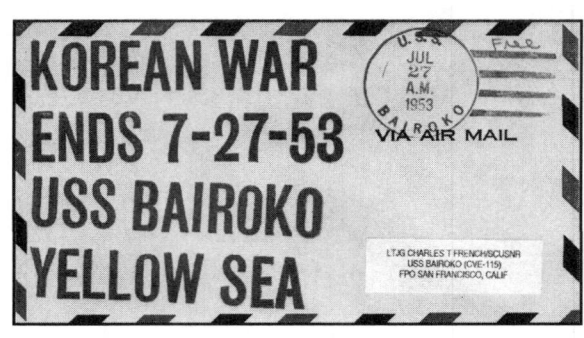

WORLD WAR II EVENT	CACHETED COVER
5th and 7th Armies Meet at Brenner Pass 5/4/45	25.00
Liberation of Copenhagen 5/5/45	25.00
Liberation of Amsterdam 5/5/45	25.00
Over a Million Nazis Surrender 5/5/45	25.00
Liberation of Oslo 5/8/45	35.00
Liberation of Prague 5/8/45	35.00
V-E Day 5/8/45	35.00
Atomic Bomb Test 5/16/45	25.00
Invasion of Borneo 6/11/45	25.00
Eisenhower Welcomed Home 6/19/45	20.00
Okinawa Captured 6/21/45	25.00
United Nations Conference 6/25/45	25.00
American Flag Raised over Berlin 7/4/45	25.00
Gen. Spatts Made Commander of Strategic Air Force in Pacific 7/5/45	20.00
Italy Declares War on Japan 7/15/45	25.00
Potsdam Conference Opens 7/17/45	25.00
3rd Fleet Hits Tokyo Bay 7/19/45	25.00
Churchill Defeated 7/26/45	25.00
Chineses Armies Retake Kweilin 7/28/45	25.00
Big Three Meet at Potsdam 8/1/45	25.00
Atomic Bomb Dropped on Hiroshima 8/6/45	70.00
Russia Declares War on Japan 8/8/45	25.00
Japan Offers To Surrender 8/10/45	25.00
Japan Capitulates 8/14/45	25.00
Hirohito Broadcasts News of Surrender 8/15/45	40.00
Hirohito Orders Cease Fire 8/16/45	25.00
Japan Signs Peace Treaty 9/1/45	50.00
Liberation of China 9/2/45	35.00
V-J Day 9/2/45	35.00
Liberation of Korea 9/2/45	35.00
MacArthur in Tokyo 9/7/45	25.00
Flag Raising over Tokyo - Gen. MacArthur Takes Over 9/8/45	25.00
Gen. Wainwright Rescued from the Japanese 9/10/45	25.00
Nimitz Post Office 9/10/45	25.00
Wainright Day 9/10/45	25.00
Marines Land in Japan 9/23/45	40.00
Nimitz Day-Washington 10/5/45	25.00
War Crimes Commission 10/18/45	25.00
Premier Laval Executed as Traitor 10/15/45	25.00
Fleet Reviewed by President Truman 10/27/45	35.00
De Gaulle Wins Election 10/27/45	25.00
Atomic Bomb and Energy Conference Opens 11/10/45	25.00
Eisenhower Named Chief of Staff 11/20/45	25.00
End of Meat and Fat Rations 11/24/45	25.00
Big 3 Conferencxe at Moscow 12/15/45	25.00
Trygue Lie Elected 1/21/46	25.00
Big 4 Meet in Paris 4/25/46	20.00
Tojo and 24 others Indicated 4/30/46	25.00
1st Anniversary of V-E Day 5/8/46	25.00
2nd Anniversary of D-Day 6/6/46	25.00
Operation Crossroads 6/30/46	100.00
Bikini Atomic Bomb Able Test 7/1/46	125.00
Philippine Republic Independence 7/3/46	25.00
Atomic Age 7/10/46	25.00
Bikini Atomic Bomb Baker Test 7/25/46	125.00
Victory Day 8/14/46	25.00
Opening of UN Post Office at Lake Success 9/23/46	25.00
Goering Commits Suicide 10/16/46	40.00
Opening Day of UN in Flushing, NY 10/23/46	25.00
Marshall is Secretary of State 1/21/47	25.00
Moscow Peace Conference 3/10/47	30.00

KOREAN WAR

KOREAN WAR EVENT	CACHETED COVER
MacArthur Takes Command of Our Army to Repel the Reds 6/27/50	40.00
US Forces From Japan go into Action in Korea 7/1/50	35.00
MacArthur Takes Supreme Command of All Land and Sea Forces in Korea Under the UN Flag 7/8/50	35.00
Red Korean Chief of Staff, Gen. Kam, Killed 9/8/50	40.00
UN Naval Ships Shell Inchon 9/14/50	40.00
US Marines Land at Inchon 9/15/50	40.00
US Flag Raised Over Seoul 9/27/50	40.00
Liberation of Seoul Completed 9/28/50	40.00
Seoul Restored as Capital of Korea 9/29/50	40.00
South Korean Troops Drive Reds Back North Across the 38th Parallel 10/1/50	40.00
UN Troops Capture Pyongyang, Capital of North Korea 10/20/50	40.00
UN Forces Recapture Seoul 3/15/51	40.00
Truman Removes MacArthur From Command of the UN Troops 4/11/51	40.00
MacArthur Departs From the Far East for USA 4/16/51	40.00
MacArthur Arrives at San Francisco, CA 4/17/51	40.00
MacArthur Addresses the Joint Session of Congress at Washington, DC 4/19/51	40.00
Operation Atomic Nevada 5/14/51	60.00
UN and Communists Meet at Kaesong to Open Formal Cease Fire Talks 7/10/51	40.00
Communists Break Off Truce Talks 8/23/51	40.00
USS New Jersey Bombarding Chansangot Region of Korea 11/13/51	40.00
1st H-Bomb Explosion 11/18/52	50.00
General Taylor Takes Command of the 8th Army with Teixeira Cachet 2/11/53	75.00
Operation Little Switch with Teixeira Cachet 4/20/53	75.00
Korean War Ends, USS Bairoko – Yellow Sea 7/27/53	60.00

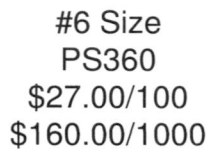

UNITED STATES SOUVENIR CARDS

ABOUT OUR SOUVENIR CARD LISTINGS

Catalog numbers are from the Souvenir Card Collectors Society catalogs.
Cancelled prices are for cards with First Day of Show or Issue Postmarks applied by the USPS or BEP Visitors Center unless designated "sc" or "F".
sc = Show cancel other than first day.
F = First day postmark applied by foreign post office.
($) = Basic design on card is from or based on Currency.
#1396 = Scott catalog number of U.S. or Canada stamp designs on cards.
Mexico = Stamps(s) from that country are depicted on that card.

(1) = "SC" Scott catalog number of this card. (N1) = "NSC" Scott Numismatic Card.

UNITED STATES POSTAL SERVICE

EXPOSICIÓN FILATÉLICA INTERNACIONAL
EFIMEX 68
MEXICO, D. F.   1-9 NOVIEMBRE, 1968

EL SELLO TRANS-MISSISSIPPI DE $1.00 "GANADO DEL OESTE DURANTE UNA TORMENTA",
DETALLE DE LA PINTURA POR J. A. MacWHIRTER CON EL TÍTULO "LA VANGUARDIA"

OBSEQUIO DEL DEPARTAMENTO DE CORREOS DE LOS ESTADOS UNIDOS DE NORTEAMÉRICA

W. Marvin Watson
MINISTRO DE CORREOS

PS2

SCCS Number	Event and Description	First Day Show/Issue	Mint Card	Cancelled Card
FPS1939Aa	Philatelic Truck with Gum	1939	50.00	..
FPS1939Ab	Philatelic Truck without Gum	1939	9.50	..
PS1	Barcelona'60-Columbus Landing ($) (2)	3/26/60	450.00	425.00
PS2	Efimex'68-#292 (4)	11/1/68	2.50	7.50
1970-1975				
PS3	Philympia - #548-550 (9)	9/18/70	1.25	15.00
PS4	Exfilima'71 - #1110, 1125, Peru (15)	11/6/71	1.25	60.00
PS5	Belgica'72 - #914, 1026, 1104 (20)	6/24/72	1.00	22.50
PS6	Olympia Philatelie Munchen'72 - #1460, 1461, 1462, C85 (21)	8/18/72	1.00	25.00
PS7	Exfilbra'72 - #C14, Brazil (22)	8/26/72	1.00	45.00
PS8	Postal Forum VI - #1396 Block (23)	8/28/72	1.00	20.00
PS9	Postal People - #1489-98 (11"x14")	1973	125.00	225.00
PS10	Ibra'73 - #C13, Germany (28)	5/11/73	1.25	10.00
PS11	Apex'73 - #C3a, Newfld., Honduras (30)	7/4/73	1.25	20.00
PS12	Polska'73 - #1488 (31)	8/19/73	1.25	175.00
PS13	Hobby Show Chicago - #1456-59 (35)	2/3/74	1.50	15.00
PS14	Internaba'74 - #1530-37 (37)	6/6/74	2.50	12.00
PS15	Stockholmia'74 - #836, Sweden (38)	9/21/74	2.50	15.00
PS15	Swedish First Day Cancel	...		22.50
PS16	Exfilmex'74 - #1157, Mexico (39)	10/26/74	2.50	37.50
PS17	Espana'75 - #233, 1271, Spain (40)	4/4/75	1.25	35.00
PS17	Spanish First Day Cancel	...		75.00
PS18	Arphila'75 - #1187, 1207, France (42)	6/6/75	2.35	35.00
1976-1980				
PS19	Weraba'76 - #1434-35 (45)	4/1/76	2.50	3.50
PS20	Science & Technology - #C76 (48)	5/30/76	2.50	3.50
PS21	Colorado Centennial - #288, 743, 1670 (50)	8/1/76	2.50	3.50
PS22	Hafnia'76 - #5, Denmark (51)	8/20/76	2.50	3.50
PS23	Italia'76 - #1168, Italy (52)	10/14/76	2.50	3.50
PS23	Italian First Day Cancel			40.00
PS24	Nordposta'76 - #689, Germany, Hamburg(53)	10/30/76	2.50	3.50
PS25	Amphilex'77 - #1027, Netherlands (56)	5/26/77	2.50	3.50
PS26	San Marino'77 - #1, 2, San Marino (57)	8/28/77	2.50	3.50
PS27	Rocpex'78 - #1706-9, Taiwan (60)	3/20/78	2.50	75.00
PS28	Naposta'78 - $555, 563, Germany (61)	5/20/78	2.50	4.00
PS28	German First Day Cancel			22.50
PS29	Brasiliana'79 - #C91-92, Brazil (63)	9/15/79	3.75	6.50
PS30	Japex'79 - #1158, Japan (64)	11/2/79	3.75	6.50
PS31	London'80 - #329 (65)	5/6/80	3.75	75.00
PS32	Norwex'80 - #620-21, Norway (66)	6/13/80	3.75	5.00
PS33	Essen'80 - #1014, German (69)	11/15/80	3.75	5.00
1981-1985				
PS34	Wipa'81 - #1252, Austria (71)	5/22/81	3.25	4.50
PS35	Stamp Collecting Month - #245, 1913 (72)	10/1/81	3.25	4.50
PS36	Philatokyo'81 - #1531, Japan (73)	10/9/81	3.25	4.50
PS37	Nordposta'81 - #923, Germany (74)	11/7/81	3.25	4.50
PS38	Canada'82 - #116, Canada #15 (76)	5/20/82	3.25	4.50
PS39	Philexfrance'82 - #1753, France (77)	6/11/82	3.25	4.50
PS40	Stamp Collecting Month - #C3a (78)	10/1/82	3.25	4.50
PS41	Espamer'82 - #801, 1437, 2024 (80)	10/12/82	3.25	4.50
PS42	U.S.-Sweden - #958, 2036, Sweden (81)	3/24/83	3.25	4.50
PS43	Concord, German Settlers - #2040, Germany (82)	4/29/83	3.25	4.50
PS44	Tembal'83 - #C71, Switzerland (83)	5/21/83	3.25	4.50

PS45

SCCS Number	Event and Description	First Day Show/Issue	Mint Card	Cancelled Card
1981-1985 (cont.)				
PS45	Brasiliana'83 - #2, Brazil (85)	7/29/83	3.25	4.50
PS46	Bangkok'83 - #210, Siam (86)	8/4/83	3.25	4.50
PS47	Philatelic Memento'83 - #1387 (87)	8/19/83	3.25	3.50
PS48	Stamp Collecting Month - #293 (88)	10/4/83	4.50	6.00
PS49	Espana'84 - #233, Spain (92)	4/27/84	3.25	5.00
PS50	Hamburg'84 - #C66, Germany (95)	6/19/84	3.25	5.00
PS51	St. Lawrence Seaway - #1131, Canada #387 (96)	6/26/84	3.25	4.50
PS52	Ausipex'84 - #290, Australia (97)	9/21/84	3.25	4.50
PS53	Stamp Collecting Month - #2104 (98)	10/1/84	3.25	4.50
PS54	Philakorea'84 - #741, Korea (99)	10/22/84	3.25	5.00
PS55	Philatelic Memento'85 - #2 (101)	2/26/85	3.25	4.50
PS56	Olymphilex'85 - #C106, Switzerland (102)	3/18/85	3.25	5.00
PS57	Israphil'85 - #566, Israel (103)	5/14/85	3.25	5.00
PS58	Argentina'85 - #1737, Argentina (107)	7/5/85	3.25	5.00
PS59	Mophila'85 - #296, Germany (108)	9/11/85	3.25	5.00
PS60	Italia'85 - #1107, Italy (109)	10/25/85	3.25	5.00
PS61	Statue of Liberty - #2147	7/18/85	32.50	25.00
1986-1992				
PS62	Statue of Liberty - #C87 (110)	2/21/86	5.75	6.75
PS62v	Stampex Overprint - #2204, Australia	8/4/86	15.00	25.00
PS63	Stockholmia'86 - #113, Sweden (113)	8/28/86	5.00	6.75
PS64	Capex'87 - #569, Canada #883 (117)	6/13/87	5.00	7.00
PS65	Hafnia'87 - #299, Denmark (118)	10/16/87	5.00	7.00
PS66	Monte Carlo - #2286, 2300, Monaco (121)	11/13/87	5.00	7.00
PS67	Finlandia'88 - #836, Finland (122)	6/1/88	5.00	7.00
PS68	Philexfrance'89 - #C120, France (125)	7/7/89	9.00	12.00
PS69	World Stamp Expo'89 - #2433 (127)	11/17/89	8.00	9.00
PS70	Stamp World London - #1, G.B. #1 (130)	5/3/90	8.00	9.00
PS71	Olymphilex'92 - #2619, 2637-41		75.00	125.00

BUREAU OF ENGRAVING AND PRINTING

SCCS Number	Event and Description	First Day Show/Issue	Mint Card	Cancelled Card
1954-1970				
F1954A	National Philatelic Museum, DC (1)	3/13/54	1875.00	..
F1966A	Sipex Scenes'66 - Washington D.C. Scenes (3)	5/21/66	150.00	160.00
B1	Sandipex - 3 Washington D.C. Scenes(5)	7/16/69	50.00	180.00
B2	ANA'69 - Eagle "Jackass" Notes ($) (N1)	8/12/69	75.00	..
B3	Fresno Fair - 3 Wash. D.C. Scenes (N2)	10/2/69	400.00	..
B4	ASDA'69 - #E4 Block (6)	11/21/69	20.00	120.00
B5	Interpex'70 - #1027, 1035, C35, C38 (7)	3/13/70	50.00	150.00
B6	Compex'70 - #C18 Block (8)	5/29/70	12.50	150.00
B7	ANA'70 - Currency Collage ($) (N3)	8/18/70	95.00	..
B8	Hapex APS'70 - #799, C46, C55 (10)	11/5/70	12.50	..
1971-1973				
B9	Interpex'71 - #1193 Block,1331-32, 1371,C76 (11)	3/12/71	1.75	50.00
B10	Westpex San Francisco - #740,852,966,997 (12)	4/23/71	1.75	130.00
B11	Napex'71 - #990-92 (13)	5/12/71	1.95	125.00
B12	ANA'71 - #Anniv. Convention ($) (N4)	8/10/71	6.75	..
B13	Texanex'71 - #938, 1043, 1242 (14)	8/26/71	1.75	250.00
B14	ASDA'71 - #C13-15 (16)	11/19/71	3.00	32.50
B15	Anphilex, Collectors Club - #1-2 (17)	11/26/71	1.50	275.00
B16	Interpex'72 - #1173 Block,976,1434-35 (18)	3/17/72	1.00	10.00
B17	Nopex, New Orleans - #1020 (19)	4/6/72	1.00	150.00
B18	ANA'72 - $2 Science Allegory ($) (N5)	8/15/72	7.50	135.00
B19	Sepad'72, SPA - #1044 Block (24)	10/20/72	1.00	30.00
B20	ASDA'72 - #863, 868, 883, 888 (25)	11/17/72	1.00	10.00
B21	Stamp Expo'72 - #C36 Block (26)	11/24/72	2.00	25.00
B22	Interpex'73 - #976 Block (27)	3/9/73	1.25	10.00
B23	Compex'73 - #245 Block (29)	5/25/73	3.00	37.50
B24	ANA'73 - $5 "America" ($) (N6)	8/23/73	10.00	25.00
B25	Napex'73 - #C3 Block, C4-6 (32)	9/14/73	2.00	35.00
B26	ASDA'73 - #908 Block, 1139-44 (33)	11/16/73	1.00	8.00
B27	Stamp Expo'73 - #C20 Block (34)	12/7/73	2.00	20.00

UNITED STATES SOUVENIR CARDS

BUREAU OF ENGRAVING AND PRINTING

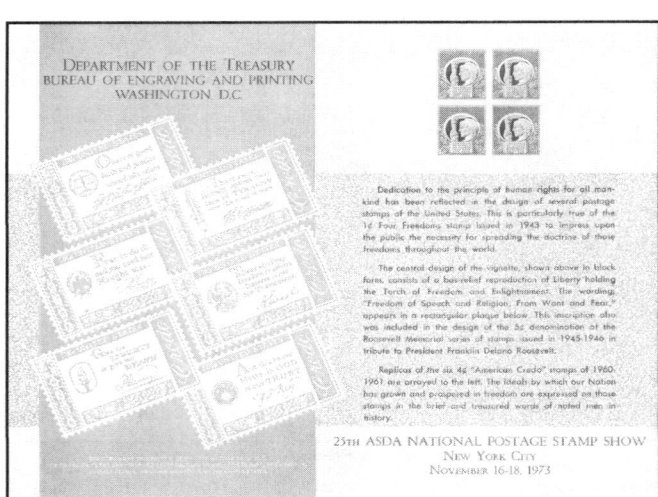

B26

SCCS Number	Event and Description	First Day Show/Issue	Mint Card	Cancelled Card
	1974-1976			
B28	Milcopex'74 - #C43 Block (36)	3/8/74	1.25	8.00
B29	ANA'74 - $10 Education ($) (N7)	8/13/74	11.00	35.00
B30	Napex'75 - #708 Block (41)	5/9/75	5.75	18.50
B31	Women's Year (with folder) - #872, 878, #959, $1 Martha Wash. ($) (43)	5/2/75	22.50	250.00
B32	ANA'75 -$1 George & Martha Wash. ($)(N8)	8/19/75	11.00	40.00
B33	ASDA'75 - #1003 Block, Washington (44)	11/21/75	22.50	50.00
B34	Interphil'76 - #120 Block, Jefferson (46)	5/29/76	5.00	15.00
B35	Card from Interphil program - #1044	5/29/76	5.50	75.00
B36	Bicentennial Expo on Science and Technology, Kitty Hawk/Space	5/30/76	5.50	150.00
B37	Stamp Expo'76, Citizen Soldier - #1348, #1348, 51, 52 (49)	6/11/76	5.50	40.00
B38	ANA'76 - $2 Fulton & Morse ($) (N9)	8/24/76	8.75	32.50
	1977-1980			
B39	Milcopex'77, Polar Theme - #733, 1128 (54)	3/4/77	2.00	15.00
B40	Rompex'77, Mountains - #1001 Block (55)	5/20/77	2.00	9.50
B41	ANA'77 - $5 Indian Chief ($) (N10)	8/23/77	11.00	13.50
B42	Puripex'77 - #801 Block, San Juan Gate(58)	9/2/77	1.25	6.00
B43	ASDA'77 - #C45 Block, Wright Bros (59)	11/16/77	2.25	6.00
B44	Paper Money Show'78 -De Soto Vign.(N11)	6/2/78	4.50	9.00
B45	Cenjex'78 - #785 Block, 646, 680, 689, #1086, 1716 (62)	6/23/78	2.00	6.00
B46	ANA'80 - $5 Grant & Sheridan ($) (N12)	2/15/80	15.00	40.00
B47	Paper Money Show'80 - 2 $10 Lewis-Clark ($) (N13)	6/6/80	22.50	35.00
B48	Napex'80 - #573 Block, Capitol (67)	7/4/80	10.00	30.00
B49	Visitor Center - Eagle & Freedom	9/8/80	6.75	15.00
B50	ASDA Stamp Festival - #962 Block, Francis S.Key (68)	9/25/80	11.50	35.00
	1981-1983			
B51	Stamp Expo'81 South - #1287 Block, 1331-32 (70)	3/20/81	13.50	37.50
B52	Visitor Center - G.Wash. & D.C.Views	4/22/81	8.00	12.00
B53	Paper Money Show'81-$20 G.Wash.($)(N14)	6/19/81	15.00	20.00
B54	ANA'81 - $5 Silver Certificate ($) (N15)	7/27/81	15.00	20.00
B55	Milcopex'82 - #1136 Block, Reuter (75)	3/5/82	12.00	25.00
B56	Paper Money Show'82 -"Brown Backs"($)(N16)	6/18/82	12.00	20.00
B57	ANA'82 - $1 Great Seal ($) (N17)	8/17/82	11.00	20.00
B58	Espamer'82 - #244 Block, Isabella (79)	10/12/82	25.00	35.00
B59	FUN'83 - $100 "Watermelon" ($) (N18)	1/5/83	22.50	22.50
B60	Texanex-Topex'83 - #776 Block, 1660 (84)	6/17/83	18.00	25.00
B61	ANA'83 - $20 1915 Note ($) (N19)	8/16/83	16.50	16.50
B62	Philatelic Show'83, Boston - #718-19 (89)	10/21/83	10.00	12.50
B63	ASDA'83 - #881, Metropolitan Opera (90)	11/17/83	10.00	20.00
	1984			
B64	FUN'84 - $1 1880 Note ($) (N20)	1/4/84	22.50	22.50
B65	Spider Press, Intaglio, Brown Eagle	1/4/84	350.00	425.00
B66	Espana'84 - #241 Block (91)	4/27/84	15.00	20.00
B67	Stamp Expo'84 - #1791-94, Torch (93)	4/27/84	20.00	18.00
B68	Compex'84 - #728 (94)	5/25/84	20.00	27.50
B69	Money Show'84, Memphis - $10,000 1878 Note ($) (N21)	6/15/84	22.50	22.50
B70	Spider Press, Intaglio, Blue Eagle	6/15/84	350.00	450.00
B71	ANA'84 - $500 1882 Gold Certificate($)(N22)	7/28/84	15.00	15.00
B72	Spider Press, Intaglio, Green Eagle	7/28/84	350.00	425.00
B73	ASDA'84 - #1470 Block, Youth (100)	11/15/84	13.00	25.00
B74	Spider Press,Intaglio,Green/Brown Liberty	11/15/84	140.00	200.00

SCCS Number	Event and Description	First Day Show/Issue	Mint Card	Cancelled Card
	1985			
B75	Long Beach'85 #954, $20 1865 Note $(104)	1/31/85	10.00	11.00
B76	Milcopex'85 - #880 Block, Sousa (105)	3/1/85	11.00	20.00
B77	Coin Club of El Paso-$50 1902 Note ($)(N23)	4/19/85	15.00	22.50
B78	Spider Press, Maroon Statue of Liberty	4/19/85	150.00	200.00
B79	Pacific NW Numismatics -$50 1914 ($)(N24)	5/17/85	15.00	22.50
B80	Napex'85 - #2014 Block, Peace Garden(106)	6/7/85	10.00	22.50
B81	Paper Money Show, Memphis - $10,000 1878 Note ($) (N25)	6/14/85	17.50	22.50
B82	ANA'85 - $500 1882 Gold Cert. ($) (N26)	8/20/85	15.00	20.00
B83	Spider Press, Green/Blue Statue-Liberty	8/20/85	150.00	200.00
B84	Paper Money Show, Cherry Hill - $10 1882 ($) (N27)	11/14/85	16.50	25.00
B85-86	Spider Press,Blue Liberty Bell with card	11/14/85	175.00	200.00
	1986-1987			
B87	FUN'86 - $100 1890 Treasury ($) (N28)	1/2/86	16.50	22.50
B88	ANA Midwinter,Salt Lake C.-$10 1901($)(N29)	2/19/86	16.50	22.50
B89	Garfield-Perry - #306 Block,Martha Wash.(111)	3/21/86	10.00	25.00
B90	Ameripex'86-#134,2052,1474, Franklin(112)	5/22/86	10.00	20.00
B91-92	Spider Press, Green Liberty Bell with card	5/22/86	65.00	100.00
B93	Paper Money Show'86 - $5 1902 ($)(N30)	6/20/86	13.00	17.50
B94	ANA'86, Milwaukee - 5¢ Fractional ($)(N31)	8/5/86	13.00	17.50
B95-96	Spider Press, Brown Liberty Bell with card	8/5/86	65.00	100.00
B97	Houpex'86 - #1035, 1041, 1044A (114)	9/5/86	12.00	25.00
B98	Lobex'86 - $10 1907 Gold Cert. ($) (115)	10/2/86	13.00	22.50
B99	NW Paper Money-Fractional Currency($)(N32)	11/13/86	13.00	22.50
B100	Dallas Expo-#550 Block,$10,000 1918($)(116)	12/11/86	16.00	22.50
B101	BEP 125th Anniv. - Cherry Blossoms	1/7/87	45.00	70.00
B101A	same, "FUN" Embossed	1/7/87	75.00	100.00
B101B	same, ANA Midwinter Seals	2/27/87	75.00	100.00
B101C	same, BEP & WMPG Seals	4/9/87	85.00	135.00
B101D	same, BEP & IPMS Seals	6/19/87	85.00	100.00
B101E	same, BEP & ANA'87 Seals	8/26/87	80.00	95.00
B101F	same, BEP & GENA Seals	9/18/87	50.00	75.00
B102	FUN'87 -$1 1874 Columbus,Wash. ($)(N33)	1/7/87	14.00	18.50
B103	ANA Midwinter'87 - $500,000,000 Treasury Note ($) (N34)	2/27/87	15.00	18.50
B104	BEP 125th Anniv., Fort Worth - $5 1902 Harrison ($) (N35)	4/25/87	20.00	115.00
B105	Paper Money Show'87-$20 1922 Seal($)(N36)	6/19/87	13.00	18.00
B106	ANA'87, Atlanta - $2 1886 ($) (N37)	8/26/87	13.00	18.00
B108	GENA'87 Numismatics - $10 1907 ($)(N38)	9/18/87	15.00	18.00
B109	Spider Press, Brown State Shields, Intaglio	9/18/87	85.00	150.00
B110	Sescal'87 - #798 Constitution (119)	10/16/87	12.50	22.50
B111	Hawaii Numismatist -$5 1923($),#C55(120)	11/12/87	22.50	30.00
	1988-1989			
B112	FUN'88 - 50¢ Fractional Currency ($) (N39)	1/7/88	12.00	17.50
B113	Spider Press, Green State Shields, Intaglio	1/7/88	85.00	150.00
B114	ANA Midwinter, Little Rock, $10,000 1882 Jackson, Gold Certificate (N40)	3/11/88	15.00	16.50
B115	Paper Money Show'88 - $5 1899 ($) (N41)	6/24/88	13.00	18.00
B116	ANA'88,Cincinnati -$2 1918 Battleship($)(N42)	7/20/88	22.50	18.00
B117	Spider Press, Blue State Shields, Intaglio	7/20/88	85.00	140.00
B118	APS Stampshow,Detroit-#835 Constitution(123)	8/25/88	11.00	20.00
B119	Illinois Numismatist - $10 1915 ($) (N43)	10/6/88	12.00	15.00
B120	Midaphil'88 - #627, Steamboat (124)	11/18/88	10.00	22.50
B121	FUN'89 - $50 1891 Seward ($) (N44)	1/5/89	13.00	20.00
B122	FUN, Indian Mourning Civilization, Intaglio	1/5/89	45.00	75.00
B124	ANA Midwinter, Colorado Springs - $5,000 1878 ($) (N45)	3/3/89	15.00	25.00
B125	Texas Numismatics, El Paso - $5,000 1918 ($) (N46)	4/28/89	14.00	25.00
B126	Paper Money Show - $5 1907 U.S. Note ($) (N47)	6/23/89	12.00	18.00
B127	Paper Money S., Agriculture Scene, Intag.	6/23/89	45.00	70.00
B129	ANA'89, Pittsburgh - $1,000 1891 ($) (N48)	8/9/89	15.00	20.00
B130	ANA, Declaration of Independence, Intag.	8/9/89	45.00	75.00
B132	APS Stampshow, Anaheim - #565, Indians (126)	8/24/89	10.00	18.00
	1990-1991			
B133	FUN'90 - $5 1897 Silver ($) (N49)	1/4/90	12.00	16.00
B134	FUN, Brown Eagle & Ships, Intaglio	1/4/90	35.00	70.00
B135	ANA Midwinter, San Diego - $2 1897 ($)(N50)	3/2/90	12.00	16.00
B136	Central States Numismatics, Milwaukee - $1 1897 Silver ($)(N51)	4/6/90	12.00	16.00
B137	CSNS, Blue Eagle & Ships, Intaglio	4/6/90	35.00	70.00
B138	Aripex'90 - #285 Trans-Mississippi (128)	4/20/90	10.00	17.50
B139	DCSE'90, Dallas - $10 1890 Note ($)(N52)	6/14/90	14.00	18.00
B140	ANA Seattle - $1,000 1891 Silver ($) (N53)	8/22/90	17.50	20.00
B141	ANA, Green Eagle & Ships, Intaglio	8/22/90	35.00	70.00
B142	APS Stampshow - #286 Trans-Mississippi (129)	8/23/90	10.00	18.00
B143	Westex Numismatic, Denver - $2 1890 ($) (N54)	9/21/90	16.50	16.00
B144	Hawaii Numis. - $50 1874 Legal Tender($) (N55)	11/1/90	16.50	25.00
B145	FUN - $20 1875 Legal Tender ($)(N56)	1/3/91	16.50	16.00
B146	FUN, Green "Freedom & Capitol, Intaglio	1/3/91	39.50	70.00
B147	ANA Midwinter - $2 1917 Legal Tender ($) (N57)	3/1/91	14.00	22.50
B148	Paper Money Show, Memphis - $20 1890 ($) (N58)	6/14/91	14.00	22.50

UNITED STATES SOUVENIR CARDS

BUREAU OF ENGRAVING AND PRINTING

B119

SCCS Number	Event and Description	First Day Show/Issue	Mint Card	Cancelled Card
1991 (continued)				
B149	ANA, Chicago - $5,000 1878 Legal T. ($) (N59)	8/13/91	19.50	35.00
B150	ANA, Gray "Freedom" & Capitol, Intaglio	8/13/91	42.50	70.00
B151	APS Stampshow, Philadelphia - #537 (131)	8/22/91	12.50	20.00
B152	Fort Worth, Five BEP Buildings	4/26/91	40.00	160.00
1992-1993				
B153	FUN - $1 1862 Legal Tender ($) (N60)	1/9/92	10.00	16.00
B154	FUN, Blue Columbus Voyage, Intaglio	1/9/92	35.00	70.00
B155	Central States Numis. - $1,000 1875 Legal Tender ($) (N61)	4/30/92	16.50	25.00
B156	World Columbian Stamp Expo - #118 (132)	5/22/92	11.00	30.00
B157	WCSE, Red Columbus Voyage, Intaglio	5/22/92	35.00	80.00
B158	Paper Money Show - $5 1914 ($) (N62)	6/19/92	12.00	16.00
B159	ANA, Orlando - $5 1865 Note ($) (N63)	8/12/92	12.50	16.00
B160	ANA, Green Columbus Voyage, Intaglio	8/12/92	35.00	85.00
B161	APS, Oakland - #118 Block (134)	8/27/92	10.00	17.00
B162	Savings Bonds - #WS7, $25 Sav. Bond (133)	6/15/92	12.50	45.00
B163	Green Fleet of Columbus 1492, Intaglio	10/13/92	35.00	75.00
B164	CFC, Red Cross - #1016 + 1155, 1263, 1385, 1425, 1438, 1549 (135)	1/13/93	11.50	50.00
B165	FUN - $1,000 1890 Treasury Note Back ($) (N64)	1/7/93	16.50	22.50
B166	FUN, 3 National Parks Scenes, Intaglio	1/7/93	55.00	90.00
B167	ANA, Colorado Springs - $2 1880 Legal Tender Back($) (N65)	3/11/93	15.00	22.50
B168	ASDA'93 - #859, 864, 869, 874, 879, 884, 889, 1¢ Famous Americans (136)	5/5/93	10.00	16.00
B169	Texas Numismatics - $100 1902 Back ($)(N66)	5/6/93	12.50	16.00
B170	Georgia Numism.-$1,000 1878 Back($)(N67)	5/13/93	16.00	22.00
B171	Paper Money Show-$500 1918 Back ($)(N69)	6/18/93	14.00	22.00
B172	IPMS, 3 National Parks Scenes,Purple, Int.	6/18/93	55.00	90.00
B173	ANA, Baltimore - $100 1914 Back ($)	7/28/93	16.00	22.00
B174	ANA, 3 National Parks Scenes, Green, Int.	7/28/93	55.00	90.00
B175	Savings Bond - #WS8, $200 Bond (137)	8/2/93	12.50	25.00
B176	Omaha Philatelic - #QE4, JQ5, E7, Newspaper (138)	9/3/93	12.00	20.00
B178	ASDA - Unfinished Masterpieces,Wash(139)	10/28/93	12.00	16.00
1994-1995				
B179	FUN'94 - $20 1923 Proposed ($) (N70)	1/6/94	10.00	16.00
B180	FUN, Justice Orlando, Intaglio	1/6/94	35.00	60.00
B181	SANDICAL - #E1 Block (140)	2/11/94	10.00	17.50
B182	ANA, New Orleans -$10 1899 Proposed($) (N71)	3/3/94	15.00	22.50
B183	European Paper Money Show, Netherlands - $100 1908 Proposed Note (N72)	4/16/94	16.00	45.00
B184	Paper Money Show - $10 Proposed Note ($) (N73)	6/17/94	15.00	22.50
B185	IPMS, Justice Memphis, Intaglio	6/17/94	40.00	65.00
B186	BEP Stamp Cent. -#246/263 Black(140A)	7/1/94	150.00	200.00
B187	ANA, Detroit - $10 1915 Prop. Back ($)(N74)	7/27/94	12.50	18.00
B188	ANA, 1915 3 Female Figures Allegory, Int	7/27/94	85.00	110.00
B189	Savings Bonds - #S1-5, Minuteman (141)	8/1/94	17.50	35.00
B190	APS, Pittsburgh - #J31, J32, J35 (142)	8/18/94	10.00	16.00
B191	ASDA, N.Y. - 1894 Newspaper Stamps(143)	11/3/94	10.00	16.00
B192	FUN'95- $1 1899 Silver Certificate($)(N75)	1/5/95	16.00	16.50
B193	FUN, Red-Brown Seated Eagle, Intaglio	1/5/95	40.00	55.00
B194	COLOPEX,Columbus,OH - #261 Block(144)	4/7/95	10.00	16.50
B195	New York Numismatics - $1 1917 ($) (N76)	5/5/95	13.50	22.50

SCCS Number	Event and Description	First Day Show/Issue	Mint Card	Cancelled Card
1995 (continued)				
B196	Paper Money Show, Memphis - $1 1880 ($) (N77)	6/16/95	15.00	18.00
B197	BEP Stamp Centennial - #246/263, Blue (13) (145)	6/30/95	90.00	150.00
B198	Savings Bond - #905, 908, 940 WWII(146)	8/16/95	10.00	25.00
B199	ANA, Anaheim - $1 1918 Back ($) (N78)	8/16/95	16.00	20.00
B200	ANA, Blue Eagle & Flag, Intaglio	8/16/95	35.00	55.00
B201	Long Beach Numism. - $1 1923 Back ($) (N79)	10/4/95	12.00	18.00
B202	ASDA, N.Y. - #292 Block and background (147)	11/2/95	10.00	18.00
1996-1997				
B203	FUN'96 - $500 1878 Silver Cert. ($) (N80)	1/4/96	12.00	20.00
B204	FUN, Miners Panning for Gold, Brown Int	1/4/96	40.00	55.00
B205	Suburban Washington / Baltimore Coin Show - $500 1878 Back Silver Cert. ($) (N81)	3/22/96	12.00	18.00
B206	Central States Numism.-$1,000 1907($)(N82)	4/25/96	12.00	18.00
B207	CAPEX'96, Toronto - #291 Block (148)	6/8/96	10.00	20.00
B208	Olymphilex, Atlanta - #718 Block (149)	7/19/96	10.00	18.00
B209	Olymphiles, Miners Panning Gold, Green Intaglio	7/19/96	35.00	55.00
B210	Savings Bond - Brown Eagle in Flight	8/12/96	11.50	25.00
B211	ANA, Denver - $1,000 1907 Back ($) (N83)	8/14/96	15.00	20.00
B212	ANA, Miners Panning for Gold, Blue Int	8/14/96	35.00	55.00
B213	Billings Stamp Club (150)	10/19/96	10.00	24.00
B214	FUN'96 20 1886 Silver Cert. ($) (N84)	1/9/97	12.00	20.00
B215	Long Beach C&C, Lock Seal (151)	2/19/97	12.00	20.00
B216	Bay State Coin Show, $20 1882 BN (N85)	4/17/97	12.00	20.00
B217	Pacific '97, Butter Revenue	5/29/97	12.00	20.00
B219	1PMS, Memphis, TN, $10 1902 ($) (N86)	6/20/97	12.00	20.00
B220	1PMS, intaglio	6/20/97	40.00	50.00
B221	ANA 106th, $100 1874 LT ($) (N87)	7/30/97	12.00	20.00
B222	Milcopex, Newspaper Stamps (153)	9/17/97	11.00	25.00
1998-1999				
B224	FUN'98 (N88)	1/8/98	11.00	25.00
B225	Okpex'98 #922 Block (154)	5/1/98	12.00	25.00
B226	IPMS, Memphis ($) (N89)	6/19/98	12.00	20.00
B227	ANA, Portland, OR ($) (N90)	8/5/98	12.00	20.00
B228	Long Beach C&C ($) (N91)	9/23/98	12.00	20.00
B229	Long Beach C&C, Trans-Mississippi (155)	9/23/98	60.00	90.00
B230	Savings Bond, Washington, DC	12/21/98	15.00	20.00
B231	FUN'99 (N92)	1/7/99	15.00	22.50
B232	Bay State Coin ($) (N93)	2/26/99	15.00	22.50
B233	1PMS, Memphis ($) (N94)	6/18/99	14.00	22.50
B234	Savings Bonds, DC	8/9/99	12.00	20.00
B235	ANA, Rosemont, IL ($) (N95)	8/11/99	12.00	20.00
B236	ANA, Intaglio	8/11/99	40.00	50.00
B237	National, King of Prussia, PA (156)	10/1/99	12.00	20.00
2000-2003				
B238	Progress, DC	1/3/00	12.00	35.00
B239	Wright Brothers, DC	2/1/00	12.00	35.00
B240	Panama Canal, DC	3/1/00	12.00	35.00
B241	Engineering, DC	4/3/00	12.00	35.00
B242	Mt. Rushmore, Perkins, DC	5/1/00	12.00	35.00
B243	Eagle & Ships, DC	6/1/00	12.00	35.00
B244	Nuclear Sub, DC	7/3/00	12.00	25.00
B245	M.L.King, Jr., DC	8/1/00	12.00	25.00
B246	Vietnam Soldier, DC	9/1/00	12.00	35.00
B247	Banking & Commerce #1577-78, DC	10/2/00	12.00	20.00
B248	Space Shuttle, DC	11/1/00	12.00	35.00
B249	Information Highway, DC	12/1/00	12.00	35.00
B251	FUN, 2001 Orlando, FL($) (N96)	1/4/01	12.00	25.00
B252	IPMS, Memphis, TN (N97)	6/15/01	12.00	20.00
B254	ANA, Atlanta,GA ($) (N98)	8/8/01	12.00	25.00
B256	Savings Bond 2001	8/8/02	12.00	25.00
B257	LBC & CEC, Long Beach, CA (N99)	10/4/01	12.00	20.00
B258	FUN, 2002 (N100)	1/20/02	12.00	25.00
B259	FUN, Intaglio	...	45.00	...
B260	Texas Numismatic, Fort Worth (N101)	5/10/02	12.00	25.00
B261	ANA, New York, NY (N102)	7/31/02	12.00	25.00
B263	LBC & CEC, Long Beach, CA (N103)	9/25/02	12.00	25.00
B264	FUN, 2003 (N104)	2003	45.00	...
B265	Georgia Numismatic (N105)	2003	45.00	...
B266	ANA, Baltimore, MD (N106)	2003	45.00	...

WASHINGTON 2006
World Philatelic Exhibition
May 27-June 3, 2006
See you there!
www.washington-2006.org

UNITED STATES SOUVENIR CARDS

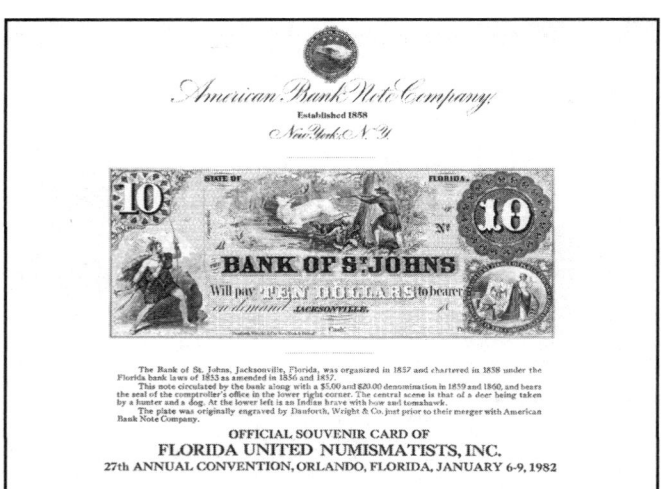

OFFICIAL SOUVENIR CARD OF
FLORIDA UNITED NUMISMATISTS, INC.
27th ANNUAL CONVENTION, ORLANDO, FLORIDA, JANUARY 6-9, 1982

SO22

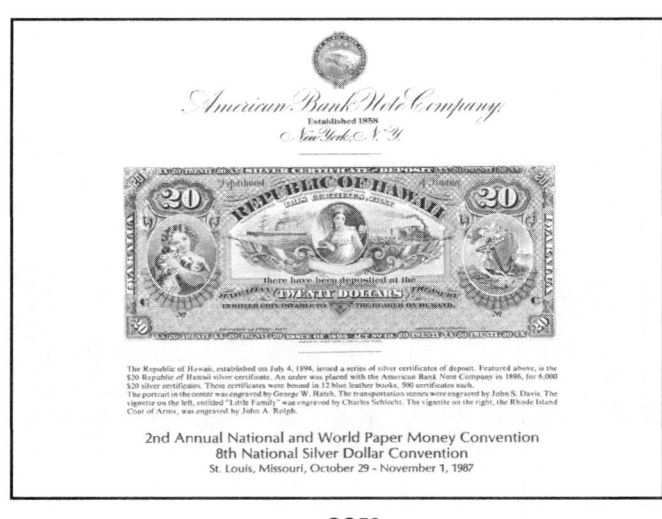

2nd Annual National and World Paper Money Convention
8th National Silver Dollar Convention
St. Louis, Missouri, October 29 - November 1, 1987

SO58

SCCS Number	Event and Description	First Day Show/Issue	Mint Card	Cancelled Card
	1966-1980			
SO1	SIPEX Miner - United States Bank Note Company	5/21/66	15.00	(sc)95.00
SO2	Interphil "America 1776-1976"	5/29/76	50.00	100.00
SO3	Interphil "Lincoln's Gettysburg Address"	5/29/76	60.00	100.00
SO4	Interphil "Awards Banquet, Scenes"	6/5/76	135.00	300.00
SO5	Interphil "Awards Banquet Menu"	6/5/76	200.00	350.00
SO9	Paper Money Show - $2 Liberty Bank of Providence, RI ($)	6/15/79	35.00	50.00
SO10	ANA'79 - $10 Exchange Bank, St.Louis ($)	7/28/79	8.00	35.00
SO11	Paper Money Show - $100 Bank of Lebanon, NH ($)	6/6/80	20.00	35.00
SO12	ANA'80 - $3 Bank of the Ohio Valley ($)	8/13/80	8.00	50.00
SO13	Bank Note Reporter - $3 Bank of the State of Kansas ($)	9/9/80	7.00	500.00
	1981-1984			
SO14	ANA Midyear, Honolulu - $5 Republic of Hawaii Silver Certificate ($)	2/5/81	15.00	85.00
SO15	Paper Money Show - $50 Bank of Selma,AL($)	6/19/81	13.50	20.00
SO16	INTERPAM - $1 Grenville County Bank of Prescott, ON & $2 Cataract City Bank of Paterson, NJ ($)	6/15/81	9.00	100.00
SO17	ANA'81 - $5,000 Canal Bank of New Orl.($)	7/28/81	12.50	22.50
SO18	ANA Building Fund - $10 Artisan Bank of Trenton, NJ ($)	7/28/81	18.50	150.00
SO20	Chester County, PA - 4 Vignettes, Green	12/10/81	9.00	95.00
SO21	Chester County, PA - 4 Vignettes, Brown	21/10/81	9.00	95.00
SO22	FUN'82 - $10 Bank of St. Johns, FL ($)	1/6/82	10.00	...
SO23	ANA Midyear, Colorado Springs - Certificate of Deposit, Bank of Ruby, CO	2/18/82	9.50	20.00
SO24	Paper Money Show - $1 Baton Rouge ($)	6/18/82	17.50	20.00
SO25	ANA'82 - $3 Tremont Bank of Boston ($)	8/17/82	11.00	20.00
SO32	ANA Midwinter, Tucson - $1 Lord & Williams Arizona Territory ($)	1/5/83	11.50	17.00
SO33	Paper Money Show - $2 White Mountains Bank of Lancaster, NH ($)	1/5/83	14.00	18.00
SO34	ANA'83 - $100 Felix Argenti & Co. ($)	8/16/83	14.00	18.00
SO35	ANA Midwinter, Colorado Springs - Colorado National Bank Advertising Card	2/23/84	17.50	35.00
SO37	Paper Money Show - $100 Bank of the State of Indiana ($)	6/15/84	16.50	25.00
SO38	Statue of Liberty, Black	7/4/84	7.75	18.00
SO39	ANA'84 - $10 Michigan State Bank ($)	7/28/84	25.00	32.50
	1985-1988			
SO40	FUN'85 - $10 Bank of Commerce at Fernandina, FL ($)	1/3/85	9.00	45.00
SO41	ANA Midwinter, San Antonio - $3 Commercial and Agricultural Bank of Galveston ($)	2/21/85	27.50	40.00
SO42	Natl. Assoc. of Tobacco Distributors	3/27/85	9.00	..
SO43	SPMC & IBNS - Hologram with Statue of Liberty	..	50.00	..
SO53	INS'87 - Statue of Liberty	2/6/87	40.00	75.00
SO54	200th Anniv.-Constitution - Independence Hall	6/19/87	10.00	20.00
SO56	AFL-CIO Trade Show - Eagle	6/19/87	175.00	200.00
SO57	ANA'87 - $10 Republic of Hawaii ($)	8/26/87	16.00	20.00

SCCS Number	Event and Description	First Day Show/Issue	Mint Card	Cancelled Card
	1985-1988 (cont.)			
SO58	NWPMC, St.Louis - $20 Rep. of Hawaii ($)	10/29/87	17.00	20.00
SO59	200th Anniv.-Constitution - 8 States & Eagle	1988	9.00	..
SO60	Paper Money Show - $50 Rep.of Hawaii($)	6/24/88	17.50	20.00
SO61	ANA'88 - $100 Republic of Hawaii ($)	7/20/88	15.00	20.00
	1989-1991			
SO62	FUN'89 - $5 Republic of Hawaii ($)	1/5/89	15.00	20.00
SO63	Miami Stamp Expo - 3 Railroad Vignettes	1/27/89	24.00	35.00
SO64	ANA'89 - #SO34 with Museum Overprint on Back($)	3/3/89	25.00	25.00
SO65	Washington Inauguration - $20 Bank of Pittsylvania ($)	3/15/89	12.00	..
SO66	200th Anniv.-Constitution - 3 States		12.00	..
SO67	Paper Money Show - $10 Rep. Hawaii ($)	6/23/89	15.00	20.00
SO68	ANA'89 - $20 Republic of Hawaii ($)	8/9/89	18.00	22.50
SO69	200th Anniv.-N.Carolina - $5 Bank of North Carolina ($)	11/2/89	13.50	....
SO71	Miami Stamp Expo - Native Americans	1/12/90	20.00	35.00
SO72	200th Anniv.-Rhode I. - $100 Bank-America($)	6/15/90	14.00	20.00
SO73	ANA'90 - #SO12 overprinted on back ($)	..	20.00	18.00
SO74	Paper Money Show -$5 City of Memphis($)	6/14/91	15.00	20.00
SO75	IPMS - America, American Flag Hologram	6/14/91	15.00	20.00
SO76	ANA'91 - $3 Marine Bank of Chicago ($)	8/13/91	15.00	20.00
SO77	Souvenir Card Collectors Soc.10th Anniv.	8/13/91	15.00	20.00
SO78	APS'91 - #114 and Railroad Scene	8/22/91	15.00	25.00
SO79	APS - William Penn Treaty with Indians	8/22/91	115.00	175.00
SO80	Baltimore Phil.Soc.- #120 Decl.of Indep.	8/31/91	15.00	25.00
SO81	ASDA - #117 and S.S.Adriatic	11/7/91	15.00	25.00
SO82	ASDA - Brooklyn Bridge Harbor Scene	11/7/91	110.00	175.00
SO83	PSNE - #118 and Landing of Columbus	11/15/91	15.00	25.00
	1992-1994			
SO84	FUN'92 - Cuban 50 Centavo Note ($)	1/9/92	15.00	25.00
SO85	FUN - Columbus with Globe Hologram	1/9/92	17.00	30.00
SO86	ANA - Costa Rica 100 Colones Gold Ct.($)	2/27/92	18.00	25.00
SO87	Interpex - Venezuela 25¢ Land.-Columbus	3/12/92	15.00	25.00
SO88	World Columbian Stamp Expo - Costa Rica 12¢ Christopher Columbus	5/22/92	15.00	25.00
SO89	WCSE - #230 1¢ Columbian	5/22/92	15.00	25.00
SO90	WCSE - 1921 El Salvador & Statue (Red)	5/22/92	110.00	165.00
SO90A	WCSE - 1921 El Salvador & Statue (Blue)	5/22/92	250.00	375.00
SO91-96	WCSE - set of 6 1893 Columbian Exposition Tickets	5/22/92	165.00	275.00
SO97	WCSE - Folder for #2624-29 with insert bearing "Landing of Columbus"	5/22/92	35.00	45.00
SO102	Paper Money Show -$10 City -Memphis($)	6/19/92	15.00	25.00
SO103	ANA, Orlando - $4 Bank of Florida ($)	8/12/92	15.00	27.50
SO104	APS, Oakland - #234, Costa Rica #122	8/27/92	15.00	25.00
SO105	APS, 3 El Salvador stamps in brown	8/27/92	70.00	100.00
SO105A	same as SO105 in Green, Purple, Orge.	8/27/92	250.00	375.00
SO106	ASDA - 2 El Salvador stamps plus vignette of Columbus	10/28/92	15.00	25.00
SO107	ASDA, Historic Event, Dominican Rep. 50 Pesos Columbus Note ($)	10/28/92	15.00	25.00
SO108	ASDA, Grey Columbus Vignette	10/28/92	100.00	175.00
SO108A	same, Maroon Hand Pulled Proof	10/28/92	250.00	375.00
SO109	Orcoexpo, Anaheim - Hawaii #79 Block	1/8/93	15.00	25.00
SO110	Orcoexpo, Iron-Horse Hologram	1/8/93	17.50	25.00
SO111	Milcopex - Hawaii #76 Block	3/5/93	15.00	25.00

UNITED STATES SOUVENIR CARDS

AMERICAN BANK NOTE COMPANY

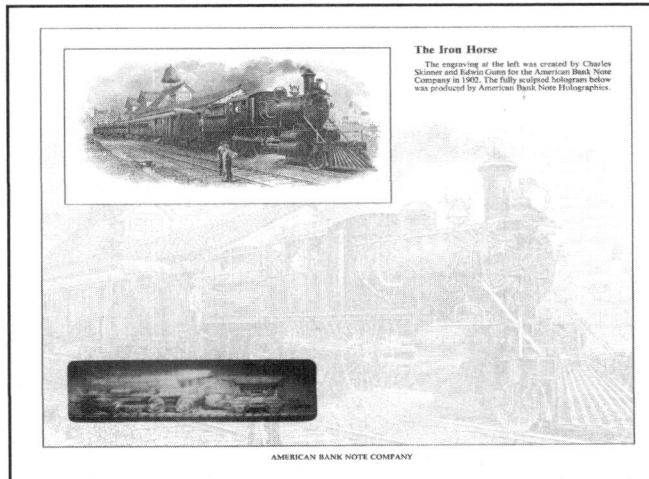

AMERICAN BANK NOTE COMPANY

SO112

PLATE PRINTERS UNION

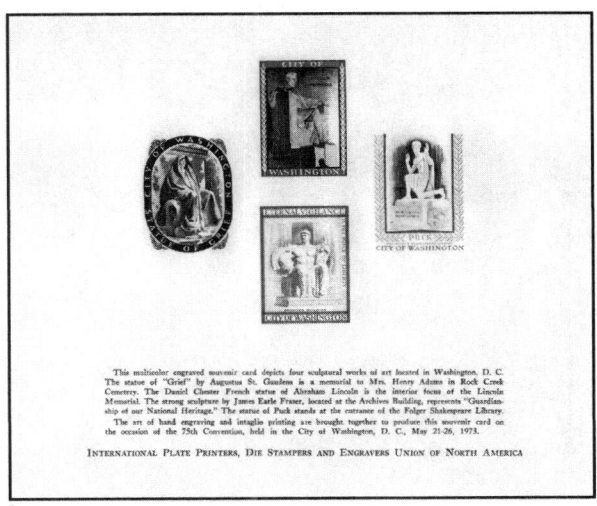

F1973B

SCCS Number	Event and Description	First Day Show/Issue	Mint Card	Cancelled Card
	1992-1994(cont.)			
SO112	ANA - 50 Peso Banco de Minero,Mexico($)	3/11/93	15.00	25.00
SO113	Plymouth, MI - Hawaii #75 Block	4/24/93	15.00	60.00
SO114	ASDA Mega Event - Hawaii #77 Block	5/5/93	15.00	25.00
SO115	Paper Money Show - $20 City-Memphis($)	6/18/93	15.00	25.00
SO116	ANA, Baltimore - $20 Peoples' Bank of Baltimore ($)	7/28/93	14.00	25.00
SO117	ANA, $100 Chesepeake Bank Proof ($)	7/28/93	80.00	120.00
SO118	APS, Houston - Hawaii #74 Block	8/19/93	14.00	22.50
SO119	APS, $1 Hawaii Revenue Blue Proof	8/19/93	70.00	110.00
SO119A	same, Black Hand pulled Proof	8/19/93	250.00	375.00
SO120	ASDA Mega Event - Hawaii #78 Block	10/28/93	13.50	22.50
SO121	ASDA - Holiday, Bank Draft for the Shetucket Bank of Norwich, CT	10/28/93	13.50	22.50
SO122	ASDA, 3 Hawaii Foreign Affairs, Green	10/28/93	80.00	120.00
SO122A	same, Green, Blue, Red Proof	10/28/93	250.00	375.00
SO123	Aripex, Mesa,AZ - U.S. #1 Franklin	1/7/94	16.00	25.00
SO124	ANA, New Orleans - 1 Peso Medellin, Colombia ($)	3/3/94	16.00	25.00
SO125	Milcopex - #73, 2¢ Andrew Jackson	3/4/94	16.00	25.00
SO126	Garfield-Perry - #13, 10¢ Washington	3/18/94	16.00	25.00
SO127	Central States Numism. - $2 Indiana's Pioneer Association ($)	4/8/94	16.00	25.00
SO128	Paper Money Show - $100 Union Bank ($)	6/17/94	16.00	25.00
SO129	ANA, Detroit - $5 Bank of the Capitol, Lansing, Michigan ($)	7/27/94	16.00	25.00
SO130	ANA - Winged Majesty / Eagle Hologram	7/27/94	20.00	30.00
SO131	ANA - $1 White Mountain Bank 0f NH ($)	7/27/94	80.00	120.00
SO132	APS, Pittsburgh - #39, 90¢ Washington	8/18/94	16.00	25.00
SO133	APS - #1 Proof of 5¢ Franklin	8/18/94	80.00	120.00
SO134	Balpex'94 - #226, 10¢ D. Webster	9/3/94	16.00	25.00
SO135	ASDA Mega Event - #122, 90¢ Lincoln	11/3/94	16.00	25.00
SO136	ASDA - #2 Proof of 10¢ Washington	11/3/94	80.00	120.00
SO137	Paper Money Show - 100 Peso El Banco of Uruguay ($)	11/11/94	16.00	25.00

Note: From 1995 on, ABNC Souvenir Cards were limited editions.

SCCS Number	Event and Description	First Day Show/Issue	Mint Card	Cancelled Card
F1973B	Four Statues with IPP Text line	5/21/73	9.50	70.00
F1981B	$2 Embarkation of the Pilgrims ($)	5/17/81	35.00	95.00
F1982A	Napex'82 - Flag with Pledge of Allegiance	7/2/82	10.00	20.00
F1982B	Balpex'82 - Great Seal	9/4/82	15.00	40.00
F1983A	IPPDS & EU - $1 North Berwick Bank($)	1983	10.00	40.00
F1983C	Napex'83 - "Medal of Honor"	6/10/83	10.00	25.00
F1983F	Balpex'83 - George Washington	9/3/83	10.00	15.00
F1984A	Napex'84 - G.Washington & U.S. Capitol	6/24/84	10.00	20.00
F1984C	"Men in Currency" 11 faces	1984	250.00	275.00
F1985D	IPPDS & EU - Eagle resting on Rock	5/12/85	30.00	..
F1987A-B	IPPDS & EU - 6 Train Vignettes on 2 cards	5/3/87	35.00	90.00
F1987G	IPPDS & EU - 6 Train Vignettes on 1 card	5/3/87	70.00	150.00
F1988C	IPPDS & EU - Canadian Parliament, Statue of Liberty, Indep'Hall, U.S. Capitol	1988	30.00	..
F1990D	Napex'90 - #F1983C with 60th Ann. Ovpt.	6/1/90	80.00	100.00
F1991F	GENA'91 - "1000" Breakfast Card	9/27/91	125.00	..
F1992A	SCCS Annual Meeting - Trolley Scene	1992	25.00	..
F1993A	GENA'93 - Woman with Sword & Shield	3/5/93	9.50	..
F1993F	ANA'93 - SCCS "$" Card	7/28/93	10.00	12.00
F1993G	SCCS'93 - Farming Scene	1993	25.00	28.50
F1993J	MANA'93 - SCCS, Eagle & Shield	1993	11.50	..

===

STAMP VENTURES SOUVENIR CARDS

SCCS Number	Event and Description	First Day Show/Issue	Mint Card	Cancelled Card
SO98	World Columbian Stamp Expo - Vignette of Columbus by Canadian Bank Note Co.	5/22/92	42.50	90.00
SO99	WCSE - Czeslae Slania, Engraver	5/22/92	75.00	80.00
SO100	WCSE - Bonnie Blair Olympic Champion	5/22/92	70.00	80.00
SO101	WCSE - Eagle in Flight Hologram	5/22/92	50.00	90.00

WASHINGTON 2006
World Philatelic Exhibition
May 27-June 3, 2006
See you there!
www.washington-2006.org

OFFICIAL SOUVENIR PAGES

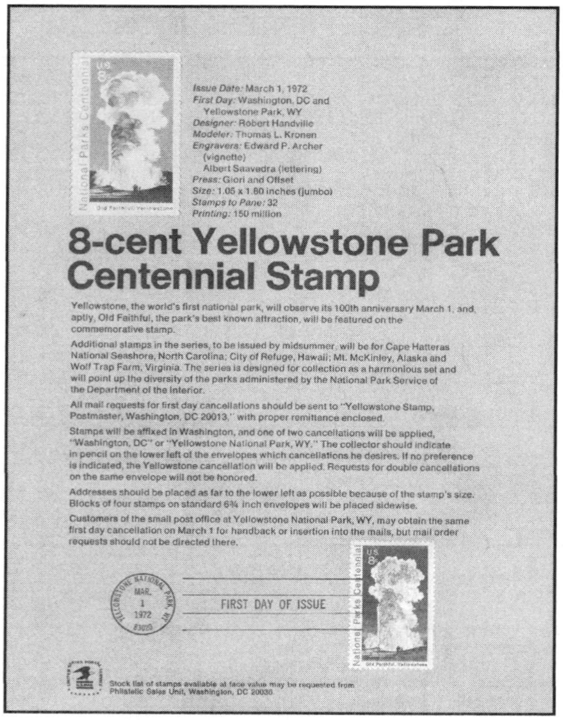
Issue Date: March 1, 1972
First Day: Washington, DC and Yellowstone Park, WY
Designer: Robert Handville
Modeler: Thomas L. Kronen
Engravers: Edward P. Archer (vignette)
Albert Saavedra (lettering)
Press: Giori and Offset
Size: 1.05 x 1.80 inches (jumbo)
Stamps to Pane: 32
Printing: 150 million
8-cent Yellowstone Park Centennial Stamp
Yellowstone, the world's first national park, will observe its 100th anniversary March 1, and, aptly, Old Faithful, the park's best known attraction, will be featured on the commemorative stamp.
Additional stamps in the series, to be issued by midsummer, will be for Cape Hatteras National Seashore, North Carolina; City of Refuge, Hawaii; Mt. McKinley, Alaska and Wolf Trap Farm, Virginia. The series is designed for collection as a harmonious set and will point up the diversity of the parks administered by the National Park Service of the Department of the Interior.
All mail requests for first day cancellations should be sent to "Yellowstone Stamp, Postmaster, Washington, DC 20013," with proper remittance enclosed.
Stamps will be affixed in Washington, and one of two cancellations will be applied, "Washington, DC" or "Yellowstone National Park, WY." The collector should indicate in pencil on the lower left of the envelopes which cancellations he desires. If no preference is indicated, the Yellowstone cancellation will be applied. Requests for double cancellations on the same envelope will not be honored.
Addresses should be placed as far to the lower left as possible because of the stamp's size. Blocks of four stamps on standard 6¾ inch envelopes will be placed sidewise.
Customers of the small post office at Yellowstone National Park, WY, may obtain the same first day cancellation on March 1 for handback or insertion into the mails, but mail order requests should not be directed there.
Yellowstone National Park, WY
MAR. 1 1972
FIRST DAY OF ISSUE
National Parks Centennial
Stock list of stamps available at face value may be requested from Philatelic Sales Unit, Washington, DC 20036

1453

Since March 1, 1972 the U.S. Postal Service has offered, by subscription, Souvenir Pages with first day cancels. They are known as "Official" Souvenir Pages. These were issued flat and unfolded.

Scott No.	Subject	Price
	1972-78 Regular Issues	
1297	3¢ Francis Parkman	6.50
1305C	$1 O'Neill coil	17.50
1305E	15¢ O.W. Holmes	5.50
1393D	7¢ Benjamin Franklin	8.50
1397	14¢ LaGuardia	125.00
1399	18¢ Eliz. Blackwell	5.00
1400	21¢ A. Giannini	6.50
	1972 Commemoratives	
1448-51	2¢ Cape Hatteras	100.00
1452	6¢ Wolf Trap Farm	40.00
1453	8¢ Yellowstone Park	130.00
1454	15¢ Mt. McKinley	30.00
1455	8¢ Family Planning	750.00
1456-59	8¢ Colonial Craftsmen	20.00
1460-62	C85 Olympics	15.00
1463	8¢ PTA	9.00
1464-67	8¢ Wildlife	10.00
1468	8¢ Mail Order	8.00
1469	8¢ Osteopathic Med	6.00
1470	8¢ Tom Sawyer	12.50
1471-72	8¢ Christmas 1972	10.00
1473	8¢ Pharmacy	10.00
1474	8¢ Stamp Collecting	8.00
	1973 Commemoratives	
1475	8¢ Love	10.00
1476	8¢ Pamphleteers	8.00
1477	8¢ Broadside	8.00
1478	8¢ Post Rider	8.00
1479	8¢ Drummer	5.00
1480-83	8¢ Boston Tea Party	10.00
1484	8¢ George Gershwin	10.00
1485	8¢ Robinson Jeffers	8.00
1486	8¢ Henry O. Tanner	9.00
1487	8¢ Willa Cather	10.00
1488	8¢ Copernicus	8.00
1489-98	8¢ Postal People	10.00
1499	8¢ Harry S. Truman	8.00
1500-02,C86	Electronics	13.00
1503	8¢ Lyndon B. Johnson	8.00
1504	8¢ Angus Cattle	5.50
1505	10¢ Chautauqua	5.00
1506	10¢ Kansas Wheat	5.00
1507-08	8¢ Christmas 1973	9.50
	1973-74 Regular Issues	
1509	10¢ Crossed Flags	5.00
1510	10¢ Jeff. Memorial	5.00
1511	10¢ Zip Code	7.00
1518	6.3¢ Bulk Rate coil	5.00
	1974 Commemoratives	
1525	10¢ VFW	5.00
1526	10¢ Robert Frost	8.00
1527	10¢ Expo '74	10.00
1528	10¢ Horse Racing	10.00

Scott No.	Subject	Price
	1974 Commemoratives (continued)	
1529	10¢ Skylab	10.00
1530-37	10¢ Univ. Postal Un	11.00
1538-41	10¢ Mineral Heritage	10.00
1542	10¢ Fort Harrod	5.00
1543-46	10¢ Cont. Congress	8.00
1547	10¢ Energy Conserv	5.00
1548	10¢ Sleepy Hollow	8.00
1549	10¢ Retarded Children	5.00
1550-52	10¢ Christmas 1974	8.00
	1975 Commemoratives	
1553	10¢ Benjamin West	6.00
1554	10¢ Paul L. Dunbar	6.00
1555	10¢ D.W. Griffith	8.00
1556	10¢ Pioneer – Jupiter	10.00
1557	10¢ Mariner 10	10.00
1558	10¢ Collective Bargain.	5.00
1559	8¢ Sybil Ludington	5.00
1560	10¢ Salem Poor	6.00
1561	10¢ Haym Salomon	6.00
1562	18¢ Peter Francisco	6.00
1563	10¢ Lexington-Concord	6.00
1564	10¢ Bunker Hill	6.00
1565-68	10¢ Military Uniforms	10.00
1569-70	10¢Apollo Soyuz	13.00
1571	10¢ Women's Year	5.00
1572-75	10¢ Postal Bicent	6.00
1576	10¢ Peace thru Law	5.00
1577-78	10¢ Bank/Commerce	6.50
1579-80	10¢ Christmas 1975	7.00
	1975-81 Americana Issues	
1581-82,84-85	1¢-4¢ Issues	5.00
1591	9¢ Right to Assemble	5.00
1592	10¢ Petition/Redress	5.00
1593	11¢ Freedom of Press	5.00
1594,1816	12¢ Conscience	5.00
1596	13¢ Eagle/Shield	6.50
1597,1618C	15¢ Ft. McHenry	5.00
1599,1619	16¢ Liberty	5.00
1603	24¢ Old No. Church	5.00
1604	28¢ Remote Outpost	5.00
1605	29¢ Lighthouse	6.00
1606	30¢ Am. Schools	6.00
1608	50¢ "Betty" Lamp	6.00
1610	$1 Rush Lamp	8.00
1611	$2 Kerosene Lamp	10.00
1612	$5 R.R. Lantern	16.00
1613	3.1¢ Non Profit coil	8.00
1614	7.7¢ Bulk Rate coil	5.00
1615	7.9¢ Bulk Rate coil	5.00
1615C	8.4¢ Bulk Rate coil	6.00
1616	9¢ Assembly coil	5.00
1617	10¢ Redress coil	5.00
1618	13¢ Liberty Bell coil	5.00

Scott No.	Subject	Price
	1975-81 Americana Issues (cont.)	
1622,25	13¢ Flag/Ind. Hall	5.00
1623c	$1 Vending bk. p. 10	32.50
	1976 Commemoratives	
1629-31	13¢Spirit of '76	8.00
1632	13¢ Interphil'76	5.00
1633-82	13¢ State Flags(5 pgs)	57.50
1683	13¢ Telephone Cent.	5.00
1684	13¢ Comm.Aviation	5.00
1685	13¢ Chemistry	5.00
1686-89	Bicentennial SS (4)	55.00
1690	13¢ Ben Franklin	5.00
1691-94	13¢ Decl.of Independ.	8.00
1695-98	13¢ Olympics	8.00
1699	13¢ Clara Maass	10.00
1700	13¢ Adolphe Ochs	5.00
1701-3	13¢ Christmas 1976	5.00
	1977 Commemoratives	
1704	13¢ Wash./Princeton	5.00
1705	13¢ Sound Recording	6.50
1706-9	13¢ Pueblo Art	9.50
1710	13¢ Lindbergh Flight	6.00
1711	13¢ Colorado	6.00
1712-15	13¢ Butterflies	8.00
1716	13¢ Lafayette	5.00
1717-20	13¢ Skilled Hands	7.00
1721	13¢ Peace Bridge	5.00
1722	13¢ Herkimer/Oriskany	5.00
1723-24	13¢ Energy	5.00
1725	13¢ Alta California	5.00
1726	13¢ Art. of Confed.	5.00
1727	13¢ Talking Pictures	6.00
1728	13¢ Saratoga	6.00
1729-30	13¢ Christmas,Omaha	5.50
1729-30	13¢ Valley Forge	5.50
	1978 Issues	
1731	13¢ Carl Sandburg	6.00
1732-33	13¢ Cook, Anchorage	6.50
1732-33	13¢ Cook, Honolulu	6.50
1734	13¢ Indian Head Penny	5.00
1735,43	(15¢)"A" Stamp (2)	8.00
1737	15¢ Roses Bklt.single	6.50
1742a	15¢ Windmills BP(1980)	13.00
1744	13¢ Harriet Tubman	8.00
1745-48	13¢ Quilts	8.50
1749-52	13¢ Dance	8.50
1753	13¢ French Alliance	5.00
1754	13¢ Dr.Papenicolaou	6.00
1755	13¢ Jimmie Rodgers	8.00
1756	15¢ George M. Cohan	6.00
1757	13¢ CAPEX'78	13.00
1758	15¢ Photography	8.00
1759	15¢ Viking Missions	10.00
1760-63	15¢ American Owls	8.00
1764-67	15¢ American Trees	6.00
1768	15¢ Madonna & Child	5.00
1769	15¢ Hobby Horse	5.00
	1979 Commemoratives	
1770	15¢ Robert F. Kennedy	6.50
1771	15¢ Martin L.King,Jr.	8.00
1772	15¢ Year of the Child	5.00
1773	15¢ John Steinbeck	10.00
1774	15¢ Albert Einstein	10.00
1775-78	15¢ PA Toleware	8.00
1779-82	15¢ Architecture	6.00
1783-86	15¢ Endangered Flora	6.00
1787	15¢ Seeing Eye Dogs	5.00
1788	15¢ Special Olympics	5.00
1789	15¢ John Paul Jones	5.00
1790	10¢ Olympics	5.50
1791-94	15¢ Summer Olympics	7.50
1795-98	15¢ Winter Olympics(80)	8.00
1799	15¢ Virgin & Child	5.00
1800	15¢ Santa Claus	5.00
1801	15¢ Will Rogers	6.00
1802	15¢ Vietnam Vets	8.00
	1980-81 Issues	
1803	15¢ W.C.Fields	8.00
1804	15¢ Ben.Banneker	6.00
1805-10	15¢ Letter Writing	6.50
1811	1¢ Quill Pen Coil	5.00
1813	3.5¢ Non Profit Coil	5.00
1818,20	(18¢) "B" Stamps	5.00
1819a	(18¢) "B" Bk.Pane	5.00
1821	15¢ Frances Perkins	5.00
1822	15¢ Dolly Madison	6.00
1823	15¢ Emily Bissell	6.00
1824	15¢ Keller/Sullivan	5.00
1825	15¢ Veterans Admin.	5.00
1826	15¢ B. de Galvez	5.00
1827-30	15¢ Coral Reefs	8.00
1831	15¢ Organized Labor	5.00
1832	15¢ Edith Wharton	5.00
1833	15¢ Education	5.00
1834-37	15¢ Indian Masks	8.50
1838-41	15¢ Architecture	6.50
1842	15¢ St.Glass Windows	5.00
1843	15¢ Antique Toys	6.00

Scott No.	Subject	Price
	1980-85 Great Americans	
1844	1¢ Dorothea Dix	5.00
1845	2¢ Igor Stravinsky	6.00
1846	3¢ Henry Clay	5.00
1847	4¢ Carl Shurz	5.00
1848	5¢ Pearl S. Buck	5.00
1849	6¢ Walter Lippmann	5.00
1850	7¢ A. Baldwin	5.00
1851	8¢ Henry Knox	5.00
1852	9¢ Sylvanus Thayer	5.00
1853	10¢ Richard Russell	5.00
1854	11¢ A. Partridge	5.00
1855	13¢ Crazy Horse	6.00
1856	14¢ Sinclair Lewis	8.00
1857	17¢ Rachel Carson	5.00
1858	18¢ George Mason	5.00
1859	19¢ Sequoyah	5.00
1860	20¢ Ralph Bunche	7.50
1861	20¢ T. Gallaudet	5.00
1862	20¢ H. Truman	5.00
1863	22¢ Audubon	6.00
1864	30¢ Dr. Laubach	5.00
1865	35¢ Dr. C. Drew	5.00
1866	37¢ R. Millikan	5.00
1867	39¢ G. Clark	5.00
1868	40¢ L. Gilbreth	5.00
1869	50¢ C. Nimitz	7.00
	1981-82 Issues	
1874	15¢ Everett Dirksen	5.00
1875	15¢ Whitney Young	8.00
1876-79	18¢ Flowers	6.50
1889a	18¢ Wildlife bk/10	10.75
1890-91	18¢ Flag	5.00
1893a	6¢ & 18¢ Flag & Stars bklt. pn	5.00
1894-95	20¢ Flag	6.00
1896a	20¢ Flag bklt. pn./6	5.25
1896b	20¢ Flag bklt. pn./10	5.50
	1981-84 Transportation Coils	
1897	1¢ Omnibus	5.00
1897A	2¢ Locomotive	7.00
1898	3¢ Handcar	5.00
1898A	4¢ Stagecoach	6.00
1899	5¢ Motorcycle	8.00
1900	5.2¢ Sleigh	8.00
1901	5.9¢ Bicycle	8.00
1902	7.4¢ Baby Buggy	5.00
1903	9.3¢ Mail Wagon	6.00
1904	10.9¢ Hansom Cab	6.50
1905	11¢ Caboose	6.50
1906	17¢ Electric Car	5.00
1907	18¢ Surrey	6.50
1908	20¢ Pumper	8.00
	1981-83 Regulars & Commems.	
1909	$9.35 Eagle bklt. sgl.	150.00
1909a	$9.35 Bklt.pane of 3	210.00
1910	18¢ Red Cross	5.00
1911	18¢ Savings & Loan	5.00
1912-19	18¢ Space Achieve	13.00
1920	18¢ Prof. Management	5.00
1921-24	18¢ Wildlife Habitats	6.50
1925	18¢ Disabled Persons	5.00
1926	18¢ St. Vincent Millay	5.00
1927	18¢ Alcoholism	5.00
1928-31	18¢ Architecture	6.50
1932	18¢ Babe Zaharias	27.50
1933	18¢ Bobby Jones	32.50
1934	18¢ Fred. Remington	8.00
1935-36	18¢ & 20¢ J. Hoban	5.00
1937-38	18¢ Yorktown/V Capes	6.00
1939	20¢ Madonna/Child.	5.00
1940	20¢ "Teddy Bear"	8.00
1941	20¢ John Hanson	5.00
1942-45	20¢ Desert Plants	6.50
1946-47	"C" sht./coil stamps	5.00
1948a	"C" bklt. pane/10	5.25
1949a	20¢ Sheep bk pn/10	6.00
	1982 Issues	
1950	20¢ F.D. Roosevelt	5.00
1951	20¢ Love	5.00
1952	20¢ G. Washington	5.00
1953/2002	20¢ State Birds & Flowers (5)	80.00
2003	20¢ Netherlands	5.00
2004	20¢ Library-Congress	5.00
2005	20¢ Consumer Coil	6.50
2006-09	20¢ World's Fair	5.00
2010	20¢ Horatio Alger	5.00
2011	20¢ Aging	5.00
2012	20¢ Barrymores	8.00
2013	20¢ Dr. Mary Walker	5.00
2014	20¢ Int'l Peace Garden	5.00
2015	20¢ Libraries	5.00
2016	20¢ Jackie Robinson	22.50
2017	20¢ Touro Synagogue	5.00
2018	20¢ Wolf Trap	5.00
2019-22	20¢ Architecture	6.50
2023	20¢ Francis of Assisi	5.00

OFFICIAL SOUVENIR PAGES

Scott No.	Subject	Price
	1982 Issues (continued)	
2024	20¢ Ponce de Leon	5.00
2025	13¢ Kitten & Puppy	6.00
2026	20¢ Madonna	6.00
2027-30	20¢ Snow Scene	6.50
	1983 Commemoratives	
2031	20¢ Science & Industry	5.00
2032-35	20¢ Balloons	5.50
2036	20¢ Sweden/US	5.00
2037	20¢ Civilian Conservat.	5.00
2038	20¢ Joseph Priestley	5.00
2039	20¢ Volunteerism ...	5.00
2040	20¢ German Immigrants	5.00
2041	20¢ Brooklyn Bridge	6.50
2042	20¢ Tenn. Valley Auth.	5.00
2043	20¢ Physical Fitness	5.00
2044	20¢ Scott Joplin	5.00
2045	20¢ Medal of Honor	10.00
2046	20¢ Babe Ruth	20.00
2047	20¢ N.Hawthorne ...	5.00
2048-51	13¢ Olympics	6.00
2052	20¢ Treaty of Paris	5.00
2053	20¢ Civil Service	5.00
2054	20¢ Metropolitan Opera	6.00
2055-58	20¢ Inventors	6.50
2059-62	20¢ Streetcars	8.00
2063	20¢ Madonna	5.00
2064	20¢ Santa Claus	5.00
2065	20¢ Martin Luther ..	8.00
	1984 Commemoratives	
2066	20¢ Alaska Statehood	5.00
2067-70	20¢ Winter Olympics	6.50
2071	20¢ FDIC	5.00
2072	20¢ Love	5.00
2073	20¢ Carter G. Woodson	6.00
2074	20¢ Soil/Water Con	5.00
2075	20¢ Credit Union Act	5.00
2076-79	20¢ Orchids	8.00
2080	20¢ Hawaii Statehood	6.00
2081	20¢ Nat'l. Archives	5.00
2082-85	20¢ Summer Olympics	6.50
2086	20¢ LA World Expo	5.00
2087	20¢ Health Research	5.00
2088	20¢ Douglas Fairbanks	8.00
2089	20¢ Jim Thorpe	16.00
2090	20¢ John McCormack	8.00
2091	20¢ St.Lawrence Seaway	5.00
2092	20¢ Migratory Bird Act	8.00
2093	20¢ Roanoke Voyages	5.00
2094	20¢ Herman Melville	6.00
2095	20¢ Horace Moses .	5.00
2096	20¢ Smokey Bear ..	17.50
2097	20¢ Roberto Clemente	20.00
2098-2101	20¢ Dogs	8.00
2102	20¢ Crime Prevention	6.00
2103	20¢ Hispanic Americans	5.00
2104	20¢ Family Unity	5.00
2105	20¢ Eleanor Roosevelt	8.00
2106	20¢ Nation of Readers	5.00
2107	20¢ Xmas Traditional	5.00
2108	20¢ Xmas Santa Claus	5.00
2109	20¢ Vietnam Vets Mem	8.00
	1985-87 Issues	
2110	22¢ Jerome Kern ...	5.00
2111-12	"D" sht./coil stamps	5.00
2113a	22¢ "D" bklt. pane/10	5.50
2114-15	22¢ Flag	6.00
2115b	22¢ Flag "T" coil	5.50
2116a	22¢ Flag bklt. bk./5	6.50
2121a	22¢ Seashells bk/10	8.00
2122	$10.75 Eagle bklt.sgl.	65.00
2122a	$10.75 Bklt. pane/3	130.00
	1985-89 Transportation Coils	
2123	3.4¢ School Bus	6.50
2124	4.9¢ Buckboard	6.00
2125	5.5¢ Star Rt. Truck	6.00
2126	6¢ Tricycle	6.00
2127	7.1¢ Tractor	5.00
2127a	7.1¢ Tractor Zip+4 .	5.00
2128	8.3¢ Ambulance	6.50
2129	8.5¢ Tow Truck	5.00
2130	10.1¢ Oil Wagon	5.00
2130a	10.1¢ Red Prec	5.00
2131	11¢ Stutz Bearcat ..	6.00
2132	12¢ Stanley Steamer	6.00
2133	12.5¢ Pushcart	5.50
2134	14¢ Iceboat	5.00
2135	17¢ Dog Sled	5.00
2136	25¢ Bread Wagon ..	6.50
	1985 Issues (cont.)	
2137	22¢ Mary Bethune .	8.00
2138-41	22¢ Duck Decoys ..	10.00
2142	22¢ Winter Special Olympics.	5.00
2143	22¢ Love	5.00
2144	22¢ Rural Electricity	5.00
2145	22¢ AMERIPEX '86	5.00
2146	22¢ Abigail Adams .	5.00

Scott No.	Subject	Price
	1985 Issues (continued)	
2147	22¢ Fred Bartholdi .	6.00
2149	18¢ G. Wash. coil ..	5.00
2150	21.1¢ Zip+4 coil	5.00
2152	22¢ Korean War Vets	7.00
2153	22¢ Social Security	5.00
2154	22¢ W War I Vets ..	8.00
2155-58	22¢ Horses	10.00
2159	22¢ Public Education	5.00
2160-63	22¢ Youth Year	9.50
2164	22¢ End Hunger	5.00
2165	22¢ Madonna	5.00
2166	22¢ Poinsettia	5.00
	1986 Issues	
2167	22¢ Arkansas Statehd	5.00
	1986-94 Great Americans	
2168	1¢ M. Mitchell	7.50
2169	2¢ Mary Lyon	5.00
2170	3¢ Dr. P.D. White ...	5.00
2171	4¢ Fr. Flanagan	5.00
2172	5¢ Hugo Black	5.75
2173	5¢ Munoz Marin	6.00
2175	10¢ Red Cloud	8.00
2176	14¢ Julia W. Howe .	5.00
2177	15¢ Buffalo Bill	6.00
2178	17¢ B. Lockwood ...	5.00
2179	20¢ Virginia Agpar .	7.00
2180	21¢ C. Carlson	5.00
2181	23¢ M. Cassatt	5.00
2182	25¢ Jack London ...	5.00
2182a	Bklt. pn./10	8.50
2183	28¢ Sitting Bull	8.00
2184	29¢ Earl Warren	5.00
2185	29¢ T. Jefferson	5.00
2186	35¢ Dennis Chavez	5.50
2187	40¢ C.L. Chennault	6.00
2188	45¢ Cushing	5.00
2189	52¢ H. Humphrey ...	5.00
2190	56¢ John Harvard ..	5.00
2191	65¢ H. Arnold	7.50
2192	75¢ Wendell Wilkie .	5.50
2193	$1 Dr. B. Revel	4.50
2194	$1 Johns Hopkins ..	6.50
2195	$2 W.J. Bryan	8.00
2196	$5 B. Harte	15.00
2197a	25¢ London, bk/6 ..	5.00
	1986 Issues	
2201a	22¢ Stamp Collect .	6.50
2202	22¢ Love	6.00
2203	22¢ Sojourner Truth	8.00
2204	22¢ Republic Texas	5.00
2209a	22¢ Fish bklt. pane/5	9.50
2210	22¢ Public Hospitals	5.00
2211	22¢ Duke Ellington .	9.50
2216-19	US Pres. shts.,4 pgs.	32.50
2220-23	22¢ Polar Explorers	8.00
2224	22¢ Statue of Liberty	6.00
2226	2¢ Locom. re-engr .	5.00
2235-38	22¢ Navajo Art	8.00
2239	22¢ T.S. Elliot	8.00
2240-43	22¢ Woodcarv Figures	8.50
2244	22¢ Madonna	5.00
2245	22¢ Christmas Trees	5.00
	1987 Issues	
2246	22¢ Michigan	6.00
2247	22¢ Pan-Am. Games	5.00
2248	22¢ Love	5.00
2249	22¢ J. Baptiste Pointe du Sable	9.50
2250	22¢ Enrico Caruso .	6.00
2251	22¢ Girl Scouts	10.00
	1987-88 Transportation Coils	
2252	3¢ Conestoga Wagon	5.00
2253,62	5¢,17.5¢	5.00
2254	5.3¢ Elevator, Prec.	5.00
2255	7.6¢ Carretta, Prec.	5.00
2256	8.4¢ Wheelchair, Prec.	5.00
2257	10¢ Canal Boat	6.00
2258	13¢ Police Wagon,Prec.	8.00
2259	13.2¢ RR Car, Prec	8.00
2260	15¢ Tugboat	5.00
2261	16.7¢ Popcorn Wag,Prec.	6.00
2263	20¢ Cable Car	6.00
2264	20.5¢ Fire Engine, Prec	8.00
2265	21¢ RR Mail Car,Prec.	8.00
2266	24.1¢ Tandem Bike,Prec.	5.00
	1987-89 Issues	
2274a	22¢ Spec. Occasions	7.50
2275	22¢ United Way	5.00
2276	222¢ Flag/Fireworks	5.00
2276a	Bklt. pair	5.00
2277,79	(25¢) "E" sheet/coil	5.00
2278	25¢ Flag/Clouds	5.00
2280	25¢ Flag/Yosemite coil	5.00
2280var	Pre-phos. paper	5.00
2281	25¢ Honeybee coil .	8.00
2282a	(25¢) "E" Bklt. Pane/10	6.50
2283a	25¢ Pheasant Bk/10	8.00

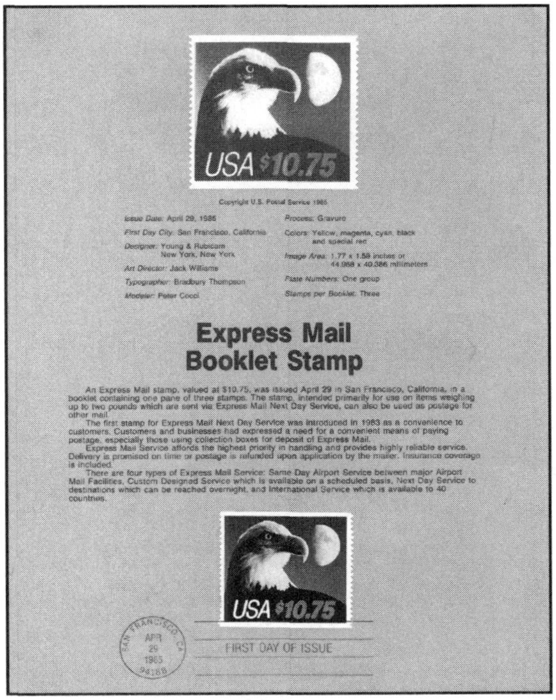

2122

Scott No.	Subject	Price
	1987-89 Issues (continued)	
2284-85b	25¢ Owl/Grosbeak. Bk	6.00
2285Ac	25¢ Flag/Clouds Bk	6.50
2286-2335	22¢ Wildlife (5) ...	45.00
	1987-90 Bicentennial Issues	
2336	22¢ Delaware	6.00
2337	22¢ Penn	5.00
2338	22¢ New Jersey	6.00
2339	22¢ Georgia	6.00
2340	22¢ Conn	6.00
2341	22¢ Mass	6.00
2342	22¢ Maryland	6.00
2343	25¢ S. Carolina	5.00
2344	25¢ New Hampshire	5.00
2345	25¢ Virginia	6.00
2346	25¢ New York	5.00
2347	25¢ North Carolina .	6.00
2348	25¢ Rhode Island ..	5.00
	1987-88 Issues	
2349	22¢ U.S.-Morocco ..	5.00
2350	22¢ W.Faulkner	10.00
2351-54	22¢ Lacemaking ...	11.00
2359a	22¢ Constitution Bklt.	6.50
2360	22¢ Signing Constit.	5.00
2361	22¢ CPA	9.50
2366a	22¢ Locomotive Bklt	13.00
2367	22¢ Madonna	5.00
2368	22¢ Ornament	5.00
2369	22¢ Winter Olympics	5.00
2370	22¢ Australia Bicent.	6.00
2371	22¢ J.W. Johnson .	6.00
2372-75	22¢ Cats	11.00
2376	22¢ Knute Rockne .	16.00
2377	25¢ Francis Ouimet	21.50
2378	25¢ Love	5.00
2379	45¢ Love	5.00
2380	25¢ Summer Olympics	5.00
2385a	25¢ Classic Cars bk	10.75
2386-89	25¢ Antarc.Explorers	6.50
2390-93	25¢ Carousel Animal	7.50
2394	$8.75 Express Mail	37.50
2396a-98a	25¢ Occas.bk.(2)	55.00
2399	25¢ Madonna	5.00
2400	25¢ Village Scene ..	5.00
	1989-90 Issues	
2401	25¢ Montana Sthd .	5.00
2402	25¢ A.P. Randolph .	6.00
2403	25¢ N.Dakota Sthd	5.00
2404	25¢ Washington Sthd.	5.00
2409a	25¢ Steamboats bklt.	10.75
2410	25¢ Wld. Stamp Exp	5.00
2411	25¢ A. Toscanini	7.50
2412	25¢ House of Reps	5.00
2413	25¢ U.S. Senate	5.00
2414	25¢ Exec.Branch/GW	5.00
2415	25¢ Supreme Ct.('90)	5.00

Scott No.	Subject	Price
	1989-90 Issues (continued)	
2416	25¢ S.Dakota Sthd.	5.00
2417	25¢ Lou Gehrig	22.50
2418	25¢ E. Hemingway .	10.00
2419	$2.40 Moon Landing	32.50
2420	25¢ Letter Carriers .	5.00
2421	25¢ Bill of Rights ...	5.00
2422-25	25¢ Prehis. Animals	13.00
2426/C121	25¢/45¢ Pre-Columbian Customs	5.00
2427,27a	25¢ Christmas Art, Sht. & Bklt. Pn	10.00
2428,29a	25¢ Christmas Sleigh, Sht. & Bklt. Pn	10.00
2431	25¢ Eagle, self-adhes	5.00
2433	90¢ WSE S/S of 4 .	18.00
2434-37	25¢ Classic Mail ...	8.00
2438	25¢ Cl.Mail S/S of 4	10.00
2439	25¢ Idaho Sthd	5.00
2440,41a	25¢ Love, sht. & bklt.	8.00
2442	25¢ Ida B. Wells	8.00
2443a	15¢ Beach Umbr., bklt.	8.00
2444	25¢ Wyoming Sthd .	6.00
2445-48	25¢ Classic Films .	13.50
2449	25¢ Marianne Moore	6.00
	1990-95 Transportation Coils	
2451	4¢ Steam Carriage .	5.00
2452	5¢ Circus Wagon ...	6.00
2452B	5¢ Wagon, gravure	8.00
2452D	5¢ Circus Wagon, (¢)Sign	6.00
2453,57	5¢/10¢ Canoe/Trailer	5.00
2454	5¢ Canoe, gravure .	6.00
2458	10¢ Tractor Trailer .	6.00
2463	20¢ Cog Railway	6.00
2464	23¢ Lunch Wagon ..	5.00
2466	32¢ Ferryboat	6.00
2468	$1.00 Seaplane coil	10.00
	1990-95 Issues	
2474a	25¢ Lighthouse bklt	13.00
2475	25¢ ATM Plastic Flag	6.00
2476,78,80	1¢/30¢ Birds	5.00
2477	1¢ Kestrel	5.00
2479	19¢ Fawn	5.00
2481	45¢ Pumpkinseed ..	6.00
2482	$2 Bobcat	8.00
2483	20¢ Blue Jay	5.00
2484a,85a	29¢ Wood Duck bklts. BEP & KCS	15.00
2486a	29¢ African Violet, booklet pane of 10 .	8.00
2487-88,93-94	Peach & Pear	8.00
2489	29¢ Red Squirrel	6.00
2490	29¢ Rose	5.00
2491	29¢ Pine Cone	5.00

OFFICIAL SOUVENIR PAGES

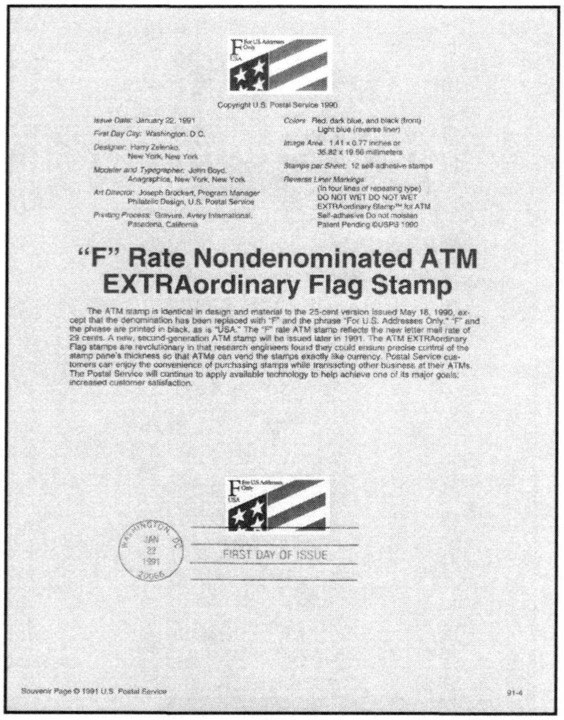
F For U.S. Addresses Only USA
Copyright U.S. Postal Service 1990
Issue Date: January 22, 1991
First Day City: Washington, D.C.
Designer: Harry Zelenko, New York, New York
Modeler and Typographer: John Boyd, Anagraphics, New York, New York
Art Director: Joseph Brockert, Program Manager Philatelic Design, U.S. Postal Service
Printing Process: Gravure, Avery International, Pasadena, California
Colors: Red, dark blue, and black (front) Light blue (reverse liner)
Image Area: 1.41 x 0.77 inches or 35.82 x 19.56 millimeters
Stamps per Sheet: 12 self-adhesive stamps
Reverse Liner Markings: (in four lines of repeating type) DO NOT WET DO NOT WET EXTRAordinary Stamp™ for ATM Self-adhesive Do not moisten Patent Pending ©USPS 1990
"F" Rate Nondenominated ATM EXTRAordinary Flag Stamp
The ATM stamp is identical in design and material to the 25-cent version issued May 18, 1990, except that the denomination has been replaced with "F" and the phrase "For U.S. Addresses Only." "F" and the phrase are printed in black, as is "USA." The "F" rate ATM stamp reflects the new letter mail rate of 29 cents. A new, second-generation ATM stamp will be issued later in 1991. The ATM EXTRAordinary Flag stamps are revolutionary in that research engineers found they could ensure precise control of the stamp pane's thickness so that ATMs can vend the stamps exactly like currency. Postal Service customers can enjoy the convenience of purchasing stamps while transacting other business at their ATMs. The Postal Service will continue to apply available technology to help achieve one of its major goals: increased customer satisfaction.
FIRST DAY OF ISSUE
Souvenir Page © 1991 U.S. Postal Service
91-4

2522

Scott No.	Subject	Price
1990-95 Issues (continued)		
2492	32¢ Pink Rose	8.00
2493-94	32¢ Peach/Pear	16.00
2496-2500	25¢ Olympics	9.50
2505a	25¢ Indian Headress	10.00
2506-07	25¢ Marshall Is. & MicronesiaJoint Issue	5.00
2508-11	25¢ Sea Creatures	10.75
2512/C127	25¢,45¢ America	5.00
2513	25¢ D.D. Eisenhower	6.00
2514,14a	25¢ Christmas sht. & Bklt. Pn./10	9.50
2515,16a	25¢ Christmas Tree sht. & Bklt. Pn./10	9.50
1991-94 Issues		
2517,18	(29¢) "F" Flower, sht. & Coil pr	5.00
2519a,20a	(29¢) "F" Flower, Bklt. Pns. of 10	16.50
2521	(4¢) Make-up rate	5.00
2522	(29¢) "F" Self Adh	5.00
2523	29¢ Flag/Rushmore	6.00
2523A	29¢ Mt. Rush, grav.	5.00
2524,27a	29¢ Flower,sht./bklt	10.00
2525	29¢ Flower coil,roulette	5.00
2526	29¢ Flower coil,perf.	5.00
2528a	29¢ Flag/Olympic Rings Bklt. pane fo 10	11.00
2529	19¢ Fishing Boat coil	8.00
2529C	19¢ Fishing Boat III	5.00
2530a	19¢ Balloons, bklt	8.00
2531	29¢ Flags on Parade	5.00
2531A	29¢ Liberty, ATM	5.00
1991 Commemoratives		
2532	50¢ Switzerland	5.00
2533	29¢ Vermont	5.00
2534	29¢ Savings Bonds	5.00
2535,36a,37	29¢,52¢ Love, shts. & Bklt.	18.50
2538	29¢ William Saroyan	10.00
1991-95 Regular Issues		
2539	$1.00 USPS/Olympics	6.50
2540	$2.90 Priority Mail	21.75
2541	$9.95 Express Mail	47.50
2542	$14.00 Express Mail	65.00
2543	$2.90 Space P.M.	15.00
2544	$3 Challenger	20.00
2544A	$10.75 Endeavor	40.00
1991 Commemoratives		
2549a	29¢ Fishing Flies bklt.	30.00
2550	29¢ Cole Porter	6.00
2551	29¢ Desert Storm/ Shield	15.00
2553-57	29¢ Summer Olympic	10.75
2558	29¢ Numismatics	8.00
2559	29¢ WW II S/S	16.00
2560	29¢ Basketball	13.00

Scott No.	Subject	Price
1991 Commemoratives (continued)		
2561	29¢ Washington, D.C.	5.00
2566a	29¢ Comedians bklt.	13.00
2567	29¢ Jan Matzeliger	9.00
2577a	29¢ Space bklt	16.00
2578,78a	29¢ Madonna,sht/bklt	15.00
2579,80, or 81,82-85	29¢ Santa Claus sht./bklt	26.50
1992-95 Regulars		
2587	32¢ James Polk	8.00
2590	$1.00 Burgoyne	8.00
2592	$5.00 Washington	18.50
2593a	29¢ Pledge bklt.	8.00
2595-97	29¢ Eagle & Shield/ Die Cut (3 Pgs.)	7.50
2598	29¢ Eagle S/A	5.00
2599	29¢ Liberty	5.00
2602	(10¢)Eagle&Shld. coil	8.00
2603-4	(10¢) BEP & SV	6.50
2605	23¢ Flag/Pre-sort	5.00
2606	23¢ USA/Pre-sort	5.00
2607	23¢ Same, BEP	6.00
2608	23¢ Same, SV	5.00
2609	29¢ Flag/W.H. Coil	5.00
1992 Commemoratives		
2611-15	29¢ Winter Olympics	8.00
2616	29¢ World Columbian	5.00
2617	29¢ W.E.B. DuBois	10.00
2618	29¢ Love	5.00
2619	29¢ Olympic Baseball	25.00
2620-23	29¢ Columbus Voyages	7.00
2624-29	1¢-$5 Columbus S/S	80.00
2630	29¢ NY Stock Exchg	5.00
2631-34	29¢ Space Accomp	10.00
2635	29¢ Alaska Highway	6.00
2636	29¢ Kentucky Sthd	5.00
2637-41	29¢ Summer Olympics	8.00
2646a	29¢ Hummingbird Pn	13.00
2647-96	29¢ Wildflowers (5)	50.00
2697	29¢ WW II S/S	10.75
2698	29¢ Dorothy Parker	6.00
2699	29¢ Dr. von Karman	10.00
2700-03	29¢ Minerals	8.00
2704	29¢ Juan Cabrillo	5.00
2709a	29¢ Wild Animals Bklt.	10.75
2710,10a	29¢ Christmas Trad. Sheet & Bklt.	16.50
2711-14,18a,19	29¢ Toys, sheet bklt.& Die Cut	11.00
2720	29¢ Chinese New Year	15.00
1993 Commemoratives		
2721	29¢ Elvis Presley	21.50
2722	29¢ Oklahoma	5.00
2723	29¢ Hank Williams	10.00
2724/30,2737a	29¢ Rock 'n Roll Bklt. & Single	45.00

Scott No.	Subject	Price
1993 Commemoratives (continued)		
2745a	29¢ Space Fantasy, Bklt. Pane of 5	15.00
2746	29¢ Perry L. Julian	8.00
2747	29¢ Oregon Trail	5.00
2748	29¢ World Games	5.00
2749	29¢ Grace Kelly	15.00
2750-3	29¢ Circus	10.00
2754	29¢ Cherokee Strip	8.00
2755	29¢ Dean Acheson	5.00
2756-9	29¢ Sports Horses	10.00
2764a	29¢ Garden Flowers, Bklt. Pane of 5	8.00
2765	29¢ WW II S/S	13.00
2766	29¢ Joe Louis	18.00
2770a	29¢ Broadway, Booklet of 4	9.00
2771/4,2778a	Country Music, Booklet & Single	26.50
2779-82	29¢ Postal Museum	6.50
2783-4	29¢ Deaf Communic.	5.00
2785-8	29¢ Youth Classics	6.00
2789,2790a	29¢ Madonna	10.75
2791/4,2798b,2799/2802,2803	29¢ Christmas	27.50
2804	29¢ Nthn. Marianas	5.00
2805	29¢ Columbus Landing in Puerto Rico	6.00
2806,2806b	29¢ AIDS	10.75
1994 Issues		
2807-11	29¢ Winter Olympics	11.00
2812	29¢ Edward R.Murrow	7.00
2813	29¢ Sunrise Love	6.00
2814a,15	29¢-52¢ Love	13.00
2814C	29¢ Love	6.00
2816	29¢ Dr. Allison Davis	9.00
2817	29¢ Chinese New Year	8.00
2818	29¢ Buffalo Soldiers	10.00
2819-28	29¢ Silent ScreenStars	13.50
2833a	29¢ Garden Flowers, Bklt. Pane of 5	13.00
2834-36	29¢-50¢ Soccer	13.00
2837	Soccer Sv. Sheet	13.00
2838	29¢ WWII S/S	10.75
2839-40	29¢ Rockwell Stamp & S/S	21.50
2841-42	29¢/$9.95 Moon	37.50
2847a	29¢ Locomotive Pn.	13.50
2848	29¢ George Meany	6.00
2849-53	29¢ Pop Singers	13.00
2854-61	29¢ Blues/Jazz	15.00
2862	29¢ J. Thurber	8.00
2863-66	29¢ Wonders-Sea	10.00
2867-68	29¢ Cranes	6.00
2869	29¢ Legends-West.	31.50
2871,71b	29¢ Madonna	15.00
2872,72a	29¢ Stocking	10.00
2873-74	29¢ Santa/Cardinal	12.50
2875	$2 BEP S/S	25.00
2876	29¢ Year of the Boar	10.00
2877,84,90,93	"G" ABNC	8.00
2878,80,82,85	"G" SVS	8.00
2879,81,83,89	"G" BEP	8.00
2886-87	"G" Self. Adh.	15.00
1995-99 Issues		
2897/2916	32¢ Flag-Porch	9.50
2902	(5¢) Butte Coil	8.00
2902B,4A, 6,10,12A,15B	Coils	9.50
2903-4	(5¢) Mountain Coil	7.50
2905	(10¢) Automobile Coil	8.00
2907,20d,21	Regulars	8.00
2908-9	(15¢) Tail Fin Coil	8.00
2911-12	(25¢) Juke Box Coil	6.00
2912B/15	Self Adhesives	9.00
2919	32¢ Flag - Field, S.A.	5.00
2933	32¢ M. Hershey	5.00
2934	32¢ Cal Farley	6.00
2935	32¢ Henry R. Luce	10.00
2936	32¢ Wallaces	8.00
2938	46¢ Ruth Benedict	6.00
2940	55¢ A. Hamilton	5.00
2941	55¢ Justin S. Morrill	10.00
2942	77¢ M. Breckenridge	10.00
2943	78¢ Alice Paul	5.00
1995 Commemoratives		
2948-49	(32¢) Love	6.00
2950	32¢ Florida	5.00
2951-54	32¢ Kids Care	6.50
2955	32¢ Richard Nixon	6.00
2956	32¢ Bessie Coleman	7.50
2957-60	32¢ - 55¢ Angel	6.00
2961-65	32¢ Recreat. Sports	15.00
2966	32¢ POW/MIA	6.00
2967	32¢ Marilyn Monroe	21.50
2968	32¢ Texas	8.00
2973a	32¢ Lighthouses Pn.	15.00
2974	32¢ U.N. Nations	5.00

Scott No.	Subject	Price
1995 Commemoratives (continued)		
2975	32¢ Civil War	27.50
2976-79	32¢ Carousel	10.00
2980	32¢ Suffrage	5.00
2981	32¢ World War II	13.00
2982	32¢ L. Armstrong	8.00
2983-92	32¢ Jazz	13.00
2997a	32¢ Garden Flowers, Pane of 5	12.50
2998	60¢ E. Rickenbacker	8.00
2999	32¢ Republic-Palau	6.00
3000	32¢ Comic Strips	27.50
3001	32¢ Naval Academy	8.00
3002	32¢ Tenn. Williams	8.00
3003,3b	32¢ Madonna	10.00
3004-7,8-11	32¢ Christmas	9.50
3012	32¢ Midnight Angel	8.00
3013	32¢ Children Sledding	8.00
3019-23	32¢ Antique Autos	10.00
1996 Commemoratives		
3024	32¢ Utah Statehood	6.00
3029a	32¢ Garden Flowers, Pane of 5	10.75
3030	32¢ Love	7.50
1996-2000 Regulars		
3031	1¢ Kestrel, SA	10.00
3032	2¢ Woodpeckers	6.00
3033	3¢ Bluebird	6.00
3036	$1 Red Fox	12.75
3045	2¢ Woodpecker	10.00
3048,53	20¢ Bluejay	8.00
3049	32¢ Yellow Rose	8.00
3050,55	20¢ Pheasant	10.00
3052	33¢ Coral Pink Rose	10.00
3052E	33¢ Coral Pink Rose	10.00
3054	32¢ Yellow Rose Coil(97)	10.00
1996 Commemoratives (cont.)		
3058	32¢ Ernest Just	9.50
3059	32¢ Smithsonian	6.00
3060	32¢ Chinese New Year	10.75
3061-64	32¢ Communications	8.00
3065	32¢ W.Fulbright	6.00
3066	50¢ J Cochran	6.00
3067	32¢ Marathon	6.00
3068	32¢ Atlanta Games	26.50
3069	32¢ Georgia O'Keefe	8.00
3070	32¢ Tennessee	6.00
3072-76	32¢ American Indian Dances	8.00
3077-80	32¢ Prehistoric Animals	8.00
3081	32¢ Breast Cancer	8.00
3082	32¢ James Dean	10.00
3083-86	32¢ Folk Heroes	8.00
3087	32¢ Olympic Games	7.50
3088-89	32¢ Iowa	7.50
3090	32¢ Rural Free Delivery	6.00
3091-95	32¢ Riverboats	110.00
3096-99	32¢ Big Band Leaders	11.00
3100-3	32¢ Songwriters	11.00
3104	32¢ F.Scott Fitzgerald	6.00
3105	32¢ Endangered Species	27.50
3106	32¢ Computer Tech	6.00
3107/12	32¢ Madonna	10.00
3108/16	32¢ Family Scenes	11.00
3117	32¢ Skaters	10.00
3118	32¢ Hanukkah	8.00
3119	50¢ Cycling S.S.	10.75
1997 Issues		
3120	32¢ Year of the Ox	12.75
3121	32¢ B.O. Davis, Jr.	10.00
3122	32¢ Liberty	9.00
3123-24	32¢-55¢ Love	9.50
3125	32¢ Children Learn.	7.50
3126-29	32¢ Merian Prints	9.50
3130-31	32¢ PAC-97 Triangles	10.00
3132-33	Linerless Coils	9.00
3134	32¢ Thorton Wilder	8.00
3135	32¢ R. Wallenberg	8.00
3136	32¢ Dinosaurs	27.50
3137a	32¢ Bugs Bunny	27.50
3139	50¢ B. Franklin Sh.	22.50
3140	60¢ G.Washington Sh	22.50
3141	32¢ Marshall Plan	8.00
3142	32¢ Aircraft	27.50
3143-46	32¢ Football Coaches	25.00
3147	32¢ Vince Lombardi	16.50
3148	32¢ Bear Bryant	16.50
3149	32¢ Pop Warner	16.50
3150	32¢ George Halas	16.50
3151	32¢ Dolls	21.75
3152	32¢ Humphry Bogart	9.00
3153	32¢ Stars & Stripes	10.00
3154-57	32¢ Opera Singers	15.00
3158-65	32¢ Composers & Conductors	18.00
3166	32¢ Felix Varela	10.00
3167	32¢ Air Force	15.00

OFFICIAL SOUVENIR PAGES

Scott No.	Subject	Price
1997 Issues (continued)		
3168-72	32¢ Movie Monsters	18.50
3173	32¢ Supersonic Flight	15.00
3174	32¢ Women in Military	10.00
3175	32¢ Kwanzaa	13.00
3176	32¢ Madonna	13.00
3177	32¢ Holly	13.00
3178	$3 Mars Pathfinder	21.00
1998 Issues		
3179	32¢ Year of the Tiger	13.50
3180	32¢ Alpine Skiing	12.50
3181	32¢ Mdm. CJ Walker	12.50
3182	32¢ 1900's	25.00
3183	32¢ 1910's	25.00
3184	32¢ 1920's	25.00
3185	32¢ 1930's	25.00
3186	33¢ 1940's (1999)	25.00
3187	33¢ 1950's (1999)	25.00
3188	33¢ 1960's (1999)	25.00
3189	33¢ 1970's (1999)	25.00
3190	33¢ 1980's (2000)	25.00
3191	33¢ 1990's (2000)	25.00
3192	32¢ Remember-Maine	13.00
3193-97	32¢ Flowering Trees	13.50
3198-3202	32¢ A. Calder	13.50
3203	32¢ Cinco de Mayo	10.00
3204a	32¢ Sylvester & Tweety	16.50
3206	32¢ Wisconsin	13.50
3207-8	Wetlands, Diner Coils	10.00
3207A,70-71	Wetlands, Eagle & Shield Coils	10.00
3208A	Diner Coil	9.00
3209	1¢-$2 Trans-Mississippi	27.50
3210	$1 Trans-Mississippi	22.50
3211	32¢ Berlin Airlift	10.00
3212-15	32¢ Folk Musicians	15.00
3216-19	32¢ Gospel Singers	13.00
3220	32¢ Spanish Sett.	9.00
3221	32¢ Stephen Benet	10.00
3222-25	32¢ Tropical Birds	16.50
3226	32¢ Alfred Hitchcock	13.50
3227	32¢ Organ & Tissue	10.00
3229	(10¢) Green Bicycle	10.00
3230-34	32¢ Bright Eyes	16.50
3235	32¢ Klondike Gold	13.00
3236	32¢ American Art	27.50
3237	32¢ Ballet	13.00
3238-42	32¢ Space Discovery	13.50
3243	32¢ Giving & Sharing	10.00
3244	32¢ Madonna & Child	10.00
3245-52	32¢ Wreaths	12.00
3257-58,60	1¢ W.Vane, 33¢ Hat	10.00
3259,63	22¢ Uncle Sam	10.00
3261	$3.20 Shuttle	25.00
3262	$11.75 Shuttle	38.75
3264,66	33¢ Hat, Coils	10.50
3267-69	33¢ Hat, Booklet Singles	11.00
1999 Issues		
3272	33¢ Year of the Rabbit	16.00
3273	33¢ Malcolm X	18.00
3274	33¢ Love	10.00
3275	55¢ Love	10.00
3276	33¢ Hospice Care	10.00
3279,80,82	33¢ Flag and City	13.00
3283	33¢ Flag-Chalkboard	10.00
3286	33¢ Irish Immigration	10.00
3287	33¢ Lunt & Fontaine	10.00
3288-92	33¢ Arctic Animals	13.50
3293	33¢ Sonoran Desert	23.50
3294-97	33¢ Berries	13.00
3294a-96a,97c	Berries (2000)	11.00
3306a	33¢ Daffy Duck	15.00
3308	33¢ Ayn Rand	13.00
3309	33¢ Cinco de Mayo	10.00
3310-13	33¢ Tropical Flowers	13.50
3314	33¢ J & W Bertram	10.00
3315	33¢ Prostrate Cancer	10.00
3316	33¢ Calif.Gold Rush	10.00
3317-20	33¢ Aquarium Fish	13.00
3321-24	33¢ Xtreme Sports	13.00
3325-28	33¢ American Glass	13.00
3329	33¢ James Cagney	13.00
3330	55¢ Billy Mitchell	13.00
3331	33¢ Those Who Served	10.00
3332	45¢ Univ.Postal Union	10.00
3333-37	33¢ All Aboard,Trains	16.50
3338	33¢ F.L.Olmstead	10.00
3339-44	33¢ Hollwd.Composers	21.50
3345-50	33¢ Bdwy.Songwriters	21.50
3351	33¢ Insects-Spiders	27.50
3352	33¢ Hanukkah	10.00
3353	22¢ Uncle Sam	10.00
3354	33¢ N.A.T.O.	10.00
3355	33¢ Madonna & Child	10.00
3356-59	33¢ Christmas Deer	11.00
3368	33¢ Kwanzaa	10.00
3369	33¢ Year 2000	10.00

Scott No.	Subject	Price
2000 Issues		
3370	33¢ Year of the Dragon	16.50
3371	33¢ P.R.Harris	12.50
3372	33¢ Submarine	13.00
3378	33¢ Pacific Coast R.F.	27.50
3379-83	33¢ Louise Nevelson	13.00
3384-88	33¢ Hubble Telescope	11.50
3389	33¢ American Samoa	10.00
3390	33¢ Library of Congress	10.00
3391a	33¢ Road Runner & Wile E. Coyote	16.50
3393-96	33¢ Disting.Soldiers	15.00
3397	33¢ Summer Sports	10.00
3398	33¢ Adoption	15.00
3399-3402	33¢ Team Sports	13.50
3403	33¢ Stars & Stripes	27.50
3408	33¢ Legends-Baseball	32.50
3414-17	33¢ Stampin-Future	13.00
2000-2 Distinguished Americans		
3420	10¢ J.W. Stilwell	9.00
3426	33¢ Claude Pepper	9.00
3431	76¢ Hattie Caraway	9.00
3433	83¢ Edna Ferber(2002)	8.00
3438	33¢ California	9.00
3439-43	33¢ Sea Creatures	11.50
3444	33¢ Thomas Wolfe	10.00
3445	33¢ The White House	9.00
3446	33¢ Edward G.Robinson	9.00
3447	(10¢) N.Y.Library Lion	9.00
3448-50	(34¢) Flag over Farm	9.00
3451-53	(34¢) Statue of Liberty	9.00
3454-57	(34¢) Flowers	9.00
2001 Issues		
3466	34¢ Liberty, SA Coil	10.00
3467/84	21¢ Bison	10.00
3468,75	21¢ Bison	10.00
3468A/78A	23¢ Washington	10.00
3469	34¢ Flag over Farm	10.00
3470	34¢ Flag over Farm	10.00
3471	55¢ Eagle	10.00
3471	57¢ Eagle	10.00
3472	$3.50 U.S. Capitol	18.50
3473	$12.25 Washington Monument	39.50
3476,77,85	34¢ Statue-Liberty	10.00
3478-81	34¢ Flowers	11.00
3482	20¢ G.Washington	10.00
3491-92	34¢ Apple & Orange	10.00
3495	34¢ Flag over Farm, Self-adhesive Booklet	10.00
3496	(34¢) Love	10.00
3497,99	34¢,55¢ Love	13.00
3500	34¢ Year of the Snake	13.50
3501	34¢ Roy Wilkins	16.50
3502	34¢ Illustrators	39.50
3503	34¢ Diabetes Aware	13.00
3504	34¢ Nobel Prize	13.00
3505	1¢-80¢ Pan-Am Inverts	26.50
3506	34¢ Great Plains	27.50
3507	34¢ Peanuts	18.75
3508	34¢ Honoring Veterans	13.00
3509	34¢ Frida Kahlo	17.50
3510-19	34¢ Baseball Fields	40.00
3520	(10¢) Atlas Coil	10.00
3521	34¢ Leonard Bernstein	13.00
3522	(15¢) Woody Wagon	10.00
3523	34¢ Lucille Ball	16.50
3524-27	34¢ Amish Quilt	13.50
3528-31	34¢ Carnivorous Plants	13.50
3532	34¢ EID, Islamic	10.00
3533	34¢ Enrico Fermi	13.00
3534a	34¢ Porky Pig	16.50
3536	34¢ Madonna	10.00
3537-40	34¢ Santa Claus	11.00
3545	34¢ James Madison	10.00
3546	34¢ Thanksgiving	10.00
3547	34¢ Hanukkah	13.00
3548	34¢ Kwanzaa	13.00
3549,50	37¢ United We Stand	20.00
3551	57¢ Love	10.00
2002-3 Issues		
3552-55	34¢ Winter Olympics	16.50
3556	34¢ Mentoring a Child	10.00
3557	34¢ Langston Hughes	15.00
3558	34¢ Happy Birthday	10.00
3559	34¢ Year of the Horse	13.50
3560	34¢ Military Academy	13.00
3561-3610	34¢ Greetings from America	50.00
3611	34¢ Pine Forest	26.50
3612	5¢ American Toleware	10.00
3613-15	3¢ Star	10.00
3616-18	23¢ George Washington	10.75
3620-23	(37¢) Flag	13.75
3626-29	(37¢) Toys	13.00
3630-31,33,35	37¢ Flag	10.00
3637	37¢ Flag Bklt.Stamp	10.00
3638-41	37¢ Toys	13.00

Scott No.	Subject	Price
2002-3 Issues (continued)		
3646	60¢ Eagle	10.00
3647	$3.85 Jefferson Meml.	18.50
3648	$13.65 Capitol Dome	40.00
3649	37¢ Photography	39.50
3650	37¢ J.J.Audubon	13.00
3651	37¢ Harry Houdini	13.00
3652	37¢ Andy Warhol	13.00
3653-56	37¢ Teddy Bears	13.50
3657-58	37¢,60¢ Love	13.50
3659	37¢ Ogden Nash	12.50
3660	37¢ Duke Kahanamoku	12.50
3661-64	37¢ Bats	13.50
3665-68	37¢ Women in Journalism	15.00
3669	37¢ Irving Berlin	12.50
3670-71	37¢ Neuter & Spay	13.00
3672	37¢ Hanukkah	12.50
3673	37¢ Kwanzaa	12.50
3674	37¢ Eid	12.50
3675	37¢ Madonna	12.50
3676-79	37¢ Snowmen	13.50
3692	37¢ Cary Grant	16.50
3693	(5¢) Sea Coast Coil	13.00
3694	37¢ Hawaiian Missionaries	18.50
3695	37¢ Happy Birthday	13.00
3696-3745	37¢ Greetings	50.00
2003 Issues		
3746	37¢ Thurgood Marshall	10.00
3747	37¢ Year of the Ram	10.00
3748	37¢ Zora Neale Hurston	10.00
3751	10¢ American Clock	10.00
3757	1¢ Tiffany Lamp Coil	10.00
3766	$1 Wisdom	12.00
3769	(10¢) N.Y. Library Lion	10.00
3771	80¢ Special Olympics	11.00
3772	37¢ American Filmmaking	14.00
3773	37¢ Ohio Statehood	10.00
3774	37¢ Pelican Is. National Wildlife Refuge	10.00
3775	(5¢) Sea Coast Pf.Coil	10.00
3776-80	37¢ Old Glory	13.00
3781	37¢ Cesar E.Chavez	10.00
3782	37¢ Louisiana Purchase	10.00
3783	37¢ Wright Brothers	10.00
3784	37¢ Purple Heart	10.00
3787-91	37¢ Southeastern Lighthouses	12.00
3792-3801	(25¢) Eagle	13.00
3802	37¢ Arctic Tundra	27.50
3803	37¢ Korean War Veterans Memorial	9.00
3804-7	37¢ Mary Casatt Paint.	11.00
3808-11	37¢ Football Heroes	11.00
3812	37¢ Roy Acuff	9.00
3813	37¢ District of Columbia	9.00
3820	37¢ Madonna	9.00
3821-24	37¢ Music Makers	11.00
3829	37¢ Snowy Egret Coil	9.00

Scott No.	Subject	Price
1998-2003 Semi-Postal		
B1	32¢+8¢ Breast Cancer	13.00
B2	(34¢+11¢) Heroes	10.00
B3	37¢+8¢ Family Violence	9.00
1973-85 Airmails		
C79	13¢ Winged Envelope	5.00
C83	13¢ Winged Env. Coil	5.00
C84	11¢ City of Refuge	115.00
C87	18¢ Stat. of Liberty	10.00
C88	26¢ Mt. Rushmore	8.00
C89-90	25¢ & 31¢ Airmails	5.00
C91-92	31¢ Wright Brothers	6.00
C93-94	21¢ Octave Chanute	6.00
C95-96	25¢ Wiley Post	6.00
C97	31¢ Olympic Games	6.50
C98	40¢ Philip Mazzei	5.00
C99	28¢ Blanche Scott	5.00
C100	35¢ Glenn Curtiss	5.00
C101-04	28¢ Olympics	6.00
C105-08	40¢ Olympics	6.00
C109-12	35¢ Olympics	7.00
C113	33¢ Alfred Verville	5.00
C114	39¢ L.& E. Sperry	6.00
C115	44¢ Transpacific Flight	5.50
C116	44¢ Father J. Serra	5.00
1988-2001 Airmails		
C117	44¢ New Sweden	5.00
C118	45¢ S.P. Langley	5.00
C119	36¢ Sikorsky	5.00
C120	45¢ French Rev	9.00
C122-25	45¢ Future Mail	10.00
C126	$1.80 Future Mail S/S	10.00
C128	50¢ Harriet Quimby	6.00
C129	40¢ William Piper	5.00
C130	50¢ Antarctic Treaty	6.00
C131	50¢ America	5.00
C133	48¢ Niagara Falls	10.00
C134	40¢ Rio Grande	10.00
C135	60¢ Grand Canyon	10.00
C136	70¢ Nine-Mile Prairie	10.00
C137	80¢ Mt. McKinley	13.50
C138	60¢ Acadia	12.50
1983-2002 Official Issues		
O127-29,30-35	1¢/$5 (5 pgs)	32.50
O129A,136	14¢&22¢ Issues	5.00
O138-39	(14¢&22¢)"D" Sht.&Coil	5.00
O138A,141	15¢,25¢ Coils	5.00
O138B	20¢ Coil	5.00
O140	(25¢) "E" Coil	5.00
O143	1¢ Offset	5.00
O144	(29¢) "F" Coil	5.00
O145,47-48	19¢,23¢,29¢ Sgls. & Coil	5.00
O146	4¢ Make-up rate	5.00
O146A	10¢ Official	5.00
O153/56	1¢/32¢ Officials	6.00
O157	33¢ Official Coil	10.00
O158	34¢ Official Coil	10.00
O159	37¢ Official Coil	10.00
1992-94 Variable Rate Coils		
CVP31	29¢ Variable Rate	6.00
CVP32	29¢ Vert. Design	8.00
CVP33	32¢ Variable Rate	8.00

AMERICAN COMMEMORATIVE PANELS

1480-83

1706-09

The U.S. Postal Service has provided panels for commemorative and Christmas issues since Scott #1464-67 (Sept. 20, 1972). Each panel features mint stamps along with appropriate steel engravings and interesting stories about the subject. Prices are for with or without the original sleeves. Please add 25% if you require sleeves.

Scott No.	Subject	Price
1972 Commemoratives		
1464-67	8¢ Wildlife	8.00
1468	8¢ Mail Order	8.00
1469	8¢ Osteopathic Med	15.00
1470	8¢ Tom Sawyer	15.00
1471	8¢ Christmas 1972	10.00
1472	8¢ 'Twas Night......	10.00
1473	8¢ Pharmacy	12.00
1474	8¢ Stamp Collecting	8.50
1973 Commemoratives		
1475	8¢ Love	10.00
1476	8¢ Pamphleteers	8.00
1477	8¢ Posting Broadside	8.00
1478	8¢ Post Rider	10.00
1479	8¢ Drummer	13.00
1480-83	8¢ Boston Tea Party	27.50
1484	8¢ George Gershwin	10.00
1485	8¢ Robinson Jeffers	8.50
1486	8¢ Henry O. Tanner	8.00
1487	8¢ Willa Cather	8.00
1488	8¢ Copernicus	8.00
1489-98	8¢ Postal People ...	9.00
1499	8¢ Harry S Truman .	12.00
1500-02,C86	Electronics	10.00
1503	8¢ Lyndon B. Johnson	10.50
1504	8¢ Angus Cattle	10.50
1505	10¢ Chautauqua (74)	10.50
1506	10¢ Kansas Wheat(74)	10.50
1507	8¢ Christmas (73) ...	14.00
1508	8¢ Needlepoint	12.50
1974 Commemoratives		
1525	10¢ Vet. Foreign Wars	8.00
1526	10¢ Robert Frost	8.00
1527	10¢ Expo '74	10.00
1528	10¢ Horse Racing ...	12.50
1529	10¢ Skylab	16.50
1530-37	10¢ Univ. Postal Un	10.00
1538-41	10¢ Mineral Heritage	13.00
1542	10¢ Fort Harrod	8.00
1543-46	10¢ Cont. Congress	10.50
1547	10¢ Energy Conserv	8.00
1548	10¢ Sleepy Hollow .	10.00
1549	10¢ Retarded Children	8.00
1550	10¢ Angel	10.00
1551	10¢ Currier & Ives .	10.00
1975 Commemoratives		
1553	10¢ Benjamin West	10.00
1554	10¢ Paul L. Dunbar	10.00
1555	10¢ D.W. Griffith ...	13.50
1556	10¢ Pioneer	15.00
1557	10¢ Mariner	18.50
1558	10¢ Coll Bargaining	7.50
1559-62	10¢ Contrib. to Cause	10.00
1563	10¢ Lexington/Concord	8.00
1564	10¢ Bunker Hill	10.00

Scott No.	Subject	Price
1975 Commemoratives (cont.)		
1565-68	10¢ Military Uniforms	10.00
1569-70	10¢ Apollo Soyuz ..	16.00
1571	10¢ Women's Year .	8.00
1572-75	10¢ Postal Bicent ..	8.00
1576	10¢ Peace thru Law	8.00
1577-78	10¢ Banking/Commerce	10.00
1579	10¢ Madonna	10.50
1580	10¢ Christmas Card	10.50
1976 Commemoratives		
1629-31	13¢ Spirit of '76 ...	12.50
1632	13¢ INTERPHIL '76	12.00
1633/82	State Flags,Blk.4 .	25.00
1683	13¢ Telephone Cent.	10.00
1684	13¢ Commer. Aviation	13.00
1685	13¢ Chemistry	10.00
1690	13¢ Benj Franklin ...	11.50
1691-94	13¢ Dec.Independence	10.00
1695-98	13¢ Olympics	12.50
1699	13¢ Clara Maass	18.50
1700	13¢ Adolph S. Ochs	14.00
1701	13¢ Copley Nativity	15.00
1702	13¢ Currier Winter Past	12.50
1977 Commemoratives		
1704	13¢ Wash.- Princeton	16.00
1705	13¢ Sound Recording	37.50
1706-09	13¢ Pueblo Art	100.00
1710	13¢ Lindbergh Flight	100.00
1711	13¢ Colorado	18.50
1712-15	13¢ Butterflies	21.50
1716	13¢ Lafayette	18.00
1717-20	13¢ Skilled Hands ..	18.00
1721	13¢ Peace Bridge ..	18.00
1722	13¢ Herkimer	18.00
1723-24	13¢ Energy	18.00
1725	13¢ Alta California .	18.00
1726	13¢ Art.Confederation	25.00
1727	13¢ Talking Pictures	21.75
1728	13¢ Saratoga	22.50
1729	13¢ Valley Forge	20.00
1730	13¢ Rural Mailbox ..	35.00
1978 Commemoratives		
1731	13¢ Carl Sandburg .	11.50
1732-33	13¢ Captain Cook ..	17.50
1744	13¢ Harriet Tubman	13.00
1745-48	13¢ Quilts	20.00
1749-52	13¢ Dance	15.00
1753	13¢ French Alliance	13.00
1754	13¢ Dr. Papanicolaou	14.00
1755	13¢ Jimmie Rodgers	15.00
1756	15¢ George M. Cohan	20.00
1758	15¢ Photography ...	16.00
1759	15¢ Viking Missions	45.00
1760-63	15¢ Owls	45.00
1764-67	15¢ Trees	37.50

Scott No.	Subject	Price
1978 Commemoratives (cont.)		
1768	15¢ Madonna	16.00
1769	15¢ Hobby Horse ...	16.00
1979 Commemoratives		
1770	15¢ Robert Kennedy	16.00
1771	15¢ Martin L. King, Jr.	13.50
1772	15¢ Year of the Child	10.75
1773	15¢ John Steinbeck	9.00
1774	15¢ Albert Einstein	13.50
1775-78	15¢ Toleware	16.00
1779-82	15¢ Architecture ...	12.00
1783-86	15¢ Endangered Flora	13.00
1787	15¢ Seeing Eye Dogs	10.75
1788	15¢ Special Olympics	10.00
1789	15¢ John Paul Jones	12.00
1790/C97	Olympic Games ...	13.50
1791-94	15¢ Summ.Olympics	12.00
1795-98	15¢ Winter Olympics(80)	10.00
1799	15¢ Virgin & Child ..	13.00
1800	15¢ Santa Claus	13.00
1801	15¢ Will Rogers	15.00
1802	15¢ Vietnam Vets ...	13.50
1980 Commemoratives		
1803	15¢ W.C. Fields	18.00
1804	15¢ Benj. Banneker	10.75
1821	15¢ Frances Perkins	8.00
1823	15¢ Emily Bissell ...	13.50
1824	15¢ Keller/Sullivan .	8.00
1825	15¢ Veterans Admin	8.00
1826	15¢ Gen. B. de Galvez	8.00
1827-30	15¢ Coral Reefs	11.75
1831	15¢ Organized Labor	8.00
1832	15¢ Edith Wharton .	8.00
1833	15¢ Amer. Education	8.00
1834-37	15¢ Indian Masks ..	18.50
1838-41	15¢ Architecture ...	10.00
1842	15¢ St. Glass Window.	13.50
1843	15¢ Antique Toys ...	13.50
1981 Commemoratives		
1874	15¢ Everett Dirksen	9.50
1875	15¢ Whitney Young	13.50
1876-79	18¢ Flowers	13.50
1910	18¢ Red Cross	10.00
1911	18¢ Savings & Loan	10.00
1912-19	18¢ Space Achieve	18.50
1920	18¢ Professional Management	8.00
1921-24	18¢ Wildlife Habitats	12.00
1925	18¢ Disable Persons	8.00
1926	18¢ E.Vincent Millay	8.50
1928-31	18¢ Architecture ...	10.00
1932-33	18¢ Jones/Zaharias	45.00
1934	18¢ Fred Remington	13.50
1935-36	18¢ & 20¢ J. Hoban	8.00
1937-38	18¢ Yorktown Capes	8.00
1939	20¢ Madonna	11.50
1940	20¢ "Teddy Bear" ...	12.75
1941	20¢ John Hanson ..	8.00
1942-45	20¢ Desert Plants ..	13.50

Scott No.	Subject	Price
1982 Commemoratives		
1950	20¢ F.D.Roosevelt .	13.00
1951	20¢ Love	16.00
1952	20¢ G. Washington	16.00
1953/2002	20¢ State Birds & Flowers Blk of 4	45.00
2003	20¢ U.S./Netherlands	17.50
2004	20¢ Library Congress	16.00
2006-09	20¢ World's Fair ...	13.50
2010	20¢ Horatio Alger ...	15.00
2011	20¢ Aging	15.00
2012	20¢ Barrymores	18.00
2013	20¢ Mary Walker	13.50
2014	20¢ Peace Garden .	15.00
2015	20¢ Libraries	14.00
2016	20¢ J.Robinson	40.00
2017	20¢ Touro Synagogue	13.50
2018	20¢ Wolf Trap Farm	16.00
2019-22	20¢ Architecture	16.00
2023	20¢ Francis Assisi .	15.00
2024	20¢ Ponce de Leon	15.00
2025	20¢ Kitten & Puppy	22.50
2026	20¢ Madonna	22.50
2027-30	20¢ Snow Scene	22.50
1983 Commemoratives		
2031	20¢ Science/Industry	8.00
2032-35	20¢ Balloons	10.00
2036	20¢ Sweden/US	8.00
2037	20¢ Conservation Corps	8.00
2038	20¢ J.Priestley	8.00
2039	20¢ Voluntarism	22.75
2040	20¢ German Immigrants	8.00
2041	20¢ Brooklyn Bridge	10.00
2042	20¢ Tenn. Valley Auth	8.00
2043	20¢ Physical Fitness	8.00
2044	20¢ Scott Joplin	10.00
2045	20¢ Medal of Honor	12.50
2046	20¢ Babe Ruth	32.50
2047	20¢ Nath. Hawthorne	8.50
2048-51	13¢ Olympics	10.75
2052	20¢ Treaty of Paris	9.00
2053	20¢ Civil Service	9.50
2054	20¢ Metropolitan Opera	12.50
2055-58	20¢ Inventors	11.50
2059-62	20¢ Streetcars	13.50
2063	20¢ Madonna	13.50
2064	20¢ Santa Claus	13.50
2065	20¢ Martin Luther ..	11.50
1984 Commemoratives		
2066	20¢ Alaska Statehood	8.00
2067-70	20¢ Winter Olympics	10.00
2071	20¢ FDIC	8.00
2072	20¢ Love	8.00
2073	20¢ Carter Woodson	10.00
2074	20¢ Soil/Water Cons.	8.00
2075	20¢ Credit Union Act	8.00
2076-79	20¢ Orchids	10.00
2080	20¢ Hawaii Statehood	10.00
2081	20¢ Nat'l. Archives	8.00
2082-85	20¢ Summer Olympics	10.00

AMERICAN COMMEMORATIVE PANELS

2381-85

2505a

Scott No.	Subject	Price
	1984 Commemoratives (cont.)	
2086	20¢ Louisiana Expo	8.50
2087	20¢ Health Research	8.00
2088	20¢ Doug Fairbanks	10.00
2089	20¢ Jim Thorpe	10.00
2090	20¢ J McCormack	10.00
2091	20¢ St. Lawr. Seaway	10.00
2092	20¢ Migratory Bird	15.00
2093	20¢ Roanoke	8.00
2094	20¢ Herman Melville	10.00
2095	20¢ Horace Moses	8.00
2096	20¢ Smokey Bear	35.00
2097	20¢ R.Clemente	45.00
2098-2101	20¢ Dogs	13.50
2102	20¢ Crime Prevention	8.00
2103	20¢ Hispanic Americans	8.00
2104	20¢ Family Unity	8.00
2105	20¢ E. Roosevelt	19.50
2106	20¢ Nation Readers	8.00
2107	20¢ Madonna	10.00
2108	20¢ Santa Claus	10.00
2109	20¢ Vietnam Vets	15.00
	1985 Commemoratives	
2110	22¢ Jerome Kern	10.00
2137	22¢ Mary M. Bethune	10.00
2138-41	22¢ Duck Decoys	27.50
2142	22¢ Winter Special Olympics	8.00
2143	22¢ Love	8.00
2144	22¢ Rural Electrific	8.00
2145	22¢ AMERIPEX '86	8.50
2146	22¢ Abigail Adams	8.00
2147	22¢ Bartholdi	13.50
2152	22¢ Korean War Vets	15.00
2153	22¢ Social Security	8.00
2154	22¢ World War I Vets	9.00
2155-58	22¢ Horses	18.50
2159	22¢ Public Education	8.00
2160-63	22¢ Youth Year	17.50
2164	22¢ Help End Hunger	8.50
2165	22¢ Madonna	10.00
2166	22¢ Poinsettias	11.00
	1986 Commemoratives	
2167	22¢ Arkansas Statehd.	8.00
2201a	22¢ Stamp Collecting	10.00
2202	22¢ Love	13.50
2203	22¢ Sojourner Truth	13.50
2204	22¢ Republic Texas	10.00
2209a	22¢ Fish booklet	12.50
2210	22¢ Public Hospitals	8.00
2211	22¢ Duke Ellington	13.50
2216-19	22¢ U.S. Presidents, 4 panels	45.00
2220-23	22¢ Polar Explorers	13.50
2224	22¢ Statue of Liberty	13.50
2235-38	22¢ Navajo Art	15.00
2239	22¢ T.S. Elliot	10.00
2240-43	22¢ Woodcarved	13.50
2244	22¢ Madonna	10.00
2245	22¢ Village	10.00

Scott No.	Subject	Price
	1987 Commemoratives	
2246	22¢ Michigan	10.00
2247	22¢ Pan-Am. Games	8.00
2248	22¢ Love	10.00
2249	22¢ J.Baptiste Sable	10.00
2250	22¢ Enrico Caruso	12.50
2251	22¢ Girls Scouts	15.00
2274a	22¢ Special Occasions	17.50
2275	22¢ United Way	8.00
2286-2335	22¢ Amer.Wildlife(5)	75.00
	1987-90 Bicentennial Issues	
2336	22¢ Delaware	13.50
2337	22¢ Pennsylvania	10.00
2338	22¢ New Jersey	10.00
2239	22¢ Georgia	10.00
2340	22¢ Connecticut	10.00
2341	22¢ Massachusetts	10.00
2342	22¢ Maryland	10.00
2343	25¢ South Carolina	10.00
2344	25¢ New Hampshire	10.00
2345	25¢ Virginia	10.00
2346	25¢ New York	10.00
2347	25¢ North Carolina	10.00
2348	25¢ Rhode Island	10.00
	1987 Commemoratives (cont)	
2349	22¢ U.S.-Morocco	8.00
2350	22¢ Faulkner	8.00
2351-54	22¢ Lacemaking	12.00
2359a	22¢ Constitution Bklt.	10.50
2360	22¢ Constitution Signing	10.00
2361	22¢ CPA	32.50
2366a	22¢ Locomotive Bklt	13.50
2367	22¢ Madonna	9.00
2368	22¢ Ornaments	8.00
	1988 Commemoratives	
2369	22¢ Winter Olympics	10.00
2370	22¢ Australia Bicent.	12.50
2371	22¢ J.W. Johnson	10.00
2372-75	22¢ Cats	13.50
2376	22¢ K. Rockne	20.75
2377	25¢ F. Ouimet	30.00
2378-79	25¢-45¢ Love	10.00
2380	25¢ Summer Olympics	10.00
2385a	25¢ Classic Cars bk	13.50
2386-89	25¢ Antarctic Explorer	10.00
2390-93	25¢ Carousel	13.50
2395-98	25¢ Special Occasions	10.00
2399-2400	25¢ Christmas	10.00
	1989 Commemoratives	
2401	25¢ Montana	10.00
2402	25¢ Randolph	13.50
2403	25¢ North Dakota	10.00
2404	25¢ Washington	10.00
2409a	25¢ Steamboats bklt.	13.50
2410	25¢ World Stamp Expo	8.00
2411	25¢ Arturo Toscanini	13.50
2412	25¢ House of Reps	13.50
2413	25¢ U.S. Senate	13.50
2414	25¢ Exec./GW Inaug.	13.50
2415	25¢ Supreme Court(90)	13.50

Scott No.	Subject	Price
	1989 Commemoratives (cont.)	
2416	25¢ South Dakota	10.00
2417	25¢ Lou Gehrig	40.00
2418	25¢ E. Hemingway	18.00
2420	25¢ Letter Carriers	10.00
2421	25¢ Bill of Rights	10.00
2422-25	25¢ Prehistoric Animals	23.50
2426/C121	25¢/45¢ Pre-Columbian Customs	10.00
2427-28	25¢ Christmas	13.50
2434-37	25¢ Classic Mail	10.00
	1990 Commemoratives	
2439	25¢ Idaho Sthd	10.00
2440,41a	25¢ Love	10.00
2442	25¢ Ida B. Wells	17.50
2444	25¢ Wyoming Sthd	10.00
2445-48	25¢ Classic Films	22.50
2449	25¢ Marianne Moore	8.00
2474a	25¢ Lighthouse bklt	23.50
2496-2500	25¢ Olympians	16.00
2505a	25¢ Indian Headdresses	16.00
2506-07	25¢ Marshalls & Micronesia Joint Issue	10.00
2508-11	25¢ Sea Creatures	20.00
2512/C127	25¢,45¢ America	13.50
2513	25¢ D.D. Eisenhower	13.50
2514,15	25¢ Christmas	13.50
	1991 Commemoratives	
2532	50¢ Switzerland	13.50
2533	29¢ Vermont	10.00
2534	29¢ Savings Bonds	9.50
2535,37	29¢ Love	12.50
2538	29¢ William Saroyan	23.50
2549a	29¢ Fishing Flies bk	20.00
2550	29¢ Cole Porter	12.00
2551	29¢ Desert Shield	40.00
2553-57	29¢ Summer Olympics	13.50
2558	29¢ Numismatics	10.00
2559	29¢ WW II	18.00
2560	29¢ Basketball	23.50
2561	29¢ Dist.of Columbia	10.00
2566a	29¢ Comedians bklt.	18.00
2567	29¢ Jan Matzeliger	13.50
2577a	29¢ Space bklt	18.00
2578-79	29¢ Christmas	15.00
2587	32¢ J. S. Polk(1995)	15.00
	1992 Commemoratives	
2611-15	29¢ Winter Olympics	13.50
2616	29¢ World Columbian	13.50
2617	29¢ W.E.B. DuBois	18.75
2618	29¢ Love	13.50
2619	29¢ Olympic Baseball	45.00
2620-23	29¢ Columbus Voyages	15.00
2624-29	1¢/$5 Columbus S/S Set of 3 Panels	250.00
2630	29¢ Stock Exchange	24.00
2631-34	29¢ Space Accomp	18.50
2635	29¢ Alaska Highway	13.00
2636	29¢ Kentucky Sthd	10.00
2637-41	29¢ Summer Olympic	13.50
2646a	29¢ Hummingbird B.Pn	18.50

Scott No.	Subject	Price
	1992 Commemoratives (cont.)	
2647-96	29¢ Wildflowers (5)	225.00
2697	29¢ WW II S/S	18.00
2698	29¢ Dorothy Parker	10.00
2699	29¢ Dr. von Karman	18.00
2700-03	29¢ Minerals	18.00
2704	29¢ Juan Cabrillo	13.50
2709a	29¢ Wild Animals Pn.	16.50
2710,14a	29¢ Christmas	18.50
2720	29¢ Year of Rooster	35.00
	1993 Commemoratives	
2721	29¢ Elvis Presley	35.00
2722	29¢ Oklahoma	12.00
2723	29¢ Hank Williams	30.00
2737b	29¢ Rock 'n Roll	35.00
2745a	29¢ Space Fantasy	21.50
2746	29¢ Percy L. Julian	18.00
2747	29¢ Oregon Trail	12.00
2748	29¢ World Games	12.00
2749	29¢ Grace Kelly	30.00
2750-3	29¢ Circus	16.00
2754	29¢ Cherokee Strip	12.00
2755	29¢ Dean Acheson	18.00
2756-9	29¢ Sports Horses	18.00
2764a	29¢ Garden Flowers	12.00
2765	29¢ WW II S/S	18.50
2766	29¢ Joe Louis	40.00
2770a	29¢ Broadway Musicals, Booklet Pane	17.50
2775-8	29¢ Country-Western	30.00
2779-82	29¢ Postal Museum	15.00
2783-4	29¢ Deaf Communicat.	15.00
2785-8	29¢ Youth Classics	18.00
2789,91-4	29¢ Christmas	18.00
2804	29¢ Northern Marianas	15.00
2805	29¢ Columbus Lands in Puerto Rico	16.00
2806	29¢ AIDS	16.00
	1994 Commemoratives	
2807-11	29¢ Winter Olympics	20.00
2812	29¢ Edward R.Murrow	13.50
2814a	29¢ Love, Bklt Pane	15.00
2816	29¢ Allison Davis	18.00
2817	29¢ Year of the Dog	20.00
2818	29¢ Buffalo Soldiers	18.50
2819-28	29¢ Silent Screen Stars	25.00
2833a	29¢ Garden Flowers, Pane of 5	16.00
2837	29¢,40¢,50¢ World Cup Soccer, S/S of 3	18.50
2838	29¢ WWII S/S	18.00
2839	29¢ Norman Rockwell	25.00
2841	29¢ Moon Landing	27.50
2847a	29¢ Locomotives, Pane of 5	18.50
2848	29¢ George Meany	11.00
2849-53	29¢ Popular Singers	18.50
2854-61	29¢ Jazz/Blues	25.00
2862	29¢ J. Thurber	11.50
2863-66	29¢ Wonders - Sea	18.00
2867-68	29¢ Cranes	19.50

AMERICAN COMMEMORATIVE PANELS

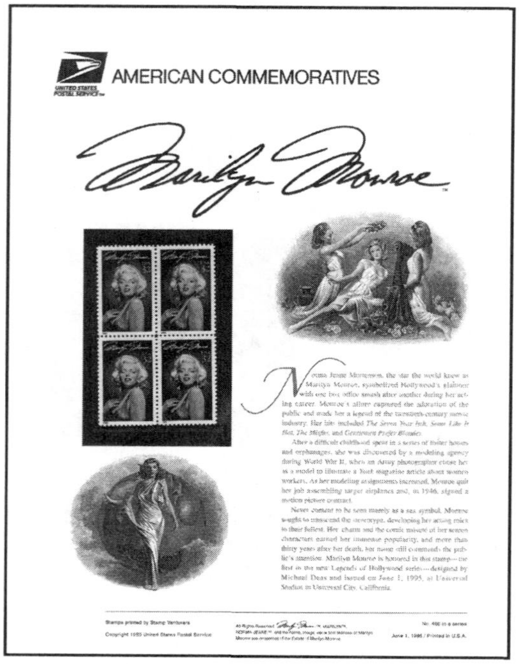

2967

Scott No.	Subject	Price
	1994 commemoratives (cont.)	
2871	29¢ Madonna	11.00
2872	29¢ Stocking	11.00
2876	29¢ Year of the Boar	18.50
	1995 Commemoratives	
2950	32¢ Florida	15.00
2951-54	32¢ Kids Care	13.50
2955	32¢ R. Nixon	25.00
2956	32¢ B. Coleman	19.50
2957-58	32¢-55¢ Love	19.00
2961-65	32¢ Recreation Sports	19.00
2966	32¢ POW/MIA	16.50
2967	32¢ M. Monroe	35.00
2968	32¢ Texas	16.50
2973a	32¢ Lighthouses	18.50
2974	32¢ United Nations	15.00
2976-79	32¢ Carousel	25.00
2980	32¢ Women's Suffrage	14.50
2981	32¢ WWII S/S	22.50
2982	32¢ L. Armstrong	25.00
2983-92	32¢ Jazz Musicians.	25.00
2997a	32¢ Garden Flowers Pane of 5	15.00
2999	32¢ Palau	15.00
3001	32¢ Naval Academy	18.50
3002	32¢ Tennessee Williams	16.50
3003	32¢ Madonna	19.50
3004-7	32¢ Christmas	18.50
3019-23	32¢ Antique Autos	25.00
	1996 Commemoratives	
3024	32¢ Utah	15.00
3029a	32¢ Garden Flowers	15.00
3058	32¢ Ernest E. Just	18.00
3059	32¢ Smithsonian	15.00
3060	32¢ Year of the Rat	25.00
3061-4	32¢ Communications	18.50
3065	32¢ Fulbright Scholar.	15.00
3067	32¢ Marathon	18.50
3068	32¢ Olympics Sheet	50.00
3069	32¢ Georgia O'Keeffe	15.00
3070	32¢ Tennessee	15.00
3072-6	32¢ Indian Dances	21.50
3077-80	32¢ Prehistoric Animals	21.50
3081	32¢ Breast Cancer	15.00
3082	32¢ James Dean	21.50
3083-86	32¢ Folk Heroes	21.50
3087	32¢ Olympic Games	16.50
3088	32¢ Iowa	15.00
3090	32¢ Rural Free Delivery	15.00
3091-95	32¢ Riverboats	21.50
3096-99	32¢ Big Band Leaders	21.50
3100-3	32¢ Songwriters	21.50
3104	32¢ Scott Fitzgerald	40.00
3105	32¢ Endangered Species	35.00
3106	32¢ Computer Tech	35.00
3107	32¢ Madonna	17.00
3108-11	32¢ Family	18.00
3118	32¢ Hanukkah	17.00

Scott No.	Subject	Price
3119	50¢ Cycling Sv. Sheet	35.00
	1997 Commemoratives	
3120	32¢ Year of the Ox	35.00
3121	32¢ Benjamin Davis	25.00
3123-24	32¢/55¢ Love	16.50
3125	32¢ Children Learning	15.00
3130-31	32¢ Triangles	20.00
3134	32¢ Thorton Wilder	18.00
3135	32¢ R. Wallenberg	17.50
3136	32¢ Dinosaurs	30.00
3137c	32¢ Bugs Bunny	25.00
3139	50¢ B. Franklin Sh	95.00
3140	60¢ G.Washington Sh.	95.00
3141	32¢ Marshall Plan	15.00
3142	32¢ Aircraft Sheet	36.50
3143-46	32¢ Football Coaches	27.50
3151	32¢ Dolls Sheet	55.00
3152	32¢ Humphrey Bogart	20.00
3153	32¢ Stars and Stripes	16.00
3154-57	32¢ Opera Singers	20.00
3158-65	32¢ Composers/ Conductors	21.50
3166	32¢ Felix Varela	16.00
3167	32¢ Air Force	21.50
3168-72	32¢ Movie Monsters	23.50
3173	32¢ Supersonic Flight	22.50
3174	32¢ Women in Military	18.50
3175	32¢ Kwanzaa	18.50
3176a	32¢ Madonna	23.50
3177a	32¢ Holly	23.50
	1998 Commemoratives	
3179	32¢ Year of the Tiger	18.50
3180	32¢ Alpine Skiing	18.50
3181	32¢ Madame CJ Walker	18.50
	1998-2000 Celebrate the Century	
3182	32¢ 1900's	27.50
3183	32¢ 1910's	27.50
3184	32¢ 1920's	27.50
3185	32¢ 1930's	30.00
3186	33¢ 1940's (1999)	30.00
3187	33¢ 1950's (1999)	27.50
3188	33¢ 1960's (1999)	27.50
3189	33¢ 1970's (1999)	27.50
3190	33¢ 1980's (2000)	27.50
3191	33¢ 1990's (2000)	27.50
	1998 Commemoratives (cont.)	
3192	32¢ Remember-Maine	20.00
3193-97	32¢ Flowering Trees	19.50
3198-3202	32¢ A. Calder	19.50
3203	32¢ Cinco de Mayo	16.00
3204c	32¢ Sylvester/Tweety	23.50
3206	32¢ Wisconsin	18.00
3209-10	Trans-Mississippi (2)	30.00
3211	32¢ Berlin Airlift	16.00
3212-15	32¢ Folk Musicians	21.50
3216-19	32¢ Gospel Singers	21.50
3220	32¢ Spanish Settlem.	17.00
3221	32¢ Stephen V. Benet	16.00
3222-25	32¢ Tropical Birds	18.50
3226	32¢ Alfred Hitchcock	21.50

Scott No.	Subject	Price
	1998 Commemoratives (cont.)	
3227	32¢ Organ & Tissue	18.00
3230-34	32¢ Bright Eyes	18.50
3235	32¢ Klondiike Gold	16.00
3236	32¢ Art	32.50
3237	32¢ Ballet	16.00
3238-42	32¢ Space Discovery	21.50
3243	32¢ Giving/Sharing	16.00
3244a	32¢ Madonna	21.00
3249-52	32¢ Wreaths	16.00
	1999 Commemoratives	
3272	33¢ Year of the Rabbit	20.00
3273	33¢ Malcolm X	20.00
3274a	33¢ Love, Pane	21.50
3275	55¢ Love	18.00
3276	33¢ Hospice Care	16.00
3286	33¢ Irish Immigration	22.50
3287	33¢ Lunt & Fontaine	16.00
3288-92	33¢ Arctic Animals	18.50
3293	33¢ Sonoran Desert	25.00
3306	33¢ Daffy Duck	25.00
3308	33¢ Ayn Rand	30.00
3309	33¢ Cinco de Mayo	18.00
3314	33¢ J & W Bartram	18.00
3315	33¢ Prostrate Cancer	18.00
3316	33¢ Calif. Gold Rush	18.00
3317-20	33¢ Aquarium Fish	18.00
3321-24	33¢ Xtreme Sports	18.00
3325-28	33¢ American Glass	18.00
3329	33¢ James Cagney	18.00
3331	33¢ Those who Served	16.00
3333-37	33¢ All Aboard,Trains	22.50
3338	33¢ F.L.Olmstead	18.00
3339-44	33¢ Hollywood Composers	20.00
3345-50	33¢ Broadway Songwriters	20.00
3351	33¢ Insects-Spiders	27.50
3352	33¢ Hanukkah	18.00
3354	33¢ N.A.T.O.	18.00
3355	33¢ Madonna and Child	18.00
3356-59	33¢ Christmas Deer	18.00
3368	33¢ Kwanzaa	18.00
3369	33¢ Millennium Year	22.50
	2000 Commemoratives	
3370	33¢ Year of the Dragon	25.00
3371	33¢ Patricia R. Harris	22.50
3372	33¢ Submarine	22.50
3378	33¢ Pacific Rain Forest	27.50
3379-83	33¢ Louise Nevelson	20.00
3384-88	33¢ Space Telescope	22.50
3389	33¢ American Samoa	18.00
3390	33¢ Library of Congress	18.00
3391	33¢ Road Runner & Wile E. Coyote	25.00
3393-96	33¢ Disting.Soldiers	22.50
3397	33¢ Summer Sports	18.00
3398	33¢ Adoption	22.50
3399-3402	33¢ Team Sports	22.50
3403	33¢ Stars & Stripes	35.00
3408	33¢ Legends- Baseball	40.00
3414-17	33¢ Stampin'the Future	20.00
3438	33¢ California	18.00
3439-43	33¢ Deep Sea Creatures	20.00
3444	33¢ Thomas Wolfe	20.00
3445	33¢ White House	18.00
3446	33¢e Ed. G. Robinson	22.50
	2001 Commemoratives	
3496	(34¢) Love Letters	20.00
3497	34¢ Love Letters	20.00
3499	55¢ Love Letters	22.50
3500	34¢ Year of the Snake	25.00
3501	34¢ Roy Wilkins	25.00
3502	34¢ Illustrators (2)	39.50
3503	34¢ Diabetes Aware.	20.00
3504	34¢ Nobel Prize	22.50
3505	1¢-80¢ Pan-Am Inverts (2)	40.00
3506	34¢ Great Plains Prairie (2)	36.50
3507	34¢ Peanuts	27.50
3508	34¢ Honoring Vets	20.00
3509	34¢ Frida Kahlo	25.00
3510-19	34¢ Baseball Fields	45.00
3521	34¢ Leonard Bernstein	22.50
3522	34¢ Lucille Ball	22.50
3524-27	34¢ Amish Quilts	22.50
3528-31	34¢ Carnivorous Plants	20.00
3532	34¢ EID, Islamic	20.00
3533	34¢ Enrico Fermi	20.00
3535c	34¢ Porky Pig	22.50
3536	34¢ Madonna	18.00
3537-40	34¢ Santa Claus	20.00
3545	34¢ James Madison	20.00
3546	34¢ Thanksgiving	20.00
3547	34¢ Hanukkah	20.00
3548	34¢ Kwanzaa	22.50

Scott No.	Subject	Price
	2001 Commemoratives (cont.)	
3551	57¢ Love	20.00
	2002 Commemoratives	
3552-55	34¢ Winter Olympics	20.00
3556	34¢ Mentoring	20.00
3557	34¢ Langston Hughes	20.00
3558	34¢ Happy Birthday	20.00
3559	34¢ Year of the Horse	25.00
3560	34¢ Military Academy	22.50
3561-3610	34¢ Greetings from America (2 pages)	57.50
3611	34¢ Longleaf Pine Forest (2 pages)	40.00
3649	37¢ Photography	45.00
3650	37¢ J.J.Audubon	22.50
3651	37¢ H.Houdini	22.50
3652	37¢ Andy Warhol	22.50
3653-56	37¢ Teddy Bears	22.50
3657	37¢ Love	18.00
3658	60¢ Love	20.00
3659	37¢ Ogden Nash	20.00
3660	37¢ Duke Kahanamoko	26.50
3661-64	37¢ Bats	25.00
3665-68	37¢ Women in Journalism	25.00
3669	37¢ Irving Berlin	20.00
3670-71	37¢ Neuter or Spay	22.50
3672	37¢ Hanukkah	22.50
3673	37¢ Kwanzaa	22.50
3674	37¢ Eid	22.50
3675	37¢ Madonna	20.00
3676-79	37¢ Snowmen	20.00
3692	37¢ Cary Grant	22.50
3694	37¢ Hawaiian Missionaries (2)	40.00
3695	37¢ Happy Birthday	18.00
3696-3745	37¢ Greetings from America (2)	57.50
	2003 Commemoratives	
3746	37¢ Thurgood Marshall	18.00
3747	37¢ Year of the Ram	20.00
3748	37¢ Zora Neale Hurston	18.00
3771	80¢ Special Olympics	21.50
3772	37¢ American Filmmaking (2 pages)	32.50
3773	37¢ Ohio Statehood	18.00
3774	37¢ Pelican Is. National Wildlife Refuge	18.00
3776-80	37¢ Old Glory Strip-5	20.00
3781	37¢ Cesar E.Chavez	18.00
3782	37¢ Louisiana Purchase	18.00
3783	37¢ Wright Brothers	18.00
3787-91	37¢ Southeastern Lighthouses	20.00
3802	37¢ Arctic Tundra	32.50
3803	37¢ Korean War Veterans Memorial	18.00
3804-7	37¢ Mary Cassatt Paint.	18.00
3808-11	37¢ Football Heroes	18.00
3812	37¢ Roy Acuff	18.00
3813	37¢ District-Columbia	18.00
3814-18	37¢ Reptiles and Amphibians	20.00
3820	37¢ Madonna & Child	18.00
3821-24	37¢ Music Makers	18.00
	1998-2003 Semi-Postal	
B1	32¢+8¢ Breast Cancer	25.00
B2	(34¢+11¢) Heroes	25.00
B3	37¢+8¢ Stop Family Violence	18.00
	Airmails	
C101-04	28¢ Olympics	10.00
C105-06	40¢ Olympics	10.00
C109-12	35¢ Olympics	12.50
C117	44¢ New Sweden	10.00
C120	45¢ French Revolution	10.00
C122-25	45¢ Future Mail	12.50
C130	50¢ Antarctic Treaty	10.00
C131	50¢ America	10.00
C136	70¢ Nine-Mile Prairie	20.00
C137	80¢ Mt. McKinley	20.00

CONFEDERATE STATES OF AMERICA

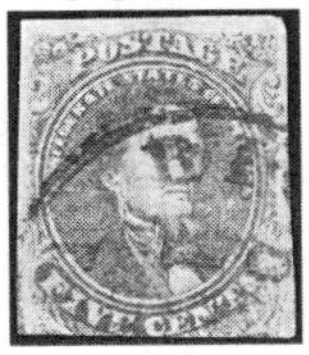
1,4

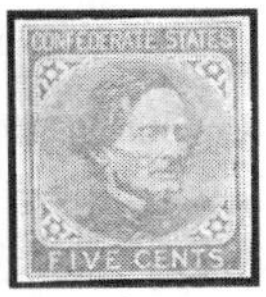
6

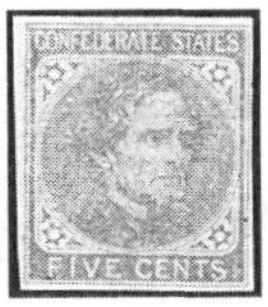
7

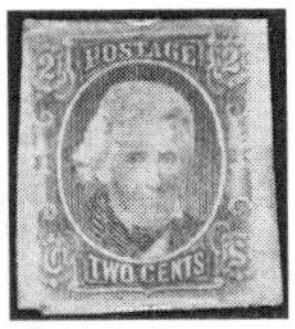
8

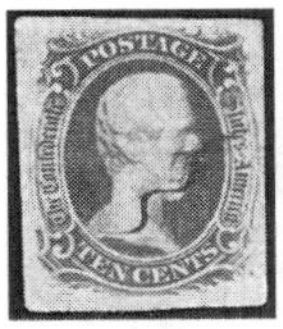
9

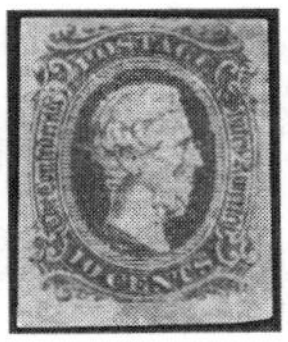
11

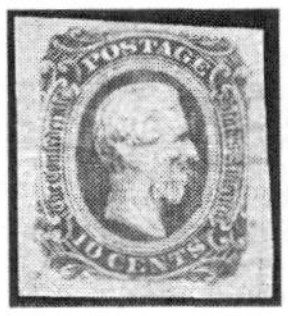
12

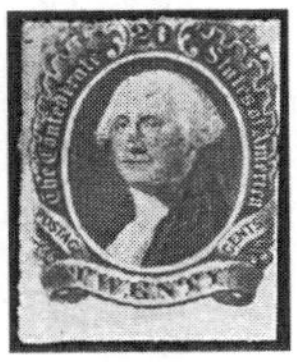
13

1861-62 VF+80% (C)

Scott's No.		Unused Fine	Unused Ave.	Used Fine	Used Ave.
1	5¢ Jefferson Davis, Green	165.00	95.00	160.00	95.00
2	10¢ T. Jefferson, Blue	195.00	120.00	200.00	125.00
3	2¢ Andrew Jackson, Green (1862)	465.00	275.00	600.00	350.00
4	5¢ Jefferson, Blue (1862)	125.00	75.00	110.00	65.00
5	10¢ T. Jefferson, Rose (1862)	950.00	575.00	450.00	275.00
6	5¢ J. Davis, London Print, Clear ('62)	9.00	5.50	25.00	16.00
7	5¢ J. Davis, Local Print, Coarse ('62)	11.50	7.00	18.75	12.00

1862-63 VF+80% (C)

Scott's No.		Unused Fine	Unused Ave.	Used Fine	Used Ave.
8	2¢ A. Jackson, Brown Red (1863)	49.50	29.50	325.00	200.00
9	10¢ J. Davis, Blue "TEN CENTS"('63)	650.00	400.00	475.00	280.00
10	10¢ Blue "10 CENTS", Frame Line	3500.00	2000.00	1300.00	775.00
11	10¢ same, No Frame Line, Die A	8.50	5.25	15.00	9.00
12	10¢ same, Filled in Corners, Die B	9.00	5.50	17.50	10.50
13	20¢ Washington, Green (1863)	32.50	20.00	375.00	225.00
14	1¢ J.C. Calhoun, Orange (unissued)	80.00	52.50	...	...

UNUSED STAMPS WITH ORIGINAL GUM

Scott No.	Original Gum Fine	Original Gum Ave.	Scott No.	Original Gum Fine	Original Gum Ave.	Scott No.	Original Gum Fine	Original Gum Ave.
1	230.00	140.00	6	13.50	8.50	11	11.75	7.00
2	275.00	165.00	7	17.50	11.00	12	12.50	7.50
3	650.00	400.00	8	67.50	40.00	13	45.00	27.50
4	175.00	105.00	9	950.00	550.00	14	110.00	75.00

CANAL ZONE

1904 U.S. 1902-03 Issue Ovptd. "CANAL ZONE" "PANAMA" VF Used + 60% (C)

Scott's No.		Unused, NH VF	Unused, NH F-VF	Unused, OG VF	Unused, OG F-VF	Used F-VF
4	1¢ Frank., Bl. Grn. (#300)	87.50	57.50	50.00	32.50	25.00
5	2¢ Wash., Carmine (#319)	72.50	47.50	42.50	27.50	23.50
6	5¢ Lincoln, Blue (#304)	260.00	160.00	150.00	95.00	70.00
7	8¢ M. Wash., V.Blk. (#306)	425.00	265.00	260.00	160.00	95.00
8	10¢ Webster,Red Brn.(#307)	435.00	270.00	265.00	165.00	100.00

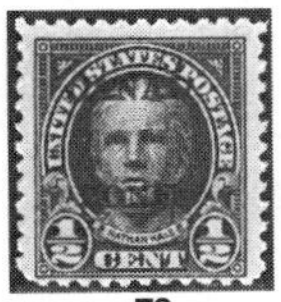
70

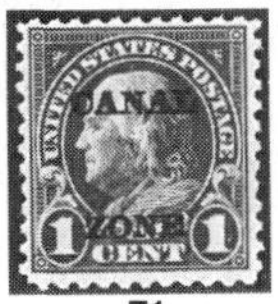
71

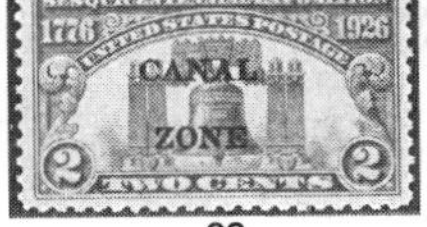
96

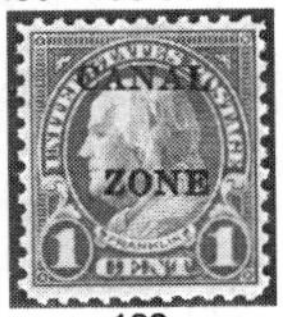
100

1924-25 U.S. Stamps of 1923-25 Overprinted "CANAL ZONE" (Flat Top "A") Flat Press, Perf. 11 VF Used + 40% (B)

Scott's No.		Unused, NH VF	Unused, NH F-VF	Unused, OG VF	Unused, OG F-VF	Used F-VF
70	½¢ N. Hale (#551)	2.35	1.60	1.40	1.00	.75
70	Plate Block of 6	37.50	26.50	23.00	16.50	...
71	1¢ Franklin (#552)	3.25	2.30	1.95	1.40	.80
71	Plate Block of 6	67.50	47.50	41.50	30.00	...
71e	1¢ Bklt. Pane of 6 (#552a)	300.00	210.00	185.00	135.00	...
72	1½¢ Harding (#553)	4.50	3.25	2.75	2.00	1.65
72	Plate Block of 6	72.50	56.50	51.50	36.50	...
73	2¢ Washington (#554)	17.50	13.00	11.00	8.00	1.65
73	Plate Block of 6	425.00	295.00	260.00	185.00	...
73a	2¢ Bklt. Pane of 6 (#554c)	435.00	325.00	275.00	200.00	...
74	5¢ T. Roosevelt (#557)	45.00	31.50	28.00	20.00	9.00
75	10¢ Monroe (#562)	87.50	65.00	56.50	40.00	24.00
76	12¢ Cleveland (#564)	80.00	55.00	50.00	35.00	30.00
77	14¢ Indian (#565)	62.50	45.00	37.50	27.50	21.00
78	15¢ Liberty (#566)	110.00	80.00	70.00	50.00	36.50
79	30¢ Buffalo (#569)	75.00	52.50	47.50	33.50	25.00
80	50¢ Amphitheater (#570)	155.00	110.00	97.50	70.00	42.50
81	$1 Lincoln Mem. (#571)	525.00	365.00	315.00	225.00	100.00

1925-28 Same as Preceding but with Pointed "A", VF Used + 40% (B)

Scott's No.		Unused, NH VF	Unused, NH F-VF	Unused, OG VF	Unused, OG F-VF	Used F-VF
84	2¢ Washington (#554)	65.00	45.00	40.00	28.50	8.25
84d	2¢ Bklt. Pane of 6 (#554c)	450.00	300.00	285.00	195.00	...
85	3¢ Lincoln (#555)	9.50	6.75	6.00	4.25	3.25
85	Plate Block of 6	425.00	275.00	240.00	175.00	...
86	5¢ T. Roosevelt (#557)	8.75	6.25	5.50	3.95	2.75
86	Plate Block of 6	365.00	260.00	225.00	160.00	...

CANAL ZONE

1925-28 Same as Preceding but with Pointed "A", VF Used + 40% (B)

Scott's No.		Unused, NH VF	Unused, NH F-VF	Unused, OG VF	Unused, OG F-VF	Used F-VF
87	10¢ Monroe (#562)	71.50	51.50	45.00	32.50	11.00
88	12¢ Cleveland (#564)	50.00	35.00	31.50	22.50	15.00
89	14¢ Indian (#565)	50.00	35.00	31.50	22.50	17.50
90	15¢ Liberty (#566)	14.50	10.50	9.00	6.50	4.25
90	Plate Block of 6	425.00	300.00	260.00	185.00	...
91	17¢ Wilson (#623)	8.75	6.50	5.50	4.00	3.00
91	Plate Block of 6	425.00	300.00	260.00	185.00	...
92	20¢ Golden Gate (#567)	15.50	11.00	9.75	7.00	3.75
92	Plate Block of 6	370.00	265.00	230.00	165.00	...
93	30¢ Buffalo (#569)	13.00	9.00	8.00	5.75	4.25
94	50¢ Amphitheater (#570)	525.00	365.00	315.00	225.00	160.00
95	$1 Lincoln Mem (#571)	260.00	185.00	160.00	115.00	55.00

1926 Sesquicentennial Issue Overprinted "CANAL ZONE" VF Used + 30% (B)

Scott's No.		Unused, NH VF	Unused, NH F-VF	Unused, OG VF	Unused, OG F-VF	Used F-VF
96	2¢ Liberty Bell (#627)	8.00	6.00	5.50	4.25	3.75
96	Plate Block of 6	175.00	130.00	110.00	80.00	...

1926-27 Rotary Press, Perf. 10, Overprinted "CANAL ZONE" VF Used + 50% (B)

Scott's No.		Unused, NH VF	Unused, NH F-VF	Unused, OG VF	Unused, OG F-VF	Used F-VF
97	2¢ Washington (#583)	135.00	87.50	85.00	55.00	11.50
98	3¢ Lincoln (#584)	20.00	13.00	12.50	8.25	5.00
98	Plate Block of 4	285.00	210.00	175.00	125.00	...
99	10¢ Monroe (#591)	41.50	26.50	26.00	17.00	7.25

1927-31 Rotary Press, Perf. 11x10½, Overprinted "CANAL ZONE" VF Used + 40% (B)

Scott's No.		Unused, NH VF	Unused, NH F-VF	Unused, OG VF	Unused, OG F-VF	Used F-VF
100	1¢ Franklin (#632)	4.15	2.85	2.95	2.10	1.35
100	Plate Block of 4	38.50	27.50	26.50	18.75	...
101	2¢ Washington (#634)	4.50	3.20	3.25	2.30	.95
101	Plate Block of 4	47.50	33.50	33.50	23.75	...
101a	2¢ Bklt. Pane of 6 (#634d)	450.00	300.00	300.00	200.00	...
102	3¢ Lincoln (#635) (1931)	9.00	6.25	6.00	4.25	3.00
102	Plate Block of 4	170.00	120.00	120.00	85.00	...
103	5¢ T. Roosevelt (#637)	56.50	40.00	38.50	27.50	10.75
103	Plate Block of 4	340.00	240.00	250.00	175.00	...
104	10¢ Monroe (#642) (1930)	37.50	26.75	25.00	18.00	11.50
104	Plate Block of 4	375.00	265.00	260.00	185.00	...

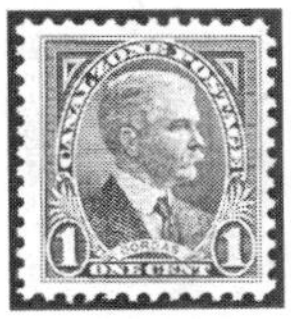
105

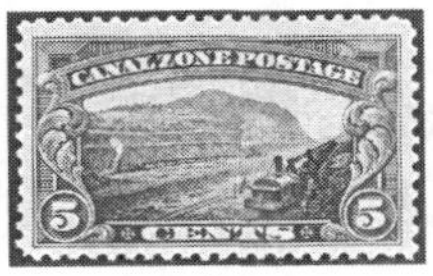
107

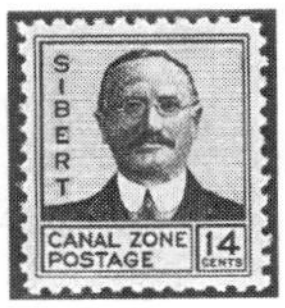

110

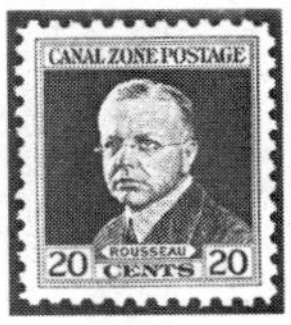

112

1928-40 Flat Plate Printing VF Used + 25% (B)

Scott's No.		Unused, NH VF	Unused, NH F-VF	Unused, OG VF	Unused, OG F-VF	Used F-VF
105-14	**Set of 10**	**12.75**	**9.50**	**9.25**	**7.25**	**4.95**
105	1¢ General Gorgas	.35	.25	.30	.20	.20
105	Plate Block of 6	3.00	2.35	2.25	1.75	...
106	2¢ General Goethels	.35	.25	.30	.20	.20
106	Plate Block of 6	3.75	3.00	2.80	2.25	...
106a	2¢ Booklet Pane of 6	25.00	20.00	19.50	15.00	...
107	5¢ Gaillard Cut (1929)	1.90	1.50	1.40	1.10	.60
107	Plate Block of 6	17.50	13.50	12.50	10.00	...
108	10¢ General Hodges (1932)	.40	.30	.35	.25	.20
108	Plate Block of 6	9.50	7.00	6.75	5.00	...
109	12¢ Colonel Gaillard (1929)	1.60	1.20	1.15	.90	.75
109	Plate Block of 6	18.00	13.50	13.00	10.50	...
110	14¢ Gen. W.L. Sibert (1937)	1.70	1.30	1.20	.95	.95
110	Plate Block of 6	22.00	17.50	16.50	13.00	...
111	15¢ Jackson Smith (1932)	.85	.65	.65	.50	.40
111	Plate Block of 6	11.75	9.25	8.75	7.00	...
112	20¢ Adm. Rousseau (1932)	1.25	1.00	.95	.75	.25
112	Plate Block of 6	12.50	10.00	9.50	7.50	...
113	30¢ Col. Williamson (1940)	1.50	1.15	1.10	.90	.85
113	Plate Block of 6	19.00	14.00	13.50	10.50	...
114	50¢ J. Blackburn (1929)	3.15	2.30	2.15	1.70	.75
114	Plate Block of 6	25.00	19.00	18.50	15.00	...

1933 Rotary Press, Perf. 11x10½ VF Used + 30% (B)

Scott's No.		Unused, NH VF	Unused, NH F-VF	Unused, OG VF	Unused, OG F-VF	Used F-VF
115	3¢ Washington (#720)	5.15	3.95	3.65	2.75	.25
115	Plate Block of 4	65.00	50.00	47.50	35.00	...
116	14¢ Indian (#695)	9.00	7.00	6.75	5.25	3.50
116	Plate Block of 4	115.00	87.50	85.00	65.00	...

1934-39 Issues VF Used + 30% (B)

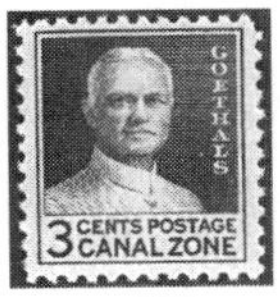

117

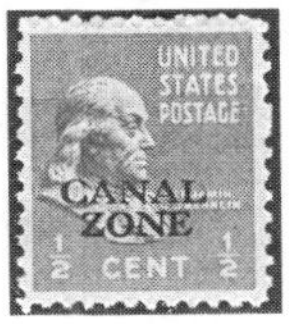

118

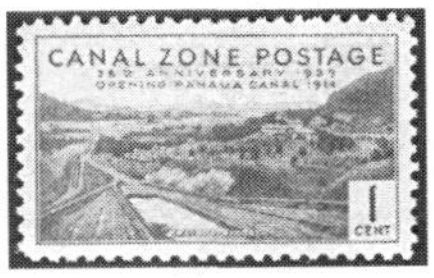

120

Scott's No.		Unused, NH VF	Unused, NH F-VF	Unused, OG VF	Unused, OG F-VF	Used F-VF
117	3¢ General Goethals	.35	.25	.30	.20	.20
117	Plate Block of 6	2.10	1.60	1.55	1.25	...
117a	3¢ Booklet Pane of 6	110.00	72.50	75.00	52.50	...
118	½¢ Franklin (#803) (1939)	.35	.25	.30	.20	.20
118	Plate Block of 4	3.85	3.00	3.25	2.50	...
119	1½¢ M. Wash. (#805) (1939)	.35	.25	.30	.20	.20
119	Plate Block of 4	3.25	2.50	2.65	2.00	...

1939 25th Anniversary Series (Used VF + 25%)

Scott's No.		Unused, NH VF	Unused, NH F-VF	Unused, OG VF	Unused, OG F-VF	Used F-VF
120-35	**Set of 16**	**145.00**	**115.00**	**115.00**	**92.50**	**72.50**
120	1¢ Balboa, before	.75	.60	.65	.50	.35
120	Plate Block of 6	16.00	12.50	12.50	10.00	...
121	2¢ Balboa, after	.80	.65	.70	.55	.45
121	Plate Block of 6	16.00	12.50	12.50	10.00	...
122	3¢ Gaillard Cut, before	.80	.65	.70	.55	.25
122	Plate Block of 6	16.00	12.50	12.50	10.00	...
123	5¢ Gaillard Cut, after	1.90	1.50	1.50	1.20	1.15
123	Plate Block of 6	27.50	21.50	21.50	17.00	...
124	6¢ Bas Obispo, before	3.75	3.00	3.00	2.40	2.50
124	Plate Block of 6	57.50	45.00	45.00	35.00	...
125	7¢ Bas Obispo, after	3.75	3.00	3.00	2.40	2.50
125	Plate Block of 6	57.50	45.00	45.00	35.00	...
126	8¢ Gatun Locks, before	5.50	4.50	4.50	3.65	3.25
126	Plate Block of 6	70.00	55.00	55.00	45.00	...
127	10¢ Gatun Locks, after	4.65	3.75	3.75	3.00	2.65
127	Plate Block of 6	70.00	55.00	55.00	45.00	...
128	11¢ Canal Channel, before	10.75	8.50	8.50	6.75	7.50
128	Plate Block of 6	160.00	125.00	125.00	100.00	...
129	12¢ Canal Channel, after	9.50	7.50	7.50	6.00	7.00
129	Plate Block of 6	125.00	100.00	100.00	80.00	...
130	14¢ Gamboa, before	9.75	7.75	7.75	6.25	6.75
130	Plate Block of 6	150.00	120.00	120.00	95.00	...
131	15¢ Gamboa, after	13.75	11.00	11.00	9.00	5.50
131	Plate Block of 6	190.00	150.00	150.00	120.00	...
132	18¢ P. Miguel Locks, before	13.00	10.50	10.50	8.50	8.25
132	Plate Block of 6	175.00	140.00	140.00	110.00	...
133	20¢ P. Miguel Locks, after	17.00	13.50	13.50	11.00	6.75
133	Plate Block of 6	225.00	180.00	180.00	140.00	...
134	25¢ Gatun Spillway, before	23.50	18.75	18.75	15.00	16.00
134	Plate Block of 6	375.00	300.00	300.00	240.00	...
135	50¢ Gatun Spillway, after	31.50	25.00	25.00	20.00	5.50
135	Plate Block of 6	415.00	325.00	325.00	265.00	...

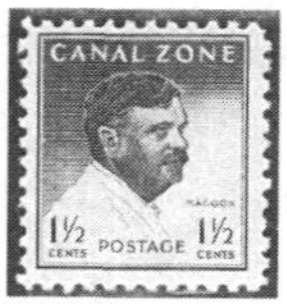

137

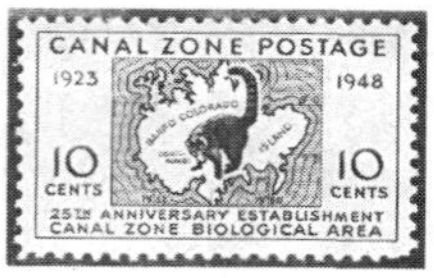

141

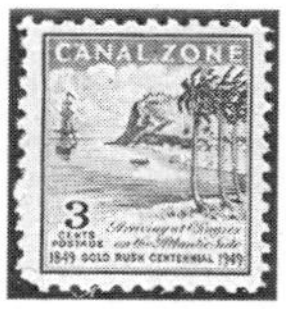

142

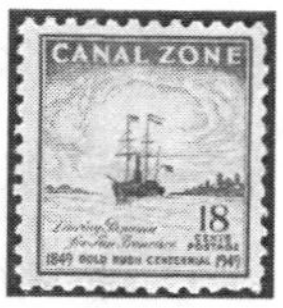

145

Scott's No.		Plate Blocks NH	Plate Blocks Unused	F-VF NH	F-VF Unused	F-VF Used
	1946-51 Issues VF + 25%					
136-40	**Set of 5**	**21.50**	**16.50**	**2.60**	**2.00**	**1.50**
136	½¢ General Davis (1948) ... (6)	3.25	2.60	.45	.35	.25
137	1½¢ Gov. Magoon (1948) .. (6)	3.25	2.60	.45	.35	.25
138	2¢ T. Roosevelt (1949) .... (6)	1.65	1.25	.25	.20	.20
139	5¢ J. Stevens, 19x22 mm .. (6)	3.50	2.75	.45	.35	.20
140	25¢ J.F. Wallace (1948) ..... (6)	11.75	8.50	1.10	.85	.75
141	10¢ Biological Area (1948) . (6)	10.00	8.00	1.50	1.20	.95
142-45	**Gold Rush (1949)**	**55.00**	**45.00**	**5.25**	**4.25**	**3.50**
142	3¢ "Forty Niners" (6)	6.50	5.00	.65	.50	.35
143	6¢ Journey to Las Cruces . (6)	7.00	5.50	.75	.60	.45
144	12¢ Las Cruces Trail (6)	22.50	18.00	1.75	1.40	1.10
145	18¢ To San Francisco (6)	22.50	18.50	2.50	2.00	1.80
146	10¢ W. Indian Labor(1951) . (6)	30.00	24.00	3.00	2.40	2.25

1955-58 Commemoratives

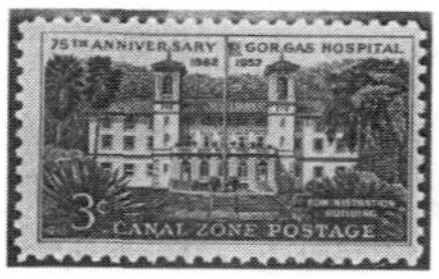

148

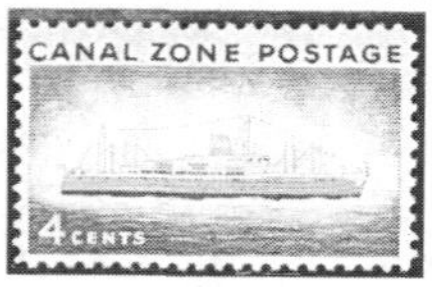

149

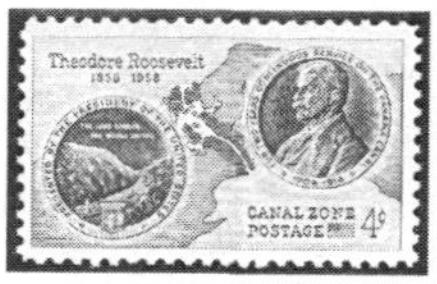

150

Scott's No.		Plate Blocks NH	F-VF NH	F-VF Used
147	3¢ Panama Railroad (6)	7.50	.75	.55
148	3¢ Gorgas Hospital (1957)	4.75	.50	.40
149	4¢ S.S. Ancon (1958)	3.75	.50	.35
150	4¢ T. Roosevelt Birth (1958)	3.50	.50	.40

1960-62 Issues

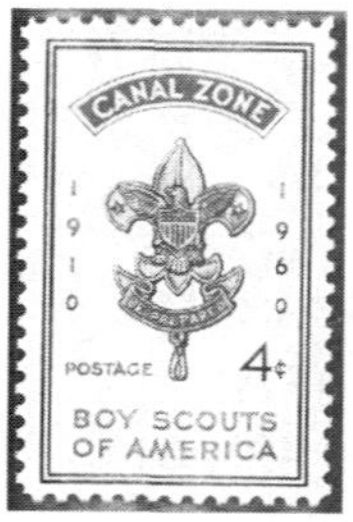

151

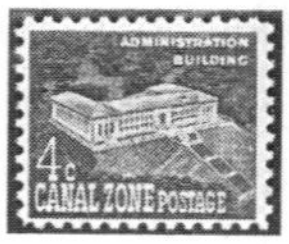

152

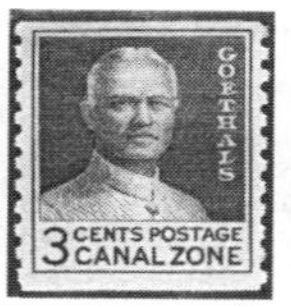

153

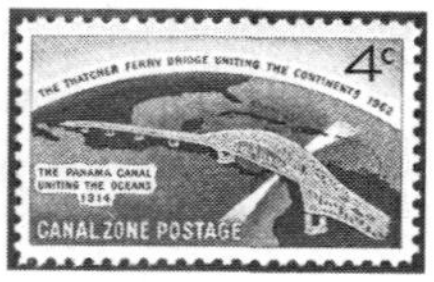

157

CANAL ZONE

Scott's No.		Plate Blocks F-VF,NH	F-VF NH	F-VF Used
151	4¢ Boy Scouts	4.50	.55	.45
152	4¢ Administration Bldg	1.25	.25	.20
		Line Pairs		
153	3¢ Goethals, Coil, Perf.10 Vert.	1.10	.25	.20
154	4¢ Admin. Bldg., Coil, Perf.10 Horiz.	1.15	.25	.20
155	5¢ Stevens, Coil, Perf.10 Vert. (1962)	1.50	.35	.30
		Plate Blocks		
156	4¢ Girl Scouts (1962)	2.75	.45	.35
157	4¢ Thatcher Ferry Bridge ('62)	3.75	.40	.30

1968-78 Issues

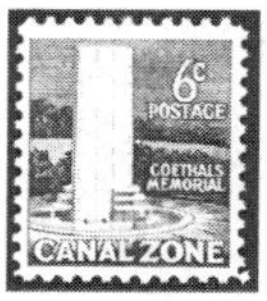

158

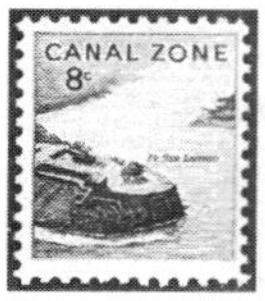

159

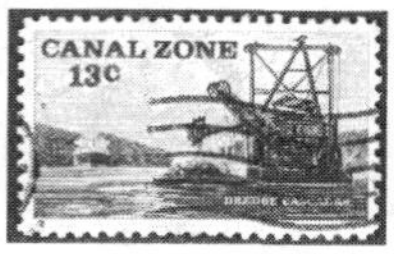

163

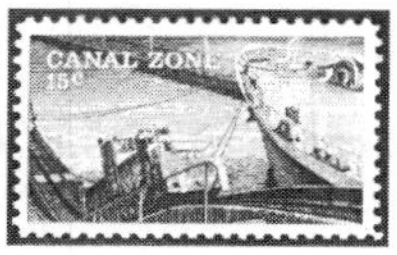

165

Scott's No.		Plate Blocks F-VF,NH	F-VF NH	F-VF Used
158	6¢ Goethals Memorial Balboa	2.25	.35	.30
159	8¢ Fort San Lorenzo (1971)	2.95	.45	.25
		Line Pairs		
160	1¢ Gorgas,Coil,Pf.10 Vert.(1975)	1.10	.20	.20
161	10¢ Hodges,Coil,Pf.10 Vert.(1975)	5.00	.75	.45
162	25¢ Wallace,Coil,Pf.10 Vert.(1975)	21.50	3.00	2.85
		Plate Blocks		
163	13¢ Dredge Cascadas (1976)	2.35	.45	.30
163a	13¢ Booklet Pane of 4	...	3.00	...
164	5¢ Stevens, Rotary, 19x22½mm (1977)	4.75	.80	.75
164a	5¢ Stevens, Tagged	...	13.00	16.00
165	15¢ Towing Locomotive (1978)	2.75	.50	.40

AIR MAIL STAMPS

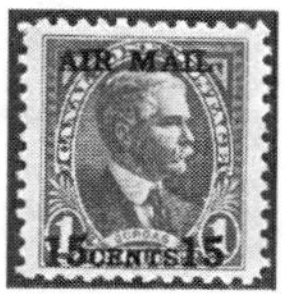

C1

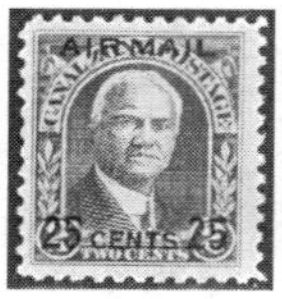

C3

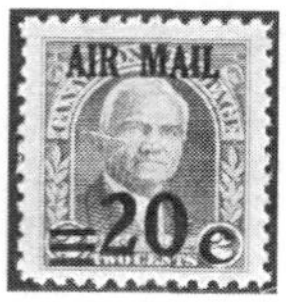

C5

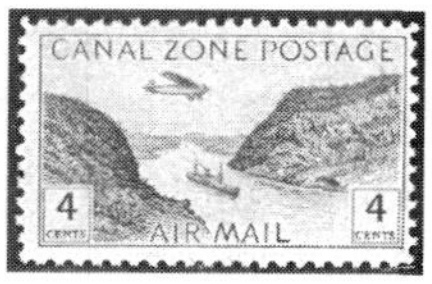

C6

Scott's No.		Unused, NH VF	Unused, NH F-VF	Unused, OG VF	Unused, OG F-VF	Used F-VF
	1929-31 Surcharges on Issues of 1928-29 VF Used + 30% (B)					
C1	15¢ on 1¢ Gorgas T.I (#105)	16.00	12.00	11.00	8.50	5.75
C1	Plate Block of 6	235.00	175.00	160.00	120.00	...
C2	15¢ on 1¢ Gorgas T.II (1931)	175.00	130.00	120.00	90.00	80.00
	Type I: Flag "5" points up. Type II: Flag of "5" is curved up.					
C3	25¢ on 2¢ Goethals (#106)	7.00	5.25	5.00	3.75	2.25
C3	Plate Block of 6	210.00	155.00	145.00	110.00	...
C4	10¢ on 50¢ Blackburn (#114)	16.00	12.00	11.00	8.25	8.00
C4	Plate Block of 6	235.00	175.00	160.00	120.00	...
C5	20¢ on 2¢ Goethals (#106)	10.50	7.75	7.25	5.50	2.00
C5	Plate Block of 6	185.00	140.00	130.00	100.00	...
	1931-49 Series Showing "Gaillard Cut" VF Used + 25% (B)					
C6-14	**Set of 9**	**33.75**	**25.00**	**24.00**	**18.50**	**6.95**
C6	4¢ Red Yellow (1949)	1.25	1.00	1.00	.80	.80
C6	Plate Block of 6	8.75	7.00	7.00	5.75	...
C7	5¢ Yellow Green	.90	.65	.65	.50	.45
C7	Plate Block of 6	6.50	5.00	4.95	4.00	...
C8	6¢ Yellow Brown (1946)	1.20	.95	.90	.70	.35
C8	Plate Block of 6	8.50	6.75	6.65	5.50	...
C9	10¢ Orange	1.50	1.20	1.15	.90	.35
C9	Plate Block of 6	15.75	12.00	11.75	9.50	...
C10	15¢ Blue	1.85	1.50	1.40	1.10	.30
C10	Plate Block of 6	16.75	12.75	12.50	10.00	...
C11	20¢ Red Violet	3.25	2.50	2.40	1.90	.30
C11	Plate Block of 6	28.00	21.50	21.00	16.50	...
C12	30¢ Rose Lake (1941)	5.25	4.00	3.75	2.95	1.10
C12	Plate Block of 6	45.00	36.50	35.00	27.50	...
C13	40¢ Yellow	5.25	4.00	3.75	2.95	1.25
C13	Plate Block of 6	45.00	36.50	35.00	27.50	...
C14	$1 Black	14.50	11.00	10.50	8.25	2.50
C14	Plate Block of 6	125.00	97.50	95.00	75.00	...
	1939 25th Anniversary of Canal Opening VF + 30%					
C15-20	**Set of 6**	**95.00**	**72.50**	**73.50**	**57.50**	**46.50**
C15	5¢ Plane over Sosa Hill	5.25	4.00	4.25	3.25	2.75
C15	Plate Block of 6	52.50	40.00	42.50	32.50	...
C16	10¢ Map of Central America	4.65	3.75	3.75	3.00	2.75
C16	Plate Block of 6	75.00	60.00	55.00	45.00	...
C17	15¢ Fort Amador	5.50	4.25	4.35	3.35	1.25
C17	Plate Block of 6	65.00	50.00	52.50	40.00	...
C18	25¢ Cristobal Harbor	19.50	15.00	15.75	12.00	8.50
C18	Plate Block of 6	295.00	225.00	225.00	175.00	...
C19	30¢ Gaillaird Cut	16.50	12.50	13.00	10.00	7.50
C19	Plate Block of 6	195.00	150.00	150.00	115.00	...
C20	$1 Clipper Landing	47.50	35.00	35.00	27.50	25.00
C20	Plate Block of 6	625.00	475.00	500.00	375.00	...

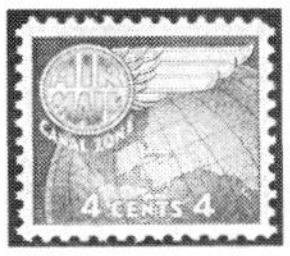

C21

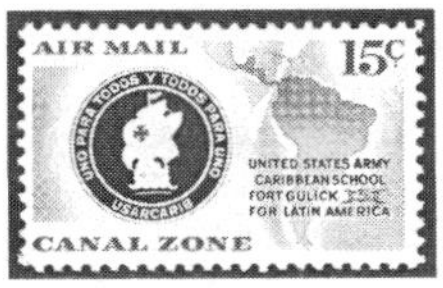

C32

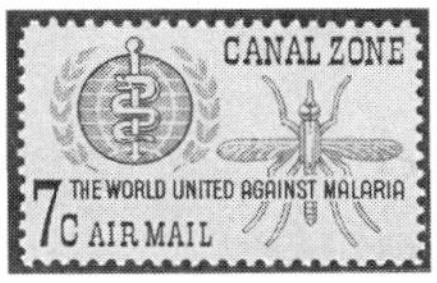

C33

1951 "Globe and Wing" Issue VF + 25%

Scott's No.		Plate Blocks NH	Plate Blocks Unused	F-VF NH	F-VF Unused	F-VF Used
C21-26	**Set of 6**	**220.00**	**175.00**	**24.50**	**19.50**	**11.00**
C21	4¢ Red Violet (6)	7.50	5.75	.85	.70	.40
C22	6¢ Brown (6)	5.75	4.50	.75	.60	.35
C23	10¢ Red Orange (6)	9.50	7.50	1.15	.90	.45
C24	21¢ Blue (6)	80.00	65.00	8.50	6.75	4.50
C25	31¢ Cerise (6)	82.50	67.50	8.50	6.75	4.25
C26	80¢ Gray Black (6)	42.50	35.00	6.25	5.00	1.75

1958 "Globe and Wing" Issue

Scott's No.		Plate Blocks F-VF NH	F-VF NH	F-VF Used
C27-31	**Set of 5**	**180.00**	**25.00**	**9.50**
C27	5¢ Yellow Green	7.00	1.25	.60
C28	7¢ Olive	6.50	1.10	.55
C29	15¢ Brown violet	35.00	4.75	2.50
C30	25¢ Orange Yellow	90.00	11.00	3.00
C31	35¢ Dark Blue	50.00	8.50	3.25
	1961-63 Issues			
C32	15¢ U.S. Army Caribbean School	15.00	1.65	.95
C33	7¢ Anti-Malaria (1962)	3.75	.65	.55
C34	8¢ Globe & Wing, Carmine (1963)	5.00	.65	.35
C35	15¢ Alliance for Progress (1963)	12.50	1.50	1.00

1964 50th Anniversary of Canal Opening

C36-41	**Set of 6**	**67.50**	**12.75**	**8.95**
C36	6¢ Jet over Cristobal	2.75	.50	.45
C37	8¢ Gatun Locks	3.25	.60	.45
C38	15¢ Madden Dam	8.00	1.40	.80
C39	20¢ Gaillard Cut	11.00	2.00	1.10
C40	30¢ Miraflores Lock	17.50	3.25	2.65
C41	80¢ Balboa	27.50	5.50	3.75

1965 Seal & Jet Plane

C42-47	**Set of 6**	**31.50**	**5.85**	**2.95**
C42	6¢ Green & Black	2.25	.40	.35
C43	8¢ Rose Red & Black	2.50	.40	.25
C44	15¢ Blue & Black	3.00	.50	.30
C45	20¢ Lilac & Black	3.50	.75	.45
C46	30¢ Reddish Brown & Black	5.00	1.00	.50
C47	80¢ Bistre & Black	16.50	3.00	1.25

1968-76 Seal & Jet Plane

C48-53	**Set of 6**	**25.75**	**4.95**	..
C48	10¢ Dull Orange & Black	1.75	.35	.25
C48a	10¢ Booklet Pane of 4 (1970)	...	4.50	...
C49	11¢ Olive & Black (1971)	2.00	.40	.25
C49a	11¢ Booklet Pane of 4	...	3.50	...
C50	13¢ Emerald & Black (1974)	5.50	1.00	.35
C50a	13¢ Booklet Pane of 4	...	6.00	...
C51	22¢ Violet & Black (1976)	5.50	1.10	1.75
C52	25¢ Pale Yellow Green & Black	4.75	1.00	.75
C53	35¢ Salmon & Black (1976)	7.50	1.30	1.75

1941-47 OFFICIAL AIRMAIL STAMPS VF Used + 30%
Issue of 1931-46 Overprinted OFFICIAL PANAMA CANAL "PANAMA CANAL" 19-20 mm long

Scott's No.		Unused, NH VF	Unused, NH F-VF	Unused, OG VF	Unused, OG F-VF	Used F-VF
CO1-7,14	**Set of 8**	**170.00**	**127.50**	**125.00**	**95.00**	**45.00**
CO1	5¢ Yellow Green (#C7)	7.75	6.00	5.75	4.50	2.00
CO2	10¢ Orange (#C9)	13.75	10.50	10.50	8.00	2.75
CO3	15¢ Blue (#C10)	17.50	13.50	13.00	10.00	3.25
CO4	20¢ Rose Violet (#C11)	21.00	16.00	15.50	12.00	5.50
CO5	30¢ Rose Lake (#C12) (1942)	26.50	20.00	19.50	15.00	6.00
CO6	40¢ Yellow (#C13)	29.50	22.50	22.00	17.00	9.00
CO7	$1 Black (#C14)	42.50	30.00	29.00	22.50	13.50
CO14	6¢ Yel. Brown (#C8) (1947)	18.00	13.75	13.00	10.00	5.75

1941 OFFICIAL AIRMAIL STAMPS
Issue of 1931-46 Overprinted OFFICIAL PANAMA CANAL "PANAMA CANAL" 17 mm long

					Used VF	Used F-VF
CO8	5¢ Yellow Green (#C7)	...	...	...	200.00	150.00
CO9	10¢ Orange (#C9)	...	...	...	325.00	250.00
CO10	20¢ Red Violet (#C11)	...	...	...	215.00	165.00
CO11	30¢ Rose Lake (#C12)	...	...	...	70.00	55.00
CO12	40¢ Yellow (#C13)	...	...	...	225.00	175.00

NOTE: ON #CO1-CO14 AND 01-9, USED PRICES ARE FOR CANCELLED-TO-ORDER. POSTALLY USED COPIES SELL FOR MORE.

POSTAGE DUE STAMPS

1914 U.S. Dues Ovptd. "CANAL ZONE", Perf. 12 VF Used + 50% (C)

Scott' No.		Unused, NH VF	Unused, NH F-VF	Unused, OG VF	Unused, OG F-VF	Used F-VF
J1	1¢ Rose Carmine (#J45a)	210.00	140.00	125.00	85.00	16.00
J2	2¢ Rose Carmine (#J46a)	675.00	450.00	375.00	250.00	50.00
J3	10¢ Rose Carmine (#J49a)	...	1375.00	...	800.00	45.00

CANAL ZONE

1924 U.S. Dues Ovptd. "CANAL ZONE", Flat "A" VF Used + 40% (B)

Scott's No.		Unused, NH VF	Unused, NH F-VF	Unused, OG VF	Unused, OG F-VF	Used F-VF
J12	1¢ Carmine Rose (#J61)	250.00	175.00	155.00	110.00	28.50
J13	2¢ Claret (#J62b)	140.00	100.00	85.00	60.00	12.00
J14	10¢ Claret (#J65b)	575.00	400.00	350.00	250.00	50.00
	1925 U.S. Ovptd. "CANAL ZONE POSTAGE DUE" VF Used + 40% (B)					
J15	1¢ Franklin (#552)	230.00	160.00	140.00	100.00	16.50
J16	2¢ Washington (#554)	57.50	40.00	35.00	25.00	7.00
J17	10¢ Monroe (#562)	110.00	75.00	67.50	47.50	11.50
	1925 U.S. Dues Ovptd. "CANAL ZONE", Sharp "A" VF Used + 40% (B)					
J18	1¢ Carmine Rose (#J61)	20.00	14.00	12.50	8.75	3.00
J18	Plate Block of 6	225.00	160.00	140.00	100.00	...
J19	2¢ Carmine Rose (#J62)	35.00	24.00	21.50	15.00	4.50
J19	Plate Block of 6	350.00	240.00	210.00	150.00	...
J20	10¢ Carmine Rose (#J65)	315.00	225.00	195.00	140.00	19.50

1929-30 Issue of 1928 Surcharged "POSTAGE DUE" VF Used + 30% (B)

J21	1¢ on 5¢ Gaillard Cut (#107)	8.50	6.25	5.50	4.25	2.00
J21	Plate Block of 6	80.00	60.00	56.50	42.50	...
J22	2¢ on 5¢ Blue	13.00	10.00	9.25	7.00	3.00
J22	Plate Block of 6	130.00	100.00	92.50	70.00	...
J23	5¢ on 5¢ Blue	13.00	10.00	9.25	7.00	3.50
J23	Plate Block of 6	130.00	100.00	92.50	70.00	...
J24	10¢ on 5¢ Blue	13.00	10.00	9.25	7.00	3.50
J24	Plate Block of 6	130.00	100.00	92.50	70.00	...

1932-41 Canal Zone Seal VF Used + 30% (B)

J25-29	**Set of 5**	**7.15**	**5.00**	**4.95**	**3.75**	**3.65**
J25	1¢ Claret	.35	.25	.30	.20	.20
J25	Plate Block of 6	3.75	2.65	3.00	2.00	...
J26	2¢ Claret	.35	.25	.30	.20	.20
J26	Plate Block of 6	5.00	3.75	3.65	2.75	...
J27	5¢ Claret	.80	.55	.55	.40	.30
J27	Plate Block of 6	6.75	5.00	5.00	3.75	...
J28	10¢ Claret	3.25	2.35	2.25	1.70	1.70
J28	Plate Block of 6	33.50	24.50	23.00	17.50	...
J29	15¢ Claret (1941)	2.65	1.90	1.80	1.35	1.25
J29	Plate Block of 6	27.50	21.00	19.50	15.00	...

1941-47 OFFICIAL STAMPS VF Used + 30% (B)
Issues of 1928-46 Overprinted "OFFICIAL PANAMA CANAL"

O1	1¢ Gorgas, Type 1 (#105)	3.00	2.25	2.30	1.75	.50
O2	3¢ Goethals, T. 1 (#117)	5.75	4.25	4.50	3.50	.90
O3	5¢ Gaillard Cut, T. 2 (#107)	...	...	...	...	35.00
O4	10¢ Hodges, Type 1 (#108)	10.00	7.50	7.50	5.75	2.40
O5	15¢ Smith, Type 1 (#111)	20.00	15.00	14.50	11.00	2.75
O6	20¢ Rousseau, T. 1 (#112)	24.75	18.75	18.50	13.75	3.50
O7	50¢ Blackburn, T. 1 (#114)	60.00	45.00	45.00	35.00	6.50
O8	50¢ Blackburn, T. 1A (#114)	...	...	...	...	700.00
O9	5¢ Stevens, T. 1 (#139) ('47)	14.50	10.75	10.50	8.00	4.25

Type 1: Ovptd. "10mm", Type 1A: Ovptd. "9mm", Type 2: Ovptd. "19½mm".

CUBA VF Used + 60% (C)

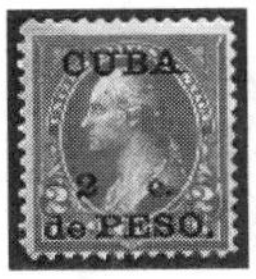

222

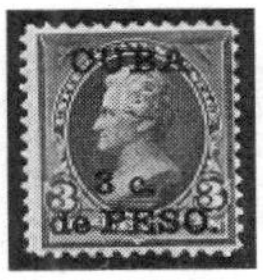

224

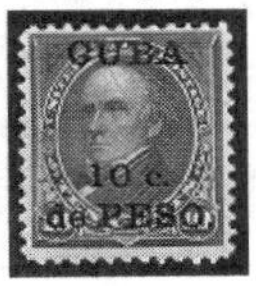

226

1899 U.S. Stamps of 1895-98 Surcharged for Use in Cuba

Scott's No.		Unused, NH VF	Unused, NH F-VF	Unused, OG VF	Unused, OG F-VF	Used F-VF
221	1¢ on 1¢ Franklin (#279)	16.00	9.50	8.00	5.00	.50
222	2¢ on 2¢ Wash. T. III (#267)	28.50	16.00	14.50	9.00	.75
222A	2¢ on 2¢ Wash. T. IV (#279B)	16.75	9.75	8.50	5.25	.50
223	2½¢ on 2¢ Wash. (#267)	14.00	8.50	7.25	4.50	.85
223A	2½¢ on 2¢ Wash. (#279B)	11.50	6.75	6.00	3.75	.85
224	3¢ on 3¢ Jackson (#268)	35.00	21.00	18.00	11.50	1.65
225	5¢ on 5¢ Grant (#281a)	35.00	21.00	18.00	11.50	2.00
226	10¢ on 10¢ Webster (#282C)	77.50	45.00	40.00	25.00	7.75
226A	10¢ on 10¢ Webster,Type II	..	..	..	..	..

1899 Issues of Republic under U.S. Military Rule, Wtmk. "US-C"

227	1¢ Statue of Columbus	10.00	6.00	5.25	3.25	.25
228	2¢ Royal Palms	10.00	6.00	5.25	3.25	.25
229	3¢ Allegory "Cuba"	10.00	6.00	5.25	3.25	.30
230	5¢ Ocean Liner	13.00	8.00	7.00	4.25	.40
231	10¢ Cane Field	31.50	18.75	16.00	10.00	.75

NOTE: A RE-ENGRAVED SET WAS ISSUED BY THE REPUBLIC OF CUBA IN 1905-07. THEY ARE UN-WATERMARKED.

1899 SPECIAL DELIVERY

E1	10¢ on 10¢ Blue (#E5)	375.00	225.00	195.00	120.00	95.00
E2	10¢ Messenger, Orange	150.00	90.00	80.00	50.00	15.00

#E2 IS INSCRIBED "IMMEDIATE". THE REPUBLIC OF CUBA ISSUED A CORRECTED VERSION IN 1902 INSCRIBED "INMEDIATA".

1899 POSTAGE DUE

J1	1¢ on 1¢ Claret (#J38)	130.00	75.00	67.50	42.50	5.00
J2	2¢ on 2¢ Claret (#J39)	130.00	75.00	67.50	42.50	5.00
J3	5¢ on 5¢ Claret (#J41)	130.00	75.00	67.50	42.50	5.00
J4	10¢ on 10¢ Claret (#J42)	90.00	55.00	47.50	30.00	2.50

GUAM VF Used + 60% (C)

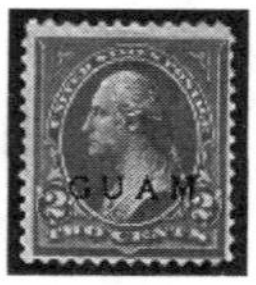
2

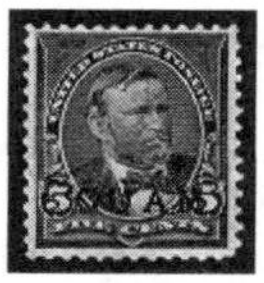
5

1899 U.S. Stamps of 1895-98 Overprinted "GUAM"

Scott's No.		Unused, NH VF	Unused, NH F-VF	Unused, OG VF	Unused, OG F-VF	Used F-VF
1	1¢ Franklin (#279)	60.00	35.00	32.50	20.00	27.50
2	2¢ Wash., Red (#279B)	55.00	32.50	30.00	18.50	26.50
2a	2¢ Rose Carmine (#279Bc)	85.00	50.00	45.00	27.50	35.00
3	3¢ Jackson (#268)	375.00	225.00	200.00	125.00	160.00
4	4¢ Lincoln (#280a)	375.00	225.00	200.00	125.00	160.00
5	5¢ Grant (#281a)	90.00	55.00	48.50	30.00	45.00
6	6¢ Garfield (#282)	350.00	210.00	185.00	115.00	185.00
7	8¢ Sherman (#272)	400.00	235.00	210.00	130.00	185.00
8	10¢ Webster,Ty.I (#282C)	140.00	80.00	72.50	45.00	55.00
9	10¢ Webster,Ty.II(#283)	...	...	3750.00	...	...
10	15¢ Clay (#284)	435.00	265.00	275.00	140.00	175.00
11	50¢ Jefferson (#275)	1000.00	575.00	525.00	325.00	385.00
12	$1 Perry, Type I (#276)	1100.00	650.00	575.00	350.00	425.00
13	$1 Perry, Type II (#276A)	...	...		3750.00	...
	1899 SPECIAL DELIVERY					
E1	10¢ Blue (on U.S. #E5)	425.00	250.00	225.00	140.00	190.00

HAWAII

1853-68 Imperforate Issues VF + 60% (C)

Scott's No.		Unused Fine	Unused Ave.	Used Fine	Used Ave.
5	5¢ Kamehameha III, Blue,Thick Paper	1500.00	900.00	1250.00	750.00
6	13¢ Dark Red, Thick Paper	650.00	400.00	1000.00	650.00
7	5¢ on 13¢ Dark Red (#6)	7500.00	4650.00	...	...
8	5¢ Kamehameha III, Blue	700.00	425.00	650.00	400.00
9	5¢ Blue, Bluish Paper	325.00	195.00	225.00	135.00
10	5¢ Blue, Reissue	22.50	13.75	...	...
10R	5¢ Blue. 1889 Reprint	70.00	50.00	...	...
11	13¢ Dull Rose, Reissue	225.00	140.00	...	...
11R	13¢ Orange Red, 1889 Reprint	275.00	175.00	...	...
	1859-65 Imperforate Numeral Issues VF +50% (C)				
12	1¢ Light Blue	8000.00	5500.00	6500.00	4500.00
13	2¢ Light Blue	5500.00	3750.00	3250.00	2150.00
14	2¢ Black, greenish blue	7000.00	4750.00	4000.00	2650.00
15	1¢ Black, Grayish	500.00	325.00	1000.00	650.00
16	2¢ Black, Grayish Paper	875.00	550.00	650.00	400.00
17	2¢ Dark blue, bluish	9000.00	5500.00	6500.00	4000.00
18	2¢ Black, blue gray	3000.00	2000.00	4500.00	3000.00
19	1¢ Black	550.00	350.00	1100.00	750.00
20	2¢ Black	700.00	450.00	1250.00	850.00
21	5¢ Blue, Bluish Paper	750.00	475.00	600.00	400.00
22	5¢ Blue, Interisland	550.00	350.00	800.00	475.00
23	1¢ Black, Laid Paper	275.00	175.00	...	...
24	2¢ Black, Laid Paper	275.00	175.00	...	...
25	1¢ Dark Blue (1865)	275.00	175.00	...	...
26	2¢ Dark Blue	275.00	175.00	...	...

UNUSED STAMPS WITH ORIGINAL GUM

Scott No.	Original Gum Fine	Ave.	Scott No.	Original Gum Fine	Ave.	Scott No.	Original Gum Fine	Ave.
15	650.00	425.00	21	1000.00	650.00	24	365.00	225.00
19	850.00	550.00	22	725.00	450.00	25	365.00	225.00
20	925.00	595.00	23	365.00	225.00	26	365.00	225.00

1861-69 Kamehameha IV (NH + 125) VF + 60% (C)

Scott's No.		Unused, OG Fine	Unused, OG Ave.	Used Fine	Used Ave.
27	2¢ Pale Rose, Horiz.Laid Paper	250.00	150.00	225.00	135.00
28	2¢ Pale Rose, Vert. Laid Paper	250.00	150.00	140.00	90.00
29	2¢ Red, Thin Wove Paper Reprint	50.00	30.00	...	...
	1864-86 Issues (NH + 125) VF + 60% (C)				
30	1¢ Victoria Kamamalu, Purple('86)	8.50	5.00	7.00	4.25
31	2¢ Kamehameha IV, Vermilion	14.50	9.00	8.50	5.75
32	5¢ Kamehameha V, Blue (1866)	160.00	110.00	27.50	16.50
33	6¢ Kamehameha V, Green (1871)	23.50	14.50	8.50	5.75
34	18¢ Kekuanaoa, Dull Rose, Gum	90.00	55.00	37.50	22.75

UNUSED STAMPS WITHOUT GUM

Scott No.	Without Gum Fine	Ave.	Scott No.	Without Gum Fine	Ave.	Scott No.	Without Gum Fine	Ave.
27	200.00	120.00	30	7.00	4.00	33	18.50	12.00
28	200.00	120.00	31	12.00	7.50	34	75.00	45.00
29	40.00	25.00	32	125.00	75.00			

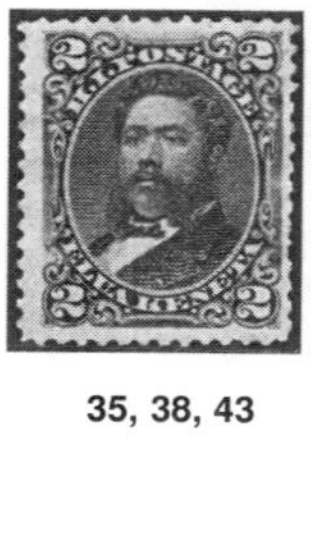
35, 38, 43

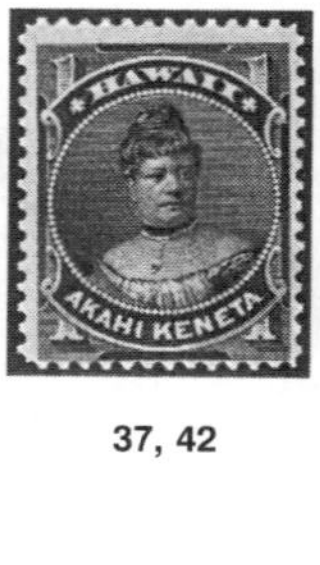
37, 42

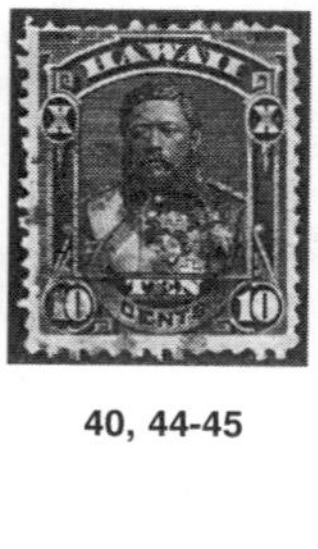
40, 44-45

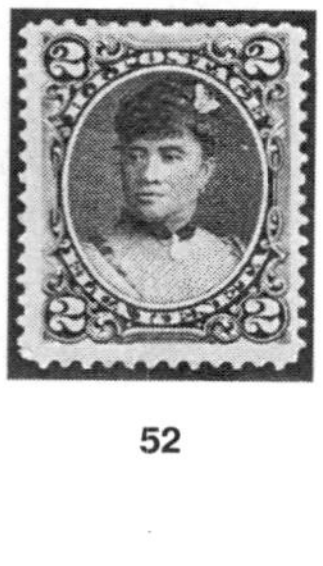
52

HAWAII

Scott's No.		NH Fine	Unused, OG Fine	Unused, OG Ave.	Used Fine	Used Ave.
	1875 Issues VF + 60% (C)					
35	2¢ Kalakaua, Brown	16.50	7.50	4.75	3.25	1.95
36	12¢ Leleiohoku, Black	110.00	50.00	30.00	30.00	18.50
	1882 Issues VF + 60% (C)					
37	1¢ Likelike, Blue	12.50	5.50	3.25	9.00	5.50
38	2¢ Kalakaua, Lilac Rose	240.00	110.00	67.50	40.00	25.00
39	5¢ Kamehameha V, Ultra	30.00	14.50	9.00	3.00	1.85
40	10¢ Kalakaua, Black	72.50	32.50	19.50	18.00	11.00
41	15¢ Kapiolani, Red Brown	110.00	50.00	30.00	25.00	15.00
	1883-86 Issues VF + 60% (C)					
42	1¢ Likelike, Green	6.00	2.75	1.65	1.75	1.10
43	2¢ Kalakaua, Rose (1886)	9.00	4.25	2.50	1.10	.65
44	10¢ Kalakaua,Red Brown('84)	60.00	27.50	17.00	9.00	5.50
45	10¢ Kalakaua, Vermilion	65.00	30.00	18.00	12.00	7.50
46	12¢ Leleiohoku, Red Lilac	150.00	70.00	42.50	31.50	19.50
47	25¢ Kamehameha I, Dk. Viol.	285.00	135.00	85.00	55.00	32.50
48	50¢ Lunalilo, Red	325.00	150.00	90.00	80.00	50.00
49	$1 Kaleleonalani, Rose Red	475.00	225.00	140.00	200.00	120.00
	1886-89 Reproductions & Reprints, Imperforate VF + 40% (B)					
50	2¢ Kamehameha,Orange Vermilion..	150.00	95.00		...	...
51	2¢ Kamehameha, Carmine(1889)...	30.00	17.50		...	...
	1890-91 Issues VF + 60% (C)					
52	2¢ Liliuokalani, Dull Violet(91)	12.75	6.00	3.75	1.40	.90
52C	5¢ KamehamehaV, D.Indigo	240.00	110.00	65.00	125.00	75.00

UNUSED STAMPS WITHOUT GUM

Scott No.	Without Gum Fine	Ave.	Scott No.	Without Gum Fine	Ave.	Scott No.	Without Gum Fine	Ave.
35	6.00	3.75	42	2.25	1.35	48	120.00	72.50
36	40.00	25.00	43	3.50	2.00	49	180.00	110.00
37	4.50	2.50	44	22.50	14.00	50	120.00	75.00
38	85.00	55.00	45	24.00	15.00	51	25.00	15.00
39	12.00	7.25	46	55.00	35.00	52	4.75	3.00
40	25.00	16.00	47	110.00	70.00	52C	85.00	52.50
41	40.00	24.00						

1893 Issues of 1864-91 Overprinted "Provisional Government 1893" VF + 50% (C)

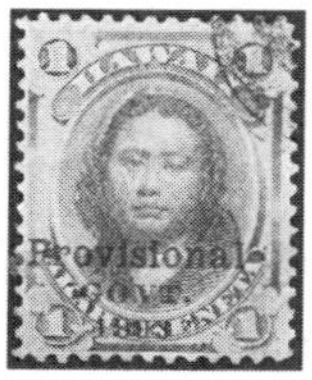
53

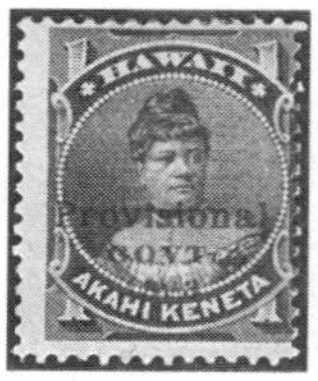
55

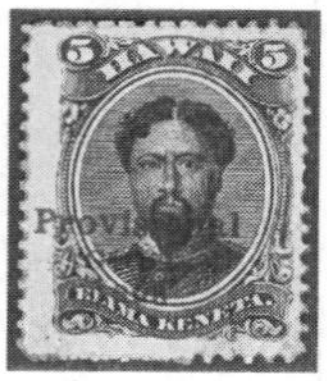
58

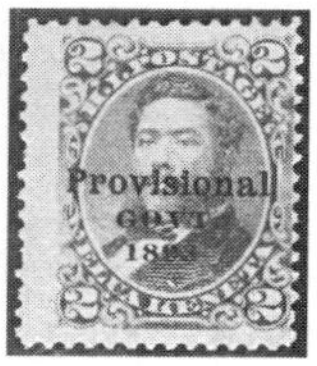
66

Scott's No.		NH Fine	Unused,OG Fine	Unused,OG Ave.	Used Fine	Used Ave.
	Red Overprints					
53	1¢ Purple (#30)	13.50	7.00	4.25	12.00	7.25
54	1¢ Blue (#37)	10.75	5.50	3.50	12.00	7.25
55	1¢ Green (#42)	2.75	1.50	.90	3.00	1.80
56	2¢ Brown (#35)	27.50	9.00	5.50	17.50	10.75
57	2¢ Dull Violet (#52)	3.25	1.75	1.10	1.25	.75
58	5¢ Deep Indigo (#52C)	19.50	10.00	6.00	22.50	13.50
59	5¢ Ultramarine (#39)	10.75	5.75	3.50	3.00	1.85
60	6¢ Green (#33)	26.50	14.00	8.50	22.50	13.50
61	10¢ Black (#40)	17.00	8.75	5.25	13.50	8.25
61B	10¢ Red Brown (#44)	...	...	...	...	...
62	12¢ Black (#36)	17.00	8.75	5.25	15.00	9.00
63	12¢ Red Lilac (#46)	270.00	140.00	85.00	225.00	135.00
64	25¢ Dark Violet (#47)	47.50	25.00	15.00	35.00	21.50
	Black Overprint					
65	2¢ Rose Vermilion (#31)	120.00	65.00	40.00	65.00	40.00
66	2¢ Rose (#43)	2.50	1.40	.85	2.25	1.35
66C	6¢ Green (#33)	...	...	...	...	...
67	10¢ Vermilion (#45)	27.00	14.00	8.50	27.50	16.50
68	10¢ Red Brown (#44)	14.50	7.50	4.50	12.00	7.50
69	12¢ Red Lilac (#46)	500.00	265.00	160.00	450.00	275.00
70	15¢ Red Brown (#41)	35.00	18.50	11.50	30.00	18.00
71	18¢ Dull Rose (#34)	47.50	25.00	15.00	35.00	21.50
72	50¢ Red (#48)	125.00	65.00	40.00	85.00	52.50
73	$1 Rose Red	210.00	110.00	67.50	175.00	110.00

UNUSED STAMPS WITHOUT GUM

Scott No.	Without Gum Fine	Ave.	Scott No.	Without Gum Fine	Ave.	Scott No.	Wthout Gum Fine	Ave.
53	5.50	3.50	60	11.00	7.00	67	11.00	7.00
54	4.50	2.85	61	7.00	4.25	68	6.00	3.75
55	1.20	.75	62	7.00	4.25	69	220.00	130.00
56	7.25	4.50	63	110.00	70.00	70	15.00	9.00
57	1.40	.90	64	20.00	12.00	71	20.00	12.00
58	8.00	4.75	65	52.50	32.50	72	52.50	32.50
59	4.75	2.85	66	1.10	.70	73	90.00	52.50

HAWAII

| 74,80 | 76 | 78 | O1 |

1894 Issues VF + 50% (B)

Scott's No.		NH Fine	Unused, OG Fine	Unused, OG Ave.	Used Fine	Used Ave.
74	1¢ Coat of Arms, Yellow	4.50	2.50	1.50	1.25	.75
75	2¢ Honolulu, Brown	5.00	2.75	1.65	.70	.40
76	5¢ Kamehameha I, Rose Lake	9.00	5.00	3.00	1.75	1.10
77	10¢ Star & Palms, Yel. Grn.	11.50	6.25	3.75	4.50	2.75
78	12¢ S.S. "Arawa", Blue	26.50	14.50	8.75	15.00	9.00
79	25¢ S. Dole, Deep Blue	26.50	14.50	8.75	15.00	9.00

1899 Issues VF + 50% (B)

Scott's No.		NH Fine	Unused, OG Fine	Unused, OG Ave.	Used Fine	Used Ave.
80	1¢ Coat of Arms, Green	3.75	2.00	1.20	1.20	.75
81	2¢ Honolulu, Rose	3.75	2.00	1.20	1.20	.75
82	5¢ Kamehameha I, Blue	12.00	6.50	3.95	3.00	1.80

1896 OFFICIALS VF + 50% (B)

Scott's No.		NH Fine	Unused, OG Fine	Unused, OG Ave.	Used Fine	Used Ave.
O1	2¢ Thurston, Green	70.00	37.50	23.00	17.50	11.00
O2	5¢ Black Brown	70.00	37.50	23.00	17.50	11.00
O3	6¢ Deep Ultramarine	80.00	45.00	28.50	17.50	11.00
O4	10¢ Bright Rose	70.00	37.50	23.00	17.50	11.00
O5	12¢ Orange	110.00	60.00	35.00	17.50	11.00
O6	25¢ Gray Violet	135.00	75.00	45.00	17.50	11.00

UNUSED STAMPS WITHOUT GUM

Scott No.	Without Gum Fine	Without Gum Ave.	Scott No.	Without Gum Fine	Without Gum Ave.	Scott No.	Without Gum Fine	Without Gum Ave.
74	2.00	1.20	79	11.50	7.00	O2	30.00	18.50
75	2.25	1.40	80	1.65	1.00	O3	36.50	22.50
76	4.00	2.50	81	1.65	1.00	O4	30.00	18.50
77	5.00	3.00	82	5.25	3.25	O5	47.50	28.00
78	11.50	7.00	O1	30.00	18.50	O6	60.00	36.50

PHILIPPINE ISLANDS VF Used + 60% (C)

| 214 | 216 | 227 |

1899 U.S. Stamps of 1894-98 Overprinted "PHILIPPINES"

Scott's No.		Unused, NH VF	Unused, NH F-VF	Unused, OG VF	Unused, OG F-VF	Used F-VF
212	50¢ Jefferson (#260)	1300.00	750.00	650.00	400.00	250.00
213	1¢ Franklin (#279)	10.00	6.00	5.25	3.25	1.00
214	2¢ Wash., Red (#279)	4.50	2.50	2.15	1.35	.65
215	3¢ Jackson (#268)	21.00	12.00	10.50	6.50	1.75
216	5¢ Grant (#281)	21.00	12.00	10.50	6.50	1.50
217	10¢ Webster Ty. I (#282C) .	65.00	39.50	33.50	21.50	4.25
217A	10¢ Webster, Ty. II (#283) .	600.00	350.00	300.00	185.00	40.00
218	15¢ Clay (#284)	120.00	67.50	60.00	37.50	8.50
219	50¢ Jefferson (#275)	375.00	220.00	195.00	120.00	40.00

1901 U.S. Stamps of 1895-98 Overprinted "PHILIPPINES"

Scott's No.		Unused, NH VF	Unused, NH F-VF	Unused, OG VF	Unused, OG F-VF	Used F-VF
220	4¢ Lincoln (#280b)	75.00	42.50	37.50	23.50	5.25
221	6¢ Garfield (#282)	95.00	55.00	47.50	30.00	7.50
222	8¢ Sherman (#272)	100.00	57.50	50.00	32.50	7.50
223	$1 Perry, Ty. I (#276)	1450.00	800.00	725.00	450.00	250.00
223A	$1 Perry, Ty. II (#276A)	...	...	3500.00	2250.00	950.00
224	$2 Madison (#277a)	...	...	800.00	500.00	325.00
225	$5 Marshall (#278)	...	...	1500.00	950.00	950.00

1903-04 U.S. Stamps of 1902-03 Overprinted "PHILIPPINES"

Scott's No.		Unused, NH VF	Unused, NH F-VF	Unused, OG VF	Unused, OG F-VF	Used F-VF
226	1¢ Franklin (#300)	14.50	8.25	7.25	4.50	.45
227	2¢ Wash. (#301)	25.00	14.50	12.75	8.00	1.85
228	3¢ Jackson (#302)	230.00	130.00	115.00	70.00	15.00
229	4¢ Grant (#303)	260.00	140.00	130.00	80.00	24.00
230	5¢ Lincoln (#304)	40.00	22.50	20.00	12.50	1.25
231	6¢ Garfield (#305)	260.00	140.00	130.00	80.00	23.50
232	8¢ M. Wash. (#306)	130.00	77.50	70.00	42.50	15.00
233	10¢ Webster (#307)	80.00	45.00	40.00	25.00	3.00
234	13¢ Harrison (#308)	120.00	70.00	60.00	37.50	18.00
235	15¢ Clay (#309)	210.00	115.00	105.00	65.00	15.00
236	50¢ Jefferson (#310)	400.00	250.00	220.00	135.00	40.00
237	$1 Farragut (#311)	1500.00	875.00	800.00	475.00	275.00
238	$2 Madison (#312)	...	...	1700.00	1050.00	825.00
239	$5 Marshall (#313)	...	...	2150.00	1300.00	...
240	2¢ Wash. (#319)	17.00	10.50	9.00	5.50	2.50

1901 SPECIAL DELIVERY U.S. #E5 Ovptd. "PHILIPPINES"

Scott's No.		Unused, NH VF	Unused, NH F-VF	Unused, OG VF	Unused, OG F-VF	Used F-VF
E1	10¢ Messenger, Dark Blue	350.00	210.00	180.00	115.00	110.00

1899-1901 POSTAGE DUES U.S. Dues Ovptd. "PHILIPPINES"

Scott's No.		Unused, NH VF	Unused, NH F-VF	Unused, OG VF	Unused, OG F-VF	Used F-VF
J1	1¢ Deep Claret (#J38)	18.75	11.00	9.50	6.00	1.75
J2	2¢ Deep Claret (#J39)	18.75	11.00	9.50	6.00	1.75
J3	5¢ Deep Claret (#J41)	40.00	25.00	21.75	13.50	3.00
J4	10¢ Deep Claret (#J42)	52.50	32.50	28.00	17.50	6.25
J5	50¢ Deep Claret (#J44)	525.00	325.00	285.00	180.00	100.00
J6	3¢ Deep Claret (#J40)	50.00	30.00	26.00	16.00	8.50
J7	30¢ Deep Claret (#J43)	600.00	365.00	325.00	200.00	110.00

PUERTO RICO VF Used + 60% (C)

| 215 | 216 |

1899 U.S. Stamps of 1895-98 Overprinted "PORTO RICO" at 36° Angle

Scott's No.		Unused, NH VF	Unused, NH F-VF	Unused, OG VF	Unused, OG F-VF	Used F-VF
210	1¢ Franklin, Y.Green (#279)	17.50	10.75	9.00	5.75	1.65
211	2¢ Washington,Red (#279Bf)	16.00	10.00	8.50	5.25	1.50
212	5¢ Grant, Blue (#281)	29.50	16.00	15.00	9.50	2.35
213	8¢ Sherman,Vl.Brown(#272)	110.00	62.50	55.00	35.00	18.00
214	10¢ Webster,Brown (#282C)	80.00	40.00	35.00	22.50	5.75

1899 U.S. Stamps of 1895-98 Overprinted "PORTO RICO" at 25° Angle

Scott's No.		Unused, NH VF	Unused, NH F-VF	Unused, OG VF	Unused, OG F-VF	Used F-VF
210a	1¢ Franklin (#279)	26.50	16.00	13.75	8.50	2.50
211a	2¢ Washington (#279Bf)	20.00	12.75	11.00	6.75	2.50
213a	8¢ Sherman (#272)	125.00	72.50	65.00	40.00	18.50

1900 U.S. Stamps of 1895-98 Overprinted "PUERTO RICO"

Scott's No.		Unused, NH VF	Unused, NH F-VF	Unused, OG VF	Unused, OG F-VF	Used F-VF
215	1¢ Franklin, Green (#279) ..	18.75	11.50	10.00	6.25	1.75
216	2¢ Wash., Red (#279B)	16.50	10.00	8.75	5.50	1.75

1899 Postage Dues; U.S. Dues Overprinted "PORTO RICO" at 36° Angle

Scott's No.		Unused, NH VF	Unused, NH F-VF	Unused, OG VF	Unused, OG F-VF	Used F-VF
J1	1¢ Deep Claret (#J38)	75.00	42.50	38.00	23.50	7.50
J2	2¢ Deep Claret (#J39)	60.00	35.00	30.00	19.00	6.75
J3	10¢ Deep Claret (#J42)	525.00	300.00	265.00	165.00	55.00

1899 Postage Dues; U.S. Dues Overprinted "PORTO RICO" at 25° Angle

Scott's No.		Unused, NH VF	Unused, NH F-VF	Unused, OG VF	Unused, OG F-VF	Used F-VF
J1a	1¢ Deep Claret (#J38)	85.00	47.50	42.50	26.50	9.00
J2a	2¢ Deep Claret (#J39)	67.50	40.00	35.00	22.50	80.00
J3a	10¢ Deep Claret (#J42)	650.00	365.00	325.00	200.00	80.00

U.S. TRUST TERRITORY OF THE PACIFIC

THE MARSHALL ISLANDS, MICRONESIA, AND PALAU WERE PART OF
THE U.S. TRUST TERRITORY OF THE PACIFIC.
THE MARSHALL'S BECAME INDEPENDENT IN 1986.

MARSHALL ISLANDS

| 31 | 35 | 50 |

1984 Commemoratives

Scott's No.		Mint Sheet	Plate Block	F-VF NH
31-34	20¢ Postal Service Inaugural, Block of 4	...	3.50	2.75

1984-85 Maps and Navigational Instruments

35-49A	1¢,3¢,5¢,10¢,13¢,14¢,20¢,22¢,28¢,30¢, 33¢,37¢,39¢,44¢,50¢,$1 Definitives (16)	...	49.50	10.95
39a	13¢ Booklet Pane of 10	...	...	9.75
40a	14¢ Booklet Pane of 10	...	...	9.75
41a	20¢ Booklet Pane of 10	...	...	10.75
41b	13¢/20¢ Bklt. Pane of 10 (5 #39, 5 #41)	...	...	12.50
42a	22¢ Booklet Pane of 10	...	...	9.75
42b	14¢/22¢ Bklt. Pane of 10 (5 #40, 5 #42)	...	...	11.75

1984 Commemoratives (continued)

50-53	40¢ U.P.U.Congress, Hamburg, Block of 4	...	4.50	3.50
54-57	20¢ Ausipex '84, Dolphins, Block of 4	...	3.00	2.25
58	20¢ Christmas, 3 Kings, Strip of 4	(16) 11.75	(8) 5.75	2.50
58	20¢ Christmas Strip of 4 with tabs		(8) 7.50	3.50
59-62	20¢ Marshall Is. Constitution, Block of 4	...	3.25	2.15

| 63-64 |

1985 Commemoratives

63-64	22¢ Audubon Bicentenary, Pair	...	2.95	1.40
65-69	22¢ Seashells, Strip of 5	...	(10) 5.50	2.40
70-73	22¢ Decade for Women, Block of 4	...	3.00	2.25
74-77	22¢ Reef and Lagoon Fish, Block of 4	...	3.00	2.25
78-81	22¢ Youth Year, Atele Nautical Museum,Block-4	...	3.00	2.25
82-85	14¢,22¢,33¢,44¢ Christmas, Missions (4)	...	15.00	2.75
86-90	22¢ Halley's Comet, Strip of 5	(15) 45.00	(10) 14.00	5.75
86-90	22¢ Halley's Comet Strip of 5 with tabs	...	...	35.00
91-94	22¢ Medicinal Plants, Block of 4	...	2.75	2.10

1986-87 Maps and Navigational Instruments

107	$2 Wotje & Erikub, 1571 Terrestrial Globe	...	25.00	5.25
108	$5 Bikini, Stick Chart	...	55.00	11.75
109	$10 Stick Chart of the Atolls(1987)	...	85.00	18.70

| 110 | 163 |

1986-87 Commemoratives

110-13	14¢ Marine Invertebrates, Block of 4	...	2.95	2.35
114	$1 Ameripex Souv.Sheet (C-54 Globester)	...	...	3.25
115-18	22¢ Operation Crossroads, Atomic Tests, Block of 4	3.00	...	2.50
119-23	22¢ Seashells, Strip of 5	...	(10) 5.75	2.50
124-27	22¢ Game Fish, Block of 4	...	2.75	2.25
128-31	22¢ Christmas, Peace Year,Block of 4	...	3.75	2.75
132-35	22¢ U.S.Whaling Ships, Block of 4 (1987)	...	3.00	2.50
136-41	33¢,39¢,44¢ Flights, Pilots, 3 Pairs	...	(12)11.50	5.25
142	$1 Amelia Earhart / CAPEX'87 Souvenir Sheet	...	...	2.95
143-51	14¢,22¢,44¢ U.S. Constitution Bicentennial, Strips of 3 (3)	(15) 25.00	...	5.00
152-56	22¢ Seashells, Strip of 5	...	(10) 5.95	2.50
157-59	44¢ Copra Industry, Strip of 3	...	(6) 6.00	2.75
160-63	14¢,22¢,33¢,44¢ Christmas, Bible Verses (4)	...	12.00	2.50

| 164 | 184 |

1988 Commemoratives

Scott's No.		Mint Sheet	Plate Block	F-VF NH
164-67	44¢ Marine Birds, Block of 4	...	4.75	4.00

1988-89 Fish Definitives

168-83	1¢,3¢,14¢,15¢,17¢,22¢,25¢,33¢,36¢, 39¢,44¢,45¢,56¢,$1,$2,$5 Fish (16)	...	110.00	22.50
170a	14¢ Booklet Pane of 10	...	...	4.25
171a	15¢ Booklet Pane of 10	...	...	6.00
173a	22¢ Booklet Pane of 10	...	...	5.50
173b	14¢ & 22¢ Bklt. Pane of 10 (5 ea.)	...	...	5.50
174a	25¢ Booklet Pane of 10	...	...	7.25
174b	15¢ & 25¢ Booklet Pane of 10	...	...	7.25
184	$10 Blue Jack (1989)	...	90.00	19.75

1988 Commemoratives (continued)

188-89	15¢-25¢ Summer Olympics Strips of 5 (2)	...	(10)10.75	4.75
190	25¢ Robert Louis Stevenson Pacific Voyages Sv.Sheet of 9	...	...	6.75
191-94	25¢ Colonial Ships and Flags, Block of 4	...	3.25	2.50
195-99	25¢ Christmas, Santa Claus & Sleigh, Strip of 5	...	(10) 6.50	3.00
200-04	25¢ John F. Kennedy, Strip of 5	(15) 10.75	...	3.50
205-08	25¢ Space Shuttle, Strip of 4	(12) 8.25	(8) 6.25	2.75
205-08	25¢ Space Shuttle Strip of 4 with tabs	...	...	3.50

1989 Commemoratives

| 209 | 222 |

209-12	45¢ Links to Japan, Block of 4	...	4.75	4.00
213-15	45¢ Alaska Statehood 30th Anniv., Strip of 3 (9)	11.00	...	2.95
216-20	25¢ Seashells, Strip of 5	...	(10) 6.75	3.00
221	$1.00 Hirohito & Akihito Enthronement Souv. Sheet	...	...	2.25
222-25	45¢ Migrant Birds, Block of 4	...	4.75	3.75
226-29	45¢ Postal History, Block of 4	...	5.00	4.00
230	25¢ PHILEXFRANCE, Postal History Souv. Sheet of 6	...	...	11.75
231	$1 Postal History, Souvenir Sheet	...	...	11.50
238a	$2.50 Moon Landing Booklet Pane of 7 (6x25¢,$1)	...	...	17.95

Also See #341-45

| 239 | 298 |

* World War II Anniversaries 1939-1989

239	25¢ Invasion of Poland	(12) 11.50	3.75	.75
240	45¢ Sinking of HMS Royal Oak	(12) 18.50	6.00	1.25
241	45¢ Invasion of Finland	(12) 18.50	6.00	1.25
242-45	45¢ Battle of River Platte, Block of 4	(16) 22.50	6.00	4.75

* World War II Anniversaries 1940-1990

246-47	25¢ Invasion of Norway & Denmark, Pair	(12) 12.75	3.00	1.35
248	25¢ Katyn Forest Massacre	(12) 8.50	3.25	.65
249-50	25¢ Bombing of Rotterdam and Invasion of Belgium, Pair	(12) 9.00	3.25	1.25
251	45¢ Churchill Becomes Prime Minister	(12) 18.00	6.00	1.25
252-53	45¢ Evacuation at Dunkirk, Pair	(12) 18.00	6.25	2.50
254	45¢ Occupation of Paris	(12) 18.00	6.00	1.25
255	25¢ Battle of Mers-el-Kebir	(12) 11.00	3.50	.75
256	25¢ Battles for Burma Road	(12) 11.00	3.50	.75
257-60	45¢ U.S. Destroyers for Gr.Britain, Block-4	(16) 22.50	6.25	5.00
261-64	45¢ Battle of Britain, Block of 4	(16) 22.50	6.25	5.00
265	45¢ Tripartite Pact, 1940	(12) 18.00	6.00	1.25
266	25¢ FDR Elected to Third Term	(12) 11.00	3.50	.75
267-70	25¢ Battle of Taranto, Block of 4	(16) 13.75	3.75	3.00

* World War II Anniversaries 1941-1991

271-74	30¢ Four Freedoms, Block of 4	(16) 16.50	4.50	3.50
275	30¢ Battle of Beda Fomm	(12) 11.50	4.00	.80
276-77	29¢ German Invasion of Greece & Yugoslavia, Pair	(12) 11.50	3.75	1.50
278-81	50¢ Sinking of the Bismarck, Block of 4	(16) 27.50	7.50	6.00
282	30¢ Germany Invades Russia	(12) 11.00	4.25	.85
283-84	29¢ Atlantic Charter, Pair	(12) 22.50	4.00	1.70
285	29¢ Siege of Moscow	(12) 11.00	4.25	.85
286-87	30¢ Sinking of USS Reuben James, Pair	(16) 12.50	4.00	1.70
288-91	50¢ Japanese Attack Pearl Harbor, Block-4	(16) 26.50	7.00	5.75
288a-91a	50¢ Pearl Harbor Reprint, Block of 4	(16) 85.00	21.00	17.50
292	29¢ Japanese Capture Guam	(12) 11.50	4.25	.85
293	29¢ Fall of Singapore	(12) 11.50	4.25	.85
294-95	50¢ Flying Tigers, Pair	(16) 23.50	6.75	2.75
296	29¢ Fall of Wake Island	(12) 11.50	4.25	.85

* World War II Anniversaries 1942-1992

297	29¢ FDR & Churchill at Arcadia Conf.	(12) 11.50	4.25	.85
298	50¢ Japanese enter Manila	(12) 19.75	7.25	1.50
299	29¢ Japanese take Rabaul	(12) 11.50	4.25	.85
300	29¢ Battle of Java Sea	(12) 11.50	4.25	.85
301	50¢ Fall of Rangoon to Japan	(12) 19.75	7.25	1.50
302	29¢ Battle for New Guinea	(12) 11.50	4.25	.85
303	29¢ MacArthur Leaves Corregidor	(12) 11.50	4.25	.85
304	29¢ Raid on Saint-Nazaire	(12) 11.50	4.25	.85
305	29¢ Surrender of Bataan/Death March	(12) 11.50	4.25	.85
306	50¢ Doolittle Raid on Tokyo	(12) 19.50	7.50	1.50

* WW II Anniversary Issues are available with tabs for an additional 50%

THE MARSHALL ISLANDS

Scott's No.		Mint Sheet	Plate Block	F-VF NH

*World War II Anniversaries 1942-1992 (continued)

Scott's No.		Mint Sheet	Plate Block	F-VF NH
307	29¢ Fall of Corregidor	(12) 11.50	4.25	.85
308-11	50¢ Battle of the Coral Sea, Block of 4	(16) 26.50	7.50	6.00
308a-11a	50¢ Coral Sea Reprint, Block of 4	(16) 70.00	18.50	15.00
312-15	50¢ Battle of Midway, Block of 4	(16) 26.50	7.50	6.00
316	29¢ Village of Lidice Destroyed	(12) 11.50	4.25	.85
317	29¢ Fall of Sevastopol	(12) 11.50	4.25	.85
318-19	29¢ Atlantic Convoys/German U-Boat, Pair	(12) 11.50	4.25	1.70
320	29¢ Marines Land on Guadalcanal	(12) 11.50	4.25	.85
321	29¢ Battle of Savo Island	(12) 11.50	4.25	.85
322	29¢ Dieppe Raid	(12) 11.50	4.25	.85
323	50¢ Battle of Stalingrad	(12) 19.50	7.50	1.50
324	29¢ Battle of Eastern Solomons	(12) 11.50	4.25	.85
325	50¢ Battle of Cape Esperance	(12) 19.50	7.50	1.50
326	29¢ Battle of El Alamein	(12) 11.50	4.25	.85
327-28	29¢ Battle of Barents Sea, Pair	(12) 11.50	4.25	1.70

* World War II Anniversaries 1943-1993

Scott's No.		Mint Sheet	Plate Block	F-VF NH
329	29¢ Casablanca Conference	(12) 11.50	4.25	.85
330	29¢ Liberation of Kharkov	(12) 11.50	4.25	.85
331-34	50¢ Battle of Bismarck Sea, Block of 4	(16) 26.50	7.50	6.00
335	50¢ Interception of Admiral Yamamoto	(12) 26.50	7.50	1.50
336-37	29¢ Battle of Kursk, Pair	(16) 17.50	5.00	2.00

See #467-563 for additional World War II Anniversary Issues

364 · **382** · **383**

1989 Commemoratives (continued)

Scott's No.		Plate Block	F-VF NH
341-44	25¢ Christmas, Angels, Block of 4	5.00	4.25
345	45¢ Milestones in Space Exploration, Sheet of 25 ...	...	39.50

1990-92 Birds Definitives

Scott's No.		Plate Block	F-VF NH
346-65A	1¢,5¢,10¢,12¢,15¢,20¢,23¢,25¢,27¢,29¢,30¢, 35¢,36¢,40¢,50¢,52¢,65¢,75¢,$1,$2 Birds (21)	165.00	29.50
361a	95¢ Essen '90 Miniature Sheet of 4 (#347,350,353,361)	...	4.75

1990 Commemoratives

Scott's No.		Plate Block	F-VF NH
366-69	25¢ Children's Games, Block of 4	4.50	3.75
376a	$2.50 Penny Black Booklet Pane of 7 (6x25¢,$1Sv.Sheet)	...	14.75
377-80	25¢ Endangered Sea Turtles, Block of 4 ...	5.75	4.75
381	25¢ Joint Issue with Micronesia & U.S. (U.S.#2507)...	8.75	1.10
382	45¢ German Reunification	5.75	1.35
383-86	25¢ Christmas, Block of 4	4.50	3.50
387-90	25¢ Breadfruit, Block of 4	4.25	3.35

1991 Commemoratives

399 · **411**

Scott's No.		Plate Block	F-VF NH
391-94	50¢ US Space Shuttle Flights, 10th Anniv., Block of 4	6.50	4.75
395-98	52¢ Flowers, Block of 4	7.50	5.25
398a	52¢ Phila Nippon, Flowers, Miniature sheet of 4...	...	5.25
399	29¢ Operation Desert Storm	8.75	1.60
406a	$2.74 Birds Booklet Pane of 7 (6x29¢,$1 Sv.Sheet)...	...	20.75
407-10	12¢,29¢,50¢ (2) Air Marshall Island Aircraft (4)	17.75	4.00
411	29¢ Admission to United Nations	8.00	.80
412	30¢ Christmas, Peace Dove	4.50	.90
413	29¢ Peace Corps in Marshall Islands	5.00	.90

425 · **426** · **427** · **428**

1992 Commemoratives

Scott's No.		Mint Sheet	Plate Block	F-VF NH
414-17	29¢ Ships, Strip of 4	(8) 10.50		4.50
424a	$4 Discovery Booklet Pane of 7 (6x50¢ + $1 Sv.Sheet)	...		16.50
425-28	29¢ Traditional Handicrafts, Strip of 4	(8)	7.50	3.25
429	29¢ Christmas			.80

1992 Birds Definitives

Scott's No.		Plate Block	F-VF NH
430-33	9¢,22¢,28¢,45¢ Birds	22.50	4.00

1993 Commemoratives

Scott's No.		Plate Block	F-VF NH
440a	$4 Reef Life Booklet Pane of 7 (6x50¢,$1 Sv.Sheet)	...	15.00

THE MARSHALL ISLANDS

1993-95 Ship Definitives

441 · **464**

Scott's No.		Plate Block	F-VF NH
441/66	10¢,14¢,15¢,19¢,20¢,23¢,24¢,29¢,30¢, 32¢,35¢,40¢,45¢,46¢,50¢,52¢,55¢,60¢, 75¢,78¢,95¢,$1,$2.90,$3 Ships (24)	170.00	35.00
463	$1.00 Walap, Eniwetok	17.50	3.25
464	$2.00 Walap, Jaluit	22.50	4.75
466A	$5.00 Tipnol, Ailuk (1994)	70.00	12.50
466B	$10.00 Racing canoes (1994)	125.00	25.00
466C	15¢,23¢,52¢,75¢ Hong Kong'94, Sailing Vessels, Souvenir Sheet of 4 (1994)	...	4.25

476 · **477**

* World War II Anniversaries 1943-1993 (continued)

Scott's No.		Mint Sheet	Plate Block	F-VF NH
467-70	52¢ Invasion of Sicily, Block of 4	(16)29.50	7.50	6.50
471	50¢ Bombing Raids on Schweinfurt ...	(12)21.50	7.50	1.50
472	29¢ Liberation of Smolensk	(12)11.50	4.25	.85
473	29¢ Landing at Bougainville	(12)11.50	4.25	.85
474	50¢ US Invasion of Tarawa	(12)21.50	7.50	1.50
475	52¢ Tehran Conference	(12)21.50	7.50	1.50
476-77	29¢ Battle of North Cape, Pair	(12)15.00	5.25	2.25

* World War II Anniversaries 1944-1994

Scott's No.		Mint Sheet	Plate Block	F-VF NH
478	29¢ Eisenhower Commands SHAEF ..	(12)11.50	4.25	.85
479	50¢ Invasion of Anzio	(12)21.50	7.50	1.50
480	52¢ Siege of Leningrad Ends	(12)21.50	7.50	1.50
481	29¢ U.S. Frees Marshall Islands	(12)11.50	4.25	.85
482	29¢ Japanese Defeat at Truk	(12)11.50	4.25	.85
483	52¢ Bombing of Germany	(12)21.50	7.50	1.50
484	50¢ Rome Falls to Allies	(12)21.50	7.50	1.50
485-88	75¢ D-Day Landings, Block of 4	(16)45.00	11.50	9.50
485a-88a	75¢ D-Day, Reprint, Block of 4	(16)90.00	25.00	19.95
489	50¢ V-1 Bombs Strike England	(12)21.50	7.50	1.50
490	29¢ Marines Land on Saipan	(12)11.50	4.25	.85
491	50¢ Battle of Philippine Sea	(12)21.50	7.50	1.50
492	29¢ U.S. Liberates Guam	(12)11.50	4.25	.85
493	50¢ Warsaw Uprising	(12)21.50	7.50	1.50
494	50¢ Liberation of Paris	(12)21.50	7.50	1.50
495	29¢ Marines Land on Peliliu	(12)11.50	4.25	.85
496	52¢ MacArthur Returns to Philippines	(12)21.50	7.50	1.50
497	52¢ Battle of Leyte Gulf	(12)21.50	7.50	1.50
498-99	50¢ Battleship "Tirpitz" Sunk, Pair	(16)31.50	8.75	3.50
500-3	50¢ Battle of the Bulge, Block of 4 ...	(16)41.50	10.50	8.50

*World War II Anniversaries 1945-1995

Scott's No.		Mint Sheet	Plate Block	F-VF NH
504	32¢ Yalta Conference	(12)18.50	6.00	1.20
505	55¢ Bombing of Dresden	(12)38.50	14.50	3.00
506	$1 Iwo Jima Invaded by Marines	(12)47.50	15.75	3.50
507	32¢ Remagen Bridge Taken	(12)18.50	6.00	1.20
508	55¢ Marines Invade Okinawa	(12)27.50	10.00	1.95
509	50¢ Death of F.D. Roosevelt	(12)27.00	10.00	1.95
510	32¢ US/USSR Troops Link	(12)17.50	5.75	1.25
511	60¢ Soviet Troops Conquer Berlin	(12)27.50	10.00	1.95
512	55¢ Allies liberate concentration camps	(12)27.50	10.00	1.95
513-16	75¢ V.E. Day, Block of 4	(16)70.00	18.50	15.00
517	32¢ United Nations Charter	(12)18.50	6.00	1.20
518	55¢ Postdam Conference	(12)27.50	10.00	1.95
519	60¢ Churchill's Resignation	(12)27.50	10.00	1.95
520	$1 Atomic Bomb dropped on Hiroshima	(12)57.50	19.75	4.25
521-24	75¢ V.J. Day, Block of 4	(16)70.00	18.75	15.75

* WW II Anniversary Issues are available with tabs for an additional 50%.

1994-95 World War II Anniversary Souvenir Sheets

Scott's No.		Mint Sheet	Plate Block	F-VF NH
562	50¢ MacArthur Returns to Philippines, Souvenir Sheet of 2	...	...	4.00
563	$1 U.N. Charter Souvenir Sheet (1995)	...	...	3.75

1993 Commemoratives (continued)

Scott's No.		Plate Block	F-VF NH
567-70	29¢ Capitol Building Complex	16.50	2.50
571	50¢ Mobil Oil Tanker Eagle Souvenir Sheet ...	...	1.00
572-75	29¢ Marshallese Life in 1800's, attd .	3.25	2.50
576	29¢ Christmas	4.50	.85

1994 Commemoratives

Scott's No.		Plate Block	F-VF NH
577	$2.90 15th Anniv. Constitution Souvenir Sheet...	...	5.75
578	29¢ 10th Anniv. Postal Service Souvenir Sheet ...	...	.70
579-80	50¢ World Soccer Cup, U.S., Pair	11.50	5.00

1994 Commemoratives (continued)

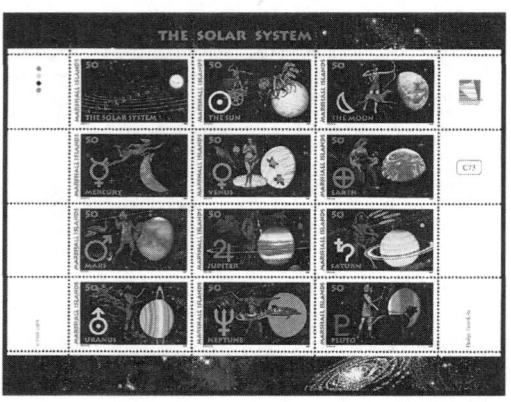

582

Scott's No.		Mint Sheet	Plate Block	F-VF NH
582	50¢ Solar System, Mythological Characters, sheet of 12	...	...	14.50
583-86	75¢ First Moon Landing, 25th Anniv. Block of 4	...	7.50	6.00
586b	75¢ First Moon Landing, Souv. Sheet of 4	...	...	6.00
587	29¢, 52¢, $1 Philakorea, Butterflies, Souv. Sheet of 3...	...	...	4.50
588	29¢ Christmas	...	4.25	.75

1995 Commemoratives

589	50¢ Year of the Boar, Souvenir Sheet	...	...	1.75
590	55¢ Underseas Glory, Marine Life Block of 4	...	9.75	7.50
591	55¢ John F. Kennedy, Strip of 6	...(12)	15.00	6.75
592	75¢ Marilyn Monroe, Block of 4	(12) 21.75	9.00	7.00
593	32¢ Cats, Block of 4	...	5.00	3.25
594	75¢ Mir-Space Shuttle Docking, Block of 4 ..	...	6.75	5.75
595	60¢ Pacific Game Fish, Block of 8	... (8)	18.00	15.00
596	32¢ Island Legends, Block of 4	...	3.25	2.85
597	32¢ Singapore '95, Orchids Min. Sheet of 4 .	...	...	2.85
598	50¢ Beijing '95, Suzhou Gardens, Souv. Sheet	...	...	1.00
599	32¢ Christmas, Shepherd	...	3.50	.75
600	32¢ Legendary Jet Fighter Planes, Min. Sheet of 25	...	...	17.50
601	32¢ Yitzhak Rabin, Israeli Prime Minister	(8) 7.00	4.25	.80

1996 Commemoratives

604 Part   608   616

602	50¢ Year of the Rat Souvenir Sheet	...	...	1.10
603	32¢ Native Birds, Block of 4	...	8.25	7.00
604	55¢ Wild Cats, Block of 4	...	7.00	5.50
605	32¢ Millennium of Navigation, Sailing Ships,Min. Sheet of 25	...	...	17.75
606	60¢ Modern Olympics, Block of 4	...	6.25	5.00
607	55¢ Marshall Island Chronology, Sheet of 12	...	...	14.75
608	32¢ Elvis Presley, Heartbreak Hotel	(20) 60.00 (6)15.00		1.85
609	50¢ China '96, Palace Museum Souv. Sheet ..	...	...	1.50
610	32¢ James Dean	(20) 45.00(6) 16.50		1.50
611	60¢ Ford Motor 100th Anniv., Souvenir Sheet of 8	...	...	9.75
612	32¢ Island Legends, Block of 4	...	3.75	2.75
613	55¢ Steam Locomotives, Sheet of 12	...	...	15.00
614	32¢ Taipei '96, Marine Life Block of 4	...	...	2.75
615	$3 Compact with U.S., Canoe and Flag	...	35.00	6.75
616	32¢ Christmas, Angels	(16) 12.50	...	.75
617	32¢ Legendary Biplanes, Sheet of 25.	...	...	16.75

621   638

1997 Commemoratives

Scott's No.		Mint Sheet	Plate Block	F-VF NH
618	32¢ Native Crafts, Block of 4	...	3.50	2.75
619	60¢ Year of the Ox, Souvenir Sheet .	...	...	1.25
620-21	32¢-60¢ Amata Kabua (2)	(8) 17.00	4.50	1.95
622	32¢ Elvis Presley, Strip of 3	(15) 12.50	(6)5.95	2.50
623-24	32¢ Hong Kong '97, Ships, Souvenir Sheets of 2 (2)	...		3.00
625	60¢ Christianity, Twelve Apostles, Sheet of 12...	...		15.00
626	$3 Christianity, Last Supper, Souvenir Sheet	...		6.50
627	60¢ 20th Century, 1900-1909, Sheet of 15	...	...	19.50
628	60¢ Deng Xiaoping, Chinese Leader .	...	6.50	1.35
629	32¢ Traditional Crafts, Self-adhesive block of 4 (2x10 design)	(20) 17.50	4.50	3.50
630	32¢ Traditional Crafts, Self-adhesive strip of 4 (4x5 design)	(20) 17.50	(8) 8.75	3.50
636a,37a	$4 Pacific '97 Booklet (6-50¢, 1-$1 Souvenir Sheet)	...		9.00
638	16¢ World Wildlife Fund, Birds, Block or Strip of 4	(16) 6.00	...	1.50
639	50¢ Bank of China, Hong Kong Souv. Sheet	...	...	1.60
640	32¢ Canoes, Block or Strip of 4	...	3.75	3.00
641	32¢ Legendary Air Force Planes, Sheet of 25...	...	...	18.50
642	32¢ U.S.S. Constitution, Old Ironsides (15)	3.75	.80
643	32¢ Island Legends, Block of 4	(8) 6.00	3.50	3.00
644	60¢ Underseas Glory, Marine Life Block of 4	(24) 32.50	6.50	5.50
645	60¢ Princess Diana, Strip of 3	(15) 22.50	...	4.50
646	60¢ 20th Century, 1910-1919,Sheet of 15	...	...	22.50
647-48	32¢ Christmas, Raphael's Angel, Pair	(16) 13.00	(8) 7.50	1.60
649	20¢ U.S. Warships of 50 States,Sheet of 50	...	...	25.00
650	50¢ Shanghai '97, Treasure Ship Souvenir Sheet	...	...	1.25

1998 Commemoratives

651	60¢ Year of the Tiger Souvenir Sheet	...	...	1.50
652	32¢ Elvis Presley TV Special,Strip of 3 (15)	12.50		2.50
653	32¢ Seashells, Strip of 4	(20) 15.75	3.85	3.25

654

654	60¢ 20th Century, 1920-29, Sheet of 15	...	...	22.50
655	32¢ Canoes of the Pacific, Sheet of 8	...	...	6.50
656	60¢ Berlin Airlift, Block of 4	(16) 23.00	7.00	5.95
657	60¢ 20th Century, 1930-39, Sheet of 15	...	...	22.50
664a	$6.60 Czar Nicholas II Booklet (6-60¢ ,1-$3 Sv.Sheet)...	...		16.50
665	32¢ Babe Ruth, Baseball	(15) 11.75	4.00	.80
666	32¢ Legendary U.S. Navy Planes Sheet of 25	...	...	19.50
667	60¢ Chevrolet Automobiles, Sheet of 8	...	...	11.75
668	33¢ Marshallese Alphabet & Language, Sheet of 24	...	...	19.50
669	33¢ New Buildings, Strip of 3	(12) 9.75(6)	5.50	2.50
670	32¢ Christmas, Angel	...	4.00	.80
677a	$6.60 John Glenn, Hero in Space Booklet (6-60¢, $3 Souvenir Sheet)	...		16.50
678	$3 Drought Relief Priority Mail Souvenir Sheet	...	...	7.50
679	60¢ 20th Century, 1940-49, Sheet of 15	...	...	22.50
680	33¢ History's Greatest Fighting Ships, Sheet of 25	...	...	19.75
681	60¢ Year of the Rabbit Souvenir Sheet	...	...	1.50

1999 Birds of the Marshall Islands Regular Issue

682-89	1¢, 3¢, 20¢, 22¢, 33¢, 55¢, $1, $10 (8)	...	125.00	28.75

1999 Commemoratives

690	33¢ Canoes of the Pacific, Sheet of 8	...	...	6.50
691-98	33¢ Canoes of the Pacific, Self-adhesive ..... 8 designs, Block of 10 with 3 #698	(20)16.75	...	8.25
699	60¢ Great American Indian Chiefs, Sheet of 12	...	...	17.50
700	33¢ Marshallese Flag	(16)12.00	3.75	.80
701	33¢ Flowers of the Pacific, Block of 6	(12) 10.00	...	4.75
702	60¢ 20th Century, 1950-59, Sheet of 15	...	...	22.50
703	$1.20 Australia '99, World Stamp Expo, "HMAS Australia" Souvenir Sheet	...	...	3.00
704	33¢ Elvis Presley, Artist of the Century	(20) 16.75	4.00	.85

226

1999 Commemoratives (continued)

705

2001 Great Marshallese Regular Issue

| 772 | 773 | 774 | 775 |

Scott's No.		Mint Sheet	Plate Block	F-VF NH
705	60¢ IBRA '99 Stamp Exh., Germany, Souvenir Sheet of 4			5.75
706	33¢ RMI Constitution 20th Anniversary ...... (6) 4.75		...	.80
707	33¢ 15th Anniv. RMI Postal Service Bk of 4(24)18.50		3.95	3.25
708	33¢ Legendary Aircraft, Sheet of 25		...	19.50
709	$1 Philexfrance '99, Transportation on Moon, Souv Sheet			2.40
710	60¢ Marshall Is. Ship Registry Souvenir Sheet	...	...	1.50
711	60¢ 20th Century, 1960-69, Sheet of 15	...	...	21.50
712	33¢ 30th Anniversary of First Men on the Moon Souvenir Sheet of 3	...	...	2.40
713	33¢ Early European Navigation,Block-4 ...... (16) 12.50		3.75	3.25

1999 Birds of the Marshall Islands Regular Issue

714-21	5¢,40¢,45¢,75¢,$1.20,$2,$3.20,$5 (8)		130.00	29.50

1999 Commemoratives (continued)

722	33¢ Traditional Christmas .... (20) 15.50		3.75	.80
723	60¢ 20th Century, 1970-79, Sheet of 15	...	...	21.50
724-25	33¢ End/Beginning of Millennium,Pair. .... (16) 12.50		3.75	1.60

2000 Commemoratives

726	60¢ 20th Century, 1980-89, Sheet of 15	...	...	21.50
727	60¢ Year of the Dragon Souvenir Sheet	...	...	1.50
728	33¢ Legendary Aircraft II Sheet of 25	...	...	19.50
729	33¢ Garden Roses, Block of 6 .... (12) 9.95		...	5.00
730	60¢ 20th Century, 1990-99, Sheet of 15	...	...	19.50
731	33¢ China Pandas, Block of 6 .... (12) 9.95		...	5.00
732-38	1¢-42¢ American Presidents, set of 7 sheets of 6 depicting each president plus White House	...	...	19.75
739	33¢ Zeppelin Flights, Block of 4 .... (16) 11.85		3.50	3.00
746a	60¢ - $1 Winston Churchill Booklet (6-60¢, 1-$1 Souvenir Sheet)	...		11.75

747

747	33¢ 225th Ann. of U.S. Military Strip-3 .... (12) 10.00(6) 5.25			2.40
748	33¢ Marshall Island Capitol, Nitijela Flag and Seal, Block of 4	(16) 11.95	3.25	3.00
749	60¢ Ships of Discovery (6)	(12) 17.00	9.50	8.75
750	60¢ Queen Mother's 100th Birthday Block of 4	(16) 22.75	6.50	5.75
751	33¢ Reef Life Sheetlet of 8	...	...	6.00
752	60¢ Butterflies Sheetlet of 12	...	...	17.50
753	33¢ Germany United 10th Anniversary ...... (16) 12.50		3.75	.80
754	33¢ U.S. Submarines, block of 4 .... (8) 6.50		3.75	3.25
755	33¢ Christmas - Palm Trees .... (20) 15.50		3.75	.80
756	$4.60 Sun Yat-Sen Booklet of 7 (6-60¢, 1-$1 Sv.Sheet)	...	...	11.75

2001 Commemoratives

757	80¢ Year of the Snake Souvenir Sheet	...	...	2.25

2001 Flower of the Month

758-69	34¢ Flowers, set of 12	82.50	50.00	10.95
758	34¢ January - Carnation .... (8)	7.25	4.35	.95
759	34¢ February - Violet .... (8)	7.25	4.35	.95
760	34¢ March - Jonquil .... (8)	7.25	4.35	.95
761	34¢ April - Sweet Pea .... (8)	7.25	4.35	.95
762	34¢ May - Lily of the Valley .... (8)	7.25	4.35	.95
763	34¢ June - Rose .... (8)	7.25	4.35	.95
764	34¢ July - Larkspur .... (8)	7.25	4.35	.95
765	34¢ August - Poppy .... (8)	7.25	4.35	.95
766	34¢ September - Aster .... (8)	7.25	4.35	.95
767	34¢ October - Marigold .... (8)	7.25	4.35	.95
768	34¢ November - Chrysanthemum .... (8)	7.25	4.35	.95
769	34¢ December - Poinsettia .... (8)	7.25	4.35	.95

2001 Sailing Canoes Regular Issue

770	$5 Walap of Jaluit	...	55.00	12.50
771	$10 Walap of Eniwetok	...	110.00	25.00

Scott's No.		Mint Sheet	Plate Block	F-VF NH
772-75	34¢ A. Kabua, 55¢ R.Reimiers, 80¢ l.Hacker, $1 D. Heine (4)	...	32.50	7.50
784	57¢ Atain Anien .... (20) 28.50		6.95	1.50

2001 Commemoratives (continued)

776	80¢ Butterflies II Sheet of 12	...	...	25.75
777	34¢ Fairy Tales, strip of 7 .... (28) 27.50		...	6.95
778	34¢ Watercraft Racing, Block of 4 ... (16) 14.50		...	3.65
779	80¢ Manned Space Flight, Block of 4 (8) 17.50		...	8.95
780	34¢ Stamp Day .... (16) 14.50		4.35	.95
780a	same, Tete-Beche Pair	...	...	1.90
781	80¢ American Achievements in Space Block of 4 .... (16) 35.00		9.95	8.95
782	34¢ Marine Life, Block of 4 .... (8) 7.25		4.25	3.65
783	34¢ Sports: Basketball, Bowling, Ping Pong, Kayaking, Block of 4 ...... (16) 14.50		4.25	3.65
785	34¢ Signs of the Zodiac, Sheet of 12	...	...	11.00
786	80¢ Philanippon 2001, Dreams Across the Globe, Sheet of 12	...	...	25.75
787	80¢ U.S. Naval Heroes of World War II, Sheet of 9	...	...	18.75

788

788	34¢ Vintage Cars, Block of 8 .... (16) 14.75		9.00	7.50
789	$3.04 In Rememberance of September 11, 2001 Booklet of 7 (6-34¢, $1 Souvenir Sheet) ...	...		7.75
790	34¢ Christmas, Vert. Strip of 4 .... (20) 17.95		(8)7.95	3.65
791	80¢ Classic Aircraft, Block of 10 ...... (20) 41.50		23.50	20.75

2002 Commemoratives

792	80¢ Year of the Horse Souvenir Sheet	...	..	1.95
793	34¢ Seashells, Block of 6 .... (12) 9.95		..	5.00
794	80¢ Elizabeth II Golden Jubilee Souvenir Sheet		..	1.95
795	34¢ United We Stand .... (16) 13.50		..	.85
796	34¢ Vintage Cars II, Block of 8 .... (16) 13.75		..	7.00
797	34¢ Gardens of the Sea Block-4 ...... (16) 13.75		..	3.50
798	80¢ Butterflies III, Sheet of 12	..	...	24.75
799	34¢ Horses from Art of World, Sheet of 12	...	...	9.95
800	80¢ Horses in Chinese Art Souvenir Sheet	...	...	1.95
801	37¢ Russian Palekh Art, The Frog Princess Fairy Tale, Sheet of 12	...	...	10.95
802	80¢ Carousel Animals, Block of 4 .... (16) 31.50		...	7.95
803	37¢ Tropical Island Birds, Sheet of 16	...	...	15.00
804	80¢ Benjamin Franklin, Pair .... (16) 31.50		...	3.95
805	37¢ Sea Turtles, Block .... (16) 15.75		...	3.95
806	80¢ IFSDA, Stamp Collecting, Block of 6 .... (12) 23.50		13.75	12.00
807	37¢ Naval Ships, Block of 6 .... (12) 10.75		...	5.50
808	23¢ Insects & Spiders, Sheet of 20 ..	...	...	11.50
809	80¢ Vintage Cars III, Block of 8 .... (16) 31.75		18.00	15.95
810	80¢ Queen Mother, Block of 4 .... (16) 31.75		9.75	7.95
811	80¢ Regal Princess Cruise Ship Souvenir Sheet		...	1.95
812	80¢ Military Heroes of WWI, Block of 8 (16) 31.75		...	15.95
813	37¢ Christmas Cookies, Pair .... (20) 18.50		...	1.85

VERY FINE COPIES OF THE STAMPS OF THE MARSHALL ISLANDS, MICRONESIA **AND** PALAU ARE AVAILABLE FOR 20% PREMIUM. MINIMUM 10¢ PER STAMP.

811

2003 Commemoratives

Scott's No.		Mint Sheet	Plate Block	F-VF NH
814	80¢ Year of the Ram Souvenir Sheet	…	…	1.80
815	60¢ U.N. Membership	…	…	1.35
816	50¢ Folktales Block of 4	(8) .9.00	…	4.50

2003 Great Marshallese Regular Issue

817-19	37¢ Oscar deBrum, $3.85 Tipne Philippo, $13.65 Henchi Balos set of 3	…	180.00	39.50

2003 Commemoratives (continued)

820

820	37¢ Heritage and Culture Blk of 8	(16) 13.50	…	6.75
821	80¢ Butterflies Sheet of 12	…	…	21.50
822	37¢ Powered Flight Block of 10	(20) 15.95	…	8.25
823	37¢ Antique Cars Block of 8	(16) 12.50	…	6.25
824	37¢ Heritage and Culture Block-8 II	(16) 12.50	…	6.25
825	37¢ Christmas Ornaments Block-4	(16) 12.75	3.75	3.25

2004 Commemoratives

…	$1 Year of the Monkey Souvenir Sheet	… …		2.25
…	37¢ Sailing Ships Strip of 3	(12) 9.50	(6) 5.25	2.40
…	37¢ Antique Cars Block of 8	(16) 13.50	…	6.75

1996 Semi-Postal

B1

Scott's No.		Mint Sheet	Plate Block	F-VF NH
B1	32¢ + 8¢ Operations Crossroads, Testing at Bikini Atoll, Sheet of 6	…	…	6.25

C8   **C9-12**

1985-89 Airmails

C1-2	44¢ Audubon, Pair	…	5.95	2.95
C3-6	44¢ Ameripex - Planes, Block of 4 (1986)	…	5.75	4.50
C7	44¢ Operation Crossroads, Souv.Sheet (1986)	…	…	4.75
C8	44¢ Statue of Liberty/Peace Year (1986)	…	5.50	1.20
C9-12	44¢ Girl Scouts, Block of 4 (1986)	…	5.00	4.00
C13-16	44¢ Marine Birds, Block of 4 (1987)	…	5.00	4.25

C17   **C22**

C17-20	44¢ Amelia Earhart/CAPEX'87, Block of 4 (1987)	…	5.25	4.50
C21	45¢ Astronaut and Space Shuttle (1988)	…	5.00	1.15
C22-25	12¢,36¢,39¢,45¢ Aircraft (4) (1989)	…	15.00	3.25
C22a	12¢ Booklet Pane of 10	…	…	3.75
C23a	36¢ Booklet Pane of 10	…	…	9.75
C24a	39¢ Booklet Pane of 10	…	…	10.75
C25a	45¢ Booklet Pane of 10	…	…	11.75
C25b	36¢-45¢ Booklet Pane of 10 (5 each)	…	…	11.50

Postal Cards

UX1	20¢ Elvis Presley (1996)	…	…	2.50
UX2-5	20¢ Canoes, Set of 4	…	…	4.75
UX6	20¢ Heavenly Angels, Christmas (1996)	…	…	1.35
UX7	32¢ Turtle (1997)	…	…	1.25

| | 1 | 21 | 22 | 142 | 160 | 179 |

1984 Commemoratives

Scott's No.		Mint Sheet	Plate Block	F-VF NH
1-4	20¢ Postal Service Inaugural, Block of 4		3.00	2.50

1984 Explorers and Views Definitives

5-20	1¢2¢,3¢,4¢,19¢,20¢,30¢,37¢ Explorers, 5¢,10¢,13¢,17¢,50¢,$1,$2,$5 Views (16)	...	95.00	22.75

1984 Commemoratives (continued)

21,C4-6	20¢,28¢,35¢,40¢ AUSIPEX'84 (4)	...	17.50	3.75
22,C7-9	20¢,28¢,35¢,40¢ Christmas (4)		23.50	4.75

1985 Commemoratives

23,C10-12	22¢,33¢,39¢,44¢ Ships (4)...........		21.50	3.75
24,C13-14	22¢,33¢,44¢ Christmas, Churches (3)	...	23.50	3.75
25-28,C15	22¢ (4),44¢ Audubon Birth Cent.(5)		9.00	3.95

1985-88 Birds, Views, Ships, Seal Definitives

31-39,C34-36	3¢,14¢,22¢.33¢,44¢,$1 Birds, 15¢,25¢,45¢ Views, 22¢,36¢ Ships, $10 Seal (12)...	130.00		27.50
33a	15¢ Booklet Pane of 10	...	...	6.95
36a	25¢ Booklet Pane of 10	...	...	7.75
36b	15¢ & 25¢ Booklet Pane of 10 (5 ea.)	...	...	8.75

1985 Commemoratives (continued)

45,C16-18	22¢,33¢,39¢,44¢ Nan Madol Ruins (4)	...	18.50	3.75

| | 52 | C31 | 63 |

1986 Commemoratives

46,C19-20	22¢, 44¢ (2) Int'l Peace Year (3) ..	...	22.75	4.75
48-51	22¢ on 20¢ Postal Service (#1-4), Block of 4		2.85	2.50
52,C21-24	22¢,33¢,39¢,44¢ AMERIPEX, Bully Hayes (4)...		25.00	5.25
53	22¢ First Passport	...	3.50	.75
54-5,C26-7	5¢,22¢,33¢,44¢ Christmas Paintings (4)		18.75	3.75

1987 Commemoratives

56,C28-30	22¢ Homeless,33¢ U.S. Currency, 39¢ American in Orbit,44¢ U.S.Constitution (4)		19.50	4.00
57	$1.00 CAPEX Souvenir Sheet	...	...	3.50
58,C31-33	22¢,33¢,39¢,44¢ Christmas (4) .... (25)110.00		18.75	3.50

1988 Commemoratives

59-62,C37-8	22¢,44¢ Colonial Flags, Block of 4 (6)		10.75	5.75
59-62,C37-8	Center Blocks of 8	...	...	17.50
63-66	25¢ Summer Olympics, attd., Two Pairs	...	6.50	2.85
67-70	25¢ Christmas Tree, Block of 4	...	2.75	2.40
71	25¢ Truk Lagoon Miniature Sheet of 18	...	...	11.50

1989 Commemoratives

72-75	45¢ Flowers, Mwarmwarms, Block of 4		5.25	4.50
76	$1.00 Hirohito, Hiroshige Painting Souv. Sheet...		...	2.50
77-80	25¢-45¢ Sharks, attd. two pair	...	8.50	3.50
81	25¢ Moon Landing, 20th Anniv., Min. Sheet of 9		...	6.00
82	$2.40 Moon Landing, 20th Anniversary	...	26.50	5.75

1989 Seashells Definitives

83-102	1¢,3¢,15¢,20¢,25¢,30¢,36¢,45¢, 50¢,$1,$2,$5 Seashell definitives (12)	...	95.00	22.75
85a	15¢ Booklet Pane of 10 (1990)	...	...	5.75
88a	25¢ Booklet Pane of 10 (1990)	...	...	9.75
88b	15¢ & 25¢ Booklet Pane of 10 (5 ea.)(1990)	...	...	9.75

1989 Commemoratives (continued)

103	25¢ World Stamp Expo, Fruits & Flowers, Sheet of 18	...		11.75
104-05	25¢,45¢ Christmas (2)	...	8.50	1.75

1990 Commemoratives

106-09	10¢,15¢,20¢,25¢ World Wildlife Fund (4)	...	30.00	5.50
110-113	45¢ Stamp World London '90, Whalers, Block of 4...		5.75	4.50
114	$1.00 S.W. London '90, Whalers, Souv.Sheet...		...	2.50
115	$1.00 Penny Black, 150th Anniv., Souv.Sheet...		...	2.50
116-20	25¢ Pohnpei Agriculture & Trade School, Strip of 5	(15) 9.75	...	3.25
121	$1.00 Int'l. Garden Expo, Osaka, Japan Souv. Sheet		...	2.50
122-23	25¢,45¢ Loading Mail, Airport & Truk Lagoon (2)		4.75	1.85
124-26	25¢ Joint issue w/Marshall Is. & U.S. Strip of 3	(12) 9.00 (6)	5.00	2.25
127-30	45¢ Moths, attd	...	5.25	4.50
131	25¢ Christmas, Miniature Sheet of 9 .	...	...	5.75

1991 Commemoratives

Scott's No.		Mint Sheet	Plate Block	F-VF NH
132	25¢,45¢ New Capital of Micronesia Souv. Sheet of 2		...	1.75
133	$1 New Capital, Souvenir Sheet		...	2.50
134-37	29¢-50¢ Turtles, attd. two pairs	...	13.75	6.25
138-41	29¢ Operation Desert Storm, Block of 4	...	3.50	2.75
142	29¢ Frigatebird, Flag		...	6.25
142a	$2.90 Frigatebird, Souvenir Sheet		...	6.50
143-44	29¢-50¢ Phila Nippon '91, Paul Jacoulet, Miniature Sheets of 3 (2)	...	...	6.50
145	$1 Phila Nippon Souvenir Sheet		...	2.75
146-48	29¢,40¢,50¢ Christmas, Handicrafts (3)	...	...	2.75
149	29¢ Pohnpei Rain Forest, Miniature sheet of 18...		...	14.50

1992 Commemoratives

150	29¢ Peace Corps, strip of 5	(15)12.75	...	3.50
151	29¢ Discovery of America, strip of 3		(6) 11.50	5.25

Note: From #151 to date, Plate Blocks have Logos instead of Plate Numbers

152-53	29¢,50¢ U.N. Membership First Anniv (2)	...	...	4.00
153a	Same, Souvenir Sheet of 2		...	4.00
154	29¢ Christmas	...	9.50	2.00

1993 Commemoratives

155	29¢ Pioneers of Flight, Tupolev+, Block of 8...		7.00	5.75

1993-94 Fish Definitives

156-67	10¢,19¢,20¢,22¢,25¢,29¢,30¢,35¢,40¢, 45¢,50¢,52¢,75¢,$1,$2,$2.90 set of 16	...	115.00	23.95

1993 Commemoratives (continued)

168	29¢ Golden Age of Sail, Mininature sheet of 12	...		17.50
172	29¢ Thomas Jefferson	...	5.25	.95
173-76	29¢ Pacific Canoes, Block of 4	...	4.50	3.75
177	29¢ Local Leaders, Strip of 4	(8)	6.75	3.00
178	50¢ Pioneers of Flight, Dryden+, Block of 8	(8)	11.50	9.75
179-80	29¢-50¢ Pohnpei, Tourism (2)	...	10.00	2.25
181	$1 Pohnpei Souvenir Sheet		...	2.40
182-83	29¢-50¢ Butterflies, two pairs	...	8.75	3.95
184-85	29¢-50¢ Christmas (2)	...	9.50	2.10
186	29¢ Yap Culture, Sheet of 18	...	...	14.75

1994 Commemoratives

| | 187 | 211 |

187-89	29¢,40¢,50¢ Kosrae, Tourism (3)	...	13.00	2.95
190	29¢-50¢ Butterflies, Hong Kong'94, sheet of 4...		...	4.75
191	29¢ Pioneers of Flight, Aldrin+. Block of 8	...	7.75	6.75
192	29¢ Micronesian Games, Block of 4 .	...	3.75	3.15
193	29¢ Native Costumes, Block of 4	...	3.75	3.15
194	29¢ 15th Anniversary of Constitution	...	8.75	1.95
195	29¢ Flowers, Strip of 4	(8)	6.95	3.15
196-97	50¢ World Cup Soccer, Pair		13.00	5.25
198	29¢ Postal Service, 10th Anniv., Block of 4	...	7.75	5.95
199	29¢, 52¢, $1 Philakorea Dinosaurs, Souvenir Sheet of 3		...	6.25
200	50¢ Pioneers of Flight, Bishop+, Block of 8		11.50	9.95
201	29¢ Migratory Birds, Block of 4	...	7.75	5.75
202-3	29¢-50¢ Christmas (2)	...	18.00	3.95
204-7	32¢ Pioneers of Unification (4)	...	27.00	5.95

1995 Commemoratives

208	50¢ Year of the Boar Souvenir Sheet	...	...	1.35
209	32¢ Chuuk Lagoon, underwater scenes, Block of 4	...	9.75	8.00
210	32¢ Pioneers of Flight, Goddard+, Block of 8 ...		6.75	6.25
211	32¢ Dogs of the World, Block of 4 ...	...	3.85	3.35

1995-96 Fish Definitives

213-26	23¢,32¢,46¢,55¢,60¢, 78¢, 95¢,$3,$5 Fish Set of 9 ..	...	130.00	26.95
227	32¢ Native Fish Sheetlet of 25 (96)	...	...	23.75

1995 Commemoratives (continued)

Scott's No.		Mint Sheet	Plate Block	F-VF NH
228	32¢ Hibiscus, Strip of 4	...	(8) 7.50	3.15
229	$1 United Nations 50th Anniv. Souv. Sheet	...	...	2.40
230	32¢ Singapore '95, Orchids Min. Sheet of 4	...	...	3.25
231	60¢ End of World War II, Block of 4 .		6.95	5.75
232	50¢ Beijing '95 Stamp & Coin Expo Souvenir Sheet		...	1.25
233	60¢ Pioneers of Flight, Dowding+, Block of 8	...	13.50	12.00
234-35	32¢-60¢ Christmas Poinsettias (2)	...	11.95	2.20

236   **239**

236	32¢ Yitzhak Rabin, Israeli P.Minister	(8) 10.95	...	1.00

1996 Commemoratives

237	50¢ Year of the Rat Souvenir Sheet ..	...	...	1.50
238	32¢ Pioneers of Flight, Doolittle+, Block of 8	...	9.50	7.50
239	32¢ Tourism in Yap, Block of 4		4.25	3.50
240	55¢ Sea Stars, Block of 4		7.00	6.00
241	60¢ Modern Olympics, Block of 4		8.25	7.00
242	50¢ China '96, Suzhou Souvenir Sheet		...	1.75
243-44	32¢ Patrol Boats, Pair		5.75	2.50
245	55¢ Ford Motor 100th Anniversary Sheet of 8	...		10.75
247	32¢ Officer Reza, Police Dog		7.50	1.40
248	50¢ Citrus Fruits, strip of 4	...	(8) 15.75	7.25
249	60¢ Pioneers of Flight, Capron+, Block of 8	...	16.00	13.75
250	32¢ Taipei '96, Fish, Block of 4		...	4.25
251-52	32¢-60¢ Christmas, Magi (2)		16.50	2.65
253	$3 Compact with US, Canoe, Flag		36.50	7.50

273   **279**

1997 Commemoratives

254	60¢ Deng Xiaoping, Sheet of 4	...	...	6.00
255	$3 Deng Xiaoping, Souvenir Sheet	...	...	7.50
256	$2 Hong Kong, Souvenir Sheet	...	...	6.00
257	32¢ Year of the Ox	...	6.00	1.15
258	$2 Year of the Ox, Souvenir Sheet ...	...	...	5.00
259	60¢ Hong Kong return to China, Sheet of 6	...	...	8.95
260	$3 Hong Kong return to China, Souv.Sheet	...	...	7.50
261	32¢ Pacific '97, Goddesses of the Sea, Sheet of 6	...	...	4.75
262-64	20¢,50¢,60¢ Hiroshige Sheets of 3 (3)	...	...	9.75
265-66	$2 Hiroshige Souvenir Sheets (2)	...	...	9.95
267	32¢ Pre-Olympics, Micronesian Games, Block of 4	(16) 12.75	4.00	3.25
268	50¢ Elvis Presley, Sheet of 6	...	...	7.50
269	32¢ Underwater Exploration, Sheet of 6	...	...	7.25
270-72	$2 Underwater Exploration, Souv. Sheets (3) ...	...	...	14.95
273	60¢ Diana, Princess of Wales, ...	(6) 8.75	...	1.50
274	50¢ WWF, Butterfly Fish, Block of 4 .	(16) 21.75	6.50	5.50
275-76	32¢ Christmas, Fra Angelico, Pair	(16) 13.75	4.25	1.75
277-78	60¢ Christmas, Simon Marmion, Pair	(16) 25.75	8.25	3.25

1998 Commemoratives

279-80	50¢ Year of the Tiger Souvenir Sheets (2)	...	...	2.50
281	$1 Micronesia's Admission to United Nations Souv. Sheet....			2.50
282	32¢ Disney "Winnie the Pooh" Sheet of 8	...	...	9.25
283-84	$2 Disney "Winnie the Pooh" Souvenir Sheets (2)	...	...	12.50
285	32¢ World Cup Soccer, Sheet of 8 ..	...	...	6.50
286-87	$2 World Cup Soccer, Souvenir Sheets (2)	...	...	9.75
288	$3 Olympics Recognition, Souvenir Sheet	...	...	7.50

1998 Commemoratives (continued)

Scott's No.		Mint Sheet	Plate Block	F-VF NH
289-91	32¢, 40¢, 60¢ Israel '98, Old Testament Bible Stories Sheets of 3 (3)	...	...	9.50
292-94	$2 Israel '98, Souvenir Sheets (3)			14.50
295	32¢ Year of the Ocean, Deep-Sea Research,Sheet of 9	...		7.25
296-98	$2 Year of the Ocean, Souvenir Sheets (3)	...	...	14.75
299	50¢ Native Birds, Block or Strip of 4	(16) 18.00		4.85
300	$3 Native Birds, Souvenir Sheet			7.50

1998 Fish Definitives

301-19	1¢,2¢,3¢,4¢,5¢,10¢,13¢,15¢,17¢,20¢,22¢, 32¢,39¢,40¢,60¢,78¢,$1,$3,$5 Fish (19) ...	...	120.00	27.50
319A	$10.75 Pinktail Triggerfish	...	100.00	23.75

1998 Commemoratives (continued)

320	32¢ F.D. Roosevelt Memorial, Fala, Sheet of 6...		...	4.75
321-22	32¢-60¢ Christmas, Madonna in 20th Century Art, Sheet of 3...			6.50
323	$2 Christmas Souvenir Sheet			5.00
324-25	60¢ John Glenn's Return to Space Sheets of 8 (2)		...	23.50
326-27	$2 John Glenn's Return to Space Souvenir Sheets (2)		...	9.75

1999 Fish Definitives

328-32	33¢,50¢,55¢,77¢,$3.20 Fish (5)	...	52.50	12.50
333	$11.75 Yellow-faced Angelfish	...	105.00	25.00

1999 Commemoratives

334	33¢ Russian Space Accomplishments, Sheet of 20	...	...	14.95
335-36	$2 Russian Space Souvenir Sheets (2)	...	...	9.50
337-38	33¢ Romance of the Three Kingdoms, Sheets of 5 (2)	...	...	7.75
339	$2 Romance of Three Kingdoms, Souvenir Sheet...	...	...	4.75

340-41

340-41	55¢ IBRA'99, Caroline Is. Stamps (2)	...	5.65	2.65
342	$2 IBRA'99, Caroline Is. Stamps, Souvenir Sheet...			4.75
343	33¢ Australia '99 World Stamp Expo, Voyages of the Pacific, Sheet of 20...		...	16.50
344	33¢ United States Space Achievements Sheet of 20	...		16.50
345-46	$2 U.S. Space Achievements Souvenir Sheets (2)...	...		9.50
347	33¢ Earth Day: Endangered, Extinct and Prehistoric Species, Sheet of 20	...		16.50
348-49	$2 Earth Day, Souvenir Sheets (2)	...	...	9.50
350-51	33¢ Hokusai Paintings, Sheets of 6 (2)	...	...	9.50
352-53	$2 Hokusai Paintings, Souvenir Sheets (2)	...	...	9.50
354	50¢ Faces of the Millennium, Princess Diana Sheet of 8 ...			9.50
355	20¢ Millennium, 12th Century, Sheet of 17	...	...	8.75
356	33¢ Millennium, Science & Technology of Ancient China, Sheet of 17	...	...	14.75
357	33¢ Costumes of the World Sheet of 20	...	...	16.50
358-60	33¢, 60¢, $2 Christmas, Van Dyck (3)	...	32.50	7.25
361	$2 Christmas Souvenir Sheet	...	...	4.75
362	33¢ First Century of Flight Sheet of 15	...	...	12.50
363-64	$2 Flight Souvenir Sheets (2)	...	...	9.50

2000 Commemoratives

365-67	33¢ Orchids Sheets of 6 (3)	...	...	14.50
368-69	$2 Orchids Souvenir Sheets (2)	...	...	9.50
370	33¢ Religious Leaders Sheet of 12 ...	...	...	9.50
371	$2 Year of the Dragon Souvenir Sheet	...	...	4.75
372-73	20¢-55¢ Butterflies Sheets of 6 (2) ...	...	...	11.00
374-76	$2 Butterflies Souvenir Sheets (3)	...	...	14.50
377	20¢ 20th Century 1920-29 Sheet of 17	...	...	8.50
378	33¢ Millennium 2000	...	...	.80
379	33¢ Peacemakers Sheet of 24	...	...	19.75
380	33¢ 20th Century Philanthropists Sheet of 16	...	...	13.75
381-82	33¢ Mushrooms Sheets of 6 (2)	...	...	9.50
383-84	$2 Mushrooms Souvenir Sheets (2) ..	...	...	9.50
385	33¢ Flowers of the Pacific Sheet of 6	...	...	4.75
386	33¢ Wildflowers Sheetlet of 6	...	...	4.75
387	$2 Flowers of the Pacific Souvenir Sheet	...	...	4.75
388	$2 Wildflowers Souvenir Sheet	...	...	4.75
389	33¢ Sydney Olympics Sheet of 4	...	...	3.00
390	33¢ Zeppelins & Airships Sheet of 6 .	...	...	4.75
391-92	$2 Zeppelin Souvenir Sheets (2)	...	...	9.50
393	33¢ Queen Mother Photomosiac Sheet of 8	...	...	6.25
394	33¢, $1 Olymphilex 2000, Olympics, Sheet of 3...	...	...	4.25
395-98	33¢ Coral Reef, Fish set of 4	...	...	3.00
399-400	33¢ Coral Reef, Fish Sheets of 9 (2)	...	...	15.00
401-2	$2 Coral Reef, Fish Souvenir Sheets (2)	...	...	9.50
403	50¢ Pope John Paul II Photomosaic Sheet of 8...	...	...	9.50
404-7	20¢, 33¢, 60¢, $3.20 Christmas (4) ..	...	...	10.75
408	33¢ Dogs Sheet of 6	...	...	4.75
409	33¢ Cats Sheet of 6	...	...	4.75
410	$2 Dogs Souvenir Sheet	...	...	4.75
411	$2 Cats Souvenir Sheet	...	...	4.75

2001 Commemoratives

Scott's No.		Mint Sheet	Plate Block	F-VF NH
412-13	60¢ Year of the Snake Souvenir Sheets (2) .	...	...	2.95
414	50¢ Pokemon Sheet of 6	...	...	7.75
415	$2 Pokemon Souvenir Sheet	...	...	5.25
416-17	50¢-60¢ Whales Sheets of 6 (2)	...	...	16.00
418-19	$2 Whales Souvenir Sheets (2)	...	...	9.50
420-21	34¢-60¢ Environment-One Earth Sheets of 6, 4(2)	...	...	10.00
422-23	$2 Environment-One Earth Souvenir Sheet 3(2)	...	...	10.00

2001 Fish Definitives

424-28	11¢,34¢,70¢,80¢,$3.50 set of 5	...	55.00	12.50
429	$12.25 Blue-Spotted Boxfish	...	130.00	27.95

2001 Commemoratives (continued)

430-35

430-35	34¢ Philanippon '01, Japanese Art (6)	...	...	4.50
436	34¢ Philanippon '01 Sheet of 6	...	...	4.75
437-38	$2 Philanippon '01 Souvenir Sheets (2)	...	...	9.50
439	60¢ Toulouse-Lautrec Sheet of 3	...	...	4.25
440	$2 Toulouse-Lautrec Souvenir Sheet	...	...	4.75
441	60¢ Queen Victoria Sheet of 6	...	...	8.25
442	$2 Queen Victoria Souvenir Sheet	...	...	4.75
443	60¢ Queen Elizabeth 75th Birthday Sheet of 6	...	...	8.25
444	$2 Queen Elizabeth 75th Birthday Souvenir Sheet	...	...	4.75
445-46	60¢ Underwater Treasures Sheets of 6 (2) ...	...	...	16.50
447-48	$2 Underwater Treasures Souvenir Sheets (2)	...	...	9.00
449-52	60¢ Prehistoric Animals set of 4	...	...	5.50
453-54	60¢ Prehistoric Animals Sheets of 6 (2)	...	...	16.00
455-56	$2 Prehistoric Animals Souvenir Sheets (2) ..	...	...	9.50
457-58	50¢ Sea Shells Sheets of 6 (2)	...	...	14.00
459-60	$2 Sea Shells Souvenir Sheets (2)	...	...	9.50
461-64	5¢, 22¢, 23¢, $2.10 Birds (4)	...	...	6.00
465-66	60¢ Birds of Micronesia Sheets of 6 (2)	...	...	16.00
467-68	$2 Birds of Micronesia Souvenir Sheets (2) ..	...	...	9.00
469-70	60¢ Nobel Prize Winners Sheets of 6 (2)	...	...	16.00
471-72	$2 Nobel Prize Winners Souvenir Sheets (2)	...	...	9.00
473-76	22¢,34¢,60¢,$1 Christmas Santa Claus (4) ..	...	...	4.75
477	$2 Christmas Santa Claus Souvenir Sheet	...	...	4.75
478-79	60¢ Pearl Harbor 60th Anniv. Sheets of 6 (2)	...	...	16.00
480-81	$2 Pearl Harbor 60th Anniv. Souvenir Sheets (2)	...	...	9.50

2002 Commemoratives

482	60¢ Year of the Horse Sheet ol 5	...	...	6.75
483	80¢ Queen Elizabeth Golden Jubilee Sheet of 4	...	...	7.25
484	$2 Queen Elizabeth Golden Jubilee Souvenir Sheet	...	...	4.50
485	$1 United We Stand, Statue of Liberty .... (4)	8.95	..	2.30
486-87	$1 Winter Olympics, large rings (2)	..	...	4.75
487a	$2 Winter Olympics Large rings Souvenir Sheet	...	...	4.75
488-89	60¢ Japanese Art Sheets of 6 (2)	...	...	16.75
490-91	$2 Japanese Art Souvenir Sheets (2)	...	...	9.50
492	80¢ Year of the Mountains Sheet of 4	...	...	7.25
493	$2 Year of the Mountains Souvenir Sheet	...	...	4.75
494	60¢ John F. Kennedy Sheet of 4	...	...	5.75
495	$2 John F. Kennedy Souvenir Sheet	...	...	4.75
496	60¢ Princess Diana Sheet of 6	...	...	8.50
497	$2 Princess Diana Souvenir Sheet	...	...	4.75
498	80¢ EcoTourism Sheet of 6	...	...	11.75
499	$2 EcoTourism Souvenir Sheet	...	...	4.75

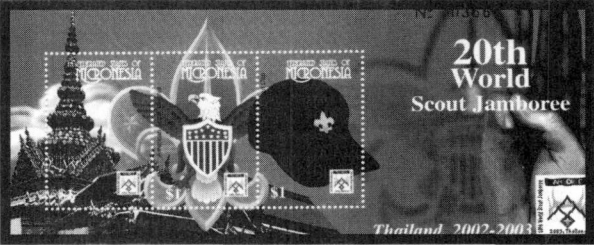

500

500	$1 Boy Scout Jamboree, Thailand Sheet of 3	...	...	7.25
501	$2 Boy Scout Jamboree Souvenir Sheet	...	...	4.75
502-3	$1 Winter Olympics, smaller rings (2)	...	...	4.75
503a	$2 Winter Olympics, smaller rings Souvenir Sheet	...	...	4.75
504	37¢ Xavier High School	...	...	.90
505	80¢ Queen Mother Memorial Sheet of 4	...	...	7.25
506	$2 Queen Mother Memorial Souvenir Sheet ..	...	...	4.75
507	80¢ Teddy Bear Centennial Sheet of 4	...	...	7.50
508	37¢ Elvis Presley Sheet of 6	...	...	5.50

2002 Commemoratives (continued)

Scott's No.		Mint Sheetlet	Plate Block	F-VF NH
509-13	15¢,37¢,55¢,80¢,$1 Christmas (5)	...	...	7.00
514	$2 Christmas Souvenir Sheet	...	...	4.75
515	37¢ Moths Sheet of 6	...	...	5.50
516	55¢ Mushrooms Sheet of 6	...	...	7.75
517	60¢ Orchids Sheet of 6	...	...	8.50
518	60¢ Butterflies Sheet of 6	...	...	8.50
519	80¢ Insects Sheet of 6	...	...	11.50
520	$2 Moths Souvenir Sheet	...	...	4.75
521	$2 Mushrooms Souvenir Sheet	...	...	4.75
522	$2 Orchids Souvenir Sheet	...	...	4.75
523	$2 Butterflies Souvenir Sheet	...	...	4.75
524	$2 Insects Souvenir Sheet	...	...	4.75

2002-03 Bird Definitives

525-35	3¢, 5¢, 21¢, 22¢, 23¢, 37¢, 60¢, 70¢, 80¢			
	$2, $3.85 Bird Definitives (11)	...	...	19.75
536	$5 Bird Definitive	...	...	9.95
537	$13.65 Bird Definitive	...	...	26.95

2003 Commemoratives

538	60¢ First Non-Stop Solo Transatlantic Flight Sheet of 6		...	7.50
539	37¢ Year of the Ram Strip of 3	(6) 4.76	...	2.40
540	37¢ In Memoriam Space Shuttle Columbia Crew Sheet of 7.....			5.50
541	$1 Queen Elizabeth II 50th Anniv. of Coronation Sheet of 3.....			6.50
542	$2 Queen Elizabeth II 50th Anniv. Souvenir Sheet	...	...	4.25
543	$1 Prince William Sheet of 3	...	...	6.50
544	$2 Prince William Souvenir Sheet	...	...	4.25
545-46	37¢ Operation Iraqi Freedom Sheets of 6 (2)		...	9.35
547	60¢ Tour de France Sheet of 4	...	...	6.00
548	$2 Tour de France Souvenir Sheet	...	...	4.25
549	$1 Fresh Water Sheet of 3	...	...	6.60
550	$2 Fresh Water Souvenir Sheet	...	...	4.25
551	55¢ Powered Flight, Aviation Sheet of 6	...	...	6.95
552	$2 Powered Flight, Aviation Souvenir Sheet ...	...	...	4.25
553-54	80¢ Circus Clowns Sheets of 4 (2)	...	...	13.50
555	80¢ Norman Rockwell/Boy Scouts Sheet of 4	...	...	6.75
556	$2 Norman Rockwell/Boy Scouts Souvenir Sheet	...	...	4.25
557	80¢ Paul Gauguin Sheet of 4	...	...	6.75
558	$2 Paul Gauguin Souvenir Sheet	...	...	4.25
559-62	37¢,55¢,60¢,$1 James M. Whistler (4)	...	...	5.50
563	$1 James M. Whistler Sheet of 3	...	...	6.50
564	$2 James M. Whistler Souvenir Sheet	...	...	4.25
565-68	37¢,60¢,80¢,$1 Christmas (4)	...	...	5.95
569	$2 Christmas Souvenir Sheet	...	...	4.25
570	80¢ Cats Sheet of 4	...	...	6.75
571	80¢ Dogs Sheet of 4	...	...	6.75
572	80¢ Birds Sheet of 4	...	...	6.75
573	80¢ Reptiles & Amphibians Sheet of 4	...	...	6.75
574	$2 Cats Souvenir Sheet	...	...	4.25
575	$2 Dogs Souvenir Sheet	...	...	4.25
576	$2 Birds Souvenir Sheeet	...	...	4.25
577	$2 Reptiles & Amphibians Souvenir Sheet ...			4.25
...	80¢ Pablo Picasso Sheet of 4	...	...	6.75
...	$2 Pablo Picasso Souvenir Sheet	...	...	4.25

2004 Issues

...	37¢ Bailey Olter	...	3.65	.80
...	50¢ Year of the Monkey	(4) 4.35	...	1.10
...	$2 Year of the Monkey Souvenir Sheet	...	...	4.25
...	22¢,37¢,80¢,$1 The Hermitage, St. Petersburg (4)	...	...	4.95
...	$2 The Hermitage, St. Petersburg Souvenir Sheet	...	...	4.25

Airmails

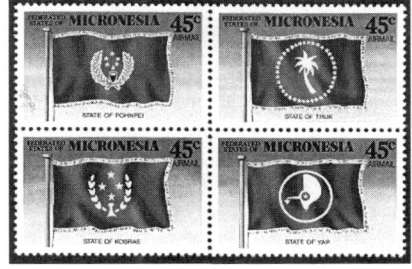

C39-42

1984-94

C1-3	28¢,35¢,40¢ Aircraft (3) (1984)	...	12.75	2.50
C25	$1.00 Ameripex, Bully Hayes Souv. Sheet (1986)	...	...	4.25
C39-42	45¢ Federated State Flags, Block of 4 (1989)	...	4.50	3.75
C43-46	22¢,36¢,39¢,45¢ Aircraft Serving Micronesia (4) (1990)	...	23.50	5.75
C47-48	40¢,50¢ Aircraft (2) (1992)	...	16.75	3.95
C49	$2.90 Moon Landing Souvenir Sheet (1994) .	...	...	6.50

Postal Stationary Entires

U1	20¢ National Flag (1984)	...	...	18.50
U2	22¢ Tall Ship Senyavin (1986)	...	...	10.75
U3	29¢ on 30¢ New Capital (1991)	...	...	4.95

Postal Cards

UX1-4	20¢ Scenes, Set of 4 (1997)	...	...	5.95

REPUBLIC OF PALAU
PALAU BECAME INDEPENDENT IN 1994.

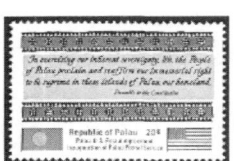

| 1 | 5 | 9 | 21 |

1983 Commemoratives

Scott's No.		Mint Sheet	Plate Block	F-VF NH
1-4	20¢ Postal Service Inaugural, Block of 4	...	3.95	3.00
5-8	20¢ Birds, Block of 4	...	2.75	2.25

1983-84 Marine Definitives

9-21	1¢,3¢,5¢,10¢,13¢,20¢,28¢,30¢,			
	37¢,50¢,$1,$2,$5 Definitives, Set of 13	...	120.00	24.75
13a	13¢ Booklet Pane of 10	...	...	12.75
13b	13¢/20¢ Bklt. Pane of 10 (5 #13, 5 #14)	...	...	14.75
14b	20¢ Booklet Pane of 10	...	...	13.75

1983 Commemoratives (continued)

24-27	20¢ World Wildlife Fund, Whales, Block of 4	...	4.75	3.75
28-32	20¢ Christmas, Charlie Gibbons Strip of 5	(10) 7.50	3.50
33-40	20¢ Captain Henry Wilson, Block of 8	...	5.75	4.75

1984 Commemoratives

41-50	20¢ Seashells, Block of 10		6.00	5.00
51-54	40¢ 19th UPU, Explorer Ships, Block of 4	...	5.25	4.25
55-58	20¢ Ausipex'84, Fishing, Block of 4	...	2.75	2.15
59-62	20¢ Christmas Flowers, Block of 4....		2.75	2.15

1985 Commemoratives

63-66	22¢ Audubon Bicentenary, Block of 4		4.25	3.50
67-70	22¢ Shipbuilding, Canoes and Rafts, Block of 4...		3.00	2.40

1985 Marine Definitives

75-81	14¢,22¢,25¢,33¢,39¢,44¢ Marine Life (6)	...	25.00	5.25
75a	14¢ Booklet Pane of 10	...	...	10.75
76a	22¢ Booklet Pane of 10	...	...	13.50
76b	14¢/22¢ Bklt. Pane of 10 (5 #75, 5 #76)	...	...	14.75
85	$10 Spinner Dolphins	...	115.00	25.00

1985 Commemoratives (continued)

86-89	44¢ Youth Year, Children, Block of 4	...	5.25	4.50
90-93	14¢,22¢,33¢,44¢ Christmas (4)	...	17.50	3.25
94	$1.00 Trans-Pacific Mail Flight Anniv. Souvenir Sheet	...		3.25
95-98	44¢ Halley's Comet, Block of 4	...	5.00	4.25

| 99 | 141 | 164 |

1986 Commemoratives

99-102	44¢ Songbirds, Block of 4	...	5.25	4.65
103	14¢ AMERIPEX Sea & Reef, Sheet of 40	...	...	42.50
104-08	22¢ Seashells, Strip of 5	(10)	7.25	3.25
109-12	22¢ Int'l. Peace Year, Block of 4	...	4.50	3.25
113-16	22¢ Reptiles, Block of 4	...	3.25	2.50
117-21	22¢ Christmas,Joy to the World,Strip-5	(15) 10.50	(10) 6.75	3.00
117-21	22¢ Christmas Strip of 5 with Tabs	...	(10) 8.25	3.75

1987 Commemoratives

121B-E	44¢ Butterflies, Block of 4	...	5.75	4.75
122-25	44¢ Fruit Bats, Block of 4	...	5.50	4.75

1987-88 Indigenous Flowers Definitives

126-42	1¢,3¢,5¢,10¢,14¢,15¢,22¢,25¢,36¢,39¢,			
	44¢,45¢,50¢,$1,$2,$5, $10 (17)	...	225.00	49.50
130a	14¢ Booklet Pane of 10	...	...	5.00
131a	15¢ Booklet Pane of 10 (1988)	...	...	4.25
132a	22¢ Booklet Pane of 10	...	...	8.25
132b	14¢/22¢ Booklet Pane of 10 (5 ea.) ..	...	...	8.25
133a	25¢ Booklet Pane of 10 (1988)	...	...	6.50
133b	15¢/25¢ Booklet Pane of 10 (5 ea.) (1988)	...	...	6.25

1987 Commemoratives (continued)

146-49	22¢ CAPEX'87, Scenes, Block of 4 ..	...	3.00	2.40
150-54	22¢ Seashells, Strip of 5	(10)	6.95	3.00
155-63	14¢,22¢,44¢ U.S. Constitution Bicentennial,			
	attd. (3 strips of 3)	(15) 26.50		5.75
164-67	14¢,22¢,33¢,44¢ Japanese Links (4)	...	13.50	2.75
168	$1 Japanese Links to Palau Souvenir Sheet	...	...	2.50
173-77	22¢ Christmas, "I Saw Three Ships" Strip of 5...	(10)	7.50	2.95
178-82	22¢ "Silent Spring" Symbiotic			
	Marine Species, Strip of 5	(15) 11.00	(10) 7.95	3.25

REPUBLIC OF PALAU

191-95

1988 Commemoratives

Scott's No.		Mint Sheet	Plate Block	F-VF NH
183-86	44¢ Butterflies & Flowers, Block of 4	...	4.75	3.95
187-90	44¢ Ground Dwelling Birds, Block of 4	...	4.75	3.95
191-95	25¢ Seashells, Strip of 5		(10) 8.00	3.25
196	25¢ Postal Independence (FINLANDIA) Souv.Sheet of 6	...		3.75
197	45¢ U.S.Possessions Philatelic Society			
	(PRAGA '88) Souvenir Sheet of 6	...	...	6.50
198-202	25¢ Christmas, Strip of 5	(15) 9.75	(10) 7.25	3.25
198-202	25¢ Christmas Strip of 5 with Tabs		(10)10.00	4.75
203	25¢ Palauan Nautilus, Miniature Sheet of 5	...		3.75

1989 Commemoratives

204-07	45¢ Endangered Birds, Block of 4		5.25	4.50
208-11	45¢ Exotic Mushrooms, Block of 4 ...	...	5.25	4.50
212-16	25¢ Seashells, Strip of 5	...	(10) 6.75	3.25
217	$1 Hirohito & Akihito, Hiroshige Souvenir Sheet...			2.50
218	25¢ Moon Landing, 20th Anniv., Souv.Sheet of 25	...		14.95
219	$2.40 Moon Landing, 20th Anniversary	...	25.75	5.75
220	25¢ Literacy, block of 10	...	6.95	5.95
221	25¢ World Stamp Expo,			
	Stilt Mangrove Fauna, Miniature sheet of 25	...		14.75
222-26	25¢ Christmas, Strip of 5	(15) 9.50	(10) 6.75	3.00
222-26	25¢ Christmas Strip of 5 with Tabs		(10)10.50	4.35

| 258 | 266 |

1990 Commemoratives

227-30	25¢ Soft Coral, Block of 4	...	2.95	2.50
231-34	45¢ Forest Birds, Block of 4	...	4.85	4.50
235	25¢ Stamp World London '90, Min.Sheet of 9 ...		...	5.75
236	$1.00 Penny Black, 150th Anniv. Souvenir Sheet	...		2.50
237-41	45¢ Orchids, Strip of 5	(15) 17.50	(10) 12.00	5.75
237-41	45¢ Orchids Strip of 5 with Tabs	...	...	6.50
242-45	45¢ Butterflies & Flowers, Block of 4	...	5.25	4.50
246	25¢ Lagoon Life, Sheet of 25	...	...	15.75
247-48	45¢ Pacifica/Mail Delivery, Pair	(10) 15.75	7.50	3.00
249-53	25¢ Christmas, Strip of 5, attd	(15) 9.75	(10)7.25	3.25
249-53	25¢ Christmas Strip of 5 with Tabs		...	3.75
254-57	45¢ U.S. Forces in Palau, 1944, Block of 4	...	5.50	4.75
258	$1 U.S. Forces in Palau, 1944, Souv.Sheet	...	...	2.75

1991 Commemoratives

259-62	30¢ Coral, Block of 4	...	3.75	3.00
263	30¢ Angaur, The Phospate Island, Sheet of 16 ...	...		12.50

1991-92 Birds Definitives

266-83	1¢,4¢,6¢,19¢,20¢,23¢,29¢,35¢,40¢,45¢,50¢,			
	52¢,75¢,95¢,$1.34,$2,$5,$10 Birds (18)	...	250.00	55.00
269b	19¢ Fantail, Booklet Pane of 10 ...	...	...	5.00
272a	29¢ Fruit Dove, Booklet Pane of 10	...	...	6.75
272b	19¢ Fantail & 29¢ Fruit Dove, Booklet Pane/10(5 ea)	...		5.75

1991 Commemoratives (continued)

288	29¢ Cent. of Christianity in Palau, Sheet of 6	...	...	4.25
289	29¢ Marine Life, Miniature Sheet of 20 ...			16.95
290	20¢ Desert Shield/Desert Storm, Miniature Sheet of 9		...	4.75
291	$2.90 Fairy tern, Yellow/Ribbon	...	...	7.25
292	$2.90 Same, Souvenir Sheet	...		7.25
293	29¢ Palau,10th Anniversary, Miniature Sheet of 8...		...	5.95
294	50¢ Giant Clam Cultivation, Min. Sheet of 5	...	...	6.25
295	29¢ Japanese Heritage, Phila Nippon,Sheet of 6	...		4.50
296	$1 Japanese Heritage Souvenir Sheet	...		2.75
297	29¢ Peace Corps in Palau, Miniature Sheet of 6 ...		...	4.50
298	29¢ Christmas, Strip of 5	(15) 10.50	(10) 7.50	3.50
298	29¢ Christmas Strip of 5 with Tabs	...	...	4.25
299	29¢ WWII in the Pacific, Miniature Sheet of 10	...	...	8.50

1992 Commemoratives

300	50¢ Butterflies, Block of 4	...	5.75	5.00
301	29¢ Seashells, Strip of 5	...	(10) 9.50	3.75
302	29¢ Columbus & Age of Discovery,			
	Miniature Sheet of 20	...	...	14.75
303	29¢ Biblical Creation, Miniature Sheet of 24	...	...	16.95

312 Part   **313 Part**

384   **399-400**

1992 Commemoratives (continued)

Scott's No.		Mint Sheets	Plate Block	F-VF NH
304-09	50¢ Summer Olympics, Souvenir Sheets (6)	...	...	7.50
310	29¢ Elvis Presley, Miniature Sheet of 9 .	...	...	8.50
312	29¢ Christmas, Strip of 5	(15) 11.50	(10) 8.25	3.95
312	Christmas Strip of 5 with Tabs	...	...	4.75

1993 Commemoratives

313	50¢ Animal Families, Block of 4	...	5.75	5.00
314	29¢ Seafood, Block of 4	...	...	3.00
315	50¢ Sharks, Block of 4	...	...	5.00
316	29¢ WWII, Pacific Theater, 1943, Miniature Sheet of 10	...	...	9.75
317	29¢ Christmas, Strip of 5	(15) 10.00	(10) 7.75	3.65
317	29¢ Christmas Strip of 5 with Tabs	...	...	4.25
318	29¢ Prehistoric & Legendary Sea Creatures, Sheet of 25	...		17.50
319	29¢ Indigenous People, Sheet of 4	...	...	2.95
320	$2.90 Indigenous People, Souvenir Sheet	...	...	7.75
321	29¢ Jonah and the Whale, Sheet of 25 ..	...	...	17.95

1994 Commemoratives

323   **364**

322	40¢ Palau Rays, Block of 4	...	...	3.95
323	20¢ World Wildlife Fund, Crocodiles, Block of 4 (16) 13.00		3.65	3.25
324	50¢ Large Seabirds, Block of 4	...	...	5.00
325	29¢ WWII, Pacific Theater, 1944, Miniature Sheet of 10	...		10.75
326	50¢ WWII, D-Day, Miniature Sheet of 10	...		14.75
327	29¢ Baron Pierre de Coubertin	...	...	.90
328-33	50¢, $1, $2 Coubertin and Winter Olympics Stars, Set of 6 Souvenir Sheets	...	...	14.75
334-36	29¢, 40¢, 50¢ Philakorea '94 Philatelic Fantasies, Wildlife, 3 Souvenir Sheets of 8	...	...	27.50
337	29¢ Apollo XI Moon Landing 25th Anniv., Miniature Sheet of 20			14.75
338	29¢ Independence Day Strip of 5	(15) 10.75	...	3.65
339	$1 "Invasion of Peleliu" Overprint Souvenir Sheet (#258)		...	2.75
340	29¢ Disney Tourism Sheet of 9	...	...	7.50
341-43	$1 (2), $2.90 Disney Tourism, 3 Souv. Sheets	...	...	13.50
344	20¢ Year of the Family, Story of Tebruchel, Miniature Sheet of 12			5.95
345	29¢ Christmas '94 Strip of 5	(15) 10.00	...	3.75
345	29¢ Christmas Strip of 5 with Tabs	...	...	4.25
346-48	29¢ (2), 50¢ World Cup of Soccer, Set of 3 Sheets of 12	...		28.75

1995 Commemoratives

350	32¢ Elvis Presley, Sheet of 9	...	...	8.00

1995 Fish Definitives

351-64	1¢,2¢,3¢,4¢,5¢,10¢,20¢,32¢,50¢, 55¢,$1,$2,$3,$5 Fish Definitives (14) ...	...	135.00	28.95
365	$10 Coral Grouper	...	100.00	22.50
366	20¢ Fish, Booklet Single	...	...	.55
366a	20¢ Fish, Booklet Pane of 10	...	...	4.75
367	32¢ Fish, Booklet Single	...	...	.85
367a	32¢ Fish, Booklet Pane of 10	...	...	7.75
367b	20¢, 32¢ Fish, Bklt. Pane of 10 (5 each)	...	...	6.75

1995 Commemoratives (continued)

368	32¢ Tourism, Lost Fleet, Sheet of 18	...	...	14.75
369	32¢ Earth Day, Flying Dinosaurs, Sheet of 18	...	...	14.75
370	50¢ Research Jet Aircraft, Sheet of 12 .	...	...	14.75
371	$2 Jet Aircraft, Souvenir Sheet	...	...	4.50
372	32¢ Underwater Ships, Sheet of 18	...	...	15.00
373	Singapore '95 Hidden Treasures, Block of 4...	...	3.75	3.25
374	60¢ U.N., FAO 50th Anniv., Block of 4 ...	...	6.85	6.00
375-76	$2 U.N. FAO 50th Anniv., Souv. Sheets (2)	...	...	9.75
377	20¢ Independence, Flags, Block of 4	...	2.50	2.00
378	32¢ Independence, Marine Life	...	3.95	.85
379	32¢ End of World War II, Sheet of 12	...	...	9.75
380	60¢ End of World War II, Sheet of 5	...	...	8.75

1995 Commemoratives (continued)

Scott's No.		Mint Sheets	Plate Block	F-VF NH
381	$3 End of World War II Souvenir Sheet	...	...	7.75
382	32¢ Christmas Strip of 5	(15) 11.50	(10) 8.50	3.75
382	32¢ Christmas with Tabs	...	...	4.25
383	32¢ Life Cycle of the Sea Turtle, Sheet of 12	...	...	12.00
384	32¢ John Lennon	(16) 19.95	...	1.25

1996 Commemoratives

385	10¢ Year of the Rat Strip of 4	(8) 4.50	...	2.10
386	60¢ Year of the Rat Min. Sheet of 2	...	...	2.95
387	32¢ 50th Anniversary of UNICEF Blk/4 ..	(16) 12.75	3.95	3.25
388	32¢ China '96 Marine Life Strip of 5	(15) 12.00	...	4.00
389	32¢ Capex '96 Circumnavigators Sheet of 9	...	...	7.00
390	60¢ Capex '96 Air & Space Sheet of 9...	...	...	13.50
391	$3 Capex '96 Air & Space Souvenir Sheet	...	...	7.50
392	$3 Capex '96 Circumnavigators Souvenir Sheet	...	...	7.50
392A-F	1¢ - 6¢ Disney Sweethearts (6)	...	...	1.25
393	60¢ Disney Sweethearts Sheet of 9	...	...	16.50
394-95	$2 Disney Sweethearts Souvenir Sheets (2)	...	...	12.00
396	20¢ 3000th Anniversary of Jerusalem Sheet of 30	...	...	15.00
397-400	40¢-60¢ Atlanta '96 Olympics, 2 Pairs ...	(20) 55.00	11.00	5.25
401	32¢ Atlanta '96, Sheet of 20	...	...	15.75
402	50¢ Lagoon Birds, Sheet of 20	...	...	25.00
403	40¢ "Spies in the Sky", Sheet of 12	...	...	12.50
404	60¢ Oddities of the Air, Sheet of 12	...	...	17.75
405	$3 Stealth Bomber, Souvenir Sheet	...	...	8.25
406	$3 Martin Marietta X-24B, Souvenir Sheet	...	...	8.25
407-8	20¢ Independence, Sekiguchi, Pair........	(16) 7.95	...	1.00
409	32¢ Christmas Trees, Strip of 5	(15) 11.75	...	3.95
409	32¢ Christmas Strip of 5 with Tabs	...	...	4.75
410	32¢ Voyages to Mars, Sheet of 12	...	...	9.75
411-12	$3 Voyages to Mars, Souvenir Sheet (2)	...	...	15.00

1997 Commemoratives

412A	$2 Year of the Ox, Souvenir Sheet	...	...	5.00
413	$1 South Pacific Commission, 50th Anniv., Souvenir Sheet ...			2.50

414   **435**   **440**

1997 Hong Kong '97, Flowers

414-19	1¢, 2¢, 3¢, 4¢, 5¢, $3 Flowers (6)	...	37.50	7.95
420-21	32¢-50¢ Shoreline Plants, Blocks of 4 (2) (16) 33.50		10.00	8.25

1997 Commemoratives (continued)

422-23	32¢-60¢ Parachutes, Sheets of 8 (2)	...	...	17.75
424-25	$2 Parachutes, Souvenir Sheets (2)	...	...	9.75
426	20¢ Native Birds, Avian Environment, Sheet of 12	...	...	6.00
427-28	32¢-60¢ UNESCO, 50th Anniversary, Sites in Japan & Germany, Sheets of 8 and 5 (2)		...	13.00
429-30	$2 UNESCO, Sites in Japan, Souvenir Sheets (2)...		...	10.00
431	32¢ Hiroshige Poetic Prints, Sheet of 5 .	...	...	4.00
432-33	$2 Hiroshige Souvenir Sheets (2)	...	...	9.75
434	32¢ Volcano Goddesses of the Pacific, Pacific '97, Sheet of 6			5.25
435	32¢ 3rd Anniv. of Independence	(12) 9.50	3.95	.80
436	32¢ Underwater Exploration, Sheet of 9 .	...	...	7.50
437-39	$2 Underwater Exploration, Souvenir Sheets (3)...		...	15.75
440	60¢ Diana, Princess of Wales, ...	(6) 10.50	...	1.75
441-46	1¢-10¢ Disney "Let's Read" (6)	...	...	1.25
447	32¢ Disney "Let's Read" Sheet of 9	...	...	7.00
448-49	$2-$3 Disney "Let's Read" Souvenir Sheets (2) ...		...	13.00
450	32¢ Christmas Carol, Strip of 5	(15) 12.75	...	4.25
450	32¢ Christmas Strip of 5 with tabs	...	...	8.25

1998 Commemoratives

451-52	50¢ Year of the Tiger Souvenir Sheets (2) ...		...	2.50
453	32¢ Hubble Space Telescope Sheetlet of 6...	...	...	4.75
454-56	$2 Hubble, Souvenir Sheets (3)	...	...	14.75

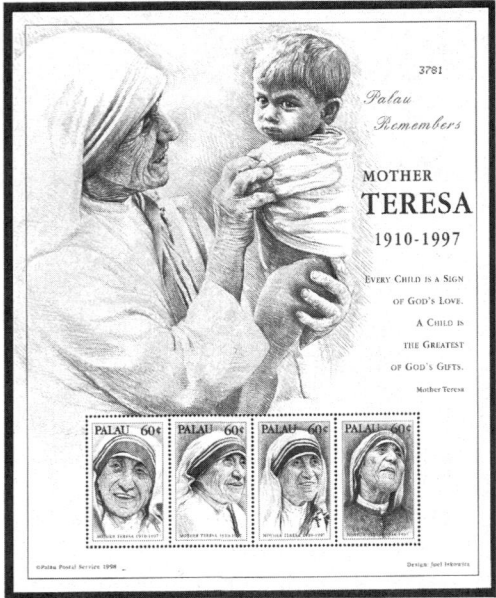

457

1998 Commemoratives (continued)

Scott's No.		Mint Sheets	Plate Block	F-VF NH
457	60¢ Mother Teresa, Souvenir Sheet of 4..	...	...	6.50
458	32¢ Deep Sea Robots Sheet of 18	...	...	15.00
459-60	$2 Deep Sea Robots, Souvenir Sheets (2)	...	...	10.75
461	20¢ "Israel 98" Overprint on Jerusalem Sheet of 30 (#396)	...		15.00
462	40¢ Legend of Orachel, Sheet of 12	...	...	12.00
463	50¢ World Cup Soccer, Sheet of 8	...	...	9.75
464	$3 World Cup Soccer, Souvenir Sheet ...	...	...	7.50
465	32¢ 4th Micronesian Games, Sheet of 9	...	...	7.25
466	32¢ Christmas, Rudolph, Strip of 5	(15) 10.50	...	3.95
467-70	20¢, 32¢, 50¢, 60¢ Disney's "A Bug's Life" Sheets of 4 (4)	...		18.00
471-74	$2 Disney's "A Bug's Life" Souvenir Sheets (4) ...	...	...	22.50
	1999 Commemoratives			
475-76	60¢ John Glenn's Return to Space Sheets of 8 (2)	...		23.50
477-78	$2 John Glenn's Return to Space Souvenir Sheets (2)	...		9.75
479	33¢ Environmental Heroes of 20th Century Sheet of 16	...		13.00
480	33¢ Mir and the Space Shuttles Sheet of 6	...	...	4.75
481-84	$2 Mir and the Space Shuttles Souvenir Sheets (4)	...		19.50

1999-2001 Famous Persons Regular Issues

490	**491**	**492**	**493**	**494**

485-94	1¢,2¢,20¢,22¢,33¢,50¢,55¢,60¢.77¢,$3.20 set of 10	... 67.50	15.00
485v.92v	1¢,60¢ "2001" Dates (2)	... ...	1.60

1999 Commemoratives (continued)

495	33¢ Australia'99, World Stamp Expo, Vanishing Turtles, Frogs and Amphibians, Sheet of 12	...		9.50
496-97	$2 Vanishing Turtles, etc. Souvenir Sheets (2) ...	...	...	9.75
498-99	55¢ IBRA '99, Caroline Is. Stamps (2)		11.50	2.65
500	$2 IBRA '99, Caroline Is. Stamps, Souvenir Sheet	...		4.95
501	33¢ Exploring Mars, Sheet of 6	...	...	4.95
502-5	$2 Exploring Mars, Souvenir Sheets (4)	...	...	20.00
506	33¢ Earth Day, Pacific Insects, Sheet of 20	...	...	16.50
507	33¢ Space Station, Sheet of 6	...	...	4.75
508-11	$2 Space Station, Souvenir Sheets (4)	...	...	19.50
512	33¢ Information Age, Visionaries of the 20th Century, Sheet of 25	...		19.50
513-14	33¢ Hokusai Paintings Sheets of 6 (2)	...	...	9.50
515-16	$2 Hokusai Paintings Souvenir Sheets (2)	...	...	9.75
517	33¢ Apollo 11 Sheet of 6	...	...	5.00
518-21	$2 Apollo ii Souvenir Sheets (4)	...	...	20.00
522	60¢ Queen Mother 100th Birthday Sheet of 4	...		5.75
523	$2 Queen Mother 100th Birthday Souvenir Sheet...	...		5.25
524	33¢ Hubble Images from Space Sheet of 6	...	...	5.25
525-28	$2 Hubble Images from Space Souvenir Sheets (4)	...		20.00
529	20¢ Christmas, Birds & Animals, Strip of 5(15) 7.50	...	...	2.50
530	33¢ Love your Dog Sheet of 10	...	...	8.50
531-32	$2 Love your Dog Souvenir Sheets (2)	...	...	10.00
	2000 Commemoratives			
533	33¢ Space Probes Sheet of 6	...	...	7.50
534-37	$2 Space Probes Souvenir Sheets (4)	...	...	19.50
538	20¢ Millennium 1800-1850 Sheet of 17	...	...	8.25
539	20¢ Millennium 1980-89 Sheet of 17 .	...	...	8.25
540	$2 Year of the Dragon Souvenir Sheet	...	...	5.00

2000 U.S. Presidents Regular Issue

Scott's No.		Mint Sheets	Plate Block	F-VF NH
541-44	$1 Clinton, $2 Reagan, $3 Ford, $5 Bush (4)	...	110.00	25.00
545	$11.75 J.F. Kennedy	...	...	25.00
	2000 Commemoratives (continued)			
546	20¢ 20th Century Discoveries about Prehistoric Life Sheet of 20			9.75
547	33¢ Summer Olympics Sheet of 4			3.25
548	33¢ Unmanned Space Craft Sheet of 6	...		5.25
549-52	$2 Unmanned Space Craft Souvenir Sheets (4)	...	...	19.00
553-54	20¢-33¢ Native Birds Sheets of 6 (2)	...		7.75
555-56	$2 Native Birds Souvenir Sheets (2) .	...	...	9.50
557	33¢ Visionaries of the 20th Century Sheet of 20			16.50
558-61	33¢ Science & Medicine Sheets of 5 (4)	...	...	16.75
562-63	$2 Sciences & Medicine Souvenir Sheets (2)	...	...	9.50
564-65	33¢ Marine Life Sheet of 6 (2)	...	...	9.50
566-67	$2 Marine Life Souvenir Sheet (2)	...	...	9.50
568-69	20¢-55¢ New Millennium Sheets of 6 (2)			11.00
570-71	33¢ New & Recovering Species Sheets of 6 (2)	...		9.50
572-73	$2 New & Recovering Species Souvenir Sheets (2)	...		9.50
574-75	20¢-33¢ Dinosaurs Sheets of 4 and 6 (2)	...	...	7.75
576-77	$2 Dinosaurs Souvenir Sheet (2)	...	...	9.50
578-79	55¢ Queen Mother, Pair	(4) 10.50	...	2.75
580	$2 Queen Mother Souvenir Sheet	...	...	4.75
581	55¢ Zeppelin Flight Sheet of 6	...	...	8.00
582-83	$2 Zeppelin Souvenir Sheets (2)	...	...	9.50
584	33¢ Underseas History & Exploration Sheet of 17			14.75
585	50¢ Pope John Paul II Photomosaic Sheet of 8	...		10.00
586-87	60¢ Year of the Snake Souvenir Sheets (2)	...		2.95
588	55¢ Pacific Ocean Marine Life Sheet of 6	...		7.95
589	20¢ Atlantic Ocean Fish Sheet of 6 ..	...		2.95
590-91	$2 Atlantic Ocean Fish Souvenir Sheets (2)	...	...	9.50
592	33¢ Pacific Arts Festival Sheet of 9 .	...	...	7.50
593	33¢ Belau Museum Sheetlet of 12	...	...	9.50
594-97	33¢ Butterflies, set of 4	...	...	3.50
598-99	33¢ Butterflies Sheetlets of 6 (2)	...	...	10.00
600-01	$2 Butterflies Souvenir Sheets (2)	...	...	9.50
602-03	33¢ Fauna and Flora Sheetl of 6 (2) .	...	...	10.00
604-05	$2 Fauna and Flora Souvenir Sheets(2)	...	...	10.00

2001 Famous Persons Regular Issue

606	11¢ Lazarus Salil	...	...	.25

607		**608**	**609**

607-9	70¢ F. MacArthur, 80¢ C. Nimitz, $12.25 John F. Kennedy, set of 3	...	...	28.50
	2001 Commemoratives			
610-12	60¢ Phila Nippon'01 Japan Sheets of 5 & 6 (3)...	...		23.75
613-15	$2 Phila Nippon'01 Souvenir Sheets (3)	...	...	14.50
616-19	20¢,21¢,80¢,$1 Moths set of 4	...		5.25
620-21	34¢-70¢ Moths Sheets of 6 (2)	...		15.00
622-23	$2 Moths Souvenir Sheets (2)	...	...	9.50
624-26	34¢, 70¢, 80¢ Nobel Prize Winners Sheets of 6 (3)	...		25.00
627-29	$2 Nobel Prize Winners Souvenir Sheets (3)	...	...	14.50
630-31	34¢, 80¢ World Cup Soccer Sheets of 6 (2)	...	...	17.00
632-33	$2 Soccer Souvenir Sheets (2)	...	...	9.50
634-35	20¢-34¢ Christmas (2)	...		1.40
636	60¢ Queen Mother Sheet of 4	...	...	6.00
637	$2 Queen Mother Souvenir Sheet	...	...	4.75
638	60¢ Year of the Horse	(4) 5.95	...	1.50
639-40	55¢-60¢ Birds Sheets of 6 (2)	...		17.50
641-42	$2 Birds Souvenir Sheets (2)	...	...	9.50
	2002 Commemoratives			
643-44	20¢, 34¢ Palau-Japan Friendship Sheet of 30 (2)	...		37.50
645	$1 United We Stand, U.S. Flag	...	...	2.50
646	80¢ Elizabeth II Golden Jubilee Sheet of 4	...		7.95
647	$2 Elizabeth II Golden Jubilee Souvenir Sheet ...	...		4.75
	2002 Bird Definitives			
648-65	1¢, 2¢,3¢,4¢,5¢,10¢,15¢,20¢,21¢,23¢ 50¢,57¢,70¢,80¢,$1,$2,$3 (18)	...		21.95
666-67	$3.50-$3.95 Bird Definitives (2)	...	...	17.50
668-69	$5-$10 Bird Definitives (2)	...	...	32.50
	2002 Commemoratives (continued)			
670-73	20¢, 34¢, 60¢, 80¢ Flowers (4)	...		4.75
674-75	60¢ Flowers Sheets of 6 (2)	...	...	17.50
676-77	$2 Flowers Souvenir Sheets (2)	...	...	9.50
678-79	$1 Winter Olympics, (2)	...	...	4.75
679a	$2 Winter Olympics Souvenir Sheet ..	...	...	4.75
680	50¢ Cats Sheet of 6	...	...	7.50
681	50¢ Dogs Sheet of 6	...	...	7.50
682	$2 Cats Souvenir Sheet	...	...	4.75
683	$2 Dogs Souvenir Sheet	...	...	4.75
684	80¢ Year of the Mountains Sheet of 4	...		7.75
685	$2 Year of the Mountains Souvenir Sheet	...		4.75
686	34¢ Flags of all States Sheet of 17 ..	...		13.95
687-88	$1 Winter Olympics, smaller rings (2)	...	...	4.75
688a	$2 Winter Olympics, smaller rings, Souvenir Sheet	...		4.75
689	60¢ EcoTourism Sheet of 6	...	...	8.75
690	$2 EcoTourism Souvenir Sheet	...	...	4.75

REPUBLIC OF PALAU

2002 Commemoratives (continued)

Scott's No.		Mint Sheets	Plate Block	F-VF NH
691	60¢ Masterpieces of Japanese Art, Kabuki Actor Portraiture Sheet of 6 ..	...	...	8.75
692-93	80¢ Masterpieces of Japanese Art Sheets of 4 (2)...		...	15.75
694-95	$2 Japanese Art Souvenir Sheets (2)			9.50
696	60¢ Popeye, Summer Sports Sheet of 6	...	...	8.75
697	$2 Popeye, Golf Souvenir Sheet	...	...	4.75
698	37¢ Elvis Presley Sheet of 6	...	...	5.50
699-703	15¢, 37¢, 55¢, 80¢, $1 Christmas (5)		...	7.00
704	$2 Christmas Souvenir Sheet	...	...	4.75
705	60¢ Teddy Bear Centennial Sheet of 4	...	...	5.75
706	80¢ Queen Mother Memorial Sheet of 4	...	...	7.75
707	$2 Queen Mother Memorial Souvenir Sheet	...	...	4.75

2003 Commemoratives

708	60¢ Boy Scouts Sheet of 6	...	...	7.50
709	$2 Boy Scouts Souvenir Sheet	...	...	4.25
710	60¢ Shells Sheet of 6	...	...	7.50
711	$2 Shells Souvenir Sheet	...	...	4.25
712	37¢ Year of the Ram Strip of 4	(8) 6.30	...	3.15
713	80¢ John F. Kennedy Sheet of 4	...	...	6.95

2003 Bird Definitives

714-15	26¢-37¢ Bird Definitives (2)			1.35

2003 Commemoratives (continued)

716	37¢ In Memoriam - Space Shuttle Columbia Sheet of 7......			5.50
717	60¢ Orchids Sheet of 6	...	...	7.50
718	$2 Orchids Souvenir Sheet	...	...	4.25
719	60¢ Insects Sheet of 6	...	...	7.50
720	$2 Insects Souvenir Sheet	...	...	4.25
721	60¢ Non-Stop Trans-atlantic Flight Sheet of 6	...	...	7.50
722	80¢ Ronald Reagan Sheet of 4	...	...	6.75

723

723	80¢ Princess Diana Sheet of 4	...	...	6.95
724	$1 Queen Elizabeth 50th Anniv. of Coronation Sheet of 3...			6.50
725	$2 Queen Elizabeth 50th Anniv. Souvenir Sheet…			4.25
726	37¢ Operation Iraqi Freedom Sheet of 6	...	...	4.75
727	$1 Prince William 21st Birthday Sheet of 3	...	...	6.50
728	$2 Prince William 21st Birthday Souvenir Sheet	...	...	4.25
729	60¢ Tour de France Sheet of 4	...	...	5.00
730	$2 Tour de France Souvenir Sheet ...	...	...	4.25
731	55¢ Powered Flight, Aviation Sheet of 6	...	...	6.95
732	$2 Powered Flight. Aviation Souvenir Sheet	...	...	4.25
733-36	37¢,55¢,60¢,$1 James M.Whistler (4)	...	...	5.50
737	80¢ James M.Whistler Sheet of 4	...	...	6.75
738	$2 James M. Whistler Souvenir Sheet	...	...	4.25
739-40	80¢ Circus Clowns Sheets of 4 (2) ..	...	...	13.50
741-44	37¢,60¢,80¢,$1 Christmas (4)	...	...	5.95
745	$2 Christmas Souvenir Sheet	...	...	4.25

746

REPUBLIC OF PALAU

2004 Commemoratives

Scott's No.		Mint Sheets	Plate Block	F-VF NH
746	60¢ Sea Turtles Sheet of 6	...	...	7.75
747	$2 Sea Turtles Souvenir Sheet	...	...	4.25
748	80¢ Norman Rockwell Sheet of 4	...	...	6.75
749	$2 Norman Rockwell Souvenir Sheet	...	...	4.25
...	80¢ Pablo Picasso Sheet of 4	...	...	6.75
...	$2 Pablo Picasso Souvenir Sheet	...	...	4.25
...	50¢ Year of the Monkey	(4) 4.35	...	1.10
...	$1 Year of the Monkey Souvenir Sheet	...	...	2.15
...	55¢ Minerals Sheet of 6	...	...	6.95
...	$2 Minerals Souvenir Sheet	...	...	4.25
...	55¢ Marine Life Sheet of 6	...	...	6.95
...	$2 Marine Life Souvenir Sheet	...	...	4.25

1988 Semi-Postals

B1-2

B1-4	25¢ + 5¢,45¢ + 5¢ Olympic Sports, 2 pairs	...	9.00	3.95

Airmails

C5   C10

1984-95

C1-4	40¢ Birds, Block of 4 (1984)	...	4.75	3.95
C5	44¢ Audubon (1985)	...	5.75	1.25
C6-9	44¢ Palau-Germany Exchange Cent., Block of 4	...	5.50	4.50
C10-13	44¢ Trans-Pacific Airmail Anniv., Block of 4	...	5.50	4.50
C14-16	44¢ Remelik Memorial, Strip of 3 (1986)	(9) 16.50	(6) 9.50	4.50
C14-16	Remelik Mem.,Strip of 3 with tabs	...	(6) 10.75	5.50

C17   C18-20

C17	44¢ Peace Year, Statue of Liberty	...	5.25	1.10
C18-20	36¢,39¢,45¢ Aircraft (3) (1989)	...	15.75	3.25
C18a	36¢ Booklet Pane of 10	...	...	8.75
C19a	39¢ Booklet Pane of 10	...	...	9.50
C20a	45¢ Booklet Pane of 10	...	...	10.50
C20b	36¢/45¢ Booklet Pane of 10 (5 each)	...	...	10.00
C21	50¢ Palauan Bai (#293a), self adhesive (1991)	...	9.75	2.10
C22	50¢ WWII in Pacific, Aircraft Sheet of 10 (1992)	...	...	13.75
C23	50¢ Birds, Block of 4 (1994)	...	...	5.00

Postal Stationery

U1	22¢ Parrotfish (1989)	...	...	4.50
U2	22¢ Spearfishing	...	...	7.95
U3	25¢ Chambered Nautilus (1991)	...	...	4.25
UC1	36¢ Birds (1985)	...	...	11.95
UX1	14¢ Giant Clam (1985)	...	...	3.50

CANADA

| 1,4 | 2,5,10 | 8 |

PROVINCE OF CANADA
1851 Laid Paper, Imperforate (OG + 75%) VF+80% (C)

Scott's No.		Unused Fine	Ave.	Used Fine	Ave.
1	3p Beaver, Red	...	...	600.00	350.00
2	6p Prince Albert, Grayish Purple	...	...	1000.00	600.00
3	12p Queen Victoria, Black	...	...	...	...

1852-1857 Wove Paper, Imperforate (OG + 50%) VF+80% (C)

4	3p Beaver, Red, Thick Paper	875.00	525.00	130.00	80.00
4d	3p Thin Paper	900.00	550.00	140.00	90.00
5	6p Prince Albert, Slate Gray	...	...	775.00	425.00
7	10p Jacques Cartier, Blue	...	...	950.00	550.00
8	½p Queen Victoria, Rose	500.00	300.00	350.00	215.00
9	7½p Queen Victoria, Green	...	...	1500.00	850.00
10	6p Prince Albert, Reddish Purple, Thick Paper	...	...	3000.00	1500.00

1858-59 Wove Paper, Perforated 11 3/4 (OG + 50%) VF+80% (C)

11	½p Queen Victoria, Rose	1700.00	1000.00	700.00	375.00
12	3p Beaver, Red	3000.00	1650.00	400.00	250.00
13	6p Prince Albert, Brown Violet	...	...	3250.00	1800.00

| 14 | 17 | 18 | 19 | 20 |

1859-64, Perf. 11 3/4 or 12 (OG + 50%) VF + 80% (C)

14	1¢ Queen Victoria, Rose	225.00	135.00	37.50	22.50
15	5¢ Beaver, Vermilion	275.00	165.00	18.00	11.00
16	10¢ Prince Albert, Black Brown	...	...	...	1500.00
17	10¢ Red Lilac	575.00	375.00	60.00	37.50
18	12½¢ Queen Victoria, Yellow Green	550.00	350.00	60.00	37.50
19	17¢ Jacques Cartier, Blue	600.00	375.00	80.00	45.00
20	2¢ Queen Victoria, Rose (1864)	325.00	210.00	160.00	100.00

PRIOR TO #21, UNUSED PRICES ARE FOR STAMPS WITH PARTIAL OR NO GUM, FOR ORIGINAL GUM, ADD % INDICATED IN ( ).

CANADA
DOMINION OF CANADA
1868-1876 Large "Cents" Issue, Perf. 12 VF + 80% (C)

| 21 | 22 | 26 | 27 | 28 |

Scott's No.		Unused, OG Fine	Ave.	Used Fine	Ave.
21	½¢ Queen Victoria, Black	65.00	40.00	30.00	16.50
21a	½¢ Perf. 11½ x 12	70.00	45.00	30.00	16.50
21c	½¢ Thin Paper	70.00	45.00	37.50	21.50
22	1¢ Brown Red	425.00	250.00	55.00	35.00
22a	1¢ Watermarked	...	...	180.00	110.00
22b	1¢ Thin Paper	450.00	265.00	55.00	35.00
23	1¢ Yellow Orange (1869)	750.00	450.00	90.00	52.50
24	2¢ Green	450.00	270.00	45.00	27.50
24a	2¢ Watermarked	1950.00	1200.00	210.00	135.00
24b	2¢ Thin Paper	500.00	300.00	55.00	33.50
25	3¢ Red	700.00	400.00	19.00	12.00
25a	3¢ Watermarked	2750.00	1700.00	210.00	135.00
25b	3¢ Thin Paper	800.00	475.00	22.50	14.00
26	5¢ Olive Green, Perf. 11½ x 12(1875)	950.00	550.00	130.00	80.00
27	6¢ Dark Brown	1100.00	675.00	55.00	35.00
27b	6¢ Watermarked	4000.00	2500.00	950.00	550.00
27c	6¢ Thin Paper	1475.00	900.00	110.00	65.00
28	12½¢ Blue	600.00	375.00	65.00	40.00
28a	12½¢ Watermarked	2100.00	1300.00	200.00	120.00
28b	12½¢ Thin Paper	800.00	500.00	85.00	52.50
29	15¢ Gray Violet	57.50	35.00	22.50	14.00
29a	15¢ Perf. 11½ x 12	800.00	500.00	120.00	72.50
29b	15¢ Red Lilac	675.00	450.00	65.00	37.50
29c	15¢ Gray Violet Wmkd	3950.00	2500.00	550.00	325.00
29e	15¢ Gray Violet, Thin Paper	525.00	325.00	85.00	50.00
30	15¢ Gray	57.50	35.00	22.50	13.50
30a	15¢ Perf. 11½ x 12	800.00	475.00	120.00	70.00

1868 Laid Paper, Perf. 12 VF +80% (C)

31	1¢ Brown Red	...	...	2750.00	1500.00
32	2¢ Green	...	...	...	...
33	3¢ Bright Red	...	...	600.00	325.00

FROM #21 THROUGH 103, UNUSED PRICES ARE FOR STAMPS WITH FULL ORIGINAL GUM. STAMPS WITH PARTIAL OR NO GUM SELL FOR 30% LESS THAN THOSE WITH FULL ORIGINAL GUM.

| 34 | 37, 41 | 38 | 44 | 47 |

Scott's No.		Unused,NH Fine	Unused, OG Fine	Ave.	Used Fine	Ave.

1870-89 Queen Victoria Small "Cents" Issue, Perf. 12 VF + 80% (C)

34	½¢ Black (1882)	16.00	7.00	4.25	5.25	3.00
35	1¢ Yellow	55.00	22.50	13.50	.75	.45
35a	1¢ Orange	160.00	65.00	40.00	6.75	4.00
35d	1¢ Orange, Pf. 11½ x 12	375.00	150.00	90.00	12.00	7.50
36	2¢ Green (1872)	80.00	32.50	20.00	1.25	.75
36d	2¢ Blue Green	130.00	55.00	32.50	3.00	1.80
36e	2¢ Green, Pf. 11½ x 12	500.00	200.00	120.00	15.00	9.25
37	3¢ Dull Red	150.00	60.00	35.00	1.80	1.00
37a	3¢ Rose	800.00	325.00	195.00	7.50	4.25
37b	3¢ Copper or Indian Red	...	850.00	525.00	30.00	17.50
37c	3¢ Orange Red	150.00	60.00	35.00	1.95	1.10
37d	3¢ Copper Red Perf. 12½	...	...	...	675.00	425.00
37e	3¢ Red, Perf. 11½ x 12	450.00	180.00	100.00	7.50	4.50
38	5¢ Slate Green (1876)	725.00	295.00	175.00	12.75	8.25
38a	5¢ Olive Green, Pf. 11½x12	...	395.00	240.00	25.00	16.50
39	6¢ Yellow Brown (1877)	675.00	275.00	160.00	13.00	8.25
39b	6¢ Brown, Perf.11½ x 12	...	450.00	275.00	22.50	14.50
40	10¢ Dull Rose Lilac (1877)	950.00	385.00	225.00	37.50	23.00
40c	10¢ Rose Lilac, Perf.11½ x 12	800.00	475.00	175.00	110.00	

1888-93 Queen Victoria Small "Cents" Issue, Perf. 12 VF + 80% (C)

41	3¢ Bright Vermilion	65.00	27.50	16.50	.55	.35
41a	3¢ Rose Carmine	675.00	275.00	160.00	8.00	4.95
42	5¢ Gray	175.00	70.00	40.00	3.00	1.85
43	6¢ Red Brown	160.00	65.00	37.50	7.50	4.15
43a	6¢ Chocolate	375.00	150.00	90.00	22.50	14.00
44	8¢ Gray shades (1893)	170.00	70.00	42.50	2.95	1.75
45	10¢ Brown Red (1891)	615.00	250.00	150.00	22.50	13.50
46	20¢ Vermilion (1893)	550.00	225.00	135.00	62.50	37.50
47	50¢ Deep Blue (1893)	550.00	225.00	135.00	60.00	35.00

1897 Queen Victoria Diamond Jubilee Issue VF Used + 70% (B)

| 56 | 58 | 61 |

Scott's No.		Unused, NH VF	F-VF	Unused, OG VF	F-VF	Used F-VF

50	½¢ Black	235.00	135.00	90.00	55.00	52.50
51	1¢ Orange	40.00	22.50	16.50	10.00	6.00
52	2¢ Green	55.00	30.00	23.50	13.50	9.50
53	3¢ Bright Rose	31.75	16.50	12.50	7.50	1.35
54	5¢ Deep Blue	100.00	55.00	40.00	25.00	15.00
55	6¢ Yellow Brown	525.00	275.00	210.00	125.00	100.00
56	8¢ Dark Violet	115.00	62.50	47.50	28.50	20.00
57	10¢ Brown Violet	220.00	120.00	92.50	55.00	50.00
58	15¢ Steel Blue	485.00	270.00	195.00	120.00	100.00
59	20¢ Vermilion	485.00	270.00	195.00	120.00	100.00
60	50¢ Ultramarine	550.00	300.00	275.00	135.00	100.00
61	$1 Lake	1600.00	900.00	650.00	400.00	400.00
62	$2 Dark Purple	2700.00	1500.00	1100.00	675.00	350.00
63	$3 Yellow Bister	3000.00	1700.00	1200.00	750.00	650.00
64	$4 Purple	3000.00	1700.00	1200.00	750.00	650.00
65	$5 Olive Green	3000.00	1700.00	1200.00	750.00	650.00

| 73 | 84 | 85-86 | 88 |

1897-1898 Issue, Maple Leaves in Four Corners, VF Used + 70% (B)

66	½¢ Queen Victoria, Black	17.50	9.50	7.00	4.25	3.50
67	1¢ Blue Green	42.50	22.50	17.00	10.00	.70
68	2¢ Purple	42.50	22.50	17.00	10.00	1.00
69	3¢ Carmine (1898)	67.50	39.50	27.00	16.50	.25
70	5¢ Dark Blue on Bluish	250.00	140.00	100.00	60.00	3.50
71	6¢ Brown	175.00	100.00	70.00	42.50	16.75
72	8¢ Orange	475.00	270.00	200.00	120.00	5.75
73	10¢ Brown Violet (1898)	575.00	315.00	230.00	135.00	45.00

Scott's No.		Unused, NH VF	F-VF	Unused,OG VF	F-VF	Used F-VF

1898-1902 Issue, Numerals in Lower Corners VF Used + 70% (B)

74	½¢ Queen Victoria, Black	8.00	4.50	3.25	2.00	1.00
75	1¢ Gray Green	47.50	26.50	19.50	11.75	.20
76	2¢ Purple	47.50	26.50	19.00	11.50	.20
77	2¢ Carmine, Die I (1899)	50.00	27.50	20.00	12.00	.20
77a	2¢ Carmine, Die II	53.50	31.50	21.50	13.50	.30
77b	2¢ Booklet Pane of 6, Die II	2250.00	1400.00	975.00	600.00	

#77 Die I Four thin lines in frame #77a Die II One thick line between 2 thin lines

78	3¢ Carmine	90.00	50.00	36.50	21.50	.40
79	5¢ Blue (1899)	350.00	195.00	145.00	85.00	1.00
80	6¢ Brown	250.00	145.00	105.00	62.50	26.50
81	7¢ Olive Yellow (1902)	210.00	110.00	85.00	50.00	12.50
82	8¢ Orange	400.00	215.00	160.00	95.00	13.75
83	10¢ Brown Violet	525.00	275.00	210.00	125.00	12.50
84	20¢ Olive Green (1900)	925.00	525.00	375.00	225.00	60.00

1898 Imperial Penny Post, Christmas Issue VF Used + 70% (B)

85	2¢ Map, Black, Lavender & Carmine	67.50	35.00	33.50	20.00	4.35
86	2¢ Black, Blue, Carmine	67.50	35.00	33.50	20.00	4.35

1899 Surcharges VF Used + 70% (B)

87	2¢ on 3¢ Carmine (on #69)	27.50	15.00	10.00	6.50	4.00
88	2¢ on 3¢ Carmine (on #78)	42.50	22.50	17.00	10.00	3.00

| 94 | 100 | 103 |

1903-1908 King Edward VII VF Used + 70% (B)

89	1¢ Green	50.00	27.50	20.00	12.00	.20
90	2¢ Carmine	52.50	28.50	21.00	12.50	.20
90b	2¢ Booklet Pane of 6	2600.00	1600.00	1050.00	650.00	...
90a	2¢ Imperforate Pair	60.00	45.00	40.00	30.00	...
91	5¢ Blue on Bluish	300.00	170.00	125.00	75.00	2.50
92	7¢ Olive Bister	250.00	135.00	100.00	60.00	2.50
93	10¢ Brown Lilac	500.00	265.00	200.00	120.00	4.75
94	20¢ Olive Green (1904)	1150.00	625.00	465.00	275.00	20.00
95	50¢ Purple (1908)	1350.00	750.00	550.00	325.00	60.00

1908 Quebec Tercentenary VF + 70% (B)

96-103	Set of 8	1500.00	850.00	595.00	350.00	265.00
96	½¢ Prince & Princess of Wales	10.00	5.50	4.25	2.50	2.50
97	1¢ Cartier & Champlain	26.50	15.00	10.75	6.50	2.60
98	2¢ Queen Alexandria & King Edward VII	45.00	25.00	17.50	10.50	.80
99	5¢ Champlain's Home	105.00	60.00	42.50	25.00	22.50
100	7¢ Montcalm & Wolfe	275.00	160.00	110.00	65.00	45.00
101	10¢ 1700 View of Quebec	275.00	160.00	110.00	65.00	45.00
102	15¢ Champlain Heads West	325.00	180.00	135.00	80.00	62.50
103	20¢ Cartier Arrival	475.00	265.00	185.00	110.00	95.00

| 104-105 | 122 | 131 | 140 |

1912-1925 King George V "Admiral Issue" Perf. 12 VF Used + 60% (B)

104-22	Set of 18	1650.00	1000.00	635.00	395.00	25.75
104	1¢ George V. Green	21.75	12.50	8.75	5.50	.15
104a	1¢ Booklet Pane of 6	47.50	27.50	23.75	15.00	...
105	1¢ Yellow, Wet, Die I (1922)	21.75	12.50	8.75	5.50	.15
105a	1¢ Booklet Pane of 4	110.00	60.00	55.00	35.00	...
105b	1¢ Booklet Pane of 6	90.00	52.50	45.00	30.00	...
105d	1¢ Chrome Yellow, Dry Printing, Die II	23.50	13.50	9.50	6.00	.25

#105 & 126b Die I "N" of "ONE" is well clear of center oval.
#105d & 126 Die II "N" of "ONE" almost touches center oval.

106	2¢ Carmine	18.75	11.75	7.00	4.50	.15
106a	2¢ Booklet Pane of 6	57.50	35.00	27.50	17.50	...
107	2¢ Yellow Green (1922)	15.00	9.00	6.00	3.75	.15
107a	2¢ Thin Paper	15.75	9.50	6.50	4.00	1.75
107b	2¢ Booklet Pane of 4	120.00	67.50	60.00	37.50	...
107c	2¢ Booklet Pane of 6	625.00	350.00	325.00	200.00	...
108	3¢ Brown (1918)	25.00	14.50	9.50	6.00	.15
108a	3¢ Booklet Pane of 4	160.00	90.00	82.50	52.50	...
109	3¢ Carmine, Die I (1923)	13.50	8.25	5.50	3.50	.15
109a	3¢ Booklet Pane of 4	110.00	62.50	55.00	35.00	...
109c	3¢ Carmine, Die II	67.50	39.50	27.50	17.50	.30

#109 & 130b Die I "R" of "THREE" is well clear of center oval.
#109c & 130b Die II "R" of "THREE" almost touches center oval.

110	4¢ Olive Bistre (1922)	65.00	37.50	26.00	16.50	2.10
111	5¢ Dark Blue	210.00	125.00	85.00	52.50	.35
112	5¢ Violet (1922)	37.50	23.50	15.75	9.75	.35
112a	5¢ Thin Paper	40.00	24.00	16.00	10.00	4.50
113	7¢ Yellow Ochre	72.50	47.50	28.50	18.50	1.80
114	7¢ Red Brown (1924)	40.00	23.50	16.00	10.00	5.25
115	8¢ Blue (1925)	60.00	37.50	24.00	15.00	4.75
116	10¢ Plum	465.00	275.00	160.00	100.00	.90
117	10¢ Blue (1922)	79.50	45.00	31.75	20.00	1.00
118	10¢ Bister Brown (1925)	72.50	42.50	28.50	18.50	1.00
119	20¢ Olive Green	160.00	95.00	65.00	40.00	.85

1912-1925 King George V "Admiral Issue" Perf. 12 VF Used + 60% (B)

Scott's No.		Unused, NH VF	Unused, NH F-VF	Unused,OG VF	Unused,OG F-VF	Used F-VF
120	50¢ Black Brown,Dry (1925) .	160.00	95.00	65.00	40.00	1.50
120a	50¢ Black, Wet Printing	325.00	190.00	130.00	80.00	4.50
122	$1 Orange (1923)	220.00	130.00	90.00	55.00	5.35

1912 Coil Stamps, Perf. 8 Horizontally VF Used + 60% (B)

123	1¢ Dark Green	175.00	110.00	80.00	50.00	35.00
123	1¢ Pair	375.00	235.00	175.00	110.00	...
124	2¢ Carmine	175.00	110.00	80.00	50.00	35.00
124	2¢ Pair	375.00	235.00	175.00	110.00	...

1912-1924 Coil Stamps, Perf. 8 Vertically VF Used + 60% (B)

125-30	**Set of 6 ....**	**250.00**	**145.00**	**125.00**	**79.50**	**10.85**
125-30	**Set of 6 Pairs ....**	**550.00**	**320.00**	**275.00**	**175.00**	**...**
125	1¢ Green	30.00	18.00	15.00	9.50	.80
125	1¢ Pair	65.00	40.00	32.50	21.00	...
126	1¢ Yellow, Die II (1923)	18.75	11.00	9.50	6.00	4.25
126	1¢ Pair	41.50	24.00	21.00	13.00	...
126a	1¢ Block of four (1924)	80.00	50.00	50.00	32.50	...
126b	1¢ Yellow, Die I	21.00	12.50	10.50	6.50	4.75
126b	1¢ Pair	45.00	27.50	23.00	14.50	...
127	2¢ Carmine	38.50	21.50	19.50	12.00	.60
127	2¢ Pair	82.50	47.50	42.50	26.00	...
128	2¢ Green (1922)	25.00	15.00	12.50	7.75	.50
128	2¢ Pair	55.00	32.75	27.50	17.00	...
128a	2¢ Block of four (1924)	80.00	50.00	50.00	32.50	...
129	3¢ Brown (1918)	18.75	11.00	9.50	6.00	.50
129	3¢ Pair	41.50	24.00	21.00	13.00	...
130	3¢ Carmine, Die I (1924)	130.00	75.00	65.00	40.00	4.50
130	3¢ Pair	285.00	165.00	145.00	90.00	...
130a	3¢ Block of four (1924)	935.00	625.00	635.00	425.00	...
130b	3¢ Carmine, Die II	160.00	90.00	80.00	50.00	8.00
130b	3¢ Pair	350.00	200.00	175.00	110.00	...

#126a,128a,130a are from Part.-Perf. Sheets - Pairs are at half block prices.

1915-1924 Coil Stamps, Perf. 12 Horizontally VF Used + 60% (B)

131-34	**Set of 4 ....**	**200.00**	**115.00**	**102.50**	**63.50**	**52.75**
131-34	**Set of 4 Pairs ....**	**435.00**	**250.00**	**225.00**	**140.00**	**...**
131	1¢ Dark Green	13.00	7.25	6.50	4.00	5.00
131	1¢ Pair	28.50	16.00	14.75	8.75	...
132	2¢ Carmine	37.50	21.50	19.00	12.00	6.00
132	2¢ Pair	82.50	47.00	42.50	26.00	...
133	2¢ Yellow Green (1924)	145.00	82.50	72.50	45.00	40.00
133	2¢ Pair	315.00	180.00	160.00	100.00	...
134	3¢ Brown (1921)	15.00	8.75	7.50	4.75	4.00
134	3¢ Pair	33.50	19.50	16.50	10.50	...

1917 50th Anniversary of Confederation VF Used + 100% (B)

135	3¢ "Fathers of Confederation" .	95.00	50.00	38.50	20.00	.70

1924 Imperforate VF Used + 30% (B)

136	1¢ Yellow	70.00	47.50	37.50	28.50	30.00
137	2¢ Green	70.00	47.50	37.50	28.50	30.00
138	3¢ Carmine	35.00	25.00	19.50	15.00	15.00

1926 Surcharges on #109 VF Used + 60% (B)

139	2¢ on 3¢ - One Line	90.00	52.50	56.50	35.00	35.00
140	2¢ on 3¢ - Two Lines	40.00	25.00	26.50	16.50	16.50

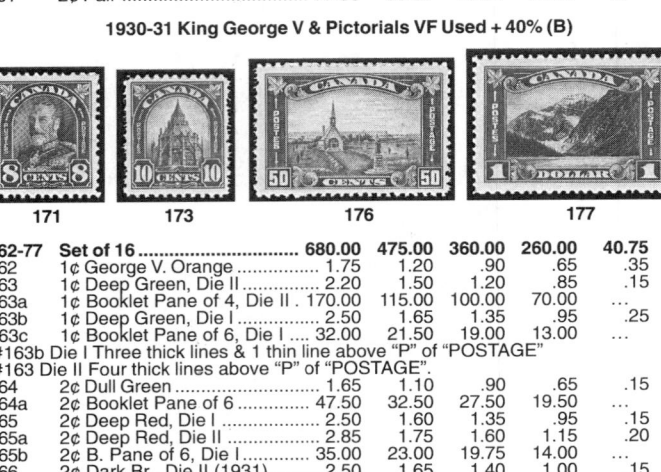

141

143

146

148

1927 60th Anniversary of Confederation Issue VF Used + 40% (B)

141-45	**Set of 5 ....**	**53.50**	**37.50**	**30.75**	**20.75**	**8.50**
141	1¢ John A. Macdonald	4.95	3.25	2.75	1.95	.65
142	2¢ "Fathers of Confederation" ...	2.85	1.95	1.65	1.20	.20
143	3¢ Parliament Buildings	12.00	8.50	7.25	5.25	3.25
144	5¢ Wilfrid Laurier	7.25	5.00	4.25	3.00	1.75
145	12¢ Map of Canada	28.50	20.00	16.00	11.50	3.25

1927 Historical Issue VF Used + 40% (B)

146-48	**Set of 3 ....**	**52.50**	**35.00**	**29.50**	**20.75**	**8.50**
146	5¢ Thomas d'Arcy McGee	6.50	4.50	3.50	2.50	1.75
147	12¢ Laurier & Macdonald	15.00	10.00	8.75	6.25	3.00
148	20¢ Baldwin & Lafontaine	33.00	22.50	18.00	13.00	4.25

1928-29 King George V Scroll Issue & Pictorials VF Used + 40% (B)

149

154

156

158

149-59	**Set of 11 ....**	**975.00**	**685.00**	**500.00**	**350.00**	**107.50**
149	1¢ George V, Orange	4.50	3.00	2.25	1.60	.25
149a	1¢ Booklet Pane of 6	31.50	21.00	18.50	13.50	...
150	2¢ Green	2.15	1.40	1.10	.80	.15
150a	2¢ Booklet Pane of 6	31.50	21.00	18.50	13.50	...
151	3¢ Dark Carmine	31.50	21.50	16.50	11.75	7.00
152	4¢ Bister (1929)	30.00	20.00	15.50	11.00	3.25
153	5¢ Deep Violet	15.75	11.00	7.75	5.50	1.70
153a	5¢ Booklet Pane of 6	165.00	115.00	110.00	75.00	...
154	8¢ Blue	21.50	14.00	10.50	7.50	3.75
155	10¢ Mount Hurd	21.50	14.00	10.50	7.50	.70

1928-29 King George V Scroll Issue & Pictorials VF Used + 40% (B)

Scott's No.		Unused, NH VF	Unused, NH F-VF	Unused,OG VF	Unused,OG F-VF	Used F-VF
156	12¢ Quebec Bridge (1929)	37.50	25.00	17.50	12.50	4.00
157	20¢ Harvesting Wheat (1929) .	55.00	40.00	26.50	19.00	7.00
158	50¢ Ship "Bluenose" (1929) ..	375.00	250.00	190.00	135.00	37.50
159	$1 Parliament Bldg. (1929) ...	450.00	300.00	230.00	165.00	45.00

1929 Coil Stamps, Perf. 8 Vertically VF Used + 40% (B)

160	1¢ George V, Orange	52.50	37.50	25.75	18.50	13.75
160	1¢ Pair	115.00	82.50	56.50	41.50	...
161	2¢ Green	35.00	25.00	17.50	12.50	1.75
161	2¢ Pair	77.50	55.00	38.50	27.50	...

1930-31 King George V & Pictorials VF Used + 40% (B)

171

173

176

177

162-77	**Set of 16 ....**	**680.00**	**475.00**	**360.00**	**260.00**	**40.75**
162	1¢ George V. Orange	1.75	1.20	.90	.65	.35
163	1¢ Deep Green, Die II	2.20	1.50	1.20	.85	.15
163a	1¢ Booklet Pane of 4, Die II .	170.00	115.00	100.00	70.00	...
163b	1¢ Deep Green, Die I	2.50	1.65	1.35	.95	.25
163c	1¢ Booklet Pane of 6, Die I	32.00	21.50	19.00	13.00	...

#163b Die I Three thick lines & 1 thin line above "P" of "POSTAGE"
#163 Die II Four thick lines above "P" of "POSTAGE".

164	2¢ Dull Green	1.65	1.10	.90	.65	.15
164a	2¢ Booklet Pane of 6	47.50	32.50	27.50	19.50	...
165	2¢ Deep Red, Die I	2.50	1.60	1.35	.95	.15
165a	2¢ Deep Red, Die II	2.85	1.75	1.60	1.15	.20
165b	2¢ B. Pane of 6, Die I	35.00	23.00	19.75	14.00	...
166	2¢ Dark Br., Die II (1931)	2.50	1.65	1.40	1.00	.15
166a	2¢ B. Pane of 4, Die II	160.00	105.00	95.00	65.00	...
166b	2¢ Dark Brown, Die I	6.95	4.50	3.85	2.75	2.75
166c	2¢ B. Pane of 6, Die I	47.50	32.50	28.50	20.00	...

#166b & 191a Die I: Small Dot of Color in "P" of "POSTAGE".
#166 & 191 Die II: Large Dot in "P" of "POSTAGE".

167	3¢ Deep Red (1931)	3.50	2.30	1.95	1.40	.15
167a	3¢ Booklet Pane of 4	55.00	36.50	31.50	22.50	...
168	4¢ Yellow Bistre	16.50	10.75	8.50	6.00	3.50
169	5¢ Dull Violet	8.75	5.75	4.65	3.25	2.50
170	5¢ Dull Blue	5.90	4.00	3.15	2.25	.20
171	8¢ Dark Blue	29.50	19.00	15.00	10.50	6.25
172	8¢ Red Orange	9.75	6.50	5.00	3.50	2.50
173	10¢ Library of Parliament	15.00	10.50	7.75	5.50	.70
174	12¢ Citadel at Quebec	27.50	18.00	13.75	9.75	3.35
175	20¢ Harvesting Wheat	41.50	27.50	21.00	15.00	.30
176	50¢ Museum-Grand Pre	295.00	200.00	150.00	110.00	7.75
177	$1 Mt. Edith Cavell	295.00	200.00	150.00	110.00	15.00

1930-31 Coil Stamps, Perf. 8½ Vertically VF Used + 40% (B)

178-83	**Set of 6 ....**	**107.50**	**72.50**	**57.50**	**41.50**	**13.75**
178-83	**Set of 6 Pairs ....**	**250.00**	**170.00**	**130.00**	**92.50**	**...**
178	1¢ George V,Orange	21.00	15.00	11.50	8.00	6.00
178	1¢ Pair	45.00	32.50	25.00	17.50	...
178	1¢ Line Pair	65.00	45.00	35.00	25.00	...
179	1¢ Green	13.00	8.75	6.75	4.75	3.25
179	1¢ Pair	28.50	19.00	15.00	10.50	...
179	1¢ Line Pair	37.50	25.00	19.50	13.50	...
180	2¢ Dull Green	8.75	6.00	4.50	3.25	2.00
180	2¢ Pair	19.50	13.50	10.00	7.00	...
180	2¢ Line Pair	35.00	20.00	18.00	11.00	...
181	2¢ Carmine	35.00	22.50	17.50	12.50	1.65
181	2¢ Pair	75.00	48.50	37.00	27.00	...
181	2¢ Line Pair	95.00	63.50	48.50	35.00	...
182	2¢ Dark Brown (1931)	18.00	12.00	9.25	6.50	.45
182	2¢ Pair	38.50	26.00	19.75	14.00	...
182	2¢ Line Pair	57.50	39.50	30.00	21.50	...
183	3¢ Deep Red (1931)	27.00	18.00	14.00	10.00	.45
183	3¢ Pair	57.50	38.50	30.00	21.50	...
183	3¢ Line Pair	80.00	55.00	41.50	29.50	...

1931 Design of 1912, Perforated 12 x 8 VF Used + 50% (B)

184	3¢ George V Carmine	9.50	6.50	4.00	2.75	2.35

190

192

194

199

1931 Cartier Issue VF +40% (B)

190	10¢ Sir Georges Cartier	16.00	11.50	7.75	5.50	.20

1932 Surcharges VF + 40% (B)

191	3¢ on 2¢ Deep Red, Die II	1.70	1.15	1.10	.75	.15
191a	3¢ on 2¢ Deep Red, Die I	3.75	2.50	2.30	1.65	1.10

1932 Imperial Economic Conference VF + 30% (B)

192-94	**Set of 3 ....**	**18.75**	**13.00**	**11.00**	**8.00**	**5.15**
192	3¢ King George V	1.20	.85	.70	.50	.20
193	5¢ Prince of Wales	8.75	6.25	5.25	3.75	1.50
194	13¢ Allegory "Britannia"	9.50	6.75	5.50	4.00	3.75

1932 George V, Medallion, VF Used + 40% (B)

Scott's No.		Unused, NH VF	F-VF	Unused,OG VF	F-VF	Used F-VF
195-201	**Set of 7**	**165.00**	**112.50**	**97.50**	**69.50**	**7.50**
195	1¢ George V. Dark Green	1.20	.85	.75	.55	.15
195a	1¢ Booklet Pane of 4	120.00	85.00	77.50	55.00	...
195b	1¢ Booklet Pane of 6	31.75	22.75	21.50	15.00	...
196	2¢ Black Brown	1.40	.90	.85	.60	.15
196a	2¢ Booklet Pane of 4	120.00	85.00	77.50	55.00	...
196b	2¢ Booklet Pane of 6	32.50	22.50	21.00	15.00	...
197	3¢ Deep Red, Die I	1.85	1.30	1.25	.90	.15
197a	3¢ Booklet Pane of 4, Die I	45.00	30.00	28.50	20.00	...
197c	3¢ Deep Red, Die II	2.00	1.50	1.40	1.00	.20

#197 Die I Bottom right curve of right "3" separate from border line.
#197c Die II Bottom right curve of right "3" joined to border line.

Scott's No.		Unused, NH VF	F-VF	Unused,OG VF	F-VF	Used F-VF
198	4¢ Ocher	60.00	40.00	35.00	25.00	3.75
199	5¢ Dark Blue	12.50	8.50	7.00	5.00	.20
200	8¢ Red Orange	42.50	30.00	25.00	18.00	2.35
201	13¢ Citadel at Quebec	55.00	37.50	31.50	22.50	1.75

203

208

209

1933 Pictorials VF + 40%

202	5¢ U.P.U. Meeting, Parliament Buildings	9.75	7.75	6.25	4.50	2.00
203	20¢ Grain Exhibition & Conference (on #175)	42.50	30.00	25.00	18.00	8.00
204	5¢ Trans-Atlantic Crossing of the "Royal William"	9.75	7.50	6.25	4.50	2.00

1933 George V "Medallion" Coil Stamps, Perf. 8½ Vertically VF + 40% (B)

205	1¢ George V. Dark Green	21.50	14.50	12.50	8.50	1.50
205	1¢ Pair	46.50	31.50	27.00	18.50	...
205	1¢ Line Pair	57.50	39.50	32.50	23.50	...
206	2¢ Black Brown	22.50	15.00	13.00	9.00	.60
206	2¢ Pair	48.50	32.50	28.50	19.50	...
206	2¢ Line Pair	65.00	42.50	37.50	27.00	...
207	3¢ Deep Red	21.50	14.50	12.50	8.50	.25
207	3¢ Pair	46.50	31.50	27.00	18.50	...
207	3¢ Line Pair	62.50	42.50	35.00	25.00	...

1934 Commemoratives VF + 40%

208	3¢ Jacques Cartier at Quebec	5.00	3.50	2.80	2.00	.80
209	10¢ Loyalists Monument	33.75	24.00	19.75	14.00	4.75
210	2¢ Seal of New Brunswick	3.35	2.40	1.95	1.40	1.00

1935 Silver Jubilee VF + 30%

211

213

214

216

Scott's No.		Plate Blocks NH	Unused	F-VF NH	F-VF Unused	F-VF Used
211-16	**Set of 6**	...	...	**22.75**	**15.00**	**7.35**
211	1¢ Princess Elizabeth (6)	8.75	6.50	.45	.30	.25
212	2¢ Duke of York (6)	7.50	5.50	.65	.45	.20
213	3¢ King George V and Queen Mary (6)	18.50	13.50	1.90	1.30	.20
214	5¢ Prince of Wales (6)	47.50	35.00	5.25	3.50	1.80
215	10¢ Windsor Castle (6)	60.00	45.00	6.50	4.25	1.65
216	13¢ Royal Yacht "Britannia" (6)	75.00	55.00	9.50	6.25	3.50

1935 George V "Bar" Issue & Pictorials VF + 30%

217

222

225

227

217-27	**Set of 11**	...	...	**153.00**	**95.00**	**12.75**
217	1¢ George V Green (8)	4.00	3.00	.25	.20	.15
217a	1¢ Booklet Pane of 4	...	...	57.50	37.50	...
217b	1¢ Booklet Pane of 6	...	...	22.50	15.00	...
218	2¢ Brown (8)	4.00	3.00	.40	.25	.15
218a	2¢ Booklet Pane of 4	...	...	57.50	37.50	...
218b	2¢ Booklet Pane of 6	...	...	20.00	13.50	...
219	3¢ Dark Carmine (8)	7.50	5.50	.60	.40	.15
219a	3¢ Booklet Pane of 4	...	...	20.00	15.00	...

1935 George V "Bar" Issue & Pictorials VF + 30%

Scott's No.		Plate Blocks NH	Unused	F-VF NH	F-VF Unused	F-VF Used
220	4¢ Yellow (6)	37.50	27.50	2.60	1.60	.35
221	5¢ Blue (6)	37.50	27.50	2.75	1.70	.20
222	8¢ Deep Orange (6)	37.50	27.50	3.25	2.00	1.30
223	10¢ Mounted Police (6)	57.50	42.50	7.75	4.75	.20
224	13¢ Charlottetown Confederation Conference (6)	65.00	47.50	8.25	5.75	.50
225	20¢ Niagara Falls (6)	160.00	120.00	25.00	15.00	.35
226	50¢ Parliament, Victoria (6)	235.00	175.00	28.00	17.00	3.25
227	$1 Champlain Monument (6)	550.00	400.00	85.00	50.00	6.75

1935 George V "Bar" Coil Stamps, Perf. 8 Vertically VF + 30% (B)

228	1¢ George V, Green	...	...	16.50	9.75	1.75
228	1¢ Pair	...	...	34.00	21.00	...
229	2¢ Brown	...	...	15.50	9.00	.60
229	2¢ Pair	...	...	33.00	19.50	...
230	3¢ Dark Carmine	...	...	14.25	8.50	.35
230	3¢ Pair	...	...	29.00	18.50	...

231

237

241

244

1937 King George VI "Mufti" Issue VF + 30% (B)

231-36	**Set of 6**	...	...	**11.00**	**6.50**	**.85**
231	1¢ George VI, Green	2.50	1.85	.40	.25	.15
231a	1¢ Booklet Pane of 4	...	...	12.75	9.00	...
231b	1¢ Booklet Pane of 6	...	...	1.95	1.35	...
232	2¢ Brown	3.00	2.25	.60	.35	.15
232a	2¢ Booklet Pane of 4	...	...	14.00	9.75	...
232b	2¢ Booklet Pane of 6	...	...	7.75	5.25	...
233	3¢ Carmine	3.75	2.75	.85	.50	.15
233a	3¢ Booklet Pane of 6	...	...	2.75	1.85	...
234	4¢ Yellow	19.00	13.50	3.00	1.80	.20
235	5¢ Blue	19.00	13.50	3.50	2.15	.20
236	8¢ Orange	19.00	13.50	3.00	1.80	.30

1937 King George VI Coronation Issue VF + 25% (B)

237	3¢ George VI and Elizabeth	2.25	1.75	.30	.20	.20

1937 King George VI Coil Stamps, Perf. 8 Vertically VF + 30% (B)

238	1¢ George VI, Green	...	...	2.25	1.30	.70
238	1¢ Pair	...	...	5.00	2.95	...
239	2¢ Brown	...	...	3.50	2.10	.25
239	2¢ Pair	...	...	7.50	4.50	...
240	3¢ Carmine	...	...	6.00	3.50	.20
240	3¢ Pair	...	...	12.50	7.50	...

1938 Pictorials VF + 30%

241-45	**Set of 5**	...	...	**120.00**	**72.50**	**7.95**
241	10¢ Memorial Hall	37.50	27.50	6.25	4.25	.20
242	13¢ Halifax Harbor	45.00	32.50	8.00	5.25	.35
243	20¢ Ft. Garry Gate, Winnipeg	95.00	65.00	14.00	8.00	.25
244	50¢ Vancouver Harbor	185.00	135.00	30.00	16.50	3.25
245	$1 Chateau de Ramesay	425.00	275.00	70.00	42.50	4.75

1939 Royal Visit VF + 25%

246

247

248

246-48	**Set of 3**	**3.65**	**2.90**	**.70**	**.50**	**.45**
246	1¢ Princesses Elizabeth & Margaret Rose	1.65	1.35	.30	.20	.20
247	2¢ War Memorial, Ottawa	1.65	1.35	.30	.20	.20
248	3¢ King George VI and Queen Elizabeth	1.65	1.35	.30	.20	.20

1942-43 King George VI War Issue VF +25%

249

250

257

262

1942-43 King George VI War Issue VF +25%

Scott's No.		Plate Blocks NH	Unused	F-VF NH	F-VF Unused	F-VF Used
249-62	Set of 14	...	...	142.00	87.50	11.50
249	1¢ George VI, Green	2.35	1.75	.35	.20	.15
249a	1¢ Booklet Pane of 4	...	...	5.50	3.50	...
249b	1¢ Booklet Pane of 6	...	...	1.50	1.10	...
249c	1¢ Booklet Pane of 3	...	...	1.40	1.00	...
250	2¢ Brown	2.75	2.00	.55	.35	.15
250a	2¢ Booklet Pane of 4 (1943)	...	...	5.75	4.00	...
250b	2¢ Booklet Pane of 6	...	...	5.00	3.50	...
251	3¢ Dark Carmine	3.15	2.25	.50	.30	.15
251a	3¢ Booklet Pane of 4	...	...	1.80	1.25	...
252	3¢ Rose Violet (1943)	2.75	2.00	.50	.30	.15
252a	3¢ Booklet Pane of 4	...	...	1.95	1.35	...
252b	3¢ Booklet Pane of 3	...	...	2.75	1.95	...
252c	3¢ Booklet Pane of 6 (1947)	...	...	2.75	1.95	...
253	4¢ Grain Elevators	9.50	7.00	1.40	.90	.50
254	4¢ George VI. Carmine(1943)	3.00	2.25	.45	.30	.15
254a	4¢ Booklet Pane of 6 (1942)	...	...	2.10	1.50	...
254b	4¢ Booklet Pane of 3 (1943)	...	...	2.50	1.80	...
255	5¢ George VI, Deep Blue ..	8.75	6.50	1.05	.75	.15
256	8¢ Farm Scene	12.50	9.00	1.60	1.00	.35
257	10¢ Parliament Buildings ...	28.50	21.50	4.40	2.75	.20
258	13¢ "Ram" Tank	37.50	27.50	5.50	3.50	2.75
259	14¢ "Ram" Tank (1943)	40.00	30.00	7.75	5.00	.25
260	20¢ Corvette	47.50	35.00	9.00	5.75	.20
261	50¢ Munitions Factory	175.00	120.00	35.00	22.50	1.50
262	$1 Destroyer	375.00	275.00	74.50	47.50	5.50

1942-43 George VI Coil Stamps, Perf. 8 Vertically VF + 25%

263-67	Set of 5	...	...	11.00	7.25	2.15
263	1¢ George VI, Green	...	...	1.10	.70	.35
264	2¢ Brown	...	...	1.65	1.10	.75
265	3¢ Dark Carmine..............	...	...	1.65	1.10	.75
266	3¢ Rose Violet (1943)	...	...	2.75	1.75	.25
267	4¢ Dark Carmine (1943) ...	...	...	4.75	3.00	.20

From 1942 to Date, Unused Coil Pairs are priced at double the single price.

1946 Reconversion "Peace" Issue VF + 25%

	268	272	273

268-73	Set of 6	...	...	68.00	43.50	4.35
268	8¢ Farm Scene	8.00	6.00	1.50	1.00	.45
269	10¢ Great Bear Lake	9.50	7.00	2.00	1.30	.20
270	14¢ Hydroelectric Station .	17.50	12.75	3.50	2.25	.20
271	20¢ Combine	20.00	15.00	4.50	2.75	.20
272	50¢ Logging	95.00	70.00	20.00	13.00	1.35
273	$1 Train Ferry	225.00	165.00	42.00	26.50	2.25

274	275	276	283

1947-48 Commemoratives

Scott's No.		Plate Blocks F-VF, NH	F-VF,NH Unused	F-VF Used
274-77,282-83	Set of 6	...	1.00	.70
274	4¢ Alexander Graham Bell	.85	.25	.15
275	4¢ Citizenship	.85	.25	.15
276	4¢ Royal Wedding,Princess Elizabeth(1948)	.85	.25	.15
277	4¢ Responsible Government, Parliament (1948)	.75	.25	.15

1948 King George VI Coils, Perf. 9½ Vertically (VF+40%)

278-81	Set of 4	...	25.00	10.50
278	1¢ Green	...	3.25	1.40
279	2¢ Brown	...	9.75	5.75
280	3¢ Rose Violet	...	6.25	1.65
281	4¢ Dark Carmine	...	7.00	2.25

1949 Commemoratives

282	4¢ Founding of Newfoundland "Matthew" ...	.95	.25	.15
283	4¢ Halifax Founding 200th Anniversary	.95	.25	.15

284	289	294	302

1949 King George VI with "Postes-Postage" In Design

Scott's No.		Plate Blocks F-VF, NH	F-VF,NH Unused	F-VF Used
284-88	Set of 5	...	3.00	.55
284	1¢ George VI, Green	.85	.25	.15
284a	1¢ Booklet Pane of 3 (1950)	...	.75	...
285	2¢ Sepia	1.40	.30	.15
286	3¢ Rose Violet	1.40	.35	.15
286a	3¢ Booklet Pane of 3 (1950)	...	1.25	...
286b	3¢ Booklet Pane of 4 (1950)	...	1.50	...
287	4¢ Dark Carmine	2.25	.55	.15
287a	4¢ Booklet Pane of 3 (1950)	...	9.50	...
287b	4¢ Booklet Pane of 6 (1950)	...	11.00	...
288	5¢ Deep Blue	5.50	1.20	.15

1950 George VI without "Postes-Postage" In Design

289-93	Set of 5	...	2.85	1.25
289	1¢ George VI, Green	.65	.25	.15
290	2¢ Sepia	2.50	.45	.15
291	3¢ Rose Violet	1.20	.30	.15
292	4¢ Dark Carmine	1.75	.40	.15
293	5¢ Deep Blue	6.75	1.65	.85

1950 Industry Regular Issue

294	50¢ Oil Wells, Alberta	55.00	12.85	1.20

1949-50 King George VI Coil Stamps, Perf. 9½ Vertically

295-300	Set of 6	...	17.50	2.95
	(without "Postes-Postage")			
295	1¢ George VI, Green	...	.70	.30
296	3¢ Rose Violet	...	1.00	.50
	(with "Postes-Postage")			
297	1¢ George VI, Green (1950)	...	.40	.25
298	2¢ Sepia (1950)	...	2.75	1.35
299	3¢ Rose Violet (1950)	...	1.75	.20
300	4¢ Dark Carmine (1950)	...	12.50	.65

1950-1951 Industry Regular Issues

301	10¢ Fur Resources, Drying Skins	4.50	1.05	.20
302	$1 Fishing Resources (1951)	300.00	72.00	10.75

303	311	314	315

1951-52 Commemoratives

303-4,11-15,17-19	Set of 10	...	5.50	2.65
	1951 Commemoratives			
303	3¢ Prime Minister Robert L. Borden	1.40	.30	.15
304	4¢ Prime Minister William L. Mackenzie King	1.50	.30	.15

1951 King George VI Color Changes (with "Postes-Postage")

305	2¢ George VI, Olive Green	.70	.25	.15
306	4¢ Orange Vermilion	1.35	.35	.15
306a	4¢ Booklet Pane of 3	...	2.00	...
306b	4¢ Booklet Pane of 6	...	2.50	...
309	2¢ Olive Green, Coil Perf. 9½ Vertically ...	...	1.55	.60
310	4¢ Orange Vermilion, Coil Pf. 9½ Vertically	...	3.00	.70

1951 "CAPEX" Philatelic Exhibition, Stamp Centennial

311-14	Set of 4	...	4.80	1.95
311	4¢ Trains of 1851 & 1951	2.70	.30	.20
312	5¢ Steamships of 1851 & 1951 ...	9.75	2.15	1.35
313	7¢ Plane & Stagecoach	5.00	1.10	.30
314	15¢ 1st Canada Stamp "Beaver"	6.50	1.20	.30
	1951 Commemoratives (continued)			
315	4¢ Royal Visit to Canada and U.S. of Duchess & Duke of Edinburgh	.95	.25	.15

316	317	320

1952 Industry Regular Issue

316	20¢ Paper Industry, Forestry Products	7.50	1.65	.20

1952 Commemoratives

317	4¢ Red Cross Conference	1.15	.25	.15
318	3¢ Prime Minister John J.C. Abbott	1.00	.25	.15
319	4¢ Prime Minister Alexander Mackenzie	1.25	.30	.15

1952-53 Industry Regular Issues

320	7¢ Canada Goose	1.70	.40	.15
321	$1 Pacific Coast Totem Pole (1953)	50.00	11.00	.80

**FROM 1947 TO PRESENT, ADD 20% FOR VERY FINE QUALITY
UNLESS OTHERWISE NOTED
Minimum of 10¢ per stamp**

322

327

330

334

1953-54 Commemoratives

Scott's No.		Plate Blocks F-VF,NH	F-VF,NH Unused	F-VF Used
322-24,35-36,49-50	**Set of 7**	...	**1.65**	**.95**
	1953 Wildlife Commemoratives			
322-24	2¢-4¢ Wildlife, Set of 3	3.50	.65	.40
322	2¢ Polar Bear	1.10	.25	.15
323	3¢ Moose	1.20	.25	.15
324	4¢ Bighorn Sheep	1.25	.30	.15
	1953 Queen Elizabeth II, Karsh Portrait Issue			
325-29	**Set of 5**	...	**1.05**	**.60**
325	1¢ Elizabeth II, Violet Brown	.50	.25	.15
325a	1¢ Booklet Pane of 3	...	1.50	...
326	2¢ Green	.60	.25	.15
327	3¢ Carmine Rose	.75	.25	.15
327a	3¢ Booklet Pane of 3	...	1.75	...
327b	3¢ Booklet Pane of 4	...	1.50	...
328	4¢ Violet	1.15	.30	.15
328a	4¢ Booklet Pane of 3	...	2.00	...
328b	4¢ Booklet Pane of 6	...	1.60	...
329	5¢ Ultramarine	1.40	.35	.15
	1953 Queen Elizabeth II Coronation Issue			
330	4¢ Elizabeth II, Karsh Portrait	.85	.25	.15
	1953 Queen Elizabeth II Coils, Perf. 9½ Vertically			
331-33	**Set of 4**	...	**6.00**	**3.15**
331	2¢ Elizabeth II, Green	...	1.50	.90
332	3¢ Carmine Rose	...	1.45	.90
333	4¢ Violet	...	3.25	1.40
	1953 Industry Regular Issue			
334	50¢ Textile Industry	19.75	3.85	.20

336

339

349

351

Scott's No.		Plate Blocks F-VF,NH	F-VF,NH Unused	F-VF Used
	1954 Wildlife Commemoratives			
335	4¢ Walrus	1.60	.30	.15
336	5¢ Beaver	1.60	.35	.15
336a	5¢ Booklet Pane of 5	...	2.00	...
	1954 Queen Elizabeth II, Wilding Portrait Issue			
337-43	**Set of 7**	...	**2.65**	**.75**
337-41p	**Set of 5 Tagged Stamps**	...	**9.75**	...
337	1¢ Elizabeth II, Violet Brown	.50	.25	.15
337a	1¢ Booklet Pane of 5 (1956)	...	1.25	...
337p	1¢ Tagged, Wide Side Bars (A) .... (Blank)	6.00	1.20	...
338	2¢ Green	.70	.25	.15
338a	2¢ Miniature Pane of 25 (1961) (Pack of 2)	9.00	4.00	...
338p	2¢ Tagged, Wide Side Bars (A) .... (Blank)	6.00	1.20	...
339	3¢ Carmine Rose	1.00	.25	.15
339p	3¢ Tagged, Wide Side Bars (A) .... (Blank)	6.00	1.20	...
340	4¢ Violet	1.00	.25	.15
340a	4¢ Booklet Pane of 5 (1956)	...	1.60	...
340b	4¢ Booklet Pane of 6 (1955)	...	3.75	...
340p	4¢ Tagged, Wide Bar in Middle (B) ... (Blank)	15.00	3.00	...
341	5¢ Bright Blue	1.10	.25	.15
341a	5¢ Booklet Pane of 5	...	1.30	...
341b	5¢ Miniature Pane of 20 (1961) (Pack of 1)	8.75	7.75	...
341p	5¢ Tagged, Wide Side Bars (A) .... (Blank)	17.50	3.50	...
342	6¢ Orange	1.95	.45	.15
343	15¢ Gannet, Gray	5.25	1.35	.15

"Tagged" Issues Tagging Variations

(A) = Wide Side Bars (B) = Wide Bar in Middle (C) = Bar at Left or Right
(D) = Narrow Bar in Middle (E) = Narrow Side Bars, General Tagging
Plate Block prices are for Blank Corner Blocks of 4.

Scott's No.		Plate Blocks F-VF,NH	F-VF,NH Unused	F-VF Used
	1954 Queen Elizabeth II Coil Stamps, Perf. 9½ Vertically			
345-48	**Set of 3**	...	**4.55**	**.55**
345	2¢ Elizabeth II, Green	...	.55	.20
347	4¢ Violet	...	1.65	.20
348	5¢ Bright Blue	...	2.50	.20
	1954 Commemoratives			
349	4¢ Prime Minister John S.D. Thompson	1.50	.35	.15
350	5¢ Prime Minister Mackenzie Bowell	1.50	.35	.15
	1955 Regular Issue			
351	10¢ Eskimo in Kayak	1.90	.45	.15

352

356

35

360

1955 Commemoratives

Scott's No.		Plate Blocks F-VF,NH	F-VF,NH Unused	F-VF Used
352-58	**Set of 7**	...	**2.20**	**.85**
352	4¢ Wildlife - Musk Ox	1.40	.35	.15
353	5¢ Wildlife - Whooping Cranes	1.50	.35	.15
354	5¢ Civil Aviation Organization (ICAO)	1.65	.40	.15
355	5¢ Alberta - Saskatchewan 50th Annv.	1.65	.40	.15
356	5¢ Boy Scout Jamboree	1.65	.40	.15
357	4¢ Prime Minister Richard B. Bennett	1.50	.35	.15
358	5¢ Prime Minister Charles Tupper	1.50	.35	.15

1956 Commemoratives

Scott's No.		Plate Blocks F-VF,NH	F-VF,NH Unused	F-VF Used
359-61,364	**Set of 4**	...	**1.25**	**.50**
359	5¢ Ice Hockey	1.50	.35	.15
360	4¢ Wildlife - Caribou	1.60	.40	.15
361	5¢ Wildlife - Mountain Goat	1.60	.40	.15

362

364

370

374

Scott's No.		Plate Blocks F-VF,NH	F-VF,NH Unused	F-VF Used
	1956 Industry Regular Issues			
362	20¢ Paper Industry	7.50	1.50	.15
363	25¢ Chemistry Industry	8.50	1.65	.15
	1956 Commemoratives (continued)			
364	5¢ Fire Prevention	1.40	.35	.15

1957 Commemoratives

Scott's No.		Plate Blocks F-VF,NH	F-VF,NH Unused	F-VF Used
365-74	**Set of 10**	...	**5.00**	**2.75**
365-68	5¢ Outdoor Recreation, attd	2.25	1.75	1.25
365-68	Set of 4 Singles	...	1.65	.80
369	5¢ Wildlife - Loon	1.50	.35	.15
370	5¢ David Thompson	1.50	.35	.15
371	5¢ U.P.U. - Parliament	1.50	.35	.15
372	15¢ U.P.U. - Post Horn	9.50	2.20	1.50
373	5¢ Mining Industry	1.25	.30	.15
374	5¢ Royal Visit	1.25	.30	.15

1958 Commemoratives

376

378

380

382

Scott's No.		Plate Blocks F-VF,NH	F-VF,NH Unused	F-VF Used
375-82	**Set of 8**	...	**2.35**	**1.00**
375	5¢ Newspaper Industry .... (Blank)	2.75	.35	.15
376	5¢ Int'l. Geophysical Year .... (Blank)	2.75	.35	.15
377	5¢ British Columbia Cent. and Miner	2.50	.35	.15
378	5¢ Sieur de la Verendrye,Explorer	1.95	.35	.15
379	5¢ Quebec Founding 350th Anniversary	4.50	.35	.15
380	5¢ National Health, Nurse	1.80	.35	.15
381	5¢ Petroleum Industry	1.80	.35	.15
382	5¢ 1st Elected Assembly 200th Anniv.	1.60	.35	.15

1959 Commemoratives

383

385

388

Scott's No.		Plate Blocks F-VF,NH	F-VF,NH Unused	F-VF Used
383-88	**Set of 6**	...	**1.75**	**.75**
383	5¢ First Flight in Canada 50th Anniv.	1.95	.35	.15
384	5¢ N.A.T.O.50th Anniversary	1.80	.35	.15
385	5¢ Country Women of the World	1.60	.35	.15
386	5¢ Royal Visit of Queen Elizabeth II	1.60	.35	.15
387	5¢ St. Lawrence Seaway Opening	4.25	.35	.15
388	5¢ Battle of Plains of Abraham 200th An.	1.60	.35	.15

1960-1961 Commemoratives

390

391

393

395

1960-61 Commemoratives

Scott's No.		Plate Blocks F-VF,NH	F-VF,NH Unused	F-VF Used
389-95	**Set of 7**	...	**2.00**	**.85**
389	5¢ Girl Guides Association 50th Anniv.	1.60	.35	.15
390	5¢ Battle of Long Sault 300th Anniv.	1.60	.35	.15
391	5¢ Northern Development (1961)	1.60	.35	.15
392	5¢ E. Pauline Johnson, Poetess (1961)	1.60	.35	.15
393	5¢ Prime Minister Arthur Meighen (1961)	1.60	.35	.15
394	5¢ Colombo Plan 10th Anniv.(1961)	1.60	.35	.15
395	5¢ Resources for Tomorrow (1961)	1.60	.35	.15

396

398

400

402

1962 Commemoratives

Scott's No.		Plate Blocks F-VF,NH	F-VF,NH Unused	F-VF Used
396-400	**Set of 5**	...	**1.40**	**.65**
396	5¢ Education. Students	1.60	.30	.15
397	5¢ Red River Settlement, Lord Selkirk	1.60	.30	.15
398	5¢ Jean Talon & Colonists	1.60	.30	.15
399	5¢ Victoria B.C. Centenary	1.60	.30	.15
400	5¢ Trans-Canada Highway	1.60	.30	.15

1962-63 Queen Elizabeth "Cameo" Issue

Scott's No.		Plate Blocks F-VF,NH	F-VF,NH Unused	F-VF Used
401-5	**Set of 5**	...	**.90**	**.60**
401-5	**Set of 5 Tagged Stamps**	...	**1.80**	...
401	1¢ Deep Brown (1963)	.50	.20	.15
401a	1¢ Booklet Pane of 5	...	3.25	...
401p	1¢ Tagged, Wide Side Bars (A) (Blank)	.60	.20	...
402	2¢ Green (1963)	2.95	.20	.15
402a	2¢ Miniature Pane of 25 (Pack of 2)	15.00	7.50	...
402p	2¢ Tagged, Wide Side Bars (A) (Blank)	2.75	.20	...
403	3¢ Purple (1963)	.70	.20	.15
403p	3¢ Tagged, Wide Side Bars (A) (Blank)	1.25	.25	...
404	4¢ Carmine (1963)	1.00	.20	.15
404a	4¢ Booklet Pane of 5	...	3.25	...
404b	4¢ Miniature Pane of 25 (Pack of 1)	11.75	10.75	...
404p	4¢ Tagged, Bar at Left or Right (C)	...	.75	...
404pa	4¢ Tagged, Narrow Bar in Middle (D) (Blank)	5.00	.75	...
404pb	4¢ Tagged, Wide Bar in Middle (B) ... (Blank)	18.75	3.75	...
405	5¢ Violet Blue	1.20	.20	.15
405a	5¢ Booklet Pane of 5	...	3.75	...
405b	5¢ Miniature Pane of 20 (Pack of 1)	13.75	12.75	...
405p	5¢ Tagged, Wide Side Bars (A) (Blank)	2.25	.50	...
405q	5¢ Tagged, Miniature Pane of 20 (Pack of 1)	50.00	45.00	...

1962-63 Queen Elizabeth II Coil Stamps, Perf. 9½ Horizontally (VF+40%)

Scott's No.		Plate Blocks F-VF,NH	F-VF,NH Unused	F-VF Used
406-9	**Set of 4**	...	**13.00**	**5.00**
406	2¢ Elizabeth, Green (1963)	...	3.25	1.75
407	3¢ Purple (1963)	...	2.75	1.35
408	4¢ Carmine (1963)	...	3.75	1.70
409	5¢ Violet Blue	...	3.75	.60

410

411

412

1963 Commemoratives

Scott's No.		Plate Blocks F-VF,NH	F-VF,NH Unused	F-VF Used
410,412-13	**Set of 3**	...	**.75**	**.35**
410	5¢ Sir Casimir S. Gzowski	1.30	.25	.15
	1963 Regular Issues			
411	$1 Export Trade, Crate & Map	65.00	11.75	2.00
	1963 Commemoratives (continued)			
412	5¢ Martin Frobisher,Explorer	1.30	.25	.15
413	5¢ First Post Route, Postrider	1.30	.25	.15
	1963-1964 Regular Issues			
414	7¢ Jet at Ottawa Airport (1964)	1.95	.40	.40
415	15¢ Canada Geese (1963)	8.75	1.85	.20

1964 Commemoratives

Scott's No.		Plate Blocks F-VF,NH	F-VF,NH Unused	F-VF Used
416,431-35	**Set of 6**	...	**1.45**	**.75**
416	5¢ "Peace on Earth" & Globe	1.30	.25	.15

418

431

433

CANADA

1964-1966 Coat of Arms & Flowers

Scott's No.		Plate Blocks F-VF,NH	F-VF,NH Unused	F-VF Used
417-29A	**Set of 14**	**16.75**	**3.15**	**2.40**
417	5¢ Canadian Unity, Maple Leaf	1.20	.25	.20
418	5¢ Ontario, White Trillium	1.20	.25	.20
419	5¢ Quebec, White Garden Lily	1.20	.25	.20
420	5¢ Nova Scotia, Mayflower/1965	1.20	.25	.20
421	5¢ New Brunswick, Purple Violet (1965)	1.20	.25	.20
422	5¢ Manitoba, Prairie Crocus (1965)	2.00	.25	.20
423	5¢ British Columbia, Dogwood (1965)	1.20	.25	.20
424	5¢ Pr. Edward I., Lady's Slipper (1965)	1.20	.25	.20
425	5¢ Saskatchewan, Prairie Lily (1966)	1.20	.25	.20
426	5¢ Alberta, Wild Rose (1966)	1.20	.25	.20
427	5¢ Newfoundland, Pitcher Plant (1966)	2.00	.25	.20
428	5¢ Yukon, Firewood (1966)	1.20	.25	.20
429	5¢ Northwest Terr., Mountain Avens (1966)	1.20	.25	.20
429A	5¢ Canada, Maple Leaf (1966)	1.20	.25	.20
	1964 Regular Issue			
430	8¢ on 7¢ Jet Aircraft (on #414) (Blank)	1.65	.35	.30
	1964 Commemoratives (continued)			
431	5¢ Charlottetown Conference Centennial	1.15	.25	.15
432	5¢ Quebec Conference Centennial	1.15	.25	.15
433	5¢ Queen Elizabeth Royal Visit	1.15	.25	.15
434	3¢ Christmas, Family & Star	.85	.25	.15
434a	3¢ Miniature Pane of 25 (Pack of 2)	17.00	8.00	...
434p	3¢ Tagged, Wide Side Bars (A) (Blank)	3.75	.75	...
434q	3¢ Tagged, Miniature Pane of 25 (Pack of 2)	23.00	11.00	...
435	5¢ Christmas, Family & Star	1.15	.25	.15
435p	5¢ Tagged, Wide Side Bars (A) (Blank)	8.50	1.10	...
	1964 Regular Issue			
436	8¢ Jet at Ottawa Airport	1.75	.35	.20

1965 Commemoratives

438

440

441

443

Scott's No.		Plate Blocks F-VF,NH	F-VF,NH Unused	F-VF Used
437-44	**Set of 8**	...	**1.65**	**1.00**
437	5¢ International Cooperation Year	1.00	.25	.15
438	5¢ Wilfred Grenfell, Author	1.00	.25	.15
439	5¢ National Flag	1.00	.25	.15
440	5¢ Winston Churchill	1.00	.25	.15
441	5¢ Inter Parliamentary Union, Ottawa	1.00	.25	.15
442	5¢ Ottawa as Capital Centennial	1.00	.25	.15
443	3¢ Christmas, Gifts of Wise Men	.80	.25	.15
443a	3¢ Miniature Pane of 25 (Pack of 2)	14.00	6.50	...
443p	3¢ Tagged, Wide Side Bars (A) (Blank)	1.35	.25	...
443q	3¢ Tagged, Miniature Pane of 25 (Pack of 2)	19.50	9.00	...
444	5¢ Christmas, Gifts of Wise Men	1.25	.25	.15
444p	5¢ Tagged, Wide Side Bars (A) (Blank)	1.75	.35	...

1966 Commemoratives

445

448

450

451

Scott's No.		Plate Blocks F-VF,NH	F-VF,NH Unused	F-VF Used
445-52	**Set of 8**	...	**1.60**	**1.00**
445	5¢ Satellite Alouette II	1.00	.25	.15
446	5¢ Sieur de laSalle Arrival 300th Anniv.	1.00	.25	.15
447	5¢ Highway Safety, Traffic Signs	1.00	.25	.15
448	5¢ London Conference Centenary	1.00	.25	.15
449	5¢ Atomic Energy, Reactor	1.00	.25	.15
450	5¢ Parliamentary Association	1.00	.25	.15
451	3¢ Christmas, Praying Hands	.70	.25	.15
451a	3¢ Miniature Pane of 25 (Pack of 2)	8.00	3.75	...
451p	3¢ Tagged, Wide Side Bars (A) (Blank)	1.35	.25	...
451q	3¢ Tagged, Miniature Pane of 25 (Pack of 2)	10.50	5.00	...
452	5¢ Christmas, Praying Hands	1.00	.25	.15
452p	5¢ Tagged, Wide Side Bars (A) (Blank)	2.25	.45	...

1967 Commemoratives

Scott's No.		Plate Blocks F-VF,NH	F-VF,NH Unused	F-VF Used
453,469-77	**Set of 10**	...	**1.90**	**1.30**
453	5¢ Canadian Confederation Centenary	1.00	.25	.15
453p	5¢ Tagged, Wide Side Bars (A) (Blank)	2.75	.40	...

1967-73 Queen Elizabeth & Centennial Regular Issue, Perforated 12

459,460

465A

465B

1967-73 Queen Elizabeth II Centennial Regular Issue, Perforated 12

Scott's No.		Plate Block F-VF,NH	F-VF,NH Unused	F-VF Used
454-65B	**Set of 14**	**...**	**14.10**	**2.50**
	#454-60h Queen Elizabeth II & Views			
454	1¢ Northern Lights, Brown	.70	.25	.15
454a	1¢ Booklet Pane of 5	...	.95	...
454d	1¢ Booklet Single, Perf. 10 (1968)	...	.25	.20
454b	1¢ Bklt. Pane of 5 (1 #454d & 4 #459), Perf. 10	...	3.00	...
454c	1¢ Bklt. Pane of 10 (5 #454d & 5 #457d) Perf.10	...	1.95	...
454e	1¢ Booklet Single, Perf. 12½ x 12 (1969)	...	.50	.20
454p	1¢ Tagged, Wide Side Bars (A) .... (Blank)	1.35	.25	...
454pa	1¢ Tagged, Wide Bar in Middle(B) ... (Blank)	1.75	.25	...
454pb	1¢ Tagged, Narrow Side Bars (E) .... (Blank)	1.00	.20	...
454ep	1¢ Tagged, Booklet Single, Perf.12½x12 (E)	...	.40	...
455	2¢ Totem Pole, Green	.75	.25	.15
455a	2¢ Booklet Pane of 8 (4 #455, 4 #456)	...	1.75	...
455p	2¢ Tagged, Wide Side Bars (A) .... (Blank)	2.00	.25	...
455pa	2¢ Tagged, Wide Bar in Middle(B) ... (Blank)	1.40	.25	...
455pb	2¢ Tagged, Narrow Side Bars (E) .... (Blank)	1.00	.20	...
456	3¢ Combine & Prairie, Purple	1.50	.25	.15
456a	3¢ Booklet Single, Perf. 12½ x 12 (1971)	...	2.75	1.25
456p	3¢ Tagged, Wide Side Bars (A) .... (Blank)	2.00	.25	...
456pa	3¢ Tagged, (E) Precancelled .... (Blank)	45.00	2.00	...
457	4¢ Seaway Lock, Carmine	1.50	.25	.15
457a	4¢ Booklet Pane of 5	...	1.40	...
457b	4¢ Miniature Pane of 25 (Pack of 1)	26.50	25.00	...
457d	4¢ Booklet Single, Perf. 10(1968)	...	.70	.25
457c	4¢ Booklet Pane of 25, Perf. 10 (1968)	...	8.00	...
457p	4¢ Tagged, Bar at Left or Right(C) (Blank)	3.50	.55	...
457pa	4¢ Tagged, Wide Bar in Middle (B) (Blank)	2.50	.45	...
457pb	4¢ Tagged, Narrow Side Bars (E) .... (Blank)	1.50	.25	...
458	5¢ Fishing Port, Blue	1.25	.20	.15
458a	5¢ Booklet Pane of 5	...	6.25	...
458b	5¢ Miniature Pane of 20 (Pack of 1)	35.00	32.50	...
458d	5¢ Booklet Single, Perf. 10 (1968)	...	.65	.25
458c	5¢ Booklet Pane of 20, Perf. 10 (1968)	...	8.25	...
458p	5¢ Tagged, Wide Side Bars (A) .... (Blank)	3.50	.60	...
458bp	5¢ Tagged, Miniature Pane of 20 (A) (Pack of 1)	62.50	57.50	...
458pa	5¢ Tagged, Wide Bar in Middle(B) ... (Blank)	3.25	.45	...
459	6¢ Transportation, Orange, Perf. 10 (1968)	3.50	.30	.15
459a	6¢ Booklet Pane of 25, Perf. 10 (1968)	...	8.75	...
459b	6¢ Orange, Perf. 12½ x 12 (1968)	2.75	.30	.15
459p	6¢ Tagged, Orange, Perf.10 (A) ...... (Blank)	3.75	.65	...
459bp	6¢ Tagged, Orange, Pf.12½x12(A) (Blank)	3.75	.65	...
460	6¢ Black, Die I, Perf. 12½ x 12 (1970)	1.75	.20	.15
460b	6¢ Die I, Booklet Pane of 25, Perf. 12½x12	...	17.50	...
460g	6¢ Black, Die I, Booklet Single, Perf. 10 (1970)	...	1.60	.35
460a	6¢ Die I, Booklet Pane of 25, Perf. 10	...	12.50	...
460f	6¢ Black, Die I, Perforated 12 (1973)	2.50	.45	.40
460p	6¢ Tagged, Black, Die I, Perforated 12½x12 (A) .... (Blank)	4.75	.35	...
460fp	6¢ Tagged, Black, Die I (B) .... (Blank)	2.50	.30	...
460fpa	6¢ Tagged, Black, Die I (E) .... (Blank)	3.25	.60	...
460c	6¢ Black, Die II. Perf. 12½ x 12 (1970)	2.25	.30	.20
460d	6¢ Die II, Booklet Pane of 4, Perf. 12½ x 12...	3.75	...	
460h	6¢ Die II, Booklet Single, Perf. 10 (1970)	...	2.50	1.25
460e	6¢ Die II, Booklet Pane of 4, Perf. 10	...	11.75	...
460cp	6¢ Tagged, Black, Die II, Perforated 12½x12 (B) .... (Blank)	5.75	.75	...
460cpa	6¢ Tagged, Black, Die II, Booklet Single (E)	...	5.50	...
	#460, 460f Die I has weak shading lines around "6" #460c Die II has lines strengthened.			
461	8¢ "Alaska Highway" by A.Y.Jackson	3.50	.30	.20
462	10¢ "The Jack Pine" by Tom Thomson	1.85	.30	.20
462p	10¢ Tagged, Wide Side Bars (A) ..... (Blank)	5.50	1.00	...
462pa	10¢ Tagged, Narrow Side Bars(E) ... (Blank)	3.75	.75	...
463	15¢ "Bylot Island" by Lawren Harris	3.00	.45	.20
463p	15¢ Tagged, Wide Side Bars (A) ..... (Blank)	5.50	1.00	...
463pa	15¢ Tagged, Narrow Side Bars(E) ... (Blank)	4.25	1.00	...
464	20¢ "The Ferry, Quebec" by J.W.Maurice	3.25	.60	.20
464p	20¢ Tagged, Wide Side Bars (A) ..... (Blank)	7.50	1.50	...
465	25¢ "The Solemn Land" by J.E.H. MacDonald	5.75	1.10	.20
465p	25¢ Tagged, Wide Side Bars (A) ..... (Blank)	35.00	6.50	...
465A	50¢ "Summer's Stores" by John Ensor	16.50	3.75	.20
465B	$1 "Oilfield, Edmonton" by H.G.Glyde	32.50	7.00	.65

"Tagged" Issues Tagging Variations

(A) = Wide Side Bars (B) = Wide Bar in Middle (C) = Bar at Left or Right
(D) = Narrow Bar in Middle (E) = Narrow Side Bars, General Tagging
Plate Block prices are for Blank Corner Blocks of 4.

1967-70 Coil Stamps, Perf. 9½ or 10 Horiz.

Scott's No.		Plate Block F-VF,NH	F-VF,NH Unused	F-VF Used
466-68B	**Set of 5**	**...**	**5.50**	**2.65**
466	3¢ Elizabeth & Prairie	...	2.00	1.10
467	4¢ Elizabeth & Seaway Lock	...	1.00	.60
468	5¢ Elizabeth & Fishing Port	...	2.10	.80
468A	6¢ Elizabeth, Orange (1969)	...	.40	.15
468B	6¢ Elizabeth, Black, Die II (1970)	...	.40	.15

1967 Commemoratives (See also #453)

469

471

473

1967 Commemoratives (continued)

Scott's No.		Plate Block F-VF,NH	F-VF,NH Unused	F-VF Used
469	5¢ Expo '67, Montreal Worlds Fair	1.00	.25	.15
470	5¢ Women's Suffrage 50th Anniversary	1.00	.25	.15
471	5¢ Royal Visit, Elizabeth II	1.00	.25	.15
472	5¢ Pan American Games, Winnipeg	1.00	.25	.15
473	5¢ Canadian Press 50th Anniversary	1.00	.25	.15
474	5¢ Georges P. Vanier, Governor-General	1.20	.25	.15
475	5¢ Toronto as Ontario Capital Centennial	1.00	.25	.15
476	3¢ Christmas, Singing Children	.80	.25	.15
476a	3¢ Miniature Pane of 25 .... (Pack of 2)	7.00	3.25	...
476p	3¢ Tagged, Wide Side Bars (A) .... (Blank)	1.25	.25	...
476q	3¢ Tagged, Miniature Pane of 25 (Pack of 2)	9.50	4.50	...
477	5¢ Christmas, Singing Children	.85	.25	.15
477p	5¢ Tagged, Wide Side Bars (A) .... (Blank)	1.50	.30	...

1968 Commemoratives

479

485

486

488

Scott's No.		Plate Block F-VF,NH	F-VF,NH Unused	F-VF Used
478-89	**Set of 12**	**...**	**4.30**	**2.50**
478	5¢ Wildlife - Gray Jays	3.75	.45	.20
479	5¢ Meteorological Readings	1.00	.25	.15
480	5¢ Wildlife - Narwhal	1.00	.25	.15
481	5¢ Hydrological Decade, Rain Gauge	1.00	.25	.15
482	5¢ Voyage of "Nonsuch" 300th Anniv.	1.25	.25	.20
483	5¢ Lacrosse Players	1.25	.25	.20
484	5¢ George Brown, Journalist and Politician, and "Globe"	1.25	.25	.20
485	5¢ Henry Bourassa - Journalist	1.15	.25	.15
486	15¢ World War I Armistice 50th Anniv.	9.00	1.85	1.20
487	5¢ John McCrae, Poet	1.15	.25	.15
488	5¢ Christmas - Eskimo Carving	.85	.25	.15
488a	5¢ Booklet Pane of 10	...	3.25	...
488p	5¢ Tagged, Wide Bar in Middle (B) .. (Blank)	1.25	.25	...
488q	5¢ Tagged, Booklet Pane of 10 (B)	...	3.75	...
489	6¢ Christmas - Mother & Infant	1.00	.25	.15
489p	6¢ Tagged, Wide Side Bars (A) .... (Blank)	1.50	.30	...

1969 Commemoratives

493

496

498

Scott's No.		Plate Block F-VF,NH	F-VF,NH Unused	F-VF Used
490-504	**Set of 15**	**...**	**10.50**	**6.85**
490	6¢ Sports - Curling	1.00	.25	.15
491	6¢ Vincent Massey, Governor-General	1.00	.25	.15
492	50¢ Aurele de Fey Suzor-Cote "Return from the Harvest Field"	16.00	3.40	2.25
493	6¢ Int'l. Labor Organization 50th Anniv.	1.25	.25	.15
494	15¢ Non-Stop Atlantic Flight	8.75	1.95	1.50
495	6¢ William Osler, Physician	1.25	.25	.15
496-98	6¢-25¢ Canadian Birds, Set of 3	13.00	2.85	2.10
496	6¢ White-Throated Sparrow	1.65	.35	.20
497	10¢ Ipswich Sparrow	3.25	.75	.45
498	25¢ Hermit Thrush	8.50	1.90	1.50
499	6¢ Charlottetown, P.E.I. Bicentennial	1.25	.25	.15
500	6¢ Canada Games	1.00	.25	.15
501	6¢ Isaac Brock, Military Leader	1.00	.25	.15
502	5¢ Christmas, Children Praying	.85	.25	.15
502a	5¢ Booklet Pane of 10	...	3.50	...
502p	5¢ Tagged, Wide Bar in Middle (B) .. (Blank)	1.50	.25	...
502q	5¢ Tagged, Booklet Pane of 10 (B)	...	3.95	...
503	6¢ Christmas, Children Praying	.85	.25	.15
503p	6¢ Tagged, Wide Side Bars (A) .... (Blank)	1.60	.30	...
504	6¢ Stephen Leacock, Humorist	1.25	.25	.15

NOTE: STARTING IN 1967, MANY PLATE BLOCKS HAVE IMPRINTS WITHOUT PLATE NUMBERS.

1970 Commemoratives

505

507

513

CANADA

1970 Commemoratives (continued)

Scott's No.		Plate Block F-VF,NH	F-VF,NH Unused	F-VF Used
505-18,531	Set of 15	...	12.25	9.75
505	6¢ Manitoba Provincial Centenary	.95	.25	.15
505p	6¢ Tagged, Wide Side Bars (A) .... (Blank)	1.75	.35	...
506	6¢ Northwest Territories Centennial	.90	.25	.15
507	6¢ Biological Program	1.15	.25	.15
508-11	25¢ Expo '70, Osaka, Japan, Block of 4 ...	10.00	9.00	8.50
508-11	25¢ Set of 4 Singles	...	8.00	8.00
508-11p	25¢ Tagged, Expo'70, Block of 4 (A)(Blank)	13.75	11.75	...
512	6¢ Henry Kelsey - Western Explorer	1.15	.25	.15
513	10¢ United Nations 25th Anniversary	3.35	.75	.60
513p	10¢ Tagged, Wide Side Bars (A) ... (Blank)	4.75	.95	...
514	15¢ United Nations 25th Anniversary	4.75	1.10	.70
514p	15¢ Tagged, Wide Side Bars (A) ..... (Blank)	9.75	1.50	...
515	6¢ Louis Riel, Metis Leader	1.15	.25	.15
516	6¢ Alexander Mackenzie - Explorer	.90	.25	.15
517	6¢ Oliver Mowat, Early Leader	1.15	.25	.15
518	6¢ Group of Seven, Artists, 50th Anniv. ...	.95	.25	.15

Note: Prices are for stamps without straight edges. Deduct 50% for straight edges.

529	530	531

1970 Christmas - Children's Designs

519-30	Set of 12 Singles	...	4.75	2.75
519-30p	Set of 12 Tagged Singles		5.25	...
519-23	5¢ Christmas, Strip of 5 .... (10)	6.75	2.75	2.50
519-23	5¢ Set of 5 Singles		1.50	.90
519-23p	5¢ Tagged, Strip of 5 (B) (Blank) (10)	9.00	3.75	...
519-23p	5¢ Tagged, Set of 5 Singles		1.75	...
524-28	6¢ Christmas, Strip of 5 .... (10)	8.00	3.25	2.75
524-28	6¢ Set of 5 Singles		1.95	.90
524-28p	6¢ Tagged, Strip of 5 (B) (Blank) (10)	11.00	4.50	...
524-28p	6¢ Tagged, Set of 5 Singles		2.25	...
529	10¢ Christ Child in Manger	1.95	.40	.30
529p	10¢ Tagged, Wide Bar in Middle (B)(Blank)	2.75	.60	...
530	15¢ Snowmobile & Trees	4.50	.90	.85
530p	15¢ Tagged, Wide Bar in Middle (B)(Blank)	5.25	1.00	...

1970 Commemoratives (continued)

531	6¢ Donald Alexander Smith, Railroads	.95	.20	.15

1971 Commemoratives

532	533	535	539

532-42,552-58	Set of 18	...	6.15	4.15
532	6¢ Emily Carr, Painter & Writer	.95	.25	.15
533	6¢ Discovery of Insulin	.95	.25	.15
534	6¢ Ernest Rutherford, Nuclear Physicist ...	.95	.25	.15
535-38	Maple Leaves in Four Seasons, Set of 4	5.00	1.15	.70
535	6¢ Spring	1.40	.30	.20
536	6¢ Summer	1.40	.30	.20
537	7¢ Autumn	1.40	.30	.20
538	7¢ Winter	1.40	.30	.20
539	6¢ Louis Papineau, Political Reformist	.95	.25	.15
540	6¢ Samuel Hearne, Explorer	.95	.25	.15
541	15¢ Radio Canada International	8.50	1.80	1.10
541p	15¢ Tagged, Wide Side Bars (A) ... (Blank)	13.50	2.75	...
542	6¢ Census Centennial	.95	.25	.15

1971-72 Queen Elizabeth II Regular Issue, Perf.12½x12

543	7¢ Transportation, Green	3.00	.30	.15
543a	Booklet Pane of 5 (1 #454a,1 #456a ,3 #543)	...	4.75	...
543b	Booklet Pane of 20 (4 #454e,4 #456a,12 #543)	...	9.00	...
543p	7¢ Tagged, Wide Side Bars (A) ..... (Blank)	3.75	.60	...
544	8¢ Parliament, Slate	2.50	.25	.15
544a	Booklet Pane of 6 (3 #454e,1 #460c,2 #544)	...	2.00	...
544b	Booklet Pane of 18 (6 #454e,1 #460c,11 #544)	...	6.75	...
544c	Booklet Pane of 10 (4 #454e,1 #460c,5 #544) (1972)	...	1.85	...
544p	8¢ Tagged, Wide Side Bars (A) ..... (Blank)	3.00	.35	...
544pa	8¢ Tagged, Narrow Side Bars (E) .. (Blank)	2.00	.30	...
544q	Tagged, Bklt.Pane of 6 (3 #454pb,1#460cpa,1#544pa)	1.75	...	...
544r	Tagged, Bklt.Pane of 18(6#454pb,1#460cpa,11#544pa)	5.75	...	...
544s	Tagged,Bklt.Pane of 10(4#454pb,1#460cpa,5#544pa)	2.50	...	...
549	7¢ Emerald Green, Coil, Perf. 10 Horiz ...	...	.35	.15
550	8¢ Slate, Coil, Perf. 10 Horiz	...	.35	.15
550p	8¢ Tagged, Coil, Narrow Side Bars (E)		.35	...

From 1942 to Date, Unused Coil Pairs are priced at double the single price.

CANADA

552	556	561

1971 Commemoratives (continued)

Scott's No.		Plate Block	F-VF NH	F-VF Used
552	7¢ British Columbia Centenary	.95	.25	.15
553	7¢ Paul Kane, Painter "Indian Encampment on Lake Huron"	2.50	.35	.20
554-57	6¢-15¢ Christmas, Set of 4 Singles	6.50	1.40	1.20
554	6¢ Snowflake	.95	.25	.15
554p	6¢ Tagged, Wide Bar in Middle (B) (Blank)	1.25	.25	...
555	7¢ Snowflake	1.00	.25	.15
555p	7¢ Tagged, Wide Side Bars (A) ..... (Blank)	1.75	.35	...
556	10¢ Snowflake	1.70	.35	.30
556p	10¢ Tagged, Wide Side Bars (A) ... (Blank)	2.50	.50	...
557	15¢ Snowflake	3.25	.70	.65
557p	15¢ Tagged, Wide Side Bars (A) ... (Blank)	4.75	.95	...
558	7¢ Pierre Laporte, Quebec Minister	2.25	.25	.15

1972 Commemoratives

559-61,582-85,606-10	Set of 12	...	10.45	8.75
559	8¢ Figure Skating Champs, Calgary	1.15	.25	.15
560	8¢ World Health Day	1.40	.30	.15
560p	8¢ Tagged, Narrow Side Bars (E) ... (Blank)	3.00	.60	...
561	8¢ Frontenac, Governor of New France ...	1.15	.25	.15
561p	8¢ Tagged, Narrow Side Bars (E).....(Blank)	4.25	.85	...

1972-76 Canadian Indians

564-65	568-69

1972 Indians of the Plains

562-63	8¢ Plains Indians, Pair	1.80	.80	.50
562-63	8¢ Set of 2 Singles, Horizontal Design	...	.70	.30
562-63p	8¢ Tagged (E), Pair .... (Blank)	2.50	1.25	...
564-65	8¢ Plains Indians, Pair	1.80	.80	.50
564-65	8¢ Set of 2 Singles, Vertical Design	...	.70	.30
564-65p	8¢ Tagged (E), Pair .... (Blank)	2.50	1.25	...

1973 Algonkian Indians

566-67	8¢ Algonkians, Pair	1.80	.80	.60
566-67	8¢ Set of 2 Singles, Horizontal Design	...	.70	.30
568-69	8¢ Algonkians, Pair	1.65	.70	.60
568-69	8¢ Set of 2 Singles, Vertical Design	...	.60	.30

1974 Pacific Coast Indians

570-71	8¢ Pacific Indians, Pair	1.50	.65	.55
570-71	8¢ Set of 2 Singles, Horizontal Design	...	.55	.30
572-73	8¢ Pacific Indians, Pair	1.50	.65	.55
572-73	8¢ Set of 2 Singles, Vertical Design	...	.55	.30

576-77	580-81

1975 Subarctic Indians

574-75	8¢ Subarctic, Pair	1.20	.55	.45
574-75	8¢ Set of 2 Singles, Horizontal Design	...	.45	.30
576-77	8¢ Subarctic, Pair	1.20	.55	.45
576-77	8¢ Set of 2 Singles, Vertical Design	...	.45	.30

1976 Iroquoian Indians

578-79	10¢ Iroquoian, Pair	1.20	.55	.45
578-79	10¢ Set of 2 Singles, Horizontal Design ...	...	.45	.30
580-81	10¢ Iroquoian, Pair	1.20	.55	.45
580-81	10¢ Set of 2 Singles, Vertical Design	...	.45	.30
562-81	Canadian Indians, set of 20	...	6.00	2.65

1972 Earth Sciences

582-85	15¢ Sciences, Block of 4		8.40	7.75
582-85	15¢ Sheet of 16	...	33.50	...
582-85	15¢ Set of 4 Singles		7.50	7.25
582-85p	15¢ Tagged (E), Block of 4 .... (Blank)	13.75	11.00	...
582-85p	15¢ Tagged, Sheet of 16	...	45.00	...

CANADA

1972-1977 Regular Issue, Line Drawings, Perf. 12 x 12½ or 12½ x 12

| 586 | 591 | 593 | 599 |

Scott's No.		Plate Block F-VF,NH	F-VF,NH Unused	F-VF Used
586-601	Set of 17	...	17.00	5.95
	#586-92 Famous People			
586	1¢ John A. Macdonald	.50	.25	.15
586a	B. Pane of 6 (3 #586,1 #591,2 #593) (1974)...		1.20	...
586b	B. Pane of 18 (6 #586,1 #591,11 #593)(1975)	...	1.85	...
586c	B. Pane of 10 (2 #586,4 #587,4 #593Ac)(1976)	...	1.40	...
587	2¢ Wilfred Laurier (1973)	.50	.25	.15
588	3¢ Robert L. Borden (1973)	.50	.25	.15
589	4¢ William L. Mackenzie King (1973)	.60	.25	.15
590	5¢ Richard B. Bennett (1973)	.80	.25	.15
591	6¢ Lester B. Pearson (1973)	.80	.25	.15
592	7¢ Louis St. Laurent (1974)	.90	.25	.15
593	8¢ Queen Elizabeth II, Perf. 12 x 12½ (1973)	1.00	.20	.15
593b	8¢ Queen Elizabeth II, Perf. 13 x 13½ (1976)	4.95	.95	.50
593A	10¢ Queen Elizabeth II, Perf. 13 x 13½ (1976)	1.20	.30	.15
593Ac	10¢ Booklet Single, Perf. 12 x 12½ (1976) .	...	.45	.25
	#594-601 Scenic Pictorials			
594	10¢ Forests, Tagged, Narrow Side Bars (E)	1.40	.30	.15
594p	10¢ Tagged, Wide Side Bars (A) ..... (Blank)	5.50	1.10	...
594a	10¢ Redrawn, Perf. 13½ (1976)	1.50	.30	.15
595	15¢ Mountain Sheep, Tagged, Narrow Side Bars(E)	1.60	.35	.15
595p	15¢ Tagged, Wide Side Bars (A) ..... (Blank)	7.00	1.35	...
595a	15¢ Redrawn, Perf. 13½ (1976)	3.50	.50	.15
596	20¢ Prairie Mosaic, Tagged, Narrow Side Bars (E)	2.10	.45	.15
596p	20¢ Tagged, Wide Side Bars (A) ..... (Blank)	8.75	1.75	...
596a	20¢ Redrawn, Perf. 13½ (1976)	2.40	.50	.15
597	25¢ Polar Bears, Tagged, Narrow Side Bars (E)	2.70	.55	.15
597p	25¢ Tagged, Wide Side Bars (A) ..... (Blank)	9.00	1.95	...
597a	25¢ Redrawn, Perf. 13½ (1976)	3.00	.65	.15
598	50¢ Seashore	5.00	1.20	.15
598a	50¢ Redrawn, Perf. 13½ (1976)	8.00	1.70	.20
599	$1 Vancouver, Revised (1973)	13.50	2.75	.50
599a	$1 Redrawn, Perf. 13½ (1977)	12.50	2.65	.35
600	$1 Vancouver, Original, Perf. 11	25.00	5.50	1.75
601	$2 Quebec Buildings, Perf. 11	21.00	5.00	2.50
604	8¢ Elizabeth II, Coil, Perf. 10 Vert (1974) .	...	.25	.15
605	10¢ Elizabeth II, Coil, Perf. 10 Vert (1976) ..	...	.30	.15

1972 Commemoratives (continued)

| 606 | 608 | 610 |

606-9	6¢-15¢ Christmas, set of 4	6.95	1.45	1.25
606	6¢ Candles	.90	.20	.15
606p	6¢ Tagged, Narrow Side Bars (E)	1.35	.25	...
606pa	6¢ Tagged, Wide Side Bars (A)	1.50	.30	...
607	8¢ Candles	1.00	.20	.15
607p	8¢ Tagged, Narrow Side Bars (E)	1.50	.30	...
607pa	8¢ Tagged, Wide Side Bars (A)	1.75	.35	...
608	10¢ Candles & Fruit	2.15	.45	.35
608p	10¢ Tagged, Narrow Side Bars (E)	3.25	.65	...
608pa	10¢ Tagged, Wide Side Bars (A)	3.50	.70	...
609	15¢ Candles & Prayer Book	3.25	.70	.70
609p	15¢ Tagged, Narrow Side Bars (E)	5.50	1.10	...
609pa	15¢ Tagged, Wide Side Bars (A)	6.25	1.25	...
610	8¢ Cornelius Krieghoff, Painter, "The Blacksmith's Shop"	2.00	.25	.15
610p	8¢ Tagged, Narrow Side Bars (E)	2.25	.35	...

1973 Commemoratives

| 615 | 616 | 617 |

CANADA

1973 Commemoratives (continued)

Scott's No.		Plate Block F-VF,NH	F-VF,NH Unused	F-VF Used
611-28	Set of 18	...	5.75	4.50
611	8¢ Monsignor de Montmorency-Laval	.90	.25	.15
612-14	8¢-15¢ Mounties, Set of 3	5.50	1.25	1.00
612	8¢ Mounties - G.A. French	.95	.25	.15
613	10¢ Mounties - Spectograph	1.60	.35	.35
614	15¢ Mounties - On Horseback	3.15	.65	.60
615	8¢ Jeanne Mance - Nurse	.90	.25	.15
616	8¢ Joseph Howe - Journalist/Politicians ..	.90	.25	.15
617	15¢ J.E.H. MacDonald - "Mist Fantasy' ...	2.80	.60	.50
618	8¢ Prince Edward I Centenary	.90	.25	.15
619	8¢ Scottish Settlers Bicentenary	.90	.25	.15
620	8¢ Royal Visit, Elizabeth II	.90	.25	.15
621	15¢ Royal Visit, Elizabeth II	2.75	.60	.55
622	8¢ Nellie McClung, Suffragette	.90	.25	.15
623	8¢ 21st Olympics Publicity	.90	.25	.15
624	15¢ 21st Olympics Publicity	2.75	.60	.50
625-28	6¢-15¢ Christmas, set of 4	5.25	1.25	1.00
625	6¢ Ice Skate	.70	.25	.15
626	8¢ Dove	.90	.25	.15
627	10¢ Santa Claus	1.25	.25	.25
628	15¢ Shepherd and Star	2.75	.60	.60

NOTE: STARTING IN 1973, ALL CANADIAN STAMPS ARE TAGGED.
#623-24, 629-32, 644-47, 656-57, 664-66, 681-89,
B1-12 = 1973-76 Montreal Olympic Games

1974 Commemoratives

| 644 | 645 | 655 |
| 646 | 647 | |

629-55	Set of 27	...	9.70	5.65
629-32	8¢ Summer Olympics "Keep Fit", Block of 4	1.80	1.50	.95
629-32	8¢ Set of 4 Singles	...	1.30	.70
633	8¢ Winnipeg Centenary	.90	.25	.15
634-39	8¢ Letter Carriers 100th Anniv., Block of 6	4.00	3.25	3.25
634-39	8¢ Set of 6 Singles	...	2.25	2.00
640	8¢ Ontario Agricultural College	.90	.25	.15
641	8¢ Telephone Invention Centenary	.90	.25	.15
642	8¢ World Cycling Championships,Montreal	.95	.20	.15
643	8¢ Mennonite Settlement Centennial	.90	.25	.15
644-47	8¢ Winter Olympics, "keep Fit", Block of 4	1.80	1.60	.95
644-47	8¢ Set of 4 Singles	...	1.30	.70
648	8¢ Universal Postal Union, Mercury	.90	.25	.15
649	15¢ Universal Postal Union, Mercury	3.50	.80	.65
650-53	6¢ Christmas, set of 4	5.75	1.35	.95
650	6¢ "Nativity"	.70	.25	.15
651	8¢ "Skaters in Hull"	.85	.25	.15
652	10¢ "The Ice Cone"	1.65	.35	.25
653	15¢ "Laurentian Village"	2.95	.65	.50
654	8¢ Guglielmo Marconi , Wireless Inventor	.90	.25	.15
655	8¢ William H. Merritt, Welland Canal	.90	.25	.15

1975 Commemoratives

| 657 | 658-59 | 664 |

656-80	Set of 25	...	15.00	10.95
656	$1 Olympic Sculptures "The Sprinter"	11.00	2.35	2.10
657	$2 Olympic Sculptures "The Plunger"	21.50	4.75	4.50
658-59	8¢ Authors Lucy Maud Montgomery & Louis Hemon, Pair	1.10	.45	.35
658-59	8¢ Set of 2 Singles	...	.40	.30
660	8¢ Marguerite Bourgeoys, Girls School	.90	.25	.15
661	8¢ Alphonse Desjardins, Journalist	.90	.25	.15
662-63	8¢ Religious Leaders, Dr. Samuel Chown & Dr. John Cook, Pair	1.10	.45	.40
662-63	8¢ Set of 2 Singles	...	.40	.35
664-66	20¢-50¢ Montreal Olympics, Set of 3	11.50	2.60	1.95
664	20¢ Olympics - Pole Vaulting	2.75	.55	.50
665	25¢ Olympics - Marathon Running	3.15	.70	.55
666	50¢ Olympics - Hurdling	6.00	1.45	1.00
667	8¢ Calgary Centennial "Untamed"	1.00	.25	.15

680   **687**

684   **692-93**   **704**

1977-82 Regular Issues, Perf.12x12½ (continued)

Scott's No.		Plate Block F-VF,NH	F-VF,NH Unused	F-VF Used
726	$1 Bay of Fundy Natl.Pari, Perf. 13½ (1979)	8.75	2.10	.50
726a	$1 Untagged(1981)	10.00	2.25	.65
727	$2 Kluane National Park, Perf.13½ (1979)	18.00	4.15	1.25
729	12¢ Parliament, Coil, Perf. 10 Vert.	...	.25	.15
730	14¢ Parliament, Coil, Perf. 10 Vert. (1978) .	...	.30	.15

NOTE: Also see #781-806

733-34   **769-70**

736   **738-39**

1977 Commemoratives (continued)

732	12¢ Endangered Wildlife - Eastern Cougar	1.20	.30	.15
733-34	12¢ Tom Thomson Paintings, Pair	1.20	.55	.40
733-34	12¢ Set of 2 Singles		.50	.30
735	12¢ Canadian-born Governor Generals	1.20	.25	.15
736	12¢ Order of Canada 10th Anniversary	1.20	.25	.15
737	12¢ Peace Bridge, Fort Erie, Ontario & Buffalo, NY - 50th Anniversary	1.20	.25	.15
738-39	12¢ Pioneers Joseph E. Bernier & Sandford Fleming, Pair	1.20	.55	.40
738-39	12¢ Set of 2 Singles	...	.50	.30
740	25¢ 23rd Parliamentary Conference	3.00	.70	.65
741-43	10¢-25¢ Christmas, Set of 3	4.40	.95	.65
741	10¢ Christmas - Christmas Star	.95	.25	.15
742	12¢ Christmas - Angelic Choir	1.20	.25	.15
743	25¢ Christmas - Christ Child	2.40	.50	.40
744-47	12¢ Sailing Ships, Block of 4	1.20	1.10	.90
744-47	12¢ Set of 4 Singles	...	.95	.75
748-49	12¢ Inuit Hunting, Pair	1.20	.50	.40
748-49	12¢ Set of 2 Singles, Hunter, Dream	...	.50	.30
750-51	12¢ Inuit Hunting, Pair	1.20	.50	.40
750-51	12¢ Set of 2 Singles, Archer, Hunters	...	.50	.30

1975 Commemoratives (continued)

Scott's No.		Plate Block F-VF,NH	F-VF,NH Unused	F-VF Used
668	8¢ International Women's Year	1.00	.25	.15
669	8¢ Supreme Court Centenary "Justice"	1.00	.25	.15
670-73	8¢ Canadian Coastal Ships, Block of 4	2.25	1.90	1.70
670-73	8¢ Set of 4 Singles	...	1.75	1.50
674-75	6¢-15¢ Christmas, set of 6	4.75	1.60	1.15
674-75	6¢ Santa Claus & Skater, Pair	.85	.50	.35
674-75	6¢ Set of 2 Singles	...	.40	.30
676-77	8¢ Child & Family, Pair	1.00	.50	.35
676-77	8¢ Set of 2 Singles	...	.40	.30
678	10¢ Gift Box	1.20	.25	.25
679	15¢ Christmas Tree	1.85	.40	.40
680	8¢ Royal Canadian Legion 50th Anniv.	1.00	.25	.15

1976 Commemoratives

681-703	Set of 23	...	19.50	13.95
681-88	8¢-$2 Montreal Olympics, Set of 8	65.00	14.95	10.75
681	8¢ Olympic Torch	.95	.20	.15
682	20¢ Olympic Opening Ceremonies	3.00	.70	.55
683	25¢ Olympic Medal Ceremonies	3.85	.90	.70
684	20¢ Olympics - Communication Arts	5.50	1.30	.65
685	25¢ Olympics - Handicraft Tools	6.50	1.55	.70
686	50¢ Olympics - Performing Arts	10.00	2.35	1.20
687	$1 Olympic Site - Notre Dame & Place Ville Marie	14.00	3.00	2.35
688	$2 Olympic Site - Olympic Stadium	26.50	6.00	4.75
689	20¢ Winter Olympic Games, Innsbruck	3.75	.90	.65
690	20¢ HABITAT - U.N. Conference	2.25	.50	.50
691	10¢ U.S. Bicentennial - Benjamin Franklin .	1.40	.30	.20
692-93	8¢ Royal Military College, Pair	1.00	.45	.40
692-93	8¢ Set of 2 Singles	...	.40	.30
694	20¢ Olympiad for Physically Disabled	2.85	.65	.55
695-96	8¢ Authors Robert Service & Germaine Guevremont, Pair	1.00	.45	.35
695-96	8¢ Set of 2 Singles	...	.40	.30
697-99	8¢-20¢ Christmas, Set of 3	3.85	.90	.65
697	8¢ Stained Glass Window, Toronto	.75	.25	.15
698	10¢ Stained Glass Window, London	1.10	.25	.15
699	20¢ Stained Glass Window	2.15	.45	.40
700-03	10¢ Canadian Inland Ships, Block of 4	1.80	1.60	1.35
700-03	10¢ Set of 4 Singles	...	1.30	1.20

Se-Tenant Issues: Se-tenants in mint sets are attached, singles in used sets.
#670-73, 700-3, 744-47, 776-79 = 1975-78 Canadian Ships

1977 Commemoratives

704,732-51	Set of 21	...	5.95	3.95
704	25¢ Queen Elizabeth II Silver Jubilee	3.25	.75	.50

1977-1982 Regular Issues, Perf. 12 x 12½

705-27	Set of 23	...	16.00	5.65
#705-12 Wildflowers				
705	1¢ Bottle Gentian	.70	.25	.15
707	2¢ Western Columbine	.70	.25	.15
708	3¢ Canada Lily	.70	.25	.15
709	4¢ Hepatica	.70	.25	.15
710	5¢ Shooting Star	.70	.25	.15
711	10¢ Lady's Slipper	.95	.25	.15
711a	10¢ Lady's Slipper, Perf.13x13½ (1978)	.95	.25	.15
712	12¢ Jewelweed, Perf. 13 x 13½ (1978)	1.50	.30	.20
713	12¢ Queen Elizabeth II, Perf. 13 x 13½	1.20	.30	.15
713a	12¢ Booklet Single, Perf. 12 x 12½	...	.35	.25
714	12¢ Parliament, Perf. 13 (1978)	1.20	.30	.15
715	14¢ Parliament, Perf. 13 (1978)	1.40	.35	.15
716	14¢ Elizabeth II, Perf.13 x 13½ (1978)	1.40	.35	.15
716a	14¢ Booklet Single, Perf. 12 x 12½ (1978)	...	.65	.50
716b	14¢ Booklet Pane of 25, Perf. 12 x 12½ (1978)	...	6.00	...
#717-21 Trees				
717	15¢ Trembling Aspen, Perf. 13½	1.85	.45	.15
718	20¢ Douglas Fir, Perf. 13½	1.85	.45	.15
719	25¢ Sugar Maple, Perf. 13½	2.25	.55	.15
720	30¢ Red Oak, Perf. 13½ (1978)	2.75	.60	.20
721	35¢ Winter Pine, Perf. 13½ (1979)	3.25	.75	.25
#723-25 Streets				
723	50¢ Prairie Town, Perf.13½ (1978)	5.25	1.25	.25
723A	50¢ "1978" on License Plate	4.75	1.10	.20
723C	60¢ Ontario, Perforated 13½ (1982)	5.50	1.25	.25
724	75¢ Row Houses, Perf. 13½ (1978)	7.00	1.60	.40
725	80¢ Maritime Scene, Perf. 13½ (1979)	7.50	1.70	.45

1978 Commemoratives

752-56,757-79	Set of 28	...	11.75	6.75
752	12¢ Endangered Wildlife, Peregrine Falcon	1.20	.25	.15
753-56	12¢ -$1.25 CAPEX'78, Set of 4	17.50	3.85	1.75
753	12p Queen Victoria (#3)	1.20	.25	.15
754	14¢ 10p Jacques Cartier (#7)	1.40	.30	.15
755	30¢ ½p Queen Victoria (#8)	2.75	.60	.40
756	$1.25 6p Prince Albert (#5)	12.50	2.90	1.10
756a	14¢, 30¢, $1.25 CAPEX Souvenir Sheet	...	4.00	3.50
757-62	14¢-30¢ Commonwealth Games, Set of 6 .	7.95	2.80	1.85
757	14¢ Games, Symbol	1.40	.30	.15
758	30¢ Games, Badminton	2.75	.60	.40
759-60	14¢ Games, Pair	1.35	.60	.40
759-60	14¢ Set of 2 Singles, Stadium,Running	...	.55	.30
761-62	30¢ Games, Pair	2.75	1.35	1.25
761-62	30¢ Set of 2 Singles, Edmonton, Lawn Bowls	...	1.20	1.10
763-64	14¢ Captain James Cook, Pair	1.35	.60	.40
763-64	14¢ Set of 2 Singles	...	.55	.30
765-66	14¢ Resource Development, Pair	1.35	.60	.40
765-66	14¢ Set of 2 Singles	...	.55	.30
767	14¢ Canadian National Exhibition 100th	1.35	.30	.15
768	14¢ Mere d'Youville, Beatified, Grey Nuns ..	1.35	.30	.15
769-70	14¢ Travels of Inuit, Pair	1.35	.60	.40
769-70	14¢ Set of 2 Singles, Woman Walking,Migration	...	.55	.30
771-72	14¢ Travels of Inuit, Pair	1.35	.60	.40
771-72	14¢ Set of 2 Singles, Plane, Dogteam & Sled	...	.55	.30
773-75	12¢-30¢ Christmas, Set of 3	4.95	1.15	.70
773	12¢ Christmas, Madonna	1.15	.25	.15
774	14¢ Christmas, Virgin & Child	1.35	.30	.15
775	30¢ Christmas, Virgin & Child	2.60	.65	.45
776-79	14¢ Sailing Ice Vessels, Block of 4	1.50	1.40	1.10
776-79	14¢ Set of 4 Singles	...	1.20	.90

1979 Commemoratives

780   **817-18**

780,813-20,833-46	Set of 23	...	8.75	4.75
780	14¢ Quebec Winter Carnival	1.35	.30	.15

1977-1983 Floral Definitives, Perf. 13 x 13½
Designs of #705-730 plus new designs

Scott's No.		Plate Block F-VF,NH	F-VF,NH Unused	F-VF Used
781-792	Set of 11	...	3.25	1.45
#781-88	Wildflowers			
781	1¢ Bottle Gentian (1979)	.50	.20	.15
781a	1¢ Booklet Single, Perf. 12 x 12½	...	.35	.20
781b	Booklet Pane of 6 (2 #781a & 4 #713a)	...	1.00	...
782	2¢ Western Columbine (1979)	.50	.25	.15
782b	2¢ Booklet Single, Perf. 12 x 12½ ('78) ..	...	.25	.15
782a	Booklet Pane of 7 (4 #782b, 3 #716a) (1978)	...	1.00	...
783	3¢ Canada Lily (1979)	.50	.25	.15
784	4¢ Hepatica (1979)	.50	.25	.15
785	5¢ Shooting Star (1979)	.60	.25	.15
786	10¢ Lady's Slipper (1979)	.80	.25	.15
787	15¢ Canada Violet (1979)	1.40	.30	.15
789	17¢ Elizabeth II ('79)	1.50	.35	.15
789a	17¢ Booklet Single, Perf. 12 x 12½ (1979) .	...	.60	.50
789b	Booklet Pane of 25, Perf. 12 x 12½ (1979) .	...	8.50	...
790	17¢ Houses of Parliament (1979)	1.50	.40	.15
791	30¢ Elizabeth II (1982)	2.50	.60	.15
792	32¢ Elizabeth II (1983)	2.75	.60	.15
797	1¢ Parliament, Booklet Single, Perf. 12 x 12½ (1979)	.65		.25
797a	Booklet Pane of 6 (1 #797,3 #800,2 #789a)...	1.30	...	
800	5¢ Parliament, Booklet Single, Perf. 12 x 12½ (1979)		.30	.20
806	17¢ Parliament Coil, Perf. 10 Vert (1978)		.35	.15

1979 Commemoratives (continued)

813	17¢ Endangered Wildlife, Soft-shell Turtle ..	1.60	.35	.15
814	35¢ Endangered Wildlife, Bowhead Whale	3.25	.70	.60
815-16	17¢ Postal Code, Pair	1.50	.70	.55
815-16	17¢ Set of 2 Singles	...	.70	.30
817-18	17¢ Author Frederick P. Grove & Poet Emile Nelligan Pair	1.50	.70	.55
817-18	17¢ Set of 2 Singles	...	.70	.30
819-20	17¢ Colonels, De Salaberry & John By, Pair	1.50	.70	.55
819-20	17¢ Set of 2 Singles	...	.70	.30
832a	17¢ Provincial & Territorial Flags, Sheetlet of 12 .		4.50	3.75
821-32	17¢ Flags, Set of 12 Singles	...	4.35	2.40
833	17¢ Canoe-Kayak World Championships	1.60	.35	.15
834	17¢ Women's Field Hockey Championships	1.60	.35	.15
835-36	17¢ Inuit, Pair	1.60	.70	.55
835-36	17¢ Set of 2 Singles, Summer Tent, Igloo ..	...	.70	.30
837-38	17¢ Inuit, Pair	1.60	.70	.55
837-38	17¢ Set of 2 Singles, Dance, Soapstone ...	...	.70	.30

839   **840**   **841**

839-41	15¢-35¢ Christmas, Set of 3	6.00	1.30	.70
839	15¢ Christmas - Antique Toy Train	1.40	.30	.15
840	17¢ Christmas - Antique Toy Horse	1.60	.35	.15
841	35¢ Christmas - Antique Knotted Doll	3.25	.70	.45
842	17¢ International Year of the Child	1.60	.35	.15
843-44	17¢ Flying Boats, Pair	1.60	.70	.55
843-44	17¢ Set of 2 Singles	...	.70	.30
845-46	35¢ Flying Boats, Pair	3.25	1.40	1.25
845-46	35¢ Set of 2 Singles	...	1.35	1.20

1980 Commemoratives

847   **848**   **855**

859   **860-61**

847-77	Set of 31	...	12.95	7.25
847	17¢ Arctic Islands Acquisition 100th Anniv.	1.60	.35	.15
848	35¢ Winter Olympics, Downhill Skier	3.25	.70	.55
849-50	17¢ Artists, Robert Harris, Louis Philippe Hebert, Pair	1.60	.70	.55
849-50	17¢ Set of 2 Singles	...	.70	.30

1980 Commemoratives (continued)

Scott's No.		Plate Block F-VF,NH	F-VF,NH Unused	F-VF Used
851-52	35¢ Artists, Thomas Fuller, Lucius O'Brien, Pair	3.25	1.40	1.25
851-52	35¢ Set of 2 Singles	...	1.35	1.10
853	17¢ Endangered Wildlife, Atlantic Whitefish	1.60	.35	.15
854	17¢ Endangered Wildlife, Greater Prairie Chicken	1.60	.35	.15
855	17¢ Montreal Flower Show	1.60	.35	.15
856	17¢ Rehabilitation Congress, Winnipeg	1.60	.35	.15
857-58	17¢ "O Canada" Centenary, Pair	1.60	.70	.55
857-58	17¢ Set of 2 Singles	...	.70	.30
859	17¢ John George Diefenbaker, Pr.Minister .	1.60	.35	.15
860-61	17¢ Musicians, Emma Albani, Healey Willan, Pair	1.60	.70	.55
860-61	17¢ Set of 2 Singles	...	.70	.35
862	17¢ Ned Hanlan, Oarsman	1.60	.35	.15
863	17¢ Saskatchewan, Wheat Field	1.60	.35	.15
864	17¢ Alberta, Strip Mining	1.60	.35	.15
865	35¢ Uranium Resources	3.25	.70	.50
866-67	17¢ Inuit Spirits, Pair	1.60	.70	.55
866-67	Set of 2 Singles, Sedna, Return of the Sun	...	.70	.30
868-69	35¢ Inuit Spirits, Pair	3.25	1.40	1.25
868-69	Set of 2 Singles, Bird Spirit, Shaman	...	1.35	1.10
870-72	15¢-35¢ Christmas, Set of 3	6.00	1.30	.70
870	15¢ Christmas, "Christmas Morning"	1.40	.30	.15
871	17¢ Christmas, "Sleigh Ride"	1.60	.35	.15
872	35¢ Christmas, "McGill Cab Stand"	3.25	.70	.45
873-74	17¢ Military Aircraft, Pair	1.60	.70	.55
873-74	Set of 2 Singles	...	.70	.30
875-76	35¢ Military Aircraft, Pair	3.25	1.40	1.25
875-76	Set of 2 Singles	...	1.35	1.10
877	17¢ E.P. Lachapelle, Notre Dame Hospital, Montreal 100th Anniversary	1.60	.35	.15

1981 Commemoratives

879-82

Scott's No.		Plate Block F-VF,NH	F-VF,NH Unused	F-VF Used
878-906	Set of 29	...	11.15	5.60
878	17¢ 18th Century Mandora	1.60	.35	.15
879-82	17¢ Feminists, Emily Stowe, Louise McKinney, Idola Saint-Jean, Henrietta Edwards, Block of 4	1.75	1.65	1.35
879-82	17¢ Set of 4 Singles	...	1.50	.90
883	17¢ Endangered Wildlife, Marmot	1.60	.35	.15
884	35¢ Endangered Wildlife, Wood Bison	3.25	.75	.70
885-86	17¢ Beatified Women, Kateri Tekakwitha & Marie de l'Incarnation, Pair	1.60	.70	.55
885-86	17¢ Set of 2 Singles	...	.70	.30
887	17¢ Marc-Aurele Fortin, Painter	1.60	.35	.15
888	17¢ Frederic H. Varley, Painter	1.60	.35	.15
889	35¢ Paul-Emile Borduas, Painter	3.25	.70	.60
890-93	17¢ Historic Maps, Strip of 4 .... (8)	3.50	1.60	1.30
890-93	17¢ Maps, Sheetlet of 16	...	5.75	...
890-93	17¢ Set of 4 Singles	...	1.45	.90
894-95	17¢ Botanists, Frere Marie-Victorin, John Macoun, Pair	1.60	.70	.55
894-95	17¢ Set of 2 Singles	...	.70	.30
896	17¢ Montreal Rose	1.60	.35	.15
897	17¢ Niagara-on-the-Lake	1.60	.35	.15
898	17¢ Acadian Congress Centenary	1.60	.35	.15
899	17¢ Aaron Mosher Labor Congress	1.60	.35	.15
900-2	15¢ Christmas, Set of 3	3.50	.70	.40
900	15¢ 1781 Christmas Tree	1.20	.25	.15
901	15¢ 1881 Christmas Tree	1.20	.25	.15
902	15¢ 1981 Christmas Tree	1.20	.25	.15
903-04	17¢ Aircraft, Pair	1.60	.75	.55
903-04	17¢ Set of 2 Singles	...	.70	.30
905-06	35¢ Aircraft, Pair	3.25	1.50	1.20
905-06	35¢ Set of 2 Singles	...	1.35	1.10

907   **914**   **915**

1981 "A" Interim Definitives

907	(30¢) "A" and Maple Leaf, ...	3.50	.80	.15
908	(30¢) "A" and Maple Leaf, Coil	...	.95	.20

CANADA

1982 Commemoratives

Scott's No.		Plate Block F-VF,NH	F-VF,NH Unused	F-VF Used
909-13,914-16,954,967-75 Set of 18		...	12.50	6.75
909-13	30¢-60¢ Youth Exhibition, Set of 5	...	3.65	2.25
909	30¢ 1851 3d Beaver (#1)	2.75	.60	.20
910	30¢ 1908 15¢ Champlain (#102)	2.75	.60	.20
911	35¢ 1935 10¢ Mountie (#223)	3.25	.70	.65
912	35¢ 1928 10¢ Mt. Hurd (#155)	3.25	.70	.65
913	60¢ 1929 50¢ Bluenose (#158)	5.75	1.30	1.00
913a	30¢-60¢ Youth Exhibition Souvenir Sheet of 5	...	4.15	3.95
914	30¢ Jules Leger, Governor-General	2.75	.60	.15
915	30¢ Marathon of Hope - Terry Fox	2.75	.60	.15
916	30¢ New Canadian Consitution	2.75	.60	.15

1982-89 Regular Issue

917   923   927   929

917-37 Set of 22		...	31.25	9.50
#917-22,927-30,932-33 Artifacts				
917	1¢ Decoy, Perf. 14 x 13½	.50	.25	.15
917a	1¢ Perf. 13 x 13½ (1985)	.85	.25	.15
918	2¢ Fishing Spear, Perf. 14 x 13½	.50	.25	.15
918a	2¢ Perf. 13 x 13½ (1984)	.50	.25	.15
919	3¢ Stable Lantern, Perf. 14 x 13½	.50	.25	.15
919a	3¢ Perf. 13 x 13½ (1985)	.75	.25	.15
920	5¢ Bucket, Perf. 14 x 13½	.60	.25	.15
920a	5¢ Perf. 13 x 13½ (1985)	.70	.25	.15
921	10¢ Weathercock, Perf. 14 x 13½	.90	.25	.15
921a	10¢ Perf. 13 x 13½ (1985)	1.30	.30	.15
922	20¢ Ice Skates	1.85	.40	.15
923	30¢ Maple Leaf, Red & Blue Pf.13x13½	2.75	.60	.15
923b	30¢ Booklet Single, Perf. 12 x 12½	...	1.40	1.30
923b	30¢ with straight edge	...	.70	.20
923a	30¢ Booklet Pane of 20, Perf. 12 x 12½	...	11.75	...
924	32¢ Maple Leaf, Red & Brown on Beige, Pf. 13 x 13½ ('83)	2.70	.60	.15
924b	32¢ Booklet Single, Perf. 12 x 12½ (1983)	...	1.00	.75
924b	32¢ with straight edge	...	.75	.35
924a	32¢ Booklet Pane of 25, Perf. 12 x 12½ (1983)	...	14.50	...
925	34¢ Parliament Library, Perf.13½x13 (1985)	2.95	.70	.15
925a	34¢ Booklet Pane of 25 (1985)	...	14.75	...
925b	34¢ Bluer sky, Pf. 13½ x 14, Booklet Single(1986)	...	1.50	.70
925b	34¢ with straight edge	...	.70	.20
925c	34¢ Bluer sky, Booklet Pane of 25 (1986)	...	14.75	...
926	34¢ Queen Elizabeth II (1985)	2.75	.65	.15
926A	36¢ Queen Elizabeth II (1987)	19.50	3.75	2.00
926B	36¢ Parliamentary Library, Pf 13½x13 (1987)	2.75	.70	.15
926Be	36¢ Booklet Single, Perf. 13½ x 14 (1987)	...	1.35	.75
926Be	36¢ with straight edge	...	.85	.30
926Bc	36¢ Booklet Pane of 10 (1987)	...	6.50	...
926Bd	36¢ Booklet Pane of 25 (1987)	...	15.75	...
927	37¢ Wooden Plough (1983)	3.25	.75	.20
928	39¢ Settle Bed (1985)	3.50	.80	.20
929	48¢ Hand Hewn Cradle (1983)	4.25	.95	.25
930	50¢ Sleigh (1985)	4.25	.95	.25
932	64¢ Wood Burning Stove (1983)	5.75	1.30	.35
933	68¢ Spinning Wheel (1985)	5.95	1.35	.35
934	$1.00 Glacier National Park (9184)	8.50	1.90	.45
935	$1.50 Waterton Lakes National Park	13.50	3.00	.60
936	$2.00 Banff National Park (1985)	17.00	4.00	1.00
937	$5.00 Point Pelee National Park (1983)	39.50	9.40	2.00

NOTE: Also see #1080-84

1982-89 Booklet Stamps

938-48 Set of 11		...	4.85	3.50
938	1¢ East Parliament, Booklet Single (1987)	...	.20	.15
939	2¢ West Parliament, Deep Green,Booklet Single (1985)		.20	.15
939a	2¢ Slate Green, Booklet Single (1989)	...	.20	.20
940	5¢ Maple Leaf, Booklet Single	...	.20	.15
941	5¢ East Parliament, Booklet Single (1985)	...	.30	.20
942	6¢ West Parliament, Booklet Single (1987)	...	.25	.15
943	8¢ Maple Leaf, Blue, Booklet Single (1983)	...	.50	.40
944	10¢ Maple Leaf, Green, Booklet Single	...	.45	.35
945	30¢ Maple Leaf, Red, Booklet Single	...	.85	.70
945a	Booklet Pane of 4 (2 #940,#944,#945) Perforated 12 x 12½	...	1.20	...
946	32¢ Maple Leaf, Brown, Booklet Single (1983)	...	.65	.40
946b	Booklet Pane of 4 (2 #940, #943, #946, Perf. 12 x 12½)	...	1.25	...
947	34¢ Center Parliament, Booklet Single(1985)	...	1.10	.70
947a	Booklet Pane of 6 (3 #939,2 #941, #947)	...	1.50	...
948	36¢ Parliament Library, Booklet Single (1987)	...	1.10	.70
948a	Booklet Pane of 5 (2 #938,2 #942, #948)	...	1.50	...

1982-87 Coil Stamps

950-53 Set of 4		...	2.75	.55
950	30¢ Maple Leaf, Red	...	.90	.20
951	32¢ Maple Leaf, Brown (1983)	...	.65	.15
952	34¢ Parliament, Red Brown (1985)	...	.65	.15
953	36¢ Parliament, Dark Red (1987)	...	.65	.15

CANADA

1982 Commemoratives (continued)

954   967   973

Scott's No.		Plate Block F-VF,NH	F-VF,NH Unused	F-VF Used
954	30¢ Salvation Army	2.75	.60	.15

1982 Provincial & Territorials Paintings

966a	30¢ Canada Day Sheetlet of 12 Paintings	...	10.00	9.50
955-66	30¢ Canada Day Set of 12 Singles	...	8.75	7.75

1982 Commemoratives (continued)

967	30¢ Regina Centennial	2.75	.60	.15
968	30¢ Henley Rowing Regatta	2.75	.60	.15
969-70	30¢ Bush Aircraft, Pair	3.50	1.60	1.20
969-70	30¢ Set of 2 Singles	...	1.40	.40
971-72	60¢ Bush Aircraft, Pair	6.00	2.65	2.25
971-72	60¢ Set of 2 Singles	...	2.40	1.80
973-75	30¢-60¢ Christmas, Set of 3	11.50	2.40	1.70
973	30¢ Christmas, Holy Family	2.75	.60	.15
974	35¢ Christmas, Shepherds	3.25	.70	.60
975	60¢ Christmas, Three Wise Men	5.75	1.20	1.00

1983 Commemoratives

976-82,993-1008 Set of 23		...	21.95	10.50
976	32¢ World Communications Year	2.75	.65	.20

977   980   981

977	$2 Commonwealth Day, Map of the Earth	39.50	9.00	3.50
978-79	32¢ Author Laure Conan, Poet E.J. Pratt, Pair	2.75	1.25	1.00
978-79	32¢ Set of 2 Singles	...	1.20	.40
980	32¢ St. John Ambulance Centennial	2.80	.60	.20
981	32¢ World University Games, Edmonton	2.80	.60	.20
982	64¢ World University Games	5.50	1.20	.95

1983 Historic Forts Commemorative Booklet

992a	32¢ Historic Forts Booklet Pane of 10	...	7.85	7.50
983-92	32¢ Forts, Set of 10 Booklet Singles	...	6.75	6.50

993   996   1005

995   1007-08

1983 Commemoratives (continued)

993	32¢ Boy Scout Jamboree, Alberta, 75th Anniversary of Scout	2.75	.60	.20
994	32¢ World Council of Churches	2.75	.60	.20
995	32¢ Sir Humphrey Gilbert	2.75	.60	.20
996	32¢ Discovery of Nickel	3.00	.65	.20
997	32¢ Josiah Henson, Underground RR	2.75	.60	.20
998	32¢ Antoine Labelle, Quebec Colonizer	2.75	.60	.20
999-1002	32¢-64¢ Locomotives, Set of 4	(3) 11.00	3.15	2.25
999-1000	32¢ Steam Locomotives, Pair	2.75	1.25	1.20
999-1000	32¢ Sheet of 25	...	14.75	...
999-1000	32¢ Set of 2 Singles	...	1.30	.50
1001	37¢ Locomotive Samson 0-6-0,	3.25	.70	.70
1001	37¢ Sheet of 25	...	17.50	...
1002	64¢ Locomotive Adam Brown 4-4-0,	5.50	1.30	1.10
1002	64¢ Sheet of 25	...	29.75	...
#999-1002, 1036-39, 1071-74, 1118-21 1983-86 Locomotives				
1003	32¢ Dalhousie Law School Centennial	2.75	.60	.20

1983 Commemoratives (continued)

Scott's No.		Mint Sheet	Plate Block	F-VF NH	F-VF Used
1004-6	32¢-64¢ Christmas, Set of 3	...	11.00	2.50	1.80
1004	32¢ Christmas, Urban Church	...	2.75	.60	.20
1005	37¢ Christmas, Family Going to Church	...	3.25	.70	.60
1006	64¢ Christmas, Rural Church	...	5.50	1.30	1.10
1007-08	32¢ Army Regiment Uniforms, Pair	...	2.75	1.35	1.10
1007-08	32¢ Set of 2 Singles	...	...	1.20	.40

1984 Commemoratives

1013

1028

1043

Scott's No.		Mint Sheet	Plate Block	F-VF NH	F-VF Used
1009-15,1028-39,1040-44 Set of 24		**...**	**...**	**16.65**	**8.35**
1009	32¢ Yellowknife 50th Anniversary ..	...	2.75	.60	.20
1010	32¢ Montreal Symphony 50th Anniv.	...	2.75	.60	.20
1011	32¢ Cartier Landing in Quebec 450th	...	2.75	.60	.20
1012	32¢ Voyage of Tall Ships Regatta .	...	2.75	.60	.20
1013	32¢ Red Cross Society 75th Anniv.	...	2.75	.60	.20
1014	32¢ New Brunswick Bicentennial ...	...	2.75	.60	.20
1015	32¢ St. Lawrence Seaway 25th Anniv.	(25)14.50	2.75	.60	.20
	1984 Provincial & Territorial Landscape Scenes				
1027a	32¢ Canada Day Sheetlet of 12 ...	...	...	9.50	8.75
1016-27	32¢ Canada Day, Set of 12 Singles.	...	...	8.25	4.75
	1984 Commemoratives (continued)				
1028	32¢ United Empire Loyalists	...	2.75	.60	.20
1029	32¢ Roman Catholic Church in Newfoundland 200th Anniversary .	...	2.75	.60	.20
1030	32¢ Papal Visit	...	2.75	.60	.20
1031	64¢ Papal Visit	...	5.50	1.20	.95
1032-35	32¢ Lighthouses, Block of 4	...	3.15	3.00	1.40
1032-35	32¢ Set of 4 Singles	...	...	2.50	.90
1036-37	32¢ Steam Locomotives, Pair	(25)16.00	2.75	1.35	1.10
1036-37	32¢ Set of 2 Singles	...	...	1.20	.40
1038	37¢ Locomotive Grand Trunk 2-6-0	(25)17.50	3.25	.70	.70
1039	64¢ Locom. Canadian Pacific 4-6-0	(25)30.00	5.75	1.30	1.10
1039a	32¢-64¢ Locomotive Souvenir Sheet of 4	...	...	4.00	3.85
1040	32¢-64¢ Christmas, Set of 3	...	11.50	2.50	1.75
1040	32¢ Christmas, Annunciation	...	2.75	.60	.20
1041	37¢ Christmas, The Three Kings ...	...	3.25	.70	.65
1042	64¢ Christmas, Snow in Bethlehem	...	5.75	1.30	1.00
1043	32¢ Royal Canadian Air Force	...	2.75	.60	.20
1044	32¢ Treffle Berthiaume, Newspaper, La Presse, 100th Anniversary	...	2.75	.60	.20

1985 Commemoratives

1045

1062

1075

1076

Scott's No.		Mint Sheet	Plate Block	F-VF NH	F-VF Used
1045-49,1060-66,1067-70,1071-76 Set of 22			**...**	**16.00**	**6.95**
1045	32¢ International Youth Year		2.75	.60	.20
1046	32¢ Canadian Astronaut, Marc Garneau		3.00	.65	.20
1047-48	32¢ Decade of Women, Feminists Therese Casgrain, Emily Murphy, Pair		2.75	1.35	1.25
1047-48	32¢ Set of 2 Singles		...	1.20	.40
1049	32¢ Gabriel Dumont, Metis, Northwest Rebellion 100th Anniversary		2.75	.60	.20
	1985 Historic Forts Commemorative Booklet				
1050-59	34¢ Historic Forts, Set of 10 Booklet Singles		...	10.25	6.75
1059a	34¢ Booklet Pane of 10		...	11.00	12.50
	1985 Commemoratives (continued)				
1060	34¢ Louis Hebert, Apothecary		3.00	.65	.20
1061	34¢ Inter-Parliamentary Union 75th Conf. ..		3.00	.65	.20
1062	34¢ Girl Guides 75th Anniversary		3.00	.65	.20
1063-66	34¢ Lighthouses, Block of 4		3.65	3.40	2.50
1063-66	34¢ Set of 4 Singles		...	3.15	1.10
1066b	34¢ Lighthouse Souvenir Sheet of 4		...	4.15	3.15
1067-70	32¢-68¢ Christmas, Set of 4	(3)12.00		3.65	2.25
1067	34¢ Santa Claus Parade		3.00	.65	.20
1068	39¢ Santa Claus Parade, Coach		3.50	.75	.65
1069	68¢ Santa Claus Parade, Tree		5.95	1.35	1.10
1070	32¢ Polar Float Booklet Single		...	1.00	.40
1070a	32¢ Christmas Booklet Pane of 10		...	9.50	8.50
1071-74	34¢-68¢ Locomotives, Set of 4	(3) 12.50		3.50	2.10
1071-72	34¢ Locomotives, Pair	(25)18.75	3.50	1.50	.75
1071-72	34¢ Set of 2 Singles		...	1.45	.50
1073	39¢ Locomotives #010a	(25)18.75	3.50	.75	.70
1074	68¢ Locomotives #H4D	(25)31.50	5.95	1.35	1.00
1075	34¢ Royal Canadian Navy 75th Anniv.		3.00	.65	.20
1076	34¢ Montreal Fine Arts Museum 120th Anniv.		3.00	.65	.20

1986 Commemoratives

1078

1084

1117

Scott's No.		Mint Sheet	Plate Block	F-VF NH	F-VF Used
1077-79,1090-1107,1108-21 Set of 32			**...**	**26.50**	**11.95**
1077	34¢ 1988 Calgary Winter Olympics,Map	(25)15.95	3.00	.65	.20
	#1077, 1111-12, 1130-31, 1152-53, 1195-96 1986-88 Calgary Winter Olympics.				
1078	34¢ EXPO '86 Vancouver Pavilion		3.00	.65	.20
1079	39¢ EXPO '86 Communications		3.50	.75	.60
	1986-87 Artifacts Regular Issue				
1080-84	**Set of 5 ....**		**...**	**14.15**	**3.35**
1080	25¢ Butter Stamp (1987)		2.30	.50	.25
1081	42¢ Linen Chest (1987)		4.15	.85	.25
1082	55¢ Iron Kettle (1987)		6.25	1.45	.35
1083	72¢ Hand-drawn Cart (1987)		8.00	1.80	.45
1084	$5 La Mauricie National Park		42.50	10.00	2.25
	1986 Commemoratives (continued)				
1090	34¢ Philippe Aubert de Gaspe, Author		3.00	.65	.20
1091	34¢ Molly Brant, Iroquois		3.00	.65	.20
1092	34¢ EXPO '86, Expo Center		3.00	.65	.20
1093	68¢ EXPO '86, Transportation		6.00	1.35	.85
1094	34¢ Canadian Forces Postal Service		3.00	.65	.20
1095-98	34¢ Indigenous Birds, Block of 4		4.25	3.65	2.75
1095-98	34¢ Set of 4 Singles		...	3.35	1.40
	#1095-98, 1591-94, 1631-34, 1710-13, 1770-77, 1839-46, 1886-93 1986-2001 Canadian Birds				
1099-1102	34¢ Transportation Inventions,Block-4	(16)11.75	3.50	3.15	2.75
1099-1102	34¢ Set of 4 Singles		...	2.90	1.40
1103	34¢ Canadian Broadcasting Corp 50th Anniv.		3.00	.65	.20
1104-07	34¢ Canada Exploration, Block of 4		3.50	3.15	2.75
1104-07	34¢ Set of 4 Singles		...	2.90	1.40
	1986-89 Exploration #1104-7, 1126-29, 1199-1202, 1233-36				
1107b	34¢ CAPEX '87, Exploration Souvenir Sheet of 4		...	3.65	3.00
1108-09	34¢ Prairie Peacemakers, Pair		3.00	1.45	1.20
1108-09	34¢ Set of 2 Singles		...	1.30	.50
1110	34¢ International Peace Year		3.00	.70	.20
1111-12	34¢ Calgary Winter Olympics, Pair		3.00	1.45	1.00
1111-12	34¢ Set of 2 Singles, Ice Hockey, Biathlon		...	1.30	.50
1113-16	29¢-68¢ Christmas, Set of 4	(3) 12.00		4.15	2.95
1113	34¢ Christmas, Angel		3.00	.65	.20
1114	39¢ Christmas, Angel		3.50	.75	.65
1115	68¢ Christmas, Angel		6.00	1.45	.95
1116	29¢ Christmas, Angel, Booklet Single Perf. 13½		...	1.30	1.25
1116a	29¢ Booklet Pane of 10, Perf. 13½		...	12.00	...
1116b	29¢ Booklet Single, Perf. 12½		...	8.00	3.00
1116c	29¢ Booklet Pane of 10, Perf. 12½		...	80.00	...
1117	34¢ John Molson		3.00	.65	.20
1118-21	34¢-68¢ Locomotives, Set of 4	(3) 15.00		4.00	2.65
1118-19	34¢ Locomotives, Pair	(20)14.75	4.25	1.50	1.10
1118-19	34¢ Set of 2 Singles		...	1.45	.50
1120	39¢ Locomotive CN U2a	(20)19.75	4.50	1.10	.90
1121	68¢ Locomotive CP H1c	(20)29.50	7.00	1.60	1.35

1987 Commemoratives

1122

1130

1134

Scott's No.		Mint Sheet	Plate Block	F-VF NH	F-VF Used
1122-25,1126-54 Set of 33			**...**	**26.00**	**11.75**
1122-25	34¢-72¢ CAPEX '87 Set of 4		...	3.35	2.35
1122	34¢ 1st Toronto Post Office		3.00	.65	.20
1123	36¢ Nelson-Miramichi Post Office		3.25	.70	.25
1124	42¢ Saint Ours Post Office		4.00	.85	.75
1125	72¢ Battleford Post Office		6.50	1.50	1.35
1125A	36¢-72¢ CAPEX'87 Souvenir Sheet of 4 ...		...	4.00	3.75
1125Ab-e	36¢-72¢ Set of 4 Singles from Souvenir Sheet		...	3.75	3.50
	#1125Ab-e have yellow green inscriptions.				
1126-29	34¢ Exploration,New France, Block of 4		3.75	3.50	2.75
1126-29	34¢ Set of 4 Singles		...	3.15	1.40
	#1130-31 1988 Calgary Winter Olympics				
1130	36¢ Speed Skating		3.25	.70	.20
1131	42¢ Bobsledding		3.95	.85	.80
1132	36¢ Volunteer Week	(25)17.50	3.25	.70	.20
1133	36¢ Law Day	(25)17.50	3.25	.70	.20
1134	36¢ Engineering Institute	(25)17.50	3.25	.70	.20
1135-38	36¢ Canada Day, Communications, Block of 4	(16)12.50	3.35	3.00	2.75
1135-38	36¢ Set of 4 Singles		...	2.80	1.20
1139-40	36¢ Steamships, Pair	(25)18.50	3.35	1.60	1.25
1139-40	36¢ Set of 2 Singles		...	1.50	.60
1141-44	36¢ Underwater Archaeology, Shipwrecks, Block of 4	(25)19.50	3.65	3.50	2.75
1141-44	36¢ Set of 4 Singles		...	3.00	1.20

FROM 1947 TO PRESENT, ADD 20% FOR VERY FINE QUALITY
UNLESS OTHERWISE NOTED. Minimum of 10¢ Per Stamp

1987 Commemoratives (continued)

1145

1148

1152-53

Scott's No.		Mint Sheet	Plate Block	F-VF NH	F-VF Used
1145	36¢ Air Canada 50th Anniversary	...	3.25	.70	.20
1146	36¢ Francophone Int'l. Summit, Quebec	...	3.25	.70	.20
1147	36¢ Commonwealth Heads of Government	...	3.25	.70	.20
1148-51	31¢-72¢ Christmas, Set of 4	...	(3) 13.25	3.70	2.75
1148	36¢ Christmas, Poinsettia	...	3.25	.70	.15
1149	42¢ Christmas, Holly Wreath	...	3.95	.85	.80
1150	72¢ Christmas, Mistletoe, Tree	...	6.50	1.50	1.25
1151	31¢ Christmas Gifts Booklet Single	...	...	.75	.70
1151a	31¢ Christmas Booklet Pane of 10	...	...	7.00	...
1152-53	36¢ Calgary Winter Olympics, Pair	...	3.35	1.60	.90
1152-53	36¢ Set of 2 Singles Cross-Country Skiing, Ski Jumping			1.40	.50
1154	36¢ Grey Cup Football, 75th Anniversary	...	3.25	.75	.20
	1987-91 Regular Issues				
1155-83	**Set of 30**	**...**	**...**	**37.00**	**12.00**
#1155-61, 1170-80 Mammals					
1155	1¢ Flying Squirrel, Pf. 13 x 13½ (1988)	...	.50	.25	.15
1155a	1¢ Perf 13 x 12 3/4 (1991)	(Blank)	19.75	3.50	1.10
1156	2¢ Porcupine (1988)	...	.50	.25	.15
1157	3¢ Muskrat (1988)	...	.50	.25	.15
1158	5¢ Varying Hare (1988)	...	.60	.25	.15
1159	6¢ Red Fox (1988)	...	.70	.25	.15
1160	10¢ Skunk, Pf. 13 x 13½ (1988)	...	.85	.25	.15
1160a	10¢ Perf. 13 x 12 3/4 (1991)	(Blank)	25.00	4.75	.45
1161	25¢ Beaver (1988)	...	2.10	.45	.15
1162	37¢ Queen Elizabeth II	...	3.50	.80	.15
1163	37¢ Parliament Perf. 13½ x 13	...	3.50	.80	.15
1163c	37¢ Booklet Single, Pf. 13½ x 14 (1988)	...	...	1.25	.50
1163c	37¢ with straight edge		...	.75	.25
1163a	37¢ Booklet Pane of 10 (1163c) (1988)	...	...	7.50	...
1163b	37¢ Booklet Pane of 25 (1163c) (1988)	...	...	18.50	...
1164	38¢ Queen Elizabeth II Perf. 13 (1988)	...	3.50	.75	.15
1164a	38¢ Booklet Single, Pf. 13 x 13½ (1988)	...	...	1.50	1.50
1164a	38¢ with straight edge		...	.80	.30
1164b	38¢ Booklet Pane of 10 + 2 labels (1988)	...	...	8.25	...

1165

1166

1167

1173

Scott's No.		Mint Sheet	Plate Block	F-VF NH	F-VF Used
1165	38¢ Parliament Clock Tower (1988)	...	3.25	.75	.15
1165a	38¢ Booklet Pane of 10 + 2 labels (1988)	...	...	7.50	...
1165b	38¢ Booklet Pane of 25 + 2 labels (1988)	...	...	21.50	...
1166	39¢ Flag & Clouds, Perf.13½x13 (1989)	...	3.50	.75	.15
1166a	39¢ Booklet Pane of 10 (1989)	...	...	7.50	...
1166b	39¢ Booklet Pane of 25 (1989)	...	...	23.75	...
1166c	39¢ Flag, Perf. 12 3/4 x 13 (1990)	(Blank)	57.50	12.25	.95
1167	39¢ Elizabeth II, Perf. 13 x 13½ (1990)	...	3.50	.75	.15
1167a	39¢ Booklet Pane of 10 (1990)	...	...	8.00	...
1167b	39¢ Perf. 13 x 12¼ (1990)	(Blank)	57.50	11.50	.75
1168	40¢ Queen Elizabeth II (1990)	...	3.50	.75	.15
1168a	40¢ Booklet Pane of 10 + 2 labels (1990)	...	...	8.75	...
1169	40¢ Flag & Mountains (1990)	...	3.50	.80	.15
1169a	40¢ Booklet Pane of 25 + 2 labels	...	...	26.50	...
1169b	40¢ Booklet Pane of 10 + 2 labels	...	...	8.75	...
1170	43¢ Lynx (1988)	...	5.35	1.15	.35
1171	44¢ Walrus Perf. 14½ x 14 (1989)	...	8.00	1.80	.25
1171a	44¢ Booklet Single Perf. 12½ x 13 (1989)	...	...	3.00	1.40
1171b	44¢ Booklet Pane of 5+label, Perf. 12½ x 13		...	13.95	...
1171c	44¢ Perf. 13½ x 13 (1989)	(Blank)	1650.00	325.00	40.00
1172	45¢ Pronghorn (1990) Perf. 14½ x 14 (1990)		4.25	1.00	.30
1172f	45¢ Booklet Single Perf. 12½ x 13 (1990)		...	3.00	.55
1172b	45¢ Booklet Pane of 5 + label, Perf. 12½ x 13		...	13.75	...
1172d	45¢ Perforated 13 (1990)	(Blank)	110.00	19.75	1.10
1172A	46¢ Wolverine, Perf. 13 (1990)	...	4.25	.95	.30
1172Ac	46¢ Booklet Single Perf. 12½ x 13 (1990)	...	...	1.50	.55
1172Ae	46¢ Booklet Pane of 5 + label, Perf. 12½x13 (1991)		...	7.75	...
1172Ag	46¢ Perforated 14½ x 14 (1990)	...	27.50	6.00	.45
1173	57¢ Killer Whale (1988)	...	5.50	1.15	.35
1174	59¢ Musk-ox, Perf. 14½ x 14 (1989)	...	5.75	1.35	.35
1174a	59¢ Perforated 13 (1989)	(Blank)	42.50	9.00	7.50

1175

1183

1185

CANADA

1987-91 Regular Issue (continued)

Scott's No.		Mint Sheet	Plate Block	F-VF NH	F-VF Used
1175	61¢ Timber Wolf, Perf. 14½ x 14 (1990)	...	5.00	1.20	.40
1175a	61¢ Perforated 13 (1990)	(Blank)	375.00	75.00	6.50
1176	63¢ Harbor Porpoise, Perf. 14½ x 14 (1990)		10.75	1.95	.40
1176a	63¢ Perforated 13 (1990)	(Blank)	40.00	9.00	4.50
1177	74¢ Wapiti (1988)	...	8.25	1.85	.70
1178	76¢ Grizzly Bear, Perf. 14½ x 14 (1989)	...	8.25	1.85	.50
1178a	76¢ Booklet Single, Perf. 12½ x 13 (1989)	...	...	3.00	2.50
1178b	76¢ Booklet Pane of 5 + label, Perf. 12½x13		...	17.50	...
1178c	76¢ Perforated 13	(Blank)	160.00	32.50	12.75
1179	78¢ Beluga Whale, Perf. 14½ x 14 (1990)	...	9.00	1.95	.65
1179c	78¢ Booklet Single, Perf. 12½ x 13 (1990)	...	...	2.95	1.75
1179a	78¢ Booklet Pane of 5, Perf. 12½ x 13	...	...	15.00	...
1179b	78¢ Perforated 13 (1990)	(Blank)	195.00	35.00	6.50
1180	80¢ Peary Caribou, Perf. 13 (1990)	9.50	2.10	.85	
1180a	80¢ Booklet Single, Perf 12½ x 13 (1990)	...	...	3.00	1.25
1180b	80¢ Booklet Pane of 5+label, Perf. 12½x13 (1991)		...	17.50	...
1180c	80¢ Perforated 14½ x 14 (1991)	...	29.50	6.50	2.25
1181	$1 Runnymede Library (1989)	...	7.75	1.85	.60
1182	$2 McAdam Train Station (1989)	...	16.50	3.95	1.25
1183	$5 Bonsecours Market (1990)	...	41.50	9.00	2.50
	1988-90 Booklet Singles and Panes				
1184-90	**Set of 7**	**...**	**...**	**5.25**	**2.50**
1184	1¢ Flag, Perforated 13½ x 14 (1990)	...	...	.20	.20
1184a	1¢ Perforated 12½ x 13 (1990)	...	...	16.50	16.50
1185	5¢ Flag, Perforated 13½ x 14 (1990)	...	...	.20	.20
1185a	5¢ Perforated 12½ x 13 (1990)	...	...	21.50	21.50
1186	6¢ Parliament (1988)	...	...	.75	.30
1187	37¢ Parliament Library (1988)	...	...	.95	.70
1187a	Booklet Pane of 4 (#938,2 #942,#1187)	...	...	1.50	...
1188	38¢ Parliament Center, (1989)	...	...	.95	.40
1188a	Booklet Pane of 5 (3 #939a, 1186, 1188)	...	...	1.50	...
1189	39¢ Canadian Flag, 13½x14 (1990)	...	...	1.10	.35
1189a	Booklet Pane of 4 (#1184,2 #1185,#1189)	...	...	1.60	...
1189b	39¢ Perforated 12½ x 13	...	...	27.50	27.50
1189c	Booklet Pane of 4 (#1184a,2 #1185a,#1189b)		...	67.50	...
1190	40¢ Canadian Flag (1990)	...	...	1.60	.60
1190a	Booklet Pane of 4 (2 #1184,1185,1190)	...	...	2.20	...

1193

1203

1204

Scott's No.		Mint Sheet	Plate Block	F-VF NH	F-VF Used
	1989-91 Self-Adhesive Stamps				
1191-93	38¢-40¢ Flag Booklet Singles, Set of 3		...	3.50	1.40
1191	38¢ Flag & Forest, Booklet Single	...	...	1.10	.50
1191a	38¢ Booklet of 12	...	...	12.75	...
1192	39¢ Flag & Prairie Scene, Booklet Single (1990)		...	1.10	.50
1192a	39¢ Booklet of 12	...	...	12.75	...
1193	40¢ Flag & Seacoast, Booklet Single (1991)...		1.40	.50	
1193a	40¢ Booklet of 12	...	...	16.50	...
	1988-90 Coil Stamps, Perf. 10 Horizontal				
1194-94C	**Set of 4**	**...**	**...**	**3.35**	**.75**
1194	37¢ Parliament Library	...	...	.90	.20
1194A	38¢ Parliament Library (1989)	...	...	1.10	.20
1194B	39¢ Canadian Flag (1990)	...	...	.85	.20
1194C	40¢ Canadian Flag (1990)	...	...	.85	.20
	1988 Commemoratives				
1195-1228	**Set of 34**	**...**	**...**	**27.50**	**11.50**
1195-98	37¢-74¢ Winter Olympics, Set of 4	...	(3) 13.00	3.85	2.15
1195-96	37¢ Calgary Winter Olympics, Pair	...	3.25	1.65	.85
1195-96	37¢ Set of 2 Singles Alpine Skiing, Curling		...	1.40	.50
1197	43¢ Winter Olympics, Figure Skating	...	3.75	.90	.65
1198	74¢ Winter Olympics,Luge	...	6.25	1.40	1.10
1199-1202	37¢ 18th Century Explorers, Block of 4	...	3.50	3.00	2.75
1199-1202	37¢ Set of 4 Singles	...	...	2.85	1.40
1203	50¢ Art, "The Young Reader" by Ozias Leduc	(16)17.50	5.00	1.20	.95
#1203, 1241, 1271, 1310, 1419, 1466, 1516,1545, 1602, 1635, 1754, 1800, 1863, 1915 - 1988-2002 Canadian Art					
1204-05	37¢ Wildlife Conservation, Pair	...	3.15	1.50	1.10
1204-05	37¢ Set of 2 Singles, Duck, Moose	...	...	1.35	.60
1206-09	37¢ Science & Technology, Block of 4	(16)12.00	3.50	3.15	2.75
1206-09	37¢ Set of 4 Singles	...	...	2.70	1.20
1210-13	37¢ Butterflies, Entomology, Block of 4	...	4.00	3.45	2.85
1210-13	37¢ Set of 4 Singles	...	...	2.70	1.40

1214

1215

1216

1988 Commemoratives (continued)

Scott's No.		Mint Sheet	Plate Block	F-VF NH	F-VF Used
1214	37¢ St. John's Newfld. City Centennial	3.25		.70	.20
1215	37¢ 4-H Clubs 75th Anniversary	3.25		.70	.20
1216	37¢ Les Forges du Saint-Maurice, Trois Rivieres, Quebec	3.25		.70	.20
1217-20	37¢ Kennel Club Centennial, Dogs, Block of 4	5.50		4.75	3.00
1217-20	37¢ Set of 4 Singles	...		4.25	1.50

1221	**1223**	**1226**	**1228**

1221	37¢ Canadian Baseball 150th Anniversary...	3.25	.75	.20
1222-25	Christmas, Icons of Eastern Church, Set of 4	(3) 13.50	4.00	2.40
1222	37¢ Conception	3.25	.75	.20
1223	43¢ Virgin and Child	3.95	.90	.65
1224	74¢ Virgin and Child	6.75	1.65	.95
1225	32¢ Nativity, Booklet Single	...	.95	.70
1225a	32¢ Booklet Pane of 10	...	9.00	...
1226	37¢ Charles Inglis, 1st Anglican Bishop	3.25	.75	.20
1227	37¢ Frances Ann Hopkins, Painter	3.25	.75	.20
1228	37¢ Angus Walters, "Bluenose" Captain	3.25	.75	.20

1989 Commemoratives

1229	**1241**	**1249**

1229-63	**Set of 34**	...	**29.35**	**13.95**
1229-32	38¢ Small Craft, Native Boats, Block of 4...	3.75	3.40	2.75
1229-32	38¢ Set of 4 Singles, Canoes and Kayak ...	...	3.15	1.40
1233-36	38¢ Explorers of Canadian North, Block of 4	3.75	3.40	2.75
1233-36	38¢ Set of 4 Singles	...	3.15	1.40
1237-40	38¢ Canada Day Photography,Block-4(16)13.00	3.75	3.40	2.75
1237-40	38¢ Set of 4 Singles	...	3.15	1.40
1241	50¢ Art, Ceremonial Frontlet .... (16)20.75	5.95	1.40	.95
1243-44	38¢ Poets, Louis H. Frechette, Archibald Lampman, Pair	3.25	1.55	1.00
1243-44	38¢ Set of 2 Singles	...	1.40	.60
1245-48	38¢ Mushrooms, Block of 4	3.75	3.45	2.75
1245-48	38¢ Set of 4 Singles	...	3.15	1.40
1249-50	38¢ Canadian Infantry Regiments, Pair	*225.00	1.80	1.40
1249-50	38¢ Set of 2 Singles	...	1.60	.70

* Printing difficulties caused a severe shortage of inscription blocks.

1251	**1252**	**1260**

1251	38¢ International Trade	3.25	.70	.20
1252-55	38¢ Performing Arts, Block of 4	4.00	3.40	2.50
1252-55	38¢ Set of 4 Singles	...	3.15	1.40
1256-59	Christmas Landscapes, Set of 4	(3) 14.50	4.50	3.35
1256	38¢ Athabasca, Perf. 13 x 13½	3.25	.75	.20
1256b	38¢ Booklet Single, Perf. 13 x 12½	...	4.50	4.25
1256a	38¢ Booklet Pane of 10, Perf. 13 x 12½	...	45.00	...
1257	44¢ Snow II	4.25	.95	.70
1257a	44¢ Booklet Pane of 5 + label	...	16.50	...
1258	76¢ Ste. Agnes	7.50	1.60	1.25
1258a	76¢ Booklet Pane of 5 + label	...	32.50	...
1259	33¢ Champ-de-Mars Booklet Single	...	1.60	1.40
1259a	33¢ Booklet Pane of 10	...	13.75	...
1260-63	38¢ World War II,1939 Events,Block-4(16)14.00	4.25	3.75	3.25
1260-63	38¢ Set of 4 Singles	...	3.35	2.20

#1260-63, 1298-1301, 1345-48, 1448-51, 1503-6, 1537-44 1989-95 World War II

CANADA

1990 Commemoratives

1264	**1270**	**1271**

Scott's No.		Mint Sheet	Plate Block	F-VF NH	F-VF Used
1264-71,1274-1301	**Set of 36**	...		**32.60**	**15.75**
1264-65	39¢ Norman Bethune, Medicine, Pair	7.50	3.75	2.50
1264-65	39¢ Set of 2 Singles	...	2.00	.80
1266-69	39¢ Small Work Boats, Block of 4	4.00	3.75	2.75
1266-69	39¢ Set of 4 Singles	...	3.25	1.40
1270	39¢ Multicultural Heritage of Canada	3.25	.75	.25
1271	50¢ Art, "The West Wind" by Tom Thomson .... (16)17.50	5.35	1.20	.85

1272-73	**1278**

1990 Regular Issue Prestige Booklet

1272-73	39¢ Postal Truck, Horizontal Pair	...	2.35	2.25
1272-73	39¢ Postal Truck Booklet Singles	...	1.70	1.00
1273a	39¢ Booklet Pane of 8 (4 English + 4 French Inscriptions)	...	7.50	...
1273b	39¢ Booklet Pane of 9 (4 English + 5 French Inscriptions)	...	9.75	...
1273a-b	Prestige Booklet with 2 #1273a & 1 #1273b...	...	24.50	...

1990 Commemoratives (continued)

1274-77	39¢ Cultural Treasures, Dolls, Block of 4 ...	4.00	3.70	3.00
1274-77	39¢ Set of 4 Singles	...	3.25	1.40
1278	39¢ Canada Day, Flag & Fireworks 25th Anniversary .... (16)11.00	3.50	.75	.25
1279-82	39¢ Prehistoric Life,Fossils,Block of 4(20)17.50	4.00	3.75	3.00
1279-82	39¢ Set of 4 Singles	...	3.25	1.40
1283-86	39¢ Forests, 19th World Cong. Block-4(20)17.50	4.00	3.75	2.75
1283-86	39¢ Set of 4 Singles	...	3.25	1.20
1283a-86b	39¢ Miniature sheets of 4 (Set of 4)	...	37.50	30.00

1287	**1288**	**1293**	**1294**

1287	39¢ Weather Observations 150th Anniv..	3.50	.75	.20
1288	39¢ International Literacy Year	3.50	.75	.20
1289-92	39¢ Canadian Folklore, Legendary Creatures, Perf.12½x13,Block of 4, ...	4.25	4.00	3.50
1289-92	39¢ Set of 4 Singles, Perf. 12½ x 13	...	3.50	3.25
1289a-92a	39¢ Folklore, Perf. 12½ x 12, Block of 4...	...	42.50	25.00
1289a-92a	39¢ Set of 4 Singles, Perf. 12½ x 12	...	37.50	16.00
1293	39¢ Agnes Macphail, 1st Woman MP	3.50	.75	.20
1294-97	34¢-78¢ Christmas, Set of 4	(3) 16.75	4.50	2.40
1294	39¢ Christmas, Virgin Mary	3.50	.75	.20
1294a	39¢ Booklet Pane of 10	...	8.75	...
1295	45¢ Christmas, Mother & Child	5.25	1.20	.80
1295a	45¢ Booklet Pane of 5 + label	...	8.50	...
1296	78¢ Christmas, Children & Raven	8.50	1.80	1.20
1296a	78¢ Booklet Pane of 5 + label	...	12.50	...
1297	34¢ Christmas, Rebirth, Booklet Single	...	1.00	.35
1297a	Bklt. Pane of 10	...	8.25	...
1298-1301	39¢ World War II,1940 Events,Blk.-4(16)13.75	4.00	3.75	3.50
1298-1301	39¢ Set of 4 Singles	...	3.25	2.50

1991 Commemoratives

1302

1310

1316

Scott's No.		Mint Sheet	Plate Block	F-VF NH	F-VF Used
1302-43,1345-48	**Set of 45**	**...**	**...**	**39.95**	**16.75**
1302-05	40¢ Physicians; Jennie K. Trout, Wilder G. Penfield, Frederick Banting, Harold L. Griffith, Block of 4	...	4.00	3.50	3.00
1302-05	40¢ Set of 4 Singles	...	...	3.25	1.40
1306-09	40¢ Prehistoric Life, Block of 4	(20)17.50	4.00	3.50	3.00
1306-09	40¢ Set of 4 Singles		...	3.25	1.40
1310	50¢ Art, "Forest,BC" by Emily Carr	(16)15.75	4.75	1.00	.90
1311-15	40¢ Public Gardens, Booklet Strip of 5	...	...	4.50	4.00
1311-15	40¢ Set of 5 Singles	...	...	4.25	1.75
1315b	40¢ Gardens, Booklet Pane of 10	...	...	8.75	...
1316	40¢ Canada Day, Maple Leaf	(20)14.75	3.50	.75	.20
1317-20	40¢ Small Craft, Pleasure Boats, Block of 4		4.00	3.50	3.00
1317-20	40¢ Set of 4 Singles	...	...	3.25	1.40
1321-25	40¢ River Heritage, Booklet Strip of 5	...	...	4.50	4.00
1321-25	40¢ Set of 5 Singles	...	...	4.25	1.75
1325b	40¢ River Booklet Pane of 10	...	...	8.75	...
#1321-25, 1408-12, 1485-89, 1511-15 - 1991-94 River Heritage					
1326-29	40¢ Ukrainian Migration-Canada,Block-4 (20)		4.00	3.50	3.00
1326-29	40¢ Set of 4 Singles	...	...	3.25	1.40
1330-33	40¢ Dangerous Public Service Organizations, Block of 4	...	5.25	4.50	3.50
1330-33	40¢ Set of 4 Singles	...	...	4.25	1.40
1334-37	40¢ Canadian Folklore, Folktales, Block of 4		4.25	3.50	3.00
1334-37	40¢ Set of 4 Singles	...	...	3.35	1.40

1338

1339

1345

Scott's No.		Mint Sheet	Plate Block	F-VF NH	F-VF Used
1338	40¢ Queen's University, Booklet Single	...	...	.85	.50
1338a	40¢ Booklet Pane of 10	...	...	8.25	...
1339-42	35¢-80¢ Christmas, Set of 4	...	(3) 15.00	4.15	2.40
1339	40¢ Christmas, Santa at Fireplace	...	4.50	.95	.20
1339a	40¢ Booklet Pane of 10		...	8.50	...
1340	46¢ Christmas,Bonhomme Noel, France	...	4.00	.85	.75
1340a	46¢ Booklet Pane of 5	...	...	4.75	...
1341	80¢ Christmas, Sinterklass, Hollandl	...	7.00	1.60	1.30
1341a	80¢ Booklet Pane of 5	...	...	8.25	...
1342	35¢ Greet More, Father Christmas, England, Booklet Single	...	...	.85	.25
1342a	35¢ Booklet Pane of 10	...	...	8.50	...
1343	40¢ Basketball Centennial		4.15	.85	.30
1344	40¢, 46¢, 80¢ Basketball Souvenir Sheet of 3		...	6.20	5.50
1344a-c	40¢-80¢ Singles from Souvenir Sheet	...	...	...	5.00
1345-48	40¢ World War II,1941 Events,Block-4	(16) 14.00	4.25	3.75	3.00
1345-48	40¢ Set of 4 Singles	...	...	3.35	1.60

1991-98 Regular Issues

1349

1356

1357

1361

Scott's No.		Mint Sheet	Plate Block	F-VF NH	F-VF Used
1349-78	**Set of 29**	**...**	**...**	**34.95**	**9.75**
#1349-55, 1361-74 Edible Berries					
1349	1¢ Blueberry (1992)	...	.50	.20	.15
1350	2¢ Strawberry (1992)	...	.50	.20	.15
1351	3¢ Crowberry (1992)	...	.50	.20	.15
1352	5¢ Rose Hip (1992)	...	.50	.20	.15
1353	6¢ Black Raspberry (1992)	...	.60	.20	.15
1354	10¢ Kinnikinnick (1992)	...	.80	.20	.15
1355	25¢ Saskatoon Berry (1992)	...	1.95	.45	.20
1356	42¢ Canadian Flag & Rolling Hills	...	3.75	.80	.15
1356a	42¢ Booklet Pane of 10	...	...	8.25	...
1356b	42¢ Booklet Pane of 50	...	...	95.00	...
1356c	42¢ Booklet Pane of 25	...	...	19.95	...
1357	42¢ Queen Elizabeth II, Karsh Portrait	...	3.75	.85	.15
1357a	42¢ Booklet Pane of 10	...	...	8.25	...

1991-98 Regular Issues (continued)

Scott's No.		Mint Sheet	Plate Block	F-VF NH	F-VF Used
1358	43¢ Queen Elizabeth II Karsh Portrait (1992)		4.00	.85	.15
1358a	43¢ Booklet Pane of 10	...	...	8.50	...
1359	43¢ Flag & Prairie, Perf. 13½ x 13 (1992)	...	4.00	.90	.15
1359a	43¢ Booklet Pane of 10, Perf. 13½ x 13	...	...	8.50	...
1359b	43¢ Booklet Pane of 25, Perf. 13½ x 13	...	...	23.50	...
1359c	43¢ Flag & Prairie, Perf. 14½ (1994)	...	5.50	1.10	.20
1359d	43¢ Booklet Pane of 10, Perf. 14½	...	...	9.95	...
1359e	43¢ Booklet Pane of 25, Perf. 14½	...	...	26.50	...
1360	45¢ Queen Elizabeth II (1995)	...	4.00	.95	.15
1360a	45¢ Booklet Pane of 10	...	...	9.50	...
1361	45¢ Flag & Office Building, Perf. 14½ (1995)		4.00	.95	.15
1361a	45¢ Booklet Pane of 10, Perf 14½	...	...	9.50	...
1361b	45¢ Booklet Pane of 25, Perf 14½	...	...	27.50	...
1361c	45¢ Flag, Booklet Single, Perf. 13½ x 13	...	...	.85	.20
1361d	45¢ Booklet Pane of 10, Perf 13½ x 13	...	...	9.00	...
1361e	45¢ Booklet Pane of 25, Perf 13½ x 13	..	...	22.75	...
1362	45¢ Flag, smaller 16 x 20mm size, Perforated 13 x 13½ (1998)	...	...	.85	.30
1362a	45¢ Booklet Pane of 10, 13 x 13½	...	...	9.50	...
1362b	45¢ Booklet Pane of 30, 13 x 13½	...	...	26.50	...
#1363-74 Fruit Trees					
1363	48¢ McIntosh Apple Tree, Perf. 13	...	4.25	.95	.25
1363a	48¢ Booklet Single, Perf. 14½x14 on 3 sides		...	1.30	.35
1363b	48¢ Booklet Pane of 5, Pf.14½x14	...	...	6.50	...
1364	49¢ Delicious Apple, Perf. 13 (1992)	...	4.75	1.00	.25
1364c	49¢ Booklet Pane of 5, Perf. 13	...	...	12.75	...
1364a	49¢ Booklet Single, Perf. 14½ x 14	...	...	1.95	.30
1364b	49¢ Booklet Pane of 5, Perf. 14½ x 14	...	...	8.75	...
1365	50¢ Snow Apple, Perf. 13 (1994)	...	4.75	1.00	.30
1365a	50¢ Booklet Pane of 5, Perf. 13	...	...	6.50	...
1365b	50¢ Booklet Single, Perf. 14½ x 14 (1995	...	...	1.75	.75
1365c	50¢ Booklet Pane of 5, Perf. 14½ x 14	...	...	9.50	...
1366	52¢ Gravenstein Apple, Perf. 13 (1995)	...	8.25	1.80	.30
1366a	52¢ Booklet Pane of 5, Perf. 13	...	...	8.50	...
1366b	52¢ Apple, Perf. 14½ x 14	...	11.75	2.50	.60
1366c	52¢ Booklet Pane of 5, Perf 14½ x 14	...	...	11.50	...
1367	65¢ Black Walnut Tree	...	6.00	1.35	.40
1368	67¢ Beaked Hazelnut (1992)	...	6.00	1.25	.40
1369	69¢ Shagbark Hickory (1994)	...	6.25	1.30	.40
1370	71¢ American Chestnut, Perf.13 (1995)	...	6.25	1.40	.40
1370a	71¢ Perf. 14½ x 14	...	50.00	8.50	.95
1371	84¢ Stanley Plum Tree, Perf. 13	...	9.50	1.70	.40
1371a	84¢ Booklet Single, Perf. 14½x14	...	...	2.40	.60
1371b	84¢ Booklet Pane of 5, Perf.14½x14	...	...	11.00	...
1372	86¢ Bartlett Pear, Perf. 13 (1992)	...	9.95	2.30	.60
1372c	86¢ Booklet Pane of 5, Perf. 13	...	...	17.50	...
1372a	86¢ Booklet Single, Perf. 14½ x 14	...	...	3.50	1.85
1372b	86¢ Booklet Pane of 5, Perf. 14½ x 14	...	...	14.50	...
1373	88¢ Westcot Apricot, Perf. 13(1994)	...	8.50	1.90	.50
1373a	88¢ Booklet Pane of 5, Perf. 13	...	...	10.00	...
1373b	88¢ Booklet Single, Perf. 14½ x 14 (1995)	...	...	3.50	1.10
1373c	88¢ Booklet Pane of 5, Perf. 14½ x 14	...	...	17.00	...
1374	90¢ Elberta Peach, Perf. 13 (1995)	...	9.75	2.30	.45
1374a	90¢ Booklet Pane of 5, Perf. 13	...	...	11.50	...
1374ii	90¢ Elberta Peach, Perf.14½x14	...	65.00	9.75	...
1374b	90¢ Booklet Single, Perf 14½ x 14	...	...	3.50	1.10
1374c	90¢ Booklet Pane of 5, Perf. 14½ x 14	...	...	14.75	...

1375

1388

1395

Scott's No.		Plate Block	F-VF NH	F-VF Used
#1375-78 Canadian Architecture				
1375	$1 Yorkton Court House Perf. 14½x 14 (1994)	8.75	1.90	.50
1375b	$1 Yorkton, Reprint, Perf. 13½ x 13	8.95	2.10	.60
1376	$2 Truro Normal School (1994) Perf. 14½x 14	16.75	4.00	1.10
1376c	$2 Truro, Reprint, Perf 13½ x 13	17.50	3.85	1.10
1378	$5 Victoria, BC Public Library (1996)	43.50	9.50	2.50

1992-93 Self-Adhesive Stamps

Scott's No.		Plate Block	F-VF NH	F-VF Used
1388	42¢ Flag & Mountains, Booklet Single.	...	1.40	.50
1388a	42¢ Booklet of 12	...	16.50	...
1389	43¢ Flag & Shoreline, Booklet Single (1993)..	...	1.40	.50
1389a	43¢ Booklet of 12	...	16.50	...

1991-95 Coil Stamps, Perf. 10 Horizontal

Scott's No.		Plate Block	F-VF NH	F-VF Used
1394-96	42¢-45¢ Flag, Set of 3	...	2.40	.80
1394	42¢ Canadian Flag, Red	...	.80	.30
1395	43¢ Canadian Flag, Olive Green (1992)	...	.85	.30
1396	45¢ Canadian Flag, Blue Green (1995)	...	.85	.25

1992 Commemoratives

1407	1413	1419

Scott's No.	Mint Sheet	Plate Block	F-VF NH	F-VF Used
1399-1407,1408-19,1432-55 Set of 45		...	**40.00**	**18.95**
1399-1403 42¢ Winter Olympics, Albertville, France, Booklet Strip of 5		...	4.75	4.25
1399-1403 42¢ Set of 5 Singles		...	4.50	2.00
1403b 42¢ Olympics Booklet Pane of 10			9.50	...
1404-7 42¢-84¢ Canada Day, Set of 4	(3) 15.75		4.15	2.40
1404-05 42¢ Montreal, 350th Anniv., Pair ..... (25) 41.50		4.00	1.70	1.25
1404-05 42¢ Set of 2 Singles		...	1.60	.60
1406 48¢ Jacques Cartier .... (25) 21.95		4.35	.90	.85
1407 84¢ Christopher Columbus .... (25) 41.50		7.75	1.70	1.10
1407a 42¢-84¢ Explorers Souvenir Sheet of 4, regular edition			4.50	4.00
1407al Special Edition, with Maisonneuve signature		...	125.00	...
1408-12 42¢ River Heritage, Booklet Strip of 5		...	4.75	4.25
1408-12 42¢ Set of 5 Singles		...	4.50	2.00
1412b 42¢ Rivers Booklet Pane of 10		...	9.50	...
1413 42¢ Alaska Highway		3.75	.80	.25
1414-18 42¢ Summer Olympics, Barcelona, Spain, Booklet Strip of 5		...	4.75	4.50
1414-18 42¢ Set of 5 Singles		...	4.50	2.00
1418b 42¢ Olympics Booklet Pane of 10		...	9.50	...
1419 50¢ Art,"Red Nasturtiums" David Milne(16)15.00		4.50	.95	.85

1992 Provincial and Territorial Landmarks Paintings

1431a 42¢ Canada Day, Miniature Sheet of 12		...	26.25	24.75
1420-31 42¢ Set of 12 Singles		...	22.75	18.50

1992 Commemoratives (continued)

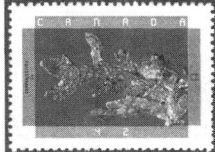

1436	1441-42

1445	1446-47	1453

1432-35 42¢ Folklore, Legendary Heroes, Block of 4	4.00	3.75	3.00
1432-35 42¢ Set of 4 Singles		...	3.25	1.40
1436-40 42¢ Minerals, Booklet Strip of 5		...	5.00	4.75
1436-40 42¢ Set of 5 Singles		...	4.00	2.00
1440b 42¢ Minerals Booklet Pane of 10		...	9.75	...
1441-42 42¢ Space Exploration, Pair .... (20)17.50		3.95	1.90	1.75
1441-42 42¢ Set of 2 Singles		...	1.70	1.60
1443 42¢ Hockey, Early Years (1917-42)		...	.80	.25
1443a 42¢ Skates, Sticks, Booklet Pane of 8		...	6.35	...
1444 42¢ Hockey, Six-Team Years(1942-67)		...	.80	.25
1444a 42¢ Team Emblems, Booklet Pane of 8		...	6.25	...
1445 42¢ Hockey, Expansion Years (1967-92) ...		...	.80	.25
1445a 42¢ Goalie's Mask, Booklet Pane of 9		...	8.25	...
1443a-45a Prestige Booklet with 1443a, 44a, 45a ...		...	21.75	...
1446-47 42¢ Order of Canada & Roland Michener, Pair .... (25)20.75		3.95	1.70	1.50
1446 42¢ Order of Canada		...	.80	.25
1447 42¢ Roland Michener		...	1.00	.35
1448-51 42¢ World War II,1942 Events,Block-4(16)14.75		4.15	4.00	3.00
1448-51 42¢ Set of 4 Singles		...	3.50	1.80
1452-55 37¢-84¢ Christmas, Set of 4 .... (3) 15.25			4.50	2.70
1452 42¢ Joouluvana, Perf. 12½		3.75	.80	.20
1452a 42¢ Booklet Single, Perf. 13½		...	.95	.25
1452b 42¢ Booklet Pane of 10, Perf. 13½		...	9.00	...
1453 48¢ La Befana		4.50	1.10	.85
1453a 48¢ Booklet Pane of 5		...	5.25	...
1454 84¢ Weihnachtsmann		7.50	1.70	1.00
1454a 84¢ Booklet Pane of 5		...	8.50	...
1455 37¢ Santa Claus, Booklet Single		...	.85	.75
1455a 37¢ Booklet Pane of 10		...	9.00	...

1993 Commemoratives

1460	1466	1484

Scott's No.	Mint Sheet	Plate Block	F-VF NH	F-VF Used
1456-71,1484-89,1491-1506 Set of 38		...	**35.25**	**15.25**
1456-59 43¢ Prominent Women, A. Hoodless, Marie-Josephine Gerin-Lajoie, P.Ashoona, Helen Kinnear, Block of 4		4.50	4.00	3.00
1456-59 43¢ Strip of 4		...	3.75	3.00
1456-59 43¢ Set of 4 Singles		...	3.50	1.40
1460 43¢ Stanley Cup Centennial .... (25)19.50		3.75	.80	.20
1461-65 43¢ Hand-crafted Textiles, Booklet Strip of 5		...	5.00	4.00
1461-65 43¢ Set of 5 Singles		...	4.25	2.00
1465b 43¢ Textiles, Booklet Pane of 10		...	8.75	...
1466 86¢ Art, Drawing for the Owl .... (16)24.75		7.25	1.70	1.00
1467-71 43¢ Historic Hotels, Booklet Strip of 5		...	5.50	4.25
1467-71 43¢ Set of 5 Singles		...	4.75	2.75
1471b 43¢ Historic Hotels, Booklet Pane of 10		...	9.75	...

1993 Canada Day - Provincial & Territorial Parks

1483a 43¢ Miniature sheet of 12		...	17.95	16.50
1472-83 43¢ Parks, Set of 12 Singles		...	16.50	10.75

1993 Commemoratives (continued)

1484 43¢ Founding of Toronto Bicentennail(25)19.50		3.75	.80	.20

1485-89 Ex.	1491-94 Example	1495-98 Example

1485-89 43¢ River Heritage, Booklet Strip of 5		...	4.75	4.00
1485-89 43¢ Set of 5 Singles		...	4.50	1.75
1489b 43¢ Rivers, Booklet Pane of 10		...	9.25	...
1490 43¢-86¢ Personal Vehicles, Souvenir Sheet of 6		...	9.00	7.75
1490a-f Set of 6 Singles, 2-43¢,2-49¢,2-86¢		...	8.25	6.50
#1490, 1527, 1552, 1604-5 - 1993-96 Historic Land Vehicles				
1491-94 43¢ Folklore, Folk Songs, Block of 4		4.00	3.75	3.00
1491-94 43¢ Set of 4 Singles		...	3.25	1.40
1495-98 43¢ Prehistoric Life,Dinosaurs,Block- 4(20)17.50		4.00	3.75	3.00
1495-98 43¢ Set of 4 Singles		...	3.25	1.40
1499-1502 38¢-86¢ Christmas Personalities, Set of 4	(3) 15.00		4.50	2.00
1499 43¢ Swiety Mikolaj, Poland		3.75	.80	.20
1499a 43¢ Booklet Pane of 10		...	8.25	...
1500 49¢ Ded Moroz, Russia		4.25	.90	.60
1500a 49¢ Booklet Pane of 5		...	6.00	...
1501 86¢ Father Christmas, Australia		7.50	1.60	.75
1501a 86¢ Booklet Pane of 5		...	9.95	...
1502 38¢ Santa Claus, North America, Booklet Single		...	.75	.60
1502a 38¢ Booklet Pane of 10		...	8.50	...
1503-06 43¢ World War II,1943 Events,Block-4.(16)15.00		4.35	4.00	3.25
1503-06 43¢ Set of 4 Singles		...	3.50	1.80

1994 Regular Issues

1507-08 43¢ Greetings, Self-adhesive		...	2.00	1.50
1508a 43¢ Booklet Pane of 10 (5 each) w/stickers		...	9.95	...

1994 Commemoratives

1509	1510	1511 Example

1509-22,1525-26,1528-40 Set of 29		...	**27.50**	**12.85**
1509 43¢ Jeanne Sauve, Governor General(20)16.50		...	.85	.30
1509 43¢ Block of 4 with 4 different tabs		4.25	3.75	3.50

1994 Commemoratives (continued)

Scott's No.		Mint Sheet	Plate Block	F-VF NH	F-VF Used
1510	43¢ T. Eaton Company, Timothy Eaton Booklet Singles			.85	.30
1510a	43¢ Prestige Booklet of 10	...	...	8.25	...
1511-15	43¢ Rivers Heritage Booklet Strip of 5	...	...	5.50	4.75
1511-15	43¢ Set of 5 Singles	...	...	5.25	2.50
1515b	43¢ Rivers, Booklet Pane of 10	...	...	10.75	...
1516	88¢ Art, "Vera, 1931" Frederick Varley(16)26.50	8.00	1.65	1.20

1522 **1529-32**

1517-22	43¢-88¢ Commonwealth Games Set of 6 ...	(4) 19.75		5.95	3.00
1517-18	43¢ Lawn Bowl and Lacrosse, Pair . (25) 20.75		3.75	1.70	1.35
1517-18	43¢ Set of 2 Singles	...	...	1.60	.60
1519-20	43¢ High Jump and Wheelchair Marathon, Pair .... (25) 20.75		3.75	1.70	1.35
1519-20	43¢ Set of 2 Singles	...	...	1.60	.60
1521	50¢ Diving.................................... (25) 24.75		4.75	1.00	.85
1522	88¢ Cycling .... (25) 41.50		8.00	1.70	1.10
1523	43¢ Year of the Family, Souvenir Sheet of 5	...	...	4.75	4.25
1523a-e	43¢ Set of 5 Singles	...	...	4.35	2.50

1994 Canada Day - Maple Trees

1524	43¢ Miniature Sheet of 12	...	...	10.75	10.00
1524a-l	43¢ Set of 12 Singles	...	...	10.50	9.50

1994 Commemoratives (continued)

1525-26	43¢ Billy Bishop, World War I Flying Ace and Mary Travers, Singers, Pair		3.70	1.70	1.30
1525-26	43¢ Set of 2 Singles	...	...	1.60	.60
1527	43¢-88¢ Public Service Vehicles, Souvenir Sheet of 6		8.00	7.50
1527a-f	43¢-88¢ Set of 6 Singles, 2-43¢,2-50¢,2-88¢	...		7.85	6.50
1528	43¢ Civil Aviation, ICAO 50th Anniv.(25) 26.50		5.00	1.10	.25
1529-32	38¢-88¢ Prehistoric Life, Mammals, Block of 4...		4.00	3.50	3.00
1529-32	43¢ Set of 4 Singles	...	...	3.25	1.40
1533-36	43¢-88¢ Christmas, Set of 4	(3) 15.00		3.85	2.50
1533	43¢ Christmas, Singing Carols		3.75	.80	.20
1533a	43¢ Booklet Pane of 10	...	...	9.50	...
1534	50¢ Christmas, Choir		4.25	.90	.60
1534a	50¢ Booklet Pane of 5	...	...	5.50	...
1535	88¢ Christmas, Caroling		7.50	1.60	1.20
1535a	88¢ Booklet Pane of 5	...	...	8.75	...
1536	38¢ Christmas, Soloist, Booklet Single	...	...	.85	.60
1536a	38¢ Booklet Pane of 10	...	...	9.50	...
1537-40	43¢ World War II,1944 Events,Block-4(16)16.00		4.50	4.00	3.25
1537-40	43¢ Set of 4 Singles	...	...	3.60	1.60

1995 Commemoratives

1541-51,1553-58,1562-66,1570-90 Set of 46 ...		...		39.70	16.50
1541-44	43¢ World War II,1945 Events,Block-4(16)16.00		4.50	4.00	3.50
1541-44	43¢ Set of 4 Singles	...	...	3.95	1.60
1545	88¢ Art, "Floraison" by Alfred Pellan(16) 25.00		7.50	1.60	1.10
1546	(43¢) Canada Flag 30th Anniversary(20) 15.75		3.75	.80	.25
1547-51	(43¢) Fortress of Louisbourg,BookletStrip of 5	...		4.50	4.25
1547-51	(43¢) Set of 5 singles	...	...	4.25	2.00
1551b	(43¢) Louisbourg, Booklet Pane of 10	...		8.75	...

1552

CANADA

1995 Commemoratives (continued)

Scott's No.		Mint Sheet	Plate Block	F-VF NH	F-VF Used
1552	43¢-88¢ Farm and Frontier Vehicles, Souvenir Sheet of 6	...		8.00	7.00
1552a-f	43¢-88¢ Set of 6 Singles, 2-43¢,2-50¢,2-88¢	...		7.75	6.50
1553-57	43¢ Golf, Booklet Strip of 5	...	...	5.25	4.50
1553-57	43¢ Set of 5 Singles	...	...	5.00	2.00
1557b	43¢ Golf, Booklet Pane of 10	...	...	10.50	...

1558 **1562**

1568-69 **1563-66**

1558	43¢ Lunenburg Academy Centennial		3.70	.80	.25
1559-61	43¢ Canada Day, The Group of Seven, Set of 3 Souvenir Sheets bearing 10 different stamps	...		9.75	11.50
1559a-c,1560a-d,1561a-c Set of 10 Singles			9.50	9.75
1562	43¢ Manitoba 125th Anniversary .... (20) 15.75		3.75	.80	.30
1563-66	43¢ Migratory Wildlife,"Aune" Block of 4(20)22.50	5.00	4.50	3.75
1563-66	43¢ Set of 4 Singles	...	...	4.25	1.40
1563/67	43¢ Migratory Wildlife revised Kingfisher Inscribed "Faune", Block of 4 .... (20)26.50		6.00	5.25	4.00
1563/67	43¢ Set of 4 singles	...	...	...	2.00

1995 Greetings Booklets

1568-69	45¢ Greetings, Self-adhesive	...	...	2.10	1.10
1569a	Booklet Pane of 10 (5 Each) w/ labels	...	...	12.00	...
1569c	Booklet Pane of 10 w/ "Canadian Memorial Chiropractic College", covers and labels ...	...		12.00	...

1995 Commemoratives (continued)

1570-73	45¢ Bridges, Block of 4 .... (20) 18.50	4.35	3.75	3.00
1570-73	45¢ Strip of 4	...	...	3.75	3.00
1570-73	45¢ Set of 4 Singles	...	...	3.50	1.40
1574-78	45¢ Canadian Arctic, Booklet Strip of 5	...		4.50	4.00
1574-78	45¢ Set of 5 Singles	...	...	4.25	2.00
1578b	45¢ Arctic, Booklet Pane of 10	...		8.75	...

1579 **1584** **1585**

1579-83	45 Comic Book Superheroes, Booklet Strip of 5	...		4.50	4.25
1579-83	45¢ Set of 5 Singles	...	...	4.25	2.10
1583b	45¢ Comic Books, Booklet Pane of 10	...		8.75	...
1584	45¢ United Nations 50th Anniversary(10) 8.35	4.00	.85	.25
1585-88	40¢-90¢ Christmas, Set of 4	(3) 15.50		4.15	2.40
1585	45¢ Capitol Sculpture, The Nativity ...		4.00	.85	.20
1585a	45¢ Booklet Pane of 10	...	...	9.00	...
1586	52¢ Capitol Sculpture,The Annunciation		4.25	.95	.60
1586a	52¢ Booklet Pane of 5	...	...	5.00	...
1587	90¢ Capitol Sculpture, Flight to Egypt ...		7.75	1.65	.90
1587a	90¢ Booklet Pane of 5	...	...	8.50	...
1588	40¢ Christmas,Holly, Booklet Single		...	.80	.80
1588a	40¢ Booklet Pane of 10	...	...	7.95	...
1589	45¢ La Francophonie 25th Anniversary(20) 16.75	4.00	.85	.25
1590	45¢ End of the Holocaust 50th Anniv.(20) 16.75	4.00	.85	.25

1996 Commemoratives

1591-98,1602-3,1606-14,1617-21,1622-29 Set of 36 ...		...		37.00	14.95
1591-94	45¢ Birds, American Kestrel, Atlantic Puffin, Woodpecker, Hummingbird, Strip of 4		4.25	3.50
1591-94	45¢ Set of 4 Singles	...	...	4.10	1.60
1591-94d	45¢ Diamond Philatelic Pane of 12	...	...	11.95	...
1591-94r	45¢ Rectangular Pane of 12	...	...	14.95	...

1996 Commemoratives (continued)

1595-98

Scott's No.		Mint Sheet	Plate Block	F-VF NH	F-VF Used
1595-98	45¢ High Technology Industries, Booklet Block of 4...			4.50	3.50
1595-98	45¢ Set of 4 Singles	...		4.25	1.60
1598b	45¢ Technology, Booklet Pane of 12	...		13.50	...

1996 Greetings Booklets

1600-1	45¢ Greetings, Self-adhesive	...		2.25	1.50
1601a	45¢ Booklet Pane of 10 (5 each) with labels	...		10.95	...

NOTE: #1600-1 are slightly larger than #1568-69 & same size as #1507-8.

1996 Commemoratives (continued)

1602	90¢ Art "The Spirit of Haidi Gwali" by Bill Reid .... (16) 25.75		7.75	1.65	1.20
1603	45¢ Aids Awareness, Joe Average . (20) 16.75		4.00	.85	.25
1604	45¢-90¢ Industrial and Commercial Vehicles Souvenir Sheet of 6	...		8.00	8.00
1604a-f	45¢-90¢ Set of 6 Singles, 2-45¢,2-52¢,2-90¢	...		7.75	7.75
1605	5¢ (10), 10¢ (4), 20¢ (10), 45¢ Canadian Vehicles Souvenir Pane of 25	...		8.50	...
1605a-y	5¢-45¢ Set of 25 Singles	...		8.25	7.75

NOTE: The above pane pictures all 24 stamps shown on the Vehicles series souvenir sheets of 6 plus one additional vehicle.

1606	45¢ Yukon Gold Rush Strip of 5 ..... (10) 11.50			5.75	5.50
1606a-e	45¢ Yukon Set of 5 Singles	...		5.50	3.00

1607   **1613**   **1614**

1607	45¢ Canada Day, Maple Leaf in stylized Quilt Design, self-adhesive			.90	.30
1607a	45¢ Canada Day Pane of 12			11.50	...
1608-12	45¢ Canadian Olympic Gold Medalists, Booklet Strip of 5			5.25	4.50
1608-12	45¢ Set of 5 Booklet Singles			5.00	2.25
1612b	45¢ Olympics, Booklet Pane of 10			10.50	...
1613	45¢ British Columbia 125th Anniv. .. (25) 19.50		4.00	.85	.25
1614	45¢ Canadian Heraldry .... (25) 19.50		4.00	.85	.25
1615-16	45¢ 100 Years of Cinema, Self-adhesive Souvenir Sheets of 5 (2)			8.75	8.50
1615a-16a	45¢ Set of 10 Singles	...		8.50	7.50

1617   **1627**   **1628**

1617	45¢ Edouard Montpetit, Educator	...	4.00	.85	.25
1618-21	45¢ Winnie the Pooh, Block of 4	...		5.00	4.50
1618-21	45¢ Set of 4 Singles	...		4.75	1.80
1618-21	45¢ Booklet of 16 (4 each design)	...		19.50	...
1621b	45¢ Winnie the Pooh, Souvenir Sheet of 4...			8.00	7.50
1622-26	45¢ Authors, Booklet Strip of 5			5.75	5.00
1622-26	45¢ Set of 5 Singles			5.50	2.00
1626b	45¢ Authors, Booklet Pane of 10			11.50	...
1627-29	45¢-90¢ UNICEF 50th Ann./Christmas,Set of 3	16.00		3.35	1.30
1627	45¢ Delivering Gifts, Sled, Perf.13½x13½...		4.00	.85	.20
1627v	45¢ Booklet Single, Perf.13½x13			1.00	.25
1627a	45¢ Booklet Pane of 10, Perf.13½x13			9.50	...
1628	52¢ Santa Claus Skiing, Perf.12½x12½		4.75	1.00	.35
1628v	52¢ Booklet Single, Perf.13½x13			1.15	.40
1628a	52¢ Booklet Pane of 5, Perf.13½x13			5.25	...
1629	90¢ Children Skating, Perf.f2½x12½		7.75	1.70	.80
1629v	90¢ Booklet Single, Perf.13½x13			2.25	.95
1629a	90¢ Booklet Pane of 5, Perf.13½x13			10.75	...

1997 Commemoratives

Scott's No.		Mint Sheet	Plate Block	F-VF NH	F-VF Used
1630, 1631-36, 1637-38, 1639-48, 1649-60, 1661-69, 1670, 1671, 1672, Set of 43		...		40.00	16.50
1630	45¢ Year of the Ox .... (25) 20.95		4.00	.85	.30
1630a	45¢ New Year Souvenir Sheet of 2	...		2.75	2.65
1630v	45¢ Hong Kong '97 Overprint Souvenir Sheet of 2	...		8.75	...
1631-34	45¢ Birds, Bluebird, Western Grebe, Gannet, Scarlet Tanager, Block of 4 .... (20) 17.50		4.00	3.50	3.00
1631-34	45¢ Strip of 4	...		3.50	3.00
1631-34	45¢ Set of 4 Singles	...		3.40	1.60
1635	90¢ Art, "York Boat on Lake Winnipeg" by Walter Joseph Phillips .... (16) 26.75		7.75	1.70	1.10
1636	45¢ Canadian Tire, 75th Anniv., Booklet Single	...		1.00	.30
1636a	45¢ Tire, Booklet of 12	...		11.50	...

1637   **1639**   **1647**

1640    **1641-44**

1637	45¢ Abbe Charles-Emile Gadbois, Composer	4.50		1.00	.30
1638	45¢ Quebec Floral Festival, "Blue Poppy" .. by Claude A. Simard, Booklet Single	...		.95	.30
1638a	45¢ Blue Poppy, Booklet Pane of 12	...		10.75	...
1639	45¢ Victorian Order of Nurses Centennial ...	4.50		1.00	.30
1640	45¢ Law Society of Upper Canada Bicent....	4.50		1.00	.30
1641-44	45¢ Ocean Water Fish, Block of 4 . (20) 18.50		4.35	3.75	3.00
1641-44	45¢ Strip of 4	...		3.75	3.00
1641-44	45¢ Set of 4 Singles	...		3.50	1.60
1645-46	45¢ Confederation Bridge, Pair .... (20) 12.75		4.00	1.80	1.50
1645-46	45¢ Set of 2 Singles	...		1.70	.70
1647	45¢ Gilles Villeneuve,Race Car Driver(16)13.50		4.00	.85	.30
1648	90¢ Gilles Villeneuve .... (16) 28.50		7.95	1.80	1.10
1648b	45¢-90¢ Gilles Villeneuve, Souvenir Sheet of 8			11.75	...
1649	45¢ John Cabot's Voyage .... (20) 16.75		4.00	.85	.30
1650-53	45¢ Scenic Highways, Block of 4 .. (20) 18.50		4.35	3.75	3.00
1650-53	45¢ Set of 4 Singles	...		3.50	1.60
1654	45¢ Canadian Industrial Designers		4.00	.85	.30
1654	45¢ Industrial, Sheet of 24 with12 different labels	...		21.50	...
1655	45¢ Highland Games 50th Anniv. ... (20) 16.75		4.00	.85	.30
1656	45¢ Knights of Columbus Centennial(20) 16.75		4.00	.85	.30
1657	45¢ World Congress PTTI Labour Un.(20) 16.75		4.00	.85	.30
1658	45¢ Year of Asia-Pacific Econ. Coop(20) 16.75		4.00	.85	.30
1659-60	45¢ Hockey Series of Century, Booklet Pair...			1.90	1.50
1659-60	45¢ Set of 2 Singles	...		1.80	.70
1660a	45¢ Hockey, Booklet Pane of 10 (5 each)…			9.00	...
1661-64	45¢ Prominent Canadians,Martha Black,Lionel Chevrier, Judy LeMarsh,Real Caouette,Bk.of 4(20)17.50		4.35	3.75	3.00
1661-64	45¢ Strip of 4	...		3.75	3.00
1661-64	45¢ Set of 4 Singles	...		3.50	1.60

1669   **1672**

1665-68	45¢ The Supernatural, Block of 4 .... (16)14.75		4.35	3.75	3.00
1665-68	45¢ Set of 4 Singles	...		3.50	1.60
1669-71	45¢-90¢ Christmas, Stained Glass Windows (3)	16.50		3.40	1.35
1669	45¢ Our Lady of the Rosary,Perf.12½x13...		4.00	.85	.20
1669v	45¢ B1100klet Single, Perf.12½ Horiz.	...		.95	.30
1669a	45¢ Booklet Pane of 10, Perf.12½ Horiz. ...			9.50	...
1670	52¢ Nativity Scene, Perf.12½x13	4.75		1.00	.40
1670v	52¢ Booklet Single, Perf.12½ Horiz.	...		1.15	.65
1670a	52¢ Booklet Pane of 5, Perf.12½ Horiz.			5.25	...
1671	90¢ Life of Blessed Virgin, Perf.12½x13 ...	8.25		1.70	.80
1671v	90¢ Booklet Single, Perf.12½ Horiz.	...		1.85	1.00
1671a	90¢ Booklet Pane of 5, Perf.12½ Horiz.			9.00	...
1672	45¢ Royal Agricultural Winter Fair 75th(20)16.75		4.00	.85	.30

1997-2002 Regular Issues

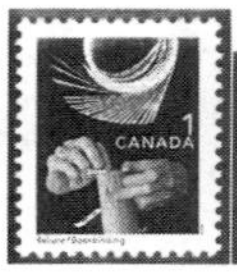

1673

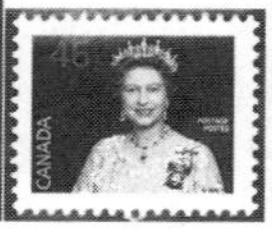

1682

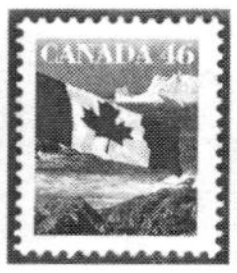

1687

1692

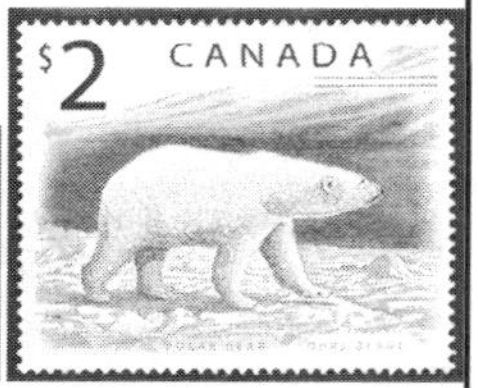

1698

Scott's No.		Mint Sheet	Plate Block	F-VF NH	F-VF Used
1673-1700	**1¢-$8 set of 17**	**...**	**...**	**27.00**	**11.25**
#1673-80 Traditional Trades					
1673	1¢ Bookbinding (1999)	...	.40	.20	.15
1674	2¢ Decorative Ironwork (1999)	...	.40	.20	.15
1675	3¢ Glass-blowing (1999)	...	.40	.20	.15
1676	4¢ Oyster Farming (1999)	...	.45	.20	.15
1677	5¢ Weaving (1999)	...	.45	.20	.15
1678	9¢ Quilting (1999)	...	.80	.20	.15
1679	10¢ Artistic Woodworking (1999)	...	.80	.20	.15
1680	25¢ Leatherworking (1999)	...	2.00	.45	.20
1682	46¢ Queen Elizabeth II (1998)	...	3.85	.85	.20
1683	47¢ Queen Elizabeth II (2000)	...	4.00	.90	.20
1687	46¢ Flag & Iceberg (1998)	...	3.85	.85	.20
1687a	46¢ Flag, Booklet Pane of 10	...	...	9.00	...
1692	55¢ Stylized Maple Leaf, (1998)	...	4.75	1.00	.30
1692a	55¢ Booklet Pane of 5	...	...	5.50	...
1694	73¢ Stylized Maple Leaf (1998)	...	6.25	1.35	.45
1696	95¢ Stylized Maple Leaf (1998)	...	8.00	1.75	.55
1696a	Maple Leaf, Booklet Pane of 5	...	...	9.50	...
1697	$1 Wildlife, Loon (1998)	...	8.25	1.80	.65
1697r	$1 Loon Reprint (2002)		8.25	1.80	1.65
1698	$2 Wildlife, Polar Bear (1998)	...	15.75	3.60	1.25
1698r	$2 Polar Bear Reprint (2002)		15.75	3.60	3.25
	Note: $1 Reprint - "LOON" & "Huard" have lighter lettering than original, "$1" is Orange red on reprint, Red on original. $2 Reprint - background and shading are lighter than on original				
1700	$8 Wildlife,Grizzly Bear,	...	67.50	14.50	6.75
1703	46¢ Canadian Flag Coil, Perf. 10 Horiz. (1998)		...	.85	.25
1705	46¢ Flag & Iceberg, S.A. Booklet Single ..		...	1.10	.70
1705a	46¢ Flag, Self-adhesive Booklet Pane of 30 (1998)...			27.50	...
1706	46¢ Maple Leaf, Self-adhesive Booklet Single		...	2.50	2.00
1706a	46¢ Maple Leaf, S.A. Booklet Pane of 18 (1998)		...	45.00	...
1707	47¢ Flag & Inunshuk, SA Booklet Single (2000)		...	.90	.30
1707a	47¢ Flag, Booklet of 10	...	...	9.00	...
1707b	47¢ Flag, Booklet of 30	...	...	26.50	...

1998 Commemoratives

Scott's No.		Mint Sheet	Plate Block	F-VF NH	F-VF Used
1708,1710-13, 1715-20, 1721-24, 1735-37, 1738-42, 1750-54, 1756-60, 1761-66	**Set of 40**	**...**	**...**	**36.50**	**17.00**
1708	45¢ Year of the Tiger	(25) 21.00	4.00	.85	.30
1708a	45¢ Year of the Tiger Souvenir Sheet of 2...		...	2.00	1.80
1708v	45¢ Overprinted Souvenir Sheet...		...	3.25	...
1709	45¢ Provincial Prime Ministers Souvenir Sheet of 10			8.75	8.25
1709a-j	45¢ Set of 10 Singles	...	...	8.65	6.50
1710-13	45¢ Birds, Hairy Woodpecker, Flycatcher, Screech-Owl, Rosy-Finch, Block of 4	(20) 18.50	4.35	3.75	3.25
1710-13	45¢ Set of 4 Singles		...	3.50	1.60

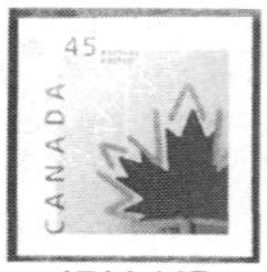

1714,14B

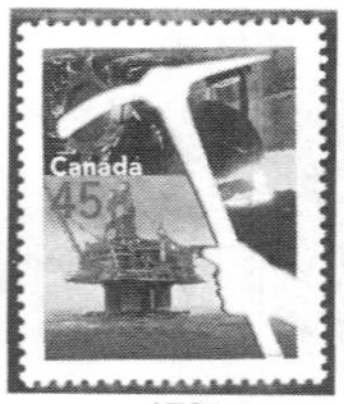

1721

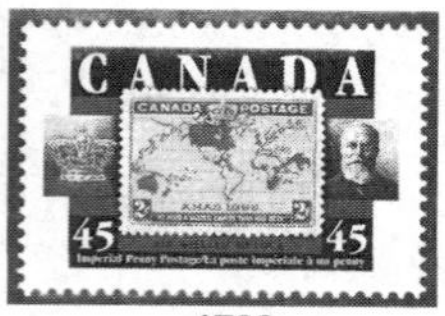

1722

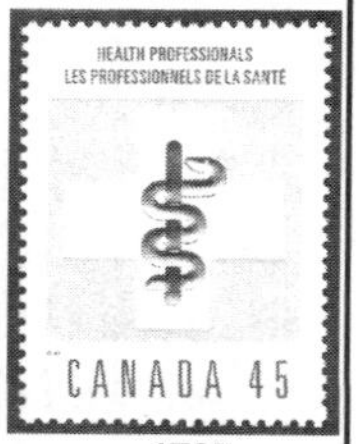

1735

1998 Self-Adhesive Stamps

Scott's No.		Mint Sheet	Plate Block	F-VF NH	F-VF Used
1714	45¢ Stylized Maple Leaf, die-cut	...	...	1.50	1.60
1714a	45¢ Sheetlet of 18		...	27.50	...
1714B	45¢ Stylized Maple Leaf Coil, die-cut	...	...	1.35	.45

1998 Commemoratives (continued)

Scott's No.		Mint Sheet	Plate Block	F-VF NH	F-VF Used
1715-20	45¢ Fishing Flies, Booklet Strip of 6	...	...	6.25	5.75
1715-20	45¢ Set of 6 Singles	...	...	6.00	3.50
1720a	45¢ Flies, Booklet Pane of 12	...	...	12.50	...
1721	45¢ Institute of Mining, Metallurgy and Petroleum Centennial	(20) 16.75	4.00	.85	.30
1722	45¢ Imperial Penny Postage Centennial, William Mulock	(14) 11.75	4.00	.85	.30
1723-24	45¢ Sumo Wrestling, Pair	(20) 17.50	4.25	1.80	1.50
1723-24	45¢ Set of 2 Singles		...	1.70	.70
1724b	45¢ Sumo, Souvenir Sheet of 2		...	3.75	3.50
1734a	45¢ Canals, Booklet of 10 Stamps	...	...	15.00	...
1725-34	45¢ Canals, Set of 10 Singles		...	14.50	6.75
1735	45¢ Health Professionals	(16) 13.50	4.00	.85	.30
1736-37	45¢ Royal Canadian Mounted Police, Pair	(20) 17.50	4.25	1.80	1.50
1736-37	45¢ Set of 2 Singles		...	1.70	.70
1737b	45¢ Mounties, Souvenir Sheet of 2	...	...	2.50	2.25
1737c	45¢ "Lt.Col.G.A.French" Overprint on Souv.Sheet		...	3.25	...
1737d	45¢ "Portugal '98" Overprint on Souv.Sheet		...	4.75	...
1737e	45¢ "Italia, '98" Overprint on Souv.Sheet ..		...	4.75	...

1998 Commemoratives (continued)

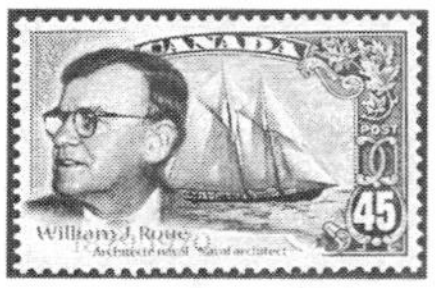

1738

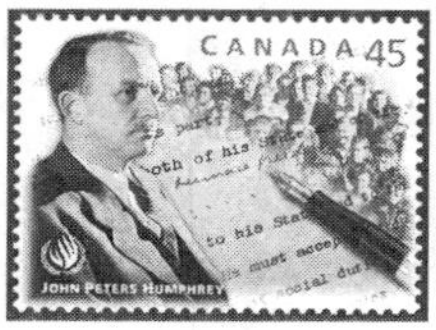

1761

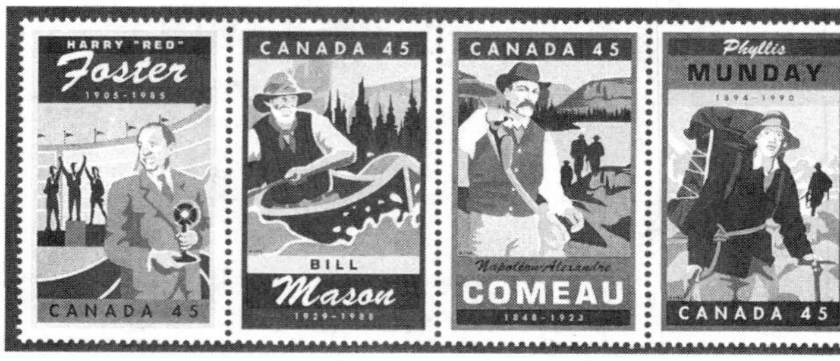

1750-53

Scott's No.		Mint Sheet	Plate Block	F-VF NH	F-VF Used
1738	45¢ William J. Roue, "Bluenose"	(25) 20.75	4.00	.85	.30
1739-42	45¢ Scenic Highways, Block of 4 ..	(20) 18.50	4.35	3.75	3.00
1739-42	45¢ Strip of 4	...	...	3.75	3.00
1739-42	45¢ Set of 4 Singles		...	3.50	1.60
1743-49	45¢ Montreal Painters, Set of 7 Singles	...	...	8.25	6.50
1749a	45¢ Montreal Painters "The Automatistes" Booklet of 7			8.50	...
1750-53	45¢ Legendary Canadians, N. Comeau, Phyllis Munday, Bill Mason. Harry "Red" Foster, Block of 4	(20) 18.50	4.35	3.75	3.00
1750-53	45¢ Strip of 4	...	...	3.75	3.00
1750-53	45¢ Set of 4 Singles	...	...	3.50	1.60
1754	90¢ Art, "The Farmers Family" by Bruno Bobak	(16) 26.50	8.00	1.70	1.00
1755	45¢ Housing in Canada, Sheetlet of 9	...	...	8.75	8.50
1755a-i	45¢ Housing, Set of 9 Singles		...	8.65	6.50
1756	45¢ University of Ottawa 150th Ann.	(20) 16.75	4.00	.85	.30
1757-60	45¢ Circus, Set of 4 Booklet Singles	...	...	4.25	3.00
1760a	45¢ Circus, Booklet of 12	...	...	12.75	...
1760b	45¢ Circus, Souvenir Sheet of 4	...	...	4.25	4.00
1757i-60i	45¢ Circus, Set of 4 Souvenir Sheet Singles			...	2.50
	#1757-60 are perforated on 3 sides #1757i-60i are perforated on all sides.				
1761	45¢ John Peters Humphrey	(20) 16.75	4.00	.85	.30
1762-63	45¢ Naval Reserve 75th Ann., Pair	(20) 17.50	4.25	1.80	1.25
1762-63	45¢ Set of 2 Singles		...	1.70	.70
1764-66	45¢-90¢ Christmas, Set of 3	...	16.00	3.40	1.50
1764	45¢ Christmas Angel, Perf.13	...	4.00	.85	.25
1764i	45¢ Booklet Single, Perf. 13	...	...	2.50	...
1764a	45¢ Booklet Pane of 10, Perf.13 ..	...	...	23.75	...
1764b	45¢ Angel, Sheet Stamp, Perf.13x13½	...	...	250.00	27.50
1764ii	45¢ Angel , Booklet Single, Perf.13x13½ ..		...	2.25	2.50
1764c	45¢ Booklet Pane of 10, Perf.13x13½	...	...	21.50	..
1765	52¢ Christmas Angel, Perf.13x13½	...	4.50	.95	.45
1765i	52¢ Angel, Booklet Single, Perf13x13½ ..	...	...	2.50	...
1765a	52¢ Booklet Pane of 5, Perf.13x13½	...	...	11.75	...
1765b	52¢ Angel, Booklet Single, Perf.13	...	...	1.25	.95
1765c	52¢ Booklet Pane of 5, Perf.13	...	...	5.95	...
1766	90¢ Christmas Angel, Perf.13x13½	...	8.00	1.70	.85
1766i	90¢ Angel, Booklet Single, Perf.13x13½ .	...	...	3.25	...
1766a	90¢ Booklet Pane of 5, Perf.13x13½	...	...	15.50	...
1766b	90¢ Angel, Booklet Single, Perf.13		...	2.10	1.10
1766c	90¢ Booklet Pane of 5, Perf.13	...	...	9.75	...

1999 Commemoratives

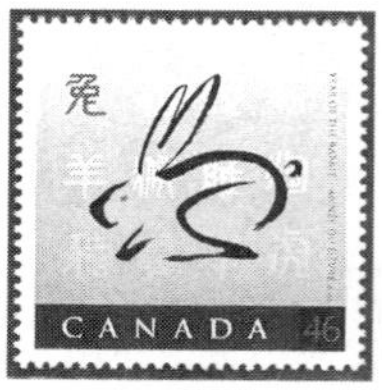

1767

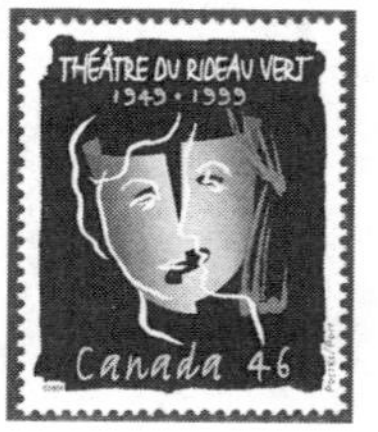

1769

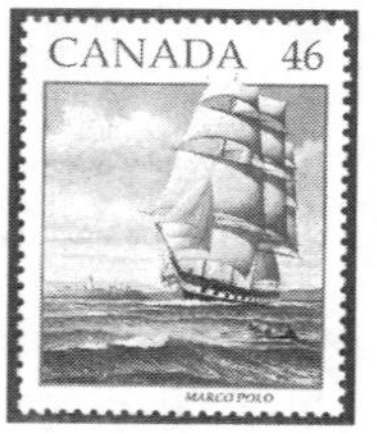

1779

Scott's No.		Mint Sheet	Plate Block	F-VF NH	F-VF Used
1767, 1769-79,1780-1806,1809-10,1812-17	**set of 47**	**...**	**...**	**42.50**	**17.50**
1767	46¢ Year of the Rabbit	(25) 20.75	4.00	.85	.30
1768	95¢ Year of the Rabbit Souvenir Sheet	...	...	2.40	2.25
1768i	95¢ China'99 Logo Overprint on #1768	...	...	2.50	...
1769	46¢ Le Theatre du Rideau Vert	(16) 13.50	4.00	.85	.30
1770-73	46¢ Birds: Goshawk, Blackbird, Goldfinch, Sandhill Crane, Block of 4	(20) 18.50	4.25	3.75	3.00
1770-73	46¢ Strip of 4	...	...	3.75	3.00
1770-73	46¢, Set of 4 singles		...	3.50	1.60
1774-77	46¢ Birds, Self-adhesive singles...	...	...	4.00	2.25
1777a	Birds, Booklet Pane, 2-1774-5, 1-1776-7	...	...	6.00	...
1777b	Birds, Booklet Pane, 1-1774-5, 2-1776-7	...	...	6.00	...
1777ab	Birds, Booklet of 12, Self-adhesive	...	...	11.95	...

1999 Commemoratives (continued)

Scott's No.		Mint Sheet	Plate Block	F-VF NH	F-VF Used
1778	46¢ UBC Museum of Anthropology (16)	13.50	4.00	.85	.30
1779	46¢ "Marco Polo",19th Century Ship (16)	13.50	4.00	.85	.30
1779a	46¢"Marco Polo" on Souvenir Sheet with 85¢ Australian Joint Issue ($1.25)	...		3.00	2.75

1780-83

1780-83	46¢ Scenic Highways, Block of 4 . (20)	18.50	4.25	3.75	3.00
1780-83	46¢ Strip of 4	...	...	3.75	3.00
1780-83	46¢ Set of 4 Singles	...		3.50	1.60
1784	46¢ Nunavit Territory Creation .... (20)	16.50	4.00	.85	.30
1785	46¢ Year of Older Persons .... (16)	13.50	4.00	.85	.30
1786	46¢ Sikh Canadians, Baisakhi New Year 300th Anniversary .... (16)	15.75	4.50	1.00	.30
1787-90	46¢ Orchids, 4 Booklet Singles	...	...	4.00	2.00
1790a	46¢ Orchids, Booklet of 12	...		11.75	
1790b	46¢ Orchids, Souvenir Sheet of 4	...		4.50	4.00
1791-94	46¢ Canadian Horses, Block of 4 .. (20)	20.75	5.00	4.25	3.25
1791-94	46¢ Strip of 4	...		4.25	3.25
1791-94	46¢ Set of 4 Singles	...		4.00	1.80
1795-98	46¢ Horses, Booklet Block of 4, SA	...		4.50	...
1795-98	46¢ Set of 4 Singles	...		4.50	2.00
1798a	46¢ Horses, Booklet of 12	...		13.50	...
1799	46¢ Barreau du Quebec, Quebec Bar Association, 150th Anniv. .... (16)	13.50	4.00	.85	.30
1800	95¢ Art "Cog Licorne" by Jean Dallaire .... (16)	28.50	8.00	1.80	1.25
1801-4	46¢ Pan-American Games, Block-4 (16)	14.75	4.25	3.75	3.00
1801-4	46¢ Set of 4 Singles	...		3.50	1.60
1805	46¢ World Rowing Championships . (20)	16.75	4.00	.85	.30
1806	46¢ Universal Postal Union 125th .. (20)	16.75	4.00	.85	.30
1807	46¢ Canadian Air Show, Souvenir Sheet of 4	...		3.85	3.50
1807a-d	46¢ Air Show, Set of 4 Singles	...		3.65	2.00
1808	46¢ Canadian Air Force 75th Anniv. Sheet of 16	...		14.50	...
1808a-p	46¢ Air Force, Set of 16 Singles	...		14.25	9.50
1809	46¢ NATO 50th Anniversary .... (16)	13.50	4.00	.85	.30

1810	1813	1814

1810	46¢ Frontier College 100th Anniv. .. (16)	13.50	4.00	.85	.30
1811a-d	46¢ Kites, SA Block of 4	...		4.50	...
1811a-d	46¢ Set of 4 Singles	...		4.50	2.00
1811	46¢ Kites, Complete Booklet of 8, SA	...		9.00	...
1812-14	46¢-95¢ Millennium, Set of 3	14.50		3.65	2.95
1812	46¢ Millennium Hologram, Dove .... (4)	3.50		.90	.55
1812i	46¢ Dove, Souvenir Sheet of 1	...		3.75	...
1813	55¢ Millennium, Girl & Dove .... (4)	4.35		1.10	1.00
1813i	55¢ Girl & Dove, Souvenir Sheet of 1	...		4.00	...
1814	95¢ Millennium, Dove on Branch .... (4)	7.50		1.80	1.50
1814i	95¢ Dove on Branch, Souvenir Sheet of 1...	...		4.75	...
1815-17	46¢-95¢ Christmas, Set of 3	17.00		3.65	1.70
1815	46¢ Christmas Angels	4.00		.85	.30
1815a	46¢ Angels Booklet Pane of 10	...		9.95	...
1816	55¢ Christmas Angels	5.00		1.10	.40
1816a	55¢ Angels Booklet Pane of 5	...		5.75	...
1817	95¢ Christmas Angels	8.25		1.80	1.10
1817a	95¢ Angels Booklet Pane of 5	...		9.50	...

1999-2000 Millennium Collection Souvenir Sheets of 4

1818-34	Set of 17 Souvenir Sheets	...		95.00	...
1818	46¢ Media Technologies: IMAX, Softimage, William Stephenson, Ted Rogers Jr.			5.75	5.75
1818a-d	46¢ Media, set of 4 singles			5.75	5.00
1819	46¢ Canadian Entertainment: Calgary Stampede, Cirque du Soleil, Hockey-forum, Hockey Night ...			5.75	5.75
1819a-d	46¢ Entertainment, set of 4 singles			5.75	5.00
1820	46¢ Extraordinary Entertainers: Portia White, Glenn Gould, Felix Leclerc, Guy Lombardo			5.75	5.75
1820a-d	46¢ Entertainers, set of 4 singles			5.75	5.00

1999-2000 Millennium Collection Souvenir Sheets of 4 (continued)

1820

Scott's No.		Mint Sheet	Plate Block	F-VF NH	F-VF Used
1821	46¢ Fostering Canadian Talent: Academy of Arts, Canada Council, Canadian Broadcasting Corp., National Film Board		...	5.75	5.75
1821a-d	46¢ Talent, set of 4 singles		...	5.75	5.00
1822	46¢ Medical Innovators: Frederick Banting, Armand Frappier, Maude Abbott, Dr. Hans Selye			5.75	5.75
1822a-d	46¢ Medical, set of 4 singles			5.75	5.00
1823	46¢ Social Progress: Les Hospitalieres, Women are Persons, Desjardins, Moses Coady			5.75	5.75
1823a-d	46¢ Social, set of 4 singles			5.75	5.00
1824	Hearts of Gold: CIDA, Lucille Teasdale, Meals and Friends on Wheels, Marathon of Hope			5.75	5.75
1824a-d	46¢ Hearts of Gold, set of 4 singles		...	5.75	5.00
1825	46¢ Humanitarians and Peacekeepers: Raoul Dandurand, Vanier and Smellie, Banning Land Mines, Lester B. Pearson			5.75	5.75
1825a-d	46¢ Humanitarians, set of 4 singles		...	5.75	5.00
1826	46¢ First Peoples: Pontiac, Tom Longboat, Healing from Within, Inuit Shamans			5.75	5.75
1826a-d	46¢ First Peoples, set of 4 singles…			5.75	5.00
1827	46¢ Cultural Fabric: L'Anse Aux Meadows, Welcome to Canada, Stratford Festival, Neptune Story ...			5.75	5.75
1827a-d	46¢ Cultural, set of 4 singles			5.75	5.00
1828	46¢ Literary Legends: W.O.Mitchell, Gratien Gelinas, Harlequin, Pierre Tisseyre			5.75	5.75
1828a-d	46¢ Literary, set of 4 singles			5.75	5.00
1829	46¢ Great Thinkers: Marshal McLuhan, Northrop Frye, Hilda Marion Neatby, Roger Lemelin ...			5.75	5.75
1829a-d	46¢ Thinkers, set of 4 singles		...	5.75	5.00
1830	46¢ Tradition of Generosity: Massey Foundation, Killam Legacy, Macdonald Stewart Foundation, Eric Lafferty Harvie			5.75	5.75
1830a-d	46¢ Generosity, set of 4 singles		...	5.75	5.00
1831	46¢ Engineering and Technological Marvels: Locomotive & Tunnel, Manic Dams, Canadian Satellites, CN Tower			5.75	5.75
1831a-d	46¢ Engineering, set of 4 singles		...	5.75	5.00
1832	46¢ Fathers of Invention: George Klein, Abraham Geiner, Alexander Graham Bell, Joseph-Armand Bombardier			5.75	5.75
1832a-d	46¢ Invention, set of 4 singles		...	5.75	5.00
1833	46¢ Food: Marquis Wheat, Pablum, Frozen Fish, McCain Foods			5.75	5.75
1833a-d	46¢ Food, set of 4 singles		...	5.75	5.00
1834	46¢ Enterprising Giants: Hudson's Bay Company, Bell Canada, Vachon Co., George Weston Ltd.			5.75	5.75
1834a-d	46¢ Giants, set of 4 singles		...	5.75	5.00
1818v-34i	Limited edition Millennium Collection hard-cover book containing the above stamp designs with slight differences from those in the souvenir sheets.		...	79.50	...

2000 Commemoratives

 1835 1836

1835-36,39-48,49-52,54-77 set of 48			...	55.00	37.50
1835	46¢ Millennium Partnership .... (16)	13.50	4.00	.85	.30
1836	46¢ Year of the Dragon .... (25)	20.75	4.00	.85	.30
1837	95¢ Year of the Dragon Souvenir Sheet	...		1.95	1.50
1838	46¢ 50th National Hockey League All-Start Game Souvenir Sheet of 6			5.50	4.95
1838a-f	46¢ Hockey, Set of 6 Singles	...		5.25	4.75
1839-42	46¢ Birds, Block of 4 .... (20)	18.50	4.25	3.75	3.00
1839-42	46¢ Strip of 4	...		3.75	3.00
1839-42	46¢ Set of 4 Singles	...		3.50	1.60

2000 Commemoratives (continued)

Scott's No.		Mint Sheet	Plate Block	F-VF NH	F-VF Used
1843-46	46¢ Canadian Birds, Booklet Singles ...		...	3.75	1.80
	#1839,43 Canada Warbler,1840,44-Osprey, 1841,45-Loon, 1842,46 Blue Jay				
1846a	46¢ Birds Bklt.Pane of 6 (2each 1843-4, 1 each 1845-6)			5.50	...
1846b	46¢ Birds Bklt.Pane of 6 (1each 1843-4, 2 each 1845-6)			5.50	...
1846ab	46¢ Birds Booklet of 12 with 2 Bklt.Panes of 6		...	11.00	...
1847	46¢ Supreme Court 125th	(16) 13.50	4.00	.85	.30
1848	46¢ Ritual of the Calling of an Engineer, Pair	(16) 13.50	4.00	.85	.30
1848a	46¢ Engineer, Tete-Beche Pair ...		...	1.70	1.50
1849-52	46¢ Rural Mailboxes, Booklet Block of 4 ...		...	3.75	3.50
1849-52	46¢ Set of 4 Booklet Singles ...		...	3.65	1.80
1852a	46¢ Mailboxes, Booklet of 12 ...		...	11.00	...
	2000 Greetings Booklet				
1853	46¢ Greetings, Picture Frames, Self-adhesive		...	.95	.50
1853a	46¢ Booklet of 5 + 5 stickers		...	4.75	...

2000 Commemoratives (continued)

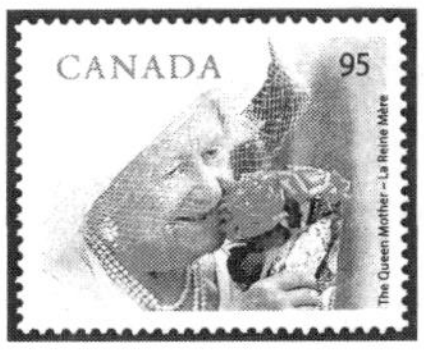
1856

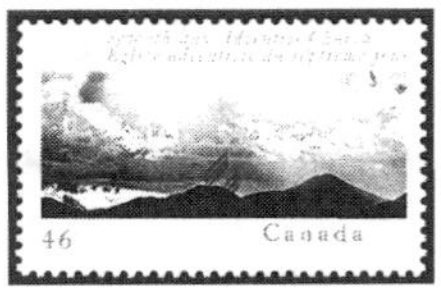
1858

Scott's No.		Mint Sheet	Plate Block	F-VF NH	F-VF Used
1854	55¢ Fresh Waters, Booklet of 5, SA ...		...	10.75	...
1854a-e	55¢ Fresh Waters, set of 5 singles ...		...	10.50	10.00
1855	95¢ Fresh Waters, Booklet of 5, SA ...		...	17.50	...
1855a-e	95¢ Fresh Waters, set of 5 singles... ...		...	17.00	15.00
1856	95¢ Queen Mother's 100th Birthday	(9) 16.00	...	1.80	1.10
1857	46¢ Boys and Girls Clubs 100th	(16) 13.50	4.00	.85	.30
1858	46¢ Seventh-Day Adventists	(16) 13.50	4.00	.85	.30
1859-62	46¢ Stampin' the Future, Block of 4	(16) 14.50	4.15	3.65	3.00
1859-62	46¢ Strip of 4 ...		...	3.65	3.00
1859-62	46¢ Set of 4 Singles ...		...	3.50	1.60
1862b	46¢ Stampin' the Future, Souvenir Sheet of 4		...	3.75	3.75
1863	95¢ Art "Artist et Niagara" by Cornelius Krieghoff	(16) 28.50	8.00	1.80	1.10
1864-65	46¢ Tall Ships visit Halifax, Pair, SA ...		...	1.90	...
1864-65	46¢ Set of 2 Singles ...		...	1.85	.90
1865b	46¢ Tall Ships Booklet of 10 ...		...	9.50	...
1866	46¢ Department of Labour Cent.	(16) 13.50	3.50	.85	.30
1867	46¢ Petro-Canada, SA ...		...	1.00	.50
1867a	46¢ Petro-Canada, Booklet Pane of 12 ...		...	11.50	...
1868-71	46¢ Whales, Block of 4	(16) 14.50	...	3.65	3.00
1868-71	46¢ Whales, Set of 4 Singles		...	3.50	1.60
1872	46¢ Christmas Greetings, Picture Frame, Booklet Single			.95	.75
1872a	46¢ Christmas Greetings Booklet of 5 ...		...	4.50	...
1873-75	46¢-95¢ Christmas Nativity, Set of 3 ...		16.00	3.65	1.80
1873	46¢ Adoration of the Shepherds ...		4.00	.85	.30
1873a	46¢ Shepherds Booklet of 10		...	9.50	...
1874	55¢ Christmas Creche ...		4.75	1.10	.60
1874a	55¢ Creche Booklet of 6 ...		...	7.00	...
1875	95¢ Flight into Egypt ...		8.00	1.80	1.00
1875a	95¢ Egypt Booklet of 6 ...		...	11.50	...
1876-77	46¢ Horse Regiments, Pair	(16) 13.50	4.00	1.75	1.50
1876-77	46¢ Regiments, set of 2 singles ...		...	1.70	.70

2000 Regular Issues, Self-Adhesive

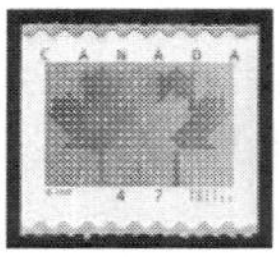
1878

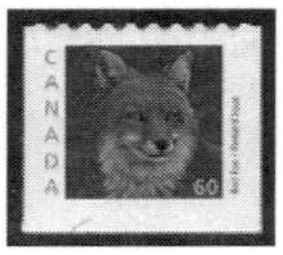
1879

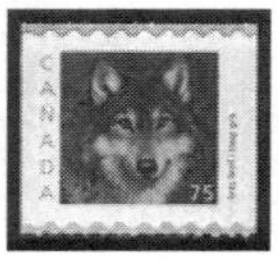
1880

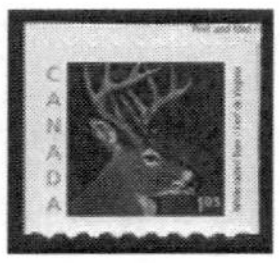
1881

Scott's No.		Mint Sheet	Plate Block	F-VF NH	F-VF Used
1878-81	**47¢-$1.05 Coils, Set of 4**		**...**	**5.50**	**1.90**
1878	47¢ Maple Leaf, Coil ...		...	.90	.30
1879	60¢ Red Fox, Coil ...		...	1.50	.50
1879v	60¢ Red Fox, Booklet Single ...		...	1.75	.75
1879a	60¢ Red Fox, Booklet Pane of 6 ...		...	10.75	...
1880	75¢ Grey Wolf, Coil ...		...	1.40	.55
1881	$1.05 White-Tailed Deer, Coil ...		...	2.00	.65
1881v	$1.05 White-Tailed Deer, Booklet Single ...		...	2.50	1.25
1881a	$1.05 White-Tailed Deer, Booklet Pane of 6...		...	14.50	...
	2000 Greetings Booklet				
1882	47¢ Picture Frames Booklet of 5 + 5 Stickers		...	4.95	...
1882a-e	47¢ Booklet Singles, set of 5 ...		...	4.75	3.00

2001 Commemoratives

Scott's No.		Mint Sheet	Plate Block	F-VF NH	F-VF Used
1883,86-1909,11-17,19-20,21a-d,22-26 set of 51			**...**	**53.95**	**27.95**
1883	47¢ Year of the Snake	(25) 22.50	4.25	.90	.35
1884	47¢ Year of the Snake Souvenir Sheet ...		...	2.25	...
1885	47¢ National Hockey League Legends Souvenir Sheet of 6 ...		...	5.25	...
1885a-f	47¢ Hockey, Set of 6 Singles ...		...	5.25	4.75
1886-89	47¢ Birds: Longspure, Arctic Tern, Golden Eagle, Rock Ptarmingan, Block of 4	(20) 18.50	4.25	3.70	3.25
1886-89	47¢ Strip of 4 ...		...	3.70	3.25
1886-89	47¢ Set of 4 Singles ...		...	3.60	1.80
1890-93	47¢ Birds, SA Block of 4 ...		...	4.00	...
1890-93	47¢ Set of 4 Singles ...		...	4.00	1.80
1893a	47¢ Birds, Booklet Pane of 6 (2-Auila Chrysaetos)...			6.00	...
1893b	47¢ Birds, Booklet Pane of 6 (2-Calcarius Lapponicus)			6.00	...
1893ab	47¢ Birds, SA Booklet of 12 ...		...	11.95	...

2001 Commemoratives (continued)

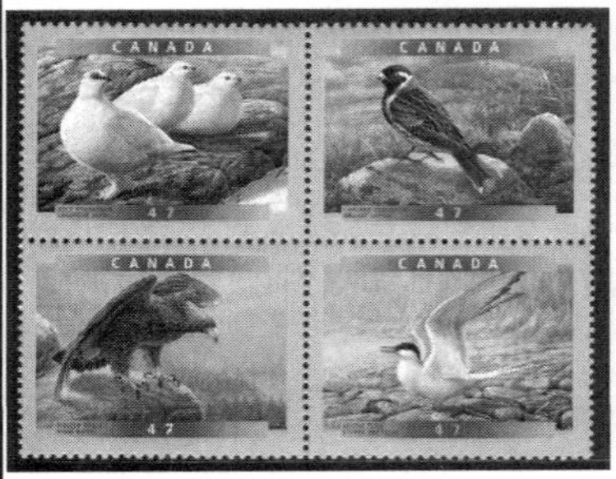

1886-89

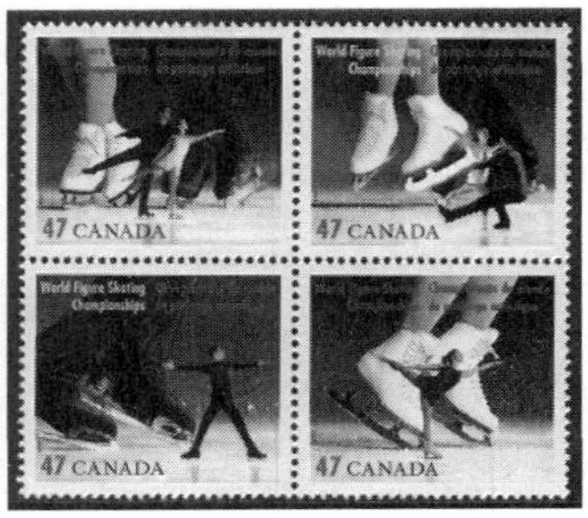

1896-99

Scott's No.		Mint Sheet	Plate Block	F-VF NH	F-VF Used
1894-95	47¢ IV Games of La Francophone Pair	(16) 14.25	4.25	1.80	1.20
1894-95	47¢ Set of 2 Singles ...		...	1.80	.80
1896-99	47¢ Figure Skating, Block of 4	(16) 14.50	4.25	3.70	3.00
1896-99	47¢ Set of 4 Singles ...		...	3.60	1.80
1900	47¢ 150th Anniversary of First Canadian Stamp, 3p Beaver, Booklet Single ...		...	.90	.35
1900v	47¢ First Canadian Stamp Booklet of 8 ...		...	7.00	...
1901	47¢ Toronto Blue Jays, SA Booklet Single...		...	.95	.40
1901a	47¢ Toronto Blue Jays Booklet of 8 ...		...	7.50	...
1902	47¢ Summit of the Americas	(16) 14.25	4.25	.90	.35
1903	60¢ Tourist Attractions, Booklet of 5, SA ...		...	6.25	...
1903a-e	60¢ Tourist, Set of 5 Booklet Singles ...		...	6.00	4.00
1904	$1.05 Tourist Attractions, Booklet of 5, SA...		...	10.50	...
1904a-e	$1.05 Tourist, Set of 5 Booklet Singles ...		...	10.25	7.50
1905	47¢ Armenian Apostolic Church	(16) 14.25	4.25	.90	.35
1906	47¢ Royal Military College 125th	(16) 14.25	4.25	.90	.35
1907-8	47¢ International Amateur Athletic Fed. World Championship; Edmonton Pair	(16) 14.25	4.25	1.80	1.20
1907-8	47¢ Set of 2 Singles ...		...	1.80	.80
1909	47¢ Pierre Trudeau, Prime Minister	(16) 14.25	4.25	.90	.35
1909a	47¢ Trudeau Souvenir Sheet of 4 ...		...	3.75	3.75
1910	47¢ Canadian Roses Souvenir Sheet of 4...		...	3.75	...
1910a-d	47¢ Roses, Set of 4 Souvenir Sheet Singles		...	3.70	2.00
1911-14	47¢ Roses, Booklet Vertical Strip of 4, SA...		...	3.65	...
1911-14	47¢ Set of 4 Booklet Singles ...		...	3.60	1.80
1914a	47¢ Roses Booklet of 12, SA ...		...	10.75	...
1915	47¢ Great Peace of Montreal 400th	(16) 14.25	4.25	.90	.35
1915	47¢ Pair with Vertical Gutter ...		...	1.80	...
1916	$1.05 Art "The Space Between Columns #21" (Italian) by Jack Shadbolt	(16) 31.50	8.75	2.00	1.00
1917	47¢ Shriners, Clown with Boy	(16) 14.25	4.25	.90	.35
	2001 Greeting Booklet				
1918	(47¢) Picture Frames, Booklet of 5 plus 5 labels		...	5.25	...
1918a-e	(47¢) Booklet Singles, set of 5 ...		...	5.00	4.50

2001 Commemoratives (continued)

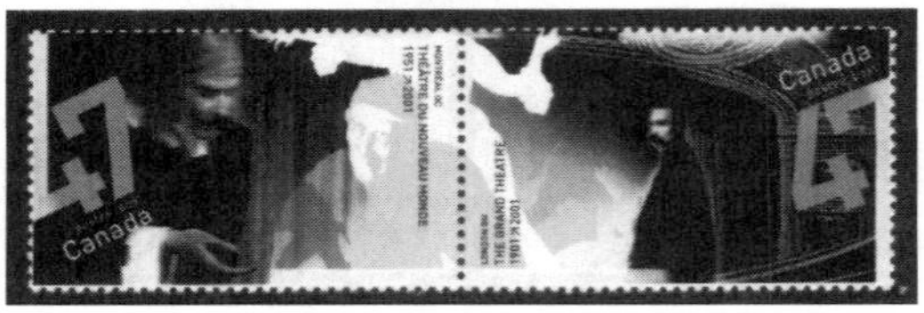

1919-20

Scott's No.		Mint Sheet	Plate Block	F-VF NH	F-VF Used
1919-20	47¢ Canadian Theaters,Pair	(16) 14.25	4.25	1.80	1.30
1919-20	47¢ Set of 2 Singles ...		...	1.80	.80
1921	47¢ Hot Air Balloons, Booklet of 8, SA ...		...	7.50	...
1921a-d	47¢ Hot Air Balloons, Set of 4 Booklet Singles		...	3.75	1.80
1922-24	Christmas Lights, Set of 3 ...		17.50	3.85	1.80
1922	47¢ Horse-drawn Sleigh	(25) 22.50	4.25	.90	.30
1922a	47¢ Sleigh Booklet Pane of 10 ...		...	9.75	...
1923	60¢ Skater	(25) 26.50	5.00	1.10	.60
1923a	60¢ Skater Booklet Pane of 6 ...		...	7.50	...
1924	$1.05 Snowman & Children	(25) 48.50	8.75	2.00	1.00
1924a	$1.05 Snowman Booklet Pane of 6 ...		...	13.00	...
1925	47¢ Y.M.C.A. 150th Anniv.	(16) 14.25	4.25	.90	.35
1926	47¢ Royal Canadian Legion 75th	(16) 14.25	4.25	.90	.35

2002 Regular Issue, Self-adhesive

Scott's No.		Mint Sheet	Plate Block	F-VF NH	F-VF Used
1927-30	**48¢-$1.25 Coils, Set of 4 ...**		**...**	**5.65**	**1.95**
1927	48¢ Maple Leaf Coil ...		...	.80	.25
1928	65¢ Jewelry Coil ...		...	1.10	.40
1928as	65¢ Jewelry, Booklet Single ...		...	1.25	.60
1928a	65¢ Jewelry, Booklet of 6 ...		...	7.50	...
1929	77¢ Basket Weaving Coil ...		...	1.25	.40
1930	$1.25 Sculpture Coil ...		...	2.00	.65
1930as	$1.25 Sculpture, Booklet Single ...		...	2.25	1.00
1930a	$1.25 Sculpture, Booklet of 6 ...		...	12.50	...
1931	48¢ Flag & Building, Booklet Single...		...	.75	.20
1931a	48¢ Flag, Booklet Pane of 10 ...		...	7.50	...
1931b	48¢ Flag, Booklet of 30 (3 #1931a)... ...		...	22.75	...

Note: Printed backing on unused booklet issue, blank backing on coils. Line of color on one or two die-cut edges on booklets, no line of color on coils.

2002 Commemoratives

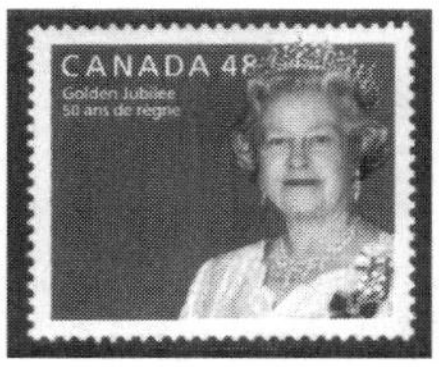

1932

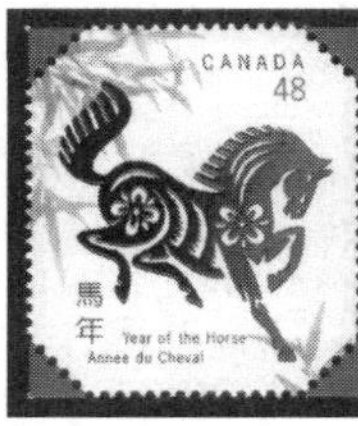

1933

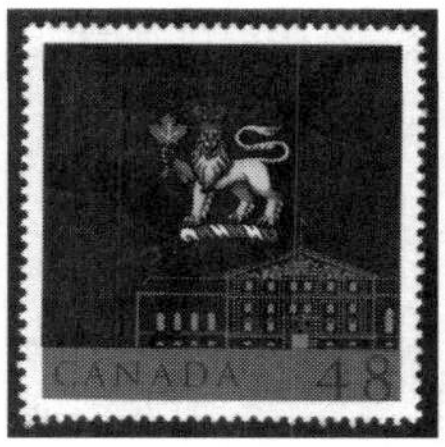

1940

Scott's No.		Mint Sheet	Plate Block	F-VF NH	F-VF Used
1932-33, 36-45, 46a-d, 48-59, 61-68 set of 44		...	...	**48.75**	**27.75**
1932	48¢ Elizabeth II Golden Jubilee	(16) 14.25	4.25	.90	.35
1933	48¢ Year of the Horse	(25 22.50	4.25	.90	.35
1934	$1.25 Year of the Horse Souvenir Sheet	...	...	2.35	2.25
1935	48¢ National Hockey League All-Stars Souvenir Sheet of 6	...	...	5.50	5.50
1935a-f	48¢ Hockey, Set of 6 Singles	...	...	5.50	4.50
1936-39	48¢ Olympic Winter Games, Salt Lake City, Block of 4	(16) 14.25	4.25	3.65	3.25
1936-39	48¢ Strip of 4	...	...	3.65	3.25
1936-39	48¢ Set of 4 Singles	...	...	3.60	1.80
1940	48¢ First Governor General 50th	(16) 14.25	4.25	.90	.35
	2002 Canadian Universities				
1941-44	48¢ Canadian Universities, Set of 4		...	3.50	1.35
1941	48¢ University of Manitoba, Booklet Single...		...	.90	.35
1941a	48¢ Manitoba, Booklet of 8	...	...	7.00	...
1942	48¢ Laval University, Booklet Single	...	...	.90	.35
1942a	48¢ Laval, Booklet of 8	...	...	7.00	...
1943	48¢ Trinity College, Booklet Single...	...	...	.90	.35
1943a	48¢ Trinity, Booklet of 8	...	...	7.00	...
1944	48¢ Saint Mary's University, Booklet Single...		...	.90	.35
1944a	48¢ Saint Mary's, Booklet of 8	...	...	7.00	...
	2002 Commemoratives (continued)				
1945	$1.25 Art, "Church & Horse" by Alex Colville	(16) 35.00	10.00	2.25	1.25
1946	48¢ Tulips, Booklet Pane of 4, SA	...	...	3.60	...
1946a-d	48¢ Set of 4 Singles	...	...	3.60	2.00
1946	48¢ Tulips, Booklet of 8, SA	...	...	7.15	...
1947	48¢ Tulips, Souvenir Sheet of 4, WA	...	...	3.75	3.50
1947a-d	48¢ Tulips, Set of 4 Souvenir Sheet Singles		...	3.70	2.40
1948-51	48¢ Corals, Perf.12½x13, Block of 4	(16) 18.50	5.50	4.75	4.25
1948-51	48¢ Set of 4 Singles, Perf.12½x13	...	...	4.75	2.00
1951b	48¢ Corals, Souvenir Sheet of 4,Perf.13½x13		...	3.75	3.65
1951c-f	48¢ Set of 4 Singles from Souv.Sheet, Perf.13½x13...			3.70	2.00
1951v	48¢ Corals Sv.Sheet, Hong Kong Overprint		...	4.25	4.25
1952	65¢ Tourist Attractions, Booklet of 5, SA	...	...	6.25	...
1952a-e	65¢ Tourist, Set of 5 Singles	...	...	6.25	5.00
1953	$1.25 Tourist Attractions, Booklet of 5, SA...		...	11.50	...
1953a-e	$1.25 Tourist, Set of 5 Singles	...	...	11.50	9.00
1954-55	48¢ Sculptors, Charles Daudelin & Leo Mol, Pair	(16) 14.25	4.25	1.80	1.30
1954-55	48¢ Set of 2 Singles	...	...	1.80	.80
1956	48¢ Canadian Postmasters and Assistants Association Centennial	(16) 14.25	4.25	.90	.35
1957	48¢ 17th World Youth Day, Toronto, Booklet Single, SA			.90	.40
1957a	48¢ Youth Day, Booklet of 8	...	...	7.15	...
1958	48¢ Public Service International World Congress, Ottawa	(16) 14.25	4.25	.90	.35
1959	48¢ Public Pensions 75th Anniv.	(16) 14.25	4.25	.90	.35
1960	48¢ Mountains, Stamp Collecting Month Souvenir Sheet of 8	...	...	9.75	...
1960a-h	48¢ Mountains, Set of 8 Singles	...	...	...	6.50
1961	48¢ World Teacher Day	(16) 14.25	4.25	.90	.35
1962	48¢ Toronto Stock Exchange	(16) 14.25	4.25	.90	.35
1963-64	48¢ Communications Technologies: Marconi/Transatlantic Radio Message & Pacific Telegraphic Cable, Pair	(16) 14.25	4.25	1.80	1.25
1963-64	48¢ Set of 2 Singles	...	...	1.80	.80
1965-67	48¢-$1.25 Christmas Aboriginal Art, Set of 3		18.75	4.25	1.90
1965	48¢ "Genesis"	(16) 14.25	4.25	.90	.30
1965a	48¢ Booklet of 10	...	...	9.50	...
1966	65¢ "Winter Travel"	(16) 16.75	5.25	1.20	.60
1966a	65¢ Booklet of 5	...	...	6.25	...
1967	$1.25 "Mary & Child"	(16) 35.00	9.75	2.25	1.10
1967a	$1.25 Booklet of 5	...	...	11.75	...
1968	48¢ Quebec Symphony	(16) 14.25	4.25	.90	.35

2003 Commemoratives

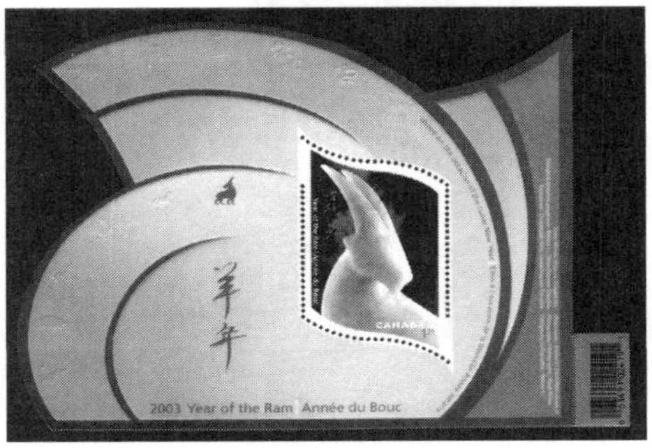

1970

CANADA

2003 Commemoratives (continued)

Scott's No.		Mint Sheet	Plate Block	F-VF NH	F-VF Used
1969,73-77,79-90,92-2002,2004-6 Set of 40		...	...	**55.00**	...
1969	48¢ Year of the Ram	(25) 22.50	4.25	.90	.35
1970	$1.25 Year of the Ram Souvenir Sheet	...	...	2.30	2.25
1971	48¢ National Hockey League All Stars Souv. Sheet of 6			5.50	...
1971a-f	48¢ Hockey League Set of 6 Singles from Souv Sheet			5.50	4.50
1972	48¢ National Hockey League All Stars Booklet Panel of 6			5.50	...
1972a-f	48¢ Hockey League Set of 6 Singles from Booklet Panel			...	4.50
	2003 Canadian Universities Booklets				
1973-77	48¢ Canadian Universities, Set of 5		...	4.35	1.70
1973	48¢ Bishop's University, Booklet Single	...	...	.90	.35
1973a	48¢ Bishop's University, Booklet of 8	...	...	7.00	...
1974	48¢ Western Ontario Booklet Single		...	.90	.35
1974a	48¢ Western Ontario Booklet of 8	...	...	7.00	...
1975	48¢ St. Francis Xavier University Booklet Single			.90	.35
1975a	48¢ St. Francis Xavier Booklet of 8	...	...	7.00	...
1976	48¢ University of Guelph's Macdonald Institute Bk. Single			.90	.35
1976a	48¢ Macdonald Institute Booklet of 8	...	...	7.00	...
1977	48¢ University of Montreal Booklet Single		...	.90	.35
1977a	48¢ University of Montreal Booklet of 8	...	...	7.00	...
	2003 Commemoratives (continued)				
1979-82	48¢ John J. Audubon's Birds, Block-4	(16)14.25	4.25	3.60	3.00
1979-82	48¢ Birds, Set of 4 Singles	...	...	3.60	1.80
1983	65¢ Audubon's Birds, Gyrfalcon SA Booklet Single...			1.20	1.20
1983a	65¢ Birds Gyrfalcon SA Booklet of 6	...	...	7.15	...
1984	48¢ Canadian Rangers	(16) 14.25	4.25	.90	.35
1985	48¢ AHEPA: American Hellenic Educational Progressive Association in Canada	(16) 14.25	4.25	.90	.35
1986	48¢ Volunteer Firefighters	(16) 14.25	4.25	.90	.35
1987	48¢ Queen Elizabeth II 50th Anniversary of Coronation	(16) 14.25	4.25	.90	.35
1988	48¢ Pedro de Silva, First Courier	(16) 14.25	4.25	.90	.35
1989	65¢ Tourist Attractions, Booklet of 5	...	...	6.25	...
1989a-e	65¢ Tourist, set of 5 singles	...	...	6.25	5.00
1990	$1.25 Tourist Attractions, Booklet of 5	...	...	11.50	...
1990a-e	$1.25 Tourist, set of 5 singles	.	...	11.50	9.00
	2003 "Vancouver 2010" Overprint Booklet				
1991	48¢ Flag & Building Booklet single	...	...	1.25	1.25
1991a	48¢ Flag & Building Booklet of 10	...	...	12.50	...
1991b	48¢ Flag & Building Booklet of 30	...	...	37.50	...
	2003 Canada-Alaska Cruise Special Issue				
1991C-D	($1.25) Blank Space Stamps, Pair..	(10) 25.00	...	5.25	...
	2003 Commemoratives (continued)				
1992	48¢ Lutheran World Federation	(16) 14.25	4.25	.90	.35
1993	48¢ Korean War Armistice	(16) 14.25	4.25	.90	.35

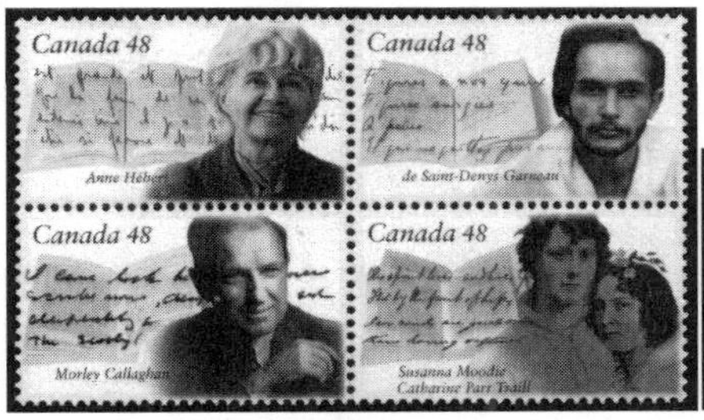

1994-97

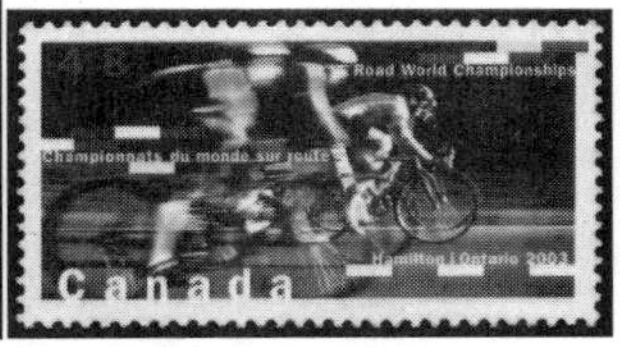

1998

1994-97	48¢ National Library of Canada: Authors, Block of 4 from Booklet	...	...	3.60	3.00
1994-97	48¢ Library, Set of 4 singles	..	...	3.60	1.80
1997a	48¢ National Library Booklet of 8	...	...	7.15	...
1998	48¢ Road World Championship Booklet single		...	.90	.35
1998a	48¢ Road World Booklet of 8	...	...	7.15	...
1999	48¢ Canadian Astronauts Booklet of 8	...	...	7.25	...
1999a-h	48¢ Canadian Astronauts Set of 8 singles...		...	...	7.15
2000-1	48¢ National Emblems of Canada and Thailand, Pair	(16) 14.25	4.25	1.80	1.50
2000-1	48¢ National Emblems, Set of 2 singles	...	...	1.80	.80
2001b	48¢ National Emblems Souvenir Sheet of 2		...	1.80	1.50
2002	48¢ Jean-Paul Riopelle, Painter & Sculptor, Sheet of 6			5.35	4.75
2002a-f	48¢ Jean-Paul Riopelle, Set of 6 singles...		...	5.25	4.25
2003	$1.25 Jean-Paul Riopelle Souvenir Sheet	...	...	2.25	2.25

2004

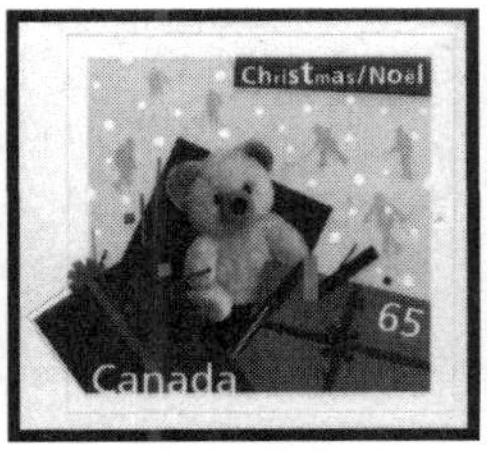

2005

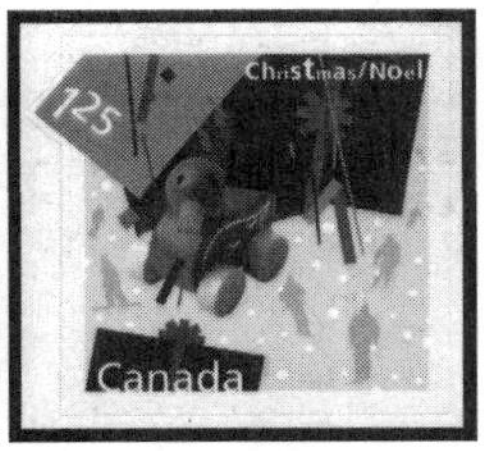

2006

2004	48¢ Christmas Gifts Booklet Single	...	...	.90	.30
2004a	48¢ Christmas Gifts Booklet Pane of 6	..	...	5.35	...
2005	65¢ Christmas Gifts Booklet Single	...	...	1.20	.75
2005a	65¢ Christmas Gifts Booklet of 6...		...	7.15	...
2006	$1.25 Christmas Gifts Booklet Single	...	...	2.25	1.50
2006a	$1.25 Christmas Gifts Booklet of 6	...	...	13.25	...

CANADA

2003 Regular Issues

| | 2008 | 2009,2013 | 2011 | 2012 |

Scott's No.		Mint Sheet	Plate Block	F-VF NH	F-VF Used
2007	$5 Moose ....(4) 36.75			8.50	7.00
2008	49¢ Maple Leaf & Samara Coil Stamp	...		.85	.30
2009	80¢ Maple Leaf & Twig Coil Stamp	...		1.40	1.25
2010	$1.40 Maple Leaf & Twig Coil Stamp	...		2.50	2.25
2011	49¢ Flag over Edmonton Booklet Single	...		.85	.30
2011a	49¢ Flag over Edmonton Booklet of 10	...		8.50	...
2012	49¢ Queen Elizabeth II Booklet Single	...		.85	.30
2012a	49¢ Elizabeth II Booklet of 10	...		8.50	...
2013	80¢ Maple Leaf & Twig Booklet Single	...		1.40	1.25
2013a	80¢ Maple Leaf & Twig Booklet of 6	...		8.25	...
2014	$1.40 Maple Leaf & Twig Booklet Single	...		2.50	2.25
2014a	$1.40 Maple Leaf & Twig Booklet of 6	...		14.75	...

2004 Commemoratives

2015	49¢ Year of the Monkey .... (25) 21.00		4.00	.85	.30
2016	$1.40 Year of the Monkey Souvenir Sheet...	...		2.50	...
2016v	$1.40 Monkey Souvenir Sheet with Show Overprint			2.75	...

| | 2017 | | | | |

2017	49¢ National Hockey League All-Star Game Gummed Sheet of 6		...	5.00	...
2017a-f	49¢ Hockey, Gummed Set of 6 singles		...	5.00	4.75
2018	49¢ National Hockey League All-Star Game Self-adhesive Sheet of 6		...	5.00	...
2018a-f	49¢ Hockey, Self-adhesive Set of 6 singles		...	5.00	4.75
2019	49¢ Quebec Winter Carnival Booklet Single		...	.85	.30
2019a	49¢ Quebec Winter Carnival Booklet of 6 .		...	5.00	...
2024	49¢ Ramon John Hnatyshun .... (16)13.50		4.00	.85	.30
2025	49¢ Royal Canadian Army Cadets Booklet Single ...		...	.85	.30
2025a	49¢ Royal Canadian Army Cadets Booklet Pane of 4...		...	3.40	...
2025b	49¢ Royal Canadian Army Cadets Booklet of 8		...	6.75	...
2026	49¢ Otto Sverdrup .... (16) 13.50		4.00	.85	.30
2027	$1.40 Otto Sverdrup Souvenir Sheet (1 stamp + 2 labels)			2.50	...
2028-31	49¢ Urban Transit Vert. Strip of 4 .. (16) 13.50 (8) 7.25			3.40	...
2028-31	49¢ Urban Transit Set of 4 singles		...	3.40	1.60
...	49¢ St. Joseph's Oratory Booklet Single		...	.85	.30
...	49¢ St. Joseph's Oratory Booklet of 6		...	5.00	...
...	49¢ 40th Anniv. of Home Hardware Booklet Single...		...	.85	.30
...	49¢ Home Hardware Booklet of 10		...	8.50	...

2004 Canadian Universities

...	49¢ Sherbrooke University Booklet Single	...		.85	.30
...	49¢ Sherbrooke University Booklet of 8 ...	...		6.75	...
...	49¢ Univ. of Prince Edward Island Booklet Single	...		.85	.30
...	49¢ Univ. of Prince Edward Island Booklet of 8	...		6.75	...
...	49¢ Montreal Children's Hospital Booklet Single	...		.85	.30
...	49¢ Montreal Children's Hospital Booklet of 8	...		6.75	...
...	49¢ John J.Audubon's Birds Block-4 (16) 13.50	4.00		3.40	...
...	49¢ John J.Audubon's Birds Set of 4 singles	...		3.40	1.60
...	80¢ John J.Audubon Lincoln's Sparrow Booklet Single			1.40	1.35
...	80¢ John J.Audubon Lincoln's Sparrow Booklet of 6...			8.35	...

2004 Canadian Universities (cont.)

Scott's No.		Mint Sheet	Plate Block	F-VF NH	F-VF Used
...	49¢ Sir Samuel Cunard and Sir Hugh Allan, Trans-atlantic Mail Service, Pair .... (16) 13.50		4.00	1.70	...
...	49¢ Cunard & Allan, Set of 2 singles		...	1.70	.80
...	49¢ Festival International de Jazz de Montreal, Booklet Single		...	.85	.30
...	49¢ Jazz Festival Booklet of 6		...	5.00	...
...	49¢ D-Day, 6/6/44 .... (16) 13.50		4.00	.85	.30
...	49¢ Lake Saint-Jean International Swimming Meet, Booklet Single		...	.85	.30
...	49¢ Lake Saint-Jean Booklet of 6		...	5.00	...
...	49¢ French Settlement in Acadia, St. Croix Island .... (16) 13.50		4.00	.85	.30

MINT CANADA COMMEMORATIVE YEAR SETS
All Fine To Very Fine, Never Hinged

Year	Scott Nos.	Qty.	F-VF NH
1947-49	274-77,82-83	6	1.00
1951-52	303-04,11-15,17-19	10	5.50
1953-54	322-24,35-36,49-50	7	1.65
1955	352-58	7	2.20
1956	359-61,64	4	1.25
1957	365-74	10	5.00
1958	375-82	8	2.35
1959	383-88	6	1.75
1960-61	389-95	7	2.00
1962	396-400	5	1.40
1963	410,12-13	3	.75
1964	416,431-35	6	1.45
1964-66	417-29A (Coats of Arms & Flowers)	14	3.15
1965	437-44	8	1.65
1966	445-52	8	1.60
1967	453,469-77	10	1.90
1968	478-89	12	4.30
1969	490-504	15	10.50
1970	505-18,531	15	12.25
1970	519-30 (Christmas)	12	4.75
1971	532-42,552-58	18	6.15
1972	559-61,582-85,606-10	12	10.45
1972-76	562-81 (Indians)	20	6.00
1973	611-28	18	5.75
1974	629-55	27	9.70
1975	656-80	25	15.00
1976	681-703	23	19.50
1977	704,732-51	21	5.95
1978	752-56,757-59	28	11.75

Year	Scott Nos.	Qty.	F-VF NH
1979	780,813-20,833-46	23	8.75
1980	847-77	31	12.95
1981	878-906	29	11.15
1982	909-13,914-16,954,967-75	18	12.50
1983	976-82,993-1008	23	21.95
1984	1009-15,1028-39,1040-4444	24	16.65
1985	1045-49,1060-66,1067-70,1071-76	22	16.00
1986	1077-79,1090-1107,1108-15,1116b,1117-21	32	26.50
1987	1122-25,1126-54	33	26.00
1988	1195-1228	34	27.50
1989	1229-63	34	29.35
1990	1264-71,1274-1301	36	32.60
1991	1302-43,1345-48	45	39.95
1992	1399-1407,1408-19,1432-55	45	40.00
1993	1456-71,1484-89,1491-1506	38	35.25
1994	1509-22,1525-26,1528-40	29	27.50
1995	1541-51,1553-58,1562-67,1570-90	47	39.70
1996	1591-98,1602-3,1606-14,1617-21,1622-29	36	37.00
1997	1630, 1631-36, 1637-38, 1639-48, 1649-60 1661-69, 1670, 1671, 1672,	43	40.00
1998	1708, 1710-13, 1715-20, 1721-24, 1735-37, 1738-42, 1750-54, 1756-60, 1761-66	40	36.50
1999	1767, 1769-79, 1780-1806, 1809-10, 1812-17	47	42.50
2000	1835-36,39-48,49-52,54-57	48	55.00
2001	1883, 86-1909, 11-17, 19-20, 21a-d, 22-26	51	53.95
2002	1932-33, 36-45, 46a-d, 48-59, 61-68	44	48.75
2003			

CANADA
SEMI-POSTALS

| B3 | B4 | B7 | B13 |

Scott's No.		Plate Block	F-VF NH	F-VF Used
B1-12	Montreal Olympics, Set of 12	...	6.15	6.15
1974 Olympic Games Symbols				
B1	8¢+2¢ Olympic Emblem, Bronze	1.60	.35	.35
B2	10¢+5¢ Olympic Emblem, Silver	2.25	.50	.50
B3	15¢+5¢ Olympic Emblem, Gold	3.25	.70	.70
1975 Olympic Games - Water Sports				
B4	8¢+2¢ Swimming	1.60	.35	.35
B5	10¢+5¢ Rowing	2.25	.50	.50
B6	15¢+5¢ Sailing	3.25	.70	.70
1975 Olympic Games - Combat Sports				
B7	8¢+2¢ Fencing	1.60	.35	.35
B8	10¢+5¢ Boxing	2.25	.50	.50
B9	15¢+5¢ Judo	3.25	.70	.70
1976 Olympic Games - Team Sports				
B10	8¢+2¢ Basketball	1.60	.35	.35
B11	10¢+5¢ Vaulting	2.25	.50	.50
B12	20¢+5¢ Soccer	3.85	.85	.85
1996 Literacy Issue				
B13	45¢ + 5¢ Literacy Singles	...	1.10	.45
B13a	Booklet Pane of 10	...	10.75	...

CANADA
AIR MAIL STAMPS

| C1 | C2 | C5 |

1928-1932 Airmail Issues VF +40% (B)

Scott's No.		Unused, NH VF	Unused, NH F-VF	Unused, OG VF	Unused, OG F-VF	Used F-VF
C1	5¢ Mercury & Allegory (1928)	18.50	13.00	10.50	7.50	2.75
C2	5¢ Globe (1930)	75.00	52.50	47.50	31.50	16.50
C3	6¢ on 5¢ Allegory (#C1) (1932)	11.00	7.50	7.00	5.00	2.50
C4	6¢ on 5¢ Ottawa (#C2) (1932)	32.75	23.50	20.75	14.75	8.50

1935-46 Airmail Issues VF + 25%

| C6 | C7 | C9 |

Scott's No.		Plate Blocks NH	Plate Blocks Unused	F-VF NH	F-VF Unused	F-VF Used
C5-9	Set of 5	...	...	12.00	7.75	2.20
C5	6¢ Daedalus	(6) 22.50	15.00	3.00	2.00	.90
C6	6¢ Steamer (1938)	18.00	13.50	2.85	2.00	.30
C7	6¢ Student Flyers (1942)	24.00	15.00	5.00	3.00	.75
C8	7¢ Student Flyers (1943)	4.00	3.00	.90	.65	.20
C9	7¢ Canada Goose (1946)	4.00	3.25	.90	.70	.20
C9a	7¢ Booklet Pane of 4	...	...	3.25	2.50	...

| CE1 | E1 |

CANADA

1942-1947 AIRMAIL SPECIAL DELIVERY VF + 25%

Scott's No.		Plate Blocks NH	Unused	F-VF NH	F-VF Unused	F-VF Used
CE1-4	Set of 4	...	...	12.95	9.50	9.15
CE1	16¢ Aerial View	13.00	9.75	2.00	1.40	1.35
CE2	17¢ Aerial View (1943)	15.00	11.75	2.70	1.95	1.85
CE3	17¢ Plane, Original Die (1946) .	23.00	18.00	4.50	3.25	3.15
CE4	17¢ Corrected Die (1947)	23.00	18.00	4.50	3.25	3.15

CE3 has circumflex (^) over second "E" of "EXPRES". CE4 has an accent (`).

AIRMAIL OFFICIAL STAMPS 1949-1950 VF + 25%

CO1	7¢ Canada Goose Overprinted "O.H.M.S." (C9)	47.50	35.00	11.00	7.95	3.85
CO2	7¢ Canada Goose Overprinted "G" (#C9) (1950)	75.00	58.50	15.00	11.00	11.00

SPECIAL DELIVERY STAMPS
1898 First Issue VF Used + 70% (B)

Scott's No.		NH VF	F-VF	Unused, OG VF	F-VF	Used F-VF
E1	10¢ Blue Green (1898)	215.00	130.00	87.50	52.50	7.50

1922-1933 Special Delivery VF Used +50% (B)

| | | | | | | |
| E2 | | E3 | | E4 | | |

E2	20¢ Carmine (1922)	165.00	110.00	70.00	47.50	6.00
E3	20¢ Confederation, Mail Transport (1927)	35.00	22.75	16.00	10.75	8.00
E4	20¢ "TWENTY CENTS" (1930) .	95.00	60.00	47.50	32.50	10.75
E5	20¢ "CENTS" (1933)	95.00	60.00	47.50	32.50	13.00

1935-1946 SPECIAL DELIVERY VF + 25%

E6		E7				
E10		E11				

Scott's No.		Plate Blocks NH	Unused	F-VF NH	F-VF Unused	F-VF Used
E6-11	Set of 6	...	...	46.00	31.50	27.50
E6	20¢ Progress .... (6)	70.00	50.00	8.25	5.50	4.50
E7	10¢ Arms, Green (1939)	35.00	25.00	5.00	3.50	2.50
E8	20¢ Arms, Carmine (1938)	210.00	140.00	31.50	21.50	19.50
E9	10¢ on 20¢ (#E8) (1939)	35.00	24.00	4.65	3.25	3.25
E10	10¢ Arms & Flags (1942)	12.50	8.75	2.35	1.65	1.40
E11	10¢ Arms (1946)	10.75	8.00	1.85	1.40	.75

1949-1950 SPECIAL DELIVERY OFFICIAL STAMPS VF + 25%

EO1	10¢ Arms Overprinted "O.H.M.S." (#E11)	90.00	65.00	13.00	9.50	9.50
EO2	10¢ Arms Overprinted "G" (#E11) (1950)	170.00	130.00	19.50	15.00	15.00

1875-1888 REGISTRATION STAMPS, Perf.12 VF + 80% (C)

Scott's No.		NH Fine	Unused, OG Fine	Ave.	Used Fine	Ave.
F1	2¢ Orange	150.00	65.00	40.00	2.25	1.40
F1a	2¢ Vermilion	175.00	75.00	45.00	7.50	4.50
F1b	2¢ Rose Carmine	...	165.00	100.00	75.00	45.00
F1d	2¢ Orange, Perf. 12 x 11½ ...	...	275.00	160.00	75.00	45.00
F2	5¢ Dark Green	225.00	90.00	50.00	3.00	1.75
F2a	5¢ Blue Green	250.00	100.00	60.00	3.25	2.00
F2b	5¢ Yellow Green	325.00	135.00	80.00	5.00	3.00
F2d	5¢ Green, Perf. 12 x 11½ ...	...	950.00	550.00	140.00	85.00
F3	8¢ Blue (1876)	...	275.00	200.00	200.00	125.00

#F1-3 UNUSED PRICES ARE FOR STAMPS WITH FULL ORIGINAL GUM. STAMPS WITH PARTIAL OR NO GUM SELL FOR 30% LESS THAN THOSE WITH FULL ORIGINAL GUM.

CANADA

| F2 | J1 | J6 | J11 |

POSTAGE DUE STAMPS
1906-1928 VF Used + 50% (B)

Scott's No.		NH VF	F-VF	Unused VF	F-VF	Used F-VF
J1-5	Set of 5	225.00	145.00	130.00	87.50	25.75
J1	1¢ Violet	25.00	15.75	14.00	9.50	3.00
J1a	1¢ Thin Paper (1924)	43.50	27.50	25.00	16.50	5.50
J2	2¢ Violet	25.00	15.75	14.00	9.50	.65
J2a	2¢ Thin Paper (1924)	50.00	31.50	28.00	18.50	7.00
J3	4¢ Violet (1928)	100.00	62.50	56.50	37.50	13.50
J4	5¢ Violet	25.00	15.75	14.00	9.50	1.10
J4a	5¢ Thin Paper (1928)	18.50	12.00	10.50	7.00	4.75
J5	10¢ Violet (1928)	67.50	41.50	37.50	25.00	9.00

1930-1932 VF Used + 40% (B)

J6-10	Set of 5	215.00	145.00	115.00	83.50	17.25
J6	1¢ Dark Violet	18.75	12.50	10.50	7.50	2.65
J7	2¢ Dark Violet	11.75	7.50	6.25	4.50	.70
J8	4¢ Dark Violet	29.50	18.50	15.75	11.00	3.00
J9	5¢ Dark Violet (1931)	24.00	16.00	13.50	9.50	4.50
J10	10¢ Dark Violet (1932)	140.00	95.00	75.00	55.00	7.00

1933-1934 VF Used + 40% (B)

J11-14	Set of 4	72.50	46.75	40.75	28.50	12.50
J11	1¢ Dark Violet (1934)	19.00	12.75	10.50	7.50	4.50
J12	2¢ Dark Violet	7.25	5.00	4.25	3.00	.80
J13	4¢ Dark Violet	16.50	10.75	9.00	6.50	4.75
J14	10¢ Dark Violet	33.50	21.00	18.50	13.00	3.75

| J15 | J23 | J28 |

1935-1965 VF + 30%

Scott's No.		Plate Block	F-VF NH	F-VF Used
J15-20	Set of 7	...	5.25	3.50
J15	1¢ Dark Violet	2.25	.25	.15
J16	2¢ Dark Violet	2.25	.25	.15
J16B	3¢ Dark Violet (1965)	17.50	2.00	1.25
J17	4¢ Dark Violet	2.75	.30	.15
J18	5¢ Dark Violet (1948)	3.50	.40	.30
J19	6¢ Dark Violet (1957)	13.75	1.95	1.50
J20	10¢ Dark Violet	3.00	.40	.15

1967 Centennial Issue Regular Size 20 x 17 mm., Perforated 12

J21-27	Set of 7	...	3.25	3.00
J21	1¢ Carmine Rose	7.00	.20	.20
J22	2¢ Carmine Rose	1.40	.25	.25
J23	3¢ Carmine Rose	1.40	.25	.25
J24	4¢ Carmine Rose	3.00	.35	.35
J25	5¢ Carmine Rose	9.75	1.60	1.40
J26	6¢ Carmine Rose	2.75	.35	.35
J27	10¢ Carmine Rose	2.50	.40	.35

1969-1970 Modular Size 20 x 15¾ mm., Perf. 12 Dextrose (Yellow Gum)

J28,J31,J32a,J34,J35,J36 (6)		...	19.75	20.00
J28	1¢ Carmine Rose (1970)	2.75	.50	.40
J31	4¢ Carmine Rose	2.25	.45	.35
J32a	5¢ Carmine Rose	85.00	17.50	17.50
J34v	8¢ Carmine Rose	2.25	.40	.25
J35	10¢ Carmine Rose	2.75	.60	.25
J36	12¢ Carmine Rose	4.75	.80	.70

1973-74 Modular Size 20 x 15¾ mm., Perf.12 White Gum

J28v,J29-30,J31v,J33,J34v,J35v,J36v,J37 (9)		...	2.40	...
J28v	1¢ Carmine Rose (1974)	2.00	.40	...
J29	2¢ Carmine Rose	1.50	.20	.20
J30	3¢ Carmine Rose (1974)	1.80	.35	.20
J31v	4¢ Carmine Rose	1.20	.25	...
J33	6¢ Carmine Rose	1.20	.25	.20
J34	8¢ Carmine Rose (1974)	1.25	.25	...
J35v	10¢ Carmine Rose	1.25	.25	...
J36v	12¢ Carmine Rose	1.50	.25	...
J37	16¢ Carmine Rose (1974)	2.25	.40	.35

1977-78 Modular Size 20 x 15¾mm.,Perf. 12½ x 12

J28a-40	Set of 9		4.65	3.50
J28a	1¢ Carmine Rose	.50	.20	.15
J31a	4¢ Carmine Rose	.60	.20	.20
J32	5¢ Carmine Rose	.75	.20	.20
J34a	8¢ Carmine Rose (1978)	2.40	.40	.20
J35a	10¢ Carmine Rose	1.30	.25	.25
J36a	12¢ Carmine Rose	11.75	1.60	.90
J38	20¢ Carmine Rose	2.50	.50	.45
J39	24¢ Carmine Rose .	2.75	.60	.45
J40	50¢ Carmine Rose	4.75	1.00	.90

CANADA

1915-1916 WAR TAX STAMPS Perforated 12 VF Used + 60% (B)

MR1 MR3

Scott's No.		Unused, NH VF	F-VF	Unused,OG VF	F-VF	Used F-VF
MR1	1¢ George V, Green	33.50	20.00	15.00	9.50	.20
MR2	2¢ Carmine	33.50	20.00	15.00	9.50	.25
MR3	2¢ + 1¢ Carmine, Die1 (1916)	47.50	26.50	21.00	13.00	.20
MR3a	2¢ + 1¢ Carmine, Die II	285.00	150.00	130.00	75.00	3.50
MR4	2¢ + 1¢ Brown, Die II	36.50	21.50	17.00	10.75	.20
MR4a	2¢ + 1¢ Brown, Die I	600.00	350.00	285.00	180.00	7.50
MR5	2¢ + 1¢ Carmine, Perf. 12 x 8	90.00	55.00	43.50	27.50	20.00

1916 War Tax Coils, Perforated 8 Vertically VF Used +60% (B)

MR6	2¢ + 1¢ Carmine	235.00	135.00	125.00	75.00	5.75
MR6	2¢ + 1¢ Pair	525.00	300.00	275.00	165.00	...
MR7	2¢ + 1¢ Brown, Die II	50.00	30.00	26.75	16.75	.75
MR7	2¢ + 1¢ Pair	110.00	65.00	57.50	37.50	..
MR7a	2¢ + 1¢ Brown, Die I	275.00	160.00	145.00	90.00	5.75
MR7a	2¢ + 1¢ Pair	600.00	350.00	325.00	200.00	..

Die I Single colored line between 2 white lines below large "T" of "1T¢".
Die II Right half of colored line is replaced by 2 short diagonal lines and 5 small dots.

OFFICIAL STAMPS

O2 O15A O19

1949-50 Issues of 1942-46 Overprinted "O.H.M.S." VF + 25%

Scott's No.		Plate Blocks NH	Unused	F-VF NH	F-VF Unused	F-VF Used
O1-10	Set of 9	...	...	250.00	185.00	140.00
O1	1¢ George VI, Green (249)	9.75	7.75	1.85	1.40	1.35
O2	2¢ George VI, Brown (250)	110.00	90.00	8.00	6.50	6.00
O3	3¢ George VI, Violet (252)	9.75	7.25	1.70	1.30	1.00
O4	4¢ George VI, Carmine (254) ...	19.00	13.50	2.50	1.80	.55
O6	10¢ Great Bear Lake (269)	22.50	18.00	2.75	2.20	.50
O7	14¢ Hydroelectric Station (270)	30.00	23.75	3.60	2.85	1.90
O8	20¢ Reaper (271)	80.00	60.00	14.00	11.00	2.65
O9	50¢ Lumbering (272)	1000.00	750.00	175.00	125.00	100.00
O10	$1 Train Ferry (273)	450.00	350.00	55.00	42.50	29.50

1950 Issues of 1949-50 Overprinted "O.H.M.S." VF + 20%

O11	50¢ Development (294)	165.00	130.00	27.50	21.50	18.50
O12-15A	George VI Set of 5	...	...	4.65	3.75	2.50
O12	1¢ Green (284)	3.65	3.00	.30	.25	.25
O13	2¢ Sepia (285)	4.50	3.50	.95	.75	.65
O14	3¢ Rose Violet (286)	5.75	4.50	1.00	.80	.45
O15	4¢ Carmine (287)	5.75	4.50	1.00	.80	.15
O15A	5¢ Deep Blue (288)	10.75	8.00	1.80	1.35	1.20

CANADA

Official Stamps (continued)

1950 Issues of 1948-50 Overprinted "G" VF + 20%

Scott's No.		Plate Blocks NH	F-VF Unused	F-VF NH	F-VF Unused	F-VF Used
O16-25	Set of 10	...	...	105.00	80.00	62.50
O16	1¢ George VI, Green (284)	2.50	2.00	.35	.25	.15
O17	2¢ George VI, Sepia (285)	5.50	4.50	1.20	.90	.70
O18	3¢ George VI, Rose Violet (286)	6.25	5.00	1.20	.90	.20
O19	4¢ George VI, Carmine (287)	6.25	5.00	1.20	.90	.15
O20	5¢ George VI, Deep Blue (288)	14.50	11.75	1.40	1.10	.75
O21	10¢ Great Bear Lake (269)	14.00	11.00	2.20	1.65	.40
O22	14¢ Hydroelectric Station (270)	33.50	26.50	4.50	3.50	2.10
O23	20¢ Reaper (271)	87.50	67.50	12.75	9.75	.90
O24	50¢ Oil Development (294)	52.50	40.00	8.25	6.50	5.25
O25	$1 Train Ferry (273)	415.00	325.00	80.00	60.00	55.00
O26	10¢ Fur Trading (301)	5.95	4.75	1.10	.90	.20

(stamp images)

O28 O36 O40 O46

1951-53 Issues of 1951-53 Overprinted G VF + 20%

O27	$1 Fisheries (302)	415.00	325.00	75.00	60.00	60.00
O28	2¢ George VI, Olive Green (305)	2.40	1.95	.50	.40	.15
O29	4¢ George VI, Orange (306)	4.75	3.50	.80	.60	.15
O30	20¢ Forestry Products (316)	12.00	9.00	2.25	1.65	.20
O31	7¢ Canada Goose (320)	16.00	12.00	3.65	2.75	1.10
O32	$1 Totem Pole (321)	85.00	65.00	16.50	12.00	9.50

1953-55 Issues of 1953-55 Overprinted G VF + 20%

O33-37	Queen Elizabeth Set of 5	...	...	1.70	1.35	.65
O33	1¢ Violet Brown (325)	1.70	1.40	.30	.25	.15
O34	2¢ Green (326)	1.70	1.40	.30	.25	.15
O35	3¢ Carmine Rose (327)	1.70	1.40	.30	.25	.15
O36	4¢ Violet (328)	2.40	1.95	.45	.35	.15
O37	5¢ Ultramarine (329)	2.40	1.95	.45	.35	.15
O38	50¢ Textile Industry (334)	27.50	21.50	4.50	3.50	1.10
O38a	50¢ Textile, Flying "G" (1961) ...	27.50	21.50	4.50	3.50	1.70
O39	10¢ Eskimo & Kayak (351)	4.75	3.75	.85	.65	.15
O39a	10¢ Eskimo, Flying "G" (1962) ..	12.50	10.00	1.75	1.40	.85

1955-56 Issues of 1955-56 Overprinted G VF + 20%

O40-45	Set of 5	...	...	3.35	2.75	.80
O40	1¢ Queen Elizabeth (337)	1.75	1.50	.30	.25	.25
O41	2¢ Queen Elizabeth (338)	1.85	1.60	.30	.25	.15
O43	4¢ Queen Elizabeth (340)	5.00	4.00	.95	.80	.15
O44	5¢ Queen Elizabeth (341)	2.75	2.25	.55	.45	.15
O45	20¢ Paper Industry (362)	8.25	6.75	1.50	1.20	.20
O45a	20¢ Paper, Flying "G" (1962)	43.50	35.00	6.50	5.25	.45

Flying "G" = Bottom right side forms thin straight line.

1963 Issue of 1962-63 Overprinted G

Scott's No.		Plate Block	F-VF NH	F-VF Used
O46-49	Set of 4	...	2.60	2.60
O46	1¢ Queen Elizabeth (401) .... (Blank)	3.50	.70	.70
O47	2¢ Queen Elizabeth (402) .... (Blank)	3.50	.70	.70
O48	4¢ Queen Elizabeth (404) .... (Blank)	7.50	.80	.80
O49	5¢ Queen Elizabeth (405) .... (Blank)	2.75	.50	.50

NOTE: NUMBER IN ( ) INDICATES CATALOG NUMBER OF BASIC STAMP WHICH WAS OVERPRINTED.

CANADA HUNTING PERMIT STAMPS

CANADA FEDERAL ISSUES

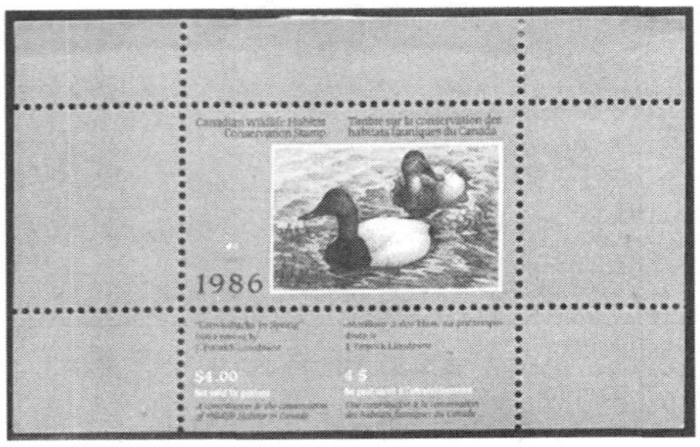

CN 1

No.	Description	Min.Sheet of 16 (B)	Bklt. NH
CN 1	1985 $4 Mallards	...	12.00
CN 2	1986 $4 Canvasbacks	165.00	12.00
CN 3	1987 $6.50 Canada Goose	275.00	11.00
CN 4	1988 $6.50 Pintails	275.00	15.00
CN 5	1989 $7.50 Snow Goose	275.00	15.00
CN 6	1990 $7.50 Wood Duck	225.00	15.00
CN 7	1991 $8.50 Black Duck	225.00	13.00
CN 7J	1991 Joint Issue with U.S.	...	35.00
CN 7JI	1991 Joint Issue with U.S., Imperf....		80.00
CN 8	1992 $8.50 Common Elders Bk.	225.00	13.00
CN 9	1993 $8.50 Hooded Merganser	195.00	13.00
CN 10	1994 $8.50 Ross' Geese	195.00	13.00
CN 11	1995 $8.50 Redheads	195.00	13.00
CN 12	1996 $8.50 Goldeneyes	195.00	13.00
CN 13	1997 $8.50 Gadwalls	195.00	13.00
CN 14	1998 $8.50 Ring Necked Duck	195.00	12.00
CN 15	1999 $8.50 Buffleheads	195.00	12.00
CN 16	2000 $8.50 Sandhill Crane	195.00	12.00
CN 17	2001 $8.50 Harlequin	195.00	12.00
CN 18	2002 $8.50 King Eiders	160.00	11.00
CN 19	2003 $8.50 Shoveler	160.00	11.00
CN 20	2004 $8.50 Mallards	160.00	11.00
Canada Complete 1985-2003(19)			**220.00**

ALBERTA

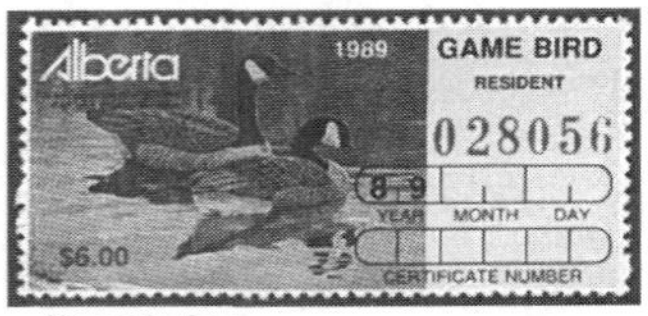

AB1

No.	Description	F-VF,NH
AB 1	1989 $6 Canada Geese	28.00
AB 2	1990 $7 Mallards	24.00
AB 3	1991 $7.71 Pintails	20.00
AB 4	1992 $7.90 Snow Geese	20.00
AB 5	1993 $7.90 Canvasbacks	18.00
AB 6	1994 $8.36 Redheads	15.00
AB 7	1995 $8.36 White Fronted Geese	15.00
AB 8	1996 $8.36 Goldeneyes	15.00
AB 9	1997 $8.36 Harlequin	15.00
Alberta Complete 1989-97 (9)		

ALBERTA HABITAT

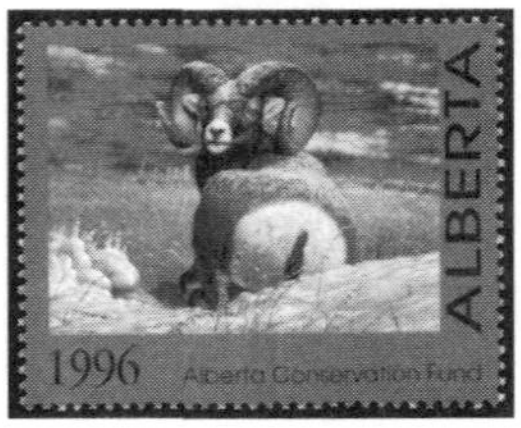

ABH 1

No.	Description	Min.Sheet of 4 (M)	F-VF NH
ABH 1	1996 $6 Big Horn Sheep	34.00	8.00
ABH 1B	1996 $6 same-Booklet Single	...	10.00
ABH 2	1997 $6 Rocky Mountain Goat	34.00	8.00
ABH 2B	1997 $6 same-Booklet Single	...	10.00
ABH 3	1998 $6 Cougar	34.00	8.00
ABH 3B	1998 $6 same-Booklet Single	...	10.00
ABH 4	1999 $6 Elk	34.00	8.00
ABH 4B	1999 $6 same-Booklet Single	...	10.00
ABH 5	2000 $6 Bald Eagle	34.00	8.00
ABH 5B	2000 $6 same-Booklet Single		10.00

No.	Description	Min.Sheet of 4 (M)	Bklt. Sgl.(B)
ABH 6	2001 $6 Bobcat Booklet	30.00	10.00
ABH 7	2002 $6 Elk Booklet	30.00	10.00
ABH 8	2003 $6 Whitetail Deer Bklt.	30.00	9.00
ABH 9	2004 $6 Cougar Booklet	30.00	9.00

BRITISH COLUMBIA

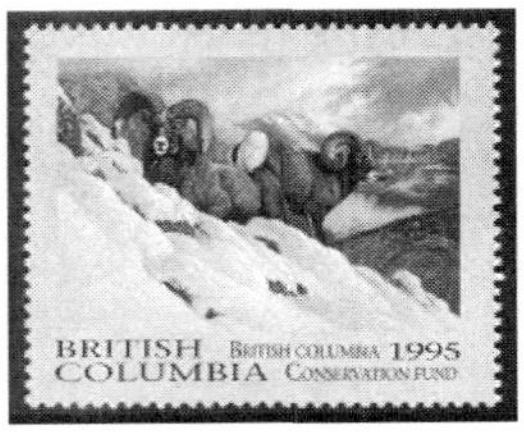

BC1

No.	Description	Min.Sheet of 4 (M)	F-VF NH
BC 1	1995 $6 Bighorn Sheep	34.00	8.00
BC 1B	1995 same, Booklet Single	...	10.00
BC 2	1996 $6 Elk	34.00	8.00
BC 2B	1996 same, Booklet Single	...	10.00
BC 3	1997 $6 Grizzly Bear	34.00	8.00
BC 3B	1997 same, Booklet Single	...	10.00
BC 4	1998 $6 Tufted Puffins	34.00	8.00
BC 4B	1998 same, Booklet Single	...	10.00
BC 5	1999 $6 Bald Eagle	34.00	8.00
BC 5B	1999 same, Booklet Single	...	10.00
BC 6	2000 $6 Mule Deer	34.00	8.00
BC 6B	2000 same, Booklet Single	...	10.00

No.	Description	Min.Sheet of 4 (M)	Bklt. Sgl.(B)
BC 7	2001 $6 Canada Goose	30.00	10.00
BC 8	2002 $6 Northern Goshawk	30.00	9.00
BC 9	2003 $6 Sea Otter.	30.00	9.00
BC 10	2004 $6 Mule Deer	30.00	9.00

MANITOBA

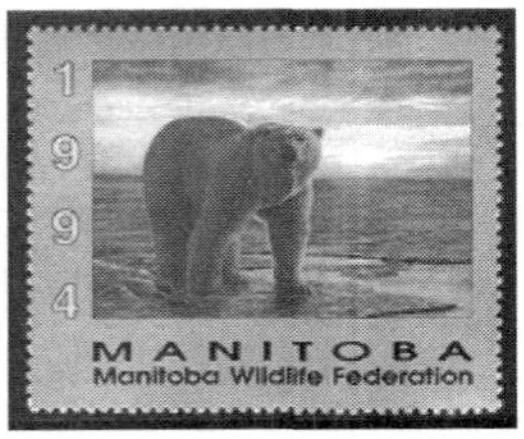

MAN 1

No.	Description	Min.Sheet of 4 (M)	F-VF NH
	Winnipeg Duck Stamp	...	13.00
	Winnipeg Duck,Flourescent Paper	...	13.00
MAN 1	1994 $6 Polar Bear	34.00	8.00
MAN 1B	1994 same, Booklet Single	...	10.00
MAN 2	1995 $6 Whitetailed Deer	34.00	8.00
MAN 2B	1995 Same, Booklet Single	...	10.00
MAN 3	1996 $6 Lynx	34.00	8.00
MAN 3B	1996 same, Booklet Single	...	10.00
MAN 4	1997 $6 Falcon	34.00	8.00
MAN 4B	1997 same, Booklet Single	...	10.00
MAN 5	1998 $6 Moose	34.00	8.00
MAN 5B	1998 same, Booklet Single	...	10.00
MAN 6	1999 $6 Buffalo	34.00	8.00
MAN 6B	1999 same, Booklet Single	...	10.00
MAN 7	2000 $6 Canada Geese	34.00	8.00
MAN 7B	2000 same, Booklet Single	...	10.00

No.	Description	Min.Sheet of 4 (M)	Bklt. Sgl.(B)
MAN 8	2001 $6 Redheads.	30.00	10.00
MAN 9	2002 $6 Eared Gerbe	30.00	10.00
MAN 10	2003 $6 Grey Squirrel	30.00	9.00
MAN 11	2004 $6 Wood Duck	30.00	9.00

NEW BRUNSWICK

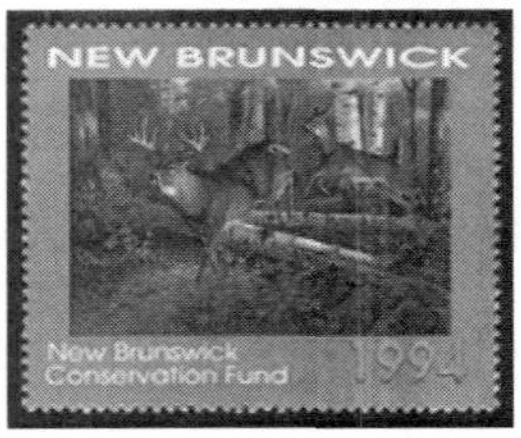

NB1

No.	Description	Min.Sheet of 4 (M)	F-VF NH
NB 1	1994 $6 White Tail Deer	34.00	8.00
NB 1B	1994 same, Booklet Single	...	10.00
NB 2	1995 $6 Cougar	34.00	8.00
NB 2B	1995 same, Booklet Single	...	10.00
NB 3	1996 $6 Moose	34.00	8.00
NB 3B	1996 same, Booklet Single	...	10.00
NB 4	1997 $6 Pheasant	34.00	8.00
NB 4B	1997 same, Booklet Single	...	10.00
NB 5	1998 $6 Rainbow Trout	34.00	8.00
NB 5B	1998 same, Booklet Single	...	10.00
NB 6	1999 $6 Wood Ducks	34.00	8.00
NB 6B	1999 same, Booklet Single	...	10.00
NB 7	2000 $6 King Eider	34.00	8.00
NB 7B	2000 same, Booklet Single	...	10.00

NEW BRUNSWICK (continued)

No.	Description	Min.Sheet of 4 (M)	Bklt. Sgl.(B)
NB 8	2001 $6 Goldeneye	30.00	10.00
NB 9	2002 $6 Whitetail Deer	30.00	9.00
NB 10	2003 $6 Green Winged Teal	30.00	9.00
NB 11	2004 $6 Pintails	30.00	9.00

NEWFOUNDLAND

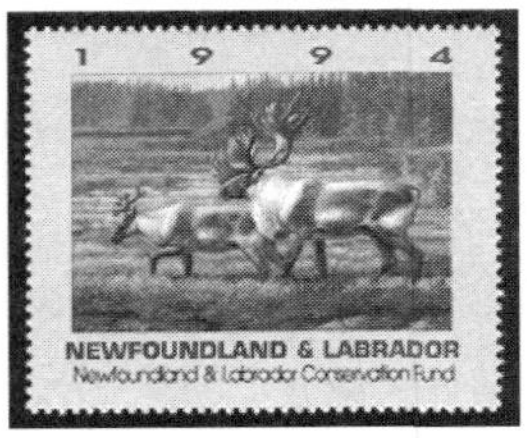

NF1

No.	Description	Min.Sheet of 4 (M)	F-VF NH
NF 1	1994 $6 Woodland Caribou	34.00	8.00
NF 1B	1994 same, Booklet Single	...	10.00
NF 2	1995 $6 Goldeneyes	34.00	8.00
NF 2B	1995 same, Booklet Single	...	10.00
NF 3	1996 $6 Moose	34.00	8.00
NF 3B	1996 same, Booklet Single	...	10.00
NF 4	1997 $6 Harlequin Duck	34.00	8.00
NF 4B	1997 same, Booklet Single	...	10.00
NF 5	1998 $6 Bear	34.00	8.00
NF 5B	1998 same, Booklet Single	...	10.00
NF 6	1999 $6 Fox	34.00	8.00
NF 6B	1999 same, Booklet Single	...	10.00
NF 7	2000 $6 King Eider	34.00	8.00
NF 7B	2000 same, Booklet Single	...	10.00

No.	Description	Min.Sheet of 4 (M)	Bklt. Sgl.(B)
NF 8	2001 $6 Moose	30.00	10.00
NF 9	2002 $6 Common Eider	30.00	10.00
NF 10	2003 $6 Bufflehead	30.00	9.00
NF 11	2004 $6 Black Bear	30.00	9.00

NORTHWEST TERRITORIES

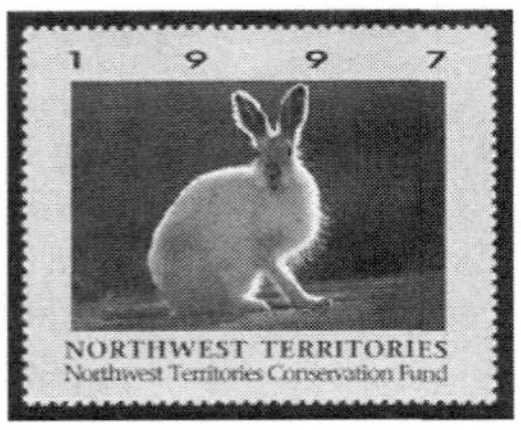

NWT1

No.	Description	Min.Sheet of 4 (M)	F-VF NH
NWT 1	1997 $6 Arctic Hare	34.00	8.00
NWT 1B	1997 same, Booklet Single	...	10.00
NWT 2	1998 $6 Snowy Owl	34.00	8.00
NWT 2B	1998 same, Booklet Single	...	10.00
NWT 3	1999 $6 Arctic Loon	34.00	8.00
NWT 3B	1999 same, Booklet Single	...	10.00
NWT 4	2000 $6 Caribou	34.00	8.00
NWT 4B	2000 same, Booklet Single	...	10.00

No.	Description	Min.Sheet of 4 (M)	Bklt. Sgl.(B)
NWT 5	2001 $6 Walrus	30.00	10.00
NWT 6	2002 $6 Moose	30.00	10.00
NWT 7	2003 $6 Black Bear	30.00	9.00
NWT 8	2004 $6 Stone Sheep	30.00	9.00

NOVA SCOTIA

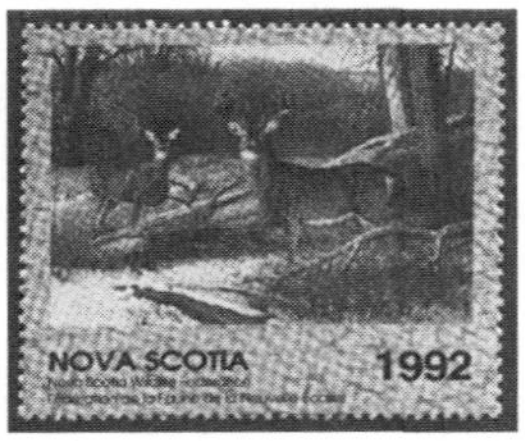

NS1

No.	Description	Min.Sheet of 4 (M)	F-VF NH
NS 1	1992 $6 Whitetail Deer	50.00	12.00
NS 1B	1992 same, Booklet Single	...	35.00
NS 2	1993 $6 Summer Pheasant	34.00	10.00
NS 2B	1993 same, Booklet Single	...	12.50
NS 3	1994 $6 Wood Duck	34.00	8.00
NS 3B	1994 same, Booklet Single	...	10.00
NS 4	1995 $6 Coyote	34.00	8.00
NS 4B	1995 same, Booklet Single	...	10.00
NS 5	1996 $6 Osprey	34.00	8.00
NS 5B	1996 same, Booklet Single	...	10.00
NS 6	1997 $6 Woodpecker	34.00	8.00
NS 6B	1997 same, Booklet Single	...	10.00

CANADA HUNTING PERMIT STAMPS

NOVA SCOTIA (continued)

No.	Description	Min.Sheet of 4 (M)	F-VF NH
NS 7	1998 $6 Blue Winged Teal	34.00	8.00
NS 7B	1998 same, Booklet Single	...	10.00
NS 8	1999 $6 Moose	34.00	8.00
NS 8B	1999 same, Booklet Single	...	10.00
NS 9	2000 $6 Bald Eagle	34.00	8.00
NS 9B	2000 same, Booklet Single	...	10.00

No.	Description	Min.Sheet of 4 (M)	Bklt. Sgl.(B)
NS 10	2001 $6 Wood Duck	30.00	10.00
NS 11	2002 $6 Bear	30.00	9.00
NS 12	2003 $6 Northern Goshawk	30.00	9.00
NS 13	2004 $6 Black Duck	30.00	9.00

NUNAVUT TERRITORY

NU1

No.	Description	Min.Sheet of 4 (M)	F-VF NH
NU 1	1999 $6 Polar Bear	34.00	8.00
NU 1B	1999 same, Booklet Single	...	10.00
NU 2	2000 $6 Arctic Loon	34.00	8.00
NU 2B	2000 same, Booklet Single	...	10.00

No.	Description	Min.Sheet of 4 (M)	Bklt. Sgl.(B)
NU 3	2001 $6 Caribou	30.00	10.00
NU 4	2002 $6 Polar Bear	30.00	9.00
NU 5	2003 $6 Musk Ox	30.00	9.00
NU 6	2004 $6 Grizzly Bear	30.00	9.00

ONTARIO

ON1

No.	Description	Min.Sheet of 4 (M)	F-VF NH
ON 1	1993 $6 Ruffed Grouse	34.00	11.00
ON 1B	1993 same, Booklet Single	...	10.00
ON 2	1994 $6 Deer	34.00	8.00
ON 2B	1994 same, Booklet Single	...	10.00
ON 3	1995 $6 Fish	34.00	8.00
ON 3B	1995 same, Booklet Single	...	10.00
ON 4	1996 $6 Blue Winged Teal	34.00	8.00
ON 4B	1996 same, Booklet Single	...	10.00
ON 5	1997 $6 Lesser Scaup	34.00	8.00
ON 5B	1997 same, Booklet Single	...	10.00
ON 6	1998 $6 River Otter	34.00	8.00
ON 6B	1998 same, Booklet Single	...	10.00
ON 7	1999 $6 Buffleheads	34.00	8.00
ON 7B	1999 same, Booklet Single	...	10.00
ON 8	2000 $6 Cardinals	34.00	8.00
ON 8B	2000 same, Booklet Single	...	10.00

No.	Description	Min.Sheet of 4 (M)	Bklt. Sgl.(B)
ON 9	2001 $6 Weasel	30.00	10.00
ON 10	2002 $6 American Kestrel	30.00	9.00
ON 11	2003 $6 Mallard	30.00	9.00
ON 12	2004 $6 Belted Kingfisher	30.00	9.00

PRINCE EDWARD ISLAND

PE1

No.	Description	Min.Sheet of 4 (M)	F-VF NH
PEI 1	1995 $6 Canada Geese	34.00	8.00
PEI 1B	1995 same, Booklet Single ...	...	10.00
PEI 2	1996 $6 Woodcock	34.00	8.00
PEI 2B	1996 same, Booklet Single	...	10.00
PEI 3	1997 $6 Red Fox	34.00	8.00
PEI 3B	1997 same, Booklet Single ...	...	10.00

PRINCE EDWARD ISLAND (continued)

No.	Description	Min.Sheet of 4 (M)	F-VF NH
PEI 4	1998 $6 Wigeon	34.00	8.00
PEI 4B	1998 same, Booklet Single ...	...	10.00
PEI 5	1999 $6 Mallard	34.00	8.00
PEI 5B	1999 same, Booklet Single ...	...	10.00
PEI 6	2000 $6 Wood Ducks	34.00	8.00
PEI 6B	2000 same, Booklet Single ...	...	10.00

No.	Description	Min.Sheet of 4 (M)	Bklt. Sgl.(B)
PEI 7	2001 $6 Northern Pintail	30.00	10.00
PEI 8	2002 $6 American Kestrel	30.00	9.00
PEI 9	2003 $6 Blue Winged Teal	30.00	9.00
PEI 10	2004 $6 Black Duck	30.00	9.00

QUEBEC

QU1

Bklt. No.	Description	Min.Sheet of 4 (M)	Single
QU 1	1988 $6 Ruffled Grouse	225.00	120.00
QU 1MI	1988 Imperforate Sheet of 4	POR	
QU 2	1989 $6 Black Ducks	140.00	37.50
QU 2MI	1989 Imperforate Sheet of 4	350.00	
QU 3	1990 $6 Common Loons	135.00	22.00
QU 3MI	1990 Imperforate Sheet of 4	350.00	
QU 4	1991 $6 Common Goldeneyes	85.00	16.00
QU 4MI	1991 Imperforate Sheet of 4	350.00	
QU 5	1992 $6.50 Lynx	90.00	12.50
QU 5MI	1992 Imperforate Sheet of 4	280.00	
QU 5A	1992 $10 Lynx Surcharge	...	25.00
QU 6	1993 $6.50 Peregrine Falcon .	60.00	12.50
QU 6MI	1993 Imperforate Sheet of 4	225.00	
QU 7	1994 $7 Beluga Whale	45.00	13.00
QU 7MI	1994 Imperforate Sheet of 4	225.00	
QU 8	1995 $7 Moose	45.00	12.00
QU 8MI	1995 Imperforate Sheet of 4	225.00	
QU 9	1996 $7.50 Blue Heron	45.00	12.00
QU 9MI	1996 Imperforate Sheet of 4	225.00	
QU 9A	1996 $10 Capex Overprint	...	17.50
QU 9B	1996 $10 WWF Overprint	...	18.00
QU 10	1997 $8.50 Snowy Owl	55.00	14.00
QU 10MI	1997 Imperforate Sheet of 4	225.00	
QU 10A	1997 $10 WWF Overprint	...	18.00
QU 11	1998 $10 Snow Goose	55.00	14.00
QU 11MI	1998 Imperforate Sheet of 4	225.00	
QU 11A	1998 $12.50 WWF Overprint	...	18.00
QU 12	1999 $10 River Otter	55.00	14.00
QU 12MI	1999 Imperforate Sheet of 4	225.00	
QU 12A	1999 $12.50 Overprint.WWF	...	18.00
QU 12AI	same, $12.50 WWF Imperforate	...	40.00
QU 13	2000 $10 Puffin/Wood Turtle ..	55.00	14.00
QU 13MI	2000 Imperforate Sheet of 4	225.00	
QU 13A	2000 $12.50 WWF Overprint	...	18.00
QU 13AI	same, $12.50 WWF Imperforate	...	35.00
QU 14	2001 $10 Blue Jay	55.00	14.00
QU 14MI	2001 Imperforate Sheet of 4	225.00	
QU 14A	2001 $12.50 WWF Overprint	...	18.00
QU 14AI	same, $12.50 WWF Imperforate	...	35.00
QU 15	2002 $10 Caribou	55.00	12.00
QU 15MI	2002 Imperforate Sheet of 4	225.00	
QU 15A	2002 $12.50 WWF Overprint	...	15.00
QU 15AI	same, $12.50 WWF Imperforate	...	35.00
QU 16	2003 $10 Arctic Fox	55.00	13.00
QU 16MI	2003 Imperforate Sheet of 4	225.00	
QU 16A	2003 $12.50 WWF Overprint	...	18.00
QU 16AI	same, $12.50 WWF Imperforate...	...	35.00
QU 17	2004 $10 Musk Ox	55.00	15.00
QU 17MI	2004 Imperforate Sheet of 4	225.00	
QU 17A	2004 $12.50 WWF Overprint	...	18.00
QU 17Ai	same, $12.50 WWF Imperforate	...	35.00

SASKATCHEWAN

SK4

No.	Description	Min.Sheet of 4 (M)	F-VF NH
SK 1	1988 $5 American Widgeon Bklt.Sgle.		40.00
SK 2	1989 $5 Bull Moose Booklet Single		40.00
SK 3	1990 $5 Sharp-taile'd Grouse Bk.Sgle		50.00
SK 4	1993 $6 Mallards	34.00	8.00
SK 4B	1993 same, Booklet Single	...	10.00
SK 5	1994 $6 Wood Ducks	34.00	8.00
SK 5B	1994 same, Booklet Single	...	10.00

SASKATCHEWAN (continued)

No.	Description	Min.Sheet of 4 (M)	F-VF NH
SK 6	1995 $6 Antelope	34.00	8.00
SK 6B	1995 same, Booklet Single	...	10.00
SK 7	1996 $6 Ruddy Duck	34.00	8.00
SK 7B	1996 same, Booklet Single	...	10.00
SK 8	1997 $6 Wigeon	34.00	8.00
SK 8B	1997 same, Booklet Single	...	10.00
SK 9	1998 $6 Swans	34.00	8.00
SK 9B	1998 same, Booklet Single	...	10.00
SK 10	1999 $6 Moose	34.00	8.00
SK 10B	1999 same, Booklet Single ...	...	10.00
SK 11	2000 $6 Pheasants	34.00	8.00
SK 11B	2000 same, Booklet Single ...	...	10.00

No.	Description	Min.Sheet of 4 (M)	Bklt. Sgl.(B)
SK 12	2001 $6 Grouse	30.00	10.00
SK 13	2002 $6 Grey Wolf	30.00	9.00
SK 14	2003 $6 Grizzly Bear	30.00	9.00
SK 15	2004 $6 Whitetail Deer	30.00	9.00

YUKON TERRITORY

YT1

No.	Description	Min.Sheet of 4 (M)	F-VF NH
YT 1	1996 $6 Bald Eagle	34.00	8.00
YT 1B	1996 same, Booklet Single	...	10.00
YT 2	1997 $6 Moose	34.00	8.00
YT 2B	1997 same, Booklet Single	...	10.00
YT 3	1998 $6 Polar Bear	34.00	8.00
YT 3B	1998 same, Booklet Single	...	10.00
YT 4	1999 $6 Rocky Mountain Goat	34.00	8.00
YT 4B	1999 same, Booklet Single	...	10.00
YT 5	2000 $6 Snowy Owl	34.00	8.00
YT 5B	2000 same, Booklet Single	...	10.00

No.	Description	Min.Sheet of 4 (M)	Bklt. Sgl.(B)
YT 6	2001 $6 Red Tailed Hawk	30.00	10.00
YT 7	2002 $6 Swan	30.00	9.00
YT 8	2003 $6 Grizzly Bear.	30.00	9.00
YT 9	2004 $6 Red Fox	30.00	9.00

ATLANTIC WATERFOWL CELEBRATION

AWC1

No.	Description	Min.Sheet of 4 (M)	F-VF NH
AWC 1	1995 $6 Green Winged Teal ...	85.00	22.00
AWC 1B	1995 same, Booklet Single ..	...	30.00
AWC 2	1996 $6 Canada Geese	34.00	10.00
AWC 2B	`1996 same, Booklet Single	...	10.00
AWC 3	1997 $6 Goldeneye	34.00	8.00
AWC 3B	1997 same, Booklet Single ..	...	10.00
AWC 4	1998 $6 Hooded Mergansers .	34.00	8.00
AWC 4B	1998 same, Booklet Single ...	...	10.00

PITT WATERFOWL MANAGEMENT

No.	Description		F-VF NH
PT 1	1990 Canvasbacks	...	8.00
PT 2	1991 Snow Goose	...	8.00
PT 3	1992 Mallard Decoy	...	8.00
PT 4	1993 Brant Goose	...	8.00
PT 5	1994 Mallard Decoy	...	6.00
PT 6	1995 Mallard Decoy	...	6.00

NEWFOUNDLAND

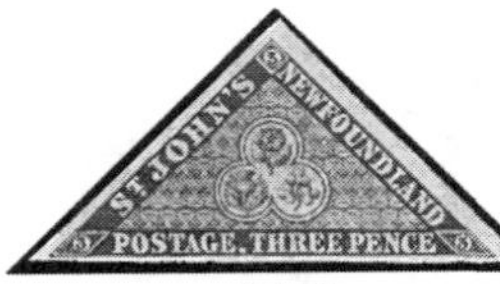

3,11A

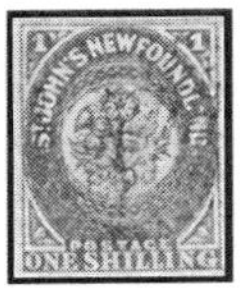

23

1857 Imperforate, Thick Porous Wove Paper, Mesh (OG + 50%) VF+50%(C)

Scott's No.		Unused Fine	Unused Ave.	Used Fine	Used Ave.
1	1p Crown & Flowers, Brown Violet ..	60.00	35.00	120.00	75.00
2	2p Flowers, Scarlet Vermilion	...	...	3500.00	2500.00
3	3p Triangle, Green	300.00	180.00	325.00	200.00
4	4p Flowers, Scarlet Vermilion	...	...	2500.00	1750.00
5	5p Crown & Flowers, Vlt. Brown	150.00	90.00	275.00	175.00
6	6p Flowers, Scarlet Vermilion	...	...	2750.00	1850.00
7	6½p Flowers, Scarlet Vermilion	2350.00	1500.00	2250.00	1450.00
8	8p Flowers, Scarlet Vermilion	175.00	110.00	275.00	180.00
9	1sh Flowers, Scarlet Vermilion	...	...	4500.00	2950.00

1860 Imperforate Thin to Thick Wove Paper, No Mesh (OG + 50%) VF+50%(C)

11	2p Flowers, Orange	200.00	130.00	300.00	190.00
11A	3p Triangle, Green	50.00	30.00	85.00	55.00
12	4p Flowers, Orange	1900.00	1300.00	750.00	500.00
12A	5p Crown & Flowers, Violet Brown ..	55.00	35.00	125.00	80.00
13	6p Flowers, Orange	2500.00	1600.00	600.00	375.00
15	1sh Flowers, Orange	...	...	6000.00	4000.00

1861-62 Imperforate Thin Wove Paper (OG + 50%) VF+50% (C)

15A	1p Crown & Flowers, Violet Brown ..	120.00	70.00	225.00	135.00
16	1p Reddish Brown	4750.00	3000.00	...	...
17	2p Flowers, Rose	110.00	65.00	150.00	95.00
18	4p Flowers, Rose	26.75	16.50	55.00	35.00
19	5p Crown & Flowers, Reddish Brown	35.00	20.00	55.00	35.00
20	6p Flowers, Rose	15.00	10.00	45.00	30.00
21	6½ Flowers, Rose	50.00	27.50	225.00	140.00
22	8p Flowers, Rose	55.00	37.50	250.00	160.00
23	1sh Flowers, Rose	25.00	13.75	175.00	110.00

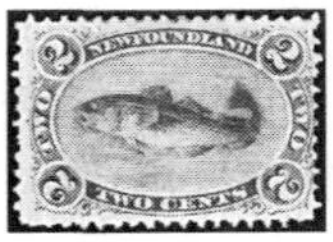

24

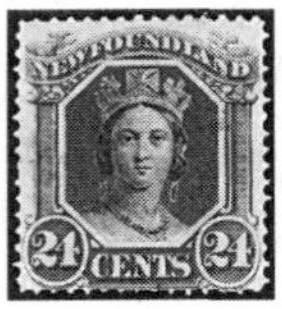

31

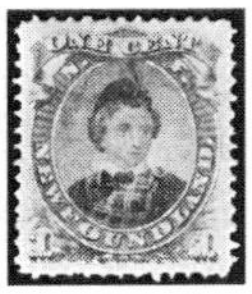

32-32A

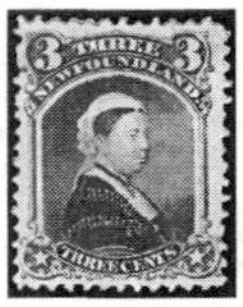

33, 34

1865-1894 Perforated 12 (NH + 150%) VF+100% (C)

Scott's No.		Unused, OG Fine	Unused, OG Ave.	Used Fine	Used Ave.
24	2¢ Codfish, Green, White Paper	45.00	30.00	25.00	15.00
24a	2¢ Green, Yellow Paper	55.00	35.00	30.00	19.00
25	5¢ Harp Seal, Brown	350.00	225.00	225.00	150.00
26	5¢ Harp Seal, Black (1868)	170.00	110.00	100.00	60.00
27	10¢ Prince Albert, Black, White Paper	115.00	75.00	37.50	22.50
27a	10¢ Black, Yellow Paper	175.00	110.00	65.00	40.00
28	12¢ Victoria, Red Brown, White Paper	32.50	17.00	30.00	16.50
28a	12¢ Red Brown, Yellow Paper	275.00	150.00	110.00	70.00
29	12¢ Brown, White Paper (1894)	30.00	18.50	30.00	18.50
30	13¢ Fishing Ship, Orange	75.00	45.00	60.00	37.50
31	24¢ Victoria, Blue	25.00	15.00	25.00	15.00

1868-1894 Perforated 12 (NH + 150%) VF+100% (C)

32	1¢ Edward, Prince of Wales, Violet .	30.00	18.00	30.00	18.00
32A	1¢ Brown Lilac (1871)	40.00	25.00	40.00	25.00
33	3¢ Victoria, Vermilion (1870)	190.00	115.00	100.00	60.00
34	3¢ Blue (1873)	175.00	110.00	20.00	12.00
35	6¢ Victoria, Dull Rose (1870)	9.50	6.00	9.50	6.00
36	6¢ Carmine Lake (1894)	11.75	7.25	11.75	7.25

1876-1879 Rouletted (NH + 150%) VF+100% (C)

37	1¢ Edward, Prince of Wales, Brown Lilac (1877)	60.00	37.50	25.00	15.00
38	2¢ Codfish, Green (1879)	90.00	55.00	30.00	18.50
39	3¢ Victoria, Blue (1877)	215.00	130.00	8.50	5.25
40	5¢ Harp Seal, Blue	125.00	80.00	8.50	5.25

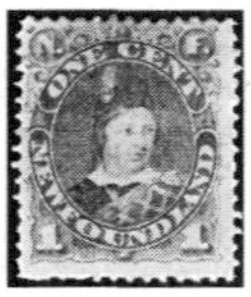

41-45

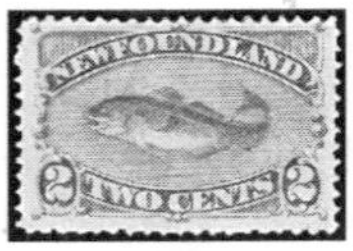

46-48

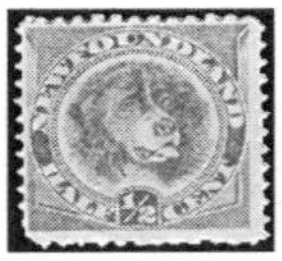

56-58

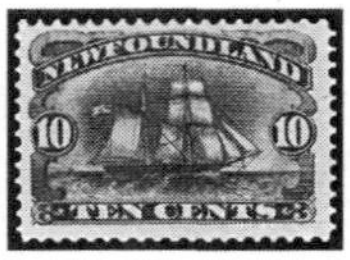

59

1880-1896 Perforated 12 VF + 80% (C)

Scott's No.		Unused,NH Fine	Unused, OG Fine	Unused, OG Ave.	Used Fine	Used Ave.
41	1¢ Edward, Prince of Wales, Violet Brown	37.50	15.00	9.00	7.50	4.25
42	1¢ Gray Brown	37.50	15.00	9.00	7.50	4.25
43	1¢ Brown (1896)	90.00	35.00	21.50	30.00	18.50
44	1¢ Deep Green (1887)	12.50	6.50	4.00	2.75	1.65
45	1¢ Green (1897)	15.00	7.00	4.25	3.00	1.85
46	2¢ Codfish, Yellow Green	50.00	20.00	12.00	11.50	7.00
47	2¢ Green (1896)	90.00	35.00	20.00	20.00	13.00

1880-1896 Perforated 12 VF + 80% (C) (continued)

Scott's No.		Unused, NH Fine	Unused, OG Fine	Unused, OG Ave.	Used Fine	Used Ave.
48	2¢ Orange (1887)	35.00	14.00	8.50	6.00	3.75
49	3¢ Queen Victoria, Blue	60.00	22.50	14.00	4.00	2.50
51	3¢ Umber Brown (1887)	40.00	16.00	10.00	3.00	1.65
52	3¢ Violet Brown (1896)	115.00	45.00	27.50	45.00	27.50
53	5¢ Harp Seal, Pale Blue	450.00	190.00	115.00	7.00	4.25
54	5¢ Dark Blue (1887)	175.00	75.00	45.00	5.25	3.25
55	5¢ Bright Blue (1894)	50.00	20.00	12.00	4.75	2.75

1887-1896 Perforated 12 VF + 80% (C)

56	½¢ Newfoundland Dog, Rose Red	12.75	6.00	3.75	5.00	3.00
57	½¢ Orange Red (1896)	90.00	37.50	23.00	30.00	18.50
58	½¢ Black (1894)	12.75	6.00	3.75	5.00	3.00
59	10¢ Schooner, Black	135.00	55.00	35.00	37.50	23.00

1890 Issue Perforated 12 VF + 80% (C)

60	3¢ Victoria, Slate	22.50	9.00	5.25	1.50	.90

FROM #24 THROUGH 60, UNUSED PRICES ARE FOR STAMPS WITH FULL ORIGINAL GUM. STAMPS WITH PARTIAL OR NO GUM SELL FOR 30% LESS THAN THOSE WITH FULL ORIGINAL GUM.

1897 John Cabot, Discovery of Newfoundland Issue VF Used + 50% (B)

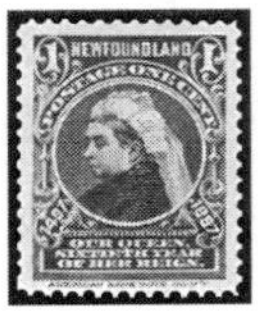

61

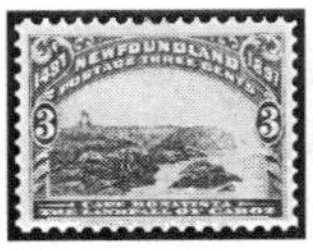

63

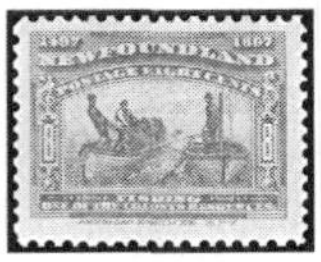

67

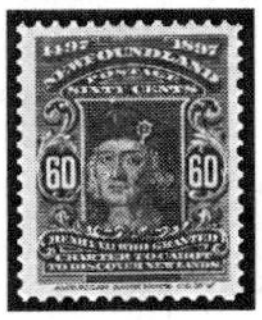

74

Scott's No.		Unused, NH VF	Unused, NH F-VF	Unused,OG VF	Unused,OG F-VF	Used F-VF
61-74	**Set of 14 ....**	**590.00**	**370.00**	**275.00**	**180.00**	**115.00**
61	1¢ Queen Victoria	4.75	3.00	2.25	1.50	1.50
62	2¢ John Cabot	5.50	3.50	2.60	1.75	1.50
63	3¢ Cape Bonavista	7.00	4.50	3.35	2.25	1.00
64	4¢ Caribou Hunting	12.50	7.50	5.75	3.75	2.25
65	5¢ Mining	17.50	11.00	8.25	5.50	2.25
66	6¢ Logging	14.00	8.50	6.50	4.25	2.50
67	8¢ Fishing	31.50	20.00	14.50	9.50	4.75
68	10¢ Ship "Matthew"	47.50	30.00	22.50	15.00	4.25
69	12¢ Willow Ptarmigan	47.50	30.00	22.50	15.00	6.25
70	15¢ Seals	47.50	30.00	22.50	15.00	6.25
71	24¢ Salmon Fishing	47.50	30.00	22.50	15.00	7.00
72	30¢ Colony Seal	90.00	55.00	41.50	27.50	27.50
73	35¢ Iceberg	215.00	130.00	100.00	65.00	45.00
74	60¢ King Henry VII	28.75	18.00	13.50	9.00	6.75

1897 Surcharges on Queen Victoria VF Used + 80% (C)

75	1¢ on 3¢ Type a (#60)	130.00	75.00	52.50	30.00	15.00
76	1¢ on 3¢ Type b (#60)	475.00	275.00	210.00	125.00	125.00
77	1¢ on 3¢ Type c (#60)	1600.00	900.00	700.00	400.00	385.00

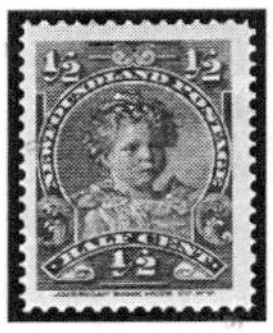

78

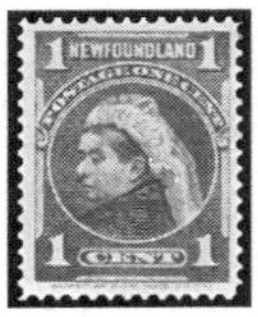

79-80

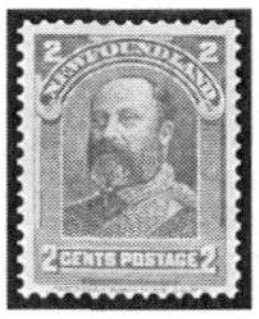

81-82

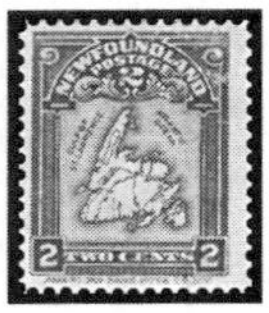

86

1897-1901 Royal Family Issue VF Used + 50% (B)

78-85	**Set of 8 ....**	**195.00**	**130.00**	**95.00**	**65.00**	**13.95**
78	½¢ Edward VII as Child	5.50	3.50	3.00	2.00	1.85
79	1¢ Queen Victoria, Carmine Rose	7.75	5.25	4.50	3.00	3.00
80	1¢ Yellow Green (1898)	8.25	5.50	4.50	3.00	.20
81	2¢ King Edward VII, Orange	7.85	5.35	4.50	3.00	2.75
82	2¢ Vermilion (1898)	23.50	15.00	11.50	7.50	.45
83	3¢ Queen Alexandria (1898) ...	39.50	25.75	19.00	12.75	.45
84	4¢ Duchess of York (1901)	53.50	35.00	26.00	17.50	3.35
85	5¢ Duke of York (1899)	62.50	40.00	30.00	20.00	2.25

1908 Map Stamp VF Used + 50% (B)

86	12¢ Map of Newfoundland	70.00	45.00	33.50	22.50	1.00

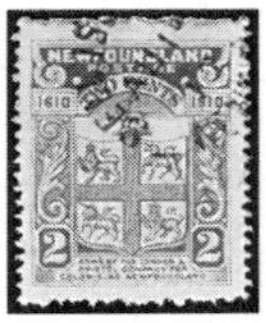

88

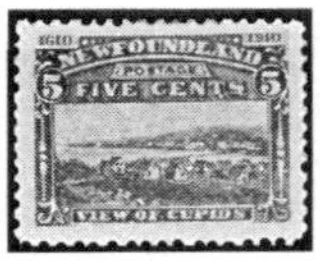

91

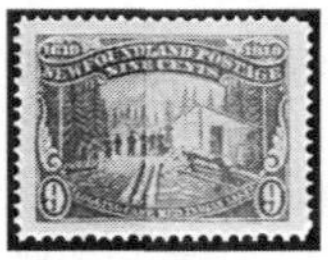

94,100

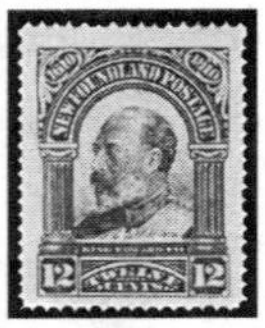

96, 102

1910 Guy Issue (Lithographed) Perf. 12 except as noted VF Used + 50% (B)

87-97	**#87-91,92A,93-97 Set of 11**	**750.00**	**485.00**	**365.00**	**240.00**	**220.00**
87	1¢ King James I,Perf. 12 x 11 ...	3.65	2.35	1.80	1.20	.80
87a	1¢ Perforated 12	8.25	5.50	4.00	2.75	1.60
87b	1¢ Perforated 12 x 14	6.00	3.95	3.00	2.00	1.75

1910 Guy Issue (Lithographed) Perf. 12 except as noted (continued)

Scott's No.		Unused, NH VF	F-VF	Unused,OG VF	F-VF	Used F-VF
88	2¢ Company Coat of Arms	14.00	9.00	6.75	4.50	.90
88a	2¢ Perforated 12 x 14	11.50	7.50	5.50	3.75	.65
88c	2¢ Perforated 12 x 11½	...	...	425.00	285.00	225.00
89	3¢ John Guy	23.50	15.75	11.50	7.75	7.75
90	4¢ The "Endeavor"	35.00	22.50	16.50	11.00	8.75
91	5¢ Cupids, Perf. 14 x 12	27.50	18.00	13.50	9.00	2.75
91a	5¢ Perforated 12	40.00	26.00	19.50	13.00	3.75
92	6¢ Lord Bacon Claret (Z Reversed)	160.00	105.00	77.50	52.50	50.00
92A	6¢ Claret (Z Normal)	56.50	36.50	27.00	18.00	18.00
#92 "Z" of "COLONIZATION" Backwards. #92A "Z" is normal.						
93	8¢ View of Mosquito, Red Brown	120.00	75.00	57.50	37.50	37.50
94	9¢ Logging Camp, Olive Green	120.00	75.00	57.50	37.50	37.50
95	10¢ Paper Mills, Black	120.00	75.00	57.50	37.50	35.00
96	12¢ Edward VII, L. Brown	120.00	75.00	57.50	37.50	37.50
97	15¢ George V, Gray Black	155.00	100.00	75.00	50.00	45.00

1911 Guy Issue (Engraved) Perforated 14 VF Used + 50% (B)

Scott's No.		Unused, NH VF	F-VF	Unused,OG VF	F-VF	Used F-VF
98-103	**Set of 6**	**715.00**	**460.00**	**350.00**	**230.00**	**245.00**
98	6¢ Lord Bacon Brown Violet	55.00	36.00	27.00	18.00	16.50
99	8¢ Mosquito, Bister Brown	125.00	80.00	60.00	40.00	42.50
100	9¢ Logging, Olive Green	110.00	70.00	52.50	35.00	40.00
101	10¢ Paper Mills, Violet Black	185.00	120.00	90.00	60.00	65.00
102	12¢ Edward VII, Red Brown	140.00	90.00	67.50	45.00	45.00
103	15¢ George V, Slate Green	140.00	90.00	67.50	45.00	45.00

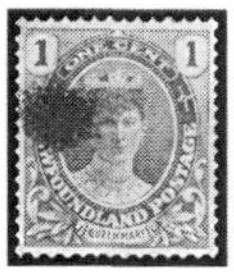
104

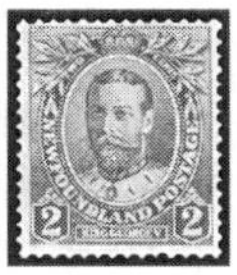
105

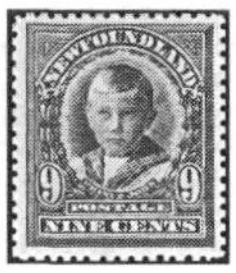
111

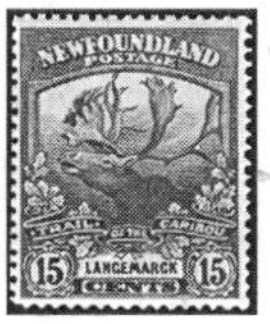

124

1911 Royal Family Coronation Issue VF Used + 50% (B)

Scott's No.		Unused, NH VF	F-VF	Unused,OG VF	F-VF	Used F-VF
104-14	**Set of 11**	**565.00**	**365.00**	**270.00**	**180.00**	**162.50**
104	1¢ Queen Mary	4.95	3.25	2.40	1.60	.25
105	2¢ King George V	4.95	3.25	2.40	1.60	.20
106	3¢ Prince of Wales	52.50	33.00	25.00	16.50	15.00
107	4¢ Prince Albert	41.50	27.00	20.00	13.50	10.75
108	5¢ Princess Mary	17.50	11.50	8.50	5.75	1.15
109	6¢ Prince Henry	47.50	30.00	22.50	15.00	15.00
110	8¢ Prince George (Aniline Blue paper)	150.00	95.00	70.00	47.50	45.00
110a	8¢ White Paper	160.00	105.00	77.50	52.50	50.00
111	9¢ Prince John	52.50	35.00	25.00	17.00	15.00
112	10¢ Queen Alexandra	80.00	50.00	37.50	25.00	22.50
113	12¢ Duke of Connaught	75.00	47.50	36.00	24.00	24.00
114	15¢ Seal of Colony	70.00	45.00	33.50	22.50	22.50

1919 Trail of the Caribou Issue, World War I Battles VF Used + 50% (B)

Scott's No.		Unused, NH VF	F-VF	Unused,OG VF	F-VF	Used F-VF
115-26	**Set of 12**	**415.00**	**280.00**	**220.00**	**150.00**	**130.00**
115	1¢ Suvla Bay	4.00	2.50	2.10	1.40	.20
116	2¢ Ubigue	4.75	2.80	2.40	1.60	.35
117	3¢ Gueudecourt	5.25	3.35	2.65	1.80	.20
118	4¢ Beaumont Hamel	8.75	5.50	4.50	3.00	.85
119	5¢ Ubigue	10.75	6.75	5.50	3.75	.85
120	6¢ Monchy	38.50	25.00	20.00	13.50	13.50
121	8¢ Ubigue	38.50	25.00	20.00	13.50	12.00
122	10¢ Steenbeck	19.50	12.50	10.00	6.75	3.25
123	12¢ Ubigue	115.00	75.00	60.00	40.00	32.50
124	15¢ Langemarck	65.00	42.50	33.50	22.50	27.50
125	24¢ Cambral	77.50	50.00	40.00	27.50	27.50
126	36¢ Combles	65.00	42.50	33.50	22.50	22.50

1920 Stamps of 1897 Surcharged VF Used + 50% (B)

Scott's No.		Unused, NH VF	F-VF	Unused,OG VF	F-VF	Used F-VF
127	2¢ on 30¢ Colony Seal (#72)	10.75	6.75	5.50	3.75	3.75
128	3¢ on 15¢ Seals, Bars 10½ Millimeters apart (#70)	475.00	315.00	250.00	170.00	160.00
129	3¢ on 15¢ Bars 13½ mm(#70)	24.00	16.00	12.50	8.50	8.50
130	3¢ on 35¢ Iceberg (#73)	20.00	12.50	10.50	7.00	7.00

1923-1924 Pictorial Issue VF Used + 50% (B)

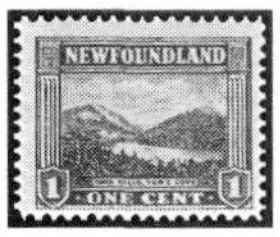

131

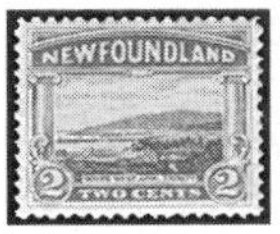

132

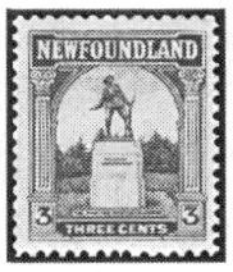

133

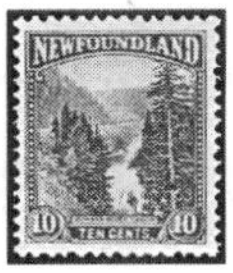

139

Scott's No.		Unused, NH VF	F-VF	Unused,OG VF	F-VF	Used F-VF
131-44	**Set of 14**	**245.00**	**160.00**	**140.00**	**92.50**	**80.00**
131	1¢ Twin Hills, Tor's Cove	2.75	1.80	1.65	1.10	.20
131a	1¢ Booklet Pane of 8	875.00	575.00	525.00	350.00	...
132	2¢ South West Arm, Trinity	2.75	1.80	1.65	1.10	.20
132a	2¢ Booklet Pane of 8	575.00	375.00	335.00	225.00	...
133	3¢ War Memorial, St. John's	3.00	2.00	1.80	1.20	.20
134	4¢ Humber River	3.75	2.50	2.25	1.50	1.40
135	5¢ Coast of Trinity	6.50	4.25	3.75	2.50	1.75
136	6¢ Upper Steadies, Humber R.	8.00	5.25	4.50	3.00	3.00
137	8¢ Quidi Vidi	6.50	4.25	3.75	2.50	2.40
138	9¢ Caribou Crossing Lake	53.50	35.00	30.00	20.00	18.50
139	10¢ Humber River Canyon	8.75	5.75	4.75	3.25	1.60
140	11¢ Shell Bird Island	11.50	7.50	6.75	4.50	4.50
141	12¢ Mt. Moriah, Bay of Island	12.00	8.00	7.00	4.75	4.75

NEWFOUNDLAND

1923-24 Pictorial Issue VF Used + 50% (B) (continued)

Scott's No.		Unused, NH VF	F-VF	Unused,OG VF	F-VF	Used F-VF
142	15¢ Humber River, Little Rapids	16.00	10.50	9.00	6.00	5.25
143	20¢ Placentia (1924)	21.00	13.50	12.00	8.00	5.50
144	24¢ Topsail Falls (1924)	100.00	65.00	57.50	37.50	35.00

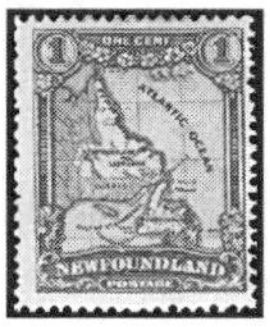

145,163,172

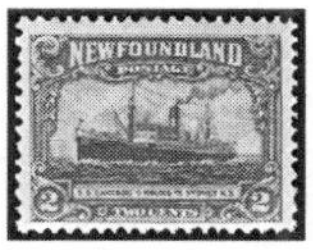

146,164,173

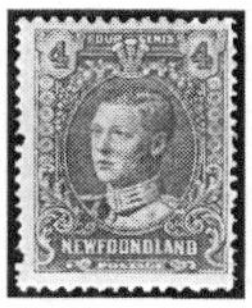

148,166,175

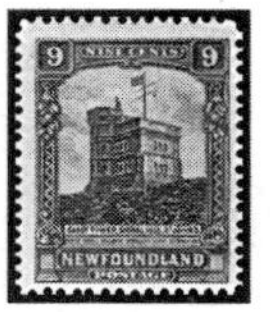

155

1928 Publicity Issue - Unwatermarked - Thin Paper VF Used + 40% (B)

Scott's No.		Unused, NH VF	F-VF	Unused,OG VF	F-VF	Used F-VF
145-59	**Set of 15**	**155.00**	**110.00**	**90.00**	**65.00**	**55.00**
145	1¢ Map of Newfoundland	2.65	1.90	1.55	1.10	.55
146	2¢ Steamship "Caribou"	3.35	2.40	1.95	1.40	.45
147	3¢ Queen Mary/King George V	3.60	2.50	2.10	1.50	.35
148	4¢ Prince of Wales	4.60	3.15	2.65	1.85	1.50
149	5¢ Express Train	9.50	6.75	5.65	4.00	3.00
150	6¢ Newfoundland Hotel	7.00	4.75	3.95	2.75	2.50
151	8¢ Heart's Content	9.00	6.25	5.25	3.75	3.50
152	9¢ Cabot Tower	10.50	7.50	6.25	4.50	4.25
153	10¢ War Memorial	10.50	7.50	6.25	4.50	4.00
154	12¢ General Post Office	8.00	5.50	4.75	3.25	2.75
155	14¢ Cabot Tower	12.00	8.25	7.00	5.00	3.50
156	15¢ First Trans-Atlantic Nonstop Flight	13.00	9.00	7.50	5.25	4.75
157	20¢ Colonial Building	10.75	7.50	6.25	4.50	3.75
158	28¢ General Post Office	47.50	33.50	27.50	19.50	17.50
159	30¢ Grand Falls	13.00	9.00	7.50	5.25	5.00

1928-31 Publicity Original and Re-engraved Identification

1¢ Map #145 Engraving lines thin and clear, "C.BAULD" is above "C.NORMAN".
#163,171 Engraving lines thicker, "C.BAULD" is below "C.NORMAN".
2¢ "Caribou" #146 Flag at stern is lower than the top of boat davit.
#164,173 Flag at stern rises above boat davits.
3¢ Mary & George V #147 Tablets with "THREE" & "CENTS" have a background of crossed lines (horizontal and vertical).
#165,174 Tablets have background of only horizontal lines.
4¢ Prince of Wales #148 Six circles at each side of portrait.
#166,175 Five roses at each side of portrait.
5¢ Express Train #149 Crossbars of telegraph pole touch the frame at the left.
#167,176 Crossbars of telegraph pole just clear the frame at the left.
6¢ Newfld. Hotel #150 Period after "John's". Numerals 1¼ mm wide.
#168,177 No Period after "John's". Numerals are 1½ mm wide.
8¢ Heart's Content #151 Four berries on the laurel branch at right.
#178 Three berries on the laurel branch at right.
10¢ War Memorial #153 Period after "ST.JOHN'S." Smaller "TEN CENTS".
#169,179 No Period after :ST.JOHN'S" Larger "TEN CENTS".
15¢ Nonstop Flight #156 "L" of "LEAVING" is below the first "A" of "AIRPLANE".
#170,180 "L" of "LEAVING" is below the "T" of "FIRST".
20¢ Colonial Building #157 Columns at sides have shading of even horizontal lines.
#171,181 Columns at sides have an almost solid shading.
30¢ Grand Falls #159 Size 19¼x24½ mm. Faint period after "FALLS".
#182 Size 19x25 mm. Clear period after "FALLS"

1929 Stamp of 1923 Surcharged VF Used + 50% (B)

Scott's No.		Unused, NH VF	F-VF	Unused,OG VF	F-VF	Used F-VF
160	3¢ on 6¢ Upper Steadies(#136)	6.25	4.00	3.75	2.50	2.50

1929-31 Publicity Issue, Re-engraved, Unwatermarked - Like Preceding but Thicker Paper VF Used + 40% (B)

Scott's No.		Unused, NH VF	F-VF	Unused,OG VF	F-VF	Used F-VF
163-71	**Set of 9**	**185.00**	**132.50**	**110.00**	**78.50**	**53.50**
163	1¢ Map of Newfoundland	3.35	2.40	2.00	1.40	.35
164	2¢ Steamship "Caribou"	3.15	2.25	1.90	1.35	.20
165	3¢ Queen Mary/King George V	3.15	2.25	1.90	1.35	.20
166	4¢ Prince of Wales	4.75	3.35	2.75	1.95	.85
167	5¢ Express Train	6.50	4.75	3.85	2.75	.95
168	6¢ Newfoundland Hotel	16.50	12.00	9.75	7.00	6.00
169	10¢ War Memorial	6.50	4.75	3.90	2.75	1.30
170	15¢ Nonstop Flight (1930)	63.50	45.00	37.50	26.50	26.50
171	20¢ Colonial Building (1931)	90.00	62.50	52.50	37.50	20.00

1931 Publicity Issue - Re-engraved - Watermarked "Coat of Arms" VF Used + 40% (B)

Scott's No.		Unused, NH VF	F-VF	Unused,OG VF	F-VF	Used F-VF
172-82	**Set of 11**	**355.00**	**250.00**	**210.00**	**145.00**	**82.50**
172	1¢ Map of Newfoundland	3.25	2.40	1.95	1.40	.75
173	2¢ Steamship "Caribou"	4.60	3.25	2.65	1.85	.95
174	3¢ Queen Mary/King George V	4.75	3.35	2.75	1.95	.75
175	4¢ Prince of Wales	6.00	4.15	3.50	2.50	1.10
176	5¢ Express Train	14.50	10.00	8.50	6.00	5.50
177	6¢ Newfoundland Hotel	33.50	23.50	20.00	13.75	12.50
178	8¢ Heart's Content	33.50	23.50	20.00	13.75	12.50
179	10¢ War Memorial	27.50	18.75	15.75	11.00	5.75
180	15¢ Nonstop Flight	80.00	55.00	47.50	32.50	21.50
181	20¢ Colonial Building	97.50	67.50	56.50	40.00	6.50
182	30¢ Grand Falls	72.50	50.00	42.50	30.00	19.50

1932-1937 Pictorial Set, Perf. 13½ or 14 VF Used + 30% Perkins Bacon Printings

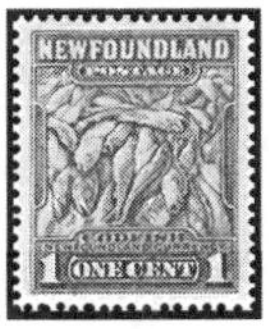

183-84,253

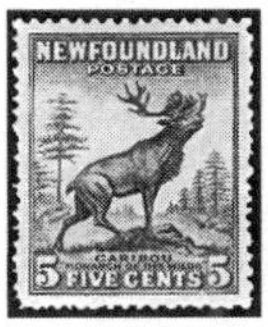

190-91,257

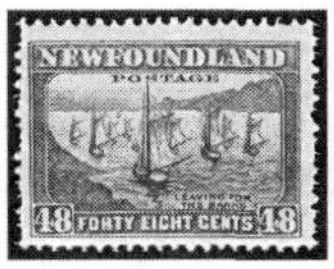

199,266

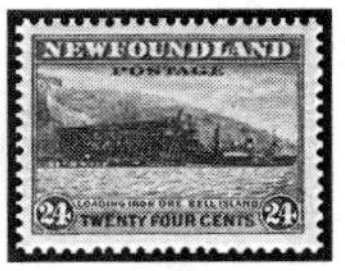

210,264

1932-37 Pictorial Set, Perf.13½ or 14 VF Used + 30% (continued)

Scott's No.		Unused, NH VF	F-VF	Unused,OG VF	F-VF	Used F-VF
183-99	**Set of 17**	**107.50**	**81.50**	**71.50**	**55.00**	**36.75**
183	1¢ Codfish, Green	2.65	2.10	1.85	1.40	.30
183a	1¢ Booklet Pane of 4, Perf.13	95.00	70.00	65.00	50.00	...
184	1¢ Gray Black	.45	.35	.35	.25	.15
184a	1¢ Bk. Pane of 4, Pf. 13½	70.00	52.50	50.00	37.50	...
184b	1¢ Bk. Pane of 4, Pf. 14	85.00	65.00	60.00	45.00	...
185	2¢ George V, Rose	2.40	1.80	1.60	1.20	.20
185a	2¢ Bk. Pane of 4, Pf.13½	52.50	40.00	36.50	27.50	...
185b	2¢ Bk. Pane of 4, Pf.13	75.00	55.00	50.00	37.50	...
186	2¢ Green	1.95	1.50	1.30	1.00	.20
186a	2¢ Bk. Pane of 4, Pf. 13½	35.00	26.50	24.50	18.50	...
186b	2¢ Bk. Pane of 4, Pf. 14	46.50	35.00	32.50	25.00	...
187	3¢ Queen Mary	1.95	1.50	1.30	1.00	.20
187a	3¢ Bk. Pane of 4, Pf. 13½	75.00	55.00	52.50	40.00	...
187b	3¢ Bk. Pane of 4, Pf. 14	85.00	65.00	60.00	45.00	...
187c	3¢ Bk. Pane of 4, Pf. 13	95.00	77.50	70.00	55.00	...
188	4¢ Prince of Wales,Deep Violet	6.75	5.25	5.00	3.75	1.25
189	4¢ Rose Lake	1.00	.75	.65	.50	.20
190	5¢ Caribou Violet Brown (I)	9.00	6.75	6.00	4.50	.85
191	5¢ Deep Violet (II)	1.50	1.10	1.00	.75	.20
191a	5¢ Deep Violet (I)	15.75	10.50	10.00	7.50	.75
	#191 Antler under "T" higher, #190,191a Antlers are even height.					
192	6¢ Princess Elizabeth	16.50	12.00	10.50	8.00	7.50
193	10¢ Salmon Leaping Falls	1.70	1.25	1.15	.85	.55
194	14¢ Newfoundland Dog	4.50	3.35	2.95	2.25	1.50
195	15¢ Harp Seal Pup	4.00	3.00	2.60	2.00	1.50
196	20¢ Cape Race	4.00	3.00	2.60	2.00	.70
197	25¢ Sealing Fleet	4.50	3.35	2.95	2.25	1.50
198	30¢ Fishing Fleet	36.50	27.00	23.50	18.00	18.00
199	48¢ Fishing Fleet (1937)	15.75	11.50	10.00	7.50	3.75

1932 New Values VF Used + 30%

208	7¢ Duchess of York	2.25	1.65	1.45	1.10	1.00
209	8¢ Corner Brook Paper Mill	1.90	1.50	1.30	1.00	.80
210	24¢ Loading Ore, Bell Island	4.00	2.95	2.60	1.95	1.95

1933 "L & S Post" Overprinted on #C9 VF Used + 30%

211	15¢ Dog Sled & Plane	12.75	9.50	8.50	6.50	6.50

1933 Sir Humphrey Gilbert Issue VF Used + 30%

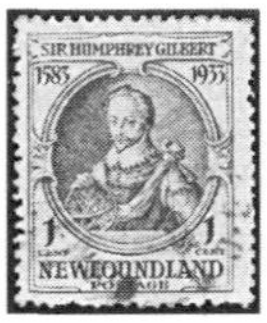

212

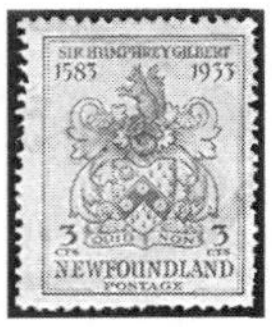

214

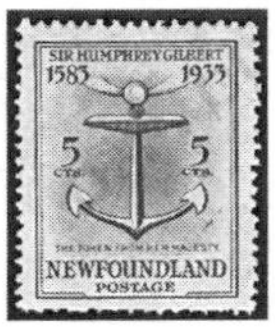

216

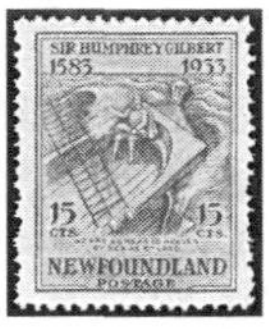

222

212-25	**Set of 14**	**205.00**	**155.00**	**135.00**	**105.00**	**95.00**
212	1¢ Sir Humphrey Gilbert	1.20	.90	.80	.60	.50
213	2¢ Compton Castle	1.70	1.25	1.15	.85	.50
214	3¢ Gilbert Coat of Arms	2.75	2.10	1.85	1.40	.45
215	4¢ Eton College	2.50	1.95	1.70	1.30	.45
216	5¢ Token from Queen Elizabeth I	3.50	2.50	2.25	1.70	.85
217	7¢ Royal Patents	22.50	16.50	15.00	11.00	11.00
218	8¢ Fleet Leaving Plymouth	13.00	9.75	8.50	6.50	6.50
219	9¢ Fleet Arriving St. John's	13.50	10.50	9.00	7.00	6.50
220	10¢ Annexation of Newfld.	13.50	10.50	9.00	7.00	6.00
221	14¢ England's Coat of Arms	26.50	20.00	17.50	13.50	12.50
222	15¢ Deck of "Squirrel"	25.00	19.00	16.50	12.75	12.00
223	20¢ 1626 Map of Newfld.	19.50	14.50	12.75	9.75	7.50
224	24¢ Queen Elizabeth I	35.00	26.50	23.50	18.00	18.00
225	32¢ Gilbert Statue at Truro	35.00	26.50	23.50	18.00	18.00

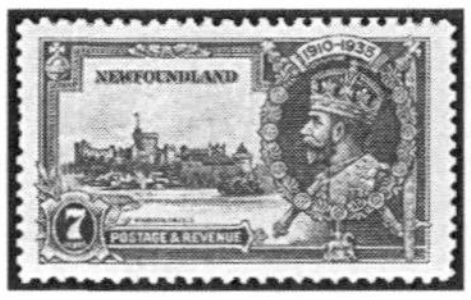

228

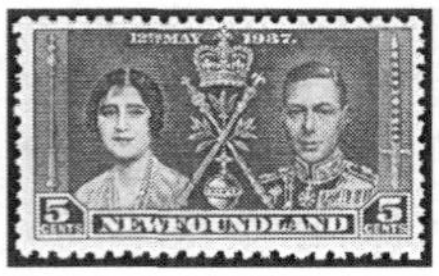

232

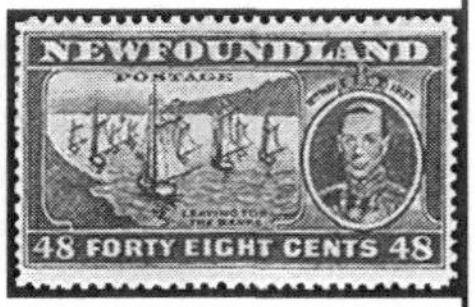

243

1935 Silver Jubilee Issue, Windsor Castle VF Used + 25%

226-29	**Set of 4**	**16.50**	**13.00**	**11.95**	**9.25**	**7.35**
226	4¢ George V, Bright Rose	1.40	1.15	1.10	.85	.50
227	5¢ Violet	1.40	1.15	1.10	.85	.65
228	7¢ Dark Blue	4.50	3.50	3.15	2.50	2.00
229	24¢ Olive Green	9.75	7.75	7.00	5.75	4.50

1937 Coronation "Omnibus" Issue VF Used + 30%

230-32	**Set of 3**	**4.75**	**3.85**	**3.50**	**2.75**	**1.40**
230	2¢ Queen Elizabeth & King George VI Deep Green	1.30	1.00	.95	.75	.45
231	4¢ Carmine Rose	1.30	1.00	.95	.75	.30
232	5¢ Dark Violet	2.40	1.85	1.80	1.40	.75

1937 Coronation Issue (Long Set) VF Used + 40%

233-43	**Set of 11**		**41.50**	**29.50**	**21.95**	**18.00**
233	1¢ Codfish	.65	.45	.50	.35	.20
234	3¢ Map of Newfoundland, Die I	2.60	1.85	1.95	1.40	.70
234a	3¢ Map, Die II	2.30	1.60	1.70	1.20	.80

3¢ Map #234 Die I Fine Printing, No Lines on Bridge of Nose.
#234a Die II Coarse Printing, Lines on Bridge of Nose.

NEWFOUNDLAND

1937 Coronation Issue (Long Set) VF Used + 40% (continued)

Scott's No.		Unused, NH VF	F-VF	Unused,OG VF	F-VF	Used F-VF
235	7¢ Caribou	2.80	2.00	2.10	1.50	1.25
236	8¢ Corner Brook Paper Mills	2.80	2.00	2.10	1.50	1.25
237	10¢ Salmon	5.15	3.65	3.85	2.75	2.35
238	14¢ Newfoundland Dog	4.50	3.25	3.35	2.40	2.25
239	15¢ Harp Seal Pup	5.00	3.50	3.75	2.65	2.25
240	20¢ Cape Race	4.15	2.85	2.95	2.10	1.50
241	24¢ Loading Iron Ore, Bell I.	4.75	3.35	3.50	2.50	2.25
242	25¢ Sealing Fleet	5.15	3.65	3.85	2.70	2.25
243	48¢ Fishing Fleet	6.25	4.50	4.70	3.25	2.50

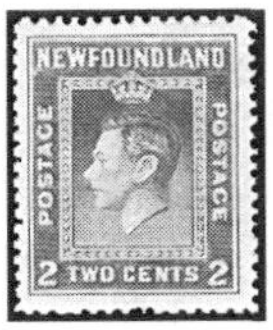

245

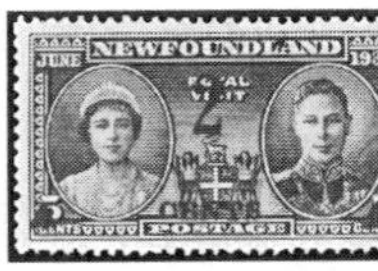

249

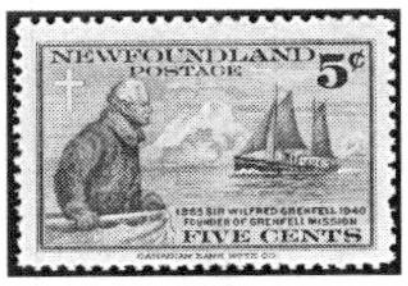

252

1938 Royal Family, Perf. 13½ VF Used + 30%

245-48	**Set of 4**	**7.85**	**6.15**	**6.25**	**4.75**	**1.50**
245	2¢ King George VI, Green	1.95	1.50	1.55	1.20	.20
246	3¢ Queen Elizabeth	1.95	1.50	1.55	1.20	.20
247	4¢ Princess Elizabeth	2.50	1.95	1.95	1.50	.20
248	7¢ Queen Mary	1.80	1.40	1.45	1.10	.95

1939 Royal Visit of King George VI & Queen Elizabeth VF Used + 20%

249	5¢ George VI & Elizabeth	1.10	.90	.90	.75	.65
249	5¢ Plate Block of 4	12.75	10.50	10.25	8.50	...

1939 Royal Visit Surcharge VF Used + 20%

250	2¢ on 5¢ (Brown) (#249)	1.30	1.10	1.05	.85	.85
250	2¢ on 5¢ Plate Block of 4	15.00	12.75	12.75	10.50	...
251	4¢ on 5¢ (Red) (#249)	1.10	.90	.90	.75	.65
251	4¢ on 5¢ Plate Block of 4	13.75	11.50	11.50	9.50	...

1941 Wilfred Grenfell Issue VF Used + 20%

252	5¢ Grenfell Mission Founding	.45	.35	.40	.30	.25
252	5¢ Plate Block of 4	3.25	2.65	2.65	2.25	...

1941-1944 Pictorial Set, Waterlow Printing, Perf. 12½ VF Used + 30%

253-66	**Set of 14**	**20.75**	**16.00**	**16.50**	**12.75**	**9.00**
253	1¢ Codfish, Dark Gray	.40	.30	.35	.25	.20
253	1¢ Plate Block of 4	3.85	3.00	3.15	2.40	...
254	2¢ King George VI, Deep Green	.40	.30	.35	.25	.20
254	2¢ Plate Block of 4	3.85	3.00	3.15	2.40	...
255	3¢ Queen Elizabeth	.40	.30	.35	.25	.20
255	3¢ Plate Block of 4	4.85	3.75	3.85	2.95	...
256	4¢ Princess Elizabeth	.80	.65	.65	.50	.20
256	4¢ Plate Block of 4	8.25	6.25	6.50	5.00	...
257	5¢ Caribou, Violet (I)	.85	.70	.70	.55	.20
257	5¢ Plate Block of 4	8.25	6.25	6.50	5.00	...
258	7¢ Queen Mary (1942)	1.45	1.15	1.15	.90	.75
259	8¢ Corner Brook Paper Mills	1.10	.80	.85	.65	.50
259	8¢ Plate Block of 4	9.75	7.50	7.75	6.00	...
260	10¢ Salmon Leaping Falls	1.10	.80	.85	.65	.45
260	10¢ Plate Block of 4	9.75	7.50	7.75	6.00	...
261	14¢ Newfoundland Dog	2.25	1.75	1.80	1.40	.90
261	14¢ Plate Block of 4	25.00	19.00	19.50	15.00	...
262	15¢ Harp Seal Pup	2.25	1.75	1.80	1.40	1.00
262	15¢ Plate Block of 4	25.00	19.00	19.50	15.00	...
263	20¢ Cape Race	1.90	1.50	1.50	1.15	.90
263	20¢ Plate Block of 4	25.00	19.00	19.50	15.00	...
264	24¢ Bell Island	2.60	2.00	2.10	1.65	1.25
264	24¢ Plate Block of 4	25.00	19.00	19.50	15.00	...
265	25¢ Sealing Fleet	2.60	2.00	2.10	1.65	1.25
265	25¢ Plate Block of 4	25.00	19.00	19.50	15.00	...
266	48¢ Fishing Fleet (1944)	3.65	2.75	2.80	2.15	1.40
266	48¢ Plate Block of 4	28.50	22.00	22.50	17.50	...

The Waterlow Printings are slightly taller than the Perkins Printings.

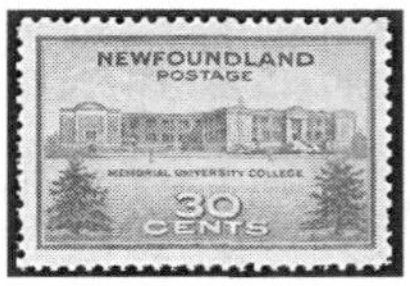

267

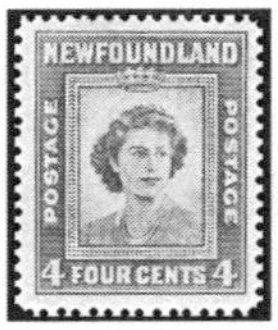

269

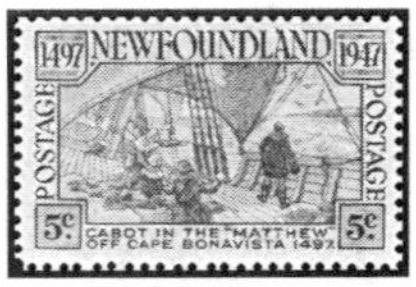

270

1943 Memorial University College Issue VF Used + 20%

267	30¢ Memorial University	1.50	1.25	1.20	1.00	.90
267	30¢ Plate Block of 4	9.50	8.00	7.75	6.50	...

1946 "TWO CENT" Provisional Surcharge VF Used + 20%

268	2¢ on 30¢ Memorial (#267)	.40	.30	.35	.25	.25
268	2¢ on 30¢ Plate Block of 4	4.25	3.50	3.60	3.00	...

1947 Issues VF Used+ 20%

269	4¢ Princess Elizabeth	.40	.30	.35	.25	.20
269	4¢ Plate Block of 4	3.25	2.75	2.75	2.25	...
270	5¢ John Cabot on the "Matthew", Discovery of Newfld, 450th	.40	.30	.35	.25	.20
270	5¢ Plate Block of 4	3.95	3.25	3.30	2.75	...

NEWFOUNDLAND

AIRMAIL STAMPS

1919 Hawker First Trans-Atlantic Flight VF Used +50% (B)

Scott's No.		Unused, NH VF	F-VF	Unused,OG VF	F-VF	Used F-VF
C1	3¢ Red brown, Overprint (#117) …	…	…	…	…	…

1919 Alcock & Brown Trans-Atlantic Flight VF Used +50% (B)

C2	$1 on 15¢ "FIRST TRANS-ATLANTIC AIR POST April, 1919. ONE DOLLAR" (#70)	350.00	225.00	200.00	135.00	135.00
C2a	$1 on 15¢ Without Comma after "POST""	385.00	250.00	225.00	150.00	165.00

1921 Halifax Airmail Issue VF Used +50% (B)

C3	35¢ Iceberg "AIR MAIL to Halifax, N.S. 1921"(#73)	250.00	165.00	150.00	100.00	110.00
C3b	35¢ With Period after "1921"	275.00	180.00	165.00	110.00	120.00

1927 De Pinedo Flight VF Used +50% (B)

C4	60¢ King Henry VII, Overprint on #74	…	…	…	…	…

1930 "Columbia" Trans-Atlantic Air Mail Flight Used +50% (B)

C5	50¢ on 36¢ Caribou, Overprint on #126	…	…	…	…	…

C7,C10   C6,C9   C8,C11

1931 Pictorials, Unwatermarked VF Used + 40% (B)

C6-8	Set of 3	150.00	105.00	95.00	67.50	67.50
C6	15¢ Dog Sled & Airplane	12.50	8.75	8.00	5.75	5.50
C7	50¢ Trans-Atlantic Plane	42.50	30.00	27.50	19.50	16.50
C8	$1 Historic Trans-Atlantic Flight Routes	97.50	70.00	62.50	45.00	47.50

1931 Pictorials, Watermarked "Coat of Arms" VF Used + 40% (B)

C9-11	Set of 3	210.00	140.00	130.00	92.50	90.00
C9	15¢ Dog Sled & Airplane	12.50	8.75	8.00	5.75	5.50
C10	50¢ Trans-Atlantic Plane	55.00	37.50	35.00	25.00	25.00
C11	$1 Flight Routes	150.00	100.00	95.00	67.50	65.00

1932 Dornier DO-X Trans-Atlantic Surcharge VF Used + 40% (B)

C12	$1.50 on $1 Routes (#C11)	415.00	300.00	270.00	195.00	195.00

NEWFOUNDLAND

C13   C19   J5

1933 Labrador Issue VF Used + 30%

Scott's No.		NH VF	F-VF	Unused,OG VF	F-VF	Used F-VF
C13-17	Set of 5	250.00	180.00	160.00	120.00	130.00
C13	5¢ "Put to Flight"	18.00	13.50	11.75	9.00	9.00
C14	10¢ "Land of Heart's Delight"	27.50	20.00	17.50	13.50	12.00
C15	30¢ "Spotting the Herd"	50.00	36.00	31.50	23.50	25.00
C16	60¢ "News from Home"	85.00	60.00	55.00	40.00	45.00
C17	75¢ "Labrador, Land of Gold"	85.00	60.00	55.00	40.00	45.00

1933 General Balbo Flight VF Used + 30%

C18	$4.50 on 75¢ (#C17)	515.00	385.00	340.00	260.00	260.00

1943 St. John's VF Used + 20%

C19	7¢ View of St. John's	.45	.35	.40	.30	.30
C19	7¢ Plate Block of 4	3.60	3.00	3.00	2.50	…

POSTAGE DUE STAMPS 1939-1949 VF Used + 25%
Unwatermarked

J1-6	Set of 6	49.50	34.50	32.75	25.00	…
J1	1¢ Yellow Green, Perf.11(1949)	5.95	4.25	3.95	3.00	3.75
J1a	1¢ Perforated 10-10½	8.50	6.00	5.65	4.25	3.95
J2	2¢ Vermillion, Perf.10-10½	9.25	6.75	6.25	4.75	3.75
J2a	2¢ Perforated 11 x 9 (1949)	9.25	6.75	6.25	4.75	4.00
J3	3¢ Ultramarine, Perf.10-10½	9.75	7.00	6.50	5.00	4.25
J3a	3¢ Perforated 11 x 9 (1949)	11.00	8.00	7.50	5.75	5.75
J3b	3¢ Perforated 9	365.00	280.00	265.00	200.00	…
J4	4¢ Yellow Orange Perf. 11x9	13.50	9.50	8.75	6.75	6.75
J4a	4¢ Perf. 10-10½ (1949)	18.50	13.00	12.50	9.50	9.50
J5	5¢ Pale Brown, Perf.10-10½	5.50	3.85	3.65	2.75	2.75
J6	10¢ Dark Violet, Perf.10-10½	5.50	3.85	3.65	2.75	2.75
J7	10¢ Watermarked, Perf. II	16.00	11.50	10.50	8.00	9.75

NOTE: PRICES THROUGHOUT THIS LIST ARE SUBJECT TO CHANGE WITHOUT NOTICE IF MARKET CONDITIONS REQUIRE. MINIMUM ORDER MUST TOTAL AT LEAST $20.00.

BRITISH COLUMBIA AND VANCOUVER ISLAND

1860 British Columbia & Vancouver I, Queen Victoria, VF+100% (C)

Scott's No.		Unused Fine	Ave.	Used Fine	Ave.
1	2½p Dull Rose, Imperforate	2500.00	1600.00	...	...
2	2½p Dull Rose, Perforated 14	225.00	135.00	165.00	100.00

1865 Vancouver Island, Queen Victoria (OG + 100%) VF+100% (C)

Scott's No.		Unused Fine	Ave.	Used Fine	Ave.
3	5¢ Rose, Imperforate	...	...	...	...
4	10¢ Blue, Imperforate	1400.00	950.00	750.00	475.00
5	5¢ Rose, Perforated 14	250.00	150.00	170.00	100.00
6	10¢ Blue, Perforated 14	250.00	150.00	170.00	100.00

1865 Seal of British Columbia (OG + 100%) VF+100% (C)

Scott's No.		Unused Fine	Ave.	Used Fine	Ave.
7	3p Blue, Perforated 14	80.00	55.00	80.00	55.00

1867-1869 Surcharges on #7 Design, Perf. 14 (OG + 100%) VF+100% (C)

Scott's No.		Unused Fine	Ave.	Used Fine	Ave.
8	2¢ on 3p Brown (Black Surcharge) ..	100.00	60.00	100.00	60.00
9	5¢ on 3p Bright Red (Black)	170.00	100.00	170.00	100.00
10	10¢ on 3p Lilac Rose (Blue)	1250.00	750.00	...	...
11	25¢ on 3p Orange (Violet)	165.00	100.00	165.00	100.00
12	50¢ on 3p Violet (Red)	625.00	375.00	625.00	375.00
13	$1 on 3p Green (Green)	1100.00	600.00	...	...

1869 Surcharges on #7 Design, Perf. 12½ (OG + 100%) VF+100% (C)

Scott's No.		Unused Fine	Ave.	Used Fine	Ave.
14	5¢ on 3p Bright Red (Black)	1350.00	850.00	1000.00	600.00
15	10¢ on 3p Lilac Rose (Blue)	825.00	500.00	825.00	500.00
16	25¢ on 3p Orange (Violet)	500.00	300.00	500.00	300.00
17	50¢ on 3p Green (Green)	675.00	400.00	675.00	400.00
18	$1 on 3p Green (Green)	1250.00	750.00	1250.00	750.00

NEW BRUNSWICK

1851 Pence Issue Imperforate, Blue Paper, (OG + 50%) VF+50% (C)

Scott's No.		Unused Fine	Ave.	Used Fine	Ave.
1	3p Crown & Flowers, Red	1250.00	750.00	300.00	185.00
2	6p Olive Yellow	2500.00	1500.00	550.00	350.00
3	1sh Bright Red Violet	...	...	3000.00	1800.00
4	1sh Dull Violet	...	...	3750.00	2250.00

1860 Charles Connell Issue (C)

Scott's No.		Unused Fine	Ave.	Used Fine	Ave.
5	5¢ Brown (Never issued)	...	...	...	...

1860-63 Cents Issue, Perf. 12, White Paper (NH + 100%) VF+100% (C)

6	7-9	10	11

Scott's No.		Unused, OG Fine	Ave.	Used Fine	Ave.
6	1¢ Locomotive, Red Lilac	22.50	13.75	22.50	13.75
6a	1¢ Brown Violet	37.50	22.50	30.00	17.00
7	2¢ Queen Victoria, Orange (1863) ...	8.00	5.00	8.00	5.00
8	5¢ Queen Victoria, Yellow Green	9.00	5.50	9.00	5.50
8b	5¢ Olive Green	80.00	50.00	17.50	10.75
9	10¢ Queen Victoria, Vermilion	30.00	18.50	30.00	18.50
10	12½¢ Steamship, Blue	40.00	25.00	40.00	25.00
11	17¢ Prince of Wales, Black	30.00	18.50	30.00	18.50

NOVA SCOTIA

1851-1857 Pence Issues, Imperforate, Blue Paper (OG + 50%) VF+50% (C)

2,3

Scott's No.		Unused Fine	Ave.	Used Fine	Ave.
1	1p Queen Victoria, Red Brown	1700.00	1000.00	350.00	225.00
2	3p Crown & Flowers, Blue	475.00	275.00	120.00	75.00
3	3p Dark Blue	600.00	375.00	140.00	85.00
4	6p Crown & Flowers,, Yellow Green ..	2500.00	1500.00	375.00	225.00
5	6p Dark Green	5000.00	3000.00	700.00	425.00
6	1sh Crown & Flowers, Reddish Violet	...	...	3000.00	1850.00
7	1sh Dull Violet	...	...	4500.00	2850.00

1860-1863 Queen Victoria, Perforated 12 (NH + 60%) VF+80% (C)

8	10	11	13

Scott's No.		Unused, OG Fine	Ave.	Used Fine	Ave.
8	1¢ Black, Yellow Paper	6.00	3.75	5.00	3.00
8a	1¢ White Paper	6.00	3.75	5.00	3.00
9	2¢ Lilac, White Paper	7.50	4.50	7.50	4.50
9a	2¢ Yellowish Paper	7.50	4.50	7.50	4.50
10	5¢ Blue, White Paper (NH+200%) ..	275.00	165.00	5.00	3.00
10a	5¢ Yellowish Paper (NH+200%)	275.00	165.00	5.00	3.00
11	8½¢ Green, Yellowish Paper	4.75	3.00	13.50	8.50
11a	8½¢ White Paper	4.75	3.00	11.00	6.75
12	10¢ Vermilion, White Paper	6.50	4.00	6.00	3.75
12a	10¢ Yellowish Paper	6.50	4.00	6.00	3.75
13	12½¢ Black, Yellowish Paper	18.50	11.00	17.50	11.00
13a	12½¢ White Paper	20.00	12.00	20.00	12.00

NEW BRUNSWICK #6-11; NOVA SCOTIA #8-13; PRINCE EDWARD I. #4-16 UNUSED PRICES ARE FOR STAMPS WITH FULL ORIGINAL GUM. STAMPS WITH PARTIAL OR NO GUM SELL FOR 30% LESS THAN THOSE WITH FULL ORIGINAL GUM.

PRINCE EDWARD ISLAND

1,5	2,6	3,7	9

1861 Queen Victoria, Perforated 9 (OG + 80%) VF+100% (C)

Scott's No.		Unused Fine	Ave.	Used Fine	Ave.
1	2p Dull Rose	300.00	180.00	150.00	90.00
2	3p Blue	700.00	425.00	350.00	215.00
3	6p Yellow Green	1200.00	750.00	700.00	425.00

1862-65 Queen Victoria, Pence Issues Perf. 11,11½,12 and Compound (NH + 80%) VF+80% (C)

Scott's No.		Unused, OG Fine	Ave.	Used Fine	Ave.
4	1p Yellow Orange	18.75	11.75	30.00	20.00
5	2p Rose, White Paper	4.75	3.00	5.50	3.50
5a	2p Yellowish Paper	4.75	3.00	5.50	3.50
6	3p Blue, White Paper	6.00	3.50	8.50	5.00
6a	3p Yellowish Paper	9.50	6.00	9.50	6.00
7	6p Yellow Green	52.50	31.50	52.50	31.50
8	9p Violet	47.50	30.00	47.50	30.00

1868-1870 Queen Victoria Pence Issues (VF + 50%, NH + 80%) (C)

Scott's No.		Unused Fine	Ave.	Used Fine	Ave.
9	4p Black, White Paper	5.75	3.50	15.00	9.50
9a	4p Yellowish Paper	11.00	7.00	17.50	11.50
10	4½p Brown (1870)	40.00	25.00	42.50	26.50

1872 Queen Victoria Cents Issue, Perf. 12,12½ (NH + 60%) VF+60% (C)

11	12	15	16

Scott's No.		Unused Fine	Ave.	Used Fine	Ave.
11	1¢ Brown Orange	3.35	2.10	5.75	3.50
12	2¢ Ultramarine	9.00	5.75	18.50	11.50
13	3¢ Rose	15.00	9.00	15.00	9.00
14	4¢ Green	3.75	2.40	8.00	5.00
15	6¢ Black	3.75	2.40	8.00	5.00
16	12¢ Violet	3.75	2.40	16.50	10.00

NOTE: PRICES THROUGHOUT THIS LIST ARE SUBJECT TO CHANGE WITHOUT NOTICE IF MARKET CONDITIONS REQUIRE. MINIMUM ORDER MUST TOTAL AT LEAST $20.00.

Welcome to
Brookman's Autograph Section

Welcome to the Wonderful World of Autograph Collecting!

We are very excited about the continued response to this sectioin of the price guide. As we suspected, there is a very significant cross-over of autograph collectors to philately and vice-versa. As we have previously mentioned, a collector interested in collecting certain famous individuals on the stamps and covers, might also want to have their autograph as well. In addition, autograph collectors, now have an opportunity to have all this information in one price guide. No other price guide offers stamps, covers and autographs all in one guide, and no other autograph guide prices autographs on cover.

As mentioned in previous issues, this was a massive project to begin with, from which we have created a huge database. This continues to be a work in progress, as we add new names in every edition, as well as the hundreds of price changes.

We wish to thank our contributing editors, particularly Phillip J. Marks, who has over 20 years experience in sports autographs including cards and sports memorabilia; I. Michael Orenstein of Aurora Galleries, a leading expert in astronaut autographs and memorabilia, and Greg Tucker who is a specialist in movie stars, celebrities and sports. A special thanks to Alexander Autographs, a premier auction house, for the original use of their autograph database, to Bob Eaton, of R and R Enterprises who contributed to the original data on entertainers and celebrities, and Scott Winslow of Scott Winslow Associates, who helped with our original pricing of Presidents, government figures, and war and military leaders.

ABBREVIATIONS USED IN THE AUTOGRAPH SECTION

ALS : Autograph Letter Signed (written and signed by the same person.)

LS : Letter Signed (body of letter written by another person.)

TLS : Typed Letter Signed

DS : Document Signed

SIG : Signature on paper or card

WH CARD : White House Card signed

COVER : For 19th century, covers are free franks. Depending on other time periods, covers can be stamped envelopes, commemorative events or First Day of Issue.

* : Hall of Fame

D : Deceased

Special Authentication Service to Brookman Price Guide Buyers

Because buyers of autographs may have little knowledge as to the authenticity of the autographs they own and in many cases not enough information is available, particularly in the philatelic field, we are offering a special service to Brookman Price Guide customers.

Greg Tucker has agreed to offer an opinion of authenticity for any autographs sent to him in his field of expertise.

To keep the cost of this service low, he will indicate on the back of the item sent whether the autograph is genuine or not. A modest fee of $45.00 per item will be charged and includes return postage.

We feel that all of our editors are extremely qualified to render the opinions and urge you to contact them for your authentication needs and mention Brookman when doing so.

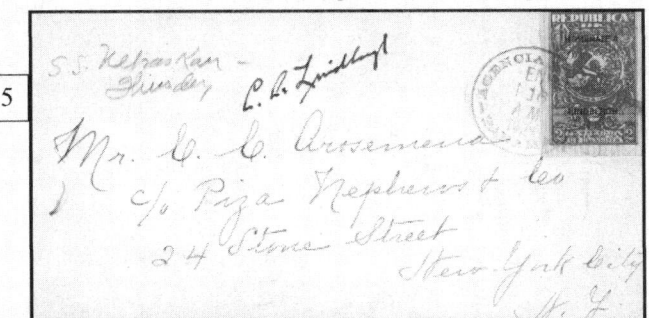

273

	PHOTO	ALS	LS/TLS	DS	SIG.	COVER
John Adams		15000	5000	5000	2000	4000
John Quincy Adams		1750	650	650	375	750
Chester A. Arthur		1500	750	750	350	700
*** David R. Atchison (Pres. only one day)		1400	850	850	375	750
James Buchanan	750	900	650	650	300	600
George Bush	275	900	900	900	150	200
George W. Bush	475	1500	850	850	315	525
Jimmy Carter	150	575	250	250	50	350
Grover Cleveland	900	750	500	500	225	450
William J. Clinton	400	1250	750	750	275	450
Calvin Coolidge	400	750	400	400	200	400
Dwight D. Eisenhower	650	1500	850	850	400	650
Millard Fillmore		2500	750	750	325	650
Gerald R. Ford	200	900	600	600	125	200
James A. Garfield	2500	900	650	650	250	500
Ulysses S. Grant	2500	1500	1250	1250	525	1050
Warren G. Harding	550	950	400	400	250	500
Benjamin Harrison	950	750	600	600	300	600
William Henry Harrison		1500	950	950	500	3000
Rutherford B. Hayes	950	650	750	750	250	500
Herbert Hoover	350	1250	275	275	195	350
Andrew Jackson		3500	1750	1750	750	1500
Thomas Jefferson		12500	5500	5500	3500	6000
Andrew Johnson	3000	2000	1500	1500	575	1150
Lyndon B. Johnson	550	2500	950	950	275	500
John F. Kennedy	2500	3500	1750	1750	900	1800
Abraham Lincoln	75000	18000	7500	7500	3500	7000
James Madison		2500	1400	1400	550	1100
William McKinley	950	2500	500	500	325	650
James Monroe		2900	900	900	400	800
Richard M. Nixon	450	2500	750	750	250	450
Franklin Pierce		950	750	750	375	750
James Polk		3000	1750	1750	500	1500
Ronald Reagan	375	1500	575	575	225	400
Franklin D. Roosevelt	900	1200	900	900	375	750
Theodore Roosevelt	1250	950	750	750	450	900
William Taft	450	750	400	400	225	450
Zachary Taylor		4000	3500	3500	900	1800
Harry S. Truman	450	2000	1200	1200	300	600
John Tyler		1500	900	900	375	750
Martin VanBuren		900	900	900	325	650
George Washington		20000	10000	10000	5000	7500
Woodrow Wilson	400	750	575	575	300	600

	PHOTO	ALS	LS/TLS	DS	SIG.	COVER
Spiro T. Agnew	95	575		150	35	75
Alben W. Barkley	75	150		75	25	75
John C. Calhoun	375	350		275	125	250
Richard Cheney	90				30	60
George Clinton		300		175	125	250
Schuyler Colfax	250			125	75	150
Charles Curtis	90	150		125	50	100
George M. Dallas		300		200	75	150
Charles G. Dawes	275	225		150	35	70
William Eustis		175		125	35	70
Charles Fairbanks	150	275		100	50	100
John N. Garner	175	250		175	65	200
Elbridge Gerry		2500		750	275	550
Alexander Hamilton		4500		3500	900	1800
Hannibal Hamlin		350		200	90	180
Thomas Hendricks		175		150	50	100
Garrett Hobart	200	225		200	75	150
Hubert H. Humphrey	65			125	45	100
Richard M. Johnson	400	350		200	100	200
William King				340	200	400
Thomas R. Marshall	175	350		175	75	150
Walter Mondale	45			35	25	75
Levi P. Morton	240	240		85	60	120
Dan Quayle	45	45			35	70
Nelson Rockefeller	50	90		75	25	50

ALS : Autograph Letter Signed (written and signed by the same person.) LS : Letter Signed (body of letter written by another person.)
TLS : Typed Letter Signed DS : Document Signed SIG : Signature on paper or card WH CARD : White House Card signed
COVER : Depending on the time period, can be franked envelope, stamped envelope, event or First Day of Issue
*: Hall of Fame D : Deceased

VICE PRESIDENTS (cont.)

	PHOTO	ALS	LS/TLS	DS	SIG.	COVER
James S. Sherman	200	275		175	75	150
Adlai E. Stevenson	150	200		150	50	100
Daniel D. Tompkins		150		125	100	200
Henry A. Wallace	100	150		125	50	200
William A. Wheeler				225	75	150
Henry Wilson		125		125	75	150
Al Gore	80				25	50

FIRST LADIES

	PHOTO	ALS	LS/TLS	DS	SIG.	COVER
Abigal Adams		4900		2500	500	1000
Louisa Catherine Adams		750		575	250	500
Ellen Lewis Arthur		1200			600	1200
Barbara Bush	75	125		100	50	100
Laura Bush	300			300	200	250
Rosalynn Carter	50	90		65	25	75
Francis Flosom Cleveland	225	200		75	50	100
Hillary Clinton						
Grace Coolidge	150	150		125	75	150
Mamie Eisenhower	50	150		125	50	125
Caroline Fillmore		1200		900	500	1000
Betty Ford	50			90	35	75
Lucretia R. Garfield		225		175	95	190
Julia Dent Grant		750		375	150	300
Florence Harding	75			125	75	150
Anna Harrison		2000		950	750	1500
Caroline S. Harrison	750	950		250	150	300
Mary Lord Harrison	125	175		125	75	150
Lucy W. Hayes	750	400		300	225	450
Lou Henry Hoover		200		100	75	150
Rachel Jackson					575	1150
Lady Bird Johnson	125	100		275	60	150
Eliza M. Johnson				1500	750	1500
Jacqueline Kennedy	1250	1500		950	450	900
Harriet Lane (acting First Lady for James Buchanan)	375		250	100	200	
Mary Lincoln		1500		900	350	700
Dolly Payne Madison		2500		1500	900	1800
Ida Saxton McKinley	500	950		600	375	750
Patricia Nixon	175	250		75	50	200
Jane M. Pierce		950		500	250	500
Sarah Polk	1200	900		500	300	600
Nancy Reagan	75	100		75	35	200
Edith K. Roosevelt	350	225		200	75	150
Eleanor Roosevelt	250	325		200	75	175
Helen M. Taft	750	325		200	90	180
Bess Truman	175	175		125	75	150
Julia G. Tyler	650			450	200	400
Martha Washington					8500	17000
Edith Bolling Wilson	200	175		200	90	180
Ellen Louise Wilson		500		300	125	250

SUPREME COURT JUSTICES

	PHOTO	ALS	LS/TLS	DS	SIG.	COVER
William Benjamin Jr.	60				40	80
Hugo Black	95	225		120	45	90
Harry Blackman	75	270		225	40	80
John Blair	48	1200		775	150	300
Samuel Blatchford		150		125	45	90
Joseph P. Bradley		200		100	55	110
Louis D. Brandeis	1200	650		400	150	300
William J. Brennan	90	155		105	65	130
David J. Brewer		160		95	75	150
Henry A. Brown		250		175	60	120
Warren E. Burger	75	195		175	50	100
Harold E. Burton	85			170	40	80
Pierce Butler	45	275		90	35	70
James F. Byrnes	55	235		125	30	60
John A. Cambell		200		150	100	200
Tom Clark	125	125		100	40	80
Nathan Clifford	150	200		175	75	150
Benjamin R. Curtis		200		150	35	70
David Davis		225		200	75	150
William O. Douglas	200	150		175	75	150
Gabriel Duval		245		115	45	90
Oliver Ellsworth		575		275	100	200

	PHOTO	ALS	LS/TLS	DS	SIG.	COVER
Stephen J. Field	225	250		150	75	150
Abe Fortas		200		150	25	100
Felix Frankfurter	750	1195		1250	145	290
Melville Fuller	175	275		150	50	100
Arthur J. Goldberg	115			145	50	150
John M. Harlan		175		95	55	110
Oliver W. Holmes	600	550		300	250	500
Charles E. Hughes	250			150	45	90
Robert H. Jackson	125			295	50	100
John Jay		2250		1750	550	1100
Lucius Lamar	200	150		100	75	150
Thurgood Marshall	175			200	115	230
John Marshall		2500		1200	600	1200
Stanley Matthews		275		150	50	100
John McLean		285		200	55	110
J.C. McReynolds	100	145		125	30	60
Samuel F. Miller		250		185	95	190
Sherman Minton	100	250		150	50	100
William H. Moody	100	175		125	50	100
Alfred Moore	RARE				3000	6000
Frank Murphy	150	250		195	65	130
Samuel Nelson		200		150	50	100
Sandra Day O'Connor	45	200		125	25	50
Rufus Peckham	125	250		125	65	130
Lewis F. Powell Jr.				100	30	60
William H. Rehnquist	100	175		150	50	100
Owen J. Roberts	100	200		150	50	100
John Rutledge	50	250		100	30	60
Antonin Scalia	45	175		125	25	75
Edward Shippin		150			50	100
George Shiras		350		250	100	200
David H. Souter	45	75		125	25	75
John Paul Stevens	150			90	40	80
Potter Stewart	90				35	70
Harlan Fiske Stone	225	250		200	75	150
Joseph Story		250		175	100	200
George Sutherland	250			150	75	150
Roger B. Taney		350		275	100	200
Clarence Thomas	40				25	50
Smith Thompson		175		150	75	150
Frederick M. Vinson	300	300		75	75	150
Morrison R. Waite	65			40	40	80
Earl Warren	250			75	75	150
Bushrod Washington		700		350	125	250
James Wayne		350		200	100	200
Byron R. White	75	150		125	55	110
Edward D. White	150	200		150	50	100
Levi Woodbury		250		150	65	130

SIGNERS OF THE CONSTITUTION

	PHOTO	ALS	LS/TLS	DS	SIG.	COVER
Abraham Baldwin		2500		1500	500	1000
Richard Bassett				700	350	700
Gunning Bedford				700	350	700
John Blair		1200		775	150	300
William Blount				900	320	640
David Brearly				800	375	750
Jacob Broom		5000		2000	1000	2000
Pierce Butler		275		90	35	70
Daniel Carroll		710		685	175	350
George Clymer		900		505	125	250
Jonathan Dayton		657		450	175	350
John Dickinson				575	200	400
William Few	1250		750	200	400	
Thomas Fitzsimons		400		315	200	400
Benjamin Franklin		25000		10000	4300	8600
Nicholas Gilman		500		300	100	200
Nathaniel Gorham		1200		425	375	750
Alexander Hamilton		3500		3000	800	1600
Jared Ingersoll		400		250	100	200
William S. Johnson		675		375	130	260
Rufus King		450		475	250	500
John Langdon		1200		400	210	420
William Livingston		1600		900	300	600

SIGNERS OF THE CONSTITUTION (cont.)

	PHOTO	ALS	LS/TLS	DS	SIG.	COVER
James Madison	2500	3000		1100	550	1100
James McHenry		1000		275	200	400
Thomas Mifflin		600		450	150	300
Gouverneur Morris		625		585	190	380
Robert Morris		750		750	325	650
Charles Pinckney Jr.		1200			450	900
Charles Coatsworth Pickney		650			175	350
George Read		1250		450	350	700
John Rutledge		1200		600	200	400
Roger Sherman		900		600	200	400
Richard Dobbs Spaight				250	100	200
George Washington		18000		10000	4500	7500
James Wilson		1400		900	700	1400

SIGNERS OF THE DECLARATION OF INDEPENDENCE

	PHOTO	ALS	LS/TLS	DS	SIG.	COVER
John Adams		15000		5000	2000	4000
Samuel Adams		3500		2000	750	1500
Josiah Bartlett		750		555	250	500
Charter Braxton		2000		550	275	550
Charles Carroll		765		679	275	550
Samuel Chase		1550		775	275	550
Abraham Clark		2500		800	320	640
George Clymer		900		505	125	250
William Ellery		785		360	175	350
William Floyd		1600		1250	450	900
Elbridge Gerry		2880		675	265	530
Button Gwinnett	RARE			250000	150000	
Lyman Hall		5000		2950	2200	4400
John Hancock		8000		4500	2200	4400
Benjamin Harrison		1800		675	450	900
John Hart		1300		644	320	640
Joseph Hewes		8500		7250	2500	5000
Thomas Heyward		1800		1300	600	1200
William Hooper	SCARCE				3000	6000
Stephen Hopkins		900		600	250	500
Francis Hopkinson		900		450	250	500
Samuel Huntington		1200		750	250	500
Thomas Jefferson (Covered under Presidents)						
Francis Lightfoot Lee		3000		1050	660	1320
Richard Henry Lee		2250		1600	450	900
Francis Lewis		2500		1250	400	800
Philip Livingston		1175		1080	288	576
Thomas Lynch, Jr.	RARE			35000	20000	40000
Thomas McKean		800		475	250	500
Arthur Middleton		25000		12000	5000	10000
Lewis Morris		1500		950	675	1350
Robert Morris		750		750	325	650
John Morton		1400		1200	500	1000
Thomas Nelson Jr.		2500		1400	550	1100
William Paca		2500		1500	750	1500
Robert Treat Paine		900		450	250	500
John Penn	RARE	5000		2000	750	1500
George Read		1250		450	350	700
Caesar Rodney		2000		900	500	1000
George Ross		950		450	250	500
Benjamin Rusk		2250			750	1500
Edward Rutledge		750		500	200	400
James Smith		1600		750	250	500
Richard Stockton	RARE			1000	500	1000
Thomas Stone		1400		775	500	1000
George Taylor		45000		20000	7500	15000
Matthew Thorton		1650		1400	625	1250
George Walton		950		650	350	700
William Whipple		1500			750	1500
William Williams		600		450	300	600
James Wilson		1400		900	700	1400
John Witherspoon				1500	600	1200
Oliver Wolcott		1200		450	200	400
George Wythe				650	450	900

HEADS OF STATE

	PHOTO	ALS	LS/TLS	DS	SIG.	COVER
Behangi Aljere						
Alexander II (Russia)	200				125	250
Alfonso XIII (Spain)	500	550			175	350
Arthur J. Balfour	90	125		100	50	100

	PHOTO	ALS	LS/TLS	DS	SIG.	COVER
Menachem Begin	150	250			80	160
David Ben-Gurion	600	1200			300	500
Jean B. Bernadotte		650		575	150	300
Simon Bolivar		4975		3075	500	1000
Joseph Bonaparte (Spain)		350		245	120	240
Willy Brandt	85	210		175	35	100
Fidel Castro	950			750	675	1350
Catherine the Great		2400		1200	600	1200
Neville Chamberlain	165	400		400	75	150
Charles I		4000		1750	625	1250
Charles II (England)		2500		2000	900	1800
Charles IV (England)				1100	245	490
Charles V (Spain)		4000		2100	580	1160
Charles VI				1200	375	750
Charles X		725		450	150	300
John Charles XIV		880		675	145	290
Charles Prince	600	1500			400	800
Chou En-Lai	2500				1250	2500
Henry Christophe (Haiti)					1200	2400
Sarah Churchill	35	30		35	20	40
Winston S. Churchill	2750	2750		1600	800	1600
George Clemenceau		175		150	150	300
Hernando Cortes				20000	6000	12000
Charles de Gaulle	2500	1500		1000	375	750
Grace de Monaco	300	450		300	165	330
Porfirio Diaz	225	250		200	100	200
Duke & Duchess of Windsor	650				400	800
Duke of Wellington		375		250	175	350
Duke of Windsor (Edward)	655			600	200	400
Sir Anthony Eden	90	200		150	50	200
Edward VII (England)				200		
Edward VIII (England)	750	650		900	300	600
Elizabeth I		30000		12000	5500	11000
Elizabeth II	775	800		775	350	700
Empress Josephine		2500		1500	750	1500
Levi Eshkol		560		250	295	590
Francisco Franco				750	500	1000
Ferdinand VIII				475	125	250
Frederick I				95	25	50
Frederick V		500		270	90	180
Frederick II (The Great)		2000		1200	400	800
Indira Gandhi		350		350	150	300
Giuseppe Garibaldi	650			370	155	310
George I (England)		2500		1000	225	450
George II (England)		1200		550	400	800
George III (England)				400	200	400
George IV (England)		550		275	125	250
George V (England)		750		475	125	250
George VI (England)	450	300		400	200	400
Mikhail Gorbachev	575	900			300	600
Gregory XIV (Pope)				1200		
Gustaf V	275					
Gustavus II (Sweden)		985		700	115	230
Henry III (France)		1250		675	250	500
Henry IV (France)				700	200	400
Henry VII (England)					1200	2400
Henry VIII				15000	3500	7000
Hirohito	12000				2000	4000
Adolf Hitler	2500			2250	1500	3000
Isabella I		5000		2500	850	1700
Isabella II (Spain)		600		400	175	350
James I				1200	800	1600
James II (England)		1700		1200	530	1060
Anson Jones		1200			350	700
Joseph II (King of Germany)		875		350	125	250
Franz Joseph (Austria)	45	140		75	40	80
Josephine (Napoleon)		2500		1500	750	1500
Juan II	150	245		120	55	110
Benito Juarez	1500	1500		1200	425	850
Chaing Kai-Shek	700	450		220	100	225
Kalakaua (Hawaiin Chief & King)	1500	850		425	100	200

ALS : Autograph Letter Signed (written and signed by the same person.) **LS** : Letter Signed (body of letter written by another person.)
TLS : Typed Letter Signed **DS** : Document Signed **SIG** : Signature on paper or card **WH CARD** : White House Card signed
COVER : Depending on the time period, can be franked envelope, stamped envelope, event or First Day of Issue
*: Hall of Fame **D** : Deceased

	PHOTO	ALS	LS/TLS	DS	SIG.	COVER
King Hussein	75	300		135	75	150
A. Kihito (Emperor of Japan)		650			400	800
Lajos Kossuth	90	475		825	125	250
Leopold I (Belgium)				475	105	210
Leopold II		625		375	100	200
Louis XII (France)				1750	800	1600
Louis XIII (France)				900	500	1000
Louis XVI				600	375	750
Louis XVIII		1250		400	200	400
Ferdinand Marcos	125			125	50	100
Maximilian (Mexico)		1250		675	400	800
Golda Meir	300	550		250	125	200
Benito Mussolini	1200			450	300	600
Napoleon I				2200	700	1400
Napoleon III		2000		700	300	600
Gamal Abdel Nasser	275	350		400	75	150
Jawaharlai Nehru	400	700		350	130	260
Nicholas I		1200				
Nicholas II (Russia)		2500				
Manuel A. Noriega		100		100	75	150
M.R. Pahlavi (Shah of Iran)	300	300		200	125	250
Tomas Estrsda Palma		45		35	20	40
Juan Peron	600	500		300	125	250
Peter I (The Great)		7500		5500		
Philip II (Spain)					250	500
Philip III (France)				750	250	500
Philip IV (Spain)		900		550	250	500
Pope John XXIII	650				500	1000
Pope Paul III				1200		
Pope Paul VI	600	900		475	300	600
Pope Pius X				700		
Pope Pius XI				950	450	900

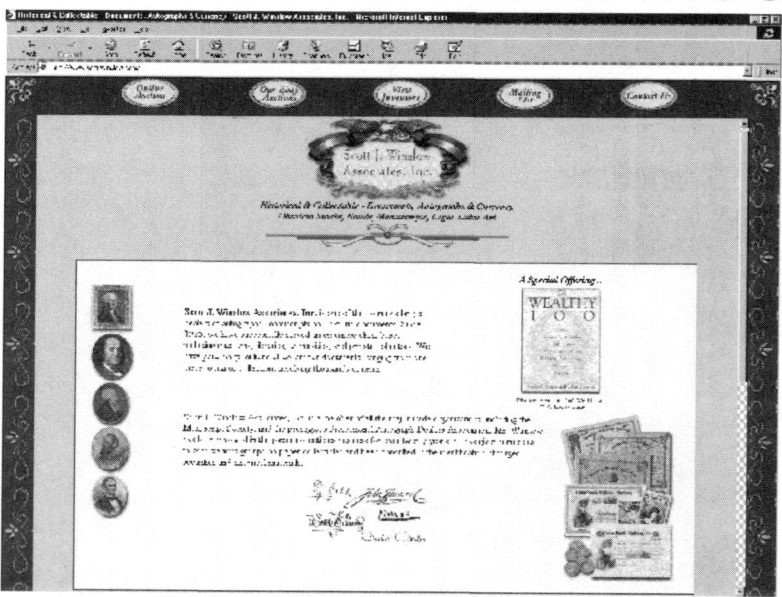

	PHOTO	ALS	LS/TLS	DS	SIG.	COVER
Prince Albert					25	50
Prince Rainier III	125	200			75	150
Queen Alexandra (England)					150	300
Queen Anne (Great Britian)		2000		1500	500	1000
Quenn Victoria	900	550		350	175	350
Rudolf I (Austria)		750				
Anwar Sadat	500	300			100	200
Haile Selassie	750	550		300	200	400
Margaret Thatcher	135	225		150	50	100
Leon Trotsky	950	2250		1500	650	1300
Arthur W. Wellington		375		250	175	350
William III (England)		2250		1400	650	1300
William IV (England)		400		300	100	200

CABINET MEMBERS-GOVERNORS-STATESMEN

	PHOTO	ALS	LS/TLS	DS	SIG.	COVER
Dean Acheson	90				35	75
Edward Bates	450	250		125	35	70
Jonathan Belcher		650		325	225	450
Francis Bernard		750		522	175	350
William Jennings Bryan	375	375			125	250
Dewitt Clinton		500		300	100	200
Henry Clinton		2200		925	425	850
Henry Clay		950		300	125	250
Benjamin Curtis		200		150	35	70
David Davis		225		200	75	150
Henry M. Dearborn		550		400	100	200
Thomas E. Dewey	50	175	100		50	
Joseph Dudley		1000		800	400	800
John Foster Dulles	75	150		120	30	100
Miriam A. Ferguson		175		150	60	120
William P. Fessenden				65	40	80
Hamilton Fish		100		95	20	40
John B. Floyd		400		320	175	350
James Forrestal	25			100	45	100
John W. Foster	140	65			25	50
Albert Gallatin		390		275	75	150
Alexander Hamilton		3500		3000	800	1600
W. Averell Harriman	50	100		70	25	50
Cordell Hull	125			135	50	150
John Jay		2250		1750	550	1100
Robert F. Kennedy	675			800	200	400
Henry Kissinger	60			125	35	100
Henry Knox		650		300	150	300
Paul Kruger	175			350	75	150
Robert T. Lincoln		325		200	100	200
Robert R. Livingston		900		400	200	400
Henry Cabot Lodge	95	200		160	45	90
William L. Marcy		225		150	50	100
John Marshall	20	35		20	10	20
James McHenry				275	200	400
Robert S. McNamara	30			45	15	30
Andrew W. Mellon	400	1200		900	250	500
John Mitchell		125		50	30	60
Timothy Pickering					10	20
William Pinkney		200		100	100	200
Caesar Rodney		2000		900	500	1000
Elihu Root	140				65	130
Dean Rusk	50			60	25	50
John Sevier		700			600	1200
William H. Seward		150		125	75	150
George P. Shultz	30	55		25	10	20
Caleb B. Smith		250		150	50	100
Hoke Smith	30			35	10	20
Edwin M. Stanton		300		160	100	200
Henry L. Stimson		50		125	40	80
Charles Thomas				600		
Daniel Webster	475	350		250	100	200
Gideon Welles	675	300		200	100	200
Edward D. White	150	200		150	50	100
Oliver Wolcott JR		350		250	75	150

ALS : Autograph Letter Signed (written and signed by the same person.) **LS** : Letter Signed (body of letter written by another person.)
TLS : Typed Letter Signed **DS** : Document Signed **SIG** : Signature on paper or card **WH CARD** : White House Card signed
COVER : Depending on the time period, can be franked envelope, stamped envelope, event or First Day of Issue
*: Hall of Fame **D** : Deceased

	PHOTO	ALS	LS/TLS	DS	SIG.	COVER
Samuel Adams		3500	2500	1700	750	1500
Lord Jefferly Amherst		1000		575	400	800
Joseph Anderson		350		225	75	150
John Andre		7500		3500	1250	2500
John Armstrong		450		250	75	150
Benedict Arnold		4500		3250	1500	3000
Moses Austin		2250		1500	575	1150
Daniel Boone		17500		11000	5000	10000
Elias Boudinot		950		750	275	550
James Bowdoin		275		200	125	250
William Bradford		450		250	125	250
William Clark		3500		2500	1000	2000
Henry Clinton		2000		950	400	800
Elias Dayton		375		200	125	250
Jonathan Dayton		650		400	175	350
Marquis de Lafayette		1100		900	375	750
Thomas Gage		950		875	225	450
Horatio Gates		1250		750	275	550
Nathaniel Green		3250		2500	900	1800
Edward Hand		1250		575	225	450
Willaim Heath		1250		250	150	300
Patrick Henry		3500		1750	850	1700
Nicholas Herkimer				3700		
Sir William Howe		750		450	200	400
David Humphreys		250		175	75	150
Jedediah Huntington		250		125	75	150
James Irvine		250		125	75	150
Henry Knox		650		450	125	250
John Langdon		950		375	200	400
Tobias Lear		300		200	75	150
Charles Lee		2000		1500	750	1500
Henry Lee		625		575	200	400
Benjamin Lincoln		500		225	100	200
George Mason				4500		
Lachlan Mcintosh		1250		950	550	1100
Samuel Meredith		275		175	100	200
John Morton		1500		1200	450	900
William Moultrie		750		475	250	500
Gen. John Nixon		325		275	125	250
James Otis		750		475	250	500
Thomas Paine		12500		5500	3500	7000
John Paterson		300		200	75	150
William Penn		7500		3000	1500	3000
William Phillips		750		500	200	400
Oliver Prescott		450		175	75	150
Rufus Putman		425		300	175	350
Edmund Randolph		750		400	200	400
Paul Revere		20000		8500	4000	8000
Robert Rogers				900	400	800
Philip Schuyler		750		450	200	400
Charles Scott		300		200	100	200
Isaac Shelby		500		300	200	400
John Stark		2000		1250	650	1300
Arthur St. Clair		950		300	175	350
Baron Von Stueben		1250		900	450	900
Gen. John Sullivan		500		375	150	300
Thomas Sumter		950		750	400	800
Charles Thomas		600				
Charles Thompson		750		450	125	250
Jonathan Trumbull		750		500	300	600
Thomas Truxton		550		300	125	250
Richard Varick		200		125	75	150
James Wadsworth		225		125	50	100
Seth Warner		1500		950	250	500
Anthony Wayne		1750		1250	750	1500
Gen. Samuel B. Webb		450		275	125	250
Jamees Wilkinson		350		275	125	250
Marinus Willett		250		125	75	150
William Williams		575		350	275	550
David Wooster				650	250	500

CIVIL WAR-CONFEDERATE STATES OF AMERICA

	PHOTO	ALS	LS/TLS	DS	SIG.	COVER
William W. Allen		550			175	350
Robert H. Anderson	1500	500		300	125	250
J.R. Anderson		3000		400		
Turner Ashby		1600			450	900

	PHOTO	ALS	LS/TLS	DS	SIG.	COVER
William Barksdale		1500			450	900
W.N.R. Beall		600		300	175	350
P.G.T. Beauregard	900	950		850	350	700
Barnard Elliott Bee		1600		700	300	600
Judah P. Benjamin		1200		800	300	600
Braxton Bragg	900	900		600	365	730
John C. Breckinridge				40	25	50
Simon B. Bucker		375			200	400
William L. Cabell				405	175	350
Bwn F. Cheatham				400	225	450
Charles Clark		350		275	110	220
Pat Cleburne				1650	1050	2100
Howell Cobb		400		200	100	200
Francis Marion Cockrell		200		110	70	140
Samuel Cooper		445		230	120	240
Jefferson Davis	2500	1750		1500	500	1000
Varian Davis	700	500		250	150	300
G.G. Dibrell		300		300	150	300
Jubal A. Early		1000		800	500	1000
Samuel W. Ferguson		550		350	180	360
Nathan Bedford Forrest	RARE	SCARCE			575	1150
Frankllin Gardner		850		215	225	450
Randall L. Gibson		600		300	100	200
S.R. Gist		1250		900	450	900
John Brown Gordon		400		200	150	300
Wade Hampton		900		550	270	540
William J. Hardee	950	1110		875	300	600
Harry T. Hays				900	300	600
Henry Heth		3500		3000	750	1500
Ambrose Powell Hill	SCARCE	SCARCE		3000	2000	4000
Ddaniel Harvey Hill		600		500	320	640
Thomas Carmichael Hindman					320	640
Robert F. Hoke		300			100	200
Theophilus H. Holms				245	205	410
John B. Hood	1000	1600		1500	800	1600
Benjamin Huger		300		250	90	180
W.Y.C. Humes		435		235	140	280
T. J. "Stonewall" Jackson	RARE	20000		10000	4000	8000
Bushrood Johnson				300	115	230
Albert S. Johnston		2000		1500	290	580
Joseph E. Johnston	1600	750		600	300	600
John Marshall Jones				650	225	450
Samuel Jones				300	95	190
William E. Jones		600		250	140	280
Thomas Jordan		350		255	80	160
John H. Kelly					475	950
Joseph Brevard Kershaw		900			200	400
James H. Lane	950	335		200	100	200
Evander M. Law		500		250	100	200
Danville Leadbetter				450	150	300
Fitzhugh Lee	500	300		200	150	300
George W. C. Lee		410			155	310
Mary Lee	475	690			150	300
Robert E. Lee	6500			3500	2000	4000
Stephen Dill Lee		400		325	125	250
Lunsford L. Lomax		370		270	100	200
James Longstreet	900	1200		900	400	800
Francis R. Lubbock	350	295		185	150	300
John B. Magruder		475		525	275	550
William Mahone		365		252	120	240
Will T. Martin		400		250	100	200
Abney H. Maury		350			100	200
Samuel Bell Maxey		250		225	125	250
Henry McCulloch				350	145	290
Fayette McLaws		400		300	175	350
Christopher Memminger		550		480	165	330
George Meade				400	300	600
Samuel P. Moore		800		725	595	1190
John T. Morgan		350		200	125	250
John S. Mosby	2750	2000		900	450	900
Johm C. Pemberton	500	400		350	150	300

ALS : Autograph Letter Signed (written and signed by the same person.) LS : Letter Signed (body of letter written by another person.)
TLS : Typed Letter Signed DS : Document Signed SIG : Signature on paper or card WH CARD : White House Card signed
COVER : Depending on the time period, can be franked envelope, stamped envelope, event or First Day of Issue
*: Hall of Fame D : Deceased

	PHOTO	ALS	LS/TLS	DS	SIG.	COVER
William Dorsey Pender					400	800
George J. Pillow		350			100	200
Leonidas Polk					300	600
Elisha F. Paxton	RARE	RARE		RARE	750	1500
Sterling Price				350	200	400
William A. Quarles				225	75	150
George W. Randolph		550		400	250	500
John H. Reagan		600		450	150	300
Robert Emmet Rodes	RARE	RARE		RARE	1000	2000
John Ross		1000		600	350	700
Thomas L. Rosser	350	350		250	125	250
Daniel Ruggles		600		300	90	180
James A. Seddon	RARE	RARE		500	250	500
Raphael Semmens	1500	1400		750	300	600
Paul Semmes		900		900	700	1400
J.O. Shelby	2000	1200			300	600
E. Kirby Smith		600			300	600
Martin Luther Smith		200		125	75	150
G.W. Smith		550		250	125	250
Alexandeer H. Stephens		500			250	500
C.L. Stevenson		400		200	100	200
J.E.B. Stuart	RARE	RARE		4500	2500	5000
Richard Taylor				675	225	450
Walter H. Taylor				100	50	100
Robert Toombs		200		200	125	250
Isaac R. Trimble		1200			400	800
David Emanuel Twiggs		750		300	150	300
Robert C. Tyler		800		500	250	500
Earl Van Dorn		700			250	500
L.P. Walker			1100	1100		
Richard Waterhouse		550	320	320	150	300
Joseph Wheeler	950	475	225	225	80	160
William Henry Whiting					200	400
Marcus Wright		200	160	160	125	250
Felix K. Zolllicoffer		540	350	350	175	350

CIVIL WAR-UNION ARMY

	PHOTO	ALS	LS/TLS	DS	SIG.	COVER
R.A. Alger	75	85	55	55	30	60
Daniel Ammen	175	85	60	60	32	64
Robert Anderson	1950	300	325	325	115	230
Christopher C. Auger		170	125	125	50	100
Addam Badeau		125	60	60	35	70
Nathaniel P. Banks		145	100	100	70	140
John Beatty		80	55	55	27	54
William Belknap		175	160	160	50	100
H.W. Benham		135	50	50	35	70
Frederick W. Benteen	2500		3500	3500		
Thomas H. Benton Jr.		205	95	95	50	100
J.D. Bingham		185	140	140	45	90
James G. Blunt			75	75	46	92
John Wilkes Booth	4500	4000	3050	3050	1500	3000
C.R. Brayton		100	65	65	40	80
John Brown	8500	3450	1700	1700	775	1550
Don C. Buell	150	175	155	155	70	140
John N. Burns	1250				350	700
Ambrose E. Burnside	725	405	375	375	110	220
Benjamin F. Butler		255	125	125	90	180
Daniel Butterfiled	450	315	260	260	55	110
Edward Canby		370	310	310	55	110
Samuel P. Chase	300	325	150	150	90	180
Cassius m. Clay		450	220	220	80	160
James B. Coit		125			25	50
P. Edward Connor			58	58	35	70
S.W. Crawford		210	85	85	48	96
George Crook	400	375	275	275	125	250
George A. Custer	13000	15000	12500	12500	3380	6760
John A. Dahlgren		415	295	295	85	170
J.J. Dana			140	140	40	80
Gustavus A. DeRussy			250	250	45	90
John A. Dix	500	170-600	110	110	60-115	120-230
Abner Doubleday		1670	675	675	285	570
Ephriam Elmer Ellsworth		2500	1500	1500	540	1080
Richard E. Ewell			395	395	190	380
Thomas Ewing		245	110	110	40	80
David G. Farragut	1500	750	290	290	100	200
James W.M. Forsyth		175	105	105	35	70

	PHOTO	ALS	LS/TLS	DS	SIG.	COVER
John C. Fremont		1025	700	700	230	460
John Gibbon		330	185	185	50	100
Gordon Granger		145	95	95	45	90
Benjamin Grierson		330	235	235	125	250
Henry W. Halleckk	200	530	300	300	150	300
Winfield Scott Hancock		250	245	245	150	300
James A. Hardie		245	205	205	55	110
Joseph Henry		245	130	130	55	110
Ethan A. Hitchcock		200	150	150	50	100
Joseph Hooker		675	400	400	180	360
Oliver O. Howard	270	285	185	185	120	240
David Hunter	250	170	130	130	55	110
Fred S. Hutchinson		130			35	70
Philip Kearney		850	650	650	360	720
Erasmus D. Keyes		275	120	120	47	94
Rufus King		355			250	500
Samuel P. Lee		275	210	210	60	120
Joseph K.F. Mansfield		410	330	330	150	300
George B. McClellan		395	275	275	200	400
Irvin McDowell	1250	595	235	235	125	250
James B. McPherson		1125			150	300
George G. Meade	350	765	345	345	245	490
Wesley Merritt		175	250	250	80	160
Nelson A. Miles		230	160	160	85	170
John G. Mitchell		140	50	50	30	60
John Newton		325			50	100
Richard James Oglesby	150	95	60	60	40	80
Edward H.C. Ord	750	210	145	145	50	100
John M. Palmer		225	140	140	80	160
John G. Parke	150		75	75	45	90
Ely S. Parker			195	195	300	600
M.R. Patrick		205	50	50	35	70
John S. Phelps		100	65	65	25	50
Alfred Pleasanton			185	185	75	150
Fitz John Porter	750	155	100	100	40	80
David Dixon Porter		410	285	285	105	210
Horace Porter		85	190	190	45	90
William Radford		30	15	15	10	20
Joseph Jones Reynolds		190	110	110	45	90
James W. Ripley		210	185	185	55	110
William S. Rosecrans		365	270	270	160	320
Lovell H. Rousseau			165	165	50	100
Eliakia P. Scammon					125	250
Winfield Scott Hancock	450	430	330	330	125	250
John Sedgwick			350	350	135	270
Truman Seymour		205	110	110	75	150
Daniel Sickles	175	290	225	225	110	220
Franz Sigel		200	115	115	45	90
Henry W. Slocum		150	75	75	50	100
William Sprague		105	90	90	75	150
George Stoneman		195	155	155	60	120
Henry D. Terry		160	100	100	45	90
George H. Thomas		435	195	195	100	200
Lorenzo Thomas		270	140	140	90	180
Henry VanRensselaer					225	450
Mary E. Walker		575			215	430
Joseph Wheeler	950	475	225	225	80	160
George Williams		40	25	25	10	20
Thomas J. Wood			105	105	45	90
John Wool		375	210	210	85	170
Marcus J. Wright		200	160	160	125	250
Horatio G. Wright		200	75	75	40	80

MILITARY

	PHOTO	ALS	LS/TLS	DS	SIG.	COVER
William Alexander		1200		600	300	600
Ethan Allen		3000		1500	750	1500
Juan N. Almonte		250			60	120
William Bainbridge		550		300	150	300
Sir John Barron		325		170	75	150
W.A. "Billy" Bishop	220	300		225	150	300

ALS : Autograph Letter Signed (written and signed by the same person.) **LS** : Letter Signed (body of letter written by another person.)
TLS : Typed Letter Signed **DS** : Document Signed **SIG** : Signature on paper or card **WH CARD** : White House Card signed
COVER : Depending on the time period, can be franked envelope, stamped envelope, event or First Day of Issue
*: Hall of Fame **D** : Deceased

	PHOTO	ALS	LS/TLS	DS	SIG.	COVER
Cpt. William Bligh		7500		3500	1500	3000
Omar Bradley	185	300		250	100	200
Lloyd Bucher	90	150		90	35	90
Arleigh Burke	100	110		60	35	70
Aaron Burr		750		650	400	800
Guy (Aaron) Carleton		800		645	250	500
Mark W. Clark	100	275		190	35	70
Lucius Clay	100	145		125	30	60
Sir Henry Clinton		2200		925	425	850
Robert Clive		1200		600	250	500
Charles Cornwallis		1200		650	175	350
Moshe Dayan	250	275		235	125	250
Stephen Decatur		4500		2700	1000	2000
Jeff Deblanc	40	45			15	30
George Dewey	300	200		150	100	200
Hugo Eckner	550	550		400	200	400
Adolf Eichmann	750	1250		500	275	550
Mariano Escobedo				225	50	100
Thomas Ferebee	100	250		125	50	100
Ferninand Foch	235	280		125	50	100
Eugene B. Fluckey	90	110			45	90
Mitsuo Fuchida		500		350	300	600
Frances Gabreski	72	125		95	35	70
James Gavin	125	275		100	45	100
Joseph Goebbels	1250	1250		1025	350	700
Charles G. Gordon	600	1217		350	110	220
Hermann Goering	1475	2425		2044	450	900
Natnanael Greene		3000		2400	900	1800
Otto Gunsche	55	85			50	100
Alexander Haig	45	50		45	20	40
William Bull-Halsey	200	225		175	75	150
Frank Hamer					110	220
Albert H. Heinrich		120			35	70
Erich Hartmann	300				125	250
Rudolf Hess	750	750		450	155	310
Heinrich Himmler	750	1500		750	250	500
Kurt Caesar Hoffman	65				25	50
Sam Houston		2200		1500	600	1200
William Howe				850	200	400
Isaac Hull		565		570	190	380
Alfred Jodl	250	550		500	150	300
J. Joffre	225	250		155	75	150
Johnny Johnson	95	120		65	30	60
Robert Johnson	80	45			25	50
John Paul Jones	RARE	65000		25000	8000	16000
Ernst Kaltenbrunner	175			500	150	300
Richard Kane	75				25	50
Mike Kawato	150				50	100
Wilhelm Keitel	650			575	350	700
Albert Kesselring	175				100	200
Husband E. Kimmel		950		575	325	800
Ernest J. King	125			100	30	125
Otto Kretschmer	185			140	45	90
Marquis De Lafayette		1600		850	400	800
Ernest Lehmann		365			100	200
Curtis Lemay	75			75	30	60
Erich Ludendorff	275	350		225	100	200
Douglas MacArthur	500	750		600	225	450
George C. Marshall	400	550		300	200	400
Anthony McAuliffe	350	175		175	85	170
David McCampbell	75	45		25	15	30
George G. Meade	450			400	300	600
Frank D. Merrill		325			225	450
Erhard Milch	175	400		250	80	160
Gen. Nelson Miles		350		285	130	260
William Mitchell	1495	975		900	200	400
Sir Bernard Montgomery	350			225	75	300
Horatio Nelson		3000		1900	800	1600
Chester Nimitz	400	350		300	125	300
Oliver North	65	175		100	35	70
George S. Patton	5000	3500		2000	950	1900
Robert Peary	600	450			150	300
Matthew Calbraitte Perry		1400		775	450	900
John J. Pershing	400	300			100	200
Philippe Petain	50			90	35	70
Colin Powell	125	300	200	100	45	100
William C. Quantrill		3500			900	1800

MILITARY (cont.)

	PHOTO	ALS	LS/TLS	DS	SIG.	COVER
Erich Raeder	125	400		175	65	130
Gunther Rall	90	125		65	40	80
Hyman C. Rickover	250	400	400	200	100	200
Matthew B. Ridgeway	125	175		195	90	180
John Rogers		350		350	150	300
Erwin Rommel	1500	RARE		1150	750	1500
Alfred Rosenberg				350	175	350
Joe Rosenthal	250	250		200	75	150
Hams Ulrich Rudel	350	RARE		300	150	300
Ftitz Sauckel				200	75	150
Norman Schwarzkoff	75	125			35	70
Winfield Scott		675		400	175	350
Otto Skorzeny	500	450			250	500
Albert Speer	150	225		150	50	100
H.R. Stark	40	75		45	15	30
Joseph Stilwell	400				175	350
Maxwell D. Taylor	65	100		75	25	75
Lorenzo Thomas		250		140	75	150
Hideki Tojo	1500	1500		550	250	500
Hoyt Vandenberg	75				25	50
James Vanfleet	45	75		65	25	50
Franz Vonpapen	175	250		150	100	200
Joachim Von Ribbentrop	325	550		450	200	400
Jonathan Wainwright	225	250		225	100	200
William Westmoreland	65	75			25	75
Earle Wheeler	50				20	40
Charles Wilkes		200		100	50	100
Katsumari Yamashiro	300				100	200
Sgt. Alvin York	425	450		250	175	350
Elmo Zumwalt	50	125		75	25	50

ARTISTS

	PHOTO	ALS	LS/TLS	DS	SIG.	COVER
Ansel Adams	200	350		200	100	200
John J. Audobon		3000			750	1500
Fabian Bacharach	75	125			50	100
Frederic A. Bartholdi	900	600		750	400	800
Albert Bierstadt		540		220	125	250
Karl Bitter	100	155		75	25	50
Rosa Bonheur		325		155	110	220
Gutzon Borgulm	800	550		375	225	450
Matthew B. Brady		4500		2500	900	2000
Benvenuto Cellini				4800	1000	2000
Marc Chagall	350			350	185	370
Giorgio Giulio Clovio		2000		1400	650	1300
John Singleton Copley				710	350	700
George Cruikshank	375	345		115	160	320
E.E. Cummings	690	500		350	200	400
Salvador Dali	850	650		450	200	400
Edgar Degas		2000			650	1300
Gustave Dore		550		150	50	100
Raqul Dufy	500	750		450	300	600
Albrecht Durer					3000	6000
Sir Jacob Epstein		392		210	150	300
Max Ernst		575		300	200	400
Erte		450		275	125	250
Paul Gauguin		3600		1250	585	1170
Charles Dana Gibson	300	200		200	80	160
Francisco Goya					2500	5000
Kate Greenaway				1500	1000	2000
George Grosz		250		250	55	110
Kieth Haring	200	95		40	25	50
William Hart	425	235		180	130	260
Childe Hassam		500		350	150	300
Herman Hesse	400	550		500	100	200
William Hogarth		3500		1665	450	900
William Morris Hunt		500		215	50	100
Peter Hurd		300		200	100	200
George Inness		425		225	75	150
William H. Jackson				110	40	80
Will James	600	400		250	75	150

ALS : Autograph Letter Signed (written and signed by the same person.) LS : Letter Signed (body of letter written by another person.)
TLS : Typed Letter Signed DS : Document Signed SIG : Signature on paper or card WH CARD : White House Card signed
COVER : Depending on the time period, can be franked envelope, stamped envelope, event or First Day of Issue
*: Hall of Fame D : Deceased

287

	PHOTO	ALS	LS/TLS	DS	SIG.	COVER
John Barthold Jongkind		750		450	200	400
Wasily Kandinsky				500	200	400
Rockwell Kent	75				40	80
Dong Kingman		100		50	25	50
Marie Laurencin		590			125	250
Sir Thomas Lawrence		200		225	150	300
Sal Lewitt	50				25	50
Rene Magritte		900		350	200	400
Aristide Maillol		800		460	200	400
Edouard Manet				2000		
Henri Matisse		1200		750	550	1100
Jean Francois Millet				450	200	400
Juan Miro	310	700		575	200	400
Claude Monet		1500		1200	450	900
Henry Moore	100	450		200	50	100
A.M.R. Moses (Grandma)	600	860		500	175	350
Thomass Nast	RARE	300		350	125	250
Leroy Neiman	75	150		150	40	80
Georgia O'Keefe		950			350	700
Maxfield Parrish		800		500	175	350
Charles Wilson Peale		750		450	250	500
Pablo Picasso	1500			1500	750	1500
Camille Pissarro		1200			250	500
Alexander Pope		600		300	150	300
Hiram Powers	150	250		150	50	100
Raphael	RARE			9000	3500	7000
Frederic Remington	1750	1750		800	575	1150
Pierre Auguste Renoir	RARE	2100		700	300	600
Diego Rivera	1200	800		550	300	600
Norman Rockwell	250			300	125	400
Auguste Rodin		475		450	250	500
George Romney		450		375	150	300
Georges Roualt	900	750		475	200	400
Theodore Rousseau		475		175	75	150
Thomas Rowlandson		800		500	250	500
Charles M. Russell		1500		750	250	500
Augustus Saint-Gaudens	1200	900			200	400
John Singer Sargent		350		250	100	200
Thomas Scully		550		375	200	400
Paul Signac		300		150	75	150
Alfred Sisley		1200		400	175	350
Alfred Stieglitz		600		450	200	400
Gilbert Stuart		750		500	200	400
Louis C. Tiffany	1500			750	400	800
Henry Toulousse-Lautrec					1200	2400
John Trumbull		750		300	100	200
Vincent Van Gogh					4000	8000
Alberto Vargas	250	350			150	300
Andy Warhol	275	475		250	150	300
George Frederic Watts		300		150	75	150
Benjamin West		1250		700	200	400
Edward H. Weston					35	70
James M. Whistler		600		450	300	600
Olaf Wieghorst	200	250		225	75	150
Grant Wood		550		400	150	300
Andrew Wyeth	950	650		450	250	500
N.C. Wyeth		800		400	150	300

ASTRONAUTS

	PHOTO	ALS	DS	SIG.	COVER
Buzz Aldrin	100	300	225	75	100
Bill Anders	700				650
Neil A. Armstrong	2300	1500	1500	175	450
Charles Bassett II					400
Alan L. Bean	50		150	40	80
Frank Borman	50		50	30	60
John Bull	125			15	30
Scott Carpenter	50	125	75	25	100
Eugene A. Cernan	200			35	70
Roger Chaffee	475			200	400
Michael Collins	500	250	150	100	200
Charles Conrad Jr.	60			35	50
Gordon Cooper	60				35
Walter Cunningham	75				35
Charlie Duke	75				35
Donn F. Eisele	75				75
Ronald Evans	150			50	100

	PHOTO	ALS	LS/TLS	DS	SIG.	COVER
Ted Freeman				400		
Yuri Gagarin	1000			350		350
John Glenn	50		150	40		75
Dick Gordon	50					50
David Griggs	140		150	60		120
Virgil "Gus" Grissom	1500		725	275		550
Fred Haise	75		50	10		35
James B. Irwin	750	500				100
Gregory B. Jarvis	1200					350
Vladamir Komarov	250					200
Alexei Leonov	100					
James A. Lovell	100					50
Ken Mattingly	375					
Christa McAuliffe	1000	1250	1000	600		700
James A. McDivitt	50			30		90
Ronald E. McNair	75			100		100
Ed Mitchell	85	150	50	20		40
Ellison S. Onizuka	225					
Mercury 7 Astronauts	4500					2500
Robert Overmyer	65			20		40
Judith A. Resnick	100		250	100		75
Sally K. Ride	65		45	15		30
Stuart Roosa	125			15		150
Walter M.Schirra	50	150	75	25		50
Harrison H. Schmitt	100		125	20		100
Dick Scobee	350	925		50		100
Dave Scott	200			50		100
Elliot M. See Jr.	150			175		350
Alan B. Shepard	100		100	60		75
Donald K. Slayton	55		100	35		70
Michael Smith	250			200		400
Thomas P. Stafford	50					60
John L. Swigert Jr.	125		75	40		150
Valentina Tereshkova	150	75				50
Konstantin Tsiolicovsky			750			
Wernher Von Braun	2200	200				250
Edward H. White II	800	550	250	400		400
Clifton "c.c." Williams	400					225
Alfred Worden	100		50			40
John Young	750	265		75		125

The following is the listing of Apollo "crew-signed" Covers, Photos, and Insurance Covers

FLIGHT	CREW	PHOTO	COVER	INS.COVER
Apollo 1	Grissom, White & Chaffee	12500	n/a	n/a
Apollo 7	Schirra, Eisele & Cuningham	850	450	
Apollo 8	Borman, Lovell & Anders	1150	750	
Apollo 9	McDivitt, Scott & Schweickart	275	300	
Apollo 10	Stafford, Young & Cernan	1550	1400	
Apollo 11	Armstrong, Collins & Aldrin	4000	2200	
Apollo 12	Conrad, Gordon & Bean	175	500	975
Apollo 13	(1) Lovell, Mattingly & Haise	650	800	3500
Apollo 13	(2) Lovell, Swigert & Haise	1750	750	
Apollo 13	(3) Lovell, Mattingly, Swigert & Haise	2100	1500	4600
Apollo 14	Shepard, Mitchell & Roosa	750	700	1450
Apollo 15	Scott, Worden & Irwin	500	700	1000
Apollo 16	Young, Duke & Mattingly	1150	1000	1150
Apollo 17	Cernan, Schmitt & Evans	750	425	1150

AUTHORS & POETS

	PHOTO	ALS	LS/TLS	DS	SIG.	COVER
Edward Albee	80				30	60
Louisa May Alcott		450			250	500
Horatio Alger	250	250			125	250
W.H. Auden	550	500			200	400
Hans Christian Andersen	1650	1250			450	900
Gertrude Atherton	75	150			30	60
John James Audubon		3000			750	1500
Francis Bacon		20000		12000	5500	11000
Sabine Baring Gould	60	200			20	40

ALS : Autograph Letter Signed (written and signed by the same person.) **LS** : Letter Signed (body of letter written by another person.) **TLS** : Typed Letter Signed **DS** : Document Signed **SIG** : Signature on paper or card **WH CARD** : White House Card signed **COVER** : Depending on the time period, can be franked envelope, stamped envelope, event or First Day of Issue *: Hall of Fame **D** : Deceased

	PHOTO	ALS	LS/TLS	DS	SIG.	COVER
James M. Barrie		250		250	85	170
John Barth	40	85		40	30	60
Katherine Lee Bates		300			75	150
Charles Baudelaire		1600		900	300	600
Frank L. Baum	RARE	4500		2750	1750	3500
Samuel Beckett		400			150	300
Stephen V. Benet	150	175		140	80	160
Sir Walter Besant		190		125	35	70
Ambrose Bierce		588		670	275	550
Earl Derr Biggers	350	400			150	300
Vincent Blasco-Ibanez	450				100	200
William Cullen Bryant	750	375		250	100	200
Pearl S. Buck	65	198		145	40	100
Ned Buntline	750	250			140	280
Robert Burns		2750		1450	500	1000
Edgar Rice Burroughs	600	750		450	225	450
John Burroughs	525	200			100	200
Lord Geo G. Byron		2750			1600	3200
Erskine Caldwell	75	210		150	35	70
Albert Camus		600		250	75	150
Truman Capote	250			225	125	250
Edgar Cayce				225	70	140
Robert W. Chambers		20		15	10	20
Paddy Chayefsky	125	250		150	75	150
John Cheever	100	250		125	45	90
Agatha Christie				400	150	300
Samuel Clemens (Mark Twain)		2000		1500	750	1500
Irvin S. Cobb	95	150		45	25	50
Jean Cocteau	600	600			125	250
Samuel Taylor Coleridge		1250		575	325	650
Wilkie Collins	1380	530		309	100	200
Joseph Conrad	1250	1450		1125	230	460
Alistair Cooke	75	140		95	20	40
James Fenimore Cooper				180	90	180
Noel Coward	275	340		200	100	200
Hart Crane	350	1500		600	130	260
Stephen Crane	RARE	4500			1500	3000
E.E. Cummings	690	500		350	200	400
Richard H. Dana Jr.		215		200	50	100
Daniel Defoe					1500	3000
Theodore Dreiser	300	300		200	75	150
Dr. Suess	250	400			75	150
Alexander Dumas	750	550		225	110	220
T.S. Eliot	750			400	175	350
Ralph Waldo Emerson		450		300	200	400
John Erskine		175		125	35	70
Mary Ann Evans (George Eliot)		1250		595	160	320
William Faulkner		2500		1500	350	700
Eugene Field	200	400		230	110	220
F. Scott Fitzgerald	SCARCE			1500	450	900
Gustave Flaubert		1500		635	175	350
Ian Fleming	1800			1500	575	1150
Robert Frost	750	1000		600	150	300
Erle Stanley Gardner	200	300		200	75	150
Andre Gide		600		350	175	350
Allen Ginsberg	75	225		200	35	70
Johann W. Goethe				2550	1200	2400
Nikolai Gogol		6500		3350	750	1500
Maksim Gorky	1200	1200		900	400	800
Horace Greeley	750	300		275	65	130
Zane Grey	400	450		200	75	150
Jacob Grimm		3760		1840	565	1130
Edward Everett Hale	225	250		200	75	150
Sarah J. Hale		225		150		
Alex Haley	140	150		125	40	80
Dashiell Hammett	RARE			1500	550	1100
Thomas Hardy	1400	1425		1000	275	550
Nathaniel Hawthorne		1750		950	400	800
Lillian Hellman				145	50	100
Ernest Hemingway	2500	3000		2000	1000	2000
John Hersey	25	125		75	20	40
Herman Hessse	400	550		500	100	200
Oliver Wendall Holmes		350		200	75	150
A.E. Housmat		600		225	75	150
Julia Ward Howe		300		150	100	200
William Dean Howells				195	75	150
Elbert Hubbard	145	275		160	50	100

	PHOTO	ALS	LS/TLS	DS	SIG.	COVER
Thomas Hughs		125			40	80
Victor Hugo	975	650		375	200	400
Washington Irving		550		385	150	300
James Jones				150	50	100
James Joyce		2500		590	400	800
Emanuel Kant					1000	2000
Helen Keller	875			400	200	400
Francis Scott Key		950		650	450	900
Joyce Kilmer				550	200	400
Stephen King	100	400		150	60	120
Charles Kinsley		160		95	45	90
Rudyard Kipling	900	700		550	200	400
Charles Lamb		550		399	125	250
Louis L'Amour	200	RARE		200	90	180
Sidney Lanier		900		590	300	600
D.H. Lawrence		2500		590	300	600
T.E. Lawrence	RARE			1250	650	1300
Edward Lear		450			150	300
Harper Lee	250			250	100	200
Mikhail Lermontov	RARE				750	1500
Sinclair Lewis	300	550		325	100	200
Vachel Lindsay	125	450		185	50	100
John Locke	RARE			1950	700	1400
Jack London				750	400	800
Henry W. Longfellow	950	600			175	350
J.H. Lowell	350	225		145	75	150
Clare Boothe Luce	40	175		100	30	75
Niccolo Machiavelli				1250	500	1000
Vladimir V. Maiakovski	RARE			795	300	600
Maurice Maeterlinck	425	205		115	35	70
Norman Mailer	75	175		125	35	70
Thomas Mann	1100	900		450	200	400
Marcel Marceau	95			70	25	50
Edwin Markham	65	140		125	35	70
Karl Marx	RARE			1500	750	1500
Edgar Lee Masters	65	250		150	50	100
W.S. Maugham	400	350		250	85	170
Herman Melville	RARE			2000	750	1500
Henry Mencken	450	350		225	100	200
James A. Mitchner	115	340		265	40	80
Edna St. Vincent Millay	1265	800		325	140	280
Arthur Miller	100	200		100	50	100
Henry Miller	150	350		160	85	170
A.A. Milne	550	750		450	225	450
Margaret Mitchell	RARE	2500		1750	750	1500
George Moore		125		150	45	90
Frank Norris	450			275	125	250
Sean O'Casey	300	400		275	100	200
John O'Hara		600		450	150	300
Eugene O'Neill	RARE			350	200	400
Thomas Paine	RARE				3500	7000
Dorothy Parker	45	75			30	60
Boris Pasternak		1600		750	400	800
Albert Pike		250		175	100	200
Luigi Pirandello	375	300		175	75	150
Edgar Allan Poe	RARE			15000		
Alexander Pope	RARE				600	1200
William S. Porter (O. Henry)		1717		850	350	700
Emily Post		125			65	130
Beatrix Potter		750			250	500
Ezra Pound		900		675	250	500
Marcel Proust		1600		875	500	1000
Joseph Pulizter		500		350	125	250
Alexander Pushkin				2600	825	1650
Mario Puzo	55			75	25	50
Ernie Pyle	350	450		300	200	400
Ayn Rand	750				500	1000
John Reed	300				200	400
James Whitcomb Riley	225	450		150	85	170
Harold Robbins	35	100		75	20	40
Dante Rossetti		550		225	150	300

ALS : Autograph Letter Signed (written and signed by the same person.) **LS** : Letter Signed (body of letter written by another person.)
TLS : Typed Letter Signed **DS** : Document Signed **SIG** : Signature on paper or card **WH CARD** : White House Card signed
COVER : Depending on the time period, can be franked envelope, stamped envelope, event or First Day of Issue
* : Hall of Fame **D** : Deceased

	PHOTO	ALS	LS/TLS	DS	SIG.	COVER
Ramon Runyon	225	350		275	125	250
Jerome David Salinger		4000		3000		
Carl Sandberg	400	300		225	100	200
George Sand		600	250		250	250
Dorothy Sayers		475		350	200	400
Arthur Schopenhauer	RARE				1500	3000
Sir Walter Scott		900		500	150	300
Rod Serling				200	125	250
George Bernard Shaw	1500	800		650	400	800
Neil Simon	50			50	25	50
Upton Sinclair	125	150			50	100
Betty Smith	75				40	80
Samuel Francis Smith	450				200	400
Mickey Spillane	125	100		75	40	80
Elizabeth Cody Stanton		400		225	150	300
Richard Steele		1200		600	200	400
Gertrude Stein	675	750		550	400	800
John Steinbeck	1250	2250		1450	400	800
Robert Louis Stevenson	RARE	1400		750	300	600
Irving Stone	40	100		45	20	40
Rex Stout	45	200		100	35	70
Harriet Stowe		550			275	550
Rabindranath Tagore	350	350		250	100	200
Ida M. Tarbell	30	75		45	20	40
Allen Tate		75		30	10	20
Bayard Taylor		125		75	25	50
Lord Alfred Tennyson	950	700			200	400
Dylan Thomas	1500	1500			500	1000
Henry David Thoreau	RARE	8500		6000	3000	6000
Leo Tolstoy	2200	RARE			1200	2400
John Updike	45	125		75	25	50
S.S. Vandine (William H. Huntington)				650		
Jules Verne	RARE	900		1400	250	500
Francois Voltaire	RARE			225	500	1000
Edgar Wallace	350	300		100	75	150
Irving Wallace	75	150		100	25	50
Robert Penn Warren	75	125		750	35	70
Noah Webster		1400			500	1000
H.G. Welles	750	400		125	175	350
E.B. White				2000	35	70
Walt Whitman	2750	2400			1200	2400
John Greenleaf Whittier		350		250	100	200
Oscar Wilde	2250	2500		1500	675	1350
William Carlos Williams	300				275	550
Tennessee Williams	350	475		300	150	300
Thomas Wolfe	RARE			2000	500	1000
Virginia Woolf		1500			450	900
Herman Wouk	125	150		100	45	90
William Butler Yeats	1500	900		600	200	400
Emile Zola		450			200	400

AVIATION

	PHOTO	ALS	LS/TLS	DS	SIG.	COVER
Clara Adams		500		600		400
John W. Alcock	600			500	300	600
Hap Arnold	175	350		175	55	150
Italo Balbo	200	200			125	250
Gerhard Barkhorn	125				60	120
Floyd Bennett	500	750		370	300	600
Jacob Beser	100			100	50	100
Louis Bleriot	500	595		500	250	500
Gregory "Pappy" Boyington	175	200		150	75	150
Arthur W. Brown	575	575		400	300	600
Richard Byrd	325	450		275	75	150
Clarence D. Chamberlin	250	375		250	50	200
Claire L. Chenault	525	600			500	1000
Jacquelince Cochran	150			175	45	100
Everett R. Cook	50			30	10	40
Douglas Corrigan				80	65	130
Dieudonne Coste	275	385		235	125	300
Glenn Curtiss	850	650		500	300	600
F.L. Dobehoff	75				25	50
Joseph Doerflinger	45	50			15	30
James H. Doolittle	200	200		150	50	100
Donald W. Douglas Sr.	360	450		295	150	300
Amelia Earhart	1500			1750	425	1200
Ira Eaker	150	100		75	35	70

	PHOTO	ALS	LS/TLS	DS	SIG.	COVER
Hugo Eckener	550	550		400	200	400
Ruth Elder	350	310		190	100	200
Thomas Ferebee	100	250		125	50	100
Anthony Fokker	500	530		295	200	400
Joe Foss	55	85		75	30	60
Mitzuo Fuchida		500		350	300	125
Harold Gatty	175	450		275	75	150
Francis Gabreski	72	125		95	35	70
Claude Grahame-White	125	250		100	75	150
Frank Hawks	250	325		135	80	160
Herman Hesse	400	550		500	100	200
Amy Johnson	200	135		85	75	150
George C. Kennedy	200				40	80
Samuel Langley		600			250	500
Hubert Latham	75	90		35	25	50
Ruth Law	100				35	75
Pierre Charles L'Enfant		1200		850	400	800
Charles A. Lindbergh	2500	2400		1250	575	1400
Alan Lockheed	150	250		150	75	200
Gunther Lutzow	450	445			175	350
Glenn L. Martin	250	265		170	75	450
Dick Merrill	75	105		55	35	70
Henry T. Merrill	100	100		45	30	60
Willy Messerschmitt	395			275	125	200
Billy Mitchell	1495	975		900	200	400
Edwin C. Musick	150	300	200	175	100	150
Ruth R. Nichols	250			250	125	250
Charles Nungesser	275					
Walter Oesau	200	400			150	300
Earle Ovington	250	200			45	100
Clyde Pangborn				150	75	150
William T. Piper	750			350	175	350
Wiley Post	275	650			350	900
Edward Rickenbacker		450		200	100	350
W. Roedel	200					
Charles Rosendahl		200		160	75	150
Claude Ryan	225				100	200
A. Santos-Dumont	750	600			300	600
William E. Scripps	40			50	15	30
Boris Sergievsky	150				75	150
Paul W. Tibbetts	75	100			25	100
Juan T. Trippe	40	200	125	100	30	40
Roscoe Turner	125				75	150
Ermst Udet	500	450		375	225	450
Theodore Van Kirk	100			85	50	100
Wolfgang VonGronau	500				200	400
Ferdinand VonZeppelin	1000	775	1045		375	750
Leigh Wade	45	100		75	30	60
Frank Whittle	45				15	30
Orville Wright	2000	1750		1250	500	1000
Wilbur Wright	4500	5000		2000	775	1550
Jeanne Yeager	35				15	50
Chuck Yeager	50	65		50	25	100

BUSINESS

	PHOTO	ALS	LS/TLS	DS	SIG.	COVER
John Jacob Astor III		800		550	200	400
William B. Astor		1200		800	250	500
Phineas T. Barnum	900	550		750	200	400
Bernard Baruch	250	550		300	75	150
Clyde Beatty	150	150		100	50	100
Nicholas Biddle		800		600	150	300
William Bingham		340		315	120	240
"Diamond" Jim Brady	650	1500		1250		2500
J.M. Browning		575				
Luther Burbank	165	298		275		550
August A. Busch	50	175		90		200
Andrew Carnegie	1110	1250		1250		2500
Auguste Chouteau		900		600		1200
Walter P. Chrysler	900	1500		1000		950
Andre Citreon	700			350		700

ALS : Autograph Letter Signed (written and signed by the same person.) LS : Letter Signed (body of letter written by another person.)
TLS : Typed Letter Signed DS : Document Signed SIG : Signature on paper or card WH CARD : White House Card signed
COVER : Depending on the time period, can be franked envelope, stamped envelope, event or First Day of Issue
*: Hall of Fame D : Deceased

	PHOTO	ALS	LS/TLS	DS	SIG.	COVER
Jay Cooke		2250		1250		2500
W.K. Coors	50	95		60		125
Erastas Corning		295		175		350
Cyrus Curtis	95	140		55		100
John Deere		1500		1500		1200
Sanford B. Dole	100	350		250		500
Frank W. Doubleday		375		185		400
Frederick S. Duesenberg				1250		2500
Charles E. Duryea	RARE	SCARCE		450		900
J. Eberhard Faber		725		500		1000
Max Factor	60	175		125		250
William G. Fargo				900		1800
Enzo Ferrari	550			550		5000
Marshall Field Jr.	75	170		110		220
Cyrus W. Field		1500		550		1100
Harvey S. Firestone	1500	1500		900		750
Malcolm Forbes	75	150		75	35	70
Edsel Ford	500			550	250	500
Henry Ford	2550	5000		3500	900	1800
Henry Ford II	55	30		15	10	40
Alfred C. Fuller	150	195			125	250
J. Paul Getty	375	1500		750	185	500
A.P.M Giannini		500		290	150	300
Bernard F. Gimbel	90	375		175	60	120
Stephen Girard		325		350	125	250
Charles Goodyear	RARE	RARE		2000	400	800
Jay Gould	1200	1500		550	250	500
W.T. Grant	275	350		125	50	100
Armand Hammer	150	275		535	50	100
William Randolph Hearst	695	950		600	150	300
Henry John Heinz	350	550			150	300
Leona Hemsley	35				10	20
Conrad Hilton	110	190		90	60	120
Ben Holladay		450		250	125	250
Johns Hopkins				500	175	350
Howard Hughes	2750	3500		2000	1250	2500
Henry E. Huntington		200		125	75	150
Lee A. Iaccoca	35			50	15	50
Robert H. Ingersoll	225	300		175	80	160
John Jay		2250		1750	550	1100
Howard Johnson	35			30	15	30
Henry J. Kaiser	375			900	200	400
W.K. Kellogg	250	400		250	125	250
Joeseph P. Kennedy	150				75	150
James C. Kraft	50	175		95	30	60
Ray Kroc	100	150			40	80
Alfred Krupp		500		450	180	360
Carl Laemmle	700	600		250	100	200
William P. Lear Sr.	100	150		100	30	60
Louis K. Liggett		350		170	90	180
Peter Lorillard		450		250	125	250
Frederick L. Maytag	200	600		275	100	200
Richard McDonald	250			275	75	150
Andrew Mellon	400	1200		900	250	500
J.P. Morgan Sr.	1200	2500		900	300	600
J.S.G. Morton	75	145		50	25	50
John K. Northrop	100	250		125	45	90
Ransom E. Olds				1200	300	600
Aristotle Onassis	225			300	175	350
Fred Pabst	400			450	150	300
J.C. Penny	300	400		300	100	200
Allen Pinkerton	RARE	1200		750	300	600
Dr. Ferdinand Porsche	550			450	225	450
Joseph Pulitzer		500		350	125	250
George M. Pullman		500		450	225	450
Orville Redenbacker	30	30		30	10	20
R.J. Reynolds				600	250	500
Albert Ringling				400	150	300
Charles Ringling				300	125	250
Henry Ringling				350	125	250
John Ringling				600	125	250
John D. Rockerfeller	1500	2250		1650	500	1000
John D. Rockerfeller Jr.	75	175		125	35	70
Washington A. Roebling		400		225	100	200
Charles S. Rolls		600			300	600
Nathan Meyer Rothschild				850	275	550
Sir Henry Royce		1200			600	1200

BUSINESS (cont.)

	PHOTO	ALS	LS/TLS	DS	SIG.	COVER
Russel Sage		1500		750	200	400
David Sarnoff	150	750		400	75	150
Harry Sinclair	200	300		175	125	250
Leland Stanford	400	2500		1750	225	450
F.O. Stanley		1200			350	700
Clement Studebaker		650		500	200	400
Seth E. Thomas		400		250	125	250
Charles L. Tiffany	1500	RARE		400	200	400
Donald J. Trump	40	75		50	15	30
Ted Turner	30	40			10	20
Cornelius Vanderbilt	3000	3500		2000	600	1200
William H. Vanderbilt	500	1500		750	250	500
Jack L. Warner	150			175	75	150
Wells & Fargo				1250	850	1700
Henry Wells		1500		750	300	600
George Westinghouse				1500	500	1000
Frank W. Woolworth	RARE	RARE		2500	550	1100
William J. Wrigley	350	400		350	150	300

CELEBRITIES

	PHOTO	ALS	LS/TLS	DS	SIG.	COVER
Ralph Abernathy	75	125			30	60
Abigail Adams		5500		2000	550	1100
Louisa C. Adams		750		500	250	500
Jane Addams	250				75	150
Susan B. Anthony	1200	600			175	350
Stephen Austin		5000		2000	800	1600
Clara Barton	800	675		450	155	310
Judge Roy Bean		7500		5000	2000	4000
Henry Ward Beecher		200			75	150
William W. Belknap		175			75	150
David Berkowitz		250			75	150
Harry Blackstone	250	450			120	240
Letizia Bonaparte		2700		1500		
Lizzie Borden	RARE	RARE		RARE	1800	3600
Margaret Bourke-White		200		75	75	150
Belle Boyd	10000	RARE		10000	2000	4000
Joseph Brant	RARE	5000		RARE	RARE	
Eva Braun		2750			1000	2000
Harry Bridges	140			125	70	140
Chief John F. Brown		350		175	100	200
John Brown	2500	2500		1600	775	1550
Ralph Bunche	125	225		130	50	100
David G. Burnet		1200		635	275	550
Al Capone	RARE	RARE		8000	3000	6000
Clementine S. Churchill	150	200		150	75	150
William Clark		2000		1500	400	800
William F. Cody	4500	2000		1500	750	1500
Capt. James Cook	RARE	RARE		8850	3800	7600
Peter Cooper		750		500	150	300
Hernando Cortez	RARE	RARE		20000	6000	12000
Davy Crockett		20000		9000	6000	12000
George Croghan		800		400	200	400
Emmett Dalton	SCARCE	3500		1600	800	1600
Clarence Darrow	1300	2200		1600	400	800
Varina H. Davis	750	500		250	150	300
James W. Denver		450		210	100	200
Thomas E. Dewey	100	150		75	40	80
Mahlon Dickerson		150		75	25	50
Jacob M. Dickinson		125		50	25	50
Dorothea L. Dix	25	45		30	15	30
Stephen A. Douglas	270	450		225	100	200
Allen W. Dulles	75	225		165	30	60
Virgil Earp		7500		4500	2000	4000
Wyatt Earp		30000		15000	5000	10000
Mary Baker Eddy	SCARCE	SCARCE		2500	1250	2500
Muhammad Elijah	425			275	175	350
Brian Epstein		750		600	350	700
James A. Farley	25	70		40	15	30
Father Flanagan	250			125	45	90
Nathan Bedford Forrest	RARE	RARE		SCARCE	750	1500

ALS : Autograph Letter Signed (written and signed by the same person.) **LS** : Letter Signed (body of letter written by another person.)
TLS : Typed Letter Signed **DS** : Document Signed **SIG** : Signature on paper or card **WH CARD** : White House Card signed
COVER : Depending on the time period, can be franked envelope, stamped envelope, event or First Day of Issue
*: Hall of Fame **D** : Deceased

	PHOTO	ALS	LS/TLS	DS	SIG.	COVER
Otto Frank				550	300	600
Sir John Franklin		610		320	125	250
James Gadsden		550		350	175	350
Gandhi	SCARCE	1500		1200	550	1100
Pat Garrett		3000		2500	SCARCE	
Geronimo	RARE	RARE		RARE	5000	10000
Joseph Goebbels	1250			1025	350	700
Samuel Gompers		450		225	150	300
Robert K. Gray	100	250		150	50	100
Horace Greeley	750	300		275	65	130
Charles J. Guiteau	SCARCE	2500		900	400	800
John N. Griggs		110		45	15	30
John Wesley Hardin	RARE	9000		3750	1800	3600
Mata Hari	RARE	RARE		1100	400	800
Lucy Webb Hayes	700	400			230	460
Patty Hearst					325	650
John Hinckley Jr.		200		150	35	70
Alger Hiss		200		65	40	80
James R. Hoffa	400				275	550
J. Edgar Hoover	145	220	200	160	60	125
L. Ron Hubbard	SCARCE	SCARCE		900	200	400
Robert G. Ingersoll	40	85		60	30	60
Jessie Jackson	35	45			15	30
Frank James		2750		1600	975	1950
Marshall Jewell		195		75	40	80
Anson Jones		1200			350	700
Alvin Karpis	100				75	150
Emmett Kelly	275			150	65	130
Ethel Kennedy	35			45	15	30
John F. Kennedy	225	500	600		200	300
Rose Kennedy	100			150	100	200
Sister Elizabeth Kenny	275				175	350
Simon Kenton					400	800
Alexander F. Ferensky	400				200	400
Martin Luther King Jr.	3000	3500		2750	1500	3000
Frederick West Lander		375		225	150	300
Marcy C. Lee	475	690			150	300
Meriwether Lewis	RARE	11500		6000	RARE	
G. A. "Pawnee Bill" Lillie	500	750		550	275	550
David Livingstone		1600		750	225	450
Martin Luther	RARE	550000		40000	15000	30000
Cotton Mather				4000		
Malcom X	RARE	14000		900	1250	2500
Thomas Robert Malthus				250	300	600
Charles Manson	200	350		175	75	150
Luther Martin		360		RARE	70	140
Bat Masterson	RARE	RARE		400	5000	10000
John Stuart Mill		850			150	300
Maria Montessori					295	590
John Montagu (Earl of Sandwich)		400		200	75	150
Lola Montez		500			200	400
Mother Teresa	275	RARE		250	125	250
Elijah Muhammad				250	100	200
Edward R. Murrow	250			300	130	260
Eliot Ness	RARE	RARE		800	375	750
Annie Oakley	7500	9000		6000	2500	5000
Judge Isaac Parker				1500	500	1000
Rosa Parks	100			100	40	80
Eva Peron		600			400	800
Jane M. Pierce		900		500	200	400
William A. Pinkerton				200	100	200
Peter B. Porter		175		150	75	150
John Profumo	100			65	40	80
Melvin Purvis	100	150		100	25	50
Buford Pusser				250	125	250
Ernie Pyle	350	450		300	200	400
James Earl Ray		200			75	150
Hiram R. Revels					500	1000
John Ross		1000		600	350	700
Jack Ruby	RARE	RARE		500	300	500
Harland (Col) Sanders		125		150	45	90
John Scopes	1500	RARE			300	600
John Selman				2500	1200	2400
Samuel Sewall	60				25	50
Sitting Bull	RARE	RARE		RARE	5750	11500
Alfred E. Smith	125				50	100
Joseph Smith				1500	750	1500

	PHOTO	ALS	LS/TLS	DS	SIG.	COVER
Ashrel Smith		450			150	300
Sir Henry M. Stanley	750	550			275	550
Elizabeth C. Stanton		400		225	150	300
Edwin M. Stanton		300		160	100	200
William Stratton (Tom Thumb)	450	375			250	500
John A. Sutter	RARE	2700		RARE	1200	2400
Henretta Szold		600		450	150	300
Isiah Thomas		750		300	150	300
William M. Tilghman		1250		850	200	400
Donald Trump	40	75		50	15	30
William M. "Boss" Tweed	750	350		200	125	250
Bartolomeo Vanzetti	RARE	RARE		1500	600	1200
Booker T. Washington	1500	700		450	300	600
Francis E. Willard		125		65	40	80
Wendell L. Willkie	125			75	35	70
Christopher Wren	RARE	RARE		RARE	1500	3000
Frank Lloyd Wright	RARE	RARE		1550	900	1800
Brigham Young	RARE	RARE		1500	650	1300
Cole Younger		7500			2000	4000
Emiliano Zapate	RARE	RARE		1500	500	1000

COMPOSERS, CONDUCTORS, OPERA & BALLET DANCERS

	PHOTO	ALS	LS/TLS	DS	SIG.	COVER
Antonio Annalord	40	35			10	20
Edmond Audran		175	85	85	45	90
Joann Sebastion Bach	50				20	40
George Balanchine	200	250			125	250
Mikhail Baryshnikov	150	130	85	85	65	130
Harold Bauer			80	80	45	90
Alan Berg		1425	485	485	135	270
Irving Berlin	1100	1420	1060	1060	230	460
Hector Berlioz		2190	785	785	245	490
Leonard Bernstein	255	525	350	350	200	400
Georges Bizet		2100	890	890	350	700
Eubie Blake	125	175	105	105	60	120
Sir Arthur Bliss		175			25	50
Arrigo Boita		325	110	110	45	90
Alexander Borodin		1100	450	450	250	500
Joannes Brahms	6200	5375	1350	1350	1000	2000
Benjamin Britten	195	650	405	405	115	230
Anton Bruckner	2500	5500	2500	2500	1200	2400
Ferruccio Busoni	425	340			120	240
John Cage	190	250	125	125	95	190
Sammy Cahn	50	125	80	80	15	30
Maria Callas	825	976	850	850	300	600
Hoagy Carmichael	110		200	200	45	90
Enrico Caruso	1265	1250	625	625	275	550
Pablo Casals	285	245	150	150	100	200
Cecile Chaminade	270	300	195	195	85	170
Gustave Charpentier	300	370	250	250	100	200
Ernest Chausson		345	145	145	50	100
Luigi Cherubini		595	375	375	175	350
George M. Cohan	280	275	185	185	85	170
Florencio Constantino	365				75	150
Aaron Copland	155	285	165	165	75	150
Peter Cornelius		325			55	110
Noel Coward	375	380	210	210	165	330
George Crumb		375			25	50
Cesar Cui		450	200	200	95	190
Walter J. Damrosch	200	115	75	75	50	100
Felicien David			500	500	100	200
Claude Debussy		1375	1000	1000	350	700
Manuel Defalla			1200	1200	425	850
Mario Delmonaco	175	125	65	65	45	90
Erno Dohnanyi		220	135	135	50	100
Gaetano Donnizetti		2150	800	800	500	1000
Isadora Duncan	825	1150			400	800
Antonin Dvorak		2500	895	895	400	800
Duke Ellington	400		325	325	125	250
Daniel D. Emmett		600	425	425	300	600
Geraldine Farrar	130	120			65	130

ALS : Autograph Letter Signed (written and signed by the same person.) LS : Letter Signed (body of letter written by another person.)
TLS : Typed Letter Signed DS : Document Signed SIG : Signature on paper or card WH CARD : White House Card signed
COVER : Depending on the time period, can be franked envelope, stamped envelope, event or First Day of Issue
*: Hall of Fame D : Deceased

	PHOTO	ALS	LS/TLS	DS	SIG.	COVER
Margot Fonteyn	200	135	45	45	40	80
Arthur Foote		195	85	85	30	60
Stephen Foster		10000	3500	3500	1000	2000
Cesar Franck		890	1100	1100	340	680
Rudolf Friml	250	325	250	250	100	200
Amelita Galli-Curci	200	385	190	190	85	170
Mary Garden	85	45	30	30	20	40
George Gershwin	4075	4650	1700	1700	900	1800
Ira Gershwin	180	1375	250	250	85	170
Beniamino Gigli	275	300	90	90	50	100
Umberto Giordano	400		400	400	250	500
Alexander Glazunov		675	365	365	225	450
Louis M. Gottschalk	SCARCE	1600		1200	500	1000
Charles Gounod	550	500	365	150	300	
Edward Grieg	1095	1125		600	350	700
Ferde Grofe	125	245		200	100	200
Oscar Hammerstein	250			250	125	250
George Frederick Handel	RARE	RARE		5800	1000	2000
W.C. Handy	450	SCARCE		475	275	550
Joseph Hayon	RARE	RARE		RARE	3500	7000
Roland Hayes	250				100	200
Jascha Heifetz	585				130	260
Hans Werner Henze	150				45	90
Victor Herbert	350	375		200	100	200
Paul Hindemith		425		295	100	200
Earl K. "Father" Hines	30				125	250
Josef C. Hofmann	150	140		100	40	80
Arthur Honegger	50	290		130	45	90
Englebert Humperdinck	250	375		225	100	200
Jacques Ibert		325			75	150
Charles E. Ives	500	1500		750	250	500
Joseph Joachim	220	337		150	95	190
Scott Joplin		2000		1200	750	1500
Walter Kent	65				40	80
Jerome Kern	2000	SCARCE		650	250	500
Zoltan Kodaly	450	450		250	125	250
Erich Korngold	100	350		200	75	150
D.J. "Nick" LaRocca	200				75	150
Franz Lehar	350	550		200	85	170
Ruggierro Leoncavallo	675	500		500	175	350
Lydia Lipkowska	325				100	200
Franz Liszt	1600	950		650	450	900
Anna Magnani	450				275	550
Gustav Mahler	RARE	3500		1200	550	1100
Henry Mancini	75			60	30	60
Pietro Mascagni	600	500		375	165	330
Jules Massenet	295	255		145	65	130
Jimmy McHugh				75	25	50
Johnny Mercer	135				50	100
Olivier Messiaen				200	70	140
Giacomo Meyerbeer	300	400		250	175	350
Julia Migenes	35				15	30
Darius Milhaud	450	300		250	150	300
Glenn Miller	450	600		400	200	400
Wolfgang A. Mozart	RARE	75000		RARE	RARE	
Ethelbert Nevin	100	300		150	75	150
Jacques Offenbach	275	450		250	145	290
Eugene Ormandy	80	90		45	25	50
Ignace J. Paderewski	450	550			175	350
Nicolo Paganini	RARE	RARE		RARE	450	900
Luciano Pavarotti	65	100			35	70
Anna Pavlona	550	450			350	700
Aureliano Pertile	125				40	80
Lily Pons	125				50	100
Cole Porter	650			450	225	450
Andre Previn	75	80		40	20	40
William Primrose	225				75	150
Serge Prokofieff	950	1200		750	400	800
Serge Rachmaninoff	475	775		600	225	450
Maurice Ravel	1600	1400			450	900
Hans Richter		450			150	300
Nikolai Rimsky-Korsakov	1500	2500		1500	600	1200
Richard Rodgers	225			250	75	150
Sigmund Romberg	225	300		200	75	150
Gioacchino Rossini	RARE	1750		1000	RARE	
Anton Rubinstein	400	300		200	75	150
Camille Saint Saens	400	400		300	150	300

COMPOSERS, CONDUCTORS, OPERA & BALLET DANCERS (cont.)

	PHOTO	ALS	LS/TLS	DS	SIG.	COVER
Alessandro Scarlatti	RARE	20000		RARE	RARE	
Ernestine Schumann-Heink	150				50	100
Robert Schumann	RARE	RARE		RARE	1000	2000
Franz Schubert	RARE	RARE		5000	2500	5000
Sara Scuderi	85				35	70
Neil Sedaka	20			20	10	20
Pete Seeger		75		50	20	40
Marcella Sembrich	200	200			100	200
Roger Sessions		90			15	30
George B. Shaw	1500	800		650	400	800
John Philip Sousa	900	400		400	125	250
William Grant Still	250	300			125	250
Leoplod Stokowski	150	150		125	65	130
Oscar Straus	200	250			150	300
Joann Strauss Jr.	RARE	900		750	450	900
Richard Strauss	700	750		450	225	450
Igor Stravinsky	750	750		550	325	650
Arthur Sullivan	1000	650		400	175	350
Set Svanholm	45				20	40
Gladys Swarthout	75			75	25	50
Marie Taglioni	RARE	RARE			300	600
Peter Tchaikovsky	RARE	RARE		3000	2000	4000
John Charles Thomas	45	55		45	25	50
Virgil Thomson	125	150		75	50	100
Arturo Toscanini	700	750		550	300	600
Ludwig Van Beethoven	RARE	50000		27500	RARE	
Guiseppe Verdi	RARE	2400		1500	1200	2400
Hans Von Bulow		65			20	40
Richard Wagner	3000	2500		1600	1200	2400
Thomas "Fats" Waller	400	RARE		275	125	250
Bruno Walter	375	150			75	150
Kurt Weil	375	900		500	250	500
John Williams	50			75	20	40

ENTERTAINERS

		PHOTO	ALS	LS/TLS	DS	SIG.	COVER
Bud	Abbot	350	450	420	350	150	200
	Abbott & Costello	1500			1000	500	600
F. Murray	Abraham	30				15	25
Maude	Adams	100	125	110	100	50	60
Nick	Adams	200	250	220	220	75	100
Isabelle	Adjani	30				15	25
Ben	Affleck	50				20	25
Christina	Aguilera	50				25	35
Brian	Aherne	35	45	38	35	20	25
Dan	Akyrod	25				10	20
Alan	Alda	60				20	25
Kim	Alexis	30				15	25
Kirstie	Aley	25				10	20
Fred	Allen	75	95	85	80	25	30
Grace	Allen	150	195	180	165	50	60
Karen	Allen	20				10	20
Woody	Allen	40				15	20
Carol	Alt	25				17	20
Don	Ameche	75	97	90	80	25	65
Gillian	Anderson	40				20	25
Loni	Anderson	20				10	20
Pamela	Anderson	50				25	35
Ursula	Andress	40				20	25
Julie	Andrews	60				20	25
Heather	Angel	50	65	60	50	20	30
Christina	Applegate	40				20	25
Roscoe	Arbuckle	950	1200	1100	1050	400	480
Richard	Arlen	75	95	85	75	35	40
George	Arliss	100	125	115	100	30	35
Robert	Armstrong	200	255	225	200	100	110
Desi	Arnez (full name)	200	260	240	220	100	120
Edward	Arnold	100	125	110	100	30	40
Roseanne	Arquette	20				10	20
Jean	Arthur	200	260	240	210	100	120
Armand	Assante	20				10	20

ALS : Autograph Letter Signed (written and signed by the same person.) **LS** : Letter Signed (body of letter written by another person.)
TLS : Typed Letter Signed **DS** : Document Signed **SIG** : Signature on paper or card **WH CARD** : White House Card signed
COVER : Depending on the time period, can be franked envelope, stamped envelope, event or First Day of Issue
*: Hall of Fame **D** : Deceased

		PHOTO	ALS	LS/TLS	DS	SIG.	COVER
Mary	Astor	75	95	90	85	25	30
Roscoe	Ates	100	115	110	100	25	30
Agnes	Ayres	100	115	110	100	25	30
Lew	Ayres	50	65	57	55	20	25
Lauren	Bacall	25				15	25
Catherine	Bach	20				10	20
Kevin	Bacon	25				10	20
Max	Baer	40				20	30
Fay	Bainter	125	160	145	125	45	55
Carroll	Baker	40				20	30
Josephine	Baker	350	450	420	385	125	150
Alec	Baldwin	35				18	25
Lucille	Ball (first name)	200	260	240	230	75	100
Lucille	Ball (full name)	400	520	480	460	125	150
Anne	Bancroft	30				15	20
Antonio	Banderas	40				30	35
Tallulah	Bankhead	150	195	180	165	50	60
John	Banner	200	255	225	200	75	85
Theda	Bara	250	325	300	275	100	120
Brigitte	Bardot	75				25	40
Lex	Barker	200	260	240	220	75	100
Roseanne	Barr	25				13	25
Diana	Barrymore	100	130	120	110	35	40
Drew	Barrymore	50				25	35
Freddie	Bartholomew	100	130	120	110	35	40
Kim	Basinger	60				25	40
Justine	Bateman	20				10	20
Kathy	Bates	30				15	25
Warner	Baxter	125	160	145	125	45	55
Stephanie	Beacham	10				5	15
Jennifer	Beals	15				8	15
Amanda	Bearse	10				5	20
Warren	Beatty	50				25	25
Scotty	Beckett	100	110	110	100	50	60
Noah	Beery	75	100	90	80	35	40
Wallace	Beery	200	260	240	220	75	100
Ed	Begley Sr.	125	160	140	125	50	60
Ralph	Bellamy	50	65	60	50	20	30
John	Belushi	550	450	360	320	300	350
William	Bendix	150	160	145	135	50	60
Joan	Bennett	50	65	60	50	20	45
Bruce	Bennett (Tarzan)	100	130	120	120	50	60
Jack	Benny	150	195	160	175	50	75
Gertrude	Berg	65	80	75	65	20	25
Edgar	Bergen	125	160	140	135	50	75
Ingrid	Bergman	225	260	240	220	100	150
Busby	Berkeley	350	450	420	400	100	120
Milton	Berle	75				40	60
Sarah	Bernhardt	250	320	300	275	100	120
Corbin	Bernsen	20				10	20
Chuck	Berry	95				40	60
Halle	Berry	40				25	35
Valerie	Bertinelli	20				10	20
Joe	Besser	100	110	110	100	50	60
Turhan	Bey	75	100	90	80	25	30
Jacqueline	Bisset	25				13	20
Shirley Temple	Black	75				25	40
Linda	Blair	20				10	20
Amanda	Blake	100	130	120	110	25	35
Clara	Blandick	2500	3200	2900	2750	700	840
Joan	Blondell	100	130	110	100	25	30
Ben	Blue	50	65	60	55	20	25
Humphrey	Bogart	2000	2600	2400	2300	900	900
Mary	Boland	50	60	55	50	20	25
Ray	Bolger	100	130	120	110	50	60
Jon	Bon Jovi	75				35	50
Ward	Bond	125	160	150	135	50	60
Tommy "Butch"	Bond	35				18	25
Lisa	Bonet	20				10	20
Edwin	Booth	200	260	240	240	75	90
Shirley	Booth	35				18	25
Ernest	Borgnine	30				15	25
Clara	Bow	400	520	480	440	125	150
David	Bowie	75				40	60
Charles	Boyer	100	130	120	110	35	40
Eddie	Bracken	50	60	55	50	20	25
Marlon	Brando	500				350	400

		PHOTO	ALS	LS/TLS	DS	SIG.	COVER
Walter	Brennen	150	190	170	160	50	60
Fanny	Brice	150	195	180	175	50	60
Lloyd	Bridges	42				18	35
Christie	Brinkley	40				20	35
Morgan	Brittany	10				5	20
Matthew	Broderick	25				13	25
Charles	Bronson	50				25	40
Clive	Brook	75	80	80	75	25	30
Louise	Brooks	400	520	480	440	200	240
Mel	Brooks	35				18	30
Garth	Brooks	50				25	35
Rand	Brooks(GWTW)	75	100	90	90	30	40
Pierce	Brosnan	50				15	25
Blair	Brown	20				10	20
Lenny	Bruce	500	650	600	600	250	300
Nigel	Bruce	350	435	400	400	225	265
Yul	Brynner	100	100	90	85	50	50
Frank	Buck	75	90	85	75	30	35
Julie	Budd	10				5	15
Jimmy	Buffett	60				35	45
Gary	Burghoff	20				10	20
Billie	Burke	200	260	240	220	100	120
Carol	Burnett	20				10	20
George	Burns	60				30	60
Burns & Allen	Burns	250				100	120
Raymond	Burr	50				25	40
Richard	Burton	125	160	150	140	50	60
Francis X.	Bushman	200	260	240	220	50	60
Bruce	Cabot	150	195	180	165	50	60
Sebastian	Cabot	150	195	180	165	75	90
Nicholas	Cage	40				18	30
James	Cagney	125	130	120	110	75	75
Michael	Caine	40				20	35
Kirk	Cameron	10				5	20
Dyan	Cannon	10				5	20
Eddie	Cantor	100	130	120	110	50	75
Frank	Capra	75	100	90	85	30	35
Kate	Capshaw	10				5	20
	Capucine	75	100	90	75	30	35
Harry	Carey Sr.	100	130	120	100	50	60
Mary	Carlise	50	60	55	50	20	25
Jean	Carmen	10				5	15
Art	Carney	35				20	30
John	Carradine	100	130	120	110	50	60
Jim	Carrey	40				20	25
Leo	Carrillo (Portrait)	100	130	120	120	40	50
Earl	Carroll	75	90	85	75	30	35
Madeleine	Carroll	100	120	110	110	35	40
Johnny	Carson	40				15	25
Linda	Carter	25				10	20
Johnny	Cash	50				25	35
David	Cassidy	20				10	20
Ted	Cassidy	200	260	240	220	100	120
Phoebe	Cates	35				18	25
Joan	Caulfield	50	60	55	50	25	35
Ruth	Chalterton	200	250	225	220	50	60
Richard	Chamberlain	20				10	20
Marilyn	Chambers	35				18	30
Jeff	Chandler	100	120	110	100	35	40
Lon	Chaney Jr.	750	975	900	900	275	330
Lon	Chaney Sr.	1500	1950	1800	1800	750	900
Charles	Chaplin	1000	1300	1200	1200	400	420
Chevy	Chase	40				20	25
	Cher	50				20	30
Maurice	Chevalier	100	130	120	110	35	40
Julie	Christie	35				18	30
Rene	Clair	100	110	110	100	40	45
Eric	Clapton	75				40	60
Mae	Clark	50	55	55	55	25	30
Andrew Dice	Clay	20				10	20
Montgomery	Clift	300	390	360	360	100	120

ALS : Autograph Letter Signed (written and signed by the same person.) LS : Letter Signed (body of letter written by another person.)
TLS : Typed Letter Signed DS : Document Signed SIG : Signature on paper or card WH CARD : White House Card signed
COVER : Depending on the time period, can be franked envelope, stamped envelope, event or First Day of Issue
*: Hall of Fame D : Deceased

		PHOTO	ALS	LS/TLS	DS	SIG.	COVER
Glenn	Close	25				13	25
Lee J.	Cobb	100	120	110	110	35	50
Charles	Coburn	50	60	55	50	20	25
Steve	Cochran	75	85	85	75	25	30
Claudette	Colbert	75	95	85	85	25	30
Joan	Collins	20				10	20
Ronald	Colman	200	260	240	230	50	60
Jerry	Colonna	75	85	85	75	20	25
Jennifer	Connelly	45				25	35
Sean	Connery (James Bond)	75				40	65
Sean	Connery (Portrait)	75				40	65
Walter	Connolly	75	85	85	75	25	30
Alice	Cooper	50				25	35
Gary	Cooper	250	325	300	300	100	125
Jackie	Cooper	35				18	30
Wendell	Corey	75	95	90	80	25	30
Katherine	Cornell	50	60	60	55	20	25
Bill	Cosby	30				15	25
Dolores	Costello	50	60	55	50	20	25
Lou	Costello	350	425	400	400	150	180
Kevin	Costner	50				25	35
Joseph	Cotton	50	60	55	55	20	40
Courtney	Cox	40				20	30
Buster	Crabbe (As Tarzan)	100	125	120	120	25	40
Yvonne	Craig	25				18	25
Jeanne	Crain	100	120	110	100	25	30
Bob	Crane	225	275	250	250	85	100
Fred	Crane	25				18	25
Broderick	Crawford	100	125	110	110	50	70
Cindy	Crawford	50				25	40
Joan	Crawford	200	250	225	225	50	70
Michael	Crawford	40				20	30
Laura Hope	Crews (GWTW)	250	300	275	275	75	90
Bing	Crosby	125	325	300	75	40	50
Cathy Lee	Crosby	35				18	25
Russell	Crowe	75				30	40
Tom	Cruise	95				40	50
Billy	Crystal	30				15	25
Macaulay	Culkin	35				18	25
Bob	Cummings	50	60	55	55	20	30
Jamie Lee	Curtis	40				20	35
John	Cusack	20				10	20
Dan	Dailey	75	90	85	75	20	25
Timothy	Dalton	40				20	25
Matt	Damon	40				20	25
Dorothy	Dandridge	250	320	300	275	100	120
Bebe	Daniels	75	90	85	75	20	25
Ted	Danson	20				10	20
Tony	Danza	20				10	20
Linda	Darnell	100	120	110	100	50	70
Marion	Davies	100	120	115	100	50	60
Geena	Davis	35				13	20
Jim	Davis	75	90	85	75	25	30
Bette	Davis	100	100	90	90	75	75
Sammy	Davis Jr.	150	160	150	140	100	125
Pam	Dawber	20				10	20
Daniel	Day-Lewis	30				15	20
James	Dean	4500	5750	5400	5250	2000	2400
Yvonne	DeCarlo	35				20	20
Olivia	DeHavilland	50	60	55	55	20	30
Dolores	Del Rio	50	60	55	50	20	30
Dana	Delaney	35				18	25
Peter	DeLuise	10				5	15
Cecil B.	DeMille	200	260	250	240	50	60
Rebecca	DeMornay	25				13	25
Robert	DeNiro	95				35	50
Johnny	Depp	40				20	35
Bo	Derek	50				25	50
Curly Joe	DeRita	75				40	60
Andy	Devine	200	250	225	225	50	60
Danny	Devito	40				20	30
Neil	Diamond	60				25	40
Leonardo	Dicaprio	60				30	40
Angie	Dickinson	35				15	25
Marlene	Dietrich	75	90	85	85	50	60
Matt	Dillon	35				15	25
Celine	Dion	50				25	40

		PHOTO	ALS	LS/TLS	DS	SIG.	COVER
Donna	Dixon	35				15	25
Shannon	Doherty	40				15	25
Robert	Donat	100	120	110	110	25	30
Diana	Dors	100	100	110	100	35	40
Kirk	Douglas	50				25	35
Melvyn	Douglas	50	60	55	55	20	25
Michael	Douglas	40				20	35
Billie	Dove	75	95	90	80	35	40
Leslie Anne	Down	25				12	20
Robert	Downey Jr.	25				12	20
Marie	Dresser	350	450	420	400	75	90
Richard	Dreyfuss	35				12	20
Eddie	Duchin	75	90	85	85	35	40
Howard	Duff	50	60	55	50	20	25
Olympia	Dukakis	20				10	15
Faye	Dunaway	40				20	30
Irene	Dunne	50	60	55	50	20	25
Jimmy	Durante	125	125	120	110	50	50
Robert	Duvall	40				20	30
Clint	Eastwood	75				40	50
Buddy	Ebsen	35				15	20
Barbara	Eden	35				15	20
Anita	Ekberg	50				25	30
Britt	Ekland	50				25	30
Robert	Englund	30				15	20
Melissa	Ethridge	40				20	25
Douglas	Fairbanks Sr.	200	250	240	220	75	90
Peter	Falk	35				15	20
Frances	Farmer	250	320	300	275	100	120
Dustin	Farnum	75	90	85	80	35	40
David	Faustino	20				10	15
Farrah	Fawcett	45				22	30
Marty	Feldman	150	150	165	150	75	90
Edith	Fellows	50	55	55	50	20	25
Jose	Ferrer	50	60	55	50	20	25
Sally	Field	35				15	20
W.C.	Fields	1250	1600	1500	1600	500	600
Peter	Finch	250	300	275	275	75	90
Larry	Fine	450	550	500	475	250	240
Linda	Fiorintino	15				5	15
Carrie	Fisher	40				20	25
Barry	Fitzgerald	300	360	330	340	100	120
Eric	Fleming	250	300	275	260	100	120
Victor	Fleming	1000	1300	1200	1150	400	500
Louise	Fletcher	15				5	15
Joe	Flynn	200	250	225	225	75	100
Errol	Flynn	500	650	600	600	300	360
Jane	Fonda	40				25	35
Henry	Fonda	125	100	90	85	75	75
Peter	Fonda	35				15	20
Joan	Fontaine	50	65	60	55	20	30
Lynn	Fontaine	85	40	40	35	20	30
Glenn	Ford	35				15	25
John	Ford	250	325	300	300	100	120
Harrison	Ford	75				35	50
John	Forsythe	25				12	20
Jodie	Foster	75				35	50
Michael J.	Fox	50				25	40
Samantha	Fox	50				25	35
William	Frawley	350	375	350	350	250	300
Morgan	Freeman	40				15	25
Clark	Gable	950	1200	1150	1100	350	420
Megan	Gallagher	20				10	15
Teri	Garber	25				15	20
Greta	Garbo	7500	9750	9000	9000	2000	2400
Andy	Garcia	40				20	25
Ava	Gardner	75	110	90	85	50	60
John	Garfield	300	375	360	350	100	120
Judy	Garland	800	975	900	900	500	550
James	Garner	35				20	30
Teri	Garr	30				15	20

ALS : Autograph Letter Signed (written and signed by the same person.) LS : Letter Signed (body of letter written by another person.)
TLS : Typed Letter Signed DS : Document Signed SIG : Signature on paper or card WH CARD : White House Card signed
COVER : Depending on the time period, can be franked envelope, stamped envelope, event or First Day of Issue
*: Hall of Fame D : Deceased

		PHOTO	ALS	LS/TLS	DS	SIG.	COVER
Greer	Garson	50				25	35
Janet	Gaynor	75	90	85	80	25	30
Gladys	George	75	90	85	75	25	30
Richard	Gere	60				25	35
Mel	Gibson	95				50	60
John	Gielgud	50				25	35
Billy	Gilbert	75	95	85	80	25	30
John	Gilbert	150	185	165	165	75	90
Melissa	Gilbert	25				10	20
William	Gillette	75	90	85	75	40	45
Lillian	Gish	50	65	60	55	30	35
Jackie	Gleason	250	260	240	240	125	150
Mark	Goddard	20				10	20
Paulette	Goddard	75	95	90	85	30	40
Arthur	Godfrey	50	65	60	55	20	35
Whoopie	Goldberg	30				15	30
Jeff	Goldblum	30				15	25
John	Goodman	30				15	20
Louis	Gossett Jr.	35				20	30
Betty	Grable	200	260	240	240	50	75
Stewart	Granger	35				20	30
Cary	Grant	450	520	480	440	200	250
Bonita	Granville	50	65	60	55	20	25
Sid	Grauman	100	125	110	100	50	60
Gilda	Gray	75	90	85	80	25	30
Sydney	Greenstreet	450	575	540	525	200	240
Jennifer	Grey	35				20	25
Richard	Grieco	20				25	40
Andy	Griffith	60				25	40
D.W.	Griffith	750	975	900	900	200	240
Melanie	Griffith	50				25	30
Charles	Grodin	20				10	15
Alec	Guiness	45				25	35
Fred	Gwynn (as Herman)	150				75	90
Shelley	Hack	15				5	15
Gene	Hackman	40				20	25
Jessica	Hahn	20				10	15
Alan	Hale jr.	200	250	240	240	75	90
Jack	Haley (Portrait)	150	195	180	180	75	90
Jack	Haley (Tin Man)	300	390	360	360	75	90
Fawn	Hall	20				10	15
Jerry	Hall	25				10	15
Huntz	Hall	50				20	25
Billy	Halop(Dead End Kids)	200	260	240	240	50	60
Margaret	Hamilton (Wiz. Oz)	200	260	240	240	75	90
Harry	Hamlin	20				10	20
Tom	Hanks	60				35	60
Daryl	Hannah	30				20	35
Oliver	Hardy	500	650	600	600	200	240
Jean	Harlow	2500	3250	3000	2750	1000	1200
Neil Patrick	Harris	25				15	20
Rex	Harrison	50	65	60	55	25	40
Lisa	Hartman	35				15	25
Laurence	Harvey	100	120	110	110	50	60
Rutger	Hauer	30				15	25
Ethan	Hawke	35				15	20
Goldie	Hawn	40				20	30
Helen	Hayes	50	60	55	55	20	30
Will H.	Hays	100	100	110	100	25	30
Susan	Hayward	250	325	300	300	100	150
Rita	Hayworth	250	325	300	275	100	150
Margaux	Hemingway	100				50	75
Sonja	Henie	100	125	120	110	40	50
Don	Henley	60				30	40
Audrey	Hepburn	250	325	300	300	100	120
Katherine	Hepburn	750	975	900	900	125	120
Barbara	Hershey	35				15	25
Charlton	Heston	35				15	30
Jon-Erik	Hexum	200	240	230	220	100	120
Alfred	Hitchcock	500	650	600	600	250	300
John	Hodiak	100	120	110	110	35	50
Dustin	Hoffman	50				25	40
Paul	Hogan	25				10	20
William	Holden	100	120	110	110	50	75
Judy	Holliday	200	260	240	240	75	100
Kane	Hooder	25				10	20
Bob	Hope	75				40	60

		PHOTO	ALS	LS/TLS	DS	SIG.	COVER
Anthony	Hopkins	50				20	30
Meriam	Hopkins	100	110	110	110	25	30
Dennis	Hopper	40				20	30
Bob	Hoskins	20				10	20
Harry	Houdini	2500	3250	3000	2750	1000	1200
Leslie	Howard	350	450	425	375	100	120
Moe	Howard	450	585	540	525	200	240
Shemp	Howard	750	975	900	850	350	420
Rock	Hudson	200	250	220	220	50	75
Josephine	Hull	200	240	220	220	50	60
Helen	Hunt	50				25	30
Holly	Hunter	30				15	25
Jeffrey	Hunter	100	110	110	100	35	50
Isabelle	Huppert	30				15	20
William	Hurt	45				25	40
Anjelica	Huston	25				15	25
John	Huston	100	110	110	110	25	40
Walter	Huston	100	110	110	110	35	50
Lauren	Hutton	25				15	25
Timothy	Hutton	25				10	20
Thomas	Ince	400	480	440	440	200	240
Jill	Ireland	50	55	55	55	20	30
Jeremy	Irons	30				15	25
Henry	Irving	250	265	265	265	100	120
Glenda	Jackson	20				10	20
Janet	Jackson	100				75	100
Kate	Jackson	50				20	35
Michael	Jackson	150				75	100
Mick	Jagger	125				75	100
Emil	Jannings	250	300	300	275	75	90
David	Janssen	200	240	220	220	50	75
Billy	Joel	60				25	35
Don	Johnson	35				15	25
Al	Jolson (Black Face)	1500	1950	1800	1800		
Al	Jolson (Portrait)	500	650	600	600	100	120
Janet	Jones	30				15	20
James E.	Jones	30				15	20
Jennifer	Jones	250	300	275	275	100	120
Boris	Karloff	500	650	600	600	250	300
Roscoe	Karns	100	110	110	110	25	30
Andy	Kaufman	200	260	240	220	100	120
Danny	Kaye	100	110	110	110	50	75
Buster	Keaton	500	650	600	550	200	
Diane	Keaton	40				20	30
Michael	Keaton (Batman)	50				25	35
Michael	Keaton (Portrait)	35				25	35
Harry	Kellar	500	600	550	550	250	300
Cecil	Kellaway	100	110	110	100	50	60
Marthe	Keller	25				10	20
Deforest	Kelly	50				25	30
Gene	Kelly	75				35	50
Grace	Kelly	450	585	540	525	200	250
Paul	Kelly	100	110	110	100	25	30
Emmett	Kelly Sr.	200	260	240	220	75	100
Edgar	Kennedy	100	100	110	100	30	35
George	Kennedy	20				25	30
Deborah	Kerr	50	60	55		20	30
Persis	Khambatta	50				25	30
Margot	Kidder	40				20	30
Val	Kilmer	60				35	40
B.B.	King	50				25	35
Cammie	King	50				25	30
Ben	Kingsley	40				20	25
Natassia	Kinski	60				35	40
Ertha	Kitt	50				25	30
Werner	Klemperer	50				25	30
Don	Knotts	25				10	15
Sylvia	Kristel	50				25	30
Kris	Kristofferson	40				20	30
Alan	Ladd	100	110	110	100	50	75
Cheryl	Ladd	40				20	25

ALS : Autograph Letter Signed (written and signed by the same person.) LS : Letter Signed (body of letter written by another person.)
TLS : Typed Letter Signed DS : Document Signed SIG : Signature on paper or card WH CARD : White House Card signed
COVER : Depending on the time period, can be franked envelope, stamped envelope, event or First Day of Issue
*: Hall of Fame D : Deceased

		PHOTO	ALS	LS/TLS	DS	SIG.	COVER
Bert	Lahr (as Cowardly Lion)	5000	6500	6000	6000		7200
Veronica	Lake	300	375	360	360	100	120
Arthur	Lake (Dagwood)	150	190	180	180	50	60
Hedy	Lamarr	75				35	40
Dorothy	Lamour	50				25	30
Burt	Lancaster	95				40	50
Elsa	Lanchester	100	110	110	110	50	60
Elissa	Landi	100	100	110	100	25	30
Carole	Landis	200	240	220	220	50	75
Michael	Landon	125	125	120	120	60	75
Diane	Lane	45				25	30
Harry	Langdon	250	300	290	275	100	120
Jessica	Lange	45				25	30
Lillie	Langtry	450	585	540	540	250	300
Angela	Lansbury	35				20	25
Charles	Laughton	250	300	290	290	75	100
Stan	Laurel	500	650	600	600	200	
	Laurel & Hardy	1500				500	1000
Peter	Lawford	300	240	230	230	100	150
Gertrude	Lawrence	100	130	120	110	25	40
Kelly	LeBrock	35				20	25
Bruce	Lee	2000	2600	2400	2400	650	1200
Gordon "Porky"	Lee	40				20	25
Gypsy Rose	Lee	200	260	240	220	50	60
Spike	Lee	30				15	20
Lila	Lee	50	55	55	50	20	25
Janet	Leigh	40				35	40
Vivien	Leigh	750	975	900	900	350	420
Jack	Lemmon	50				35	40
Jay	Leno	30				15	20
David	Letterman	40				20	25
Elmo	Lincoln (Tarzan)	1000	1300	1200	1200	300	360
Jenny	Lind	400	500	450	450	100	120
Mary	Livingston	100	120	110	110	50	60
Emily	Lloyd	25				12	15
Harold	Lloyd	350	450	400	375	100	120
Heather	Locklear	50				25	30
Robert	Loggia	20				10	15
Gina	Lollobrigida	50				25	30
Carole	Lombard	750	975	900	900	300	360
Shelley	Long	35				15	20
Jennifer	Lopez	50				25	40
Sophia	Loren	50				20	25
Peter	Lorre	350	450	400	400	200	240
Anita	Louise	50	60	55	50	20	25
Bessie	Love	75	85	80	75	25	30
Rob	Lowe	45				20	25
Myrna	Loy	50	60	55	50	20	25
George	Lucas	75				40	50
Bella	Lugosi (Dracula)	2000	2600	2400	2400		
Bella	Lugosi (Portrait)	1000	1300	1200	1200	400	480
Paul	Lukas	150	180	165	165	30	35
Alfred	Lunt	50	60	55	55	20	25
Kelly	Lynch	25				12	20
Carol	Lynley	35				20	30
Bert	Lytell	50	55	55	50	20	25
Ralph	Macchio	25				15	25
Andie	MacDowell	30				15	20
Marion	Mack	35				15	20
Shirley	MacLaine	45				20	30
Fred	MacMurray	75	60	55	55	35	50
Virginia	Madsen	35				15	20
Anna	Magnani	300	390	360	360	100	120
Jock	Mahoney (Tarzan)	100	130	120	120	40	50
Marjorie	Main	200	260	240	240	75	90
Jayne	Mansfield	450	520	480	450	250	300
Frederic	March	100	120	110	110	50	60
Ann	Margaret	50				20	18
Enid	Markey (First Jane)	250	325	300	275	100	120
Mae	Marsh	100	110	110	100	25	30
Dean	Martin	100				50	75
Mary	Martin	50	60	55	50	20	25
Pamela Sue	Martin	30				15	20
Ricky	Martin	50				25	35
Steve	Martin	40				20	30
Lee	Marvin	150	120	110	110	75	75
Chico	Marx	350	420	400	420	200	240

		PHOTO	ALS	LS/TLS	DS	SIG.	COVER
Groucho	Marx	400	450	420		200	240
Harpo	Marx	400	520	480	480	200	240
Zeppo	Marx	250	325	300	325	100	120
	Marx Brothers	2500				1000	1200
James	Mason	75	90	85	80	25	30
Raymond	Massey	50	60	55	55	20	25
Mary S.	Masterson	30				15	20
Marlee	Matlin	30				15	25
Victor	Mature	50				25	30
Louis	Mayer	250	325	300	300	100	120
David	McCallum	30				15	20
Hattie	Mcdaniel (Portrait)	750	975	900	900		
Hattie	Mcdaniel (Portrait)	1000	1300	1200	1200	450	550
Roddy	McDowell	60				30	35
Reba	McEntire	35				15	20
Kelly	McGillis	30				20	25
Elizabeth	McGovern	30				15	20
Ali	McGraw	25				12	20
Tim	McGraw	35				15	20
Nancy	Mckeon	25				12	20
Kyle	McLachlin	25				12	20
Victor	Mclaglen	200	250	225	225	75	90
Butterfly	McQueen	50				25	30
Steve	McQueen	400	450	425	375	250	300
Adolph	Menjou	75	90	85	80	20	25
Una	Menkel	75	90	85	80	20	25
Burgess	Meredith (Penquin)	75				35	40
Burgess	Meredith (Portrait)	35				20	30
Ethel	Merman	75	100	90	80	25	30
Robert	Merrill	30				15	25
Bette	Midler	50				25	50
Alyssa	Milano	40				15	20
Vera	Miles	25				12	25
Ray	Milland	50	60	55	55	20	25
Marilyn	Miller	125	150	140	130	50	60
Denny	Miller (Tarzan)	50	60	55	60	20	25
Donna	Mills	25				12	20
Sal	Mineo	200	260	240	240	75	90
Liza	Minnelli	40				20	30
Carmen	Miranda	200	260	240	240	100	120
Cameron	Mitchell	50	60	55	50	20	25
Robert	Mitchum	60				30	40
Richard	Moll	20				10	20
Marilyn	Monroe	5000	6500	6000	6000	1500	1800
Maria	Montez	250	325	300	300	75	90
Robert	Montgomery	50	60	55	55	20	25
Colleen	Moore	50	60	55	50	20	25
Dudley	Moore	60				25	30
Grace	Moore	50	60	55	55	20	25
Mary Tyler	Moore	35				20	30
Demi	Moore	75				40	50
Roger	Moore (007)	65				35	50
Roger	Moore (Portrait)	50				25	35
Rick	Moranis	20				10	20
Antonio	Moreno	75	85	80	75	25	30
Frank	Morgan (Portrait)	450	585	540	525	250	300
	Morganna	25				12	20
Pat	Morita	20				10	20
Chester	Morris	50	60	55	50	20	25
Vic	Morrow	200	240	225	230	75	90
Kate	Mulgrew	40				20	25
Bill	Mumy	35				15	20
Caroline	Munro	75				35	40
Audie	Murphy	350	390	360	360	250	300
Eddie	Murphy	75				40	50
George	Murphy	50	60	55	55	10	12
Mike	Myers	40				20	25
Jim	Nabors	35				20	25
Conrad	Nagel	75	90	85	80	15	18
J. Carrol	Naish	100	115	110	110	20	25
Nita	Naldi	100	120	110	110	25	30

ALS : Autograph Letter Signed (written and signed by the same person.) LS : Letter Signed (body of letter written by another person.)
TLS : Typed Letter Signed DS : Document Signed SIG : Signature on paper or card WH CARD : White House Card signed
COVER : Depending on the time period, can be franked envelope, stamped envelope, event or First Day of Issue
*: Hall of Fame D : Deceased

		PHOTO	ALS	LS/TLS	DS	SIG.	COVER
Alla	Nazimova	200	240	225	225	75	90
Patricia	Neal	35				15	25
Pola	Negri	200	260	240	240	75	90
Ozzie	Nelson	200	240	230	230	50	75
Paul	Newman	125				60	75
Julie	Newmar	35				15	20
Olivia	Newton John	35				15	25
Michelle	Nichols	35				15	20
Jack	Nicholson (Portrait)	65				35	50
Stevie	Nicks	75				40	50
Bridgette	Nielson	25				15	25
Leonard	Nimoy	60				30	40
David	Niven	50	60	55	55	25	30
Nick	Nolte	30				15	25
Mabel	Normand	500	625	600	600	250	300
Chuck	Norris	25				12	20
Jay	North	30				15	20
Kim	Novak	35				15	25
Edmond	O'Brien	100	115	110	110	35	40
Pat	O'Brien	50	60	55	55	20	25
Carroll	O'Connor	40				20	25
Rosie	O'Donnell	40				20	25
Tatum	O'Neal	35				15	20
Ed	O'Neill	20				10	20
Maureen	O'Sullivan	40				20	25
Maureen	O'Sullivan (as Jane)	50	65	60	60	25	30
Peter	O'Toole	75	90	85	80	25	30
Merle	Oberon	100	120	110	110	50	60
Warner	Oland	250	325	300	300	100	120
Lena	Olin	25				12	20
Lawrence	Olivier	100	100	90	90	50	60
Ozzy	Osborne	75				30	50
Maria	Ouspenskaya	375	485	450	425	200	240
Al	Pacino	75				40	50
Geraldine	Page	50	60	55	55	20	25
Debra	Paget	50				25	30
Gwyneth	Paltrow	50				20	35
Larry	Parks	200	260	240	240	50	60
Butch	Patrick	30				15	20
Gregory	Peck	50				25	35
Sean	Penn	40				20	25
George	Peppard	40				20	35
Elizabeth	Perkins	20				10	20
Tom	Petty	60				30	40
Michelle	Pfeiffer	75				35	40
River	Pheonix	200				100	125
Lou Diamond	Phillips	30				15	20
Michelle	Phillips	25				12	20
Mary	Pickford	75	90	85	85	25	35
Walter	Pidgeon	75	90	85	85	20	30
James	Pierce (Tarzan)	100	130	120	110	20	25
Brad	Pitt	60				25	35
Susanne	Pleshette	25				12	20
Martha	Plimpton	25				12	20
Christopher	Plummer	30				15	20
Sidney	Poitier	50				25	40
Lily	Pons	100	120	110	110	20	30
Markie	Post	30				15	20
Dick	Powell	100	120	110	110	20	30
Jane	Powell	35				15	25
William	Powell	150	195	175	165	50	60
Tyrone	Power	200	260	240	230	75	90
Otto	Preminger	75	100	90	90	20	30
Elvis	Presley	1200	2000	1000	1000	600	1000
Priscilla	Presley	40				20	25
Kelly	Preston	25				12	25
Robert	Preston	50	60	55	55	20	30
Vincent	Price	75	100	90	90	35	40
Freddie	Prinze	250	325	300	300	100	120
Jan	Provost	35				15	20
Dennis	Quaid	40				20	25
Anthony	Quinn	60				35	40
Gilda	Radner	200	240	220	220	100	120
George	Raft	100	130	120	110	25	35
Luise	Rainer	75	100	90	90	20	25
Claude	Rains	250	325	300		100	120
Esther	Ralston	65	75	70	70	20	25

		PHOTO	ALS	LS/TLS	DS	SIG.	COVER
Vera	Ralston	50	60	55	55	20	30
Sally	Rand	65	75	70	70	20	25
Basil	Rathbone (Portrait)	500	650	600	600	150	100
Basil	Rathbone (S.H.)	2000	2600	2400	2400		
Martha	Raye	30				15	25
Robert	Redford	95				40	50
Vanessa	Redgrave	40				20	25
Donna	Reed	125	160	150	135	50	75
Christopher	Reeve (Portrait)	75				35	40
Christopher	Reeve (Superman)	150				75	75
Keanu	Reeves	50				25	30
George	Reeves (as Superman)	3000	3900	3600	3600		
George	Reeves (Portrait)	1000	1300	1200	1200	500	600
Wallace	Reid	300	350	330	300	100	120
Burt	Reynolds	35				15	25
Cynthia	Rhodes	25				12	20
Donna	Rice	25				12	20
Keith	Richards	75				40	60
Molly	Ringwald	30				15	20
John	Ritter	20				10	20
Thelma	Ritter	150	180	165	160	50	60
Joan	Rivers	20				10	25
Hal	Roach	100	110	110	100	50	50
Marty	Robbins	100	110	110	100	50	60
Julia	Roberts	75				35	25
Tanya	Roberts	40				20	30
Cliff	Robertson	25				12	25
Paul	Robeson	300	390	360	360	100	120
Edward G.	Robinson	200	180	165	165	100	125
May	Robson	50	55	55	50	20	25
	Rochester (Eddie Anderson)	200	260	240	220	75	90
Ginger	Rogers	95	95	85	80	60	60
Mimi	Rogers	25				15	25
Will	Rogers	400	520	480	480	200	240
Gilbert	Roland	40				20	30
Cesar	Romero	50				25	35
Micky	Rooney	40				20	30
S.O.	Roselline	35				15	20
Mickey	Rourke	35				15	25
Alma	Rubens	100	110	110	100	50	60
Jane	Russell	40				20	35
John	Russell	50	55	55	50	20	25
Kurt	Russell	40				20	25
Lillian	Russell	200	240	220	220	75	90
Rosalind	Russell	100	110	110	100	25	30
Rene	Russo	40				20	25
Ann	Rutherford	40				20	25
Ann	Rutherford (GWTW)	75	95	90	90	20	25
Meg	Ryan	75				35	40
Robert	Ryan	100	110	110	100	20	35
Irene	Ryan (as Granny)	200	260	240	240	100	120
Winona	Ryder	75				35	40
	Sabu	200	260	240	240	50	60
Katey	Sagal	25				10	20
S.Z.	Sakall	150	180	165	160	50	60
Emma	Samms	20				10	20
George	Sanders	150	180	165	160	50	60
Adam	Sandler	35				15	20
Laura	Sangiacomo	30				15	20
Carlos	Santana	50				25	35
Susan	Sarandon	30				15	25
Fred	Savage	25				12	20
Maximillian	Schell	45				22	30
Claudia	Schiffer	50				25	30
Arnold	Schwarzenegger	100				50	60
Paul	Scofield	45				22	35
Tracy	Scoggins	30				15	20
Gordon	Scott	35				15	20
Zachary	Scott	125	150	140	135	35	40
Steven	Segal	40				20	30
Jerry	Seinfeld	50				25	35

ALS : Autograph Letter Signed (written and signed by the same person.) LS : Letter Signed (body of letter written by another person.)
TLS : Typed Letter Signed DS : Document Signed SIG : Signature on paper or card WH CARD : White House Card signed
COVER : Depending on the time period, can be franked envelope, stamped envelope, event or First Day of Issue
*: Hall of Fame D : Deceased

		PHOTO	ALS	LS/TLS	DS	SIG.	COVER
Connie	Sellecca	30				15	20
Tom	Selleck	40				20	25
Peter	Sellers	200	250	240	225	100	120
David O.	Selznick	250	320	300	275	75	90
Mack	Sennett	500	650	600	600	200	240
Joan	Severance	25				10	20
Jane	Seymour	40				20	30
William	Shatner (Star Trek)	75				40	45
Norma	Shearer	100	120	110	110	35	50
Ally	Sheedy	35				17	25
Charles	Sheen	35				17	25
John "Boy"	Sheffield	35				15	20
Cybil	Shepherd	40				20	35
Ann	Sheridan	150	180	165	160	50	60
Nicollette	Sheridan	40				20	25
Brooke	Shields	40				20	30
Simone	Signoret	100	120	110	110	20	40
Jay	Silverheels	400	520	480	480	200	240
Phil	Silvers	100	110	110	100	50	60
Red	Skelton	75	90	85	85	40	60
Christian	Slater	45				22	30
Jaclyn	Smith	40				20	30
Maggie	Smith	35				17	25
Suzanne	Somers	40				20	25
Elke	Sommer	35				20	25
Sissy	Spacek	50				25	50
Kevin	Spacey	60				35	40
Britney	Spears	75				35	40
Steven	Spielberg	100				50	60
Bruce	Springsteen	75				40	60
Robert	Stack	25				12	20
Sylvester	Stallone	75				35	40
John	Stamos	30				15	20
Barbara	Stanwyck	75	90	85	85	25	40
Ringo	Starr	125				75	100
Rod	Steiger	40				20	25
Trish	Sterling	25				12	20
Inger	Stevens	200	240	220	210	75	90
Stella	Stevens	25				12	20
Patrick	Stewart	50				25	35
Rod	Stewart	60				35	40
James	Stewart (Portrait)	75				35	50
James	Stewart (Rabbit sketch)	400				200	240
	Sting	50				25	35
Dean	Stockwell	25				12	20
Sharon	Stone	75				35	50
Dorothy	Stratten	750	920	900	900	500	600
Meryl	Streep	75				35	50
Ed	Sullivan	100	110	110	100	25	30
Slim	Summerville	75	85	75	75	20	25
Donald	Sutherland	40				20	30
Frank	Sutton	125	110	100	100	50	50
Hillary	Swank	40				20	25
Gloria	Swanson	100	130	120	110	35	40
Patrick	Swayze	40				20	25
George	Takei	35				17	20
Jessica	Tandy	40				20	30
Lilyan	Tashman	50	55	50	50	25	30
Sharon	Tate	1000	1300	1200	1200	500	600
Elizabeth	Taylor	250				125	150
Robert	Taylor	100	110	100	100	45	60
Shirley	Temple (Pre 1950's)	250	325	300	300	100	125
Irving	Thalberg	500	650	600	600	200	240
Heather	Thomas	40				20	25
Lea	Thompson	35				17	20
	Three Stooges (W/ Curley)	2500				1250	1500
Howard	Thurston	450	550	500	500	100	120
Cheryl	Tiegs	35				17	25
Gene	Tierney	75	90	85	85	30	50
Meg	Tilly	35				15	20
Thelma	Todd	400	480	440	440	200	240
Sidney	Toler (as Chan)	400	520	480	480	200	240
Spencer	Tracy	400	520	480	480	200	250
Kathleen	Turner	35				15	25
Lana	Turner	75				35	50
Lana	Turner	75	95	85	80	25	50
Janine	Turner	25				15	20

310

		PHOTO	ALS	LS/TLS	DS	SIG.	COVER
Tina	Turner	60				35	40
Ben	Turpin	300	390	360	360	100	120
Shania	Twain	40				20	25
Shannon	Tweed	35				15	25
Tracy	Ullman	20				10	20
Rudolph	Valentino	1500	1950	1800	1800	500	600
Vivian	Vance	300	390	360	360	200	240
Mamie	VanDoren	40				20	25
Conrad	Veidt	200	250	225	225	50	60
Lupe	Velez	250	325	275	275	50	60
Jon	Voight	35				17	25
Erich	Von Stroheim	400	520	480	440	75	90
Robert	Wagner	35				17	30
Ken	Wahl	30				15	20
Christopher	Walken	45				25	30
Burt	Ward	45				22	25
Rachel	Ward	40				20	30
Jack	Warden	20				10	20
Jack	Warner	200	260	220	220	35	40
Denzel	Washington	50				25	35
David	Wayne	30				15	20
Carol	Wayne	150	125			35	120
John	Wayne (Portrait)	800	1000		800	400	450
Shawn	Weatherly	20				10	20
Charles	Weaver						60
Sigourney	Weaver	35				17	25
Jack	Webb	100			75	45	60
Johnny	Weissmuller (Tarzan)	400			300	150	200
Raquel	Welch	50				25	35
Orson	Welles	350			450	125	150
Adam	West	45				25	30
Diane	West	30				15	20
Mae	West	250			115	55	70
Joanne	Whalley-Kilmer	30				15	20
Gene	Wilder	35				17	25
Esther	Williams	50				25	40
Van	Williams	45				22	30
Bruce	Willis	75				40	50
Debra	Winger	40				25	35
Roland	Winters (as Chan)	75	75		45	30	60
Anna May	Wong	175	150		150	75	60
Natalie	Wood	100	125	125			120
Joanne	Woodward	35				15	25
Fay	Wray	75				40	50
Fay	Wray (King Kong)	50	75	75		25	30
Teresa	Wright	50				25	30
Jane	Wyman	35	50	50		15	25
Ed	Wynn	50	75	75	35	25	30
Sean	Young	30				15	20
Loretta	Young	50	50	50		25	30
Gig	Young	75	75		50	30	50
Florence	Ziegfield Jr.	300	500		350	200	250
Daphne	Zuniga	30				15	20

GROUP AUTOGRAPHS

	PHOTO
Don Adams & B. Feldon	75
Addams Family, The	500
All In The Family	100
Andy Griffith Show (Complete)	500
Andy Griffith Show (3)	200
Fred Astaire/Ginger Rogers	350
Barnaby Jones	75
Barney Miller	350
Batman & Joker (Nicholson, Keaton)	75
Batman & Robin (West, Ward)	75
Beverely Hillbillies (4)	200
Big Valley	400
Bob Cummings Show	75
Bonanza	600
Charles Bronson/Jill Ireland	75
Cagney & Lacey	75
Charlies Angels (Original)	200
Crosby & Rashad	75
Dallas (Original)	300
Designing Women (4) (Original)	100
Family Ties	100
Father Knows Best	200
Gilligan's Island (Original)	500
Golden Girls	100
Gone With the Wind (DeHavilland, Brooks, McQueen, & Rutherford)	200
Grease (Travolta, Olivia Newton-John)	100

GROUP AUTOGRAPHS

	PHOTO
Happy Days (Howard & Winkler)	75
Honeymooners, The	400
I Dream of Jeannie	150
Knot's Landing (6)	100
LA Law (3)	75
Laugh In (Rowan & Martin)	100
Leave it to Beaver	200
Lost in Space	350
Lucy & Desi (First Name)	250
Lucy & Desi (Full Names)	450
Dean Martin/Jerry Lewis	275
Mash	500
Midnight Caller (5)	100
Moonlighting	100
"Munsters, The"	500
Nabors & Knotts	100
Odd Couple	75
Perfect Strangers	75
Psycho (Perkins & Leigh)	200
Shatner & Nimoy	100
Smothers Brothers	50
Star Trek (3)	125
Star Trek (6)	500
Steel Magnolias	100
Jessica Tandy & Morgan Freeman	75
Three Amigos	100
Young Guns	250

311

	PHOTO	ALS	LS/TLS	DS	SIG.	COVER
Louis J.R. Agassiz	600	250			100	200
George Airy	50	250				
Andre Marie Ampere		1000			250	500
Charles Babbage		550			200	400
John Logie Baird	450			300	150	300
Frederick S. Banting	900	1500		1000	600	1200
Alexander Graham Bell	2500	1800		1200	500	1000
Jons Jakob Berzelius		475		165	75	150
Theodor Billroth		295		225	75	150
Aage Niels Bohr	55				25	50
William Bond		350		190	45	90
Max Born		575		350	175	350
William Henry Bragg				95	45	90
Robert W. Bunsen	1250	900		400	175	350
Luther Burbank	165	290		275	115	230
David Bushnell		1250		750	250	500
Richard E. Byrd	325	450		275	75	150
Rachel Carson	275	285		205	70	140
George Washington Carver	1750	700			200	400
Edith Cavell		750		375	225	450
Dr. Charles A. Cheever	75			100	40	80
Robert A. Chesebrough		50		30	15	30
Samul Colt		2750		2000	500	1000
George W. Corner	100			150	75	150
Marie Curie	SCARCE	2600		1550	1050	2100
Harvey Cushing		675		475	165	330
Louis J. Daguerre		1250		490	250	500
Charles Darwin	RARE	1750		1600	750	1500
Dr. Lee Dubridge	50	145		100	30	60
Charles Duryea	RARE	SCARCE		450	150	300
James Buchanan Eads		450		300	100	200
George Eastman	1500	3000		1200	800	1200
Arthur Eddington		150		125	25	50
Thomas A. Edison	2500	2000	1200	750	400	1400
Alexandre G. Eiffel	1250	900		600	300	600
Albert Einstein	2750	3500		1800	900	1800
Havelock Ellis	275	155			35	70
John Ericson		400		195	75	150
Michael Faraday	650	450			175	350
John Flamstead				975	800	1600
John Ambrose Fleming		145		65	25	50
Sir Alexander Fleming	900	750		600	225	450
Sigmund Freud	6000	4500		3500	1650	3300
Robert Fulton	RARE	2500		1300	325	650
Richard J. Gatling		2500		1200	400	800
Robert H. Goddard	SCARCE	1425		1750	450	900
Joseph Guillotin	SCARCE	SCARCE		SCARCE	275	550
Johannes Hagen		100		40	15	30
Otto Hahn	350	SCARCE		300	150	300
George Hale				100	25	50
Joseph Henry		250		200	55	110
John Herschel		675		475	150	300
William Herschel		675		475	150	300
Werner Heisenberg		650		225	75	150
Elias Howe	SCARCE	SCARCE		SCARCE	400	800
Edwin Hubble				60	20	40
Thomas H. Huxley		235		150	65	130
Edward Jenner	SCARCE	SCARCE		850	450	900
Sir William Jenner		295		110	35	70
Karl Gustav Jung		3500		1500	600	1200
Hogo Junker		300			50	100
Dr. Alfred Kinsey	250	350		225	150	300
Robert Koch	1500	2200		1200		
Simon Lake		450		150	60	120
Antoine Lavoisier	RARE	RARE		RARE	750	1500
Carolus Linnaeus	RARE	RARE		RARE	925	1850
Joseph Lister		600		400	225	450
Sir Oliver J. Lodge	250	225		130	90	180
Nevil Maskelyne		405		250	85	170
Hudson Maxim	175	175		150	60	120
Sir Hiram S. Maxim	300	375		190	95	190
Dr. Charles H. Mayo	475	380		290	140	280
Dr. William J. Mayo	475	380		290	105	210
Cyrus H. McCormick		2000		850	350	700
Gregor Mendel		2000		850	400	800
Karl Menninger	60	75		65	30	60
Albert Michelson		450			120	240

	PHOTO	ALS	LS/TLS	DS	SIG.	COVER
Robert Millikan	200	400		200	100	200
Maria Montessori		900			295	590
Samuel F.B. Morse	RARE	1250			550	1100
John Muir		1950		1450	600	1200
Sir Isaac Newton	RARE	25000		12000	4000	8000
Florence Nightingale		750		750	450	900
Alfred Nobel	450	400			250	500
John H. Northrop	100			150	50	100
Herman Oberth	250			200	72	144
Louis Pasteur	RARE	1750		900	500	1000
Linus Pauling	125	400		250	60	120
Emile Picard		400		200	75	150
Julian Pond		300			100	200
Joseph Priestly		1400		900	350	700
George M. Pullman		500		450	225	450
Sir William Ramsey		450		300	150	300
Otto Rank		400			200	400
Walter Reed	675	RARE		750	400	800
David Rittenhouse	RARE	RARE		1100	850	1700
Wilhelm Roentgen		2400		1300	650	1300
Dr. Jonas Salk	200	250		150	45	90
Dr. Albert Schweitzer	750	550			150	300
Glenn Seaborg	75	150		75	40	80
Ignaz Semmelweis	RARE	RARE		900	500	1000
Herlow Shapley		150		150	50	100
William Shockley	100	150		100	45	90
Igor Sikorsky	275	300		225	85	170
Herbert Spencer		200		125	50	100
Dr. Benjamin Spock	50	100		75	35	70
Charles Steinmetz		300		150	75	150
George Stephenson		750		350	225	450
William Talbot		900			300	600
Edward Teller	90	250		125	35	75
Nikola Tesla	1250	1250		850	400	800
James VanAllen	100	200		100	40	80
Alessandro Volta	RARE	2500		1400	600	1200
Dr. Hugo Voneckener	550	550		400	200	400
Werner Vonbraun	400	550		400	150	300
Mary E. Walker	RARE	550			300	600
Benjamin Waterhouse		1650		600	250	500
James Watt		1400		750	400	800
Eli Whitney	RARE	3500		2500	750	1500

WESTERN - BUSINESS & FINANCIAL FIGURES

	PHOTO	ALS	LS/TLS	DS	SIG.	COVER
James G. Fair		110		145	30	60
John Mackay		200		100	50	100
D.O. Mills		2000		750	250	500
William Sharon		200		100	50	100
Francis M. "Borax" Smith		75		60	30	60
Adolph Sutro		150		90	35	70
Orion Clemens		200			125	250
James W. Nye		75		125	75	150
William M. Stewart		65		45	30	60

WESTERN-VINTAGE & DECEASED

	PHOTO	ALS	LS/TLS	DS	SIG.	COVER
Buddy Allen	100				50	60
Gene Autry	100				50	75
Don "Red" Berry	75				25	30
Dan Blocker (Bonanza)	300				100	125
Richard Boone (Paladin)	200				100	125
Bill Boyd	275				100	115
Johnny Mack Brown	200				50	60
Smiley Burnette	200				50	60
Rod Cameron	100				35	40
Yakima Canutt	100				35	40
Leo Carrillo (Pancho)	250				50	60
Sunset Carson	75				25	30
Chuck Connors	75				25	35
Jim Davis	75				25	30

ALS : Autograph Letter Signed (written and signed by the same person.) **LS** : Letter Signed (body of letter written by another person.)
TLS : Typed Letter Signed **DS** : Document Signed **SIG** : Signature on paper or card **WH CARD** : White House Card signed
COVER : Depending on the time period, can be franked envelope, stamped envelope, event or First Day of Issue
*: Hall of Fame **D** : Deceased

	PHOTO	ALS	LS/TLS	DS	SIG.	COVER
Andy Devine	200				50	60
Wild Bill Elliott	250				50	60
Hoot Gibson	300				100	125
Kirby Grant	75				25	30
Lorne Greene	75				25	30
William S. Hart	225				50	60
Russell Hayden	75				25	30
Gabby Hayes	350				100	115
Jack Holt	75				50	55
Tim Holt	200				75	85
Buck Jones	400				125	140
Bob Livingston	75				25	30
Ken Maynard	200				50	55
Tim McCoy	200				50	60
Joel McCrea	50				25	30
Tom Mix	450				200	225
Slim Pickens	75				25	30
Duncan Renaldo (Cisco Kid)	125				50	60
Tex Ritter	100				40	50
Randolph Scott	100				25	35
Jay Silverheels	400				200	250
Charles Durango Starrett	50				25	30
Bob Steele	75				25	35
Tom Tyler	250				100	115
Lee Van Cleef	75				30	35
Jimmy Wakely	75				30	35
John Wayne	750				400	450
Chill Wills	50				25	30

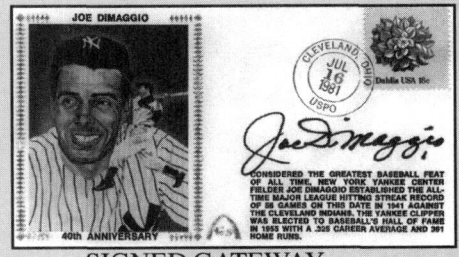

		SIG.(CUT)	3X5 CARD	PHOTO	SIG BBC	DS/TLS	* PLAK	SIG. CHK	COVER	BALL
*	Hank Aaron	20	40	60	40	100	45	45	40	75
	Roberto Alomar	5	15	25	10					35
*-D	Grover C. Alexander	325	650	1250	1250	2000	2000		750	8000
*-D	Walt Alston	20	40	100	40	100	175	75	50	750
*	Sparky Anderson	5	10	25	10		35		25	35
*-D	Cap Anson	1250	2000			2500		5000		
*	Luis Aparicio	12	20	25	15	75	20	300	25	30
*-D	Luke Appling	5	10	30	20	50	20		35	75
*-D	Richie Ashburn	5	15	25	15	75	30	60	30	75
*-D	Earl Averill Sr.	10	15	75	20	100	25	275	50	500
	Jeff Bagwell	5	15	30	10					35
*-D	Franklin "Home Run" Baker	200	350	750	600	1200	1250	2000	500	4000
*-D	Dave Bancroft	60	120	400	250	400	1000		200	3250
*	Ernie Banks	10	20	40	25	75	20	45	30	75
*-D	Al Barlick	5	15	25	20	75	20	40	25	50
*-D	Ed Barrow	50	150	300		300		150	150	3000
*-D	Jake Beckley	2000				4000				
*-D	James"Cool Papa" Bell	10	20	50	30	300	40	400	50	250
	Albert Belle	10	25	40	25					40
*	Johnny Bench	15	25	30	15	50	30	500	30	40
*-D	Chief Bender	175	350	500		750		900	400	3500
D	Moe Berg	100	250	600	400	1500		400		2000
*-D	Yogi Berra	10	15	40	20	50	25		30	60
	Wade Boggs	10	20	25	15				35	45
	Barry Bonds	35	60	95	60				75	150
*-D	Jim Bottomley	150	300	750	450	850		2250	500	4000
D	Ken Boyer	25	50	200	125	250			125	650
*	Lou Boudreau	5	10	25	10	50	12	45	25	30
*-D	Roger Breshnahan	400	800			1500			1500	12500
*	George Brett	15	30	40	25	100	80		40	75
*	Lou Brock	5	15	25	15	50	15	250	25	40
*-D	Dan Brouthers	4000				7500				
*-D	Mordecai Brown (3 finger)	300	550	1250		1500			750	5000
*-D	Morgan Bulkeley	2200				5000		3000		
*	Jim Bunning	5	15	25	15	50	25		25	40
*-D	Jesse Burkett	450	750	2500	1250	1000	2000	2500	800	5000
*-D	Roy Campanella (Pre Accid.)	300	500	1500	800	1500			800	4500
*-D	Roy Campanella (Post Accid.)	150	250	500	300		500		500	
	Jose Canseco	10	20	30	20				40	45
*	Rod Carew	10	25	40	15	50	25		25	50
*-D	Max Carey	15	30	150	50	125	75	50	75	500
*	Gary Carter	5	20	30	20		40		25	45
*-D	Alexander Cartwright	1200				2000		3000		
D	Norm Cash	30	65	175	60				100	750
*	Orlando Cepeda	5	10	20	15	50	30		25	30
*-D	Henry Chadwick	2000				4000				
*-D	Frank Chance	900				3000				
*-D	Albert "Happy" Chandler	12	25	50	25	100	25	150	40	75
*-D	Oscar Charleston	1250	2000			5000				
*-D	Jack Chesbro	1250	2000			4000		15000		
*-D	Nestor Chylak	150	300	800	400	500			600	2200
D	Eddie Cicotte (1919 CWS)	200	300	500		2500			500	2000
	Will Clark	5	10	25	15				25	30
*-D	Fred Clarke	150	275	500	500	1000	800		300	2500
*-D	John Clarkson	2500				4000				
	Roger Clemens	15	40	60	30				75	100
*-D	Roberto Clemente	300	650	1250	700	2000		1400	750	4000
*-D	Ty Cobb	300	600	2500	1000	2500	1750	1000	1000	7500
*-D	Mickey Cochrane	100	225	600	400	1500	900	250	250	4000
	Rocky Colavito	5	15	25	15			30	30	40
*-D	Eddie Collins	150	350	1000		400	3500	2000	600	4000
*-D	Jimmy Collins	800	1500			3000				5000

* : Hall of Fame D : Deceased

		SIG.(CUT)	3X5 CARD	PHOTO	SIG BBC	DS/TLS	* PLAK	SIG. CHK	COVER	BALL
*-D	Earle Combs	35	75	300	75	500	175	175	150	1500
*-D	Charles Comiskey	600	900	2000		1750		6500		
	David Cone	5	10	20	10				25	30
D	Tony Conigliaro	50	100	250	100				175	500
*-D	Jocko Conlan	10	15	35	20	75	25		35	100
*-D	Thomas Connolly	300	500			750	1750		1500	4000
*-D	Roger Connor	5000				10000				
*-D	Stan Coveleski	10	15	75	30	100	35		40	400
*-D	Sam "Wahoo" Crawford	100	200	500	400	1500	300		200	2500
*-D	Joe Cronin	15	30	75	50	100	50	150	75	600
*-D	Candy Cummings	5000				10000				
*-D	Hazen "Kiki" Cuyler	250	500	1000		2000		2500	500	5000
*-D	Ray Dandridge	8	15	30	25	150	25	50	50	75
	Alvin Dark		5	25	10	50			25	35
*-D	George Davis	5000				20000				
D	Jake Daubert	1000	2000			4000				
D	Andre Dawson	5	10	20	10			30	20	30
*-D	Leon Day	10	30	50	25	200		100	50	100
*-D	"Dizzy" Dean	75	125	375	275	500	175		200	850
*-D	Ed Delehanty	5000				10000				
*-D	Bill Dickey	20	30	50	40	150	50	150	75	200
*-D	Martin DiHigo	1200				3500				5000
	Dom DiMaggio	5	15	25	20			50	35	50
*-D	Joe Dimaggio	75	150	150	150	500	200	750	175	250
D	Vince DiMaggio	30	50	100	100				100	250
*-D	Larry Doby	5	20	35	30	100	45	100	45	75
*	Bobby Doerr		5	12	10	40	10	30	20	25
*-D	Don Drysdale	10	25	60	25	100	40	300	40	125
*-D	Hugh Duffy	250	450	1000		2500	1500		800	3500
*-D	Leo Durocher	10	35	50	35	200		300	50	150
*	Dennis Eckersley	10	20	35	25	75	40		40	50
*-D	Billy Evans	175	300	1000		500			500	4000
*-D	John Evers	400	650	2000		3000		2500	1250	5000
*-D	Buck Ewing	5000				10000				
*-D	Urban "Red" Faber	30	60	175	100	200	125		125	1500
*	Bob Feller		5	10	10	40	10	200	20	25
*-D	Rick Ferrell	5	10	30	20	75	15	35	35	60
	Cecil Fielder	5	10	25	15				25	35
*	Rollie Fingers	5	10	20	10	50	15	40	20	40
*	Carlton Fisk	10	25	40	25	100	50		45	70
*-D	Elmer Flick	40	75	250	250	300	400		175	1000
*	Whitey Ford	10	20	30	25	1075	25	35	30	35
*-D	Rube Foster	3000				7500				
*-D	Willie Foster	1500	2500	3500	2500	5000				
*-D	Nellie Fox	90	225	400	225	1500		1000	300	1500
*-D	Jimmy Foxx	250	600	1250	900	2500	2500		1200	8000
*-D	Ford Frick	35	70	250	100	500	175		150	1500
*-D	Frankie Frisch	50	75	250	200	300	250	275	150	1700
D	Carl Furillo (55BKN)	20	50	75	100				100	250
	Andre Gallaraga	5	10	25	10				25	30
*-D	"Pud" Galvin	3000				6000				
	Nomar Garciaparra	5	20	50	30				40	75
*-D	Lou Gehrig	1500	2500	9000	5000	15000		12500	3500	18000
*-D	Charles Gehringer	10	20	50	30	150	25	250	50	150
D	Bart Giamatti	20	50	125		200			100	500
*	Bob Gibson	5	10	35	15	50	20		25	50
*-D	Josh Gibson	1250				5000				7500
*-D	Warren Giles	30	50	100	75	250		750	100	500
D	Jim Gilliam(55BKN)	45	75	200	75					600
	Tom Glavine	5	10	25	10				25	30
*-D	"Lefty" Gomez	10	20	60	35	100	30	150	50	175
	Juan Gonzalez	5	20	30	15				30	35
	Dwight Gooden	5	10	25	15				25	30
*-D	"Goose" Goslin	75	150	250	250	750	750		300	1500
	Mark Grace	5	10	20	10				20	25
*-D	Hank Greenberg	45	100	275	100	350	125	1000	150	1450
	Ken Griffey JR.	15	30	50	45				50	75
	Ken Griffey SR.	5	10	20	10				25	25
*-D	Clark Griffith	100	200	500		1500	1000	1500	400	4000
*-D	Burleigh Grimes	10	20	75	30	100	25	75	50	300

		SIG.(CUT)	3X5 CARD	PHOTO	SIG BBC	DS/TLS	* PLAK	SIG. CHK	COVER	BALL
*-D	Robert "Lefty" Grove	25	50	250	125	500	125	175	100	1500
	Tony Gwynn	5	20	35	20				25	35
*-D	Chick Hafey	30	50	200	100	200	300		100	1500
*-D	Jessie "Pop" Haines	20	30	150	75	250	125	100	75	1200
*-D	Billy Hamilton	2000	3500			7500			3000	7500
*-D	Ned Hanlon	2500				4000				
*-D	William Harridge	50	100	250	125	200			200	3000
*-D	Bucky Harris	50	75	200	100	200	150		125	1200
*-D	Gabby Hartnett	50	80	250	125	350	250	300	150	1750
*-D	Harry Heilmann	250	450	1000		5000		1500	750	4000
	Ricky Henderson	10	30	50	25				35	75
*-D	Billy Herman	10	15	35	20	75	15	75	40	75
D	Don Hoak (55BKN/60PIR)	100	200	350	250			250	800	
D	Gil Hodges	150	275	500	300	600			450	2500
*-D	Harry Hooper	20	30	125	75	125	150	100	75	750
*-D	Rogers Hornsby	200	400	1000	500	3500	900	7000	600	5000
D	Elston Howard	50	125	250	125	350			250	1200
*-D	Waite Hoyt	10	20	95	40	100	35	150	50	400
*-D	Cal Hubbard(Also FB *)	50	75	200	200	250	1000	200	200	800
*-D	Carl Hubbell (Pre Stroke)	10	20	50	35	150	35	100	75	200
*-D	Carl Hubbell (Post Stroke)	5	10	25	20	75	20		35	100
*-D	Miller Huggins	900	1250	2500		7500				5000
*-D	William Hulbert	7500				10000				
*-D	Jim "Catfish" Hunter	10	30	40	25	150	45	250	50	75
*	Monte Irvin	5	10	20	15	50	15	40	25	30
	Bo Jackson	10	25	40	25				50	60
D	Joe Jackson (1919 CWS)	7500				17500				40000
*	Reggie Jackson	25	45	50	25	100	60	200	50	75
*-D	Travis Jackson	20	30	100	40	250	50	500	50	350
*	Ferguson Jenkins		5	15	10	50	20	25	20	25
*-D	Hugh Jennings	1000	2200	2500		7500				7500
D	Jackie Jensen	15	30	75	75			100	75	200
	Derek Jeter	10	30	75	45				75	100
*-D	Ban Johnson	300				600		3000		
*-D	Judy Johnson	15	30	75	40	250	40	400	50	200
	Randy Johnson	5	20	40	25				30	75
*-D	Walter Johnson	350	700	2000		3000		1000	1250	6000
	Chipper Jones	5	15	40	20				25	60
*-D	Addie Joss	10000	(only one or two known to exist)							
*	Al Kaline	5	15	25	15	50	15		30	35
*-D	Tim Keefe	5000				7500				10000
*-D	Willie Keeler	4000				7500				
*	George Kell		5	20	10	40	10	35	25	30
*-D	George "Highpockets" Kelly	10	20	40	40	150	35	75	50	200
*-D	Joe Kelley	1500	2500			7500			4000	10000
*-D	Mike "King" Kelly	7500				25000				
*	Harmon Killebrew	10	20	25	25	75	20	250	30	50
*	Ralph Kiner	10	15	20	15	50	15		25	40
*-D	Chuck Klein	400	650	1500	500	5000		7500	1250	4000
*-D	Bill Klem	350	400	1000		1000			900	3500
D	Ted Kluszewski	15	40	75	50				75	300
*	Sandy Koufax	25	60	90	75	350	80		60	150
	Tony Kubek	10	35	50	50				50	100
D	Harvey Kuenn	10	20	60	25				40	600
*-D	Larry Lajoie	350	500	1500		5000	1250		1000	5000
*-D	Kenesaw Landis	250	400	800		2500		3000	1000	4000
	Barry Larkin	5	10	25	10				25	30
	Don Larsen	10	15	20	15	40	15		20	40
*	Tommy Lasorda	5	15	25	10	100	60	250	30	60
*-D	Anthony Lazzeri	700	1000	1750	2500	5000		3000	1250	5000
*-D	Bob Lemon	5	10	25	15	75	20	250	30	50
*-D	Buck Leonard	10	20	50	20	150	35	50	50	75
*-D	Fred Lindstrom	20	30	150	75	150	60	500	75	600
*-D	John H."Pops" Lloyd	2500	5000							10000
*	Al Lopez	5	15	40	25	100	35		40	75

* : Hall of Fame D : Deceased

		SIG.(CUT)	3X5 CARD	PHOTO	SIG BBC	DS/TLS	* PLAK	SIG. CHK	COVER	BALL
*-D	Ted Lyons	10	15	75	30	150	35	75	50	350
*-D	Connie Mack	200	350	700	500	750	1000		600	2500
*-D	Larry MacPhail	100	200	300		500		1000	250	2000
*	Lee MacPhail	15	30	50		75	50	250	75	100
	Greg Maddux	5	20	40	20				30	50
*-D	Mickey Mantle	75	175	175	150	750	175	1500	175	250
*-D	Heinie Manush	40	75	250	150	250	250	350	200	1750
*-D	"Rabbit" Maranville	250	400	750	500	1000	1250		800	3000
*	Juan Marichal	10	25	35	20	100	25	250	35	50
*-D	"Rube" Marquard	20	30	100	50	125	50		75	500
D	Roger Maris	100	250	550	300				400	1500
D	Billy Martin	30	70	100	75				100	250
D	Pepper Martin	50	125	350	200	450			250	1000
	Tino Martinez	5	15	30	15				30	40
	Pedro Martinez	5	20	50	25				30	75
*-D	Eddie Mathews	10	25	40	30	100	30		40	65
*-D	Christy Mathewson	1500				10000		10000		20000
	Don Mattingly	10	25	40	20				40	50
*	Bill Mazeroski	5	15	25	15	50		250	30	40
*	Willie Mays	20	50	60	35	500	50	750	50	75
*-D	Joe McCarthy	25	40	150	50	150	100	500	75	1000
*-D	Thomas McCarthy	1500				7500				
*	Willie McCovey	10	20	30	25	100	25	50	35	50
*-D	"Bid" McPhee	5000	10000			25000				
*-D	Joseph McGinnity	1500				5000				25000
*-D	Wiiliam McGowan	400	500			3500			1000	5000
*-D	John McGraw	500	900			10000		7500		7500
	Fred McGriff	5	10	25	10				25	35
	Mark McGwire	35	75	100	100	500			150	250
*-D	William McKechnie JR.	100	200	500	300	2500			500	2500
*-D	Joe Medwick	35	60	200	100	200	150		150	1000
*-D	Johnny Mize	5	15	25	15	100	20	150	30	50
*	Paul Molitor	10	20	35	15				35	40
*	Joe Morgan	10	20	30	15	50	30	250	35	40
D	Thurman Munson	200	500	800	450	1000			800	3000
*	Eddie Murray	10	30	50	35		80		40	75
*	Stan Musial	10	25	40	30	100	30	100	45	60
*-D	Hal Newhouser	5	15	25	15	100	20	50	35	50
*-D	Charles"Kid" Nichols	350	500	1000		3500	1500	5000	1000	10000
*	Phil Niekro	5	10	20	10	75	25			
D	Walter O'Malley	75	125	400		200			200	1000
*-D	Mel Ott	300	600	1750	1000	1750	2500		1250	10000
*-D	Satchel Paige	75	125	350	150	750	150		250	1200
	Rafael Palmeiro	5	15	40	15				25	75
*	Jim Palmer	5	15	25	15	100	30	250	30	40
*-D	Herb Pennock	250	500	800		900		900	800	4000
*	Tony Perez	5	15	25	15	75	35		30	40
*	Gaylord Perry		5	20	10	50	15	25	25	30
	Mike Piazza	10	20	50	30				40	75
*-D	Eddie Plank	3000				5000				12500
*	Kirby Puckett	5	20	35	25	125	75		40	50
	Albert Pujols		20	50	40				40	75
	Manny Ramirez	5	15	30	25				30	45
*-D	Pee Wee Reese	20	35	50	25	150	50	500	50	100
*-D	Sam Rice	40	60	250	100	200	175	500	125	1250
	Bobby Richardson		10	25	15				25	35
*-D	Branch Rickey	125	250	1000	350	400			400	2500
	Cal Ripken JR.	20	50	60	35				75	75
D	Swede Risberg (1919 CWS)	300	500	2000						
*-D	Eppa Rixey	125	250	500	500	500			500	2500
*	Phil Rizzuto	10	20	30	20	100	30	250	35	50
*	Robin Roberts	5	10	20	10	75	15		20	30
*	Brooks Robinson	5	10	20	10	75	15	25	25	30
*	Frank Robinson	5	20	30	25	100	25	100	30	60
*-D	Jackie Robinson	250	450	1250	450	3500	900	675	750	3500
*-D	Wilbert Robinson	1000				2500				
	Alex Rodriguez	10	35	60	40				75	100
	Ivan Rodriguez	5	20	35	25				30	35

		SIG.(CUT)	3X5 CARD	PHOTO	SIG BBC	DS/TLS	* PLAK	SIG. CHK	COVER	BALL
*-D	"Bullett" Joe Rogan	2500								10000
	Pete Rose	10	25	40	25	250			35	40
*-D	Edd Roush	5	10	50	25	100	25	175	40	200
*-D	Red Ruffing	20	35	100	35	200	60		100	600
*-D	Amos Rusie	2500	4000			10000				
*-D	Babe Ruth	1500	2750		5000	6000				10000
*-D	G.H. Ruth (Legal Sig)	1000	1750			4000		2750	3000	6500
*	Nolan Ryan	20	40	50	35	250	60		50	60
*-D	Ray Schalk(1919 CWS)	75	125	200		250	275		150	2000
*	Mike Schmidt	20	40	50	35	100	60		50	60
*	Red Schoendienst	5	15	25	10	50	15	250	25	30
*	Tom Seaver	10	30	35	20	150	50	300	45	50
*-D	Frank Selee	5000								
*-D	Joe Sewell	5	10	30	15	75	20	25	30	75
D	Urban Shocker	3000								
*-D	Al Simmons	175	400	800	600	1000	1000	900	750	3500
*-D	George Sisler	40	75	150	125	400	150	300	125	2000
*-D	Enos Slaughter		5	20	10	50	10	25	25	30
*	Ozzie Smith	5	15	35	15				30	60
	John Smoltz	5	10	25	10				25	30
*	Duke Snider	5	15	25	15	75	15	50	30	40
	Sammy Sosa	25	50	75	50				75	100
*-D	Warren Spahn	5	12	25	15	75	15	75	35	55
*-D	Albert Spalding	1250				5000		5000		
*-D	Tris Speaker	275	500	1000		750	1000		800	7000
*-D	Willie Stargell	10	35	35	20	150	35	300	45	75
*-D	Casey Stengel	75	125	300	150	375	200	750	250	1000
	Darryl Strawberry	10	25	30	25				40	50
*	Don Sutton		5	20	10	100	30		20	30
	Ichiro Suzuki	20	60	75	60					100
*-D	Bill Terry	10	40	50	25	100	25	125	50	175
*-D	Sam Thompson	3500				7500				
	Bobby Thomson (The Shot)	5	10	20	10			35	25	30
*-D	Joe Tinker	350	550	2000		3000		5000	1000	5000
	Alan Trammel		5	20	10				20	30
*-D	Harold"Pie" Traynor	125	300	450	400	750	600	750	400	2000
*-D	Dazzy Vance	150	300	500	400	1000	1500		500	2500
D	Johnny Vandermeer	5	15	40	15			45	30	60
*-D	Arky Vaughan	250	450	750		2500			800	4000
	Mo Vaughn	5	10	25	10				25	35
*-D	Bill Veeck SR.	75	150	200		150		250	175	600
*-D	Rube Waddell	7500				15000				
*-D	Honus Wagner	300	550	1500	900	5000	2000	1750	800	3500
	Larry Walker		10	20	15				20	30
*-D	R.J."Bobby" Wallace	200	400	1250	500	3500	1750		800	3500
*-D	Ed Walsh (Sr.)	200	350	1000	500	1000	750		800	3500
*-D	Lloyd Waner	10	20	150	30	200	40		50	350
*-D	Paul Waner	125	250	400	300	750	1000			5000
*-D	John M. Ward	4000				10000				
*-D	Willie Wells	200	500	750		1000				
*-D	Zack Wheat	50	75	200	150	250	300	700	150	2500
*-D	Hoyt Wilhelm	5	10	20	10	75	25	100	25	35
	Bernie Williams	10	40	50	30				40	75
*	Billy Williams	5	10	20	15	75	15	300	25	35
*-D	"Smokey" Joe Williams	7500	12500							
*-D	Ted Williams	50	125	150	100	750	150	2000	150	200
*-D	Vic Willis	4000	5000			10000				20000
*-D	Hack Wilson	600	900	3500		5000		1500		7500
*	Dave Winfield	5	25	30	20	150			35	45
D	"Smokey Joe" Wood	10	20	75	35			25	50	400
*-D	George Wright	1000				3000				
*-D	Harry Wright	2500				5000				
*-D	Early Wynn	10	25	40	25	150	30	125	40	50
*	Carl Yastrzemski	10	40	40	30	150	40	250	40	75
*-D	Thomas Yawkey	95	225	400		250			250	1500
*-D	Cy Young	300	600	1500		2500	1500		800	7500
*-D	Ross Youngs	3000	6000			7500				
*	Robin Yount	15	30	45	25	200	50		40	60

* : Hall of Fame D : Deceased

		3X5 CARD	PHOTO	COVER	SIGN.BSKB
*	Kareem Abdul Jabbar	40	50	75	150
*	Lew Alcindor	150	400	300	500
*	Nate Archibald	5	15	15	75
*	Paul Arizin	10	20	15	75
	Charles Barkley	25	35	40	100
*	Rick Barry	10	25	25	100
*	Elgin Baylor	15	30	25	100
*	Walt Bellamy	5	15	15	75
*	Dave Bing	10	20	15	100
	Larry Bird	40	75	75	175
*	Bill Bradley	50	100	75	175
*	Carl Braun	10	25	15	75
*	Larry Brown	-	-	-	-
	Kobe Bryant	40	85	75	200
*	Lou Carneseca	10	20	20	75
	Vince Carter	25	40	40	100
*-D	Wilt Chamberlain	125	250	250	750
*	John Chaney	10	25	20	75
	Doug Collins	10	20	20	75
*	Bob Cousy	10	25	20	100
*	Dave Cowens	10	25	20	100
*	Billy Cunningham	15	25	25	100
*	Bob Davies	25	50	50	200
*-D	Dave DeBusschere	15	30	25	125
*	Clyde Drexler	20	30	30	100
	Tim Duncan	25	40	40	125
*	Julius "dr.J" Erving	30	50	50	150
	Patrick Ewing	50	125	100	275
*	Walt Frazier	10	20	15	100
*-D	Joe Fulks	50	125	100	1000
	Kevin Garnett	25	40	40	125
*-D	"Pop" Gates	10	15	15	100
*	George Gervin	10	20	20	100
	Artis Gilmore	10	15	20	75
*	Tom Gola	5	15	15	75
*	Gail Goodrich	5	15	15	75
*	Hal Greer	10	20	20	100
D	Albert Groza	30	75	50	250
*	Clifford Hagan	5	15	15	75
	Anfernee Hardaway	15	25	25	100
*	John Havlicek	15	30	30	150
*	Connie Hawkins	10	20	20	100
*	Elvin Hayes	10	20	20	100
	Spencer Haywood	10	20	20	75
	Walt Hazzard	5	15	15	75
*	Tommy Heinsohn	15	30	25	125
	Grant Hill	20	35	35	100
*-D	Nat Holman	20	40	35	125
*-D	Red Holzman	15	30	25	75
	"Hot Rod" Hundley	15	35	35	100
*-D	Henry Iba	30	75	60	250
*	Dan Issel	10	25	20	100
	Alan Iverson	35	60	50	150
	Phil Jackson	35	50	50	250
*	Buddy Jeannette	5	15	15	75
	Irvin "Magic" Johnson	50	75	75	250
	Kevin Johnson	20	30	30	125
	Bobby Jones	10	20	20	75
	Eddie Jones	10	20	25	100
*	K.C. Jones	10	20	15	100
*	Sam Jones	10	20	15	125
	Michael Jordan	125	250	250	400
	Johnny "Red" Kerr	10	20	15	75
	Jason Kidd	20	30	30	100
*	Bobby Knight	15	35	25	150
*	Mike Krzyzewski(Duke)				
	Toni Kukoc	20	35	35	125
*	Bob Lanier	10	20	20	125
*	Clyde Lovellette	5	15	15	75
*	Jerry Lucas	5	20	15	75

* : Hall of Fame **D** : Deceased

321

		3X5 CARD	PHOTO	COVER	SIGN.BSKB
	Maurice Lucas	10	20	20	75
*	Ed MacCauley	10	20	15	75
	Karl Malone	25	50	40	200
*	Moses Malone	10	25	25	100
*	"Pistol Pete" Maravich (Full)	250	500	400	1000
*	"Pistol Pete"	100	250	200	500
	Stephon Marbury	20	30	30	125
*	Slater Martin	10	20	15	75
	Bob McAdoo	10	20	20	100
*	Dick McGuire	5	15	15	75
	Kevin McHale	25	35	25	125
*	George Mikan	20	40	40	150
*-D	Vernon Mikkelsen	5	35	15	100
	Reggie Miller	20	40	35	150
*	Earl "The Pearl" Monroe	5	15	20	100
	Alonzo Mourning	25	40	40	150
	Chris Mullin	20	35	35	125
*	Calvin Murphy	10	20	20	100
*	"Stretch" Murphy	20	50	40	200
*-D	James Naismith	1000	3000	-	-
	Shaq O'Neal	40	75	75	200
	(H)Akeem Olajuwon	25	40	40	150
	Gary Payton	25	35	35	125
*-D	Drazen Petrovic	50	100	75	300
*	Bob Pettit	5	15	15	75
*-D	Andy Phillip	10	20	15	75
	Scottie Pippen	40	50	50	200
*-D	James Pollard	40	75	50	250
*	Frank Ramsey	5	15	15	75
*	Willis Reed	10	30	20	150
*	Oscar Robertson "Big O"	25	60	40	175
	David Robinson	25	40	40	150
	Dennis Rodman	40	75	75	200
*	Bill Russell	75	125	100	350
	Cazzie Russell	5	15	15	75
*	Dolph Schayes	10	20	15	100
*	William Sharman	15	35	25	150
	John Stockton	35	75	75	250
*-D	Maurice Stokes	500	1500		3500
	Isiah Thomas	25	40	40	150
*	David Thompson	15	30	25	100
*	Nate Thurmond	5	15	15	100
	Rudy Tomjanovich	10	15	15	75
*	Jack Twyman	5	15	15	75
*	Wes Unseld	5	15	15	100
*	Bill Walton	20	40	35	175
	Chris Webber	20	35	35	125
*	Jerry West	25	50	40	200
	Paul Westphal	10	20	15	100
	Dominique Wilkins	20	35	30	125
*	Lenny Wilkins	10	25	20	100
*-C	John Wooden	20	40	40	150
	James Worthy	20	35	35	125
	Max Zaslofsky	20	35	35	125

* : Hall of Fame **D** : Deceased

		3X5 CARD	PHOTO	DS/TLS	SIG FBC	GL ART	COVER
*	Herb Adderly	5	10		10	25	15
	Troy Aikman	30	45		30		50
*-D	George Allen	200	350	300			250
*	Marcus Allen	25	50		30	75	45
*	Lance Alworth	10	25		15	25	25
D	Lyle Alzado	60	125		100		150
D	Alan Ameche	60	125		125		150
*	Doug Atkins	5	10		10	20	15
*-D	Red Badgro	10	25		20	50	30
*	Lem Barney	10	15		15	25	20
*-D	Cliff Battles	60	250		100		150
*	Sammy Baugh	25	50		50	50	50
*	Chuck Bednarik	8	15		15	25	15
*-D	Bert Bell	250	500	500	(Checks 300)		
*	Bobby Bell	10	15		10	25	20
*	Raymond Berry	10	15		10	25	20
*	Elvin Bethea	10	30		15		
*-D	Charles Bidwill	1000	2500				
*	Fred Biletnikoff	10	15		10	25	20
*	George Blanda	10	30		15	40	25
	Drew Bledsoe	12	25		15		30
*	Mel Blount	12	20		15	25	20
*	Terry Bradshaw	30	60		25	60	50
	John Brodie	15	25		20		25
*	Bob Brown	20	40		30		30
*	Jim Brown	35	60		30	40	75
*-D	Paul Brown	60	125	200	75	125	150
*	Roosevelt Brown	10	20		10	25	20
	Tim Brown (Raiders)	10	25		15		20
*	Willie Brown	5	12		10	20	15
	Mark Brunell	25	35		25		40
*-D	Buck Buchanan	35	60		60	100	75
*	Nick Buoniconti	5	20		10	45	20
*	Dick Butkus	25	45		15	60	30
*	Earl Campbell	10	25		20	30	25
*-D	Tony Canadeo	12	25		25	40	25
*-D	Joe Carr	750 cut			1500 NFL letter		
	Chris Carter	15	35		20		30
*	Dave Casper	15	25		20	40	25
*-D	Guy Chamberlin	250	400	500			
*-D	Jack Christensen	50	150		75		150
*-D	"Dutch" Clark	65	200		150		150
D	Charles Conerly	25	75		50		50
*-D	George Connor	5	20		10	40	15
*-D	Jim Conzelman	250	750	1000			
	Tim Couch	20	40		20		40
*	Lou Creekmur	5	12		10	20	15
*	Larry Csonka	15	30		15	40	35
	Randall Cunningham	20	30		15		35
*	Al Davis	100	200	400	100	300	200
	Terrell Davis	20	35		25		40
*	Willie Davis	10	20		10	25	20
*	Lenny Dawson	10	20		20	25	25
*	Joe DeLamiellenre	10	30		15		
*	Eric Dickerson	20	30		20	40	30
*	Dan Dierdorf	20	35		20	40	35
*	Mike Ditka	15	30		20	35	30
*	Art Donovan	15	25		20	30	25
*	Tony Dorsett	15	35		25	40	35
*-D	"Paddy" Driscoll	275	500	500			
	Fred Dryer (Also Actor)	15	30		15		30
*-D	Bill Dudley	10	25		20	30	15
*-D	Al "Turk" Edwards	200	400	500			400
*	Carl Eller	15	25		15	40	25
*	John Elway	40	75		35		75
*-D	Weeb Ewbank	25	40		35	50	40
	Marshall Faulk	20	50		25		40
	Brett Favre	30	65		50		60
*-D	Tom Fears	15	40		30	50	40
*-D	Jim Finks	300	500	500	500		500

* : Hall of Fame D : Deceased

		3X5 CARD	PHOTO	DS/TLS	SIG FBC	GL ART	COVER
*-D	Ray Flaherty	25	50		40	75	20
*-D	Lenny Ford	500	1000	1000	500		750
	Doug Flutie	20	35		25		40
*-D	Dan Fortmann	40	75		100	RARE	50
*	Dan Fouts	15	25		25	30	30
	Roman Gabriel	5	15		15		15
*	Frank Gatski	5	15		15	20	15
*-D	Bill George	100	250		100		200
	Eddie George	20	35		25		30
*	Joe Gibbs	20	35		25	45	30
*	Frank Gifford	30	50		35	50	50
*-D	Sid Gillman	10	30		20	50	35
*-D	Otto Graham	20	40		25	55	45
*-D	"Red" Grange	75	200	250	125	200	175
*	Bud Grant	15	25		15	40	20
	Darrell Green	10	25		15		20
*	Joe Greene	10	20		15	30	25
*	Forrest Gregg	10	25		20	25	25
*	Rosie Grier	15	25		15	30	30
*	Bob Griese	20	35		25	50	40
*-D	Lou Groza	10	20		15	30	20
	Ray Guy	10	15		10		15
*-D	Joe Guyon	150	300	250			200
	Pat Haden	15	25		10		30
	John Hadl	10	20		10		15
*-D	George Halas	75	200	100	125		150
	Charles Haley	10	20		15		20
*	Jack Ham	10	20		15	30	25
*	Dan Hampton	10	20		10		15
*	Franco Harris	20	40		25	50	50
*-D	Bob Hayes	25	50		25		40
*-D	Ed Healy	100	350	300			250
*-D	Mel Hein	15	40		25	200	20
*	Ted Hendricks	15	25		10	40	30
*-D	Pete Henry	Only Avail Check 600 Check Cut 350					
*-D	Arnie Herber	250	500				350
*-D	Bill Hewitt	1000		2500			
*-D	Clark Hinkle	50	90	225			50
*-D	Elroy Hirsch	10	20		15	30	25
*	Paul Hornung	20	30		20	35	30
*	Ken Houston	10	20		10	20	20
*-D	Cal Hubbard (also BB)	75	250		200		200
*	Sam Huff	10	25		20	35	25
*-D	Don Hutson	40	100		60	150	75
	Bo Jackson	25	50		25		50
*	Jimmy Johnson	15	35		20		35
*	John Henry Johnson	5	12		10	20	15
	Keyshawn Johnson	20	35		20		30
*	Charlie Joiner	5	15		10	25	15
*	Deacon Jones	10	20		10	25	20
*	Stan Jones	10	15		10	20	15
*-D	Henry Jordan	350	600	1000	450		500
*	Lee Roy Jordan	5	15		10	20	15
*	Sonny Jurgensen	10	25		20	35	30
	Alex Karras	15	25		20		25
*	Jim Kelly	20	40		30	75	45
*	Leroy Kelly	10	20		15	25	25
	Jack Kemp	50	100		75		100
*-D	Walter Kiesling	600	1250	1000			
*-D	Frank Kinard	100	500	300			
	Jerry Kramer	10	20		10		20
*	Paul Krause	10	15		10	30	15
*-D	Curly Lambeau	500	1000	1000			750
*	Jack Lambert	15	30		20	35	25
*-D	Tom Landry	25	50	100	25	80	50
*-D	Dick Lane	15	25		20	40	30
*	Jim Langer	5	15		10	20	15
*	Willie Lanier	10	15		10	25	20
*	Steve Largent	15	35		20	50	40
*	Yale Lary	10	20		10	25	15
*	Dante Lavelli	5	15		10	25	15

* : Hall of Fame D : Deceased

324

		3X5 CARD	PHOTO	DS/TLS	SIG FBC	GL ART	COVER
*-D	Bobby Layne	75	200		100		150
*-D	"Tuffy" Leemans	200	500	300	200		250
*	Marv Levy	10	20		20	45	40
*	Bob Lilly	5	15		15	20	15
D	Gene Lipscomb	150	300	400	250		350
*	Larry Little	10	15		15	20	20
*	James Lofton	15	35		20		25
*-D	Vince Lombardi	250	500	400	(check 275)		
*	Howie Long (TV)	25	50		40	75	40
*	Ronnie Lott	15	30		15	40	30
*-D	Sid Luckman	25	50		40	75	40
*-D	Link Lyman	175	500	400			250
*	Tom Mack	5	12		10	20	15
*	John Mackey	5	12		10	20	15
	John Madden	30	50		30		50
*	Gino Marchetti	10	15		10	25	20
	Peyton Manning	25	40		25		40
	Ed Marinaro(Also Actor)	25	40		20		35
*-D	Tim Mara	400		1500			
*	Wellington Mara	10	25	75	35	35	35
	Dan Marino	40	60		30		75
*-D	George P. Marshall	400	800	1000			
	Jim Marshall	10	15		10		15
*	Ollie Matson	10	20		15	20	20
*	Dan Maynard	10	20		15	20	20
*	George McAfee	5	12		10	20	15
*	Mike McCormack	5	12		10	20	15
*	Tommy McDonald	5	12		10	20	15
*	Hugh McElhenney	10	15		15	25	15
	Jim McMahon	20	35		20		40
	Steve McNair	15	35		15		30
*-D	John McNally	350	500				500
	Don Meredith	25	50		40		50
*-D	Mike Michalske	75	200				100
*-D	Wayne Millner	75	300	250	150		150
*	Bobby Mitchell	5	12		10	20	15
*	Ron Mix	10	15		15	20	15
	Art Monk	15	25		15		20
*	Joe Montana	40	75		40	110	75
	Warren Moon	15	25		20		30
*	Lenny Moore	10	20		15	20	15
	Craig Morton	10	15		10		15
	Randy Moss	20	40		35		40
*-D	Marion Motley	20	30		40	45	40
*	Mike Munchak	5	10		10	35	
*	Anthony Munoz	10	15		15	35	20
*-D	George Musso	10	20		25	40	25
*-D	Bronko Nagurski	50	200		100		125
*-D	Earle "Greasy" Neale	150	750	400			275
*	Joe Namath	50	75		50	80	75
*-D	Ernie Nevers	75	250				125
*	Ozzie Newsome	10	25		15	30	20
*-D	Ray Nitschke	20	45		30	75	35
*	Chuck Noll	10	25		15	25	30
*-D	Leo Nomellini	10	20		25	30	25
*	Merlin Olsen	10	25		15	25	25
*	Jim Otto	10	15		10	20	20
*-D	Steven Owen	500	1500	1500			
*	Alan Page	15	25		15	35	25
	Jack Pardee	10	20		15		20
*	Clarence "Ace" Parker	5	12		10	20	15
*	Jim Parker	5	12		10	20	15
	"Babe" Parilli	10	15		15		15
*-D	Walter Payton	60	150		75	125	150
*	Joe Perry	10	20		10	25	20
D	Brian Piccolo	400	1000		750		1000
*	Pete Pihos	5	12		10	20	15
	Jim Plunkett	10	20		15		25
*-D	Hugh "Shorty" Ray	850	1500	2000			
	Andre Reed	10	25		15		25
*-D	Daniel Reeves	300	500	500			500

* : Hall of Fame D : Deceased

325

		3X5 CARD	PHOTO	DS/TLS	SIG FBC	GL ART	COVER
*	Mel Renfro	10	20		10	20	15
	Jerry Rice	25	60		30		60
*	John Riggins	50	125		75	150	100
*	Jim Ringo	10	20		10	30	20
*	Andy Robustelli	5	15		10	20	15
*-D	Knute Rockne	500	2000	1500			
*-D	Art Rooney	75	175				150
*	Dan Rooney	20	40	75	40	50	40
D	Kyle Rote	10	15		25		20
*-D	Pete Rozelle	40	100		75	175	75
*	Bob St.Clair	5	12		10	20	15
*	Barry Sanders	30	60		25		50
	Deion Sanders	25	60		25		50
	Warren Sapp	10	20		15		15
*	Gale Sayers	15	40		25	40	40
*	Joe Schmidt	5	12		10	20	15
*-D	Tex Schramm	10	25		15	30	20
	Junior Seau	10	25		15		25
*	Leroy Selmon	10	20		15	25	25
*	Billy Shaw	5	12		10	20	15
*	Art Shell	15	25		20	35	25
*	Don Shula	15	25		25	50	40
	Phil Simms	15	30		15		35
*	O.J. Simpson	50	100		75	75	100
*	Mike Singletary	10	25		15	40	25
*	Jackie Slater	5	20		10	40	20
	Bruce Smith	20	30		20		35
	Bubba Smith	10	20		15		20
	Emmitt Smith	40	95		50		75
*	Jackie Smith	5	12		10	20	15
	Steve Spurrier	20	25		25		35
	Ken Stabler	15	25		25		25
*	John Stallworth	10	25		12	40	15
*	Bart Starr	30	60		45	85	50
*	Roger Staubach	25	50		40	60	50
*	Ernie Stautner	5	12		10	20	15
*	Jan Stenerud	10	20		12	20	20
*	Dwight Stephenson	10	15		15	25	15
*	Hank Stram	20	50		30	50	50
*-D	Ken Strong	75	200	250	100		150
*-D	Joe Stydahar	75	250	250	150		150
*	Lynn Swann	40	60		50	175	50
	George Taliaferro	5	12		10		15
*	Fran Tarkenton	20	35		20	40	40
*	Charlie Taylor	10	20		15	25	20
*	Jim Taylor	10	25		15	30	25
*	Lawrence Taylor	25	50		25	50	50
	Vinny Testaverde	15	25		15		30
	Joe Theismann	15	35		15		40
D	Derrick Thomas	40	100		60		75
	Thurman Thomas	15	30		15		40
*-D	Jim Thorpe	900	2000	5000			1500
*	Y.A. Tittle	10	25		15	30	25
*-D	George Trafton	200	500	500			400
*	Charley Trippi	5	12		10	20	15
*-D	Emlen Tunnell	100	200	300	125		200
*-D	"Bulldog" Turner	20	40		40	60	50
*-D	Johnny Unitas	25	50		35	100	45
*	Gene Upshaw	10	25		15	35	25
*-D	Norman Van Brocklin	90	250	200	150		200
*	Steve VanBuren	12	25		15	20	25
*-D	Doak Walker	15	50		25	75	50
	Herschel Walker	20	30		20		35
*	Bill Walsh	25	40		25	50	40
*	Paul Warfield	10	20		15	20	20
	Kurt Warner	20	50		35		40
*-D	Bob Waterfield	75	175		150		150
	Ricky Watters	10	25		15		25
*-D	Mike Webster	20	40		30	55	35
*-D	Arnie Weinmeister	10			15	60	30

* : Hall of Fame D : Deceased

		3X5 CARD	PHOTO	DS/TLS	SIG FBC	GL ART	COVER
	Danny White	10	20		12		20
*	Randy White	10	20		15	25	20
	Reggie White	15	30		20		30
*	Bill Willis	10	15		10	20	15
*	Larry Wilson	10	15		10	25	15
*	Kellen Winslow	10	25		15	25	25
*-D	Alex Wojciechowicz	15	40		20	1250	40
*	Willie Wood	10	20		10	25	20
	Rob Woodson	10	20		15		25
*	Ron Yary	5	20		15	35	30
D	George Young	30	75	100	50		50
	Steve Young	25	50		35		60
*	Jack Youngblood	10	20		10	35	15

COLLEGE FOOTBALL

		3x5 CARD	PHOTO	COVER
D	Harry Agganis	400	1000	1000
	"Reds" Bagnell	10	25	20
	Angelo Bertelli	15	30	25
	"Doc" Blanchard	20	30	35
	Bobby Bowden	10	25	20
	Frank Broyles	10	20	20
D	Paul Bear Bryant	100	350	200
	John Cappellitti	20	30	35
	Hopalong Cassady	10	25	20
D	Jim Crowley	200	500	300
D	Ernie Davis	500	1500	
	Glenn Davis	10	25	20
	Dan Devine	25	50	40
D	George Gipp "The Gipper"	1000		
D	Tom Harmon	50	125	100
D	Woody Hayes	125	250	200
D	John Heisman	2000		
D	Cecil Isbell	60	200	100
D	Vic Janowicz	25	50	40
D	Johnny Lattner	15	30	25
D	Elmer Layden	50	125	100
D	Frank Leahy	75	175	150
	Johnny Lujack	10	20	25
D	Don Miller	200	500	350
	Tom Osborne	15	25	30
	Ara Parseghian	10	25	20
	Joseph Paterno	25	50	50
D	Fritz Pollard	100	250	
	Mike Reid	10	25	20
	Eddie Robinson (Grambling)	20	30	40
	Darrell Royal	10	20	20
	Bo Schembechler	15	25	30
D	Amos Alonzo Stagg	125	400	175
D	Harry Stuhldreher	100	500	300
D	"Pop" Warner	150	400	
D	Bud Wilkinson	25	50	50

BOXING

		3x5 CARD	PHOTO	COVER
	Muhammad Ali	75	100	75
	Ray Arcel	10	25	25
	Alexis Arguello	15	35	25
D	Henry Armstrong	100	200	125
	Bob Arum	10	25	15
D	Abe Attel	100	250	
D	Max Baer	150	500	
	Wilfredo Benitez	10	25	20
	Riddick Bowe	15	35	25
D	James J. Braddock	250	600	
D	Tommy Burns	500	2000	
	Hector "Macho Man" Camacho	15	35	30
D	Tony Canzoneri	75	200	
D	Primo Carnera	250	400	
D	Marcel Cerdan	850	2000	

BOXING (cont.)

		3x5 CARD	PHOTO	COVER
D	Ezzard Charles	150	300	200
	Julio"Cesar"Chavez	20	40	40
D	"Kid" Chocolate	200	400	
	Gil Clancy	10	25	15
	Cassius Clay	100	250	200
D	Billy Conn	35	100	50
	Gerry Cooney	10	15	15
D	James J. Corbett	500	1000	
D	Cus D'Amato	100	250	
	Oscar De Lahoya	25	50	50
D	Jack Dempsey	100	250	150
	Angelo Dundee	10	20	20
D	Johnny Dundee	60	150	
	Roberto Duran	20	45	40
D	Bob Fitzsimmons	3000		
	George Foreman	25	40	40
	Joe Frazier	10	25	25
	Eddie Futch	20	40	40
D	Kid Galivan	20	40	40
D	Joe Gans	1000		
	Joey Giardello	10	25	25
D	Rocky Graziano	40	100	75
D	Harry Greb			
	Marvin Hagler	15	30	25
D	Marvin Hart	2500	5000	
	Thomas Hearns	15	35	30
	Larry Holmes	15	35	30
	Evander Holyfield	25	50	40
D	James J. Jeffries	400	2000	
	Ingemar Johansson	20	40	40
D	Jack Johnson	1000	3000	
	Roy Jones Jr.	20	40	40
D	Stanley Ketchel			
	Don King	15	35	30
	Jake Lamotta	15	30	30
D	Benny Leonard	150	500	
D	"Sugar Ray" Leonard	20	40	35
	Lennox Lewis	25	50	50
D	Sonny Liston	750	2000	
D	Joe Louis	250	500	
D	Rocky Marciano	400	1250	
D	Joey Maxim	10	30	25
D	"Kid"McCoy(The Real)	75	175	
	Arthur Mercante	10	25	
D	Carlos Monzon	75	200	150
	Archie Moore	20	50	30
	Ken Norton	15	35	30
	Floyd Patterson	15	35	30
	Eusebio Pedroza	10	25	20
D	Willie Pep	20	40	30
	Aaron Pryor	15	35	30
D	Jerry Quarry	75	200	100
D	Tex Rickard	225	500	
D	Sugar Ray Robinson	100	250	200
	Luis Rodriquez	15	35	30

* : Hall of Fame D : Deceased

327

BOXING (cont.)

		3x5 CARD	PHOTO	COVER
D	Maxie Rosenbloom	50	100	75
	Luis Rodriquez	15	35	30
D	Maxie Rosenbloom	50	100	75
D	Barney Ross	50	100	75
	Mike Rossman	10	25	20
D	Salvador Sanchez	50	125	
D	Max Schmeling	40	75	75
	Jack Sharkey	40	75	60
	Michael Spinks	20	45	35
	Leon Spinks	10	25	20
	Emanuel Steward	10	25	15
D	John L. Sullivan	1500	7500	
D	Lew Tendler	100	250	
	Gene Tunney	100	250	150
	Mike Tyson	40	75	60
D	Pancho Villa	50	125	75
D	Jersey Joe Walcott	40	100	75
D	Mickey Walker	60	175	
D	Jess Willard	400	1500	
	Ike Williams	15	35	30
D	Tony Zale	15	30	25

GOLF

		3x5 CARD	PHOTO	COVER
D	Tommy Armour	400	800	
	Paul Azinger	10	25	20
	Seve Ballestros	10	25	20
	Jerry Barber	5	20	20
	Miller Barber	10	25	20
LPGA	Patty Berg	10	20	20
LPGA	Pat Bradley	10	20	20
*	Jack Burke JR	20	40	50
LPGA	Donna Caponi	10	20	20
LPGA	JoAnne Carner	10	20	20
	Billy Casper	10	20	20
*	Harry Cooper	20	40	30
	Fred Couples	20	50	35
	Ben Crenshaw	15	35	30
LPGA	Beth Daniel	10	20	20
*	Jimmy Demaret	175	500	
	David Duval	25	40	50
	Lee Elder	10	20	20
	Ernie Els	10	25	25
	Nick Faldo	20	30	35
	Ray Floyd	20	30	35
	Sergio Garcia	20	50	40
*-D	Ralph Guldahl	175	350	
*-D	Walter Hagen	800	2000	
LPGA	Sandra Haynie	10	20	20
*-D	Ben Hogan	75	250	200
LPGA	Julie Inkster	10	20	20
	Hale Irwin	10	25	25
D	Tony Jacklin	15	30	30
LPGA	Betty Jameson	10	20	20
*-D	Bobby Jones	1500	3000	
	Robert Trent Jones	35	75	50
LPGA	Betsy King	10	20	20
	Tom Kite	10	25	25
	Tom Lehman	10	25	25
	Justin Leonard	10	35	30
D	Lawson Little	75	200	150
*	Gene Littler	15	30	20
*-D	Bobby Locke	200	500	
LPGA	Nancy Lopez-Knight	20	35	40
	Davis Love III	10	25	25
LPGA	Carol Mann	10	20	20
	Phil Mickelson	15	35	30
	Johnny Miller	10	25	25
	Dr. Gil Morgan	5	20	20
*	Byron Nelson	20	40	50
*	Jack Nicklaus	50	75	75
	Greg Norman	35	50	50
	Jose Maria Olazabel	10	25	25

GOLF (cont.)

		3x5 CARD	PHOTO	COVER
	Mark O'Meara	10	25	25
*-D	Francis Ouimet	500	1250	
	Arnold Palmer	40	75	75
	Gary Player	15	30	30
	Nick Price	10	25	25
LPGA	Judy Rankin	10	20	20
LPGA	Betsy Rawls	10	20	20
	Chi Chi Rodriguez	20	50	35
*-D	Gene Sarazen	15	30	30
LPGA	Patti Sheehan	10	20	20
	Charlie Sifford	5	20	20
	Vijay Singh	10	25	25
D	Horton Smith	500	1000	750
D	Sam Snead	40	75	50
LPGA	Annika Sorenstam	10	25	25
	Craig Stadler	10	20	25
LPGA	Jan Stephenson	15	40	30
D	Payne Stewart	50	150	125
	Curtis Strange	10	25	25
	Hal Sutton	10	25	25
	Lee Trevino	20	40	35
*-D	Harry Vardon	1000	2500	
	Ken Venturi	15	30	30
	Lanny Wadkins	10	20	20
	Tom Watson	20	40	30
	Tom Weiskopf	5	20	20
LPGA	Kathy Whitworth	10	20	20
	Tiger Woods	275	450	375
LPGA	Mickey Wright	25	50	50
*-D	Babe Zaharias(L)	600	2000	
	Fuzzy Zoeller	10	20	20

HOCKEY

		3X5 CARD	PHOTO	COVER
*-D	Syl Apps	20	50	40
*-D	Ace Bailey	75	275	
*	Bill Barber	5	20	15
*	Jean Beliveau	10	25	25
*-D	Toe Blake	75	150	150
*-D	Mike Bossy	10	25	25
*	Ray Bourque	30	45	40
*	Scotty Bowman	30	50	40
	Martin Brodeur	15	35	30
*	Johnny Bucyk	5	15	20
*-D	Clarence Campbell	400		
*-D	King Clancy	125	400	
*-D	Bobby Clarke	15	20	30
*	Paul Coffey	25	40	40
*	Yvan Cournoyer	10	25	25
	John Davidson	10	25	25
*	Marcel Dionne	10	25	20
*	Ken Dryden	25	40	50
*	Phil Esposito	20	30	35
*	Tony Esposito	15	25	25
	Sergei Federov	25	40	50
*	Bernie Federko	15	25	25
*	Viacheslav Fetisov	15	30	20
*	Grant Fuhr	20	35	40
*	Ed Giacomin	10	25	25
*	Rod Gilbert	10	25	25
*	Clark Gillies	15	25	25
*	Wayne Gretzky	75	75	250
*-D	Gene Hart	15	30	25
*-D	Doug Harvey	150	275	
	Dominik Hasek	25	40	50
*	Dale Hawerchuck	10	20	15
*-D	Bryan Hextall	50	100	125
*-D	Tim Horton	250	500	500
*	Gordie Howe	35	50	50
*	Bobby Hull	25	40	40
	Brett Hull	15	30	40

* : Hall of Fame **D** : Deceased

HOCKEY(cont.)		3X5 CARD	PHOTO	COVER
*-D	Punch Imlach	30	75	
	Jaromir Jagr	25	40	40
*	Dave Keon	10	25	25
*	Jari Kurri	20	40	30
*	Guy Lafleur	15	25	25
*	Pat LaFontaine	10	25	25
*	Rod Langway	15	25	25
*	Mario Lemieux	30	50	75
	Eric Lindros	30	50	50
	Mark Messier	40	75	75
*	Stan Mikita	10	20	20
*-D	Howie Morenz	1000		
*	Larry Murphy	25	40	40
*	Rodger Neilson	20	30	30
*	Bobby Orr	35	60	50
*	Bernie Parent	10	15	20
*	Brad Park	10	20	20
*-D	Frank Patrick	100		
*-D	Lester Patrick	250		
*-D	Jacques Plante	150	500	300
*-D	Maurice Richard	30	50	50
	Patrick Roy	25	40	40
	Joe Sakic	15	25	25
*	Glenn Sather	10	25	25
*-D	Terry Sawchuk	250	500	500
*-D	Eddie Shore	150	300	250
*	Darryl Sittler	15	25	25
*	Billy Smith	10	25	25
*-D	Conn Smythe	250		
*	Allan Stanley	10	25	25
*-D	Lord Stanley of Preston	1500		
*	Peter Stastny	15	30	25
*	Vladislav Tretiak	20	40	40
*	Bryan Trottier	10	20	20
*-D	Georges Vezina	600	2000	
*	Gump Worsley	10	25	25
	Steve Yzerman	25	50	40

TENNIS		3X5 CARD	PHOTO	COVER
	Andre Agassi	50	75	75
D	Arthur Ashe	100	250	200
	Boris Becker	25	40	40
	Bjorn Borg	20	40	40
D	Don Budge	25	40	40
	Jennifer Capriati	10	25	25
	Michael Chang	15	30	30
	Jimmy Connors	30	50	45
	Margaret Court	15	30	25
	Lindsay Davenport	15	30	30
	Chris Evert	15	30	30
D	Vitas Gerulaitis	50	125	100
D	Althea Gibson	45	100	60
	Steffi Graf	30	50	50
	Martina Hingis	20	40	40
	Helen Jacobs	35	75	50
	Billy Jean King	20	30	30
	Anna Kournikova	25	50	50
	Rod Laver	10	25	25
	Ivan Lendl	25	40	40
	John McEnroe	30	50	50
	Ile Nastase	25	40	40
	Martina Navratilova	25	40	40
	John Newcombe	10	25	25
	Pat Rafter	10	25	25
D	Bobby Riggs	50	100	100
	Gabriella Sabatini	20	35	30
	Peter Sampras	40	65	50
	Monica Seles	25	45	35
*-D	Bill Tilden	250	500	400
	Mats Wilander	5	20	25
	Serena Williams	25	50	40
	Venus Williams	25	50	40

MISC. SPORTS		3X5 CARD	PHOTO	COVER
	Bobby Allison	10	25	20
D	Davy Allison	40	100	50
	Mario Andretti	20	40	30
	Lance Armstrong	45	100	65
	Roger Bannister	20	35	25
D	Dale Earnhardt	60	50	250
	Peggy Fleming	25	40	30
	A.J. Foyt	15	35	25
	Jeff Gordon	20	50	30
	Curt Gowdy	20	40	30
	Andy Granatelli	20	40	30
D	Sonja Henie	75	200	125
D	Graham Hill	75	125	100
D	Willie Hoppe	125	300	
	Bruce Jenner	25	40	35
	Rafer Johnson	15	35	25
	Parnelli Jones	15	30	20
	Evel Knievel	40	75	50
	Greg Lemond	25	50	40
	Carl Lewis	40	75	50
	Greg Louganis	25	50	40
	Mark Martin	15	25	20
	Bob Mathias	15	35	30
	Jim Mckay	10	30	20
D	Minnesota Fats	75	175	100
	Willie Mosconi	25	50	35
	Brent Musburger	15	35	25
D	Barney Oldfield	300	750	
D	Jessie Owens	125	500	200
D	Johnny Parsons	50	100	75
	Pele	50	125	100
	Richard Petty	25	50	35
	Cathy Rigby	10	25	20
	Jim Ryun	10	25	20
	Alberto Salazar	10	25	20
	Vin Scully	25	50	40
D	Willie Shoemaker	50	100	75
	Mark Spitz	20	40	30
	Danny Sullivan	15	25	20
	Al Unser	20	35	30
	Bobby Unser	20	35	30
	Rusty Wallace	15	25	20

* : Hall of Fame D : Deceased

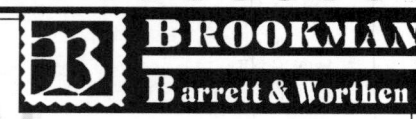

$5   THIS COUPON   **$5**
IS WORTH
$5.00
Towards any First Day Cover order over
$55.00 from this
2005 Brookman Price Guide

ONE COUPON PER ORDER

Brookman Cover Company

P.O. Box 6208
Louisville, KY 40206

$5   **$5**

$10   THIS COUPON   **$10**
IS WORTH
$10.00
Towards any First Day Cover order over
$110.00 from this
2005 Brookman Price Guide

ONE COUPON PER ORDER

Brookman Cover Company

P.O. Box 6208
Louisville, KY 40206

$10   **$10**

$10   THIS COUPON   **$10**
IS WORTH
$10.00
Towards any First Day Cover order over
$110.00 from this
2005 Brookman Price Guide

ONE COUPON PER ORDER

Brookman Cover Company

P.O. Box 6208
Louisville, KY 40206

$10   **$10**

$10   THIS COUPON   **$10**
IS WORTH
$10.00
Towards any First Day Cover order over
$110.00 from this
2005 Brookman Price Guide

ONE COUPON PER ORDER

Brookman Cover Company

P.O. Box 6208
Louisville, KY 40206

$10   **$10**

$25   THIS COUPON   **$25**
IS WORTH
$25.00
Towards any First Day Cover order over
$275.00 from this
2005 Brookman Price Guide

ONE COUPON PER ORDER

Brookman Cover Company

P.O. Box 6208
Louisville, KY 40206

$25   **$25**

$40   THIS COUPON   **$40**
IS WORTH
$40.00
Towards any First Day Cover order over
$450.00 from this
2005 Brookman Price Guide

ONE COUPON PER ORDER

Brookman Cover Company

P.O. Box 6208
Louisville, KY 40206

$40   **$40**

HOW TO WRITE YOUR COVER ORDER - PLEASE US THE ORDER BLANK.

Please send the items listed below for which I enclose: $ 128.00   Date: 8/2/2004

SHIP TO:
Name: Alissa Ryan
Address: PO Box 246

City: Asburn
State: VA   Zip: 20147

CREDIT CARD BILLING ADDRESS:

City:
State: Zip:

Phone: (999) 555-1234   Check Enclosed _____
Please charge my: Visa_____ MasterCard __✓__ American Express_____ Discover_____
Card#: 4432-998-321-640   Expir. Date: 7/06   3- or 4-digit security code on back of card 526

From Page#	Quantity Wanted	Country and items ordered: Specify Scott Numbers plus first day cover, souvenir card, plate block, mint sheet or other description	Quality Wanted	Unused	Used	Price Each	Total	Leave Blank
160	1	1030-53 FDC set of 27, cacheted				100.00		
163	1	1381 FDC cacheted				12.00		
175	1	3499 Convertible Bklt pane of 20 cacheted				20.00		

1. Fill out date, phone #.
2. Print name and address, information including ZIP CODE. Please make sure to include your credit card billing address.
3. Note: Minimum order of $20.00

4. If ordering by credit card, please indicate charge # and expiration date, and security code.
5. If paying by check, please make payments in U.S. funds.
6. Example of how to write up your orders above.

PAY SHIPPING/INSURANCE AS FOLLOWS:

Stamps only - $ 4.00
Other orders:
$20.00 to $49.99 - $ 4.00
$50.00 to $199.99 - $ 6.00
$200.00 & over - $ 8.00

Total this page	132	00
Total from reverse		
Total order	132	00
Less any discounts, refund checks, coupons, etc.	-10	00
SUBTOTAL	122	00
Sales Tax (if any)		
Shipping/Insurance (see chart at left)	6	00
TOTAL ENCLOSED	128	00

SATISFACTION GUARANTEED
MINIMUM ORDER MUST TOTAL AT LEAST $20.00
On orders outside the U.S. additional postage will be billed if necessary

$5 THIS COUPON **$5**
IS WORTH $5.00
Towards any stamp order over $55.00 from
this 2005 Brookman Price Guide

ONE COUPON PER ORDER
Available from:

Brookman Stamp Co.
Vancouver, WA
98666-0090
$5 **$5**

$10 THIS COUPON **$10**
IS WORTH $10.00
Towards any stamp order over $110.00 from
this 2005 Brookman Price Guide

ONE COUPON PER ORDER

Available from:

Brookman Stamp Co.
Vancouver, WA
98666-0090
$10 **$10**

$10 THIS COUPON **$10**
IS WORTH $10.00
Towards any stamp order over $110.00 from
this 2005 Brookman Price Guide

ONE COUPON PER ORDER

Available from:

Brookman Stamp Co.
Vancouver, WA
98666-0090
$10 **$10**

$10 THIS COUPON **$10**
IS WORTH $10.00
Towards any stamp order over $110 from
this 2005 Brookman Price Guide

ONE COUPON PER ORDER

Available from:

Brookman Stamp Co.
Vancouver, WA
98666-0090
$10 **$10**

$25 THIS COUPON **$25**
IS WORTH $25.00
Towards any stamp order over $275.00 from
this 2005 Brookman Price Guide

ONE COUPON PER ORDER

Available from:

Brookman Stamp Co.
Vancouver, WA
98666-0090
$25 **$25**

$40 THIS COUPON **$40**
IS WORTH $40.00
Towards any stamp order over $450.00 from
this 2005 Brookman Price Guide

ONE COUPON PER ORDER

Available from:

Brookman Stamp Co.
Vancouver, WA
98666-0090
$40 **$40**

HOW TO WRITE YOUR STAMP ORDER - PLEASE US THE ORDER BLANK.

Please send the items listed below for which I enclose: $ 128.00   Date: 5/15//2003

SHIP TO:
Name: Benjamin Christopher
Address: 96 Pond Rd.

City: Franklin
State: MA   Zip: 02038

Phone: (999) 444-7777   Check Enclosed _____
Please charge my: Visa_____ MasterCard__✓__ American Express_____ Discover_____
Card#: 4432-998-321-640   Expir. Date: 10/06   3- or 4-digit security code on back of card 526

CREDIT CARD BILLING ADDRESS:

City:
State: Zip:

From Page#	Quantity Wanted	Country and items ordered: Specify Scott Numbers plus first day cover, souvenir card, plate block, mint sheet or other description	Quality Wanted	Unused	Used	Price Each	Total	Leave Blank
18	1	692-701 set of 10	FVFNH			140.00		
23	1	855 Plate Block	FVFNH			11.00		
209	1	B261 Souvenir Card	Mint			12.00		

1. Fill out date, phone #.
2. Print name and address, information including ZIP CODE. Please make sure to include your credit card billing address.
3. Note: Minimum order of $20.00

4. If ordering by credit card, please indicate charge #, expiration date, and security code.
5. If paying by check, please make payments in U.S. funds.
6. Example of how to write up your orders above.

PAY SHIPPING/INSURANCE AS FOLLOWS:			
	Total this page	163	00
	Total from reverse		
Stamps only - $ 4.00	Total order	163	00
Other orders:	Less any discounts, refund checks, coupons, etc.	-10	00
$20.00 to $49.99 - $ 4.00			
$50.00 to $199.99 - $ 6.00	**SUBTOTAL**	153	00
$200.00 & over - $ 8.00	Sales Tax (if any)		
	Shipping/Insurance (see chart at left)	6	00
	TOTAL ENCLOSED	159	00

SATISFACTION GUARANTEED
MINIMUM ORDER MUST TOTAL AT LEAST $20.00
On orders outside the U.S. additional postage will be billed if necessary

EASY ORDER FORM – 2005 EDITION

Please send the items listed below for which I enclose: $_____ Date:_____

SHIP TO:

Name: _____

Address: _____

_____

City:_____

State: _____ Zip:_____

Phone: _____ Check Enclosed _____

Please charge my: Visa_____ MasterCard_____ American Express_____ Discover_____

Card#:_____ Expir. Date:_____ 3- or 4-digit security code on back of card _____

CREDIT CARD BILLING ADDRESS:

_____

_____

_____

City:_____

State: _____ _____ Zip:_____

From Page#	Quantity Wanted	Country and items ordered: Specify Scott Numbers plus first day cover, souvenir card, plate block, mint sheet or other description	Quality Wanted	Unused	Used	Price Each	Total	Leave Blank

PAY SHIPPING/INSURANCE AS FOLLOWS:

Stamps only - $ 4.00
Other orders:
$20.00 to $49.99 - $ 4.00
$50.00 to $199.99 - $ 6.00
$200.00 & over - $ 8.00

Total this page	_____	_____
Total from reverse	_____	_____
Total order	_____	_____
Less any discounts, refund checks, coupons, etc.	_____	_____
SUBTOTAL	_____	_____
Sales Tax (if any)	_____	_____
Shipping/Insurance (see chart at left)	_____	_____
TOTAL ENCLOSED	_____	_____

SATISFACTION GUARANTEED
MINIMUM ORDER MUST TOTAL AT LEAST $20.00
On orders outside the U.S. additional postage will be billed if necessary

From Page#	Quantity Wanted	Country and items ordered: Specify Scott Numbers plus first day cover, souvenir card, plate block, mint sheet or other description	Quality Wanted	Unused	Used	Price Each	Total	Leave Blank
			Total This Page					

Easy Order Form (continued)

Easy Order Form (continued)

Easy Order Form (continued)

EASY ORDER FORM – 2005 EDITION

Please send the items listed below for which I enclose: $_____   Date:_____

SHIP TO:

CREDIT CARD BILLING ADDRESS:

Name: _____   _____

Address: _____   _____

_____   _____

City:_____   City:_____

State: _____ Zip:_____   State: _____ _____ Zip:_____

Phone: _____ Check Enclosed _____

Please charge my: Visa_____   MasterCard_____   American Express_____   Discover_____

Card#:_____ Expir. Date:_____ 3- or 4-digit security code on back of card _____

From Page#	Quantity Wanted	Country and items ordered: Specify Scott Numbers plus first day cover, souvenir card, plate block, mint sheet or other description	Quality Wanted	Unused	Used	Price Each	Total	Leave Blank

PAY SHIPPING/INSURANCE AS FOLLOWS:

Stamps only - $ 4.00
Other orders:
$20.00 to $49.99 - $ 4.00
$50.00 to $199.99 - $ 6.00
$200.00 & over - $ 8.00

Total this page		
Total from reverse		
Total order		
Less any discounts, refund checks, coupons, etc.		
SUBTOTAL		
Sales Tax (if any)		
Shipping/Insurance (see chart at left)		
TOTAL ENCLOSED		

SATISFACTION GUARANTEED
MINIMUM ORDER MUST TOTAL AT LEAST $20.00
On orders outside the U.S. additional postage will be billed if necessary

Easy Order Form (continued)

From Page#	Quantity Wanted	Country and items ordered: Specify Scott Numbers plus first day cover, souvenir card, plate block, mint sheet or other description	Quality Wanted	Unused	Used	Price Each	Total	Leave Blank
			Total This Page					

338

EASY ORDER FORM – 2005 EDITION

Please send the items listed below for which I enclose: $_____   Date:_____

SHIP TO: **CREDIT CARD BILLING ADDRESS:**

Name: _____   _____

Address: _____   _____

_____   _____

City:_____   City:_____

State: _____ Zip:_____   State: _____ _____ Zip:_____

Phone: _____ Check Enclosed _____

Please charge my: Visa_____ MasterCard_____ American Express_____ Discover_____

Card#:_____ Expir. Date:_____ 3- or 4-digit security code on back of card _____

From Page#	Quantity Wanted	Country and items ordered: Specify Scott Numbers plus first day cover, souvenir card, plate block, mint sheet or other description	Quality Wanted	Unused	Used	Price Each	Total	Leave Blank

PAY SHIPPING/INSURANCE AS FOLLOWS:	
Total this page	
Total from reverse	
Stamps only - $ 4.00	Total order	
Other orders:	Less any discounts, refund checks, coupons, etc.	
$20.00 to $49.99 - $ 4.00	**SUBTOTAL**	
$50.00 to $199.99 - $ 6.00	Sales Tax (if any)	
$200.00 & over - $ 8.00	Shipping/Insurance (see chart at left)	
	TOTAL ENCLOSED	

SATISFACTION GUARANTEED
MINIMUM ORDER MUST TOTAL AT LEAST $20.00
On orders outside the U.S. additional postage will be billed if necessary

From Page#	Quantity Wanted	Country and items ordered: Specify Scott Numbers plus first day cover, souvenir card, plate block, mint sheet or other description	Quality Wanted	Unused	Used	Price Each	Total	Leave Blank
			Total This Page					

A Serious Hobby
Deserves A Serious Home.

Stamp collecting is a unique, personal pursuit. But stamp collectors are part of a larger, vibrant community, as well: the world of philately. And that world is represented by an organization whose activities embody the goals and aspirations of its worldwide membership: the American Philatelic Society.

As the premier philatelic organization, when looking for an appropriate location for our American Philatelic Center – and a new home for our world-renowned American Philatelic Research Library – we looked beyond just another office building.

And we found the perfect site. It's an historic restoration nestled within a historic community – to help honor the history of tradition and preservation which our pursuit honors.

We are in the midst of bringing that dream to life. But we can't succeed without your help. Plans have been laid, restoration has begun. In August, 2003 the Phase 1 dedication was held – but much remains to be accomplished.

Help us succeed. Contribute now.

We know you take pride in your passion for collecting. And we know you take pride in your American Philatelic Society membership. That's why we're asking for your contribution to help us turn this dream into a bricks and mortar reality.

**Our goal is $10,000,000 in 10 years.
We can't complete this historic
task without your help.
Contribute today.
Simply call 814-237-3803, ext. 218
Or visit our web site at www.stamps.org**

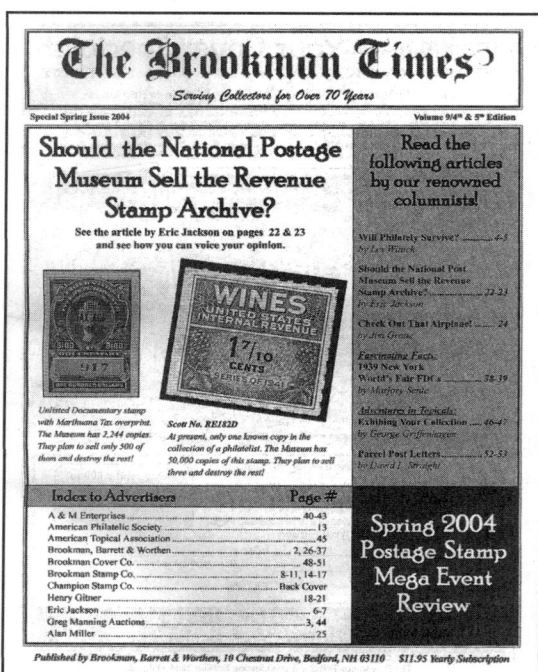

MINT UNITED NATIONS SETS & MORE
PURCHASE COMPLETE COUNTRY COLLECTIONS AT SPECIAL SAVINGS
OR CHOOSE INDIVIDUAL YEAR SETS AND SOUVENIR SHEETS.

NEW YORK ISSUES		GENEVA	VIENNA
1951-2003 COMPLETE **#1-852,B1,C1-23 WITH #38** OUR REGULAR UNIT DISCOUNT PRICE IS $965.00 *SALE PRICE* **$825.00**	**1951-2003 COMPLETE** **#1-37,39-852,B1,C1-23** **WITHOUT #38** REGULAR UNIT PRICE $795.00 *SALE PRICE* **$675.00**	**1969-2003 COMPLETE** **#1-417, B1** OUR REGULAR UNIT DISCOUNT PRICE IS $795.00 *SALE PRICE* **$675.00**	**1979-2003 COMPLETE** **#1-340, B1** OUR REGULAR UNIT DISCOUNT PRICE IS $685.00 *SALE PRICE* **$585.00**

YEAR SETS DO NOT INCLUDE SOUVENIR SHEETS OR WORLD FLAGS

NEW YORK YEAR SETS

Scott No.	Year	Normal Retail	Sale Price
1-11	1951 Regs. 11)	13.75	11.75
12-14	1952 (3)	.90	.60
15-22	1953 (8)	4.95	2.75

Scott No.	Year	Normal Retail	Sale Price
23-30	1954 (8)	20.00	11.95
31-37,39-40	1955 (9)	6.50	3.95
41-48	1956 (7)	2.15	1.20
49-58	1957 (10)	1.60	.85
59-68	1958 (10)	1.40	.75
69-76	1959 (8)	1.25	.65
77-84,86-7	1960 (10)	1.40	.75
88-99	1961 (12)	2.65	1.50
100-13	1962 (14)	2.95	1.60
114-22	1963 (9)	2.10	1.30
123-36	1964 (14)	3.35	1.95
137-44,146-53	1965(16)	5.25	3.25
154-63	1966 (10)	1.80	1.00
164-78,180	1967 (16)	2.75	1.50
181-91	1968 (11)	3.95	2.25
192-202	1969 (11)	2.40	1.40
203-11,13-14	1970 (11)	2.50	1.75
215-25	1971 (11)	3.50	2.25
226-33	1972 (8)	3.65	2.85
234-43	1973 (10)	2.50	1.80
244-55	1974 (12)	3.50	2.40
256-61,63-66	1975 (10)	3.75	2.35
267-80	1976 (14)	7.25	5.25
281-90	1977 (10)	3.75	2.50
291-303	1978 (13)	6.25	4.25
304-15	1979 (12)	4.25	2.50
316-23,41-42	1980 (10)	4.50	3.50
343-49,66-67	1981 (9)	5.00	3.95
368-73,90-91	1982 (8)	5.35	4.15
392-98,415-6	1983 (9)	5.95	4.85
417-24,41-42	1984 (10)	8.50	5.95
443-48,66-67	1985 (8)	11.25	8.85
468-76	1986 (9)	12.75	9.95
494-98,515-18	1987 (9)	9.50	7.50
519-27,44	1988 (10)	13.00	10.50
546-53,70-71	1989 (10)	15.00	12.00
572-78,80-83	1990 (11)	17.50	13.95
584-600	1991 (17)	33.50	26.95
601-17	1992 (17)	23.75	19.75
618-36	1993 (19)	26.75	22.50
637-54	1994 (18)	27.75	23.50
655-64, 66-68	1995 (13)	16.00	13.50
671-84, 86-89	1996 (18)	21.50	18.00
698-707,9-17	1997 (19)	20.75	16.75
727-33,35,37-42	1998 (14)	10.75	8.95
752-55,57-62,64-68, 770-71	1999 (17)	26.50	20.75
772-80,82,84-5,87	2000 (13)	12.50	9.95

Scott No.	Description	Normal Retail	Sale Price
789-94,803-6,8-10, 812-16	2001 (18)	17.75	14.95
817-33, 35	2002 (17)	20.75	16.75
837-51	2003 (15)	13.50	10.95
C1-23	1951-77 Airs (23)	8.50	6.25

NEW YORK WORLD FLAGS
Year sets of single stamps

Scott No.	Description	Normal Retail	Sale Price
325-40	1980 set of 16	4.75	3.25
350-65	1981 set of 16	6.50	4.95
374-89	1982 set of 16	6.50	5.25
399-414	1983 set of 16	7.50	5.95
425-40	1984 set of 16	12.00	9.50
450-65	1985 set of 16	13.75	10.95
477-92	1986 set of 16	12.75	10.50
499-514	1987 set of 16	12.75	10.50
528-43	1988 set of 16	11.50	9.95
554-69	1989 set of 16	12.50	10.75
690-97	1997 set of 8	6.95	5.95
719-26	1998 set of 8	7.50	6.25
744-51	1999 set of 8	6.75	5.75
795-802	2001 set of 8	5.95	5.25

NEW YORK SOUVENIR SHEETS

Scott	Description	Normal Retail	Sale Price
38	1955 10th Anniv.	185.00	150.00
85	1960 15th Anniversary	1.95	1.25
145	1965 20th Anniversary	.75	.40
179	1967 Chagall Window	.90	.50
212	1970 25th Anniversary	1.20	.70
262	1975 30th Anniversary	1.10	.65
324	1980 35th Anniversary	1.35	.85
449	1985 40th Anniversary	2.50	1.95
493	1986 WFUNA	4.75	2.95
545	1988 Human Rights	2.95	1.85
579	1990 45th Anniversary	10.75	8.50
665	1995 50th Anniversary	4.50	3.75
669	1995 50th A..Sheetlet-12	18.75	15.75
685	1996 Sport & Environ.	3.50	2.95
708	1997 Earth Summit	3.50	2.75
734	1998 Year of the Ocean Miniature Sheet of 12	9.75	8.25
736	1998 Rainforests	5.25	4.35
763	1999 UNISPACE III	5.95	4.95
769	1999 In Memoriam	2.75	2.30
781	2000 55th Anniversary	3.25	2.75
783	2000 United Nations in 21st Century Sheet of 6	5.95	5.25
788	2000 Refugees	2.40	2.00
811	2001 UNPA 50th Anniv.	5.25	4.50
836	2003 Latin America Sh-6	5.00	4.25
B1	2002 AIDS Awareness	1.25	1.00

GENEVA YEAR SETS

Scott	Description	Normal Retail	Sale Price
1-14	1969-70 Regs.(14)	17.95	13.50
15-21	1971 (7)	5.15	2.95
22-29	1972 (8)	7.25	4.75
30-36	1973 (7)	6.15	4.25
37-45	1974 (9)	8.25	5.25
46-51,53-56	1975 (10)	9.50	6.50
57-63	1976 (7)	9.75	6.95
64-72	1977 (9)	9.95	6.95

Scott No.	Description	Normal Retail	Sale Price
73-81	1978 (9)	9.00	5.85
82-88	1979 (7)	8.95	6.25
89-94,96-7	1980 (8)	8.25	5.95
98-104	1981 (7)	7.25	5.00
105-12	1982 (8)	8.25	5.75
113-20	1983 (9)	9.50	6.85
121-28	1984 (8)	9.50	7.25
129-36,38-9	1985 (10)	10.75	8.25
140-49	1986 (10)	18.00	14.75
151-61	1987 (11)	15.50	11.50
162-71	1988 (10)	18.75	14.95
173-81	1989 (9)	15.75	12.50
182-89,91-94	1990 (12)	28.50	21.75
195-210	1991 (16)	33.50	27.50
211-25	1992 (15)	33.75	27.75
226-43	1993 (18)	36.50	29.75
244-61	1994 (18)	36.50	29.75
262-71, 73-74	1995 (12)	25.00	19.50
277-90, 92-95	1996 (18)	36.50	29.75
296-305,7-15	1997 (19)	26.75	22.50
317-21,23,25-30	1998 (12)	21.75	16.75
332-34,36-41,43-47, 349-50	1999 (16)	25.00	19.75
351-59,62-3,65	2000 (12)	20.00	15.95
367-74,76-78,80-4	2001 (16)	29.75	23.50
385-401,403-4	2002 (19)	38.50	31.50
406-16	2003 (11)	19.50	15.75

GENEVA SOUVENIR SHEETS

Scott	Description	Normal Retail	Sale Price
52	1975 30th Anniversary	1.95	1.15
95	1980 35th Anniversary	1.50	.85
137	1985 40th Anniversary	2.50	1.50
150	1986 WFUNA	4.50	3.50
172	1988 Human Rights	3.50	2.50
190	1990 45th Anniversary	6.75	5.50
272	1995 50th Anniversary	6.50	5.25
275	1995 50th Ann. Sheet12	21.50	17.95
291	1996 Sport & Environmt.	4.50	3.65
306	1997 Earth Summit	3.50	2.95
322	1998 Ocean Mn.Sheet-12	13.75	11.50
324	1998 Rainforests	5.75	4.75
342	1999 UNISPACE III	4.75	3.65
348	1999 In Memoriam	3.50	2.85
360	2000 55th Anniversary	4.25	3.50
361	2000 21st Century Sheet-6	7.50	6.25
366	2000 Refugees	3.25	2.65
379	2001 UNPA 50th Anniv.	5.75	4.50
405	2003 Latin America Sh-6	9.75	7.95
B1	2002 AIDS Awareness	2.50	2.15

VIENNA YEAR SETS

Scott No.	Description	Normal Retail	Sale Price
1-6	1979 Regs.(6)	3.50	2.50
7-13,15-16	1980 (9)	8.25	5.75
17-23	1981 (7)	6.50	4.75
24-29	1982 (6)	5.75	4.25
30-38	1983 (9)	8.95	6.25
39-47	1984 (9)	10.50	7.95
48-53,55-6	1985 (8)	12.50	9.25
57-65	1986 (9)	15.00	11.50
67-77	1987 (11)	15.75	11.75
78-86	1988 (9)	15.75	11.95
88-96	1989 (9)	17.75	13.95
97-104,106-9	1990 (12)	22.75	18.75
110-24	1991 (15)	30.75	24.75
125-40	1992 (16)	31.75	25.95
141-59	1993 (19)	42.50	33.75
160-77	1994 (18)	40.75	32.50
178-87, 89-90	1995 (12)	26.50	21.75
193-206,8-11	1996 (18)	32.75	27.50
212-21, 23-31	1997 (19)	31.50	25.75
233-38,40,42-47	1998 (13)	17.50	14.50
249-51,53-58,60-64, 266-67	1999 (16)	25.75	20.75
268-76,79-80,82	2000 (12)	19.75	15.75
284-91,93-5,97-301	2001 (16)	24.50	19.75
302-23, 25	2002 (23)	36.50	29.50
327-39	2003 (13)	24.75	19.75

VIENNA SOUVENIR SHEETS

Scott	Description	Normal Retail	Sale Price
14	1980 35th Anniversary	2.00	1.25
54	1985 40th Anniversary	3.50	2.25
66	1986 WFUNA	5.00	3.75
87	1988 Human Rights	2.50	1.60
105	1990 45th Anniversary	6.00	4.95
188	1995 50th Anniversary	7.50	6.25
191	1995 50th Ann.Sht-12	23.50	19.75
207	1996 Sport & Environmt.	4.00	3.25
222	1997 Earth Summit	3.75	2.95
239	1998 Ocean Min.Sh.-12	10.75	8.75
241	1998 Rainforests	5.50	4.75
259	1999 UNISPACE III	4.25	3.50
265	1999 In Memoriam	3.50	2.85
277	2000 55th Anniversary	3.85	3.15
278	2000 21st Century Sheet-6	5.50	4.50
283	2000 Refugees	4.50	3.65
296	2001 50th UNPA Anniv.	5.50	4.50
326	2003 Latin America Sh-6	7.50	6.25
B1	2002 AIDS Awareness	2.50	2.10

ASK FOR OUR LATEST FREE UNITED NATIONS PRICE LIST INCLUDING INDIVIDUAL SETS, PRESTIGE BOOKLETS, POSTAL STATIONERY AND SOUVENIR CARDS

Topicals - The FUN and EDUCATIONAL
way to collect postage stamps!

Pick a topic -
ANY topic!

By collecting stamps on your favorite topic, you will add to your enjoyment while nourishing your mind!

BUT -- To get the most out of your collecting, join the *American Topical Association*.

Reap the benefits of membership in a world-class society. You'll get six issues of the ATA's bi-monthly magazine, where you'll find:

* Outstanding, informative articles on topicals by advanced collectors from around the world
* The most comprehensive publication reviews of any philatelic publication.
* Sources from whom you can obtain quality stamps on your topical.
* Updates on postmarks, meters and postal stationery that will help round out your collection.
* News on the ATA, the National Topical Stamp Show and other philatelic organizations.

PLUS...

Your new membership will also get you the following:
* A **FREE** how-to booklet on topical collecting
* Five **FREE** philatelic covers with your new member packet.
* Checklists on over 400 topics will be made available to you as an ATA member.
* Your membership card that identifies you to all dealers.

ACT SOON, and we'll give you an EXTRA ISSUE of TOPICAL TIME at no additional cost! Contact us at our new address:

American Topical Association
P.O. Box 57 - Arlington, TX 76004-0057

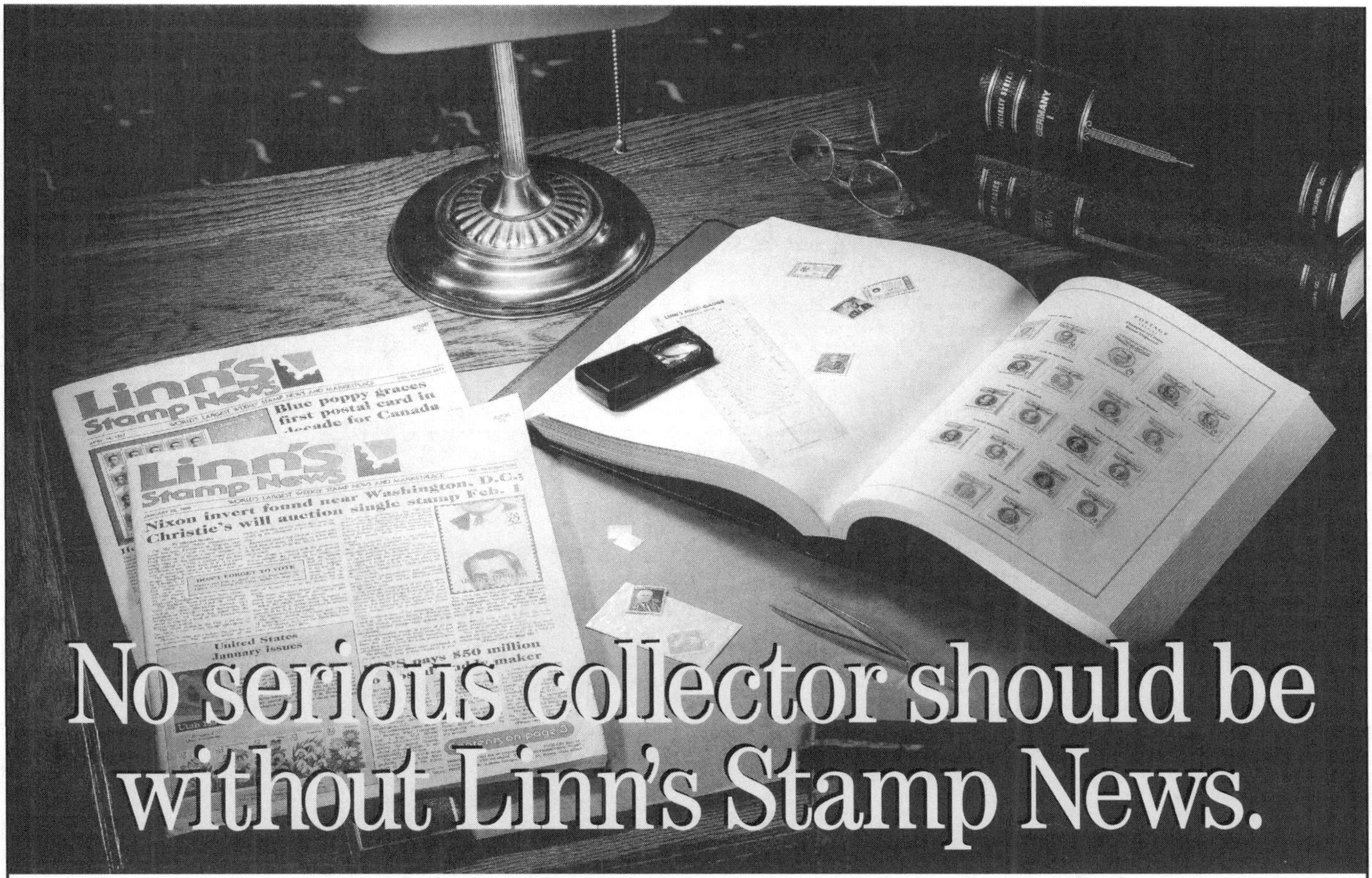

Collecting's Real Value Isn't Determined by a Catalogue

LINN'S COMPLETE STAMP COLLECTING BASICS

Whether it's the thrill of the hunt, thoughts of exotic locales, or learning something new, stamp collecting can be an adventure filled with wonderful memories. Share this passion or explore new collecting interests in this easy-to-read, fully illustrated guide, Linn's Stamp Collecting Basics.

Written by Scott Stamp Monthly editor Michael Baadke, this comprehensive book will help you start enjoying the stamp hobby and will serve as an essential reference for years to come. With a complete subject index and an extensive glossary that explains the most commonly used stamp hobby terminology, Linn's Complete Stamp Collecting Basics is an all-in-one information source that every stamp collector will enjoy.

ITEM	PRICE
LIN76	$13.99

To Order Call 1-800-572-6885
www.amosadvantage.com

We Buy All Stamp Collections

PHILATELY
–THE
INTERNATIONAL
HOBBY

UNITED
NATIONS

44c

Valued from $200 to $2 Million and up...
What are <u>your</u> stamps worth?

If the value of your stamp collection falls anywhere between $200 and $2 million or more, Mystic is ready to buy it.

We're looking for the following...

- ☑ Rare/High-quality stamps, U.S. and worldwide
- ☑ Award-winning collections
- ☑ Entire stamp dealer stocks, store inventory, show dealer and mail order dealer stocks
- ☑ United States stamp collections
- ☑ Worldwide country or topical collections
- ☑ Error stamps
- ☑ Accumulations and mixed stamps (they don't need to be organized)
- ☑ Postage lots
- ☑ First Day Covers

We Pay More for Your Stamps
Call 800-835-3609

Name _____

Street _____

City _____ State _____ Zip _____

Phone Number (include area code)_____

❏ United States ❏ Worldwide ❏ Collection ❏ Accumulation

Approximate value _____

Based on _____

Brief description of stamps _____

_____

Mystic Stamp Company
Attention: Buying Department
9700 Mill Street, Camden, N.Y. 13316
Phone: 1-800-835-3609 Fax: 1-800-385-4919
StampBuyer@MysticStamp.com

BA515

349

Brookman's Classifieds

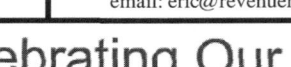

Brookman's Classifieds

351

352